WILLS, TRUSTS, AND ESTATES

WILLS, TRUSTS, AND ESTATES

Jesse Dukeminier

Late Maxwell Professor of Law
University of California, Los Angeles

Stanley M. Johanson

Fannie Coplin Regents Professor of Law
University of Texas

James Lindgren

Benjamin Mazur Research Professor of Law
Northwestern University

Robert H. Sitkoff

Associate Professor of Law
Northwestern University

111 Eighth Avenue, New York, NY 10011
www.aspenpublishers.com

Aspen Publishers
Attn: Permissions Department
111 Eighth Avenue, 7th Floor
New York, NY 10011-5201

Printed in the United States of America.

1 2 3 4 5 6 7 8 9 0

ISBN 0-7355-3695-3

Library of Congress Cataloging-in-Publication Data

Wills, trusts, and estates / Jesse Dukeminier . . . [et al.]. — 7th ed.
   p.   cm.
Rev. ed. of: Wills, trusts, and estates / Jesse Dukeminier, Stanley M. Johanson. 6th ed. c2000.
   ISBN 0-7355-3695-3 (hardcover : alk. paper)
   1. Wills — United States — Cases. 2. Estate planning — United States — Cases. 3. Future interests — United States — Cases. 4. Trusts and trustees — United States — Cases. I. Dukeminier, Jesse.
II. Dukeminier, Jesse. Wills, trusts, and estates.
KF753.A7D8 2005
346.7305 — dc22   2005007687

For Jesse Dukeminier,
teacher to us all

Jesse Dukeminier, 1925-2003

SUMMARY OF CONTENTS

*Chapter 14 was revised for the Seventh Edition principally by Stephanie J. Willbanks, Professor of Law at Vermont Law School.

CONTENTS

Chapter 7. Restrictions on the Power of Disposition: Protection of the Spouse and Children   417

*Chapter 14 was revised for the Seventh Edition principally by Stephanie J. Willbanks, Professor of Law at Vermont Law School.

LIST OF ILLUSTRATIONS

PREFACE

As trusts and estates lawyers, we are in the business of succession. The passing of Jesse Dukeminier in April of 2003 reminds us of this reality in a deeply personal way. In this seventh edition, we begin the process of authorship succession with James Lindgren and Robert H. Sitkoff joining the book.

Wills, Trusts, and Estates is designed for use in a course on trusts and decedents' estates and as an introduction to estate planning. Our basic aim in this seventh edition remains as before: to produce not merely competent practitioners in the trusts and estates field, but lawyers who think critically about problems in family wealth transmission and compare alternative solutions. Trusts and estates is a vibrant field whose difficult policy questions demand careful consideration.

Since the 1960s, the law of wills has been undergoing a thorough renovation. Initially, the change was brought on by a swelling public demand for cheaper and simpler ways of transferring property at death, avoiding expensive probate. Imaginative scholars then began to ventilate this ancient law of the dead hand, challenging assumptions and suggesting judicial and legislative innovation to simplify and rationalize it. Medical science complicated matters by creating varieties of parentage and death-deferring machines unheard of a generation ago. And legal malpractice in drawing wills and trusts arrived with a bang. Scholars, science, and malpractice liability are a potent combination for driving law reform.

The use of trusts to transmit family wealth has become commonplace, not only for rich clients, but also for those of modest wealth. In expanding, the law of private trusts has annexed the law of future interests and powers of appointment, reducing these two subjects largely to problems in drafting and construing trust instruments. The teachings of modern finance theory and the shifting locus of wealth from land to financial assets has put pressure on the law of trust investment and administration, which evolved in simpler times. As a result, the fiduciary obligation has eclipsed limitations on the trustee's powers as the principal device for safeguarding the beneficiary from mismanagement or abuse by the trustee. Meanwhile, the burgeoning tort liability of modern times has spawned an asset protection industry and with it nascent but radical change in the rights of creditors to trust assets.

Taxation of donative transfers has changed dramatically. The unlimited marital deduction — which permits spouses to make unlimited tax-free gifts and bequests to each other — is now a central feature of estate planning. In 1986, Congress enacted the generation-skipping transfer tax, implementing a policy of wealth transfer taxation at each generation. This tax, like an invisible boomerang, is delivering potentially lethal blows to the Rule against Perpetuities. In 2001, Congress enacted legislation that phases out the federal wealth transfer taxes by 2010, but then in 2011 these taxes will revert to their pre-2001 form. Surely this will not be Congress's last word on the subject.

Throughout the book we emphasize the basic theoretical structure and the general philosophy and purposes that unify the field of donative transfers. We are interested in function, not form. To this end we have pruned away mechanical matters (such as a step-by-step discussion of how to probate a will and settle an estate, which is essentially local law, easily learned from a local practice book). At the same time, we have sought historical roots of modern law. Understanding how the law became the way it is illuminates both the continuing growth of the law and the sometimes exasperating peculiarities inherited from the past.

Although we organize the material in topical compartments, we have also sought a more penetrating view of the subject as a tapestry of humanity. Every illustration included, every behind-the-scenes peek, every quirk of the parties' behavior has its place, as a piece of ornament fitting into the larger whole. Understanding the ambivalences of the human heart and the richness of human frailty, and realizing that even the best-constructed estate plans may, with the ever-whirling wheels of change, turn into sand castles, are essential to being a *counselor* at law, as opposed to being a mere attorney.

As we said in the first edition of this book, in 1972:

> In this book we deal with people, the quick as well as the dead. There is nothing like the death of a moneyed member of the family to show persons as they really are, virtuous or conniving, generous or grasping. Many a family has been torn apart by a botched-up will. Each case is a drama in human relationships — and the lawyer, as counselor, draftsman, or advocate, is an important figure in the dramatis personae. This is one reason the estates practitioner enjoys his work, and why we enjoy ours.

This observation remains true today. In a changing reality the human drama abides. Trusts and estates is a field concerned fundamentally with people.

For their sage advice on this revision, we thank David Becker, Karen Boxx, Eric Chason, Ronald Chester, Judith Daar, Joseph Dodge, Susan French, Philip Hamburger, Howard Helsinger, Adam Hirsch, Kenneth Joyce, Robert Katz, John Langbein, Ray Madoff, Bruce Mann, Geoffrey Manne, Alan Newman, Richard Primus, Randy Roth, Jeffrey Sherman, Ethan Stone, and Joshua Tate. In addition, we must single out two colleagues: Stephanie Willbanks for her assistance with tax matters throughout the book and her taking the lead in revising Chapter 14, and Helene Shapo for her ongoing encouragement and stimulation. We owe a great debt to Georgia Alexakis, Ericka Schnitzer, Jeremy Sitkoff, and Cathy Yu for superb research assistance, and to Kathryn Hensiak and Amy Mangan for additional research support. We thank Melody Davies, Sarah

Hains, Eric Holt, Carol McGeehan, and Carmen Reid at Aspen for bringing rich intelligence and sound judgment to this project. Finally, we thank our partners, David Sanders, Gerrie Johanson, Valerie Lindgren, and Tamara Sitkoff, for their support — both substantive and emotional — in bringing out this new edition.

Jesse Dukeminier, 1925-2003
Stanley M. Johanson
James Lindgren
Robert H. Sitkoff

January 2005

Editors' note: All citations to state statutes and the United States Code are to such statutes as they appear on Lexis or Westlaw on the date cited. Footnotes are numbered consecutively from the beginning of each chapter. Most footnotes in quoted materials are omitted. Authorities cited in quoted materials are sometimes omitted or edited for readability. Editors' footnotes added to quoted materials are indicated by the abbreviation: — Eds.

ACKNOWLEDGMENTS

Books and Articles

American Law Institute, Restatement (Second) of Trusts (1959), Restatement (Third) of Trusts (1992), Restatement (Third) of Trusts (2003), Restatement (Third) of Property (1999), Restatement (Third) of Property (2003). © 1959, 1992, 1999, 2003 by the American Law Institute. Reprinted by permission of the American Law Institute.

Ascher, Mark L., Curtailing Inherited Wealth, 89 Mich. L. Rev. 69 (1990). Reprinted by permission of the author and the Michigan Law Review.

Blum, Walter, & Harry Kalven, The Uneasy Case for Progressive Taxation, 19 U. Chi. L. Rev. 417 (1952). © 1952 by the University of Chicago. Reprinted by permission of Professor Blum and the University of Chicago Law Review.

Buck, Estate of. California Superior Court Opinion, 21 U.S.F. L. Rev. 691 (1987). Reprinted by permission of the University of San Francisco Law Review.

de Bruxelles, Simon, Baby Conceived After 60th Birthday Celebration, The (London) Times, Jan. 16, 1998. © 1998 by Times Newspapers Limited. Reprinted by permission of News International Syndication.

Dukeminier, Jesse, and James Krier, The Rise of the Perpetual Trust, 50 UCLA L. Rev. 1303 (2003). Reprinted by permission of Professor Krier and the UCLA Law Review.

Gray, Francine du Plessix, The New "Older Woman," N.Y. Times, §7 (Book Review), Jan. 15, 1978, p.3. © 1978 by the New York Times. Reprinted by permission of Georges Borchardt, Inc.

Gulliver, Ashbel, & Catherine Tilson, Classification of Gratuitous Transfers, 51 Yale L.J. 1 (1941). © 1941 by the Yale Law Journal. Reprinted by permission of Professor Gulliver, The Yale Law Journal Co., and Fred B. Rothman & Co.

Halbach, Edward C., Jr., An Introduction to Chapters 1-4, in Death, Taxes and Family Property (E. Halbach ed. 1977). © 1977 by West Publishing Co. Reprinted by permission of the author and West Publishing Co.

Kristol, Irving, Taxes, Poverty, and Equality, The Public Interest 26-28 (no. 37, Fall 1974). © 1974. Reprinted by permission.

Landers, Ann. Column. Reproduced by permission of Esther P. Lederer and Creators Syndicate, Inc.

Langbein, John H., Substantial Compliance with the Wills Act, 88 Harv. L. Rev. 489 (1975). © 1975 by the Harvard Law Review Association. Reprinted by permission of the author and the Harvard Law Review.

————, Living Probate: The Conservatorship Model, 77 Mich. L. Rev. 63 (1978). © 1978 by the Michigan Law Review. Reprinted by permission of the author and the Michigan Law Review.

————, Excusing Harmless Errors in the Execution of Wills: A Report on Australia's Tranquil Revolution in Probate Law, 87 Colum. L. Rev. 1 (1987). © 1987 by the Directors of the Columbia Law Review Association, Inc. All rights reserved. Reprinted by permission of the author and the Columbia Law Review.

————, The Twentieth-Century Revolution in Family Wealth Transmission, 86 Mich. L. Rev. 722 (1988). Reprinted by permission of the author and the Michigan Law Review.

————, Curing Execution Errors and Mistaken Terms in Wills: The Reinstatement of Wills Delivers New Tools (and Duties) to Probate Lawyers, Probate and Property, Vol. 18, No. 1, January/February, 2004. © 2004. Reprinted by permission of the American Bar Association.

Margolick, David, Undue Influence (1993). © 1993 by David Margolick. Excerpts reprinted by permission of HarperCollins Publishers.

National Conference of Commissioners on Uniform State Laws (NCCUSL), excerpts from the Uniform Probate Code (1969, 1990), Uniform Prudent Investor Act (1994), Uniform Statutory Rule Against Perpetuities (1986), Uniform Transfers to Minors Act (1983, 1986), Uniform Testamentary Additions to Trusts Act (1991), and Uniform Trust Code (2000). © 1969, 1983, 1986, 1990, 1991, 1993, 2000, 2001, 2003, 2004 by NCCUSL. Reprinted by permission of NCCUSL.

Plotz, David, Judicial Restraint: Sol Wachtler's Worthy Sentiments on Prison, Slate, April 16, 1997. Reprinted by permission of United Media.

Posner, Richard A., Economic Analysis of Law (6th ed. 2003). © 2003 Richard A. Posner. Reprinted by permission of Judge Posner.

Scott, Austin W., The Law of Trusts, vol. 1 (William Fratcher 4th ed. 1987). © 1987 by the Estate of Austin Wakeman Scott. Reprinted by permission of Aspen Publishers, Inc.

With His Wife in Limbo, Husband Can't Move, the New York Times, Nov. 2, 2003, §1, at 18. Reprinted by permission of Georges Borchardt, Inc.

Photographs and Illustrations

Barnes Foundation Gallery. © The Barnes Foundation. Photograph. Reproduced by permission of The Barnes Foundation.

Bogert, George G. Photograph. Reprinted by permission of the University of Chicago Library, Special Collections.

Bok, Chip. Cartoon. © 2003 ChipBok and Creators Syndicate, Inc. Reproduced by permission of Chip Bok and Creators Syndicate, Inc.

Coolidge, Calvin. Photograph. Jan. 31, 1923. Photograph by Herbert E. French, National Photo Company Collection, Library of Congress, Prints and Photographs Division, Digital Reproduction Number cph 3a35018.

Dana, Marie, with Samantha. Photograph. Los Angeles Times photo by Anacleto Rapping. Reproduced by permission of TMS Reprints.

Devine, Father. Photograph by Otto Bettmann. © Bettmann/CORBIS. Reproduced by permission.

Duke, Doris. Photograph of signature on her will. From Surrogate's Court, New York County, New York.

Duke, Doris, and her butler. Photograph by Marina Garnier. Reproduced by permission of Marina Garnier.

Dukeminier, Jesse. Photograph. Reproduced by permission of David Sanders.

Easterbrook, Frank H. Photograph. Reproduced by permission of Judge Easterbrook.

Fletcher, Betty B. Photograph. Reproduced by permission of Judge Fletcher.

Ginsburg, Ruth Bader. Photograph. Photograph by Steven Petteway, Supreme Court of the United States. Reproduced from the Collection of the Supreme Court of the United States through the Curator's Office (202) 479-3298. Reproduced by permission of Justice Ginsburg.

Hannen, James. Etching. Reproduced by permission of the National Portrait Gallery.

Janes, Rodney. Photograph from the New York Red Book, 1940 Edition. © New York Legal Publishing Corp. Reproduced by permission.

Johnson, Seward. Photograph of signature on will. From Surrogate's Court, New York County, New York.

Johnson, Seward and Basia. Photograph. Reproduced by permission of David Margolick.

Kenkut dispenser. Photograph. Reproduced by permission of Kenkut Products, Inc.

Kuralt, Charles, with Patricia Shannon. Photograph. Reproduced by permission of AP/World Wide Photos.

Landers, Ann. Photograph. Reproduced by permission of Creators Syndicate, Inc.

Langbein, John H. Photograph. Reproduced by permission of the Yale Law School Office of Public Affairs and Professor Langbein.

Leach, W. Barton. Photograph. Courtesy of Art & Visual Materials, Special Collections Department, Harvard Law School Library.

Markowitz, Harry M. Photograph. Reproduced by permission of Professor Markowitz.

New Yorker, The. The New Yorker Magazine, Inc., holds copyrights in the following cartoons: (1) cartoon by Peter Arno © 1940, 1968, 1996; (2) cartoon by Peter Arno © 1942, 1970, 1998; (3) cartoon by Leo Cullum © 1995; (4) cartoon by Wm. Hamilton © 1977; (5) cartoon by Frank Modell © 1972; (6) cartoon by Mick Stevens © 1994. These cartoons are reprinted by permission of the Cartoon Bank, a division of The New Yorker Magazine (cartoonbank.com). All rights reserved.

WILLS, TRUSTS, AND ESTATES

1
INTRODUCTION TO ESTATE PLANNING

SECTION A. THE POWER TO TRANSMIT PROPERTY AT DEATH: ITS JUSTIFICATION AND LIMITATIONS

1. The Right to Inherit and the Right to Convey

THOMAS JEFFERSON, 7 JEFFERSON'S WORKS 454 (Monticello ed. 1904): "The earth belongs in usufruct to the living; the dead have neither powers nor rights over it. The portion occupied by any individual ceases to be his when he himself ceases to be, and reverts to society." (Letter to James Madison dated Sept. 6, 1789.)

2 William Blackstone, Commentaries
*10-13

The right of inheritance, or descent to the children and relations of the deceased, seems to have been allowed much earlier than the right of devising by testament. We are apt to conceive, at first view, that it has nature on its side; yet we often mistake for nature what we find established by long and inveterate custom. It is certainly a wise and effectual, but clearly a political, establishment; since the permanent right of property, vested in the ancestor himself, was no *natural*, but merely a *civil* right. . . . It is probable that [the right of inheritance arose] . . . from a plainer and more simple principle. A man's children or nearest relations are usually about him on his death-bed, and are the earliest witnesses of his decease. They become, therefore, generally the next immediate occupants, till at length, in process of time, this frequent usage ripened into general law. And therefore, also, in the earliest ages, on failure of children, a man's servants, born under his roof, were allowed to be his heirs; being immediately on the spot when he died. For we find the old patriarch Abraham expressly declaring that "since God had given him no seed, his steward Eliezer, one born in his house, was his heir."[1]

While property continued only for life, testaments were useless and unknown: and, when it became inheritable, the inheritance was long indefeasible, and the children or heirs at law were incapable of exclusion by will; till at length it was found, that so strict a rule of inheritance made heirs disobedient and headstrong, defrauded creditors of their just debts, and prevented many provident fathers from dividing or charging their estates as the exigencies of their families required. This introduced pretty generally the right of disposing of one's property, or a part of it, by *testament*; that is, by written or oral instructions properly *witnessed* and authenticated, according to the *pleasure* of the deceased, which we, therefore, emphatically style his *will*. This was established in some countries much later than in others. With us in England, till modern times, a man could only dispose of one-third of his movables from his wife and children; and in general, no will was permitted of lands till the reign of Henry VIII; and then only of a certain portion: for it was not till after the Restoration that the power of devising real property became so universal as at present.

Wills, therefore, and testaments, rights of inheritance and successions, are all of them creatures of the civil or municipal laws, and accordingly are in all respects regulated by them; every distinct country having different ceremonies and requisites to make a testament completely valid; neither does anything vary more than the right of inheritance under different national establishments.

John Locke, *Two Treatises of Government*
Book 1, Ch. 9, §88 (Peter Laslett ed., 1988)

It might reasonably be asked here, how come Children by this right of possessing, before any other, the properties of their Parents upon their Decease. For it being Personally the Parents, when they dye, without actually Transferring their Right to another, why does it not return again to the common stock of Mankind? 'Twill perhaps be answered, that common consent hath disposed of it, to the Children. Common Practice, we see indeed does so dispose of it but we cannot say, that it is the common consent of Mankind; for that hath never been asked, nor actually given: and if common tacit Consent hath establish'd it, it would make but a positive and not Natural Right of Children to Inherit the Goods of their Parents: But where the Practice is Universal, 'tis reasonable to think the Cause is Natural. The ground then, I think, to be this. The first and strongest desire God Planted in Men, and wrought into the very Principles of their Nature being that of Self-preservation, that is the Foundation of a right to the Creatures, for the particular support and use of each individual Person himself. But next to this, God Planted in

---

1. Genesis 15:3. [The words put in quotation marks are Blackstone's paraphrase of two verses of the Bible, which no one has yet translated from the original Hebrew to everyone's satisfaction. Blackstone's statement that servants took as heirs in the absence of children has been disputed by many scholars. "Israel does not know a general rule like this for regulating the inheritance." Gerhard Von Rad, Genesis 178 (John H. Marks trans. 1961). Cf. Richard H. Hiers, Transfer of Property by Inheritance and Bequest in Biblical Law and Tradition, 10 J.L. & Relig. 121, 127 (1994). Abraham's declaration was never put to the test for thereafter, when Abraham was 100 years old and his wife Sarah was 90, Sarah gave birth to a son, Isaac. Genesis 17:15. — Eds.]

Men a strong desire also of propagating their Kind, and continuing themselves in their Posterity, and this gives Children a Title, to share in the *Property* of their Parents, and a Right to Inherit their Possessions. Men are not Proprietors of what they have meerly for themselves, their Children have a Title to part of it, and have their Kind of Right joyn'd with their Parents, in the Possession which comes to be wholly theirs, when death having put an end to their Parents use of it, hath taken them from their Possessions, and this we call Inheritance.

Until the 1980s, the views of Jefferson and Blackstone prevailed over those of Locke. It was generally accepted that the right to pass property at death was neither a natural right nor was it constitutionally protected. Thus in Irving Trust Co. v. Day, 314 U.S. 556, 562 (1942), the Supreme Court said:

> Rights of succession to property of a deceased, whether by will or by intestacy, are of statutory creation, and the dead hand rules succession only by sufferance. Nothing in the Federal Constitution forbids the legislature of a state to limit, condition, or even abolish the power of testamentary disposition over property within its jurisdiction.

But Hodel v. Irving, decided in the 1980s when the Court revived its interest in protecting private property through the Just Compensation Clause, changed all that.

Hodel v. Irving
Supreme Court of the United States, 1987
481 U.S. 704

O'CONNOR, J.   The question presented is whether the original version of the "escheat" provision of the Indian Land Consolidation Act of 1983, Pub. L. 97-459, Tit. II, 96 Stat. 2519, effected a "taking" of appellees' decedents' property without just compensation.

I

Towards the end of the 19th century, Congress enacted a series of land Acts which divided the communal reservations of Indian tribes into individual allotments for Indians and unallotted lands for non-Indian settlement. This legislation seems to have been in part animated by a desire to force Indians to abandon their nomadic ways in order to "speed the Indians' assimilation into American society," Solem v. Bartlett, 465 U.S. 463, 466 (1984), and in part a result of pressure to free new lands for further white settlement. Ibid. . . . [In 1889, by an Act of Congress] each male Sioux head of household took 320 acres of land and most other individuals 160 acres. 25 Stat. 890. In order to protect the allottees from the improvident disposition of their lands to white settlers, the Sioux allotment statute provided that the allotted lands were to be held in trust by the United States. Id., at 891. Until 1910 the lands of deceased allottees passed to their heirs "according to the laws of the State or Territory" where the land was located, ibid., and after 1910, allottees were permitted to dispose of their interests by will in accordance with regulations promulgated by

Justice Sandra Day O'Connor

the Secretary of the Interior. 36 Stat. 856, 25 U.S.C. §373. Those regulations generally served to protect Indian ownership of the allotted lands.

The policy of allotment of Indian lands quickly proved disastrous for the Indians. Cash generated by land sales to whites was quickly dissipated and the Indians, rather than farm the land themselves, evolved into petty landlords, leasing their allotted lands to white ranchers and farmers and living off the meager rentals. . . . The failure of the allotment program became even clearer as successive generations came to hold the allotted lands. Thus 40-, 80-, and 160-acre parcels became splintered into multiple undivided interests in land, with some parcels having hundreds and many parcels having dozens of owners. Because the land was held in trust and often could not be alienated or partitioned the fractionation problem grew and grew over time.

A 1928 report commissioned by the Congress found the situation administratively unworkable and economically wasteful. L. Meriam, Institute for Government Research, The Problem of Indian Administration 40-41. Good, potentially productive, land was allowed to lie fallow, amidst great poverty, because of the difficulties of managing property held in this manner. . . . In discussing the Indian Reorganization Act of 1934, Representative Howard said:

> It is in the case of the inherited allotments, however, that the administrative costs become incredible. . . . On allotted reservations, numerous cases exist where the shares of each individual heir from lease money may be 1 cent a month. Or one heir may own minute fractional shares in 30 or 40 different allotments. The cost of leasing, bookkeeping, and distributing the proceeds in many cases far exceeds the total income. The Indians and the Indian Service personnel are thus trapped in a meaningless system of minute partition in which all thought of the possible use of land to satisfy human needs is lost in a mathematical haze of bookkeeping. 78 Cong. Rec. 11728 (1934) (remarks of Rep. Howard).

In 1934, in response to arguments such as these, the Congress acknowledged the failure of its policy and ended further allotment of Indian lands. Indian Reorganization Act of 1934, ch. 576, 48 Stat. 984, 25 U.S.C. §461 et seq.

But the end of future allotment by itself could not prevent the further compounding of the existing problem caused by the passage of time. Ownership continued to fragment as succeeding generations came to hold the property, since, in the order of things, each property owner was apt to have more than one heir. In 1960, both the House and the Senate undertook comprehensive studies of the problem. . . . These studies indicated that one-half of the approximately 12 million acres of allotted trust lands were held in fractionated ownership, with over 3 million acres held by more than six heirs to a parcel. Further hearings were held in 1966, but not until the Indian Land Consolidation Act of 1983 did the Congress take action to ameliorate the problem of fractionated ownership of Indian lands.

Section 207 of the Indian Land Consolidation Act — the escheat provision at issue in this case — provided:

> No undivided fractional interest in any tract of trust or restricted land within a tribe's reservation or otherwise subjected to a tribe's jurisdiction shall descendent [sic] by intestacy or devise but shall escheat to that tribe if such interest represents 2 per centum or less of the total acreage in such tract and has earned to its owner less than $100 in the preceding year before it is due to escheat. 96 Stat. 2519.

Congress made no provision for the payment of compensation to the owners of the interests covered by §207. The statute was signed into law on January 12, 1983, and became effective immediately.

The three appellees — Mary Irving, Patrick Pumpkin Seed, and Eileen Bissonette — are enrolled members of the Oglala Sioux Tribe. They are, or represent, heirs or devisees of members of the Tribe who died in March, April, and June 1983. Eileen Bissonette's decedent, Mary Poor Bear-Little Hoop Cross, purported to will all her property, including property subject to §207, to her five minor children in whose name Bissonette claims the property. Chester Irving, Charles Leroy Pumpkin Seed, and Edgar Pumpkin Seed all died intestate. At the time of their deaths, the four decedents owned 41 fractional interests subject to the provisions of §207. The Irving estate lost two interests whose value together was approximately $100; the Bureau of Indian Affairs placed total values of approximately $2,700 on the 26 escheatable interests in the Cross estate and $1,816 on the 13 escheatable interests in the Pumpkin Seed estates. But for §207, this property would have passed, in the ordinary course, to appellees or those they represent.

Appellees filed suit in the United States District Court for the District of South Dakota, claiming that §207 resulted in a taking of property without just compensation in violation of the Fifth Amendment. The District Court concluded that the statute was constitutional. It held that appellees had no vested interest in the property of the decedents prior to their deaths and that Congress had plenary authority to abolish the power of testamentary disposition of Indian property and to alter the rules of intestate succession.

The Court of Appeals for the Eighth Circuit reversed. Irving v. Clark, 758 F.2d 1260 (1985). Although it agreed that appellees had no vested rights in the decedents' property, it concluded that their decedents had a right, derived from the original Sioux allotment statute, to control disposition of their property at death. The Court of Appeals held that appellees had standing to invoke that right and that the taking of that right without compensation to decedents' estates violated the Fifth Amendment. . . .

II

[The Court held that the plaintiffs had standing under Article III of the Constitution.]

III

The Congress, acting pursuant to its broad authority to regulate the descent and devise of Indian trust lands, Jefferson v. Fink, 247 U.S. 288, 294 (1918), enacted §207 as a means of ameliorating, over time, the problem of extreme fractionation of certain Indian lands. By forbidding the passing on at death of small, undivided interests in Indian lands, Congress hoped that future generations of Indians would be able to make more productive use of the Indians' ancestral lands. We agree with the Government that encouraging the consolidation of Indian lands is a public purpose of high order. The fractionation problem on Indian reservations is extra-ordinary and may call for dramatic action to encourage consolidation. The Sisseton-Wahpeton Sioux Tribe, appearing as amicus curiae in support of the Secretary of the Interior, is a quintessential victim of fractionation. Forty-acre tracts on the Sisseton-Wahpeton Lake Traverse Reservation, leasing for about $1,000 annually, are commonly subdivided into hundreds of undivided interests, many of which generate only pennies a year in rent. The average tract has 196 owners and the average owner undivided interests in 14 tracts. The administrative headache this represents can be fathomed by examining Tract 1305, dubbed "one of the most fractionated parcels of land in the world." Lawson, Heirship: The Indian Amoeba, reprinted in Hearing on S. 2480 and S. 2663 before the Senate Select Committee on Indian Affairs, 98th Cong., 2d Sess., 85 (1984). Tract 1305 is 40 acres and produces $1,080 in income annually. It is valued at $8,000. It has 439 owners, one-third of whom receive less than $.05 in annual rent and two-thirds of whom receive less than $1. The largest interest holder receives $82.85 annually. The common denominator used to compute fractional interests in the property is 3,394,923,840,000. The smallest heir receives $.01 every 177 years. If the tract were sold (assuming the 439 owners could agree) for its estimated $8,000 value, he would be entitled to $.000418. The administrative costs of handling this tract are estimated by the Bureau of Indian Affairs at $17,560 annually. Id., at 86, 87. See also Comment, Too Little Land, Too Many Heirs—The Indian Heirship Land Problem, 46 Wash. L. Rev. 709, 711-713 (1971). . . .

Section 207 provides for the escheat of small undivided property interests that are unproductive during the year preceding the owner's death. Even if we accept the Government's assertion that the income generated by such parcels may be properly thought of as de minimis, their value may not be. While the Irving estate lost two interests whose value together was only approximately $100, the Bureau of Indian Affairs placed total values of approximately $2,700 and $1,816 on the escheatable interests in the Cross and Pumpkin Seed estates. These are not trivial sums. . . . Of course, the whole of appellees' decedents' property interests were not taken by §207. Appellees' decedents retained full beneficial use of the property during their lifetimes as well as the right to convey it inter vivos. There is no question, however, that the right to pass on valuable property to one's heirs is itself a valuable right. Depending on the age of the owner, much or most of the value of the parcel may inhere in this "remainder" interest. See 26 CFR §20.2031-7(f) (Table A) (1986) (value of remainder interest when life tenant is age 65 is approximately 32% of the whole).

The extent to which any of appellees' decedents had "investment-backed expec-tations" in passing on the property is dubious. Though it is conceivable that some of these interests were purchased with the expectation that the owners might pass on the remainder to their heirs at death, the property has been held in trust for the Indians for 100 years and is overwhelmingly acquired by gift, descent, or devise. Because of the highly fractionated ownership, the property is generally held for lease rather than improved and used by the owners. None of the appellees here can point to any specific investment-backed expectations beyond the fact that their ancestors agreed to accept allotment only after ceding to the United States large parts of the original Great Sioux Reservation.

Also weighing weakly in favor of the statute is the fact that there is something of an "average reciprocity of advantage," Pennsylvania Coal Co. v. Mahon, 260 U.S. 393, 415 (1922), to the extent that owners of escheatable interests maintain a nexus to the Tribe. Consolidation of Indian lands in the Tribe benefits the members of the Tribe. All members do not own escheatable interests, nor do all owners belong to the Tribe. Nevertheless, there is substantial overlap between the two groups. The owners of escheatable interests often benefit from the escheat of others' fractional interests. Moreover, the whole benefit gained is greater than the sum of the burdens imposed since consolidated lands are more productive than fractionated lands.

If we were to stop our analysis at this point, we might well find §207 constitutional. But the character of the Government regulation here is extraordinary. In Kaiser Aetna v. United States, 444 U.S. 164, 176 (1979), we emphasized that the regulation destroyed "one of the most essential sticks in the bundle of rights that are commonly characterized as property — the right to exclude others." Similarly, the regulation here amounts to virtually the abrogation of the right to pass on a certain type of property — the small undivided interest — to one's heirs. In one form or another, the right to pass on property — to one's family in particular — has been part of the Anglo-American legal system since feudal times. See United States v. Perkins, 163 U.S. 625, 627-628 (1896). The fact that it may be possible for the owners of these interests to effectively control disposition upon death through complex inter vivos transactions such as revocable trusts, is simply not an adequate substitute for the rights taken, given the nature of the property. Even the United States concedes that total abrogation of the right to pass property is unprecedented and likely unconstitutional. Moreover, this statute effectively abolishes both descent and devise of these property interests even when the passing of the property to the heir might result in consolidation of property — as for instance when the heir already owns another undivided interest in the property. Cf. 25 U.S.C. §2206(b) (1982 ed., Supp. III). Since the escheatable interests are not, as the United States argues, necessarily de minimis, nor, as it also argues, does the availability of inter vivos transfer obviate the need for descent and devise, a *total* abrogation of these rights cannot be upheld. But cf. Andrus v. Allard, 444 U.S. 51 (1979) (upholding abrogation of the right to sell endangered eagles' parts as necessary to environmental protection regulatory scheme).

In holding that complete abolition of both the descent and devise of a particular class of property may be a taking, we reaffirm the continuing vitality of the long line of cases recognizing the States', and where appropriate, the United States', broad authority to adjust the rules governing the descent and devise of property without implicating the guarantees of the Just Compensation Clause. See, e.g., Irving Trust Co. v. Day, 314 U.S. 556, 562 (1942); Jefferson v. Fink, 247 U.S., at 294. The difference in this case is the fact that both descent and devise are completely abolished; indeed they are abolished even in circumstances when the governmental purpose sought to be advanced, consolidation of ownership of Indian lands, does not conflict with the further descent of the property.

There is little doubt that the extreme fractionation of Indian lands is a serious public problem. It may well be appropriate for the United States to ameliorate fractionation by means of regulating the descent and devise of Indian lands. Surely it is permissible for the United States to prevent the owners of such interests from further subdividing them among future heirs on pain of escheat. See Texaco, Inc. v. Short, 454 U.S. 516, 542 (1982) (Brennan, J., dissenting). It may be appropriate to minimize further compounding of the problem by abolishing the descent of such interests by rules of intestacy, thereby forcing the owners to formally designate an heir to prevent escheat to the Tribe. What is certainly not appropriate is to take the extraordinary step of abolishing both descent and devise of these property interests even when the passing of the property to the heir might result in consolidation of property. Accordingly, we find that this regulation, in the words of Justice Holmes, "goes too far." Pennsylvania Coal Co. v. Mahon, 260 U.S., at 415. The judgment of the Court of Appeals is

Affirmed.

NOTES AND QUESTIONS

1. Almost all the controlling cases cited by Justice O'Connor involve governmental regulation of land use. Why should tests that were designed to determine when compensation must be given for land use regulation be used when inheritance is regulated? A fundamental issue in the former area is whether the government is "forcing some people alone to bear public burdens which, in all fairness and justice, should be borne by the public as a whole." Armstrong v. United States, 364 U.S. 40, 49 (1960). Is this relevant to regulation of inheritance? To §207 of the Indian Land Consolidation Act?

In Hodel v. Irving, the Court's opinion appears to rest on the assumption that the right to transmit property at death is a separate, identifiable stick in the bundle of rights called property, and, if this right is taken away, compensation must be paid. The Court does not look at the impact of the statute upon the value of the whole bundle of property rights, including lifetime use, but only at the impact of the statute upon the right to transmit the property at death. If the issue is the amount of economic loss suffered by the property owner as a consequence of the statute, as it is in regulatory taking cases, should the court consider the impact of the statute on the whole bundle of rights or only on one stick? Either one is extremely difficult to measure, particularly because inter vivos transfer of the fractional interest is not prohibited by the statute. The Court cites as evidence of the value of the right to pass property at death only the value of a remainder interest, which is the value of the *right to receive*, not the value of the *right to transmit*.

For an interesting comment on Hodel v. Irving, see Ronald Chester, Inheritance in American Legal Thought, *in* Inheritance and Wealth in America 23 (Robert K. Miller, Jr. & Stephen J. McNamee eds., 1998).

2. If a legislature decides to abolish transmission of property by will or intestate succession, to be effective it is also necessary to abolish or severely limit donative transfers during life, which seems difficult, if not impossible. In the United States, several kinds of inter vivos transfers serve the same function as a will and are widely used: joint tenancy; gift of a remainder interest, reserving a life

estate, often in a revocable trust; designating a death beneficiary on a contract, pension plan, or bank account. Indeed, more property passes at death to survivors by way of these inter vivos arrangements than by way of will or intestacy.

3.   In Hodel v. Irving, the Court says, somewhat disingenuously, "The fact that it may be possible for the owners of these interests to effectively control disposition upon death through complex inter vivos transactions such as revocable trusts, is simply not an adequate substitute for the rights taken, given the nature of the property." Perhaps the Court has in mind revocable trusts prepared for Rockefellers and the like, but in fact a revocable trust can be very simple. A signed writing providing, "I hereby declare that I hold my fractional interest in Sioux Tribal lands in a revocable trust, for my benefit for my life, and on my death the interest is to go to Patrick Pumpkin Seed," is a valid and sufficient revocable trust (see pages 299-307). The donor now holds the property in trust, and it will go to Patrick Pumpkin Seed on the donor's death, without probate, unless the donor revokes the trust. There is nothing inherently more complex about an inter vivos trust than about a will.

4.   In many societies wills are not permitted. With respect to Native American tribal lands, for example, wills were unknown until Congress forced individual allotments on the tribes. Even then, before 1910, Native American allottees were not permitted to devise their lands.

In some countries, on the continent of Europe for example, children cannot be disinherited. They are "forced heirs." In Anglo-American history, the right to devise property has always been in uneasy tension with forced succession. As Lawrence M. Friedman, The Law of the Living, The Law of the Dead: Property, Succession, and Society, 1966 Wis. L. Rev. 1, 14, observes, "Practically speaking, forced succession means succession within the family — to the wife, children and other dependents. Forced succession . . . converts private property at death to family property." In early feudal times, forced succession had the upper hand. Prior to 1540, when the Statute of Wills was enacted, a will of land was not permitted at law in England. The legal title to land owned at death passed to the eldest son, subject to the surviving spouse's dower or curtesy. In the United States, married women could not devise land without the consent of their husbands until the enactment of Married Women's Property Acts in the late nineteenth century. By the twentieth century, forced succession reappeared when statutes were enacted giving the surviving spouse a forced share of one-third or one-half of the decedent's estate, which the surviving spouse may not be deprived of by the decedent spouse's will. In Louisiana, where the civil law of France was introduced, minor and disabled children may not be disinherited. (On protection of spouse and children, see Chapter 7.)

Although §207 of the Indian Land Consolidation Act speaks of "escheat" to the tribe, in effect the section makes the tribe the successor to, or heir of, the Native American owner of the affected fractioned land. Why is forced succession by a tribe not constitutionally permissible when forced succession by family members would be? If the Native Americans wanted tribal ownership restored, is there any way to change back to tribal ownership without paying individuals for their allotted lands? Is there any way to get the genie back in the bottle?

5.   While Hodel v. Irving was being argued in the Eighth Circuit Court of Appeals, Congress amended §207 of the Indian Land Consolidation Act to provide: "Nothing in this section shall prohibit the devise of such an escheatable

fractional interest to any other owner of an undivided fractional interest in such parcel or tract of trust or restricted land." 25 U.S.C. §2206(b). The amendment was not retroactive and hence did not affect the operation of §207 on the property involved in the case.

The amended statute was held unconstitutional in Babbitt v. Youpee, 519 U.S. 234 (1997), on the ground that the statute permits devise only among a very limited group (other owners of the parcel), which is not likely to include a lineal descendant of the decedent, usually the primary object of the decedent's bounty.

Litigation over Native American lands held in trust continues. For example, in United States v. White Mt. Apache Tribe, 537 U.S. 465 (2003), the Supreme Court held that, although the federal government was authorized to operate Fort Apache on lands held in trust for the White Mountain Apache Tribe, the government still owed duties under trust law to manage the property for the beneficiaries and to avoid damage to it.

6.   For further reading on the changing institution of inheritance in this country, from its earliest days to the present, see Carole Shammas, Marylynn Salmon & Michel Dahlin, Inheritance in America: From Colonial Times to the Present (1987); Marvin B. Sussman, Judith N. Cates & David T. Smith, The Family and Inheritance (1970).

For a fascinating study of the legal minefield of devising property to slaves in the antebellum South, see Adrienne D. Davis, The Private Law of Race and Sex: An Antebellum Perspective, 51 Stan. L. Rev. 221 (1999). The fundamental challenge was how to uphold testamentary freedom without disrupting racial hierarchies. Slaves were regarded as property, and the idea of property owning property was baffling. Professor Davis examines the wills of white men who devised property to their children by slave women, or to the women themselves, and the tensions and contradictions in legal doctrine these devises caused.

2.   *The Policy of Passing Wealth at Death*

TALCOTT PARSONS ET AL., THE "GIFT OF LIFE" AND ITS RECIPROCA-TION, 39 SOC. RES. 367, 369 (1972): "[I]t is biologically normal for all individual organisms to die. Death is now understood to be an important mechanism enhancing the adaptive flexibility of the species through the sacrifice of individuals; i.e., it makes certain that the bearers of newly emergent genetic patterns will rapidly succeed the bearers of older ones. Death may be even more critically important in contributing to cultural growth and flexibility than in supporting genetic change. Thus, we may regard death as a major contributor to the evolutionary enhancement of life, and thereby it becomes a significant part of the aggregate "gift of life" that all particular lives should end in death."

––––––––––––––––––

Why do we allow the passing of property at death? After a person dies, there are several things that could happen to his or her property. Suppose that when Marlon Brando died he left a leather jacket that he wore in a film, or that Kurt Cobain (of Nirvana) left one of his favorite guitars, or that Princess Diana, the Duchess of Wales, left a valuable necklace. What, for example, are the options regarding

Diana's necklace? Among the possibilities are: (1) destroying it; (2) burying it along with the Princess, as was often done with valuable jewelry in ancient Egypt; (3) treating it as unowned and allowing a free-for-all in which the first person to grab it is the new owner; (4) confiscation by the government; and (5) honoring Diana's wishes. Since mandatory destruction is wasteful and a free-for-all would encourage people to hover around a dying person like vultures, the alternatives worth serious consideration are some form of confiscation and the current system of private succession (limited somewhat by estate taxes and, as we shall see, perhaps a mandatory share for one's surviving family). This debate raises questions about the inequality of wealth in American society and the desirability — and feasibility — of a more confiscatory approach.

JOHN A. BRITTAIN, INHERITANCE AND THE INEQUALITY OF MATERIAL WEALTH 13 (1978): "The less the rewards of wealth are associated with one's own contribution, the better the case for taxing them. . . . Inheritance remains one of the purest forms of 'getting something for nothing.'"

Edward C. Halbach, Jr., An Introduction to Death, Taxes and Family Property
in Death, Taxes and Family Property 3, 5-7 (Edward C. Halbach, Jr., ed., 1977)[2]

What justifications are there for the private transmission of wealth from generation to generation? And how do we rationalize allowing only some individuals, selected by accident of birth, to enjoy significant comforts and power they have not earned?

Many arguments are offered in support of the institution of inheritance. One is simply that, in a society based on private property, it may be the least objectionable arrangement for dealing with property on the owner's death. Another is that inheritance is natural and proper as both an expression and a reinforcement of family ties, which in turn are important to a healthy society and a good life. After all, a society should be concerned with the total amount of happiness it can offer, and to many of its members it is a great comfort and satisfaction to know during life that, even after death, those whom one cares about can be provided for and may be able to enjoy better lives because of the inheritance that can be left to them. Furthermore, it is argued, giving and bequeathing not only express but beget affection, or at least responsibility. Thus, society is seen as offering a better and happier life by responding to the understandable desire of an individual to provide for his or her family after death.

Just as individuals may be rewarded through this desire, it can also be used by society, via inheritance rights, to serve as an incentive to bring forth creativity, hard work, initiative and ultimately productivity that benefits others, as well as encouraging individual responsibility — encouraging those who can to make provision that society would otherwise have to make for those who are or may be dependents. Of course, some doubt the need for such incentives, at least beyond modest levels of achievement and wealth accumulation, relying on the quest for

2. Reprinted from Death, Taxes and Family Property (Edward C. Halbach, Jr., ed., 1977) with permission of the West Publishing Company. Copyright © 1977 by West Publishing Co.

power (or for recognition) and other motivations—not to mention habit. Long after these forces have taken over to stimulate the industry of such individuals, however, society may continue to find it important to offer property inducements to the irrepressibly productive to save rather than to consume, and to go on saving long after their own lifelong future needs are provided for. And what harm is there if individuals, through socially approved channels, pursue immortality and psychological satisfactions? The direct and indirect (e.g., through life insurance and through corporate accumulations) savings of individuals are vital to the economy's capital base and thus to its level of employment and to the productivity of other individuals.

Consequently, it is concluded, inheritance may grant wealth to *donees* without regard to their competence and performance, but the economic reasons for allowing inheritance are viewed in terms of proper rewards and socially valuable incentives to the *donor*. In fact, some philosophers would insist, these rewards are required by ideals of social justice as the fruits of one's labors.

JEREMY BENTHAM, THE THEORY OF LEGISLATION 184 (C.K. Ogden ed., 1950): "[W]hen we recollect the infirmities of old age, we must be satisfied that it is necessary not to deprive it of this counterpoise of factitious attractions [prospects of inheritance by the younger giving care to the older]. In the rapid descent of life, every support on which man can lean should be left untouched, and it is well that interest serve as a monitor to duty."

Melvin L. Oliver, Thomas M. Shapiro & Julie E. Press, "Them That's Got Shall Get": Inheritance and Achievement in Wealth Accumulation
in 5 Research in Politics and Society: The Politics of Wealth and Inequality 69, 73-74
(Richard E. Ratcliff, Melvin L. Oliver & Thomas M. Shapiro eds., 1995)

The role and extent of inherited wealth is an important issue that occupies considerable attention among economists. However, their theoretically driven models of the importance of inherited wealth support a wide and quite contradictory range of findings. One end estimates that 80 percent of great wealth is inherited. The other end estimates that inherited wealth comprises only 20 percent of the wealthy's stockpile and 80 percent is earned the old fashioned way. In any event the amount and meaning of inherited wealth is considerable. For example, the wealthiest generation of elderly people in America's history is in the process of passing along its wealth.

Between 1987 and 2011 the baby boom generation stands to inherit an estimated 6.8 trillion dollars.[3] Much of this wealth was built by their parents between the late 1940s and the late 1960s when real wages and savings rates were higher and housing costs were considerably lower. For the elderly middle class, the

---

3. A more recent study projects that between 1998 and 2017 some $11.6 to $17.5 trillion will pass from decedents' estates. John J. Havens & Paul G. Schervish, Millionaires and the Millennium: New Estimates of the Forthcoming Wealth Transfer and the Prospects for a Golden Age of Philanthropy, Boston College Social Welfare Institute (1999).—Eds.

escalation of real estate prices over the last 20 years has meant a significant boon to their assets. Of course not all will benefit equally, or at all. The richest one percent will divide one-third of the worth of estates, each inheritance per estate receiving an average inheritance of $6 million; the next richest nine percent will divide another third for an average inheritance of about $396,000. Much of this wealth will be property. Philosopher Robert Nozick says that this "sticks out as a special kind of unearned benefit that produces unequal opportunities."

De Tocqueville warned the first new nation about the social and political dangers of inherited wealth becoming the basis of enduring privilege. He wrote: "What is the most important for democracy is not that great fortunes should not exist, but that great fortunes should not remain in the same hands. In that way there are rich men, but they do not form a class."

Forbes Magazine, in its 2003 annual report on the 400 richest Americans, listed 400 individuals from Bill Gates with $46 billion to five people with $600 million, the minimum to qualify for the list. Forbes designated inheritance as the source of wealth for less than one-third of the 400 richest, though in reading the fuller descriptions, a majority appear to have inherited most of their wealth. For example, the ten richest Americans include Sam Walton's widow Helen Walton and their four children, but the source of their fortune is given as Wal-Mart, not inheritance.

Using standard estimates of wealth that ignore human capital and most entitlements, Professor Repetti reviews the trends:

> Wealth concentration in the United States decreased from 1929 to 1979. The share of our country's net worth held by the top one percent of wealthiest households declined from more than 44.2% in 1929 to 20.5% in 1979. During the same period, productivity grew rapidly. Beginning in the early 1980s, however, the share of net worth held by the top 1% increased markedly, and by 1989, it had grown to 35.7%. After 1989, the concentration of wealth held steady. The result was that at the end of the twentieth century, wealth was more concentrated in the United States than in the United Kingdom. This was a reversal from the early years of the twentieth century when the U.S. tradition of "economic democracy" had resulted in a much lower concentration than the "royalist legacy" of Britain. [James R. Repetti, Democracy, Taxes and Wealth, 76 N.Y.U.L. Rev. 825, 825-826 (2001).]

Wealth is sometimes defined by economists as a discounted future income stream. If wealth measures were complete, however, they would include human capital, such as a law or medical school degree, as well as expected entitlement benefits, such as social security, pensions, and government income assistance. Yet even if these were included, differences in wealth remain stark. Professor Langbein explains:

> These calculations presuppose that financial instruments, business interests, and real property are the only important components of wealth. Because this way of measuring wealth excludes the capitalized value of the income streams generated by human capital, and because it excludes the capitalized value of the private-pension and Social Security income streams, it materially overstates the disparity between the top wealth holders and the rest of the populace. These calculations also overlook

what economists call the life-cycle effect: University of Michigan law students who will have six-figure incomes within a decade are currently reckoned as paupers. Nevertheless, the underlying point is undeniable. The top sliver of wealth holders is indeed very affluent . . . . [John H. Langbein, The Twentieth-Century Revolution in Family Wealth Transmission, 86 Mich. L. Rev. 722, 729 (1988).]

The most powerful argument against permitting transmission of wealth is that the transfer of great fortunes perpetuates wide disparities in the distribution of wealth, concentrates inherited economic power in the hands of a few, and denies equality of opportunity to the poor. It also tends to reward not merit or productivity but the chance of fortunate birth. For insightful discussions of these problems, see Ronald Chester, Inheritance, Wealth and Society (1982); Remi Clignet, Death, Deeds and Descendants: Inheritance in Modern America (1992); Edward J. McCaffery, The Uneasy Case for Wealth Transfer Taxation, 104 Yale L.J. 283 (1994); Inheritance and Wealth in America (Robert K. Miller, Jr. & Stephen J. McNamee eds., 1998); Edward N. Wolff, Top Heavy: A Study of the Increasing Inequality of Wealth in America (1995); William G. Gale & John Karl Scholz, Intergenerational Transfers and the Accumulation of Wealth, 8 J. Econ. Persp. (No. 4) 145 (1994).

In the United States, this argument once found a receptive ear in Congress, which for most of the last century imposed substantial estate and gift taxes on the rich. In a bizarre bit of economic planning, however, Congress is phasing out the federal estate tax, which drops to zero in 2010, but then is restored in full the following year. Most observers expect this scheme to be altered in the future, but whether we will have an estate tax in 2011 and beyond is unclear. In 2005, estate taxes are imposed on estates worth $1.5 million or more, with the exclusion rising to $2 million in 2006-2008, $3.5 million in 2009, and an unlimited amount in 2010. Rates for the taxable portion of estates range from 37 to 47 percent in 2005. Federal estate, gift, and generation-skipping taxes are dealt with in Chapter 14 of this book.

Mark L. Ascher, Curtailing Inherited Wealth
89 Mich. L. Rev. 69, 72-76 (1990)

About $150 billion pass at death each year. Yet in 1988 the federal wealth transfer taxes raised less than $8 billion. Obviously, these taxes could raise much more. If, to take the extreme example, we allowed the government to confiscate all property at death, we could almost eliminate the deficit with one stroke of a Presidential pen. This nation, however, rarely has used taxes on the transfer of wealth to raise significant revenue. Our historical hesitancy in this regard strongly suggests that we as a nation are unwilling to abolish inheritance in order to raise revenue. Nonetheless, thinking about using the federal wealth transfer taxes to abolish inheritance may not be entirely futile. It may permit an entirely new type of analysis. Conventional attempts to reform the federal wealth transfer taxes inevitably bog down in the Anglo-American tradition of freedom of testation. As begrudged intruders upon a general rule, these taxes necessarily end up playing an inconsequential role. One willing, for purposes of analysis, to discard freedom of testation could start from the proposition that property rights should end at death. Inheritance then would be tolerated only as an exception to that general rule. This article does just that. I invite the reader to join me in speculating whether it might not make sense to use the federal wealth transfer taxes to curtail inheritance, thereby increasing equality of opportunity while raising revenue.

My proposal views inheritance as something we should tolerate only when necessary — not something we should always protect. My major premise is that all property owned at death, after payment of debts and administration expenses, should be sold and the proceeds paid to the United States government. There would be six exceptions. A marital exemption, potentially unlimited, would accrue over the life of a marriage. Thus, spouses could continue to provide for each other after death. Decedents would also be allowed to provide for dependent lineal descendants. The amount available to any given descendant would, however, depend on the descendant's age and would drop to zero at an age of presumed independence. A separate exemption would allow generous provision for disabled lineal descendants of any age. Inheritance by lineal ascendants (parents, grandparents, etc.) would be unlimited. A universal exemption would allow a moderate amount of property either to pass outside the exemptions or to augment amounts passing under them. Thus, every decedent would be able to leave something to persons of his or her choice, regardless whether another exemption was available. Up to a fixed fraction of an estate could pass to charity. In addition, to prevent circumvention by lifetime giving, the gift tax would increase substantially.

My proposal strikes directly at inheritance by healthy, adult children. And for good reason. We cannot control differences in native ability. Even worse, so long as we believe in the family, we can achieve only the most rudimentary successes in evening out many types of opportunities. And we certainly cannot control many types of luck. But we can — and ought to — curb one form of luck. Children lucky enough to have been raised, acculturated, and educated by wealthy parents need not be allowed the additional good fortune of inheriting their parents' property. In this respect, we can do much better than we ever have before at equalizing opportunity. This proposal would leave "widows and orphans" essentially untouched. The disabled, grandparents, and charity would probably fare better than ever before. But inheritance by healthy, adult children would cease immediately, except to the extent of the universal exemption.

This proposal sounds radical, perhaps even communistic. Inheritance does seem to occupy a special place in the hearts of many Americans, even those who cannot realistically expect to inherit anything of significance. . . . My proposal . . . reaches the conclusion that substantial limitations on inheritance would contribute meaningfully to the equality of opportunity we offer our children. It also concludes that such limitations are fully consistent with our notions of private property. Neither conclusion is new. What is new is a $200 billion deficit. Now, as at few other times in this nation's history, our government needs new sources of revenue. Accordingly, I suggest changes in the federal wealth transfer taxes that would curtail inheritance and raise revenue. If we cannot, or will not, control the deficit, this generation's primary bequest to its children will be the obligation to pay their parents' debts. . . .

My proposal starts from the proposition that inheritance should be permitted only where public policy clearly justifies it. I find that justification in six different contexts. Spousal inheritance would always be allowed, but the amount would depend upon the length of the marriage. Inheritance by dependent lineal descendants would be permitted, subject to limitations based on the beneficiary's age [under 25 years]. Large trusts for disabled lineal descendants would be encouraged. Inheritance by lineal ascendants would be unlimited. Charity could take up to 20%. And, in any event, $250,000 would be exempt [and could be spread among anyone]. Thus, many types of inheritance would continue. In fact, my proposal leaves untouched estates of $250,000 or less.

Irving Kristol, Taxes, Poverty, and Equality
Pub. Int. 26-28 (No. 37, Fall 1974)

Large disparities of income, leading in turn to large concentrations of wealth, and these leading in turn to large *inherited* concentrations of wealth — such, it has long been recognized, compose a very special problem for democracy. The primal nightmare of the democracy is the emergence of an oligarchy that would, through the power associated with wealth, perpetuate itself, and eventually constitute a kind of aristocracy. So the question of the distribution of wealth is a proper concern for any democratic society. Whether, in the United States today, this question is acute is a matter of opinion and controversy. Since our economic historians tell us that, over the past 150 years, the distribution of wealth has probably become less unequal, it is not obvious that the subject should exercise us unduly. But let us assume, for the moment, that we decided it *was* acute enough (or was widely perceived to be acute enough) for us to do something about it. What might we do?

The question, oddly enough, is quite easy to answer: We should discourage the inheritance of large fortunes. This is a quite traditional liberal idea — Montesquieu and Jefferson would both have approved of it — nor is that such a difficult task. All we have to do is decide — and legislate — that no large fortunes should outlast the lifetime of the man who made it, but rather that such a large fortune should dissolve into much smaller fortunes upon his death. Thus, we could make it a matter of public policy and law that no individual could inherit, in a lifetime, more than one million dollars — and any possessor of a large fortune must distribute it, prior to death or by testament, to his children, his relatives, his friends, anyone, but no one receiving more than that maximum legacy, which would be tax-free. (Institutional donations, of course, could be of any size.) Should he fail to do so, a government would levy a 100 percent tax on the undistributed portion of his estate.

There would seem to the many advantages to such a policy. It does not discourage the incentive to invest and make money — anyone can still become enormously rich in his lifetime. Moreover, the foreknowledge that he would have to distribute his riches means that the wealthy man would, in his lifetime, be the recipient of much flattering attention and of many honors. He would, in addition, have the pleasure associated with the plenary power disposing of his wealth as he saw fit — rewarding some, failing to reward others. No large fortune what outlast a generation; but there would still be enough wealthy people around to support charities, private educational institutions, unpopular political causes, and minority cultural tastes — in other words, to act as a useful counterbalance to the ever-increasing weight of government and the public sector. Even the children of the rich would benefit, since it has long been recognized that the inheritance of large sums of money tends to distort the motivations and corrupt the characters of young people.

It can be predicted that any such proposal would provoke the hostility of the wealthy, who really do — it is perfectly natural — have dreams of their families moving through oligarchy to eventual aristocracy. But it can also be predicted that any such proposal would be contemptuously dismissed by great many liberal reformers. Why? The explanation is simple: when modern liberals talk about "the redistribution of income," they rarely mean a simple redistribution among individuals — more often they mean a redistribution *to the state*, which will then take a proper egalitarian measures. No proposal for the redistribution of large fortunes will get liberal support unless that money goes into the public treasury, where liberals will have much to say as to how it should be spent. That is the "dirty little secret" — the hidden agenda — behind the current chatter about the need for redistribution. The talk is about equality, the substance is about power.

QUESTIONS

In 1990, Professor Ascher proposed limiting the size of estates to be passed down to $250,000 (nearly $400,000 in 2005 dollars), with partial or complete exceptions for property passing to spouses, parents, children under the age of 25, disabled persons, and charities. In 1974, Irving Kristol explored the possibility of limiting the amount that someone could inherit to $1 million (nearly $4 million in 2005 dollars). Kristol says that it would be easy to implement his system, and though Ascher recognizes some obvious problems with his proposal, such as corresponding restrictions on gifts, he too presents his system as feasible. What would be the likely effects of an attempt to implement either approach? How would bargain sales and sweetheart employment contracts be distinguished from legitimate sales and employment contracts? How would family and business relations change? What sorts of legal and illegal avoidance mechanisms would arise? What might you advise a client wanting to provide more generously for his family? In the long run, what might be the general economic effects of such reforms?

NOTE: INHERITANCE IN THE ERSTWHILE SOVIET UNION

In 1918 the Soviet Bolsheviks, carrying out the teaching of Marx and Engels, abolished inheritance. The 1918 law, translated into English, read: "Inheritance, testate and intestate, is abolished. Upon the death of the owner his property (movable and immovable) becomes the property of the R.S.F.S.R." [1918] 1 Sob. Uzak., RSFSR, No. 34, item 456, Apr. 26, 1918. Within four years, however, inheritance was reestablished. The abolition of inheritance proved unpopular, and the Soviet rulers, on second thought, decided it was an institution encouraging savings and an incentive to work. Inheritance was also viewed as a method of providing for dependents of the deceased, relieving the state of this burden, and of furthering family unity and stability. Before the dissolution of the Soviet Union, the Soviet law of inheritance did not substantially differ from the civil law of inheritance found in Western Europe. See Frances Foster, The Development of Inheritance Law in the Soviet Union and the People's Republic of China, 33 Am. J. Comp. L. 33 (1985); Comment, Soviet Inheritance Law: Ideological Consistency or a Retreat to the West?, 23 Gonz. L. Rev. 593 (1988).

"Having a fine old name really has been enough for me."

Drawing by Wm. Hamilton.
© The New Yorker Collection 1977 William Hamilton from cartoonbank.com.
All Rights Reserved.

Inequality may result not only from inherited wealth, but also from the creation of human capital in children. The following excerpts make this point brilliantly and raise the following question: If economic inheritance were abolished, would it be even more difficult to break up an upper class?

Walter J. Blum & Harry Kalven, Jr., The Uneasy Case
for Progressive Taxation
19 U. Chi. L. Rev. 417, 501-504 (1952)

There is still another road leading to the problem of equality. Almost everybody professes to be in favor of one kind of equality — equality of opportunity. What remains to be investigated is the relationship between this kind of equality and economic equality. . . . In terms of the justice of rewards, the point is that no race can be fair unless the contestants start from the same mark. . . .

It might simplify matters somewhat to go directly to the heart of the problem — the children. . . . The important inequalities of opportunity are inequalities of environment, in its broadest sense, for the children. It is the inequalities in the worlds which the children inherit which count, and this inheritance is both economic and cultural.

. . . The critical economic inheritance consists of the day to day expenditures on the children; it is these expenditures which add up to money investments in the children's health, education and welfare which in the aggregate are, at least in our society, gravely disparate. No progressive inheritance tax, or combination of gift and inheritance taxes, can touch this source of economic inequalities among children. On the other hand a progressive income tax can, as one of its effects, help to minimize this form of unequal inheritance. It is income, not wealth, which is the important operative factor here, and by bringing incomes closer together the tax tends to bring money investments in children closer together.

But the gravest source of inequality of opportunity in our society is not economic but rather what is called cultural inheritance for lack of a better term. Under modern conditions the opportunities for formal education, healthful diet and medical attention to some extent can be equalized by economic means without too greatly disrupting the family. However, it still remains true that even today much of the transmission of culture, in the narrow sense, occurs through the family, and no system of public education and training can completely neutralize this form of inheritance. Here it is the economic investment in the parents and the grandparents, irrevocably in the past, which produces differential opportunities for the children. Nor is this the end of the matter. It has long been recognized that the parents make the children in their own image, and modern psychology has served to underscore how early this process begins to operate and how decisive it may be. The more subtle and profound influences upon the child resulting from love, integrity and family morale form a kind of inheritance which cannot, at least for those above the minimum subsistence level, be significantly affected by economic measures, or possibly by any others. If these influences on the members of the next generation are to be equalized, nothing short of major changes in the institution of the family can possibly suffice. At a minimum such changes would include socializing decisions not only about how children are to be raised but who is to raise them. And this in turn would call into question the very having of children.

John H. Langbein, The Twentieth-Century Revolution in Family Wealth Transmission
86 Mich. L. Rev. 722, 723, 732-733, 736 (1988)

The main purpose of this article is to [call attention to] the ways in which . . . changes in the nature of wealth have become associated with changes of perhaps comparable magnitude in the timing and in the character of family wealth transmission. My first theme . . . concerns human capital. Whereas of old, wealth transmission from parents to children tended to center upon major items of patrimony such as the family farm or the family firm, today for the broad middle classes, wealth transmission centers on a radically different kind of asset: the investment in skills. In consequence, intergenerational wealth transmission no longer occurs primarily upon the death of the parents, but rather, when the children are growing up, hence, during the parents' lifetimes. . . .

My thesis is quite simple, and, I hope, quite intuitive. I believe that, in striking contrast to the patterns of last century and before, in modern times the business of educating children has become the main occasion for intergenerational wealth transfer. Of old, parents were mainly concerned to transmit the patrimony — prototypically the farm or the firm, but more generally, that "provision in life" that rescued children from the harsh fate of being a mere laborer. In today's economic order, it is education more than property, the new human capital rather than the old physical capital, that similarly advantages a child. . . .

From the proposition that the main parental wealth transfer to children now takes place inter vivos, there follows a corollary: Children of propertied parents are much less likely to expect an inheritance. Whereas of old, children did expect the transfer of the farm or firm, today's children expect help with educational expenses, but they do not depend upon parental wealth transfer at death. Lengthened life expectancies mean that the life-spans of the parents overlap the life-spans of their adult children for much longer than used to be. Parents now live to see their children reaching peak earnings potential, and those earnings often exceed what the parents were able to earn. Today, children are typically middle-aged when the survivor of their two parents dies, and middle-aged children are far less likely to be financially needy. It is still the common practice within middle- and upper-middle-class families for parents to leave to their children (or grandchildren) most or all of any property that happens to remain when the parents die, but there is no longer a widespread sense of parental responsibility to abstain from consumption in order to transmit an inheritance.

———————————

For stimulating further discussion of arguments for and against inheritance, see Stephen R. Munzer, A Theory of Property 380-418 (1990); Adam J. Hirsch & William K.S. Wang, A Qualitative Theory of the Dead Hand, 68 Ind. L.J. 1, 6-14 (1992). Both studies cite many earlier contributions to the literature.

3. An Introduction to the Problem of the Dead Hand

During life, a person can use her wealth to influence the conduct of her friends and family. To what extent should a person be able to use wealth to influence behavior after death? Arthur Hobhouse wrote over 100 years ago in condemning the "cold and numbing influence of the Dead Hand":

> A clear, obvious, natural line is drawn for us between those persons and events which the Settlor knows and sees, and those which he cannot know and see. Within the former province we may push his natural affections and his capacity of judgment to make better dispositions than any external Law is likely to make for him. Within the latter, natural affection does not extend, and the wisest judgment is constantly baffled by the course of events. . . . What I consider to be not conjectural, but proved by experience in all human affairs, is, that people are the best judges of their own concerns; or if they are not, that it is better for them, on moral grounds, that they should manage their own concerns for themselves, and that it cannot be wrong continually to claim this liberty for every Generation of mortal men. [Arthur Hobhouse, The Dead Hand 188, 183-185 (1880).]

Restatement (Third) of Property: Wills and Other Donative Transfers (2003)

§10.1 Donor's Intention Determines the Meaning of a Donative Document
        and Is Given Effect to the Maximum Extent Allowed by Law

The controlling consideration in determining the meaning of a donative document is the donor's intention. The donor's intention is given effect to the maximum extent allowed by law.

COMMENT:

a. Rationale. The organizing principle of the American law of donative transfers is freedom of disposition. Property owners have the nearly unrestricted right to dispose of their property as they please. . . .

c. Effect of a donative document. Unless disallowed by law, the donor's intention not only determines the meaning but also the effect of a donative document.

American law does not grant courts any general authority to question the wisdom, fairness, or reasonableness of the donor's decisions about how to allocate his or her property. The main function of the law in this field is to facilitate rather than regulate. The law serves this function by establishing rules under which sufficiently reliable determinations can be made regarding the content of the donor's intention.

American law curtails freedom of disposition only to the extent that the donor attempts to make a disposition or achieve a purpose that is prohibited or restricted by an overriding rule of law. . . .

Among the rules of law that prohibit or restrict freedom of disposition in certain instances are those relating to spousal rights; creditors' rights; unreasonable restraints on alienation or marriage; provisions promoting separation or divorce; impermissible racial or other categoric restrictions; provisions encouraging illegal activity; and the rules against perpetuities and accumulations.

Shapira v. Union National Bank

Ohio Court of Common Pleas, Mahoning County, 1974
39 Ohio Misc. 28, 315 N.E.2d 825

HENDERSON, J.   This is an action for a declaratory judgment and the construction of the will of David Shapira, M.D., who died April 13, 1973, a resident of this county. By agreement of the parties, the case has been submitted upon the pleadings and the exhibit.

The portions of the will in controversy are as follows:

Item VIII. All the rest, residue and remainder of my estate, real and personal, of every kind and description and wheresoever situated, which I may own or have the right to dispose of at the time of my decease, I give, devise and bequeath to my three (3) beloved children, to wit: Ruth Shapira Aharoni, of Tel Aviv, Israel, or wherever she may reside at the time of my death; to my son Daniel Jacob Shapira, and to my son Mark Benjamin Simon Shapira in equal shares, with the following qualifications: . . .

   (b) My son Daniel Jacob Shapira should receive his share of the bequest only, if he is married at the time of my death to a Jewish girl whose both parents were Jewish. In the event that at the time of my death he is not married to a Jewish girl whose both parents were Jewish, then his share of this bequest should be kept by my executor for a period of not longer than seven (7) years and if my said son Daniel Jacob gets married within the seven year period to a Jewish girl whose both parents were Jewish, my executor is hereby instructed to turn over his share of my bequest to him. In the event, however, that my said son Daniel Jacob is unmarried within the seven (7) years after my death to a Jewish girl whose both parents were Jewish, or if he is married to a non Jewish girl, then his share of my estate, as provided in item 8 above should go to The State of Israel, absolutely.

The provision for the testator's other son Mark, is conditioned substantially similarly. Daniel Jacob Shapira, the plaintiff, alleges that the condition upon his inheritance is unconstitutional, contrary to public policy and unenforceable because of its unreasonableness, and that he should be given his bequest free of the restriction. Daniel is 21 years of age, unmarried and a student at Youngstown State University.

CONSTITUTIONALITY

Plaintiff's argument that the condition in question violates constitutional safeguards is based upon the premise that the right to marry is protected by the Fourteenth Amendment to the Constitution of the United States. Meyer v. Nebraska (1923), 262 U.S. 390; Skinner v. Oklahoma (1942), 316 U.S. 535; Loving v. Virginia (1967), 388 U.S. 1. . . . In Loving v. Virginia, the court held unconstitutional as violative of the Equal Protection and Due Process Clauses of the Fourteenth Amendment an antimiscegenation statute under which a black person and a white person were convicted for marrying. In its opinion the United States Supreme Court made the following statements, 388 U.S. at page 12.

> There can be no doubt that restricting the freedom to marry solely because of racial classifications violates the central meaning of the Equal Protection Clause.
> . . . The freedom to marry has long been recognized as one of the vital personal rights essential to the orderly pursuit of happiness by free men.
> Marriage is one of the "basic civil rights of man," fundamental to our very existence and survival. . . . The Fourteenth Amendment requires that the freedom of choice to marry not be restricted by invidious racial discriminations. Under our Constitution, the freedom to marry, or not to marry, a person of another race resides with the individual and cannot be infringed by the State.

From the foregoing, it appears clear, as plaintiff contends, that the right to marry is constitutionally protected from restrictive state legislative action. Plaintiff submits, then, that under the doctrine of Shelley v. Kraemer (1948), 334 U.S. 1, the constitutional protection of the Fourteenth Amendment is extended from direct state legislative action to the enforcement by state judicial proceedings of private provisions restricting the right to marry. Plaintiff contends that a judgment of this court upholding the condition restricting marriage would, under Shelley v. Kraemer, constitute state action prohibited by the Fourteenth Amendment as much as a state statute.

In Shelley v. Kraemer the United States Supreme Court held that the action of the states to which the Fourteenth Amendment has reference includes action of state courts and state judicial officials. Prior to this decision the court had invalidated city ordinances which denied blacks the right to live in white neighborhoods. In Shelley v. Kraemer owners of neighboring properties sought to enjoin blacks from occupying properties which they had bought, but which were subjected to privately executed restrictions against use or occupation by any persons except those of the Caucasian race. Chief Justice Vinson noted, in the course of his opinion at page 13: "These are cases in which the purposes of the agreements were secured only by judicial enforcement by state courts of the restrictive terms of the agreements."

In the case at bar, this court is not being asked to enforce any restriction upon Daniel Jacob Shapira's constitutional right to marry. Rather, this court is being asked to enforce the testator's restriction upon his son's inheritance. If the facts and circumstances of this case were such that the aid of this court were sought to enjoin Daniel's marrying a non-Jewish girl, then the doctrine of Shelley v. Kraemer would be applicable, but not, it is believed, upon the facts as they are. . . .

Basically, the right to receive property by will is a creature of the law, and is not a natural right or one guaranteed or protected by either the Ohio or the United States constitution. . . . It is a fundamental rule of law in Ohio that a testator may legally entirely disinherit his children. . . . This would seem to demonstrate that, from a constitutional standpoint, a testator may restrict a child's inheritance. The court concludes, therefore, that the upholding and enforcement of the provisions of Dr. Shapira's will conditioning the bequests to his sons upon their marrying Jewish girls does not offend the Constitution of Ohio or of the United States. United States National Bank of Portland v. Snodgrass (Or. 1954), 275 P.2d 860; Gordon v. Gordon (Mass. 1955), 124 N.E.2d 228; 54 Mich. L. Rev. 297 (1955); cf. 39 Minn. L. Rev. 809 (1955).

PUBLIC POLICY

The condition that Daniel's share should be "turned over to him if he should marry a Jewish girl whose both parents were Jewish" constitutes a partial restraint upon marriage. If the condition were that the beneficiary not marry anyone, the restraint would be general or total, and, at least in the case of a first marriage, would be held to be contrary to public policy and void. A partial restraint of marriage which imposes only reasonable restrictions is valid, and not contrary to public policy: . . . The great weight of authority in the United States is that gifts conditioned upon the beneficiary's marrying within a particular religious class or faith are reasonable. . . .

Plaintiff contends, however, that in Ohio a condition such as the one in this case is void as against the public policy of this state. . . . Plaintiff's position that the free choice of religious practice cannot be circumscribed or controlled by contract is substantiated by Hackett v. Hackett (Ohio App. 1958), 150 N.E.2d 431. This case held that a covenant in a separation agreement, incorporated in a divorce decree, that the mother would rear a daughter in the Roman Catholic faith was unenforceable. However, the controversial condition in the case at bar is a partial restraint upon marriage and not a covenant to restrain the freedom of religious practice; and, of course, this court is not being asked to hold the plaintiff in contempt for failing to marry a Jewish girl of Jewish parentage. . . .

It is noted, furthermore, in this connection, that the courts of Pennsylvania distinguish between testamentary gifts conditioned upon the religious faith of the beneficiary and those conditioned upon marriage to persons of a particular religious faith. In In re Clayton's Estate (1930), 13 Pa. D. & C. 413, the court upheld a gift of a life estate conditioned upon the beneficiary's not marrying a woman of the Catholic faith. In its opinion the court distinguishes the earlier case of Drace v. Klinedinst (Pa. 1922), 118 A. 907, in which a life estate willed to grandchildren, provided they remained faithful to a particular religion, was held to violate the public policy of Pennsylvania.[4] In *Clayton's Estate*, the court said that the condition concerning marriage did not affect the faith of the beneficiary, and that the condition, operating only on the choice of a wife, was too remote to be regarded as coercive of religious faith. . . .

The only cases cited by plaintiff's counsel in accord with [plaintiff's contention] are some English cases and one American decision. In England the courts have held that partial restrictions upon marriage to persons not of the Jewish faith, or of Jewish parentage, were not contrary to public policy or invalid. Hodgson v. Halford (1879 Eng.) L.R. 11 Ch. Div. 959. Other cases in England, however, have invalidated forfeitures of similarly conditioned provisions for children upon the basis of uncertainty or indefiniteness. . . . Since the foregoing decisions, a later English case has upheld a condition precedent that a granddaughter-beneficiary marry a person of Jewish faith and the child of Jewish parents. The court . . . found . . . no difficulty with indefiniteness where the legatee married unquestionably outside the Jewish faith. Re Wolffe, [1953] 1 Week. L.R. 1211, [1953] 2 All Eng. 697.[5]

The American case cited by plaintiff is that of Maddox v. Maddox (1854), 52 Va. (11 Grattan's) 804. The testator in this case willed a remainder to his niece if she remain a member of the Society of Friends. When the niece arrived at a marriageable age there were but five or six unmarried men of the society in the neighborhood in which she lived. She married a non-member and thus lost her own membership. The court held the condition to be an unreasonable restraint upon marriage and void, and that there being no gift over upon breach of the condition, the condition was in terrorem, and did not avoid the bequest. It can be seen that while the court considered the testamentary condition to be a restraint upon marriage, it was primarily one in restraint of religious faith. The court said that with the small number of eligible bachelors in the area the condition would have operated as a virtual prohibition of the niece's marrying, and that she could not be expected to "go abroad" in search of a helpmate or to be subjected to the chance of being sought after by a stranger. . . . The other ground upon which the Virginia court rested its decision, that the condition was in terrorem because of

4. In In re Estate of Laning, 339 A.2d 520 (Pa. 1975), the court stated that the *Drace* case was correctly decided on the ground that the testator sought to require his grandchildren to "remain true" to the Catholic religion, and that the enforcement of a condition that they remain faithful Catholics would require the court to determine the doctrines of the Catholic church. "Such questions are clearly improper for a civil court to determine." The court went on to uphold a provision in Laning's will that the gift be distributed to certain relatives who held "membership in good standing" in the Presbyterian church; the court construed the provision to mean only a formal affiliation with the specified church, thus avoiding improper inquiry into church doctrine. — Eds.

5. In In re Tuck's Settlement Trusts, [1977] 2 W.L.R. 411, a trust was set up by the first Baron Tuck, a Jew, for the benefit of his successors in the baronetcy. Anxious to ensure that his successors be Jewish, he provided for payment of income to the baronet for the time being if and when and as long as he should be of the Jewish faith and married to a wife of Jewish blood and of the Jewish faith. The trust also provided that in case of any dispute the decision of the Chief Rabbi of London would be conclusive. The court held that the conditions were not void for uncertainty. Lord Denning was of the view that if there was any uncertainty, it was cured by the Chief Rabbi clause. The other two judges declined to reach that issue.

The question — who is a Jew — is not easy to answer, not even in Israel where it has provoked continuing controversy. See Mark J. Altschul, Israel's Law of Return and the Debate of Altering, Repealing, or Maintaining Its Present Language, 2002 U. Ill. L. Rev. 1345; Meryl Hyman, Who Is a Jew? (1998).

See generally Peter Butt, Testamentary Conditions in Restraint of Religion, 8 Sydney L. Rev. 400 (1977); Francis M. Nevins, Jr., Testamentary Conditions: The Principle of Uncertainty and Religion, 18 St. Louis U.L.J. 563 (1974). — Eds.

the absence of a gift over, is clearly not applicable to the case at bar, even if it were in accord with Ohio law, because of the gift over to the State of Israel contained in the Shapira will.

In arguing for the applicability of the Maddox v. Maddox test of reasonableness to the case at bar, counsel for the plaintiff asserts that the number of eligible Jewish females in this county would be an extremely small minority of the total population especially as compared with the comparatively much greater number in New York, whence have come many of the cases comprising the weight of authority uphold-ing the validity of such clauses. There are no census figures in evidence. While this court could probably take judicial notice of the fact that the Jewish community is a minor, though important segment of our total local population, nevertheless the court is by no means justified in judicial knowledge that there is an insufficient number of eligible young ladies of Jewish parentage in this area from which Daniel would have a reasonable latitude of choice.[6] And of course, Daniel is not at all confined in his choice to residents of this county, which is a very different circumstance in this day of travel by plane and freeway and communication by telephone, from the horse and buggy days of the 1854 Maddox v. Maddox decision. Consequently, the decision does not appear to be an appropriate yardstick of reasonableness under modern living conditions.

Plaintiff's counsel contends that the Shapira will falls within the principle of Fineman v. Central National Bank (1961 Ohio Com. Pleas), 175 N.E.2d 837, holding that the public policy of Ohio does not countenance a bequest or device conditioned on the beneficiary's obtaining a separation or divorce from his wife. Counsel argues that the Shapira condition would encourage the beneficiary to marry a qualified girl just to receive the bequest, and then to divorce her afterward. This possibility seems too remote to be a pertinent application of the policy against bequests conditioned upon divorce. . . . Indeed, in measuring the reason-ableness of the condition in question, both the father and the court should be able to assume that the son's motive would be proper. And surely the son should not gain the advantage of the avoidance of the condition by the possibility of his own impropriety.

Finally, counsel urges that the Shapira condition tends to pressure Daniel, by the reward of money, to marry within seven years without opportunity for mature reflection, and jeopardizes his college education. It seems to the court, on the contrary, that the seven year time limit would be a most reasonable grace period, and one which would give the son ample opportunity for exhaustive reflection and fulfillment of the condition without constraint or oppression. Daniel is no more being "blackmailed into a marriage by immediate financial gain," as suggested by counsel, than would be the beneficiary of a living gift or conveyance upon con-sideration of a future marriage—an arrangement which has long been sanctioned by the courts of this state. Thompson v. Thompson (1867), 17 Ohio St. 649.

In the opinion of this court, the provision made by the testator for the benefit of the State of Israel upon breach or failure of the condition is most significant

6. The American Jewish Yearbook of 1976 estimates the Jewish population of Youngstown, Ohio, to be 5,400 in 1974. Taking into consideration other U.S. census data about the male-to-female ratio and the ages of the population in Youngstown, we estimate that about 540 Jewish females were in the 15-24 age group. If this estimate is correct, do you think this gives Daniel "a reasonable latitude of choice"?—Eds.

for two reasons. First, it distinguishes this case from the bare forfeitures in . . . Maddox v. Maddox (including the technical in terrorem objection), and, in a way, from the vagueness and indefiniteness doctrine of some of the English cases. Second, and of greater importance, it demonstrates the depth of the testator's conviction. His purpose was not merely a negative one designed to punish his son for not carrying out his wishes. His unmistakable testamentary plan was that his possessions be used to encourage the preservation of the Jewish faith and blood, hopefully through his sons, but, if not, then through the State of Israel. Whether this judgment was wise is not for this court to determine. But it is the duty of this court to honor the testator's intention within the limitations of law and of public policy. The prerogative granted to a testator by the laws of this state to dispose of his estate according to his conscience is entitled to as much judicial protection and enforcement as the prerogative of a beneficiary to receive an inheritance.

It is the conclusion of this court that public policy should not, and does not preclude the fulfillment of Dr. Shapira's purpose, and that in accordance with the weight of authority in this country, the conditions contained in his will are reasonable restrictions upon marriage, and valid.

NOTES, QUESTIONS, AND PROBLEMS

Judge Richard A. Posner

1. What social objectives are accomplished by honoring control of a beneficiary's behavior by the dead hand, a hand that does not have a live mind controlling it and making a continuously informed judgment as circumstances change, that can no longer be affected by the opinions of mankind, and that does not suffer the consequences? Compare Richard A. Posner, Economic Analysis of Law §18.7 (6th ed. 2003):

Suppose a man leaves money to his son in trust, the trust to fail however if the son does not marry a woman of the Jewish faith by the time he is 25 years old. The judicial approach in such cases is to refuse to enforce the condition if it is unreasonable. In the case just put it might make a difference whether the son was 18 or 24 at the time of the bequest and how large the Jewish population was in the place where he lived.

This approach may seem wholly devoid of an economic foundation, and admittedly the criterion of reasonableness is here an unilluminating one. Consider, however, the possibilities for modification that would exist if the gift were inter vivos rather than testamentary. As the deadline approached, the son might come to his father and persuade him that a diligent search had revealed no marriageable Jewish girl who would accept him. The father might be persuaded to grant an extension or otherwise relax the condition. But if he is dead, this kind of "recontracting" is impossible, and the presumption that the condition is a reasonable one fails. This argues for applying the cy pres approach in private as well as charitable trust cases unless the testator expressly rejects a power of judicial modification.

You are Judge Posner. Daniel Shapira appears before you six-and-a-half years after his father's death and alleges that he has found no Jewish girl whom he desires who will accept him. What do you do?

In 1994 the editors asked the attorney who represented Daniel Shapira for information about the aftermath of the case. The attorney contacted Mr. Shapira, who declined to give any information. It was a bitter experience, he said, which he wanted to forget.

2. Restatement (Second) of Property: Donative Transfers §6.2 (1983) provides that a restraint to induce a person to marry within a religious faith is valid "if, and only if, under the circumstances, the restraint does not unreasonably limit the transferee's opportunity to marry." Comment a provides that "the restraint unreasonably limits the transferee's opportunity to marry if a marriage permitted by the restraint is not likely to occur. The likelihood of marriage is a factual question, to be answered from the circumstances of the particular case." The motive or purpose of the testator is irrelevant. Suppose that Daniel Shapira were gay. Would the get-married provision in Dr. Shapira's will be enforceable?

3. In *Shapira*, the court distinguished the *Maddox* case of 1854 on the ground that "in this day of travel by plane and freeway and communication by telephone," precedents on reasonableness from the "horse and buggy days" have lost their vitality. The question thus arises, would *Shapira* be an easier case today thanks to the availability of popular Jewish internet dating services such as JDate.com? See Amy Harmon, Online Dating Sheds Its Stigma as Losers.com, N.Y. Times, June 29, 2003, at 1.

4. A will or trust provision is ordinarily invalid if it is intended or tends to encourage disruption of a family relationship. Thus, provisions encouraging separation or divorce have usually been held invalid, unless the dominant motive of the testator is to provide support in the event of separation or divorce. See Restatement (Second) of Property: Donative Transfers §7.1 (1983); In re Estate of Donner, 623 A.2d 307 (N.J. Super. 1993) (upholding father's trust denying daughter trust income or principal until age 65 unless her husband's death or a divorce should earlier occur, on ground that the decedent had a reasonable economic basis to withhold support unless daughter became breadwinner of family). Cf. Hall v. Eaton, 631 N.E.2d 805 (Ill. App. 1994).

In Girard Trust Co. v. Schmitz, 20 A.2d 21 (N.J. Ch. 1941), the court held invalid a condition that the testator's brothers and sisters must not communicate, either orally or in writing, with a brother and sister disliked by the testator. The court said it would not "lend its hand to help the testator use the power of his wealth to disrupt this family. . . . [S]ociety condemns all acts, be they contractual or testamentary, which tend to disturb the peace and harmony of families and to make inharmonious that which the state is interested in creating and preserving. 'As are families, so is society.'" Id. at 37. Accord, Estate of Romero, 847 P.2d 319 (N.M. App. 1993) (voiding condition discouraging youthful children from living with their mother, testator's former wife).

5. Frederick Foagy has a daughter-in-law who goes by the name of Nicole Bates-Foagy, coupling her maiden name, Bates, with that of her husband, Arthur Foagy. Frederick, no feminist, doesn't cotton to women using double-barreled

names. Frederick dies. His will leaves $100,000 to Nicole on condition that she legally change her name to Nicole Foagy and use only that name. Is this condition enforceable? See Restatement (Second) of Property: Donative Transfers §7.2, reporter's notes 5 & 6 (1983).

6. *Destruction of property at death.* A fundamental justification of private property is that society's total wealth usually is maximized by permitting private individuals to decide what is the best use of their property. Each individual, we ordinarily assume, makes rational choices to maximize her wealth; that economic loss from foolish or wrong decisions falls on the individual acts as a deterrent to irrational decisions. Hence a person can, if she wishes, destroy her property during life (unless it is subject to historic preservation or similar laws). For if she does, she bears most of the economic consequences of her decision, plus or minus. The question thus arises: Should a testator be permitted to order the destruction of property at death when the main economic loss is not visited upon the testator but on others? On the other hand, if a testator expects that her wishes for post-death destruction of her property will not be followed, will she suffer a loss (in money or pleasure) during life resulting from her expectation that her destructive wishes will not be honored after her death? Consider the following:

(a) The testator's will directs his executor to tear down the testator's house because the testator does not want anyone else to live in it. Can the executor tear down the house? Should a court order the house destroyed? See Eyerman v. Mercantile Trust Co., 524 S.W.2d 210 (Mo. App. 1975) ("a well-ordered society cannot tolerate" waste). If the testator had anticipated this result, might he have destroyed his house during life, earlier than would have given him the most pleasure?

(b) A photographer wants his executor to destroy all of his negatives because he fears that they will be used to create cheap copies of his best photos, thus diminishing the value of the genuine prints that he created in his darkroom. If the photographer anticipates that his destructive wishes might be ignored, will he be tempted to destroy his negatives too early in his life, when he could have received money or pleasure from their continued existence? See Lior Jacob Strahilevitz, The Right to Destroy, 114 Yale L.J. 781 (2005).

(c) Justice Hugo L. Black of the U.S. Supreme Court was of the view that private notes of the justices relating to Court conferences should not be published posthumously. Justice Black feared publication might inhibit free and vigorous discussion among the justices. Black was struck ill, destroyed his conference notes, resigned from the Court, and died a few weeks later. Suppose that Justice Black had died suddenly while on the bench and that his will had directed his executor to destroy his conference notes. Could the executor do this without a court order? Should a court order destruction of the notes, which might have enormous value to a Court historian? Who would have standing to object?

(d) Franz Kafka bequeathed his diaries, manuscripts, and letters to his friend Max Brod, directing him to burn everything. Brod declined to do so on the ground that Kafka's unpublished work was of great literary value. Should Brod have ordered a bonfire? See Max Brod, Postscript, *in* Franz Kafka, The Trial 326 (1925, Mod. Lib. ed. 1956), discussed in William R. Bishin & Christopher D. Stone, Law, Language, and Ethics 1-9 (1972). Suppose that Franz Schubert and Giacomo Puccini had ordered their unfinished works destroyed at death, thus depriving the world of Schubert's unfinished Symphony in B Minor and Puccini's unfinished opera Turandot. Should a court order destruction?

(e) Professor John Orth calls to our attention that Virgil left instructions to destroy the Aeneid ("Arms and the man I sing"), which he left unfinished. The Emperor Augustus ordered the executors to disregard the order. See Moses Hadas, A History of Latin Literature 142 (1952). Orth asks: "The course of Western literature would be unimaginable without 'arms and the man'! Who would have guided Dante in Hell?"

Building on the insight of Professor Shavell and others that, before death, the living do internalize some of the future costs of excessive or seemingly wasteful dead-hand control, Professor Strahilevitz argues for a nearly absolute rule favoring the right to destroy property after death. See Steven Shavell, Foundations of Economic Analysis of Law 67-72 (2004); Strahilevitz, supra. Strahilevitz argues that, by refusing while alive to sell the item to be destroyed, the testator internalizes the relevant costs. But does she? Strahilevitz's analysis assumes that testators are fully rational and perfectly informed, rather than subject to systematic biases that tend to prevent them from internalizing the full costs to all parties of their destructive wishes. Moreover, he does not deal squarely with the main argument against allowing post-death destruction, that such destruction tends, *on balance*, to promote economic waste even if it is not always economically wasteful.[7]

7.   Restatement (Third) of Trusts §29(c) (2003) invalidates trusts that are "contrary to public policy." The comments and reporter's notes contain an extensive discussion of the issues raised above. Generally, the Restatement (Third) frowns on restraints on beneficiary behavior, including restraints on marriage or religious freedom, disrupting family relationships, and choice of careers, but calls for balancing of conflicting social values. The reporter's notes include this account of an incentive for unhealthy behavior from a 1993 Associated Press story from Romania:

> A man who was nagged by his wife to stop smoking has left her everything—but only if she takes up his habit as punishment for 40 years of "hell," newspapers reported Saturday.
>
> Marin Cemenescu, who died last week in his hometown of Timisoara at age 76, stipulated in his will that to inherit his house and $30,000 estate, his 63-year-old wife Aneta must smoke five cigarets a day for the rest of her life, the Romania Libera daily reported.
>
> "She could not stand to see me with a cigaret in my mouth, (and) I ended up smoking in the bathroom like a schoolboy," Cemenescu reportedly wrote in his will.
>
> "My life was hell," he wrote.
>
> The report said that Mrs. Cemenescu plans a legal challenge to the conditions of the will. "I'd rather lose everything than touch a cigaret," she told the newspaper.
>
> The report did not specify the cause of Cemenescu's death or say whether it was related to his smoking.

8.   For a penetrating analysis of testamentary gifts conditioned upon specified conduct by the beneficiary, see Jeffrey G. Sherman, Posthumous Meddling: An Instrumentalist Theory of Testamentary Restraints on Conjugal and Religious

---

7. That the economic effect of destruction could be positive or negative was noted in the 2000 Sixth Edition of this casebook. Yet in one portion of his 2005 article, Strahilevitz uses as a straw man an excerpt from the 1983 Third Edition.

Choices, 1999 U. Ill. L. Rev. 1273. Professor Sherman rejects the balancing test of "contrary to public policy" and makes a principled analysis of why testation should be permitted and under what limitations. He concludes that testamentary conditions calculated to restrain legatees' personal conduct should not be enforced. The article is especially readable because it is laced with Sherman's delicious wit.

SECTION B.   TRANSFER OF THE DECEDENT'S ESTATE

1.   *Probate and Nonprobate Property*

All the decedent's assets at death can be divided into probate and nonprobate property. *Probate property* is property that passes under the decedent's will or by intestacy. *Nonprobate property* is property passing under an instrument other than a will. People often have the idea that probate under a will or intestacy is the usual way to pass property at death, but this is false. Most property is transferred at death outside of probate, through nonprobate transfers. Nonprobate property includes the following:

(a) *Joint tenancy property, both real and personal.* Under the theory of joint tenancy, the decedent's interest vanishes at death. The survivor has the whole property relieved of the decedent's participation. No interest passes to the survivor at the decedent's death. In order for the survivor to perfect title to real estate, all the survivor need do is file a death certificate of the decedent. Bank accounts, brokerage and mutual fund accounts, and real estate are often held in joint tenancy, particularly between married couples.

(b) *Life insurance.* Life insurance proceeds of a policy on the decedent's life are paid by the insurance company to the beneficiary named in the insurance contract. The company will pay upon receipt of a death certificate of the insured.

(c) *Contracts with payable-on-death provisions.* A decedent may have a contract with a bank, an employer, or some other person or corporation to distribute the property held under the contract at the decedent's death to a named beneficiary. Pension plans often provide survivor benefits. Tax-deferred investment plans (IRAs, Keoghs, and the like) often name a death beneficiary. In nearly all states, it is possible to put a death beneficiary on stock custodian accounts held in a brokerage firm. To collect property held under a payable-on-death contract, all the beneficiary need do is file a death certificate with the custodian holding the property.

(d) *Interests in trust.* When property is transferred in trust, the trustee holds the property for the benefit of the named beneficiaries, who may have life estates or remainders or other types of interests. The property is distributed to the beneficiaries by the trustee in accordance with the terms of the trust instrument. The trust may have been created by the decedent during life or by some other person. If created by the decedent, the trust may be revocable or irrevocable. If the decedent has a testamentary power of appointment over assets in the trust, the decedent's will must be admitted to probate, but the trust assets are distributed directly by the trustee to the beneficiaries named in the will and do not go through probate.

As indicated above, distribution of nonprobate assets does not involve a court proceeding, but is made in accordance with the terms of a contract or trust or deed. Distribution of probate assets under a will or to intestate successors may require a court proceeding involving probate of a will or a finding of intestacy followed by appointment of a personal representative to settle the probate estate. Nonprobate transfers are dealt with in Chapter 5 of this book. See also John H. Langbein, The Nonprobate Revolution and the Future of the Law of Succession, 97 Harv. L. Rev. 1108 (1984).

2. Administration of Probate Estates

a. History and Terminology

When a person dies and probate is necessary, the first step is the appointment of a *personal representative* to oversee the winding up of the decedent's affairs. The principal duties of the personal representative are (1) to inventory and collect the assets of the decedent; (2) to manage the assets during administration; (3) to receive and pay the claims of creditors and tax collectors; (4) to clear any titles to cars, real estate, or other assets; and (5) to distribute the remaining assets to those entitled. If the decedent dies testate and in the will names the person who is to execute (that is, carry out the terms of) the will and administer the probate estate, such personal representative is called an *executor*. When the person in charge of administering the estate is not named in the will, the personal representative is called an *administrator*. Personal representatives are appointed by, under the control of, and accountable to a court, generally referred to as a *probate court.*

One of the advantages of writing a will is that the testator can designate who is to administer the estate.[8] If a person dies intestate or leaves a will that fails to name an executor who qualifies, the administrator is selected from a statutory list of persons who are to be given preference, typically in the following order: surviving spouse, children, parents, siblings, creditors.

The person appointed as administrator must give bond. In most states, if the will names an individual rather than a corporate fiduciary as executor, the executor also must give bond unless the will waives the bond requirement, which is routinely waived in most wills. Thus, another reason for writing a will is that the expense of a fiduciary bond can be eliminated if that appears desirable.

Historically, in England, three courts had jurisdiction over probate. The king's common law courts controlled succession to land, which was the base of power in the feudal system. The ecclesiastical courts controlled succession to personal property, which, before the time of the Tudors and the rise of England as a trading power, was of little value (cows, sheep, utensils, personal ornaments, and such made up the personal property of medieval life). During the course of the sixteenth century, after Henry VIII's break with Rome, the ecclesiastical courts declined drastically in power. When Parliament attempted to strengthen the

---

8. In a number of states, nonresident corporate fiduciaries cannot be appointed as executor, and in a few states this prohibition extends to nonresident individuals. See Jeffrey A. Schoenblum, 2004 Multistate Guide to Estate Planning at Tables 3.01 & 3.03.

ecclesiastical courts a hundred years later by enacting the Statute of Distributions (1670), it was too late. A basic shift in the public's attitude toward the proper role of the church in secular affairs had already occurred, and the common law courts and chancery continued to impede the clergy's control of administration of personal property. With its flexible procedure and its power to enforce personal duties, chancery gradually took over the administration of personal property. Ecclesiastical jurisdiction over decedents' estates was finally abolished in 1857, when a court of probate was established in chancery. However, the common law courts' jurisdiction over the succession to land continued. Not until 1925, with the Administration of Estates Act, was one English court given sole jurisdiction over succession to real and personal property.

Today, in the United States, one court in each county has jurisdiction over administration of decedents' estates. The name of the court varies from state to state. It may be called the surrogate's court, the orphan's court, the probate division of the district court or chancery court, or something else. But all of these differently named courts are referred to collectively as probate courts. And "to go through probate" means to have an estate administered in one of these courts.

One needlessly complicating factor in this field is that we have two legal vocabularies—one applicable to real property, the other to personal property. It is often suggested that these parallel vocabularies are traceable to the historic fact that the English common law courts had jurisdiction over succession to real property whereas ecclesiastical courts controlled succession to personal property in England until the nineteenth century. But in most instances this is not provable. Take *last will and testament*. A common belief is that this phrase arose because a *will* disposed of real property and a *testament* disposed of personal property; therefore one instrument disposing of both was a will and testament. The belief that *testament* referred to personal property is based on its Latin origin (testamentum). It is assumed that the Latin-trained ecclesiastical courts introduced *testament* into the language to refer to an instrument disposing of property over which they had jurisdiction. It is then assumed that *will*, an old English word, was used by the common law courts and by a process of association came to relate to land, the type of property over which these courts had jurisdiction. The evidence does not support these assumptions. As far back as the records go, the words have sometimes been used interchangeably. To speak of a testament disposing of land or of a will disposing of a cow would not have sounded strange to the medieval ear. Professor Mellinkoff believes the phrase *last will and testament* is traceable to the law's habit of doubling Old English words with synonyms of Old French or Latin origin (for example, *had and received, mind and memory, free and clear*), "helped along by a distinctive rhythm." David Mellinkoff, The Language of the Law 331 (1963). In any case, the myth that a will disposes of land and a testament disposes of chattels dies terribly, terribly slowly. Today, it is perfectly proper to use the single word *will* to refer to an instrument disposing of both real and personal property.

A person dying testate *devises* real property to *devisees* and *bequeaths* personal property to *legatees*. Using devise to refer to land and bequest to refer to personalty became a lawyerly custom little more than a hundred years ago,[9] although the distinction, like that between will and testament, is sometimes erroneously thought

---

9. Cf. William Shakespeare, King John, act I, scene 1, line 109: "Upon his death-bed he by will bequeath'd/His lands to me. . . ."

to have had more ancient roots in the different courts handling the decedent's property. Although these linguistic distinctions still have currency, there are signs that synonymous usage is returning in respectable circles. The Restatement of Property applies *devise* to both realty and personalty. In drafting wills, "I give" is an excellent substitute for "I devise," "I bequeath," and "I give, devise, and bequeath." "I give" effectively transfers any kind of property, and no fly-specking lawyer can ever fault you for using the wrong verb.

When intestacy occurs we use different words to describe what happens to the intestate's real property and what happens to his personal property. We say real property *descends to heirs*; personal property is *distributed to next-of-kin*. At common law, heirs and next-of-kin were not necessarily the same. For example, when primogeniture, which applied only to land, was in effect, real property descended to the eldest son, but personal property was distributed equally among all the children. Today, in almost all states, a single *statute of descent and distribution* governs intestacy. The same persons are named as intestate successors to both real and personal property. Thus, today the word *heirs* usually means those persons designated by the applicable statute to take a decedent's intestate property, both real and personal. *Next-of-kin* usually means exactly the same thing.

At common law, a spouse was not an heir; he or she had only what were called *curtesy* or *dower* rights (rights to take a share of some of the spouse's property). Today, in all states the statutes of descent and distribution name the spouse as a possible intestate successor, depending upon who else survives, and a spouse thus may be an heir.

In this book, we do not use the Latin suffix indicating feminine gender for women playing important roles in our cast: testator, executor, and administrator. Although *testatrix*, *executrix*, and *administratrix* are still in current fashion, other *-trix* forms either have disappeared from use (for example, *donatrix, creditrix*) or would sound odd to the contemporary ear (for example, *public administratrix*).[10] And of course it does not matter whether the person in the given role is a man or a woman.[11] We have tried to avoid words that assign a role to one sex, but we dare not hope that we have succeeded in a field so long dominated by assumptions of male superiority in property management. We believe it was Bentham who observed, "Error is never so difficult to be destroyed as when it has its root in language."

b.   A Summary of Probate Procedure

(1)   Opening probate

Though the general pattern of administering decedents' probate estates is quite similar in all jurisdictions, there are widespread variations in the procedural details. In each state, the procedure is governed by a collection of statutes and court rules giving meticulous instructions for each step in the process. Happily, this precludes our being concerned about specific rules and procedures and enables us to advise you that you can safely postpone any concern about the

---

10. See *-trix* in Oxford English Dictionary (1989).

11. The Supreme Court has held unconstitutional a statute giving preference to a male to serve as executor or administrator. Reed v. Reed, 404 U.S. 71 (1971).

mechanics of probating a will and administering an estate until you can "learn by doing" when that first estate file comes across your desk. When that day comes, you will find that there are available in most jurisdictions excellent probate practice books, which will be of assistance. The purpose of the following description is to provide background information necessary for estate planning.

Probate performs three functions: (1) it provides evidence of transfer of title to the new owners by a probated will or decree of intestate succession; (2) it protects creditors by requiring payment of debts; and (3) it distributes the decedent's property to those intended after the creditors are paid. Probate procedures are designed with these functions in mind.

The will should first be probated, or letters of administration should first be sought, in the jurisdiction where the decedent was domiciled at the time of death. This is known as the *primary* or *domiciliary* jurisdiction. If real property is located in another jurisdiction, *ancillary administration* in the jurisdiction is required. The purpose of requiring ancillary administration is to prove title to real property in the situs state's recording system and to subject those assets to probate for the protection of local creditors. Ancillary administration may be costly because the state may require that a resident be appointed personal representative, with a local attorney. Executor's commissions and attorney's fees will be paid to them for handling the ancillary assets.

Each state has a detailed statutory procedure for issuance of *letters testamentary* to an executor or *letters of administration* to an administrator authorizing the person to act on behalf of the estate. Several states, mainly east of the Mississippi, follow the procedure formerly used by the English ecclesiastical courts in distinguishing between contentious and noncontentious probate proceedings. Under the English system, the executor had a choice of probating a will *in common form* or *in solemn form*. Common form probate was an ex parte proceeding in which no notice or process was issued to any person. Due execution of the will was proved by the oath of the executor or such other witnesses as might be required. The will was admitted to probate at once, letters testamentary were granted, and the executor began administration of the estate. If no one raised any questions or objections, this procedure sufficed. However, within a period of years thereafter an interested party could file a caveat, compelling probate of the will in solemn form. Under probate in solemn form, notice to interested parties was given by citation, due execution of the will was proved by the testimony of the attesting witnesses, and administration of the estate involved greater court participation. Ex parte or common form procedure is recognized in many states, sometimes preserving the common form/solemn form terminology, but more often not.

The majority of states do not permit ex parte proceedings but require prior notice to interested parties before the appointment of a personal representative or probate of a will. In these states, the petition for letters must be accompanied by an affidavit stating that the statutory notice requirements have been met (personal service, mailing, or publishing). At the hearing, if a will is to be probated, it must be proved by the testimony or affidavits of the witnesses. The hearing may be before the probate judge or a clerk.

The Uniform Probate Code (UPC), originally promulgated in 1969, revised in 1990, and adopted in a number of states, is representative of statutes regulating probate procedures. It provides for both ex parte probate and notice probate. The former is called *informal probate* (rather than common form probate), the latter *formal probate* (rather than solemn form probate). The person asking for letters can choose informal or formal probate; the theory is that one may be more useful in a particular estate than another and a choice should be available. UPC §3-301 (1990) sets forth the requirements for informal probate. Without giving notice to anyone, the representative petitions for appointment; the petition contains pertinent information about the decedent and the names and addresses of the spouse, the children or other heirs, and, if a will is involved, the devisees. If the petition is for probate of a will, the original will must accompany the petition; the executor swears that, to the best of his or her knowledge, the will was validly executed; proof by the witnesses is not required. A will that appears to have the required signatures and that contains an attestation clause showing that requirements of execution have been met is probated by the registrar without further proof. UPC §3-303 (1990). Within 30 days after appointment, the personal representative has the duty of mailing notice to every interested person, including heirs apparently disinherited by a will. UPC §3-705 (1990).

Formal probate under the UPC is a judicial determination *after notice* to interested parties. Any interested party can demand formal probate. A formal proceeding may be used to probate a will, to block an informal proceeding, or to secure a declaratory judgment of intestacy. Formal proceedings become final judgments if not appealed.

No proceeding, formal or informal, may be initiated more than three years from the date of death. UPC §3-108 (1990). If no will is probated within three years after death, the presumption of intestacy is conclusive. The three-year statute of limitations of the UPC changes the common law, which permits a will to be probated at any time, perhaps many years after the testator's death. See Annot., 2 A.L.R.4th 1315 (1980).

For a description of estate administration under the UPC, see Paul G. Haskell, Preface to Wills, Trusts and Administration 181-224 (2d ed. 1994).

Time for contest. The time for contesting probate of a will is dependent upon a statute in the particular jurisdiction. The period of limitations for filing a will contest is ordinarily jurisdictional and is not tolled by any fact not provided by statute. If the constitutional and statutory requirements for notice are complied with, when the period of limitation passes, the probate court no longer has jurisdiction to revoke probate. Probate of a will thereby becomes final. See Larkin v. Ruffin, 398 So. 2d 676 (Ala. 1981) (holding order admitting will to probate cannot be set aside three-and-a-half years later when evidence is discovered showing will had been revoked). The rules on will contests under the UPC are in §§3-401 to 3-414.

Barring creditors of the decedent. Every state has a statute requiring creditors to file claims within a specified time period; claims filed thereafter are barred. These are known as *nonclaim statutes*. They come in two basic forms: either (1) they bar claims not filed within a relatively short period after probate proceedings are begun, generally two to six months (four months under the UPC); or (2), whether or not probate proceedings are commenced, they bar claims not filed within a longer period after the decedent's death, generally one to five years (one year under the UPC). UPC §3-803 (1997). Under short-term statutes, creditors usually are notified of the requirement to file claims only by publication in a newspaper after probate proceedings are opened. The Supreme Court has held, however, that the Due Process Clause requires that known or reasonably ascertainable creditors receive actual notice before they are barred by a short-term statute running from the commencement of probate proceedings. Tulsa Prof. Collection Servs., Inc. v. Pope, 485 U.S. 478 (1988) (statute barring known creditors two months after newspaper publication objectionable). A one-year statute of limitations running from the decedent's death, barring creditors filing claims thereafter, is believed to be constitutional even without notice to creditors. Most states have such a statute. See also Sarajane Love, Estate Creditors, the Constitution, and the Uniform Probate Code, 30 U. Rich. L. Rev. 411 (1996); Mark Reutlinger, State Action, Due Process, and the New Nonclaim Statutes: Can No Notice Be Good Notice if Some Notice Is Not?, 24 Real Prop., Prob. & Tr. J. 433 (1990).

(2) *Supervising the representative's actions*

In many states, the actions of the personal representative in administering the estate are supervised by the court. This supervision can be time-consuming and costly. The court must approve the inventory and appraisal, payment of debts, family allowance, granting options on real estate, sale of real estate, borrowing of funds and mortgaging of property, leasing of property, proration of federal estate tax, personal representative's commissions, attorney's fees, preliminary and final distributions, and discharge of the personal representative. The sale of real estate may require several trips to the courthouse to get an order to sell, to file notice of all offers received, to give notice that a previous low bidder has overbid the previous high bid, and, finally, to get approval of the terms of the sale to the highest bidder.

In some states, the practice is for the personal representative to handle all these matters informally without court order, provided the interested parties are adults and approve the fiduciary's account and release the fiduciary from liability. If minors are involved, judicial supervision is ordinarily necessary.

The UPC authorizes unsupervised administration as well as supervised administration. If any interested party demands supervised administration, the probate court supervises the personal representative. But if no party demands it, administration is independent of the court. Under independent administration, after appointment, the personal representative administers the estate without going back into court. The representative has the broad powers of a trustee in dealing with the estate property and may collect assets, clear titles, sell property, invest in other assets, pay creditors, continue any business of the decedent, and distribute the estate—all without court approval. UPC §3-715 (1990). The estate may be closed by the personal representative filing a sworn statement that he has published notice to creditors, administered the estate, paid all claims, and sent a statement and accounting to all known distributees. UPC §3-1003 (1990). If at any time during independent administration an interested party is dissatisfied with the personal representative's actions, he may compel the representative to obtain court supervision. UPC §3-502 (1990).

(3) *Closing the estate*

The personal representative of an estate is expected to complete the administration and distribute the assets as promptly as possible. Even if all the beneficiaries are amicable, several things that must be done may prolong administration. Creditors must be paid. Titles must be cleared. Taxes must be paid and tax returns audited and accepted by the appropriate tax authorities. Real estate or a sole proprietorship may have to be sold.

Judicial approval of the personal representative's action is required to relieve the representative from liability, unless some statute of limitations runs upon a cause of action against the representative. The representative is not discharged from fiduciary duties until the court grants discharge.

c.   Is Probate Necessary?

Much is heard nowadays about the excessive cost of probate—or, as some have put it, the high cost of dying. The administrative costs of probate are mainly probate court fees, the commission of the personal representative, the attorney's fee, and sometimes appraiser's and guardian ad litem's fees. In most states, the personal representative's commission is set by statute at a fixed percentage of the probate estate. The fee of the attorney for the personal representative is sometimes set by statute, but more often it is determined by the court by reference to a number of factors (including customary charges for probate work, complexity of the estate, and time and labor required). These fees are deductible for federal estate tax or income tax purposes. Federal estate taxes begin on estates of $1.5 million in the year 2005 (with the exemption rising to $2 million in 2006-2008, $3.5 million in 2009, and an unlimited amount in 2010) with graduated rates from 37 percent to 47 percent in 2005. Hence, the net cost of probate fees in large estates may be substantially less than it appears. See Robert A. Stein & Ian G. Fierstein, The Role of the Attorney in Estate Administration, 68 Minn. L. Rev. 1107 (1984).

In most jurisdictions, a lawyer who serves as executor is entitled to fees for serving in both offices. See Cal. Prob. Code §10804 (2004); William M. McGovern, Jr. & Sheldon F. Kurtz, Wills, Trusts and Estates §12.5, at 535-536 (3d ed. 2004).

A 1988 study examined fees for estate attorneys in ten large states. For an ordinary $100,000 estate, fees ranged from $2,000 in Florida to $5,000 in New York and Pennsylvania. For an ordinary $600,000 estate, the fees ranged from $9,000 in Texas and Virginia to $22,000 in New York and Pennsylvania. Fees in California, Georgia, Illinois, Michigan, and Ohio were within these extremes. These numbers do not include the executor's commission, which was roughly the same amount as the attorney's fees. These estimates assume probate of a relatively simple estate with a house and no major valuation issues or disputes. Cal. L. Revision Commn. Rep. No. L-1036/1055, at 7, Oct. 26, 1988.

In view of the costs of probate and the attendant delays, the question is often asked: Can probate be avoided? The answer is Yes, provided the property owner during life transfers all his or her property into a joint tenancy or a revocable or irrevocable trust or, in many states, executes a contract providing for distribution of contract assets to named beneficiaries on the owner's death. As you will discover later, however, it is quite difficult for a rich person with a wide variety of assets to dispose of *all* property by nonprobate methods. Some property is not suitable for joint tenancy or trust or is not subject to disposition by contract. And, in any case, a will serves a backup function to catch overlooked property or property acquired after inter vivos changes in ownership have been made. Hence, even though a large portion of a person's assets can be arranged so as to avoid probate, probate administration may be necessary for some assets that pass by will or intestacy.

Nonetheless, even with property transferred by will or intestacy, probate is not always necessary. As a practical matter, establishment of the transferee's title is not necessary for many items of personal property, such as furniture or personal effects. A purchaser will assume that the possessor has title. But for items of personal property for which ownership is evidenced by a document, such as an automobile certificate of title or a stock certificate, the transferee needs some official recognition of his rights in order to transfer those rights. Statutes in all states permit heirs to avoid probate where the amount of property involved is small, but the states differ as to how much and what kind of property can be transferred without a formal administration. Among statutes commonly found are statutes permitting collection of small bank accounts or wage claims, or transfer of an automobile certificate of title to the decedent's heirs, upon affidavit by the heirs. By filling out the appropriate forms and presenting them to the bank, the employer, or the department of motor vehicles, the heir is able to collect the decedent's property or acquire a new certificate of title.

In addition, many states permit close relatives of the decedent to obtain possession of the decedent's personal property by presenting an affidavit to the holder of the property if the estate does not exceed a certain figure. The figure defining a *small estate*, which can be collected upon affidavit, ranges from $5,000 to over $100,000. The affidavit procedure authorized by these *collection statutes* does not give title to the recipient of the property, only possession. It merely permits those presumptively entitled to the decedent's property to collect it expeditiously and without a cumbersome estate proceeding. Possession of some types of property is tantamount to ownership.

Finally, statutes in some states permit filing a will for probate solely as a title document, with no formal administration to follow. And in some states, title insurance companies will insure real property sold by heirs if a certificate of death and affidavit of heirship is filed; probate proceedings are not required.

A study of five states found that the percentage of decedents' estates that underwent probate administration ranged from 20 percent in California to 34 percent in Massachusetts. Robert A. Stein & Ian G. Fierstein, The Demography of Probate Administration, 15 U. Balt. L. Rev. 54 (1985). Thus, by one way or another, the large majority of decedents manage to avoid probate.

PROBLEMS

1. Aaron Green died three weeks ago. His wife has come to your law firm with Green's will in hand: The will devises Green's entire estate "to my wife, Martha, if she survives me; otherwise to my children in equal shares." The will names Martha

Green as executor. An interview with Mrs. Green reveals that the Green family consists of two adult sons and several grandchildren and that Green owned the following property:

Furniture, furnishings, other items of tangible personal property (estimated value)	$10,000
Savings account in name of Aaron Green	5,000
Joint checking account on which Aaron and Martha Green were both authorized to write checks	1,500
Employer's pension plan, naming Martha Green for survivor's benefits	Life Annuity
Government bonds, payable to "Aaron or Martha Green"	5,000
Ordinary life insurance policy naming Martha Green as primary beneficiary	25,000
Ford car	7,500

Green owned no real property; he and his wife lived in a rented apartment. Green's debts consisted of last month's utility bills ($40) plus the usual consumer charge accounts: Visa card ($300 balance), the local department store ($125), Exxon ($35). There is also a funeral bill ($1,225) and the cost of a cemetery lot ($300). Mrs. Green wants your advice: What should she do with the will? Must it be offered for probate? Must there be an administration of her husband's estate?

2.   Same facts as in Problem 1 except that Green died intestate, and the state's statute of descent and distribution provides that where a decedent is survived by a spouse and children, one-half of his real and personal property shall descend to the spouse and the remaining one-half shall descend to the children.

3.   Same facts as in Problem 1 except that Green also owned a house and lot worth $85,000 and another lot worth $8,000. The deeds to both tracts name Aaron Green as grantee. The residential property is subject to a mortgage with a current balance of $42,000; title to the other lot is free of encumbrances. Must (should?) Green's will be probated and his estate formally administered?

4.   Let us look at Aaron Green's problem from another perspective. Suppose Green comes to you and tells you that he does not have a will. He describes his family situation and the assets owned by him: the assets listed in Problem 1 but not the real estate described in Problem 3. His question: In view of his family situation and his modest estate, does he really need a will?

d. Universal Succession

The English system of court-supervised administration of estates, which we inherited, was designed to protect creditors and to protect beneficiaries from an untrustworthy executor or heir. On the continent of Europe and in Louisiana, an entirely different system exists that rarely involves a court at all.

It is known as *universal succession,* meaning that the heirs or the residuary devisees succeed to the title of all of the decedent's property; there is no personal representative appointed by a court.

The heirs or the residuary devisees step into the shoes of the decedent at the decedent's death, taking the decedent's title and assuming all the decedent's liabilities and the obligation of paying legacies according to the decedent's will. If, for example, *O* dies intestate, leaving *H* as *O*'s heir, *H* succeeds to ownership of *O*'s property and must pay all of *O*'s creditors and any taxes resulting from *O*'s death. If *O* has three heirs, they hold as tenants in common at *O*'s death, with the ordinary rights of tenants in common. The payment of a commission to a fiduciary is not necessary, and a lawyer need not be employed unless the heirs decide they need legal advice. A system of universal succession can have enormous advantages where the heirs or the residuary devisees are all adults. See European Succession Laws (David Hayton ed., 2d ed. 2002).

The UPC authorizes universal succession as an alternative to probate administration. Under UPC §§3-312 to 3-322, the heirs or the residuary devisees may petition the court for universal succession. If the court ascertains that the necessary parties are included and that the estate is not subject to any current contest or difficulty, it issues a written statement of universal succession. The universal successors then have full power of ownership to deal with the assets of the estate. They assume the liabilities of the decedent to creditors, including tax liability. The successors are personally liable to other heirs omitted from the petition or, in the case of residuary devisees, to other devisees for the amount of property due them. No state has yet adopted these provisions of the UPC.

Universal succession is already available to a limited extent in the United States. Under California law, property that passes to the surviving spouse by intestacy or by will is not subject to administration unless the surviving spouse elects to have it administered. If the surviving spouse chooses not to have the property administered, the surviving spouse takes title to the property and assumes personal liability for the decedent's debts chargeable against the property. Cal. Prob. Code §§13500-13650 (2004). This exemption from probate raises an interesting question: If probate is not necessary for property passing to a surviving spouse, why is it necessary for property passing to adult children?

SECTION C. AN ESTATE PLANNING PROBLEM

1. *The Client's Letter and Its Enclosures*

January 15, 20___

Dear _____:

For some time now, Wendy and I have been considering the rewriting of our wills since we now have very simple wills giving our property to each other in case of death and then to our children when the survivor of us dies. However, in this day of air crashes where Wendy and I might die simultaneously, the problems of settling our estate might be complicated.

These, in general, are the assets with which we are concerned:

Residence	cost $125,000	($70,000 mtge.)
Lot, cabin, Lake Murray, ME	cost 20,000	worth more
Chevrolet station wagon	5,000	
Honda	3,000	
Household furniture, etc.	???	
Checking account	2,000 to 4,000	
Savings account	7,000	
Certificate of deposit	20,000	
IRA	30,000	
Stocks	170,000	
Mutual funds	70,000	
My life insurance	125,000	
Wendy's life insurance	100,000	
Mother's house at death	???	
Pension	???	

Wendy and I think our main objectives should be to avoid probate and to eliminate as many inheritance taxes as possible. I am enclosing copies of our present wills. These are some of the questions we would like your help on:

1.   It may be that we do not need wills at all. Can we let our property pass by inheritance or by joint and survivor arrangements? Our bank accounts and some of our stocks are set up to pass by a joint and survivor arrangement.

2.   As a sort of corollary to that first question, we have read in various places that it would be a good idea to set up a living trust to pass our house, cars, etc. With the use of a trust plus the joint and survivor arrangements, could we avoid the need for wills and probate entirely?

3.   If you think we should have wills, are our present ones all right? If not, how should they be changed?

Please let us hear from you at your earliest convenience.

Sincerely yours,

/s/ Howard Brown

Howard Brown

Last Will and Testament of Howard Brown

I, Howard Brown, of the city of Springfield, County of _____, and State of _____, do hereby make, publish, and declare this to be my Last Will and Testament, hereby revoking any and all other wills and codicils thereto, which I have heretofore made.

FIRST: I hereby direct that all of my just debts, funeral expenses, and expenses of administration of my estate be paid out of my estate as soon as may be practicable after my death.

SECOND: I name and appoint my wife, Wendy Brown, to be the executor of this my Last Will and Testament, and I direct that she not be required to give bond or other security.

THIRD: I give my remainder interest in my mother's house at 423 Elm St., Concord, Delaware, to my sister, Carol Gould.

FOURTH: I give, devise, and bequeath all the rest of my property, both real and personal, of whatever kind and nature and description, and wherever located, which I now own or may own at the time of my death, to my wife, Wendy Brown, should she survive me. Should she not survive me, I then give, devise, and bequeath all of my property, to my children.

FIFTH: I authorize and empower my Executor, or anyone appointed to administer this my Last Will and Testament, to sell and convert into cash any and all of my personal property without a court order and to convey any such real estate by deed without the necessity of a court order authorizing such conveyance or approving such deed.

SIXTH: In the event that my wife, Wendy Brown, predeceases me, I name and appoint my wife's sister, Lucy Preston Lipman, of San Francisco, California, as legal guardian of my children during their respective minorities.

IN TESTIMONY WHEREOF I have hereunto set my hand and seal this 27th day of November, 2002.

/s/ Howard Brown
_____
Howard Brown

The above instrument, consisting of two typewritten pages, of which this is the second, with paragraphs FIRST through SIXTH, inclusive, was on the 27th day of November, 2002, signed by Howard Brown, in our presence, and he did then declare this to be his Last Will and Testament, and we at his request and in his presence and in the presence of each other, did sign this instrument as witnesses thereunto and as witnesses to his signature thereto.

WITNESSES:

/s/ Michael Wong
_____

/s/ Patricia Muñoz Garcia
_____

[Wendy Brown's will contains reciprocal provisions, with the exception of the remainder interest in Howard's mother's house. Wendy leaves everything of hers to Howard if he survives, and if he does not survive her, to her children.]

2. Some Preliminary Questions Raised by Brown's Letter

From time to time, we shall refer back to the Brown estate planning situation in the context of the substantive areas being considered. But before we embark on our studies, it may be profitable to reflect on some of the questions raised in, and by, Brown's letter.

PROBLEMS

1. Examine Howard Brown's present will in the context of the asset and family situation described in his letter. Can you detect any problems that may be raised or any contingencies that are not provided for by the will provisions? Here are a few:

Article FIRST: Does the "just debts" clause require the executor to pay off the mortgage on the Browns' home? Would this be desirable? See In re Estate of Miller, 127 F. Supp. 23 (D.D.C. 1955); In re Estate of Keil, 145 A.2d 563 (Del. 1958). See also discussion of exoneration of liens, pages 413-414.

Would death taxes incurred at Howard Brown's death be "just debts," making this a tax apportionment clause requiring payment of all taxes, including those on the remainder interest in his mother's house, out of Howard's residuary estate? See Thompson v. Thompson, 230 S.W.2d 376, 380 (Tex. Civ. App. 1950); Estate of Kyreazis, 701 P.2d 1022 (N.M. App. 1985); Internal Revenue Code of 1986, §§2206, 2207.

Articles SECOND and FIFTH: Has suitable provision been made for appointment of an executor in case Wendy Brown dies before Howard? Does the executor have sufficiently broad powers to enable her to administer the estate effectively?

Article FOURTH: Is the dispositive plan provided by Howard's will a sound one? Should he make an outright distribution of his entire estate to Wendy, or should he consider making some other distribution?

Which of the assets listed in Howard Brown's letter will be governed by his will, and which will pass as nonprobate assets unaffected by the will?

Article SIXTH: If both Howard and Wendy Brown die before all their children attain majority, a guardianship administration will be required. Is this desirable? See pages 116-118.

2. In view of the Browns' asset and family situation, do they need wills at all? Will the intestacy laws of their home state provide a satisfactory distributive scheme for their assets at death?

Should the Browns consider alternatives to a will or intestacy, such as joint and survivor arrangements and inter vivos trusts, as a means of transferring their property at death?

Perhaps it has occurred to you by now that we don't really know very much about the Brown family or the assets they own. Without further information, we cannot answer these questions. What further information should we obtain from the clients before we can proceed further?

3. Additional Data on the Browns' Family and Assets

Following receipt of the letter from Howard Brown asking for a review of the present wills of Howard and Wendy Brown, a conference was held with the clients, and the following additional information was obtained.

a. Family Data

Members of Immediate Family		Age	Birth Date	Health
Husband	Howard Brown	43	7/12/—	good
Wife	Wendy Brown	41	6/1/—	"

Members of Immediate Family		Age	Birth Date	Health
Child of Wendy	Michael Walker	20	9/25/—	"
Child	Sarah Brown	14	11/19/—	"
Child	Stephanie Brown	11	8/22/—	"

Howard Brown is an industrial design engineer and manager of a department at Tresco Machine Tool Company in Springfield. He has been with this firm for the past eight years and feels that he has a secure and responsible position with the firm. His annual salary is $70,000.

Wendy Brown has a degree in modern languages and during the early years of their marriage taught German and French at a secondary school in Springfield. She then worked for several years only in the home. Four years ago Wendy decided to go to law school. Last year she finished law school and received a J.D. degree. (She did *not* take a course in wills and trusts.) Wendy has just accepted a position as an associate of Hanlon & Putz, a medium-size law firm. Her annual salary is $65,000.

Michael is Wendy's son by her first husband, Brian Walker, whom Wendy divorced when Michael was three years old. A year later, Wendy and Howard married, and Howard has raised Michael as a member of his family, though never formally adopting him. Brian stopped making child support payments a couple of years after the divorce and moved out of state. He has not been heard from in many years. Michael has left home and is living with (but not married to) an older woman, Candace Robinson, age 33. They have a child, Andy, age 1.

Residence

Home address: 2220 Casino Lane, Springfield. 477-5882
Period of residence in this state: All of life since college.
Note: No problems regarding domicile. Also, note that none of present assets acquired while residing in another state. Howard owns out-of-state property — a lot in Maine and a remainder interest in his mother's house in Delaware.

Parents; collateral relatives

Howard's parents. Howard Brown's father, Frank, died of a heart attack at age 60. His mother, Margaret Brown, a widow, is 63 years old, is in good health, and lives in Concord, Delaware. Howard stated that his mother has a modest but comfortable income from property left by her husband and from social security. Howard says his father devised his home to his wife Margaret for life, and on her death to Howard and his sister, Carol Gould.

Howard estimated that his mother owns property worth about $240,000, of which $75,000 is represented by her residence. Howard is familiar with the terms of his mother's will; it provides for an equal distribution between himself and Carol Gould. Howard is named as executor under the will.

Howard's collateral relatives. Howard has a younger sister, Carol Gould, who is a police officer with the Concord police department. Carol is divorced and lives with her mother; Carol has no children.

Wendy's parents. Wendy Brown's parents (Robert Preston, age 65, and Zoë Preston, age 62) are both living. Wendy stated that her father is a well-known doctor in Boston and is quite well off. When asked how well off, Wendy said he is probably "worth" around $900,000 (probably a conservative estimate). Wendy may acquire a substantial inheritance upon the death of her parents.

Wendy's collateral relatives. Wendy Brown's siblings: one sister, Lucy Preston Lipman, a writer, lives in San Francisco with her husband, Jonathan Lipman. They have two children. Her brother, Simon Preston, is married to Antonia Preston, has no children, and is a salesman. Her other sister, Ruth Preston, unmarried, is a professor of archeology at Swarthmore.

Wendy Brown also has a maternal aunt, Fanny Fox of Lexington, Kentucky. Aunt Fanny is a rich widow without children and has a large house full of antiques, paintings, silver — things she and her husband collected during their marriage. Wendy will likely inherit some of Aunt Fanny's things and possibly a substantial sum of money.

Special family problems

Michael is a stepchild of Howard. Michael has an out-of-wedlock child, Andy.

b.   Assets

The Browns have lived in Springfield since they were married 16 years ago. Since neither brought into the marriage any property of substantial value, there appears to be no problem in establishing their marital rights in the property they now own. All life insurance policies were taken out after the Browns married.

Tangible personal property

Tangible personalty consists of the usual furnishings in a family residence, two automobiles, outboard motor boat, personal effects such as clothing and jewelry, and other miscellaneous items. No items of unusual value. Estimated value: $20,000

Real estate

(1) Family residence. The Browns purchased their home at 2220 Casino Lane, Springfield, 15 years ago. Although the purchase price for the property was $125,000, Howard believes that it is now worth around $160,000, but this is a guesstimate. Present balance on mortgage loan (note held by Springfield Federal Savings & Loan Assn.) is $70,000. The deed shows that title to the property was taken by "Howard Brown and Wendy Brown, as joint tenants with right of survivorship and not as tenants in common." $160,000

(2) Lot and cabin, Lake Murray, Maine. Twelve years ago the Browns purchased a lot and cabin on Lake Murray for $20,000. Title to the land was taken in Howard Brown's name alone. Based on current values, the Browns believe they could sell the property for at least $75,000. No mortgage indebtedness.   75,000

(3) Mother's house. Howard has a remainder interest in 423 Elm St., Concord, Delaware, with his sister. House worth about $75,000. Howard's remainder roughly valued at $20,000.   20,000

Bank accounts

(1) Checking account, Springfield National Bank. The account balance fluctuates from around $2,000 to $4,000 each month. Howard and Wendy Brown are both authorized to draw checks on the account; the balance is payable to the survivor. $ 3,000

(2) Savings account, Springfield Federal Savings & Loan Assn. The account is in the name of Wendy Brown.   7,000

(3) Certificate of deposit, Springfield Federal Savings & Loan Assn., at 6 percent for four years. CD was issued in the name of "Howard Brown and Wendy Brown, as joint tenants with right of survivorship."   20,000

(4) IRA (Individual Retirement Account), Springfield Federal Savings & Loan Assn. Established by Howard Brown in 1990. Income taxes on contributions are deferred until the money is withdrawn or Howard reaches $70\frac{1}{2}$ or sooner dies. Current balance is $30,000. If Howard dies before withdrawal, balance is payable to Wendy Brown.   30,000

Securities

(1) 1,600 shares, General Corporation common stock. Given to Howard under his aunt's will six years ago. Current value: $50 per share. Registered in the name of Howard Brown as owner. $80,000

(2) 1,000 shares, Varoom Mutual Fund. When Howard's father died five years ago, his mother gave each of her children $7,500. Howard used all of this money to purchase 400 shares of the Varoom Fund, which has appreciated in value since his purchase. Howard has reinvested the ordinary income and capital gains dividends paid by the fund and now owns an additional 600 shares. Present value is $30 per share. Registered in the name of Howard Brown as owner.   30,000

(3) 1,000 shares, American Growth Mutual Fund. Over the years the Browns have invested in the American Growth Fund under some form of monthly investment plan. Their objective was to establish an educational fund for their children. The purchase price has fluctuated over the years from $28 to $42 a share. Present price is $40 a share. Howard says that he has kept records on the price of the shares as purchased. Registered in the name of "Howard Brown and Wendy Brown, as joint tenants with right of survivorship and not as tenants in common."   40,000

(4) 1,200 shares, Union National Bank common stock. Was given to Wendy Brown by her parents. Registered in the name of Wendy Brown as owner. 90,000

Life insurance

(1) Mutual of New York policy #624-05-91, ordinary life, participating, acquired 14 years ago. Annual premium $2,050. Cash surrender value this year $20,500; CSV is increasing at about $1,600/year. $100,000

(2) Aetna Life Group policy, group term. Premiums are paid by Howard Brown's employer. 25,000

(3) Prudential Life policy, group term. Premiums are paid by Wendy Brown's employers. 100,000

Policies (1) and (2) name Howard Brown as "insured" and "owner." The policies name Wendy Brown as primary beneficiary and the estate of Howard Brown as contingent beneficiary. Policy (3) names Wendy Brown as "insured" and "owner." The policy names Howard Brown as beneficiary. It names Wendy's children as secondary beneficiaries.

Employee benefits of Howard Brown

In addition to the group insurance mentioned above, Howard Brown's employer provides medical insurance, disability insurance, and a qualified pension plan. The plan will provide substantial retirement benefits to Howard, under a formula based on his years of service and his average annual salary. The present projection is that Howard would be able to retire at age 65 with an annuity of about $45,000.

The pension plan provides survivor benefits for the surviving spouse. If Howard survives to retirement age, the pension is payable as a joint and survivor annuity to Howard and his surviving spouse.

Employee benefits of Wendy Brown

In addition to the group insurance mentioned above, Wendy's law firm, Hanlon & Putz, provides group medical coverage. There are no pension benefits for associates, only for partners. Wendy Brown has been in practice for only a month. It is likely that her income will substantially exceed Howard's in a few years.

c. Liabilities

Real estate mortgages: $70,000 mortgage loan, Springfield Federal Savings & Loan Assn.

Other notes to banks, etc.: None.

Loans on insurance policies: None.

Accounts to others: "Usual" store, etc. accounts.

Other: None.

d. Assets and Liabilities: Summary

(1) Estate of Howard and Wendy Brown[12]

Tangible personalty	$ 20,000
Realty:	
Residence (joint tenancy)	160,000
Lake Murray property (in Howard's name)	75,000
Remainder interest in mother's home (Howard)	20,000*
Bank accounts:	
Checking (joint and survivor)	3,000
Savings (in Wendy's name)	7,000
Certificate of deposit (joint tenancy)	20,000
IRA (Howard's, payable on death to Wendy)	30,000
Securities:	
Varoom Mutual Fund (in Howard's name)	30,000*
General Corp. common (in Howard's name)	80,000*
American Growth Mutual Fund (joint tenancy)	40,000
Union Natl. Bank common (in Wendy's name)	90,000*
Life insurance on Howard 125,000	
Life insurance on Wendy 100,000	
Tresco pension plan (Howard's contributions)	10,000
	$810,000

(2) Liabilities

Mortgage loan, Springfield Federal Savings & Loan Assn.	$70,000

(3) Other factors:

Probable inheritance by Howard Brown of about $120,000 from his mother. Probability of substantial inheritance by Wendy Brown from her parents and her Aunt Fanny — but no knowledge of whether this would be outright or in some form of trust arrangement.

SECTION D. PROFESSIONAL RESPONSIBILITY

Trusts and estates practice is mined with conflicts of interest arising from duties to clients and their intended beneficiaries. Forewarned is forearmed.

---

12. Items marked by asterisk were acquired by gift or inheritance from Howard's and Wendy's respective relatives. All other assets are attributable to Howard Brown's earnings during their marriage. In a community property state, property acquired with a spouse's earnings is community property unless the spouses have changed it into another form of ownership.

1. Duties to Intended Beneficiaries

Simpson v. Calivas
Supreme Court of New Hampshire, 1994
139 N.H. 1, 650 A.2d 318

HORTON, J. The plaintiff, Robert H. Simpson, Jr., appeals from a directed verdict, grant of summary judgment, and dismissal of his claims against the lawyer who drafted his father's will. The plaintiff's action, sounding in both negligence and breach of contract, alleged that the defendant, Christopher Calivas, failed to draft a will which incorporated the actual intent of Robert H. Simpson, Sr. to leave all his land to the plaintiff in fee simple. Sitting with a jury, the Superior Court (Dickson, J.) directed a verdict for the defendant based on the plaintiff's failure to introduce any evidence on . . . breach of duty. The trial court also granted summary judgment on collateral estoppel grounds based on findings of the Strafford County Probate Court and dismissed the action, ruling that under New Hampshire law an attorney who drafts a will owes no duty to intended beneficiaries. We reverse and remand.

In March 1984, Robert H. Simpson, Sr. (Robert Sr.) executed a will that had been drafted by the defendant. The will left all real estate to the plaintiff except for a life estate in "our homestead located at Piscataqua Road, Dover, New Hampshire," which was left to Robert Sr.'s second wife, Roberta C. Simpson (stepmother). After Robert Sr.'s death in September 1985, the plaintiff and his stepmother filed a joint petition in the Strafford County Probate Court seeking a determination, essentially, of whether the term "homestead" referred to all the decedent's real property on Piscataqua Road (including a house, over one hundred acres of land, and buildings used in the family business), or only to the house (and, perhaps, limited surrounding acreage). The probate court found the term "homestead" ambiguous, and in order to aid construction, admitted some extrinsic evidence of the testator's surrounding circumstances, including evidence showing a close relationship between Robert Sr. and plaintiff's stepmother. The probate court, however, did not admit notes taken by the defendant during consultations with Robert Sr. that read: "House to wife as a life estate remainder to son, Robert H. Simpson, Jr. . . . Remaining land . . . to son Robert A. [*sic*] Simpson, Jr." The probate court construed the will to provide Roberta with a life estate in all the real property. After losing the will construction action — then two years after his father's death — the plaintiff negotiated with his stepmother to buy out her life estate in all the real property for $400,000.

The plaintiff then brought this malpractice action, pleading a contract count, based on third-party beneficiary theory, and a negligence count. . . .

The plaintiff raises . . . [these] issues on appeal: (1) whether the trial court erred in ruling that under New Hampshire law a drafting attorney owes no duty to an intended beneficiary; (2) whether the trial court erred in ruling that the findings of the probate court on testator intent collaterally estopped the plaintiff from bringing a malpractice action. . . .

We reverse and remand.

I. DUTY TO INTENDED BENEFICIARIES

In order to recover for negligence, a plaintiff must show that "there exists a duty, whose breach by the defendant causes the injury for which the plaintiff seeks to recover." Goodwin v. James, 595 A.2d 504, 507 (N.H. 1991). The critical issue, for purposes of this appeal, is whether an attorney who drafts a testator's will owes a duty of reasonable care to intended beneficiaries. We hold that there is such a duty.

As a general principle, "the concept of 'duty' . . . arises out of a relation between the parties and the protection against reasonably foreseeable harm." Morvay v. Hanover Insurance Co., 506 A.2d 333, 334 (N.H. 1986). The existence of a contract between parties may constitute a relation sufficient to impose a duty to exercise reasonable care, but in general, "the scope of such a duty is limited to those in privity of contract with each other." Robinson v. Colebrook Savings Bank, 254 A.2d 837, 839 (N.H. 1969). The privity rule is not ironclad, though, and we have been willing to recognize exceptions particularly where, as here, the risk to persons not in privity is apparent. Id. In *Morvay*, for example, we held that investigators hired by an insurance company to investigate the cause of a fire owed a duty to the insureds to perform their investigation with due care despite the absence of privity. Accordingly, the insureds stated a cause of action by alleging that the investigators negligently concluded that the fire was set, thereby prompting the insurance company to deny coverage. *Morvay*, 506 A.2d at 335; see also Spherex, Inc. v. Alexander Grant & Co., 451 A.2d 1308 (N.H. 1982) (accountants may be liable in negligence to those who reasonably rely on their work despite lack of privity); *Robinson*, 254 A.2d at 837 (bank owes duty to beneficiary of account with survivorship feature set up by depositor).

Because this issue is one of first impression, we look for guidance to other jurisdictions. The overwhelming majority of courts that have considered this issue have found that a duty runs from an attorney to an intended beneficiary of a will. R. Mallen & J. Smith, Legal Malpractice 3d. §26.4, at 595 (1989 & Supp. 1992). A theme common to these cases, similar to a theme of cases in which we have recognized exceptions to the privity rule, is an emphasis on the foreseeability of injury to the intended beneficiary. As the California Supreme Court explained in reaffirming the duty owed by an attorney to an intended beneficiary:

> When an attorney undertakes to fulfill the testamentary instructions of his client, he realistically and in fact assumes a relationship not only with the client but also with the client's intended beneficiaries. The attorney's actions and omissions will affect the success of the client's testamentary scheme; and thus the possibility of thwarting the testator's wishes immediately becomes foreseeable. Equally foreseeable is the possibility of injury to an intended beneficiary. In some ways, the beneficiary's interests loom greater than those of the client. After the latter's death, a failure in his testamentary scheme works no practical effect except to deprive his intended beneficiaries of the intended bequests.

Heyer v. Flaig, 449 P.2d 161, 164-65 (Cal. 1969). We agree that although there is no privity between a drafting attorney and an intended beneficiary, the obvious foreseeability of injury to the beneficiary demands an exception to the privity rule.

The defendant in his brief, however, urges that if we are to recognize an exception to the privity rule, we should limit it to those cases where the testator's intent as expressed in the will—not as shown by extrinsic evidence—was frustrated by attorney error. See Kirgan v. Parks, 478 A.2d 713, 719 (Md. App. 1984) ("testamentary beneficiary . . . has no cause of action against the testator's attorney for alleged negligence in drafting the will when . . . the will is valid, the testamentary intent as expressed in the will has been carried out, and there is no concession of error by the attorney"); see also Ventura Cty. Humane Soc. for P.C.C. & A., Inc. v. Holloway, 115 Cal. Rptr. 464 (App. 1974); Espinosa v. Sparber, Shevin, Shapo, Rosen & Heilbronner, 586 So. 2d 1221, 1223 (Fla. App. 1991); Schreiner v. Scoville, 410 N.W.2d 679, 683 (Iowa 1987). Under such a limited exception to the privity rule, a beneficiary whose interest violated the rule against perpetuities would have a cause of action against the drafting attorney, but a beneficiary whose interest was omitted by a drafting error would not. Similarly, application of such a rule to the facts of this case would require dismissal even if the allegations — that the defendant botched Robert Sr.'s instructions to leave all his land to his son — were true. We refuse to adopt a rule that would produce such inconsistent results for equally foreseeable harms, and hold that an intended beneficiary states a cause of action simply by pleading sufficient facts to establish that an attorney has negligently failed to effectuate the testator's intent as expressed to the attorney.

We are not the only court to reject the distinction urged by the defendant. In Ogle v. Fuiten, 466 N.E.2d 224, 225 (Ill. 1984), for example, nephews of the testator sued the testator's attorney for failing to provide in the will for the possibility that the testator's wife might not die in a common disaster, but might nonetheless fail to survive him by thirty days. The testator's wife died in the period not dealt with in the will, and without a provision in the will providing for this situation, the estate devolved by intestacy. On appeal after the dismissal of the nephews' claims, the court flatly rejected the argument that intended beneficiaries do not state a cause of action where the testator's alleged intent does not appear in the will. Id. at 227; see also Teasdale v. Allen, 520 A.2d 295, 296 (D.C. 1987) (expressly rejecting *Kirgan* and *Ventura*).

The plaintiff also argues that the trial court erred in failing to recognize that the writ stated a cause of action in contract. We agree.

The general rule that a nonparty to a contract has no remedy for breach of contract is subject to an exception for third-party beneficiaries. Arlington Trust Co. v. Estate of Wood, 465 A.2d 917, 918 (N.H. 1983). Third-party beneficiary status necessary to trigger this exception exists where "the contract is so expressed as to give the promisor reason to know that a benefit to a third party is contemplated by the promisee as one of the motivating causes of his making the contract." Tamposi Associates, Inc. v. Star Market Co., 406 A.2d 132, 134 (N.H. 1979). We hold that where, as here, a client has contracted with an attorney to draft a will and the client has identified to whom he wishes his estate to pass, that identified beneficiary may enforce the terms of the contract as a third-party beneficiary. See Stowe v. Smith, 441 A.2d at 84; Ogle v. Fuiten, 466 N.E.2d at 227; Hale v. Groce, 744 P.2d at 1292.

Because we hold that a duty runs from a drafting attorney to an intended beneficiary, and that an identified beneficiary has third-party beneficiary status, the trial court erred by dismissing the plaintiff's writ.

II.   COLLATERAL ESTOPPEL

The defendant insists, however, that even if a duty runs from a testator's attorney to an intended beneficiary, the superior court properly granted summary judgment on collateral estoppel grounds. We disagree. . . .

The primary question is whether the issues before the probate and superior courts were identical. We agree with defendant that comparison of the respective evidence which each court was competent to hear is one factor, but note that an identity of evidence is not dispositive of an identity of issues. Instead, determination of "identity" necessarily requires inquiry into each court's role and the nature of the respective findings.

The principal task of the probate court is to determine the testator's intent, In the Matter of Shirley's Estate, 379 A.2d 1261, 1262 (N.H. 1977), limited by the requirement that it determine the "intention of the testator as shown by the language of the whole will. . . ." Dennett v. Osgood, 229 A.2d 689, 690 (N.H. 1967). In this effort, the probate court is always permitted to consider the "surrounding circumstances" of the testator, id.; Royce v. Denby's Estate, 379 A.2d 1256 (N.H. 1977), and where the terms of a will are ambiguous, as here, extrinsic evidence may be admitted to the extent that it does not contradict the express terms of the will. In re Estate of Sayewich, 413 A.2d 581, 584 (N.H. 1980). Direct declarations of a testator's intent, however, are generally inadmissible in all probate proceedings. Id.; 4 Page on the Law of Wills §32.9 (Bowe-Parker ed. 1961). The defendant argues that even though his notes of his meeting with the decedent recorded the decedent's direct declarations of intent, they could have been admissible as an exception to the general rule had there been a proper proffer. We need not reach the issue of whether the defendant's notes fall within an exception to the general rule because even assuming admissibility and therefore an identity of evidence, there remain distinct issues. Quite simply, the task of the probate court is a limited one: to determine the intent of the testator as expressed in the language of the will. Obviously, the hope is that the application of rules of construction and consideration of extrinsic evidence (where authorized) will produce a finding of expressed intent that corresponds to actual intent. Further, the likelihood of such convergence presumably increases as the probate court considers more extrinsic evidence; however, even with access to all extrinsic evidence, there is no requirement or guarantee that the testator's intent as construed will match the testator's actual intent.

The defendant, however, insists that whether or not required to do so, the probate court in this case did make an explicit finding of actual intent when it concluded: "There is nothing to suggest that [the testator] intended to grant a life estate in anything less than the whole." We need not reach the issue of whether this language constitutes a finding of actual intent because collateral estoppel will not lie anyway. Collateral estoppel is only applicable if the finding in the first proceeding was essential to the judgment of that court. Restatement (Second) of Judgments §27. Inasmuch as the mandate of the probate court is simply to determine and give effect to the intent of the testator as expressed in the language of the will, a finding of actual intent is not necessary to that judgment. Accordingly, even an explicit finding of actual intent by a probate court cannot be the basis for collateral estoppel. . . .

Reversed and remanded.

NOTES

1. The large majority of courts that have considered malpractice suits against the attorney-drafter has concluded that the suit may be based on either the tort

theory or the contract theory or both, as did the New Hampshire court. In 2003 there were only nine states which continued to hold that the lack of strict privity of contract between the drafter and the beneficiaries prevents a malpractice action by the beneficiaries: Alabama, Arkansas, Maine, Maryland, Nebraska, New York, Ohio, Texas, and Virginia. See Martin D. Begleiter, The Gambler Breaks Even: Legal Malpractice in Complicated Estate Planning Cases, 20 Ga. St. U.L. Rev. 277, 282 (2003). Recent cases maintaining the privity bar include Rovello v. Klein, 757 N.Y.S.2d 496 (App. Div. 2003); Robinson v. Benton, 842 So. 2d 631 (Ala. 2002); and Pettus v. McDonald, 36 S.W.3d 745 (Ark. 2001).

The argument against the privity defense was stated succinctly by Vice Chancellor Megarry of England in rejecting the privity defense.

> In broad terms, the question is whether solicitors who prepare a will are liable to a beneficiary under it if, through their negligence, the gift to the beneficiary is void. The solicitors are liable, of course, to the testator or his estate for a breach of the duty that they owed to him, though as he has suffered no financial loss it seems that his estate could recover no more than nominal damages. Yet it is said that however careless the solicitors were, they owed no duty to the beneficiary, and so they cannot be liable to her. If this is right, the result is striking. The only person who has a valid claim has suffered no loss, and the only person who has suffered a loss has no valid claim. [Ross v. Caunters, 3 All Eng. Rep. 580, 582 (Ch. 1980).]

See also Bradley E.S. Fogel, Attorney v. Client — Privity, Malpractice, and the Lack of Respect for the Primacy of the Attorney-Client Relationship in Estate Planning, 68 Tenn. L. Rev. 261 (2001).

2. In Simpson v. Calivas, the validity and construction of the will were matters for the probate court to decide. The negligence of the lawyer was a matter for a court of general jurisdiction. This is true in most states.

Historically, probate courts were inferior courts, with jurisdiction limited to determining the will's validity and supervising administration of the decedent's estate. Legislatures were often unwilling to provide suitable compensation and clerical assistance, particularly in rural areas, because of the small amount of business. In some states, probate judges may be laypersons, without legal training. Anyone can run for the office. The National Law Journal, Dec. 24, 1984, at 39, reported the election of an 18-year-old man, just six months out of high school, as probate judge for Valencia County, New Mexico. Because of lack of confidence in probate judges, their powers were curtailed. In the twentieth century, in most states probate courts were appropriately staffed and the badges of inferiority removed. They were authorized to pass on more questions regarding wills, including construction of wills.

Nonetheless, even though probate courts are now authorized to construe wills, most courts, like the New Hampshire Supreme Court, reject the claim that conclusions reached by the probate court as to the testator's intent in a construction suit are determinative in a malpractice suit. The issues and the evidentiary rules for proving intent applied in the two proceedings are different.

3. Smith v. Lewis, 530 P.2d 589 (Cal. 1975):

> As the jury was correctly instructed, an attorney does not ordinarily guarantee the soundness of his opinions and, accordingly, is not liable for every mistake he may make in his practice. He is expected, however, to possess knowledge of those plain and

elementary principles of law which are commonly known by well informed attorneys, and to discover those additional rules of law which, although not commonly known, may readily be found by standard research techniques. If the law on a particular subject is doubtful or debatable, an attorney will not be held responsible for failing to anticipate the manner in which the uncertainty will be resolved. But even with respect to an unsettled area of the law, we believe an attorney assumes an obligation to his client to undertake reasonable research in an effort to ascertain relevant legal principles and to make an informed decision as to a course of conduct based upon an intelligent assessment of the problem. [Id. at 595.]

It is the duty of an attorney who is a general practitioner to refer the client to a specialist if the attorney cannot handle the matter with reasonable skill and care. If the attorney fails to refer to or consult a specialist when a specialist is needed, the attorney may be held to the standard of skill ordinarily possessed by a specialist. See Horne v. Peckham, 158 Cal. Rptr. 714 (Cal. App. 1979).

4. Sometimes attorneys who make drafting errors in wills have more to fear from their incompetence than a mere suit for malpractice. Because a Tennessee lawyer (a former judge who specialized in probate) mistakenly used the phrase "all monies" to refer to the residue of an estate, the testator's ex-husband was not awarded the testator's stock investments even though the testator had wanted him to take her stock. In view of what amounted to a $100,000 mistake, the testator's ex-husband became unhinged and shot and killed the lawyer—as well as a life insurance agent who at the time of the murder had the misfortune to be trying to sell an insurance policy to the 81-year-old lawyer. See Angela K. Brown, One Word Enraged Lawyer's Killer, Comm. App., Mar. 20, 1999, at B2.

2. Conflicts of Interest

Hotz v. Minyard
Supreme Court of South Carolina, 1991
304 S.C. 225, 403 S.E.2d 634

GREGORY, J. This appeal is from an order granting respondents summary judgment on several causes of action. We reverse in part and affirm in part.

Respondent Minyard (Tommy) and appellant (Judy) are brother and sister. Their father, Mr. Minyard, owns two automobile dealerships, Judson T. Minyard, Inc. (Greenville Dealership), and Minyard-Waidner, Inc. (Anderson Dealership). Tommy has been the dealer in charge of the Greenville Dealership since 1977. Judy worked for her father at the Anderson Dealership beginning in 1983; she was also a vice-president and minority shareholder. In 1985, Mr. Minyard signed a contract with General Motors designating Judy the successor dealer of the Anderson Dealership.

Respondent Dobson is a South Carolina lawyer practicing in Greenville and a member of respondent Dobson & Dobson, P.A. (Law Firm). Dobson is also a certified public accountant, although he no longer practices as one. In 1985, Dobson sold the tax return preparation practice of Law Firm to respondent Dobson, Lewis & Saad, P.A. (Accounting Firm). Although his name is included in Accounting Firm's name, Dobson is merely a shareholder and director and does not receive remuneration as an employee.

Dobson did legal work for the Minyard family and its various businesses for many years. On October 24, 1984, Mr. Minyard came to Law Firm's office to execute a will with his wife, his secretary, and Tommy in attendance. At this meeting he signed a will which left Tommy the Greenville Dealership, gave other family members bequests totalling $250,000.00, and divided the remainder of his estate equally between Tommy and a trust for Judy after his wife's death. All present at the meeting were given copies of this will. Later that afternoon, however, Mr. Minyard returned to Dobson's office and signed a second will containing the same provisions as the first except that it gave the real estate upon which the Greenville Dealership was located to Tommy outright. Mr. Minyard instructed Dobson not to disclose the existence of the second will. He specifically directed that Judy not be told about it.

In January 1985, Judy called Dobson requesting a copy of the will her father had signed at the morning meeting on October 24, 1984. At Mr. Minyard's direction, or at least with his express permission, Dobson showed Judy the first will and discussed it with her in detail.

Judy testified she had the impression from her discussion with Dobson that under her father's will she would receive the Anderson Dealership and would share equally with her brother in her father's estate. According to Dobson, however, he merely explained Mr. Minyard's intent to provide for Judy as he had for Tommy when and if she became capable of handling a dealership. Dobson made a notation to this effect on the copy of the will he discussed with Judy. Judy claimed she was led to believe the handwritten notes were part of her father's will.

In any event, Judy claims Dobson told her the will she was shown was in actuality her father's last will and testament. Although Dobson denies ever making this express statement, he admits he never told her the will he discussed with her had been revoked.

In January 1986, Mr. Minyard was admitted to the hospital for various health problems. In April 1986, he suffered a massive stroke. Although the date of the onset of his mental incompetence is disputed, it is uncontested he is now mentally incompetent.

Judy and Tommy agreed that while their father was ill, Judy would attend to his daily care and Tommy would temporarily run the Anderson Dealership until Judy returned. During this time, Tommy began making changes at the Anderson Dealership. Under his direction, the Anderson Dealership bought out another dealership owned by Mr. Minyard, Judson Lincoln-Mercury, Inc., which was operating at a loss. Tommy also formed a holding company which assumed ownership of Mr. Minyard's real estate leased to the Anderson Dealership. Consequently, rent paid by the dealership was greatly increased.

Judy questioned the wisdom of her brother's financial dealings. When she sought to return to the Anderson Dealership as successor dealer, Tommy refused to relinquish control. Eventually, in August 1986, he terminated Judy from the dealership's payroll.

Judy consulted an Anderson law firm concerning her problems with her brother's operation of the Anderson Dealership. As a result, on November 15, 1986, Mr. Minyard executed a codicil removing Judy and her children as beneficiaries under his will. Judy was immediately advised of this development by letter.

In March 1987, Judy met with Tommy, her mother, and Dobson at Law Firm's office. She was told if she discharged her attorneys and dropped her plans for a lawsuit, she would be restored under her father's will and could work at the Greenville Dealership with significant fringe benefits. Judy testified she understood restoration under the will meant she would inherit the Anderson Dealership and receive half her father's estate, including the real estate, as she understood from her 1985 meeting with Dobson. Judy discharged her attorneys and moved to Greenville. Eventually, however, Tommy terminated her position at the Greenville Dealership.

As a result of the above actions by Tommy and Dobson, Judy commenced this suit alleging various causes of action. The causes of action against Tommy for tortious interference with contract, a shareholder derivative suit for wrongful diversion of corporate profits, and fraud survived summary judgment and are not at issue here. Judy appeals the trial judge's order granting summary judgment on the remaining causes of action against Tommy, Dobson, and the professional associations. We address only the trial judge's ruling on the cause of action against Dobson for breach of fiduciary duty.

ANALYSIS

Judy's complaint alleges Dobson breached his fiduciary duty to her by misrepresenting her father's will in January 1985. As a result, in March 1987 she believed she would regain the Anderson Dealership if she refrained from pursuing her claim against her brother. This delay gave Tommy additional time in control of the Anderson Dealership during which he depleted its assets. Law Firm and Accounting Firm are charged with vicarious liability for Dobson's acts.

The trial judge granted Dobson, Law Firm, and Accounting Firm summary judgment on the ground Dobson owed Judy no fiduciary duty because he was acting as Mr. Minyard's attorney and not as Judy's attorney in connection with her father's will. We disagree.

We find the evidence indicates a factual issue whether Dobson breached a fiduciary duty to Judy when she went to his office seeking legal advice about the effect of her father's will. Law Firm had prepared Judy's tax returns for approximately twenty years until September 1985 and had prepared a will for her she signed only one week earlier. Judy testified she consulted Dobson personally in 1984 or 1985 about a suspected misappropriation of funds at one of the dealerships and as late as 1986 regarding her problems with her brother. She claimed she trusted Dobson because of her dealings with him over the years as her lawyer and accountant.

A fiduciary relationship exists when one has a special confidence in another so that the latter, in equity and good conscience, is bound to act in good faith. Island Car Wash, Inc. v. Norris, 358 S.E.2d 150, 152 (S.C. App. 1987). An Attorney/client relationship is by nature a fiduciary one. In re Green, 354 S.E.2d 557 (S.C. 1987). Although Dobson represented Mr. Minyard and not Judy regarding her father's will, Dobson did have an ongoing attorney/client relationship with Judy and there is evidence she had "a special confidence" in him. While Dobson had no duty to disclose the existence of the second will against his client's (Mr. Minyard's) wishes, he owed Judy the duty to deal with her in good faith and not actively misrepresent the first will. We find there is a factual issue presented whether Dobson breached a fiduciary duty to Judy. We conclude summary judgment was improperly granted Dobson on this cause of action.

Similarly, we find evidence to present a jury issue whether Law Firm should be held vicariously liable for Dobson's conduct since Dobson was acting in his capacity as a lawyer when he met with Judy to discuss the will in January 1985. There is no evidence, however, that Dobson was acting in his capacity as an accountant on that occasion since he was giving legal advice and not rendering accounting services. We find no basis for vicarious liability against Accounting Firm. Accordingly, we reverse the granting of summary judgment on this cause of action as to Dobson and Law Firm and affirm as to Accounting Firm. . . .

Reversed in part; affirmed in part.

A. v. B., 726 A.2d 924 (N.J. 1999): The estate planning section of Hill Wallack, a 60-person New Jersey law firm, represented both a husband, *B*, and his wife, *W*, who executed wills leaving all the property of each to the survivor, in the reasonable expectation that the survivor would care for any joint children. During the course of preparing these wills for *B* and *W*, the family law section of Hill Wallack mistakenly took on another client, a woman, *A*, who sued *B* for paternity for a child whom *B* recently had with her. The existence of this additional child was relevant to the design of *W*'s estate plan. If *B*, her husband, were to survive her, he might pass assets that he inherited from *W* to that other child. When the firm discovered its conflict of interest, it withdrew from the paternity suit and ordered *B* to tell his wife *W* of his other child, or the firm itself would notify her. *B* sued Hill Wallack to prevent disclosure. The court held that disclosure to the wife was permitted under New Jersey's version of Model Rule of Professional Conduct 1.6, which governs confidentiality. The firm was not permitted to identify the child or its mother *A*; disclosure was limited to the fact that *B* had fathered a child with another woman.

NOTES

1.   Estate planning lawyers commonly represent multiple members of the same family, such as a husband and wife, in drafting wills and trusts. In such cases it is important to discuss with them at the outset possible conflicts of interests and the ground rules for sharing information. A good practice is to speak with each client separately early in the representation to ferret out any hidden conflicts and to assure each party that the will or trust to be drafted must reflect the wishes of each, not the wishes of the spouse or other family member. A written representation agreement including possible waivers of conflicts of interest might be required in some situations. For an excellent discussion of estate planning under the ABA Model Rules of Professional Conduct, see American College of Trust and Estate Counsel, ACTEC Commentaries on the Model Rules of Professional Conduct (3d ed. 1999), particularly Model Rules of Prof. Conduct R. 1.2 (scope of representation), 1.6 (confidentiality), and 1.7 (conflicts of interest).

2.   Some years ago it was predicted that legal malpractice liability would prove to be a strong force for reform of property law. Jesse Dukeminier, Cleansing the Stables of Property: A River Found at Last, 65 Iowa L. Rev. 151 (1979). And so it is turning out. The fear of malpractice liability is fueling movements to excuse errors in will execution (see pages 233-235); correct mistakes by lawyers in drafting instruments to carry out the client's intent (see pages 374-385); cure perpetuities violations by judicial reformation of the instrument, adoption of the wait-and-see doctrine,

or abolition of the Rule against Perpetuities (see pages 697-704); and reform wills and trusts after the decedent's death to obtain tax advantages lost by the lawyer's mistake (see pages 578-579).

3. Probate matters are a common source of ethics complaints against attorneys. In Illinois in 2003, probate was fifth among 19 fields in the frequency of disciplinary complaints filed. 2003 Annual Report of the [Illinois] Attorney Registration and Disciplinary Commission.

For useful student texts covering the materials in this book, see Roger W. Andersen, Understanding Trusts and Estates (3d ed. 2003); Gerry W. Beyer, Wills, Trusts, and Estates: Examples and Explanations (3d ed. 2005); Lucy A. Marsh, Wills, Trusts, and Estates: Practical Applications of the Law (1998); William M. McGovern & Sheldon F. Kurtz, Principles of Wills, Trusts & Estates (2005); Mark Reutlinger, Wills, Trusts, and Estates, Essential Terms and Concepts (2d ed. 1998); and Paul G. Haskell, Preface to Wills, Trusts, and Administration (2d ed. 1994).

2

INTESTACY: AN ESTATE PLAN
BY DEFAULT

SECTION A. THE BASIC SCHEME

1. Introduction

Some people die leaving a will stating their wishes for giving away their property at death. Others die *intestate*, that is, without a valid will. In a 1950 poll, only 19 percent of American adults reported having made a will. In surveys taken in the last 10 years, 39 to 48 percent of adults claim to have a will.[1] Among those who claim to have a will, about one-fifth did not obtain the assistance of a lawyer in the will's preparation.[2]

When clients seek estate planning advice from lawyers, they are almost always advised to avoid intestacy by executing a will (and often a trust as well). Besides identifying who will take your probate assets, wills can be used to designate guardians for children, to select a trustworthy fiduciary to administer your estate, to save money in probate fees by waiving a bond (or surety on a bond), and to achieve tax savings. Accordingly, intestacy is the background law that lawyers plan around—what in legal theory is called a *default rule*.

Nonetheless, about half the population dies intestate, forsaking wills and legal advice. Why do many people of moderate wealth not seek legal advice and make wills? One reason, of course, is that most people cannot accept and plan for the fact of their own deaths; insurers call death insurance "life insurance," and agents are careful to omit the word *death* from their discussions with clients ("If anything

---

1. The 1950 poll was conducted by the Gallup Organization on Aug. 18, 1950. The more recent results are from various surveys collected in the Public Opinion Online database of the Roper Center for Public Opinion Research, University of Connecticut. In national polls of exclusively older and wealthier groups, up to 69 percent of respondents report having wills, and if one further separates the respondents by income, even higher percentages of the wealthiest subgroups report having wills. See also Marsha A. Goetting & Peter Martin, Characteristics of Older Adults with Written Wills, 22 J. Fam. & Econ. Issues 243 (2001) (66 percent of elderly sample, skewed toward the wealthy, had wills).

2. Roper ASW, 2003 Consumer Experience Survey, Public Opinion Online database of the Roper Center for Public Opinion Research, University of Connecticut (survey of 1,500 adults 45 and older for AARP).

59

should happen to you . . ." *If*, indeed!). As Freud wrote, "Our own death is indeed unimaginable, and whenever we make the attempt to imagine it we can perceive that we really survive as spectators. Hence . . . at bottom no one believes in his own death, or to put the same thing in another way, in the unconscious every one of us is convinced of his own immortality." Sigmund Freud, Our Attitude Towards Death, *in* 4 Collected Papers 304 (1925).

Another reason people do not make wills is the cost involved. It seems like a "big deal" to go to a lawyer. And, of course, many people arrange to transfer their property at death by way of joint tenancy, payable-on-death designations on life insurance, pension plans, and such, or revocable trusts created during life, avoiding probate and wills (indeed, more property is passed outside probate than through probate). Whatever the reasons, people who do not make wills or dispose of all of their property by nonprobate transfers accept the intestacy law as their estate plans by default.

The distribution of the probate property of a person who dies without a will, or whose will does not make a complete disposition of the estate, is governed by the statute of descent and distribution of each state. If a will is so poorly drafted that it disposes of only part of the probate estate, then the result is *partial intestacy*. Generally speaking, the law of the state where the decedent was domiciled at death governs the disposition of personal property, and the law of the state where the decedent's real property is located governs the disposition of her real property.

Since it is a safe bet that the law of intestacy is not exactly the same in all details in any two states, it is essential that you become familiar with the intestacy statutes of the state in which you intend to practice. It is quite impossible to answer any specific question about who succeeds to property without looking at the statutes of a particular state. We reproduce here the intestacy provisions of the Uniform Probate Code (UPC) and later, throughout the book, the UPC provisions relevant to the particular topic under discussion.

The UPC was originally promulgated in 1969. Subsequently, about one-third of the states adopted laws substantially conforming to major parts of the 1969 Code, and several other states enacted particular sections of the Code. Article VI of the Code, dealing with nonprobate transfers, was substantially revised in 1989. Article II of the Code, dealing with intestacy, wills, and donative transfers, was overhauled in 1990. See John H. Langbein & Lawrence W. Waggoner, Reforming the Law of Gratuitous Transfers: The New Uniform Probate Code, 55 Alb. L. Rev. 871 (1992). Some of the Code sections have since been revised further. You should compare the probate code provisions of your own state with the revised UPC and think carefully about whether the UPC solution is better than the one adopted in your state and better than any you can come up with. It is our object to help you develop an independent critical judgment about matters in this field, including the UPC. Legislatures have been selective in enacting sections of the 1990 revised Code, as they were with the 1969 Code.

Uniform Probate Code (1990)

§2-101. INTESTATE ESTATE

(a) Any part of a decedent's estate not effectively disposed of by will passes by intestate succession to the decedent's heirs as prescribed in this Code, except as modified by the decedent's will.

(b) A decedent by will may expressly exclude or limit the right of an individual or class to succeed to property of the decedent passing by intestate succession. If that individual or a member of that class survives the decedent, the share of the decedent's intestate estate to which that individual or class would have succeeded passes as if that individual or each member of that class had disclaimed his [or her] intestate share.

§2-102. SHARE OF SPOUSE[3]

The intestate share of a decedent's surviving spouse is:

    (1) the entire intestate estate if:

        (i) no descendant or parent of the decedent survives the decedent; or

        (ii) all of the decedent's surviving descendants are also descendants of the surviving spouse and there is no other descendant of the surviving spouse who survives the decedent;

    (2) the first [$200,000], plus three-fourths of any balance of the intestate estate, if no descendant of the decedent survives the decedent, but a parent of the decedent survives the decedent;

    (3) the first [$150,000], plus one-half of any balance of the intestate estate, if all of the decedent's surviving descendants are also descendants of the surviving spouse and the surviving spouse has one or more surviving descendants who are not descendants of the decedent;

    (4) the first [$100,000], plus one-half of any balance of the intestate estate, if one or more of the decedent's surviving descendants are not descendants of the surviving spouse.

§2-103. SHARE OF HEIRS OTHER THAN SURVIVING SPOUSE

Any part of the intestate estate not passing to the decedent's surviving spouse under Section 2-102, or the entire intestate estate if there is no surviving spouse, passes in the following order to the individuals designated below who survive the decedent:

    (1) to the decedent's descendants by representation;

    (2) if there is no surviving descendant, to the decedent's parents equally if both survive, or to the surviving parent;

    (3) if there is no surviving descendant or parent, to the descendants of the decedent's parents or either of them by representation;

    (4) if there is no surviving descendant, parent, or descendant of a parent, but the decedent is survived by one or more grandparents or descendants of grandparents, half of the estate passes to the decedent's paternal grandparents equally if both survive, or to the surviving paternal grandparent, or to the descendants of the decedent's paternal grandparents or either of them if both are deceased, the descendants taking by representation; and the other half passes to the decedent's maternal relatives in the same manner; but if there is no surviving grandparent or descendant of a grandparent on either

---

3. The UPC's alternate section for community property states (§2-102A) provides for the same distribution of separate property as is provided in §2-102 and further provides that all community property passes to the surviving spouse whether or not the decedent is survived by issue or parents. — Eds.

the paternal or the maternal side, the entire estate passes to the decedent's relatives on the other side in the same manner as the half.

§2-105.   NO TAKER

If there is no taker under the provisions of this Article, the intestate estate passes to the [state].

QUESTION

Under all intestate succession statutes, parents are not heirs if the decedent leaves a child. Why should this be so if the child is an adult? Why aren't the decedent's assets used to support aging parents rather than an able-bodied child? Why must support of the poor or incapacitated elderly come from public resources rather than from a child's estate?

NOTE: THE MEANING OF HEIRS AND THE TRANSFER
OF AN EXPECTANCY

In the eyes of the law no living person has heirs; to use the Latin phrase: *nemo est haeres viventis*. The persons who would be the heirs of *A*, a living person, if *A* died within the next hour, are not the heirs of *A* but the *heirs apparent*. They have a mere *expectancy*. This expectancy can be destroyed by *A*'s deed or will. It is not a legal "interest" at all. *A*'s heirs will be identified at *A*'s death by reference to the applicable statute of descent and distribution.

Not being an interest, an expectancy cannot be transferred at law. However, a purported transfer of an expectancy, for an adequate consideration, may be enforceable in equity as a contract to transfer if the court views it as fair under all the circumstances. Equity scrutinizes such transactions to protect prospective heirs from unfair bargains.[4] See Ware v. Crowell, 465 S.E.2d 809 (Va. 1996). See also Katheleen R. Guzman, Releasing the Expectancy, 34 Ariz. St. L.J. 775 (2002), advancing several thoughtful arguments for the proposition that a release of an expectancy to the donor should be subjected to less judicial scrutiny than the transfer of an expectancy to a third party.

2.   *Share of Surviving Spouse*

What policies are involved in framing an intestacy statute? The primary policy is to carry out the probable intent of the average intestate decedent. Thus we must decide what persons who die intestate would most likely want. But how can we tell? One way is to look at the dispositions made in probated wills. Another approach is to ask adults

---

4. Undoubtedly, the most famous sale of an expectancy was the sale of Esau's birthright to Jacob for a bowl of pottage. Genesis 25:29-34. Whether this sale was enforceable under Hebrew law has been much debated by biblical scholars. See David Daube, Studies in Biblical Law 191-200 (1947); Reuben Ahroni, Why Did Esau Spurn the Birthright? 29 Judaism 323 (1980). Under modern American law, was Esau's promise enforceable as a fair bargain?

to whom they would want to leave their property. For an insightful review of intestate succession law in view of default rule theory, see Adam J. Hirsch, Default Rules in Inheritance Law: A Problem in Search of Its Context, 73 Fordham L. Rev. 1031 (2004).

In the last 50 years, several empirical studies have been done to determine popular preferences for intestate succession. Although these studies do not always agree, they unanimously support the conclusion that the spouse's share given by most traditional intestacy statutes is too small. The studies show that, when there are no children from a prior marriage, most persons want everything to go to the surviving spouse, thus excluding parents and brothers and sisters — and children. This preference is particularly strong among persons with moderate estates, who believe the surviving spouse will need the entire estate for support. The richer the person, the greater the desire that children or collaterals share with the spouse in the estate. See Mary L. Fellows, Rita J. Simon & William Rau, Public Attitudes About Property Distribution at Death and Intestate Succession Laws in the United States, 1978 Am. B. Found. Res. J. 319, 348-364; Allison Dunham, The Method, Process and Frequency of Wealth Transmission at Death, 30 U. Chi. L. Rev. 241, 251-253 (1963); Comment, A Comparison of Iowans' Dispositive Preferences with Selected Provisions of the Iowa and Uniform Probate Codes, 63 Iowa L. Rev. 1041, 1078-1100 (1978). Earlier studies are cited in these publications. An empirical study by John R. Price, The Transmission of Wealth at Death in a Community Property Jurisdiction, 50 Wash. L. Rev. 277 (1975), supports giving the surviving spouse all of the decedent's interest in community property.

Under current law, the surviving spouse usually receives at least a one-half share of the decedent's estate. There are many variations in the specifics, however, such as giving the surviving spouse a lump sum plus one-half of the remainder, or giving the surviving spouse a one-half share if only one child or issue of one child survives, and a one-third share if more than one child or one child and issue of a deceased child survive.[5]

The current UPC provision for the surviving spouse (§2-102) is more generous than the current provisions for the surviving spouse under most state intestacy laws. Observe that, under the UPC, if all the decedent's descendants are also descendants of the surviving spouse, and the surviving spouse has no other descendants, the surviving spouse takes the entire estate to the exclusion of the decedent's descendants. Giving everything to the spouse and nothing to the children, under these circumstances, was a novel statutory solution, but it is supported by studies showing that in estates with minor children, that is the usual practice of those leaving wills. Thanks in large part to the influence of the UPC, intestacy statutes that give the surviving spouse the entirety of the decedent's estate are no longer uncommon. The provisions in subsections (3) and (4), giving the surviving spouse less when either spouse has a child by someone other than the other spouse, were also unusual when originally proposed. The theory of §2-102 is discussed in Lawrence M. Waggoner, The Multiple-Marriage Society and Spousal Rights Under the Revised Uniform Probate Code, 76 Iowa L. Rev. 223, 229-235 (1991). See also Martin L. Fried, The Uniform Probate Code: Intestate Succession and Related Matters, 55 Alb. L. Rev. 927, 929-933 (1992).

---

5. In Kentucky and Vermont, if there are surviving descendants, the intestacy statute leaves nothing to the surviving spouse; the descendants take the entire intestate estate. The spouse, however, is not left without recourse — the spouse remains entitled to take an elective share (see Chapter 7).

If there is no descendant, nearly half of the states provide, as does the UPC, that the spouse share with the decedent's parents, if any. If no parent survives, the spouse usually takes all to the exclusion of collateral kin, as the UPC provides, but in a number of states the spouse shares with brothers and sisters and their descendants.

A secondary policy of the intestacy laws is family protection — preserving the economic health of the family after a death. With respect to spouses, a related consideration is the recognition that marriage involves an economic partnership. Hence the law of intestate succession influences the discourse over the extent to which testators should be free to disinherit their spouses and other family members. For example, in Chapter 7, when we examine the mandatory minimum share to which the law entitles a surviving spouse in spite of a contrary will by the decedent, the question arises, should the surviving spouse's *elective share* (or *forced share*) be the same as what the spouse would have taken in intestacy? If not, what should it be? Why? For an interesting article documenting the reach of family policy in inheritance law and criticizing this focus on the family, see Frances H. Foster, The Family Paradigm of Inheritance Law, 80 N.C.L. Rev. 199 (2001).

In recent years some commentators have argued that advancing the public policy of the state and fostering positive social norms also should be relevant considerations in designing intestate succession statutes. For a discussion and critique of these goals, see Adam J. Hirsch, Default Rules in Inheritance Law: A Problem in Search of Its Context, 73 Fordham L. Rev. 1031 (2004).

PROBLEMS AND QUESTION

1.   Refer back to the estate planning problem of Howard and Wendy Brown on pages 40-48. Howard has two children by Wendy. Wendy has two children by Howard and a child by a previous marriage. If Howard dies before Wendy intestate, what will be Wendy's share under UPC §2-102 (1990)? If Wendy dies before Howard intestate, what will be Howard's share? Do the different amounts provided under §2-102(3) and (4) have a rational basis?

If Howard dies intestate, and Wendy does not have a child by a previous marriage, Wendy takes all of Howard's estate under UPC §2-102(1)(ii). But because Wendy has a child by a previous marriage, Wendy's share is cut back to $150,000 plus one-half of the balance. Does this carry out Howard's wishes?

One of the virtues of UPC §2-102(1), giving all to the surviving spouse, is that a guardianship of minor children is avoided. But in the Browns' case, because of the existence of a stepchild, guardianship may be necessary for the two minor children if one of the spouses dies intestate. On the disadvantages of guardianship, see pages 116-118.

2.   *H* and *W* have been married one year. *H* dies, survived by *W* and a brother, but no parent. What is *W*'s share? Compare the elective share provisions of UPC §2-202(a) (1990, as amended 1993) at page 427, which give the surviving spouse of a one-year marriage only 3 percent of the decedent's estate if the decedent leaves a will and the spouse elects to take against will. Why does the UPC take into account

the length of the marriage in determining the spouse's forced share but not the spouse's intestate share? Is this sound? Should it matter whether *H* and *W* are age 55 or age 25 when they marry? In Arkansas, if the decedent has no descendants, a spouse of fewer than three years takes a one-half share, and a spouse of three or more years takes the entire estate. See Ark. Code Ann. §28-9-214 (2004).

3.   Henry dies intestate. Anne, with whom he has been living, claims a spouse's share. Is Anne entitled to such a share if she married Henry, but the marriage is bigamous? If she did not marry Henry, but common law marriage is recognized? See William M. McGovern, Jr. & Sheldon F. Kurtz, Wills, Trusts and Estates §2.11 (3d ed. 2004). If Anne and Henry did not marry because they perceived, as did the Princess of Cleves long ago, that there's nothing like marriage to spoil a perfect love, but Henry promised to take care of Anne? See pages 286-288, dealing with contracts to make wills. Suppose that Henry and Anne had married, but Henry had moved out and filed for divorce. What result?

In a few states, statutes disqualify a spouse from inheritance if the spouse abandoned or refused to support the decedent. See, e.g., N.Y. Est. Powers & Trusts Law §5-1.2 (2004); Ky. Rev. Stat. Ann. §392.090 (2004); Va. Code Ann. §64.1-16.3 (2004). Compare Chinese inheritance law, which punishes bad behavior, page 131.

NOTE: DOMESTIC PARTNERS AND INTESTATE SUCCESSION

Should cohabiting domestic partners be treated like spouses for purposes of intestate succession? The chief policies that underpin the spousal intestate share — giving effect to the probable intent of the decedent and protecting those whom the decedent treated as family — seem also to apply to domestic partners. The number of unmarried domestic partners living together is growing rapidly. According to the 2000 Census, about 8 percent of the nation's cohabiting couples were unmarried, opposite-sex pairs, and about 1 percent were unmarried, same-sex pairs. If domestic partners are given an intestate share, what should be the criteria for qualifying as a domestic partner? Should the intestate share be given to same-sex partners as well as opposite-sex partners? For a thorough discussion, see Mary L. Fellows, Monica K. Johnson, Amy Chiericozzi, Ann Hale, Christopher Lee, Robin Preble & Michael Voran, Committed Partners and Inheritance: An Empirical Study, 16 Law & Ineq. J. 1 (1998); T.P. Gallanis, Inheritance Rights for Domestic Partners, 79 Tul. L. Rev. 55 (2004). The Fellows et al. study concludes that a substantial majority of committed partners want the surviving partner to take a share of the decedent's estate, and this preference is even greater among same-sex partners.

The law of domestic partners is in flux, which is related to the current uncertainty that surrounds the status of same-sex marriage. In exit polls during the 2004 election, 25 percent of voters favored making same-sex marriages legal, while 35 percent favored civil unions and only 37 percent favored no legal recognition of same-sex couples. N.Y. Times, Nov. 5, 2004, at A22.

In 1996 Congress passed the Defense of Marriage Act, restricting the extension of spousal rights to same-sex couples under federal programs and providing that states could not be forced to recognize same-sex marriages performed in other states. 1 U.S.C. §7 (2004). In response, 35 states enacted similar statutes and 3 banned same-sex marriages in their state constitutions.

On the other hand, since 1996, 3 states enacted legislation granting same-sex couples inheritance and other spousal-type rights: (1) Hawaii for "reciprocal beneficiaries" in 1997, (2) Vermont for "civil unions" in 2000, and (3) California for "domestic partners" in 2000. In Hawaii, reciprocal beneficiaries are given many (but not all) of the benefits of surviving spouses, including intestacy and elective share rights that match those of legal spouses. Haw. Rev. Stat. Ann. §§560:2-102, 2-201 to 2-214 (2004). Like Hawaii's reciprocal beneficiaries, civil unions in Vermont are open only to same-sex couples, but give many of the same rights as marriage gives legal spouses. Vt. Stat. Ann. tit. 15, §§1201-1207 (2004). California's domestic partnership statute, which gives full rights to a spousal intestate or elective share, applies to same-sex partners of any age and opposite-sex couples in which at least one of the partners is 62 or older. Cal. Fam. Code Ann. §297 (2004).

More recently, Massachusetts joined Belgium and Canada in allowing same-sex marriages, but only for Massachusetts residents. See Gallanis, supra, at 70-73; Goodridge v. Department of Pub. Health, 798 N.E.2d 941 (Mass. 2003); Opinion of the Justices to the Senate, 802 N.E.2d 565 (Mass. 2004). The Massachusetts legislature, however, has proposed an amendment to the Massachusetts constitution that would authorize civil unions, not marriages, for same-sex couples. In addition, in response to the Massachusetts *Goodridge* decision, which recognized same-sex marriages, opponents of same-sex marriage launched efforts in most states to amend their state constitutions to prohibit the recognition of same-sex marriages. Most of these proposals failed initially in the state legislatures, but in November 2004 same-sex marriages were banned by popular vote in 13 states. See Gallanis, supra, at 75.

In 1995 Professor Waggoner proposed an amendment to the UPC—to become UPC §2-102B—that would have provided an intestate share for "committed partners." A committed partner was defined as a person "sharing a common household with the decedent in a marriage-like relationship." Although Waggoner's proposal was never adopted by the Uniform Law Commissioners, it was never rejected either. In 2002 the Joint Editorial Board for Uniform Trusts and Estates Acts revisited Waggoner's proposal, appointing Professor Gallanis as special reporter for the project and tasking him with the preparation of a study on, and a model statute for, inheritance rights of domestic partners. The JEB then abandoned the project in 2004, but it consented to Gallanis's publishing his study and model statute. Under the Gallanis proposal, both same-sex and opposite-sex domestic partners would be entitled to spousal rights to inheritance and an elective share. Whether the Gallanis proposal will influence the ongoing debate in the state legislatures, and whether the Uniform Law Commission will ever take an official position on this issue, remains to be seen.

In a state that gives domestic partners spousal inheritance rights, would amounts passing to a domestic partner be entitled to the more favorable tax treatment under federal law that is afforded to property that passes to a surviving spouse? If a same-sex couple was married in Massachusetts but then moved to another state, would the surviving same-sex spouse be entitled to take an intestate share under that other state's law? Under Massachusetts law? See Jennifer Seidman, Functional Families and Dysfunctional Laws: Committed Partners and Intestate Succession, 75 U. Colo. L. Rev. 211 (2004); Barbara J. Cox, Making the Case to Go Forward: Using an "Incidents of Marriage" Analysis When Considering Interstate Recognition of Same-Sex Couples' Marriages, Civil Unions, and Domestic Partnerships, 13 Widener L.J. 699 (2004); Anita Y. Woudenberg, Giving DOMA Some Credit: The Validity of Applying Defense of Marriage Acts to Civil Unions under the Full Faith and Credit Clause, 38 Val. U.L. Rev. 1509 (2004).

PROBLEM

Suppose *H* marries *W*, a transsexual who was born a man, but had her birth certificate legally changed after undergoing sex-change surgery. Is *W* entitled to an intestate share in *H*'s estate? See Estate of Gardiner, 42 P.3d 120 (Kan. 2002) (no); Melissa Aubin, Defying Classification: Intestacy Issues for Transsexual Surviving Spouses, 82 Or. L. Rev. 1155 (2003).

Simultaneous death. A person succeeds to the property of a decedent only if the person survives the decedent for an instant of time. With the advent of the automobile and the airplane came an increase in deaths of closely related persons in common disasters, particularly husbands and wives. Thus the question arose: When a person dies simultaneously with his heir or devisee, does the heir or devisee succeed to the person's property? If two people die in a common disaster, there is little reason to have their property pass to each other's estates. The other, being dead, would have no use for the property, which instead will pass to the takers of the other's estate, possibly subject to a second round of taxation along the way.

The original Uniform Simultaneous Death Act (USDA) (1940, revised 1953), drafted to deal with this problem, provided that if "there is no sufficient evidence" of the order of deaths, the beneficiary is deemed to have predeceased the donor. Thus, neither inherits from the other. The act further provided that if two joint tenants, *A* and *B*, die simultaneously, one-half of the property is distributed as if *A* survived and one-half is distributed as if *B* survived. The same rule is applied to property held in tenancy by the entirety or community property. With respect to life insurance, when the insured and the beneficiary die simultaneously, the proceeds are distributed as if the insured survived the beneficiary. Although the USDA was at first thought to offer an elegant solution to the simultaneous death problem, the courts were soon faced with the ghastly interpretive question of what constitutes "sufficient evidence" of the order of deaths. The tragic case of Janus v. Tarasewicz, infra, is illustrative. Because of cases such as *Janus*, the act was revised in 1991, as we shall see (pages 72-73).

Before turning to Janus v. Tarasewicz, however, it bears emphasis that the problem of simultaneous death arises not only in intestacy, but also under wills, trusts, insurance policies, and other nonprobate transfers. We nevertheless locate our discussion of it here, in connection with spousal intestate succession rights, for two reasons. First, the simultaneous death problem arises more often in intestacy than elsewhere, because well-drafted instruments typically require a beneficiary to survive the decedent by 30 or 60 days. Under such a provision, a beneficiary who dies in a common disaster with the donor does not qualify to take. Second, because husbands and wives often travel together and are commonly the first takers of the estates of the other, the typical simultaneous death case involves spouses.

Janus v. Tarasewicz

Illinois Appellate Court, First District, 1985
135 Ill. App. 3d 936, 482 N.E.2d 418

O'CONNOR, J.   This non-jury declaratory judgment action arose out of the death of a husband and wife, Stanley and Theresa Janus, who died after ingesting Tylenol capsules which had been laced with cyanide by an unknown perpetrator prior to its sale in stores. Stanley Janus was pronounced dead shortly after he was admitted to the hospital. However, Theresa Janus was placed on life support systems for almost two days before being pronounced dead. Claiming that there was no sufficient evidence that Theresa Janus survived her husband, plaintiff Alojza Janus, Stanley's mother, brought this action for the proceeds of Stanley's $100,000 life insurance policy which named Theresa as the primary beneficiary and plaintiff as the contingent beneficiary. Defendant Metropolitan Life Insurance Company paid the proceeds to defendant Jan Tarasewicz, Theresa's father and the administrator of her estate. The trial court found sufficient evidence that Theresa survived Stanley Janus. We affirm.

The facts of this case are particularly poignant and complex. Stanley and Theresa Janus had recently returned from their honeymoon when, on the evening of September 29, 1982, they gathered with other family members to mourn the death of Stanley's brother, Adam Janus, who had died earlier that day from what was later determined to be cyanide-laced Tylenol capsules. While the family was at Adam's home, Stanley and Theresa Janus unknowingly took some of the contaminated Tylenol. Soon afterwards, Stanley collapsed on the kitchen floor.

Theresa was still standing when Diane O'Sullivan, a registered nurse and a neighbor of Adam Janus, was called to the scene. Stanley's pulse was weak so she began cardiopulmonary resuscitation (CPR) on him. Within minutes, Theresa Janus began having seizures. After paramedic teams began arriving, Ms. O'Sullivan went into the living room to assist with Theresa. While she was working on Theresa, Ms. O'Sullivan could hear Stanley's "heavy and labored breathing." She believed that both Stanley and Theresa died before they were taken to the ambulance, but she could not tell who died first.

Ronald Mahon, a paramedic for the Arlington Heights Fire Department, arrived at approximately 5:45 P.M. He saw Theresa faint and go into a seizure. Her pupils did not respond to light but she was breathing on her own during the time that he worked on her. Mahon also assisted with Stanley, giving him drugs to stimulate heart contractions. Mahon later prepared the paramedic's report on Stanley. One entry in the report shows that at 18:00 hours Stanley had "zero blood pressure, zero pulse, and zero respiration." However, Mahon stated that the times in the report were merely approximations. He was able to say that Stanley was in the ambulance en route to the hospital when his vital signs disappeared.

When paramedic Robert Lockhart arrived at 5:55 P.M., both victims were unconscious with non-reactive pupils. Theresa's seizures had ceased but she was in a decerebrate posture in which her arms and legs were rigidly extended and her arms were rotated inward toward her body, thus, indicating severe neurological dysfunction. At that time, she was breathing only four or five times a minute and, shortly thereafter, she stopped breathing on her own altogether. Lockhart intubated them both by placing tubes down their tracheae to keep their air passages open. Prior to being taken to the ambulance, they were put on "ambu-bags" which is a form of artificial respiration whereby the paramedic respirates the patient by squeezing a bag. Neither Stanley nor Theresa showed any signs of being able to breathe on their own while they were being transported to Northwest Community Hospital in Arlington Heights, Illinois. However, Lockhart stated that when Theresa was turned over to the hospital personnel, she had a palpable pulse and blood pressure.

The medical director of the intensive care unit at the hospital, Dr. Thomas Kim, examined them when they arrived in the emergency room at approximately 6:30 P.M. Stanley had no blood pressure or pulse. An electrocardiogram detected electrical activity in Stanley Janus' heart but there was no synchronization between his heart's electrical activity and its pumping activity. A temporary pacemaker was inserted in an unsuccessful attempt to resuscitate him. Because he never developed spontaneous blood pressure, pulse or signs of respiration, Stanley Janus was pronounced dead at 8:15 P.M. on September 29, 1982.

Like Stanley, Theresa Janus showed no visible vital signs when she was admitted to the emergency room. However, hospital personnel were able to get her heart beating on its own again, so they did not insert a pacemaker. They were also able to establish a measurable, though unsatisfactory, blood pressure. Theresa was taken off the "ambu-bag" and put on a mechanical respirator. In Dr. Kim's opinion, Theresa was in a deep coma with "very unstable vital signs" when she was moved to the intensive care unit at 9:30 P.M. on September 29, 1982.

While Theresa was in the intensive care unit, numerous entries in her hospital records indicated that she had fixed and dilated pupils. However, one entry made at 2:32 A.M. on September 30, 1982, indicated that a nurse apparently detected a minimal reaction to light in Theresa's right pupil but not in her left pupil.

On September 30, 1982, various tests were performed in order to assess Theresa's brain function. These tests included an electroencephalogram (EEG) to measure electrical activity in her brain and a cerebral blood flow test to determine whether there was any blood circulating in her brain. In addition, Theresa exhibited no gag or cord reflexes, no response to pain or other external stimuli. As a result of these tests, Theresa Janus was diagnosed as having sustained total brain death, her life support systems then were terminated, and she was pronounced dead at 1:15 P.M. on October 1, 1982.

Death certificates were issued for Stanley and Theresa Janus more than three weeks later by a medical examiner's physician who never examined them. The certificates listed Stanley Janus' date of death as September 29, 1982, and Theresa Janus' date of death as October 1, 1982. Concluding that Theresa survived Stanley, the Metropolitan Life Insurance Company paid the proceeds of Stanley's life insurance policy to the administrator of Theresa's estate.

On January 6, 1983, plaintiff brought the instant declaratory judgment action against the insurance company and the administrators of Stanley and Theresa's estates, claiming the proceeds of the insurance policy as the contingent beneficiary of the policy. Also, the administrator of Stanley's estate filed a counterclaim against Theresa's estate seeking a declaration as to the disposition of the assets of Stanley's estate.

. . . Dr. Kenneth Vatz, a neurologist on the hospital staff, was called as an expert witness by plaintiff. Although he never actually examined Theresa, he had originally read her EEG as part of hospital routine. Without having seen her other hospital records, his initial evaluation of her EEG was that it showed some minimal electrical activity of living brain cells in the frontal portion of Theresa's brain. After reading her records and reviewing the EEG, however, he stated that the electrical activity measured by the EEG was "very likely" the result of interference from surrounding equipment in the intensive care unit. He concluded that Theresa was brain dead at the time of her admission to the hospital but he could not give an opinion as to who died first.

The trial court also heard an evidence deposition of Dr. Joseph George Hanley, a neurosurgeon who testified as an expert witness on behalf of the defendants. Based on his examination of their records, Dr. Hanley concluded that Stanley Janus died on September 29, 1982. He further concluded that Theresa Janus did not die until her vital signs disappeared on October 1, 1982. His conclusion that she did not die prior to that time was based on: (1) the observations by hospital personnel that Theresa Janus had spontaneous pulse and blood pressure which did not have to be artificially maintained; (2) the instance when Theresa Janus' right pupil allegedly reacted to light; and (3) Theresa's EEG which showed some brain function and which, in his opinion, could not have resulted from outside interference. At the conclusion of the trial, the court held that the evidence was sufficient to show that Theresa survived Stanley, but the court was not prepared to say by how long she survived him. Plaintiff and the administrator of Stanley's estate appeal. In essence, their main contention is that there is not sufficient evidence to prove that both victims did not suffer brain death prior to their arrival at the hospital on September 29, 1982.

Dual standards for determining when legal death occurs in Illinois were set forth in the case of In re Haymer, 450 N.E.2d 940 (Ill. App. 1983). There, the court determined that a comatose child attached to a mechanical life support system was legally dead on the date he was medically determined to have sustained total brain death, rather than on the date that his heart stopped functioning. . . . In a footnote, the court stated that widely accepted characteristics of brain death include: (1) unreceptivity and unresponsivity to intensely painful stimuli; (2) no spontaneous movement or breathing for at least one hour; (3) no blinking, no swallowing, and fixed and dilated pupils; (4) flat EEGs taken twice with at least a 24-hour intervening period; and (5) absence of drug intoxication or hyperthermia. . . .

Regardless of which standard of death is applied, survivorship is a fact which must be proven by a preponderance of the evidence by the party whose claim depends on survivorship. In re Estate of Moran, 395 N.E.2d 579 (Ill. 1979). The operative provisions of the Illinois version of the Uniform Simultaneous Death Act provides in pertinent part:

> If the title to property or its devolution depends upon the priority of death and there is no sufficient evidence that the persons have died otherwise than simultaneously and

there is no other provision in the will, trust agreement, deed, contract of insurance or other governing instrument for distribution of the property different from the provisions of this Section:

    (a) The property of each person shall be disposed of as if he had survived. . . .

    (d) If the insured and the beneficiary of a policy of life or accident insurance have so died, the proceeds of the policy shall be distributed as if the insured had survived the beneficiary.

Ill. Rev. Stat. 1981, ch. 110 1/2, par. 3-1. . . .

Although the use of sophisticated medical technology can also make it difficult to determine when death occurs, the context of this case does not require a determination as to the exact moment at which the decedents died. Rather, the trial court's task was to determine whether or not there was sufficient evidence that Theresa Janus survived her husband. Our task on review of this factually disputed case is to determine whether the trial court's finding was against the manifest weight of the evidence. . . . We hold that it was not.

In the case at bar, both victims arrived at the hospital with artificial respirators and no obvious vital signs. There is no dispute among the treating physicians and expert witnesses that Stanley Janus died in both a cardiopulmonary sense and a brain death sense when his vital signs disappeared en route to the hospital and were never reestablished. He was pronounced dead at 8:15 P.M. on September 29, 1982, only after intensive procedures such as electro-shock, medication, and the insertion of a pacemaker failed to resuscitate him.

In contrast, these intensive procedures were not necessary with Theresa Janus because hospital personnel were able to reestablish a spontaneous blood pressure and pulse which did not have to be artificially maintained by a pacemaker or medication. Once spontaneous circulation was restored in the emergency room, Theresa was put on a mechanical respirator and transferred to the intensive care unit. Clearly, efforts to preserve Theresa Janus' life continued after more intensive efforts on Stanley's behalf had failed.

It is argued that the significance of Theresa Janus' cardiopulmonary functions, as a sign of life, was rendered ambiguous by the use of artificial respiration. In particular, reliance is placed upon expert testimony that a person can be brain dead and still have a spontaneous pulse and blood pressure which is indirectly maintained by artificial respiration. The fact remains, however, that Dr. Kim, an intensive care specialist who treated Theresa, testified that her condition in the emergency room did not warrant a diagnosis of brain death. In his opinion, Theresa Janus did not suffer irreversible brain death until much later, when extensive treatment failed to preserve her brain function and vital signs. . . .

There was also other evidence presented at trial which indicated that Theresa Janus was not brain dead on September 29, 1982. Theresa's EEG, taken on September 30, 1982, was not flat but rather it showed some delta waves of extremely low amplitude. Dr. Hanley concluded that Theresa's EEG taken on September 30 exhibited brain activity. Dr. Vatz disagreed. Since the trier of fact determines the credibility of expert witnesses and the weight to be given to their testimony . . . , the trial court in this case could have reasonably given greater weight to Dr. Hanley's opinion than to Dr. Vatz'. . . .

In conclusion, we believe that the record clearly established that the treating physicians' diagnoses of death with respect to Stanley and Theresa Janus were made in accordance with "the usual and customary standards of medical practice." Stanley Janus was diagnosed as having sustained irreversible cessation of circulatory and respiratory functions on September 29, 1982. These same physicians concluded that Theresa Janus' condition on that date did not warrant a diagnosis of death and, therefore, they continued their efforts to preserve her life. Their conclusion that Theresa Janus did not die until October 1, 1982, was based on various factors including the restoration of certain of her vital signs as well as other neurological evidence. The trial court found that these facts and circumstances constituted sufficient evidence that Theresa Janus survived her husband. It was not necessary to determine the exact moment at which Theresa died or by how long she survived him, and the trial court properly declined to do so. Viewing the record in its entirety, we cannot say that the trial court's finding of sufficient evidence of Theresa's survivorship was against the manifest weight of the evidence. . . .

Accordingly, there being sufficient evidence that Theresa Janus survived Stanley Janus, the judgment of the circuit court of Cook County is affirmed.

Affirmed.

PROBLEMS, QUESTIONS, AND NOTE

1. Suppose that *H* and *W* both drown in a boating accident. The evidence shows that *W* was a better swimmer and in better health than *H*. In addition, the autopsy shows *W* drowned after a violent death struggle while *H* passively submitted to death. Is there sufficient evidence of *W*'s survival? See In re Estate of Campbell, 641 P.2d 610 (Or. App. 1982).

H and *W* are killed in the crash of a private airplane. An autopsy reveals *W*'s brain is intact and there is carbon monoxide in her bloodstream; *H*'s brain is crushed and there is no carbon monoxide in his bloodstream. Is there sufficient evidence of *W*'s survival? See In re Bucci, 293 N.Y.S.2d 994 (Sur. 1968).

If you are interested in whether a severed head retains feeling and consciousness for a few moments after severance and therefore arguably remains alive for that period, the experiments carried on by French doctors after the invention of the guillotine are instructive. The doctors were trying to discover if death by guillotine was really instantaneous and painless, as Dr. Guillotin, the inventor, claimed. See Alister Kershaw, A History of the Guillotine 80-89 (1958) (severed heads had looks of indignation or astonishment or, as agreed in advance of decapitation, winked in response to questions). See also Antonia Fraser, Mary Queen of Scots 539 (1969), reporting that Mary's lips moved for a quarter of an hour after she was beheaded.

2. Of what possible purpose is litigation such as in *Janus*? In obtaining life insurance for Theresa's benefit, what do you think was Stanley's likely purpose, for Theresa to use the money while alive, or for her to convey it to her family to the exclusion of his? Consider that Stanley named his mother as the alternate taker under the policy if Theresa did not survive him. Is the cost of litigating this case and hiring experts money well spent?

3. The cause of the gruesome litigation in *Janus* and similar cases is the "no sufficient evidence" language of the original Uniform Simultaneous Death Act (USDA) (1940, revised 1953). To remedy the "no sufficient evidence" problem,

UPC §§2-104 and 2-702 (1990) provide that an heir or devisee or life insurance beneficiary who fails to survive by 120 hours (5 days) is deemed to have predeceased the decedent. The USDA was amended in 1991 to require survivorship by 120 hours, making it parallel with the UPC. Under both the amended UPC and USDA, a claimant must establish survivorship by 120 hours by clear and convincing evidence, not merely by some "sufficient evidence" as provided in the original UPC and USDA.

Is survivorship by 120 hours long enough? Suppose someone is lacking in higher brain function, but the family insists that the patient's heart and lungs be kept working on a ventilator for more than 120 hours, long enough to allow the patient to inherit from someone else who died in the same common disaster. Would the 30-, 60-, or 90-day survivorship clauses common in well-drafted wills work better?

3.   Shares of Descendants

In all jurisdictions in this country, after the spouse's share (if any) is set aside, children and issue of deceased children take the remainder of the property to the exclusion of everyone else. When one of several children has died before the decedent, leaving descendants, all states provide that the child's descendants shall *represent* the dead child and divide the child's share among themselves.

The following diagram involves this situation. Assume that the intestate decedent, *A*, a widow, has three children. One of her three children, *C*, dies before *A*, survived by a husband and two children. The decedent is survived by two children, *B* and *D*, and by five grandchildren, *E, F, G, H,* and *I.* Thus:

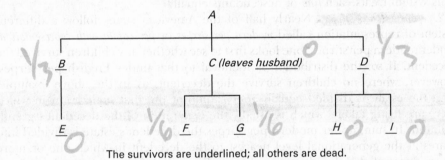

The survivors are underlined; all others are dead.

C's children take *C*'s share by *representation* of their dead parent. Therefore *A*'s heirs are *B* (1/3), *D* (1/3), *F* (1/6), and *G* (1/6). Observe that *E, H,* and *I* take nothing because their parents are living. (Observe also that *C*'s spouse, the decedent's son-in-law, takes nothing. Sons-in-law and daughters-in-law are excluded as intestate successors in virtually all states. Legislatures have decided that the decedent's property should escheat to the state before allowing a son-in-law or daughter-in-law to inherit.)

In other, more complicated contexts, there are different views about what taking by representation means. The fundamental issue is whether the division into shares should begin at the generational level immediately below the decedent *or* at the closest generational level with a descendant of the decedent alive. To see this, take this case: *A* has two children, *B* and *C. B* predeceases *A,* leaving a child *D.*

C predeceases *A*, leaving two children, *E* and *F*. *A* dies intestate leaving no surviving spouse, and survived by *D*, *E*, and *F*. Thus:

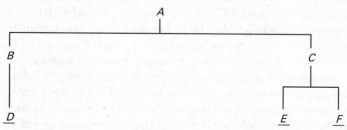

The survivors are underlined; all others are dead.

How is *A*'s estate distributed? There are three basic systems.

1. *English per stirpes*. In England, *A*'s property is divided into two shares at the level of *A*'s children, and *D* takes *B*'s one-half by representation and *E* and *F* split *C*'s one-half by representation. The *English distribution per stirpes* ("by the stocks") is to divide the property into as many shares as there are living children of the designated person and deceased children who have descendants living. The children of each descendant represent their deceased parent and are moved into their parent's position beginning at the first generation below the designated person. This system of representation owes much to the English system of primogeniture, in which the son represented the deceased father, and the grandson represented the deceased son. In 2004 the English system of per stirpes distribution among descendants was followed in about 14 states.[6] It is sometimes called *strict per stirpes*. This system treats each *line* of descendants equally.

2. *Modern per stirpes*. Nearly half of the American states follow a different system of representation called *modern per stirpes* or *per capita with representation*. Under modern per stirpes, one looks first to see whether any children survived the decedent. If so, the distribution is identical to that under English per stirpes. However, where no children survive the decedent, as in the above example, then the estate is divided equally (per capita) at the first generation in which there are living takers, which is usually the generation of the decedent's grandchildren. In sum, under modern per stirpes the decedent's estate is divided into shares at the generational level nearest to the decedent in which one or more descendants of the decedent are alive and provides for representation of any deceased descendant on that level by his or her descendants.

In the above example, where *B* and *C* are dead, *D*, *E*, and *F* are all grandchildren of equal degree of kinship to *A*, and *A*'s estate is divided equally among them in thirds. If *F* had predeceased *A*, leaving descendants, *F*'s descendants would represent *F* and take *F*'s one-third. Thus representation is used only to bring the surviving descendants of deceased descendants up to the level where a descendant is alive. This system treats each *line beginning at the closest living generation* equally.

---

6. For our counts in this section we relied on Jeffrey A. Schoenblum, 2004 Multistate Guide to Estate Planning; Restatement (Third) of Property: Wills and Other Donative Transfers §§2.2-2.3, statutory notes (1999); and reference to the text of the statutes themselves to resolve inconsistencies between Schoenblum and the Restatement. Unfortunately, because of idiosyncrasies in the statutes, several resist simple classification.

The original UPC (1969) defined representation in a manner that accords with the modern per stirpes system in all but rare cases.[7] Two studies have indicated that an overwhelming majority of people prefer the modern system of per stirpes distribution, dividing the stocks at the level where someone is alive. See Mary L. Fellows, Rita J. Simon, Teal E. Snapp & William D. Snapp, An Empirical Study of the Illinois Statutory Estate Plan, 1976 U. Ill. L.F. 717, 741 (95 percent of the persons interviewed); Comment, A Comparison of Iowans' Dispositive Preferences with Selected Provisions of the Iowa and Uniform Probate Codes, 63 Iowa L. Rev. 1041, 1111 (1978) (87 percent).

3. *Per capita at each generation (1990 UPC).* A more complicated system of distribution known as *per capita at each generation* has been advocated by Professor Waggoner since the early 1970s. See Lawrence W. Waggoner, A Proposed Alternative to the Uniform Probate Code's System for Intestate Distribution among Descendants, 66 Nw. U.L. Rev. 626 (1971).

Section 2-106(b) of the 1990 UPC, for which Waggoner was the reporter, adopts this approach:

> (b) [Decedent's Descendants.] If, under Section 2-103(1), a decedent's intestate estate or a part thereof passes "by representation" to the decedent's descendants, the estate or part thereof is divided into as many equal shares as there are (i) surviving descendants in the generation nearest to the decedent which contains one or more surviving descendants and (ii) deceased descendants in the same generation who left surviving descendants, if any. Each surviving descendant in the nearest generation is allocated one share. The remaining shares, if any, are combined and then divided in the same manner among the surviving descendants of the deceased descendants as if the surviving descendants who were allocated a share and their surviving descendants had predeceased the decedent.

Under 1990 UPC §2-106(b), the initial division of shares is made at the level where one or more descendants are alive (as under modern per stirpes), but the shares of deceased persons on that level are treated as one pot and are dropped down and divided equally among the representatives on the next generational level. Thus in the situation pictured below, *D* takes a one-third share; the two-thirds that would have passed to *B* and *C* had they been living is divided equally among all the children of *B* and *C*. *E, F,* and *G* each take a two-ninths share.

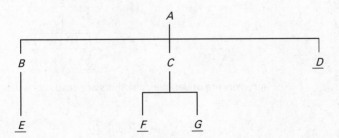

The survivors are underlined; all others are dead.

---

7. On the rare case in which the 1969 UPC produces a different result, see Restatement, supra, §2.3, cmts. e-f.

Professor Lawrence W. Waggoner

This system treats *each taker at each generation equally with the other takers at that generation*. The premise of this approach is that those equally related to the decedent should take equal shares: "Equally near, equally dear."

The per capita at each generation system is applied to descendants of parents and grandparents of the decedent, when they are entitled to take, as well as to descendants of the decedent. UPC §2-106(c) (1990). By 2004, UPC §2-106 had been adopted in about a dozen states, including Arizona, Colorado, Michigan, New York, and North Carolina.

PROBLEM AND QUESTIONS

1. *A* has two children, *B* and *C*. *B* predeceases *A*, leaving a child *D*. *C* predeceases *A*, leaving two children, *E* and *F*. *E* predeceases *A*, leaving two children, *G* and *H*, who survive *A*. Thus:

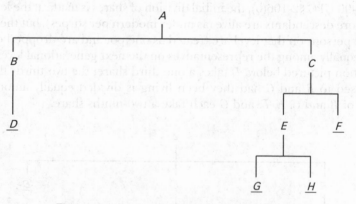

The survivors are underlined; all others are dead.

A dies intestate leaving no surviving spouse. How is *A*'s estate distributed under the modern per stirpes system? Under the English per stirpes system? Under the 1990 UPC? Under the intestacy statute of your state?

2.   Assume the same facts as in Problem 1 except that *A* has another child, *Z*, and *F* has a child *I*. *Z* predeceases *A*, leaving no descendants. *F* survives *A*, as does *F*'s child *I*. Thus:

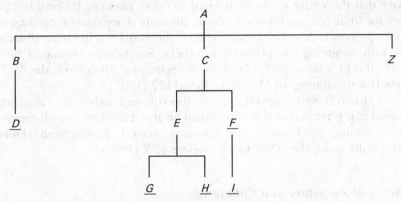

The survivors are underlined; all others are dead.

Does the presence in the family tree of the surviving *I* and the deceased *Z* change the results under any of the intestacy systems? The answer is No. *I* does not take because her parent *F* is alive, and inasmuch as no one in *Z*'s line remains, it is ignored.

3.   Which of the three systems do you prefer? Which would your parents prefer? Are you sure? Perhaps you'd better ask. More importantly, which would most decedents prefer? A questionnaire developed by one of the UPC advisors, to which 75 responses from targeted lawyers and their clients were received, revealed that 85 percent of the lawyers responding, perhaps reflecting their law school training in English property law, believed their clients wanted the English per stirpes distribution, but that 71 percent of the clients themselves wanted distribution per capita at each generation. Raymond H. Young, Meaning of "Issue" and "Descendants," 13 ACTEC Prob. Notes 225 (1988). Although this sampling is small and the methodology problematic, it provides evidence that some lawyers assume what their clients want without explaining the options to the clients. See Roger W. Andersen, Informed Decisionmaking in Office Practice, 28 B.C.L. Rev. 225 (1987), arguing that a lawyer has a duty to allow a client to make informed decisions on most estate planning issues rather than assuming that the lawyer knows best.

4.   Suppose that a will devises property "to the descendants of *A* per stirpes." Which of the three systems would a court apply in interpreting the will? Unfortunately, the answer varies depending on the state. In yet another example of the influence of intestate succession rules outside of intestacy, in some states the will may be interpreted to call for the same representational system provided by the state's intestacy laws. See pages 652-655.

NOTE: NEGATIVE DISINHERITANCE

In anger many parents have threatened to disinherit their children, but few do it by *negative disinheritance*, an express statement in their wills disinheriting a child. Yet many children are effectively disinherited when their parents leave their estates to the surviving spouse rather than to the children.

An old rule of American inheritance law says that disinheritance is not possible by a declaration in a will that "my son John shall receive none of my property." To disinherit John—that is, to prevent John from taking an intestate share—it is also necessary that the entire estate be devised to other persons. If there is a partial intestacy for some reason, John will take an intestate share notwithstanding such a provision in a will. A testator cannot alter the statutory intestate distribution scheme without giving the property to others. See Cook v. Estate of Seeman, 858 S.W.2d 114 (Ark. 1993); Frederic S. Schwartz, Models of the Will and Negative Disinheritance, 48 Mercer L. Rev. 1137 (1997).

UPC §2-101(b) (1990), page 60, changes this rule and authorizes a negative will. The barred heir is treated as if he disclaimed his intestate share, which means he is treated as having predeceased the intestate. Accord, Restatement (Third) of Property: Wills and Other Donative Transfers §2.7 (1999).

4.   *Shares of Ancestors and Collaterals*

When the intestate decedent is survived by a descendant, the decedent's ancestors and collaterals do not take. When there is no descendant, after deducting the spouse's share, in nearly half the states the rest of the intestate's property is usually distributed to the decedent's parents, as under the UPC.

If there is no spouse or parent, the decedent's heirs will be more remote ancestors or collateral kindred. All persons who are related by blood to the decedent but who are not descendants or ancestors are called *collateral kindred*. Descendants of the decedent's parents, other than the decedent and the decedent's issue, are called *first-line collaterals*. Descendants of the decedent's grandparents, other than decedent's parents and their issue, are called *second-line collaterals*. The reason for this terminology is seen by glancing at the Table of Consanguinity on page 79, which has lines descending from the decedent's ancestors.

If the decedent is not survived by a spouse, descendant, or parent, in all jurisdictions intestate property passes to brothers and sisters and their descendants. The descendants of any deceased brothers and sisters (nephews and nieces) take by representation in the same manner as decedent's descendants, discussed at pages 73-77. See, e.g., UPC §2-106(c) (1990), which is substantially identical with UPC §2-106(b), page 75, and calls for representation per capita at each generation. Hence:

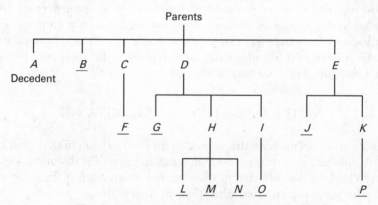

The survivors are underlined; all others are dead.

TABLE OF CONSANGUINITY

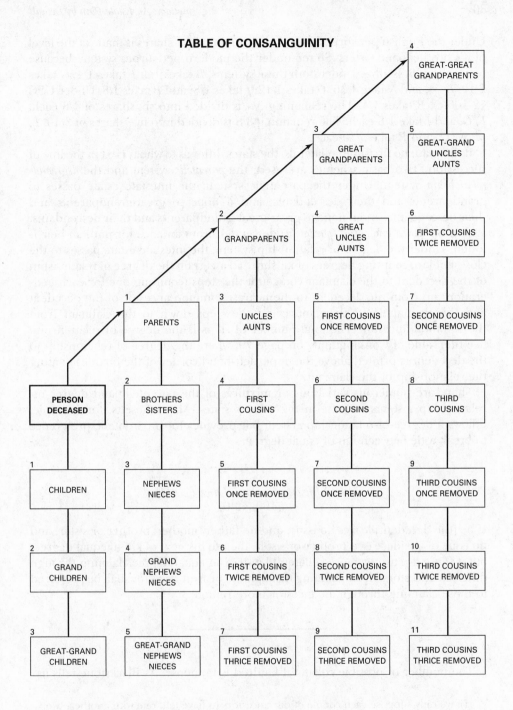

				4 GREAT-GREAT GRANDPARENTS
			3 GREAT GRANDPARENTS	5 GREAT-GRAND UNCLES AUNTS
		2 GRANDPARENTS	4 GREAT UNCLES AUNTS	6 FIRST COUSINS TWICE REMOVED
	1 PARENTS	3 UNCLES AUNTS	5 FIRST COUSINS ONCE REMOVED	7 SECOND COUSINS ONCE REMOVED
PERSON DECEASED	2 BROTHERS SISTERS	4 FIRST COUSINS	6 SECOND COUSINS	8 THIRD COUSINS
1 CHILDREN	3 NEPHEWS NIECES	5 FIRST COUSINS ONCE REMOVED	7 SECOND COUSINS ONCE REMOVED	9 THIRD COUSINS ONCE REMOVED
2 GRAND CHILDREN	4 GRAND NEPHEWS NIECES	6 FIRST COUSINS TWICE REMOVED	8 SECOND COUSINS TWICE REMOVED	10 THIRD COUSINS TWICE REMOVED
3 GREAT-GRAND CHILDREN	5 GREAT-GRAND NEPHEWS NIECES	7 FIRST COUSINS THRICE REMOVED	9 SECOND COUSINS THRICE REMOVED	11 THIRD COUSINS THRICE REMOVED

Under the English per stirpes system, division into four shares is made at the level of A's brothers and sisters. So too under the modern per stirpes system, because one sibling, B, is alive. Under both these systems, B takes 1/4; F takes 1/4; G takes 1/12; L, M, and N take 1/36; O takes 1/12; J takes 1/8; and P takes 1/8. Under UPC §2-106(c), B takes 1/4. The remaining 3/4 is divided into six shares of 1/8 each. F, G, and J take 1/8 each. The remaining 3/8 is divided into five shares of 3/40. L, M, N, O, and P take 3/40 each.

If there are no first-line collaterals, the states differ as to who is next in the line of succession. Two basic schemes are used: the *parentelic* system and the *degree-of-relationship* system. Under the parentelic system, the intestate estate passes to grandparents and their descendants, and if none to great-grandparents and their descendants, and if none to great-great-grandparents and their descendants, and so on down each line (*parentela*) descended from an ancestor until an heir is found. Under the degree-of-relationship system, the intestate estate passes to the closest of kin, counting degrees of kinship. To ascertain the degree of relationship of the decedent to the claimant you count the steps (counting one for each generation) up from the decedent to the nearest common ancestor of the decedent and the claimant, and then you count the steps down to the claimant from the common ancestor. The total number of steps is the degree of relationship. See the Table of Consanguinity on page 79, where the degree of relationship to the decedent is printed above the upper left-hand corner of the box designating the relationship of the claimant.

There are numerous variations or mixtures of the parentelic and degree-of-relationship systems in force in the various states. Massachusetts, for example, follows a degree-of-relationship system but provides for a parentelic preference to break a tie between kin of equal degree.

Massachusetts General Laws (2004)
ch. 190, §3(6)

If he [the decedent] leaves no issue, and no father, mother, brother or sister, and no issue of any deceased brother or sister, then to his next of kin in equal degree; but if there are two or more collateral kindred in equal degree claiming through different ancestors, those claiming through the nearest ancestor shall be preferred to those claiming through an ancestor more remote.

———————

The number of possible collateral kindred is immense. As Blackstone tells us:

[I]f we only suppose each couple of our ancestors to have left, one with another, two children; and each of those children on an average to have left two more, (and, without such a supposition, the human species must be daily diminishing;) we shall find that all of us have now subsisting near two hundred and seventy millions of kindred in the fifteenth degree; at the same distance from the several common ancestors as ourselves are; besides those that are one or two descents nearer to or farther from the common stock, who may amount to as many more. And if this calculation should appear incompatible with the number of inhabitants on the earth, it is because, by intermarriages among the several descendants from the same ancestor, a hundred or a thousand modes of consanguinity may be consolidated in one person, or he may be related to us a hundred or a thousand different ways. [William Blackstone, Commentaries *205. Blackstone also observes that if you go back 20 generations you have 1,048,576 ancestors (disregarding the possibility of intermarriage among relatives)!]

Should the law permit intestate succession by these remote collaterals, known to lawyers as "laughing heirs" (that is, persons so distantly related to the decedent as to suffer no sense of bereavement, laughing all the way to the bank)? This question was brought into sharp focus by three famous cases in the early part of the twentieth century, where hordes of fortune seekers appeared on death. These were the cases of Ella Wendel, Ida Wood, and Henrietta Garrett, all of whom died during the Great Depression:

(1) Ella Wendel, a recluse, died in 1931, leaving a will devising most of her $40 million estate to charity. The only persons who may contest a will are those persons who would take if the will is held invalid. Some 2,303 fortune hunters strove to establish they were her next of kin, so that they might contest her will as her intestate successors. Reams of evidence were fabricated, birth and death certificates altered, and tales spun of incest and children born out of wedlock. One man was sent to jail for fabricating evidence, and Surrogate Foley referred the activities of six lawyers to the Grievance Committee of the Bar. Ultimately nine persons were established to be her cousins, and they settled out of court with the charities. In re Wendel, 257 N.Y.S. 87 (Sur. 1932); 262 N.Y.S. 41 (Sur. 1933); 287 N.Y.S. 893 (Sur. 1936). The late Justice Harlan's participation in the *Wendel* litigation is traced in Cloyd Laporte, John M. Harlan Saves the Ella Wendel Estate, 59 A.B.A.J. 868 (1973).

(2) Ida Wood, the widow of a U.S. congressman from New York, died intestate in 1932. For more than 20 years, she and her two sisters (who predeceased her) had barricaded themselves in a New York hotel room, into which no one was permitted to enter. During her life Ida had spun a web of deceit to hide who she really was. The evidence finally accepted by the court showed she had been born Ellen Walsh in Ireland, had moved with her parents to Boston, and had been her husband's mistress for ten years before they married. Once married and propelled into high society, Ida drew a curtain across her past. She made up vague stories of having been born a Mayfield and brought up in New Orleans. Her mother, and some other members of her family, took the name Mayfield, and Ida carved "Mayfield" on their tombstones. Fearful of a depression, Ida kept $500,000 in cash tied around her waist. When she died, some 1,100 persons claimed to be her next of kin—including a great many persons named Mayfield from Louisiana. Ultimately, the court established as Ida's next of kin some first cousins once removed (none of whom Ida had seen since her marriage to Wood 65 years before). In re Wood, 299 N.Y.S. 195 (Sur. 1937). The whole fascinating story is recounted in Joseph A. Cox, The Recluse of Herald Square (1964).

(3) Henrietta E. Garrett died intestate in Philadelphia in 1930, leaving an estate of over $17 million. Nearly 26,000 claims were filed by persons claiming to be her heirs. The testimony covered 390 volumes and over 115,000 pages. Finally, three persons were found to be first cousins of Henrietta. In 1953, after 23 years of litigation, the Supreme Court of Pennsylvania finally ordered the Garrett estate closed. Estate of Garrett, 94 A.2d 357 (Pa. 1953).

With these cases in mind, Professor Cavers predicted that the rules of succession would be revised to abolish laughing heirs. David F. Cavers, Change in the

American Family and the "Laughing Heir," 20 Iowa L. Rev. 203, 208 (1935). A substantial minority of jurisdictions has done so. UPC §2-103 (1990), page 61, is typical. It does not permit inheritance by intestate succession beyond grand-parents and their descendants. It eliminates inheritance by more remote relatives traced through great-grandparents and other more remote ancestors.

Some legislatures have moved in the opposite direction—permitting step-children and kin of a predeceased spouse to inherit when the decedent leaves no blood relatives. In California, the probate code extends intestate succession not only to stepchildren but also to mothers-in-law, fathers-in-law, brothers-in-law, and sisters-in-law—but not to sons-in-law or daughters-in-law! Cal. Prob. Code §6402(e)-(g) (2004). If *A*'s mother-in-law can inherit from *A*, but *A* cannot inherit from *A*'s mother-in-law, does this have a rational basis?

If the intestate leaves no survivors entitled to take under the intestacy statute, the intestate's property *escheats* to the state. Escheats of substantial estates are rare. Relatives usually keep tabs on kinfolk of obvious wealth, and thus the larger the estate, the more likely it is that there will be heirs claiming it. Moreover, heir-hunting firms seek out unknown or uninformed heirs, offering to disclose the name of an estate to which the person may be an heir in exchange for a share of the inheritance. See Estate of Wright, 108 Cal. Rptr. 2d 572 (App. 2001) (just over one-third of estate). See also Monte Burke, Good Will Hunting, Forbes, Nov. 27, 2000 (reporting that "heir hunting is a booming business").

PROBLEMS AND NOTE

1. The decedent is survived by his mother, his sister, and two nephews (children of a deceased brother). How is the decedent's estate distributed under UPC §2-103 (1990), page 61? Under the intestacy statute of your state?

2. The decedent is survived by one first cousin on his mother's side and by two first cousins on his father's side. How is the decedent's estate distributed under UPC §2-103? Under an intestacy statute of your state? Recall that UPC §2-106 (1990), page 75, which defines representation, is based upon a goal of providing equal shares to those equally related. Is the UPC treatment of the three first cousins consistent with that goal? Why are three grandchildren or three grand-nephews (remember: "equally near, equally dear") treated alike but not three first cousins?

3. The decedent is survived by *A*, the first cousin of the decedent's mother, and by *B*, the granddaughter of the decedent's first cousin. (You can locate these on the Table of Consanguinity, page 79.) How is the decedent's estate distributed under UPC §2-103? Under Mass. Gen. Laws ch. 190, §3(6) (2004), page 80? Under the intestacy statute of your state?

4. Those interested in genealogy puzzles might like to try the one posed by Charles Lutwidge Dodgson, the English writer and mathematician better known as Lewis Carroll, author of Alice's Adventures in Wonderland (1865). The problem: The Governor of Kgovjni wants to give the very smallest dinner party possible and at the same time invite his father's brother-in-law, his brother's father-in-law, his father-in-law's brother, and his brother-in-law's father. To do this, how many guests is it absolutely necessary to invite? The answer: One. If you cannot figure

how this is done using a genealogical tree of only 14 people, see Lewis Carroll, The Complete Works of Lewis Carroll 1031 (Mod. Lib. ed. 1936).

NOTE: HALF-BLOODS

In England, which put great weight on whole-blood relations, the common law courts wholly excluded relatives of the half-blood from inheriting land through intestate succession. This rule has long been abolished in all American states. In a large majority of states, a relative of the half-blood (e.g., a half-sister) is treated the same as a relative of the whole-blood. This is the position of UPC §2-107 (1990). In a few states, a half-blood is given a half share; this was the Scottish rule and was introduced in this country in Virginia. Va. Code Ann. §64.1-2 (2004). In a few other states, a half-blood takes only when there are no whole-blood relatives of the same degree. See Miss. Code Ann. §91-1-5 (2004). In Oklahoma, half-bloods are excluded when there are whole-blood kindred in the same degree and the inheritance came to the decedent by an ancestor and the half-blood is not a descendant of the ancestor. See Okla. Stat. tit. 84, §222 (2004); Nancy I. Kenderdine, Oklahoma's Archaic Half-Blood Inheritance Statute, 49 Okla. L. Rev. 81 (1996).

PROBLEM

M has one child, *A*, by her first marriage and two children, *B* and *C*, by her second marriage. *M* and her second husband die. Then *C* dies intestate, unmarried, and without descendants. How is *C*'s property distributed under the UPC? Under Va. Code Ann. §64.1-2, supra? Under Miss. Code Ann. §91-1-5, supra?

SECTION B.   TRANSFERS TO CHILDREN

1.   Meaning of Children

a.   Adopted Children

Hall v. Vallandingham
Court of Special Appeals of Maryland, 1988
75 Md. App. 187, 540 A.2d 1162

GILBERT, C.J. Adoption did not exist under the common law of England,[8] although it was in use "[a]mong the ancient peoples of Greece, Rome, Egypt and Babylonia." M. Leary and R. Weinberg, Law of Adoption (4th ed. 1979) 1; Lord Mackenzie, Studies in Roman Law, 130-34 (3rd ed. 1870). The primary

---

8. According to J.W. Madden, Handbook of the Law of Persons and Domestic Relations (Wash. 1931) §106, adoption in the sense of the term as used in this country was not a part of the English law until 1926.

purpose for adoption was, and still is, inheritance rights, particularly in "France, Greece, Spain and most of Latin America." Leary and Weinberg, Law of Adoption, 1. Since adoption was not a part of the common law, it owes its existence in this State, and indeed in this nation, to statutory enactments.

The first two general adoption statutes were passed in Texas and Vermont in 1850. Leary and Weinberg, Law of Adoption, 1. Maryland first enacted an Adoption Statute in Laws 1892, Ch. 244, and that law has continued in existence, in various forms, until the present time. The current statute, Maryland Code, Family Law Article Ann. §5-308 provides, in pertinent part:

> (b) [A]fter a decree of adoption is entered:
>   (1) the individual adopted:
>   (i) is the child of the petitioner for all intents and purposes;[9] and
>   (ii) is entitled to all the rights and privileges of and is subject to all the obligations of a child born to the petitioner in wedlock;
>   (2) each living natural parent of the individual adopted is:
>   (i) relieved of all parental duties and obligations to the individual adopted; and
>   (ii) divested of all parental rights as to the individual adopted; and
>   (3) *all rights of inheritance between the individual adopted and the natural relations shall be governed by the Estates and Trusts Article*. (Emphasis supplied.)

The applicable section of the Md. Estates and Trusts Code Ann. §1-207(a), provides:

> An adopted child shall be treated as a natural child of his adopted parent or parents. On adoption, a child no longer shall be considered a child of either natural parent, except that upon adoption by the spouse of a natural parent, the child shall be considered the child of that natural parent.[10]

With that "thumbnail" history of adoption and the current statutes firmly in mind, we turn our attention to the matter sub judice.

Earl J. Vallandingham died in 1956, survived by his widow, Elizabeth, and their four children. Two years later, Elizabeth married Jim Walter Killgore, who adopted the children.

In 1983, twenty-five years after the adoption of Earl's children by Killgore, Earl's brother, William Jr., died childless, unmarried, and intestate. His sole heirs were his surviving brothers and sisters and the children of brothers and sisters who predeceased him.

Joseph W. Vallandingham, the decedent's twin brother, was appointed Personal Representative of the estate. After the Inventory and First Accounting were filed, the four natural children of Earl J. Vallandingham noted exceptions, alleging that they were entitled to the distributive share of their natural uncle's estate that their natural father would have received had he survived William. Est. & Trusts Art. §3-104(b).

---

9. Notwithstanding Maryland law, a child who is eligible for social security survivor's benefits through a deceased natural parent under Federal law does not lose eligibility for the continuation of those benefits because of a subsequent adoption. 42 U.S.C. §402(d).

10. Although the statute speaks in terms of the "adopted child," the person who is adopted need not be a minor child. See Family Law Art. §5-307(a).

The Orphan's Court transmitted the issue to the Circuit Court for St. Mary's County. That tribunal determined that the four natural children of Earl, because of their adoption by their adoptive father, Jim Walter Killgore, were not entitled to inherit from William M. Vallandingham Jr.

Patently unwilling to accept that judgment which effectively disinherited them, the children have journeyed here where they posit to us:

> Did the trial court err in construing Maryland's current law regarding natural inheritance by adopted persons so as to deny the Appellants the right to inherit through their natural paternal uncle, when said Appellants were adopted as minors by their stepfather after the death of their natural father and the remarriage of their natural mother?

When the four natural children of Earl J. Vallandingham were adopted in 1958 by Jim Killgore, then Md. Ann. Code art. 16, §78(b) clearly provided that adopted children retained the right to inherit from their natural parents and relatives.[11] That right of inheritance was removed by the Legislature in 1963 when it declared: "Upon entry of a decree of adoption, the adopted child shall lose all rights of inheritance from its parents and from their natural collateral or lineal relatives." Laws 1963, Ch. 174. Subsequently, the Legislature in 1969 enacted what is the current, above-quoted language of Est. & Trusts Art. §1-207(a). Laws 1969, Ch. 3, §4(c).

The appellants contend that since the explicit language of the 1963 Act proscribing dual inheritance by adoptees was not retained in the present law, Est. & Trusts Art. §1-207(a) implicitly permits adoptees to inherit from natural relatives, as well as the adoptive parents.

The right to receive property by devise or descent is not a natural right but a privilege granted by the State. . . . Every State possesses the power to regulate the manner or term by which property within its dominion may be transmitted by will or inheritance and to prescribe who shall or shall not be capable of receiving that property. A State may deny the privilege altogether or may impose whatever restrictions or conditions upon the grant it deems appropriate. Mager v. Grima, 49 U.S. 490 (1850).[12]

Family Law Art. §5-308(b)(1)(ii) entitles an adopted person to all the rights and privileges of a natural child insofar as the adoptive parents are concerned, but adoption does not confer upon the adopted child *more* rights and privileges than those possessed by a natural child. To construe Est. & Trusts Art. §1-207(a) so as to allow dual inheritance would bestow upon an adopted child a superior status. That status was removed in Laws 1963, Ch. 174 which, as we have said, expressly disallowed the dual inheritance capability of adopted children by providing that "the adopted child shall lose all rights of inheritance from its parents and from their natural collateral or lineal relatives." We think that the current statute, Est. & Trusts Art. §1-207(a), did not alter the substance of the 1963 act which eliminated dual inheritance. Rather, §1-207(a) merely "streamlined" the wording while retaining the meaning.

---

11. "[N]othing in this subtitle shall be construed to prevent the person adopted from inheriting from his natural parents and relatives. . . ."

12. Since the Legislature is elected by the people, it is answerable to the people, and that is the best safeguard against unreasonable laws concerning inheritance.

Family Law Art. §5-308 plainly mandates that adoption be considered a "rebirth" into a completely different relationship. Once a child is adopted, the rights of both the natural parents and relatives are terminated. L.F.M. v. Department of Social Services, 507 A.2d 1151 (Md. App. 1986). Est. & Trusts Art. §1-207(a) and Family Law Art. §5-308 emphasize the clean-cut severance from the natural bloodline. Because an adopted child has no right to inherit *from* the estate of a natural parent who dies intestate, it follows that the same child may not inherit *through* the natural parent by way of representation. What may not be done directly most assuredly may not be done indirectly. The elimination of dual inheritance in 1963 clearly established that policy, and the current language of §1-207(a) simply reflects the continuation of that policy.

We hold that because §1-207(a) eliminates the adopted child's right to inherit from the natural parent it concomitantly abrogated the right to inherit through the natural parent by way of representation.

"The Legislature giveth, and the Legislature taketh away."

Judgment affirmed.

Uniform Probate Code (1990)

§2-113.   INDIVIDUALS RELATED TO DECEDENT THROUGH TWO LINES

An individual who is related to the decedent through two lines of relationship is entitled to only a single share based on the relationship that would entitle the individual to the larger share.

§2-114.   PARENT AND CHILD RELATIONSHIP

(a) Except as provided in subsections (b) and (c), for purposes of intestate succession by, through, or from a person, an individual is the child of his [or her] natural parents, regardless of their marital status. The parent and child relationship may be established under [the Uniform Parentage Act] [applicable state law] [insert appropriate statutory reference].

(b) An adopted individual is the child of his [or her] adopting parent or parents and not of his [or her] natural parents, but adoption of a child by the spouse of either natural parent has no effect on (i) the relationship between the child and that natural parent or (ii) the right of the child or a descendant of the child to inherit from or through the other natural parent.

(c) Inheritance from or through a child by either natural parent or his [or her] kindred is precluded unless that natural parent has openly treated the child as his [or hers], and has not refused to support the child.[13]

---

13. UPC §2-114(c) is a minority rule, originally applied only to nonmarital fathers. Is it a good idea to extend it to marital as well as nonmarital parents? If so, why not extend it to adoptive parents? Does permitting adoptive parents, but not natural parents, who do not support the child to inherit from the child have a rational basis? See Paula A. Monopoli, "Deadbeat Dads": Should Support and Inheritance Be Linked?, 49 U. Miami L. Rev. 257 (1994); Anne-Marie E. Rhodes, Abandoning Parents Under Intestacy: Where We Are, Where We Need to Go, 27 Ind. L. Rev. 517 (1994). See also the note on Chinese law, page 131. — Eds.

NOTES, PROBLEMS, AND QUESTIONS

1.   Inheritance rights of an adopted child vary considerably from state to state. In some states, as in Maryland, an adopted child inherits only from adoptive parents and their relatives; in others, for example in Texas, an adopted child inherits from both adoptive parents and natural parents and their relatives; in still others, as provided in the UPC, an adopted child inherits from adoptive relatives and also from natural relatives if the child is adopted by a stepparent. And there are many statutory variations on these three basic schemes. See Restatement (Third) of Property: Wills and Other Donative Transfers §2.5(2) (1999).

In view of the diversity and complexities of contemporary family relations created by adoptions, multiple marriages, and single parenthood, it is not easy to discern what the average person (the hypothetical intestate decedent) would want in many of these situations. Professor Gary proposes a new statute that offers an additional way, in addition to formal adoption, to establish a parent-child relationship for purposes of inheritance — namely, a functional inquiry that looks at such things as economic and emotional support, how old the child was when the relationship arose, and whether the parent held out the child as her own. See Susan N. Gary, Adapting Intestacy Laws to Changing Families, 18 Law & Ineq. J. 1 (2000).

For analysis of the issues involved in framing a statute dealing with inheritance rights of adopted children, with citations to state laws, see Jan E. Rein, Relatives by Blood, Adoption, and Association: Who Should Get What and Why?, 37 Vand. L. Rev. 711 (1984). For discussion of stepparent adoption, see Margaret M. Mahoney, Stepfamilies in the Law of Intestate Succession and Wills, 22 U.C. Davis L. Rev. 917 (1989); Patricia G. Roberts, Adopted and Nonmarital Children — Exploring the Uniform Probate Code's Intestacy and Class Gift Provisions, 32 Real Prop., Prob. & Tr. J. 539 (1998).

2.   If UPC §2-114(b) had been applicable in Hall v. Vallandingham, Earl's children, adopted by their stepfather, would have inherited from their natural father's brother, William Jr. But observe that William Jr. would not be able to inherit from Earl's children under the UPC. In a stepparent adoption, the children can inherit from their natural relatives, but the natural relatives cannot inherit from them. Is this fair?

3.   *Switched at birth*. A few cases have arisen where babies have been inadvertently switched at the hospital when born. Here's a story widely reported in the newspapers in 1993. Baby girl Kimberly was switched at birth. Her birth mother was Mrs. Twigg, but Mrs. Twigg took home another baby, believing it to be hers. Mrs. Mays took home Kimberly, mistakenly believing Kimberly was hers. When Kimberly was 14 the mixup was discovered, and scientific evidence showed that Kimberly was the genetic daughter of Mr. and Mrs. Twigg, not Mr. and Mrs. Mays. Kimberly continued to live with Mr. Mays, Mrs. Mays having died. When Kimberly refused to move into the Twiggs' home, the Twiggs sued for custody of Kimberly. Whose child is Kimberly? See Twigg v. Mays, 1993 WL 330624 (Fla. Cir. 1993) (barring the Twiggs' attempt to prove Kimberly was not Mays' legal child on ground not in best interest of child). Subsequent to the lawsuit, Kimberly changed her mind and moved out of Mays' home and moved in with the Twiggs. Will Kimberly inherit from Mr. and Mrs. Twigg or from Mr. Mays? Consider this statement by a

Connecticut court: "We also reject the claim ... that the child's birth certificate conclusively established that the plaintiff (not genetically or gestationally related to child) is her mother. One does not gain parental status by virtue of false information on a birth certificate." Jane Doe v. John Doe, 710 A.2d 1297, 1319 (Conn. 1998).

4. *Adult adoption.* The overwhelming majority of inheritance statutes draw no distinction between the adoption of a minor and the adoption of an adult. See Tinney v. Tinney, 799 A.2d 235 (R.I. 2002) (84-year-old Newport woman adopts 38-year-old man and he shares in her intestate estate).

Occasionally, the adoption of an adult may be useful in preventing a will contest. The only persons who have standing to challenge the validity of a will are those persons who would take if the will were denied probate. If the testator adopts a child, the testator's collateral relatives cannot contest the will on the ground that they would inherit by intestacy. Hence, if a person wishes to leave property to a friend, under some circumstances it might be wise to adopt the friend as a child. In Greene v. Fitzpatrick, 295 S.W. 896 (Ky. 1927), a wealthy bachelor adopted a married woman who had been his secretary for many years and with whom, it was alleged, the bachelor had a sexual relationship. In Collamore v. Learned, 50 N.E. 518 (Mass. 1898), a 70-year-old man adopted three persons of ages 43, 39, and 25 respectively. In both cases it was held that the adoptions could not be set aside by the persons who would have been the heirs but for the adoptions. In the second case, Holmes, J., remarked that adoption for the purpose of preventing a will contest was "perfectly proper." (Of course the relatives can attack an adoption decree on grounds of mental incapacity or undue influence and, if they succeed in setting aside the adoption, then attack a will leaving property to the adoptee. See, e.g., In re Adoption of Sewell, 51 Cal. Rptr. 367 (App. 1966) (adoption of woman, 45, by man, 72, attacked).)

In the large majority of states, an adult person, married or unmarried, may adopt any other person, minor or adult, but the adoption of a spouse or lover may not be allowed. See Ralph C. Brashier, Children and Inheritance in the Nontraditional Family, 1996 Utah L. Rev. 93. See also Uniform Adoption Act §5-101(a)(1) (1994), which permits adult adoption, but bars adoption of one's spouse.

In New York, the adoption of an adult lover is not possible. In In re Robert Paul P., 471 N.E.2d 424 (N.Y. 1984), the court held that a homosexual male, age 57, could not legally adopt his lover, age 50, although New York statutes permit the adoption of adults. The court thought that a sexual relationship was incompatible with a parent-child relationship. For a case contrary to the New York view, see In re Adoption of Swanson, 623 A.2d 1095 (Del. 1993), holding a 66-year-old man could adopt a 51-year-old man, his companion for 17 years, to prevent claims against their estates by collateral relatives. The Delaware court expressly rejected the New York holding. See William M. McGovern, Jr. & Sheldon F. Kurtz, Wills, Trusts and Estates §2.10 (3d ed. 2004), for other restrictions on adult adoptions across the states.

_____

Adoption and the interpretation of wills and trusts. Is a child adopted by A entitled to share in a gift in a will or trust by T to the "children," "issue," "descendants," or "heirs" of *A*? Inasmuch as this question is often resolved in accord with intestacy principles, as under UPC §2-705 (1990, as amended 1991), we broach it first here (see also pages 652-655).

Because adoption was unknown to the common law, "children" and "issue" necessarily connoted a blood relationship. Thus, when adoption laws were enacted in the second half of the nineteenth century, courts were faced not only with the question of an adopted child's intestacy rights, but also whether an adopted child took under the will of a person who was not the adoptive parent. The early cases were heavily influenced by the inherited reverence for blood relationships; they held an adopted child could not take. These cases gave rise to the *stranger-to-the-adoption* rule: The adopted child is presumptively barred, whatever generic word is used, except when the donor is the adoptive parent. As adoption became more common and more socially acceptable, courts began to carve exceptions to the stranger-to-the-adoption rule. For example, an adopted child might be permitted to take if adopted before, but not after, the testator's death. Some courts also drew distinctions between a gift to "*A*'s children" and a gift to "*A*'s issue" or the "heirs of *A*'s body." Unlike the latter terms, which were thought to have a biological connotation, a gift to "*A*'s children" presumptively included *A*'s adopted children. Where judicial decisions were found unsatisfactory, legislatures began to intervene in favor of the adopted child. But the legislation was seldom retroactive and was sometimes ambiguous.

In most states today, adopted children are presumptively included in gifts by *T* to the "children," "issue," "descendants," and "heirs" of *A*. See Restatement (Third) of Property: Wills and Other Donative Transfers §14.5(2) (T.D. No. 4, 2004). But the law of many states is likely to have been developed by changing judicial decisions and statutes over the twentieth century, and, since the change may not be retroactive, whether the adopted child is included may depend on what the law was at testator's death in, say, 1955. See First Natl. Bank of Chicago v. King, 651 N.E.2d 127 (Ill. 1995); Annot., 71 A.L.R.4th 374 (1989, rev. 2000).

The following case involves both the adoption of an adult and the ancillary effect of intestacy statutes on the interpretation of dispositions under wills and trusts.

Minary v. Citizens Fidelity Bank & Trust Co.
Court of Appeals of Kentucky, 1967
419 S.W.2d 340

OSBORNE, J.   [Amelia S. Minary died in 1932, leaving a will devising her residuary estate in trust, to pay the income to her husband and three sons, James, Thomas, and Alfred, for their respective lives. The trust was to terminate upon the death of the last surviving beneficiary, at which time the corpus was to be distributed as follows:

> After the Trust terminates, the remaining portion of the Trust Fund shall be distributed to my then surviving heirs, according to the laws of descent and distribution then in force in Kentucky, and, if no such heirs, then to the First Christian Church, Louisville, Kentucky.

The husband died, then James died without issue, then Thomas died leaving two children: Thomas Jr. and Amelia Minary Gant. In 1934, Alfred married Myra, and in 1959 he adopted her as his child. The trust terminated upon Alfred's death without natural issue in 1963.]

The question herein presented is, "Did Alfred's adoption of his wife Myra make her eligible to inherit under the provisions of his mother's will?" More specifically, the question is, "Is Myra included in the term 'my then surviving heirs according to the laws of descent and distribution in force in Kentucky'?"

This has revived a lively question in the jurisprudence of this state and presents two rather difficult legal problems. The first being under what conditions, if any, should an adopted child inherit from or through its adoptive parent? We have encountered little difficulty with the problem of inheriting from an adoptive parent but the question of when will an adoptive child inherit through an adoptive parent has given us considerable trouble. As late as 1945 in Copeland v. State Bank and Trust Company, 188 S.W.2d 1017 (Ky.), we held without hesitation or equivocation that the words "heirs" and "issue" as well as "children" and all other words of similar import as used in a will referred only to the natural blood relations and did not include an adopted child.

In 1950, in Isaacs v. Manning, 227 S.W.2d 418 (Ky.), we adopted the contrary position and held that an adopted child was included in the phrase "heirs at law" wherein a will devised property to designated children and then upon their death to their heirs at law. In the course of the opinion, we said, "where no language [shows] a contrary intent . . . an adopted daughter clearly falls within the class designated." In this case we distinguish the *Copeland* case, supra.

In 1953, in Major v. Kammer, 258 S.W.2d 506, we again held that an adopted child was included in the term "heirs at law," basing our decision upon the legislative changes made in the adoption laws and overruling Copeland v. State Bank and Trust Company, supra. In Edmands v. Tice, Ky., 324 S.W.2d 491, which was decided in 1959, we held that where testator used the word children, an adopted child could inherit through an adopted parent the same as if heirs at law or issue had been used. . . .

From the foregoing we conclude that when Amelia S. Minary used the phrase, "my then surviving heirs according to the laws of descent and distribution then in force in Kentucky," she included the adoptive children of her sons. This leaves us with the extremely bothersome question of: "Does the fact that Myra Minary was an adult and the wife of Alfred at the time she was adopted affect her status as an 'heir' under the will?" KRS 405.390 provides: "An adult person . . . may be adopted in the same manner as provided by law for the adoption of a child and with the same legal effect. . . ."

KRS 199.520 provides: "From and after the date of the judgment the child shall be deemed the child of petitioners and shall be considered for purposes of inheritance and succession and for all other legal considerations, the natural, legitimate child of the parents adopting it the same as if born of their bodies."

It would appear from examination of the authorities that the adoption of an adult for the purpose of making him an heir has been an accepted practice in our law for many years. However, here it should be pointed out that the practice in its ancient form made the person so adopted the legal heir of the adopting party only. This court has dealt with the problem of adopting adults for the purpose of making them heirs on several occasions. . . .

In 1957, in Bedinger v. Graybill's Executors, Ky., 302 S.W.2d 594, we had before us a case almost identical to the one here under consideration. In that case Mrs. Lulu Graybill, in 1914, set up a trust for her son Robert by will. She then provided after the death of the son that the trust "be paid over and distributed by the Trustee to the heirs at law of my said son according to the laws of descent and distribution in force in Kentucky at the time of his death." There was a devise over to others in the event that Robert died without heirs. Robert having no issue adopted his wife long after his mother's death. We held that the wife should inherit the same as an adopted child, there being no public policy against the adoption of a wife. However, it will be noted that in the course of the opinion it is carefully pointed out that the will directed the estate be paid to the "heirs at law of Robert" and did not provide that the estate should go to "my heirs," "his children" or to "his issue," indicating by this language that if the phrase had been one of the others set out the results might have been different. . . .

This case could properly be distinguished from Bedinger v. Graybill's Executors, supra, on the basis of the difference in language used in the two wills[;] however, no useful purpose could be served by so distinguishing them. The time has come to face again this problem which has persistently perplexed the court when an adult is adopted for the sole purpose of making him or her an heir and claimant to the estate of an ancestor under the terms of a testamentary instrument known and in existence at the time of the adoption. Even though the statute permits such adoption and even though it expressly provides that it shall be "with the same legal effect as the adoption of a child," we, nevertheless, are constrained to view this practice to be an act of subterfuge which in effect thwarts the intent of the ancestor whose property is being distributed and cheats the rightful heirs. We are faced with a situation wherein we must choose between carrying out the intent of deceased testators or giving a strict and rigid construction to a statute which thwarts that intent. In the *Bedinger* case there is no doubt but what the intent of the testatrix, as to the disposition of her property, was circumvented. It is our opinion that by giving a strict and literal construction to the adoption statutes, we thwarted the efforts of the deceased to dispose of her property as she saw fit.

When one rule of law does violence to another it becomes inevitable that one must then give way to the other. It is of paramount importance that a man be permitted to pass on his property at his death to those who represent the natural objects of his bounty. This is an ancient and precious right running from the dawn of civilization in an unbroken line down to the present day. Our adoption statutes are humanitarian in nature and of great importance to the welfare of the public. However, these statutes should not be given a construction that does violence to the above rule and to the extent that they violate the rule and prevent one from passing on his property in accord with his wishes, they must give way. Adoption of an adult for the purpose of bringing that person under the provisions of a pre-existing testamentary instrument when he clearly was not intended to be so covered should not be permitted and we do not view this as doing any great violence to the intent and purpose of our adoption laws.

For the foregoing reasons the action of the trial court in declaring Myra Galvin Minary an heir of Amelia S. Minary is reversed.

The judgment is reversed.

NOTES AND PROBLEMS

1. Wills and trusts often use language from intestacy statutes to indicate which family members should take property. In *Minary*, the trust distributed to "surviving heirs, according to the laws of descent and distribution *then* in force in Kentucky." Why leave it to future legislatures to determine who will be the beneficiaries of your trust? Why not distribute according to the laws in force on the date the trust is created?

2. *Adult adoption revisited*. The cases are split over whether adult adoptees are included within gifts to classes such as children, issue, or descendants. Compare Commerce Bank v. Blasdel, 141 S.W.3d 434 (Mo. 2004) (six stepchildren adopted as adults share in trust for "lineal descendants"); In re Trust of Lane, 660 N.W.2d 421 (Minn. 2003) (grandson adopted his nephew to allow the nephew to take from a mutual ancestor's trust for "issue"), with Ehrenclou v. Macdonald, 12 Cal. Rptr. 3d 411 (App. 2004); Cross v. Cross, 532 N.E.2d 486 (Ill. App. 1988).

If adult adoptees are included within class gifts in will and trust dispositions, is there any reason for excluding a spouse-adopted-as-a-child from such a gift? See In re Belgard's Trust, 829 P.2d 457 (Colo. App. 1992) (holding adopted adult wife not a proper beneficiary of her mother-in-law's trust despite language in the trust defining a "child" to include "persons legally adopted by my son"; however, adopted wife was entitled to inherit her husband-father's estate through intestacy as his child). See also Uniform Adoption Act §5-101(a)(1) (1994), which permits adult adoption, but bars adoption of one's spouse.

3. *Children "adopted out."* T bequeaths a fund in trust "for my wife for life, then to my issue then living per stirpes." After T's death, his son A dies, leaving a wife and a minor child, B. A's wife remarries, and her second husband adopts B, which in many states would sever B's intestacy rights to take from T. T's wife then dies. Is B entitled to share in T's trust fund? Compare Newman v. Wells Fargo Bank, 926 P.2d 969 (Cal. 1996) (looking at intestacy law as it existed at time of T's death to determine T's intent; B excluded), with Lockwood v. Adamson, 566 N.E.2d 96 (Mass. 1991) (B shares under T's will even though B would not inherit from T under intestacy law).

4. The use of the adoption procedure for the purpose of creating a child to come within a class gift is in effect using adoption as a *special power of appointment* (discussed in Chapter 9). If Amelia Minary had given her sons such a power to appoint at least a life estate to their spouses, Alfred's desperate shenanigans would not have been necessary and his wife would not have ended up impoverished. It is hard to believe Alfred's mother would have wanted his widow to live in penury. Likely her lawyer did not suggest a special power of appointment to her because in 1932, when she died, special powers were relatively unknown except among lawyers for the rich in urban states. Speaking of the testator's intent is something of a fiction if her lawyer never brought up the subject of her sons' widows.

5. Adoption, unlike marriage, is not revocable if the relationship turns sour. In 1988 Doris Duke, 75, one of the world's richest women, adopted Chandi

Heffner, 35. Chandi had taken her name from the Hindu deity, Chandi, and was a Hare Krishna when Doris met her at a dance class. Doris Duke was the life beneficiary of two trusts created by her father, James Buchanan ("Buck") Duke, in 1917 and 1924. After Doris's death, the income from the trusts was to be payable to Doris's children. Doris had no natural children. Subsequent to the adoption, Doris Duke had a falling out with her adopted daughter Chandi and tried to exclude Chandi from her father's trust in her will.

Doris Duke died in 1993, a billionaire. She left her fortune to a charitable foundation, over which she put her barely-literate butler, Bernard Lafferty, in charge. After embarking on an extended spending spree, far exceeding the $500,000 a year Doris left him, the butler dropped dead some three years after Doris died. Doris's will provided:

TWENTY-ONE: As indicated in Article SEVEN, it is my intention that Chandi Heffner not be deemed to be my child for purposes of disposing of property under this my Will (or any Codicil thereto). Furthermore, it is not my intention, nor do I believe that it was ever my father's intention, that Chandi Heffner be deemed to be a child or lineal descendant of mine for purposes of disposing of the trust estate of the May 2, 1917 trust which my father established for my benefit or the Doris Duke Trust, dated December 11, 1924, which my father established for the benefit of me, certain other members of the Duke family and ultimately for charity.

I am extremely troubled by the realization that Chandi Heffner may use my 1988 adoption of her (when she was 35 years old) to attempt to benefit financially under the terms of either of the trusts created by my father. After giving the matter prolonged and serious consideration, I am convinced that I should not have adopted Chandi Heffner. I have come to the realization that her primary motive was financial gain. I firmly believe that, like me, my father would not have wanted her to have benefitted under the trusts which he created, and similarly, I do not wish her to benefit from my estate.

Doris Duke in 1991, with her butler, Bernard Lafferty

Her signature was shaky but bold:

IN WITNESS WHEREOF, I have hereunto set my hand and affix my seal to this my Last Will and Testament on this *5ᵗʰ* day of April, 1993.

Upon Doris Duke's death, Chandi Heffner sued the trustees of the Doris Duke Trust created by her father, Buck Duke, demanding that they pay her income as the successive life beneficiary of the Doris Duke Trust, worth $170 million at Doris's death. The trial court ruled against her, on the ground that an adult adoptee was not considered a child of the adopting parent when the trust is created by another. In re Trust of Duke, 702 A.2d 1008 (N.J. Super. 1995). Chandi Heffner also sued the trustees of the other trust created by Buck Duke and the executors of Doris Duke, claiming that Doris had promised to support her. While the litigation was proceeding, the parties settled. Chandi Heffner received $60 million from the James Buchanan Duke trusts in settlement of her claim to be a child of Doris and $5 million from the Doris Duke estate. One very expensive adoption!

For more on the Doris Duke litigation, see In re Duke, 663 N.E.2d 602 (N.Y. 1996); N.Y. Times, May 16, 1996, at B8; N.Y. Times, Nov. 5, 1996, at B8; N.Y. Times, Jan. 24, 1997, at B1 (reporting the feeding frenzy of lawyers); Susan Hansen, The Butler's Lawyers, Am. Law., Apr. 1995, at 53 (reporting sensational but unproved charges against Duke's lawyers and butler).

Thus far we have explored explicit adoptions. But the recognition of a more informal *equitable adoption* (sometimes called *virtual adoption*) can also determine the distribution of property in intestacy and under wills and trusts.

O'Neal v. Wilkes

Supreme Court of Georgia, 1994
263 Ga. 850, 439 S.E.2d 490

FLETCHER, J.   In this virtual adoption action, a jury found that appellant Hattie O'Neal had been virtually adopted by the decedent, Roswell Cook. On post-trial motions, the court granted a judgment notwithstanding the verdict to appellee Firmon Wilkes, as administrator of Cook's estate, on the ground that the paternal aunt who allegedly entered into the adoption contract with Cook had no legal authority to do so. We have reviewed the record and conclude that the court correctly determined that there was no valid contract to adopt.

O'Neal was born out of wedlock in 1949 and raised by her mother, Bessie Broughton, until her mother's death in 1957. At no time did O'Neal's biological father recognize O'Neal as his daughter, take any action to legitimize her, or provide support to her or her mother. O'Neal testified that she first met her biological father in 1970.

For four years after her mother's death, O'Neal lived in New York City with her maternal aunt, Ethel Campbell. In 1961, Ms. Campbell brought O'Neal to Savannah, Georgia, and surrendered physical custody of O'Neal to a woman identified only as Louise who was known to want a daughter. Shortly thereafter, Louise determined she could not care for O'Neal and took her to the Savannah home of Estelle Page, the sister of ONeal's biological father. After a short time with Page, Roswell Cook and his wife came to Savannah from their Riceboro, Georgia home to pick up O'Neal. Page testified that she had heard that the Cooks wanted a daughter and after telling them about O'Neal, they came for her. [Mr. and Mrs. Cook were divorced in the 1970s.]

Although O'Neal was never statutorily adopted by Cook, he raised her and provided for her education and she resided with him until her marriage in

1975. While she never took the last name of Cook, he referred to her as his daughter and, later, identified her children as his grandchildren.

In November 1991, Cook died intestate. The appellee, Firmon Wilkes, was appointed as administrator of Cook's estate and refused to recognize O'Neal's asserted interest in the estate. In December 1991, O'Neal filed a petition in equity asking the court to declare a virtual adoption, thereby entitling her to the estate property she would have inherited if she were Cook's statutorily adopted child.

1. The first essential of a contract for adoption is that it be made between persons competent to contract for the disposition of the child. Winder v. Winder, 128 S.E.2d 56 (Ga. 1962); Rucker v. Moore, 199 S.E. 106 (Ga. 1938). A successful plaintiff must also prove:

> Some showing of an agreement between the natural and adoptive parents, performance by the natural parents of the child in giving up custody, performance by the child by living in the home of the adoptive parents, partial performance by the foster parents in taking the child into the home and treating [it] as their child, and . . . the intestacy of the foster parent.

Williams v. Murray, 236 S.E.2d 624 (Ga. 1977), quoting Habecker v. Young, 474 F.2d 1229, 1230 (5th Cir. 1973). The only issue on this appeal is whether the court correctly determined that Page was without authority to contract for O'Neal's adoption.

2. O'Neal argues that Page, a paternal aunt with physical custody of her, had authority to contract for her adoption and, even if she was without such authority, any person with the legal right to contract for the adoption, be they O'Neal's biological father or maternal aunts or uncles, ratified the adoption contract by failing to object.

As a preliminary matter, we agree with O'Neal that although her biological father was living at the time the adoption contract was allegedly entered into, his consent to the contract was not necessary as he never recognized or legitimized her or provided for her support in any manner. See Williams v. Murray, 236 S.E.2d 624 (Ga. 1977) (mother alone may contract for adoption where the father has lost parental control or abandoned the child); OCGA §19-7-25, Code 1933, §74-203 (only mother of child born out of wedlock may exercise parental power over the child unless legitimized by the father); see also OCGA §19-8-10 (parent not entitled to notice of petition of adoption where parent has abandoned the child). What is less clear are the rights and obligations acquired by Page by virtue of her physical custody of O'Neal after her mother's death.

3. The Georgia Code defines a "legal custodian" as a person to whom legal custody has been given by court order and who has the right to physical custody of the child and to determine the nature of the care and treatment of the child and the duty to provide for the care, protection, training, and education and the physical, mental, and moral welfare of the child. OCGA §15-11-43, Code 1933, §24A-2901. A legal custodian does not have the right to consent to the adoption of a child, as this right is specifically retained by one with greater rights over the child, a child's parent or guardian. OCGA §15-11-43, Code 1933, §24A-2901 (rights of a legal custodian are subject to the remaining rights and duties of the child's parents or guardian); Skipper v. Smith, 238 S.E.2d 917 (Ga. 1977) (right to consent to adoption is a residual right retained by a parent notwithstanding the transfer of legal custody of the child to another person); Jackson v. Anglin, 19

S.E.2d 914 (Ga. 1942) (parent retains exclusive authority to consent to adoption although child is placed in temporary custody of another); Carey v. Phillips, 224 S.E.2d 870 (Ga. App. 1976) (parent's consent is required for adoption of child although child is in physical custody of another).

O'Neal concedes that, after her mother's death, no guardianship petition was filed by her relatives. Nor is there any evidence that any person petitioned to be appointed as her legal custodian. Accordingly, the obligation to care and provide for O'Neal, undertaken first by Campbell, and later by Page, was not a legal obligation but a familial obligation resulting in a custodial relationship properly characterized as something less than that of a legal custodian. Such a relationship carried with it no authority to contract for O'Neal's adoption. See *Skipper*, 238 S.E.2d at 919. While we sympathize with O'Neal's plight, we conclude that Page had no authority to enter into the adoption contract with Cook and the contract, therefore, was invalid.

4. Because O'Neal's relatives did not have the legal authority to enter into a contract for her adoption, their alleged ratification of the adoption contract was of no legal effect and the court did not err in granting a judgment notwithstanding the verdict in favor of the appellee. See Foster v. Cheek, 96 S.E.2d 545 (Ga. 1957) (adoption contract made between persons not competent to contract for child's adoption specifically enforceable where the parent with parental power over the child acquiesced in and ratified the adoption contract).

Judgment affirmed.

SEARS, J., dissenting.   I disagree with the majority's holding that O'Neal's claim for equitable adoption is defeated by the fact that her paternal aunt was not a person designated by law as one having the authority to consent to O'Neal's adoption.

1. In Crawford v. Wilson, 78 S.E. 30 (Ga. 1913), the doctrine of equitable or virtual

adoption was recognized for the first time in Georgia. Relying on the equitable principle that "equity considers that done which ought to have been done," id. at 32; see OCGA §23-1-8, we held that "an agreement to adopt a child, so as to constitute the child an heir at law on the death of the person adopting, performed on the part of the child, is enforceable upon the death of the person adopting the child as to property which is undisposed of by will," id. We held that although the death of the adopting parents precluded a literal enforcement of the contract, equity would "enforce the contract by decreeing that the child is entitled to the fruits of a legal adoption." Id. In *Crawford*, we noted that the full performance of the agreement by the child was sufficient to overcome an objection that the agreement was

Justice Leah Sears
**Appointed to the Georgia Supreme Court
in 1992 at age 36.**

unenforceable because it violated the statute of frauds. Id. We further held that

> [w]here one takes an infant into his home upon a promise to adopt such as his own child, and the child performs all the duties growing out of the substituted relationship of parent and child, rendering years of service, companionship, and obedience to the foster parent, upon the faith that such foster parent stands in loco parentis, and that upon his death the child will sustain the legal relationship to his estate of a natural child, there is equitable reason that the child may appeal to a court of equity to consummate, so far as it may be possible, the foster parent's omission of duty in the matter of formal adoption. [Id. at 33.]

Although the majority correctly states the current rule in Georgia that a contract to adopt may not be specifically enforced unless the contract was entered by a person with the legal authority to consent to the adoption of the child, *Crawford* did not expressly establish such a requirement, and I think the cases cited by the majority that have established this requirement are in error.

Instead, I would hold that where a child has fully performed the alleged contract over the course of many years or a lifetime and can sufficiently establish the existence of the contract to adopt, equity should enforce the contract over the objection of the adopting parents' heirs that the contract is unenforceable because the person who consented to the adoption did not have the legal authority to do so. Several reasons support this conclusion.

First, in such cases, the adopting parents and probably their heirs know of the defect in the contract and yet voice no objection to the contract while the child fully performs the contract and the adopting parents reap the benefits thereof. Under these circumstances, to hold that the contract is unenforceable after the child has performed is to permit a virtual fraud upon the child and should not be countenanced in equity. See 2 Corbin on Contracts, §429 (1950). Equity does not permit such action with regard to contracts that are initially unenforceable because they violate the statute of frauds, but instead recognizes that the full performance of the contract negates its initial unenforceability and renders it enforceable in equity. See 2 Corbin, supra, §§420, 421, 429, 432; Harp v. Bacon, 150 S.E.2d 655 (Ga. 1966).

Moreover, the purpose of requiring consent by a person with the legal authority to consent to an adoption, where such a person exists, is to protect that person, the child, and the adopting parents. See generally Clark, The Law of Domestic Relations, Vol. 2, Section 21.11 (2nd ed. 1987). However, as equitable adoption cases do not arise until the death of the adopting parents, the interests of the person with the [right to] consent to adopt and of the adopting parents are not in jeopardy. On the other hand, the interests of the child are unfairly and inequitably harmed by insisting upon the requirement that a person with the consent to adopt had to have been a party to the contract. That this legal requirement is held against the child is particularly inequitable because the child, the course of whose life is forever changed by such contracts, was unable to act to insure the validity of the contract when the contract was made.

Furthermore, where there is no person with the legal authority to consent to the adoption, such as in the present case, the only reason to insist that a person be appointed the child's legal guardian before agreeing to the contract to adopt would be for the protection of the child. Yet, by insisting upon this requirement after the adopting parents' deaths, this Court is harming the very person that the requirement would protect.

For all the foregoing reasons, equity ought to intervene on the child's behalf in these types of cases, and require the performance of the contract if it is sufficiently proven. See OCGA §23-1-8. In this case, I would thus not rule against O'Neal's claim for specific performance solely on the ground that her paternal aunt did not have the authority to consent to the adoption.

2. Moreover, basing the doctrine of equitable adoption in contract theory has come under heavy criticism, for numerous reasons. See Clark, supra, at 676-78; Rein, Relatives by Blood, Adoption, and Association: Who Should Get What and Why (The Impact of Adoptions, Adult Adoptions, and Equitable Adoptions on Intestate Succession and Class Gifts), 37 Vand. L. Rev. 710, 770-75, 784-86 (1984). For instance, as we acknowledged in *Wilson*, supra, the contract to adopt is not being specifically enforced as the adopting parents are dead; for equitable reasons we are merely placing the child in a position that he or she would have been in if he or she had been adopted. See Rein at 774. Moreover, it is problematic whether these contracts are capable of being enforced in all respects during the child's infancy. See Rein at 773-74; Clark at 678. Furthermore, because part of the consideration for these contracts is the child's performance thereunder, the child is not merely a third-party beneficiary of a contract between the adults involved but is a party thereto. Yet, a child is usually too young to know of or understand the contract, and it is thus difficult to find a meeting of the minds between the child and the adopting parents and the child's acceptance of the contract. Rein at 772-73, 775. I agree with these criticisms and would abandon the contract basis for equitable adoption in favor of the more flexible and equitable theory advanced by the foregoing authorities. That theory focuses not on the fiction of whether there has been a contract to adopt but on the relationship between the adopting parents and the child and in particular whether the adopting parents have led the child to believe that he or she is a legally adopted member of their family. Rein at 785-87; Clark at 678, 682.

3. Because the majority fails to honor the maxim that "[e]quity considers that done which ought to be done," §23-1-8, and follows a rule that fails to protect a person with superior equities, I dissent. I am authorized to state that Justice Hunstein concurs in the result reached by this dissent.

PROBLEM, NOTES, AND QUESTION

1. Suppose that H and W take baby A into their home and raise A as their child but do not formally adopt A. Under such circumstances, in some states A may be able to inherit from H and W under the doctrine of *equitable adoption*. Under this doctrine, an oral agreement to adopt A, between H and W and A's natural parents, is inferred and specifically enforced in equity against H and W. As against H and W, equity treats A as if the contract had been performed by H and W; they are estopped to deny a formal adoption took place.

Equitable adoption permits an equitably adopted child to inherit from the foster parents. Lankford v. Wright, 489 S.E.2d 604 (N.C. 1997). On the other hand, the foster parents (and their relatives) cannot inherit from the child. Having failed to perform the contract, they have no claim in equity. Estate of Riggs, 440 N.Y.S.2d 450 (Sur. 1981). In Board of Educ. v. Browning, 635 A.2d 373 (Md. 1994), the court held that an equitably adopted child could not inherit from her adoptive parent's sister even though the sister's estate thus escheated. The court concluded that the effect of equitable adoption should be limited to inheritance from the parent who is estopped. Compare First Natl. Bank in Fairmont v. Phillips, 344 S.E.2d 201 (W. Va. 1985), holding that an equitably adopted child could inherit from another child of the foster parent.

2. In Welch v. Wilson, 516 S.E.2d 35 (W. Va. 1999), a woman who was raised by her grandmother and step-grandfather was treated as having been equitably adopted by the step-grandfather, allowing her to inherit his entire estate. The court did not require an explicit contract, nor did it mention estoppel, though it did note that the step-grandparent was listed as the woman's parent on school records. Mostly, however, the court focused on the ample evidence of their having had a close, loving parent-child relationship.

3. In O'Neal v. Wilkes, suppose that the Juvenile Court had placed Hattie in the custody of Mr. and Mrs. Cook. The Juvenile Court has power to consent to adoption of Hattie by the Cooks. Same result? See Welch v. Welch, 453 S.E.2d 445 (Ga. 1995) (holding no equitable adoption, by a 4 to 3 vote).

4. Hattie O'Neal was African American, and the country town of Riceboro, Georgia, where she went to live, has a population of 767, of whom 751 are African Americans. There is no lawyer in Riceboro, but there are several lawyers in the county seat, Hinesville, 17 miles away. Does this affect your view of the *O'Neal* case? See Lynda Richardson, Adoptions that Lack Papers, Not Purpose, N.Y. Times, Nov. 25, 1993, at C1, discussing the history and prevalence of informal adoptions in the African American community ("of the estimated one million black children in this country who do not live with a biological parent, nearly 800,000 have been informally adopted, usually by a grandparent").

In the *O'Neal* case, the court was divided 5 to 2. Joining Justice Sears in her dissent was a white woman justice; the majority were all men, including one African American. Might women look at equitable adoption as less an application of abstract principles and more as a judgment about whether the responsibilities and care involved in a parent-child relationship had been satisfied in a particular case? See the views of Professor Rein, cited in Justice Sears's opinion; Carol Gilligan, In a Different Voice: Psychological Theory and Women's Development (1982).

5. In re Estate of Ford, 82 P.3d 747 (Cal. 2004), involved a foster child who was raised from the age of two by the decedent and continued to live with the decedent even after getting married. The court rejected the foster child's claim to an intestate share of the decedent's estate, giving the property instead to a nephew and niece who had not seen the decedent for 15 years. The court held that, under California law, equitable adoption was based on contract, and the promise or intention to adopt must be proved by clear and convincing evidence.

b. Posthumous Children

The typical posthumous child case involves a child who is conceived before, but born after, her father's death. Where, for purposes of inheritance or of determining property rights, it is to a child's advantage to be treated as in being from the time of conception rather than from the time of birth, the child will be so treated if born alive. The principle is an ancient one. See 1 William Blackstone, Commentaries *130.

Courts have established a rebuttable presumption that the normal period of gestation is 280 days (10 lunar months). If the child claims that conception dated more than 280 days before birth, the burden of proof is usually upon the child. On supposed periods of gestation beyond 280 days, the modern record for a protracted pregnancy apparently belongs to a woman from North Carolina. In Byerly v. Tolbert, 108 S.E.2d 29 (N.C. 1959), a child was born to the decedent's widow 322 days after his death. The child (through a guardian ad litem, of course) claimed an intestate share. The trial court held as a matter of law that the infant was not the decedent's child. On appeal, the case was reversed. Although there is a presumption that a child born more than 280 days after death is not the decedent's child, the presumption is not irrebuttable, and the child was entitled to have the issue submitted to a jury.

Uniform Parentage Act §204 (2002) establishes a rebuttable presumption that a child born to a woman within 300 (rather than 280) days after the death of her husband is a child of that husband.

c. Nonmarital Children

Although innocent of any sin or crime, children of unmarried parents were given harsh, pitiless treatment by the common law.[14] A child born out of wedlock was *filius nullius*, the child of no one, and could inherit from neither father nor mother. Only the child's spouse and descendants could inherit from the child. If the child died intestate and left neither spouse nor descendants, the child's property escheated to the king or other overlord.

All of our states have alleviated this unsympathetic treatment of nonmarital children. All jurisdictions permit inheritance from the mother, but the rules respecting inheritance from the father vary. In Trimble v. Gordon, 430 U.S. 762 (1977), the Supreme Court held unconstitutional, as a denial of equal protection, an Illinois statute denying a nonmarital child inheritance rights from the father. The Court held that state discrimination against nonmarital children, although not a suspect classification subject to the strict scrutiny test, must have a substantial justification as serving an important state interest. The valid state interest recognized by the Court is obtaining reliable proof of paternity. The Court found that total statutory disinheritance from the father was not rationally related to this objective. See also Lalli v. Lalli, 439 U.S. 259 (1978), upholding a New York statute permitting inheritance by a nonmarital child from the father only if the father had married the mother or had been formally adjudicated the father by a court during the father's lifetime.

In the wake of these two cases, most states have amended their intestacy statutes to liberalize inheritance by nonmarital children. Most permit paternity to be established by evidence of the subsequent marriage of the parents, by acknowledgment by the father, by an adjudication during the life of the father, or by clear and convincing proof after his death.

The Uniform Parentage Act (UPA) (2002) is built upon the concept of a parent-child relationship, on which the law confers rights and obligations. The parent-child relationship extends to every parent and child, regardless of the marital status of the parents. When the father and mother do not marry or attempt to marry, a parent-child

---

14. For a description of the legal position at common law of what was called an illegitimate child, see 1 William Blackstone, Commentaries *454 ff.; 2 id. *247 ff. In the first book of Blackstone (1 id. *457) you may find out, if you care to, how a child could be "more than ordinarily legitimate."

relationship is presumed to exist between a father and a child if (1) while the child is less than age two, the father lives in the same household as the child and openly holds out the child as his natural child, or (2) the father acknowledges his paternity in a writing that is filed with an appropriate court or administrative agency. UPA §§204, 301-305.

Can a father of a child born out of wedlock inherit from the child? The authorities are split. See Katheleen Guzman, What Price Paternity?, 53 Okla. L. Rev. 77 (2000).

QUESTION AND NOTE

1. Should state courts develop an equitable legitimation doctrine (similar to equitable adoption) so that where a formal adjudication of paternity is required by statute for inheritance, a nonmarital child can inherit from the father if there is clear and convincing evidence of paternity and of the father's intent that the child be treated as an heir? See Prince v. Black, 344 S.E.2d 411 (Ga. 1986) (announcing equitable legitimation doctrine) (*Georgia*, did you say? Compare O'Neal v. Wilkes, page 94); James R. Robinson, Untangling the "Loose Threads": Equitable Adoption, Equitable Legitimation, and Inheritance in Extralegal Family Arrangements 48 Emory L.J. 943 (1999).

2. In Brancato v. Moriscato, 34 Conn. L. Rptr. 208 (Super. 2003), the plaintiff alleged that she was the daughter and intestate heir of Dominic Conti, who had been buried by the time of the suit. The plaintiff petitioned the court for an order to disinter Conti so that paternity might be proven by DNA testing of his remains. The court granted the petition over the objection of the administrator of Conti's estate. In New York, on the other hand, while post-death DNA testing has been allowed on stored samples, the courts have been reluctant to order exhumation for this purpose. Compare In re Estate of Bonanno, 745 N.Y.S.2d 813 (Sur. 2002) (allowing post-mortem DNA testing of a blood sample retained by the coroner), with In re Estate of Janis, 600 N.Y.S.2d 416 (Sur. 1993) (refusing to order exhumation for DNA testing). As DNA analysis has made paternity testing both fairer and more accurate, the clear trend is toward allowing it, even if exhumation of the body is required, as in *Brancato*. See Kate Schuler, Note, The Liberalization of Posthumous Paternity Testing—Expanding the Rights of Illegitimate Children, 17 Quinnipiac Prob. L.J. 150 (2003).

In Sudwischer v. Estate of Hoffpauir, 589 So. 2d 474 (La. 1991), a person claiming to be the naturally conceived daughter of the decedent was granted an order requiring the decedent's other daughter, who had been born in wedlock, to submit to a blood test to obtain the DNA composition of her blood. But see Moore v. Metropolitan Life Ins., 2000 WL 559219 (N.D. Ill. 2000), refusing to order the decedent's surviving kin to submit to DNA testing.

d. Reproductive Technology and New Forms of Parentage

At issue in Hecht v. Superior Court, 20 Cal. Rptr. 2d 275 (App. 1993), was William Kane's devise to his girlfriend Deborah Hecht of 15 vials of his sperm that were on deposit in a sperm bank. Kane's two adult children contested the devise and sought an order that the sperm be destroyed. The court ruled in favor of Hecht, awarding her Kane's sperm.

Would a child conceived through the use of Kane's sperm qualify as Kane's heir under applicable intestacy statutes? Recall that a posthumous child (a child *en ventre sa mere*) is treated as "in being" from the time of conception rather than from the time of birth if it is to the child's advantage to do so and the child is born alive (see page 99). The posthumously-conceived child (a child *en ventre sa frigidaire*) differs from the posthumous child in that the former is born *and conceived after* the death of one or both of the child's genetic parents. Hence a posthumously-conceived child is, by definition, a nonmarital child even though the child's parents, when both alive, might have been married. The California courts were able to elide the question in the subsequent litigation over Hecht's sperm,[15] but the issue has been since confronted squarely.

Woodward v. Commissioner of Social Security

Supreme Judicial Court of Massachusetts, 2002
435 Mass. 536, 760 N.E.2d 257

MARSHALL, C.J.   The United States District Court for the District of Massachusetts has certified the following question to this court.

> If a married man and woman arrange for sperm to be withdrawn from the husband for the purpose of artificially impregnating the wife, and the woman is impregnated with that sperm after the man, her husband, has died, will children resulting from such pregnancy enjoy the inheritance rights of natural children under Massachusetts' law of intestate succession?

We answer the certified question as follows: In certain limited circumstances, a child resulting from posthumous reproduction may enjoy the inheritance rights of "issue" under the Massachusetts intestacy statute. . . .

I

The undisputed facts and relevant procedural history are as follows. In January, 1993, about three and one-half years after they were married, Lauren Woodward and Warren Woodward were informed that the husband had leukemia. At the time, the couple was childless. Advised that the husband's leukemia treatment

---

15. After the 1993 decision in the *Hecht* case, the Kane children continued their litigation to deny Hecht the vials of sperm, raising arguments about legal capacity and undue influence, but chiefly claiming that Hecht had agreed to a settlement under which she received 20 percent of the estate's "residual assets." The children claimed that under this agreement Hecht was to receive only 3 of the 15 vials of sperm. After two unsuccessful tries at impregnation by 2 vials, Hecht, passing the age of 40, sought all the rest of the vials. Finally, in Hecht v. Superior Court, 59 Cal. Rptr. 2d 222 (App. 1996), the court, expressing exasperation at the children's effort to frustrate their father's will, dismissed all the children's claims and held the property settlement giving Hecht 20 percent of the estate's residual assets did not apply to sperm specifically bequeathed to Hecht. The court ordered all 15 vials of sperm distributed to Deborah Hecht without further delay. The court said, "We do not have before us the many legal questions raised by the possible birth of a child of Hecht through use of Kane's sperm. Thus, we do not decide, for instance, whether that child would be entitled to inherit any property as Kane's heir."

Michayla and Mackenzie Woodward, conceived with their father's sperm after his death. Defending the court's decision, their mother Lauren said, "Look at them and tell me that's not right."

AP/Salem News/Amy Sweeney

might leave him sterile, the Woodwards arranged for a quantity of the husband's semen to be medically withdrawn and preserved, in a process commonly known as "sperm banking." The husband then underwent a bone marrow transplant. The treatment was not successful. The husband died in October, 1993, and the wife was appointed administratrix of his estate.

In October, 1995, the wife gave birth to twin girls. The children were conceived through artificial insemination using the husband's preserved semen. In January, 1996, the wife applied for two forms of Social Security survivor benefits: "child's" benefits . . . and "mother's" benefits.

The Social Security Administration (SSA) rejected the wife's claims on the ground that she had not established that the twins were the husband's "children" within the meaning of the Act [because] . . . they "are not entitled to inherit from [the husband] under the Massachusetts intestacy and paternity laws." . . .

The wife appealed to the United States District Court for the District of Massachusetts, seeking a declaratory judgment to reverse the commissioner's ruling.

The United States District Court judge certified the above question to this court because "[t]he parties agree that a determination of these children's rights under the law of Massachusetts is dispositive of the case and . . . no directly applicable Massachusetts precedent exists."

II

A

We have been asked to determine the inheritance rights under Massachusetts law of children conceived from the gametes of a deceased individual and his or her surviving spouse.[16] We have not previously been asked to consider whether our intestacy statute accords inheritance rights to posthumously conceived genetic children. Nor has any American court of last resort considered, in a published opinion, the question of posthumously conceived genetic children's inheritance rights under other States' intestacy laws.

. . . [T]he parties have articulated extreme positions. The wife's principal argument is that, by virtue of their genetic connection with the decedent, posthumously conceived children must *always* be permitted to enjoy the inheritance rights of the deceased parent's children under our law of intestate succession. The government's principal argument is that, because posthumously conceived children are not "in being" as of the date of the parent's death, they are *always* barred from enjoying such inheritance rights.

Neither party's position is tenable. In this developing and relatively uncharted area of human relations, bright-line rules are not favored unless the applicable statute requires them. The Massachusetts intestacy statute does not. . . . On the other hand, with the act of procreation now separated from coitus, posthumous reproduction can occur under a variety of conditions that may conflict with the purposes of the intestacy law and implicate other firmly established State and individual interests. We look to our intestacy law to resolve these tensions.

B

. . . Section 1 of the intestacy statute directs that, if a decedent "leaves issue," such "issue" will inherit a fixed portion of his real and personal property, subject to debts and expenses, the rights of the surviving spouse, and other statutory payments not relevant here. See G.L. c. 190, §1. To answer the certified question, then, we must first determine whether the twins are the "issue" of the husband.

The intestacy statute does not define "issue." However, in the context of intestacy the term "issue" means all lineal (genetic) descendants, and now includes both marital and nonmarital descendants. The term "'[d]escendants' . . . has long been held to mean persons 'who by consanguinity trace their lineage to the designated ancestor.'" Lockwood v. Adamson, 566 N.E.2d 96 (Mass. 1991).

. . . We must therefore determine whether, under our intestacy law, there is any reason that children conceived after the decedent's death who are the decedent's direct genetic descendants—that is, children who "by consanguinity trace their lineage to the designated ancestor"—may not enjoy the same succession rights as

16. Although the certified question asks us to consider an unsettled question of law concerning the paternity of children conceived from a deceased male's gametes, we see no principled reason that our conclusions should not apply equally to children posthumously conceived from a deceased female's gametes. [Recent advances have made the freezing of eggs a technological possibility. See Michael K. Elliot, Tales of Parenthood from the Crypt: The Predicament of the Posthumously Conceived Child, 39 Real Prop., Prob. & Tr. J. 47 (2004). See also Claudia Kalb, Fertility and the Freezer, Newsweek, Aug. 2, 2004, at 52.—Eds.]

children conceived before the decedent's death who are the decedent's direct genetic descendants.

To answer that question we consider whether and to what extent such children may take as intestate heirs of the deceased genetic parent consistent with the purposes of the intestacy law, and not by any assumptions of the common law. In the absence of express legislative directives, we construe the Legislature's purposes from statutory indicia and judicial decisions in a manner that advances the purposes of the intestacy law.

The question whether posthumously conceived genetic children may enjoy inheritance rights under the intestacy statute implicates three powerful State interests: [1] the best interests of children, [2] the State's interest in the orderly administration of estates, and [3] the reproductive rights of the genetic parent. Our task is to balance and harmonize these interests to effect the Legislature's over-all purposes.

1. First and foremost we consider the overriding legislative concern to promote the best interests of children. "The protection of minor children, most especially those who may be stigmatized by their 'illegitimate' status . . . has been a hallmark of legislative action and of the jurisprudence of this court." Repeatedly, forcefully, and unequivocally, the Legislature has expressed its will that all children be "entitled to the same rights and protections of the law" regardless of the accidents of their birth. Among the many rights and protections vouchsafed to all children are rights to financial support from their parents and their parents' estates. See G.L. c. 119A, §1 ("It is the public policy of this commonwealth that dependent children shall be maintained, as completely as possible, from the resources of their parents, thereby relieving or avoiding, at least in part, the burden borne by the citizens of the commonwealth"); G.L. c. 191, §20 (establishing inheritance rights for pretermitted children); G.L. c. 196, §§1-3 (permitting allowances from estate to widows and minor children); G.L. c. 209C, §14 (permitting paternity claims to be commenced prior to birth). See also G.L. c. 190, §§1-3, 5, 7-8 (intestacy rights).

We also consider that some of the assistive reproductive technologies that make posthumous reproduction possible have been widely known and practiced for several decades. In that time, the Legislature has not acted to narrow the broad statutory class of posthumous children to restrict posthumously conceived children from taking in intestacy. Moreover, the Legislature has in great measure affirmatively supported the assistive reproductive technologies that are the only means by which these children can come into being. See G.L. c. 46, §4B (artificial insemination of married woman). See also G.L. c. 175, §47H; G.L. c. 176A, §8K; G.L. c. 176B, §4J; G.L. c. 176G, §4 (insurance coverage for infertility treatments). We do not impute to the Legislature the inherently irrational conclusion that assistive reproductive technologies are to be encouraged while a class of children who are the fruit of that technology are to have fewer rights and protections than other children.

In short, we cannot, absent express legislative directive, accept the commissioner's position that the historical context of G.L. c. 190, §8, dictates as a matter of law that all posthumously conceived children are automatically barred from taking under their deceased donor parent's intestate estate. We have consistently construed statutes to effectuate the Legislature's overriding purpose to promote the welfare of all children, notwithstanding restrictive common-law rules to the contrary. Posthumously conceived children may not come into the world the way the majority of children do. But they are children nonetheless. We may assume that the Legislature intended that such children be "entitled," in so far as possible, "to the same rights and protections of the law" as children conceived before death. See G.L. c. 209C, §1.

2. However, in the context of our intestacy laws, the best interests of the post-humously conceived child, while of great importance, are not in themselves conclusive. They must be balanced against other important State interests, not the least of which is the protection of children who are alive or conceived before the intestate parent's death. In an era in which serial marriages, serial families, and blended families are not uncommon, according succession rights under our intestacy laws to posthumously conceived children may, in a given case, have the potential to pit child against child and family against family. Any inheritance rights of posthumously conceived children will reduce the intestate share available to children born prior to the decedent's death. Such considerations, among others, lead us to examine a second important legislative purpose: to provide certainty to heirs and creditors by effecting the orderly, prompt, and accurate administration of intestate estates.

The intestacy statute furthers the Legislature's administrative goals in two principal ways: (1) by requiring certainty of filiation between the decedent and his issue, and (2) by establishing limitations periods for the commencement of claims against the intestate estate. In answering the certified question, we must consider each of these requirements of the intestacy statute in turn.

First, . . . our intestacy law mandates that, absent the father's acknowledgment of paternity or marriage to the mother, a nonmarital child must obtain a judicial determination of paternity as a prerequisite to succeeding to a portion of the father's intestate estate. . . .

Because death ends a marriage, posthumously conceived children are always nonmarital children. And because the parentage of such children can be neither acknowledged nor adjudicated prior to the decedent's death, it follows that, under the intestacy statute, posthumously conceived children must obtain a judgment of paternity as a necessary prerequisite to enjoying inheritance rights in the estate of the deceased genetic father. Although modern reproductive technologies will increase the possibility of disputed paternity claims,[17] sophisticated modern testing techniques now make the determination of genetic paternity accurate and reliable. . . .

We now turn to the second way in which the Legislature has met its administrative goals: the establishment of a limitations period for bringing paternity claims against the intestate estate. Our discussion of this important goal, however, is necessarily circumscribed by the procedural posture of this case and by the terms of the certified question. [The parties stipulated that, in this dispute over Social Security benefits, timeliness was not at issue.] . . .

---

17. It is now possible for a child to be born by means of reproductive technologies in circumstances in which several people could claim or be claimed to be the child's legal parents: an egg donor, a sperm donor, a gestational carrier, and one or two people who are not biologically related to the child but who have arranged for the contributions of the others and who intend to raise the child. See Helene S. Shapo, Matters of Life and Death: Inheritance Consequences of Reproductive Technologies, 25 Hofstra L. Rev. 1091, 1102 (1997).

Nevertheless, the limitations question is inextricably tied to consideration of the intestacy statute's administrative goals. In the case of posthumously conceived children, the application of the one-year limitations period of G.L. c. 190, §7 is not clear; it may pose significant burdens on the surviving parent, and consequently on the child. It requires, in effect, that the survivor make a decision to bear children while in the freshness of grieving. It also requires that attempts at conception succeed quickly. Cf. Commentary, Modern Reproductive Technologies: Legal Issues Concerning Cryopreservation and Posthumous Conception, 17 J. Legal Med. 547, 549 (1996) ("It takes an average of seven insemination attempts over 4.4 menstrual cycles to establish pregnancy"). Because the resolution of the time constraints question is not required here, it must await the appropriate case, should one arise.

3. Finally, the question certified to us implicates a third important State interest: to honor the reproductive choices of individuals. We need not address the wife's argument that her reproductive rights would be infringed by denying succession rights to her children under our intestacy law. Nothing in the record even remotely suggests that she was prevented by the State from choosing to conceive children using her deceased husband's semen. The husband's reproductive rights are a more complicated matter.

In A.Z. v. B.Z., 725 N.E.2d 1051 (Mass. 2000), we . . . recognized that individuals have a protected right to control the use of their gametes. Consonant with the principles identified in A.Z. v. B.Z., a decedent's silence, or his equivocal indications of a desire to parent posthumously, "ought not to be construed as consent." See Anne Reichman Schiff, Arising from the Dead: Challenges of Posthumous Procreation, 75 N.C.L. Rev. 901, 951 (1997). The prospective donor parent must clearly and unequivocally consent not only to posthumous reproduction but also to the support of any resulting child. After the donor-parent's death, the burden rests with the surviving parent, or the posthumously conceived child's other legal representative, to prove the deceased genetic parent's affirmative consent to both requirements for posthumous parentage: posthumous reproduction and the support of any resulting child.

This two-fold consent requirement arises from the nature of alternative reproduction itself. It will not always be the case that a person elects to have his or her gametes medically preserved to create "issue" posthumously. A man, for example, may preserve his semen for myriad reasons, including, among others: to reproduce after recovery from medical treatment, to reproduce after an event that leaves him sterile, or to reproduce when his spouse has a genetic disorder or otherwise cannot have or safely bear children. That a man has medically preserved his gametes for use by his spouse thus may indicate only that he wished to reproduce after some contingency while he was alive, and not that he consented to the different circumstance of creating a child after his death. Uncertainty as to consent may be compounded by the fact that medically preserved semen can remain viable for up to ten years after it was first extracted, long after the original decision to preserve the semen has passed and when such changed circumstances as divorce, remarriage, and a second family may have intervened.

Such circumstances demonstrate the inadequacy of a rule that would make the mere genetic tie of the decedent to any posthumously conceived child, or the decedent's mere election to preserve gametes, sufficient to bind his intestate estate for the benefit of any posthumously conceived child. Without evidence that the deceased intestate parent affirmatively consented (1) to the posthumous reproduction and (2) to support any resulting child, a court cannot be assured that the intestacy statute's goal of fraud prevention is satisfied. . . .

C

The certified question does not require us to specify what proof would be sufficient to establish a successful claim under our intestacy law on behalf of a posthumously conceived child. Nor have we been asked to determine whether the wife has met her burden of proof. . . .

It is undisputed in this case that the husband is the genetic father of the wife's children. However, for the reasons stated above, that fact, in itself, cannot be sufficient to establish that the husband is the children's legal father for purposes of the devolution and distribution of his intestate property. In the United States District Court, the wife may come forward with other evidence as to her husband's consent to posthumously conceive children. She may come forward with evidence of his consent to support such children. We do not speculate as to the sufficiency of evidence she may submit at trial. . . .

III

. . . As these technologies advance, the number of children they produce will continue to multiply. So, too, will the complex moral, legal, social, and ethical questions that surround their birth. The questions present in this case cry out for lengthy, careful examination outside the adversary process, which can only address the specific circumstances of each controversy that presents itself. They demand a comprehensive response reflecting the considered will of the people.

In the absence of statutory directives, we have answered the certified question by identifying and harmonizing the important State interests implicated therein in a manner that advances the Legislature's over-all purposes. In so doing, we conclude that limited circumstances may exist, consistent with the mandates of our Legislature, in which posthumously conceived children may enjoy the inheritance rights of "issue" under our intestacy law. These limited circumstances exist where, as a threshold matter, the surviving parent or the child's other legal representative demonstrates a genetic relationship between the child and the decedent. The survivor or representative must then establish both that the decedent affirmatively consented to posthumous conception and to the support of any resulting child. Even where such circumstances exist, time limitations may preclude commencing a claim for succession rights on behalf of a posthumously conceived child. In any action brought to establish such inheritance rights, notice must be given to all interested parties.

[The clerk of the court was ordered to transmit an attested copy of this opinion to the district court.]

NOTES AND QUESTIONS

1. The court in *Woodward* was asked to determine the intestacy rights of the decedent's posthumously-conceived children, not for the purpose of distributing the decedent's estate, but because under the Social Security Act state intestacy law

determines rights to social security benefits for a dependent child. A child of the father is eligible for social security dependent benefits due the father's children only if the child inherits from the father under state law. In this context, at least two other courts have ruled that posthumously-conceived children are intestate heirs. See Gillett-Netting v. Barnhart, 371 F.3d 593 (9th Cir. 2004) (Arizona law); Estate of Kolacy, 753 A.2d 1257 (N.J. Super. 2000) (New Jersey law). Of course, neither *Woodward* nor these other decisions announce a national rule, as all three rest on the intestacy law of the relevant state. The question thus arises, what result in a state in which a posthumously-conceived child would not be an intestate heir?

In the early 1990s, this question was litigated in Louisiana, which requires that a successor "exist at the death of the decedent." La. Civ. Code art. 939 (2004). However, in 1996, while the case was pending, the Commissioner of Social Security ordered that survivor's benefits be paid, thereby mooting the litigation. The Commissioner's justification: "Recent advances in modern medical practice, particularly in the field of reproductive medicine, . . . should involve the executive and legislative branches, rather than the courts." Gloria J. Banks, Traditional Concepts and Nontraditional Conceptions: Social Security Survivors Benefits for Posthumously Conceived Children, 32 Loy. L.A.L. Rev. 251, 255-256 (1999). Despite this plea, the Social Security Act has not yet been amended to account for the possibility of posthumous conception.

2. The court in *Woodward* rejected the view that a child conceived after the decedent's death is not an heir of the decedent, opting instead for a balancing test in which the court considers (1) the best interests of the child, (2) the state's interest in the orderly administration of estates (which comprises both an interest in ensuring certainty of filiation and a limitations period), and (3) the deceased's reproductive rights. Inasmuch as it requires proof that the decedent "affirmatively consented" to posthumous conception, *Woodward* does not appear to invite a free-for-all, though it remains to be seen what evidence will suffice to prove affirmative consent. See Ronald Chester, Inheritance Rights of the Posthumously Conceived Child: What Exactly Does Lauren Woodward v. Commissioner of Social Security Decide?, 87 Mass. L. Rev. 49 (2002).

A more relaxed rule is advanced by Restatement (Third) of Property: Wills and Other Donative Transfers §2.5, cmt. 1 (1999): "[T]o inherit from the decedent, a child produced from genetic material of the decedent by assisted reproductive technology must be born within a reasonable time after the decedent's death in circumstances indicating that the decedent would have approved of the child's right to inherit. A clear case would be that of a child produced by artificial insemination of the decedent's widow with his frozen sperm."

Uniform Parentage Act (UPA) §707 (2002) states a stricter rule: "If an individual who consented in a record to be a parent by assisted reproduction dies before placement of eggs, sperm, or embryos, the deceased individual is not a parent of the resulting child unless the deceased spouse consented in a record that if assisted reproduction were to occur after death, the deceased individual would be a parent of the child."

A California statute enacted in 2004 and slated to take effect on January 1, 2005, grants posthumously-conceived children intestacy rights, but under more limited conditions than either the UPA or the Restatement (Third). Under Cal. Prob.

Code §249.5 (2005), "a child of the decedent conceived after the death of the decedent shall be deemed to have been born in the lifetime of the decedent" provided that (a) there is clear and convincing evidence that the decedent specified in a writing signed by a witness that a designated person could use the decedent's genetic material for posthumous conception; (b) within four months of the decedent's death notice of the possibility of posthumous conception is served upon "a person who has the power to control the distribution" of the decedent's property; and (c) the child "was in utero within two years of the" decedent's death. The California statute expressly excludes clones from its coverage.

The Joint Editorial Board for Uniform Trust and Estate Acts is now studying potential amendments to the Uniform Probate Code to account for posthumous conception. For a proposed amendment to §2-108 that would require "consent in a record" by the "putative parent," would establish a three-year limitations period, and would provide for a set-aside in the decedent's estate for later born, posthumously-conceived children, see Ronald Chester, Posthumously Conceived Heirs Under a Revised Uniform Probate Code, 38 Real Prop., Prob. & Tr. J. 727 (2004).

For criticism of the "ad hoc approach by the judiciary," see Laurence C. Nolan, Critiquing Society's Response to the Needs of Posthumously Conceived Children, 82 Or. L. Rev. 1067 (2003).

3. What are the problems in extending property rights to posthumously conceived children? The New York Times carried a story of a woman in Los Angeles giving birth to a girl using the sperm retrieved from her dead husband 30 hours after the man's death. N.Y. Times, Mar. 27, 1999, at A11. Under the *Woodward* decision, would the girl be entitled to inherit from her father, who did not give his consent? Under the Restatement (Third)? Under the UPA? Under Cal. Prob. Code §249.5? For more on the extraction of sperm from dead or comatose men who do not consent, and the use of such sperm by wives, girlfriends, and parents, see Lori B. Andrews, The Sperminator (a term coined for such a father), N.Y. Times Mag., Mar. 28, 1999, at 62. The author suggests that the practice has now become "common." See also Ronald Chester, Double Trouble: Legal Solutions to the Medical Problems of Unconsented Sperm Harvesting and Drug-Induced Multiple Pregnancies, 44 St. Louis U.L.J. 451, 453-462 (2000).

4. Suppose a man preserves his sperm but, after he dies, there is a dispute whether he consented to posthumous conception with his widow. What proof would show that the man "affirmatively consented" under *Woodward*? Under the Restatement (Third), what sort of "circumstances" would indicate "that the decedent would have approved of the child's right to inherit"? What would qualify as "consent in a record" under the UPA? Is the requirement of a witnessed writing under Cal. Prob. Code §249.5 (2005) a sensible solution to this problem?

Suppose a man preserves his sperm and records in writing his consent to posthumous conception with his widow, and then his widow gives birth to his posthumously conceived daughter 21 years later? Cf. Celia Hall, Baby Boy Born from Sperm Frozen for 21 Years, Daily Telegraph (London), May 25, 2004, at 01. Under the *Woodward* decision, would the girl be entitled to inherit from her father? Under the Restatement (Third)? Under the UPA? What if the birth were two years after the father's death? Five years later? Ten years? Fifty years? At what point does the state's interest in finality—and the interest in finality of the other potential takers—trump the interests of a later born, posthumously-conceived child? Cal. Prob. Code §249.5 (2005) requires notice of the potential for posthumous conception within four months and the child to be in utero within two years of the decedent's death. Does the California approach represent a sound compromise?

5.   Posthumously-conceived children raise problems of interpretation not only under intestacy laws, but also under wills and trusts. Suppose that a testator devises his property in trust for his children for their lives, remainder to his grandchildren. Should a posthumously-conceived child share in the trust and the children of such a child share in the remainder? Does it matter whether the testator had other children at death? For a thoughtful examination of these issues, see Kristine S. Knaplund, Postmortem Conception and a Father's Last Will, 46 Ariz. L. Rev. 91, 108-114 (2004). See also Restatement (Third) of Property: Wills and Other Donative Transfers §14.8, cmt. h (T.D. No. 4, 2004). A related question is whether the possibility of posthumous conception should be considered in assessing the validity of future interests under the Rule against Perpetuities. See pages 680-681. Many of these issues are avoided by addressing the possibility of posthumous conception when drafting your clients' wills and trusts.

6.   Other countries are also confronting the question of succession rights for posthumously-conceived children. In Margaret Ward Scott, Comment, A Look at the Rights and Entitlements of Posthumously Conceived Children: No Surefire Way to Tame the Reproductive Wild West, 52 Emory L.J. 963, 970-971 (2003), the author summarizes the law abroad, both within and without the common law world. See also E. Donald Shapiro & Benedene Sonnenblick, The Law and the Sperm: The Law of Post-Mortem Insemination, 1 J.L. & Health 229 (1986-1987), discussing Parpalaix c. CECOS (1984), decided by the French Tribunal de grand instance, which is the first reported judicial decision on the issue.

NOTE: SURROGATE MOTHERHOOD AND MARRIED COUPLES

Who is the parent of a child born by surrogate motherhood? Surrogate motherhood can involve (1) an egg of the wife fertilized by the husband's sperm; (2) an egg of the wife fertilized by the sperm of a third party donor; (3) an egg of the surrogate mother fertilized by the husband's sperm; (4) an egg of a third party donor fertilized by the husband's sperm; (5) an egg of a third party donor fertilized by the sperm of a third party donor. As you can see, there may be a genetic connection of both husband and wife to the child, or a genetic connection of only one of them to the child, or no genetic connection between the husband and wife and the child. The law is evolving on who is a parent, and courts are by no means in agreement.

In Johnson v. Calvert, 851 P.2d 776 (Cal. 1993), a husband and wife signed a contract with a woman surrogate providing that an egg of the wife fertilized by the husband's sperm would be implanted in the surrogate woman and, after the child was born, it would be taken into the home of the husband and wife as their child. The surrogate agreed to relinquish all parental rights to the child. The surrogate later changed her mind, claiming parental rights. The court held that parenthood in surrogate mother cases should not be determined by who gave birth or who contributed genetic material, but should turn on the intent of the parties as shown by the surrogacy contract. The court declared the husband and wife the sole parents. The court rejected the argument that the child has two legal mothers.

In many states, surrogacy agreements are prohibited or are enforceable only under certain specified conditions. This complicates matters. For example, in J.R. v. Utah, 261 F. Supp. 2d 1268 (D. Utah 2003), the biological parents sought parental rights for a child carried and born to a surrogate under a contract, but a Utah statute conclusively denied parental rights to biological parents in this situation. The court struck down the statute, holding that it violated the biological parents' liberty interests under the Fourteenth Amendment to the U.S. Constitution. See also R.R. v. M.H., 689 N.E.2d 790 (Mass. 1998) (consent of surrogate mother *A*, whose egg was fertilized by sperm of husband of *B*, void because given for compensation; surrogate mother *A* and husband of *B* were parents; *B* cannot adopt child without consent of *A*).

In In re Marriage of Buzzanca, 72 Cal. Rptr. 2d 280 (App. 1998), husband and wife agreed to have an embryo genetically unrelated to either of them (third party donor's egg fertilized by third party donor's sperm) implanted in a woman surrogate. Before birth of the child, the husband and wife split up; the husband petitioned for divorce. The surrogate mother did not claim parenthood. The wife claimed motherhood and claimed also that her erstwhile husband was the father and had to support the child. The husband claimed that the wife was not the mother and he was not the father because neither was genetically related to the child. The court held that both the wife and husband were parents because they had consented to the artificial insemination that created the child. Compare Jane Doe v. John Doe, 710 A.2d 1297 (Conn. 1998) (surrogate mother inseminated with sperm of wife's husband surrendered child at birth to husband and wife; upon subsequent divorce, court held the husband was the father but the wife was not a parent because she was neither genetically nor gestationally related to the child; however, wife could be granted custody of the child if in best interests of child).

Is a determination of who is a parent in custody cases and child support cases res judicata as to inheritance rights? Are the policies in the cases cited above, which are heavily influenced by the best interests of the child, the same as govern inheritance? See Helene S. Shapo, Matters of Life and Death: Inheritance Consequences of Reproductive Technologies, 25 Hofstra L. Rev. 1091 (1997).

In England, the law of parentage of children born to surrogate mothers appears to be more settled than in this country, but is it better? See Principles of Medical Law 602-603 (Ian Kennedy & Andrew Grubb eds., 1998): "Where a child is born as a result of a surrogacy arrangement, who are his/her parents? Legally the child's mother will always be the surrogate; the woman of the commissioning couple is not the mother even if her eggs were used. Where the surrogate is married, her husband is the father unless he can prove that he did not consent to the procedure and the man of the commissioning couple is not the father even if his sperm is used." In order for the genetic mother to become the legal mother, she must legally adopt the child.

See generally Naomi R. Cahn, Parenthood, Genes, and Gametes: The Family Law and Trusts and Estates Perspectives, 32 U. Mem. L. Rev. 563 (2002); James E. Bailey, An Analytical Framework for Resolving the Issues Raised by the Interaction Between Reproductive Technology and the Law of Inheritance, 47 DePaul L. Rev. 743 (1998); Randy Frances Kandel, Which Came First? The Mother or the Egg: A Kinship Solution to Gestational Surrogacy, 47 Rutgers L. Rev. 165 (1994); Alexa E. King, Solomon Revisited: Assigning Parenthood in the Context of Collaborative Reproduction, 5 UCLA Women's L.J. 329 (1995); Murray L. Manus, The Proposed Model Surrogate Parenthood Act: A Legislative Response to the Challenges of Reproductive Technology, 29 U. Mich. J.L. Reform 671 (1996);

Martha J. Stone, Tick . . . Tick . . . Tick: As Biological Clocks Wind Down, the Laws Governing Inheritance and Parental Rights Issues Heat Up, 43 S. Tex. L. Rev. 233 (2001); Helene S. Shapo, Frozen Pre-Embryos and the Right to Change One's Mind, 12 Duke J. Comp. & Intl. L. 75 (2002).

For a comprehensive discussion of whether a parent-child relationship exists for inheritance purposes with regard to nonmarital children, adopted children, and children of reproductive technologies, and also the rights of spouses and unmarried cohabitants, see Ralph C. Brashier, Inheritance Law and the Evolving Family (2004).

NOTE: ASSISTED REPRODUCTION AND SAME-SEX COUPLES

In Adoption of Tammy, 619 N.E.2d 315 (Mass. 1993), noted in 107 Harv. L. Rev. 751 (1994), the court approved the adoption of the child, conceived by artificial insemination, of Dr. Susan Love, the eminent breast cancer surgeon, by her lesbian partner, also a surgeon. The court held that both the natural mother and the adoptive mother had post-adoptive rights and that the adopted child would inherit from and through both mothers as the child of each. A similar adoption was approved in In re Jacob, 660 N.E.2d 397 (N.Y. 1995). Suppose that the jurisdiction has enacted UPC §2-114 (1990). If the natural mother thereafter dies, survived by the child and the adoptive mother, is the child the natural mother's heir? See Laura M. Padilla, Flesh of My Flesh But Not My Heir: Unintended Disinheritance, 36 J. Fam. L. 219 (1997).

"You just wait until your other mother gets home, young man!"

Drawing by M. Stevens.

Suppose a lesbian couple, *A* and *B*, go through a civil commitment ceremony. *A* then gives birth to a child after being artificially inseminated with sperm from a donor. *A* and *B* later break up. Does *B* have a right to joint custody of the child or full visitation? In King v. S.B., 818 N.E.2d 126 (Ind. App. 2004), the sperm was donated by *B*'s brother, so both *A* and *B* had a genetic relationship to the child. The court concluded that "when two women involved in a domestic relationship agree to bear and raise a child together by artificial insemination of one of the partners with donor semen, both women are the legal parents of the resulting child." Id. at 131-132.

For more on lesbian partners where partner *A* donated eggs for artificial insemination, see West v. Superior Court, 69 Cal. Rptr. 2d 160 (App. 1997) (court denied partner *B* custody or visitation rights with child when *A* and *B* split, even though *A* and *B* had jointly agreed to have the child and raise the child together; the contract was not controlling); In re Lynda A.H. v. Diane T.O., 673 N.Y.S.2d 989 (App. Div. 1998) (accord). See also Fred A. Bernstein, This Child Does Have Two Mothers . . . And a Sperm Donor with Visitation, 22 N.Y.U. Rev. L. & Soc. Change 1 (1996); Nancy D. Polikoff, This Child Does Have Two Mothers: Redefining Parenthood to Meet the Needs of Children in Lesbian-Mother and Other Nontraditional Families, 78 Geo. L.J. 459 (1990); Richard F. Storrow, Parenthood by Pure Intention: Assisted Reproduction and the Functional Approach to Parentage, 53 Hastings L.J. 597 (2002).

2.   *Advancements*

If any child wishes to share in the intestate distribution of a deceased parent's estate, the child must permit the administrator to include in the determination of the distributive shares the value of any property that the decedent, while living, gave the child by way of an *advancement*. At common law, any lifetime gift to a child was presumed to be an advancement — in effect, a prepayment — of the child's intestate share. To avoid application of the doctrine, the child had the burden of establishing that the lifetime transfer was intended as an absolute gift that was not to be counted against the child's share of the estate. The doctrine is based on the assumption that the parent would want an equal distribution of assets among the children and that true equality can be reached only if lifetime gifts are taken into account in determining the amount of the equal shares. When a parent makes an advancement to the child and the child predeceases the parent, the amount of the advancement is deducted from the shares of the child's descendants if other children of the parent survive.

If a gift is treated as an advancement, the donee must allow its value to be brought into *hotchpot* if the donee wants to share in the decedent's estate. Here is how hotchpot works: Assume the decedent leaves no spouse, three children, and an estate worth $50,000. One daughter, *A*, received an advancement of $10,000. To calculate the shares in the estate, the $10,000 gift is added to the $50,000, and the total of $60,000 is divided by three. *A* has already received $10,000 of her share; thus she receives only $10,000 from the estate. Her siblings each take a $20,000 share. If instead *A* had been given property worth $40,000 as an advancement, *A* would not have to give back a portion of this amount (we know that the decedent wanted *A* to have at least $40,000). *A* will stay out of hotchpot, and decedent's $50,000 will be equally divided between the other two children.

PROBLEMS, QUESTIONS, AND NOTE

1.   Suppose that *O* has two children, *A* and *B*. *A* owns a successful business. *B* is a single parent who struggles to make ends meet. *O* makes regular gifts to *B*, but not *A*, because *B* is in greater need. If *O*'s lifetime transfers to *B* are deemed to be advancements, then *A* will inherit more than *B* on the death of *O*. Is this result consistent with *O*'s probable intent? Why does the law regard favorable lifetime treatment of a child as a reason to disfavor that child at the parent's death? Is not favorable lifetime treatment good evidence that the decedent would have wanted the favored child to receive at least the same share of her estate as her other children? The common law of advancements answers this question in the negative.

2.   *O* has three children by his first marriage and six children by his second marriage. After his second marriage, *O* gives each of the children by his first marriage a tract of land. *O* subsequently dies intestate. Are these gifts advancements? In re Martinez's Estate, 633 P.2d 727 (N.M. App. 1981).

3.   *O* has three children. One daughter, *A*, does not leave home but lives with *O* on *O*'s farm until *O* dies. A few years before death, *O* deeds the farm to *A*. *O* dies intestate. *A* claims the gift is not an advancement but an extra gift for extraordinary services rendered *O*. What result? Thomas v. Thomas, 398 S.W.2d 231 (Ky. 1965).

Suppose that *O* gives his son *B* $20,000. *B* is ill and unable to work and support his family. Is this an advancement?

Suppose that *O*'s daughter *C* is smart, goes to Yale Medical School, and acquires an M.D. degree. *O* pays the tuition ($130,000). Is this an advancement?

4.   Largely because of problems of proof of the donor's intent, many states have reversed the common law presumption of advancement. In these states, a lifetime gift is presumed *not* to be an advancement unless it is shown to have been intended as such. In other states, statutes declare that a gift is not an advancement unless it is declared as such in a writing signed by the grantor or grantee. See Carolyn S. Bratt, Kentucky's Doctrine of Advancements: A Time for Reform, 75 Ky. L.J. 341 (1987).

Uniform Probate Code (1990)

§2-109.   ADVANCEMENTS

(a) If an individual dies intestate as to all or a portion of his [or her] estate, property the decedent gave during the decedent's lifetime to an individual who, at the decedent's death, is an heir[18] is treated as an advancement against the heir's intestate share only if (i) the decedent declared in a contemporaneous writing or

---

18. UPC §2-109 applies to advancements made to spouses and collaterals (such as nephews and nieces) as well as to lineal descendants. In most states, only gifts to lineal descendants are considered advancements. — Eds.

the heir acknowledged in writing that the gift is an advancement or (ii) the decedent's contemporaneous writing or the heir's written acknowledgment otherwise indicates that the gift is to be taken into account in computing the division and distribution of the decedent's intestate estate.

(b) For purposes of subsection (a), property advanced is valued as of the time the heir came into possession or enjoyment of the property or as of the time of the decedent's death, whichever first occurs.

(c) If the recipient of the property fails to survive the decedent, the property is not taken into account in computing the division and distribution of the decedent's intestate estate, unless the decedent's contemporaneous writing provides otherwise.

Observe that UPC §2-109(c) changes the common law if the recipient does not survive the decedent. In that case, the advancement is not taken into account in determining the share of the recipient's issue.

Because it requires the formality of a writing to evidence an advancement, the UPC virtually eliminates the doctrine of advancements from the law of intestate succession. See also Restatement (Third) of Property: Wills and Other Donative Transfers §2.6 (1999) (requiring a writing as in UPC §2-109). On the one hand, this avoids contentious litigation between family members about little-remembered lifetime gifts. On the other hand, persons who do not write wills or consult lawyers and die intestate will rarely know that a lifetime gift must be stated in writing to be an advancement to be charged against the donee's intestate share. See Mary L. Fellows, Concealing Legislative Reform in the Common-Law Tradition: The Advancements Doctrine and the Uniform Probate Code, 37 Vand. L. Rev. 671 (1984), proposing a statute requiring *all* gifts to be treated as advancements absent written evidence of a contrary intent (the opposite of the UPC).

QUESTION

Which of the following rules do you think is best?

1. Gifts to children are presumptively advancements.
2. Gifts to children are presumptively not advancements.
3. Gifts to children are not advancements unless so stated in writing.
4. Gifts to children are advancements unless stated not to be in writing.

3. Guardianship and Conservatorship of Minors

A minor has neither the legal capacity to manage property nor the power to make most choices about how and where to live. Ordinary liberties that adults enjoy are not open to minors. When clients with young children plan for death, you should advise them to provide for the possibility that their children might be orphaned — a problem that must be confronted by rich and poor clients alike. It is now time to speak of guardians, conservators, and how best to avoid them if possible.

a.   Guardian of the Person

A guardian of the person has responsibility for the minor child's custody and care. As long as one parent of the child is living and competent, that parent is the natural guardian of the child's person. Thus, if only one of two parents dies, there is no need to appoint a guardian of the person (though there may be a need for a conservator or guardian of the property if the minor receives property by reason of the parent's death). If both parents die while a child is a minor and their wills do not designate a guardian, the court will appoint a guardian of the person from among the nearest relatives. This person may not be whom the parents would want to have custody of the child.

Accordingly, for a parent with a minor child, one of the principal reasons for having a will is to designate a guardian of the person. This guardian of the person decides where the minor lives, how the minor is raised and educated, and when the minor receives medical care. A guardianship of the person terminates when the minor reaches the age of majority, dies before becoming an adult, or is adopted. See, e.g., UPC §5-210 (1998). In choosing a guardian, most testators select a family member (often a brother or sister) or sometimes a friend. It is a good idea to select not only a first choice but also an alternate for the possibility that the first choice cannot serve. For a review of the state statutes, see Peter Mosanyi II, Comment: A Survey of State Guardianship Statutes: One Concept, Many Applications, 18 J. Am. Acad. Matrimonial L. 253 (2002).

b.   Property Management Options

Another important reason that a parent with a minor child should have a will is to deal with the management of the child's property. A guardian of the person has no authority to deal with the child's property.

Several alternatives for property management are available: guardianship of the property, conservatorship, custodianship, and trusteeship. Trusts are available only to persons who create them during lifetime or who die testate, creating them by will. If a parent dies intestate, leaving property to a minor child, often a guardian of the property or a conservator must be appointed by a court, unless state law allows payment instead to a custodian under the Uniform Transfers to Minors Act or to the person who has custody of the child. Let us examine these alternatives for managing a minor's property.

(1) Guardianship of the property

In feudal times the guardian of a minor ward (usually the overlord) took possession of the ward's lands. The guardian had the duty of supporting the ward, but all income from rents in excess of the amount necessary for support belonged to the guardian personally. Thus guardianships (then known as wardships) were very profitable for the guardian.

After the feudal incidents, including wardship, were abolished in 1660, a new kind of guardianship was recognized, giving the ward the rents from the property and the guardian only a management fee. Nonetheless, the historical odor remained. A guardian of property was looked upon with suspicion and was required to account annually to a court of chancery. To avoid a disagreeable contest later with the ward or chancellor, guardians sought approval for their actions in advance from the chancellor. The product of history is a system wherein the guardian is straitjacketed and the process expensive. Indeed, guardianship for a minor's property is somewhat like going through a continuous probate until the child reaches the age of majority (usually 18).

First, the guardian of property, who does not have title to the ward's property, usually cannot change investments without a court order. The guardian has the duty of preserving the specific property left the minor and delivering it to the ward at age 18, unless the court approves a sale, lease, or mortgage. Second, the guardian ordinarily can use only the income from the property to support the ward; the guardian has no authority to go into principal to support the ward, unless the court approves. Strict court supervision over many of the guardian's acts is burdensome and time-consuming. Each trip to court costs money — for the attorney's fees and court costs. The ward often ends up with less property at the end of a guardianship than at the beginning.

(2) Conservatorship

The expense and inflexibility of guardianship for handling property has led to a major reform — the replacement of the guardian of the property system with a *conservator* system. Following the lead of UPC Article V (1998) and the Uniform Guardianship and Protective Proceeding Act (1997), in many states guardianship laws have been revised to allow a more trust-like treatment. The guardian of the property has been renamed the *conservator* and given "title as trustee" to the protected person's property, as well as investment powers similar to those of trustees. Appointment and supervision by a court is still required, but the conservator has far more flexible powers than a guardian, and only one trip to the courthouse annually for an accounting may be necessary.

The conservatorship system permits a more streamlined administration of the estate, allowing a higher net return on the assets, more flexibility in investments, and a greater chance of meeting the financial needs of the child, both while a minor and on termination of the conservatorship. The conservatorship terminates when the minor reaches the age of majority or dies before then. UPC §5-431 (1998).

In states without modern conservatorship laws, the only effective way to handle guardianship administrations is to avoid them. And, indeed, we conclude that even in states with modern conservatorship laws, the alternative arrangements of custodianship or trusteeship for a minor are preferable because the court does not become involved unless the minor contests the custodian's or trustee's actions.

(3) Custodianship

A *custodian* is a person who is given property to hold for the benefit of a minor under either the Uniform Transfers to Minors Act (UTMA) (1983, finalized 1986) or its predecessor, the Uniform Gifts to Minors Act (UGMA) (1956, revised 1966). Under these acts, some form of which has been enacted in every state, property may be transferred to a person (including the donor) as *custodian* for the benefit of the minor. A devise or gift may be made to X "as custodian for (name of minor) under the (name of state) Uniform Transfers to Minors Act," thereby incorporating the provisions of the state's uniform act and eliminating the necessity of drafting a trust instrument.

The creation of a custodianship is thus quite simple. Most banks, brokers, and other financial institutions have standard forms that can be filled out by a donor making a gift to a minor or by a fiduciary making a distribution to a minor. In a similar vein, well-drafted wills and trusts often include a *facility of payment clause* under which assets to be distributed outright to a minor may be paid instead to a custodian or even to the parent or guardian of the minor.

If no such power to transfer assets to a custodian is given in a will or trust, the Uniform Transfers to Minors Act, but not the earlier Uniform Gifts to Minors Act, allows the fiduciary to make payments to a custodian nonetheless. Uniform Transfers to Minors Act §6. Payments to custodians over $10,000, however, require court approval.

Under Uniform Transfers to Minors Act §14(a), the custodian has discretionary power to expend

> for the minor's benefit so much of the custodial property as the custodian considers advisable for the use and benefit of the minor, without court order and without regard to (i) the duty or ability of the custodian personally or any other person to support the minor; or (ii) any other income or property of the minor which may be applicable or available for that purpose.

To the extent that the custodial property is not so expended, the custodian is required to transfer the property to the minor on his attaining the age of 18 or 21, depending on the nature of the property, or, if the minor dies before attaining the age of 18 or 21, to the estate of the minor.

The custodian has the right to manage the property and to reinvest it. However, the custodian is a fiduciary and is subject to "the standard of care that would be observed by a prudent person dealing with property of another." UTMA §12. The custodian is not under the supervision of a court — as is a guardian or conservator — and no accounting to the court annually or at the end of the custodianship is necessary, but an interested party may require one if she wishes. UTMA §§12(e), 19. A custodianship is ideal for modest gifts to a minor and is helpful in other cases when used to avoid a conservatorship or guardianship, but when a large amount of property is involved, a trust is usually preferable. For further analysis of the UTMA, see Jani Maurer, Uniform Transfers to Minors Act Accounts — Progress, Potential, and Pitfalls, 28 Nova L. Rev. 745 (2004).

(4) Trusts

The fourth alternative for property management on behalf of a minor is to establish a trust. A trust is the most flexible of all property arrangements, and a good part of this book is later devoted to the law of trusts (see Chapters 8-13). The testator can tailor the trust specifically to family circumstances and the testator's particular desires. Under a guardianship or conservatorship, the child must receive the property at 18 and, under a custodianship, at 18 or 21, but a trust can postpone possession until the donor thinks the child is competent to manage the property. For an examination of guardianship, custodianship, and trusts, concluding the last is preferable in most situations, see William M. McGovern, Jr., Trusts, Custodianships, and Durable Powers of Attorney, 27 Real Prop., Prob. & Tr. J. 1, 3-17 (1992).

Even when the testator has no children or the testator's children are fully grown, most well-drafted wills provide for a *contingent trust* for any minor beneficiary. The reason: the named adult beneficiaries might predecease the testator, leaving minor children as contingent or substitute takers. Thus, in many law firms there is no such thing as a "simple will." A well-drafted will typically includes at least a contingent trust with extensive trust provisions.

(5) Variations on transfers to minors

Most jurisdictions allow guardians or conservators for limited purposes or limited times, such as a *guardian ad litem* for litigation. Some federal agencies, including the Social Security Administration and Veterans' Administration, allow the designation of a *representative payee* or *substitute payee* to receive benefit checks on behalf of a minor or incompetent. See Lawrence A. Frolik & Alison McChrystal Barnes, Elder Law: Cases and Materials 495 (3d ed. 2003).

If the testator wants to make a cash bequest to a beneficiary who is now a minor, and the testator does not want to create a custodianship or trust, the will can provide that any cash bequest to a minor beneficiary may be distributed to the beneficiary's parents or those having custody of the child (this is known as a *facility of payment clause*). Likewise, if the will so authorizes, a bequest of other property to a minor can be satisfied by delivery to the minor's parents. Even if there is no will or if the will does not expressly authorize payment to the child's parents, many states have laws permitting the personal representative to pay small sums from the decedent's estate to the custodial parent or to an account in the child's name alone without requiring the appointment of a guardian or conservator. See UPC §5-104 (1998) (sums not exceeding $5,000 per year). In addition, as noted above, the UTMA authorizes administrators of intestate estates (and executors without authority in a will) to transfer up to $10,000 to a custodian without a court order, and an unlimited amount with a court order. These devices reflect the trend in recent years to avoid the clumsier and more expensive alternatives of guardianship and conservatorship.

PROBLEM

Refer back to the estate planning problem involving Howard and Wendy Brown (pages 40-48). Assume that Howard Brown dies intestate. After payment of debts, taxes, and expenses of administration, the assets of his estate include:

	Property acquired from H's earnings during marriage[19]	*H's property acquired by gift*[19]
Tangible personalty:	$ 20,000	
Real estate:		
Residence (title is in "Howard Brown and Wendy Brown, as joint tenants with right of survivorship and not as tenants in common"); subject to mortgage of $70,000	160,000	
Lot and cabin, Lake Murray (title is in Howard alone)	75,000	
Remainder interest in mother's home		$ 20,000
Bank accounts:		
Checking (joint and survivor account with wife)	3,000	
Certificate of deposit ("Howard Brown and Wendy Brown, as joint tenants with right of survivorship")	20,000	
IRA (Howard's, payable on death to Wendy)	30,000	
Securities:		
General Corp. stock (registered in Howard's name)		80,000
Varoom Mutual Fund (registered in Howard's name)		30,000
American Growth Mutual Fund ("Howard Brown and Wendy Brown, as joint tenants with right of survivorship and not as tenants in common")	40,000	
Life insurance:		
(Wendy is named primary beneficiary; Howard's estate is named contingent beneficiary)	125,000	
	$453,000	$130,000

Brown is survived by his wife and two minor children and a stepson. How is Brown's estate distributed under the UPC? Under the intestacy statute of your state? Should Howard have left a will?

19. The source of the property is irrelevant for intestate distribution in common law property states; how title is held at death is controlling. In community property states, property acquired from a spouse's earnings during marriage is community property and at the spouse's death passes under a different intestate scheme from separate property.

AN EXERCISE IN LAWYERING

Wendy Brown writes you:

Dear _____:

We've had some changes in our family since we wrote our wills and our wills need changing.

Two months ago our son, Zachary, was born. A bundle of joy—and sleepless nights! As you know, Howard and I want our property to go absolutely to the survivor, and the main reason for having wills is to provide for the children in case we die in a common disaster or before the survivor can make a will for the children.

You drafted our wills to create a trust for our children if we die and a child is under 25. Do you think we should continue to have a single trust for all the children or should we have separate trusts for each child, permitting each child to receive the principal of the child's trust upon reaching 25? Is a "family trust" or separate trusts fairer to our newborn son? What are the pros and cons of these?

Another problem is my sister Lucy has separated from her husband, Jonathan, and has taken up with a man we don't like at all, Bill Hyde. She says she intends to marry him. Bill is a slick operator with a mysterious source of income. We're sick over this, because we love Lucy and hate for her to get mixed up with this guy. But if she marries Bill, we wouldn't want our children to move into their home if we die in a common disaster. My brother Simon and his wife Antonia don't have children, they both work, and wouldn't want to be in charge of a baby. Ruth is always off on digs in Turkey. Do you have any advice about who should be guardian for our children?

I enclose a copy of Howard's will that you drafted. Mine is the same, with appropriate changes in names, and except for the devise of his mother's house. Please give us your advice about these two matters.

Sincerely,

_____
/s/ *Wendy Brown*
Wendy Brown

[For more on Wendy and Howard Brown's family, see pages 40-48.]

Will of Howard Brown
(With Testamentary Trust)

ARTICLE 1

I, Howard Brown, hereby make my will, and I revoke all other wills and codicils that I have previously made.

ARTICLE 2

I give all my jewelry, clothing, household furniture and furnishings, personal automobiles, books, and other tangible articles of a household or personal nature, or my interest in any such property, not otherwise specifically disposed of by this or in any other manner, together with any insurance on the property, to my wife, Wendy Brown, if she survives me; but if my wife does not survive me, then to my children who survive me, in substantially equal shares as they may select on the basis of valuation. These gifts shall be free of all death taxes.

The executor shall represent any child under age 18 in matters relating to any distribution of tangible personal property, including selecting the assets that shall constitute that child's share. In the executor's absolute discretion, the executor may (1) sell all or part of such child's share which the executor deems unsuitable for the child's use, (2) distribute the proceeds to the Children's Trust or share of such trust for the child's benefit, or (3) deliver the unsold property without bond to the minor if sufficiently mature or to any suitable person with whom the child resides or who has control or care of the child.

ARTICLE 3

I give all my right, title, and interest in my mother's house at 423 Elm St., Concord, Delaware, to my sister Carol Gould.

ARTICLE 4

I give the residue of my estate to my wife, Wendy Brown, if she survives me. If my wife does not survive me and all my children are 25 years of age or older at my death, I give the residue of my estate to my children and to the descendants of any then-deceased child by right of representation. If my wife does not survive me and any of my children is under the age of 25 at my death, I give the residue of my estate to the trustee of the Children's Trust set forth in Article 5.

ARTICLE 5

The trustee of the Children's Trust shall hold, administer, and distribute all property allocated to the Children's Trust for the benefit of my children as follows: The trustee shall pay to or for any child as much of the income as is necessary for the child's health, education, support, or maintenance to maintain the child's accustomed manner of living. The trustee shall add to principal any net income not so distributed.

If the trustee considers the income insufficient, the trustee shall pay to or for a child as much of the principal as the trustee considers reasonably necessary for the child's health, education, support, maintenance, comfort, welfare, or happiness to maintain, at a minimum, the child's accustomed manner of living.

In making distributions, the trustee (1) may consider any other income or resources of the child, including the child's ability to obtain gainful employment and the obligation of others to support the child, known to the trustee and reasonably available for the purposes stated here, (2) may pay more to or apply more for some children than others and may make payments to or applications of benefits for one or more children to the exclusion of others, (3) may consider the value of the trust assets, the relative needs, both present and future, of each child, and the tax consequences to the trust and to any child, and (4) shall charge distributions of income and principal against the entire trust estate and not against the share of the child to whom or for whom the distribution was made.

The trustee, in the trustee's reasonable discretion, may from time to time make preliminary distributions of principal to any of my children who have attained the age of 25, if the trustee finds valid and productive reasons for making the distribution, such as the purchase of a residence or establishment of a business, and if the remaining principal and income will be adequate for the health, support, maintenance, and education of my other children. The trustee shall deduct such preliminary distributions without interest from the share ultimately distributed to such child or to such child's descendants. In the aggregate, the value of any preliminary distributions shall not exceed 50 percent of that child's putative share. The term *putative share* shall mean that portion of the entire trust estate that would be distributable to a particular child, after considering all previous loans and advances, if the entire trust were divided into separate trusts on the date that the distribution to be measured against the putative share is made.

When every child of mine has reached the age of 25 or died before reaching that age, the trustee shall divide the trust into as many equal shares as there are children of mine then living and children of mine then deceased with descendants then living.

On the division of the Children's Trust into shares, the trustee shall distribute each living child's share outright to the child and each deceased child's share to the deceased child's then-living descendants by right of representation.

ARTICLE 6

I nominate as trustee of the Children's Trust Lucy Preston Lipman. If Lucy Preston Lipman fails to qualify or ceases to act, I nominate as successor trustee [the lawyer who drew this will].

The trustee may employ custodians, attorneys, accountants, investment advisers, corporate fiduciaries, or any other agents or advisers to assist the trustee in the administration of this trust, and the trustee may rely on the advice given by these agents. The trustee shall pay reasonable compensation for all services performed by these agents from the trust estate out of either income or principal as the trustee in the trustee's reasonable discretion shall determine. These payments shall not decrease the compensation of the trustee.

No trustee shall be liable to any person interested in this trust for any act or default unless it results from the trustee's bad faith, willful misconduct, or gross negligence.

The trustee shall have the power to continue to hold any property or to abandon any property that the trustee receives or acquires.

The trustee shall have the power to retain, purchase, or otherwise acquire unproductive property.

The trustee shall have the power to manage, control, grant options on, sell (for cash or on deferred payments with or without security), convey, exchange, partition, divide, improve, and repair trust property.

The trustee shall have the power to lease trust property for terms within or beyond the terms of the trust and for any purpose, including exploration for and removal of gas, oil, and other minerals, and to enter into oil leases, pooling, and utilization agreements.

The trustee shall have the power to invest and reinvest the trust estate in every kind of property, real, personal, or mixed, and every kind of investment, specifically including, but not by way of limitation, corporate obligations of every kind, preferred or common stocks, shares in investment trusts, investment companies, mutual funds, money market funds, index funds, and mortgage participations, which persons of prudence, discretion, and intelligence acquire for their own account, and any common trust fund administered by the trustee.

The trustee shall have all the rights, powers, and privileges of an owner of the securities held in trust, including, but not by way of limitation, the power to vote, give proxies, and pay assessments; the power to participate in voting trusts and pooling agreements (whether or not extending beyond the terms of the trust); the power to enter into shareholders' agreements; the power to consent to foreclosure, reorganizations, consolidations, merger liquidations, sales, and leases, and, incident to any such action, to deposit securities with and transfer title to any protective or other committee on such terms as the trustee may deem advisable; and the power to exercise or sell stock subscription or conversion rights.

The trustee shall have the power to hold securities or other property in the trustee's name as trustee under this trust, in the trustee's own name, in the name of a nominee, or in unregistered form so that ownership will pass by delivery.

The trustee shall have the power to carry, at the expense of the trust, insurance of such kinds and in such amounts as the trustee deems advisable to protect the trust estate against any damage or loss and to protect the trustee against liability with respect to third parties.

The trustee shall have the power to loan to any person, including a trust beneficiary or the estate of a trust beneficiary, at interest rates and with or without security as the trustee deems advisable.

Upon termination of the trust, the approval of the accounts of the trustee in an instrument signed by all the adult beneficiaries and guardians of any minor beneficiaries shall be a complete discharge and release of the trustee with respect to the administration of the trust property and shall be binding on all persons.

ARTICLE 7

If my wife, Wendy Brown, does not survive me and if at my death any of my children are minors, I nominate as guardian of the persons and the property of my minor children Lucy Preston Lipman.

ARTICLE 8

The terms *child* and *children* as used in this will refer to my stepson, Michael Walker, and to my children, Sarah Brown and Stephanie Brown, and also to any child or children hereafter born to me.

ARTICLE 9

I nominate as executor of this will my wife, Wendy Brown. If for any reason she fails to qualify or ceases to act I nominate Lucy Preston Lipman to serve as executor.

My executor shall have the same powers granted the trustee under Article 6 to be exercised without court order, as well as any other powers that may be granted by law. I direct that no bond or other security shall be required of any person, including nonresidents named in this will, acting as executor, trustee, or guardian.

I have signed this will, which is typewritten on _____ sheets of paper, on this _____ day of _____, 20 _____, and, for the purposes of identification, I have also written my name on the margin of all pages before this signature page.

_____

Howard Brown

On the _____ day of _____, 20 _____, Howard Brown declared to us, the undersigned, that the foregoing instrument was his last will, and he requested us to act as witnesses to it and to his signature thereon. He then signed the will in our presence, we being present at the same time. We now, at his request, in his presence, and in the presence of each other, hereunto subscribe our names as witnesses, and each of us declares that in his or her opinion this testator is of sound and disposing mind and memory.

_____	_____
Name	Address
_____	_____
Name	Address

QUESTIONS

Note the contingent trust for children in Article 4 of Howard Brown's will. Why do you think it uses 25 as the contingent age, rather than 18 or 21? Is the contingency, limited only to Howard's children under 25, broad enough? Suppose Howard's only surviving beneficiary is a minor grandchild. Would Howard's devise of his entire estate to that minor grandchild trigger a conservatorship? How might Article 4 be redrafted to deal with this problem?

SECTION C.   BARS TO SUCCESSION

1. *Homicide*

In re Estate of Mahoney
Supreme Court of Vermont, 1966
126 Vt. 31, 220 A.2d 475

SMITH, J.   The decedent, Howard Mahoney, died intestate on May 6, 1961, of gunshot wounds. His wife, Charlotte Mahoney, the appellant here, was tried for the murder of Howard Mahoney in the Addison County Court and was convicted by jury of the crime of manslaughter in March, 1962. She is presently serving a sentence of not less than 12 nor more than 15 years at the Women's Reformatory in Rutland.

Howard Mahoney left no issue, and was survived by his wife and his father and mother. His father, Mark Mahoney, was appointed administrator of his estate which at the present time amounts to $3,885.89. After due notice and hearing, the Probate Court for the District of Franklin entered a judgment order decreeing the residue of the Estate of Howard Mahoney, in equal shares, to the father and mother of the decedent. An appeal from the judgment order and decree has been taken here by the appellant widow. The question submitted is whether a widow convicted of manslaughter in connection with the death of her husband may inherit from his estate.

The general rules of descent provide that if a decedent is married and leaves no issue, his surviving spouse shall be entitled to the whole of decedent's estate if it does not exceed $8,000. 14 V.S.A. §551(2). Only if the decedent leaves no surviving spouse or issue does the estate descend in equal shares to the surviving father and mother. 14 V.S.A. §551(3). There is no statutory provision in Vermont regulating the descent and distribution of property from the decedent to the slayer. The question presented is one of first impression in this jurisdiction.

In a number of jurisdictions, statutes have been enacted which in certain instances, at least, prevent a person who has killed another from taking by descent or distribution from the person he has killed. . . .

Courts in those states that have no statute preventing a slayer from taking by descent or distribution from the estate of his victim, have followed three separate and different lines of decision.

(1) The legal title passed to the slayer and may be retained by him in spite of his crime. The reasoning for so deciding is that devolution of the property of a decedent is controlled entirely by the statutes of descent and distribution; further, that denial of the inheritance to the slayer because of his crime would be imposing an additional punishment for his crime not provided by statute, and would violate the constitutional provision against corruption of blood. Carpenter's Estate, 32 A. 637 (Pa. 1895); Wall v. Pfanschmidt, 106 N.E. 785 (Ill. 1914); Bird v. Plunkett et al., 95 A.2d 71 (Conn. 1953).

(2) The legal title will not pass to the slayer because of the equitable principle that no one should be permitted to profit by his own fraud, or take advantage and profit as a result of his own wrong or crime. Riggs v. Palmer, 22 N.E. 188 (N.Y. 1889); Price v. Hitaffer, 165 A. 470 (Md. 1933); Slocum v. Metropolitan Life Ins., 139 N.E. 816 (Mass. 1923). Decisions so holding have been criticized as judicially engrafting an exception on the statute of descent and distribution and being "unwarranted judicial legislation." Wall v. Pfanschmidt, supra.

(3) The legal title passes to the slayer but equity holds him to be a constructive trustee for the heirs or next of kin of the decedent. This disposition of the question presented avoids a judicial engrafting on the statutory laws of descent and distribution, for title passes to the slayer. But because of the unconscionable mode by which the property is acquired by the slayer, equity treats him as a constructive trustee and compels him to convey the property to the heirs or next of kin of the deceased.

The reasoning behind the adoption of this doctrine was well expressed by Mr. Justice Cardozo in his lecture on "The Nature of the Judicial Process." "Consistency was preserved, logic received its tribute, by holding that the legal title passed, but it was subject to a constructive trust. A constructive trust is nothing but 'the formula through which the conscience of equity finds expression.' Property is acquired in such circumstances that the holder of legal title may not in good conscience retain the beneficial interest. Equity, to express its disapproval of his conduct, converts him into a trustee."

The New Hampshire court was confronted with the same problem of the rights to the benefits of an estate by one who had slain the decedent, in the absence of a statute on the subject. Kelley v. State, 196 A.2d 68 (N.H. 1963). Speaking for an unanimous court, Chief Justice Kenison said: "But, even in the absence of statute, a court applying common law techniques can reach a sensible solution by charging the spouse, heir or legatee as a constructive trustee of the property where equity and justice demand it." Kelley v. State, supra, at 69, 70. We approve of the doctrine so expressed.

However, the principle that one should not profit by his own wrong must not be extended to every case where a killer acquires property from his victim as a result of the killing. One who has killed while insane is not chargeable as a constructive trustee, or if the slayer had a vested interest in the property, it is property to which he would have been entitled if no slaying had occurred. The principle to be applied is that the slayer should not be permitted to improve his position by the killing, but should not be compelled to surrender property to which he would have been entitled if there had been no killing. The doctrine of constructive trust is involved to prevent the slayer from profiting from his crime, but not as an added criminal penalty. Kelley v. State, supra, p.70; Restatement of Restitution, §187(2), Comment a.

The appellant here was, as we have noted, convicted of manslaughter and not of murder. She calls to our attention that while the Restatement of Restitution approves the application of the constructive trust doctrine where a devisee or legatee murders the testator, that such rules are not applicable where the slayer was guilty of manslaughter. Restatement of Restitution, §187, Comment e.

The cases generally have not followed this limitation of the rule but hold that the line should not be drawn between murder and manslaughter, but between voluntary and involuntary manslaughter. Kelley v. State, supra; Chase v. Jennifer, 150 A.2d 251, 254 (Md. 1959).

We think that this is the proper rule to follow. Voluntary manslaughter is an intentional and unlawful killing, with a real design and purpose to kill, even if such killing be the result of sudden passion or great provocation. Involuntary manslaughter is caused by an unlawful act, but not accompanied with any intention to take life. State v. McDonnell, 32 Vt. 491, 545 (1860). It is the intent to kill, which when accomplished, leads to the profit of the slayer that brings into play the constructive trust to prevent the unjust enrichment of the slayer by reason of his intentional killing.

In Vermont, an indictment for murder can result in a jury conviction on either voluntary or involuntary manslaughter. State v. Averill, 81 A. 461 (Vt. 1911). The legislature has provided the sentences that may be passed upon a person convicted of manslaughter, but provides no definition of that offense, nor any statutory distinction between voluntary and involuntary manslaughter. 13 V.S.A. §2304.

The cause now before us is here on a direct appeal from the probate court. Findings of fact were made below from which it appears that the judgment of the probate court decreeing the estate of Howard Mahoney to his parents, rather than to his widow, was based upon a finding of the felonious killing of her husband by Mrs. Mahoney. However, the appellees here have asked us to affirm the decree below by imposing a constructive trust on the estate in the hands of the widow.

But the Probate Court did not decree the estate to the widow, and then make her a constructive trustee of such estate for the benefit of the parents. The judgment below decreed the estate directly to the parents, which was in direct contravention of the statutes of descent and distribution. The Probate Court was bound to follow the statutes of descent and distribution and its decree was in error and must be reversed.

The Probate Court was without jurisdiction to impose a constructive trust on the estate in the hands of the appellant, even if it had attempted to do so. Probate courts are courts of special and limited jurisdiction given by statute and do not [have powers to establish] . . . purely equitable rights and claims. . . .

However, the jurisdiction of the court of chancery may be invoked in probate matters in aid of the probate court when the powers of that court are inadequate, and it appears that the probate court cannot reasonably and adequately handle the question. The jurisdiction of the chancery court in so acting on probate matters is special and limited only to aiding the probate court. The Probate Court, in making its decree, used the record of the conviction of the appellant for manslaughter for its determination that the appellant had feloniously killed her husband. If the jurisdiction of the court of chancery is invoked by the appellees here it will be for the determination of that court, upon proof, to determine whether the appellant wilfully killed her late husband, as it will upon all other equitable considerations that may be offered in evidence, upon charging the appellant with a constructive trust. "The fact that he is convicted of murder in a criminal case does not dispense with the necessity of proof of the murder in a proceedings in equity to charge him as a constructive trustee." Restatement of Restitution, §187, Comment d.

The jurisdiction over charging the appellant with a constructive trust on the estate of Howard Mahoney lies in the court of chancery, and not in the probate court.

Decree reversed and cause remanded, with directions that the proceedings herein be stayed for sixty days to give the Administrator of the Estate of Howard Mahoney an opportunity to apply to the Franklin County Court of Chancery for relief. If application is so made, proceedings herein shall be stayed pending the final determination thereof. If application is not so made, the Probate Court for the District of Franklin shall assign to Charlotte Mahoney, surviving wife, the right and interest in and to the estate of her deceased husband which the Vermont Statutes confer.[20]

NOTES AND PROBLEMS

1. Almost all states have statutes dealing with the rights of a killer in the estate of a victim. These statutes vary in many details and usually fail to deal with one or more aspects of the problem. Among the issues arising under these statutes, the following appear to give rise to the most litigation:

(a) Does the statute apply to nonprobate transfers (joint tenancy, life insurance, pensions, and so on) as well as to wills and intestacy or only to the latter? If only to the latter, will a court apply to nonprobate transfers a common law slayer's rule or a constructive trust to prevent the beneficiary from profiting by killing? UPC §2-803 (1997), a well-drafted slayer statute, bars the killer from succeeding to nonprobate as well as probate property. It also provides that a "wrongful acquisition" of property must be treated in accordance with the equitable principle that a killer cannot profit from his wrong.

(b) If the killer is barred from taking, who takes? The usual view is that the killer is treated as having predeceased the victim. UPC §2-803 provides that the killer is treated as having disclaimed the property, and under the UPC disclaimer statute, §2-1106, the disclaimant is treated as having predeceased the decedent.

If the killer is treated as having predeceased the victim, should a court give effect to a gift in the victim's will to the killer's heirs if the killer does not survive the

---

20. In 1972, a statute was enacted in Vermont providing that an heir, devisee, or legatee who "stands convicted in any court . . . of intentionally and unlawfully killing the decedent" shall forfeit any share in the decedent's estate. Vt. Stat. Ann. tit. 14, §551(6) (2004). — Eds.

victim? In Estate of Covert, 761 N.E.2d 571 (N.Y. 2001), Edward fatally shot his wife Kathleen and then turned the gun on himself, completing the tragic murder-suicide. Applying the New York slayer rule, which was established per Cardozo, J., in the famous case of Riggs v. Palmer, 22 N.E. 188 (N.Y. 1889), the court held that Edward could not take from Kathleen's estate. However, inasmuch as Edward's devisees were "innocent" of Edward's crime, the court allowed them to take from Kathleen's estate.

The court took a similar approach in Primerica Life Ins. Co. v. Suter, 945 S.W.2d 554 (Mo. App. 1997). In *Suter* the husband named his wife primary beneficiary of his life insurance policy and her father as contingent beneficiary if the wife did not survive the husband. Subsequently, the wife was convicted of complicity in killing her husband and was therefore barred and treated as having predeceased her husband. The court, applying the general rule, gave the life insurance proceeds to the wife's father on the grounds that it would be inappropriate speculation to try to ascertain intent. It was better to have a rule of general application than to try each case seeking the decedent's intent.

The court took a different approach in Estate of Mueller, 655 N.E.2d 1040 (Ill. App. 1995). There, the decedent by will left 60 percent of his estate to his second wife and if she predeceased him to her children by a prior marriage. The husband was killed by a man solicited by the wife to commit the murder. The wife was barred under Illinois's slayer statute, which provided that the killer should be treated as having predeceased the victim. The court refused to apply the statute literally on the ground that this might result in the killer profiting from her wrong (inheriting from her daughters). The court held the devised property passed to the decedent's heirs. It opined that a gift over to the killer's heirs in a will if the killer predeceased the victim would be given effect if the killer's heirs were also the victim's heirs. The court cited cases from other states also refusing to apply the statute literally. See also Bennett v. Allstate Ins. Co., 722 A.2d 115 (N.J. 1998).

In Heinzman v. Mason, 694 N.E.2d 1164 (Ind. 1998), there was no express gift over to the killer's heirs. The husband shot and killed his wife of 13 years, after she filed for divorce, and then killed himself. His wife was the stepmother of the husband's four children, whom she had raised; she had no children of her own. The husband was named as sole beneficiary of the wife's life insurance policy and of her bank accounts. The Indiana slayer statute provided that a convicted killer was treated as having predeceased the victim, but it was inapplicable because the dead husband had not been convicted. The court, applying principles of equity, held that neither the killer nor his heirs could benefit from his wrongdoing. Thus his children were barred from inheriting their stepmother's estate, which went instead to her aunts and uncles and their issue.

(c) Is a criminal conviction required? UPC §2-803(g) provides that a criminal conviction of a felonious and intentional killing is conclusive. Acquittal, however, is not dispositive of the acquitted individual's status as a slayer. In the absence of a conviction, upon application of an interested person, the court must determine whether, under the *preponderance of evidence standard* (not the criminal law standard of beyond a reasonable doubt), the individual would be found criminally accountable for the killing. If so found, the individual is barred. The reason for use of a lower or civil standard of evidence is that probate law is concerned about a killer not profiting from his wrong, whereas criminal law is concerned with protection of the accused. Where the killer commits suicide, the killer may be barred under this section.

The UPC section appears to follow the majority view. See In re Estate of Cotton, 662 N.E.2d 63 (Ohio App. 1995), where the husband pled guilty to involuntary manslaughter in killing his wife. The court barred the husband on the ground that even though he was not convicted of an intentional and felonious killing, the civil trial court concluded that he intentionally and feloniously killed his wife and therefore the common law barred him from profiting from his wrong. Thus, a plea of guilty to a lesser crime than specified in the slayer's statute did not prevent the killer from being barred in a civil proceeding. See also Dill v. Southern Farm Bureau Life Ins. Co., 797 So. 2d 858 (Miss. 2001), where the husband was not prosecuted for homicide but was barred from collecting on his wife's life insurance policy in view of the overwhelming evidence that he arranged to have her murdered.

2.   For comprehensive discussion of these and other matters, with statutory citations, see Jeffrey G. Sherman, Mercy Killing and the Right to Inherit, 61 U. Cin. L. Rev. 803, 844-874 (1993) (arguing for an exception to permit inheritance by a killer who "proves by clear and convincing evidence that he killed the decedent with the intention of relieving the decedent's suffering attributable to the decedent's affliction").

3.   For an interesting murder-suicide case exploring the interplay between the slayer statute and the simultaneous death statute, see Miller v. Miller, 840 So. 2d 703 (Miss. 2003).

The Chinese system. In the United States, unworthy heirs — whose conduct bars inheritance — are usually limited to killers of the decedent. In a few states, spouses who abandon the decedent are barred (page 65), and in a few parents are barred for failure to support a child decedent (page 86 n.13). Otherwise, inheritance is by a mechanical rule of status (kinship, marriage, adoption).

The People's Republic of China has an entirely different scheme of inheritance, which punishes bad behavior and rewards good behavior. In an illuminating article, Frances H. Foster, Towards a Behavior-Based Model of Inheritance? The Chinese Experiment, 32 U.C. Davis L. Rev. 77 (1998), Professor Foster examines the Chinese system. The Chinese system encompasses a broad range of misconduct, and it permits courts to reduce or eliminate a wrongdoer's share. It also rewards good behavior, even by worthy nonrelatives at the expense of the decedent's family members who do not support the decedent. It is "highly time-and-labor intensive, requiring courts to evaluate on a case-by-case basis the conduct of all potential claimants and the most appropriate division of each estate. The flexibility that is the hallmark of the behavior-based model today may prove to be its greatest drawback in the future . . . [when] increased social mobility, accumulation of private property, and a rise in the popular use of courts will bring about an increase in the number and complexity of inheritance disputes." Id. at 84-85.

Nonetheless, Foster concludes that the Chinese system has "significant advantages" over the American system, which does not penalize unworthy heirs. And it "recognizes the reality of support relationships today. It rewards contributions to the decedent's welfare by individuals outside the nuclear family, including blended and extended family members, nonmarital partners, and other unrelated parties."

Id. at 125-126. Foster suggests the Chinese system may provide guidance for reforming the American inheritance system to deal with problems of parental and child neglect and rewarding exemplary conduct by, for instance, personally caring for a disabled person. See also Frances H. Foster, Linking Support and Inheritance: A New Model from China, 1999 Wis. L. Rev. 1199.

California Probate Code (2004)

§259. . . . Abuse of Elder or Dependent Adult Decedent

(a) Any person shall be deemed to have predeceased a decedent . . . where all of the following apply:

(1) It has been proven by clear and convincing evidence that the person is liable for physical abuse, neglect, or fiduciary abuse of the decedent, who was an elder or dependent adult.

(2) The person is found to have acted in bad faith.

(3) The person has been found to have been reckless, oppressive, fraudulent, or malicious in the commission of any of these acts upon the decedent.

(4) The decedent, at the time those acts occurred and thereafter until the time of his or her death, has been found to have been substantially unable to manage his or her financial resources or to resist fraud or undue influence. . . .

2. Disclaimer

Sometimes an heir or a devisee will decline to take the property, a refusal that is called a *disclaimer*.[21] Disclaimers allow for post-mortem estate planning. The most common motivations for disclaimer are to reduce taxes or to keep property from creditors.

Under the common law, when a person dies intestate, title to real and personal property passes to the decedent's heirs by operation of law. An intestate successor cannot prevent title from passing to him or her. The original reason for this rule was that there must always be someone seised of the land who was liable for the feudal obligations—a reason once valid but of no importance today. Nonetheless, if the heir refuses to accept (or, more precisely, to keep) the inheritance, the common law treats the heir's renunciation as if title had passed to the heir and then from the heir to the next intestate successor.

On the other hand, if a person dies testate, the devisee can refuse to accept the devise, thereby preventing title from passing to the devisee. Any gift, whether inter vivos or by will, requires acceptance by the donee. These different conceptions of how title passes at death formerly produced unexpectedly different tax results. If an heir renounced his inheritance and the common law rule applied, the situation was treated as though the heir had received the intestate share and then made a

---

21. By traditional usage, an heir *renounces*; a will beneficiary *disclaims*. Today, the two words are used interchangeably; they are considered synonymous. The term *disclaimer* is the one more commonly used to describe the formal refusal to take by either an heir or a beneficiary.

taxable gift to the persons who took by reason of the renunciation. Hardenburgh v. Commissioner, 198 F.2d 63 (8th Cir. 1952). By contrast, if a devisee disclaimed a testamentary gift, there were no gift tax consequences. Brown v. Routzahn, 63 F.2d 914 (6th Cir. 1933).

To eliminate the difference between disclaiming an intestate share and a devise, almost all states have enacted disclaimer legislation that provides that the disclaimant is treated as having predeceased the decedent. Thus the decedent's property does not pass to the disclaimant, and under state law the disclaimant makes no transfer of it (see UPC §§2-1105, 2-1106 (2002)).

The fiction that a disclaimant is treated as having predeceased the decedent can be used to the disclaimant's advantage. Here are some examples.

1. *Saving estate taxes.* Suppose that O dies intestate, survived by one sister, A. If A disclaims, A is treated as having predeceased O, and O's estate will pass under the intestacy law to A's child, B, who is O's niece. Thus, to pass the property on to A's child without a gift or estate tax being levied on it when it leaves A's hands, A may decide to disclaim the inheritance. Moreover, if B is taxed at a lower income tax rate than A, then A's disclaiming the inheritance will also save income taxes because any returns on the property will be taxable at B's lower rate.

Most state disclaimer statutes require that a disclaimer be made within nine months of the creation of the interest being disclaimed. However, the Uniform Disclaimer of Property Interests Act (UDPIA) (1999, last amended 2002), which in 2002 was assimilated into the UPC as §§2-1101 through 2-1107, does not contain a time limit on when a disclaimer must be made.

The origin of the nine-month time limit was not an implementation of a considered state property law policy, but rather a reaction to the passage of Internal Revenue Code §2518 in 1976. Under §2518, only "qualified disclaimers" will avoid gift tax liability by the disclaimant. Even if a person disclaims under applicable state law, if the disclaimer is not "qualified" under the federal tax code, gift tax liability results. Section 2518 requires a qualified disclaimer to be made within nine months after the interest is created or after the donee reaches 21, whichever is later. Hence, in the above example, if A disclaims a year after O's death, A is treated under the tax laws as having accepted the property and having made a taxable gift to B. Given that disclaimers are often used for post-mortem tax planning, the decoupling of the time requirement under the UDPIA from IRC §2518 has become one of the main points of contention between the act's supporters and its critics.[22]

Because disclaimer offers possibilities for post-mortem estate planning, it must be kept in mind by the lawyer handling the estate. A disclaimer can remedy a defective estate plan and correct a drafter's error, saving the estate hundreds of thousands of dollars. In recent years, a rash of cases has arisen charging a lawyer for the estate with malpractice when the lawyer did not advise the beneficiaries of

---

22. For debate on the UDPIA's pros and cons by its leading critic (Professor Hirsch) and its principal drafter (Professor LaPiana), compare Adam J. Hirsch, Revisions in Need of Revising: The Uniform Disclaimer of Property Interests Act, 29 Fla. St. U.L. Rev. 109 (2001); Adam J. Hirsch & Richard R. Gans, Perfecting Disclaimer Reform: Suggestions for a Revised Uniform Act, 31 Est. Plan. 185 (2004); Adam J. Hirsch, The Uniform Disclaimer of Property Interests Act: Opportunities and Pitfalls, 28 Est. Plan. 571 (2001) (including practice suggestions), with William P. LaPiana, Some Property Law Issues in the Law of Disclaimers, 38 Real Prop., Prob. & Tr. J. 207 (2003); William P. LaPiana, Uniform Disclaimer of Property Interests, Prob. & Prop., Jan./Feb. 2000, at 57. See also T.P. Gallanis, The Future of Future Interests, 60 Wash. & Lee L. Rev. 513, 526-529 (2003) (examining the Hirsch/LaPiana debate in the context of future interests).

the tax advantages of a disclaimer. See Kinney v. Shinholser, 663 So. 2d 643 (Fla. App. 1995), noted at page 896.

2. *Avoiding creditors.* Most disclaimer statutes provide that a disclaimer relates back *for all purposes* to the date of the decedent's death. The Uniform Disclaimer of Property Interests Act "continues the effect of the relation back doctrine, not by using the specific words, but by directly stating what the relation back doctrine has been interpreted to mean." UPC §2-1106, cmt. Thus, in an intestate estate, the disclaimer "takes effect . . . as of the time of the intestate's death." UPC §2-1106(b)(1).

In the example above, if *A* disclaims, most cases have held that *A*'s ordinary creditors cannot reach her share in *O*'s estate because the statute provides that the disclaimer relates back for all purposes to the date of death of the decedent. The disclaimed property is treated as passing directly to others, bypassing the disclaimant. In a minority of states, however, an insolvent debtor may not disclaim to avoid creditors. See Pennington v. Bigham, 512 So. 2d 1344 (Ala. 1987). See also UPC §2-1113 and the comment thereto. For further discussion, see Adam J. Hirsch, The Problem of the Insolvent Heir, 74 Cornell L. Rev. 587 (1989) (arguing that tort creditors and child support and alimony creditors should be permitted to veto the debtor's disclaimer).

PROBLEM

O has two children, *A* and *B*. *B* dies, survived by one child, *C*. Then *O*, a widow, dies intestate. *O*'s heirs are *A* and *C*. *A* has four children. *A* disclaims. What distribution is made of *O*'s estate? UPC §2-1106(b)(3)(A) provides:

[T]he disclaimed interest passes as if the disclaimant had died immediately before the time of distribution. However, if, by law or under the instrument, the descendants of the disclaimant would share in the disclaimed interest by any method of representation had the disclaimant died before the time of distribution, the *disclaimed interest* passes only to the descendants of the disclaimant who survive the time of distribution. [Emphasis added.]

────────────────

While in most states individual creditors cannot reach disclaimed assets, Uncle Sam as a creditor is treated differently.

DRYE v. UNITED STATES, 528 U.S. 49 (1999): Irma Deliah Drye died intestate, leaving her son, Rohn F. Drye, Jr. ("Drye"), as the sole heir to her $233,000 estate. Prior to his mother's death, Drye had run up an unpaid $325,000 tax bill, prompting the IRS to file tax liens against all of Drye's "property and rights to property." Accordingly, to keep his mother's estate away from the IRS, Drye disclaimed his interest. This allowed the entire estate to pass to his daughter, Theresa, who was next in line under the applicable state intestacy statute.

Theresa Drye then used the estate's proceeds to fund [a] Trust . . . of which she and, during their lifetimes, her parents are the beneficiaries. Under the Trust's terms, distributions are at the discretion of the trustee, Drye's counsel Daniel M. Traylor, and may be made only for the health, maintenance, and support of the beneficiaries. The Trust is spendthrift, and under state law, its assets are therefore shielded from creditors seeking to satisfy the debts of the Trust's beneficiaries.[23]

The question before the Court was whether Drye's disclaimer was effective to pass the property to his daughter free from the federal tax lien. Under the applicable state disclaimer law, disclaimed property bypasses the disclaimant, who is treated as having predeceased the decedent. Thus Drye argued "that state law is the proper guide to the critical determination whether his interest in his mother's estate constituted 'property' or 'rights to property.'" If so, his disclaimed interest would pass to his daughter free of the tax liens. Speaking for a unanimous Court, Justice Ruth Bader Ginsburg rejected Drye's argument:

The disclaiming heir . . . inevitably exercises dominion over the property. He determines who will receive the property—himself if he does not disclaim, a known other if he does. See Adam J. Hirsch, The Problem of the Insolvent Heir, 74 Cornell L. Rev. 587, 607-608 (1989). This power to channel the estate's assets warrants the conclusion that Drye held "property" or a "right to property" subject to the Government's liens. . . .

Drye had the unqualified right to receive the entire value of his mother's estate . . . or to channel that value to his daughter. The control rein he held under state law, we hold, rendered the inheritance "property" or "rights to property belonging to him within the meaning of [federal law], and hence subject to the federal tax liens that sparked this controversy.

Justice Ruth Bader Ginsburg

'Hottie'

QUESTION AND NOTE

1.   Suppose that Irma Deliah Drye had executed a valid will that left her entire estate to her granddaughter Theresa, thereby disinheriting her insolvent son Rohn. Under these facts, would the IRS have had any recourse against the assets of Irma's estate? See Robert T. Danforth, The Role of Federalism in Administering a National System of Taxation, 57 Tax Law. 625, 641-642 (2004).

2.   For a discussion of problems in applying *Drye* in subsequent cases, see William H. Baker, Drye and Craft—How Two Wrongs Can Make a Property Right, 64 U. Pitt. L. Rev. 745 (2003); Steve R. Johnson, The Good, the Bad, and the Ugly in Post-Drye Tax Lien Analysis, 5 Fla. Tax Rev. 415 (2002).

---

23. Spendthrift trusts are addressed in Chapter 8 at pages 547-557.—Eds.

Troy v. Hart

Maryland Court of Special Appeals, 1997
116 Md. App. 468, 697 A.2d 113

THIEME, J.   This appeal is from an order of the Circuit Court for Washington County (Sharer, J.) denying an attempt by appellant, Richard E. Troy, Personal Representative of the Estate of Paul H. Lettich, to rescind the decedent's renunciation and disclaimer of his inheritance.

. . . The question before us is whether the court erred in holding that the Medicaid recipient could disclaim his inheritance. Our answer to that question is "No," and we shall therefore affirm the judgment of the circuit court.

FACTS

Paul Lettich (Lettich) became a resident of the Cardinal Sheehan Center for the Aging, Stella Maris Hospice (Stella Maris), in April 1992. Prior to his admission, Lettich appointed Richard Troy (Troy) as his attorney in fact and granted him power of attorney, on 4 February 1992.

In conjunction with his duties, Troy applied for medical assistance on behalf of Lettich when Lettich's resources were exhausted. Lettich was ultimately deemed qualified to receive those benefits on or about 1 January 1995. All medical expenses were paid by Medicare and Medicaid from that day forward. On 25 February 1995, Lettich's sister, Alta Mae Lettich (Alta Mae) died intestate, leaving an estate in excess of $300,000. Alta Mae was survived by Lettich and two sisters, Mildred Hart (Hart) and Gladys McGlaughlin (McGlaughlin). To say that personal contact between Lettich and his sisters was sparse is hyperbole. Troy, however, kept family members abreast of Lettich's status, including, specifically, financial and administrative matters such as Troy's legal relationship with Lettich.

On 22 March 1995, Hart was appointed personal representative of Alta Mae's estate with the consent of the surviving siblings. On 28 April 1995, Hart, undeterred by Troy's capacity as Lettich's attorney in fact, visited Lettich and assisted him in executing a disclaimer to his share of his sister's estate. During that visit, Hart overlooked advising Lettich of the ramifications of the disclaimer on his Medicaid status. As a result of dividing Lettich's $100,000 share between themselves,[24] Hart and McGlaughlin each became $50,000 richer. The following month, Troy was notified by Stella Maris's business office that Lettich had renounced his inheritance. Troy promptly retained counsel, on Lettich's behalf, who filed in the orphans' court on 24 June 1995 a petition seeking to rescind the disclaimer and remove Hart as personal representative of Alta Mae's estate.

Hart retained Robert Veil, Jr., Esq., to defend her. On 24 August 1995, one day prior to the deadline for filing Hart's answer to the petition, Veil visited Lettich and requested him to execute a motion to strike the orphans' court petition so as to remove the possible irritation of an attorney, and also to execute a revocation of Troy's power of attorney. A vigilant Stella Maris social worker intervened and suggested that Troy be consulted. When notified, Troy contacted his current counsel, who immediately called Stella Maris and advised Veil that she represented

---

24. . . . [By his will], Lettich's estate was to be distributed among his surviving sisters and his lifelong friend and companion, Hernel Gruber.

Lettich and that Veil was forbidden to speak to Lettich. For reasons not clear from the record, Veil acquiesced.

Lettich died on 20 September 1995.

Subsequent to the orphans' court's denial of the petition, Troy sought a de novo appeal in the Circuit Court for Washington County. The court granted Hart's motion for judgment with respect to the attempt to have her removed as personal representative of the estate and dismissed the portion of the petition seeking to rescind Lettich's disclaimer. Troy timely filed a notice of appeal.

DISCUSSION ...

MEDICAID CONSIDERATIONS

Under English Poor Law, [if one could not pay for one's own care, one's kin could be required to do so.] ... Today, however by 42 U.S.C. §1396a(a)(17)(D), Congress has abrogated the legal duty to support one's parents, and even a cursory perusal of this, or other sections of 42 U.S.C. §1396 (the subsection of the Social Security Act with which we will be attempting to deal), will demonstrate Congress's indifference to the simplicity and clarity of the Elizabethan language.[25]

Medicaid is a "means-tested" program, that is to say, eligibility for Medicaid depends on meeting various income and resource tests. Maryland's Department of Health and Mental Hygiene (DHMH) administers the local aspect of the program and requires, as a condition of eligibility for benefits, that applicants disclose all available assets to the Department of Social Services (DSS). COMAR [Code of Maryland Regulations] 10.09.24.04. An applicant must satisfy asset limits in order to receive coverage.

Once an individual is receiving benefits, it is not inconceivable that his eligibility status might change due to a multitude of financial circumstances. COMAR dictates, as a post-eligibility requirement, that recipients or their representatives shall notify the department "within 10 working days of changes affecting ... eligibility. ..." COMAR 10.09.24.12(B)(1). If one fails to disclose such a change, the shadow of fraud surfaces.

Upon his acquisition of an equitable interest in his sister's estate, Lettich — personally, or through his attorney ... — had the legal obligation to notify DSS of the inheritance in light of its potential ramifications on Lettich's eligibility. ...

Lettich's failure to notify DSS constituted a violation of applicable Medicaid law and deprived both state and federal governments of an opportunity to reassess his eligibility.

GENERAL POLICY CONSIDERATIONS

What this Court is more broadly faced with is the propriety of the disclaimer in light of societal interest and overall policy considerations. What is ludicrous, if not repugnant, to public policy is that one who is able to regain the ability to be

---

25. "The Social Security Act is among the most intricate ever drafted by Congress. Its Byzantine construction, as Judge Friendly has observed, makes the Act 'almost unintelligible to the uninitiated.'" Schweiker, Secretary of Health and Human Services, et al. v. Gray Panthers, 453 U.S. 34, 43 (1981) (quoting Friedman v. Berger, 547 F.2d 724, 727 n.7 (CA2 1976)). ... [T]he District Court in the same case described the Medicaid statute as "an aggravated assault on the English language, resistant to attempts to understand it." 453 U.S. at 43 n.14.

financially self-sufficient, albeit for a temporary or even brief period of time, may voluntarily relinquish his windfall.[26]

While we are mindful that social agencies are "skewered through and through with office pens, and bound hand and foot with red tape,"[27] this acknowledgment does not vitiate a legal obligation to report a recipient's change in financial status. Lettich had a legal obligation to "pay his own way" (by means of the inheritance) until such time as his resources were exhausted. Had the disclaimed funds actually been acquired and exhausted, Lettich most certainly would have been eligible to resume his receipt of Medicaid benefits.

In Molloy v. Bane, 631 N.Y.S.2d 910 (A.D. 1995), the Supreme Court of New York, Appellate Division, confronted the same issue now before this Court. Molloy, a resident of a nursing home, was a recipient of medical assistance. Upon the death of her daughter, Molloy, pursuant to intestacy law, was entitled to her statutory share of the estate. Prior to disposition of the estate, Molloy renounced her interest in it. Acknowledging that the right to renounce an intestate share is irreconcilable with the principle that public aid is of a limited nature and should only be afforded to those who demonstrate legitimate need, id., 631 N.Y.S.2d at 911, the court found that "[Molloy]'s renunciation of a potentially available asset was the functional equivalent of a transfer of an asset since by refusing to accept it herself, she effectively funneled it to other familial distributees." Id. at 913.

Applying this analysis to the case sub judice, we adopt the reasoning of the New York court. The result of such a transfer prior to application for benefits is that the transferee enjoys a "windfall" for which the applicant/transferor is penalized against the inception of his eligibility. So too should this penalty result in a circumstance in which a Medicaid recipient disclaims or otherwise transfers an inheritance that if accepted would result in a loss of eligibility.

If a recipient renounces an inheritance that would cause him to be financially disqualified from receiving benefits, the renunciation should incur the same penalty of disqualification that acceptance would have brought about, and should render the recipient liable for any payments incorrectly paid by the State in consequence. To permit disclaimed property to pass to transferees free and clear of any obligation would be a violation of public policy. That is precisely the situation before this Court. Lettich's failure to disclose resulted in the improper payment of Medicaid benefits by the State on behalf of Lettich after the expiration of the grace period (during which disclosure was compelled), inasmuch as the inheritance would have caused DHMH/DSS to reassess Lettich's eligibility in light of his changed financial circumstance. COMAR indicates that an applicant/recipient's breach of this particular duty may result in the initiation of criminal or civil action by the State, including the seeking of reimbursement from the recipient. COMAR 10.09.24.12(B)(6). Because initial eligibility must be established by a lack of financial resources, an action for reimbursement against the recipient or his estate would undoubtedly be futile and similar to attempting to draw blood from a stick. The lack of a mechanism to effectuate the State's interest in reimbursement

---

26. Analogously, in divorce cases this Court has refused to award support to a spouse who has voluntarily impoverished himself. See John O. v. Jane O., 601 A.2d 149, 156 (Md. App. 1991). ("In the context of a divorce proceeding, the term "voluntarily impoverished" means: "freely, or by an act of choice, to reduce oneself to poverty or deprive oneself of resources with the intention of avoiding . . . obligations.")

27. Charles Dickens, David Copperfield.

essentially emasculates the duty to disclose a change in financial status, as there exists no meaningful recourse against individuals who fail to comply.

The effect of Lettich's execution of the disclaimer was to transfer his intestate interest in Alta Mae's estate to his surviving sisters. Accepting the inheritance would have made him financially ineligible for Medicaid. The result of our decision today is that Lettich's disclaimer is valid under Est. & Tr. §9-205. Thus, Mildred Hart and Gladys McGlaughlin will divide the estate of Alta Mae Lettich according to the laws of intestacy. We suggest that this interest should be taken subject to any claim(s) that the State may have against Lettich's estate for any Medicaid benefits improperly paid as a result of Lettich's failure to inform DSS of his acquisition of property while receiving Medicaid benefits.[28]

This Court recently stated that "[a] constructive [trust] is a remedy employed by the courts to convert the holder of legal title to property into a trustee 'for one who in good conscience should reap the benefits of the possession of said property.'" Dulany v. Taylor, 660 A.2d 1046, 1054 (Md. App. 1995). "The remedy is applied by operation of law where . . . the circumstances render it inequitable for the party holding the title to retain it." Wimmer v. Wimmer, 414 A.2d 1254, 1258 (Md. 1980). "The purpose of imposing a constructive trust is to prevent the unjust enrichment of the title holder." *Dulany*, 660 A.2d at 1054.

In Mass Transit Administration v. Granite Constr. Co., 471 A.2d 1121 (Md. App. 1984), we explained:

> The doctrine of unjust enrichment applies where "'the defendant, upon the circumstances of the case, is obliged by the ties of natural justice and equity to refund the money.'" Dobbs, Handbook on the Law of Remedies, §4.2 (1973), quoting Lord Mansfield in Moses v. MacFerlan, 97 Eng. Rep. 676 (K.B. 1760). This policy against unjust enrichment is the theory behind the restitutionary remedies. Those remedies serve to "deprive the defendant of benefits that in equity and good conscience he ought not to keep, even though he may have received those benefits quite honestly in the first instance, and even though the plaintiff may have suffered no demonstrable losses." Dobbs, supra, §4.1.

We think it clear that the State has an equitable and practical interest in both the changed circumstances of a recipient as well as the instrumentality that gives rise to such a change. The "10-day disclosure period" affords the State notice and opportunity to intervene and assert any potential claim(s) against the property or an equitable interest therein. The failure to [disclose] . . . clearly deprives the State of its ability to exercise its rights and may well result in the unjust enrichment of those who surreptitiously dine upon the fruits of inheritance while cloaked by the veil of non-disclosure.

Judgment affirmed.

NOTES AND QUESTIONS

1.   The Medicaid program is a cooperative state-federal program intended to provide medical assistance to needy people. The Medicaid program pays for

---

28. At oral argument, Hart's counsel stated that he would be acquiescent to reimbursing the State for any Medicaid benefits erroneously paid for the benefit of her late brother.

more than 50 percent of all nursing home patients in the United States. The applicant for Medicaid assistance must meet strict income and resource requirements, which vary from state to state. To qualify for Medicaid, the applicant must "spend down" his assets to a few thousand dollars. Giving away property to children before applying for Medicaid may result in disqualification of the applicant for a substantial period of time, depending upon the amount transferred. Certain transfers are exempt, such as home transfers to a spouse and trust transfers for certain disabled persons. In some states, the Medicaid applicant or recipient is required to take steps to get the property back. If a Medicaid recipient dies leaving a probate estate or nonprobate death transfers (such as life insurance), the state may look to these assets to recover benefits already paid the Medicaid recipient. See Alison Barnes, An Assessment of Medicaid Planning, 3 Hous. J. Health L. & Poly. 265 (2003); Janel C. Frank, How Far Is Too Far? Tracing Assets in Medicaid Estate Recovery, 79 N.D.L. Rev. 111 (2003); Jan Ellen Rein, Misinformation and Self-Deception in Recent Long-Term Care Policy Trends, 12 J.L. & Pol. 195 (Spring 1996).

Professor Miller describes the general problem:

> Increasingly, middle-class and upper middle-class elderly Americans voluntarily impoverish themselves in order to obtain the government benefit known as Medicaid. "Medicaid planning," as this widely discussed estate planning technique is known, has several variations and is highly controversial. Congress was so incensed by the practice of voluntary impoverishment to obtain Medicaid that it made it a crime both for citizens to practice it and for lawyers to advise their clients how to do so. Anger over this "Granny Goes to Jail" Act led Congress to amend the statute, specifically repealing the portions that targeted the elderly. Likewise, courts have rejected the statute as it targets lawyers. There remains, however, a variety of moral, legal, and policy controversies surrounding the practice of voluntary impoverishment. [John A. Miller, Voluntary Impoverishment to Obtain Government Benefits, 13 Cornell J.L. & Pub. Poly. 81, 81-82 (2003).]

The Kennedy-Kassebaum Health Reform Bill of 1996, which Miller and other critics referred to as the "Granny Goes to Jail" law, made it a federal crime to give away assets or set up trusts with the purpose of qualifying for Medicaid. Although this provision was repealed in 1997, the statute was amended to criminalize the behavior of a person who "for a fee knowingly and wilfully counsels or assists an individual to dispose of assets" to become eligible for Medicaid "if disposing of the assets results in the imposition of a period of ineligibility." 42 U.S.C. §1320a-7(b)(a)(6) (2004).

Would the actions of attorney Robert Veil, Jr., in his visit with Lettich on August 24, 1995, constitute criminal behavior under 42 U.S.C. §1320a-7(b)(a)(6)? If not, were his actions ethical? See Miller, supra, at 82 n.5; American College of Trust and Estate Counsel, Commentaries on the Model Rules of Professional Conduct (3d ed. 1999) (Commentary on Model Rule 2.2).

2.   For discussion of the use of trusts in Medicaid planning, see pages 569-572.

3

WILLS: CAPACITY AND CONTESTS

SECTION A. MENTAL CAPACITY

1. The Test of Mental Capacity

In the law of wills, the requirements for mental capacity are minimal. To be competent to make a will, the testator must be an adult (age 18 or older[1]) and "must be capable of knowing and understanding in a general way [1] the nature and extent of his or her property, [2] the natural objects of his or her bounty, and [3] the disposition that he or she is making of that property, and must also be capable of [4] relating these elements to one another and forming an orderly desire regarding the disposition of the property." Restatement (Third) of Property: Wills and Other Donative Transfers §8.1 (2003).

Observe that the test is one of *capability*, not one of actual knowledge. If the test were one of actual knowledge, a reasonable mistake about whether one of your children was alive would render you mentally incompetent since you would not know the natural objects of your bounty (your family). Nor must the testator be of average intelligence, as this would incapacitate almost half the population, but the testator must have mind and memory relevant to the four matters mentioned.

In re Estate of Wright

Supreme Court of California, 1936
7 Cal. 2d 348, 60 P.2d 434

SEAWELL, J.   The petition for admission to probate of the will of Lorenzo B. Wright, deceased, having been denied on the ground of testamentary incapacity, the executrix named in said will herewith appeals to this court. The grounds urged

---

1. In almost all states, the age of majority is 18. In many states, those who are under 18 may make a will if they are married or are legally emancipated.

for reversal are that the evidence is insufficient to sustain the judgment and order. . . .

The testator, Lorenzo B. Wright, died at Venice, California, May 2, 1933, at the age of sixty-nine years. Maud Wright Angell, the contestant, is his daughter and the nearest of kin. He left no other children. . . . Testator's wife died in 1921.

The decedent left an estate consisting of two improved parcels of land situated in Venice, California, and an interest in an estate situated in Salt Lake City, his former home, and some inconsequential personal property of unknown value. The petition for probate alleges that the total value of his estate does not exceed the sum of $10,000. His will was formally executed one year and four months prior to his death. By its terms he devised to Charlotte Josephine Hindmarch, fifty years of age and whom he describes as his friend, his house located at 722 Nowita Place and all his personal "belongings, monies, collateral, notes or anything of value"; he devised to his daughter, the contestant herein, the house located on lot nine, at 724 Nowita Place, and to his granddaughter, Marjorie Jean Angell, his interest in an estate in Salt Lake City. He gave to his grandson, his son-in-law and several other persons, relatives or friends, one dollar each.

We have in this proceeding the unusual spectacle of the drawer of the will, a notary public and realtor, and the two subscribing witnesses testifying that they were of the opinion that the testator was of unsound mind. The testimony of these three witnesses, like the testimony given by all the others, is far too weak and unsubstantial to support the judgment. To a great extent the grounds upon which the witnesses base their opinions are mere trivialities. If it could be said that the testimony of the three persons who participated in the creation of the will and who by their solemn acts gave the stamp of approval and verity to its due execution, and afterwards attempted to repudiate all they had done, had any convincing force or any substantial factual basis, their testimony would nevertheless be subject to the scrutiny and suspicion which courts rightfully exercise in considering the testimony of persons who out of their own mouths admit their guilt of self-stultification. It has been said that such testimony is simply worthless. Courts, whenever called upon to express themselves on this subject, have not been sparing in the use of forceful language. In Werstler v. Custer, 46 Pa. 502 (1864), the court said: "The legal presumption is always in favor of sanity, especially after attestation by subscribing witnesses, for, as was said by Parsons, C.J., in Buckminster v. Perry, 4 Mass. 593, 594 (1808), it is the duty of the subscribing witnesses to be satisfied of the testator's sanity before they subscribe the instrument. No honest man will subscribe as a witness to a will, or any other instrument executed by an insane man, an imbecile, an idiot, or a person manifestly incompetent for any reason to perform, with legal effect, the act in question. A duty attaches to the witness to satisfy himself of the competency of the party before he lends his name to attest the act. Like a magistrate who takes an acknowledgment of a deed, he is to be reasonably assured of the facts he undertakes to verify, else he makes himself instrumental in a fraud upon the public."

Our own court, in the Estate of Motz, 69 P. 294, 295 (Cal. 1902), made the observation which must be in the mind of every person who gives any thought to the subject. We said: "When a witness has solemnly subscribed his name to a will as an attesting witness, knowing the nature of his act, and that deceased would rely upon his name as a part of the execution of the will, undertakes by his evidence to overthrow or cast suspicion upon it, his evidence should be closely scrutinized." . . .

It appears without contradiction that Lorenzo B. Wright, testator, met Mrs. Grace Thomas, a notary public and realtor with whom he had transacted business and whom he had known for many years, in the post office and asked her what her charge would be for drawing his will. He told her he was coming to her office to have her prepare his will. About three weeks thereafter he came alone to her office, bringing with him memoranda sheets upon which he had written the names of the persons whom he wished to enjoy his property and the specific shares thereof after his death. She prepared the will accordingly. She was not acquainted with any of the persons whose names appeared on the memoranda prepared by him. She testified that she believed at the time he executed the will that he was of unsound mind. Pressed for the grounds of her opinion she said it was the "funniest will she had ever seen" in that it gave $1 to each of a number of different persons she did not know; that she had thought him queer for a long time; that he did not have in mind the legal description of the property but that she had it listed for sale and rent. The above contains the entire substance of her testimony.

James Thomas, a witness to the will, was next called by the contestant. It does not appear what relation he bears, if any, to Mrs. Grace Thomas, the scrivener, or who solicited him to become a witness. He stated that he "believed" the testator was not of sound mind; that in his opinion testator had not been of sound mind for some years prior to the execution of the will. He seemed unable to give a single reason supporting his opinion.

G.W. Madden, the other subscribing witness, when pressed for the reason of his opinion that the testator "was not of sound mind" at the time he signed the will, was also unable to say more than that he considered him of unsound mind for some time prior to the making of the will.

Mrs. Brem had known testator for sixteen years and said it was her belief that he was of unsound mind on the day the will was executed. Pressed for the reasons of her opinion, she said he had had a serious operation some years prior; he once told her he had lost $50,000 in some bank failure and she was sure from the way he lived alone in his little shack, with all the dirt and junk he had, that he was not right; he once gave her a fish (he spent much time in fishing) which he said he had caught and she found it had been soaked in kerosene and when he asked her how she liked it he laughed and said he had put the kerosene on it before he brought it to her; once he came to her house and insisted on buying her household furniture and when told it was not for sale and that she had not offered it for sale he insisted on buying it anyway. Mr. Brem testified substantially as his wife had testified, but added the statement that "Mr. Wright often chased the children out of his yard and turned the hose on them and that children in the neighborhood were afraid of Mr. Wright." He did not explain why they often returned to his yard if they feared him.

Mrs. Daisy Smith, a cousin not named in the will, testified that she believed him to be unsound in mind. Her reasons were that he drank and was drunk much of the time since his wife died; that some years ago he suffered an injury to his head and several stitches were required to close the wound; that the injury seemed to change him; that he had a serious operation in 1921; on one or more occasions he ran out of the house only partly dressed and they had to follow him and had difficulty in getting him back to bed; that he picked up silverware and other articles from the garbage cans and hid these things around the house; that he picked up paper flowers from the garbage cans, and waste, and pinned them on rose bushes in his yard and took the witness to look at his roses; that he went away with a blanket wrapped around him and was gone several days and made no explanation as to where he went; that he took from his daughter's house a radio which the witness said he had given to his daughter and granddaughter without making any explanation as to why he did so; that she knew he had been quite sick a number of times and that he did not have much care or attention; that he suffered a great deal.

Marjorie Jean Angell, a granddaughter, placed her belief that testator was unsound of mind on the ground that he acted funny and queer; that he told a number of persons that he had sent Christmas presents and a turkey to them when he had not done so; she related the removal of the radio from her mother's home which they claimed he had given to them; at times he would pass her on the street without speaking and at other times he would speak and seem friendly; one time he told her she had on too much rouge and powder or paint, when she did not have any amount on; that her mother often invited him to their home for dinner. He would say he would come but he did not appear. He collected old articles from the rubbish and garbage wagon when he drove the garbage wagon and had them about the house and he had a lot of old stuff hidden in the house. [For a number of years the testator drove a garbage wagon in Venice, California.]

Cloyd Angell, the grandson, thought testator of unsound mind. His reasons were: He had seen him fishing on the wharf at Venice and he did not tell his friends and acquaintances on the pier that witness was his grandson; neither did the witness tell his friends that testator was his grandfather. He had often seen him drunk on the pier. Some eight or ten years before his death his grandfather seemed fond of him and he used to ride with him on the garbage wagon, but his attitude changed in later years, for no reason of which he was aware, and he did not have much to do with him; he had a lot of junk and old empty liquor bottles hidden around the house.

Hariett E. McClelland said she had known testator for a number of years. She believed him to be of unsound mind. . . . The witness related an ailment which the testator had while living at her house during which he would be prone, hold his breath and appear to be dead; that when she returned from her quest for help she would find him up and walking about; that he said he did this to scare his neighbors and make them think he was dead. . . .

Maud Wright Angell, daughter of testator and contestant herein, testified . . . that testator was of unsound mind [based] on his changed attitude toward her and her family which she says took place some ten years prior to his death, occasioned by the injury to his head. She said that he drank a good deal. After he was taken to the hospital and just before he died he sent for her and he was "very usual and normal." . . .

The foregoing sets forth the full strength of contestant's case. Tested by the decisions of this court the judgment is wholly without evidentiary support. There is no evidence that testator suffered from settled insanity, hallucinations or delusions. Testamentary capacity cannot be destroyed by showing a few isolated acts, foibles, idiosyncrasies, moral or mental irregularities or departures from the normal unless they directly bear upon and have influenced the testamentary act. No medical testimony as to the extent of any injury the testator had received or its effect upon him either physically or mentally was introduced in the case. The burden was upon contestant throughout the case. Taking all the evidence adduced by contestant as true, it falls far below the requirements of the law as constituting satisfactory rebuttal of the inference of testamentary capacity. No proof whatever was offered tending to rebut the testator's ability to transact or conduct his business or to care for himself except in a few cases of illness brought about by natural causes or excesses or by accident. He went alone to the scrivener's with a list of beneficiaries prepared by himself, giving his daughter one piece of improved real property and Charlotte Josephine Hindmarch, whom he designated as his friend, the other. To his granddaughter he bequeathed his undivided interest in an estate known as the Brazier Estate, and he named seven others to whom he made nominal bequests. There is no evidence that he did not appreciate his relations and obligations to others, or that he was not mindful of the property which he possessed. The opinions or beliefs of those who testified that he was not of sound mind rest upon testimony of the most trivial character and do not establish testamentary incapacity at the time he executed his will.

It does not appear that his daughter or members of her family were concerned as to his comfort or well-being, as the testimony of some of the witnesses shows that he lived a portion of his time in a condition of squalor and that he was cared for when ill by others. The attention given to his comfort by Charlotte Josephine Hindmarch does not appear [in the record we are reviewing], as the appeal is based solely upon the evidence adduced by contestant in support of her claim that he lacked testamentary capacity. . . .

For the foregoing reasons the judgment and order are reversed.

NOTES AND QUESTION

1.   Did Grace Thomas, the nonlawyer scrivener, act unethically in drafting a will for a man whom she considered incompetent? For lawyers, to draft a will for an incompetent person is a breach of legal ethics. The lawyer, however, may rely on her own judgment regarding the client's capacity; she does not have to make an investigation of it. Logotheti v. Gordon, 607 N.E.2d 1015 (Mass. 1993). See Jan E. Rein, Ethics and the Questionably Competent Client: What the Model Rules Say and Don't Say, 9 Stan. L. & Poly. Rev. 241 (1998).

2.   The fact that a person has been declared incompetent and put under a conservator does not necessarily mean the person has no capacity to execute a will thereafter. Capacity to make a will is governed by a different legal test and requires less mental ability than to manage one's investments, to make a contract, or to make a gift. The law has the objective of protecting the incompetent contractor or donor from suffering economic loss during lifetime, which might result in impoverishment. To make an irrevocable lifetime gift, not only must one meet all the elements for making a will, but one "must also be capable of understanding the effect that the gift may have on the future financial security of the donor and of anyone who may be dependent on the donor." Restatement (Third) of Property: Wills and Other Donative Transfers §8.1 (2003).

Protecting a dead person from economic loss is of course not a consideration. Thus, in Lee v. Lee, 337 So. 2d 713 (Miss. 1976), the testator was placed under a conservatorship in 1968 because of age and physical incapacity. On May 9, 1970, testator executed a *will;* on that same date he executed and delivered a *deed* purporting to convey real property. The Mississippi Supreme Court held that the *deed* was void because one under a conservatorship is without the necessary contractual power to execute a deed but held the *will* valid. The court stated that one whose property is under a conservatorship may write a valid will if the trial court finds, as the trial court did here, that the will was written during a *lucid interval*. See also Restatement, supra, cmt. m.

Legal capacity to make a will requires a greater mental competency than is required for marriage, however. Estate of Park, [1953] 2 All E.R. 408, 411, is authority for the proposition that a person may have insufficient capacity to make a will on the same day as the person has sufficient capacity to marry. Thus, an old man suffering from cerebral arteriosclerosis may be able to marry but not make a will. Marriage alone will give the surviving spouse a share of the senile spouse's estate, even though he has no capacity to devise it to her. See Hoffman v. Kohns, 385 So. 2d 1064 (Fla. App. 1980) (housekeeper marries senile man; will made one day later set aside, but marriage held valid).

2. Why Require Mental Capacity?

To make a will a person must be of sound mind. But why should this be so? Why is not the power of testation extended to all persons regardless of their mental capacity? The requirement that the testator have mental capacity is an ancient one. It goes back at least as far as the Romans, who invented the will as we know it. Three explanations are usually given for the requirement, all owing something to how persons and property have been viewed in history.

The first explanation is that a will should be given effect only if it represents the testator's true desires. In ancient times, mad folk were viewed as possessed by an evil spirit or a devil. John tells us of the reaction of the Jews to Jesus' claim to be the good shepherd of the Twenty-third Psalm: "And many of them said, He hath a devil, and is mad; why hear ye him?" John 10:20. Equating madness with possession lasted well into the eighteenth century. In the twentieth century, psychiatrists replaced priests as exorcists, and modern psychiatric concepts and discoveries about mental disorders took over. Some psychiatric theories posit that there is a rational self and an irrational self. Freud, for example, held the view that a person might have and act upon unconscious desires of a destructive and irrational kind that overcome the conscious and rational self. Under such a theory, it might make sense to deny probate to an "irrational" will that does not represent the testator's rational desires.

The second explanation for the mental capacity requirement is that a mentally incompetent man or woman is not defined as a "person." Since the post-renaissance, with its strong emphasis on the individual as the only recognized legal entity (as opposed to the family or clan), philosophers have sought to understand what it means to be a person. As Professor Radin has written, "the concepts of sanity and personhood are intertwined: At some point we question whether the insane person is a person at all." Margaret J. Radin, Property and Personhood, 34 Stan. L. Rev. 957, 969 (1982).

The third explanation is that the law requires mental capacity to protect the decedent's family. In many ancient societies, property was viewed as tribal property or family property, not owned by individuals. Although individual ownership in time developed, indeed triumphed, the notion persisted that the family was an economic unit with some claim on the family property. Giving effect to the

"His will reads as follows: 'Being of sound mind and disposition, I blew it all.'"

Drawing by Frank Modell.

expectations of inheritance tends to preserve the family as a unit for mutual support. The institution of inheritance, through the principle of reciprocity, functions as a system for providing care and support for the aged. See Claude Lévi-Strauss, The Principle of Reciprocity, *in* The Elementary Structures of Kinship 52-97 (rev. ed. 1969); Jeffrey P. Rosenfeld, The Legacy of Aging: Inheritance and Disinheritance in Social Perspective (1979).

Close family members — ordinarily those described as heirs in intestacy statutes — usually render services and give love and comfort to the aging relative. An inheritance is a delayed payment in reciprocity. By giving an economic incentive to heirs apparent, whose expectations cannot be defeated by the testator's insanity, society furthers its objective of caring for the aged in a humane manner. The principle of reciprocity is recognized when the court considers, sometimes *sub silentio*, the fairness of a disposition as a factor in mental capacity cases.

In addition to these three explanations deriving from history, several other possible justifications for the requirement of mental capacity come to mind.

Fourth, to a large extent the public acceptance of law rests upon a belief that legal institutions, including inheritance, are legitimate, and legitimacy cannot exist unless decisions are reasoned. Hence, it is important that the succession to property be perceived as a responsible, reasoned act, according the survivors their just deserts.

Fifth, the requirement of mental capacity assures a sane person that the disposition the person desires will be carried out even if the person later becomes insane and makes another will. This gives a person of sound mind the advantage of being able, while in a rational mind, to choose what will happen to his property in the future and to have confidence that this choice will be carried out.

Sixth, the requirement of mental capacity may protect society at large from irrational acts. This justification is dubious inasmuch as courts can and do strike down particular "anti-social" dispositions as against public policy (see pages 21-30). Then too, if society is not protected from a sane person acting irresponsibly, why is it protected against similar acts by a mad person?

Finally, requiring mental capacity may protect a senile or incompetent testator from exploitation by cunning persons. If the incompetent could make wills, then many institutionalized people would be subject to imposition by the unscrupulous. Keep in mind, however, that what may look like exploitation to some may give the testator much pleasure. Also, exploitation may be adequately remedied by setting aside transfers on the ground of undue influence.

For discussions of the reasons for the requirement of mental capacity and the theoretical underpinning of it, see Jane B. Baron, Empathy, Subjectivity, and Testamentary Capacity, 24 San Diego L. Rev. 1043 (1987); Alexander M. Meiklejohn, Contractual and Donative Capacity, 39 Case W. Res. L. Rev. 307 (1989); Milton D. Green, Public Policies Underlying the Law of Mental Incompetency, 38 Mich. L. Rev. 1189 (1940).

3. *Insane Delusion*

A person may have sufficient mental capacity generally to execute a will but may be suffering from an *insane delusion* so as to cause a particular provision in a will—or perhaps the entire will—to fail for lack of testamentary capacity. Only the part of the will caused by the insane delusion fails; if the entire will was caused by the insane delusion, the entire will fails. If insane delusions are shown, but they do not affect the dispositions, then the entire will stands. For example, in Breeden v. Stone, 992 P.2d 1167 (Colo. 2000), an intoxicated testator, "excessively worried" about threats by friends and the government against him and his dog, penned a holographic will. Two days later, he shot himself. His will was held valid because testator's "insane delusions regarding his friends, government agencies, and others, did not affect or influence the disposition of his property."

An insane delusion is a legal, not a psychiatric, concept. A delusion is a false conception of reality. An example is a belief that all Irishmen have red hair. An insane delusion—which impairs testamentary capacity—is one to which the testator adheres against all evidence and reason to the contrary. Some courts have held that if there is any factual basis at all for the testator's delusion, it is not deemed insane. The majority view, however, is that a delusion is insane even if there is some factual basis for it if a rational person in the testator's situation could not have drawn the conclusion reached by the testator. Insane delusion cases often involve some false belief about a member of the testator's family. See In re Estate of Raney, 799 P.2d 986 (Kan. 1990) (a penny-dreadful tale of an angry and mentally disturbed father and his children, who put him under a conservatorship; believing his children were plotting against him for his money, the father disinherited them by a will executed while he was in jail under a drunken driving charge; the will was upheld against a claim of insane delusion).

In re Strittmater

Court of Errors and Appeals of New Jersey, 1947
140 N.J. Eq. 94, 53 A.2d 205

On appeal from a decree of the Prerogative Court, advised by Vice-Ordinary Bigelow, who filed the following opinion:

"This is an appeal from a decree of the Essex County Orphans Court admitting to probate the will of Louisa F. Strittmater. Appellants challenge the decree on the ground that testatrix was insane.

"The only medical witness was Dr. Sarah D. Smalley, a general practitioner who was Miss Strittmater's physician all her adult life. In her opinion, decedent suffered from paranoia of the Bleuler type of split personality.[2] The factual evidence justifies the conclusion. But I regret not having had the benefit of an analysis of the data by a specialist in diseases of the brain.

"The deceased never married. Born in 1896, she lived with her parents until their death [in] about 1928, and seems to have had a normal childhood. She was devoted to both her parents and they to her. Her admiration and love of her parents persisted after their death to 1934, at least. Yet four years later she wrote: 'My father was a corrupt, vicious, and unintelligent savage, a typical specimen of the majority of his sex. Blast his wormstinking carcass and his whole damn breed.' And in 1943, she inscribed on a photograph of her mother 'That Moronic she-devil that was my mother.'

"Numerous memoranda and comments written by decedent on the margins of books constitute the chief evidence of her mental condition. Most of them are dated in 1935, when she was 40 years old. But there are enough in later years to indicate no change in her condition. The Master who heard the case in the court below, found that the proofs demonstrated 'incontrovertably her morbid aversion to men' and 'feminism to a neurotic extreme.' This characterization seems to me not strong enough. She regarded men as a class with an insane hatred. She looked forward to the day when women would bear children without the aid of men, and all males would be put to death at birth. Decedent's inward life, disclosed by what she wrote, found an occasional outlet such as the incident of the smashing of the clock, the killing of the pet kitten,[3] vile language, etc. On the other hand,—and I suppose this is the split personality,—Miss Strittmater, in her dealings with her lawyer, Mr. Semel, over a period of several years, and with her bank, to cite only two examples, was entirely reasonable and normal.

"Decedent, in 1925, became a member of the New Jersey branch of the National Women's Party. From 1939 to 1941, and perhaps later, she worked as a volunteer one day a week in the New York office, filing papers, etc. During this period, she spoke of leaving her estate to the Party. On October 31, 1944, she executed her last will, carrying this intention into effect.[4] A month later, December 6, she died.

2. Eugen Bleuler (1857-1930), a Swiss psychiatrist, analyzed and named the condition schizophrenia, dividing it into several types, including paranoid. Bleuler believed that intense ambivalence (e.g., experiencing both love and hate toward an object) was a primary symptom of schizophrenia. He also observed that even normal persons, when preoccupied or distracted, show a number of schizophrenic symptoms, such as peculiar associations, logical blunders, and stereotypes.—Eds.

3. The opinion's silence leads us to wonder whether the clock was a "grandfather clock" or the kitten a "tomcat."—Eds.

4. Louisa Strittmater's intended beneficiary, the National Woman's Party, was founded in 1916 by Alice Paul. It was the most radical of the leading organizations that lobbied for the Nineteenth

Her only relatives were some cousins of whom she saw very little during the last few years of her life.

"The question is whether Miss Strittmater's will is the product of her insanity. Her disease seems to have become well developed by 1936. In August of that year she wrote, 'It remains for feministic organizations like the National Women's Party, to make exposure of women's "protectors" and "lovers" for what their vicious and contemptible selves are.' She had been a member of the Women's Party for eleven years at that time, but the evidence does not show that she had taken great interest in it. I think it was her paranoic condition, especially her insane delusions about the male, that led her to leave her estate to the National Women's Party. The result is that the probate should be set aside."

PER CURIAM.   The decree under review will be affirmed, for the reasons stated in the opinion of Vice-Ordinary Bigelow.

QUESTIONS

If the *Strittmater* case were to be decided today, would it come out the same way? To what extent are notions of capacity and insane delusion based on social constructions of what is "normal"?

In re Honigman
Court of Appeals of New York, 1960
8 N.Y.2d 244, 168 N.E.2d 676, 203 N.Y.S.2d 859

DYE, J.   Frank Honigman died May 4, 1956, survived by his wife, Florence. By a purported last will and testament, executed April 3, 1956, just one month before his death, he gave $5,000 to each of three named grandnieces, and cut off his wife

---

Amendment to the U.S. Constitution, which in 1920 granted women the right to vote. After being convicted and imprisoned in 1917 for nonviolent protests in front of the White House, Paul went on

Alice Paul, founder of the National Woman's Party

a hunger strike. She was then taken to the prison hospital's psychopathic ward and treated as mentally ill—an irony given the New Jersey Supreme Court's treatment of Louisa Strittmater 30 years later. See Doris Stevens, Jailed for Freedom 215-228 (1920).

In 1921 Alice Paul drafted the Equal Rights Amendment (ERA): "Equality of Rights under the law shall not be denied or abridged by the United States or any state on account of sex." Introduced in every Congress from 1923 through the early 1970s, the ERA finally passed in 1972. The ERA was then sent to the states for ratification, but it failed because not enough states ratified it before the 1982 deadline imposed by Congress. Paul, who had a Ph.D. in economics and three law degrees (LL.B., LL.M., and D.C.L.), was a leader in lobbying Congress to add sex discrimination to the protections of Title VII in the 1964 Civil Rights Act. Until the sex amendment to Title VII passed the House of Representatives in February 1964, the National Woman's Party was the only national women's organization that favored adding the prohibition of sex discrimination to that statute. See Jo Freeman, How "Sex" Got into Title VII: Persistent Opportunism as a Maker of Public Policy, 9 Law & Ineq. 1 (1990).

Alice Paul died in 1977 at the age of 92.—Eds.

with a life use of her minimum statutory share plus $2,500, with direction to pay the principal upon her death to his surviving brothers and sisters and to the descendants of any predeceased brother or sister, per stirpes. The remaining one half of his estate was bequeathed in equal shares to his surviving brothers and sisters and to the descendants of any predeceased brother or sister, per stirpes, some of whom resided in Germany.

When the will was offered for probate in Surrogate's Court, Queens County, the widow Florence filed objections. A trial was had on framed issues, only one of which survived for determination by the jury, namely: "At the time of the execution of the paper offered for probate was the said Frank Honigman of sound and disposing mind and memory?" The jury answered in the negative, and the Surrogate then made a decree denying probate to the will.

Upon an appeal to the Appellate Division, Second Department, the Surrogate's decree was reversed upon the law and the facts, and probate was directed. Inconsistent findings of fact were reversed and new findings substituted.

We read this record as containing more than enough competent proof to warrant submitting to the jury the issue of decedent's testamentary capacity. By the same token the proof amply supports the jury findings, implicit in the verdict, that the testator, at the time he made his will, was suffering from an unwarranted and insane delusion that his wife was unfaithful to him, which condition affected the disposition made in the will. The record is replete with testimony, supplied by a large number of disinterested persons, that for quite some time before his death the testator had publicly and repeatedly told friends and strangers alike that he believed his wife was unfaithful, often using obscene and abusive language. Such manifestations of suspicion were quite unaccountable, coming as they did after nearly 40 years of a childless yet, to all outward appearances, a congenial and harmonious marriage, which had begun in 1916. During the intervening time they had worked together in the successful management, operation and ownership of various restaurants, bars and grills and, by their joint efforts of thrift and industry, had accumulated the substantial fortune now at stake.

The decedent and his wife retired from business in 1945 because of decedent's failing health. In the few years that followed he underwent a number of operations, including a prostatectomy in 1951, and an operation for cancer of the large bowel in 1954, when decedent was approximately 70 years of age. From about this time, he began volubly to express his belief that Mrs. Honigman was unfaithful to him. This suspicion became an obsession with him, although all of the witnesses agreed that the deceased was normal and rational in other respects. Seemingly aware of his mental state, he once mentioned that he was "sick in the head" ("Mich krank gelassen in den Kopf"), and that "I know there is something wrong with me" in response to a light reference to his mental condition. In December, 1955 he went to Europe, a trip Mrs. Honigman learned of in a letter sent from Idlewild Airport after he had departed, and while there he visited a doctor. Upon his return he went to a psychiatrist who Mr. Honigman said "could not help" him. Finally, he went to a chiropractor with whom he was extremely satisfied.

On March 21, 1956, shortly after his return from Europe, Mr. Honigman instructed his attorney to prepare the will in question. He never again joined Mrs. Honigman in the marital home.

To offset and contradict this showing of irrational obsession the proponents adduced proof which, it is said, furnished a reasonable basis for decedent's belief, and which, when taken with other factors, made his testamentary disposition understandable. Briefly, this proof related to four incidents. One concerned an anniversary card sent by Mr. Krauss, a mutual acquaintance and friend of many years, bearing a printed message of congratulation in sweetly sentimental phraseology. Because it was addressed to the wife alone and not received on the anniversary date, Mr. Honigman viewed it as confirmatory of his suspicion. Then there was the reference to a letter which it is claimed contained prejudicial matter — but just what it was is not before us, because the letter was not produced in evidence and its contents were not established. There was also proof to show that whenever the house telephone rang Mrs. Honigman would answer it. From this Mr. Honigman drew added support for his suspicion that she was having an affair with Mr. Krauss. Mr. Honigman became so upset about it that for the last two years of their marriage he positively forbade her to answer the telephone. Another allegedly significant happening was an occasion when Mrs. Honigman asked the decedent as he was leaving the house what time she might expect him to return. This aroused his suspicion. He secreted himself at a vantage point in a nearby park and watched his home. He saw Mr. Krauss enter and, later, when he confronted his wife with knowledge of this incident, she allegedly asked him for a divorce. This incident was taken entirely from a statement made by Mr. Honigman to one of the witnesses. Mrs. Honigman flatly denied all of it. Their verdict shows that the jury evidently believed the objectant. Under the circumstances, we cannot say that this was wrong. The jury had the right to disregard the proponents' proof, or to go so far as to hold that such trivia afforded even additional grounds for decedent's irrational and unwarranted belief. The issue we must bear in mind is not whether Mrs. Honigman was unfaithful, but whether Mr. Honigman had any reasonable basis for believing that she was.

In a very early case we defined the applicable test as follows:

> If a person persistently believes supposed facts, which have no real existence except in his perverted imagination, and against all evidence and probability, and conducts himself, however logically, upon the assumption of their existence, he is, so far as they are concerned, under a morbid delusion; and delusion in that sense is insanity. Such a person is essentially mad or insane on those subjects, though on other subjects he may reason, act and speak like a sensible man. (American Seamen's Friend Soc. v. Hopper, 33 N.Y. 619, 624-625 (1865).)

It is true that the burden of proving testamentary incapacity is a difficult one to carry (Dobie v. Armstrong, 55 N.E. 302 (N.Y. 1899)), but when an objectant has gone forward, as Mrs. Honigman surely has, with evidence reflecting the operation of the testator's mind, it is the proponents' duty to provide a basis for the alleged delusion. We cannot conclude that as a matter of law they have performed this duty successfully. When, in the light of all the circumstances surrounding a long and happy marriage such as this, the husband publicly and repeatedly expresses suspicions of his wife's unfaithfulness; of misbehaving herself in a most unseemly fashion, by hiding male callers in the cellar of her own home, in various closets, and under the bed; of hauling men from the street up to her second-story bedroom by use of bed sheets; of making contacts over the household telephone; and of passing a clandestine note through the fence on her brother's property — and when he claims to have heard noises which he believed to be men running about his home, but which he had not investigated, and which he could not verify—the courts should have no hesitation in placing the issue of sanity in the jury's hands. To hold to the contrary would be to take from the jury its traditional function of passing on the facts.

. . . Mr. Honigman persisted over a long period of time in telling his suspicions to anyone who would listen to him, friends and strangers alike. That such belief was an obsession with him was clearly established by a preponderance of concededly competent evidence and, prima facie, there was presented a question of fact as to whether it affected the will he made shortly before his death.

The proponents argue that, even if decedent was indeed laboring under a delusion, the existence of other reasons for the disposition he chose is enough to support the validity of the instrument as a will. The other reasons are, first, the size of Mrs. Honigman's independent fortune, and, second, the financial need of his residuary legatees. These reasons, as well as his belief in his wife's infidelity, decedent expressed to his own attorney. We dispelled a similar contention in American Seamen's Friend Soc. v. Hopper, supra, where we held that a will was bad when its "dispository provisions were or *might have been* caused or affected by the delusion" (emphasis supplied). . . .

We turn now to alleged errors committed by the Surrogate when he overruled objections based on section 347 of the Civil Practice Act.[5] Much of Mrs. Honigman's testimony, which should have been excluded as incompetent since it was evidence "concerning a personal transaction or communication between the witness [an interested party] and the deceased person," was admitted because the Surrogate believed that the proponents, by failing to object to such testimony at the earliest opportunity, irrevocably waived their right to protest on that ground. In de Laurent v. Townsend (152 N.E. 699 (N.Y. 1926)) this court was unanimous in holding that the rule as to waiver of objections under section 347 was to be found in that statute "and not elsewhere" (p. 700). The statute provides an exception "where the executor, administrator, survivor, committee or person deriving title or interest is examined in his own behalf, or the testimony of the lunatic or deceased person is given in evidence, concerning the same transaction or communication." Since the exception is inapplicable to the circumstances here present, it was error not to exclude Mrs. Honigman's testimony whenever objections based on the prohibition of section 347 were appropriately raised.

Finally, since there is to be a new trial of the issues, the Surrogate's ruling with regard to the clergyman-penitent privilege deserves mention. Father Heitz, a Catholic priest, was called by the objectant, who sought to elicit from him a

---

5. New York Civil Practice Act §347, now N.Y. Civ. Prac. Law & R. §4519 (2004), is New York's dead man's statute. The statute excludes the testimony of a survivor "concerning a personal transaction or communication between the witness and the deceased person." In most states—but not in New York—the dead man's statute is not applicable to proceedings to probate a will on the theory that the testator's will is not a "transaction or communication" between the testator and the legatees. The purpose of the statute is to protect estates of deceased persons from creditors and others making false claims respecting business transactions when testator's lips are sealed, and the statute excludes testimony only in suits upon claims between other persons and the deceased existing prior to his death. See Annot., 28 A.L.R.3d 994 (1969, rev. 1993); Annot., 8 A.L.R.2d 1094 (1949, rev. 1993). In New York, however, it was early held that the dead man's statute applied to probate of a will. In re Smith, 95 N.Y. 516 (1884).

Dead man's statutes are highly unpopular with evidence scholars and have been abolished in many states. Where they exist, most courts construe them narrowly. See 2 John H. Wigmore, Evidence §578 (James H. Chadbourn rev. 1979).—Eds.

conversation he had had with the deceased at a time when the latter wanted advice concerning his marital problems. Although Father Heitz was willing, he was not permitted to testify to the conversation, "Specifically on the ground that any conversation with a priest, although not in the confessional, is privileged." There is nothing in the record to indicate the nature of the testimony sought. In this posture it cannot be determined whether such testimony falls within the privilege created by section 351 of the Civil Practice Act.

The order appealed from should be reversed and a new trial granted, with costs to abide the event.

FULD, J. (dissenting).   I am willing to assume that the proof demonstrates that the testator's belief that his wife was unfaithful was completely groundless and unjust. However, that is not enough; it does not follow from this fact that the testator suffered from such a delusion as to stamp him mentally defective or as lacking in capacity to make a will. "To sustain the allegation," this court wrote in the *Clapp* case (34 N.Y. 190, 197 (1866)),

> it is not sufficient to show that his suspicion in this respect was not well founded. It is quite apparent, from the evidence, that his distrust of the fidelity of his wife was really groundless and unjust; but it does not follow that his doubts evince a condition of lunacy. The right of a testator to dispose of his estate, depends neither on the justice of his prejudices nor the soundness of his reasoning. He may do what he will with his own; and if there be no defect of testamentary capacity, and no undue influence or fraud, the law gives effect to his will, though its provisions are unreasonable and unjust.

As a matter of fact, in the case before us, a goodly portion of the widow's testimony bearing on her husband's alleged delusion should have been excluded, as the court itself notes, by reason of section 347 of the Civil Practice Act. And, of course, if such testimony had not been received in evidence, a number of items of proof upon which the widow relies would not have been available, with the consequence that the record would have contained even less basis for her claim of delusion.

Moreover, I share the Appellate Division's view that other and sound reasons, quite apart from the alleged [delusion], existed for the disposition made by the testator. Indeed, he himself had declared that his wife had enough money and he wanted to take care of his brothers and sisters living in Europe.

In short, the evidence adduced utterly failed to prove that the testator was suffering from an insane delusion or lacked testamentary capacity. The Appellate Division was eminently correct in concluding that there was no issue of fact for the jury's consideration and in directing the entry of a decree admitting the will to probate. Its order should be affirmed.

NOTES AND QUESTIONS

1. In The Myth of Testamentary Freedom, 38 Ariz. L. Rev. 235 (1996), Professor Melanie B. Leslie argues that

> many courts do not exalt testamentary freedom above all other principles. Notwithstanding frequent declarations to the contrary, many courts are as committed

to insuring that testators devise their estates in accordance with prevailing normative views as they are to effectuating testamentary intent. Those courts impose upon testators a duty to provide for those whom the court views as having a superior moral claim to the testator's assets, usually a financially dependent spouse or persons related by blood to the testator. Wills that fail to provide for those individuals typically are upheld only if the will's proponent can convince the fact-finder that the testator's deviation from normative values is morally justifiable. This unspoken rule, seeping quietly, but fervently from case law, directly conflicts with the oft-repeated axiom that testamentary freedom is the polestar of wills law.

Courts impose and enforce this moral duty to family through the covert manipulation of doctrine. [Id. at 236.]

Leslie attempts to prove her thesis by examining cases on undue influence and cases determining whether the testator has met the technical formal requirements for a will. Would testamentary capacity also be ripe for examination under her microscope?

To this end, consider *In re Honigman*. Under New York law applicable in 1956, when an intestate was survived by a spouse and brothers and sisters (as in the *Honigman* case), the spouse took one-half and the brothers and sisters the other half. Thus, if Mr. Honigman's will was struck down because of an insane delusion, his estate would go by intestacy one-half to his wife and one-half to his brothers and sisters. What statements by the majority support Mrs. Honigman's moral claim to half her husband's fortune outright?

Since the *Honigman* case, New York law has been amended to give the surviving spouse the entire estate of an intestate decedent if the decedent leaves no issue. N.Y. Est. Powers & Trusts Law §4-1.1(a)(2) (2004). If Mr. Honigman died today and were found to have an insane delusion, Mrs. Honigman would receive everything by intestacy. If he were not found to have an insane delusion, Mrs. Honigman would have a right to take half of the estate as her elective share (see pages 425-428). How do you think the case would come out today?

As you read the cases in this book, consider the merits of Professor Leslie's hypothesis and how you might modify it.

2.   The law draws a distinction between an insane delusion and a mistake. An insane delusion is a belief not susceptible to correction by presenting the testator with evidence indicating the falsity of the belief. A mistake is susceptible to correction if the testator is told the truth. As a general rule, courts do not reform or invalidate wills because of mistake (though this rule is changing, see pages 374-385), whereas they do invalidate wills resulting from an insane delusion. Suppose, for example, that the testator falsely believes that her son has been killed and therefore executes a will leaving all her property to her daughter. In fact the son is alive. The testator is mistaken, not under an insane delusion, and the will is entitled to probate. See Bowerman v. Burris, 197 S.W. 490 (Tenn. 1917). Cf. UPC §2-302(c) (1990), giving a child an intestate share where the testator mistakenly believes the child is dead.

3.   A study of California cases some years ago indicated that when mental capacity or undue influence was in issue, the jury found for the contestant in 77 percent of the cases, and over half of the verdicts for contestants were reversed by the supreme court upon appeal on grounds of insufficient evidence. Note, Will Contests on Trial, 6 Stan. L. Rev. 91, 92 (1953). See also Estate of Fritschi, 384

P.2d 656, 659 (Cal. 1963), complaining that a "legion" of appellate decisions have been necessary to reverse juries who invalidate wills based on nothing more than "their own concepts of how testators should have disposed of their properties." See also Note, Undue Influence — Judicial Implementation of Social Policy, 1968 Wis. L. Rev. 569, which finds that in Wisconsin, where the trial judge, not a jury, finds facts in will contests, appellate courts rarely reverse the trial judge's decision in undue influence cases.

In a study of contested wills over a nine-year period in Davidson County (Nashville), Tennessee, Professor Schoenblum confirmed what other studies have found: Juries are considerably more favorable to contestants than are judges. Jeffrey A. Schoenblum, Will Contests — An Empirical Study, 22 Real Prop., Prob. & Tr. J. 607 (1987). See also Comment, The Pros and Cons of Jury Trials in Will Contests, 1990 U. Chi. Legal F. 529 (proposing abolishing jury trials in will contests over mental capacity or undue influence); Jeffrey P. Rosenfeld, Will Contests, Legacies of Aging and Social Change, *in* Inheritance and Wealth in America 173 (Robert K. Miller, Jr. & Stephen J. McNamee eds., 1998) (reporting that divorce and remarriage and the lessening of a cohesive family life have increased estate litigation among stepfamilies and siblings).

Statutes in Arkansas, North Dakota, and Ohio permit probate of a will during the testator's life. These statutes authorize a person to institute during life an adversary proceeding to declare the validity of a will and the testamentary capacity and freedom from undue influence of the person executing the will. All beneficiaries named in the will and all testator's heirs apparent must be made parties to the action. Ark. Code Ann. §28-40-202 (2004); N.D. Cent. Code §30.1-08.1-01 (2004); Ohio Rev. Code Ann. §2107.081 (2004). This procedure is known as "living probate" or "ante-mortem probate."

John H. Langbein, Living Probate: The Conservatorship Model
77 Mich. L. Rev. 63, 64-66 (1978)

Discussion of living probate must begin with the problem of the will contest alleging testamentary incapacity. Although we do not have comparative data directly on point, the impression is widespread that such litigation occurs more frequently in the United States than on the Continent or in England. We may point to several factors that bear upon the differential:

(1) In civil law countries, children as well as the spouse have a forced share entitlement in the estate of a parent. The disinherited child, who is the typical plaintiff in American testamentary capacity litigation, is unknown to European law. The European parent can leave his heir disgruntled with the statutory minimum, but that share will often be large enough by comparison with the potential winnings from litigation to deaden the incentive to contest.

(2) Many American jurisdictions permit will contests on the question of capacity to be tried to a jury, which may be more disposed to work equity for the disinherited than to obey the directions of an eccentric decedent who is in any event

beyond suffering. Civil jury trial has disappeared from English estate law; it was never known on the Continent.

(3) American law is unique among Western civil procedural systems in failing to charge a losing plaintiff with the attorney fees and other costs incurred by the defendant in the course of resisting the plaintiff's unjustified claim. In testamentary capacity litigation the American rule has the effect of requiring decedents' estates to subsidize the depredations of contestants. Put differently, the American rule diminishes the magnitude of a contestant's potential loss, which diminishes his disincentive to litigate an improbable claim.

(4) Civil law systems provide for the so-called authenticated will, which is executed before a quasi-judicial officer called the notary. This is not the only means of making a valid will in European countries, and because it is costly it is not widely used. But the notarial procedure does permit a testator who fears a post-mortem contest to generate during his lifetime and have preserved with the will evidence of exceptional quality regarding, *inter alia*, his capacity. The notary before whom the testator executes his will is not a judge; he does not adjudicate capacity. But he is a legally qualified and experienced officer of the state who is obliged to satisfy himself of the testator's capacity as a precondition for receiving or transcribing the testament. The authenticated will is, therefore, extremely difficult for contestants to set aside for want of capacity in post-mortem proceedings. . . .

A major reason that the impact of capacity litigation in America is so difficult to measure is that most of it is directed towards provoking pretrial settlements, typically for a fraction of what the contestants would be entitled to receive if they were to defeat the will. Especially when such tactics succeed, they do not leave traces in the law reports. Thus, the odor of the strike suit hangs heavily over this field. The beneficiaries named in the will are likely to be either charitable organizations whom the testator preferred to his relatives, or else those of his relatives and friends whom he loved most and who are most likely to want to spare his reputation from a capacity suit. They are typically put to the choice of defending a lawsuit in which a skilled plaintiff's lawyer will present evidence to a jury at a public trial touching every eccentricity that might cast doubt upon the testator's condition, or compromising the suit, thereby overriding the disposition desired by the testator and rewarding the contestants for threatening to besmirch his name.

NOTE

For more on ante-mortem probate as a prophylactic against later will contests, see Gregory S. Alexander & Albert M. Pearson, Alternative Models of Ante-Mortem Probate and Procedural Due Process Limitations on Succession, 78 Mich. L. Rev. 89 (1979); Mary L. Fellows, The Case Against Living Probate, 78 Mich. L. Rev. 1066 (1980); Aloysius A. Leopold & Gerry W. Beyer, Ante-Mortem Probate: A Viable Alternative, 43 Ark. L. Rev. 131 (1990); Dara Greene, Antemortem Probate: A Mediation Model, 14 Ohio St. J. Disp. Resol. 663 (1999). On adapting parts of the civil law system, see Nicole M. Reina, Protecting Testamentary Freedom in the United States by Introducing into Law the Concept of the French Notaire, 22 N.Y.L. Sch. J. Intl. & Comp. L. 427 (2003).

SECTION B. UNDUE INFLUENCE

Undue influence is one of the most bothersome concepts in all the law. It cannot be precisely defined. More than a hundred years ago Lord Hannen gave the classic explanation of what kind of influence is undue in the eyes of the law:

Lord Justice Hannen

We are all familiar with the use of the word "influence"; we say that one person has an unbounded influence over another, and we speak of evil influences and good influences, but it is not because one person has unbounded influence over another that therefore when exercised, even though it may be very bad indeed, it is undue influence in the legal sense of the word. To give you some illustrations of what I mean, a young man may be caught in the toils of a harlot, who makes use of her influence to induce him to make a will in her favour, to the exclusion of his relatives. It is unfortunately quite natural that a man so entangled should yield to that influence and confer large bounties on the person with whom he has been brought into such relation; yet the law does not attempt to guard against those contingencies. A man may be the companion of another, and may encourage him in evil courses, and so obtain what is called an undue influence over him, and the consequence may be a will made in his favour. But that again, shocking as it is, perhaps even worse than the other, will not amount to undue influence.

To be undue influence in the eye of the law there must be — to sum it up in a word — coercion. . . . It is only when the will of the person who becomes a testator is coerced into doing that which he or she does not desire to do, that it is undue influence.

The coercion may of course be of different kinds, it may be in the grossest form, such as actual confinement or violence, or a person in the last days or hours of life may have become so weak and feeble, that a very little pressure will be sufficient to bring about the desired result, and it may even be, that the mere talking to him at that stage of illness and pressing something upon him may so fatigue the brain, that the sick person may be induced, for quietness' sake, to do anything. This would equally be coercion, though not actual violence.

These illustrations will sufficiently bring home to your minds that even very immoral considerations either on the part of the testator, or of some one else offering them, do not amount to undue influence unless the testator is in such a condition, that if he could speak his wishes to the last, he would say, "this is not my wish, but I must do it." [Wingrove v. Wingrove, 11 Prob. Div. 81 (U.K. 1885).]

Undue influence may occur where there is a confidential relationship between the parties or where there is no such relationship. Proof may be wholly inferential and circumstantial. The influence may be that of a beneficiary or that of a third person imputed to the beneficiary.

In more recent times judges have tried to cabin this unruly concept by saying that, to establish undue influence, it must be proved (1) that the testator was *susceptible* to undue influence, (2) that the influencer had the *disposition* or *motive* to exercise undue influence, (3) that the influencer had the *opportunity* to exercise undue influence, and (4) that the disposition is the *result* of the influence. But this formulation begs the question because it does not tell us what influence is undue. Perhaps the only satisfactory way of acquiring a lawyer's feel about the contours of undue influence is to immerse yourself in the cases.

ESTATE OF LAKATOSH, 656 A.2d 1378 (Pa. Super. 1994): In March 1988, Roger Jacobs befriended the decedent Rose Lakatosh, who was then in her 70s, living alone with only an occasional visit from her sister. "Roger lived just a few miles from Rose and visited her at least once a day and sometimes as often as two or three times a day. Roger assisted Rose around her house and drove Rose to various appointments and took her on various errands. These facts suggest that this elderly woman came to depend on Roger as the only person with whom she really had substantial contact."

A few months after they met, Roger suggested that Rose give him a power of attorney. On November 11, 1988, she executed both a power of attorney and a new will leaving all but $1,000 of her $268,000 estate to Roger, who was not present at the execution. The lawyer who drafted the will was Roger's second cousin, to whom Roger had referred Rose on an unrelated lawsuit. A tape recording of the execution ceremony showed that, while Rose may not have lacked competence entirely, she was easily distracted and had a "weakened intellect." On the tape, "Rose also repeatedly claimed that her nephew, Dean Berg, threatened to rob and kill her and that he was persecuting and torturing her."

Roger took advantage of this confidential relationship:

> Concerning Rose's finances and Roger's power of attorney, Roger unlawfully converted $128,565.29 in assets from Rose's estate for his own benefit or for the benefit of others, not including Rose, from September, 1988 to June, 1990. Among other improper conversions, Roger caused approximately $72,000.00 of Rose's assets to be transferred to Patricia Fox, a woman who had been friends with Roger since February of 1984, but who was not known by Rose personally.
>
> In June, 1990, Rose was living in squalor and filth and had fallen behind in the payment of certain household bills including water/sewer bills, and County and City property taxes. On June 18, 1990 Rose executed a general revocation of the power of attorney placed in Roger Jacobs. On September 4, 1993, Rose died.

The court applied the test set out in Estate of Reichel, 400 A.2d 1268, 1270 (Pa. 1979):

> When the proponent of a will proves that the formalities of execution have been followed, a contestant who claims that there has been undue influence has the burden of proof. *The burden may be shifted so as to require the proponent to disprove undue influence.* To do so, the contestant must prove by clear and convincing evidence [1] that there was a confidential relationship, [2] that the person enjoying such relationship received the bulk of the estate, and [3] that the decedent's intellect was weakened.

These three elements were easily met. First, the confidential relationship was established by Rose's dependency on Roger and the power of attorney. Second, Roger received the bulk of the estate. Third, Rose's intellect was weakened:

> [S]he was an elderly woman; helpless and unable to prevent the consumption of her assets by Roger during the period before and after the execution of her will, from September, 1988, to June, 1990, when she finally had Roger's power of attorney revoked. Also, Rose was living in filth in the spring of 1990, with her bills not having been paid, and, after a house fire, it was discovered that her house was in shambles with trash throughout and dead cats found in her freezer and bathtub.

> All of this goes to establish that Rose suffered from a weakened intellect at the time the November 11, 1988 will was executed. As a result, the burden of disproving undue influence shifted to Roger. "Once the burden of disproving undue influence shifts to the proponent [of the will], it is incumbent upon the proponent to demonstrate the absence of undue influence by clear and convincing evidence." Burns v. Kabboul, 595 A.2d 1153, 1163 (Pa. Super. 1991).

> Consequently, we conclude that the trial court's findings rest on legally competent evidence and the trial court did not commit error or abuse its discretion in finding that Rose's will should be revoked because Roger failed to carry his burden of proving the absence of undue influence.

The Superior Court of Pennsylvania affirmed the order of the trial court, revoking the probate of Rose's will and imposing a constructive trust on Roger in the amount of $128,565.29.

Restatement (Third) of Property: Wills and Other Donative Transfers (2003)

§8.3   UNDUE INFLUENCE, DURESS, OR FRAUD

(a) A donative transfer is invalid to the extent that it was procured by undue influence, duress, or fraud.

(b) A donative transfer is procured by undue influence if the wrongdoer exerted such influence over the donor that it overcame the donor's free will and caused the donor to make a donative transfer that the donor would not otherwise have made.

COMMENT H TO §8.3.   SUSPICIOUS CIRCUMSTANCES

The existence of a confidential relationship is not sufficient to raise a presumption of undue influence. There must also be suspicious circumstances surrounding the preparation, execution, or formulation of the donative transfer. Suspicious circumstances raise an inference of an abuse of the confidential relationship between the alleged wrongdoer and the donor.

In evaluating whether suspicious circumstances are present, all relevant factors may be considered, including:

(1)   the extent to which the donor was in a weakened condition, physically, mentally, or both, and therefore susceptible to undue influence;

(2)   the extent to which the alleged wrongdoer participated in the preparation or procurement of the will or will substitute;

(3)   whether the donor received independent advice from an attorney or from other competent and disinterested advisors in preparing the will or will substitute;

(4) whether the will or will substitute was prepared in secrecy or in haste;

(5) whether the donor's attitude toward others had changed by reason of his or her relationship with the alleged wrongdoer;

(6) whether there is a decided discrepancy between a new and previous wills or will substitutes of the donor;

(7) whether there was a continuity of purpose running through former wills or will substitutes indicating a settled intent in the disposition of his or her property; and

(8) whether the disposition of the property is such that a reasonable person would regard it as unnatural, unjust, or unfair, for example, whether the disposition abruptly and without apparent reason disinherited a faithful and deserving family member.

NOTES AND QUESTIONS

1. In most jurisdictions, the rules about undue influence are complicated by nice questions about the burden of proof (or, more specifically, the burden of persuasion). The proponent of a will has the burden of proving its validity, but this is easily done in most cases by showing due execution. The person contesting the will then has the burden of proving undue influence directly or by proving facts that would give rise to a presumption of undue influence. To trigger this presumption, the contestant must establish the existence of a *confidential relationship* between the influencer and the testator — plus something more. In some jurisdictions, the other element that is necessary for a presumption of undue influence is that the influencer procured the will. In other jurisdictions, to trigger the presumption the contestant must show both a confidential relationship and *suspicious circumstances* such as the ones listed in Comment h, supra, to the Restatement (Third). In still other jurisdictions, such as Pennsylvania in the *Lakatosh* case, the extra elements are that the person in the confidential relationship received the bulk of the estate and that the decedent had a weakened intellect. See William M. McGovern, Jr. & Sheldon F. Kurtz, Wills, Trusts and Estates §7.3, at 306-308 (3d ed. 2004).

If the presumption of undue influence is triggered, the burden shifts back to the proponent to negate undue influence. But what must the proponent show to overcome the presumption? A pair of recent decisions by the Iowa Supreme Court illustrate the difficulties that arise in this exercise.

In a confused 1998 opinion, the court held that, to rebut the presumption, the proponent must disprove all the basic elements of undue influence: "(1) the grantor's lack of susceptibility," "(2) the want of opportunity to exercise" influence, "(3) the lack of a disposition to influence unduly," and "(4) a result clearly unaffected by undue influence." In re Estate of Todd, 585 N.W.2d 273, 277 n.5 (Iowa 1998). But why should the proponent be required to disprove, for example, susceptibility? If the other elements are disproved, is not the will reliable? Should not susceptible people be permitted to make wills favoring those close to them? See Ronald R. Volkmer, Rebutting Presumption of Undue Influence, 31 Est. Plan. 352 (2004).

In 2003, the Iowa court came to its senses, holding that "the rule for rebutting the presumption of undue influence arising from a confidential relationship only requires the grantee of a transaction to prove by clear, satisfactory, and convincing evidence that the grantee acted in good faith throughout the transaction and the grantor acted freely, intelligently, and voluntarily." Jackson v. Schrader, 676

N.W.2d 599, 605 (Iowa 2003). In other words, the proponent need not disprove all the elements of undue influence, but rather must prove the ultimate issue, that the will is free of such influence, as well as establishing his own clean hands. See Volkmer, supra.

2. Do the undue influence standards for wills apply to lifetime gifts or non-probate transfers such as revocable inter vivos trusts or life insurance? There is a split of authority. Compare Restatement (Third) of Property: Wills and Other Donative Transfers §8.3 (2003) (all donative transfers use the same rule), with Upman v. Clarke, 753 A.2d 4 (Md. 2000) (undue influence easier to establish for lifetime gifts than for wills or revocable trusts).

3. If part of a will is the product of undue influence, those portions of the will that are the product of such influence may be stricken and the remainder of the will allowed to stand, if the invalid portions of the will can be separated without defeating the testator's intent or destroying the testamentary scheme. Williams v. Crickman, 405 N.E.2d 799 (Ill. 1980).

Lipper v. Weslow
Texas Court of Civil Appeals, 1963
369 S.W.2d 698

McDONALD, C.J. This is a contest of the will of Mrs. Sophie Block, on the ground of undue influence. Plaintiffs, Julian Weslow, Jr., Julia Weslow Fortson and Alice Weslow Sale, are the 3 grandchildren of Mrs. Block by a deceased son; defendants are Mrs. Block's 2 surviving children, G. Frank Lipper and Irene Lipper Dover (half brother and half sister of plaintiffs' deceased father). (The will left the estate of testatrix to her 2 children, defendants herein; and left nothing to her grandchildren by the deceased son, plaintiffs herein.) Trial was to a jury, which found that Mrs. Block's will, signed by her on January 30, 1956, was procured by undue influence on the part of the proponent, Frank Lipper. The trial court entered judgment on the verdict, setting aside the will.

Defendants appeal, contending there is no evidence, or insufficient evidence, to support the finding that the will was procured by undue influence.

Testatrix was married 3 times. Of her first marriage she had one son, Julian Weslow (who died in 1949), who was father of plaintiffs herein. After the death of her first husband testatrix married a Mr. Lipper. Defendants are the 2 children of their marriage. After Mr. Lipper's death, testatrix married Max Block. There were no children born of this marriage. Max Block died several months after the death of testatrix.

On 30 January, 1956, Sophie Block executed the will in controversy. Such will was prepared by defendant, Frank Lipper, an attorney, one of the beneficiaries of the will, and Independent Executor of the will. The will was witnessed by 2 former business associates of Mr. Block. Pertinent provisions of the will are summarized as follows:

"That I, Mrs. Sophie Block, . . . do make, publish and declare this my last will and testament, hereby revoking all other wills by me heretofore made."

1, 2, 3 AND 4
(Provide for payment of debts; for burial in Beth Israel Cemetery; and for minor bequests to a servant, and to an old folks' home.)

5
(Devises the bulk of testatrix's estate to her 2 children, Mrs. Irene Lipper Dover and Frank Lipper (defendants herein), share and share alike.)

6
(States that $7000. previously advanced to Mrs. Irene Lipper Dover, and $9300. previously advanced to Frank Lipper be taken into consideration in the final settlement of the estate; and cancels such amounts "that I gave or advanced to my deceased son, Julian.")

7
(Appoints G. Frank Lipper Independent Executor of the estate without bond.)

8
(Provides that if any legatee contests testatrix's will or the will of her husband, Max Block, that they forfeit all benefits under the will.)

9
"My son, Julian A. Weslow, died on August 6, 1949, and I want to explain why I have not provided anything under this will for my daughter-in-law, Bernice Weslow, widow of my deceased son, Julian, and her children, Julian A. Weslow, Jr., Alice Weslow Sale, and Julia Weslow Fortson, and I want to go into sufficient detail in explaining my relationship in past years with my said son's widow and his children, before mentioned, and it is my desire to record such relationship so that there will be no question as to my feelings in the matter or any thought or suggestion that my children, Irene Lipper Dover and G. Frank Lipper, or my husband, Max, may have influenced me in any manner in the execution of this will. During the time that my said son, Julian, was living, the attitude of his wife, Bernice, was at times, pleasant and friendly, but the majority of the years when my said son, Julian, was living, her attitude towards me and my husband, Max, was unfriendly and frequently months would pass when she was not in my home and I did not hear from her. When my said son, Julian, was living he was treated the same as I treated my other children; and, my husband, Max, and I gave to each of our children a home and various sums of money from time to time to help in taking care of medical expenses, other unusual expenses, as well as outright gifts. Since my said son Julian's death, his widow, Bernice, and all of her children have shown a most unfriendly and distant attitude towards me, my husband, Max, and my 2 children G. Frank Lipper and Irene Lipper Dover, which attitude I cannot reconcile as I have shown them many kindnesses since they have been members of my family, and their continued unfriendly attitude towards me, my husband, Max, and my said children has hurt me deeply in my declining years, for my life would have been much happier if they had shown a disposition to want to be a part of the family and enter into a normal family relationship that usually exists with a daughter-in-law and grandchildren and great grandchildren. I have not seen my grandson, Julian A. Weslow, Jr. in several years, neither have I heard from him.[6] My granddaughter, Alice Weslow Sale, I have not seen in several years and I have not heard from her, but I heard a

6. Julian Weslow, Jr., became a professional dog trainer, famed throughout Texas and the Southwest for "snake proofing" hunting dogs. The dog is given a zap of electricity through an electric collar when the dog sniffs a defanged rattlesnake, which strikes at the dog simultaneously. Sometimes the dog leaps two feet straight up, but in any case the dog quickly learns to give snakes a wide berth thereafter. " 'This collar gives a good jolt,' explains Julian. 'But it's certainly a lot better than a good jolt of venom.' " De-Snaking Your Dog, Life Adventures Magazine (2002). More than 10,000 dogs die each year from snake bite. See L.A. Times, Sept. 25, 1991, at C6. — Eds.

report some months ago that she was now living in California and has since married William G. Sale. My granddaughter, Julia Weslow Fortson, wife of Ben Fortson, I have not seen in several years and I was told that she had a child born to her sometime in December 1952, and I have not seen the child or heard from my said granddaughter, Julia, up to this writing, and was informed by a friend that Julia has had another child recently and is now living in Louisiana, having moved from Houston; and needless to say, my said daughter-in-law, Bernice, widow of my deceased son, Julian, I have not seen in several years as she has taken little or no interest in me or my husband, Max, since the death of my son, Julian, with the exception that Christmas a year ago, if I remember correctly, she sent some flowers, which I acknowledged, and I believe she had sent some greeting cards on some occasions prior to that time. My said daughter-in-law, Bernice Weslow, has expressed to me, on several occasions, an intense hatred for my son, G. Frank Lipper, and my daughter, Irene Lipper Dover, which I cannot understand, as my said children have always shown her and her children every consideration when possible, and have expressed a desire to be friendly with her, and them. My said children, G. Frank Lipper, and Irene Lipper Dover, have at all times been attentive to me and my husband, Max, especially during the past few years when we have not been well. I will be 82 years old in June of this year and my husband, Max, will be 80 years of age in October of this year, and we have both been in failing health for the past few years and rarely leave our home, and appreciate any attention that is given us, and my husband, Max, and I cannot understand the unfriendly and distant attitude of Bernice Weslow, widow of my said son, Julian, and his children, before mentioned."

10
(Concerns personal belongings already disposed of.)
   "In Testimony Whereof, I have hereunto signed my name. . . .

                                                                    (S) *Sophie Block*"
(Here follows attestation clause and signature of the 2 witnesses.)

   The record reflects that the will in question was executed 22 days before testatrix died at the age of 81 years. By its terms, it disinherits the children of testatrix's son, who died in 1949. Defendant, Frank Lipper, gets a larger share than would have been the case if the plaintiffs were not disinherited. Defendant Lipper is a lawyer, and is admittedly the scrivener of the will. There is evidence that defendant Lipper bore malice against his dead half brother. He lived next door to testatrix, and had a key to her house. The will was not read to testatrix prior to the time she signed same, and she had no discussion with anyone at the time she executed it. There is evidence that the recitations in the will that Bernice Weslow and her children were unfriendly, and never came about testatrix, were untrue. There is also evidence that the Weslows sent testatrix greeting cards and flowers from 1946 through 1954, more times than stated in the will.

   Plaintiffs offered no direct evidence pertaining to the making and execution of the will on January 30, 1956, and admittedly rely wholly upon circumstantial evidence of undue influence to support the verdict.

   All of the evidence is that testatrix was of sound mind at the time of the execution of the will; that she was a person of strong will; that she was in good physical health for her age; and that she was in fact physically active to the day of her death.

   Mrs. Weslow's husband died in 1949; and after 1952 the Weslows came about testatrix less often than before.

   The witness Lyda Friberg, who worked at the home of testatrix from 1949 to 1952, testified that in *1952* she had a conversation with Bernice Weslow in which

Mrs. Weslow told her if her children didn't get their inheritance she would "sue them through every court in the Union"; that she told testatrix about this conversation, and that testatrix told her "she would have those wills fixed up so there would be no court business," and that she wasn't going to "leave them (the Weslows) a dime." The foregoing was prior to the execution of the will on January 30, 1956.

Subsequent to the execution of the will, testatrix had a conversation with her sister, Mrs. Levy. Mrs. Levy testified:

Q. Who did she say she was leaving her property to?
A. She was leaving it to her son and her daughter.
Q. What else did she say about the rest of her kin, if anything?
A. Well she said that Julian's children had been very ugly to her; that they never showed her any attention whatever; they married and she didn't know they were married; they had children and they didn't let her know. After Julian passed away, she never saw any of the family at all. They never came to see her.
Q. Did she make any statement?
A. Yes she did. When she passed away, she didn't want to leave them anything; that they did nothing for her when she was living.

Shortly before she passed away, testatrix told Mrs. Augusta Roos that she was going to leave her property to her 2 children, and further:

Q. Did she give any reason for it?
A. Yes. She said that Bernice had never been very nice to her and the children never were over.

Again, subsequent to the making of her will, testatrix talked with Effie Landry, her maid. Mrs. Landry testified:

Q. Did Mrs. Block on any occasion ever tell you anything about what was contained in her will?
A. Yes.
Q. What did she tell you about that?
A. She said she wasn't leaving the Weslow children anything.

The only question presented is whether there is any evidence of undue influence. The test of undue influence is whether such control was exercised over the mind of the testatrix as to overcome her free agency and free will and to substitute the will of another so as to cause the testatrix to do what she would not otherwise have done but for such control. Scott v. Townsend, 166 S.W. 1138 (Tex. 1914); Curry v. Curry, S.W.2d 208 (Tex. 1954); Boyer v. Pool, 280 S.W.2d 564 (Tex. 1955).

The evidence here establishes that testatrix was 81 years of age at the time of the execution of her will; that her son, defendant Lipper, who is a lawyer, wrote the will for her upon her instruction; that defendant Lipper bore malice against his deceased half brother (father of plaintiffs); that defendant Lipper lived next door to his mother and had a key to her home; that the will as written gave defendant Lipper a larger share of testatrix's estate than he would otherwise have received;

that while testatrix had no discussion with anyone at the time she executed the will, she told the witness Friberg, prior to executing the will, that she was not going to leave anything to the Weslows; and subsequent to the execution of the will she told the witnesses Mrs. Levy, Mrs. Roos, and Mrs. Landry that she had not left the Weslows anything, and the reason why. The will likewise states the reasons for testatrix's action. The testatrix, although 81 years of age, was of sound mind and strong will; and in excellent physical health. There is evidence that the recitation in testatrix's will about the number of times the Weslows sent cards and flowers were incorrect, to the extent that cards and flowers were in fact sent oftener than such will recites.

The contestants established a confidential relationship, the opportunity, and perhaps a motive for undue influence by defendant Lipper. Proof of this type simply sets the stage. Contestants must go forward and prove in some fashion that the will as written resulted from the defendant Lipper substituting his mind and will for that of the testatrix. Here the will and the circumstances might raise suspicion, but it does not supply proof of the vital facts of undue influence — the substitution of a plan of testamentary disposition by another as the will of the testatrix. Boyer v. Pool, supra.

All of the evidence reflected that testatrix, although 81 years of age, was of sound mind; of strong will; and in excellent physical condition. Moreover, subsequent to the execution of the will she told 3 disinterested witnesses what she had done with her property in her will, and the reason therefor. A person of sound mind has the legal right to dispose of his property as he wishes, with the burden on those attacking the disposition to prove that it was the product of undue influence. Long v. Long, 125 S.W.2d 1034, 1035 (Tex. 1939); Curry v. Curry, 270 S.W.2d 208 (Tex. 1954).

Testatrix's will did make an unnatural disposition of her property in the sense that it preferred her 2 children over the grandchildren by a deceased son. However, the record contains an explanation from testatrix herself as to why she chose to do such. She had a right to do as she did, whether we think she was justified or not.

Plaintiffs contend that the record supports an inference that testatrix failed to receive the cards and flowers sent to her, or in the alternative that she failed to know she received same, due to conduct of defendant Lipper. Here again, defendant Lipper had the opportunity to prevent testatrix from receiving cards or flowers from the Weslows, but we think there is no evidence of probative force to support the conclusion that he in fact did such. Moreover, the will itself reflected that *some* cards and flowers were in fact received by the testatrix, the dispute in this particular area, going to the number of times that such were sent, rather than to the fact that any were sent. See also: Rothermel v. Duncan et al., 369 S.W.2d 917 (Tex. 1963).

We conclude there is no evidence of probative force to support the verdict of the jury. The cause is reversed and rendered for defendants.

QUESTIONS

Mrs. Block's will included a statement or recital (article 9) setting forth the reasons why she was not making provision for Julian's children. When the possibility of a will contest is anticipated, is this a desirable practice to follow? Or does it create litigable issues of fact? Given the stilted legalese of "said" recital, who do you think probably wrote it?

NOTE: NO-CONTEST CLAUSES

A *no-contest clause* provides that a beneficiary who contests the will shall take nothing, or a token amount, in lieu of the provisions made for the beneficiary in the will. A no-contest clause is designed to discourage will contests. In dealing with these clauses, courts have been pulled in several directions by conflicting policies. On the one hand, enforcement of a no-contest clause discourages unmeritorious litigation, family quarrels, and defaming the reputation of the testator. On the other hand, enforcement of a no-contest clause could inhibit a lawsuit proving forgery, fraud, or undue influence and nullify the safeguards built around the testamentary disposition of property.

The majority of courts enforce a no-contest clause unless there is probable cause for the contest. The probable cause rule is adopted by UPC §§2-517 and 3-905 (1990) and by Restatement (Third) of Property: Wills and Other Donative Transfers §8.5 (2003). See also In re Estate of Shumway, 9 P.3d 1062 (Ariz. 2000) (applying the probable cause standard). In a minority of jurisdictions, courts enforce no-contest clauses unless the contestant alleges forgery or subsequent revocation by a later will or codicil, or the beneficiary is contesting a provision benefitting the drafter of the will or any witness thereto. These jurisdictions believe a probable cause rule encourages litigation and shifts the balance unduly in favor of contestants. See Burch v. George, 866 P.2d 92 (Cal. 1994) (California provides a procedure for a declaratory judgment that a particular suit will thwart the intention of the testator and trigger a no-contest clause, which will be strictly enforced). See generally Martin D. Begleiter, Anti-Contest Clauses: When You Care Enough to Send the Final Threat, 26 Ariz. St. L.J. 629 (1994) (arguing in favor of the minority rule). See also Gerry W. Beyer, Rob G. Dickinson & Kenneth L. Wake, The Fine Art of Intimidating Disgruntled Beneficiaries with In Terrorem Clauses, 51 SMU L. Rev. 225 (1998); Annot., 23 A.L.R.4th 369 (1983, rev. 2003).

The lawyer with a client who wishes to contest a will with a no-contest clause must investigate the local law carefully because there are subtle differences from state to state, particularly as to what constitutes a "contest." See Restatement (Third), supra, statutory and reporter's notes to §8.5.

NOTE: BEQUESTS TO ATTORNEYS

Undue influence. The will in Lipper v. Weslow was drafted by Mrs. Block's son, an attorney and a principal beneficiary under the will. Many courts, concerned with the appearance of impropriety, hold that a presumption of undue influence arises when an attorney-drafter receives a legacy, except when the attorney is related to the testator. The presumption can be rebutted only by clear and convincing evidence provided by the attorney. See Clarkson v. Whitaker, 657 N.E.2d 139 (Ind. App. 1995); Kirschbaum v. Dillon, 567 N.E.2d 1291 (Ohio 1991) (citing cases).

In New York, upon probate, the surrogate must investigate any bequest to the attorney who drafted the will. The attorney must submit an affidavit explaining the

"My goodness! Your dear old uncle seems to have left everything to <u>me</u>."

Drawing by Peter Arno.

facts and circumstances of the gift, and if the surrogate is not satisfied with the explanation a hearing is held to determine whether the attorney's bequest was the result of undue influence.

In re Henderson, 605 N.E.2d 323 (N.Y. 1992), the court held that a substantial bequest to the testator's long-time attorney, who suggested the client employ another lawyer to draft the will, which she did, was also subject to judicial inquiry since it could be inferred from the facts that the client did not have the full benefit of independent counsel. "Such scrutiny is especially important when attorney-beneficiaries are involved, since the intensely personal nature of the attorney-client relationship, coupled with the specialized training and knowledge that attorneys have, places attorneys in positions that are uniquely suited to exercising a powerful influence over their clients' decision." Id. at 327. The court rejected a per se rule that would create a presumption of undue influence whenever a bequest is given an attorney with whom the testator has had a professional relationship in the past. The court thought such a rule could unduly restrict freedom of testators to give property to attorneys who have been kind and helpful, "evok[ing] reciprocal sentiments of gratitude and affection" by the client.

In California, after a Los Angeles Times reporter investigated the practices of a lawyer who opened up an office adjacent to Leisure World, where he acquired 7,000 clients and prepared numerous wills leaving him millions of dollars, the legislature enacted a statute invalidating any bequest to a lawyer who drafts the will unless the lawyer is related by blood or marriage to the testator. Cal. Prob. Code §21350 (2004). There is an exception permitting a bequest to a nonrelated lawyer-drafter if the client consults an independent lawyer who attaches to the document a "Certificate of Independent Review," which must state that the reviewing lawyer concludes the gift is not due to undue influence, fraud, or duress. Id. §21351(b). For the investigation that brought on this statute, see Davan Maharaj, Lawyer Inherited Millions in Stock, Cash from Clients, L.A. Times, Nov. 22, 1992, at A1.

Unethical conduct. Should an attorney who draws a will containing a bequest to herself be subjected to disciplinary action? See Model Rules of Prof. Conduct R. 1.8(c) (1983) (adopted in a majority of states):

CONFLICT OF INTEREST: PROHIBITED TRANSACTIONS

A lawyer shall not prepare an instrument giving the lawyer or a person related to the lawyer as parent, child, sibling, or spouse any substantial gift from a client, including a testamentary gift, except where the client is related to the donee.

The comment to Rule 1.8 further advises:

A lawyer may accept a gift from a client, if the transaction meets general standards of fairness. For example, a simple gift such as a present given at a holiday or as a token of appreciation is permitted. If effectuation of a substantial gift requires preparing a legal instrument such as a will or conveyance, however, the client should have the detached advice that another lawyer can provide. Paragraph (c) recognizes an exception where the client is a relative of the donee or the gift is not substantial.

John D. Randall, president of the American Bar Association in 1959-1960, was disbarred by the Iowa Supreme Court in 1979 for naming himself the beneficiary of a client's $4.5 million estate. Committee on Prof. Ethics v. Randall, 285 N.W.2d 161 (Iowa 1979). In Attorney Griev. Commn. v. Brooke, 821 A.2d 414 (Md. 2003), an attorney was suspended from practice indefinitely for drafting a will for a longtime friend that gave the lawyer all of the estate even though the court determined that there had been no undue influence. Because the friend did not have the advice of independent counsel, the court held that the lawyer-beneficiary violated Rule 1.8(c).

For further discussion, see Joseph W. de Furia, Jr., Testamentary Gifts from Client to the Attorney-Draftsman: From Probate Presumption to Ethical Prohibition, 66 Neb. L. Rev. 695 (1987); Ronald C. Link, Developments Regarding the Professional Responsibility of the Estate Administration Lawyer: The Effect of the Model Rules of Professional Conduct, 26 Real Prop., Prob. & Tr. J. 1 (1991); William M. McGovern, Jr., Undue Influence and Professional Responsibility, 28 Real Prop., Prob. & Tr. J. 643 (1994).

In re Will of Moses

Supreme Court of Mississippi, 1969
227 So. 2d 829

[Fannie Traylor Moses was thrice married; each of her husbands died. During the second marriage, she struck up a friendship with Clarence Holland, an attorney 15 years her junior. After the death of her third husband, Holland became Mrs. Moses's lover as well as attorney, and this relationship continued for several years until Mrs. Moses died at age 57. During the six or seven years preceding her death, Mrs. Moses suffered from serious heart trouble, had a breast removed because of cancer, and became an alcoholic. Three years before death she made a will devising almost all of her property to Holland. This will was drafted by a lawyer, Dan Shell, who had no connection with Holland, and who did not tell Holland of the will. Mrs. Moses's closest relative was an elder sister. The sister attacked the will on the ground of undue influence. The chancellor found undue influence and denied probate. Holland appealed.]

SMITH, J.   A number of grounds are assigned for reversal. However, appellant's chief argument is addressed to the proposition that even if Holland, as Mrs. Moses' attorney, occupied a continuing fiduciary relationship with respect to her on May 26, 1964, the date of the execution of the document under which he claimed her estate, the presumption of undue influence was overcome because, in making the will, Mrs. Moses had the independent advice and counsel of one entirely devoted to her interests. It is argued that, for this reason, a decree should be entered here reversing the chancellor and admitting the 1964 will to probate. . . .

The evidence supports the chancellor's finding that the confidential or fiduciary relationship which existed between Mrs. Moses and Holland, her attorney, was a subsisting and continuing relationship, having . . . ended only with Mrs. Moses' death. Moreover, its effect was enhanced by the fact that throughout this period, Holland was in almost daily attendance upon Mrs. Moses on terms of the utmost intimacy. There was strong evidence that this aging woman, seriously ill, disfigured by surgery, and hopelessly addicted to alcoholic excesses, was completely bemused by the constant and amorous attentions of Holland, a man 15 years her junior. There was testimony too indicating that she entertained the pathetic hope that he might marry her.[7] Although the evidence was not without conflict and was, in some of its aspects, circumstantial, it was sufficient to support the finding that the relationship existed on May 26, 1964, the date of the will tendered for probate by Holland.

The chancellor's factual finding of the existence of this relationship on that date is supported by evidence and is not manifestly wrong. Moreover, he was correct in his conclusion of law that such relationship gave rise to a presumption of undue influence which could be overcome only by evidence that, in making the 1964 will, Mrs. Moses had acted upon the independent advice and counsel of one entirely devoted to her interest.

Appellant takes the position that there was undisputed evidence that Mrs. Moses, in making the 1964 will did, in fact, have such advice and counsel. He relies upon the testimony of the attorney in whose office that document was prepared to support his assertion.

___

7. The court perhaps has forgotten the wife of Bath in Chaucer's Canterbury Tales, who had five husbands, the last one 20 years younger than she. She craved another young and healthy husband who could satisfy her hearty sexual appetites, and no reader of Chaucer can doubt she got one. — Eds.

This attorney was and is a reputable and respected member of the bar, who had no prior connection with Holland and no knowledge of Mrs. Moses' relationship with him. He had never seen nor represented Mrs. Moses previously and never represented her afterward. He was acquainted with Holland and was aware that Holland was a lawyer.

A brief summary of his testimony, with respect to the writing of the will, follows:

Mrs. Moses had telephoned him for an appointment and had come alone to his office on March 31, 1964. She was not intoxicated and in his opinion knew what she was doing. He asked her about her property and "marital background." He did this in order, he said, to advise her as to possible renunciation by a husband. She was also asked if she had children in order to determine whether she wished to "pretermit them." As she had neither husband nor children this subject was pursued no further. He asked as to the values of various items of property in order to consider possible tax problems. He told her it would be better if she had more accurate descriptions of the several items of real and personal property comprising her estate. No further "advice or counsel" was given her.

On some later date, Mrs. Moses sent in (the attorney did not think she came personally and in any event he did not see her), some tax receipts for purposes of supplying property descriptions. He prepared the will and mailed a draft to her. Upon receiving it, she telephoned that he had made a mistake in the devise of certain realty, in that he had provided that a relatively low valued property should go to Holland rather than a substantially more valuable property which she said she wanted Holland to have. He rewrote the will, making this change, and mailed it to her, as revised, on May 21, 1964. On the one occasion when he saw Mrs. Moses, there were no questions and no discussion of any kind as to Holland being preferred to the exclusion of her blood relatives. Nor was there any inquiry or discussion as to a possible client-attorney relationship with Holland. The attorney-draftsman wrote the will according to Mrs. Moses' instructions and said that he had "no interest in" how she disposed of her property. He testified "I try to draw the will to suit their purposes and if she (Mrs. Moses) wanted to leave him (Holland) everything she had, that was her business as far as I was concerned. I was trying to represent her in putting on paper in her will her desires, and it didn't matter to me to whom she left it . . . I couldn't have cared less."

When Mrs. Moses returned to the office to execute the will, the attorney was not there and it was witnessed by two secretaries. . . .

The attorney's testimony supports the chancellor's finding that nowhere in the conversations with Mrs. Moses was there touched upon in any way the proposed testamentary disposition whereby preference was to be given a nonrelative to the exclusion of her blood relatives. There was no discussion of her relationship with Holland, nor as to who her legal heirs might be, nor as to their relationship to her, after it was discovered that she had neither a husband nor children.

It is clear from his own testimony that, in writing the will, the attorney-draftsman, did no more than write down, according to the forms of law, what Mrs. Moses told him. There was no meaningful independent advice or counsel touching upon the area in question and it is manifest that the role of the attorney in writing the will, as it relates to the present issue, was little more than that of scrivener. The chancellor was justified in holding that this did not meet the burden nor overcome the presumption.

The sexual morality of the personal relationship is not an issue. However, the intimate nature of this relationship is relevant to the present inquiry to the extent that its existence, under the circumstances, warranted an inference of undue influence, extending and augmenting that which flowed from the attorney-client relationship. Particularly is this true when viewed in the light of evidence indicating its employment for the personal aggrandizement of Holland.

. . . [T]he decree of the chancery court will be affirmed.

ROBERTSON, J. (dissenting).   . . . Mrs. Fannie T. Moses was the active manager of commercial property in the heart of Jackson, four apartment buildings containing ten rental units, and a 480-acre farm until the day of her death. All of the witnesses conceded that she was a good businesswoman, maintaining and repairing her properties with promptness and dispatch, and paying her bills promptly so that she would get the cash discount. She was a strong personality and pursued her own course, even though her manner of living did at times embarrass her sisters and estranged her from them.

It was not contended in this case that Holland was in any way actively concerned with the preparation or execution of the will. Appellees rely solely upon the finding of the chancellor that there were suspicious circumstances. However, the suspicious circumstances listed by the chancellor in his opinion had nothing whatsoever to do with the preparation or execution of the will. These were remote antecedent circumstances having to do with the meretricious relationship of the parties, and the fact that at times Mrs. Moses drank to excess and could be termed an alcoholic, but there is no proof in this long record that her use of alcohol affected her will power or her ability to look after her extensive real estate holdings. . . .

The majority was indeed hard put to find fault with . . . [the actions of Dan Shell, the attorney who drew the will,] on behalf of his client. . . . He ascertained that Mrs. Moses was competent to make a will; he satisfied himself that she was acting of her own free will and accord, and that she was disposing of her property exactly as she wished and intended. No more is required.

There is not one iota of testimony in the voluminous record that Clarence Holland even knew of this will, much less that he participated in the preparation or execution of it. The evidence is all to the contrary. The evidence is undisputed that she executed her last will after the fullest deliberation, with full knowledge of what she was doing, and with the independent consent and advice of an experienced and competent attorney whose sole purpose was to advise with her and prepare her will exactly as she wanted it.

In January 1967, about one month before her death and some two years and eight months after she had made her will, she called W.R. Patterson, an experienced, reliable and honorable attorney who was a friend of hers, and asked him to come by her home for a few minutes. Patterson testified:

> She said, "Well, the reason I called you out here is that I've got an envelope here with all of my important papers in it, and *that includes my last will and testament*," and says, "I would like to leave them with you if you've got a place to lock them up in your desk somewhere there in your office."
>
> . . . [A]nd she said, "*Now, Dan Shell drew my will for me two or three years ago*," and she says, "*It's exactly like I want it*," and says, "*I had to go to his office two or three times to get it the way I wanted it, but this is the way I want it*, and if anything happens to me I want you to

take all these papers and give them to Dan," and she says, "He'll know what to do with them." (Emphasis added.)

What else could she have done? She met all the tests that this Court and other courts have carefully outlined and delineated. The majority opinion says that this still was not enough, that there were "suspicious circumstances" . . . , but even these were not connected in any shape, form or fashion with the preparation or execution of her will. They had to do with her love life and her drinking habits and propensities. . . .

If full knowledge, deliberate and voluntary action, and independent consent and advice have not been proved in this case, then they just cannot be proved. . . .

I think that the judgment of the lower court should be reversed and the last will and testament of Fannie T. Moses executed on May 26, 1964, admitted to probate in solemn form.

QUESTIONS

1.   Why is evidence of a sexual relationship outside of marriage admissible in undue influence cases? In In re Kelly's Estate, 46 P.2d 84, 92 (Or. 1935), the court suggested the reason was that a sexual relationship casts a suspicion of deceit and "cautions the court to examine the evidence with unusual care."

Inasmuch as a person ordinarily has a sustained sexual relationship only with a partner for whom there is considerable affection, perhaps even love, why does not evidence of such a relationship indicate that the partner is a natural object of the decedent's bounty? In view of the increase of committed couples living together without marriage, why should sensual pleasures without benefit of clergy continue to be evidence of *undue* influence? See Joseph W. de Furia, Jr., Testamentary Gifts Resulting from Meretricious Relationships: Undue Influence or Natural Benef- icence?, 64 Notre Dame L. Rev. 200 (1989); Lawrence A. Frolik, The Bio- logical Roots of the Undue Influence Doctrine: What's Love Got to Do with It?, 57 U. Pitt. L. Rev. 841 (1996).

2.   If in the *Moses* case, Fannie Moses had been a man named Frank, and Clarence had been a woman named Clara, but otherwise the facts were essentially the same, would the result be the same? See In re Launius, 507 So. 2d 27 (Miss. 1987) (sexual relationship between male testator and younger female beneficiary did not give rise to confidential relationship because testator was "strong-willed and emotionally and physically sound at the time the will was executed"; legal test used partly overruled in Mullins v. Ratcliff, 515 So. 2d 1183 (Miss. 1987)); Arlene Derenski & Sally B. Landsberg, The Age Taboo: Older Women-Younger Men Relationships (1981). See also Francine du Plessix Gray, The New "Older Woman," N.Y. Times, §7 (Book Review), Jan. 15, 1978, at 3:

Americans' traditional unease with [Older Woman and Younger Man] alliances is not only based on a complex network of puritanical hangups but vastly reinforced by our literature. There is a remarkable dearth of these liaisons in British or American fic- tion; and novels, for better or for worse, have always fueled our most passionate romantic fantasies and erotic expectations. . . . [The] absence [of the Older Woman and Younger Man theme] from English language fiction since the birth of the novel two and a half centuries ago is most striking compared to its abundant presence on the Continent. The theme is central to . . . classics of European literature, . . . and most particularly the work of Colette. . . .

After centuries of calmly approving the myriad 70-year-old Dr. Spocks who take 24-year-old women to their marriage beds, and condoning vast networks of sugar daddies who heap trinkets on their molls, are we any readier for Colette's radically anti-Calvinist vision of the passive, unemployed younger man who ripens in the shelter of a powerful older woman? In the light of the new egalitarianism, in what sense is it more suspect to be a gigolo, or a man of modest employment living with a successful older woman, than to be a kept woman or a housewife? The taboos still hovering over such relationships may never be lifted until all present notions of traditional "masculinity" and of male dominance are radically demythologized. [Id.]

IN RE KAUFMANN'S WILL, 247 N.Y.S.2d 664 (App. Div. 1964), aff'd, 205 N.E.2d 864 (N.Y. 1965): In 1948, at the age of 34, Robert Kaufmann, a multi-millionaire by inheritance, seeking an independent life away from his family, moved from Washington to New York City. There he took up oil painting, engaged a psychoanalyst, the eminent and sought-after Dr. Janet Rioch, and met Walter Weiss, age 39, a man without material assets of consequence. Within a year after their meeting, Robert employed Walter as his financial consultant and had all his records moved to New York from the Kaufmann family office in Washington. More or less at the same time Walter moved into Robert's apartment. In 1951 Robert bought an expensive townhouse at 42 East 74th Street. He remodeled the top floor into an office for Walter. The rest of the house was lavishly furnished as a home for Robert and Walter. Walter ran the household, overseeing the cooking, cleaning, and entertaining, answering the mail and the telephone, paying bills from Robert's bank account, recommending doctors for Robert's various complaints. Robert was a talented artist and spent much of his time painting; he opened an art gallery where he exhibited his works and those of other artists. In their social life, Robert and Walter appeared as a couple, entertaining on a grand scale and exhibiting much love, affection, and mutual esteem. (Of course that is not to say that neither had a roving eye. Once, when Robert took a young man off to Paris, Walter followed unannounced a few days later and threw the young man out of the hotel, while Robert stood by silently.) In business matters, Robert gave Walter (who had a law degree but did not practice) his complete confidence and trust. Walter took charge of Robert's bank accounts and investments as if they belonged to the both of them. The two men lived together until 1959, when Robert died unexpectedly.[8]

Beginning in 1951, Robert made wills in successive years, each will increasing Walter's share of his estate. In 1958, Robert executed a will, drafted by a prominent New York law firm, which left substantially all his property to Walter. Accompanying it was a letter addressed to Robert's family signed by Robert in

---

8. A rather similar household was The Pines, the celebrated villa occupied by Algernon Charles Swinburne, English poet, novelist, and sage, and Theodore Watts-Dunton, a country solicitor. In 1879, at the age of 42, Swinburne moved in with Watts-Dunton, who had rescued him from delirium tremens and from a house of pleasure in St. John's Wood where a couple of blondes flagellated the customers. Watts-Dunton laid down the rules, managed all of Swinburne's business affairs, ran the household, and doled out the pin money. Swinburne stayed at home and wrote. Watts-Dunton eventually married and his wife moved into The Pines with them. In 1909, Swinburne died, leaving everything to Watts-Dunton. Swinburne's family was hurt and indignant, but no one sued. Mollie Panter-Downs, At the Pines (1971).

1951 and passed along with each subsequent will. This letter might be described as a "coming out of the closet at death" letter. It stated that when Robert met Walter, Robert was "terribly unhappy, highly emotional and filled to the brim with a grandly variegated group of fears, guilt and assorted complexes." It stated that Walter encouraged Robert to submit to psychoanalysis and went on to say:

> Walter gave me the courage to start something which slowly but eventually permitted me to supply for myself everything my life had heretofore lacked: an outlet for my long-latent but strong creative ability in painting . . . , a balanced, healthy sex life which before had been spotty, furtive and destructive; an ability to reorientate myself to actual life and to face it calmly and realistically. All of this adds up to Peace of Mind. . . . I am eternally grateful to my dearest friend—best pal, Walter A. Weiss. What could be more wonderful than a fruitful, contented life and who more deserving of gratitude now, in the form of an inheritance, than the person who helped most in securing that life? I cannot believe my family could be anything else but glad and happy for my own comfortable self-determination and contentment and equally grateful to the friend who made it possible.
>
> Love to you all,
Bob

In 1952, Robert executed a document granting Walter exclusive power over Robert's corporeal remains and the authority to make all funeral arrangements; in addition, in the event Robert was incapacitated, Walter was granted the power to consent in Robert's behalf to the performance of any operation he deemed necessary after consultation with Robert's physicians. The instrument provided that Walter was to act as "though he were my nearest relative . . . and that his instructions and consents shall be controlling, regardless of who may object to them." The document in effect gave Walter the power that a legal spouse would have over these matters.

Robert's family in Washington deeply resented Walter's presence and his interfering business advice about the family-owned Kay Jewelry Stores, in which Robert was a major shareholder. The 1951 letter appeared to confirm the family's suspicion that a homosexual relationship existed between Robert and Walter. Upon Robert's death, his brother Joel sued to have the 1958 will set aside on the ground of undue influence. In his pretrial deposition, Walter denied that a homosexual relationship existed between the two men, but the appellate judges, and probably the jury as well, suspected that this was a lie. Walter did not take the stand at the trial and, therefore, was not subject to cross-examination.

After two jury trials, both finding undue influence, the majority of the appellate division agreed that the evidence was sufficient "to find that the instrument of June 19, 1958, was the end result of an unnatural, insidious influence operating on a weak-willed, trusting, inexperienced Robert whose natural warm family attachment had been attenuated by false accusations against Joel, subtle flattery suggesting an independence he had not realized and which, in fact, Weiss had stultified, and planting in Robert's mind the conviction that Joel and other members of the family were resentful of and obstructing his drive for independence." Although the earlier wills were not directly in issue, the majority thought the undue influence began before 1951 and tainted all the prior wills and gifts to Walter. The letter signed by Robert, mentioned above, was deemed to be "cogent evidence of his complete domination by Weiss," as was Walter's termination of Robert's dalliance in Paris while Robert stood mute.

The court of appeals affirmed, saying:

> Where, as here, the record indicates that testator was pliable and easily taken advantage of, as proponent admitted, that there was a long and detailed history of dominance and subservience between them, that testator relied exclusively upon proponent's knowledge and judgment in the disposition of almost all of the material circumstances affecting the conduct of his life, and proponent is willed virtually the entire estate, we consider that a question of fact was presented concerning whether the instrument offered for probate was the free, untrammeled and intelligent expression of the wishes and intentions of testator or the product of the dominance of the beneficiary.

QUESTION AND NOTES

1. If, in In re Kaufmann's Will, Robert had been a woman named Roberta, would the result be the same? What if the cohabitants had been married? See Jeffrey G. Sherman, Undue Influence and the Homosexual Testator, 42 U. Pitt. L. Rev. 225, 239-248 (1981). See also Ray D. Madoff, Unmasking Undue Influence, 81 Minn. L. Rev. 571 (1997), arguing that the undue influence doctrine denies freedom of testation to those testators who deviate from prescribed testamentary norms in failing to provide for their families, and E. Gary Spitko, Gone But Not Conforming: Protecting the Abhorrent Testator from Majoritarian Cultural Norms Through Minority Culture Arbitration, 49 Case W. Res. L. Rev. 275 (1999), suggesting that a homosexual testator be permitted to direct that any will contest be adjudicated by an arbitrator appointed by the testator.

For an analysis of *Kaufmann*, applying psychoanalytic theory and concluding that Walter consciously and wrongfully manipulated the transference to him that gave Robert emotional security, see Thomas L. Shaffer, Death, Property, and Lawyers 243-257 (1970). But compare Theodor Reik, Masochism in Modern Man 159, 164 (1941), pointing out that it takes two to tango and that, contrary to appearances, it is the submissive partner who calls the tune and sets the limits of what the dominant one can do.

2. For a case upholding a jury finding of no undue influence, on facts similar to those in *Kaufmann*, see Estate of Sarabia, 270 Cal. Rptr. 560 (App. 1990). See also Evans v. May, 923 S.W.2d 712 (Tex. App. 1996), holding no undue influence where one man left all his estate to his male "lifemate," with whom he had lived for 30 years.

AN EXERCISE IN LAWYERING:
SEWARD JOHNSON'S ESTATE

The facts of this exercise are taken from David Margolick's book, Undue Influence: The Epic Battle for the Johnson & Johnson Fortune (1993). The book offers a fascinating glimpse of estates and trusts practice by New York lawyers

*Seward and Basia frolicking at Children's Bay Cove, the Bahamas,
mid-1970s.*

for the very rich in a compelling story of greed and wasted lives of people with too
much money.

The story begins in 1968, when Barbara Piasecka, 31, a pretty and shapely
immigrant from Poland, secured a job as a cook at the New Jersey estate of
J. Seward Johnson, the fabulously rich heir to the Johnson & Johnson Company
fortune (baby powder, Band-Aids, and so on). As a cook, Barbara (called Basia—
BAH-sha—by her friends) turned out to be a disaster, but Essie Johnson, Seward's
wife, took pity on her and made her an upstairs maid, where she caught the eye of
Essie's randy septuagenarian husband. Seward, who nearly ran his boat aground
when he spotted her sunning in a bikini, hired Basia as his personal art curator (she
had studied art history in Poland), made her his scuba partner, took her traveling
abroad, and set her up in a fancy apartment on Manhattan's Sutton Place, where he
joined her. His batteries recharged by Basia, Seward lavished gifts on her—a
$500,000 trust fund, a house on the Mediterranean, artwork, furs, and jewels.

Essie Johnson, not terribly unhappy to be rid of the philandering Seward,
agreed to a divorce for $20 million and a couple of houses. Eight days later, in
1971, Seward, age 76, and Basia, age 34, married and began the construction in
Princeton of Basia's $25 million dream house, called Jasna Polana, costing more
than any American house since William Randolph Hearst's San Simeon. One thing
about Basia, she took immediately to the swank and hauteur of *les grands riches*, and
Seward indulged her every whim.

In June 1972, Seward had Robert Myers, his Washington-based lawyer, revise
his will to increase Basia's trust to $50 million; the bulk of his estate went to Harbor

Branch Foundation, an oceanographic research center he had set up, and presided over, in Fort Pierce, Florida. He left nothing to his six children, for whom he had earlier created trusts of Johnson & Johnson stock that, if still held, would have mushroomed in value to $110 million each. Seward rarely saw his children; they returned his lack of interest; they had been omitted from his wills since the mid-1960s. He revised his will several more times, always increasing Basia's share.

Meanwhile Seward directed Basia to Shearman & Sterling, one of New York's oldest and most prestigious law firms, for her own legal work. There Basia's matters were attended to primarily by Nina Zagat, a recent graduate of Yale Law School (and better known as a co-founder of Zagat's Restaurant Survey). Nina, who was level-headed, meticulous, and deliberate, almost the opposite of the mercurial and explosive Basia, became Basia's best friend. She served the Johnsons and their foundations (including Harbor Branch) loyally, reliably, and honestly. She traveled with them on vacations, oversaw the legal work generated by their multifarious activities, and more than once extricated Basia from hot water into which her impulsive, impetuous nature had flung her. Nina had a power of attorney over Seward's bank account and paid the Johnson's bills, including millions for Basia's art and antiques purchases.

After eight years as an associate in Shearman & Sterling, Nina was passed over for partnership in 1975. She was given the option of remaining as a permanent associate, making about $115,000 a year, with the right to keep all executor's and trustee's fees she earned, which, as a partner she would have had to contribute to the firm's kitty. Not long after this snub, in 1976 Seward began fiddling around with his estate plan again. He executed a new will, much like the previous one Myers had drawn, only this time he created a $20 million trust for Basia's newly born nephew, Seward Piasecka, and Nina, not Myers, prepared the draft. Knowing that Nina had been denied partnership, Seward decided that Nina should be a co-executor and trustee and handwrote her name into his will, to serve along with Basia and Seward Junior. "I hope this will be helpful to you," he told her. And it would be helpful indeed: a $375,000 executor's fee at his death plus substantial trustee's fees annually during Basia's life.

When Shearman & Sterling took a close look at the executors' compensation clause in Seward's 1976 will (copied by Nina from the will drafted by Myers), they decided it could lead to problems. Myers had kept a tight lid on administrative costs and had limited total executors' commissions and legal fees to 1.5 percent of the estate, requiring the executors to decide how to divvy it up, and perhaps leaving little for the executors after the lawyers got paid. Nina's superiors told her she should suggest to Seward that the compensation formula be changed, so that each executor receive the full statutory percentage provided by New York law in default of a negotiated fee. And she did.

In 1981 Seward, ailing from some as yet undiagnosed condition, finally got around to following Nina's suggestion. He had Nina prepare a codicil to his will providing that she and his two other executors were each to receive the percentage given by the New York statute — 2 percent of the estate each. As Seward's estate was then worth $200 million, this would amount to executor's commissions of $4 million for each executor. In addition, Nina would collect $500,000 annually in trustee's fees for Basia's life. No record was made as to Seward's motives in vastly increasing Nina's executor's fee. The codicil was witnessed by Nina and Jay Gunther, another senior associate at Shearman & Sterling.

Only a few days after signing this codicil Seward Johnson was diagnosed with cancer.

Two years later, his health failing, Seward retired to his house in Florida with nurses around the clock and an in-residence doctor. He advised Nina that he wanted to make further changes in his will. The story continues with further estate planning changes, as told in David Margolick's book Undue Influence:

"By March 10 Nina and Gunther were back in Fort Pierce, with a newly revised will. After lunch . . . Nina went over the latest changes with Seward. Then he signed his latest will. Yet there were still more things on his mind. . . . [H]e raised a more sensitive subject. Would it be possible, he asked Nina, for any of his children to contest the will? . . .

"Nina proceeded to recite for Seward something that sounded like *The Golden Book of Will Contests.* A will, she explained, could be challenged on several grounds. One was that it had not been properly executed. Clearly, such a claim could never prevail; she and Jay Gunther had been through the drill innumerable times. Another was lack of competence; the children could say Seward had not known what he was doing when he'd signed the will. But the mere fact that they were conversing intelligently now took care of that, Nina reassured him; one had almost to be deranged to be considered incompetent. Finally, the children could claim Basia had coerced Seward into doing what he did. But claims of 'undue influence,' like claims of incompetence, rarely held up in court, particularly against a wife. In short, the children wouldn't have a leg to stand on. . . .

[On several earlier occasions, Nina had asked Seward whether his children knew they would receive nothing on his death. Always Seward assured her they did, and expected nothing. Yet until Seward broached the issue, Nina] "had never taken the threat of a will contest seriously, in part because Seward himself hadn't. Once she'd gotten back to New York, Nina hastily huddled with her Shearman & Sterling colleagues [including partner Tom Ford] to devise additional ways to safeguard what was by any standard the most important will in the firm's vault. One suggested the inclusion of an *'in terrorem'* clause. Under it, Seward would leave each child a pittance — say, a mere million or two — then threaten to take away even that if they contested things. Nina and Ford rejected that idea because Seward already had; he refused to give them anything, even to buy peace posthumously. Sensing that what they craved still more than money was paternal approval, Nina suggested killing the children with kindness. Up to now, the wills said little about them except, in so many words, that they were being left out of it. Henceforth, they would contain the following words of synthetic solace: 'It was my wish to provide my children with financial independence at an early age, and, accordingly, I created a substantial trust for each of them during my lifetime. It has been a source of pleasure to me to see my children pursue their interests independent of me and in a way that would not have been possible if I had not provided for them in this way.' It was a polite, legalistic way of saying 'You've already gotten yours. Get lost.'[9]

---

9. Margolick's book contains vignettes of the six Johnson children. Two of them were much in the news.

Seward's eldest son, Seward Johnson, Jr., who was forced out of the management of Johnson & Johnson after a lurid and humiliating divorce had fed the tabloids for months, is a well-known sculptor, who casts super-realistic life-like bronzes of people doing ordinary things (a man sitting on a bench reading a newspaper, for instance). Although scorned by the art elite as kitsch grown-up versions of baby shoes in bronze, the pieces appear to have found favor with the general public.

[On the day Seward's final will was executed, he had a slight disagreement with Nina over one of its provisions, but Nina persuaded him.] "Nina then reviewed the forty-eight-page will with Seward, piece by piece but perfunctorily; the document was basically boilerplate, and for the most part was identical to its predecessors. Seward's responses were equally cursory: a 'yes' here, an 'all right' there, a simple nod of the head. . . .

"It was already past lunchtime, and the formal signing was put off until everyone had eaten. . . . [After four o'clock, Seward was up from his afternoon nap, and so he was rolled into the living room in his wheelchair.] The time had come once more to execute a will.

"Nina began reviewing the document again. It left Basia almost everything tangible: the artwork, the airplane, the houses, Seward's clothing and personal effects, jewelry, automobiles, boats, silverware, china, livestock, and farm implements. Some $225 million went to the Barbara P. Johnson Trust, from which she could draw the income, plus up to $1 million annually of principal for herself, plus up to $20 million during her lifetime for her relatives (but only, Seward specified, if they no longer lived in a Marxist state). The will authorized Basia's trustees — Basia herself, plus Junior and Nina — to withdraw whatever they deemed appropriate for her welfare. Junior got Seward's house in Chatham plus $1 million; the other children got nothing except the solace of Nina's new more friendly disinheritance language. Anyone who'd worked for the Johnsons between five and ten years collected five thousand dollars; ten-year veterans got twice that. The rest — approximately $75 million — would be in [a] . . . trust, whose interest went to Basia for life, then, depending on how she felt at the time, either to charity, Harbor Branch, or Seward's kith and kin.

"Once again Seward said 'yes' or 'that's correct' or 'good' or simply nodded as Nina reviewed the will. When she finished, she asked Seward whether it reflected his wishes, and he said it did. She then yielded to Gunther, who turned to its last page. The document had the crisp, grainy, quality-bond feel of a newly minted dollar bill. But whoever cranked it out of Shearman & Sterling's word processor had neglected to change the 'March' left over from the previous will to 'April.' 'Can we all agree that it is April fourteenth?' Gunther asked. They did. Seward fumbled with the pen Nina had given him, then asked Basia for another, the one with which he sometimes practiced signing his name on the tablet he kept by his bed. Where the blank in 'IN WITNESS WHEREOF, I have hereunto set my hand and seal this day of March, 1983' appeared, Seward wrote '14,' his *1* wavy and perilously close to the preceding *s*. Then, with two strokes of his pen he scratched out 'March' and

---

Seward's eldest daughter, Mary Lea Johnson Ryan D'Arc Richards, whose likeness was immortalized on the Johnson baby powder can, claimed — after her father's death — to be the victim of incest with her father. When her children were young, she fed them whisky and sleeping pills to keep them quiet. When they grew up, Mary Lea sent them cocaine for Christmas. Mary Lea was a Broadway angel, backing plays, some hits (like Stephen Sondheim's Sweeney Todd and Jerry Herman's La Cage Aux Folles), some turkeys. According to Margolick, she made no bones about her kinky sexual tastes — ménages à trois, sometimes with men, sometimes with women, and a priapic chauffeur whom she shared with her second husband. When she caught the husband and the chauffeur in a plot to murder her, she divorced her husband, and the chauffeur was sent to jail.

Seward's other children stayed out of the news. But from Margolick's account they appear to be a pretty feckless lot. As Seward told a workman at Jasna Polana, only one — a son — was any good. "The others," he said, "aren't worth shit." Id. at 123. — Eds.

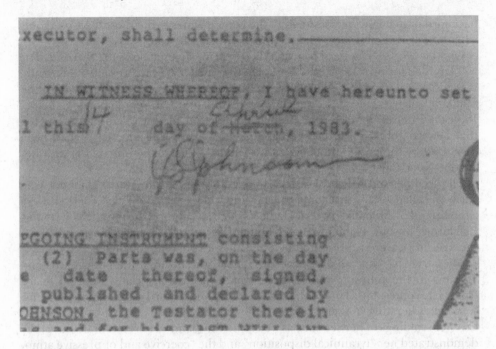

wrote 'April' on top of it. Had it appeared elsewhere, it would have been barely legible, the *A* broken in two and the *i* endowed with an extra loop; in context, it was the crabbed but comprehensible script of a very old man. Gunther asked Seward to sign the will, and it became clear that all Seward's practicing hadn't helped. He started vigorously with a robust 'JSJ . . .' then trailed off asymptotically over the course of 'ohnson.'

"'Mr. Johnson, do you declare this to be your will?' Gunther asked.

"'Yes, this is my will,' Seward replied.

"'Do you ask the two of us to sign as witnesses?' Gunther continued. 'And do you ask us to do an affidavit saying that we have done all these things?'

"'Yes,' Seward replied, 'would you be so kind?'

"Gunther and [Shearman and Sterling associate James] Hoch signed their names and addresses, thereby vouching for the soundness of Seward's mind and the propriety of the procedure. Seward sat back in his wheelchair. 'That will solve a lot of problems,' he said. It was unclear just what he meant by that, and no one pressed him to explain.

[After the execution ceremony, Seward's doctor, Dr. Schilling,] "greeted Seward by the poolside, then examined him in the bedroom. He asked the old man the usual questions: how he felt, how his night had been, how his bowels were doing. It was a routine examination, over in twenty or twenty-five minutes. 'Past two days — weaker,' the doctor wrote in his log book. 'Today more active and alert.' When Schilling completed his examination, Nina approached him in the hallway and handed him the form she'd prepared, in which he'd certify that Seward was 'of sound mind and memory and aware of his acts.' Schilling, who had never been asked to do anything like that before, perused it quickly, remarked that Seward's mental condition was 'first-rate,' and signed it. It required no deliberation; sure, there were fancier ways to test a person's mental capacity — having him count backward or to name the president of the United States — but those were used only when one had doubts, and he had none." [Id. at 140-158.]

On May 23, 1983, Seward Johnson died, leaving an estate of $402,824,972. The will was filed for probate in New York. On the value of Seward's estate at his death, Nina Zagat now stood to collect $8 million in executor's commissions and $900,000 in trustee's fees annually for Basia's life. On September 30, the six Johnson children and Harbor Branch Foundation filed a will contest, alleging that Seward Johnson lacked the capacity to make a will and that it had been produced by the undue influence of his widow, Basia, acting in concert with her lawyer, Nina Zagat.

The trial began on February 18, 1986, before Surrogate Marie Lambert, who early on called Basia "that tomato," showing where she stood. The children were represented by Milbank, Tweed, Hadley & McCloy, and Harbor Branch by Dewey, Ballantine, Bushby, Palmer & Wood, both top New York law firms. Basia and Nina, the executors, were represented by Sullivan & Cromwell, equally prestigious.

The jury trial went on and on — the nurses, the doctors, the bodyguards and servants in the Johnson homes, guests, and business associates were all heard from. The contestants claimed that Basia dominated Seward with temper tantrums, sometimes berating him and calling him "stupid old man." They further claimed that her scoldings of her servants as well as her husband were relevant because they demonstrated her "tyrannical disposition" and the "coercive and oppressive atmo-sphere" in which Seward spent his final years. Surrogate Lambert routinely admitted almost all evidence the contestants wanted in, including a tape recording of Basia screaming at a maid she fired (recorded by the maid), which electrified the trial. On the other hand, the Surrogate would not admit some of the proponents' most important evidence. She ruled that Basia's lawyers could not tell the jury about the value of the trusts Seward had set up for his children during his life (even the poorest of the siblings had trust assets of about $23 million). Nina was nervous and unappealing as a witness, searching every question for an ambiguity or misstate-ment and speaking so slowly and deliberately that the Surrogate chastised her. She was subjected to a withering cross-examination attacking her credibility, motives, and legal work. Neither she nor her gentlemanly counsel from Sullivan & Cromwell was a match for the tough Milbank attorney with the killer instinct who pictured her as Basia's agent and accomplice, devoted more to Basia's interests and her own than to her client Seward's. Basia said, "It's a pity Kafka isn't here to see this. He would understand the reality of it all."

As the trial wore on, Sullivan & Cromwell despaired of winning the verdict before the egregiously biased judge, and Milbank was frightened of losing the appeal. So, on June 2, after three months in combat, the parties decided to settle. Under the settlement each child got $6 million tax free, and Seward Junior got $7 million to make up for his lost executor's fees (he gave up the executorship when he contested the will). Harbor Branch got $20 million, less $1 million it owed Dewey, Ballantine in fees. Surrogate Lambert terminated the trusts for Basia, giving her $340 million outright, thus eliminating Nina's trustee's fees; Nina's executor's commission was slashed to $1.8 million. Milbank, Tweed collected $10 million in lawyer's fees; Sullivan & Cromwell got $7.3 million. After the set-tlement, Surrogate Lambert attended a celebration by the children and their lawyers. A juror told the judge he wasn't sure how he and his colleagues would have ruled on undue influence. "You wouldn't have had any doubts after I'd finished with my charge!" she replied.

Although she had won $340 million, and flashed a V-for-victory sign for the newspaper reporters, Basia bitterly resented having had to go through a trial, particularly one that cost her $80 million when her counsel had at the beginning advised her she had zero chance of losing. She refused to pay Shearman & Sterling's bill for $4 million and sued the firm and Nina for malpractice. But eventually, after running up more millions in lawyers' fees and tiring of litigation, Basia paid Shearman & Sterling's bill as well as Nina's $1.8 million executor's fee.

After the contest, Basia returned to Poland for a visit, where she impulsively offered to buy the Lenin Shipyard in Gdansk for $100 million and save the workers' jobs. But after worker resistance to her capitalistic reforms, the negotiations collapsed. Instead, she bought herself a Polish castle. According to Forbes Magazine, Oct. 2004, Basia is tied for 74th place among the 400 richest Americans, with $2.6 billion. Basia, who is listed as living in Monaco, is tied with Donald Trump (real estate), Stephen Spielberg (films), and Steven Jobs (Apple Computer). She is richer than the richest Rockefeller (David Rockefeller, Sr.) — a fairy tale ending for the penniless Polish farmer's daughter!

For more on the will contest, particularly the cross-examination of Nina Zagat, see Ellen J. Pollock, The Eight Million Dollar Associate, Am. Law., May 1986, at 33.

NOTES AND QUESTIONS

1.   If a will contest had been foreseeable, what omissions or mistakes did Shearman & Sterling make in preparing for it? Consider whether Seward's attorney should have taken these precautions:

(a) The attorney requests the client to write, in the client's handwriting, a letter to the attorney setting forth in detail the disposition the client wishes to make. Upon receipt of the letter, the attorney replies, detailing the consequences of the disposition on the client's heirs and emphasizing the disinheritance of one or more of them, and asks for a letter setting forth the reasons for the disposition. After receipt of this letter, the will is drafted as the client wants. The letters are kept in the attorney's files to show any prospective contestant or to enter into evidence at trial, if necessary. This procedure is recommended by Leon Jaworski, The Will Contest, 10 Baylor L. Rev. 87, 91-93 (1958). Compare the letter written by Robert Kaufmann, at his attorney's request, page 175.

(b) The attorney videotapes or records a discussion between the testator and the attorney before witnesses wherein the testator explains why he wants to dispose of the property in the manner provided in his will. The discussion may include why the testator wants to disinherit an heir (but, remember, any facts stated by the testator as justifying disinheritance may be contradicted by contestants, alleging a mistake, and the elderly and infirm often look worse on television). The witnesses execute affidavits reciting why they believe the testator is of sound mind and acting freely. Henry Ford II left a videotape that explained the dispositions in his will when he died in December 1987. See Gerry W. Beyer & William R. Buckley, Videotape and the Probate Process: The Nexus Grows, 42 Okla. L. Rev. 43 (1989); Comment, Videotaped Wills: An Evidentiary Tool or a Written Will Substitute?,

77 Iowa L. Rev. 1187 (1992). In Estate of Peterson, 439 N.W.2d 516 (Neb. 1989), and Hammer v. Powers, 819 S.W.2d 669 (Tex. Civ. App. 1991), videotapes were found to be convincing evidence of mental capacity and no undue influence.

(c) Substantial documentation of Seward's mental capacity is made each time he signs a will after his health begins to fail. If the attorney does not document mental capacity, so as to ward off a foreseeable lawsuit, it may be malpractice. Rathblott v. Levin, 697 F. Supp. 817 (D.N.J. 1988).

(d) The will contains a no-contest clause. The will gives each child $1 or $2 million, which is forfeited if they contest the will. See page 167.

(e) "The best defense against the allegation that Basia and Nina conspired to impose Basia's scheme upon Seward's will should have been a videotape or an affidavit, in which Seward explained not only why he favored Basia and disinherited his children, but also why he chose to lavish millions on avoidable executor fees for Nina." John H. Langbein, Will Contests, 103 Yale L.J. 2039, 2047-2048 (1994) (review of David Margolick, Undue Influence).

For a comprehensive discussion of precautionary measures, see Gerry W. Beyer, Estate Planning ch. 9 (2d ed. 2000). See also Dennis W. Collins, Avoiding a Will Contest—The Impossible Dream?, 34 Creighton L. Rev. 7 (2000).

2. Were any of Nina Zagat's actions unethical? Is it unethical for a lawyer to draft or witness a will naming the lawyer executor or trustee? Was it unethical for Nina to suggest to Seward that the executors' commission be increased to the amount provided by New York's statutory fee schedule? In State v. Gulbankian, 196 N.W.2d 733 (Wis. 1972), the court warned that a routine practice by an attorney to name the attorney as executor was suspicious and decided that it was unethical for the attorney-drafter to suggest, directly or indirectly, that the attorney be named as executor or lawyer for the executor. See also In re Estate of Weinstock, 351 N.E.2d 674 (N.Y. 1976).

To deal with the problem of lawyers naming themselves or an affiliated lawyer as the executor under a client's will, in 1995 New York enacted a statute that limits the lawyer-executor's commissions to one-half the statutory rate unless the testator executes a separate form, which must be witnessed, indicating that the testator understood she had the option to name someone other than the lawyer as executor and to provide for a commission less than the default statutory rate. N.Y. Sur. Ct. Proc. Act §2307-a (2004).

See generally Gerald P. Johnston, An Ethical Analysis of Common Estate Planning Practices—Is Good Business Bad Ethics?, 45 Ohio St. L.J. 57, 60-86 (1984); Paula A. Monopli, American Probate: Protecting the Public, Improving the Process 27-37 (2003); Edward D. Spurgeon & Mary J. Ciccarello, The Lawyer in Other Fiduciary Roles: Policy and Ethical Considerations, 62 Fordham L. Rev. 1357 (1994); Report of the ABA Special Committee on Professional Responsibility, Preparation of Wills and Trusts That Name Drafting Lawyer as Fiduciary, 28 Real Prop., Prob. & Tr. J. 803 (1994).

3. At one of the many will execution ceremonies, Nina Zagat did not want to be a witness. Why? Could she act as both a witness and as a lawyer for the estate? See Larkin v. Pirthauer, 700 So. 2d 182 (Fla. App. 1997); In re Estate of Giantasio, 661 N.Y.S.2d 935 (Sur. 1997); Ronald C. Link, Developments Regarding the Professional Responsibility of the Estate Administration Lawyer: The Effect of the Model Rules of Professional Conduct, 26 Real Prop., Prob. & Tr. J. 1, 93-98 (1991).

It is common in some states for the drafting attorney to name herself as attorney for the executor. Is this enforceable? Is it ethical? See Johnston, supra, at 101-114. It is also common for lawyers named as executor to hire themselves or an affiliated lawyer to handle the estate's legal work. Is this ethical? In New York, under N.Y. Surr. Ct. Proc. Act §2307-a, supra, the testator's signed acknowledgment must disclose the possibility that the executor could hire herself or an affiliated lawyer.

4.   What conflicts of interest did Shearman & Sterling have in the Johnson family affairs? Observe that Shearman & Sterling were counsel for Seward, his wife Basia, and the Harbor Branch Foundation (Seward's charitable beneficiary, which received less and less while Basia received more and more by successive wills). Should Seward and Basia have had separate lawyers for their estate planning? See American College of Trust and Estate Counsel, Commentaries on the Model Rules of Professional Conduct (3d ed. 1999) (Commentary on Model Rule 1.7); Report of the ABA Special Committee on Professional Responsibility, Comments and Recommendations on the Lawyer's Duties in Representing Husband and Wife, 28 Real Prop., Prob. & Tr. J. 765 (1994).

5.   *More on New York Surrogate's Courts.* New York Surrogates hand out millions upon millions of dollars annually to lawyers appointed as guardians ad litem for minors or incompetents. Guardians ad litem are required by New York law if a minor or incompetent person is beneficially interested in the estate. Many of these plums go to the elected surrogate's friends and supporters. Mayor Fiorello H. LaGuardia called the surrogate's court "the most expensive undertaking establishment in the world" when, during his anti-Tammany administration, he found himself unable to cut off this source of patronage to Tammany lawyers.

In the late 1980s, the federal government opened an investigation into charges that Surrogate Lambert awarded millions of dollars in fees to a small clique of lawyers in return for possible kickbacks. In her last week in office, Lambert awarded a fee of $345,000 in an estate worth $1.5 million. Several lawyers receiving her patronage were convicted of tax evasion, mail fraud, money laundering, and stealing from their wards' estates. Newsday, April 19, 1994, at A26. The prestigious New York law firms, counsel for the superrich whose wealth passes through the Manhattan Surrogate's Court, have never evinced much interest in cleaning up the abuses of guardianships. Why do you suppose not? See David Margolick, Undue Influence 313 (1993).

6.   *Mediation.* The nastiness of squabbles over estates has led to a burgeoning literature urging family mediation or arbitration of contested probate matters. These approaches have the potential to reduce litigation costs and perhaps to leave more family members speaking to each other. Should a probate court require the parties to enter into mediation (as in divorce or family disputes) before going to trial? Should you add a clause to your will requiring mediation before trial or even providing for binding arbitration of any disputes? Would courts enforce these clauses? For a discussion of these approaches, see Ray D. Madoff, Mediating Probate Disputes: A Study of Court Sponsored Programs, 38 Real Prop., Prob. & Tr. J. 697 (2004); Mary F. Radford, Advantages and Disadvantages of Mediation in Probate, Trust, and Guardianship Matters, 1 Pepp. Disp. Resol. L.J. 241 (2002); E. Gary Spitko, Gone but Not Conforming: Protecting the Abhorrent Testator from Majoritarian Cultural Norms Through Minority-Culture Arbitration, 49 Case W. Res. L. Rev. 275 (1999); Ronald Chester, Less Law, but More Justice?;

Jury Trials and Mediation as Means of Resolving Will Contests, 37 Duq. L. Rev. 173 (1999); Susan N. Gary, Mediation and the Elderly: Using Mediation to Resolve Disputes over Guardianship and Inheritance, 32 Wake Forest L. Rev. 397 (1997).

SECTION C.   FRAUD

It is fairly easy to state the test for *fraud* but often difficult to apply it to particular facts. Fraud occurs where the testator is deceived by a misrepresentation and does that which the testator would not have done had the misrepresentation not been made. It is usually said that the misrepresentation must be made with both the *intent* to deceive the testator and the *purpose* of influencing the testamentary disposition. A provision in a will procured by fraud is invalid. The remaining portion of the will stands unless the fraud goes to the entire will or the portions invalidated by fraud are inseparable from the rest of the will.

Where the probate court cannot do justice by refusing probate, the will may be probated and then a court with equity powers can impose a constructive trust on one or more of the beneficiaries to remedy the unjust enrichment caused by the fraud.

If fraud occurs in the testamentary setting, it is usually either fraud in the inducement or fraud in the execution. *Fraud in the inducement* occurs when a person misrepresents facts, thereby causing the testator to execute a will, to include particular provisions in the wrongdoer's favor, or to refrain from executing or revoking a will. Thus:

> *Case 1.* O's heir apparent, H, induces O not to execute a will in favor of A by promising O that H will convey the property to A. At the time H makes the promise, H has no intent to convey the property to A. This is fraud in the inducement. If, on the other hand, at the time of his promise H had intended to convey the property to A, but H had changed his mind after O's death and had refused to convey to A, no fraud is involved. However, A still may be able to recover from H on the theory of a secret trust. See page 532.

Questions of whether the legacy is the fruit of the fraud are particularly tricky. A fraudulently procured inheritance or bequest is invalid only if the testator would not have left the inheritance or made the bequest had the testator known the true facts. The interesting question, of course, is: What would the testator have done if the true facts had been known?

Estate of Carson, 194 P. 5 (Cal. 1920), is a dramatic illustration of the problem. In this case one J. Gamble Carson went through a marriage ceremony with Alpha O. Carson, which she believed was a real wedding. After living together thereafter happily for a year, Alpha died, devising most of her estate "to my husband J. Gamble Carson." It then came to light that Alpha had been "seduced by a marital adventurer into a marriage with him which was no marriage in the eyes of the law because of the fact, which he concealed from her, that he had already had at least one, if not more, spouses, legal and illegal, who were still living and undivorced."

But was the devise the fruit of the fraud? That causation issue was the question. Said the court:

> Now a case can be imagined where, nothing more appearing, as in this case, than that the testatrix had been deceived into a void marriage and had never been undeceived, it might fairly be said that a conclusion that such deceit had affected a bequest to the supposed husband would not be warranted. If, for example, the parties had lived happily together for 20 years, it would be difficult to say that the wife's bequest to her supposed husband was founded on her supposed legal relation with him, and not primarily on their long and intimate association. It might well be that if undeceived at the end of that time her feeling would be, not one of resentment at the fraud upon her, but of thankfulness that she had been deceived into so many years of happiness. But, on the other hand, a case can easily be imagined where the reverse would be true. If in this case the will had been made immediately after marriage, and the testatrix had then died within a few days, the conclusion would be well-nigh irresistible, in the absence of some peculiar circumstance, that the will was founded on the supposed legal relation into which the testatrix had been deceived into believing she was entering. Between these two extreme cases come those wherein it cannot be said that either one conclusion or the other is wholly unreasonable, and in those cases the determination of the fact is for the jury. Of that sort is the present. [194 P. at 8-9.]

Fraud in the execution occurs when a person misrepresents the character or contents of the instrument signed by the testator, which does not in fact carry out the testator's intent. Thus:

> *Case 2. O*, with poor eyesight, asks her heir apparent, *H*, to bring her the document prepared for her as a will so that she can sign it. *H* brings *O* a document that is not *O*'s intended will, knowing it is not the document *O* wants. *O* signs it, believing it to be her will. This is fraud in the execution.

PUCKETT v. KRIDA, 1994 Tenn. App. LEXIS 502 (1994): Nurses Laverne Krida and Mattie Ruth Reeves were hired to provide round-the-clock care for the testator, Nancy Porch Hooper, after she returned home from being hospitalized for Alzheimer's. While under the nurses' care, Hooper's condition improved, but the nurses persuaded Hooper that her relatives were wasting her money and wanted to put her in a nursing home. Neither was true.

The trial court set aside both a deed and a will favoring the nurses as the products of fraud and undue influence. On appeal, the Court of Appeals of Tennessee affirmed, holding that the nurses had a confidential relationship with Hooper for two reasons, each sufficient on its own: (1) their status as nurses, and (2) Krida's status as Hooper's attorney-in-fact under a power of attorney. This confidential relationship, when coupled with the underlying encouragement of Hooper's false beliefs, was enough to raise a presumption of undue influence and fraud. The nurses did not successfully rebut the presumption. Said the court:

> In the instant case, the evidence shows that at the time the defendants were employed, the deceased loved her family and was very close to them. She was frugal and conservative, but entrusted the management of her financial affairs to her niece, Jean Law. The evidence is that Mrs. Law carefully managed these finances and promised to keep the deceased out of a nursing home, making every effort to do so. She never reimbursed herself for any of her expenses.

Subsequent to the defendants' employment, the deceased began to believe that Jean Law wanted to put her in a nursing home and that Ms. Law had misappropriated funds. The evidence shows that neither of these beliefs were true. The evidence further shows that these false beliefs originated with the defendants who systematically separated the deceased from her family and friends and isolated her from all those individuals with whom she had previously dealt, personally and professionally. All of this was done in order to perpetuate the fraud.

Defendants, either individually or collectively, made false statements to the deceased and concealed facts from her. The deceased was led to believe that her family wasted her money. When the defendants arrived in the deceased's life, her greatest fear was going to a nursing home. The evidence shows that these defendants suddenly began to exert control over the deceased by listening in on her telephone conversations and by deluding her into believing that her family intended to place her in a nursing home. Once this fear was planted, defendants fostered and nurtured it until the deceased firmly opposed those formerly most dear to her. The deceased was told by the defendants that her niece was wasting or misappropriating funds and was reimbursing herself for airline expenses and to rent fancy cars. Defendants told the deceased that her niece was wasting money and that the deceased would be left penniless. The defendants offered no proof to refute these statements, and the trial court found that Jean Law, the deceased's niece, kept meticulous records. When the defendants accepted employment to provide around-the-clock care for the deceased, they entered into a fiduciary or confidential relationship with her, and the defendant Krida assumed additional fiduciary obligations under the unrestricted power of attorney she obtained.

"Since frauds are generally secret [they] have to be tracked by the footprints, marks, and signs made by the perpetrators and discovered by the light of the attending facts and circumstances." Henry R. Gibson, Gibson's Suits in Chancery, §448 (William H. Inman, ed., 7th ed. 1988).

By limiting information available to the deceased and by concealing their acts from the critical examination of those whom the deceased had previously known and trusted, the defendants isolated the deceased and controlled access to her. The defendants terminated the deceased's former legal and financial relationships and arranged new ones. They made her neighbors feel unwelcome and threatened her family with legal action. They replaced her long-time tenant with a family member of one of the defendants. Furthermore, the defendants made detrimental decisions regarding the sale of the deceased's real property, to avoid contact with a realtor who had previously handled the deceased's affairs.

The dealings with the deceased's money by the defendants was irregular and unusual. Defendants offered no suitable explanation at trial to account for any of the cash funds that the deceased received while the defendant Krida managed the financial affairs.

PROBLEMS

1. Suppose *H* asks *W* for his will, intending to destroy it. *W* holds up an envelope, pretends that it contains *H*'s will, and then burns the envelope and its contents. After *H*'s death, *W* probates *H*'s will, the one she had purportedly destroyed, under which she takes *H*'s entire estate. Are *H*'s other heirs entitled to a constructive trust over so much of the assets as exceed what *W*'s intestate share would have been? See Brazil v. Silva, 185 P. 174 (Cal. 1919).

2. *T*'s first will devised everything to her favorite niece, Jean, who lived in a distant city. *T*'s second will, executed in the hospital two days before she died,

revoked her prior will and devised everything to her friend, Carol. After *T*'s death a nurse in the hospital testifies that the day before the will was executed he heard Carol tell *T* that Jean had died. "In that case," *T* said, "I want you [Carol] to have everything." In fact, as Carol knew, Jean was alive. What result? See 5 Austin W. Scott, Trusts §489.3 (William F. Fratcher 4th ed. 1989).

SECTION D. DURESS

When undue influence becomes overtly coercive, it becomes *duress*. "A donative transfer is procured by duress if the wrongdoer threatened to perform or did perform a wrongful act that coerced the donor into making a donative transfer that the donor would not otherwise have made." Restatement (Third) of Property: Wills and Other Donative Transfers §8.3(c) (2003). The law invalidates transfers compelled by duress.

Latham v. Father Divine
Court of Appeals of New York, 1949
299 N.Y. 22, 85 N.E.2d 168, 11 A.L.R.2d 802

DESMOND, J. The amended complaint herein has, in response to a motion under rule 106 of the Rules of Civil Practice, been dismissed for insufficiency. Its principal allegations are these: plaintiffs are first cousins, but not distributees [next of kin], of Mary Sheldon Lyon, who died in October, 1946, leaving a will, executed in 1943, which gave almost her whole estate to defendant Father Divine,[10] leader of a religious cult, and to two corporate defendants in some way connected with that cult, and to an individual defendant (Patience Budd) said to be one of Father Divine's active followers; that said will has been, after a

---

10. Father Divine, a charismatic religious leader during the Depression who proclaimed his own divinity, attracted thousands of believers, mostly African American, but some, like Mary Sheldon Lyon, white. Whatever the merits of his claim, Father Divine was a master of theater. His inspirational sermons at a Harlem church roused his followers to spirited expression; his exuberant and melodious services were standing room only. Father Divine went beyond the spiritual; he preached racial equality and social action against segregation. He established communes ("heavens") and religious cooperatives around the country, often in white neighborhoods, where African Americans from the ghetto could move to find work and food. Father Divine taught there was only one race, no "Negro" and "white"; people just had darker or lighter complexions. The press of the time disparaged Father Divine as a con man of the cloth. Yet, in the last few decades, scholars searching for the roots of the African American churches' commitment to social action have come to reevaluate Father Divine. Many now view him as an influential and serious religious leader who gave his followers a feeling of goodness and worth, who crystallized the commitment of African American churches to the struggle for racial justice, and who stuck his thumb in the eye of the white establishment: He rode around in a chauffeured Rolls-Royce or, alternatively, a Duesenberg, inhabited the fanciest houses, hosted sumptuous feasts, and claimed for African Americans every perquisite of rich whites. See Jill M. Watts, God, Harlem U.S.A.: The Father Divine Story (1992); Robert Weisbrot, Father Divine and the Struggle for Racial Equality (1983).

The turn in Father Divine's fortunes, which transformed him from a minor religious figure into an adored incarnation of God, came as a result of a brush with the law in 1932. Father Divine had bought a large house in Sayville on the south shore of Long Island. On Sundays, flocks of the faithful from Harlem gathered there for some joyous prayer sessions. The white neighbors objected. Father Divine was arrested for disturbing the peace and conducting a public nuisance. This event was picked

contest instituted by distributees, probated under a compromise agreement with the distributees, by the terms of which agreement, to which plaintiffs were not parties, the defendants just above referred to will receive a large sum from the estate; that after the making of said will, decedent on several occasions expressed "a desire and a determination to revoke the said will, and to execute a new will by which the plaintiffs would receive a substantial portion of the estate," "that shortly prior to the death of the deceased she had certain attorneys draft a new will in which the plaintiffs were named as legatees for a very substantial amount, totalling approximately $350,000"; that "by reason of the said false representations, the said undue influence and the said physical force" certain of the defendants "prevented the deceased from executing the said new Will"; that, shortly before decedent's death, decedent again expressed her determination to execute the proposed new will which favored plaintiffs, and that defendants "thereupon conspired to kill, and did kill, the deceased by means of a surgical operation performed by a doctor engaged by the defendants without the consent or knowledge of any of the relatives of the deceased."

Nothing is better settled than that, on such a motion as this, all the averments of the attacked pleading are taken as true. For present purposes, then, we have a case where one possessed of a large property and having already made a will leaving it to certain persons, expressed an intent to make a new testament to contain legacies to other persons, attempted to carry out that intention by having a new will drawn which contained a large legacy to those others, but was, by means of misrepresentations, undue influence, force, and indeed, murder, prevented, by the beneficiaries named in the existing will, from signing the new one. Plaintiffs say that those facts, if proven, would entitle them to a judicial declaration, which their prayer for judgment demands, that defendants, taking under the already probated will, hold what they have so taken as constructive trustees for plaintiffs, whom decedent wished to, tried to, and was kept from, benefiting.

We find in New York no decision directly answering the question as to whether or not the allegations above summarized state a case for relief in equity. But reliable texts, and cases elsewhere, see 98 A.L.R. 477 et seq., answer it in the affirmative. Leading writers, 3 Scott on Trusts, pp. 2371-2376; 3 Bogert on Trusts and Trustees, part 1, §§473-474, 498, 499; 1 Perry on Trusts and Trustees [7th ed.], pp. 265, 371, in one form or another, state the law of the subject to be about as it is expressed in Comment i under section 184 of the Restatement of the Law of Restitution: "*Preventing revocation of will and making new will.* Where a devisee or legatee under a will already executed prevents the testator by fraud,

---

up by the national press. Father Divine was pictured as a martyr to racial prejudice. At trial, the jury found Father Divine guilty as charged. Some of Father Divine's partisans warned the judge that if he sent Father Divine to jail something terrible would happen to him. The judge, unheeding, gave Father Divine the maximum sentence of a year in jail. Three days later, the judge keeled over and died. "When the warden and the guards found out about it in the middle of the night," writes Professor Henry Louis Gates, Jr., "they raced to Father Divine's cell and woke him up. Father Divine, they said, your judge just dropped dead of a heart attack. Without missing a beat, Father Divine lifted his head and told them: 'I *hated* to do it.'" Henry L. Gates, Jr., Whose Canon Is It Anyway?, N.Y. Times, Feb. 20, 1989, §7 (Book Review), at 1. Although the story has been questioned, its repetition established Father Divine — among the believers — as an authentic voice of God.

Father Divine left New York in the 1950s and retired to a 72-acre estate outside Philadelphia. His apparent powers of retribution faded. Judge Desmond, who wrote the opinion in *Latham*, died in 1987, at the age of 91. — Eds.

Father Divine, calling the faithful to dinner.

duress or undue influence from revoking the will and executing a new will in favor of another or from making a codicil, so that the testator dies leaving the original will in force, the devisee or legatee holds the property thus acquired upon a constructive trust for the intended devisee or legatee."

A frequently-cited case is Ransdel v. Moore, 53 N.E. 767, 771 (Ind. 1899), where, with listing of many authorities, the rule is given thus: "when an heir or devisee in a will prevents the testator from providing for one for whom he would have provided but for the interference of the heir or devisee, such heir or devisee will be deemed a trustee, by operation of law, of the property, real or personal, received by him from the testator's estate, to the amount or extent that the defrauded party would have received had not the intention of the deceased been interfered with. This rule applies also when an heir prevents the making of a will or deed in favor of another, and thereby inherits the property that would otherwise have been given such other person." To the same effect, see 4 Page on Wills [3d ed.], p. 961.

While there is no New York case decreeing a constructive trust on the exact facts alleged here, there are several decisions in this court which, we think, suggest such a result and none which forbids it. Matter of O'Hara's Will, 95 N.Y. 403 (1884); Trustees of Amherst College v. Ritch, 45 N.E. 876 (N.Y. 1897); Edson v. Bartow, 48 N.E. 541 (N.Y. 1897), and Ahrens v. Jones, 62 N.E. 666 (N.Y. 1902), which need not be closely analyzed here as to their facts, all announce, in one form or another, the rule that, where a legatee has taken property under a will, after agreeing outside the will, to devote that property to a purpose intended and declared by the testator, equity will enforce a constructive trust to effectuate that purpose, lest there be a fraud on the testator. In Williams v. Fitch, 18 N.Y. 546 (1859), a similar result was achieved in a suit for money had and received. In each of those four cases first above cited in this paragraph, the particular fraud consisted of the legatee's failure or refusal to carry out the testator's designs, after tacitly or expressly promising so to do. But we do not think that a breach of such an engagement is the only kind of fraud which will impel equity to action. A constructive trust will be erected whenever necessary to satisfy the demands of justice. Since a constructive trust is merely "the formula through which the conscience of equity finds expression," Beatty v. Guggenheim Exploration Co., 122 N.E. 378, 380 (N.Y. 1919) . . . , its applicability is limited only by the inventiveness of men who find new ways to enrich themselves unjustly by grasping what should not belong to them. Nothing short of true and complete justice satisfies equity, and always assuming these allegations to be true, there seems no way of achieving total justice except by the procedure used here. . . .

This is not a proceeding to probate or establish the will which plaintiffs say testatrix was prevented from signing. . . . The will Mary Sheldon Lyon did sign has been probated and plaintiffs are not contesting, but proceeding on, that probate, trying to reach property which has effectively passed thereunder. . . .

We do not agree with appellants that Riggs v. Palmer, 22 N.E. 188 (N.Y. 1889), completely controls our decision here. That was the famous case where a grandson, overeager to get the remainder interest set up for him in his grandfather's will, murdered his grandsire. After the will had been probated, two daughters of the testator who, under the will, would take if the grandson should predecease testator, sued and got judgment decreeing a constructive trust in their favor. It may be, as respondents assert, that the application of Riggs v. Palmer, supra, here would benefit not plaintiffs, but this testator's distributees. We need not pass on that now. But Riggs v. Palmer, supra, is generally helpful to appellants, since it forbade the grandson profiting by his own wrong in connection with a will; and, despite an already probated will and the Decedent Estate Law, Riggs v. Palmer, supra, used the device or formula of constructive trust to right the attempted wrong, and prevent unjust enrichment. . . .

This suit cannot be defeated by any argument that to give plaintiffs judgment would be to annul those provisions of the Statute of Wills requiring due execution by the testator. Such a contention, if valid, would have required the dismissal in a number of the suits herein cited. The answer is in Ahrens v. Jones, 62 N.E. at 668, supra:

> The trust does not act directly upon the will by modifying the gift, for the law requires wills to be wholly in writing; but it acts upon the gift itself as it reaches the possession of the legatee, or as soon as he is entitled to receive it. The theory is that the will has full effect by passing an absolute legacy to the legatee, and that then equity, in order to defeat fraud, raises a trust in favor of those intended to be benefited by the testator, and compels the legatee, as a trustee ex maleficio, to turn over the gift to them.

The judgment of the Appellate Division, insofar as it dismissed the complaint herein, should be reversed, and the order of Special Term affirmed, with costs in this court and in the Appellate Division.

NOTES

1.   Another view of the contest of Mary Sheldon Lyon's will is presented by a biographer of Father Divine: Sara Harris, Father Divine 278-281 (1953). Harris says that Mary Sheldon Lyon was a devotee of Father Divine from 1938 to 1946 and took the spiritual name of Peace Dove. "She was sweet goodness personified. That was why, when she attended banquets, she was always granted a holy seat at God's own table. That was why the followers made a fuss over her." Harris reports that, after Father Divine lost in the court of appeals and after subsequent lower court rulings adverse to him, a settlement was reached giving Father Divine a small fraction of the amount bequeathed him. Harris suggests that the court rulings were motivated, at least in part, by racial prejudice against Father Divine and a belief that his church (called a "cult" by the court) was not quite a legitimate religious group.

2.   A constructive trust is sometimes said to be a "fraud-rectifying" trust. But a constructive trust may be imposed where no fraud is involved if the court thinks that unjust enrichment would result if the person retained the property. Moreover, a constructive trust is not really a trust but rather is an equitable remedy. As Judge Cardozo, speaking for the Court of Appeals of New York, said: "A constructive trust is the formula through which the conscience of equity finds expression. When property has been acquired in such circumstances that the holder of the legal title may not in good conscience retain the beneficial interest, equity converts him into a trustee." Beatty v. Guggenheim Exploration Co., 122 N.E. 378, 386 (N.Y. 1919). Once converted into a constructive trustee, the holder of the property must transfer it to the constructive beneficiary. Thus, to repeat, the constructive trust is a remedy that employs the language of trusteeship. It is not itself a trust in which property is managed by a trustee for a beneficiary subject to a fiduciary obligation. On constructive trusts imposed where there is interference with willmaking, see 5 Austin W. Scott, Trusts §§489-489.6 (William F. Fratcher 4th ed. 1989).

3.   In Pope v. Garrett, 211 S.W.2d 559 (Tex. 1948), some, but not all, of Carrie Simmons's expectant heirs "by physical force or by creating a disturbance" prevented Carrie from executing a will in favor of her friend, Claytonia Garrett. Shortly after this incident, Carrie lapsed into a coma and died. The court imposed a constructive trust in favor of Claytonia, not only on the heirs who had participated in the disturbance but also on the innocent heirs. The court reasoned that the innocent heirs would be unjustly enriched if they were permitted to keep the property since, but for the wrongful acts, they would have inherited nothing. See Scott, supra, §489.5.

4.   Observe that if, in *Latham*, a constructive trust were to be imposed on Father Divine's churches, the court would *in effect* be distributing property according to a completely unexecuted will, a will that Mary Lyon might never have signed or, having signed, might later revoke. Keep this in mind as you consider the cases in the next chapter, where courts refuse to give effect to signed wills clearly intended as wills, but defectively executed for some reason. In these cases there is far more certainty than in *Latham* that the testator intended the document to be his or her will.

SECTION E.   TORTIOUS INTERFERENCE WITH EXPECTANCY

In Latham v. Father Divine, supra, the plaintiffs asked for a constructive trust to be imposed upon the defendants to rectify alleged fraud or undue influence. Another theory that can be used is tortious interference with an expectancy or intentional interference with economic relations. Restatement (Second) of Torts §774B (1979) includes intentional interference with an expected inheritance or gift as a valid cause of action. This theory extends to expected inheritances the protection courts have accorded commercial expectancies, such as the prospect of obtaining employment or customers. Under this theory, the plaintiff must prove that the interference involved conduct tortious in itself, such as fraud, duress, or undue influence. Accordingly, the theory cannot be used when the challenge is based on the testator's mental incapacity.

MARSHALL v. MARSHALL, 275 B.R. 5 (C.D. Cal. 2002): In 1991, Anna Nicole Smith, age 24, met J. Howard Marshall, age 86 and sickly, when she gave him a lap dance at a strip club. They were married in 1994, and J. Howard, one of the richest men in Texas, died 18 months later on August 4, 1995. Lavishing gifts on Smith (whose real name is Vickie Lynn Marshall), J. Howard Marshall repeatedly promised to give her half of his considerable oil wealth.[11]

---

11. The court described not only how J. Howard made his fortune in oil but also the background of his marriage to Smith:

> Born in 1905, J. Howard attended private schools in the northeast part of the United States, including the George School, an exclusive New England prep school, Haverford College, an elite liberal arts college, and Yale Law School, one of the nation's leading law schools, from which he graduated *magna cum laude* in 1931. Although he often derided his undergraduate liberal arts education, he took great pride in the legal training he received at Yale. Upon graduation, he worked as an associate in a New York firm for two years. Subsequently he returned to Yale Law School to teach and later became the Assistant Dean. [One of the subjects he taught at Yale was wills and trusts.] . . .
>
> A. The Meeting of J. Howard and Vickie
>
> In October 1991, Vickie was dancing at Gigi's, a Houston strip club. Dan Manning was J. Howard's driver who frequented Gigi's and had seen Vickie dance. Manning and J. Howard had talked about going to a burlesque bar and in October, Manning drove his boss to Gigi's to cheer him up. Because of J. Howard's age and physical condition, he did not go out at night, and thus they arrived during the day-shift, when Vickie worked [because she was "big-boned," Anna/Vickie was denied the more lucrative evening shift]. Manning approached Vickie and asked her to dance for J. Howard. According to Vickie, when she saw J. Howard, "he looked terrible, he looked like he had lost his will to live." While Vickie danced, J. Howard tried to grab her breasts. Thus began J. Howard's aggressive pursuit of Vickie's affection. He asked her to have lunch with him the next day. . . .
>
> B. The Courtship
>
> J. Howard initially took Vickie to a restaurant hotel and ordered room service. He told Vickie . . . [personal] and funny stories about himself. When she became concerned about her job, he gave her an envelope with a thousand dollars in cash and told her not to go to work. . . . J. Howard was soon paying all of Vickie's bills. . . .
>
> Within a week of their meeting, J. Howard told Vickie that he was going to marry her. He had been re-invigorated by Vickie. . . . He called her "the light of his life." He told his attorney Harvey Sorensen numerous times that he wanted to marry Vickie.
>
> According to Vickie, J. Howard asked her to marry him "tons of times." She contends that the proposals were usually accompanied by the same assurance that once they were married, she would have half of everything he had. His proposals occurred frequently, and are confirmed by numerous friends, employees and professional associates. . . . Vickie put off J. Howard almost three years before she finally accepted his proposals.
>
> Shortly after they met, Vickie saw an ad in the newspaper to audition for *Playboy Magazine*. After meeting with a scout, Vickie was quickly hired and two weeks later was doing a test shoot in

J. Howard Marshall and Vickie Marshall (Anna Nicole Smith)
sharing a tender moment

California. In March 1992, Vickie made her *Playboy* debut, appearing on the cover. In May 1992, she was named *Playboy* Playmate of the Month.

Vickie was contacted by Guess Jeans to be part of its national advertising campaign. She became their top spokes-model for a one-year period from 1993-94. During this time, she appeared in numerous other magazines and in 1993 was named the *Playboy* Playmate of the Year. Vickie had achieved the level of international sex symbol, and was one of the most recognized print models in the world. Her stardom only encouraged J. Howard to pursue her with a newfound vigor. . . .

Vickie testified that his money was a factor in her decision to marry J. Howard, but contends that she would have married him anyway. Vickie sought security for her and her son, and what he might lack in youth, vigor, and looks, J. Howard made up for with his great wealth. Although she has often been portrayed to the Court as a gold-digger and predator, she did hold a certain regard for J. Howard, and was willing to compromise her prime modeling years for someone who showered her with gifts and offered financial security. . . .

E. Illness and Death of J. Howard . . .

[J. Howard's various ailments are recounted, as are Vickie's efforts to document their intimacy.] On another occasion, Vickie brought a tape recorder and sought to tape J. Howard. She climbed into his bed, exposed her breasts and asked J. Howard: "Do you miss your rosebuds?" . . .

On August 4, 1995, J. Howard died at the age of 90. He was survived by his two sons, his wife, and an unprecedented volume of litigation.

In sum, their lives were intertwined in need, driven by greed and lust. Nevertheless, the Court is convinced of his love for her. J. Howard referred to Vickie as the "light of my life," and the lady that saved his life. His relationship with her provided the happiest moments of his last few years. He considered Vickie his reason for living, and the joy that she brought him undoubtedly helped him live another four years. There is no question that he showered her with gifts, that he sought to protect her and provide for her.

The Court is more cautious about her love for him. J. Howard became Vickie's knight in shining armor. His help propelled her to the highest levels of stardom, something unimaginable for a girl from her background. She cherished the protection and security that he afforded her and the lavish gifts that he gave to her in order to win her affection. J. Howard used his money to get Vickie to fall in love with him, and in her own way, Vickie loved J. Howard. [275 B.R. at 11, 20-25.]

Despite the receipt of generous gifts from J. Howard, Anna/Vickie spent so heavily that, when Marshall's other relatives restricted her access to his money, she wound up in bankruptcy court. At issue in the bankruptcy proceedings was whether J. Howard's son, E. Pierce Marshall, had tortiously interfered with J. Howard's inter vivos gifts to Anna/Vickie. Among other things, Pierce depleted his father's assets, to keep them from Anna/Vickie, by purchasing deferred annuities on J. Howard's life. These annuities could be justified only if the seriously ill 90-year-old had been likely to survive for at least another five years.

In confirming the bankruptcy court's ruling in favor of Anna/Vickie, the district court awarded her $44,292,767.33 in compensatory damages, another $44,292,767.33 in punitive damages, and also reimbursement for her litigation costs.

Citing Doughty v. Morris, 871 P.2d 380 (N.M. 1994), the court applied the following test for tortious interference with her expectancy:

> A plaintiff must prove (1) the existence of an expectancy; (2) a reasonable certainty that the expectancy would have been realized but for the interference; (3) intentional interference with that expectancy; (4) tortious conduct involved with the interference; and (5) damages.

In imposing punitive damages, the court explained:

> Pierce and [lawyer Edwin] Hunter's actions of slowly draining J. Howard of assets in order to prevent a gift to Vickie were egregious in nature. What is worse, however, is that many of the documents at issue in the case were destroyed, backdated, altered, or prepared and presented to J. Howard under false pretenses. This was done in order to prevent Vickie from receiving funds, out of fear that J. Howard might sign a will or other gift instrument at Vickie's behest, and to avoid the legal consequence of important dates in J. Howard's final years including his marriage to Vickie and the appointment of a guardian ad litem to manage his affairs.
>
> The backdating and altering of the documents was done with the full knowledge of Pierce. Most of the backdated documents were prepared by [lawyer] Edwin Hunter, whose brilliant machinations on estate planning Pierce relied on to devise the necessary actions.

NOTES

1. *Aftermath.* This bankruptcy litigation, which concerned only inter vivos transfers, is but one strand of a larger web of litigation, fought also in Louisiana and Texas state courts, involving Anna Nicole Smith and her stepson Pierce Marshall, who at last report was worth $1.6 billion.

Having prevailed in much of the state court litigation, Pierce appealed the decision excerpted above. During the pendency of that appeal, Anna remained resolute, boasting that she was in the process of losing one pound for each million of the $89 million dollars she expected to collect: "I've shed one big, hefty load so I can walk into court looking sensational to collect a big, hefty load of money. . . . I don't give a rat's ass what people say. I loved him and he loved me. He died a very happy man and he'd be turning in his grave at the thought of what his family has put me through." Mike Parker, Anna Nicole Vows to Wow Courtroom, Daily Star, July 11, 2004, at 32.

Things did not work out as Anna had hoped. On December 30, 2004, as this book was being finalized for publication, the Ninth Circuit vacated the district court's opinion, ordering the case dismissed for want of jurisdiction under the probate exception to the federal jurisdiction.[12] See In re Vickie Lynn Marshall, 392 F.3d 1118 (9th Cir. 2004). Anna was not pleased: "The judges were so paid off," she told a reporter. Norm Clarke, Just Another Boring New Year's Eve in Vegas, Jan. 2, 2005, at A4A. Anna's lawyer promised to seek review by the Supreme Court.

2. The cases are split on whether to recognize a cause of action for tortious interference with an expected inheritance or gift. Compare Golden v. Golden, 382 F.3d 348 (3d Cir. 2004) (recognizing the tort under Pennsylvania law), and Allen v. Hall, 974 P.2d 199 (Or. 1999) (allowing tortious interference with inheritance to be litigated under tort of intentional interference with economic advantage), with Economopoulos v. Kolaitis, 528 S.E.2d 714 (Va. 2000) (refusing to recognize the tort under Virginia law). See also Diane J. Klein, The Disappointed Heir's Revenge, Southern Style: Tortious Interference with Expectation of Inheritance—A Survey with Analysis of State Approaches in the Fifth and Eleventh Circuits, 55 Baylor L. Rev. 79 (2003); Annot., 22 A.L.R.4th 1229 (1983, rev. 2004).

3. An action for tortious interference with an expectancy is not a will contest. It does not challenge the probate or validity of a will but rather seeks to recover tort damages from a third party for tortious interference. The action is not subject to the typically short state statute of limitations on will contests, but the tort statute of limitations starts running on the action at the time the plaintiff discovered or should have discovered the fraud or undue influence. Most courts require the plaintiff to pursue probate remedies first, if they are adequate, and failure to do so may result in barring a tortious interference suit. Compare Keith v. Dooley, 802 N.E.2d 54 (Ind. App. 2004) (upholding the dismissal of a tort action because a will contest was pending and the remedies available in the contest were "substantially the same" as those sought in the tort suit), with Martin v. Martin, 687 So. 2d 903 (Fla. App. 1997) (holding testator's sons did not have an adequate remedy in contesting the testator's will in probate when testator transferred $8 million into an inter vivos trust for a second wife and poured over $300,000 into it by will, all through the alleged undue influence of the second wife, and thus could sue second wife in tort). If the plaintiff contests the will and loses, ordinarily the plaintiff is barred by the principle of res judicata from suing later in tort. See Annot., 18 A.L.R.5th 211 (1994, rev. 2004).

Since a suit for tortious interference with an expectancy is not a will contest, a no-contest clause (page 167) does not apply to such a suit. Punitive damages may be recovered against the wrongdoer in a suit in tort (as in *Marshall*) but not, of course, in a suit seeking to prevent probate of a will on the ground of undue influence or fraud.

---

12. "The probate exception is one of the most mysterious and esoteric branches of the law of federal jurisdiction." Dragon v. Miller, 679 F.2d 712, 713 (7th Cir. 1982) (Posner, J.). The principle holds that a federal court may not probate a will or entertain a suit that could undermine or contradict the judgment of a state probate court. However, the federal courts may entertain a probate-related suit if the parties could have litigated it in a state court of general jurisdiction. See Golden v. Golden, 382 F.3d 348, 358 (3d Cir. 2004). The exception has been defended as promoting certainty and judicial economy in probate matters. See 15 Moore's Federal Practice §102.92 (3d ed. 2004).

4

WILLS: FORMALITIES AND FORMS

SECTION A. EXECUTION OF WILLS

1. Attested Wills

a. The Function of Formalities

Jane B. Baron, Gifts, Bargains, and Form
64 Ind. L.J. 155, 157 (1989)

Despite the benevolent motives and family settings usually associated with gifts, the accepted justification of donative formality assumes that, in giving, people are fundamentally unreliable and deceitful. Despite the self-interested aims and arm's length relationships usually associated with bargains, the accepted justification of the consideration doctrine assumes that, in business, people are trusting and trustworthy. These justifications turn the world topsy-turvy. We are to be suspected when we give, relied on when we trade.

James Lindgren, The Fall of Formalism
55 Alb. L. Rev. 1009, 1009 (1992)

People are not stupid. Yet for hundreds of years the law of wills has treated them as if they were. Sure, they don't know the law, but they usually know what they want. The fear that they might improvidently give away their property at death has left a legacy of formalism unmatched in American law.

In the law of wills, the story told about people is that their seriously intended statements about their property can't be trusted. They are so weak, old, feeble, and subject to pressure that they need extraordinary protection from themselves. Their spoken words are completely worthless. Their written statements are without meaning unless they're witnessed by two people. Even then, the witnesses must sign in the presence of the giver. And so on.

In the law of contracts, on the other hand, the story is completely different. People are intelligent and competent. They know their own mind. Other people can rely on their seriously made statements. They don't need protection from themselves. Their spoken words are enough to convey millions of dollars. And their written statements have meaning without witnesses.

Ashbel G. Gulliver & Catherine J. Tilson,
Classification of Gratuitous Transfers
51 Yale L.J. 1, 2-5, 9-10 (1941)

One fundamental proposition is that, under a legal system recognizing the individualistic institution of private property and granting to the owner the power to determine his successors in ownership, the general philosophy of the courts should favor giving effect to an intentional exercise of that power. . . .

If this objective is primary, the requirements of execution, which concern only the form of the transfer — what the transferor or others must do to make it legally effective — seem justifiable only as implements for its accomplishment, and should be so interpreted by the courts in these cases. They surely should not be revered as ends in themselves, enthroning formality over frustrated intent. Why do these requirements exist and what functions may they usefully perform? . . .

In the first place, the court needs to be convinced that the statements of the transferor were deliberately intended to effectuate a transfer. People are often careless in conversation and in informal writings. Even if the witnesses are entirely truthful and accurate, what is a court to conclude from testimony showing only that a father once stated that he wanted to give certain bonds to his son John? Does this remark indicate *finality of intention to transfer*, or rambling meditation about some future disposition. . . . Or suppose the evidence shows, without more, that a writing containing dispositive language was found among papers of the deceased at the time of his death? Does this demonstrate a deliberate transfer, or was it merely a tentative draft of some contemplated instrument, or perhaps random scribbling? . . . Dispositive effect should not be given to statements which were not intended to have that effect. The formalities of transfer therefore generally require the performance of some ceremonial for the purpose of impressing the transferor with the significance of his statements and thus justifying the court in reaching the conclusion, if the ceremonial is performed, that they were deliberately intended to be operative. This purpose of the requirements of transfer may conveniently be termed their *ritual function*.

Secondly, the requirements of transfer may increase the reliability of the proof presented to the court. The extent to which the quantity and effect of available evidence should be restricted by qualitative standards is, of course, a controversial matter. Perhaps any and all evidence should be freely admitted in reliance on such safeguards as cross-examination, the oath, the proficiency of handwriting experts, and the discriminating judgment of courts and juries. On the other hand, the inaccuracies of oral testimony owing to lapse of memory, misinterpretation of the statements of others, and the more or less unconscious coloring of recollection in the light of the personal interest of the witness or of those with whom he is friendly, are very prevalent; and the possibilities of perjury and forgery cannot be disregarded. These difficulties are entitled to especially serious consideration in prescribing requirements for gratuitous transfers, because the issue of the validity of the transfer is almost always raised after the alleged trans-feror is dead, and therefore the main actor is usually unavailable to testify, or to clarify or contradict other evidence concerning his all-important intention. At any rate, whatever the ideal solution may be, it seems quite clear that the existing requirements of transfer emphasize the purpose of supplying satisfactory evidence to the court. This purpose may conveniently be termed their *evidentiary function.*

Thirdly, some of the requirements of the statutes of wills have the stated prophylactic purpose of safeguarding the testator, at the time of the execution of the will, against undue influence or other forms of imposition. . . . It may conveniently be termed the *protective function.* . . . This [protective function] is difficult to justify under modern conditions. . . . The protective provisions first appeared in the Statute of Frauds, from which they have been copied, perhaps sometimes blindly, by American legislatures. While there is little direct evi-dence, it is a reasonable assumption that, in the period prior to the Statute of Frauds, wills were usually executed on the death bed. A testator in this unfortu-nate situation may well need special protection against imposition. His powers of normal judgment and of resistance to improper influences may be seriously affected by a decrepit physical condition, a weakened mentality, or a morbid or unbalanced state of mind. Furthermore, in view of the propinquity of death, he would not have as much time or opportunity as would the usual inter vivos transferor to escape from the consequences of undue influence or other forms of imposition. Under modern conditions, however, wills are probably executed by most testators in the prime of life and in the presence of attorneys. [Emphasis added.]

Professor Langbein suggests that in addition to serving the cautionary function (Langbein's term for the ritual function), the evidentiary function, and the pro-tective function, the formalities requirements of the Wills Act serve a *channeling function.* Much as it is easier to determine whether a coin is a quarter if every quarter is the same size and has the same markings on it, it is easier to determine a person's wishes at death if they are channeled into a will with standardized formalities. Will formalities create a safe harbor, which provides the testator with assurance that his wishes will be carried out.

> Compliance with the Wills Act formalities for executing witnessed wills results in considerable uniformity in the organization, language, and content of most wills. Courts are seldom left to puzzle whether the document was meant to be a will. . . .
> The standardization of testation achieved under the Wills Act also benefits the testator. He does not have to devise for himself a mode of communicating his testamentary wishes to the court, and to worry whether it will be effective. Instead, he has every inducement to comply with the Wills Act formalities. The court can process his estate routinely, because his testament is conventionally and unmistakably expressed and evidenced. The lowered costs of routinized judicial administration benefit the estate and its ultimate distributees. [John H. Langbein, Substantial Compliance with the Wills Act, 88 Harv. L. Rev. 489, 494 (1975).]

Establishing that a formality serves a particular purpose is, however, just the beginning of determining whether we should make it a minimum requirement for a valid will:

> In determining the proper level of formalities, we shouldn't ask whether this formality or that would serve the accepted purposes of formalities. Any formality would. If we required a secret handshake for willmaking that only lawyers knew, that would serve the cautionary or ritual function. In early Bavaria, to convey real property one had to box the ears of young boys.[1] Without that formality, conveyances were ineffective, even where possession occurred and the deal was never repudiated by the parties. This strange formality served all the main functions of formalities: ritual or cautionary, evidentiary, protective, and channeling. Yet it was a perverse and silly formality. Other formalities more reliably evidenced transfers.
>
> Instead of asking whether a formality serves a function of formalities, we should ask instead whether it promotes the intent of the testator at an acceptable administrative cost. We should not box the ears of little children just because it serves the ritual function; this is misplaced formalism. [James Lindgren, The Fall of Formalism, 55 Alb. L. Rev. 1009, 1033 (1992).]

The most basic formalities for an attested will are three: (1) writing, (2) signature by the testator, and (3) attestation by witnesses. But these basic requirements for execution of wills vary considerably in detail from state to state. Some of these variations result from England having had two acts governing the execution of wills, the Statute of Frauds (1677) and the Wills Act (1837), both of which served as models for American legislation.

Prior to enactment of the Statute of Frauds, personal property was transferable at death by either a written or oral will, perhaps given to the priest as part of the last confession.[2] Land was made devisable "by last will and testament in writing" by the Statute of Wills in 1540, but the statute required no signature or other formalities. The Statute of Frauds, coming 137 years later, required a written will signed by the testator in the presence of three witnesses for testamentary disposition of land. Less stringent formalities, which need not concern us here, applied to testamentary dispositions of personalty. Having different requirements for wills of realty and for wills of personalty proved unsatisfactory, and in 1837 England passed a Wills Act requiring the same formalities for all wills.

The formalities required by the Wills Act of 1837 were in some ways stricter than those required by the Statute of Frauds. Under the Statute of Frauds, the

---

1. Boxing the ears refers to striking someone hard on the side of the head. The idea was that, by creating a painful memory, the young boys would be good witnesses if a dispute later arose as to the validity of the transfer. See Celia Wasserstein Fassberg, Form and Formalism: A Case Study, 31 Am. J. Comp. L. 627 (1983). — Eds.

2. A minority of states permit nuncupative (oral) wills under very limited circumstances. Typically, these wills can be made only during a person's "last sickness" and can be used only to devise personal property of small value (say, up to $1,000); the will must be uttered before three persons, who must reduce the declaration to writing within a specified period. Military personnel and mariners at sea are, in some states, granted the privilege of making an oral will under limited circumstances. Oral wills admitted to probate are extremely rare. For a list of state nuncupative will statutes, see Restatement (Third) of Property: Wills and Other Donative Transfers §3.2, statutory note 3 (1999).

three witnesses did not have to be present at the same time; each could attest separately — and the testator did not have to sign at any particular place on the document. The 1837 Wills Act reduced the number of necessary witnesses to two, but it provided that the witnesses must both be present when the will is signed or acknowledged; in addition, the will must be signed "at the foot or end" of the will, which is called *subscription*. (The exact language of the 1837 Wills Act is set out in the court's opinion in *Groffman*, page 204.) These two additional requirements of the Wills Act have given rise to much litigation.

Some states copied the English Statute of Frauds; others copied the Wills Act of 1837. In a few states, the legislature added a requirement that the testator must *publish* the will by declaring before the witnesses that the instrument is his will. For each of the three main formalities — writing, signature, and attestation by witnesses — the Uniform Probate Code generally adopts the less strict requirements of the Statute of Frauds but reduces the required number of witnesses to two.[3]

COMPARISON OF STATUTORY FORMALITIES
FOR FORMAL WILLS

Statute of Frauds (1677) (land)	*Wills Act (1837)*	*Uniform Probate Code (1990)*
Writing	Writing	Writing
Signature	Subscription	Signature
Attestation & subscription by three witnesses	Attestation & signature by two witnesses	Attestation & signature by two witnesses

b.   The Formalities in Action

Uniform Probate Code (1990)

§2-502.   Execution; Witnessed Wills; Holographic Wills

(a) Except as provided in subsection (b) and in Sections 2-503, 2-506, and 2-513, a will must be:

(1) in writing;

(2) signed by the testator or in the testator's name by some other individual in the testator's conscious presence and by the testator's direction; and

(3) signed by at least two individuals, each of whom signed within a reasonable time after he [or she] witnessed either the signing of the will as described in paragraph (2) or the testator's acknowledgment of that signature or acknowledgment of the will.

(b) A will that does not comply with subsection (a) is valid as a holographic will, whether or not witnessed, if the signature and material portions of the document are in the testator's handwriting.

---

3. Formerly a number of states required three witnesses. Now, only Vermont requires three witnesses rather than two. Vt. Stat. Ann. tit. 14, §5 (2004). Louisiana requires two witnesses plus a notary. La. Civ. Code Ann. art. 1577 (2004). For a list of state witnessing requirements, see Jeffrey A. Schoenblum, 2004 Multistate Guide to Estate Planning at Table1.

(c) Intent that the document constitute the testator's will can be established by extrinsic evidence, including, for holographic wills, portions of the document that are not in the testator's handwriting.

We are concerned at this point only with UPC §2-502(a), dealing with attested wills. Holographic wills, authorized by §2-502(b), are treated later.

IN RE GROFFMAN, HIGH COURT OF JUSTICE, ENGLAND, [1969] 2 All E.R. 108: Charles Groffman died three years after executing a will at the home of his friends, the Blocks. After his death, Groffman's widow challenged the will. "My Charlie wouldn't have done that to me," she is reported to have said. If the will had been validly executed, Groffman's children from his first marriage would share in the estate, but if the will were invalid, his widow would take the entire estate in intestacy. The dispute centered on the fact that Groffman and both witnesses were not present together when Groffman acknowledged his signature. The applicable statute — the English Wills Act of 1837 — provided as follows:

> [N]o will shall be valid unless it shall be in writing and executed in manner hereinafter mentioned; . . . it shall be signed at the foot or end thereof by the testator, or by some other person in his presence and by his direction; and such signature shall be made or acknowledged by the testator in the presence of two or more witnesses present at the same time, and such witnesses shall attest and shall subscribe the will in the presence of the testator, but no form of attestation shall be necessary.

Under this statute a testator is permitted *either* to acknowledge his prior signature to both witnesses "at the same time" *or* to sign the will before both witnesses. Although Groffman asked his friends, Julius Leigh and David Block, together to witness his will, he did not acknowledge his signature to them both simultaneously. Instead, Groffman and the first witness, Block, left the Blocks' lounge and went into the adjacent dining room, where Block signed the will as a witness in Groffman's presence. Then, after Block returned to the lounge, the other witness, Leigh, went into the dining room and witnessed the will with Groffman present, but without Block, the first witness, also present.

Even though the court was "perfectly satisfied that the document was intended by the deceased to be executed as his will," it nevertheless refused to admit the will to probate:

> [W]e are left with this situation — that the signature of the deceased was on the document before he asked either Mr. Block or Mr. Leigh to act as his witnesses; that Mr. Block signed his name in the presence of the deceased but not in the presence of Mr. Leigh; and that Mr. Leigh signed his name in the presence of the deceased but not in the presence of Mr. Block. The deceased did not sign in the presence of either of them; and the question is whether he acknowledged his signature in the presence of both of them. . . . As must appear from the fact that I have been satisfied that the document does represent the testamentary intentions of the deceased, I would gladly find in its favour; but I am bound to apply the statute. . . . [A]lthough I would gladly accede to the arguments for the plaintiffs if I could consistently with my judicial duty, in my view there was no acknowledgment or signature by the testator in the presence

of two or more witnesses present at the same time; and I am bound to pronounce against this will.

Stevens v. Casdorph
West Virginia Supreme Court of Appeals, 1998
203 W. Va. 450, 508 S.E.2d 610

PER CURIAM. ... On May 28, 1996, the Casdorphs took Mr. Homer Haskell Miller to Shawnee Bank in Dunbar, West Virginia, so that he could execute his will.[4] Once at the bank, Mr. Miller asked Debra Pauley, a bank employee and public notary, to witness the execution of his will. After Mr. Miller signed the will, Ms. Pauley took the will to two other bank employees, Judith Waldron and Reba McGinn, for the purpose of having each of them sign the will as witnesses. Both Ms. Waldron and Ms. McGinn signed the will. However, Ms. Waldron and Ms. McGinn testified during their depositions that they did not actually see Mr. Miller place his signature on the will. Further, it is undisputed that Mr. Miller did not accompany Ms. Pauley to the separate work areas of Ms. Waldron and Ms. McGinn.

Mr. Miller died on July 28, 1996. The last will and testament of Mr. Miller, which named [his nephew] Mr. Paul Casdorph as executor, left the bulk of his estate to the Casdorphs.[5] The Stevenses, [who as] nieces of Mr. Miller [would share in his intestate estate], filed the instant action to set aside the will. The Stevenses asserted in their complaint that Mr. Miller's will was not executed according to the requirements set forth in W. Va. Code §41-1-3 (1995). After some discovery, all parties moved for summary judgment. The circuit court denied the Stevenses' motion for summary judgment, but granted the Casdorphs' cross motion for summary judgment. From this ruling, the Stevenses appeal to this Court. ...

The Stevenses' contention is simple. They argue that all evidence indicates that Mr. Miller's will was not properly executed. Therefore, the will should be voided. The procedural requirements at issue are contained in W. Va. Code §41-1-3 (1997). The statute reads:

> No will shall be valid unless it be in writing and signed by the testator, or by some other person in his presence and by his direction, in such manner as to make it manifest that the name is intended as a signature; and moreover, unless it be wholly in the handwriting of the testator, *the signature shall be made or the will acknowledged by him in the presence of at least two competent witnesses, present at the same time; and such witnesses shall subscribe the will in the presence of the testator, and of each other,* but no form of attestation shall be necessary. (Emphasis added.)

The relevant requirements of the above statute calls for a testator to sign his/her will or acknowledge such will in the presence of at least two witnesses at the same time, and such witnesses must sign the will in the presence of the testator and each other. In the instant proceeding the Stevenses assert, and the evidence supports, that Ms. McGinn and Ms. Waldron did not actually witness Mr. Miller signing his

---

4. Mr. Miller was elderly and confined to a wheelchair.
5. Mr. Miller's probated estate exceeded $400,000.00. The will devised $80,000.00 to Frank Paul Smith, a nephew of Mr. Miller. The remainder of the estate was left to the Casdorphs.

will. Mr. Miller made no acknowledgment of his signature on the will to either Ms. McGinn or Ms. Waldron. Likewise, Mr. Miller did not observe Ms. McGinn and Ms. Waldron sign his will as witnesses. Additionally, neither Ms. McGinn nor Ms. Waldron acknowledged to Mr. Miller that their signatures were on the will. It is also undisputed that Ms. McGinn and Ms. Waldron did not actually witness each other sign the will, nor did they acknowledge to each other that they had signed Mr. Miller's will. Despite the evidentiary lack of compliance with W. Va. Code §41-1-3, the Casdorphs argue that there was substantial compliance with the statute's requirements, insofar as everyone involved with the will knew what was occurring. The trial court found that there was substantial compliance with the statute because everyone knew why Mr. Miller was at the bank. The trial court further concluded there was no evidence of fraud, coercion or undue influence. Based upon the foregoing, the trial court concluded that the will should not be voided even though the technical aspects of W. Va. Code §41-1-3 were not followed.

Our analysis begins by noting that "the law favors testacy over intestacy." Syl. pt. 8, In re Teubert's Estate, 298 S.E.2d 456 (W. Va. 1982). However, we clearly held in syllabus point 1 of Black v. Maxwell, 46 S.E.2d 804 (W. Va. 1948), that "testamentary intent and a written instrument, executed in the manner provided by [W. Va. Code §41-1-3], existing concurrently, are essential to the creation of a valid will." *Black* establishes that mere intent by a testator to execute a written will is insufficient. The actual execution of a written will must also comply with the dictates of W. Va. Code §41-1-3. The Casdorphs seek to have this Court establish an exception to the technical requirements of the statute. In Wade v. Wade, 195 S.E. 339 (W. Va. 1938), this Court permitted a narrow exception to the stringent requirements of the W. Va. Code §41-1-3. This narrow exception is embodied in syllabus point 1 of Wade:

> Where a testator acknowledges a will and his signature thereto in the presence of two competent witnesses, one of whom then subscribes his name, the other or first witness, having already subscribed the will in the presence of the testator but out of the presence of the second witness, may acknowledge his signature in the presence of the testator and the second witness, and such acknowledgment, if there be no indicia of fraud or misunderstanding in the proceeding, will be deemed a signing by the first witness within the requirement of Code, 41-1-3, that the witnesses must subscribe their names in the presence of the testator and of each other.

. . . *Wade* stands for the proposition that if a witness acknowledges his/her signature on a will in the physical presence of the other subscribing witness *and the testator*, then the will is properly witnessed within the terms of W. Va. Code §41-1-3. In this case, none of the parties signed or acknowledged their signatures in the presence of each other. This case meets neither the narrow exception of *Wade* nor the specific provisions of W. Va. Code §41-1-3. . . .

In view of the foregoing, we grant the relief sought in this appeal and reverse the circuit court's order granting the Casdorphs' cross-motion for summary judgment.

Reversed.

WORKMAN, J., dissenting. The majority once more takes a very technocratic approach to the law, slavishly worshiping form over substance. In so doing, they not only create a harsh and inequitable result wholly contrary to the indisputable intent of Mr. Homer Haskell Miller, but also a rule of law that is against the spirit and intent of our whole body of law relating to the making of wills.

There is absolutely no claim of incapacity or fraud or undue influence, nor any allegation by any party that Mr. Miller did not consciously, intentionally, and with full legal capacity convey his property as specified in his will. The challenge to the will is based solely upon the allegation that Mr. Miller did not comply with the requirement of West Virginia Code 41-1-3 that the signature shall be made or the will acknowledged by the testator in the presence of at least two competent witnesses, present at the same time. The lower court, in its very thorough findings of fact, indicated that Mr. Miller had been transported to the bank by his nephew Mr. Casdorph and the nephew's wife. Mr. Miller, disabled and confined to a wheelchair, was a shareholder in the Shawnee Bank in Dunbar, West Virginia, with whom all those present were personally familiar. When Mr. Miller executed his will in the bank lobby, the typed will was placed on Ms. Pauley's desk, and Mr. Miller instructed Ms. Pauley that he wished to have his will signed, witnessed, and acknowledged. After Mr. Miller's signature had been placed upon the will with Ms. Pauley watching, Ms. Pauley walked the will over to the tellers' area in the same small lobby of the bank. Ms. Pauley explained that Mr. Miller wanted Ms. Waldron to sign the will as a witness. The same process was used to obtain the signature of Ms. McGinn. Sitting in his wheelchair, Mr. Miller did not move from Ms. Pauley's desk during the process of obtaining the witness signatures. The lower court concluded that the will was valid and that Ms. Waldron and Ms. McGinn signed and acknowledged the will "in the presence" of Mr. Miller.

In Wade v. Wade, 195 S.E. 339 (W. Va. 1938), we addressed the validity of a will challenged for such technicalities and observed that "a narrow, rigid construction of the statute should not be allowed to stand in the way of right and justice, or be permitted to defeat a testator's disposition of his property." 195 S.E.2d at 340-341. We upheld the validity of the challenged will in *Wade*, noting that "each case must rest on its own facts and circumstances to which the court must look to determine whether there was a subscribing by the witnesses in the presence of the testator; that substantial compliance with the statute is all that is required. . . ." 195 S.E. at 340. A contrary result, we emphasized, "would be based on illiberal and inflexible construction of the statute, giving preeminence to letter and not to spirit, and resulting in the thwarting of the intentions of testators even under circumstances where no possibility of fraud or impropriety exists." 195 S.E. at 341.

The majority's conclusion is precisely what was envisioned and forewarned in 1938 by the drafters of the *Wade* opinion: illiberal and inflexible construction, giving preeminence to the letter of the law and ignoring the spirit of the entire body of testamentary law, resulting in the thwarting of Mr. Miller's unequivocal wishes. . . .

The majority embraces the line of least resistance. The easy, most convenient answer is to say that the formal, technical requirements have not been met and that the will is therefore invalid. End of inquiry. Yet that result is patently absurd. That manner of statutory application is inconsistent with the underlying purposes of the statute. Where a statute is enacted to protect and sanctify the execution of a will to prevent substitution or fraud, this Court's application of that statute should further such underlying policy, not impede it. When, in our efforts to strictly apply legislative language, we abandon common sense and reason in favor of technicalities, we are the ones committing the injustice.

QUESTIONS, NOTES, AND PROBLEMS

1. Specifically, why were Mr. Groffman's and Mr. Miller's wills denied probate? In each case, what formalities required by the Wills Act were not satisfied?

2. Were the ritual, evidentiary, protective, and channeling policies underpinning the Wills Act substantially satisfied by the manners in which Groffman's and Miller's wills were executed and attested? If so, should their wills have been denied probate?

3. In *Casdorph*, the majority found that the witnesses did not sign at the request of the testator. Is this necessarily so?

4. *Presence.* What does *presence* mean in will execution? In England and in some American states, the requirement that the witnesses sign in the presence of the testator is satisfied only if the testator is capable of seeing the witnesses in the act of signing. Under this *line of sight test*, the testator does not actually have to see the witnesses sign but must be able to see them were the testator to look. 1 Thomas Jarman, Wills 138 (8th ed. 1951). An exception is made for a blind person, where the test is usually whether she would have been able to see the witnesses sign if she had the power of sight. In other American states, the line of sight rule has been rejected in favor of the *conscious presence test*. Under this test, the witness is in the presence of the testator if the testator, through sight, hearing, or general consciousness of events, comprehends that the witness is in the act of signing. UPC §2-502(a), page 203, dispenses altogether with the requirement that the witnesses sign in the testator's presence. See generally Restatement (Third) of Property: Wills and Other Donative Transfers §3.1 cmt. p (1999).

Consider these two problems concerning presence:

a. Suppose that *T*'s attorney takes *T*'s will to *T*'s home, where *T* signs the will and the attorney attests as a witness. The attorney returns to her office with the will and has her secretary call *T* on the phone. By telephone, *T* requests the secretary to witness his will; the secretary then signs as an attesting witness. Can the will be probated? See In re Jefferson, 349 So. 2d 1032 (Miss. 1977); In re McGurrin, 743 P.2d 994 (Idaho App. 1987).

b. Suppose that the president of a bank draws a will for a depositor. The depositor, seriously ill, drives to the bank's drive-in teller window and parks. The president takes the will to the depositor's car, where the depositor signs the will propped on his steering wheel. The bank teller, seated at a teller window overlooking the car, watches the depositor sign. The president signs as a witness in the car, then takes the will inside the teller's office where the teller, sitting in the window, signs as witness and waves to the depositor. The president then takes the will outside and shows it to the depositor, who asks the president to keep it. Has the teller signed as a witness in the presence of the testator? See In re Weber's Estate, 387 P.2d 165 (Kan. 1963), which held, 4 to 3, No, because though the testator could see the teller, the testator could not see the pen and will on the teller's desk as the teller signed. The court thought to apply the conscious presence test on these facts would permit it "to run wild."

5. *Order of signing.* A few days before his death, George Colling, in the hospital, made a will. He started to write his signature in the presence of two witnesses — Jackson, the patient in the bed next to his, and Sister Newman, a nurse. Although they were both present when the testator started to sign, before the testator finished writing "Colling," Sister Newman had to attend to a patient in

another part of the ward. In her absence Colling completed his signature, and Jackson witnessed the will in Colling's presence. Sister Newman then returned. Both Colling and Jackson acknowledged their signatures to her, and she then signed as the second witness. May the will be probated? Held: No. The signature is not sufficient because the testator did not complete his signature while both witnesses were present; the later acknowledgment does not suffice because the testator must sign or acknowledge his signature before either of the witnesses attest. In re Colling, [1972] 1 W.L.R. 1440. Accord, In re Estate of Wait, 306 S.W.2d 345 (Tenn. App. 1957) (testator, old and feeble, was unable to complete her signature, because her hand was shaking, until after witnesses left; will denied probate).

Compare Wheat v. Wheat, 244 A.2d 359 (Conn. 1968), holding that the attestation requirement necessitates that the testator sign first, with Waldrep v. Goodwin, 195 S.E.2d 432 (Ga. 1973), upholding a will if the testator and the witnesses all sign while assembled in a room, regardless of the order of signing.

6. *Signature.* A lawyer prepared a will for Patrick Mangeri, who was very ill. Underneath the signature line was typed "Patrick Mangeri." The will was taken to Mangeri in his hospital room. Mangeri signed with an "X" because his hands were too shaky to write his name. The two attesting witnesses then signed. Can the will be probated? See In re Estate of McCabe, 274 Cal. Rptr. 43 (App. 1990). Suppose that Mangeri had written a shaky "Pat" rather than an "X." Same result? In re Young, 397 N.E.2d 1223 (Ohio App. 1978), held that the letter *J* subscribed by Joseph Young was sufficient when Joseph was partially paralyzed from a stroke.

Suppose that, since Mangeri had trouble holding the pen, a witness said, "Here, I'll help you," and assisted Mangeri in signing his name. Can the will be probated? Would it make any difference if Mangeri had asked the witness for help? See In re Estate of DeThorne, 471 N.W.2d 780 (Wis. App. 1991).

Suppose *T* has digitized a scan of his handwritten signature. In front of two witnesses, *T* adds this digitized signature to the word processing document that is to be his will. *T* then prints the document, which includes his digital signature, and the witnesses sign and attest. Is the will valid? See Taylor v. Holt, 134 S.W.3d 830 (Tenn. App. 2003) (Yes, under statute that defines "signature" to include "any other symbol or methodology executed or adopted by a party with intention to authenticate a writing."). Suppose instead *T* affixed a rubber stamp signature to the will. What result then?

7. *Addition after signature.* Statutes in several states have adopted the Wills Act requirement that the testator sign the will "at the foot or end thereof," a requirement that is often called *subscription*. Suppose that a typewritten will is found on which is written in the testator's handwriting, below the testator's signature and above the witnesses' signatures, the following line: "I give Karen my diamond ring." Is the will entitled to probate? Initially, the answer depends upon whether the line was on the will when it was signed by the testator. If the handwritten line was added *after* the testator signed the will, the will would be admitted to probate, and the line would be ineffective as a subsequent unexecuted codicil. If added *before* the testator signed her name, would the will be admitted? Would it matter if the handwritten addition had not made a disposition of the testator's property but had said: "I appoint Emily executor"? See Clark v. National Bank of Commerce, 802 S.W.2d 452 (Ark. 1991); N.Y. Est. Powers & Trusts Law §3-2.1(a)(1) (2004).

8. *Videotaped or electronic wills*. Suppose that Robert Reed videotapes his spoken will before two witnesses. Then he puts it in a sealed envelope, on which he writes, "To be played in the event of my death only, Robert Reed," and the two witnesses sign their names. Does this comply with the requirement that the will be a "signed writing"? Is a voice print a writing? See Estate of Reed, 672 P.2d 829 (Wyo. 1983) (held No); Gerry W. Beyer & William R. Buckley, Videotape and the Probate Process: The Nexus Grows, 42 Okla. L. Rev. 43 (1989). Suppose Reed had prepared the filmed will using animated letters and words. Same result?

The Uniform Probate Code is agnostic on whether a videotape could constitute a "document or writing" sufficient to be admitted under its "dispensing power," a reform doctrine (discussed on pages 233-235) that allows a defectively executed document to be admitted to probate if there is clear and convincing evidence that it was intended to be a will.

What about a will in the form of a computer file with a unique electronic signature? In 2001, Nevada enacted a statute authorizing electronic wills, subject to some strict requirements, including a single original and some way of determining if the original has been altered. Nev. Rev. Stat. §133.085 (2004). An electronic will probably does not satisfy the writing or signature requirement of the Wills Act, but an electronic will might nonetheless be allowed under substantial compliance or the dispensing power. Substantial compliance, like the dispensing power, is a reform doctrine examined on pages 233-235.

In Rioux v. Coulombe, 19 Est. & Tr. Rep. 2d 201 (Quebec 1996), Jaqueline Rioux left a suicide note directing the police

> to an envelope which contained a computer diskette marked "this is my will/Jaqueline Rioux/february 1, 1996." The information on the diskette, when later printed out, contained unsigned directions of a testamentary nature. The testatrix had noted in her diary that she had written her will on a computer. The diskette itself contained only one file which had been saved to memory on the same day that the deceased had noted in her diary that she had made a will on computer.

The court allowed probate of the electronic will under a Quebec substantial compliance statute. The statute, however, required that the "essential" formalities be met. Were they? See Nicholas Kasirer, From Written Record to Memory in the Law of Wills, 29 Ottawa L. Rev. 39 (1997/1998).

See generally Christopher J. Caldwell, Comment, Should "E-Wills" Be Wills: Will Advances in Technology Be Recognized for Will Execution?, 63 U. Pitt. L. Rev. 467 (2002).

9. *Attestation clause*. An attestation clause recites that the will was duly executed. For an example, see paragraph 7 on page 217. No state's statute requires the use of an attestation clause. The requirement of due execution can be satisfied merely by having the witnesses sign below the testator's signature as "witnesses." An attestation clause is, however, very important. Indeed, we consider it professional malpractice not to include one. The attestation clause makes out a prima facie case that the will was duly executed; thus the will may be admitted to probate even though the witnesses predecease the testator or cannot recall the events of execution. See Gardner v. Balboni, 588 A.2d 634 (Conn. 1991); In re Estate of Collins, 458 N.E.2d 797 (N.Y. 1983). Moreover, if one of the attesting witnesses testifies that the steps for due execution were not satisfied, the attestation clause gives the will proponent's attorney ammunition for a vigorous cross-examination, and the will can be admitted to probate on the presumption of due execution despite such testimony.

10. *Delayed attestation*. Suppose that the witnesses do not get around to signing the will until after the testator dies. Is it too late? Must the witnesses sign while the testator is alive? Compare In re Estate of Royal, 826 P.2d 1236 (Colo. 1992) (holding witness must attest before the testator's death), with Estate of Eugene, 128 Cal. Rptr. 2d 622 (App. 2002) (holding that witness may attest eight years after original execution, where witness mistakenly failed to sign one of two wills being executed at the same ceremony). See also UPC §2-502(a), page 203, providing that witnesses must sign within reasonable time; N.Y. Est. Powers & Trusts Law §3-2.1(a)(4) (2004), requiring witnesses to sign within 30 days.

11. *Notarization*. Most states require that a deed be notarized to be recorded in the county recorder's office; witnessing does not suffice. Why must deeds be *notarized* and wills *witnessed*? Would it be a good idea to permit a will to be *either* witnessed or notarized?

Suppose that there were only one witness to the will itself (instead of the two required), but both the one witness and a notary signed an attached affidavit on the following page. Can the notary count as the second witness? Compare Estate of Friedman, 6 P.3d 473 (Nev. 2000) (yes), with Estate of Alfaro, 703 N.E.2d 620 (Ill. App. 1998) (no, unless the notary was intending to act as a witness rather than a notary). See also In re Will of Ranney, page 226. In most civil law countries, testators may go to a quasi-judicial public officer to have a notarial will executed. On the other hand, a European notary is a more substantial figure than an American notary public. See Nicole M. Reina, Protecting Testamentary Freedom in the United States by Introducing into Law the Concept of the French Notaire, 19 N.Y.L. Sch. J. Hum. Rts. 427 (2003).

12. For a learned and wide-ranging critique of the inconsistencies of the execution requirements among the states, see Adam J. Hirsch, Inheritance and Inconsistency, 57 Ohio St. L.J. 1057 (1997).

For a useful compendium of will execution requirements, with citations to statutes and cases, see Jeffrey A. Schoenblum, 2004 Multistate Guide to Estate Planning at Table 1.

Estate of Parsons

California Court of Appeal, First District, 1980
103 Cal. App. 3d 384, 163 Cal. Rptr. 70

GRODIN, J.   This case requires us to determine whether a subscribing witness to a will who is named in the will as a beneficiary becomes "disinterested" within the meaning of Probate Code section 51 by filing a disclaimer of her interest after the testatrix' death. While our own policy preferences tempt us to an affirmative answer, we feel constrained by existing law to hold that a disclaimer is ineffective for that purpose.

I

Geneve Parsons executed her will on May 3, 1976. Three persons signed the will as attesting witnesses: Evelyn Nielson, respondent Marie Gower, and Bob Warda, a notary public. Two of the witnesses, Nielson and Gower, were named in the will as beneficiaries. Nielson was given $100; Gower was given certain real property.

Mrs. Parsons died on December 13, 1976, and her will was admitted to probate on the petition of her executors, respondents Gower and Lenice Haymond. On September 12, 1977, Nielson filed a disclaimer of her $100 bequest. Appellants [Mrs. Parsons's heirs] then claimed an interest in the estate on the ground that the devise to Gower was invalid. The trial court rejected their argument, which is now the sole contention on appeal.

Appellants base their claim on Probate Code section 51, which provides that a gift to a subscribing witness is void "unless there are two other and disinterested subscribing witnesses to the will."[6] Although Nielson disclaimed her bequest after subscribing the will, appellants submit that "a subsequent disclaimer is ineffective to transform an interested witness into a disinterested one." Appellants assert that because there was only one disinterested witness at the time of attestation, the devise to Gower is void by operation of law.

Respondents contend that appellants' argument is "purely technical" and "completely disregards the obvious and ascertainable intent" of the testatrix. They urge that the property should go to the person named as devisee rather than to distant relatives who, as the testatrix stated in her will, "have not been overlooked, but have been intentionally omitted." They stress that there has been no suggestion of any fraud or undue influence in this case, and they characterize Nielson's interest as a "token gift" which she relinquished pursuant to the disclaimer statute. (Prob. Code, §190 et seq.) Finally, respondents point to the following language of Probate Code section 190.6: "In every case, the disclaimer shall relate back for all purposes to the date of the creation of the interest." On the basis of that language, respondents conclude that Nielson "effectively became disinterested" by reason of her timely disclaimer. According to respondents, the conditions of Probate Code section 51 have therefore been satisfied, and the devise to Gower should stand.

II

This appears to be a case of first impression in California, and our interpretation of Probate Code section 51 will determine its outcome. We are required to construe the statute "so as to effectuate the purpose of the law." (Select Base Materials v. Board of Equal. (Cal. 1959) 335 P.2d 672.) To ascertain that purpose, we may consider its history.

At common law a party to an action, or one who had a direct interest in its outcome, was not competent to testify in court because it was thought that an interested witness would be tempted to perjure himself in favor of his interest. Centuries ago, this principle concerning the competence of witnesses in litigation was injected into the substantive law of wills. The statute of frauds of 1676 required that devises of land be attested and subscribed "by three or four credible witnesses, or else they shall be utterly void and of none effect." (29 Car. II, ch. 3, §5.) The word "credible" was construed to mean "competent" according to the common law

---

6. Probate Code section 51 reads as follows: "All beneficial devises, bequests and legacies to a subscribing witness are void unless there are two other and disinterested subscribing witnesses to the will, except that if such interested witness would be entitled to any share of the estate of the testator in case the will were not established, he shall take such proportion of the devise or bequest made to him in the will as does not exceed the share of the estate which would be distributed to him if the will were not established."

principles then prevailing, and "competent" meant "disinterested"—so that persons having an interest under the will could not be "credible witnesses" within the meaning of the statute. The entire will would therefore fail if any one of the requisite number of attesting witnesses was also a beneficiary. In 1752 Parliament enacted a statute [called a "purging statute"] which saved the will by providing that the interest of an attesting witness was void. (25 Geo. II, ch. 6, §I.) Under such legislation, the competence of the witness is restored by invalidating his gift. The majority of American jurisdictions today have similar statutes; and California Probate Code section 51 falls into this category.

The common law disabilities to testify on account of interest have long been abolished. Having become a part of the substantive law of wills, Probate Code section 51, on the other hand, survives. Our task is to ascertain and effectuate its present purpose. When a court seeks to interpret legislation, "the various parts of a statutory enactment must be harmonized by considering the particular clause or section in the context of the statutory framework as a whole." (Moyer v. Workmen's Comp. Appeals Bd. (Cal. 1973) 514 P.2d 1224.) We therefore turn to the Probate Code.

In order to establish a will as genuine, it is not always necessary that each and every one of the subscribing witnesses testify in court. Moreover, Probate Code section 51 does not by its terms preclude any witness from testifying; nor does the section void the interest of a subscribing witness when "two other and disinterested" witnesses have also subscribed the will. It is therefore entirely conceivable and perfectly consistent with the statutory scheme that a will might be proved on the sole testimony of a subscribing witness who is named in the will as a beneficiary; and if the will had been attested by "two other and disinterested subscribing witnesses," the interested witness whose sole testimony established the will would also be permitted to take his gift, as provided in the instrument. If Probate Code section 51 serves any purpose under such circumstances, its purpose must necessarily have been accomplished before the will was offered for probate. Otherwise, in its statutory context, the provision would have no effect at all.

The quintessential function of a subscribing witness is performed when the will is executed. We believe that Probate Code section 51 looks in its operation solely to that time. The section operates to ensure that at least two of the subscribing witnesses are disinterested. Although disinterest may be a token of credibility, as at common law, it also connotes an absence of selfish motives. We conclude that the purpose of the statute is to protect the testator from fraud and undue influence at the very moment when he executes his will, by ensuring that at least two persons are present "who would not be financially motivated to join in a scheme to procure the execution of a spurious will by dishonest methods, and who therefore presumably might be led by human impulses of fairness to resist the efforts of others in that direction." (Gulliver & Tilson, Classification of Gratuitous Transfers (1941) 51 Yale L.J. 1, 11.) No other possible construction which has been brought to our attention squares so closely with the statutory framework.

III

Because we hold that Probate Code section 51 looks solely to the time of execution and attestation of the will, it follows that a subsequent disclaimer will be ineffective to transform an interested witness into a "disinterested" one within the meaning of that section. If the execution of a release or the filing of a disclaimer after the will has been attested could effect such a transformation, the purpose of the statute as we have defined it would be undermined. . . .

In this case, when the will was executed and attested, only one of the subscribing witnesses was disinterested. The gifts to the other witnesses were therefore void, by operation of law. (Prob. Code, §51.) Nielson's disclaimer was a nullity, because she had no interest to disclaim.

Respondents' concern for the intentions of the testatrix is likewise misplaced. The construction of the will is not at issue here. We are faced instead with the operation of Probate Code section 51, which makes no reference to the intentions of the testatrix. Legislation voiding the interest of an attesting witness "often upsets genuine expressions of the testator's intent." (Chaffin, Execution, Revocation, and Revalidation of Wills: A Critique of Existing Statutory Formalities (1977) 11 Ga. L. Rev. 297, 317.) But that legislation controls the outcome of this case.

It has been said that statutes such as this are ill suited to guard against fraud and undue influence. "If the potential malefactor does not know of the rules, he will not be deterred. If he does know of them, which is unlikely, he will realize the impossibility of the financial gain supposed to be the motive of the legatee witness, and so will probably escape the operation of the remedy against himself." (Gulliver & Tilson, supra, 51 Yale L.J. at pp. 12-13.) Lord Mansfield observed over 200 years ago, "In all my experience at the Court of Delegates, I never knew a fraudulent will, but what was legally attested; and I have heard the same from many learned civilians." (Wyndham v. Chetwynd (K.B. 1757) 96 Eng. Rep. 53.) Yet Probate Code section 51 remains the law in California.

We are mindful that there has been no suggestion of any fraud or other misconduct in the case before us, and it may well be that "the vast majority of testators in modern society do not need the type of 'protection' that is afforded by our statute." (Chaffin, Improving Georgia's Probate Code (1970) 4 Ga. L. Rev. 505, 507.) "[T]he reported decisions give the impression that the remedies are employed more frequently against innocent parties who have accidentally transgressed the requirement than against deliberate wrongdoers, and this further confirms the imaginary character of the difficulty sought to be prevented." (Gulliver & Tilson, supra, 51 Yale L.J. at p.12.) But the Legislature has spoken here, and in matters such as this, "the legislature has a wide discretion in determining the conditions to be imposed." (Estate of Mintaberry (Cal. 1920) 191 P. 909.)

Respondents note that a growing number of states have enacted statutes similar to Uniform Probate Code section 2-505, which dispenses with the rule contained in the California statute.[7] Perhaps statutes like California Probate Code section 51 represent a "mediaeval point of view" concerning the proper function of an attesting witness; and perhaps "the question whether he has abused his position should be made one of fact, like any other question having to do with the motives and conduct of parties who take part in the testamentary transaction." (Mechem, Why Not a Modern Wills Act? (1948) 33 Iowa L. Rev. 501, 506-507.) We cannot ignore

---

7. Uniform Probate Code section 2-505 provides: "(a) Any person generally competent to be a witness may act as a witness to a will. [¶] (b) A will or any provision thereof is not invalid because the will is signed by an interested witness."

what the statute commands, however, "merely because we do not agree that the statute as written is wise or beneficial legislation." (Estate of Carter (Cal. 1935) 50 P.2d 1057.) Any remedial change must come from the Legislature.

That portion of the judgment from which this appeal is taken is therefore reversed.

NOTE: PURGING STATUTES

Under Uniform Probate Code §2-505, referred to in footnote 7 in the *Parsons* case, an interested witness does not forfeit a devise under the will. In 1983 California adopted its own version of UPC §2-505, which instead imposes a rebuttable presumption that the devise to an interested witness was "procured by duress, menace, fraud, or undue influence." Cal. Prob. Code §6112 (2004).

Since UPC §2-505 has been adopted in little more than one-third of the states, however, it is useful to probe further into the operation of purging statutes. Old California Probate Code §51, referred to in footnote 6 of the *Parsons* case, is substantially similar to purging statutes in many states, which purge the witness only of the benefit the witness receives that exceeds the benefit the witness would have received if the will had not been executed (that is, the "extra benefit"). For a list of state purging statutes, see Jeffrey A. Schoenblum, 2004 Multistate Guide to Estate Planning at Table 1.

The Massachusetts purging statute, derived from the 1752 English statute referred to in the *Parsons* opinion, is different. It simply voids any devise to an attesting witness, who takes nothing under the will. Thus:

> Any person of sufficient understanding shall be deemed to be a competent witness to a will, notwithstanding any common law disqualification for interest or otherwise; but a beneficial devise or legacy to a subscribing witness or to the husband or wife of such witness shall be void unless there are two other subscribing witnesses to the will who are not similarly benefited thereunder. [Mass. Gen. Laws ch. 191, §2 (2004).]

Suppose that the testator devised a house to the spouse of a witness. Is the devise void? See Dorfman v. Allen, 434 N.E.2d 1012 (Mass. 1982) (holding statute purging devise to witness's spouse constitutional, as having a rational purpose, and voiding devise, but implying a substitute gift to the devisee's children).

RECOMMENDED METHOD OF EXECUTING A WILL

In executing a will, a lawyer should not rely on the formalities required by the statute in the client's home state. The client's will may be offered for probate in another state. The client may be domiciled elsewhere at death or may own real property in another state, or the will may exercise a power of appointment governed by the law of another state. Under the usual conflict of laws rules, the law of the decedent's domicile at death determines the validity of the will insofar as it disposes of personal property. The law of the state where real property is located determines the validity of a disposition of real property. If a person domiciled in Illinois executes a will, then moves to New Jersey and dies there, owning Florida real estate, some tangible personal property, and some stocks and bonds, the law of Illinois does not govern the validity of the will at all. New Jersey law determines the validity of the disposition of the tangible and intangible personalty, and Florida law governs the validity of the disposition of the real estate.[8] Most states have statutes recognizing as valid a will executed with the formalities required by (1) the state where the testator was domiciled at death, (2) the state where the will was executed, or (3) the state where the testator was domiciled when the will was executed. See, e.g., UPC §2-506 (1990). These statutes, where enacted, are not all uniform, however, and sometimes contain ambiguities and internal conflicts. A lawyer should draft wills so that there is no need to resort to such an act. Hence, the careful lawyer in our highly mobile society draws a will and has it executed in a manner that satisfies the formal requirements in all states.[9]

If the procedure set forth below[10] is followed, the instrument will be valid in all states, no matter in which state the testator is domiciled at the date of execution or at death or where the property is located. If all these steps are not followed to the letter, in one or more states the will may be either invalid or extremely difficult to prove as a properly executed will.

(1) If the will consists of more than one page, the pages are fastened together securely. The will specifies the exact number of pages of which it consists.

(2) The lawyer should be certain that the testator has read the will and understands its contents.

(3) The lawyer, the testator, three[11] disinterested witnesses, and a notary public are brought together in a room from which everyone else is excluded. (If the lawyer is a notary, an additional notary is unnecessary.) The door to the room is closed. No one enters or leaves the room until the ceremony is finished.

8. The Hague Convention of 1989 discards the situs rule for real property and the domicile rule for personal property, replacing them with very different choice of law rules. The Hague Convention has not been ratified by the United States and is sharply criticized by Professor Schoenblum, this country's leading choice of law scholar in estate planning matters. See Jeffrey A. Schoenblum, Choice of Law and Succession to Wealth: A Critical Analysis of the Ramifications of the Hague Convention on Succession to Decedents' Estates, 32 Va. J. Intl. L. 83 (1991).

9. If the client owns property in a foreign country or may die domiciled there, the law of the foreign country should be examined and the will executed in compliance with such law. See Jeffrey A. Schoenblum, Multistate and Multinational Estate Planning §§15.01-15.06 (2d ed. 1999); Donald D. Kozusko & Jeffrey A. Schoenblum, International Estate Planning: Principles and Strategies (1991). See also Uniform International Wills Act, found in UPC §§2-1001 to 2-1010 (1990) and adopted in many states, which sets out the procedure to be followed to comply with the 1973 Washington Convention on Wills. The procedure recommended in the text complies with the International Wills Act, except the self-proving affidavit at the end differs slightly from the affidavit required for an international will. For further discussion of the Washington Convention, ratified by the Senate in 1991, see Recent Development, The Resurgence of the International Will: A Call for Federal Legislation, 26 Vand. J. Transnatl. L. 417 (1993).

10. This procedure is an up-to-date version of the format recommended by Professor W. Barton Leach in his Cases on Wills 44 (2d ed. 1949) and subsequently refined by Professor A. James Casner in his work, 1 Estate Planning §3.1.1 (6th ed. 2004 with Jeffrey N. Pennell).

11. Vermont is the only state that still requires three witnesses, but Louisiana requires two witnesses plus a notary; see page 203, n.3. Both of these states have statutes providing that a will executed out of state is valid if it is valid either in the state where executed or in the state of the testator's domicile. La. Stat. Ann. §9.2401 (2004); Vt. Stat. Ann. tit. 14, §112 (2004). Yet even in states requiring two witnesses, using three witnesses is common—among other reasons, to reduce the harm should an interested witness be among the three. Pennsylvania is the only state that does not require witnesses at all for formal wills, so long as the testator's signature is not by a simple mark or signed by someone else at the testator's direction. Pa. Cons. Stat. tit. 20, §3132 (2004).

(4) The lawyer asks the testator the following three questions:

(a) "Is this your will?"[12]
(b) "Have you read it and do you understand it?"
(c) "Does it dispose of your property in accordance with your wishes?"

After each question the testator should answer "Yes" in a voice that can be heard by the three witnesses and the notary. It is neither necessary nor customary for the witnesses to know the terms of the will. If, however, the lawyer foresees a possible will contest, added precautions might be taken at this time. See pages 183-184.

(5) The lawyer asks the testator the following question. "Do you request _____, _____, and _____ (the three witnesses) to witness the signing of your will?" The testator should answer "Yes" in a voice audible to the witnesses.

(6) The witnesses should be standing or sitting so that all can see the testator sign. The testator signs on the margin of each page of the will. This is done for purposes of identification and to prevent subsequent substitution of pages. The testator then signs his or her name at the end of the will.

(7) One of the witnesses reads aloud the *attestation clause*, which attests that the foregoing things were done. Here is an example: "On the _____ day of _____, 20 ____, Wendy Brown declared to us, the undersigned, that the foregoing instrument was her last Will, and she requested us to act as witnesses to it and to her signature thereon. She then signed the Will in our presence, we being present at the same time. We now, at her request, in her presence, and in the presence of each other, hereunto subscribe our names as witnesses, and each of us declares that in his or her opinion this testator is of sound mind."

(8) Each witness then signs and writes his or her address next to the signature.

(9) A *self-proving affidavit*, typed at the end of the will, swearing before a notary public that the will has been duly executed, is then signed by the testator and the witnesses before the notary public, who in turn signs and attaches the required seal. Why attach a self-proving affidavit? Due execution of a will is usually proved after the testator's death by the witnesses testifying in court or executing affidavits. If the witnesses are dead or cannot be located or have moved far away, a self-proving affidavit reciting that all the requirements of due execution have been complied with permits the will to be probated. The will is valid without such an affidavit,[13] but the affidavit makes it easy to probate the will. The affidavit must be executed in front of a notary. Almost all states recognize self-proving affidavits, an invention of the UPC that has proven very popular.

UPC §2-504 (1990) authorizes two kinds of self-proving affidavits. UPC §2-504(a) authorizes a *combined* attestation clause and self-proving affidavit, so that

---

12. The testator's declaration that the instrument is his will is called *publication*. The purpose of publication is to assure that the testator is under no misapprehension as to the instrument that the testator is signing and to impress upon the witnesses the importance of the act and their consequent duties to vouch for the validity of the instrument. Nonetheless, the requirement of publication, a formality mandated in some states, is rarely a bar to probate since the testator may indicate to the witnesses that the instrument is a will by words, signs, or conduct; even the words of another saying it is the testator's will are sufficient. It is only necessary that the evidence show that the testator and the witnesses understand that the instrument is a will. Jackson v. Patton, 952 S.W.2d 404 (Tenn. 1997).

13. But see footnote 11, supra, for Louisiana law.

the testator and the witnesses (and the notary) sign their names only once; hence this is called a "one-step" self-proving affidavit. UPC §2-504(b) authorizes a self-proving affidavit to be affixed to a will already signed and attested, an affidavit that must be signed by the testator and witnesses in front of a notary *after* the testator has signed the will and the witnesses have signed the attestation clause. In our recommended procedure, we have followed this "two-step" process authorized by UPC §2-504(b), which is permitted in more states than is the combined attestation clause and self-proving affidavit.

Observe that in Will of Ranney, page 226, the lawyer included at the end of the will a self-proving affidavit authorized for use in a two-step procedure but failed to include before it an attestation clause for the witnesses to sign. The witnesses signed only the self-proving affidavit. They did not sign an attestation clause as witnesses to the will.

UPC §3-406 provides that, if a will is self-proved, compliance with signature requirements for execution is conclusively presumed. In states adopting the UPC, a self-proved will cannot be attacked on grounds of failure to comply with signature requirements but may, of course, be attacked on other grounds such as undue influence or lack of capacity. In states that permit self-proved wills but have not adopted UPC §3-406, a self-proved will may give rise to only a rebuttable presumption of due execution. See Bruce H. Mann, Self-Proving Affidavits and Formalism in Wills Adjudication, 63 Wash. U.L.Q. 39 (1985).

(10) Although not required, after the ceremony the lawyer supervising the execution should make photocopies of the original executed will. In a quiet moment after everyone has left, the lawyer should review the will to check that all the signatures are in the correct places and each page is initialed or signed in the margin. If an error was made, it is easier to correct by redoing the execution ceremony than by litigation after death. The lawyer should then write a short memo to the file noting that the firm's usual execution practices were followed and noting any problems. If the firm is retaining possession of the original (as we recommend in states where this is not expressly discouraged by local courts), the lawyer should place the original in the vault or safe-deposit box and place the copies in the client files. Many law firms then send a booklet to the client containing a photocopy of the will (marked "copy"), a cover letter stating where the original will be stored, and a copy of any earlier letters describing the estate scheme, so that after death the family might find both a copy of the will and the address of the firm having custody of the original.

NOTE: SAFEGUARDING A WILL

What should be done with the client's will after it has been executed? A common practice is to give the will to the client together with instructions that it be kept in a safe place, such as in a safe-deposit box or among valuable papers at the client's home. This is not usually the most desirable practice, however. The many reported cases involving notations, interlineations, or other markings on wills indicate that over the years a disturbing number of testators have attempted partial revocations or, perhaps, have used their wills as memo pads on which contemplated modifications have been noted. Also, an occasional testator has taken too seriously the lawyer's advice on safeguarding the will, with the result that the will cannot be located after death.[14] These potential difficulties have prompted some attorneys to follow the practice of retaining the client's will in their files. The client is given a photocopy of the will, on which the location of the original will is noted. However, keeping client's wills may have the appearance of soliciting business, an unethical practice. In State v. Gulbankian, 196 N.W.2d 733 (Wis. 1972), the Wisconsin court discussed the ethics of this practice and said:

> Nor do we approve of attorneys' "safekeeping" wills. In the old days this may have been explained on the ground many people did not have a safe place to keep valuable papers, but there is little justification today because most people do have safekeeping boxes, and if not, sec. 853.09, Stats., provides for the deposit of a will with the register in probate for safekeeping during the lifetime of the testator. The correct practice is that the original will should be delivered to the testator, and should only be kept by the attorney upon specific unsolicited request of the client. [196 N.W.2d at 736.]

Do you agree with the Wisconsin court? Can you think of a justification for the lawyer keeping the will not mentioned by the Wisconsin court? See Gerald P. Johnston, An Ethical Analysis of Common Estate Planning Practices — Is Good Business Bad Ethics?, 45 Ohio St. L.J. 57, 124-133 (1984); Report, Developments Regarding the Professional Responsibility of the Estate Planning Lawyer: The Effect of the Model Rules of Professional Conduct, 22 Real Prop., Prob. & Tr. J. 1, 28 (1987).

Like Wisconsin, many states have statutes permitting deposit of wills with the clerk of the probate court before death. UPC §2-515 (1990) provides for the deposit of a will in court for safekeeping. Depositing a will with a probate court clerk is a rare practice, however. Most persons do not know such a depository is available, and lawyers usually recommend leaving the will in the law firm's safe or safe deposit box if the client decides not to take the will home.

---

14. Consider the case of Oscar P.'s will, a true story told in a letter to one of the editors from Mr. A.J. Robinson, an attorney in Amarillo, Texas. Mr. Robinson was counsel for one group of claimants under the will.

> Two men walked into our office in late August and told us that they were Mr. P.'s nephews. They were completely covered with chigger bites from the top of their shoes to their belts. Their legs were swollen and red all over. They told us that their uncle had died in East Texas on a 40-acre farm. They said that he was found dead in his old house that did not have any doors or windows and that the floor was about to fall in, that he kept his eggs in a bucket hanging from a tree limb by wire to keep the snakes from stealing them, that he hung his milk from a tree limb, dangling in a creek, that there was no stove in the house and that he had a wheel barrow with the wheel running at about a 45 degree angle that he pushed to and from town to carry all his supplies. They had been informed that their uncle had left a will, and the entire family had descended on the place over the weekend to hunt for it. They had spent two days digging in every place that they could think of on the entire 40 acres, hunting for the will that they assumed was buried somewhere. When they were about to quit, someone decided to dig up the floor of the chicken house. Underneath the chicken house floor they found a gallon jar, and in the gallon jar was a half-gallon jar, and in the half-gallon was a quart, and in the quart was a pint, and in the pint was a half-pint, and in the half-pint was a key which appeared to fit some safe-deposit box. Upon checking all the banks in the neighboring towns, they finally found a bank that had a safe-deposit box that the key would fit. Upon opening the safe-deposit box they found P.'s holographic will. The first sentence recited that this was Oscar P.'s last will. The second sentence read: "You will find the key to my safety deposit box in a jar under the floor in the chicken house."

Oscar P. left a substantial estate.

In re Pavlinko's Estate

Supreme Court of Pennsylvania, 1959
394 Pa. 564, 148 A.2d 528

BELL, J.   Vasil Pavlinko died February 8, 1957; his wife, Hellen, died October 15, 1951. A testamentary writing dated March 9, 1949, which purported to be the will of Hellen Pavlinko, was signed by Vasil Pavlinko, her husband. The residuary legatee named therein, a brother of Hellen, offered the writing for probate as the will of Vasil Pavlinko, but probate was refused. The Orphans' Court, after hearing and argument, affirmed the decision of the Register of Wills.

The facts are unusual and the result very unfortunate. Vasil Pavlinko and Hellen, his wife, retained a lawyer to draw their wills and wished to leave their property to each other. By mistake Hellen signed the will which was prepared for her husband, and Vasil signed the will which was prepared for his wife, each instrument being signed at the end thereof. The lawyer who drew the will and his secretary, Dorothy Zinkham, both signed as witnesses. Miss Zinkham admitted that she was unable to speak the language of Vasil and Hellen, and that no conversation took place between them. The wills were kept by Vasil and Hellen. For some undisclosed reason, Hellen's will was never offered for probate at her death; in this case it was offered merely as an exhibit.

The instrument which was offered for probate was short. It stated: "I, *Hellen* Pavlinko, of . . . , do hereby make, publish and declare this to be *my* Last Will and Testament. . . ."

In the first paragraph she directed her executor to pay her debts and funeral expenses. In the second paragraph she gave her entire residuary estate to "my husband, Vasil Pavlinko . . . absolutely." She then provided:

> Third: If my aforesaid husband, Vasil Pavlinko, should predecease me, then and in that event, I give and bequeath:
>
> (a) To my brother-in-law, Mike Pavlinko, of McKees Rocks, Pennsylvania, the sum of Two Hundred ($200) Dollars.
>
> (b) To my sister-in-law, Maria Gerber, (nee Pavlinko), of Pittsburgh, Pennsylvania, the sum of Two Hundred ($200) Dollars.
>
> (c) The rest, residue and remainder of *my* estate, of whatsoever kind and nature and wheresoever situate, I give, devise and bequeath, absolutely, to *my brother*, Elias Martin, now residing at 520 Aidyl Avenue, Pittsburgh, Pennsylvania.
>
> I do hereby nominate, constitute and appoint my husband, Vasil Pavlinko, as Executor of this my Last Will and Testament.

It was then mistakenly signed "Vasil Pavlinko [Seal]."

While no attempt was made to probate, as Vasil's will, the writing which purported to be his will but was signed by Hellen, it could not have been probated as Vasil's will, because it was not signed by him at the end thereof.

The Wills Act of 1947 provides in clear, plain and unmistakable language in §2: "Every will, . . . shall be in writing and shall be signed *by the testator* at the end thereof," 20 P.S. §180.2, with certain exceptions not here relevant. The Court below correctly held that the paper which *recited* that it was the will of Hellen Pavlinko and intended and purported to give Hellen's estate to her husband, could not be probated as the will of Vasil and was a nullity.

In order to decide in favor of the residuary legatee, almost the entire will would have to be rewritten. The Court would have to substitute the words "Vasil Pavlinko" for "Hellen Pavlinko" and the words "my wife" wherever the words "my husband" appear in the will, and the relationship of the contingent residuary legatees would likewise have to be changed. To consider this paper — as written — as Vasil's will, it would give his entire residuary estate to "my husband, Vasil Pavlinko, absolutely" and "Third: If my husband, Vasil Pavlinko, should predecease me, then . . . I give and bequeath my residuary estate to my brother, Elias Martin." The language of this writing, which is signed at the end thereof by *Vasil* Pavlinko, is unambiguous, clear and unmistakable, and it is obvious that it is a meaningless nullity. . . .

Once a Court starts to ignore or alter or rewrite or make exceptions to clear, plain and unmistakable provisions of the Wills Act in order to accomplish equity and justice in that particular case, the Wills Act will become a meaningless, although well intentioned, scrap of paper, and the door will be opened wide to countless fraudulent claims which the Act successfully bars.

Decree affirmed. Each party shall pay their respective costs.

MUSMANNO, J. (dissenting).[15]   Vasil Pavlinko and his wife, Hellen Pavlinko, being unlettered in English and unlearned in the ways of the law, wisely decided to have an attorney draw up their wills, since they were both approaching the age when

15. Justice Musmanno was a striking individualist, sometimes injudicious, always colorful. In dissenting from a majority holding that Henry Miller's Rabelaisian Tropic of Cancer was not obscene, Musmanno wrote:

> "Cancer"is not a book. It is a cesspool, an open sewer, a pit of putrefaction, a slimy gathering of all that is rotten in the debris of human depravity. And in the center of all this waste and stench, besmearing himself with its foulest defilement, splashes, leaps, cavorts and wallows a bifurcated specimen that responds to the name of Henry Miller. One wonders how the human species could have produced so lecherous, blasphemous, disgusting and amoral a human being as Henry Miller. One wonders why he is received in polite society. . . . From Pittsburgh to Philadelphia, from Dan to Beersheba, and from the ramparts of the Bible to Samuel Eliot Morison's Oxford History of the American People, I dissent. [Commonwealth v. Robin, 218 A.2d 546, 561 (Pa. 1966).]

In his first five years on the Pennsylvania Supreme Court, Musmanno filed more dissenting opinions than all the other members of that court had collectively filed in the preceding 50 years. One dissent got him into a lawsuit. In another case, Chief Justice Stern ordered that Musmanno's dissent not be published in the official state reports because he had not circulated it among the court. Musmanno sought mandamus to compel the state reporter to publish his dissent. The supreme court denied the writ, Musmanno not sitting. Musmanno v. Eldredge, 114 A.2d 511 (Pa. 1955). Justice Musmanno then moved his case to the court of last resort, the law reviews. His side of the controversy can be found in Michael A. Musmanno, Dissenting Opinions, 60 Dick. L. Rev. 139 (1956). When asked whether he read Musmanno's dissents, Stern, C.J., replied that he was not "interested in current fiction." New Republic, Feb. 3, 1968, at 14.

Musmanno's ancestors came from Italy, and he was a leading force in establishing Columbus Day as a special day for Italian Americans. When Yale accepted the Vinland map as evidence that Norsemen and not an Italian, Christopher Columbus, had discovered America, Musmanno immediately rose to the attack. He dropped all his duties and went to Yale to dispute the archeologists, embarked on a six-month speaking tour attacking the authenticity of the Vinland map, and wrote a book, Columbus Was First! (1966). In 1974 the Yale Library pronounced the Vinland map a fake, based primarily on the report of a firm that found titanium in the ink, but the firm did not test authentic pre-Columbian documents for comparison, some of which have since been tested and found to contain titanium. In 1995 Yale changed its mind and announced that the Vinland map may be authentic after all. Its authenticity continues to be debated by scholars based on a range of problems besides the ink. Notwithstanding the map, scholars have reached a consensus that Musmanno's larger contention— that "Columbus Was First!"—is false. See Paul Saenger, Vinland Re-read, 50 Imago Mundi 199 (1998); R.A. Skelton, Thomas E. Marston & George D. Painter, The Vinland Map and the Tartar Relation (1995); Michael A. Fuoco, Continuing Vinland Map Feud Might Make Musmanno Smile, Pitt. Post-Gazette, Feb. 29, 2000, at A-1.

reflecting persons must give thought to that voyage from which there is no return. They explained to the attorney, whose services they sought, that he should draw two wills which would state that when either of the partners had sailed away, the one remaining ashore would become the owner of the property of the departing voyager. Vasil Pavlinko knew but little English. However, his lawyer, fortunately, was well versed in his clients' native language, known as Little Russian or Carpathian. The attorney thus discussed the whole matter with his two visitors in their language. He then dictated appropriate wills to his stenographer in English and then, after they had been transcribed, he translated the documents, paragraph by paragraph, to Mr. and Mrs. Pavlinko, who approved of all that he had written. The wills were laid before them and each signed the document purporting to be his or her will. The attorney gave Mrs. Pavlinko the paper she had signed and handed to her husband the paper he had signed. In accordance with customs they had brought with them from the old country, Mrs. Pavlinko turned her paper over to her husband. It did not matter, however, who held the papers since they were complementary of each other. Mrs. Pavlinko left her property to Mr. Pavlinko and Mr. Pavlinko left his property to Mrs. Pavlinko. They also agreed on a common residuary legatee, Elias Martin, the brother of Mrs. Pavlinko. . . .

We have also said time[s] without number that the intent of the testator must be gathered from the four corners of his will. Whether it be from the four corners of the will signed by Vasil Pavlinko or whether from the eight corners of the wills signed by Vasil and Hellen Pavlinko, all set out before the court below, the net result is always the same, namely that the residue of the property of the last surviving member of the Pavlinko couple was to go to Elias Martin.

. . . Even if we accept the Majority's conclusion . . . that all provisions in the Pavlinko will, which refer to himself, must be regarded as nullities, . . . it does not follow that the residuary clause must perish. The fact that some of the provisions in the Pavlinko will cannot be executed does not strike down the residuary clause, which is meaningful and stands on its own two feet. We know that one of the very purposes of a residuary clause is to provide a catch-all for undisposed-of or ineffectually disposed-of property. . . . I see no insuperable obstacle to probating the will signed by Vasil Pavlinko. Even though it was originally prepared as the will of his wife, Hellen, he did adopt its testamentary provisions as his own. Some of its provisions are not effective but their ineffectuality in no way bars the legality and validity of the residuary clause which is complete in itself. I would, therefore, probate the paper signed by Vasil Pavlinko. . . .

Justice Musmanno's last opinion was a freewheeling dissent to a reversal of a rape conviction. The majority held that it was error for the judge to tell the jurors they would have to answer to God for their actions. Commonwealth v. Holton, 247 A.2d 228 (Pa. 1968). Wrote Musmanno:

> God is not dead, and judges who criticize the invocation of Divine Assistance had better begin preparing a brief to use when they stand themselves at the Eternal Bar of Justice on Judgment Day. . . . I am perfectly willing to take my chances with [the trial judge] . . . at the gates of Saint Peter and answer on our voir dire that we were always willing to invoke the name of the Lord in seeking counsel. . . . Miserere nobis Omnipotens Deus! [247 A.2d at 242-243.]

The next day, Columbus Day 1968, Justice Musmanno dropped dead and presumably this voir dire took place. — Eds.

In re Snide

Court of Appeals of New York, 1981
52 N.Y.2d 193, 418 N.E.2d 656, 437 N.Y.S.2d 63

WACHTLER, J.[16]   This case involves the admissibility of a will to probate. The facts are simply stated and are not in dispute. Harvey Snide, the decedent, and his wife, Rose Snide, intending to execute mutual wills at a common execution ceremony, each executed by mistake the will intended for the other. There are no other issues concerning the required formalities of execution, nor is there any question of the decedent Harvey Snide's testamentary capacity, or his intention and belief that he was signing his last will and testament. Except for the obvious differences in the names of the donors and beneficiaries on the wills, they were in all other respects identical.

The proponent of the will, Rose Snide, offered the instrument Harvey actually signed for probate. The Surrogate decreed that it could be admitted, and further that it could be reformed to substitute the name "Harvey" wherever the name "Rose" appeared, and the name "Rose" wherever the name "Harvey" appeared. The Appellate Division reversed on the law, and held under a line of lower court cases dating back into the 1800's, that such an instrument may not be admitted to probate. We would reverse.

It is clear from the record, and the parties do not dispute the conclusion, that this is a case of a genuine mistake. It occurred through the presentment of the wills to Harvey and Rose in envelopes, with the envelope marked for each containing the will intended for the other. The attorney, the attesting witnesses, and Harvey and Rose, all proceed[ed] with the execution ceremony without anyone taking care to read the front pages, or even the attestation clauses of the wills, either of which would have indicated the error.

Harvey Snide is survived by his widow and three children, two of whom have reached the age of majority. These elder children have executed waivers and have consented to the admission of the instrument to probate. The minor child, however, is represented by a guardian ad litem who refuses to make such a concession. The reason for the guardian's objection is apparent. Because the will of Harvey would pass the entire estate to Rose, the operation of the intestacy statute after a denial of probate is the only way in which the minor child will receive a present share of the estate.

---

16. Judge Sol Wachtler was one of the most respected state court judges in the country until his conviction for sending threatening letters under a false name to his former mistress, apparently partly to harass her and partly to ingratiate himself by offering his help in protecting her from the fictional harasser.

In November 1992, he was New York state's chief judge and a rising star in the Republican party, famed for his monstrous ego, his political ambition, and his jousts with Gov. Mario Cuomo. Then he was arrested for stalking his former mistress, Joy Silverman, and charged with extortion, interstate racketeering, and blackmail, among other crimes. Wachtler had written her harassing letters in the guise of a fictional alter ego, and mailed a condom to her young daughter. The judge claimed mental incapacitation: Jilted by Silverman, he'd succumbed to a manic depression that was exacerbated by an addiction to prescription amphetamines. Wachtler pled guilty to sending threats through the mail. In September 1993—less than a year after he'd presided over New York's Court of Appeals—the 63-year-old first-time offender began serving an 11-month term in federal prison. [David Plotz, Judicial Restraint: Sol Wachtler's Worthy Sentiments on Prison, Slate, Apr. 1-16, 1997, http://slate.msn.com/id/2976/.]

—Eds.

The gist of the objectant's argument is that Harvey Snide lacked the required testamentary intent because he never intended to execute the document he actually signed. This argument is not novel, and in the few American cases on point it has been the basis for the denial of probate (see Nelson v. McDonald, 61 Hun. 406; Matter of Cutler, 58 N.Y.S.2d 604; Matter of Bacon, 165 Misc. 259; see, also, Matter of Pavlinko, 394 Pa. 564; Matter of Goettel, 184 Misc. 155). However, cases from other common-law jurisdictions have taken a different view of the matter, and we think the view they espouse is more sound (Matter of Brander, 4 DOM L. Rep. 688 [1952]; Guardian, Trust & Executor's Co. of New Zealand v. Inwood, 65 N.Z.L. Rep. 614 [1946] [New Zealand]; see Wills, 107 U. of Pa. L. Rev. 1237, 1239-1240; Kennedy, Wills-Mistake-Husband and Wife Executing Wills Drawn for Each Other — Probate of Husband's Will With Substitutions, 31 Can. Bar Rev. 185).

Of course, it is essential to the validity of a will that the testator was possessed of testamentary intent, however, we decline the formalistic view that this intent attaches irrevocably to the document prepared, rather than the testamentary scheme it reflects. Certainly, had a carbon copy been substituted for the ribbon copy the testator intended to sign, it could not be seriously contended that the testator's intent should be frustrated (Matter of Epstein, 136 N.Y.S.2d 884). Here the situation is similar. Although Harvey mistakenly signed the will prepared for his wife, it is significant that the dispositive provisions in both wills, except for the names, were identical.

Moreover, the significance of the only variance between the two instruments is fully explained by consideration of the documents together, as well as in the undisputed surrounding circumstances. Under such facts it would indeed be ironic — if not perverse — to state that because what has occurred is so obvious, and what was intended so clear, we must act to nullify rather than sustain this testamentary scheme. The instrument in question was undoubtedly genuine, and it was executed in the manner required by the statute. Under these circumstances it was properly admitted to probate (see Matter of Pascal, 309 N.Y. 108, 113-114).

In reaching this conclusion we do not disregard settled principles, nor are we unmindful of the evils which the formalities of will execution are designed to avoid; namely, fraud and mistake. To be sure, full illumination of the nature of Harvey's testamentary scheme is dependent in part on proof outside of the will itself. However, this is a very unusual case, and the nature of the additional proof should not be ignored. Not only did the two instruments constitute reciprocal elements of a unified testamentary plan, they both were executed with statutory formality, including the same attesting witnesses, at a contemporaneous execution ceremony. There is absolutely no danger of fraud, and the refusal to read these wills together would serve merely to unnecessarily expand formalism, without any corresponding benefit. On these narrow facts we decline this unjust course.

Nor can we share the fears of the dissent that our holding will be the first step in the exercise of judicial imagination relating to the reformation of wills. Again, we are dealing here solely with identical mutual wills both simultaneously executed with statutory formality.

For the reasons we have stated, the order of the Appellate Division should be reversed, and the matter remitted to that court for a review of the facts.

JONES, J., dissenting. . . . On the basis of commendably thorough world-wide research, counsel for appellant has uncovered a total of 17 available reported cases involving mutual wills mistakenly signed by the wrong testator. Six cases arise in New York, two in Pennsylvania, three in England, one in New Zealand and five in Canada. With the exception of the two recent Surrogate's decisions (*Snide* and *Iovino*) relief was denied in the cases from New York, Pennsylvania and England. The courts that have applied the traditional doctrines have not hesitated, however, to express regret at judicial inability to remedy the evident blunder. Relief was granted in the six cases from the British Commonwealth. In these cases it appears that the court has been moved by the transparency of the obvious error and the egregious frustration of undisputed intention which would ensue from failure to correct that error. . . .

I would adhere to the precedents, and affirm the order of the Appellate Division.

PROBLEM AND NOTE

1.   In *Pavlinko*, the error was not discovered when Hellen died, but only later when Vasil died. Why might this have happened? Now suppose that after Hellen Pavlinko died, the lawyer-drafter discovered the wrong wills had been signed. If Vasil were competent, he could have simply executed a new will. But suppose Vasil were then incompetent. If the lawyer photocopied the signature of Vasil on the will prepared for Hellen, superimposed it on the will prepared for Vasil, and photocopied the document, could the photocopied document be probated? Is this attempt to fix the mistake ethical? See In re Grant, 936 P.2d 1360 (Kan. 1997) (lawyer censured). What would you, as the lawyer to the now-incompetent Vasil, do to avoid a malpractice suit against you after Vasil's death?

2.   Both *Pavlinko* and *Snide* raise the same issue, yet reach opposite results. Why? Both also implicitly involve two different modes of correcting mistakes in wills. If you want to correct the error in *Pavlinko* and *Snide*, one option is to probate the will that the decedent *intended* to sign but didn't. The obvious difficulty under this approach is that the document offered for probate was not signed by the decedent. The other option is to probate the will that the decedent did sign and then to reform its terms to make sense. Under this approach, in *Pavlinko* the court would substitute the name "Vasil" for "Hellen," and in *Snide* the court would substitute "Rose" for "Harvey." We return to reformation of wills for mistake in Chapter 6.

c.   Curative Doctrines

The traditional rule is that the formalities required by the Wills Act must be complied with strictly, and almost any mistake in execution will invalidate the will. Uniform Probate Code §2-503, in what some have called a "revolutionary" change in wills formalities law, departs from this tradition by giving a court the power to dispense with formalities if there is clear and convincing evidence that the decedent intended the document to be his will.

Uniform Probate Code (1990, as amended 1997)

§2-503. HARMLESS ERROR

Although a document or writing added upon a document was not executed in compliance with Section 2-502, the document or writing is treated as if it had been executed in compliance with that section if the proponent of the document or writing establishes by clear and convincing evidence that the decedent intended the document or writing to constitute (i) the decedent's will, (ii) a partial or complete revocation of the will, (iii) an addition to or an alteration of the will, or (iv) a partial or complete revival of his [or her] formerly revoked will or of a formerly revoked portion of the will.

In re Will of Ranney

Supreme Court of New Jersey, 1991
124 N.J. 1, 589 A.2d 1339

[A traditional formal will ends with the testator's signature, followed by an attestation clause and the signatures of the witnesses. To make wills easier to prove in probate, most lawyers add a self-proving affidavit, which comes in two forms. A two-step self-proving will appends a separate affidavit to the end of the will; the witnesses (and sometimes the testator) must sign the affidavit in addition to signing the will itself, after which the affidavit is notarized. For a one-step self-proving will, the testator and the attesting witnesses sign only once, with the language of an affidavit being folded into the attestation clause, after which the will is notarized. Under either a one- or a two-step approach, the will is said to be self-proving because the affidavit provides sworn evidence of the validity of the will. Execution of a self-proving affidavit is included in the model will execution ceremony outlined on pages 215-218.

In this case, the lawyers omitted the attestation clause and used instead an affidavit designed for a two-step self-proving will. Thus, when the witnesses signed the document, they did not attest to the execution of a will but rather signed an affidavit swearing that they had previously signed their names as witnesses during a stage in the execution ceremony that never actually occurred.

Specifically, in the presence of his wife Betty, the testator Russell G. Ranney signed on the signature line of the fourth page of his will, which, to repeat, did not contain an attestation clause. The fifth page of the will was an affidavit stating that

> the Testator signed and executed the instrument as his Last Will and Testament and that he signed willingly and that he executed it as his free and voluntary act for the purposes therein expressed; and that each witness states that he or she signed the Will as witnesses in the presence and hearing of the Testator and that to the best of his or her knowledge, the Testator was at the time 18 or more years of age, of sound mind and under no constraint or undue influence.

Ranney, the two witnesses, and a notary then signed this affidavit, but the witnesses had not in fact signed the will itself as attesting witnesses, contrary to the assertions in the affidavit. If the lawyers had chosen the New Jersey form for a one-step self-proving will, which would have integrated the attestation clause and the affidavit together, then the witnesses would have been required to sign only once, simultaneously as witnesses to the will and as affiants asserting that they participated in the proper execution of that will. Unfortunately, the lawyers supervising the execution ceremony, who had executed many wills before, did not realize that the witnesses' signature on the affidavit alone did not meet New Jersey statutory formalities.]

POLLOCK, J.   . . . The acknowledgment and affidavit is almost identical to the language suggested by N.J.S.A. 3B:3-5 for a self-proving affidavit *signed subsequent to the time of execution*. The form for making a will self-proved at the time of execution, as occurred here, is set forth in the preceding section, N.J.S.A. 3B:3-4. Although the subject affidavit was executed simultaneously with the execution of the will, *the affidavit refers to the execution of the will in the past tense and incorrectly states that the witnesses had already signed the will* [emphasis added]. . . .

Russell's will gives Betty a life estate in their apartment in a building at 111 Avenue of Two Rivers in Rumson, the rental income from other apartments in that building, and the tuition and rental income from the Rumson Reading Institute, which was merged into the Ranney School after the execution of Russell's will. The will further directs that on Betty's death, the Avenue of Two Rivers property and the proceeds of the Institute are to be turned over to the trustees of the Ranney School. Additionally, Betty receives all of Russell's personal property except that necessary for the operation of the Institute.

The residue of Russell's estate is to be paid in trust to Betty, Kantor, and Henry Bass, Russell's son-in-law, who were also appointed as executors. Betty and Harland Ranney and Suzanne Bass, Russell's two children, are to receive thirty-two percent each of the trust income, and are to share equally the net income from the operation of Ransco Corporation. Nancy Orlow, Betty's daughter and Russell's step-daughter, is to receive the remaining four percent of the trust income. Russell's will provides further that after Betty's death the income from Ransco Corporation is to be distributed equally between Harland Ranney and Suzanne Bass, and on their deaths is to be distributed to the Ranney School.

Russell died on April 4, 1987, and the Monmouth County Surrogate admitted the will to probate on April 21, 1987. . . . Subsequently, Betty . . . contested the probate of Russell's will. . . . Her sole challenge was that the will failed to comply literally with the formalities of N.J.S.A. 3B:3-2. Suzanne R. Bass, Harland Ranney, Henry Bass, and the Ranney School urged that the will be admitted to probate. . . .

Although the Appellate Division "decline[d] to hold that the placement of the witnesses' signatures is immaterial," it ruled that the self-proving affidavit was part of the will and that the witnesses' signatures on the affidavit constituted signatures on the will . . . .

We disagree with the Appellate Division that signatures on the subsequently-executed self-proving affidavit literally satisfied the requirements of N.J.S.A. 3B:3-2 as signatures on a will. We further hold, however, that the will may be admitted to probate if it substantially complies with these requirements.

II

The first question is whether Russell's will literally complies with the requirements of N.J.S.A. 3B:3-2, which provides:

> [E]very will shall be in writing, signed by the testator or in his name by some other person in his presence and at his direction, and shall be signed by at least two persons each of whom witnessed either the signing or the testator's acknowledgment of the signature or of the will.

In holding that signatures on the self-proving affidavit satisfy N.J.S.A. 3B:3-2, the Appellate Division relied on out-of-state decisions that permitted the probate of wills when the witnesses signed a self-proving affidavit, but not the will. The rationale of those cases is that a self-proving affidavit and an attestation clause are sufficiently similar to justify the conclusion that signatures on a self-proving affidavit, like signatures on the attestation clause, satisfy the requirement that the signatures be on the will. The Appellate Division found that the similarity between self-proving affidavits and attestation clauses warrants treating the affidavit attached to Russell's will as the equivalent of an attestation clause. Noting that the absence of an attestation clause does not void a will, but merely requires the proponents to prove due execution, the Appellate Division could find "no reason, either in logic or policy, to deny a similar opportunity to the proponents" of Russell's will. . . .

Self-proving affidavits and attestation clauses, although substantially similar in content, serve different functions. Mann, Self-Proving Affidavits and Formalism in Wills Adjudication, 63 Wash. U.L.Q. 39, 41 (1985). Attestation clauses facilitate probate by providing "prima facie evidence" that the testator voluntarily signed the will in the presence of the witnesses. 5 A. Clapp, N.J. Practice: Wills and Administration §133 at 335 (3d ed. 1982). An attestation clause also permits probate of a will when a witness forgets the circumstances of the will's execution or dies before the testator. Id. at 337.

Self-proving affidavits, by comparison, are sworn statements by eyewitnesses that the will has been duly executed. Mann, supra, 63 Wash. U.L.Q. at 40. The affidavit performs virtually all the functions of an attestation clause, and has the further effect of permitting probate without requiring the appearance of either witness. Id. at 41; 8 A. Clapp, supra, §2063 at 9, Comment 1. Wills may be made self-proving simultaneously with or after execution. N.J.S.A. 3B:3-4, -5. One difference between an attestation clause and a subsequently-signed, self-proving affidavit is that in an attestation clause, the attestant expresses the present intent to act as a witness, but in the affidavit, the affiant swears that the will has already been witnessed. This difference is more apparent than real when, as here, the affiants, with the intent to act as witnesses, sign the self-proving affidavit immediately after witnessing the testator's execution of the will.

The Legislature first authorized self-proving affidavits in the 1977 amendments to the Probate Code, specifically N.J.S.A. 3A:2A-6. Nothing in the statutory language or history intimates that the Legislature contemplated a subsequently-executed affidavit as a substitute for the attestation clause. Instead, the 1977 amendments indicate that the Legislature envisioned the will, including the attestation clause, as independent from such an affidavit. Hence, the form provided in N.J.S.A. 3B:3-5 for a subsequently-signed affidavit refers to the will as a separate instrument and states that the testator and witnesses have signed the will. Thus, the Legislature indicated its intention that subsequently-executed, self-proving affidavits be used solely in conjunction with duly-executed wills. Although the execution of Russell's will and of the self-proving affidavit apparently were contemporaneous, the affidavit follows the form provided in N.J.S.A. 3B:3-5. Consequently, the signatures of the witnesses on the subject self-proving affidavit do not literally comply with the statutory requirements.

That finding does not end the analysis. As we stated in In re Estate of Peters, 526 A.2d 1005 (N.J. 1987), in limited circumstances a will may be probated if it substantially complies with those requirements.

Scholars . . . have supported the doctrine of substantial compliance. Langbein, Substantial Compliance with the Wills Act, 88 Harv. L. Rev. 489 (1975); Nelson & Starck, Formalities and Formalism: A Critical Look at the Execution of Wills, 6 Pepperdine L. Rev. 331, 356 (1979). At the 1990 annual conference, the Commissioners on Uniform State Laws added a section to the Uniform Probate Code explicitly advocating the adoption of the doctrine. Uniform Probate Code §2-503 (National Conference of Commissioners on Uniform State Laws 1990). That section, 2-503, provides:

> Although a document . . . was not executed in compliance with §2-502 [enumerating the wills formalities], the document . . . is treated as if it had been executed in compliance with that section if the proponent of the document . . . establishes by clear and convincing evidence that the decedent intended the document to constitute . . . the decedent's will. . . .

In the 1990 edition of the Restatement (Second) of Property (Donative Transfers) (Restatement), moreover, the American Law Institute encourages courts to permit probate of wills that substantially comply with will formalities. §33.1 Comment g (Tentative Draft No. 13) (approved by the American Law Institute at 1990 annual meeting). The Restatement concludes that in the absence of legislative action, courts "should apply a rule of excused noncompliance, under which a will is found validly executed if the proponent establishes by clear and convincing evidence that the decedent intended the document to constitute his or her will." . . .

III

Substantial compliance is a functional rule designed to cure the inequity caused by the "harsh and relentless formalism" of the law of wills. Langbein, supra, 88 Harv. L. Rev. at 489. . . . The underlying rationale is that the

> finding of a formal defect should lead not to automatic invalidity, but to a further inquiry: does the noncomplying document express the decedent's testamentary intent, and does its form sufficiently approximate Wills Act formality to enable the court to conclude that it serves the purposes of the Wills Act? [Langbein, supra, 88 Harv. L. Rev. at 489.]

Scholars have identified various reasons for formalities in the execution of wills. The primary purpose of those formalities is to ensure that the document reflects the uncoerced intent of the testator. Id. at 492; Mann, supra, 63 Wash. U.L.Q. at 49. Requirements that the will be in writing and signed by the testator also serve an evidentiary function by providing courts with reliable evidence of the terms of the will and of the testamentary intent. Gulliver & Tilson, Classification of Gratuitous Transfers, 51 Yale L.J. 1, 6-7 (1941). Additionally, attestation requirements prevent fraud and undue influence. Id. at 9-10; In re Estate of Peters, supra, 526 A.2d 1005. Further, the formalities perform a "channeling function" by requiring a certain degree of uniformity in the organization, language, and content of wills. Langbein, supra, 88 Harv. L. Rev. at 494. Finally, the ceremony serves as a ritual that impresses the testator with the seriousness of the occasion. Gulliver & Tilson, supra, 51 Yale L.J. at 5.

Rigid insistence on literal compliance often frustrates these purposes. Restatement, supra, §33.1 Comment g (strict compliance has in many cases led courts to results that defeated the intent of the testator). To avoid such frustration, some courts, although purporting to require literal compliance, have allowed probate of technically-defective wills. See In re Estate of Bochner, 464 N.Y.S.2d 958, 959 (Sur. 1983); In re Will of Leitstein, 260 N.Y.S.2d 406, 408 (Sur. 1965). Other courts have refused to probate wills because of technical defects despite evidence that the testator meant the document to be a will. See In re Estate of Sample, 572 P.2d 1232, 1234 (Mont. 1977) (refusing to probate will signed only on attached self-proving affidavit); Boren v. Boren, 402 S.W.2d 728, 729 (Tex. 1966) (same). Leading authorities have criticized the *Boren* rule, finding no basis in logic or policy for its blind insistence on voiding wills for "the most minute defect[s] in formal compliance . . . no matter how abundant the evidence that the defect [is] inconsequential." Langbein, supra, 88 Harv. L. Rev. at 489; accord In re Estate of Charry, 359 So. 2d 544, 545 (Fla. App. 1978) (declining to follow *Boren* rule because it elevated form over substance); Mann, supra, 63 Wash. U.L.Q. at 39-40 (characterizing *Boren* line of cases as "odd and rather perverse"); Nelson & Starck, supra, 6 Pepperdine L. Rev. at 356-57.

We agree with those authorities. Compliance with statutory formalities is important not because of the inherent value that those formalities possess, but because of the purposes they serve. Mann, supra, 63 Wash. U.L.Q. at 60; Nelson & Starck, supra, 6 Pepperdine L. Rev. at 355. It would be ironic to insist on literal compliance with statutory formalities when that insistence would invalidate a will that is the deliberate and voluntary act of the testator. Such a result would frustrate rather than further the purpose of the formalities. Nelson & Starck, supra, 6 Pepperdine L. Rev. at 353-55. . . .

The execution of a last will and testament, however, remains a solemn event. A careful practitioner will still observe the formalities surrounding the execution of wills. When formal defects occur, proponents should prove by clear and convincing evidence that the will substantially complies with statutory requirements. See Uniform Probate Code, supra, §2-503; Restatement, supra, §33.1 Comment g. Our adoption of the doctrine of substantial compliance should not be construed as an invitation either to carelessness or to chicanery. The purpose of the doctrine is to remove procedural peccadillos as a bar to probate.

Furthermore, as previously described, a subsequently-signed self-proving affidavit serves a unique function in the probate of wills. We are reluctant to permit the signatures on such an affidavit both to validate the execution of the will and to render the will self-proving. Accordingly, if the witnesses, with the intent to attest, sign a self-proving affidavit, but do not sign the will or an attestation clause, clear and convincing evidence of their intent should be adduced to establish substantial compliance with the statute. For that reason, probate in these circumstances should proceed in solemn form. See N.J.S.A. 3B:3-23; R. 4:84-1. Probate in solemn form, which is an added precaution to assure proof of valid execution, may be initiated on an order to show cause, R. 4:84-1(b), and need not unduly delay probate of a qualified will.

. . . If, after conducting a hearing in solemn form, the trial court is satisfied that the execution of the will substantially complies with the statutory requirements, it may reinstate the judgment of the Surrogate admitting the will to probate.

The judgment of the Appellate Division is affirmed, and the matter is remanded to the Chancery Division, Probate Part.

In re Estate of Hall

Supreme Court of Montana, 2002
310 Mont. 486, 51 P.3d 1134

REGINIER, J. . . .   James Mylen Hall ("Jim") died on October 23, 1998. At the time of his death, he was 75 years old and lived in Cascade County, Montana. His wife, Betty Lou Hall ("Betty"), and two daughters from a previous marriage, Sandra Kay Ault ("Sandra") and Charlotte Rae Hall ("Charlotte"), survived him.

Jim first executed a will on April 18, 1984 (the "Original Will"). Approximately thirteen years later, Jim and Betty's attorney, Ross Cannon, transmitted to them a draft of a joint will (the "Joint Will").[17] On June 4, 1997, Jim and Betty met at Cannon's office to discuss the draft. After making several changes, Jim and Betty apparently agreed on the terms of the Joint Will. Jim and Betty were prepared to execute the Joint Will once Cannon sent them a final version.

At the conclusion of the meeting, however, Jim asked Cannon if the draft could stand as a will until Cannon sent them a final version. Cannon said that it would be valid if Jim and Betty executed the draft and he notarized it. Betty testified that no one else was in the office at the time to serve as an attesting witness. Jim and Betty, therefore, proceeded to sign the Joint Will and Cannon notarized it without anyone else present.

When they returned home from the meeting, Jim apparently told Betty to tear up the Original Will, which Betty did. After Jim's death, Betty applied to informally probate the Joint Will. Sandra objected to the informal probate and requested formal probate of the Original Will.

On August 9, 2001, Judge McKittrick heard the will contest. He issued the Order admitting the Joint Will to probate on August 27, 2001. Sandra appealed. . . .

In contested cases, the proponent of a will must establish that the testator duly executed the will. See §72-3-310, MCA. For a will to be valid, two people typically must witness the testator signing the will and then sign the will themselves. See §72-2-522(1)(c), MCA. If two individuals do not properly witness the document, §72-2-523, MCA, provides that the document may still be treated as if it had been

---

17. A joint will is one instrument executed by two persons as the will of both — that is, one will for two people. See page 288. — Eds.

executed under certain circumstances. One such circumstance is if the proponent of the document establishes by clear and convincing evidence that the decedent intended the document to be the decedent's will. See §72-2-523, MCA.[18]

Sandra urges this Court not to use §72-2-523, MCA, "to circumvent the statute requiring two witnesses to the execution of a will." Jim and Betty's failure to use witnesses, according to Sandra, was not an innocent omission on their part. . . . She primarily argues . . . that the Joint Will should be invalid as a matter of law because no one properly witnessed it.

Sandra's numerous arguments about why the will was improperly witnessed are irrelevant to this appeal. Neither party disputes that no witnesses were present at the execution of Jim and Betty's Joint Will as required by §72-2-522, MCA. In the absence of attesting witnesses, §72-2-523, MCA, affords a means of validating a will for which the Montana Legislature expressly provides. The only question before this Court, therefore, is whether the District Court erred in concluding that Jim intended the Joint Will to be his will under §72-2-523, MCA. We conclude that the court did not err.

The District Court made several findings of fact that supported its conclusion. In particular, it noted that the Joint Will specifically revoked all previous wills and codicils made by either Jim or Betty. Furthermore, the court found that, after they had executed the Joint Will, Jim directed Betty to destroy the Original Will.

Sandra does not dispute any of the court's factual findings. She argues only that Betty testified that she and Jim had not executed the will even after they had signed it. In making this argument, she points to the following testimony:

> *Question:* Do you know if [Jim] gave [Sandra and Charlotte] a copy of the new will?
> *Answer:* I don't believe he did, no.
> *Question:* Do you know why?
> *Answer:* Well, I guess because we didn't have the completed draft without all the scribbles on it.
> *Question:* So he thought that will was not good yet?
> *Answer:* No, he was sure it was good, but he didn't give it to the girls. And we didn't give it to my son. We didn't give it to anybody.
> *Question:* Why?
> *Answer:* Because it wasn't completely finished the way Ross was going to finish it.

This testimony may suggest that Betty believed that the Joint Will was not in a final form because of "all the scribbles on it." Nevertheless, she immediately goes on to state that she believed the will was good. When asked if it were Jim's and her intent for the Joint Will to stand as a will until they executed another one, she responded, "Yes, it was." The court could reasonably interpret this testimony to mean that Jim and Betty expected the Joint Will to stand as a will until Cannon

---

18. Section 72-2-523 is the Montana enactment of UPC §2-503 (1990).—Eds.

provided one in a cleaner, more final form. Sandra points to no other evidence that suggests that Jim did not intend for the Joint Will to be his will.

For these reasons, we conclude that the District Court did not err in admitting the Joint Will into final probate. Because Jim directed Betty to destroy the Original Will, we also conclude that the District Court did not err in finding that these acts were acts of revocation of the Original Will under §72-2-527, MCA.

Affirmed.

NOTES AND QUESTIONS

1. The architect of both *substantial compliance* (adopted in *Ranney*) and the *dispensing power* (authorized by UPC §2-503 and applied in *Hall*) is Professor John Langbein of Yale. Langbein first proposed substantial compliance to correct execution defects but later came to believe that a dispensing power was better. The story of these curative doctrines begins with Langbein's classic 1975 article, Substantial Compliance with the Wills Act, 88 Harv. L. Rev. 489 (1975). Langbein proposed that courts develop a substantial compliance doctrine to cure will execution errors. Under *substantial compliance*, if there is clear and convincing evidence (generally the highest evidentiary standard in civil litigation) that the purposes of formalities — the evidentiary, cautionary, protective, and channeling functions — were served despite a defective execution, the will is admitted to probate. Langbein viewed substantial compliance as a broad palliative that would excuse most innocent execution defects, especially those involving missing or defective attestation by witnesses. In 1981, the Australian state of Queensland enacted a statute providing for probate of a will that substantially complies with the will formalities. Queensland Succession Act of 1981, §9(a), 1981 Queensl. Stat. No. 69.

In the same year that Langbein published his substantial compliance article, South Australia enacted a *dispensing power* statute providing for the probate of a document that was not properly executed if the court "is satisfied that there can be no reasonable doubt that the deceased intended the document to constitute his will." S. Austl. Wills Act Amendment Act (No. 2) of 1975, §9, amending Wills Act of 1936, §12(2), 8 S. Austl. Stat. 665. This act excuses noncompliance with the Wills Act. It gives a court a dispensing power — the power to validate a document the decedent intended to be a will even though the formalities are not complied with.

After observing the South Australian experience with the dispensing power and the Queensland experience with substantial compliance, in 1987 Langbein concluded that the dispensing power was preferable to the substantial compliance doctrine. The reason was that the "courts read into their substantial compliance doctrine a near-miss standard, ignoring the central issue of whether the testator's conduct evidenced testamentary intent." John H. Langbein, Excusing Harmless Errors in the Execution of Wills: A Report on Australia's Tranquil Revolution in Probate Law, 87 Colum. L. Rev. 1, 53 (1987). For example, Langbein had intended that substantial compliance would allow most wills with defective attestation to be probated, but the Queensland courts applied substantial compliance so narrowly that, because attestation generally served the purposes of formalities, they were unwilling to overlook most defects in attestation.

In South Australia, however, the dispensing power fared much better. From examining the first 41 South Australian cases after 1975, Langbein concluded:

> Implicitly, this case law has produced a ranking of the Wills Act formalities. Of the three main formalities—writing, signature, and attestation—writing turns out to be indispensable. Because section 12(2) requires a "document," nobody has tried to use the dispensing power to enforce an oral will. Failure to give permanence to the terms of your will is not harmless. Signature ranks next in importance. If you leave your will unsigned, you raise a grievous doubt about the finality and genuineness of the instrument. An unsigned will is presumptively only a draft, . . . but that presumption is rightly overcome in compelling circumstances such as in the switched-wills cases. By contrast, attestation makes a more modest contribution, primarily of a protective character, to the Wills Act policies. But the truth is that most people do not need protecting, and there is usually strong evidence that want of attestation did not result in imposition. The South Australian courts have been quick to find such evidence and to excuse attestation defects under the dispensing power.
>
> In devaluing attestation while insisting on signature and writing, the South Australian legislation and case law has brought the South Australian law of wills into a kind of alignment with the American law of will substitutes, that is, with our nonprobate system, where business practice has settled the forms for transfer. In life insurance beneficiary designations; in bank transfer arrangements such as pay-on-death accounts, joint accounts, and Totten trusts; in pension accounts; and in revocable inter vivos trusts, writing is the indispensable formality of modern practice, and signature is nearly as universal. Attestation, however, is increasingly uncommon. . . .
>
> Americans should . . . shudder that we still inflict upon our citizens the injustice of the traditional law, and we should join in this movement to rid private law of relics so embarrassing. [Id. at 52-54.]

Professor John H. Langbein

In 1990, the dispensing power was codified in the UPC, albeit with a change in the standard of proof from the criminal law standard (no reasonable doubt, as in South Australia) to what is usually the highest evidentiary standard in American civil litigation (clear and convincing evidence). Under UPC §2-503, courts are directed to look not at whether the purposes of formalities were served (as in substantial compliance), but at whether "the decedent intended the document or writing to constitute . . . the decedent's will." UPC §2-503 has been adopted in Colorado, Hawaii, Michigan, Montana, South Dakota, and Utah. Measures similar to UPC §2-503 have been enacted in other Australian states, Manitoba, Saskatchewan, and Israel. The official comment to the Israeli Succession

Law of 5725-1965, §25, adopting a dispensing power, notes: "Jewish Law demands on the one hand strict compliance with certain formulae. . . . [O]n the other hand it developed the concept of 'a . . . *mitzvah*[19] to carry out the wishes of the deceased.'" Israel Misrad ha-Mishpatim, Hatzaat Hok ha-Yerushah 73 (5712-1952).

Restatement (Third) of Property: Wills and Other Donative Transfers §3.3 (1999) also adopts the dispensing power: "A harmless error in executing a will may be excused if the proponent establishes by clear and convincing evidence that the decedent adopted the document as his or her will."

For discussion of the dispensing power and the substantial compliance doctrine, see, in addition to Langbein's articles, Emily Sherwin, Clear and Convincing Evidence of Testamentary Intent: The Search for a Compromise Between Formality and Adjudicative Justice, 34 Conn. L. Rev. 453 (2002); Lloyd Bonfield, Reforming the Requirements for Due Execution of Wills: Some Guidance from the Past, 70 Tul. L. Rev. 1893 (1996); Melanie B. Leslie, The Myth of Testamentary Freedom, 38 Ariz. L. Rev. 235, 258-290 (1996); James Lindgren, The Fall of Formalism, 55 Alb. L. Rev. 1009 (1992); Bruce H. Mann, Formalities and Formalism in the Uniform Probate Code, 142 U. Pa. L. Rev. 1033 (1994); C. Douglas Miller, Will Formality, Judicial Formalism, and Legislative Reform: An Examination of the New Uniform Probate Code "Harmless Error" Rule and the Movement toward Amorphism, 43 Fla. L. Rev. 167 (pt. 1), 599 (pt. 2) (1991).

2.   If attestation defects can be excused by a court, as in *Hall,* and serve only a modest Wills Act function, as Langbein suggests, why not abolish the attestation requirement entirely? In his 1987 study, Langbein finds that in every South Australian case involving attestation defects, the will was nonetheless reliable enough to be admitted to probate. If in almost every case attestation defects are going to be excused, then why not use a *rule* (no attestation requirement) rather than a litigation-breeding *standard* (the dispensing power)?

Since the 1700s, Pennsylvania has not required attestation for formal wills. Yet practitioners there continue to use attested wills and there is no evidence that fraud has run wild in Pennsylvania. As long as self-proving wills are easier to probate, well-counseled testators will continue to use witnesses. For an argument that the minimum formalities for a will should be reduced to a writing (typed or handwritten) signed by the testator, see James Lindgren, Abolishing the Attestation Requirement for Wills, 68 N.C. L. Rev. 541 (1990); Lindgren, The Fall of Formalism, supra, at 1024-1033.

3.   Suppose that a signed, handwritten, but unwitnessed will is offered for probate. Apparently, this document could be probated under UPC §2-503, just as South Australian cases have probated handwritten unwitnessed wills. Would the adoption of UPC §2-503 mean that holographic wills are permitted in jurisdictions having no statute authorizing them? See Langbein, Excusing Harmless Errors, supra, at 18-22.

---

19. The term *mitzvah* resists straightforward English translation, but the basic idea is a mix of commandment and good deed. — Eds.

2. Holographic Wills

The Jolly Testator Who Makes His Own Will[20]

Ye lawyers who live upon litigants' fees,
And who need a good many to live at your ease,
Grave or gay, wise or witty, whate'er your degree,
Plain stuff or Queen's Counsel, take counsel of me:
When a festive occasion your spirit unbends,
You should never forget the profession's best friends;
So we'll send round the wine, and a light bumper fill
To the jolly testator who makes his own will.
He premises his wish and his purpose to save
All dispute among friends when he's laid in the grave;
Then he straightway proceeds more disputes to create
Than a long summer's day would give time to relate.
He writes and erases, he blunders and blots,
He produces such puzzles and Gordian knots,
That a lawyer, intending to frame the thing ill,
Couldn't match the testator who makes his own will.

LORD NEAVES

In slightly over half of the states, primarily in the South and West, holographic wills are permitted.[21] A holographic will is a will written by the testator's hand and signed by the testator; attesting witnesses are not required. Holographic wills are of Roman origin and are recognized by the Code Napoleon and civil law countries. They were introduced into this country by a Virginia statute of 1751 and by the reception of the civil law into Louisiana. See generally R.H. Helmholz, The Origin of Holographic Wills in English Law, 15 Leg. Hist. 97 (1994).

ASHBEL G. GULLIVER & CATHERINE J. TILSON, CLASSIFICATION OF GRATUITOUS TRANSFERS, 51 Yale L.J. 1, 13-14 (1941): "The exemption of holographic wills from the usual statutory requirements seems almost exclusively justifiable in terms of the evidentiary function. The requirement that a holographic will be entirely written in the handwriting of the testator furnishes more complete evidence for inspection by handwriting experts than would exist if

---

20. We reproduce only the first two stanzas of Lord Neaves's poem. For the entire poem, see William L. Prosser, The Judicial Humorist 246 (1952). — Eds.

21. The states are Alaska, Arizona, Arkansas, California, Colorado, Hawaii, Idaho, Kentucky, Louisiana, Maine, Michigan, Mississippi, Montana, Nebraska, Nevada, New Jersey, North Carolina, North Dakota, Oklahoma, Pennsylvania, South Dakota, Tennessee, Texas, Utah, Virginia, West Virginia, and Wyoming. In Maryland and New York, holographic wills are permitted for soldiers and sailors. For a list of state statutes, see Jeffrey A. Schoenblum, 2004 Multistate Guide to Estate Planning at Table 1.

Suppose that the testator writes a holographic will in a state recognizing such a will, and then the testator moves to a state that does not recognize holographic wills and dies there. On this matter, states that do not recognize holographs are split. Some permit probate of a holographic will if valid where executed; other states deny probate.

only the signature were available, and consequently tends to preclude the probate of a forged document. . . . While there is a certain ritual value in writing out the document, casual off-hand statements are frequently made in letters. The relative incompleteness of the performance of the functions of the regular statute of wills, and particularly the absence of any ritual value, may account for the fact that holographic wills are not recognized in the majority of the states, and for some decisions, in states recognizing them, requiring the most precise compliance with specified formalities."

Kimmel's Estate

Supreme Court of Pennsylvania, 1924
278 Pa. 435, 123 A. 405

SIMPSON, J. One of decedent's heirs at law appeals from a decree of the orphans' court, directing the register of wills to probate the following letter:

Johnstown, Dec. 12.
The Kimmel Bro. and Famly

    We are all well as you can espec fore the time of the Year. I received you kind & welcome letter from Geo & Irvin all OK glad you poot your Pork down in Pickle it is the true way to keep meet every piece gets the same, now always poot it down that way & you will not miss it & you will have good pork fore smoking you can keep it from butchern to butchern the hole year round. Boys, I wont agree with you about the open winter I think we are gone to have one of the hardest. Plenty of snow & Verry cold verry cold! I dont want to see it this way but it will come see to the old sow & take her away when the time comes well I cant say if I will come over yet. I will wright in my next letter it may be to ruff we will see in the next letter if I come I have some very valuable papers I want you to keep fore me so if enny thing hapens all the scock money in the 3 Bank liberty lones Post office stamps and my home on Horner St goes to George Darl & Irvin Kepp this letter lock it up it may help you out. Earl sent after his Christmas Tree & Trimmings I sent them he is in the Post office in Phila working.

                                     Will clost your Truly,
                                     Father.

This letter was mailed by decedent at Johnstown, Pa., on the morning of its date — Monday, December 12, 1921 — to two of his children, George and Irvin, who were named in it as beneficiaries; the envelope being addressed to them at their residence in Glencoe, Pa. He died suddenly on the afternoon of the same day.

    Two questions are raised: First. Is the paper testamentary in character? Second. Is the signature to it a sufficient compliance with our Wills Act? Before answering them directly, there are a few principles, now well settled, which, perhaps, should be preliminarily stated.

    While the informal character of a paper is an element in determining whether or not it was intended to be testamentary (Kisecker's Estate, 190 Pa. 476), this becomes a matter of no moment when it appears thereby that the decedent's purpose was to make a posthumous gift. On this point the court below well said: "Deeds, mortgages, letters, powers of attorney, agreements, checks, notes, etc., have all been held to be, in legal effect, wills. Hence, an assignment (Coulter v. Shelmadine, 204 Pa. 120, . . . a deed (Turner v. Scott, 51 Pa. 126), a letter of instructions (Scott's Estate, 147 Pa. 89), a power of attorney (Rose v. Quick, 30 Pa. 225), and an informal letter of requests (Knox's Estate, 131 Pa. 220), were all held as wills."

It is equally clear that where, as here, the words "if enny thing hapens," condition the gift, they strongly support the idea of a testamentary intent; indeed they exactly state what is expressed in or must be implied from every will. True, if the particular contingency stated in a paper, as the condition upon which it shall become effective, has never in fact occurred, it will not be admitted to probate. Morrow's Appeal, 116 Pa. 440; Forquer's Estate, 216 Pa. 331. In the present case, however, it is clear the contingency, "if enny thing hapens," was still existing when testator died suddenly on the same day he wrote and mailed the letter; hence, the facts not being disputed, the question of testamentary intent was one of law for the court. Davis' Estate, 275 Pa. 126.

As is often the case in holographic wills of an informal character, much of that which is written is not dispositive; and the difficulty, in ascertaining the writer's intent, arises largely from the fact that he had little, if any, knowledge of either law, punctuation, or grammar. In the present case this is apparent from the paper itself; and in this light the language now quoted must be construed:

> I think we are gone to have one of the hardest [winters]. Plenty of snow & Verry cold verry cold! I dont want to see it this way but it will come . . . well I cant say if I will come over yet. I will wright in my next letter it may be to ruff we will see in the next letter if I come I have some very valuable papers I want you to keep fore me so if enny thing hapens all . . . [the real and personal property specified] goes to George Darl and Irvin Kepp this letter lock it up it may help you out.

When resolved into plainer English, it is clear to us that all of the quotation, preceding the words "I have some very valuable papers," relate to the predicted bad weather, a doubt as to whether decedent will be able to go to Glencoe because of it, and a possible resolution of it in his next letter; the present one stating "we will see in the next letter if I come." This being so, the clause relating to the valuable papers begins a new subject of thought, and since the clearly dispositive gifts which follow are made dependent on no other contingency than "if enny thing hapens," and death did happen suddenly on the same day, the paper, so far as respects those gifts, must be treated as testamentary.

It is difficult to understand how the decedent, probably expecting an early demise — as appears by the letter itself, and the fact of his sickness and inability to work, during the last three days of the first or second week preceding — could have possibly meant anything else than a testamentary gift, when he said "so if enny thing hapens [the property specified] goes to George Darl and Irvin"; and why, if this was not intended to be effective in and of itself, he should have sent it to two of the distributees named in it, telling them to "Kepp this letter lock it up it may help you out."

The second question to be determined . . . [is whether] the word "Father," when taken in connection with the contents of the paper, show that it was "signed by him?" . . . If the word "Father" was intended as a completed signature to this particular character of paper, it answers all the purposes of the Wills Act. That it was so intended we have no doubt. It was the method employed by decedent in signing all such letters, and was mailed by him as a finished document.

. . . True, a formal will would not be so executed; but this is not a formal will. It is a letter, signed by him in the way he executed all such letters, and, from this circumstance, his "intent to execute is apparent" beyond all question.

Decree affirmed and appeal dismissed, the costs in this court to be paid by the estate of Harry A. Kimmel, deceased.

QUESTIONS AND NOTES

1.   If you had asked Mr. Kimmel before he died whether his letter was a will, what would he have answered?

2.   In Kimmel's Estate, the will was upon the condition, "if enny thing hapens," meaning "if I die." Suppose the will is written to become operative if death from a stated event occurs, such as death from a surgical operation or death while on a journey. Does the testator want the will to be effective only if the event happens or to be effective at the testator's death regardless of whether his death is related to the event? There seems little reason to suppose that the testator would want to favor one set of family members if he dies on a trip but another set of family members if he returns and then dies.

In Eaton v. Brown, 193 U.S. 411 (1904), the testator wrote a holographic will saying: "I am going on a journey and may not return. If I do not, I leave everything to my adopted son." The testator returned from her journey and died some months later. The Supreme Court, per Holmes, J., ordered the will probated. "Obviously the first sentence, 'I am going on a journey and may not ever return,' expresses the fact which was on her mind as the occasion and inducement for writing it. . . . She was thinking of the possibility of death or she would not have made a will. But that possibility at that moment took the specific shape of not returning from her journey, and so she wrote 'if I do not return,' before giving her last commands." Id. at 414.

Most of the cases on conditional wills are in accord with Eaton v. Brown. They presume the language of condition does not mean that the will is to be probated only if the stated event happens but is, instead, merely a statement of the inducement for execution of the will, which can be probated upon death from any cause. See Estate of Martin, 635 N.W.2d 473 (S.D. 2001) ("If anything should happen to me on this trip to Rapid City . . . [e]verything I own is to go to" one of T's three daughters and that daughter's family.).

3.   Holographic wills are often written *in extremis*, when the testator is close to death, and sometimes under heart-rendering circumstances. Consider Estate of Harris, reported in W.M. Elliott, Wills — Writing Scratched on Tractor Fender — Granting of Probate, 26 Can. B. Rev. 1242 (1948):

Recently the Surrogate Court of the Judicial District of Kerrobert in Saskatchewan granted Letters of Administration with Will Annexed of a holograph writing scratched on a tractor fender (the Estate of Cecil George Harris). . . .

The facts of the Harris case were as follows. The deceased, a married man with two small children, was a wheat farmer. At noon on June 8th, 1948, he set out with a tractor and one-way disc to summer-fallow, telling his wife that he intended to work through the day and probably would not be back until almost ten in the evening. About an hour later he stopped the implements to do some oiling and make adjustments. After stepping down from the tractor seat, he put the tractor by mistake into reverse gear. As a result, it moved backwards pinning him between the two implements with his left leg caught under the left rear wheel of the tractor and the lower part of his body caught between the implements. Although he had the freedom of his arms, he was unable to reach the controls of the tractor. Eventually, the tractor engine died. He was still in this position some nine hours later when his wife, wondering at his absence, discovered him. She summoned help from the neighbors and at about 10:30 p.m. he was released and rushed to the hospital where he died, as a result of his injuries, within forty-eight hours.

When the deceased was discovered he was conscious and able to give instructions for releasing him. He remained conscious until given medical attention and stated that he had been conscious during the whole of the time he was imprisoned.

On June 10th . . . [a neighbor] noticed the writing scratched on the fender. It read: "In case I die in this mess, I leave all to the wife. Cecil Geo. Harris." [Id. at 1242-1243.]

The knife used to scratch the will was discovered in Harris's clothes. The fender was taken to the solicitor's office and ultimately the piece containing the will was cut off, admitted to probate, and stored with the case files. The testator's handwriting was proved by affidavit.

4. Purported holographic wills have taken myriad forms — and shapes. In addition to tractor fenders, wills have been written on a nurse's petticoat, a chest of drawers, and a bedroom wall,[22] as well as tattooed on a person's back and inscribed on an eggshell. See Virgil M. Harris, Ancient, Curious and Famous Wills (1911, reprint 1981); Robert S. Menchin, The Last Caprice (1963); Elmer Million, Wills: Witty, Witless, and Wicked, 7 Wayne L. Rev. 335 (1960).

To be valid, a holographic will must be written by the testator's hand and signed by the testator. Out of this simple formulation, however, arises two important interpretive problems: (a) the nature of the requirement that the testator sign the holograph, and (b) whether the entirety, or if not, how much, of the holograph must be in the testator's handwriting.

(a) Signature. In almost all states permitting holographs, a holograph may be signed at the end, at the beginning, or anywhere on the will, but if not signed at the end there may be doubt about whether the decedent intended his name to be a signature. For example, in Estate of Fegley, 589 P.2d 80 (Colo. App. 1978), the court denied probate to a handwritten instrument reading, "I, Henrietta Fegley, being of sound mind and disposing memory, declare this instrument to be my last will," but not otherwise signed. But see Estate of MacLeod, 254 Cal. Rptr. 156 (App. 1988), reaching a contrary result on virtually identical facts.

22. Herman Schmidt wrote a note on a bedroom wall to his fiancé, a belly dancer, Genevieve Decker. The 18 inch square piece of plaster containing the note was cut from the wall and offered as a will in a Philadelphia probate court. The purported will read:

Genevieve: You take care of all my belongings. This give's you authority. Love, Herman, 8-14-1968. [Austin (Texas) American Statesman, Oct. 15, 1968.]

(b) Extent written in the testator's own handwriting. On the issue of how much of the holograph must be written by the testator's hand, the statutes fall into three categories:

1. First generation statutes: "entirely, written, signed, and dated." The first generation of holographic will statutes required that holographs be "entirely, written, signed, and dated" in the handwriting of the testator. Under these statutes holographs were sometimes struck down even when they included only one or two printed words. For example, in Estate of Thorn, 192 P. 19 (Cal. 1920), the court struck down the testator's handwritten will because he had stamped the name of his home, Cragthorn, twice within its text.

In Estate of Dobson, 708 P.2d 422 (Wyo. 1985), the testator took her signed handwritten will to her local banker to discuss it with him. To make the will clearer, the banker penciled in certain numbers and parentheses and added to the devise of a tract of land, "including all mineral and oil rights," all with the consent of the testator. The court held the will could not be probated because it was not entirely in the handwriting of the decedent. On the other hand, some courts have ignored the printed portions and probated only the handwritten portions of the will. See Estate of Mulkins, page 242.

Some courts interpreted the first generation statutes as requiring that the will be "entirely dated," so that simply writing "May 1948" or "1965" was insufficient to allow probate. See Estate of Carson, 344 P.2d 612 (Cal. App. 1959) (although "May 1948" was clear, the day of the month between the month and year was illegible; date insufficient); Estate of Hazelwood, 57 Cal. Rptr. 332 (App. 1967) ("1965" insufficient). Nine states still require that a holograph be entirely in the handwriting of the testator, but only two of these states require this also for the date.[23]

2. Second generation statutes (1969 UPC): "material provisions." The inconsistent and harsh results under statutes requiring that the entire holograph be handwritten led the drafters of the original 1969 Uniform Probate Code to require only that "the signature and the material provisions" of the holograph be in the testator's handwriting. Still, courts struggled with wills that were partially typed and partially handwritten because sometimes a material dispositive provision was wholly or partly printed and sometimes the language that indicated testamentary intent was printed rather than written out by the testator. Although some courts were willing to look to the printed words to establish testamentary intent, others were not. Five states still have holographic will statutes based on the 1969 UPC.[24]

3. Third generation statutes (1990 UPC): "material portions" and extrinsic evidence allowed. Unhappy with courts continuing to strike down seemingly reliable holographs, the drafters of the 1990 UPC tried yet again to make it easier to make a valid holograph. The requirement that the "material provisions" be handwritten was changed to "material portions": "A will ... is valid as a holographic will, whether or not witnessed, if the signature and material portions of the document are in the testator's handwriting." UPC §2-502(b). Although this would seem like a trivial change, it was apparently intended to allow the probate of a holograph even if "immaterial" parts such as the "date" or "introductory wording" are printed. UPC §2-502(b) cmt. As an example, the comment to §2-502(b) states that language

---

23. Arkansas, Kentucky, Louisiana (also requires a handwritten date), Mississippi, North Carolina, Oklahoma (also requires a handwritten date), Texas, Virginia, and Wyoming.

24. California, Idaho, Maine, New Jersey, and Tennessee.

such as "I give, devise and bequeath to" in a preprinted will form should not disqualify the instrument as a valid holograph if the testator fills in the rest by hand.

The 1990 UPC also explicitly allows extrinsic evidence to be used to establish testamentary intent, thus further encouraging courts to look at the printed words in addition to the handwritten ones. "Intent that the document constitute the testator's will can be established by extrinsic evidence, including, for holographic wills, portions of the document that are not in the testator's handwriting." UPC §2-502(c). At least nine states have adopted a variant of UPC §2-502(c) (1990).[25]

A recurring problem under the heading of whether the entirety, or if not, how much, of the holograph must be in the testator's handwriting is the testator who writes her will on a preprinted will form but fails to have the form properly witnessed. If the instrument therefore fails as an attested will, can it be probated as a holograph? On this question courts have reached surprisingly inconsistent conclusions, even within the same jurisdiction. Consider the following three cases from Arizona.

ESTATE OF MULKINS, 496 P.2d 605 (Ariz. App. 1972): This case was decided under a first generation holographic will statute requiring that the will be entirely in the handwriting of the testator. Although the court found that the printed portions of the will were intended to be part of the will, it rejected using an "intent theory." Instead, the court treated the preprinted language as "mere surplusage" to be ignored. The dispositive language handwritten on the printed will form read as follows:

> I hereby make my will to Lettie Smith as Sister now living in Flint Michigan at 2222 on Oklahoma Ave. and Betty Hart Elkins at Rt. 1. Box 267 36 St. Just North of Southern Ave Phoenix, Ariz. about a block. I have 10 acres on Rincon Road. The South 330 feet of the Northwest quarter of the Northeast quarter of Section Twenty six 26 of township eight 8 North range 5 West of the Gila and Salt River base and Meridian Yavapai County of Arizona this 8 day of April 1966.

Without the printed language, this handwritten portion is hard to follow. Nonetheless, the court held that the "important thing is that the *testamentary* part of the will be wholly written by the testator and of course signed by him." Applying this standard, the court found that the printed words of the will were not essential to the meaning of the handwritten words and thus the holograph was upheld.

ESTATE OF JOHNSON, 630 P.2d 1039 (Ariz. 1981): The testator wrote his will on a stationer's form, filling in certain blanks in his own handwriting and then signing it. The will was also notarized, but it did not qualify as an attested will for lack of the required two witnesses. Because this case arose after Arizona adopted the 1969 UPC, the question was whether the "material provisions" of the will were in the testator's handwriting.

---

25. Alaska, Arizona (but with "material provisions"), Colorado, Hawaii, Michigan, Montana, North Dakota, South Dakota, and Utah.

Despite working with a more permissive statute than was in force in *Mulkins*, the court held that the will could not be admitted to probate on the ground that the printed words of the will were essential to establish testamentary intent and hence were material provisions. If you delete the printed words, you have only these words in the handwriting of the testator:

Arnold H. Johnson   Mesa Arizona   Maricopa
My six living children as follows

>   To John M. Johnson   1/8 of my Estate
>   Helen Marchese   1/8
>   Sharon Clements   1/8
>   Mirriam Jennings   1/8
>   Mary D. Korman   1/8
>   A. David Johnson   1/8
>   To W.V. Grant[26]   1/8
>   To Barton Lee McLain and Marie Gansels   1/8
>   Address 901 E. Broadway Mesa

Mirriam Jennings my Daughter
Nashville   Tenn.   ress   Address
1247 Saxon Drive   Nashville   Tenn.
22   March   77   Arnold H. Johnson
22   March   77

The court was not impressed with the argument that "To John M. Johnson 1/8 of my Estate" expressed a testamentary intent:

Appellants argue that the purported will here should thus be admitted to probate, since all the key dispositive provisions essential to its validity as a will are in the decedent's own handwriting; and further, when all the printed provisions are excised, the requisite intent to make a will is still evidenced. We do not agree. In our opinion, the only words which establish this requisite testamentary intent on the part of the decedent are found in the *printed* portion of the form. . . . Though the decedent here used the word "estate," this word alone is insufficient to indicate an animus testandi.

ESTATE OF MUDER, 765 P.2d 997 (Ariz. 1988): In this case, the court had before it a will handwritten on a printed will form, signed and notarized but not

---

26. W.V. Grant is a television evangelist and faith healer who has been richly successful in raising money from his believers. In the early 1990s, he lived in a $900,000 home in Dallas (7,000 square feet with nine baths and three bars), drove two Ferraris, and wore $1,500 suits. In 1991 ABC's Diane Sawyer looked into this TV evangelist and his empire, which she essayed into a funny and sad and shocking hour on PrimeTime Live (Nov. 21, 1991).

> One favorite ruse is claiming to have an orphanage in Haiti, and soliciting donations from viewers by showing them photos of starving toddlers. Grant in fact claims to have 64 Haitian orphanages, but Diane Sawyer couldn't find them. . . .
> In some ways, exposing frauds in the televangelical racket is a lost cause. The faithful, who insist on investing hope and money in these tricksters, may not care where the money really does go. [Tom Shales, The Money Changers, Wash. Post, Nov. 21, 1991, at D13.]

In 1996 W.V. Grant was sent to federal prison for income tax fraud. But now he's back in business. As of late 2004, one could follow W.V. Grant's ministry and buy his tapes from his web site: http://www.wvgrant.com.

witnessed. The relevant handwritten dispositive language, inserted in a printed paragraph saying "I give to," read:

> My wife Retha F. Muder, our home and property in Shumway, Navajo County, car — pick up, travel trailer, and all other earthly possessions belonging to me, livestock, cattle, sheep, etc. Tools, savings accounts, checking accounts, retirement benefits, etc.

The court, 3 to 2, upheld the will as a holograph under the same statute as was at issue in *Johnson*:

> In the instant case, there is no question as to the testator's intent. We hold that a testator who uses a preprinted form, and *in his own handwriting* fills in the blanks by designating his beneficiaries and apportioning his estate among them and signs it, has created a valid holographic will. Such handwritten provisions may draw testamentary context from both the printed and the handwritten language on the form. We see no need to ignore the preprinted words when the testator clearly did not, and the statute does not require us to do so.

NOTES AND QUESTIONS

1.   Is the *Johnson* case consistent with the earlier *Mulkins* case or the later *Muder* case? Do the handwritten words in *Mulkins* or *Muder* more clearly express testamentary intent?

2.   In *Muder*, the majority cited but did not discuss, approve, or disapprove of Estate of Johnson. The question thus arises, is *Johnson* still good law in Arizona? Citing *Muder*, Restatement (Third) of Property: Wills and Other Donative Transfers §3.2, reporter's note 2 (1999), says No.

The official comment to UPC §2-502(c), page 204, says that holographs may be written on a printed will form if the material portions of the document are handwritten. See also Restatement (Third) of Property, supra, §3.2, illust. 4.

3.   *Statutory form wills*. Perceiving a public demand for a legally valid do-it-yourself will that can be written on a printed form available at stationery stores, several states have authorized simple statutory "fill-in-the-form wills." These are short wills, with the wording spelled out in a statute. The will provides spaces for the testator to fill in the names of the beneficiaries. A jurisdiction may have several forms of statutory wills — one to leave everything to a spouse; another to leave everything in trust for the spouse for life, remainder to the children; and still another to leave property in trust for children until they reach majority. See, e.g., Cal. Prob. Code §6240 (2004); Mich. Stat. Ann. §27.5123(3) (2004).

Statutory wills must be signed and attested in the same manner as any attested will. A large number of statutory fill-in wills fail in probate because they are improperly completed or executed. See Gerry W. Beyer, Statutory Fill-in Will Forms, 72 Or. L. Rev. 769 (1993); Herbert T. Krimmel, A Criticism of the California Statutory Will, 19 W. St. U.L. Rev. 77 (1991). See also Uniform Statutory Will Act (1984).

In re Estate of Kuralt

Supreme Court of Montana, 2000
303 Mont. 335, 15 P.3d 931

[Charles Kuralt, who became a homespun American icon, was born in North Carolina in 1934. From 1970 through 1994, Kuralt was the host of CBS News Sunday Morning. He was known particularly for his "On the Road" stories based on his travels around the country in a mobile home. Kuralt specialized in "big-hearted essays on topics others thought tiny," reporting "on horse-traders and a 93-year-old brickmaker, on the wonders of nature and the nature of other wonders, like the sharecropper in Mississippi who put nine children through college or the 103-year-old entertainer who performed at nursing homes." Joe Sexton, Charles Kuralt, 62, Is Dead, N.Y. Times, July 5, 1997, at 24. Kuralt went through six motor homes while doing over 500 On the Road stories. When in 1994 the beloved Kuralt retired from CBS News Sunday Morning, Saturday Night Live did a scathing satire in which Norm MacDonald as Kuralt bid farewell, saying that he would miss all the people he had met over the years—and had sex with.[27]

Sometimes life imitates art. In 1968, six years into his marriage to Suzanne Baird (who was known as Petie), Kuralt met a woman named Pat Baker (later she went by Pat Shannon) while doing an On the Road story in Reno on her efforts to build a park for African American children. Smitten, Kuralt asked her out to dinner, arriving to pick her up with a bouquet of roses in hand. A long-term romance ensued. Over the years Kuralt saw or spoke to Shannon frequently, and he provided financial support for her and her family—including buying her a vacation home in Ireland. According to Shannon, when she moved from Reno to the San Francisco Bay area in the early 1970s, she and Kuralt "went on picnics and we went sail[ing] and, you know, we acted like a family." In 1985 she moved to a log cabin that Kuralt had built for them in Montana. Larry King Live, Charles Kuralt's Longtime Companion Speaks Out, CNN, Feb. 14, 2001, http://edition.cnn.com/TRANSCRIPTS/0102/14/lkl.00.html.

Kuralt died on the Fourth of July in 1997 of either a heart attack or lupus (or both), after a short illness. Two weeks before he died, however, he wrote Shannon a letter assuring her that he would see to it that she would inherit his property in Montana. This opinion was the second decision by the Montana Supreme Court on whether that letter was a valid holographic codicil, a codicil being a testamentary instrument that amends rather than replaces an earlier will.]

Trieweiler, J.   . . . Charles Kuralt and Elizabeth Shannon maintained a long-term and intimate personal relationship. Kuralt and Shannon desired to keep their

---

27. The SNL sketch began with Norm MacDonald as Charles Kuralt talking in Kuralt's folksy manner about how much he would miss life "On the Road." After noting the beauty of the countryside, he confessed that it was the prospect of sex that had lured him to the road 37 years before and that he would miss the most. He then recounted a string of sexual conquests, including the wife of Old Ned Harrigan, known for his ball of twine that was 67 feet around, and 75-year-old Thelma Ober, famous for her pumpkin pies. Saturday Night Live, Sunday Morning with Charles Kuralt, April 9, 1994, http://www.fakenews.net/archive/impressions/kuralt_94_04_09.html. — Eds.

Elizabeth (Pat) Shannon and Charles Kuralt, bundled against the chilly weather on Angel Island near San Francisco in the early 1970s, sharing a picnic of wine, cheese, and fruit.

AP/World Wide Photos

relationship secret, and were so successful in doing so that even though Kuralt's wife, Petie, knew that Kuralt owned property in Montana, she was unaware, prior to Kuralt's untimely death, of his relationship with Shannon.

Over the nearly 30-year course of their relationship, Kuralt and Shannon saw each other regularly and maintained contact by phone and mail. Kuralt was the primary source of financial support for Shannon and established close, personal relationships with Shannon's three children. Kuralt provided financial support for a joint business venture managed by Shannon and transferred a home in Ireland to Shannon as a gift.

In 1985, Kuralt purchased a 20-acre parcel of property along the Big Hole River in Madison County, near Twin Bridges, Montana. Kuralt and Shannon constructed a cabin on this 20-acre parcel. In 1987, Kuralt purchased two additional parcels along the Big Hole which adjoined the original 20-acre parcel. These two additional parcels, one upstream and one downstream of the cabin, created a parcel of approximately 90 acres and are the primary subject of this appeal.

On May 3, 1989, Kuralt executed a holographic will which stated as follows:

May 3, 1989

In the event of my death, I bequeath to Patricia Elizabeth Shannon all my interest in land, buildings, furnishings and personal belongings on Burma Road, Twin Bridges, Montana.

Charles Kuralt
34 Bank St.
New York, N.Y. 10014

Although Kuralt mailed a copy of this holographic will to Shannon, he subsequently executed a formal will on May 4, 1994, in New York City. This Last Will and Testament, prepared with the assistance of counsel, does not specifically mention any of the real property owned by Kuralt. The beneficiaries of Kuralt's Last Will and Testament were his wife, Petie, and the Kuralts' two children. Neither Shannon nor her children are named as beneficiaries in Kuralt's formal will. Shannon had no knowledge of the formal will until the commencement of these proceedings.

On April 9, 1997, Kuralt deeded his interest in the original 20-acre parcel with the cabin to Shannon. The transaction was disguised as a sale. However, Kuralt supplied the "purchase" price for the 20-acre parcel to Shannon prior to the transfer. After the deed to the 20-acre parcel was filed, Shannon sent Kuralt, at his request, a blank buy-sell real estate form so that the remaining 90 acres along the Big Hole could be conveyed to Shannon in a similar manner. Apparently, it was again Kuralt's intention to provide the purchase price. The second transaction was to take place in September 1997 when Shannon, her son, and Kuralt agreed to meet at the Montana cabin.

Kuralt, however, became suddenly ill and entered a New York hospital on June 18, 1997. On that same date, Kuralt wrote the letter to Shannon which is now at the center of the current dispute:

June 18, 1997

Dear Pat—

Something is terribly wrong with me and they can't figure out what. After cat-scans and a variety of cardiograms, they agree it's not lung cancer or heart trouble or blood clot. So they're putting me in the hospital today to concentrate on infectious diseases. I am getting worse, barely able to get out of bed, but still have high hopes for recovery . . . if only I can get a diagnosis! Curiouser and curiouser! I'll keep you informed. I'll have the lawyer visit the hospital to be sure you inherit the rest of the place in MT. if it comes to that.

   I send love to you & [your youngest daughter,] Shannon. Hope things are better there!

   Love,
   C.

Enclosed with this letter were two checks made payable to Shannon, one for $8000 and the other for $9000. Kuralt did not seek the assistance of an attorney to devise the remaining 90 acres of Big Hole land to Shannon. Therefore, when Kuralt died unexpectedly, Shannon sought to probate the letter of June 18, 1997, as a valid holographic codicil to Kuralt's formal 1994 will.

The Estate opposed Shannon's Petition for Ancillary Probate based on its contention that the June 18, 1997 letter expressed only a future intent to make a will. The District Court granted partial summary judgment for the Estate on May 26, 1998. Shannon appealed from the District Court order which granted partial summary judgment to the Estate. This Court, in In re Estate of Kuralt (*Kuralt I*), 981 P.2d 771 (Mont. 1999), reversed the District Court and remanded the case for trial in order to resolve disputed issues of material fact.[28] Following an abbreviated evidentiary hearing, the District Court issued its Findings and Order. The District Court held that the June 18, 1997 letter was a valid holographic codicil to Kuralt's formal will of May 4, 1994 and accordingly entered judgment in favor of Shannon. The Estate now appeals from that order and judgment. . . .

Did the District Court err when it found that the June 18, 1997 letter expressed a present testamentary intent to transfer property in Madison County?

The Estate contends that the District Court made legal errors which led to a mistaken conclusion about Kuralt's intent concerning the disposition of his Montana property. The Estate argues that the District Court failed to recognize the legal effect of the 1994 will and therefore erroneously found that Kuralt, after his May 3, 1989 holographic will, had an uninterrupted intent to transfer the Montana property to Shannon. The Estate further argues that Kuralt's 1994 formal will revoked all prior wills, both expressly and by inconsistency. This manifest change of intention, according to the Estate, should have led the District Court to the conclusion that Kuralt did not intend to transfer the Montana property to Shannon upon his death.

Montana courts are guided by the bedrock principle of honoring the intent of the testator. On remand, the District Court resolved the factual question of whether Kuralt intended the letter of June 18, 1997 to effect a testamentary disposition of the Montana property. As we stated in *Kuralt I*, the "question of whether that letter contains the necessary animus testandi becomes an issue suitable for resolution by the trier of fact."[29] 981 P.2d at 778. The argument on appeal, while clothed as a legal argument, addresses factual findings made by the District Court. However, if the

---

28. In dissent in *Kuralt I*, Chief Justice Turnage wrote:

The letter of June 18, 1997, and the record in this case does not meet the standard of clear and convincing evidence. . . . The June 18, 1997 letter, as set forth in the majority opinion, contains this—and only this—language relating to the question of a holographic will: "I'll have the lawyer visit the hospital to be sure you inherit the rest of the place in MT. if it comes to that." That language clearly indicates that decedent Kuralt did not intend the letter to operate as a holographic will but, rather, expressed his intent that at a future date he would have a lawyer visit him in the hospital to be sure that Patricia Shannon would, by a document thereafter to be executed, inherit "the rest of the place in MT." Such language is precatory and expresses only a desire or wish. It certainly does not constitute imperative, direct terms of bequest. [*Kuralt I*, 981 P.2d at 778.]

—Eds.

29. Montana had enacted the 1990 UPC, including the provisions on:

1. *holographic wills* ("A will that does not comply with [formalities] is valid as a holographic will, whether or not witnessed, if the signature and material portions of the document are in the testator's handwriting.");
2. *proving testamentary intent* ("Intent that the document constitute the testator's will may be established by extrinsic evidence, including, for holographic wills, portions of the document that are not in the testator's handwriting."); and
3. *the dispensing power* (allowing an instrument to be admitted as a will if "the proponent of the document or writing establishes by clear and convincing evidence that the decedent intended the document or writing to constitute . . . the decedent's will").

Mont. Code Ann. §§72-2-522 to -523 (2004).—Eds.

factual findings of the District Court are supported by substantial credible evidence and are not otherwise clearly erroneous, they will not be reversed by this Court.

The record supports the District Court's finding that the June 18, 1997 letter expressed Kuralt's intent to effect a posthumous transfer of his Montana property to Shannon. Kuralt and Shannon enjoyed a long, close personal relationship which continued up to the last letter Kuralt wrote Shannon on June 18, 1997, in which he enclosed checks to her in the amounts of $8000 and $9000. Likewise, Kuralt and Shannon's children had a long, family-like relationship which included significant financial support.

The District Court focused on the last few months of Kuralt's life to find that the letter demonstrated his testamentary intent. The conveyance of the 20-acre parcel for no real consideration and extrinsic evidence that Kuralt intended to convey the remainder of the Montana property to Shannon in a similar fashion provides substantial factual support for the District Court's determination that Kuralt intended that Shannon have the rest of the Montana property.

The June 18, 1997 letter expressed Kuralt's desire that Shannon inherit the remainder of the Montana property. That Kuralt wrote the letter *in extremis* is supported by the fact that he died two weeks later. Although Kuralt intended to transfer the remaining land to Shannon, he was reluctant to consult a lawyer to formalize his intent because he wanted to keep their relationship secret. Finally, the use of the term "inherit" underlined by Kuralt reflected his intention to make a posthumous disposition of the property. Therefore, the District Court's findings are supported by substantial evidence and are not clearly erroneous. Accordingly, we conclude that the District Court did not err when it found that the letter dated June 18, 1997 expressed a present testamentary intent to transfer property in Madison County to Patricia Shannon. . . .

[W]e agree with the District Court's conclusion that the June 18, 1997 holograph was a codicil to Kuralt's 1994 formal will. Admittedly, the June 18, 1997 letter met the threshold requirements for a valid holographic will. Moreover, the letter was a codicil as a matter of law because it made a specific bequest of the Montana property and did not purport to bequeath the entirety of the estate. See Official Comments to §72-2-527, MCA ("when the second will does not make a complete disposition of the testator's estate, the second will is more in the nature of a codicil to the first will"). The District Court was therefore correct when it concluded that the June 18, 1997 letter was a codicil. . . .

Accordingly, we affirm the judgment of the District Court.

NOTES AND QUESTIONS

1. *Epilogue.* A codicil is a testamentary instrument that amends a prior will; it does not replace it. In this case Kuralt's 1994 formal will, which remained operative to the extent not amended by his 1997 letter to Shannon, provided that all taxes were to be paid by the estate, thus reducing the share of the residuary takers. Since Kuralt's wife and children were the beneficiaries of the residue, not only did they lose the land in Montana, but in effect they were forced to pay the taxes on it even though it passed to Shannon. See In re Estate of Kuralt, 68 P.3d 662 (Mont. 2003).

2. If you had asked Kuralt whether his June 18, 1997, letter was a will, what do you think he would have answered? Suppose that Kuralt had sent several letters

over the years concerning his plans to redraft wills. If he then executed a new will but failed to revoke those letters, would they still be in force as wills to the extent they were not inconsistent with the later will?

3. Once one admits extrinsic evidence and goes searching for the testator's dispositive intent, are there any limits on where we might search? *Kuralt* presents a case in which there is excellent written evidence of whom Kuralt intended to benefit, but a serious question whether he intended the 1997 letter itself to be a will. Why do we have a requirement that testamentary directions be left in a will? Why not have an open-ended inquiry in every case into what each decedent intended? Is the safe harbor of a will jeopardized by giving effect to letters not intended to be wills but that contain good evidence of the decedent's intended beneficiaries?

4. In the few states that have adopted the dispensing power (allowing a court to dispense with any formality as long as a will was clearly intended), the effective minimum requirement for admitting a document as a will has been reduced to little more than the intent that the document be a will. Accordingly, much more pressure is put on the concept of testamentary intent. If intent is all that is required, then

> the subject of litigation will shift. More casual documents will have to be examined to determine whether they were intended to be a will. . . . Unfortunately, testamentary intent is not well understood or defined. Often the requirement is described in such broad terms that it can just as easily apply to a will substitute, such as a trust. At other times, the doctrine is described so narrowly that, unless the testator intended to fall within the legal category called will, he wouldn't meet the requirement. Neither extreme is true. . . . [A] more coherent body of law [might emerge] if we had more precise terminology for the different strands of testamentary intent that might be present in a will. [James Lindgren, The Fall of Formalism, 55 Alb. L. Rev. 1009, 1018-1019 (1992).]

There are many possible components to testamentary intent, which no one has yet sorted out: intent that a document be used as evidence after death, intent that the document convey no present interest, intent that it be a will, intent that it not be a will substitute, intent to execute a document, intent that it be final unless later revoked, intent that certain beneficiaries receive certain property, and so on. For a fumbling attempt to disentangle these threads, see id. at 1019. On finding testamentary intent, see Emily Sherwin, Clear and Convincing Evidence of Testamentary Intent: The Search for a Compromise Between Formality and Adjudicative Justice, 34 Conn. L. Rev. 453 (2002).

5. In Estate of Wong, 47 Cal. Rptr. 2d 707 (App. 1995), the following hand-written document was offered for probate:

All Tai-Kin Wong's → Xi Zhao, my best half

/s/ *TKW*
——————————————
12/31/92

Tai-Kin Wong was a 44-year-old bachelor, and Xi Zhao was his girlfriend with whom he had lived for three years. The document was found in a sealed envelope in Wong's office, to which rainbow stickers reading "You're Special" and "Love

You" had been added. The court denied probate because the document did not refer to any property of Tai-Kin Wong and did not contain a word indicating a gift. The arrow was deemed not a word but a symbol of no fixed meaning.

Wong died suddenly late on New Year's Eve, 1992, the day the document was signed. The court made much of the fact that Xi Zhao was that very evening dining at a fancy French restaurant with a man she moved in with two and one-half months later, a rendezvous she had concealed from Wong. Just des(s)ert?

6. A few months after the death of her husband in March 1984, Esther Smith delivered to Harry Fass, her 84-year-old attorney, a writing that read:

> My entire estate is to be left *jointly* to my step-daughter, Roberta Crowley, and my step-son, David J. Smith.
>
> <div align="right">/s/ <i>Esther L. Smith</i></div>

According to the attorney's testimony, when Mrs. Smith handed him the writing, which was on a 5″ × 7″ piece of paper torn from a notebook, she said, "this is my will, this is the way I want my estate to go." The attorney, however, did not treat the paper as a will. He did not put the paper in his safe. He stapled the paper to the probate file of her husband. He wrote on the paper, "Extor-David," meaning David was to be the executor. In September 1984, the attorney wrote Mrs. Smith that he was retiring: "Your file and/or Last Will and Testament in my office is at your disposal if you do not care to retain [the attorney to whom he was transferring his practice]."

Mrs. Smith died in October 1984. Her heirs are her first cousins. Is the paper entitled to probate? See In re Will of Smith, 528 A.2d 918 (N.J. 1987) (denying probate).

Was Fass's delay in executing Esther Smith's estate plan malpractice? Compare White v. Jones, [1995] 1 All E.R. 691 (House of Lords) (holding solicitor liable to intended will beneficiaries where solicitor instructed to prepare a new will is negligent in delaying its preparation and securing the client's signature), with Krawczyk v. Stingle, 543 A.2d 733 (Conn. 1988) (week's delay in preparing a revocable trust not malpractice; "[i]mposition of liability would create an incentive for an attorney to exert pressure on a client to complete and execute estate planning documents summarily."), and Sisson v. Jankowski, 809 A.2d 1265 (N.H. 2002) (negligent failure to execute a will for a dying person does not give rise to liability to beneficiaries).

Should the document Esther Smith handed to Harry Fass be probated as her will under UPC §2-503?

SECTION B.   REVOCATION OF WILLS

1. *Revocation by Writing or Physical Act*

A will is an ambulatory document, which means that it is subject to modification or revocation by the testator during his or her lifetime. All states permit revocation of a will in one of two ways: (1) by a subsequent *writing* executed with testamentary formalities,[30] or (2) by a *physical act* such as destroying, obliterating, or burning the

---

30. UPC §1-201(56) (1990) defines a *will* to include a codicil and any testamentary instrument that merely appoints an executor or revokes or revises another will.

will. On the assumption that oral revocations would open the door wide for fraud, an oral declaration that a will is revoked, without more, is inoperative in all states. *If a duly executed will is not revoked in a manner permitted by statute, the will is admitted to probate.*[31]

The UPC's revocation section is fairly representative of statutes setting forth methods of permissible revocation.

Uniform Probate Code (1990)

§2-507. REVOCATION BY WRITING OR BY ACT

(a) A will or any part thereof is revoked:

(1) by executing a subsequent will that revokes the previous will or part expressly or by inconsistency; or

(2) by performing a revocatory act on the will, if the testator performed the act with the intent and for the purpose of revoking the will or part or if another individual performed the act in the testator's conscious presence and by the testator's direction. For purposes of this paragraph, "revocatory act on the will" includes burning, tearing, canceling, obliterating, or destroying the will or any part of it. A burning, tearing, or canceling is a "revocatory act on the will," whether or not the burn, tear, or cancellation touched any of the words on the will.

PROBLEM: REVOCATION BY INCONSISTENCY

A subsequent will wholly revokes the previous will by inconsistency if the testator intends the subsequent will to replace rather than supplement the previous will. A subsequent will that does not expressly revoke the prior will but makes a complete disposition of the testator's estate is presumed to replace the prior will and revoke it by inconsistency. If the subsequent will does not make a complete disposition of the testator's estate, it is not presumed to revoke the prior will but is viewed as a codicil. A codicil supplements a will rather than replacing it. See UPC §2-507(b)-(d) (1990); Restatement (Third) of Property: Wills and Other Donative Transfers §4.1, cmts. b-c (1999).

In 2003, *T* executes a will that gives all her property to *A*. In 2004, *T* executes a will that gives her diamond ring to *B* and her car to *C*. It contains no words of revocation. Even though the 2004 will makes no reference to the earlier will, the 2004 will is ordinarily called a *codicil*.

(a) In early 2005, *T* destroys the 2004 codicil with the intention of revoking it; *T* dies later in 2005. The 2003 will is offered for probate. Should it be admitted? See In re Estate of Hering, 166 Cal. Rptr. 298 (App. 1980).

(b) Suppose, instead, that *T* destroys the 2003 will with the intention of revoking it. After *T*'s death, the codicil is offered for probate. Should it be admitted? See Comment, Wills — Revocation by Act to the Document — Effect on Codicil, 60 Mich. L. Rev. 82 (1961).

In states recognizing holographic wills, a holograph can revoke a typewritten, attested will — a principle that is implicit in Estate of Kuralt, pages 244-249.

31. Just as UPC §2-503 (1990) excuses harmless errors in execution, it likewise excuses harmless errors in revocation.

Harrison v. Bird

Supreme Court of Alabama, 1993
621 So. 2d 972

HOUSTON, J.   The proponent of a will appeals from a judgment of the Circuit Court of Montgomery County holding that the estate of Daisy Virginia Speer, deceased, should be administered as an intestate estate and confirming the letters of administration granted by the probate court to Mae S. Bird.

The following pertinent facts are undisputed:

Daisy Virginia Speer executed a will in November 1989, in which she named Katherine Crapps Harrison as the main beneficiary of her estate. The original of the will was retained by Ms. Speer's attorney and a duplicate original was given to Ms. Harrison. On March 4, 1991, Ms. Speer telephoned her attorney and advised him that she wanted to revoke her will. Thereafter, Ms. Speer's attorney or his secretary, in the presence of each other, tore the will into four pieces. The attorney then wrote Ms. Speer a letter, informing her that he had "revoked" her will as she had instructed and that he was enclosing the pieces of the will so that she could verify that he had torn up the original. In the letter, the attorney specifically stated, "As it now stands, you are without a will."

Ms. Speer died on September 3, 1991. Upon her death, the postmarked letter from her attorney was found among her personal effects, but the four pieces of the will were not found. Thereafter, on September 17, 1991, the Probate Court of Montgomery County granted letters of administration on the estate of Ms. Speer, to Mae S. Bird, a cousin of Ms. Speer. On October 11, 1991, Ms. Harrison filed for probate a document purporting to be the last will and testament of Ms. Speer and naming Ms. Harrison as executrix. . . .

Thereafter, the circuit court ruled (1) that Ms. Speer's will was not lawfully revoked when it was destroyed by her attorney at her direction and with her consent, but not in her presence, see Ala. Code 1975, §43-8-136(b); (2) that there could be no ratification of the destruction of Ms. Speer's will, which was not accomplished pursuant to the strict requirements of §43-8-136(b); and (3) that, based on the fact that the pieces of the destroyed will were delivered to Ms. Speer's home but were not found after her death, there arose a presumption that Ms. Speer thereafter revoked the will herself.

. . . [F]inding that the presumption in favor of revocation of Ms. Speer's will had not been rebutted and therefore that the duplicate original will offered for probate by Ms. Harrison was not the last will and testament of Daisy Virginia Speer, the circuit court held that the estate should be administered as an intestate estate and confirmed the letters of administration issued by the probate court to Ms. Bird.

If the evidence establishes that Ms. Speer had possession of the will before her death, but the will is not found among her personal effects after her death, a presumption arises that she destroyed the will. See Barksdale v. Pendergrass, 319 So. 2d 267 (Ala. 1975). Furthermore, if she destroys the copy of the will in her possession, a presumption arises that she has revoked her will and all duplicates, even though a duplicate exists that is not in her possession. See Stiles v. Brown, 380 So. 2d 792 (Ala. 1980); see, also, Snider v. Burks, 4 So. 225 (Ala. 1887). However, this presumption of revocation is rebuttable and the burden of rebutting the presumption is on the proponent of the will. See *Barksdale*, supra.

Based on the foregoing, we conclude that under the facts of this case there existed a presumption that Ms. Speer destroyed her will and thus revoked it. Therefore, the burden shifted to Ms. Harrison to present sufficient evidence to rebut that presumption — to present sufficient evidence to convince the trier of fact that the absence of the will from Ms. Speer's personal effects after her death was not due to Ms. Speer's destroying and thus revoking the will. See Stiles v. Brown, supra.

From a careful review of the record, we conclude, as did the trial court, that the evidence presented by Ms. Harrison was not sufficient to rebut the presumption that Ms. Speer destroyed her will with the intent to revoke it. We, therefore, affirm the trial court's judgment. We note Ms. Harrison's argument that under the particular facts of this case, because Ms. Speer's attorney destroyed the will outside of Ms. Speer's presence, "[t]he fact that Ms. Speer may have had possession of the pieces of her will and that such pieces were not found upon her death is not sufficient to invoke the presumption [of revocation] imposed by the trial court." We find that argument to be without merit.

Affirmed.

PROBLEMS

1. In Harrison v. Bird, if the torn four pieces of the testator's will had been found at her death, would her attorney be liable for malpractice? Suppose the torn pieces of the will had been found among the testator's papers in a file labeled "revoked will." What result?

2. Suppose that the testator's lawyer sends her home with the only executed copy of the testator's will. The will leaves all her property to *A*. After the testator's death, her heir goes in her house looking for her will. The heir reports that she couldn't find a will, and no will is found. What result? See Estate of King, 817 A.2d 297 (N.H. 2003) (presumption of revocation rebutted by testimony that the testator had recently referred to the will being in effect); Estate of Travers, 589 P.2d 1314 (Ariz. 1978) (opportunity of disinherited heir to destroy will does not rebut presumption of revocation); Lonergan v. Estate of Budahazi, 669 So. 2d 1062 (Fla. App. 1996) (presumption of revocation of lost will disinheriting husband rebutted where husband lived in house with wife and the couple had been fighting before she died); Annots., 70 A.L.R.4th 323 (1989), 84 A.L.R.4th 531 (1991).

NOTE: PROBATE OF LOST WILLS

In the absence of statute, a will that is lost, or is destroyed without the consent of the testator, or is destroyed with the consent of the testator but not in compliance with the revocation statute can be admitted into probate if its contents are proved. A lost will can be proved by a copy in the lawyer-drafter's office or by other clear and convincing evidence.

The attacks on the World Trade Center on September 11, 2001, led to a large number of destroyed wills that were stored in these and nearby buildings — with resulting problems. Because those wills were not destroyed by the testators with the intent to revoke, they can still be probated if their terms can be proved from other copies, which will be possible in some cases but not others.

In a few states, statutes prohibit the probate of a lost or destroyed will unless the will was "in existence" at the testator's death (and destroyed thereafter) or was "fraudulently destroyed" during the testator's life. Theoretically, under such a statute a will accidentally tossed out by a housekeeper during the testator's life cannot be probated. Thus, on its face, such a statute is in conflict with the state's will revocation statute, since under it a will not legally revoked is nevertheless barred from probate. Courts have chosen to give effect to the will revocation statutes and have gutted the proof statutes by holding *either* that a will not lawfully revoked continues in "legal existence" until the testator's death (and the word "existence" in the statute means "legal existence") *or* that a will destroyed by a method not permitted by the will revocation statute has been "fraudulently destroyed." See Estate of Irvine v. Doyle, 710 P.2d 1366 (Nev. 1985). Compare Sheridan v. Harbison, 655 N.E.2d 256 (Ohio App. 1995) (peculiar statute forbidding probate if will lost or destroyed prior to testator's death with the knowledge of the testator).

Thompson v. Royall
Supreme Court of Virginia, 1934
163 Va. 492, 175 S.E. 748

HUDGINS, J.   The only question presented by this record is whether the will of Mrs. M. Lou Bowen Kroll had been revoked shortly before her death.

The uncontroverted facts are as follows: On the 4th day of September, 1932, Mrs. Kroll signed a will, typewritten on the five sheets of legal cap paper; the signature appeared on the last page duly attested by three subscribing witnesses. H.P. Brittain, the executor named in the will, was given possession of the instrument for safe-keeping. A codicil typed on the top third of one sheet of paper dated September 15, 1932, was signed by the testatrix in the presence of two subscribing witnesses. Possession of this instrument was given to Judge S.M.B. Coulling, the attorney who prepared both documents.

On September 19, 1932, at the request of Mrs. Kroll, Judge Coulling and Mr. Brittain took the will and the codicil to her home where she told her attorney, in the presence of Mr. Brittain and another, to destroy both. But, instead of destroying the papers, at the suggestion of Judge Coulling, she decided to retain them as memoranda, to be used as such in the event she decided to execute a new will. Upon the back of the manuscript cover, which was fastened to the five sheets by metal clasps, in the handwriting of Judge Coulling, signed by Mrs. Kroll, there is the following notation:

> This will null and void and to be only held by H.P. Brittain instead of being destroyed as a memorandum for another will if I desire to make same. This 19 Sept. 1932.
>
> *M. Lou Bowen Kroll*

The same notation was made upon the back of the sheet on which the codicil was written, except that the name S.M.B. Coulling was substituted for H.P. Brittain; this was likewise signed by Mrs. Kroll.

Mrs. Kroll died October 2, 1932, leaving numerous nephews and nieces, some of whom were not mentioned in her will, and an estate valued at approximately $200,000. On motion of some of the beneficiaries, the will and codicil were offered for probate. All the interested parties including the heirs at law were convened, and on the issue devisavit vel non [whether the purported will is valid or not] the jury found that the instruments dated September 4 and 15, 1932, were the last will and testament of Mrs. M. Lou Bowen Kroll. From an order sustaining the verdict and probating the will this writ of error was allowed.

For more than 100 years, the means by which a duly executed will may be revoked have been prescribed by statute. These requirements are found in section 5233 of the 1919 Code, the pertinent parts of which read thus:

> No will or codicil, or any part thereof, shall be revoked, unless . . . by a subsequent will or codicil, or by some writing declaring an intention to revoke the same, and executed in the manner in which a will is required to be executed, or by the testator, or some person in his presence and by his direction, cutting, tearing, burning, obliterating, canceling, or destroying the same, or the signature thereto, with the intent to revoke.

The notations, dated September 19, 1932, are not wholly in the handwriting of the testatrix, nor are her signatures thereto attached attested by subscribing witnesses; hence under the statute they are ineffectual as "some writing declaring an intention to revoke." The faces of the two instruments bear no physical evidence of any cutting, tearing, burning, obliterating, canceling, or destroying. The only contention made by appellants is that the notation written in the presence, and with the approval, of Mrs. Kroll, on the back of the manuscript cover in the one instance, and on the back of the sheet containing the codicil in the other, constitute "canceling" within the meaning of the statute.

Both parties concede that to effect revocation of a duly executed will, in any of the methods prescribed by statute, two things are necessary: (1) The doing of one of the acts specified, (2) accompanied by the intent to revoke — the animo revocandi. Proof of either, without proof of the other, is insufficient. Malone v. Hobbs, 1 Rob. (40 Va.) 346. The proof established the intention to revoke. The entire controversy is confined to the acts used in carrying out that purpose. The testatrix adopted the suggestion of her attorney to revoke her will by written memoranda, admittedly ineffectual as revocations by subsequent writings, but appellants contend the memoranda, in the handwriting of another, and testatrix' signatures, are sufficient to effect revocation by cancellation. To support this contention, appellants cite a number of authorities which hold that the modern definition of cancellation includes "any act which would destroy, revoke, recall, do away with, overrule, render null and void, the instrument."

Most of the authorities cited that approve the above or a similar meaning of the word were dealing with cancellation of simple contracts, or other instruments that require little or no formality in execution. However, there is one line of cases which apply this extended meaning of "canceling" to the revocation of wills. The leading case so holding is Warner v. Warner's Estate, 37 Vt. 356. In this case proof of the intent and the act were a notation on the same page with, and below the signature of, the testator, reading: "This will is hereby cancelled and annulled. In full this 15th day of March in the year 1859," and written lengthwise on the back of the fourth page of the foolscap paper, upon which no part of the written will appeared, were these words, "Cancelled and is null and void. (Signed) I. Warner." It was held this was sufficient to revoke the will under a statute similar to the one here under consideration.

In Evans' Appeal, 58 Pa. 238, the Pennsylvania court approved the reasoning of the Vermont court in Warner v. Warner's Estate, supra, but the force of the opinion is weakened when the facts are considered. It seems that there were lines drawn through two of the three signatures of the testator appearing in the Evans will, and the paper on which material parts of the will were written was torn in four places. It therefore appeared on the face of the instrument, when offered for probate, that there was a sufficient defacement to bring it within the meaning of both obliteration and cancellation. The construction of the statute in Warner v. Warner's Estate, supra, has been criticized by eminent text-writers on wills, and the courts in the majority of the states in construing similar statutes have refused to follow the reasoning in that case. Jarman on Wills (6th Ed.) 147, note 1; Schouler on Wills (5th Ed.) §391; Redfield on the Law of Wills (4th Ed.) 323-325; 28 R.C.L. 180; 40 Cyc. 1173; Dowling v. Gilliland, 122 N.E. 70. . . .

The above, and other authorities that might be cited, hold that revocation of a will by cancellation within the meaning of the statute contemplates marks or lines across the written parts of the instrument or a physical defacement, or some mutilation of the writing itself, with the intent to revoke. If written words are used for the purpose, they must be so placed as to physically affect the written portion of the will, not merely on blank parts of the paper on which the will is written. If the writing intended to be the act of canceling does not mutilate, or erase, or deface, or otherwise physically come in contact with, any part of written words of the will, it cannot be given any greater weight than a similar writing on a separate sheet of paper, which identifies the will referred to, just as definitely as does the writing on the back. If a will may be revoked by writing on the back, separable from the will, it may be done by a writing not on the will. This the statute forbids. . . .

The attempted revocation is ineffectual, because testatrix intended to revoke her will by subsequent writings not executed as required by statute, and because it does not in any wise physically obliterate, mutilate, deface, or cancel any written parts of the will.

For the reasons stated, the judgment of the trial court is affirmed.

QUESTIONS AND PROBLEMS

1. If the facts in Thompson v. Royall had occurred in 2005, would Judge Coulling be liable to Mrs. Kroll's heirs for malpractice? Although no one sued for legal malpractice in the 1930s, we have been told by Judge Coulling's grandson that for the rest of his life Judge Coulling suffered greatly from shame and loss of reputation in his community because of the probate of Mrs. Kroll's unrevoked will.

2. What policy is served by the court's decision in the *Thompson* case? Given the clear and uncontroverted evidence of Mrs. Kroll's intention that her will be revoked, how can the court's decision be justified?

UPC §2-507, page 252, would change the result in Thompson v. Royall. It provides: "A burning, tearing, or canceling is a 'revocatory act on the will,' whether or not the burn, tear, or cancellation touched any of the words on the will." Words of cancellation must, however, be written on the will, whether or not they touch the words of the will. They cannot be written on another document.

3. Suppose that Mrs. Kroll's will had attached to it a self-proving affidavit and that the notation signed by Mrs. Kroll had been written across the self-proving affidavit. Has the cancellation touched any words of the will? See In re Estate of Dickson, 590 So. 2d 471 (Fla. App. 1991).

4. Suppose that Mrs. Kroll had written, on the left-hand margin of each page of the will, "Cancelled. 19/9/32. M. Kroll." Would this be a valid revocation by physical act? See Kronauge v. Stoecklein, 293 N.E.2d 320 (Ohio App. 1972). Would this be a valid revocation in states permitting holographic wills? See McCarthy v. Bank of Cal., 668 P.2d 481 (Or. App. 1983) (valid holographic revocation); but cf. In re Estate of Johnson, page 242, dealing with *execution* of holographic will.

5. Suppose that the testator writes "VOID" across the face of an unexecuted photocopy of his will. Is this a valid revocation by physical act? In Estate of Tolin, 622 So. 2d 988 (Fla. 1993), the testator showed a photocopy of a codicil (with a formal blue backing) to his will to a friend, a retired lawyer, telling the friend he wanted to revoke the codicil. The friend, mistaking the photocopy for the original, told him he could revoke the codicil by tearing up the document. The testator did so. After the testator died, the lawyer who drafted his will and codicil produced the originals. The court held that revocation of a copy is not a valid revocation. However, because of the testator's mistake of fact, believing he was destroying the original, the court imposed a constructive trust on the codicil beneficiary for the benefit of the will beneficiary. Is this an application of the substantial compliance doctrine to the revocation of wills in the guise of a constructive trust to prevent unjust enrichment? Or is it another step toward correcting mistakes in execution and revocation of wills? In a later case, Allen v. Dalk, 826 So. 2d 245 (Fla. 2002), the Florida Supreme Court refused to extend *Tolin* to allow probate of a will that the testator erroneously thought she had signed along with other documents.

Partial revocation by physical act. Although UPC §2-507 and the statutes of many states authorize partial revocation by physical act, in several states a will cannot be revoked in part by an *act* of revocation; it can be revoked in part only by a subsequent instrument. The reasons for prohibiting partial revocation by physical act are two. First, canceling a gift to one person necessarily results in someone else taking the gift, and this "new gift" — like all bequests — can be made only by an attested writing. Second, permitting partial revocation by physical act offers opportunity for fraud. The person who takes the "new gift" may be the one who made the canceling marks. If partial revocation by act is not recognized, the will must be admitted to probate in the form in which it was originally executed if the original language can be ascertained. See Frederic S. Schwartz, Models of Will Revocation, 39 Real Prop., Prob. & Tr. J. 135 (2004).

PROBLEM

T executes a will that devises the residue of her estate to four named relatives. After *T*'s death some years later, her will is found in a stack of papers on her desk. One of the four names in the residuary clause has been lined out with a pencil. There is no direct evidence that *T* marked out the name.

(a) What result in a state having a statute similar to UPC §2-507? See In re Byrne's Will, 271 N.W. 48 (Wis. 1937). Compare In re Estate of Funk, 654 N.E.2d 1174 (Ind. App. 1995).

In Estate of Malloy, 949 P.2d 804 (Wash. 1997), the court discussed the fundamental inconsistency between allowing partial revocation by physical acts and requiring bequests to be attested, and held that partial revocation by physical act would not be permitted where the intent and effect of the change would result in a substantial enhancement of another bequest. A few cases have held that the testator can revoke a complete devise ("my car to *A*"), but cannot rearrange the shares in a single devise to increase the other devisee's gift. Example: "$10,000 to *A* and *B*, residue to *C*." *T* later lines out *B*'s name. *A*'s gift cannot be increased this way. The $5,000 given to *B* falls into the residuary and goes to *C*.

Restatement (Third) of Property: Wills and Other Donative Transfer §4.1, cmt. i (1999), disapproves of the *Malloy* approach and "any distinction between revocation of a complete devise and rearranging shares within a single devise or otherwise rewriting the terms of the will by deleting selected words. It is a classic example of a distinction without a difference. It is not supported by the language of the statutes specifically authorizing the revocation by act. . . . The legislature not only granted broad approval of deleting words but of the natural consequence of doing so — giving effect to the will as if the deleted words were not present."

(b) What result in a state that does not permit partial revocation by physical act? See Hansel v. Head, 706 So. 2d 1142 (Ala. 1997) (name obliterated with correction fluid); In re Estate of Haurin, 605 P.2d 65 (Colo. App. 1979).

(c) Suppose that *T*'s will is a holographic will in a jurisdiction permitting holographic wills. What result? See La Rue v. Lee, 60 S.E. 388 (W. Va. 1908).

2.   Dependent Relative Revocation and Revival

Simply put, the doctrine of dependent relative revocation is this: If the testator purports to revoke his will upon a mistaken assumption of law or fact, the revocation is ineffective if the testator would not have revoked his will had he known the truth. The usual case involves a situation where the testator destroys his will under a belief that a new will is valid but for some reason the new will is invalid. If the court finds that the testator would not have destroyed his old will had he known the new will was ineffective, the court, applying the doctrine of dependent relative revocation, will cancel the revocation and probate the destroyed prior will. The doctrine is one of presumptive intent, not actual intent. On dependent relative revocation generally, see George E. Palmer, Dependent Relative Revocation and Its Relation to Relief for Mistake, 69 Mich. L. Rev. 989 (1971). See also Kroll v. Nehmer, 705 A.2d 716 (Md. 1998); Carter v. First United Methodist Church of Albany, 271 S.E.2d 493 (Ga. 1980).

LaCroix v. Senecal
Supreme Court of Connecticut, 1953
140 Conn. 311, 99 A.2d 115

[The testator, Celestine Dupre, executed a will leaving the residue of her estate in equal shares, half to her nephew and half to a friend, Aurea Senecal. Dupre then executed a codicil revoking the residuary clause of her will and replacing it with an almost identical clause, the only difference being that in the original will she had referred to her nephew by his nickname and in the codicil she referred to him by both his nickname and his given name. The dispositive schemes were identical. Unfortunately, Senecal's husband witnessed the codicil. Under the applicable purging statute, the codicil would be valid, but the gift to Senecal would be struck down. Would Dupre have revoked the devises in her earlier will if she had known that she could not substitute the same devises in her codicil? Enter the doctrine of dependent relative revocation.]

BROWN J.   . . . The testatrix, Celestine L. Dupre, died in Putnam on April 19, 1951, leaving as her heir at law and next of kin her niece, the plaintiff. The testatrix left a will dated March 26, 1951, and a codicil thereto dated April 10, 1951. These instruments were admitted to probate on May 22, 1951. Item five of the will reads as follows:

> All the rest, residue and remainder of my property of whatsoever the same may consist and wheresoever the same may be situated, both real and personal, I give, devise and bequeath one-half to my nephew, Nelson Lamoth of Taftville, Connecticut, to be his absolutely; the other one-half to Aurea Senecal of 200 Providence Street, Putnam, Connecticut, to be hers absolutely.

The codicil reads as follows:

> 1. I hereby revoke Item Five of said will and substitute for said Item Five the following: Item Five: All the rest, residue and remainder of property of whatsoever the same may consist and wheresoever the same may be situated, both real and personal, I give, devise and bequeath one-half to my nephew Marcisse Lamoth of Taftville, Connecticut, also known as Nelson Lamoth, to be his absolutely; the other one-half to Aurea Senecal of 200 Providence Street, Putnam, Connecticut to be hers absolutely.
> 2. I hereby republish and confirm my said will in all respects except as altered by this Codicil.

Aurea Senecal is not related to the testatrix. One of the three subscribing witnesses to the codicil was Adolphe Senecal, who at the time he witnessed the codicil was, and still is, the husband of Aurea Senecal. Section 6952 of the General Statutes, so far as material, provides as follows: "Every devise or bequest given in any will or codicil to a subscribing witness, or to the husband or wife of such subscribing witness, shall be void unless such will or codicil shall be legally attested without the signature of such witness . . . ; but the competency of such witness shall not be affected by any such devise or bequest." As the court pointed out in its memorandum of decision, any bequest to Aurea Senecal in item five of the codicil was void because her husband was a subscribing witness. The question left to be answered, therefore, was whether the devise or bequest to the defendant Aurea under item five of the original will stands. It is to be noted that the only difference between item five of the will and item five of the codicil is the substitution for the words "my nephew, Nelson Lamoth of Taftville, Connecticut," in the former, of the words "my nephew Marcisse Lamoth of Taftville, Connecticut, also known as Nelson Lamoth," in the latter. It is also to be noted that by the second paragraph of the codicil the testatrix confirmed the will "in all respects except as altered by this Codicil."

The defendants' brief suggests that the issue on this appeal is whether the doctrine of dependent relative revocation may be invoked to sustain a gift by will, when such gift has been revoked in a codicil which substantially reaffirmed the gift but was void as to it under §6952 by reason of the interest of a subscribing witness. The gist of the doctrine is that if a testator cancels or destroys a will with a present intention of making a new one immediately and as a substitute and the new will is not made or, if made, fails of effect for any reason, it will be presumed that the testator preferred the old will to intestacy, and the old one will be admitted to probate in the absence of evidence overcoming the presumption. The rule has been more simply stated in these words: "[W]here the intention to revoke is conditional and where the condition is not fulfilled, the revocation is not effective." Matter of Macomber, 87 N.Y.S.2d 308 (App. Div. 1949). As is stated in that opinion at page 727, the doctrine has had wide acceptance in both England and the United States. It is a rule of presumed intention rather than of substantive law; and is applicable in cases of partial as well as total revocation. That it can only apply when there is a clear intent of the testator that the revocation of the old is made conditional upon the validity of the new is well brought out in Sanderson v. Norcross, 136 N.E. 170 (Mass. 1922), and in Estate of Kaufman, 155 P.2d 831 (Cal. 1945), where many cases are cited.

The doctrine has long been accepted in Connecticut, notwithstanding the plaintiff's claim that we should adopt the contrary view. In 1898, Justice Simeon E. Baldwin stated in a case involving a question of this nature: "It being [the testator's] manifest intention to revoke the provision in the will only for this purpose, so far as the purpose fails of effect, the revocation must fall with it. . . . The revocation of his former provision . . . was indissolubly coupled with the creation of the substituted provision." . . .

So far as the factual situation is concerned, it would be difficult to conceive of a more deserving case for the application of the doctrine of dependent relative revocation than the one before us. There is no room for doubt that the sole purpose of the testatrix in executing the codicil was, by making the very minor change in referring to her nephew, to eliminate any uncertainty as to his identity. Obviously, it was furthest from her intention to make any change in the disposition of her residuary estate. When the will and codicil are considered together, as they must be, to determine the intent of the testatrix, it is clear that her intention to revoke the will was conditioned upon the execution of a codicil which would be effective to continue the same disposition of her residuary estate. Therefore, when it developed that the gift under the codicil to the defendant Aurea was void, the conditional intention of the testatrix to revoke the will was rendered inoperative, and the gift to Aurea under the will continued in effect. The situation is well summed up in this statement by the court in a case on all fours with the one at bar: "When a testator repeats the same dispositive plan in a new will, revocation of the old one by the new is deemed inseparably related to and dependent upon the legal effectiveness of the new." Estate of Kaufman, 155 P.2d 831 (Cal. 1945). In short, in the words of the court in Matter of Macomber, 87 N.Y.S.2d 308 (App. Div. 1949), "the facts here fit well within the classic pattern of the rule in its most reliable aspect, and it ought to be applied to the facts of this case." . . .

There is no error.

NOTES AND PROBLEMS

1. Clause 5 of *T*'s typewritten will provides: "I bequeath the sum of $1,000 to my nephew, Charles Blake." *T* crosses out the "$1,000" and substitutes therefore "$1,500." *T* then writes her initials and the date in the right-hand margin opposite this entry. After *T*'s death some years later, her will is admitted to probate. Blake contends that he is entitled to $1,500 or, in the alternative, $1,000.

(a) What result in a state that recognizes holographic wills? See Estate of Phifer, 200 Cal. Rptr. 319 (App. 1984); but cf. McCarthy v. Bank of Cal., page 258; In re Estate of Muder, page 243.

(b) What result in a state that does not permit partial revocation by physical act?

(c) What result in a state that permits partial revocation by physical act? Should the doctrine of dependent relative revocation be applied? See Carpenter v. Wynn, 67 S.W.2d 688 (Ky. 1934).

(d) Suppose that *T* had crossed out "$1,000" and substituted "$500." In a state that permits partial revocation by physical act, should the doctrine of dependent relative revocation be applied? See Ruel v. Hardy, 6 A.2d 753 (N.H. 1939).

2. In his typewritten will, which contains a legacy of $5,000 to "John Boone," *T* crosses out "John" and writes in "Nancy." Nancy cannot take because the gift to her is not attested. In a state permitting partial revocation by physical act, should the legacy to John be given effect under the doctrine of dependent relative revocation? See In re Houghten's Estate, 17 N.W.2d 744 (Mich. 1945); Estate of Lyles, 615 So. 2d 1186 (Miss. 1993). Suppose John were Nancy's father. How would this affect your analysis?

In a state that recognizes holographic wills, the change from John to Nancy is not a valid holograph even though *T* signs his name on the margin. Standing alone, the handwritten words are insufficient to constitute a will. Estate of Phifer, supra. On the other hand, if *T*'s will were entirely handwritten and a valid holograph, the change from John to Nancy would be permitted. See Stanley v. Henderson, 162 S.W.2d 95 (Tex. 1942); Estate of Archer, 239 Cal. Rptr. 137 (App. 1987).

3. In *Body Heat*, a steamy 1981 *film noir* set in Florida, Matty Walker (Kathleen Turner), a silky blonde bent on doing away with her rich older husband, entraps a not-so-smart young lawyer, Ned Racine (William Hurt), to do the dirty work. The husband's existing will leaves half his fortune to Matty and half to his 10-year-old niece, Heather. After the husband is done in by Ned, Matty—a sometime legal secretary—produces a second will, written by Matty on stationery stolen from Ned's office, to which she has forged the signatures of her husband and—to his astonishment—Ned as a witness. (The second witness is—well, it takes too long to explain: You'll have to rent the DVD.) This second will leaves half to Matty, but it puts Heather's half in a trust that violates the Rule against Perpetuities. At a family conference, the husband's lawyer, oozing unction at every pore, pronounces the second will void. As a result, the lawyer says, the husband died intestate, and

under Florida law Matty takes her husband's entire estate. Little Heather and her mother meekly acquiesce and disappear from the movie. Matty ends up on an island paradise with all her husband's money and a new lover; the dupe Ned is left languishing in jail.

Before the movie was made, Florida had adopted wait-and-see for perpetuities violations (see page 702). Hence the husband's lawyer was too quick on the trigger; the trust for Heather might not turn out to be void. Apart from this oversight by the screenwriter, what other legal doctrine did the writer overlook that could have saved Heather's share? See In re Estate of Jones, 352 So. 2d 1182 (Fla. App. 1977). Though wills lawyers might grouse, these flaws seem not to have been noticed by the critics. The movie was boffo at the box office.

Courts have set limits on the dependent relative revocation doctrine. With rare exceptions, courts have held that DRR applies only (1) where there is an alternative plan of disposition that fails or (2) where the mistake is recited in the terms of the revoking instrument or, possibly, is established by clear and convincing evidence. The alternative plan of disposition is usually in the form of another will, either duly or defectively executed. By so limiting the doctrine, the kind of extrinsic evidence that can be looked at is narrowed.

NOTE AND PROBLEM

1. Preparing to make a new will, *T* writes "VOID" across her duly executed will. Several days later she shows the defaced will to her lawyer and instructs the lawyer to prepare a new will. The lawyer prepares a draft of the new will, but when it is shown to *T*, *T* tells the lawyer that it wrongly describes some property and is wrong in some other ways and must be changed. Before the draft can be corrected and executed, *T* dies. The lawyer testifies who the beneficiaries were to be under the new will. Does dependent relative revocation apply so as to cancel the revocation of the earlier will? In In re Estate of Ausley, 818 P.2d 1226 (Okla. 1991), the court refused to apply dependent relative revocation because the lawyer's testimony was insufficient evidence of a definite alternative plan of disposition. After In re Estate of Kuralt, page 244, would a Montana court reach the same result?

2. *T*'s will bequeaths $5,000 to his old friend, Judy, and the residue of his estate to his brother Mark. *T* later executes a codicil as follows: "I revoke the legacy to Judy, since she is dead." In fact, Judy is still living and survives *T*. Does Judy take $5,000? In Campbell v. French, 30 Eng. Rep. 1033 (Ch. 1797), on similar facts, the court held that there was no revocation, "the cause being false."

Suppose that the codicil had read: "I revoke the legacy to Judy, since I have already given her $5,000." In fact, the testator did not give Judy $5,000 during life. What result? See Witt v. Rosen, 765 S.W.2d 956 (Ark. App. 1989).

Suppose that the codicil had read: "I revoke the legacy to Judy." Evidence is offered that shows that three weeks prior to execution of the codicil *T* was told by a friend that Judy had died, believing it to be true. In fact, Judy survives *T*. What result? See In re Salmonski's Estate, 238 P.2d 966 (Cal. 1951) (holding DRR not applicable because mistake not recited on face of will); Estate of Anderson, 65 Cal.

Rptr. 2d 307 (App. 1997) (DRR applicable when mistake inferable from dispositive instruments and supported by lawyer-drafter's testimony).

On dependent relative revocation, see generally Restatement (Third) of Property: Wills and Other Donative Transfers §4.3 (1999) (renaming it the doctrine of ineffective revocation).

Estate of Alburn

Supreme Court of Wisconsin, 1963
18 Wis. 2d 340, 118 N.W.2d 919

Ottilie L. Alburn, a resident of the city of Fort Atkinson, Jefferson county, died on November 13, 1960, at the age of eighty-five years. On December 5, 1960, Adele Ruedisili, a sister of deceased, filed a petition for appointment of an administrator of the estate, which petition alleged that deceased died intestate. Thereafter, Viola Henkey, a grandniece of the deceased, filed a petition for the probate of a will which deceased executed at Milwaukee, Wisconsin, in 1955 (hereinafter the "Milwaukee will"), in which Viola Henkey was named a legatee and also executrix. After the filing of these two petitions, Lulu Alburn and Doris Alburn filed a petition for the probate of a will which deceased executed at Kankakee, Illinois, in 1959 (hereinafter the "Kankakee will"). Neither of these last-named petitioners is a next-of-kin of the deceased but Lulu Alburn is a sister-in-law of deceased. Objections were filed to both the Milwaukee and Kankakee wills.

The county court held a joint hearing on all three petitions.... The court determined that the Kankakee will had been destroyed by deceased under the mistaken belief that by so doing she would revive the Milwaukee will which had been revoked by the revocation clause of the Kankakee will. The court applied the doctrine of dependent relative revocation and held that the Kankakee will was entitled to probate. By a judgment (denominated an "Order") entered December 28, 1961, the Kankakee will was admitted to probate. Adele Ruedisili has appealed this judgment. The proponents of the Milwaukee will have not appealed. Further facts will be stated in the opinion.

CURRIE, J. This court is committed to the doctrine of dependent relative revocation. Estate of Eberhardt (Wis. 1957), 85 N.W.2d 483, and Estate of Callahan (Wis. 1947), 29 N.W.2d 352. The usual situation for application of this doctrine arises where a testator executes one will and thereafter attempts to revoke it by making a later testamentary disposition which for some reason proves ineffective. In both the *Eberhardt* and *Callahan* cases, however, the doctrine was applied to the unusual situation in which a testator revokes a later will under the mistaken belief that by so doing he is reinstating a prior will. In this unusual situation, the doctrine of dependent relative revocation is invoked to render the revocation ineffective. The basis of the doctrine is stated in Estate of Callahan, supra, as follows (29 N.W.2d at p.355):

> The doctrine of dependent relative revocation is based upon the testator's inferred intention. It is held that as a matter of law the destruction of the later document is intended to be conditional where it is accompanied by the expressed intent of reinstating a former will and where there is no explanatory evidence. Of course if there is

evidence that the testator intended the destruction to be absolute, there is no room for the application of the doctrine of dependent revocation.

The sole question raised by appellant on this appeal is whether the finding of the trial court that deceased revoked the Kankakee will under the mistaken belief that she was thereby reinstating the prior Milwaukee will is against the great weight and clear preponderance of the evidence. This requires that we review the pertinent evidence.

Testatrix was born in Wisconsin. For about thirty years she had resided in San Francisco, California, and later in Cleveland, Ohio. As a widow without children, she came to Milwaukee in the fall of 1954 and lived there with Viola Henkey, her grandniece. While so residing she executed the Milwaukee will on August 12, 1955. The original of this will was left with Attorney George R. Affeldt of Milwaukee, who had drafted it, where it remained until the death of testatrix. Sometime shortly prior to May 22, 1959, testatrix moved to Kankakee, Illinois, and resided there with her brother, Robert Lehmann. On May 22, 1959, she executed the Kankakee will.

On June 28, 1960, testatrix left Kankakee and came to Fort Atkinson, Wisconsin, and lived there with another brother, Edwin Lehmann, until her death in November of 1960. Testatrix was a patient at a hospital in Fort Atkinson during part of October and November of that year. Edwin testified that he had learned of the execution of the Kankakee will prior to the arrival of testatrix on June 28, 1960. On the evening of her arrival, he asked her what she had done with that will, and she replied, "What do you suppose, I got rid of it."[32] The next morning testatrix came downstairs with the torn pieces of the Kankakee will tied up in a handkerchief. Edwin provided her with a paper sack in which she deposited the pieces of the will. Edwin then took the sack with the garbage to the dump. There he opened the sack and let the pieces fly in the wind as testatrix had directed him to do.

Edwin was not questioned about any statement regarding the Milwaukee will which testatrix might have made in his presence at Fort Atkinson. He did testify that after her death he searched through her effects for a will but failed to find one. In view of the following testimony given by Olga Lehmann, his wife, this gives rise to an inference that Edwin was searching for the Milwaukee will.

Olga Lehmann was called as a witness by counsel for proponents of the Kankakee will. . . . Olga Lehmann was then asked the following questions and gave the following answers thereto:

Q. Did the deceased ever discuss in your presence the matter of the Milwaukee will at any other time other than the time we are just now referring to?
A. Yes.
Q. Who was present at that time?
A. Just myself.
Q. What did she tell you concerning the Milwaukee will?

32. The trial court in its memorandum decision found that the attempted revocation of the Kankakee will took place in Illinois but held that Wisconsin law rather than Illinois law controlled the question of whether the doctrine of dependent relative revocation should be invoked. This ruling is in accord with Restatement, Conflicts, p. 389, §307, which states: "Whether an act claimed to be a revocation of a will is effective to revoke it as a will of movables is determined by the law of the state in which the deceased was domiciled at the time of his death."

A. That was the one she wanted to stand.

Q. Can you tell me in point of time when this might have been?

A. No, we talked often.

We deem it significant that counsel for appellant did not cross-examine Olga Lehmann with respect to her testimony that testatrix said she wanted the Milwaukee will to stand. Therefore, Olga Lehmann's testimony was not qualified or limited in any way.

This statement by testatrix clearly occurred after her destruction of the Kankakee will. Appellant now attacks this statement on the ground that it was not made contemporaneously with such destruction. In Estate of Callahan, supra, however, the only evidence regarding the intent of testatrix when she destroyed her 1944 will was her husband's statement in her presence after the destruction and her silence indicating acquiescence. The husband stated that they both had destroyed their 1944 wills because they desired to put their son back in the position he occupied under their 1940 wills. Upon this evidence this court determined the doctrine of dependent relative revocation applied and affirmed the judgment of the county court which had admitted the 1944 will of testatrix to probate.

The plan of testamentary disposition under the two wills was in part as follows: The Milwaukee will contained specific bequests of jewelry and household furnishings to Viola Henkey, the grandniece of testatrix, and directed that any indebtedness owing deceased by Viola Henkey and her husband be deemed satisfied. The residuary clause bequeathed one fourth of the estate to her friend Olga Olson, one fourth to Doris Alburn, one fourth to Lulu Alburn, and one fourth to Viola Henkey. The Kankakee will included a bequest to Olga Olson of 38 shares of stock in the Bank of America National Trust & Savings Association and bequests of jewelry to Lulu and Addie Alburn. The remainder of the estate was bequeathed as follows: four tenths to Lulu Alburn, five tenths to Doris Alburn, and one tenth to Robert Lehmann, brother of testatrix. The Alburns are not related to testatrix but are relatives of her deceased husband. Viola Henkey, although a blood relative of testatrix, is not one of her next-of-kin who would inherit in the event testatrix had died intestate. The next-of-kin consist of four surviving brothers and one sister plus a large number of nieces and nephews of testatrix, the children of four deceased sisters and one deceased brother. Thus under the Milwaukee will, none of the next-of-kin were named as legatees, whereas under the Kankakee will, the only next-of-kin named a legatee was Robert, her brother. His share under the Kankakee will is somewhat less than the one-tenth share of the entire estate which he would receive if testatrix had died intestate. The bulk of the estate under both wills was bequeathed to the Alburns and Olga Olson. This plan of testamentary disposition extended as late as May, 1959.

There is no evidence of any change of circumstances occurring thereafter that would indicate any reason why testatrix should die intestate and nine tenths of her estate go to next-of-kin not named in either will. The one change in circumstance was her leaving the home of her brother Robert and moving in with her brother Edwin. This move might provide a reason for her desiring to revoke the Kankakee will, but certainly not for her wishing to die intestate. The learned trial judge, in the supplemental memorandum decision of December 26, 1961, stated, "I have a strong conviction that decedent did not want to die intestate." The evidence fully supports this conclusion despite the fact that testatrix took no steps between June 29, 1960, and her death nearly five months later to draft a new will. We deem that a reasonable inference, to be drawn from the competent evidence in this case, for her failure to make a new will is her evident belief that her Milwaukee will was still operative. Testatrix must have known that the original of the Milwaukee will was still in possession of Attorney Affeldt and believed that the only impediment to this will was the revocation clause of the Kankakee will. She also knew that the Kankakee will had been destroyed by tearing it in pieces and scattering the pieces so that they could not be found.[33]

We are constrained to conclude that the statement made to Olga Lehmann that testatrix wished her Milwaukee will to stand, the inference that she did not wish to die intestate, and the fact that she took no steps following the destruction of the Kankakee will to make a new will are sufficient evidence to support the finding that she destroyed the Kankakee will under the mistaken belief that the Milwaukee will would control the disposition of her estate. Furthermore there is no evidence which controverts this finding. Therefore, it is not against the great weight and clear preponderance of the evidence.

Counsel for respondents Alburn request a review by this court of several rulings by the trial court which excluded certain evidence pursuant to objections made by counsel for appellant Ruedisili. This excluded evidence related to further statements made by testatrix, after destruction of the Kankakee will, that she then considered her Milwaukee will to be in effect or desired this result. In view of our conclusion that the trial court's determination may be sustained upon the evidence admitted, we find it unnecessary to review these rulings.

Judgment affirmed.

NOTE: REVIVAL

Under Wisconsin law at the time, the will executed by Ottilie Alburn in Milwaukee in 1955 could not be revived after it had been expressly revoked by the 1959 Kankakee will. Why not? The explanation requires a brief discussion of the doctrine of revival.

The question of revival typically arises under the following facts (which were present in Estate of Alburn): Testator executes will #1. Subsequently testator executes will #2, which revokes will #1 by an express clause or by inconsistency. Later testator revokes will #2. Is will #1 revived?

The American states tend to fall within one of three groups. A few states take the view of the English common law courts that will #1 is not revoked unless will #2 remains in effect until the testator's death. The theory is that, since a will does not operate until the testator's death, will #2 is not legally effective during the testator's life. Therefore will #1 is not "revoked" by will #2. Technically, this theory does not involve "revival" at all because the first will has never been revoked.

---

33. The contents of the Kankakee will were proved by a carbon copy in the possession of the lawyer who had drafted it at Kankakee, Illinois.

The large majority of jurisdictions assumes that will #2 legally revokes will #1 at the time will #2 is executed. But they divide into two groups. A majority of states holds that upon revocation of will #2, will #1 is revived if the testator so intends. The testator's intent may be shown from the circumstances surrounding revocation of will #2 or from the testator's contemporaneous or subsequent oral declarations that will #1 is to take effect. Wisconsin is now in this group of states. See Restatement (Third) of Property: Wills and Other Donative Transfers §4.2, statutory note (1999).

A minority of states takes the view that a revoked will cannot be revived unless reexecuted with testamentary formalities or republished by being referred to in a later duly executed testamentary writing. At the time of the *Alburn* case, Wisconsin had this rule. See In re Eberhardt's Estate, 85 N.W.2d 483 (Wis. 1957).

UPC §2-509 has been adopted in a substantial number of states, either in its 1969 or 1990 version.

Uniform Probate Code (1990)

§2-509.   REVIVAL OF REVOKED WILL

(a) If a subsequent will that wholly revoked a previous will is thereafter revoked by a revocatory act under Section 2-507(a)(2), the previous will remains revoked unless it is revived. The previous will is revived if it is evident from the circumstances of the revocation of the subsequent will or from the testator's contemporary or subsequent declarations that the testator intended the previous will to take effect as executed.

(b) If a subsequent will that partly revoked a previous will is thereafter revoked by a revocatory act under Section 2-507(a)(2), a revoked part of the previous will is revived unless it is evident from the circumstances of the revocation of the subsequent will or from the testator's contemporary or subsequent declarations that the testator did not intend the revoked part to take effect as executed.

(c) If a subsequent will that revoked a previous will in whole or in part is thereafter revoked by another, later, will, the previous will remains revoked in whole or in part, unless it or its revoked part is revived. The previous will or its revoked part is revived to the extent it appears from the terms of the later will that the testator intended the previous will to take effect.

NOTE, QUESTIONS, AND PROBLEM

1.   Under UPC §2-509(a), if a subsequent will that *wholly* revoked the previous will is itself revoked by physical act, the presumption is that the previous will remains revoked. On the other hand, under UPC §2-509(b), if a subsequent will that *partly* revoked the previous will is itself revoked, the presumption is that the previous will is revived.

Suppose that Ottilie Alburn's Kankakee will, executed in 1959, had not contained an express revocation clause. Under UPC §2-509, would the presumption be that the 1955 will was revived? Does the 1959 will wholly or only partly revoke the 1955 will?

2. In 2000 *T* dies. *T*'s heir is *H*. *T*'s safe-deposit box contains the following three documents, all duly signed and witnessed according to law:

(1)   A will executed in 1995 devising all *T*'s property to *A*.
(2)   A will executed in 1996 devising all *T*'s property to *B*.
(3)   A document executed in 1999 reading: "I hereby revoke my 1996 will."

Under UPC §2-509(c), who takes *T*'s property?

3. In a state that has enacted UPC §§2-509 on revival and 2-503 to correct harmless errors in execution, is dependent relative revocation still necessary? See UPC §2-507, cmt. (1990).

3.   Revocation by Operation of Law: Change in Family Circumstances

In all but a tiny handful of states, statutes provide that a divorce revokes any provision in the decedent's will for the divorced spouse. In the remaining states, revocation occurs only if divorce is accompanied by a property settlement. These revocation statutes ordinarily apply only to wills, not to life insurance policies, pension plans, or other nonprobate transfers.

UPC §2-804 (1990) applies to nonprobate transfers as well as to wills. The term "governing instrument" in §2-804 is defined in UPC §1-201(19) to mean a deed, will, trust, insurance or annuity policy, account with a payable-on-death designation, pension plan, or similar nonprobate donative transfer.

Uniform Probate Code (1990, as amended in 1997)

§2-804.   REVOCATION OF PROBATE AND NONPROBATE TRANSFERS BY DIVORCE; NO
REVOCATION BY OTHER CHANGES OF CIRCUMSTANCES

(a) [Definitions.] [Omitted.]

(b) [Revocation Upon Divorce.] Except as provided by the express terms of a governing instrument, a court order, or a contract relating to the division of the marital estate made between the divorced individuals before or after the marriage, divorce, or annulment, the divorce or annulment of a marriage:

(1) revokes any revocable (i) disposition or appointment of property made by a divorced individual to his [or her] former spouse in a governing instrument and any disposition or appointment created by law or in a governing instrument to a relative of the divorced individual's former spouse, (ii) provision in a governing instrument conferring a general or nongeneral power of appointment on the divorced individual's former spouse or on a relative of the divorced individual's former spouse, and (iii) nomination in a governing instrument, nominating a divorced individual's former spouse or a relative of the divorced individual's former spouse to serve in any fiduciary or representative capacity, including a personal representative, executor, trustee, conservator, agent, or guardian; and

(2) severs the interests of the former spouses in property held by them at the time of the divorce or annulment as joint tenants with the right of

survivorship, transforming the interests of the former spouses into equal tenancies in common. . . .

(d) [Effect of Revocation.] Provisions of a governing instrument are given effect as if the former spouse and relatives of the former spouse disclaimed all provisions revoked by this section or, in the case of a revoked nomination in a fiduciary or representative capacity, as if the former spouse and relatives of the former spouse died immediately before the divorce or annulment. . . .

(f) [No Revocation for Other Change of Circumstances.] No change of circumstances other than as described in this section and in Section 2-803 [dealing with homicide] effects a revocation.

PROBLEM AND NOTE

1. *T* executes a will devising all his property to his wife, and if his wife does not survive him to his wife's son (*T*'s stepson). *T* divorces his wife and then dies. *T*'s heirs are his children by a prior marriage. A state statute revokes all provisions in a will for a divorced spouse and treats the divorced spouse as having predeceased the testator. Does the stepson take *T*'s property? Bloom v. Selfon, 555 A.2d 75 (Pa. 1989); In re Group Life Ins. Proceeds of Mallory, 872 S.W.2d 800 (Tex. App. 1994).

Who takes under UPC §2-804?

2. In Egelhoff v. Egelhoff, p. 336, the U.S. Supreme Court held that federal law preempts the application of state revocation-on-divorce statutes to federally regulated pension benefits.

Marriage. If the testator executes his will and subsequently marries, a large majority of states have statutes giving the spouse her intestate share, unless it appears from the will that the omission was intentional or the spouse is provided for in the will or by a will substitute with the intent that the transfer be in lieu of a testamentary provision. See UPC §2-301, page 465, which is a typical statute. In effect, this kind of statute revokes the will to the extent of the spouse's intestate share. See Estate of Shannon, 274 Cal. Rptr. 338 (App. 1990), page 462.

Where the spouse omitted from a premarital will does not take an intestate share because mentioned in the will, the spouse may take a "forced share" of the decedent's estate, which is given to all spouses whether intentionally or unintentionally disinherited. See page 425.

Birth of children. A small minority of states, either by statute or judicial decision, follow the common law rule that marriage followed by birth of issue revokes a will executed before marriage, but this rule has not been incorporated in the UPC and is rapidly disappearing. However, almost all states have pretermitted child statutes, giving a child born after execution of the parent's will, and not provided for in the will, a share in the parent's estate. See UPC §2-302 and page 480. Sometimes, pretermitted child statutes include children born before the execution of the will as well as children born thereafter. A pretermitted child statute, if applicable to the testator's will, results in a revocation of the will to the extent of the child's share.

SECTION C.   COMPONENTS OF A WILL

In Section A of this chapter, we considered the formalities with which a will must be executed. We saw that if a state's Wills Act is not complied with in all its particulars, a testamentary instrument may not be entitled to probate, no matter how clearly it reflects the testator's intention that it be a will. Yet despite these formal requirements of transfer, it is possible for documents and acts not executed with testamentary formalities to have the effect of determining *who* takes *what* property belonging to the testator. In this section, we are primarily concerned with two doctrines that can have this effect, two doctrines that permit extrinsic evidence to resolve the identity of persons or property: (1) the doctrine of incorporation by reference and (2) the doctrine of acts of independent significance. Before we consider these doctrines, we must examine two others that are sometimes confused with them.

1.   Integration of Wills

Wills are often written on more than one sheet of paper. Under the doctrine of *integration*, all papers present at the time of execution, intended to be part of the will, are integrated into the will. See Restatement (Third) of Property: Wills and Other Donative Transfers §3.5 (1999).

Hence the question may arise: Which sheets of paper, present at the time of execution, comprise the testator's duly executed will? Typically, there is no problem, for the pages of the will are physically connected with a staple or ribbon, or, failing this, there is a sufficient connection of language carrying over from page to page to show an internal coherence of the provisions. The attorney can prevent any problem from arising under the integration doctrine by seeing to it that the will is fastened together before the testator signs and by having the testator sign or initial each numbered page of the will for identification. The litigated cases involving integration arise when, for example, the pages are not physically connected and there is no internal coherence, or there is evidence that a staple has been removed, or one page is typed with elite type whereas the rest of the will is in pica.

In re Estate of Beale, 113 N.W.2d 380 (Wis. 1962), is illustrative of the integration cases. In that case, the testator, a history professor at the University of Wisconsin, planning to take a trip to Russia, dictated his will to his secretary in Madison. He had three sons, 16, 15, and 10, and his earlier will treated the three sons equally. In this new will, the testator left all his property to his wife and two older sons, disinheriting the youngest son. The will consisted of 14 pages, and the secretary gave the testator three carbon copies plus the original. The testator took all these sheets with him to New York on his way to Moscow. At a festive goodbye party in New York, given by a history professor at Columbia, the testator produced his will and asked three of his friends, all professors at eastern colleges, to witness his will. He laid "a pile" of papers on the table, declaring it was his will, and the testator and witnesses signed the last page. After the testator's death, none of the witnesses could identify any page except the signature page, but all pages of the will had the testator's initials on the margin. On the same day as the party, either before or after the execution ceremony, the testator wrote his secretary from

New York asking her to retype pages 12 and 13 and to make certain changes, including changing the executor from his wife to a friend. The letter to her enclosed pages 12 and 13. These pages were retyped by the secretary after the testator's death, and, as retyped, they too had the testator's initials on the margin! Noting that "the question is one of inference," the court upheld the trial court's decision to admit the will to probate as the will existed before any changes were made.

An oddball Indiana case, Keener v. Archibald, 533 N.E.2d 1268 (Ind. App. 1989), holds that the doctrine of integration is not the law in Indiana, but such a doctrine would seem to be necessary unless wills are required to be written on one page. One suspects that the judges were confused.

2. *Republication by Codicil*

Publication of a will is the testator's statement to the witnesses, by words or by action, that a document is the testator's will. Under the doctrine of *republication by codicil*, a will is treated as reexecuted (*re*published) as of the date of the codicil: "A will is treated as if it were executed when its most recent codicil was executed, whether or not the codicil expressly republishes the prior will, unless the effect of so treating it would be inconsistent with the testator's intent." Restatement (Third) of Property: Wills and Other Donative Transfers §3.4 (1999).

Updating the original will in this manner can have important consequences. For example, suppose that the testator revokes a first will by a second will and then executes a codicil to the first will. The first will is republished, and thus the second will is revoked by implication ("squeezed out"). See In re Estate of Stormont, 517 N.E.2d 259 (Ohio App. 1986).

The doctrine of republication by codicil is not applied automatically but only where updating the will carries out the testator's intent. Case 1 is illustrative.

> *Case 1.* The jurisdiction has an interested witness statute purging any gift to an attesting witness. In 1998 *T* executes a will devising all his property to *A*. *A* and *B* are witnesses to the will. In 1999 *T* executes a codicil bequeathing $5,000 to *C*. *C* and *D* are witnesses to the codicil. In 2000 *T* executes a second codicil bequeathing *C* a diamond ring. *D* and *E* are witnesses to the second codicil. Under the doctrine of republication by codicil, the will and first codicil are deemed to be reexecuted in 2000 by the second codicil, which has two disinterested witnesses. *A* and *C* are not purged of their gifts. See King v. Smith, 302 A.2d 144 (N.J. Super. 1973).

The fundamental difference between republication by codicil and the doctrine of incorporation by reference, discussed below, is that republication applies only to a prior validly executed will, whereas incorporation by reference can apply to incorporate into a will language or instruments that have never been validly executed. In the few jurisdictions that do not recognize incorporation by reference, courts have sometimes used the republication doctrine to give effect to wills that are invalid for some reason other than faulty execution. In New York, for example, which does not in general permit incorporation of unattested documents into a will, a codicil can republish and thereby give testamentary effect to a will that was invalid because of mental incapacity or undue influence, but a codicil cannot republish an instrument never duly executed with the required formalities.

3.   Incorporation by Reference

Uniform Probate Code (1990)

§2-510.   INCORPORATION BY REFERENCE

Any writing in existence when a will is executed may be incorporated by reference if the language of the will manifests this intent and describes the writing sufficiently to permit its identification.

Clark v. Greenhalge
Supreme Judicial Court of Massachusetts, 1991
411 Mass. 410, 582 N.E.2d 949

NOLAN, J.   We consider in this case whether a probate judge correctly concluded that specific, written bequests of personal property contained in a notebook maintained by a testatrix were incorporated by reference into the terms of the testatrix's will.

We set forth the relevant facts as found by the probate judge. The testatrix, Helen Nesmith, duly executed a will in 1977, which named her cousin, Frederic T. Greenhalge, II, as executor of her estate. The will further identified Greenhalge as the principal beneficiary of the estate, entitling him to receive all of Helen Nesmith's tangible personal property upon her death except those items which she "designate[d] by a memorandum left by [her] and known to [Greenhalge], or in accordance with [her] known wishes," to be given to others living at the time of her death.[34] Among Helen Nesmith's possessions was a large oil painting of a farm scene signed by T.H. Hinckley and dated 1833. The value of the painting, as assessed for estate tax purposes, was $1,800.00.

In 1972, Greenhalge assisted Helen Nesmith in drafting a document entitled "MEMORANDUM" and identified as "a list of items of personal property prepared with Miss Helen Nesmith upon September 5, 1972, for the guidance of myself in the distribution of personal tangible property." This list consisted of forty-nine specific bequests of Ms. Nesmith's tangible personal property. In 1976, Helen Nesmith modified the 1972 list by interlineations, additions and deletions. Neither edition of the list involved a bequest of the farm scene painting.

Ms. Nesmith kept a plastic-covered notebook in the drawer of a desk in her study. She periodically made entries in this notebook, which bore the title "List to be given Helen Nesmith 1979." One such entry read: "Ginny Clark farm picture hanging over fireplace. Ma's room." Imogene Conway and Joan Dragoumanos, Ms. Nesmith's private home care nurses, knew of the existence of the notebook and had observed Helen Nesmith write in it. On several occasions, Helen Nesmith orally expressed to these nurses her intentions regarding the disposition of particular pieces of her property upon her death, including the farm scene painting. Helen Nesmith told Conway and Dragoumanos that the farm scene painting was to be given to Virginia Clark, upon Helen Nesmith's death.

---

34. The value of Ms. Nesmith's estate at the time of her death exceeded $2,000,000.00, including both tangible and nontangible assets.

Virginia Clark and Helen Nesmith first became acquainted in or about 1940. The women lived next door to each other for approximately ten years (1945 through 1955), during which time they enjoyed a close friendship. The Nesmith-Clark friendship remained constant through the years. In more recent years, Ms. Clark frequently spent time at Ms. Nesmith's home, often visiting Helen Nesmith while she rested in the room which originally was her mother's bedroom. The farm scene painting hung in this room above the fireplace. Virginia Clark openly admired the picture.

According to Ms. Clark, sometime during either January or February of 1980, Helen Nesmith told Ms. Clark that the farm scene painting would belong to Ms. Clark after Helen Nesmith's death. Helen Nesmith then mentioned to Virginia Clark that she would record this gift in a book she kept for the purpose of memorializing her wishes with respect to the disposition of certain of her belongings.[35] After that conversation, Helen Nesmith often alluded to the fact that Ms. Clark someday would own the farm scene painting.

Ms. Nesmith executed two codicils to her 1977 will: one on May 30, 1980, and a second on October 23, 1980. The codicils amended certain bequests and deleted others, while ratifying the will in all other respects.

Greenhalge received Helen Nesmith's notebook on or shortly after January 28, 1986, the date of Ms. Nesmith's death. Thereafter, Greenhalge, as executor, distributed Ms. Nesmith's property in accordance with the will as amended, the 1972 memorandum as amended in 1976, and certain of the provisions contained in the notebook.[36] Greenhalge refused, however, to deliver the farm scene painting to Virginia Clark because the painting interested him and he wanted to keep it. Mr. Greenhalge claimed that he was not bound to give effect to the expressions of Helen Nesmith's wishes and intentions stated in the notebook, particularly as to the disposition of the farm scene painting. Notwithstanding this opinion, Greenhalge distributed to himself all of the property bequeathed to him in the notebook. Ms. Clark thereafter commenced an action against Mr. Greenhalge seeking to compel him to deliver the farm scene painting to her.

The probate judge found that Helen Nesmith wanted Ms. Clark to have the farm scene painting. The judge concluded that Helen Nesmith's notebook qualified as a "memorandum" of her known wishes with respect to the distribution of her tangible personal property, within the meaning of Article Fifth of Helen Nesmith's will.[37] The judge further found that the notebook was in existence at the time of the execution of the 1980 codicils, which ratified the language of Article Fifth in its entirety. Based on these findings, the judge ruled that the notebook was

35. According to Margaret Young, another nurse employed by Ms. Nesmith, Ms. Nesmith asked Ms. Young to "print[ ] in [the] notebook, beneath [her] own handwriting, 'Ginny Clark painting over fireplace in mother's bedroom.'" Ms. Young complied with this request. Ms. Young stated that Ms. Nesmith's express purpose in having Ms. Young record this statement in the notebook was "to insure that [Greenhalge] would know that she wanted Ginny Clark to have that particular painting."

36. Helen Nesmith's will provided that Virginia Clark and her husband, Peter Hayden Clark, receive $20,000.00 upon Helen Nesmith's death. Under the terms of the 1972 memorandum, as amended in 1976, Helen Nesmith also bequeathed to Virginia Clark a portrait of Isabel Nesmith, Helen Nesmith's sister with whom Virginia Clark had been acquainted. Greenhalge honored these bequests and delivered the money and painting to Virginia Clark.

37. Article Fifth of Helen Nesmith's will reads, in pertinent part, as follows: "that [Greenhalge] distribute such of the tangible property to and among such persons *as I may designate by a memorandum left by me and known to him, or in accordance with my known wishes,* provided that said persons are living at the time of my decease" (emphasis added).

incorporated by reference into the terms of the will. Newton v. Seaman's Friend Soc'y, 130 Mass. 91, 93 (1881). The judge awarded the painting to Ms. Clark.

. . . We . . . now hold that the probate judge correctly awarded the painting to Ms. Clark.

A properly executed will may incorporate by reference into its provisions any "document or paper not so executed and witnessed, whether the paper referred to be in the form of . . . a mere list or memorandum, . . . if it was in existence at the time of the execution of the will, and is identified by clear and satisfactory proof as the paper referred to therein." Newton v. Seaman's Friend Soc'y, supra at 93. The parties agree that the document entitled "memorandum," dated 1972 and amended in 1976, was in existence as of the date of the execution of Helen Nesmith's will. The parties further agree that this document is a memorandum regarding the distribution of certain items of Helen Nesmith's tangible personal property upon her death, as identified in Article Fifth of her will. There is no dispute, therefore, that the 1972 memorandum was incorporated by reference into the terms of the will. *Newton*, supra.

The parties do not agree, however, as to whether the documentation contained in the notebook, dated 1979, similarly was incorporated into the will through the language of Article Fifth. Greenhalge advances several arguments to support his contention that the purported bequest of the farm scene painting written in the notebook was not incorporated into the will and thus fails as a testamentary devise. The points raised by Greenhalge in this regard are not persuasive. First, Greenhalge contends that the judge wrongly concluded that the notebook could be considered a "memorandum" within the meaning of Article Fifth, because it is not specifically identified as a "memorandum." Such a literal interpretation of the language and meaning of Article Fifth is not appropriate.

"The 'cardinal rule in the interpretation of wills, to which all other rules must bend, is that the intention of the testator shall prevail, provided it is consistent with the rules of law.'" Boston Safe Deposit & Trust Co. v. Park, 29 N.E.2d 977 (Mass. 1940), quoting McCurdy v. McCallum, 72 N.E. 75 (Mass. 1904). The intent of the testator is ascertained through consideration of "the language which [the testatrix] has used to express [her] testamentary designs," Taft v. Stearns, 125 N.E. 570 (Mass. 1920), as well as the circumstances existing at the time of the execution of the will. The circumstances existing at the time of the execution of a codicil to a will are equally relevant, because the codicil serves to ratify the language in the will which has not been altered or affected by the terms of the codicil.

Applying these principles in the present case, it appears clear that Helen Nesmith intended by the language used in Article Fifth of her will to retain the right to alter and amend the bequests of tangible personal property in her will, without having to amend formally the will. The text of Article Fifth provides a mechanism by which Helen Nesmith could accomplish the result she desired; i.e., by expressing her wishes "in a memorandum." The statements in the notebook unquestionably reflect Helen Nesmith's exercise of her retained right to restructure the distribution of her tangible personal property upon her death. That the notebook is not entitled "memorandum" is of no consequence, since its apparent purpose is consistent with that of a memorandum under Article Fifth: It is a written instrument which is intended to guide Greenhalge in "distribut[ing] such of [Helen Nesmith's] tangible personal property to and among . . . persons [who] are living at the time of her decease." In this connection, the distinction between the notebook and "a memorandum" is illusory. The appellant acknowledges that the subject documentation in the notebook establishes that Helen Nesmith wanted Virginia Clark to receive the farm scene painting upon Ms. Nesmith's death. The appellant argues, however, that the notebook cannot take effect as a testamentary instrument under Article Fifth, because the language of Article Fifth limits its application to "a" memorandum, or the 1972 memorandum. We reject this strict construction of Article Fifth. The language of Article Fifth does not preclude the existence of more than one memorandum which serves the intended purpose of that article. As previously suggested, the phrase "a memorandum" in Article Fifth appears as an expression of the manner in which Helen Nesmith could exercise her right to alter her will after its execution, but it does not denote a requirement that she do so within a particular format. To construe narrowly Article Fifth and to exclude the possibility that Helen Nesmith drafted the notebook contents as "a memorandum" under that Article, would undermine our long-standing policy of interpreting wills in a manner which best carries out the known wishes of the testatrix. See Boston Safe Deposit & Trust Co., supra. The evidence supports the conclusion that Helen Nesmith intended that the bequests in her notebook be accorded the same power and effect as those contained in the 1972 memorandum under Article Fifth. We conclude, therefore, that the judge properly accepted the notebook as a memorandum of Helen Nesmith's known wishes as referenced in Article Fifth of her will. . . .

. . . The judge further found that the notebook was in existence on the dates Helen Nesmith executed the codicils to her will [which republished her will], . . . and that it thereby was incorporated into the will pursuant to the language and spirit of Article Fifth. . . .

Lastly, the appellant complains that the notebook fails to meet the specific requirements of a memorandum under Article Fifth of the will, because it was not "known to him" until after Helen Nesmith's death. For this reason, Greenhalge states that the judge improperly ruled that the notebook was incorporated into the will. One of Helen Nesmith's nurses testified, however, that Greenhalge was aware of the notebook and its contents, and that he at no time made an effort to determine the validity of the bequest of the farm scene painting to Virginia Clark as stated therein. There is ample support in the record, therefore, to support the judge's conclusion that the notebook met the criteria set forth in Article Fifth regarding memoranda.

We note, as did the Appeals Court, that "one who seeks equity must do equity and that a court will not permit its equitable powers to be employed to accomplish an injustice." Pitts v. Halifax Country Club, Inc., 476 N.E.2d 222 (Mass. App. 1985). To this point, we remark that Greenhalge's conduct in handling this controversy fell short of the standard imposed by common social norms, not to mention the standard of conduct attending his fiduciary responsibility as executor, particularly with respect to his selective distribution of Helen Nesmith's assets. We can discern no reason in the record as to why this matter had to proceed along the protracted and costly route that it did.[38]

Judgment affirmed.

---

38. And it had a costly aftermath for Greenhalge, the executor and residuary beneficiary of Helen Nesmith's estate. A letter from Thomas D. Burns, counsel for Virginia Clark, to Jesse Dukeminier dated

SIMON v. GRAYSON, 102 P.2d 1081 (Cal. 1940): The testator's will, dated March 25, 1932, left $4,000 to his executors "to be paid by them as shall be directed by me in a letter that will be found in my effects and which will be addressed to my executors and dated March 25, 1932." A codicil to the will was executed November 25, 1933, which made a small change not relevant here and otherwise reaffirmed the will. After the testator's death, a letter dated July 3, 1933, addressed to the executors, was found in the testator's safe-deposit box. It stated: "In my will I have left you $4,000 to be paid to a person named in a letter. I direct you to pay the $4,000 to Esther Cohn." No letter dated March 25, 1932, was found.

The court held that the letter found in the safe-deposit box was the letter referred to in the will, despite the discrepancy in dates. It was incorporated by reference into the will, becoming an integral part of the will. Since the letter was dated prior to the date of the codicil, which republished the will, it complied with the requirement that an incorporated document be in existence on the date of the republished will. The court directed the executors to give the $4,000 to Esther Cohn's estate (she died seven days after testator).

If the testator intended to make a secret gift to Esther Cohn, he failed. A document incorporated by reference becomes part of the probate files, open to the public.

NOTES AND PROBLEMS

1. In Clark v. Greenhalge, suppose that the entry in the notebook, "Ginny Clark farm picture," had been made after the 1980 codicils. Could it have been given effect? Could it have been given effect under UPC §2-503 or the substantial compliance doctrine? Under UPC §2-513, page 278?

2. The testator executed a deed to his farm that named his niece as grantee. The deed was sealed in an envelope and placed by the testator in his safe-deposit box at a local bank, where it remained until his death. Sometime later, the testator executed a will containing the following provision: "Sixth: I have already deeded my farm to my niece, Alta J. Pullman, and for that reason I do not devise my farm to her in this Will." After the testator's death, it was held that the deed was not effective to convey title to the niece because it was not delivered by the grantor during his lifetime. The niece contends that the deed was incorporated by reference by the language of clause Sixth of the will. What result? See Estate of Dimmitt, 3 N.W.2d 752 (Neb. 1942) (deed incorporated by reference!). Since the court could not openly correct the mistake by adding words to the will,

Sept. 27, 1993, reveals:

> While the picture was later appraised at about $35,000, its stated value by the executor Greenhalge in the inventory was only $1500. I was awarded a fee of $80,000 by the Probate Court, which I settled for $70,000 to avoid an appeal. The executor, who was a very terrible guy, refused to give up the picture and I thought the case would be on a pro bono basis, but the Probate Judge who heard the case was so incensed by Greenhalge's conduct, he awarded me my full hourly rate upon application.

— Eds.

the court did so in effect by a generous application of the incorporation doctrine. On correcting mistakes in wills, see Chapter 6.

3.   The doctrine of incorporation by reference is not recognized, as a general rule, in Connecticut,[39] Louisiana, and New York. To fill this lacuna, New York courts have stretched the doctrines of republication by codicil (see page 273) and integration to carry out the testator's intent. As for the latter, if, for example, the testator refers in his will to a separate memorandum disposing of his tangible personal property, and if such memorandum is attached to the other pages of his will and was present at execution, such memorandum is entitled to probate under the doctrine of integration. In re Will of Hall, 300 N.Y.S.2d 813 (Sur. 1969). Indeed, even if the memorandum is attached after the signature page, it will be deemed constructively inserted before the signature page so as to comply with the requirement that a will be signed at the end. In re Will of Powell, 395 N.Y.S.2d 334 (Sur. 1977).

Uniform Probate Code (1990)

§2-513.   Separate Writing Identifying Bequest of Tangible Property

Whether or not the provisions relating to holographic wills apply, a will may refer to a written statement or list to dispose of items of tangible personal property not otherwise specifically disposed of by the will, other than money. To be admissible under this section as evidence of the intended disposition, the writing must be signed by the testator and must describe the items and the devisees with reasonable certainty. The writing may be referred to as one to be in existence at the time of the testator's death; it may be prepared before or after the execution of the will; it may be altered by the testator after its preparation; and it may be a writing that has no significance apart from its effect on the dispositions made by the will.

---

39.   Hathaway v. Smith, 65 A. 1058 (Conn. 1907), established that the doctrine of incorporation by reference does not exist in Connecticut. An earlier, more interesting case suggested that ultimate result. In Bryan's Appeal, 58 A. 748 (Conn. 1904), the testator, Philo S. Bennett, was a rich Connecticut friend and political ally of the Great Commoner and scourge of eastern capitalists, William Jennings Bryan, who thrice ran unsuccessfully for the presidency on the Democratic ticket. ("You shall not press down upon the brow of labor this crown of thorns. You shall not crucify mankind on a cross of gold.") While on a visit to Bryan at Lincoln, Nebraska, Bennett, with Bryan's assistance, prepared his will. The will was duly executed on May 22, 1900. It provided: "I give and bequeath unto my wife, Grace Imogene Bennett, the sum of fifty thousand dollars (50,000), in trust, however for the purposes set forth in a sealed letter which will be found with this will." Found with the will, at testator's death, was a letter dated "5/22/1900" addressed to "My Dear Wife," which referred to the $50,000 bequest in the will and stated that the $50,000 conveyed to her in trust was to be paid to William Jennings Bryan inasmuch "as his political work prevents the application of his time and talents to money making." Largely because Bennett left $20,000 to his mistress, Mrs. Bennett, angered by the will, refused to carry out Bennett's desires. Bryan sued and lost. The court held that even if incorporation by reference were recognized, the reference in the will was so vague as to be incapable of being applied to any particular instrument.

Bryan then sued Mrs. Bennett a second time, alleging that she held the $50,000 in a constructive trust for him (see page 532 on semisecret testamentary trusts). The court held that no trust arose because Mrs. Bennett had never been apprised of the terms of the will and had made no promise, an essential ingredient of a semisecret testamentary trust. Bryan v. Bigelow, 60 A. 266 (Conn. 1905).

It may be that Bryan's Appeal is an example of the old adage that hard cases make bad law. Bryan, a graduate of Northwestern University School of Law, had acted indelicately — perhaps even unethically — in participating in this secret gift to himself, and the court was probably not disposed to rule in his favor.

Johnson v. Johnson
Supreme Court of Oklahoma, 1954
279 P.2d 928

PER CURIAM. This is an appeal from a judgment of the District Court of Oklahoma County affirming the County Court of Oklahoma in denying probate to an instrument purporting to be the last will and testament of Dexter G. Johnson, who was sometimes known as D.G. Johnson.

The instrument in question was on a single sheet of paper and contained three typewritten paragraphs, started out with the words, "I, D.G. Johnson also known as Dexter G. Johnson, of Oklahoma City, Oklahoma County, State of Oklahoma do hereby make, publish and declare this to be my last Will and Testament . . ." and made numerous bequests and devises and concluded with recommending the employment of a certain attorney to probate the will. This typewritten portion was not dated nor did the testator sign his name at the conclusion thereof nor was it attested by two witnesses. At the end of the typewritten portion, at the bottom of [the] sheet of paper, appears the following, admitted to be in the handwriting of the deceased:

> To my brother James I give ten dollars only. This will shall be complete unless here- after altered, changed or rewritten. Witness my hand this April 6, 1947. Easter Sunday, 2:30 P.M.
> D.G. Johnson
> Dexter G. Johnson

On trial de novo in the District Court the proponents of this purported will, plaintiffs in error here, introduced evidence over objections (which objections were never ruled on by the court) showing that Dexter G., or D.G. Johnson for many years was a practicing attorney in Oklahoma City; that during his practice he prepared many wills, all in proper form, for various clients; that in October, 1946, deceased told Jack G. Wiggins, his insurance counselor, that he had a will but it was out of date and needed changing; that in March, 1947, deceased told this insurance counselor that he was working on his will, making changes, and expected to complete it right away and told Mr. Wiggins in general the disposition he intended to make of his property; that in the latter part of 1946 Lowell M. Wickham, deceased's rental agent, was shown the instrument here in question at which time it had only the typewritten portions on it; that at that time deceased told him that was his will and he wanted Wickham to witness it, but he and deceased started discussing other business and neglected to do it at that time; that when Wickham left the paper was lying on deceased's desk; that some months later Wickham asked deceased about witnessing the will and deceased replied he had changed his will by codicil and did not need Wickham to sign it as witness; an offer by statement of counsel was made to show the intention of the testator in leaving his property to the persons he named as beneficiaries which was rejected by the court and is not helpful in deciding the questions raised here.

The above is a summary of all the testimony that appears in the record. None of the testimony presented to the County Court appears in the record; defendant below, contestant of the will and defendant in error here, offered no testimony.

129067

I, D. G. Johnson also known as Dexter G. Johnson, of Oklahoma City, Oklahoma County, State of Oklahoma do hereby make, publish and declare this to be my last Will and Testamnt and revoke all former wills and codocils by me made.

FIRST: I direct my Executor to pay my just debts, last illness and burial expense.

SECOND: I give, devise and bequeath to my sister Beulah Johnson also known as Beulah J. Johnson and my brother V. C. Johnson also known as Victor C. Johnson all of the rest, residue and rrmainder of my estate, real, personal and mixed propertt, wherever situated and whatsoever kind and/or character, subject only to the following requests of my said brother and sister, namely and specifically that at a time when in the jydgment of my said sister and brother they shall deem the cpndition of the estate in a proper and suitable condition so to do without material injuxxxxxx damage to or otherwise detrimental to said estate and the properties reasonably disposed of to pay into a trust fund to be governed by my said sister and brother the sum of Fifty thousand dollars to be used for the erection of a new church in Montrose,Effingham County, State of Illinois on the site where the present church now stands being the church formerly attended by our family regularily and to build a parsonage of not less than six rooms,nor more than eight rooms on the lots owned by me across the street from said church site and said lots to be deeded to said church organization for the use of the minister to preside over the church aforesaid; also to use any sum remaining for a mauseloeum or suitable arrangement as my said sister and brother may determine proper and fitting for the graves of our family now buried there and any sum then remaining to generally improve said cemetery a ll as my said sister and brother may determine; if there be difference of opinions or desires in any matter, then the will and desire of my sister shall prevail. and further that a fund of Ten thousand dollars to be set up and invested in SAFE SECURITIES with reasonable rate of interest, for the use and benefit of my great neice Joanna Johnson and a similiar sum for Joanna's sister with same conditions and to be paid to each of them in monthly payments of Seventy-five dollars each month beginning on their seventeenth birthday and thereafter until exhausted ans each shall have received the full sum together with it's accruals of ten thousand dollars or a total of twenty thousand dollars; I also request that a fund of ten thousand dollars be set up for the purpose of paying to my brother Joseph Evera d Johnson a monthoy stipend of fifty dollars each and every month during his life to begin ninety days after my death and to end with the death of my said brother or the exhaustizn of the funds if they shall. exhaust prior to his death with any sum remaining to remine to the use and benefit of my brother Victor C. Johnson and sister Beulah J. Johnson, and yhe further sum of Five yhousand dollars to be paid within reasonable time to Alma L. Kloss friend of my sister Beulah J.Johnson in appreciation for her kindness and sincere friendship to and for my sister Beulah J. Johnson with the request that said Alma L. Kloss invest same in some good securities, government bonds or annuity, sxkinxxxk. I further suggest that my said sister and brother employ Claude Monnett, attorney and friend of mine be employed for a reasonable fee, to be agreed upon by ixxxxxxxxxx my sister, brother and Mr. Monnett for complete service but should they not agree then my said brother and sister shall employ whomsoever they may desire, being contious that nothing to be done without their consent and knowledge

To my brother James I give ten dollars only

This will shall be complete unless except altered changed or renewtten

Witness My Hand this

April 6, 1947

Easter Sunday 2 30 Pm

B J Johnson

Dexter G Johnson

Reproduction of the actual will (or wills) in Johnson.

Is this instrument one complete, integrated writing, partly typed and partly handwritten; or is it an unexecuted nonholographic will to which is appended a valid holographic codicil? If it be the former it cannot be admitted to probate because it was not signed in the presence of two subscribing witnesses as required by law.

Defendant in error urges that the instrument shows on its face that it is but one instrument and that it cannot be divided into two parts, one, the typewritten part to be called a will and the other, the handwritten part, to be called a codicil. In support of his contention he says that the typewritten portion standing alone is not a will because, though admittedly testamentary in character, it is not dated, signed, nor witnessed; that it takes the handwritten portion to complete the instrument; that by definition to have a codicil there must first be a will.

There is no question in this case that the typewritten instrument which was not signed, dated, nor attested was prepared by D.G. Johnson and that it is testamentary in character, or that he intended same as his will or that it effectively makes complete disposition of his estate. A will may be so defective, as here, that it is not entitled to probate but if testamentary in character it is a will, nonetheless. . . . Nor is there any question that the handwritten words were wholly in the handwriting of the testator.

The question next arises, do these words meet the requirements of a codicil? By definition a codicil is a supplement to, an addition to or qualification of, an existing will, made by the testator to alter, enlarge, or restrict the provisions of the will, to explain or republish it, or to revoke it, and it must be testamentary in character. In re Whittier's Estate, 176 P.2d 281 (Wash. 1947). A codicil need not be called a codicil, In re Carr's Estate, 209 P.2d 956 (Cal. App. 1949); In re Atkinson's Estate, 294 P. 425 (Cal. App. 1930). The intention to add a codicil is controlling. Allgeier v. Brown, 251 S.W. 851 (Ky. 1952); Stewart v. Stewart, 59 N.E. 116 (Mass. 1900). The handwritten words are admittedly testamentary in character. It is clear that they made an addition to the provisions of the will theretofore existing. This codicil is on the same sheet of paper and the terms thereof, the circumstances surrounding it, as shown by the evidence indicate that the testator intended it as an addition to and republication of his will.

If it be a codicil, then, is it a valid one? It is written, dated, and signed by the testator. It meets all the requirements of a valid holographic codicil. The fact that the codicil was written on the same piece of paper as the typewritten will will not invalidate the codicil. In re Atkinson's Estate, supra.

It is admitted that a codicil republishes a previous will as modified by the codicil as of the date of the codicil. Can a valid, holographic codicil republish and validate a will which was theretofore inoperative because not dated, signed, or attested according to law?

The general principle of law is that a codicil validly executed operates as a republication of the will no matter what defects may have existed in the execution of the earlier document, that the instruments are incorporated as one, and that a proper execution of the codicil extends also to the will. Twenty-two states and England so hold. For citation of cases see Annotations 21 A.L.R.2d 823. That a properly executed codicil will give effect to a will which has never been signed has been specifically held in Kentucky, New Jersey, and England. See Beall v. Cunningham, 1843, 42 Ky. 390, in which it appeared that a paper wholly written by testator dated 1825 was denied probate, and thereafter there was offered for probate a typewritten will dated in 1827,[40] which was unsigned and unattested, together with a codicil dated 1832 on the same sheet of paper which was signed and attested; the opinion holds that the properly executed codicil had the effect of giving operation to the whole as one will. See also Hurley v. Blankinship, 229 S.W.2d 963 (Ky. 1950), in which a holographic will which was not signed was held validated by properly executed holographic codicils; Doe v. Evans, 1832, 149 Eng. Reprint 307, in which an unsigned typewritten will was held validated by a properly executed codicil on the same sheet of paper; see also McCurdy v. Neall, 7 A. 566 (N.J. Prerog. 1886), and Smith v. Runkle, 98 A. 1086 (N.J. App. 1916), in both of which the signatures to the wills were defective because not placed on the will in the presence of witnesses but it was held that valid codicils thereafter executed gave operation to the entire will and codicils; Rogers v. Agricola, 3 S.W.2d 26 (Ark. 1928), in which an invalid typewritten will (due to only one witness) was held validated by a subsequent holographic codicil; In re Plumel's Estate, 90 P. 192 (Cal. 1907), an invalid holographic will because of printing thereon was held validated by a subsequent holographic codicil written on the back of the will. . . .[41]

The only exception is New York which modifies the general rule by holding that a properly executed codicil validates a will originally invalid for want of testamentary capacity, undue influence, or revocation but does not validate a will defectively executed because of improper attestation. It will be noted, however, that Justice Cardozo in Re Fowles, 118 N.E. 611 (N.Y. 1918), stated that the rule was malleable and uncertain and he anticipated that New York would abandon its limitations on the rule. . . .

We therefore hold that the valid holographic codicil incorporated the prior will by reference and republished and validated the prior will as of the date of the codicil, thus giving effect to the intention of the testator.

Reversed with directions to enter the will for probate.

CORN, J. (concurring specially).[42]   I concur in the per curiam opinion. In so doing I have in mind the purpose of our law-makers in enacting statutes regulating the

---

40. Typewritten will in 1827? The first typewriters were placed on the market in 1874. Later in this paragraph the court refers to a typewritten will in Doe v. Evans, decided in 1832. In neither Beall v. Cunningham nor in Doe v. Evans was there mention of any typewriting. This anachronism was called to our attention by John Cutcher, J.D. Vanderbilt 1987, whose sharp eyes spotted it while a student in Professor Jeffrey Schoenblum's wills course at Vanderbilt.—Eds.

41. Examine carefully the facts of the cases cited in this paragraph. Do you see why the cases cited are properly analyzed as applications of either incorporation by reference or integration and that republication by codicil is not involved?—Eds.

42. In 1964, Justices Corn and Welch were convicted of federal income tax evasion and sentenced to prison terms of 18 months and 3 years respectively. N.Y. Times, July 19, 1964, at 44; id., Nov. 14, 1964, at 14. Corn and Welch resigned their judicial positions. Subsequently Corn signed a statement in which Corn said Welch, Johnson, and he had accepted more than $150,000 in bribes for throwing cases. In 1965 Justice Johnson was convicted of corruption in office and removed from the court by the Oklahoma legislature. Id., May 14, 1965, at 40.

The newspaper accounts did not mention any evidence of bribery in the principal case of Johnson v. Johnson. Yet when a judge has been convicted of bribery in one case, the public may suspect there was bribery in others. (Indeed, when Corn was asked if he could remember any year, in the 24 he served as Justice, when he did not take money for his votes, he replied: "Well, I don't know." Id., May 11, 1965, at 18.) The votes of Corn, Welch, and Johnson were decisive in Johnson v. Johnson. Although there is no report of bribery in this case, *and none is to be inferred from this note*, does the mere appearance of possible impropriety require that the case now be reheard upon petition of the losing party?

making of a Will. They require certain steps to be taken in the execution of a Will solely for the purpose of permitting a person to dispose of his property by Will, to take effect after his death the way he desired, and to prevent someone, through fraud or by other means, from permitting this to be done. It was the purpose of our law-makers, in passing the Act, to make it impossible for fraud or undue influence to be practiced in the execution of the Will, and in the disposition of the property disposed of by the Will. It was not the intent of our lawmakers, in enacting these statutes, if substantially complied with, to ever allow a miscarriage of justice by a wrongful disposition of the testator's property contrary to his intent. 84 O.S. 1951 §151 provides: "Intention of testator governs. — A will is to be construed according to the intention of the testator. . . ."

In the instant case, the intent expressed by the testator in the written instrument which he prepared, while of sound mind and disposing memory, is clear and beyond any question of doubt, free from fraud or undue influence of any kind. The only objection raised is that the statutes were not strictly complied with in the execution of the Will. I am of the opinion, when a person dies leaving a written instrument which he intended to be his last Will, and it is free from fraud or undue influence and in harmony with the purpose of our law-makers for enacting statutes regulating the execution of Wills, . . . it would be a miscarriage of justice to not admit the Will to probate, and thereby allow the property to be disposed of contrary to the testator's intent.[43]

To hold otherwise would, in effect, permit a contrary disposition of testator's property against the purpose for which the statutory provisions were aimed.

HALLEY, C.J., dissenting. . . . Counsel for the proponents of the purported will have come up with the ingenious idea that this instrument which is partly

---

In Johnson v. Johnson, 424 P.2d 414 (Okla. 1967), the executor of the losing party in the original case (who had since died) petitioned to have the 1954 decision vacated in view of Justice Corn's participation in that decision. Five of the supreme court justices who were on the court in 1954 disqualified themselves, and five special justices were appointed in their stead. In a unanimous decision, the court denied the petition since there was no allegation of wrongdoing in the particular case. Among the reasons given were the practical consequences of a contrary decision:

> It is apparent that if our holding were in the affirmative every decision from 1938 to January of 1959 in which Corn cast the deciding vote would have to be set aside. There are more than one thousand such cases. Rights of every kind have been settled by the decisions in such cases. Marriages have been contracted upon the basis of divorces granted, titles have been transferred and judgments paid. To now go back and reopen every such case for a possible new decision requiring new arguments and new hearings would cast intolerable and unjust burdens upon all the parties. Titles and status long thought put at rest would be thrown open to doubt. It would indeed create a "shambles" as Respondent contends. And this would be so in every case in which Corn cast the deciding vote even though no corruption occurred in such case.
>
> To us this result seems unthinkable and contrary to the most elementary principles of justice. We think it more just that those cases in which no corruption can be found should be allowed to stand, at the same time giving full right to any person who believes that any such decision has been corruptly obtained, to petition this Court for a hearing, in which, if corruption can be shown, the decision may be set aside.

Cf. Electric Auto-Lite Co. v. P. & D. Mfg. Co., 109 F.2d 566 (2d Cir. 1940), where a rehearing was granted "because of the disqualification of one member of the original court [Judge Martin T. Manton, convicted of bribery in 1939], not known at the time." — Eds.

43. Is Justice Corn's view in concord with a substantial compliance doctrine or the dispensing power of UPC §2-503, page 226 — Eds.

in typewriting and partly in handwriting is valid and should be admitted to probate for the fantastic reason that the handwriting is a codicil to the typewriting. It is my position that the typewritten part is not a will and the handwritten part is not a codicil. The handwritten part is only a continuation of the typewritten part and, combined, they constitute a will which was not attested and therefore cannot properly be admitted to probate.

. . . [T]here was nothing in the handwriting which referred to a previous will. It spoke of "this will" and not of a previous will. There is nothing about this handwriting to indicate that the testator intended it to be a codicil. He was completing his will with the handwriting.

I think he intended the typewritten portion to be a part of his will, not the completed will. A will is to be interpreted by what is found in its "four corners" and there is nothing to indicate that the testator intended it to be anything but one instrument. Parol or extrinsic evidence should not be admitted to show the contrary when the signed will is one instrument.

Under no circumstances should this be considered a codicil and I can never subscribe to the proposition that a holographic codicil will validate as a will an instrument that is typewritten, unfinished as to content, undated, unsigned and unattested. Not a case has been cited where a holographic codicil validates an instrument as a will which was not dated, signed or attested and no reference made in the purported codicil to the preceding will. . . . Something is attempted to be made of the fact that the testator was a lawyer but that would prove nothing as many eminent lawyers have failed to properly prepare and execute their own wills. The will of Samuel J. Tilden is a notable example.

This will was one complete will unattested and therefore not admissible to probate and to give this will the construction that the majority has placed upon it is wholly unwarranted. Why make a mockery of the plain provision of our statutes? Property may only descend by will when the will is executed in conformity with the statutes.

I dissent.

PROBLEMS AND NOTE

1. The court determined that there were two wills written on the same page with the second will (a handwritten codicil) incorporating the first will (the typed will). Looking at the picture of the wills and their language, do you agree? In the purported second will, is there a reference to the first will as such to justify application of the incorporation by reference doctrine? The language "this will" refers to—well—*this* will, not a prior will on the same page. If the only reference to the typewritten portions are the words "this will," does not this undermine the court's premise that there were two wills?

2. Would the court have any problem probating Johnson's typed will if the handwritten portion had appeared on the back of the typed sheet rather than on the bottom? Could the handwritten portion incorporate the typed material on the back by reference, or are the front and back of a sheet integrated? See In re Estate of Plumel, 90 P. 192 (Cal. 1907).

3. In Estate of Nielson, 165 Cal. Rptr. 319 (App. 1980), the testator drew lines through the dispositive provisions of his typewritten will and wrote between the

lines: "Bulk of Estate—1.—Shrine Hospital for Crippled Children—Los Angeles, $10,000—2. Society for Prevention of Cruelty to Animals." Near the margin of these cancellations and interlineations were the testator's initials and date. At the top and bottom of the will were the handwritten words, "Revised by Lloyd M. Nielson November 29, 1974." The court held the handwritten words constituted a holographic codicil because they did not intend to incorporate the attested typed material. The holographic codicil republished the typewritten will, as modified.

But compare In re Estate of Sola, 275 Cal. Rptr. 98 (App. 1990), and In re Estate of Foxley, 575 N.W. 2d 150 (Neb. 1998), holding that handwritten words written across an attested will did not constitute a holographic codicil because they made no sense apart from the typewritten words. Compare also Estate of Johnson, 630 P.2d 1039 (Ariz. 1981), page 242.

4. Acts of Independent Significance

Now we turn to another doctrine permitting extrinsic evidence to identify the will beneficiaries or property passing under the will. If the beneficiary or property designations are identified by acts or events that have a lifetime motive and significance apart from their effect on the will, the gift will be upheld under the doctrine of acts of independent significance (also called the doctrine of nontestamentary acts). This is true even though the phrasing of the will leaves it in the testator's power to alter the beneficiaries or the property by a nontestamentary act.

Case 2 illustrates some common applications of the acts of independent significance doctrine.

> *Case 2. T*'s will devises "the automobile that I own at my death" to her nephew *N*, and gives $1,000 "to each person who shall be in my employ at my death." At the time the will is executed, *T* owns an old Toyota. Shortly before her death, *T* trades the Toyota in for a new Cadillac, with the result that *T* dies owning a $40,000 automobile rather than one worth $4,000. In the year before her death, *T* fires two long-time employees and hires three new ones. The gifts are valid. While *T*'s act in buying the Cadillac had the practical effect of increasing the value of her gift to *N*, it is unlikely that this is what motivated her purchase. It is more probable that she bought the car because she wanted to drive a Cadillac. Similarly, *T*'s acts in hiring and firing various employees were doubtless prompted by business needs rather than a desire to make or unmake legatees under the will. Indeed, cases involving this form of devise typically assume the validity of the gift without discussion of the acts of independent significance doctrine.

Uniform Probate Code (1990)

§2-512.   EVENTS OF INDEPENDENT SIGNIFICANCE

A will may dispose of property by reference to acts and events that have significance apart from their effect upon the dispositions made by the will, whether they occur before or after the execution of the will or before or after the testator's death. The execution or revocation of another individual's will is such an event.

PROBLEMS

1.   *T* bequeaths the contents of the right-hand drawer of her desk to *A*. In the drawer at *T*'s death are a savings bank passbook in *T*'s name, a certificate for 100 shares of General Electric common stock, and a diamond ring. Does *A* take these items?

T bequeaths the contents of her safe-deposit box in Security Bank to *B* and the contents of her safe-deposit box in First National Bank to *C*. Do *B* and *C* take the items found in the respective boxes? See Annot., 5 A.L.R.3d 466 (1966).

T's will provides: "I have put in my safe-deposit box in Continental Bank shares of stock in several envelopes. Each envelope has on it the name of the person I desire to receive the stock contained in the envelope." At *T*'s death, several envelopes are found in *T*'s safe-deposit box with the name of a person written on the envelope. Inside each is a stock certificate. For example, in one envelope is a certificate for 200 shares of Coca-Cola stock and on the envelope is written "For Ruth Moreno." Do Ruth Moreno and the other persons take the stock in the envelopes bearing their names? See Will of Le Collen, 72 N.Y.S.2d 467 (Sur. 1947); Smith v. Weitzel, 338 S.W.2d 628 (Tenn. App. 1960).

2.   In 2000 Sarah executes her will devising the residue of her estate to any charitable trust established by the last will and testament of her brother, Barney. In 2001 Barney executes his will, devising his property to the Barney Educational Trust, a charitable trust established by his will. In 2004, Barney dies. In 2005, Sarah dies. Is the Barney Educational Trust entitled to the residue of Sarah's estate? See First Natl. Bank v. Klein, 234 So. 2d 42 (Ala. 1970); In re Will of Tipler, 10 S.W.3d 244 (Tenn. App. 1998). Suppose that Barney had survived Sarah. What result? See Restatement (Third) of Property: Wills and Other Donative Transfers §3.8, statutory note (1999).

SECTION D.   CONTRACTS RELATING TO WILLS

A person may enter into a contract *to make a will* or a contract *not to revoke a will*. Contract law, not the law of wills, applies. The contract beneficiary must sue under the law of contracts and prove a valid contract. If, after a contract becomes binding, a party dies leaving a will not complying with the contract, the will is probated but the contract beneficiary is entitled to a remedy for the broken contract. Although the courts are not uniform in their description of the applicable remedies — many impress a constructive trust upon the estate or the successors of the defaulting party, some purport to award specific performance, and still others call the remedy damages — in the usual case the remedy, regardless of characterization, amounts to either (1) an award to the contract beneficiary of "the value of the property which was to come to" her under the contractual will, or (2) an order compelling the decedent's "successors to transfer the property to the [contract beneficiary] in accordance with the deceased's agreement." Thomas E. Atkinson, Handbook of the Law of Wills §48, at 218–219 (2d ed. 1953).

1. *Contracts to Make a Will*

Questions respecting contracts to make a will may arise in a variety of fact situations, such as a claimed promise to make a will in exchange for an agreement to marry, or to serve as nurse and housekeeper, or not to contest a will. To ameliorate problems of proof, many states now subject contracts to make a will to a Statute of Frauds provision, thus requiring such contracts to be in writing to be enforceable. In these states, however, if the contract beneficiary is not entitled to enforce the contract because of noncompliance with the Statute of Frauds, the beneficiary may nonetheless be entitled to restitution of the value to the decedent of services rendered (quantum meruit). Atkinson, supra, at 219. See generally E. Allan Farnsworth, Contracts §6.11, at 402 (4th ed. 2004). In the context of a promise to make a will in return for services to be rendered, the value the decedent put on the services in the oral agreement ("I promise to leave you half of my estate") is evidence of the reasonable value of those services. See Hastoupis v. Gargas, 398 N.E.2d 745 (Mass. App. 1980).

PROBLEMS

1. *T* makes a contract with *A* to leave everything to *A* at death if *A* will take care of *T* for life. *T* executes a will leaving her estate to *A*. Subsequently, *A* changes her mind and decides not to care for *T*. *T* rescinds the contract. Upon *T*'s death, is *A* entitled to take under *T*'s will? See Trotter v. Trotter, 490 So. 2d 827 (Miss. 1986).

2. *A* dies of AIDS. After *A*'s death, *A*'s roommate, *B*, claims half of *A*'s estate. *B* alleges that *A* promised to leave *B* half his estate if *B* cared for *A* for his life. *B* produces a document typed by *B* and signed by *A* and one witness devising one-half of his estate to *B*. The jurisdiction has enacted UPC §2-514, page 289, requiring that the contract be evidenced by a writing signed by the decedent. Is *B* entitled to one-half of *A*'s estate? See Estate of Fritz, 406 N.W.2d 475 (Mich. App. 1987).

3. If *W* promises *H* to take care of him for his life in consideration of *H* devising her Blackacre, and *H* dies, devising Blackacre to *A*, is the contract enforceable by *W*? Is consideration given by *W*? See Borelli v. Brusseau, 16 Cal. Rptr. 2d 16 (App. 1993) (unenforceable because no consideration; *W* had legal duty to care for *H*). Compare Byrne v. Laura, 60 Cal. Rptr. 2d 908 (App. 1997) (promise by man to his live-in lover gives rise to claim for quantum meruit), with In re Estate of Braaten, 96 P.3d 1125 (Mont. 2004) (stepson did not rebut presumption that personal services rendered to a decedent by a relative are gratuitous; quantum meruit claim denied).

*". . . and to my faithful valet, Sidney, whom I promised to remember
in my will — 'Hi there, Sidney' – –!"*

QUESTION

Does Sidney have an enforceable claim against his employer's estate?

2. Contracts Not to Revoke a Will

Questions respecting contracts not to revoke a will typically arise where a husband
and a wife have executed a joint will or mutual wills. A *joint will* is one instrument
executed by two persons as the will of both — that is, one will for two people. When
one testator dies, the instrument is probated as the testator's will; when the other
testator dies, the instrument is again probated, this time as the other testator's will.
A joint will is relatively uncommon; well-counseled testators do not use them.
Mutual wills, on the other hand, are the separate wills of two or more persons
that contain similar or reciprocal (mirror-image) provisions. Mutual or reciprocal
wills are quite common because spouses often want to favor each other, followed

by the same set of other beneficiaries. A *joint and mutual will* refers to a joint will in which the respective testators make similar or reciprocal provisions.[44] See Atkinson, supra, §49, at 222-224.

There are no legal consequences peculiar to joint or mutual wills unless they are executed pursuant to a contract between the testators not to revoke their wills. The initial problem is proof of the contract. Most courts hold that the mere execution of a joint or mutual will does not give rise to a presumption of contract; a contract not to revoke is unenforceable unless it is proved by clear and convincing evidence. The difficulty, however, is that in the case of a joint will, the use of a jointly executed instrument implies an understanding or agreement and thus invites a claim of contract, the terms of which can be inferred from the will. Similarly, some courts also find an implied contract in the existence of a common dispositive scheme in mutual (reciprocal) wills, an implication that is usually without basis. Considerable litigation results. A line of cases developed in which the courts searched the language of the joint or mutual will for language of agreement, sometimes finding that the use of plural first-person pronouns such as *we* and *our* implied a contract not to revoke. See, e.g., Glass v. Battista, 374 N.E.2d 116 (N.Y. 1978). The danger of a lawsuit can be reduced by inserting in every joint or mutual will a provision declaring that the will was or was not executed pursuant to a contract, but the lawyer who is astute enough to be aware of this problem doubtless also knows that joint wills are notorious litigation-breeders that should not be used at all.

To extricate the courts from this unhappy interpretive exercise, many states have enacted a Statute of Frauds provision applicable to all agreements concerning contracts relating to wills. See Estate of Lubins, 656 N.Y.S.2d 851 (Sur. 1997) (a lucid recounting of the prior case law and the emergence of the New York statute).

Uniform Probate Code (1990)

§2-514. CONTRACTS CONCERNING SUCCESSION

A contract to make a will or devise, or not to revoke a will or devise, or to die intestate, if executed after the effective date of this Article, may be established only by (i) provisions of a will stating material provisions of the contract, (ii) an express reference in a will to a contract and extrinsic evidence proving the terms of the contract, or (iii) a writing signed by the decedent evidencing the contract. The execution of a joint will or mutual wills does not create a presumption of a contract not to revoke the will or wills.

A contract not to revoke a will is breached if, after the contract becomes binding, a party dies leaving a will that does not comply with the contract. In the usual case, this occurs because the testator affirmatively revoked the contractual will, typically by leaving a later will with different terms. But what about the case where the

---

44. Unfortunately, the term *joint and mutual will* is also occasionally—and confusingly—used by courts to describe a joint will that devises the property in accordance with a contract. See, e.g., Kinkin v. Marchesi, 604 N.E.2d 957 (Ill. App. 1992).

testator's contractual will is revoked by operation of law arising from a change in family circumstances?

Via v. Putnam
Supreme Court of Florida, 1995
626 So. 2d 460

OVERTON, J.   We have for review Putnam v. Via, 638 So. 2d 981 (Fla. 2d DCA 1994). This case involves a dispute between a decedent's surviving spouse, who claimed a share of the decedent's estate under the pretermitted spouse statute,[45] and the children of the decedent's first marriage, who claimed that the mutual wills executed by their parents, naming them residuary beneficiaries of their parents' estates, gave rise to a creditor's contract claim that had priority against the surviving spouse's claim against the estate. The Second District Court of Appeal held that the surviving spouse's right to receive either an elective share or pretermitted spouse's share of the decedent's estate has priority over the claims of the decedent's children. The district court acknowledged conflict with Johnson v. Girtman, 542 So. 2d 1033 (Fla. 3d DCA 1989). We have jurisdiction. Art. V, §3(b)(3), Fla. Const.

For the reasons expressed in this opinion, we approve the decision of the district court and find that Florida has a strong public policy concerning the protection of the surviving spouse of the marriage in existence at the time of the decedent's death. This policy has been continuously expressed in the law of this state and is controlling. We agree with the district court's reasoning and conclude that the children, as third-party beneficiaries under the mutual wills of their parents, should not be given creditor status under section 733.707, Florida Statutes (1993), when their interests contravene the interests of the surviving spouse under the pretermitted spouse statute.

The record reveals the following facts. On November 15, 1985, Edgar and Joann Putnam executed mutual wills, each of which contained the following provision:

> I acknowledge that this is a mutual will made at the same time as my [spouse's] Will and each of us have executed this Will with the understanding and agreement that the survivor will not change the manner in which the residuary estate is to be distributed and that neither of us as survivors will do anything to defeat the distribution schedule set forth herein, such as disposing of assets prior to death by way of trust bank accounts, trust agreements, or in any other manner.

Each will devised that spouse's entire estate to the survivor and provided that the residuary estate would go to the children upon the survivor's death. Joann Putnam died without having done anything to defeat the terms of her mutual will. Edgar Putnam later remarried and failed to execute a subsequent will to provide for his second wife, Mary Rachel Putnam (Rachel Putnam).

Upon Edgar Putnam's death, his mutual will was admitted to probate. Rachel Putnam filed both a Petition to Determine Share of Pretermitted Spouse and an

---

45. §732.301, Fla. Stat. (1993).

Election to Take Elective Share. In response, the children filed claims against the estate alleging that, by marrying Rachel Putnam, Edgar had breached his contract not to defeat the distribution schedule set forth in his mutual will by subjecting his assets to the statutes governing homestead property, exempt property, pretermitted share, and family allowance. . . . The trial judge, during the course of these proceedings, made the following findings. First, he found that: (a) the mutual will provision previously quoted "constituted a binding contractual agreement," of which the children are third-party beneficiaries; (b) the children properly filed a claim against the estate based upon the decedent's breach of the mutual will; and (c) the surviving spouse, Rachel Putnam, is the pretermitted spouse of Edgar Putnam. Second, the trial judge entered a summary judgment expressly finding that "Edgar J. Putnam breached his joint and mutual will that he made with Joann Putnam when he married Rachel Putnam without taking appropriate steps to protect the interests of the third-party beneficiaries under said will" and that the claims of the children "are class 7 obligations pursuant to §733.707, Florida Probate Code." The trial judge concluded that "any pretermitted spouse share or elective share that Rachel Putnam may have is subject to the class 7 obligations of this estate."

On appeal, the district court reversed and noted that, if the children's residuary beneficiary status in the mutual wills allowed them to assert creditor status against the estate, the surviving spouse in this instance would "receive nothing except family allowance and any exempt property that may pass to her free from claims of creditors." *Putnam*, 638 So. 2d at 982. The district court's decision relied on the reasoning in Shimp v. Huff, 556 A.2d 252, 263 (Md. 1989), in which Maryland's highest court, on facts essentially identical to the facts in this case, found that the public policy surrounding the marriage relationship and the elective share statute required it to rule in favor of protecting the surviving spouse's right to receive an elective share. Likewise, the Second District Court of Appeal stated that "the statutes of Florida pertaining to a surviving spouse's elective share or pretermitted share in cases discussing those rights and their predecessor, dower, suggest a strong public policy in favor of protecting a surviving spouse's right to receive an elective share or a pretermitted share." *Putnam*, 638 So. 2d at 984. The district court recognized that its holding conflicts with the Third District Court's decision in Johnson v. Girtman, 542 So. 2d 1033 (Fla. 3d DCA 1989).

. . . [The elective share statute gives the surviving spouse the right to elect against the decedent's will and take a forced share of the decedent's net estate.] The statute reads as follows:

> The elective share shall consist of an amount equal to 30 percent of the fair market value, on the date of death, of all assets referred to in §732.206, computed after deducting from the total value of the assets:
>> (1) All valid claims against the estate paid or payable from the estate; and
>> (2) All mortgages, liens, or security interests on the assets.

§732.207, Fla. Stat. (1993).

. . . [T]he pretermitted spouse statute . . . reads as follows:

> When a person marries after making a will and the spouse survives the testator, the surviving spouse shall receive a share in the estate of the testator equal in value to that

which the surviving spouse would have received if the testator had died intestate,[46] unless:

>   (1) Provision has been made for, or waived by, the spouse by prenuptial or postnuptial agreement;
>
>   (2) The spouse is provided for in the will; or
>
>   (3) The will discloses an intention not to make provision for the spouse.

The share of the estate that is assigned to the pretermitted spouse shall be obtained in accordance with §733.805.

§732.301, Fla. Stat. (1993).

The children argue that they are third-party beneficiaries of the contract between the decedent and their mother and that they deserve creditor status under section 733.707. As creditors, they would have priority over the share of the pretermitted spouse and would receive the entire estate. Under this scheme, the second wife would receive only a family allowance, the exempt property, and a life estate in the homestead. . . . [I]t is our view that the legislature did not intend . . . to allow creditors' claims by third-party beneficiaries of previously executed mutual wills to take priority over the statutory rights of a pretermitted spouse and deny the pretermitted spouse any share in the decedent's estate.

We acknowledge that other jurisdictions and the Third District Court of Appeal in *Johnson* take the view that a surviving spouse's statutory share of an estate can be subordinated to claims of third-party beneficiaries of previously executed mutual wills. See *Johnson;* see also Gregory v. Estate of Gregory, 866 S.W.2d 379 (Ark. 1993); In re Estate of Stewart, 444 P.2d 337 (Cal. 1968); Keats v. Cates, 241 N.E.2d 645 (Ill. App. 1968); Baker v. Syfritt, 125 N.W. 998 (Iowa 1910); Lewis v. Lewis, 178 P. 421 (Kan. 1919); Rubenstein v. Mueller, 225 N.E.2d 540 (N.Y. 1967); Robison v. Graham, 799 P.2d 610 (Okla. 1990). These courts have advanced four different rationales for giving priority to the contract beneficiaries: (1) The surviving spouse's marital rights attach only to property legally and equitably owned by the deceased spouse, and the will contract entered into before the marriage deprives the deceased spouse of equitable title and places it in the contract beneficiary. *Lewis.* (2) When the surviving testator accepts benefits under the contractual will, an equitable trust is impressed upon the property in favor of the contract beneficiaries, and the testator is entitled to only a life estate in the property with the remainder going to the beneficiaries upon the testator's death. *Rubenstein; Gregory; Keats; Baker; Robison.* (3) When the surviving testator accepts benefits under the contractual will, the testator becomes estopped from making a different disposition of the property, despite any subsequent marriage. *Stewart.* (4) Finally, as expressed in *Johnson,* when the surviving testator breaches the will contract, the contract beneficiaries are entitled to judgment creditor status, thus giving them priority over the rights of the surviving spouse under the applicable state probate code. It is this last theory that the trial judge adopted in ruling for

---

46. Under Fla. Stat. §732. 101(1)(c), the intestate share of a surviving spouse is one-half when the decedent leaves lineal descendants, as in this case. Therefore, in Florida the widow can elect against her husband's will and receive 30 percent of his estate, or, if his will is executed before their marriage, she can claim half his estate under the pretermitted spouse statute.

If the husband executes a will after marriage, which leaves his wife 10 percent, 50 percent, all, or nothing of his estate, she has no claim as a pretermitted spouse. She is entitled only to a 30 percent share under the elective share statute. — Eds.

the children in the instant case. Under these four theories, it makes no difference whether the surviving spouse was married to the decedent for one year or twenty-five years; the surviving spouse would be entitled to no interest in the deceased spouse's probatable estate if the third-party beneficiaries' claim consumed the estate.

The Court of Appeals of Maryland, that state's highest court, recently made a detailed analysis of this issue in an opinion by Chief Judge Murphy. See Shimp v. Huff, 556 A.2d 252 (Md. 1989). That court, after reviewing the theories identified above, found that

> the question of priorities between a surviving spouse and beneficiaries under a contract to make a will should be resolved based upon the public policy which surrounds the marriage relationship and which underlies the elective share statute. . . .
>
> In addition to the public policy underlying these statutes, the public policy surrounding the marriage relationship also suggests that the surviving spouse's claim to an elective share should be afforded priority over the claims of beneficiaries of a contract to make a will. Like the majority of other courts, we have recognized the well settled principle that contracts which discourage or restrain the right to marry are void as against public policy.

556 A.2d at 263. Similar views have been expressed by other courts. See e.g., Patecky v. Friend, 350 P.2d 170 (Or. 1960); In re Arland's Estate, 230 P. 157 (Wash. 1924). The *Shimp* court concluded that the contract that gave rise to the claim of the third-party beneficiaries included an implied limitation. It stated: "[W]e find that the respondent's rights under the contract were limited by the possibility that the survivor might remarry and that the subsequent spouse might elect against the will." *Shimp*, 556 A.2d at 263.

The district court of appeal in the instant case found the reasoning and analysis in *Shimp* to be persuasive. We agree. . . . We emphasize that the justification for the elective share and pretermitted spouse statutes is to protect the surviving spouse of the marriage in existence at the time of death of his or her spouse. The legislature has made these shares of a deceased spouse's estate a part of the marriage contract.

Florida's pretermitted spouse statute applies only "[w]hen a person marries after making a will and the spouse survives the testator." §732.301, Fla. Stat. (1993). The statute sets forth three specific circumstances when a pretermitted spouse would not be entitled to a share of the decedent's estate: (1) when "[p]rovision has been made for, or waived by, the spouse by prenuptial or postnuptial agreement"; (2) when "[t]he spouse is provided for in the will"; or (3) when "[t]he will discloses an intention not to make provision for the spouse." Id. The trial judge found that none of these exceptions applied and that the surviving spouse in this case was a pretermitted spouse under the statute. To hold as suggested by the children would essentially amend the statutory exceptions to the pretermitted spouse statute and add a fourth exception. The legislature enacted these exceptions based on the public policy of protecting the surviving spouse of the marriage contract in existence at the time of the decedent's death. The legislature has clearly taken into account when this provision should apply and when it should not apply. We conclude that we have no authority to judicially modify the public policy protecting a surviving spouse's interest in the deceased spouse's estate by adopting this creditor-theory approach as an exception to the pretermitted spouse statute.

Accordingly, we approve the decision of the district court of appeal in this case and disapprove the decision of the Third District Court of Appeal in *Johnson* to the extent that it conflicts with this opinion. It is so ordered.

NOTES AND PROBLEMS

1. On will contracts and their intersection with spousal rights to inheritance, see Carolyn L. Dessin, The Troubled Relationship of Will Contracts and Spousal Protection: Time for an Amicable Separation, 45 Cath. U.L. Rev. 435 (1996). See also Adam J. Hirsch, Cognitive Jurisprudence, 76 S. Cal. L. Rev. 1331, 1352-1358 (2003) (criticizing Via v. Putnam).

2. Tricky questions of interpretation arise under contracts between spouses not to revoke their wills. For example, suppose that the majority rule (the third party beneficiaries prevail over the second wife) is followed in this state. After Joann Putnam's death, what are Edgar's rights in the property during his lifetime? How is he restricted in what he can do with his own property and the property received from Joann? See Flohr v. Walker, 520 P.2d 833 (Wyo. 1974) (survivor entitled to "income and reasonable portions of principal for his support and ordinary expenditures, . . . but cannot dissipate the estate or alienate by inter vivos transfers . . . to defeat the contract"); Schwartz v. Horn, 290 N.E.2d 816 (N.Y. 1972) (inter vivos gifts permitted provided that they are not inconsistent with, or defeat the purpose of, the contract); Estate of Chayka, 176 N.W.2d 561 (Wis. 1970) (inter vivos gifts by survivor can be set aside if not made in good faith). Suppose that Edgar thinks that a round-the-world cruise will be the perfect wedding present for his new bride. Is that permitted? Suppose he wants to buy Rachel an emerald bracelet from Tiffany's. Is that okay?

In a similar vein, does the contract in *Putnam* apply only to Edgar's property owned at Joann's death and to property inherited from her, or does it also cover property acquired by Edgar thereafter? Suppose that Edgar inherits property from his brother after Joann died or he wins the lottery a year after Joann died. Does the contract apply to this property? See Estate of Maloney v. Carsten, 381 N.E.2d 1263 (Ind. App. 1978). Does the contract apply to nonprobate property, such as life insurance? See Bergheger v. Boyle, 629 N.E.2d 1168 (Ill. App. 1994).

3. *H* and *W* have children by prior marriages. They want the survivor to have "everything" and "be comfortable," and they want all their property divided equally among their children upon the death of the survivor. But, knowing that the survivor will have closer ties to his or her own children, they feel uncomfortable leaving the disposition entirely in the survivor's hands. This is the basic dilemma suggested by many contractual wills. When you study trusts later in this course, you will find that *H* and *W*'s desires can be better realized, with fewer problems, by creating a trust rather than by using contractual wills.

Suppose *H* and *W* do enter into a contract not to revoke their respective wills, and then *H* dies, having performed on the contract by not changing his will. If *W* executes a new will that excludes *H*'s children, and then *W* dies, *H*'s children can enforce the contract against *W*'s estate or successors as *third party beneficiaries* of the contract between *H* and *W*. This is a standard application of third party beneficiary standing in contract law. See Seaver v. Ransom, 120 N.E. 639 (N.Y. 1918); E. Allan Farnsworth, Contracts §§10.2-10.3 (4th ed. 2004).

5

NONPROBATE TRANSFERS AND PLANNING FOR INCAPACITY

In this chapter we treat revocable inter vivos trusts, life insurance, pension accounts, and other modes of transfer that have the effect of passing property at death but avoid probate. We also examine the problem of planning for incapacity, including the use of powers of attorney and health care directives. It is convenient to locate the two in a single chapter because there is overlap between them, particularly in the use of revocable inter vivos trusts.

SECTION A.   AN INTRODUCTION TO WILL SUBSTITUTES

The point of departure in assaying nonprobate transfers and the rise of the will substitute is to ask: What is a will substitute, and why do people find nonprobate transfer advantageous?

John H. Langbein, The Nonprobate Revolution and the
Future of the Law of Succession
97 Harv. L. Rev. 1108, 1108-1116 (1984)

Over the course of the twentieth century, persistent tides of change have been lapping at the once-quiet shores of the law of succession. Probate, our court-operated system for transferring wealth at death, is declining in importance. Institutions that administer noncourt modes of transfer are displacing the probate system. Life insurance companies, pension plan operators, commercial banks, savings banks, investment companies, brokerage houses, stock transfer agents, and a variety of other financial intermediaries are functioning as free-market competitors of the probate system and enabling property to pass on death without probate and without will. The law of wills and the rules of descent no longer govern succession to most of the property of most decedents. . . .

In order to validate will-like modes of transfer that lack Wills Act formality and that operate without the mechanisms and protections of probate, we have been pretending that the will substitutes are lifetime transfers. In truth, will substitutes are simply "nonprobate wills" — "wills" that need not comply with the Wills Act. . . .

I. THE WILL SUBSTITUTES

Four main will substitutes constitute the core of the nonprobate system: life insurance, pension accounts, joint accounts, and revocable trusts. When properly created, each is functionally indistinguishable from a will — each reserves to the owner complete lifetime dominion, including the power to name and to change beneficiaries until death. These devices I shall call "pure" will substitutes, in contradistinction to "imperfect" will substitutes (primarily joint tenancies), which more closely resemble completed lifetime transfers. The four pure will substitutes may also be described as mass will substitutes: they are marketed by financial intermediaries using standard form instruments with fill-in-the-blank beneficiary designations.

The typical American of middle- or upper-middle-class means employs many will substitutes. The precise mix of will and will substitutes varies with individual circumstances — age, family, employment, wealth, and legal sophistication. It would not be unusual for someone in mid-life to have a dozen or more will substitutes in force, whether or not he had a will.

A. LIFE INSURANCE

A propertied person of middle years commonly has several life insurance policies that he has acquired at different times — one or two purchased individually, others obtained as group policies that typically arise out of employment. The beneficiary designation in a life insurance policy serves precisely the function of the designation of a devisee in a will. The label aside, life insurance is functionally indistinguishable from a will, for it satisfies the twin elements of the definition of a will. We say that a will is revocable until the death of the testator and that the interests of the devisees are ambulatory — that is, nonexistent until the testator's death. Unless specially restricted by contract, the life insurance beneficiary designation operates identically.

In the 1960's, Spencer Kimball wrote about "the close similarity" of the execution of a life insurance beneficiary designation "to the making of a will. . . . Just as the will is 'ambulatory,' taking effect only on death, so the beneficiary designation can be changed until death."

B. PENSION ACCOUNTS

Any American who has spent much time in the work force since World War II is likely to have acquired rights in one or more pension accounts, depending upon his employment history and the features of the plans in force where he has worked. The tax laws have also been encouraging him to create supplementary retirement accounts, sometimes arranged through his employer, otherwise in the form of IRA accounts or Keogh plans with any of the many financial intermediaries that offer them. All these pension accounts contain will substitutes — beneficiary designations that pass the owner's interest to the persons of his choice in the event that he dies before exhausting the account in its retirement payout phase.

C. BANK, BROKERAGE, AND MUTUAL FUND ACCOUNTS

In arranging their personal banking, Americans meet another raft of invitations to execute will substitutes. Married persons in particular elect these options widely. The purest of the bank-operated will substitutes are accounts over which the depositor retains explicit lifetime dominion while designating beneficiaries to take on his death. Where local law permits, such arrangements may assume the blatant form of the P.O.D. ("pay on death") account, which was pioneered by the United States Treasury for selling government bonds. . . .

More commonly, the joint bank account — whether savings or checking — is manipulated to do the work of a will. In theory, joint accounts differ from other pure will substitutes: they look more like gifts than like wills. When the owner of property arranges to take title jointly, he supposedly creates a present interest in his donee-cotenant. In the prototypical joint tenancy of realty, the donee receives an interest equal to the donor's, and the donor loses the power to revoke the transfer. Moreover, the commonality-of-use rule requires that the cotenants act together in order to transfer the realty. Joint accounts of personalty, however, "differ from the true joint tenancies as defined in [real] property law, for by the privilege of withdrawal either [cotenant] may consume the account." Accordingly, a depositor may name a cotenant on a bank account but deal with the account as though it were his own. The cotenant may not even know that he has been designated. Depending on his contract with the bank, the depositor may revoke and alter cotenancy designations as freely as he would beneficiary designations under any of the other will substitutes. He may also achieve the same result by closing the account, as he pleases. In this way, joint accounts may be used to approximate the incidents of a will; the cotenancy designation is effectively revocable and ambulatory.

Brokerage houses apply the same mechanism to so-called street accounts. In an account that is nominally joint, the beneficial owner of the securities may deal with them as though he has not made the cotenancy designation, but on the owner's death the cotenant succeeds to the securities or other account proceeds. Investment companies have extended the practice to mutual fund accounts. . . .

D. THE REVOCABLE INTER VIVOS TRUST

Although the revocable trust is the fundamental device that the estate-planning bar employs to fit the carriage trade with highly individuated instruments, the revocable trust also keeps company with the mass will substitutes. Standard-form revocable trusts with fill-in-the-blank beneficiary designations are widely offered in the banking industry and were at one time aggressively promoted in the mutual fund industry. . . .

Either by declaration of trust or by transfer to a third-party trustee, the appropriate trust terms can replicate the incidents of a will. The owner who retains both the equitable life interest and the power to alter and revoke the beneficiary designation has used the trust form to achieve the effect of testation. Only nomenclature distinguishes the remainder interest created by such a trust from the mere expectancy arising under a will. Under either the trust or the will, the interest of the beneficiaries is both revocable and ambulatory.

E. IMPERFECT WILL SUBSTITUTES

The "pure" will substitutes are not the only instruments of the nonprobate revolution; "imperfect" will substitutes — most prominent among them the common-law joint tenancy — also serve to transfer property at death without probate. Joint tenancies in real estate and in securities are quite common; joint tenancies in automobiles and other vehicles are also fairly widespread. Because they ordinarily effect lifetime transfers, joint tenancies are "imperfect" rather than "pure" will substitutes. When the owner of a house, a car, a boat, or a block of IBM common stock arranges to take title jointly, his cotenant acquires an interest that is no longer revocable and ambulatory. Under the governing recording act or stock transfer act, both cotenants must ordinarily join in any subsequent transfer. Yet like the pure will substitutes, joint tenancy arrangements allow the survivor to obtain marketable title without probate: under joint tenancy, a death certificate rather than a probate decree suffices to transfer title.

. . . By providing a nonprobate mode of transfer for realty and securities, the joint tenancy operates in conjunction with the pure will substitutes to make total avoidance of probate feasible for persons of ordinary or even substantial means. . . .

II. THE HIDDEN CAUSES OF THE NONPROBATE REVOLUTION

The typical propertied decedent in modern America leaves a will and many will substitutes. The will substitutes differ from the ordinary "last will and testament" in three main ways. First, most will substitutes — but not all — are asset-specific: each deals with a single type of property, be it life insurance proceeds, a bank balance, mutual fund shares, or whatever. Second, property that passes through a will substitute avoids probate. A financial intermediary ordinarily takes the place of the probate court in effecting the transfer. Third, the formal requirements of the Wills Act — attestation and so forth — do not govern will substitutes and are not complied with. Of these differences, only probate avoidance is a significant advantage that transferors might consciously seek.

The principal legal questions raised by the increasing use of will substitutes are two. First, inasmuch as they effect a testamentary disposition, are will substitutes valid in spite of their lack of Wills Act formalities? Second, should the subsidiary law of wills be applied to will substitutes? The subsidiary law of wills, including creditor's rights, antilapse, simultaneous death, slayer, and revocation rules, reflects long experience with the problems that arise in administering testamentary dispositions. On the other hand, will substitutes are already governed by their own separate bodies of law (such as contract or trust law). Both of these issues will recur throughout the material that follows. See also Restatement (Third) of Property: Wills and Other Donative Transfers §§7.1-7.2 (2003).

SECTION B.   REVOCABLE TRUSTS

1. Introduction

Revocable inter vivos trusts have come into widespread use, particularly among the moderately and very wealthy. A revocable inter vivos trust is the most flexible of all will substitutes because the donor can draft both the dispositive and the administrative provisions precisely to the donor's liking. Thus, although trusts in general receive extended treatment in Chapters 8 through 13, we examine here the use of revocable inter vivos trusts as will substitutes.

Under the typical revocable inter vivos trust involving a *deed of trust*, the creator of the trust, known as the *settlor*, transfers legal title to property to another person as *trustee* pursuant to a writing in which the settlor retains the power to revoke, alter, or amend the trust and the right to trust income during lifetime.[1] On the settlor's death, the trust assets are to be distributed to or held in further trust for other beneficiaries. While several early cases held these revocable trusts invalid unless executed with Wills Act formalities, by statute or judicial decision all jurisdictions (with one possible exception[2]) now recognize the validity of a trust where property is transferred to another person as trustee and the settlor reserves the power to revoke the trust during life. The settlor may also reserve an income interest and a testamentary power of appointment.

The second context in which the question of validity arises is where there is a *revocable declaration of trust*, under which the settlor declares himself trustee for the benefit of himself during lifetime, with the remainder to pass to others at his death. Since there is little discernible change in the settlor's relation to the property during lifetime, should the courts give effect to this arrangement to the extent that it causes assets to pass to others at the settlor's death without complying with Wills Act formalities?

Farkas v. Williams
Supreme Court of Illinois, 1955
5 Ill. 2d 417, 125 N.E.2d 600

HERSHEY, J.   ... The plaintiffs asked the court to declare their legal rights, as co-administrators, in four stock certificates issued by Investors Mutual Inc. in the

---

1. Revocable deeds of land not in trust are dangerous will substitutes that should never be used. The cases are split as to whether revocable deeds of land are testamentary and therefore void for failure to comply with the Wills Act. Since land can be put in a revocable trust, no knowledgeable lawyer ever uses a revocable deed delivered to the grantee.

2. In Arnold v. Davis, 2004 Tenn. App. LEXIS 389, an oddball decision designated by the court as "not for citation" and for which permission to appeal to the Tennessee Supreme Court was denied, the court held that an irrevocable inter vivos trust that provided for dispositions at the death of the settlor was testamentary and thus void for want of compliance with Wills Act formalities. However, because Tennessee's adoption of the Uniform Trust Code took effect two weeks after this decision was rendered, see Tenn. Code Ann. §35-15-401 (2004), the *Arnold* decision is likely to amount to nothing more than "an isolated deviation from the strong current of precedents — a derelict on the waters of the law." Lambert v. California, 355 U.S. 225, 232 (1957) (Frankfurter, J., dissenting). We understand from Professor Jeffrey Schoenblum of Vanderbilt that legislation confirming that *Arnold* is not good law is slated for introduction in the legislature in 2005.

name of "Albert B. Farkas, as trustee for Richard J. Williams" and which were issued pursuant to written declarations of trust. The decree of the circuit court found that said declarations were testamentary in character, and not having been executed with the formalities of a will, were invalid, and directed that the stock be awarded to the plaintiffs as an asset of the estate of said Albert B. Farkas. Upon appeal to the Appellate Court, the decree was affirmed. See 121 N.E.2d 344 (Ill. App. 1954). We allowed defendants' petition for leave to appeal.

Albert B. Farkas died intestate at the age of sixty-seven years, a resident of Chicago, leaving as his only heirs-at-law brothers, sisters, a nephew and a niece. Although retired at the time of his death, he had for many years practiced veterinary medicine and operated a veterinarian establishment in Chicago. During a considerable portion of that time, he employed the defendant Williams, who was not related to him.

On four occasions (December 8, 1948; February 7, 1949; February 14, 1950; and March 1, 1950) Farkas purchased stock of Investors Mutual, Inc. At the time of each purchase he executed a written application to Investors Mutual, Inc., instructing them to issue the stock in his name "as trustee for Richard J. Williams." Investors Mutual, Inc., by its agent, accepted each of these applications in writing by signature on the face of the application. Coincident with the execution of these applications, Farkas signed separate declarations of trust, all of which were identical except as to dates. The terms of said trust instruments are as follows:

> Declaration of Trust — Revocable. I, the undersigned, having purchased or declared my intention to purchase certain shares of capital stock of Investors Mutual, Inc. (the Company), and having directed that the certificate for said stock be issued in my name as trustee for Richard J. Williams as beneficiary, whose address is 1704 W. North Ave. Chicago, Ill., under this Declaration of Trust Do Hereby Declare that the terms and conditions upon which I shall hold said stock in trust and any additional stock resulting from reinvestments of cash dividends upon such original or additional shares are as follows:
>
> (1) During my lifetime all cash dividends are to be paid to me individually for my own personal account and use; provided, however, that any such additional stock purchased under an authorized reinvestment of cash dividends shall become a part of and subject to this trust.
>
> (2) Upon my death the title to any stock subject hereto and the right to any subsequent payments or distributions shall be vested absolutely in the beneficiary.
>
> (3) During my lifetime I reserve the right, as trustee, to vote, sell, redeem, exchange or otherwise deal in or with the stock subject hereto, but upon any sale or redemption of said stock or any part thereof, the trust hereby declared shall terminate as to the stock sold or redeemed, and I shall be entitled to retain the proceeds of sale or redemption for my own personal account and use.
>
> (4) I reserve the right at any time to change the beneficiary or revoke this trust, but it is understood that no change of beneficiary and no revocation of this trust except by death of the beneficiary, shall be effective as to the Company, for any purpose unless and until written notice thereof in such form as the Company shall prescribe is delivered to the Company at Minneapolis, Minnesota. The decease of the beneficiary before my death shall operate as a revocation of this trust.
>
> (5) In the event this trust shall be revoked or otherwise terminated, said stock and all rights and privileges thereunder shall belong to and be exercised by me in my individual capacity.

. . . The applications and declarations of trust were delivered to Investors Mutual, Inc., and held by the company until Farkas' death. The stock certificates were issued in the name of Farkas as "trustee for Richard J. Williams" and were discovered in a safety-deposit box of Farkas after his death, along with other securities, some of which were in the name of Williams alone. . . .

It is conceded that the instruments were not executed in such a way as to satisfy the requirements of the statute on wills; hence, our inquiry is limited to whether said trust instruments created valid inter vivos trusts effective to give the purported beneficiary, Williams, title to the stock in question after the death of the settlor-trustee, Farkas. To make this determination we must consider: (1) whether upon execution of the so-called trust instruments defendant Williams acquired an interest in the subject matter of the trusts, the stock of defendant Investors Mutual, Inc., (2) whether Farkas, as settlor-trustee, retained such control over the subject matter of the trusts as to render said trust instruments attempted testamentary dispositions.

First, upon execution of these trust instruments did defendant Williams presently acquire an interest in the subject matter of the intended trusts?

If no interest passed to Williams before the death of Farkas, the intended trusts are testamentary and hence invalid for failure to comply with the statute on wills. Oswald v. Caldwell, 80 N.E. 131 (Ill. 1906); Troup v. Hunter, 133 N.E. 56 (Ill. 1921); Restatement of the Law of Trusts, §56. But considering the terms of these instruments we believe Farkas did intend to presently give Williams an interest in the property referred to. For it may be said, at the very least, that upon his executing one of these instruments, he showed an intention to presently part with some of the incidents of ownership in the stock. Immediately after the execution of each of these instruments, he could not deal with the stock therein referred to the same as if he owned the property absolutely, but only in accordance with the terms of the instrument. He purported to set himself up as trustee of the stock for the benefit of Williams, and the stock was registered in his name as trustee for Williams. Thus assuming to act as trustee, he is held to have intended to take on those obligations which are expressly set out in the instrument, as well as those fiduciary obligations implied by law. In addition, he manifested an intention to bind himself to having this property pass upon his death to Williams, unless he changed the beneficiary or revoked the trust, and then such change of beneficiary or revocation was not to be effective as to Investors Mutual, Inc., unless and until written notice thereof in such form as the company prescribed was delivered to them at Minneapolis, Minnesota. An absolute owner can dispose of his property, either in his lifetime or by will, in any way he sees fit without notifying or securing approval from anyone and without being held to the duties of a fiduciary in so doing.

It seems to follow that what incidents of ownership Farkas intended to relinquish, in a sense he intended Williams to acquire. . . . It is difficult to name this interest of Williams, nor is there any reason for so doing so long as it passed to him immediately upon the creation of the trust.[3] As stated in 4 Powell, The Law of Real Property, at page 87: "Interests of beneficiaries of private express trusts run the

---

3. The idea of an interest smaller than any interest you can name, but nonetheless an interest, brings to mind the mathematical concept of the infinitesimal, developed by Isaac Newton and Gottfried Wilhelm von Leibniz. Although scorned by Bishop Berkeley as "ghosts of departed quantities," infinitesimals proved very useful in differential calculus.

gamut from valuable substantialities to evanescent hopes. Such a beneficiary may have any one of an almost infinite variety of the possible aggregates of rights, privileges, powers and immunities."

An additional problem is presented here, however, for it is to be noted that the trust instruments provide: "The decease of the beneficiary before my death shall operate as a revocation of this trust." The plaintiffs argue that the presence of this provision removes the only possible distinction which might have been drawn between these instruments and a will. Being thus conditioned on his surviving, it is argued that the "interest" of Williams until the death of Farkas was a mere expectancy. Conversely, they assert, the interest of Farkas in the securities until his death was precisely the same as that of a testator who bequeaths securities by his will, since he had all the rights accruing to an absolute owner.

Admittedly, had this provision been absent the interest of Williams would have been greater, since he would then have had an inheritable interest in the lifetime of Farkas. But to say his interest would have been greater is not to say that he here did not have a beneficial interest, properly so-called, during the lifetime of Farkas. The provision purports to set up but another "contingency" which would serve to terminate the trust. The disposition is not testamentary and the intended trust is valid, even though the interest of the beneficiary is contingent upon the existence of a certain state of facts at the time of the settlor's death. (Restatement of the Law of Trusts, section 56, Comment f.) In an example contained in the previous reference, the authors of the Restatement have referred to the interest of a beneficiary under a trust who must survive the settlor (and where the settlor receives the income for life) as a contingent equitable interest in remainder. . . .

Second, did Farkas retain such control over the subject matter of the trust as to render said trust instruments attempted testamentary dispositions?

In each of these trust instruments, Farkas reserved to himself as settlor the following powers: (1) the right to receive during his lifetime all cash dividends; (2) the right at any time to change the beneficiary or revoke the trust; and (3) upon sale or redemption of any portion of the trust property, the right to retain the proceeds therefrom for his own use.

Additionally, Farkas reserved the right to act as sole trustee, and in such capacity, he was accorded the right to vote, sell, redeem, exchange or otherwise deal in the stock which formed the subject matter of the trust.

We shall consider first those enumerated powers which Farkas reserved to himself as settlor.

It is well established that the retention by the settlor of the power to revoke, even when coupled with the reservation of a life interest in the trust property, does not render the trust inoperative for want of execution as a will. . . .

A more difficult problem is posed, however, by the fact that Farkas is also trustee, and as such, is empowered to vote, sell, redeem, exchange and otherwise deal in and with the subject matter of the trusts. . . .

In the instant case the plaintiffs contend that Farkas, as settlor-trustee, retained complete control and dominion over the securities for his own benefit during his

---

Would it be a good idea for the Illinois legislature to settle the matter by passing a statute providing that, if a settlor retained the powers Farkas retained, the beneficiary would be deemed to receive an infinitesimal interest? Should the legislature give the interest a name, such as a *farkas*, since the court finds naming so difficult? — Eds.

lifetime. It is argued that he had the power to deal with the property as he liked so long as he lived and owed no enforceable duties of any kind to Williams as beneficiary. . . .

That the retention of the power by Farkas as trustee to sell or redeem the stock and keep the proceeds for his own use should not render these trust instruments testamentary in character becomes more evident upon analyzing the real import and significance of the powers to revoke and to amend the trust, the reservation of which the courts uniformly hold does not invalidate an inter vivos trust.

It is obvious that a settlor with the power to revoke and to amend the trust at any time is, for all practical purpose, in a position to exert considerable control over the trustee regarding the administration of the trust. For anything believed to be inimicable to his best interest can be thwarted or prevented by simply revoking the trust or amending it in such a way as to conform to his wishes. Indeed, it seems that many of those powers which from time to time have been viewed as "additional powers" are already, in a sense, virtually contained within the overriding power of revocation or the power to amend the trust. Consider, for example, the following: (1) the power to consume the principal; (2) the power to sell or mortgage the trust property and appropriate the proceeds; (3) the power to appoint or remove trustees; (4) the power to supervise and direct investments; and (5) the power to otherwise direct and supervise the trustee in the administration of the trust. Actually, any of the above powers could readily be assumed by a settlor with the reserved power of revocation through the simple expedient of revoking the trust, and then, as absolute owner of the subject matter, doing with the property as he chooses. Even though no actual termination of the trust is effectuated, however, it could hardly be questioned but that the mere existence of this power in the settlor is sufficient to enable his influence to be felt in a practical way in the administration of the trust. . . .

In the case at bar, the power in Farkas to vote, sell, redeem, exchange or otherwise deal in the stock was reserved to him as trustee, and it was only upon sale or redemption that he was entitled to keep the proceeds for his own use. Thus, the control reserved is not as great as in those cases where said power is reserved to the owner as settlor. For as trustee he must so conduct himself in accordance with standards applicable to trustees generally. It is not a valid objection to this to say that Williams would never question Farkas' conduct, inasmuch as Farkas could then revoke the trust and destroy what interest Williams has. Such a possibility exists in any case where the settlor has the power of revocation. Still, Williams has rights the same as any beneficiary, although it may not be feasible for him to exercise them. Moreover, it is entirely possible that he might in certain situations have a right to hold Farkas' estate liable for breaches of trust committed by Farkas during his lifetime. In this regard, consider what would happen if, without having revoked the trust, Farkas as trustee had given the stock away without receiving any consideration therefor, had pledged the stock improperly for his own personal debt and allowed it to be lost by foreclosure or had exchanged the stock for another security or other worthless property in such manner as to constitute gross impropriety and gross negligence. In such instances, it would seem in accordance with the terms of these instruments that Williams would have had an enforceable claim against Farkas' estate for whatever damage had been suffered. Contrast this with the rights of a legatee or devisee under a will. The testator could waste the property or do anything with it he wished during his lifetime without incurring any liability to those designated by the will to inherit the property. . . .

Another factor often considered in determining whether an inter vivos trust is an attempted testamentary disposition is the formality of the transaction. Restatement of the Law of Trusts, §57, Comment g; Stouse v. First National Bank, 245 S.W.2d 914 (Ky. App. 1951); In re Sheasley's Trust, 77 A.2d 448 (Pa. 1951). Historically, the purpose behind the enactment of the statute on wills was the prevention of fraud. The requirement as to witnesses was deemed necessary because a will is ordinarily an expression of the secret wish of the testator, signed out of the presence of all concerned. The possibility of forgery and fraud are ever present in such situations. Here, Farkas executed four separate applications for stock of Investors Mutual, Inc., in which he directed that the stock be issued in his name as trustee for Williams, and he executed four separate declarations of trust in which he declared he was holding said stock in trust for Williams. The stock certificates in question were issued in his name as trustee for Williams. He thus manifested his intention in a solemn and formal manner.

For the reasons stated, we conclude that these trust declarations executed by Farkas constituted valid inter vivos trusts and were not attempted testamentary dispositions. It must be conceded that they have, in the words of Mr. Justice Holmes in Bromley v. Mitchell, 30 N.E. 83 (Mass. 1892), a "testamentary look." Moreover, it must be admitted that the line should be drawn somewhere, but after a study of this case we do not believe that point has been reached. . . .

Reversed and remanded, with directions.

NOTES AND PROBLEM

1. A *trust* is a management relation whereby the *trustee* manages property for the benefit of one or more *beneficiaries*. The trustee holds legal title to the property and, in the usual trust, can sell the trust property and replace it with property thought more desirable. The beneficiaries hold equitable title. We call the beneficiaries' interest in a trust "equitable title" because an equity court enforces their rights against the trustee (and third parties). To safeguard the beneficiaries against mismanagement or misappropriation by the trustee, the trustee is held to a *fiduciary* standard of conduct. The fiduciary obligation in trust law comprises duties of *loyalty, prudence*, and a host of *subsidiary rules* that reinforce the duties of loyalty and prudence (see Chapter 13). If the trustee breaches one of these duties, the trustee may be held personally liable to the beneficiaries.

The trustee can be one of the beneficiaries of the trust. If, however, the trustee is the *sole* beneficiary, there is no trust, because the trustee owes no duties to anyone except himself. It would be silly for a court to entertain a lawsuit by A, the sole beneficiary, charging A, the trustee, with malfeasance in office, and asking for damages. The law rejects this idea by saying that, where one person is the sole beneficiary and the trustee, the equitable and legal titles *merge*, leaving that one person with absolute legal title. This rarely happens, however, because most trusts have different beneficiaries at some point in the life of the trust.

2. In *Farkas*, what duties did Farkas as trustee owe Williams as beneficiary? What equitable interest was created in Williams? The court applied two tests: (1) whether Williams acquired a present interest when the trust was created,

and (2) whether Farkas retained too much control over the trust assets. What is the difference?

Uniform Trust Code §603(a) (2000, rev. 2004) provides (brackets in original): "While a trust is revocable [and the settlor has capacity to revoke the trust], rights of the beneficiaries are subject to the control of, and the duties of the trustee are owed exclusively to, the settlor." Under this provision, would Farkas as trustee owe any duties to Williams as beneficiary? Suppose Farkas named a third party trustee who looted the trust without Farkas's knowledge but while Farkas was alive and competent. If Farkas dies without having discovered the looting, would Williams have no recourse against the trustee?

3.   In *Estate of Brenner*, 547 P.2d 938 (Colo. App. 1976), R. Forrest Brenner executed a revocable declaration of trust (captioned "The R. Forrest Brenner Trust") of certain real property for the benefit of himself for life, remainder to his children by a prior marriage and a niece. On the date the trust instrument was executed, Brenner did not own the real property in question, but five days later this property was conveyed to "R. Forrest Brenner, Trustee for R. Forrest Brenner." On Brenner's death, the validity of the trust was challenged. The court held the trust valid, stating:

> [W]e hold that the conveyance of the real property to Brenner as trustee five days after he executed the trust instrument effectively validated the trust. Where, as here, an individual manifests an intention to create a trust in property to be acquired in the future, and thereafter confirms this intent by taking the steps necessary to transfer the property to the trust, the property so transferred becomes subject to the terms of the trust. For reasons stated hereafter, we do not believe that the foregoing rule is inapplicable merely because Brenner was settlor, trustee, and lifetime beneficiary of the trust. Appellant contends, in effect, that the evidence failed to establish Brenner's intent to establish a trust. In support of this contention, appellant relies upon evidence, inter alia, that Brenner failed to prepare and file the requisite Colorado and federal tax forms relative to a trust, that he failed to keep separate books, records, and bank accounts relative to the trust property, that he reported income and expenses from trust property on an individual income tax form, and that he did not advise either [his wife] Evelyn or his accountant of the existence of the trust. However, other evidence established that Brenner took title to the property described in the "exhibit" as trustee, that he acquired additional real estate as trustee, and that he executed a contract as trustee relating to both properties. The evidence and inferences therefrom being in conflict, the trial court's determination that Brenner intended to create a trust and thereby provide for his children and niece, as natural objects of his bounty, may not be disturbed on review.
>
> Appellant next contends that the declaration of trust was invalid by reason of the extensive control retained over the trust property by Brenner through his appointment as trustee, his reservation of all income during his lifetime, the right to revoke, alter, or amend the trust, and the sole power to invest, reinvest, manage, and control the trust property. We disagree. See *Farkas v. Williams*, supra. [547 P.2d at 941.]

4.   The revocable declaration of trust—sometimes called a *living trust*—is the key feature of Norman F. Dacey's book, How to Avoid Probate!, which finally went out of print after the fifth edition (1993). Upon its publication in 1965, the book became a runaway best-seller. In the first edition, Dacey opens

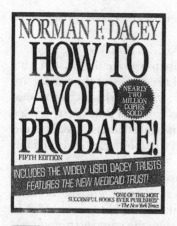

his book with a slashing attack on lawyers who profit from the probate system. He charges:

> The probate system, conceived generations ago as a device for protecting heirs, has now become their greatest enemy. Almost universally corrupt, it is essentially a form of private taxation levied by the legal profession upon the rest of the population. All across the land, both large and small estates are being plundered by lawyers specializing in "probate practice." [1st ed. at 15.]

After denouncing the "extortionate legal fees" and delays of probate, Dacey offers a way to avoid probate: Declare yourself trustee of your property by using a revocable declaration of trust, with the trust property to pass to named beneficiaries upon your death. In other words, do what Albert Farkas did in Farkas v. Williams. Dacey's book contains all kinds of do-it-yourself trust and will forms designed for various kinds of assets and different family situations.

The legal profession was not amused by Dacey's book. After publication of the first edition, the New York County Lawyers' Association sought an injunction to ban sale of the book on the ground that Dacey (a nonlawyer) was giving legal advice. The New York Court of Appeals held that Dacey's readers were not his clients because the book was sold to the public at large and no relationship of personal trust and confidence arose. New York County Lawyers' Assn. v. Dacey, 234 N.E.2d 459 (N.Y. 1967). After this victory, Dacey retaliated by suing the New York County Lawyers' Association for $5 million in damages for interfering with his right to free speech. He lost. Dacey v. New York County Lawyers' Assn., 423 F.2d 188 (2d Cir. 1969). Dacey also unsuccessfully sued the Florida Bar Association for publishing a book review that Dacey thought was libelous. Dacey v. Florida Bar, Inc., 427 F.2d 1292 (5th Cir. 1970). Subsequently, to avoid income tax on royalties on 2.5 million copies sold, Dacey moved to Ireland, but lawyers had their revenge when the Commissioner of Internal Revenue (a lawyer!) pursued Dacey and forced him to cough up hundreds of thousands of dollars in taxes and penalties because he remained a U.S. citizen. Dacey v. Commissioner, T.C. Memo 1992-187. In 1988, Dacey renounced his U.S. citizenship and became a citizen of Ireland. Norman Dacey died in London in 1994.

Since Dacey first published his book, there has been a groundswell of public demand for a simpler and less costly probate system. Reform has occurred in many states, often in the form of adoption of the Uniform Probate Code (UPC). It is fair to suggest that How to Avoid Probate!, and its astonishing reception by the public, served as a catalyst for probate reform. The reforms to date, however, have not deprived the revocable trust of its advantage in bypassing probate. Probate remains costly, time-consuming, and public. See Paula A. Monopoli, American Probate: Protecting the Public, Improving the Process (2003).

5.   For further discussion of the revocable trust, particularly of its function as a will substitute, see Restatement (Third) of Trusts §25 (2003).

In Farkas v. Williams, the court grappled with the question whether a revocable inter vivos trust should be allowed to have a testamentary effect despite its noncompliance with Wills Act formalities. Because it found the trust valid under the law of trusts, the court answered Yes. The next question is whether the subsidiary law of wills should be applied to revocable inter vivos trusts.

IN RE ESTATE AND TRUST OF PILAFAS, 836 P.2d 420 (Ariz. App. 1992): In 1982 Steve J. Pilafas executed a will and revocable inter vivos trust. Twice he updated both, the last revisions coming about a month before his death. Pilafas named himself as trustee, and he funded the trusts with substantial assets, including "a Phoenix residence and his interest in a note and deed of trust on a mobile home park to himself as trustee under the trust agreement. The trust corpus also included other real property, an agreement of sale, and, eventually, a promissory note payable to the trustee and secured by a deed of trust on real property that decedent acquired on June 2, 1988."

The lawyer who drafted the final will and revised trust documents gave both to Pilafas after their execution. Pilafas died in 1988. "Subsequently, the decedent's son, appellee James S. Pilafas, unsuccessfully searched decedent's house and belongings for the original will and trust documents. No information of record indicates their possible whereabouts." Because the will and trust documents were last known to be in possession of the decedent, the question thus arose, would a presumption of revocation apply to one or both instruments?

> Appellees claim that decedent revoked his will because that document could not be found in a diligent search of his personal effects and papers after his death. This argument relies on the common law presumption that a testator destroyed his will with the intention of revoking it if the will is last seen in the testator's possession and cannot be found after his death.[4]
>
> In response, appellants contend that the common law presumption never arose in this case because appellees proffered insufficient evidence that the will was last seen in decedent's possession or that it could not be found after decedent's death. We disagree. In support of their motion for summary judgment, appellees submitted affidavits tending to prove that decedent took possession of his original will after he executed it; that he meticulously kept important documents; and that appellee James S. Pilafas diligently searched decedent's home after his death and was unable to find the original will. In response, appellants offered no evidence undermining the factual basis for the common law presumption. In our opinion, the trial court correctly determined that decedent revoked his will and died intestate. . . .
>
> Appellees ask us to extend to revocable inter vivos trusts the common law presumption that a will last seen in the testator's possession that cannot be found after his death has been revoked. Appellees' reliance on this common law presumption is misplaced, however, if decedent's trust agreement was not susceptible to revocation by physical destruction.
>
> Unlike the execution of a will, the creation of a trust involves the present transfer of property interests in the trust corpus to the beneficiaries. George G. Bogert and George T. Bogert, Trusts & Trustees §998 (2d ed. rev. 1983). "These interests cannot be taken from [the beneficiaries] except in accordance with a provision of the trust instrument, or by their own acts, or by a decree of a court." Id. Even a revocable trust vests the trust beneficiary with a legal right to enforce the terms of the trust. The terms of the trust also limit the powers of the settlor and trustee over the trust corpus, even when the settlor declares himself trustee for the benefit of himself and others.

4. On the presumption of revocation, see page 252.—Eds.

The terms of decedent's trust agreement governing revocation provide: "The Settlor may at any time or times during the Settlor's lifetime by instrument in writing delivered to the Trustee amend or revoke this Agreement in whole or in part." Appellants argue that under this provision decedent could exercise his power to revoke the trust only through an "instrument in writing delivered to the Trustee." We agree. . . .

Appellees claim to discern a trend in the law toward wholesale application of the law of wills to revocable trusts. This trend is logical and justified, appellees argue, because revocable trusts often serve as substitutes for wills and the same rules should apply to both. As evidence of this trend, appellees cite decisions that apply statutory rules affecting lapsed bequests and post-will divorce to provisions in revocable inter vivos trusts. See, e.g., Clymer v. Mayo, 473 N.E.2d 1084, 1093-94 (Mass. 1985); Miller v. First Nat'l Bank & Trust Co., 637 P.2d 75, 77-78 (Okla. 1981). These decisions, however, involve trust provisions that as a practical matter operate only after the settlor's death. In contrast, the provisions of decedent's inter vivos trust transferred present remainder interests to the trust beneficiaries, who are entitled to insist on full compliance with the terms of the trust instrument. We see no cogent reason the settled and predictable common law rules governing the revocation of trusts should be generally displaced by the distinct statutory rules for the revocation of wills.[5]

Because appellees presented no evidence showing that decedent complied with the required method of revocation, the inter vivos trust was not revoked and remained valid.

PROBLEM

Suppose that Steve J. Pilafas, the settlor in the preceding case, had executed a will expressly revoking the inter vivos trust. This will is found among Pilafas's papers at death. Does it revoke the trust? Has it been delivered to the settlor-trustee? See In re Estate of Lowry, 418 N.E.2d 10 (Ill. App. 1981). Suppose that a bank were trustee. Same result? See Connecticut Gen. Life Ins. Co. v. First Natl. Bank of Minneapolis, 262 N.W.2d 403 (Minn. 1977). Suppose Pilafas tore both his will and trust into many pieces. What result as to the will? What result as to the trust? See Salem United Methodist Church v. Bottorff, 138 S.W.3d 788 (Mo. 2004).

Restatement (Third) of Trusts §63 (2003) provides that a revocable trust may be revoked, "Absent contrary provision in the terms of the trust, . . . in any way that provides clear and convincing evidence of the settlor's intention to do so," which includes revocation by will. Uniform Trust Code §602(c) (2000) is to similar effect.

STATE STREET BANK & TRUST CO. v. REISER, 389 N.E.2d 768 (Mass. App. 1979): In 1971 Wilfred A. Dunnebier created a revocable inter vivos trust funded with stock from five closely-held corporations. In 1972 he borrowed $75,000 from the State Street Bank in the form of an unsecured loan. Four months later Dunnebier died. Before Dunnebier's death, under traditional doctrine,

---

5. Because we hold that the decedent's trust agreement could not have been revoked by physical destruction, we need not decide whether the common law presumption that a lost will last seen in the testator's possession was revoked by physical destruction may apply under some circumstances to revocable inter vivos trusts. We also need not decide whether Arizona's Statute of Frauds, A.R.S. §44-101, would have required a written instrument to revoke the decedent's trust.

the bank could have reached the entire trust corpus to satisfy Dunnebier's debt because the trust was self-settled and its entire corpus was available to Dunnebier.[6] "When a person creates for his own benefit a trust for support or a discretionary trust, his creditors can reach the maximum amount which the trustee, under the terms of the trust, could pay to him or apply for his benefit." Hence the question presented was whether the trust assets were likewise reachable by the bank after Dunnebier's death.

   We . . . face the question whether Dunnebier's death broke the vital chain. His powers to amend or revoke the trust, or to direct payments from it, obviously died with him, and the remainder interests of the beneficiaries of the trust became vested. The contingencies which might defeat those remainder interests could no longer occur. . . .

   As an estate planning vehicle, the inter vivos trust has become common currency. Frequently, as Dunnebier did in the instant case, the settlor retains all the substantial incidents of ownership because access to the trust property is necessary or desirable as a matter of sound financial planning. Psychologically, the settlor thinks of the trust property as "his," as Dunnebier did when he took the bank's officer to visit the real estate owned by the corporation whose stock he had put in trust. . . . In other circumstances, persons place property in trust in order to obtain expert management of their assets, while retaining the power to invade principal and to amend and revoke the trust. It is excessive obeisance to the form in which property is held to prevent creditors from reaching property placed in trust under such terms.

   This view was adopted in United States v. Ritter, 558 F.2d 1165, 1167 (4th Cir. 1977). In a concurring opinion in that case Judge Widener observed that it violates public policy for an individual to have an estate to live on, but not an estate to pay his debts with. Id. at 1168. The Internal Revenue Code institutionalizes the concept that a settlor of a trust who retains administrative powers, power to revoke or power to control beneficial enjoyment "owns" that trust property and provides that it shall be included in the settlor's personal estate. I.R.C. §§2038 and 2041.

   We hold, therefore, that where a person places property in trust and reserves the right to amend and revoke, or to direct disposition of principal and income, the settlor's creditors may, following the death of the settlor, reach in satisfaction of the settlor's debts to them, to the extent not satisfied by the settlor's estate, those assets owned by the trust over which the settlor had such control at the time of his death as would have enabled the settlor to use the trust assets for his own benefit.

NOTES AND PROBLEMS

1. In *Reiser*, had Dunnebier not transferred his stock to the trust, then as an asset owned by him at death it would have been included in his probate estate. As such, it would have been subject to the claims of his creditors. The same result obtains under the court's holding that the trust assets were subject to the claims of Dunnebier's creditors to the extent that those claims could not be satisfied out of his probate estate. This is the prevailing view. See In re Estate of Nagel, 580 N.W.2d 810 (Iowa 1998) (tort creditors can reach revocable trust after settlor's

---

6. For more on the rights to trust assets of the beneficiary's creditors, see Chapter 8 at page 557.

death); In re Marriage of Perry, 68 Cal. Rptr. 2d 445 (App. 1997) (revocable trust held liable, after settlor's death, to claim for child support in divorce decree); Nathaniel W. Schwickerath, Note, Public Policy and the Probate Pariah: Confusion in the Law of Will Substitutes, 48 Drake L. Rev. 769, 782 (2000). Both Restatement (Third) of Trusts §25, cmt. e (2003), and Uniform Trust Code §505(a)(3) (2000), are in accord.

2. With creditors' rights in revocable trusts, compare creditors' rights in other nonprobate assets. Nonprobate assets are not all treated alike. Life insurance proceeds or retirement benefits are usually exempt from the insured's creditors if payable to a spouse or child. U.S. savings bonds with a payable-on-death (P.O.D.) beneficiary may be exempt. The creditors of a joint tenant holding a joint tenancy in land cannot reach the land after the joint tenant's death because the deceased joint tenant's interest has vanished.

UPC §6-215 (1990) expressly permits the decedent's creditors to reach P.O.D. bank accounts and joint bank accounts, if the probate estate is insufficient. With respect to liability of other nonprobate assets, see UPC §6-102 (1998 amendment); Wash. Rev. Code §11.18.200 (2004).

2. Pour-Over Wills

Along with the increasing use of the revocable trust as an estate planning arrangement has come the development of the *pour-over will*. In concept it is simple. *O* sets up a revocable inter vivos trust naming *X* as trustee. *O* transfers to *X*, as trustee, his stocks and bonds. *O* then executes a will devising the residue of his estate to *X*, as trustee, to hold under the terms of the inter vivos trust. The *pour-over* by will of probate assets into an inter vivos trust is a useful device where *O* wants to establish an inter vivos trust of some of his assets and wants to merge after his death his testamentary estate, insurance proceeds, and other assets into a single receptacle subject to unified trust administration. The testators in both *Pilafas* and *Reiser* executed pour-over wills to transfer their residuary estates to the inter vivos trusts they had created.

Two theories were found useful in validating a pour-over of probate assets into an inter vivos trust when pour-overs first developed. The first is *incorporation by reference*. A will can incorporate by reference a trust instrument in existence at the time the will is executed, but it cannot incorporate trust amendments made after the will is executed. See page 273. Hence, if the trust is amended after the will is executed, the probate assets will either be disposed of in accordance with the terms of the trust instrument as it stood at the time of execution of the will and not as subsequently amended, *or*, if this would not be in accordance with testator's intent, pass by intestacy.

The second theory for validating pour-overs is the doctrine of *independent significance* (see page 285). Under this doctrine a will may dispose of property by referring to some act that has significance apart from disposing of probate assets — in this context, by reference to an inter vivos trust that disposes of assets transferred to the trust during life. Under this doctrine the trust instrument does not have to be in existence when the will is executed, but the trust must have some assets in it before the time of the testator's death. Note the difference between independent significance and incorporation by reference: Independent significance requires that the inter vivos trust have some *property transferred to it during life*, which the trust disposes of; incorporation by reference requires that the *trust instrument be in existence at the time the will is executed.*

Under the doctrine of independent significance, the assets poured over into the inter vivos trust, like the assets transferred to the trust during life, are subject to the terms of (and are treated as an addition to) the inter vivos trust. The will can pour over assets to the trust as amended after execution of the will.

Because of the limitations and uncertainties of these doctrines and frequent embarrassing errors by lawyers, estate planners sought the enactment of legislation permitting a will to pour over probate assets into an inter vivos trust as amended on the date of death, even if that trust had not otherwise been funded. The 1960 Uniform Testamentary Additions to Trusts Act (UTATA) or an equivalent statute has been enacted in all jurisdictions. The UTATA was revised in 1990 and incorporated into the UPC as §2-511.

Uniform Probate Code (1990)

§2-511. TESTAMENTARY ADDITIONS TO TRUSTS

(a) A will may validly devise property to the trustee of a trust established or to be established (i) during the testator's lifetime by the testator, by the testator and some other person, or by some other person, including a funded or unfunded life insurance trust, although the settlor has reserved any or all rights of ownership of the insurance contracts, or (ii) at the testator's death by the testator's devise to the trustee, if the trust is identified in the testator's will and its terms are set forth in a written instrument, other than a will, executed before, concurrently with, or after the execution of the testator's will or in another individual's will if that other individual has predeceased the testator, regardless of the existence, size, or character of the corpus of the trust. The devise is not invalid because the trust is amendable or revocable, or because the trust was amended after the execution of the will or the testator's death.

(b) Unless the testator's will provides otherwise, property devised to a trust described in subsection (a) is not held under a testamentary trust of the testator, but it becomes a part of the trust to which it is devised, and must be administered and disposed of in accordance with the provisions of the governing instrument setting forth the terms of the trust, including any amendments thereto made before or after the testator's death.[7]

(c) Unless the testator's will provides otherwise, a revocation or termination of the trust before the testator's death causes the devise to lapse.

The Uniform Testamentary Additions to Trusts Act, as originally drafted, validated a pour-over of probate assets into an inter vivos trust only if the trust

---

7. Compare N.Y. Est. Powers & Trusts Law §§7-1.17 & 3-3.7 (2004), which require that the trust and any amendments be executed with the formalities required for recording a deed (i.e., notarized) or for executing a will in order to pour over into a trust as amended. — Eds.

instrument was executed (signed) before or concurrently with the will. In this respect, the uniform act resembled the doctrine of incorporation by reference, which requires that the incorporated document be in existence at the time the will is executed; the uniform act differed slightly in that it required the document to be in existence and signed when the will is executed. The original uniform act did not require that some property be transferred to the inter vivos trust during life, as is required by the doctrine of independent significance. If the trust instrument was executed before or concurrently with the will, the probate assets could be poured over into the inter vivos trust as subsequently amended. The trust funded at death by the pour-over was treated as an inter vivos trust — that is, as having come into existence before the testator's death! The purpose of this magical transformation is to give pour-over trusts the advantages of inter vivos trusts (see pages 318-320).

The 1990 revision to the uniform pour-over act deleted the requirement in the original act that the trust instrument be executed before or concurrently with the will. The revised act permits the trust instrument to be executed after the will. Thus, a testator's will can pour over the testator's probate assets to "a trust with the First National Bank as trustee, which I will execute," if the testator thereafter executes the trust instrument.

QUESTIONS, PROBLEM, AND NOTE

1. Inasmuch as the 1990 revision to the Uniform Testamentary Additions to Trusts Act permits a pour-over to a trust to be created *after* the will is executed, why does UPC §2-510 (the doctrine of incorporation by reference, page 273) continue to require a writing to be in existence when it is incorporated into a will? Is there any reason why a signed letter or other document should be treated differently from a signed trust instrument?

2. Suppose that the UTATA is the law in this jurisdiction. Refer back to the Brown family estate planning problem, pages 40-48. Wendy Brown's Aunt Fanny, who has a house full of things, executes a trust deed that names Wendy as trustee and provides that Wendy shall distribute the trust property in equal shares to Wendy Brown, Lucy Lipman, Simon Preston, and Ruth Preston. The trust deed provides that the trust can be revoked or amended at any time by a written or oral communication to Wendy from Aunt Fanny. No property is transferred to the trust during Aunt Fanny's life. Aunt Fanny subsequently makes a will pouring over all her property into this trust. Then, Aunt Fanny invites Wendy for a visit and tells Wendy exactly what item she wants to go to whom. After Wendy returns home, Aunt Fanny writes Wendy a letter saying that she is preparing a memorandum about the family silver and heirlooms that will state who is to get what. Upon Aunt Fanny's death, such a memorandum is found. What disposition is made of Aunt Fanny's estate? See Estate of Kirk, 907 P.2d 794 (Idaho 1995). Is it possible to have an oral will by executing a will pouring over probate assets into an inter vivos trust amendable by oral instructions?

3. A will speaks at death and disposes of property acquired by the testator after the will is executed. Thus a devise of "all of my personal property to *A*" includes personal property acquired after the will is executed. A revocable trust, however, can dispose only of property transferred to the trust during life, and a settlor cannot transfer to the trust property the settlor does not have. Thus *T* cannot

use a revocable trust to dispose of after-acquired property unless *T* conveys that property to the trust before death. But if *T* executes a will that pours over after-acquired property into the trust, then *T* can, in effect, dispose of all her property via the terms of the trust. From this bit of information, you doubtless see why a pour-over will is a good idea when the settlor wants the revocable trust to dispose of all her property at her death.

CLYMER v. MAYO, 473 N.E.2d 1084 (Mass. 1985): In this complex but much discussed case, Clara Mayo, a professor of psychology at Boston University, executed a will in 1963 designating her husband James as the primary beneficiary. In 1964 she named James as the beneficiary of her B.U. group life insurance policy. In 1965 she made him the beneficiary of her B.U. retirement plans, which were administered by TIAA-CREF, the leading company administering university pensions in the United States. On February 2, 1973, Clara executed a new will and a new revocable trust. Under the new will, the bulk of her estate was to pour over into the new revocable trust. James was the principal beneficiary under the trust.

On the same day that she executed her new will and trust, Clara named the trustees as the beneficiary of her B.U. life insurance policy. Later she designated the trustees as the beneficiary of her TIAA-CREF retirement plans. In so doing, Clara unified the disposition of all of her property through her new revocable trust.

In 1978 Clara and James divorced. Clara thereupon changed the beneficiary designation of her life insurance to Marianne LaFrance, but left the trust as the beneficiary of her pension plans, and left James as the principal beneficiary under the trust. In 1981 Clara died, leaving her parents as her only heirs.

The first issue was the validity of the trust. If the trust was valid, James would take as the named beneficiary. If the trust was invalid, then the devise in Clara's will to the trust would fail, and Clara's parents would take as her intestate heirs. Under traditional principles, a trust must contain property, known as the *res*, to be valid. However, the Uniform Testamentary Additions to Trusts Act (UTATA) validates unfunded trusts that are intended to be funded by a pour-over will if the trust agreement is executed before the testator's death. Applying the Massachusetts version of the UTATA, the court held that the inter vivos trust was valid even though unfunded. As an alternative holding, the court concluded that this trust did have a res, namely, the right to receive the insurance and pension plan proceeds.

The next issue was whether James's interest in the trust was revoked as a result of the divorce. Like many states, Massachusetts statutory law revokes an ex-spouse's interests under the testator's will. The question here was whether this statute, which by its terms spoke only of wills, should be applied to Clara's inter vivos revocable trust inasmuch as Clara employed the trust as a will substitute.

> [T]he trust had no practical significance until her death in 1981. The decedent executed both her will and indenture of trust on February 2, 1973. She transferred no property or funds to the trust at that time. The trust was to receive its funding at the decedent's death, in part through her life insurance policy and retirement benefits, and in part through a pour-over from the will's residuary clause. [James], the proposed executor and sole legatee under the will, was also made the primary beneficiary of the trust. . . .

During her lifetime, the decedent retained power to amend or revoke the trust. Since the trust was unfunded, her cotrustee was subject to no duties or obligations until her death. Similarly, it was only as a result of the decedent's death that [James] could claim any right to the trust assets. It is evident from the time and manner in which the trust was created and funded, that the decedent's will and trust were integrally related components of a single testamentary scheme. For all practical purposes the trust, like the will, "spoke" only at the decedent's death. For this reason Mayo's interest in the trust was revoked by operation of G.L. c. 191, §9 [providing that divorce revokes an ex-spouse's interests under a will], at the same time his interest under the decedent's will was revoked.

". . . Divorce usually represents a stormy parting, where the last thing one of the parties wishes is to have an earlier will carried out giving everything to the former spouse." Young, Probate Reform, 18 B.B.J. 7, 11 (1974). To carry out the testator's implied intent, the law revokes "any disposition or appointment of property made by the will to the former spouse." It is indisputable that if the decedent's trust was either testamentary or incorporated by reference into her will, Mayo's beneficial interest in the trust would be revoked by operation of the statute. . . .

[We conclude] that the legislative intent under G.L. c. 191, §9, is that a divorced spouse should not take under a [revocable] trust executed in these circumstances. In the absence of an expressed contrary intent, that statute implies an intent on the part of a testator to revoke will provisions favoring a former spouse. It is incongruous then to ignore that same intent with regard to a trust funded in part through her will's pour-over at the decedent's death. As one law review commentator has noted, "[t]ransferors use will substitutes to avoid probate, not to avoid the subsidiary law of wills. The subsidiary rules are the product of centuries of legal experience in attempting to discern transferors' wishes and suppress litigation. These rules should be treated as presumptively correct for will substitutes as well as for wills." Langbein, The Nonprobate Revolution and the Future of the Law of Succession, 97 Harv. L. Rev. 1108, 1136-1137 (1984).

Restricting our holding to the particular facts of this case—specifically the existence of a revocable pour-over trust funded entirely at the time of the decedent's death—we conclude that G.L. c. 191, §9, revokes Mayo's interest under [the trust].[8]

NOTES AND PROBLEM

1. Where a settlor names the trustee of her inter vivos trust as the beneficiary of her life insurance policy but does not add any other funds or assets to the trust, the inter vivos trust is called an *unfunded life insurance trust*. If the settlor adds other assets to the inter vivos trust, it is called a *funded inter vivos trust*. An unfunded life insurance trust as well as a funded trust is a valid inter vivos trust.

In the former case, the trust res or property (traditionally a necessary ingredient of a valid trust, see page 508) is the trustee's contingent right to receive the proceeds of the policy. This interest is potentially valuable, for if the insured dies

---

8. As an alternative ground the appellants argue that the terms of the Mayos' divorce settlement, in which Mayo waived "any right, title or interest" in the assets that later funded the decedent's trust, amount to a disclaimer of his trust interest. We decline to base our holding on such reasoning because a disclaimer of rights "must be clear and unequivocal," Second Bank-State St. Trust Co. v. Yale Univ. Alumni Fund, 156 N.E.2d 57, 59 (Mass. 1959), and we find no such disclaimer in the Mayos' divorce agreement.

without changing the policy beneficiary, the trustee will be entitled to the policy proceeds. This is true even though the right is fragile in the sense that the insured, while still alive, might change the beneficiary designation.

That the trust in Clymer v. Mayo did in fact have a res was not essential to the validity of Clara Mayo's devise to its trustees in her will. Under the UTATA, if the testator executes the trust agreement during life, then its trustee is a permissible taker under the testator's will. See In re Estate of Canales, 837 S.W.2d 662, 666 (Tex. App. 1992): "The purpose of the statute was to make standby trusts available as an estate planning tool, to receive assets from a pour-over will."

2. *Revocation by divorce*. Statutes in some states provide that divorce revokes any provision in a revocable trust for the ex-spouse, who is deemed to have predeceased the settlor. See, e.g., Ohio Rev. Code Ann. §1339.62 (2004); Okla. Stat. Ann. tit. 60, §175 (2004). Had Clymer v. Mayo involved one of these statutes, the question of whether the divorce revoked James's interest in Clara's trust would have been easier.

UPC §2-804 (1990), excerpted at page 269, provides that divorce revokes dispositions in favor of the divorced spouse in revocable inter vivos trusts as well as in other will substitutes such as life insurance, pension plans, pay on death (P.O.D.) contracts, and transfer on death (T.O.D.) securities. UPC §2-804 also revokes any provision for a relative of the divorced spouse. But the reach of §2-804 has been limited by Egelhoff v. Egolhoff (pages 336-341), which holds that federal law preempts the applicability of state revocation-on-divorce statutes to federally regulated pension benefits. See also Susan N. Gary, Applying Revocation-on-Divorce Statutes to Will Substitutes, 18 Quinnipiac Prob. L.J. 83 (2004).

3.   Suppose Pablo executes an unfunded inter vivos trust naming Eduardo as beneficiary. Pablo also executes a will pouring over all his assets into the trust. The will contains a no-contest clause (see page 167) providing that any person contesting the will shall forfeit any interest given by the will. Subsequently Pablo amends his trust to name Maria as a beneficiary of half of the trust. Upon Pablo's death, Eduardo contests the trust amendment on the ground that Pablo lacked mental capacity when the trust was amended. The court holds there is no probable cause for Eduardo's lawsuit. Does Eduardo forfeit his beneficial interest under the trust instrument? See In re Lindstrom, 236 Cal. Rptr. 376 (App. 1987) (not applying no-contest clause in the will to the trust). See also Briggs v. Wyoming Natl. Bank, 836 P.2d 263 (Wyo. 1992) (enforcing no-contest clause in the trust); Jo Ann Englehardt, In Terrorem Inter Vivos: Terra Incognita, 26 Real Prop., Prob. & Tr. J. 535 (1991).

4.   The unfunded revocable life insurance trust coupled with a will pouring over probate assets into the trust is one means of creating a unified trust of both life insurance proceeds and probate assets. The trust that results is an inter vivos trust. Another method is to create a trust in the will and designate as beneficiary of the insurance proceeds "the trustee named in my will." The resulting unified trust is a testamentary trust because created by the will, not by an inter vivos instrument. Under the latter method, the insurance proceeds are not payable to the executor of the testator's estate, but to the trustee named in the will. Hence the proceeds do not "go through probate," as do assets under the executor's control.

The insurance proceeds may also be payable to "the estate of the insured." In this event, the proceeds would be payable to the executor, would be treated as probate assets, and would be distributed under the testator's will in the same manner as other property.

3. Use of Revocable Trusts in Estate Planning

a. Introduction

A revocable trust can be created by a *declaration of trust*, whereby the settlor becomes the trustee of the trust property. In the trust instrument, the settlor should name a successor trustee to take over the trusteeship upon the settlor's death or incompetency. Where the trust is to end on the settlor's death, and the trust is merely a means of avoiding probate, the death beneficiary should ordinarily be named successor trustee. At the settlor's death, the successor trustee automatically takes over, without a court order, and distributes the property to the trust beneficiaries. A revocable declaration of trust was involved in Farkas v. Williams, page 299, and in Estate and Trust of Pilafas, page 307.

A revocable trust can also be created by a *deed of trust*, naming a third party as trustee. The settlor can be co-trustee, if desired. A revocable trust can be funded, as in State Street Bank & Trust Co. v. Reiser, page 308, where the settlor transferred his stock to the trust; or the trust can be unfunded, as were some of the trusts in Estate of Canales, 837 S.W.2d 662 (Tex. App. 1992).

The terms of a revocable trust may call for distribution of the trust assets at the settlor's death. Or the revocable trust may provide the main vehicle for the disposition of the settlor's estate, either outright or in further trust after his death; assets in the settlor's probate estate can be poured over into the revocable trust to bring about a uniform disposition of the settlor's assets. In fact, if unified control of assets is desired during life, the settlor can change all the beneficiary designations on the settlor's nonprobate assets to make them payable to the revocable trust and also execute a will pouring over all probate assets to the revocable trust. After doing this, the settlor has consolidated under one document his dispositive plan for all his assets. He can later amend it as he could amend a will. Under this scheme, the revocable trust, with amendments, functions as a will did in the days before the proliferation of will substitutes.

It is rather ironic that a generation after the will began to lose its dominance because of the public's desire to avoid probate, the revocable trust has replaced it as a document with almost all the same attributes of a will, but without probate. Perhaps we should think anew about making probate optional, as it is in California for all transfers to a spouse.

Now let us take a closer look at the advantages and disadvantages of revocable trusts (often called living trusts, particularly in the popular literature). While the revocable trust may have advantages for many clients, for some it will be unsuitable.

b. Consequences During Life of Settlor

(1) *Property management by fiduciary.* A third party trustee may be selected to manage a funded revocable trust. The settlor may want to be relieved of the burdens of financial management. Although a custodianship account for securities or other assets is often used for this purpose, a custodianship is an agency relationship and terminates on the disability or death of the principal. By contrast, a revocable trust continues during the settlor's incapacity and can provide for

disposition of the trust assets at the settlor's death. The settlor can evaluate the trustee's performance and name a new trustee if not satisfied — an opportunity not available to the settlor's executor.

On the other hand, when property is put in trust, some inconveniences may arise upon sale or mortgage of the property. Third parties such as banks and transfer agents may want to see copies of the trust instrument to determine whether the trustee has power to engage in the transaction. It is not as easy to conduct some transactions when title to the property is in a trustee as it is when title is in a private individual.

(2) *Keeping title clear.* A revocable trust is useful in keeping separate and apart property that a husband or wife or both want not to be commingled with their other assets. A husband and wife, for example, may want to establish separate revocable trusts of property that each brings to the marriage or acquires by inheritance. This may prevent ambiguities of ownership from developing later, with consequent problems upon divorce or death.

Spouses who move from a community property state to a separate property state may create a revocable trust for their community property in order to avoid a stepped-up income tax basis on all the property when one spouse dies (see page 460).

(3) *Income and gift taxes.* Under the federal income, gift, and estate taxes, assets in a revocable trust are treated as still owned by the settlor. When the revocable trust is created, it is not treated as a completed gift to the beneficiaries under the federal gift tax (see page 853). Because of the retained power to revoke, trust income is taxable to the settlor regardless of to whom it is paid. Internal Revenue Code of 1986 §676(a). There are no federal tax advantages in creating a revocable trust.

(4) *Dealing with incompetency.* Increased longevity has brought with it an increased chance that a person's last days (or perhaps months or years) may be spent in a state of mental or physical disability, requiring some form of fiduciary administration of the person's assets. Many persons are reluctant to have a spouse or parent formally adjudicated an incompetent. Moreover, guardianship or conservatorship proceedings are cumbersome and expensive, and invite unwanted publicity. Even the modern UPC §5-406 stipulates an elaborate court procedure protecting the alleged incompetent. When Groucho Marx was in his 80s, he was declared incompetent by a court, against his wishes. At the time he was living with a woman named Erin Fleming, who said he preferred her as his guardian if he had to have one. After a messy court fight, with the newspapers titillating readers with intimate family details, a relative of Marx was appointed guardian.

A revocable trust can be used in planning for the contingency of incapacity. The settlor may be co-trustee, with the trust instrument providing that either trustee alone may act on behalf of the trust. Or the trust instrument may provide that the other co-trustee shall act as sole trustee if the settlor becomes incompetent. An alternative to a revocable trust is a durable power of attorney, described on page 346.

QUESTION

In drafting revocable trust provisions dealing with incompetency, what provisions would you make for determining when the settlor is incompetent?

c. Consequences at Death of Settlor: Avoidance of Probate

(1) *Costs*. Assets transferred during life to a revocable trust avoid probate because legal title to the assets passes to the trustee, and there is no need to change the title to the trust assets by probate administration on the settlor's death. Although trustee's fees may be payable if a third party trustee is named, these fees will be considerably smaller than court costs, attorney's fees, and executor's commissions incurred in probate.

Against the savings in probate fees, certain other costs must be offset. Lawyers charge more to draft a revocable trust than a will, particularly when there are related pour-over documents. These documents are more complicated than a will. In addition, transferring title of assets to the trustee may entail certain costs, for example, stock transfer fees.

(2) *Delays*. In an estate administration, the assets may be in the executor's possession and control for a substantial period of time. A typical estate takes 18 to 24 months to settle. Under a revocable trust, income and principal can be disbursed to the beneficiaries much more quickly.

In some states, executors (viewed as temporary "caretakers") are restricted to purchasing very safe investments. On the other hand, trustees are viewed as managers governed only by the prudent investor rule. Because rules governing trustees are often more liberal than rules applicable to executors, it is usually simpler for a trustee rather than an executor to deal with an ongoing business in the form of a partnership or sole proprietorship, and for a trustee to exercise options, borrow money, and participate in reorganizations.

(3) *Creditors*. In probate a short-term statute of limitations is applicable to creditors (see page 36). If creditors do not file claims within a short period after the testator's death, the creditors are forever barred. There is no short-term statute of limitations applicable to revocable trusts; the limitations period is the normal one applicable to the particular claim. Where it is important to cut off the rights of creditors — as might be true with professionals such as doctors or lawyers where the statute of limitations on malpractice runs from discovery — probate holds an advantage over the revocable trust. On creditors' rights against revocable trusts, see State Street Bank & Trust Co. v. Reiser, page 308.

(4) *Publicity*. A will is a public record, open to disappointed heirs, newspaper reporters, and the just plain curious. Any inventory of property and the named beneficiaries are there for all the world to see. An inter vivos trust is not recorded in a public place. The identity and amount of the settlor's property and the names of the beneficiaries need not be disclosed to any public officials except the tax authorities (whose records are private). Hence, revocable trusts are especially attractive to persons desiring secrecy. Such persons include personalities trying to keep out of the tabloids and persons of great wealth who fear kidnapping or other victimization of their beneficiaries or theft of their art collections, jewels, or other property. For example, in In re Estate of Hearst, 136 Cal. Rptr. 821 (App. 1977), William Randolph Hearst had created a testamentary trust to care for his descendants and relatives. After Patty Hearst was kidnapped by the Symbionese Liberation Army, the trustees asked the court to cut off public access to the probate files in Hearst's estate, fearing that radicals would find hitherto unnoticed members of the family and the location of their homes and properties. The court agreed to restrict public access while the Hearst family was in danger of attack.

If W.R. Hearst had created a revocable inter vivos trust of his property, the family records would have been kept private.

(5) *Ancillary probate*. If the settlor owns real property located outside the domiciliary state, any will passing title to that property must be probated in the state where the land is located. To avoid ancillary probate, which may be cumbersome and expensive, land in another state can be transferred to a revocable inter vivos trust. Through this device, title to the land is changed to the trustee during the owner's life.

(6) *Avoiding restrictions protecting family members*. In many states the surviving spouse is given by statute an elective share in the decedent's probate estate only. In these states, the elective share does not extend by statute to revocable trusts created by the decedent spouse. Courts in most of these jurisdictions, however, exercising equity powers, have permitted the surviving spouse to reach the assets in a revocable trust created by the decedent spouse. See pages 438-450. Nonetheless, a disgruntled spouse might be able to create a funded revocable trust in another state not recognizing the spouse's right to reach the trust and thereby defeat a spouse's elective share.

A funded revocable trust may be used to put assets beyond the reach of a child born out of wedlock, protected by a pretermission statute, whom the client does not wish to mention in his will. Pretermission statutes apply only to probate property. See pages 479-480.

(7) *Avoiding restrictions on testamentary trusts*. A testamentary trust is a trust created by a will. It is sometimes called a court trust because it comes into being by an order of the probate court that supervises the administration of the estate, and in many states this court continues to supervise the administration of the testamentary trust after the estate is closed. An inter vivos trust, on the other hand, created by the settlor during lifetime, comes into being without any court order. It is not subject to any court supervision unless the beneficiary or the trustee comes into court to settle some trust matter.

Inasmuch as a testamentary trust is created by a court order, the trustee may have the duty to account to the court. Judicial approval of a trustee's accounts is often a time-consuming and expensive procedure. It may require the appointment of guardians ad litem to represent unborn and unascertained beneficiaries. To avoid this, the will may provide that certain beneficiaries (perhaps all adult, competent beneficiaries) have the power to approve the trustee's accounts without a court proceeding. Although such a provision would be effective in an inter vivos trust, whether it is effective in testamentary trusts varies from jurisdiction to jurisdiction. In some states, the probate court, having brought the testamentary trust into being, may refuse to be deprived of its authority to oversee the trustee's work. To avoid judicial accounting, the settlor may create a revocable inter vivos trust.

In some states, a nondomiciliary bank or a nonresident person cannot serve as testamentary trustee under the will of a testator who was a domiciliary of the state. See Jeffrey A. Schoenblum, 2004 Multistate Guide to Estate Planning at Tables 3.01 & 3.03. By contrast, the settlor of an inter vivos trust can name as trustee a person or bank in another state. Where the beneficiaries reside in another state, the settlor may wish to appoint a trustee in their state, particularly where the trustee is given discretionary powers that can be soundly exercised only on the basis of personal contact with the beneficiaries.

(8) *Choosing the law of another jurisdiction to govern*. As a general rule, the settlor of an inter vivos trust of personal property may choose the state law that is to govern the trust. (If a trust asset is land, the law of the state where the land is located governs.) The settlor may choose the law of the domicile of the settlor or of the beneficiaries, or the law of the state where the trust is administered. A testator may not have this freedom of choice. Many states apply the law of the settlor's domicile to a testamentary trust because it was created by a will probated in that state, regardless of the testator's intent that the law of another state apply. Hence, to avoid some local restriction on trusts, the settlor may want to create an inter vivos trust in another state.

The settlor of an inter vivos trust can create a trust in a state that has the most permissive period of perpetuities. Alaska, Delaware, Illinois, South Dakota, and a host of other states have effectively abolished the Rule against Perpetuities as applied to trusts (see page 711). As we shall see, a perpetual trust for the settlor's descendants, which incurs no federal estate or generation-skipping transfer taxes at the expiration of each generation, can be created in these states. Persons domiciled in other states can take advantage of these permissive laws by creating inter vivos trusts in these states.

UPC §2-703 (1990) changes the old law and provides that the testator may select the state law to govern the meaning and legal effect of his will, including trusts created by will, unless that law is contrary to the domiciliary state's law protecting the surviving spouse or any other public policy of the domiciliary state. This provision aligns testamentary choice of law rules with those generally used for inter vivos trusts, and, where adopted, it lessens the need to create an inter vivos trust to achieve some benefit available in some other state. It is not wholly clear, however, when applying foreign law to the will of a domiciliary testator would violate public policy of the domiciliary state.

(9) *Lack of certainty in the law*. Where a revocable trust is used as a substitute for a will, the law may be more uncertain in solving a problem that arises than it would be in case of a will. Wills rules developed over the centuries — for dealing with divorce, adoption, lapse, ademption, simultaneous death, apportionment of death taxes, and creditor's rights — may or may not apply to revocable trusts. Most of these issues can be solved by appropriate drafting if the drafter is awake to the problems.

(10) *Avoiding will contests*. A revocable trust, like a will, can be contested for lack of mental capacity and undue influence. In practice, however, it is more difficult to set aside a funded revocable trust than a will on these grounds. In the first place, the heirs of the decedent are not entitled to see the trust instrument, which is not a public document but a private document available only to the trust beneficiaries.[9] If the heirs bring suit, they will be able to learn the trust terms, but they are thereby forced to commit themselves to legal fees in a lawsuit without a realistic appraisal of their chances of winning. Second, if a trust continues as an ongoing operation for several years, generating monthly or yearly statements, sales of assets and reinvestments, a jury or a court will be reluctant to set the trust aside. Do you see why? If a will contest is foreseen, creating a revocable trust of the client's assets may be advisable.

---

9. On the rights of trust beneficiaries to examine the trust instrument, see Chapter 13 at pages 832-838.

(11) *Estate taxation*. As mentioned above, there are no significant federal tax advantages to a revocable trust. The assets of a revocable trust are included in the gross estate of the settlor under §2038 of the Internal Revenue Code of 1986. See page 837.

(12) *Controlling surviving spouse's disposition*. When one spouse wants some assurance that the surviving spouse's property will be disposed of in accordance with a mutual estate plan, both spouses can create a revocable trust of their property — to become irrevocable upon the death of one spouse. The trust may provide, for example, that all the income shall be payable to the surviving spouse, with the right of the surviving spouse to dip into principal if necessary to support him, and upon the surviving spouse's death the trust principal shall be divided equally between the husband's son and the wife's daughter by prior marriages. This use of the revocable trust may be especially attractive in second marriages and is much preferable to trying to control the surviving spouse's disposition by contract (see pages 288-294).

(13) *Custodial trusts*. An alternative to an individually tailored revocable trust, in states that have enacted the Uniform Custodial Trust Act (1987), is a statutory custodial trust. The act provides a statutory trust for the support of the beneficiary. The terms of the trust are spelled out in the statute. Someone other than the beneficiary must be named trustee. Until the beneficiary is incapacitated, the trustee must pay so much or all of the trust property as the beneficiary directs. If the beneficiary becomes incapacitated, the trustee may use the trust property for the support of the beneficiary and for the beneficiary's dependents. Upon the death of the beneficiary, the trust terminates and the trust assets are transferred to the persons designated by the beneficiary in a written document delivered to the trustee. The trust can be created by a transfer of property "to *X* as custodial trustee for *A*, under the (state) Uniform Custodial Trust Act."

The custodial trust is designed for elderly persons of modest means who consult attorneys in general practice, not estate planning specialists, and who want an inter vivos trust for management of assets in the event of incapacity. Because the terms of a custodial trust are fixed by statute, there is little flexibility. Most lawyers will have trust forms of their own and will prefer to draft a trust for the particular client's objectives rather than use an invariable form. But, where that is impracticable, a custodial trust is better than a guardianship upon a person's incapacity. See Gerry W. Beyer, Simplification of Inter Vivos Trust Instruments — From Incorporation by Reference to the Uniform Custodial Trust Act and Beyond, 32 S. Tex. L. Rev. 203 (1991). See also pages 432-433.

NOTE: MARKETING OF LIVING TRUSTS

Because of the public demand for living (or revocable) trusts, in some states a living trust industry has developed, run by bankers and financial consultants, sometimes in consultation with lawyers. These nonlawyers market living trusts to the public. Lawyers have begun to fight these purveyors of living trusts, alleging unauthorized practice of law. In Florida Bar v. American Senior Citizens Alliance, Inc., 689 So. 2d 255 (Fla. 1997), the court ruled that a for-profit corporation managed by nonlawyers in the business of selling complex estate planning documents, including wills, living trusts, and durable powers of attorney, was engaged in the unauthorized practice of law. The court also thought that lawyer participation in such living trust marketing schemes compromised the lawyer's duty of loyalty to the lawyer's client and independent professional judgment. Accord, Akron Bar Assn. v. Miller, 684 N.E.2d 288 (Ohio 1997). In 1993, Illinois enacted a statute providing that the assembly, drafting, and execution of a living trust by a nonlawyer or by a corporation not authorized to do trust business is an unlawful business practice. 815 Ill. Comp. Stat. Ann. §505/2BB (2004). For further discussion, see Angela M. Vallario, Living Trusts in the Unauthorized Practice of Law: A Good Thing Gone Bad, 59 Md. L. Rev. 595 (2000).

What about a will-drafting computer program, such as Quicken Family Lawyer, or an online web site such as LegalZoom.com, both of which generate will and trust forms according to answers that the user gives to a set of standard questions? The Texas State Bar won an injunction against the sale of Quicken Family Lawyer in Texas, but the legislature quickly changed the law to allow computer drafting programs provided that they "clearly and conspicuously state that the products are not a substitute for the advice of an attorney." See Unauthorized Practice of Law Comm. v. Parsons Tech., Inc., 1999 WL 47235 (N.D. Tex.), vacated, 179 F.3d 956 (5th Cir. 1999). See also Catherine J. Lanctot, "What Needs Fixing?": Scriveners in Cyberspace: Online Document Preparation and the Unauthorized Practice of Law, 30 Hofstra L. Rev. 811 (2002); Legal Advice on the Web, N.Y. Times, May 23, 2002, at G10 (letter to the editor).

The rise of a lay industry to meet consumer demand for living trusts to avoid probate contains an obvious lesson: Reform probate and the law of wills so that a will can have all the attributes of a living trust if desired. If this were done, the living trust business would collapse. But until it is done, suppressing nonlawyers who are giving the public what it wants, while lawyers are not, is not likely to be a rousing success.

SECTION C.   LIFE INSURANCE, PENSION ACCOUNTS, BANK ACCOUNTS, AND OTHER PAYABLE-ON-DEATH ARRANGEMENTS

Life insurance contracts, pension plans, bank and brokerage accounts, and a host of other contract-based arrangements regularly provide for the disposition of assets at death. These free market competitors to the probate system typically involve neutral financial institutions, which ensure reliable evidence of the decedent's wishes and provide some protection against fraud or imposition. In this section we examine some of the more common payable-on-death arrangements in contemporary estate planning, paying attention to their use in practice, trouble spots in their enforceability, and the applicability to them of the subsidiary law of wills.

1.   Life Insurance

Life insurance is a euphemism for death insurance. The principal purpose of life insurance is to shift the financial risk of dying young to an insurance company. By buying into a pool with other people worried about the same risk, those who die older in effect pay off those who die younger. Accordingly, by dying young, the insured wins her bet with the insurance company—a small consolation, perhaps.

Of all the financial risks associated with dying young, life insurance is particularly effective at replacing lost income. For those with dependents, experts typically recommend purchasing life insurance totaling at least six to ten times annual income so that someone who makes $50,000 a year should have at least $300,000 to $500,000 in life insurance. This rule of thumb is designed not to generate a figure that will replace all lost income, but rather to achieve a sensible level of insurance against the risk of lost income from an early death. We tend to favor amounts toward the high end of that range (or even more). Life insurance is also commonly purchased to protect a partnership or closely held corporation, either by giving the partnership or corporation enough money to buy out the decedent's share, or by giving the decedent's family enough cash to pay the estate taxes on the business without having to liquidate it.

Whole life insurance, also called *ordinary* or *straight* life insurance, is a combination product involving both life insurance and a savings plan. The person insured is covered for his entire life. In most policies, after many years the policies become *paid up* or *endowed*, after which no further premiums are owed. These policies "include a forced savings feature. Although the risk of death increases with the age of the life insured, the premiums remain fixed at the same amount ('level') throughout the time that they are payable." Robert J. Lynn & Grayson M.P. McCouch, Introduction to Estate Planning 124-125 (5th ed. 2004). There are newer variations on whole life policies, called *universal* life or *variable* life, which also combine life insurance with a savings account but that allow more investment options or greater flexibility.

The other primary type of life insurance is called *term life* insurance. Professors Lynn and McCouch explain:

> "Term" life insurance is sometimes referred to as pure insurance—it has no savings feature. If the life insured dies while the contract is in force, that is, during the term of the policy—commonly one year or five years—a stated sum is payable to the designated beneficiary. Because term insurance has no savings feature, it has no cash surrender value. And once the current term expires, the insurance policy is no longer in force unless it is renewed. Nonetheless, term insurance often plays an important role in estate planning. The lack of a savings feature means that a term policy can be purchased for considerably less than a whole life policy with a comparable face amount. . . . The term insurance contract might by its terms provide for optional renewal of insurance coverage for an additional term without regard to the life insured's state of health at the time of renewal. The policy might also give the policyholder the option to convert the policy from term insurance to a more permanent type of life insurance, without regard to the life insured's state of health at the time of conversion. [Id. at 126-127.]

NOTES

1. Consider the following life insurance industry statistics for 2003:

- The total face value of all life insurance in force was $16.8 trillion, of which $9.4 trillion was in the form of individual policies and $7.2 trillion was in the form of group policies.
- There were roughly 370 million life insurance policies in force.

- Individual life insurance policies averaged $56,000 in face value per policy.
- Group life insurance policies averaged $44,000 in face value per policy.
- Among individual life insurance policies sold in 2003, term life policies averaged $193,000 in face value and whole life policies averaged $72,000. See American Council of Life Insurers, 2004 Life Insurer's Fact Book.

To put these figures in perspective, observe that the 2003 Gross Domestic Product was roughly $11 trillion, about $6 trillion less than the face value of all life insurance in force. There are more domestic life insurance policies in force (370 million) than people alive in the country (about 300 million).

2.   Two features of term life insurance bear further emphasis. First, because it is more affordable than other forms of life insurance, it is often an especially sensible option for young couples who have (or plan to have) children. Healthy young adults can usually obtain twenty-year term policies at reasonable cost. Such a policy would cover the years of acute vulnerability — namely, the years before the couple's children are self-sufficient. Second, if the term policy includes a conversion option whereby it can be made more permanent, it protects the insured against the inability to obtain insurance in the future, after the policy would have otherwise expired, if the insured's health declines.

Yet insurance agents sell more whole life than term policies. This is not an accident. Because whole life policies combine savings with insurance, for a young adult a whole life policy will cost three to six times more in annual premiums than term insurance with the same face amount of coverage. As a result, many young families with whole life insurance are spending more on premiums and getting less insurance coverage than they need. Indeed, despite the rule of thumb that one should insure at six to ten times one's annual income, the average amount of insurance in force per individual policy is a low $44,000 to $56,000. Note also that among new policies sold in 2003, those purchasing whole life insurance (or other policies with savings components) bought only $72,000 of insurance, while those purchasing term life insurance policies bought $193,000 of coverage.

Depending on the policy terms, the owner of the life insurance policy or the beneficiary may select different *settlement options* for the receipt of death benefits, including a lump-sum payment, an annuity for the rest of the beneficiary's life, interest for years followed by payment of the principal, and periodic payments of interest and principal. For modest estates these settlement options can provide some of the flexibility that trusts provide for more substantial estates. Moreover, because these options are still treated as life insurance, they avoid the problem of effecting a testamentary disposition without Wills Act formalities. Life insurance contracts have long been recognized as valid notwithstanding their testamentary effect. Problems may still arise, however, when there is ambiguity whether a particular arrangement qualifies as a life insurance contract. If not, the question arises whether to enforce payable-on-death contracts more generally.

Wilhoit v. Peoples Life Insurance Co.
United States Court of Appeals, Seventh Circuit, 1955
218 F.2d 887

MAJOR, J.   The plaintiff, Robert Wilhoit, instituted this action against the defendants, Peoples Life Insurance Company (sometimes referred to as the company) and Thomas J. Owens, for the recovery of money held by the company. Roley Oscar Wilhoit was the insured and Sarah Louise Wilhoit, his wife, the beneficiary in a life insurance policy in the amount of $5,000, issued by Century Life Insurance Company of Frankfort, Indiana. Mr. Wilhoit died prior to October 22, 1930 (the exact date not disclosed by the record), without having changed the beneficiary designated in the policy, and the proceeds thereof became due to and payable to Mrs. Wilhoit. The amount due was paid to her and the policy surrendered, as is evidenced by the following receipt appearing on the back of the policy:

$4,749.00

Indianapolis, Ind.,
Oct. 22-1930.

Received from Century Life Insurance Company Forty Seven hundred forty nine Dollars in full for all claims under the within policy, terminated by death of Roley O. Wilhoit.

Sarah Louise Wilhoit

The main body of the policy contained a provision entitled "The Investment" as follows:

Upon the maturity of this policy, the amount payable hereunder, or any portion thereof, not less than One Thousand Dollars, may be left on deposit with the Company, and the Company will pay interest annually in advance upon the amount so left on deposit at such rate as the Company may declare on such funds so held by it, but never at a rate less than three percent, so long as the amount shall remain on deposit with the Company. The said deposit may be withdrawn at the end of any interest year; or upon the death of the payee of the amount of said deposit will be paid to the executors, administrators or assigns of the payee.[10]

On November 14, 1930, Mrs. Wilhoit (twenty-three days after she had acknowledged receipt of the amount due her under the policy) from her home in Indiana signed and addressed a letter to the company in the same State, which in material parts reads as follows:

I hereby acknowledge receipt of settlement in full under Policy No. C172 terminated by the death of Roley O. Wilhoit, the Insured, and I direct that the proceeds of $4,749.00 be held in trust[11] by the Peoples Life Insurance Company under the following conditions:

10. This settlement option is known as an *interest option*. — Eds.
11. Although Mrs. Wilhoit directed that the proceeds be held "in trust" and ordered that "this trust fund" be payable to Robert G. Owens upon her death, and the company accepted the agreement creating "a trust fund," the company did not set up a trust fund. A trust involves a duty to manage

(1) Said amount or any part thereof (not less than $100.00) to be subject to withdrawal on demand of the undersigned.

(2) While on deposit, said amount or part thereof shall earn interest at the rate of 3 1/2%, compounded annually, plus any excess interest authorized by the Board of Directors of the Company. Interest may be withdrawn at the end of each six months period or whenever the principal of the fund is withdrawn or may be allowed to accumulate compounded annually. Interest on this trust fund shall begin as of October 9th, 1930.

(3) In the event of my death, while any part of this trust fund is still in existence, the full amount, plus any accrued interest, shall be immediately payable to Robert G. Owens (Relationship) Brother.

The proposal contained in this letter was, on November 17, 1930, accepted by the company in the following form:

> The above agreement creating a trust fund is hereby accepted and we acknowledge receipt of the deposit of $4,749.00 under the above specified conditions.

Robert G. Owens, a brother of Mrs. Wilhoit and the person mentioned in her November 14 letter to the company, died January 23, 1932, and Mrs. Wilhoit died April 12, 1951, each leaving a last will and testament. The will of the former by a general clause devised all his property to Thomas J. Owens, a defendant, and was admitted to probate in Marion County, Indiana. The will of Mrs. Wilhoit was admitted to probate in Edgar County, Illinois, and contained the following provision:

> I now have the sum of Four Thousand Seven Hundred Forty Nine Dollars ($4,749.00), or approximately that amount, which is the proceeds of an insurance policy on the life of my deceased husband, Oscar Wilhoit, on deposit with the insurance company, the Peoples Life Insurance Company of Frankfort, Indiana. This I give and bequeath to Robert Wilhoit, now of Seattle, Washington, who is another son of my said stepson, the same to be his property absolutely. . . .

The fund in controversy, deposited with the company by Mrs. Wilhoit on November 17, 1930, remained with the company continuously until the date of her death, April 12, 1951. The company refused to recognize the claim to the fund made by Robert Wilhoit, the legatee named in the will of Mrs. Wilhoit and the plaintiff in the instant action. . . . [The defendant] Thomas J. Owens claimed the fund as the legatee under the will of Robert G. Owens. . . . The District Court, on March 11, 1954, without opinion sustained the motion of the plaintiff for summary

---

specific property. A debt involves merely a personal obligation to pay a sum of money. One could argue that in this case a debt was created. The parties may not have intended for the company to segregate $4,749 from its general assets and keep it as separate trust property; they probably intended the company to mix the money with its general assets. On the other hand, one could argue that the company *should* have set aside the funds in a trust, a breach for which they could be liable. Supporting the first interpretation of a debt is that the company was required to pay interest at a fixed rate of 3 1/2 percent, not all the income it earned on $4,749. This suggests that the parties intended the company to have the use of the money for its own purposes and to be under a personal liability to repay the sum to Mrs. Wilhoit. Thus the company is probably best viewed as a debtor, not a trustee. See the discussion of differences between a debt and a trust at page 511. — Eds.

judgment. . . . Thereupon, judgment was entered in favor of the plaintiff in the sum of $4,749.00, together with interest and costs. . . .

Defendants . . . advance two theories in support of their argument for reversal, both of which are firmly grounded upon the premise that the agreement of November 17, 1930, between Mrs. Wilhoit and the company, was an insurance contract or a contract supplemental thereto. Thus premised, they argue (1) that the rights of the parties must be determined by the law of insurance and not by the statute of wills, and (2) that Mrs. Wilhoit as a primary beneficiary named Robert G. Owens as the successor beneficiary irrevocably, without right to revoke or change and without a "pre-decease of beneficiary" provision, and that as a result the rights of such successor beneficiary upon his death prior to the death of the primary beneficiary did not lapse but passed on to the heirs and assigns of such successor beneficiary.

On the other hand, plaintiff argues, in support of the judgment, that the disposition of the fund is not controlled by the law of insurance because the agreement between Mrs. Wilhoit and the company was not an insurance contract or a supplement thereto but was nothing more than a contract of deposit, and that the provision in the agreement by which Robert G. Owens was to take the funds in the event of her death was an invalid testamentary disposition. Further, it is argued that in any event any interest acquired by Robert G. Owens was extinguished upon his death, which occurred prior to that of Mrs. Wilhoit.

Defendants cite many cases from numerous jurisdictions which have held under a variety of circumstances that the proceeds of a life insurance policy are to be disposed of in accordance with its provisions, and that a beneficiary, if authorized by the policy, may designate a successor beneficiary to take on the death of the primary beneficiary. . . .

Other cases are cited, some from Indiana, to the effect that the beneficiary designated in a life insurance policy acquires a vested interest therein. However, these cases as well as those cited above are based upon the premise that the agreement under discussion was either an insurance contract or a supplemental agreement characterized as such because a successor beneficiary had been designated by the primary beneficiary under authority contained in the policy.

Obviously, defendants' contention is without merit and the cases cited in support thereof are without application unless we accept the premise upon which the contention is made, that is, that the agreement between Mrs. Wilhoit and the company was an insurance contract or an agreement supplemental thereto. While there may be room for differences of opinion, we have reached the conclusion that the premise is not sound, that the arrangement between the parties was the result of a separate and independent agreement, unrelated to the terms of the policy. . . .

The "investment" provision was an offer by the company by which Mrs. Wilhoit, on maturity of the policy, could have left the proceeds with the company on the terms and conditions therein stated. It is plain, however, that she did not take advantage of this offer. Instead, she accepted the proceeds, surrendered the policy and receipted the company in full "for all claims under the within policy," and presumably the proceeds were paid to her at that time. At any rate, it was not until twenty-three days later that she, by letter, made her own proposal to the company, which differed materially from that contained in the policy. The company proposed to pay interest annually in advance on the amount left on deposit, at a rate of interest not less than 3%. Her proposal provided for interest at the rate of

3 1/2%, compounded annually, with a right to withdraw interest at the end of any six-month period. The company proposal provided that Mrs. Wilhoit could withdraw the deposit only at the end of any interest year, it made no provision for the withdrawal of any amount less than the total on deposit, while the offer of Mrs. Wilhoit provided for the right to withdraw, on demand, any amount or part thereof (not less than $100). Undoubtedly the company was obligated, upon request by Mrs. Wilhoit, to comply with the terms of the investment provision and, upon refusal, could have been forced by her to do so. On the other hand, it was under no obligation to accept the proposal made by her and, upon its refusal, she would have been without remedy.

. . . [We have] concluded that the agreement between Mrs. Wilhoit and the company was neither an insurance contract nor an agreement supplemental thereto. . . . Mrs. Wilhoit deposited her money with the company, which obligated itself to pay interest and return the principal to her on demand. Only "in the event of her death" was the deposit, if it still remained, to Robert G. Owens. If Mrs. Wilhoit had deposited her money with a bank rather than with the insurance company under the same form of agreement, we think it would have constituted an ineffectual disposition because of failure to comply with the Indiana statute of wills.

In conclusion, we think it not immaterial to take into consideration what appears to have been the intention of the parties. . . . As already shown, Robert G. Owens, through whom defendants claim, died in 1932, and in his will made no mention of the funds in controversy. . . . On the other hand, Mrs. Wilhoit in her will specifically devised the fund in controversy to plaintiff, Robert Wilhoit. It thus appears plain that Mrs. Wilhoit did not intend that the fund go to the successors of Robert G. Owens but that after his death she thought she had a right to dispose of the fund as she saw fit, as is evidenced by the specific bequest contained in her will. We recognize that the intention of the parties or the belief which they entertained relative to the fund is not controlling, but under the circumstances presented, we think it is entitled to some consideration.

The judgment of the District Court is affirmed.

NOTE

The court in *Wilhoit* struck down a payable-on-death (P.O.D.) designation in a contract of deposit because it was a testamentary act not executed with the formalities required by the Wills Act. The *Wilhoit* case applies the traditional rule, still followed in a few states, that P.O.D. designations in many contracts other than life insurance are invalid. The materials that follow concern the reform of this traditional rule by courts and legislatures.

Estate of Hillowitz
Court of Appeals of New York, 1968
22 N.Y.2d 107, 238 N.E.2d 723, 291 N.Y.S.2d 325

FULD, C.J. This appeal stems from a discovery proceeding brought in the Surrogate's Court by the executors of the estate of Abraham Hillowitz against his widow, the appellant herein. The husband had been a partner in an "investment club" and, after his death, the club, pursuant to a provision of the partnership agreement, paid the widow the sum of $2,800, representing his interest in the partnership. "In the event of the death of any partner," the agreement recited, "his share will be transferred to his wife, with no termination of the partnership." The executors contend in their petition that the above provision was an invalid attempt to make a testamentary disposition of property and that the proceeds should pass under the decedent's will as an asset of his estate. The widow maintains that it was a valid and enforceable contract. Although the Surrogate agreed with her, the Appellate Division held that the agreement was invalid as "an attempted testamentary disposition" (264 N.Y.S.2d 868 (A.D. 1965)).

A partnership agreement which provides that, upon the death of one partner, his interest shall pass to the surviving partner or partners, resting as it does in contract, is unquestionably valid and may not be defeated by labeling it a testamentary disposition. . . . We are unable to perceive a difference in principle between an agreement of this character and one, such as that before us, providing for a deceased partner's widow, rather than a surviving partner, to succeed to the decedent's interest in the partnership. . . .

These partnership undertakings are, in effect, nothing more or less than third-party beneficiary contracts, performable at death. Like many similar instruments, contractual in nature, which provide for the disposition of property after death, they need not conform to the requirements of the statute of wills. . . . Examples of such instruments include (1) a contract to make a will . . . ; (2) an inter vivos trust in which the settlor reserves a life estate . . . ; and (3) an insurance policy. . . .

In short, members of a partnership may provide, without fear of running afoul of our statute of wills, that, upon the death of a partner, his widow shall be entitled to his interest in the firm. This type of third-party beneficiary contract is not invalid as an attempted testamentary disposition.

The executors may derive little satisfaction from McCarthy v. Pieret (24 N.E.2d 102 (N.Y. 1939)),[12] upon which they heavily rely. In the first place, it is our considered judgment that the decision should be limited to its facts. And, in the second place, the case is clearly distinguishable from the one now before us in that the court expressly noted that the "facts . . . indicate a mere intention on the part of the mortgagee to make a testamentary disposition of the property and not an intention to convey an immediate interest" and, in addition, that the named beneficiaries "knew nothing of the provisions of the extension agreement" (24 N.E.2d at 104).

The order of the Appellate Division should be reversed, with costs in this court and in the Appellate Division, and the order of the Surrogate's Court reinstated.

QUESTIONS AND NOTE

1.   In *Hillowitz*, the court analogized a partnership agreement under which a deceased partner's interest passes to the surviving partners with one in which

---

12. In McCarthy v. Pieret, a mortgage provided that if any installments remained unpaid at the mortgagee's death they should be paid to *A*. The provision was held to be testamentary and void. — Eds.

a deceased partner's interest passes to his or her surviving spouse. Yet in the first arrangement the surviving partners take pursuant to a bargained-for exchange, whereas in the second arrangement the spouse takes as the donee of a gratuitous transfer. Is this relevant? Are there any better rationales that the court might have used?

2.   A more recent nonprobate transfer involving partnership interests, which is driven by tax considerations, involves what is known as a *family limited partnership* (FLP). In an FLP, the decedent transfers assets (usually the majority of his assets) to the partnership in exchange for a limited partnership interest. The decedent's family likewise transfers assets (usually minimal assets, however) to the partnership in exchange for limited partnership interests. The general partner is a corporation owned by the decedent and his family. The reason for creating an FLP is that, when the decedent's limited partnership interests pass to his family, the value of those interests are discounted for estate tax purposes because of their lack of control rights and nonmarketability. We discuss the tax ramifications of FLPs at page 886.

The Uniform Probate Code in 1969 authorized P.O.D. designations in all contracts, and all but a few states have followed suit. The current P.O.D. provision in the Code, rewritten in 1989, follows.

Uniform Probate Code (1990)

§6-101.   Nonprobate Transfers on Death

(a) A provision for a nonprobate transfer on death in an insurance policy, contract of employment, bond, mortgage, promissory note, certificated or uncertificated security, account agreement, custodial agreement, deposit agreement, compensation plan, pension plan, individual retirement plan, employee benefit plan, trust, conveyance, deed of gift, marital property agreement, or other written instrument of a similar nature is nontestamentary. This subsection includes a written provision that:

(1) money or other benefits due to, controlled by, or owned by a decedent before death must be paid after the decedent's death to a person whom the decedent designates either in the instrument or in a separate writing, including a will, executed either before or at the same time as the instrument, or later;

(2) money due or to become due under the instrument ceases to be payable in the event of death of the promisee or the promisor before payment or demand; or

(3) any property controlled by or owned by the decedent before death which is the subject of the instrument passes to a person the decedent designates either in the instrument or in a separate writing, including a will, executed either before or at the same time as the instrument, or later.

(b) This section does not limit rights of creditors under other laws of this State.

NOTE AND QUESTIONS

1.   Return to the *Wilhoit* case. Why did the court in *Wilhoit* try to put the trans-action into a legal pigeonhole—trust, will, insurance, or contract of deposit—when the decedent was not thinking in legal categories? Why did the court choose a legal category that invalidates the transaction, rather than one that would have carried out Mrs. Wilhoit's intent at the time the transaction occurred?

2.   How would the *Wilhoit* case be decided in a jurisdiction that has enacted UPC §6-101? Should the court imply a requirement that Robert Owens survive Mrs. Wilhoit in order to take? Observe that UPC §6-101 is silent on whether a death beneficiary named in a contract must survive the contracting benefactor.

Under the law of wills, a devisee is required to survive the testator in order to take; if the devisee predeceases, the gift "lapses." Should the rule applied to wills—that the beneficiary must survive the testator in order to take—be applied to all will substitutes, including contracts? Although UPC §6-101 does not require survivorship by P.O.D. beneficiaries of contracts, when the beneficiary is a close relative of the benefactor, the UPC includes an antilapse provision for P.O.D. designations, which substitutes the issue of the named beneficiary who does not survive the benefactor. See UPC §2-706 (1990), which parallels the UPC antilapse provision for wills (§2-603, discussed on pages 396-397). In the *Wilhoit* case, the P.O.D. beneficiary was Robert Owens, the decedent's brother. If he was survived by issue—if Thomas J. Owens was his descendant, as seems likely—then Robert Owens's issue would be substituted for Robert as beneficiaries under the contract by UPC §2-706. They would be entitled to the money on deposit. Is this what Mrs. Wilhoit intended?

3.   If Robert Owens had survived and Mrs. Wilhoit had not changed her mind about giving him the fund, would the court still have held the attempted gift testamentary and void? Is there a legal approach other than the one the court took that would accord with the testator's intent regardless of whether Robert Owens had survived? Perhaps Mrs. Wilhoit should have had the power to change a P.O.D. beneficiary by will, an issue raised in the next case.

COOK v. EQUITABLE LIFE ASSURANCE SOCIETY, 428 N.E.2d 110 (Ind. App. 1981): Douglas Cook purchased a whole life insurance policy, naming his wife at the time, Doris Cook, as the beneficiary. Douglas and Doris divorced. The divorce decree made no mention of the life insurance policy, and Douglas failed to change the beneficiary designation after the divorce. Nine months later, on Christmas Eve, Douglas married Margaret, with whom he later had a son Daniel. Eleven years later Douglas made a holographic "Last Will & Testimint" leaving "all my Worldly posessions" to Margaret and Daniel, including specifically his life insurance policy. Douglas died three years later. Because the court assumed that Douglas's designation of Doris as the beneficiary of his life insurance policy was not revoked by their subsequent divorce, the issue was whether Douglas could change the beneficiary designation by will. The policy terms required a written notice to the company to change the beneficiary.

Clearly it is in the interest of insurance companies to require and to follow certain specified procedures in the change of beneficiaries of its policies so that they may pay over benefits to persons properly entitled to them without subjection to claims by others of whose rights they had no notice or knowledge. Certainly it is also in the interest of beneficiaries themselves to be entitled to prompt payment of benefits by insurance companies which do not withhold payment until the will has been probated in the fear of later litigation which might result from having paid the wrong party. . . .

[In this case there has been no] showing that the insured had done all within his powers or all that reasonably could have been expected of him to comply with the policy provisions respecting a change of beneficiary, but that through no fault of his own he was unable to achieve his goal. . . . There is no indication that Douglas took any action in the fourteen years between his divorce from Doris and his death, other than the making of the will, to change the beneficiary of his life insurance policy from Doris to Margaret and Daniel. Surely, if Douglas had wanted to change the beneficiary he had ample time and opportunity to comply with the policy requirements. . . .

We may be sympathetic to the cause of the decedent's widow and son, and it might seem that a departure from the general rule in an attempt to do equity under these facts would be noble. Nevertheless, such a course is fraught with the dangers of eroding a solidly paved pathway of the law and leaving in its stead only a gaping hole of uncertainty. Public policy requires that the insurer, insured, and beneficiary alike should be able to rely on the certainty that policy provisions pertaining to the naming and changing of beneficiaries will control except in extreme situations. We, therefore, invoke a maxim equally as venerable as the one upon which appellants rely in the determination of this cause: Equity aids the vigilant, not those who slumber on their rights.

NOTES AND QUESTIONS

1. The *Cook* case is followed in a large majority of states. See McCarthy v. Kapcar, 704 N.E.2d 557 (N.Y. 1998).

2. In *Cook*, we see once again the problem of a nonprobate transfer to an ex-spouse. In most states, the statute that revokes a will provision for a divorced spouse does not apply to the designation of the divorced spouse as a life insurance beneficiary. UPC §2-804 (1990), excerpted at page 269, provides that divorce revokes the designation of the divorced spouse as beneficiary of an insurance policy or pension plan or other P.O.D. contract, though its application to insurance beneficiary designations made before the effective date of the statute is questionable. Compare Hill v. Dewitt, 54 P.3d 849 (Colo. 2002) (statute based on §2-804 revokes life insurance beneficiary designation made before act was passed), with Whirlpool Corp. v. Ritter, 929 F.2d 1318 (8th Cir. 1991) (retroactive application of statute held to be unconstitutional). In addition, the application of statutes such as UPC §2-804 to federally regulated pension accounts is preempted by federal law. See Egelhoff v. Egelhoff, page 336. See also Susan N. Gary, Applying Revocation-on-Divorce Statutes to Will Substitutes, 18 Quinnipiac Prob. L.J. 83 (2004).

Regardless of the state of the statutory law, good matrimonial practice normally includes attending to this problem explicitly in the divorce agreement as well as rewriting the will and changing the nonprobate beneficiary designations.

3. *A superwill?* In view of the proliferation of nonprobate transfers, would it be a good idea to permit a *superwill*? A superwill would annul the beneficiaries named in various nonprobate instruments and name a new beneficiary. Can you think of situations where a superwill would be useful? What are the drawbacks? There is precedent for the superwill concept. A power to revoke an inter vivos trust created

by the decedent can be exercised by will, if the trust so provides. And a power of appointment given the decedent over a trust created by another person can be exercised by the will of the decedent. If the decedent can change the beneficiary of trust assets by will, why not beneficiaries of contracts? See Cynthia J. Artura, Superwill to the Rescue? How Washington's Statute Falls Short of Being a Hero in the Field of Trust and Probate Law, 74 Wash. L. Rev. 799 (1999); Roberta R. Kwall & Anthony J. Aiello, The Superwill Debate: Opening the Pandora's Box?, 62 Temp. L. Rev. 277 (1989). See also Wash. Rev. Code §§11.11.003-11.11.901 (2004) (superwill statute).

2.   Pension Accounts

Federal law has fueled the payable-on-death revolution. First, the federal government has long permitted a death beneficiary to be put on U.S. savings and war bonds. Second, beginning in the early 1960s, Congress has given favorable tax treatment to various types of savings plans for retirement. Federal law permits death beneficiaries to be put on these plans, including pension and profit-sharing plans, Keogh plans, 401(k) plans, and individual retirement accounts (IRAs). Let us examine the pension account phenomenon more closely. By 2002, pension funds held roughly $10 trillion dollars, nearly equal to the Gross Domestic Product of all goods and services in the United States.

John H. Langbein, The Twentieth-Century Revolution in Family Wealth Transmission
86 Mich. L. Rev. 722, 739-746 (1988)

Pension funds are [an] artifact of the new forms of wealth that arose in consequence of the breakup of older, family-centered modes of production. Neither on the prairie nor in the cities of Abraham Lincoln's day had anybody ever heard of a pension fund. Your life expectancy was such that you were unlikely to need much in the way of retirement income. If you did chance to outlive your period of productive labor, you were in general cared for within the family.

Not only is the need for a retirement income stream relatively recent, but so too is the mode of wealth that now supplies it. Pension funds are composed almost entirely of financial assets — the instruments of financial intermediation — that distinctively modern form of property that was still of peripheral importance in the last century. . . .

A.   THE ENHANCEMENT OF LIFE EXPECTANCY

The way to begin thinking about the pension revolution is to grasp the magnitude of the underlying demographic phenomena that brought it about. Life expectancy a hundred years ago was about forty-five years. Today, it is seventy-five years and climbing. . . .

Not only have the demographics altered so that the elders are routinely surviving for long intervals beyond their years of employment, but in consequence of the transformation in the nature of wealth, their property has taken on a radically altered character. That family farm or family firm that was the source of intrafamilial support in former times has become ever more exceptional. Most parental wealth (apart from the parents' own human capital) now takes the form of financial assets, which embody claims upon those large-scale enterprises that have replaced family enterprise.

B. PENSION WEALTH

In propertied families, today's elderly no longer expect much financial support from their children. The shared patrimony in farm or firm that underlay that reverse transfer system in olden times has now largely vanished. Instead, people of means are expected to foresee the need for retirement income while they are still in the workforce, and to conduct a program of saving for their retirement. Typically, these people have already undertaken one great cycle of saving and dissaving in their lives — that program by which they effected the investment in human capital for their children. Just as that former program of saving was oriented toward a distinctively modern form of wealth, human capital, so this second program centers on the other characteristic form of twentieth-century wealth, financial assets.

A priori, we might expect that individuals would be left to save for retirement without government guidance, much as they are left alone to save and spend for other purposes, but that has not been the case. Instead, the federal government has intervened by creating irresistible tax incentives to encourage people to conduct much or most of their retirement saving in a special mode, the tax-qualified pension plan.

There are three crucial advantages to conducting retirement saving through a tax-qualified pension plan. First, most contributions to the plan are tax-deferred. When my employer contributes to a qualified pension or profit-sharing plan on my behalf, or when I contribute to a defined contribution plan such as a 401(k) or, in the case of academic personnel, a 403(b), I am saving with pretax dollars. If I am in the 25-percent bracket, the Treasury is contributing to my pension savings plan 25 cents in foregone taxation for my 75 cents in foregone consumption. The second great tax advantage is that the earnings on qualified plan investments accrue and compound on a tax-deferred basis. It is not until the employee retires and begins to receive distributions of his pension savings that he pays income tax on the sums distributed. The third major advantage associated with pension taxation is that, because most retirees have lower taxable income in their retirement years than in their peak earning years, they find that distributions from pension accounts are usually taxed at lower marginal rates. As the progressivity of the income tax has abated in recent years, however, this attribute of the system has become less significant.

As a matter of tax policy, it is open to serious question whether Congress should be granting the level of tax subsidy for pension saving that it now does, but that is a topic for another day. The present point is that the tax attractions of conducting retirement saving through the medium of a tax-qualified pension plan are simply overwhelming. These advantages explain why employers incur the regulatory costs incident to sponsoring these plans; and why employees, especially those in higher tax brackets, prefer to take compensation in the form of pension saving rather than cash wages. The private pension system — this [in 2002 ten]-trillion-dollar savings scheme — is tax driven.

C. ANNUITIZATION ELIMINATES SUCCESSION

From the standpoint of our interest in the patterns of family wealth transmission, what is especially important about the pension system is that it has been deliberately designed to promote lifetime exhaustion of the accumulated capital. The same body of federal law that encourages pension saving also tries to ensure that pension wealth will be consumed over the lives of the worker and his spouse. I do not mean to say that the federal policy in favor of lifetime consumption of retirement savings cannot be defeated for particular clients using appropriately designed plans; indeed, that is one of the major avenues of tax and estate planning for the carriage trade that has arisen with the pension system. My point is simply that, in the main, the federal policy achieves its goal, and only a negligible fraction of pension wealth finds its way into intergenerational transfer.

The mechanism by which pension wealth is consumed is annuitization. Just as life insurance is insurance against dying too soon, annuitization insures against living too long. Annuitization allows people to consume their capital safely, that is, without fear of running out of capital while still alive. Annuitization requires a large pool of lives, which is achieved by various methods of aggregating the pension savings of many workers. Sometimes the employer runs the pool, sometimes an intermediary such as an insurance company or (for multiemployer plans) a labor union. Annuitization requires assets that can be liquidated predictably as distribution requires. That is a trait characteristic of financial assets. Annuitization is wonderfully effective in allowing a person to consume capital without fear of outliving his capital, but the corollary is also manifest: Accounts that have been annuitized disappear on the deaths of the annuitants. Not so much as a farthing remains for the heirs.

NOTE AND PROBLEMS

1. *Annuities.* In its pure form, an annuity is a payment every year for the rest of the beneficiary's life. Its main purpose is to shift the financial risk of living too long (we should all have such problems!) to a pension fund or insurance company. By buying into a pool with other people worried about the same risk, those who die younger pay those who die older. An annuity thus reflects the opposite bet from that of life insurance: with an annuity, if you die sooner than expected, you lose; with life insurance, if you die sooner, you win (albeit a Pyrrhic victory[13]).

Since Professor Langbein's article appeared in 1988, the prominence of annuitization as the mode of payout in pension plans has diminished in part because there has been a shift from defined benefit plans to defined contribution plans. In a *defined benefit plan*, the employer promises to pay an annuity on retirement — for example, 40 percent of the employee's top three years of income. In a *defined contribution plan*, usually both the employee and the employer make contributions to a specific pension account for the employee. Because the employee and her family are entitled to all the accumulation in this account, these plans often lead to lump-sum payouts on the death of the worker and her spouse. In such a case the

---

13. The expression *Pyrrhic victory* is allusion to King Pyrrhus of Epirus. After defeating the Romans in a bloody battle at Asculum in 279 B.C.E., King Pyrrhus is reported to have said: "Another such victory and we are lost."

defined contribution plan operates (in effect) as a tax-advantaged savings account that concludes with a nonprobate transfer. Thanks to the increasing popularity of defined contribution plans, "It's becoming a lump-sum world." Alicia Munnell et al., The Impact of Defined Contribution Plans on Bequests 268, *in* Death and Dollars: The Role of Gifts and Bequests in America (Alicia H. Munnell & Annika Sunden, eds., 2003). See also Edward A. Zelinsky, The Defined Contribution Paradigm, 114 Yale L.J. 451 (2004).

2. In 2000, *O*, a 65-year-old man with a life expectancy of 15 years, buys an annuity of $50,000 per year for a one-time payment $600,000. If *O* lives for another 15 years, then at age 80 his new life expectancy would be an additional 7 years. Having exceeded his life expectancy when he bought the annuity, is *O* still entitled to receive $50,000 a year for the rest of his life?

Now suppose instead that *O* dies at age 66, after receiving only one year of annuity payments. Would *O*'s heirs or devisees receive anything? Under a pure annuity, the answer is No. For this reason, annuitants (such as *O*) often buy an annuity with slightly reduced payments in return for a promise from the insurance company to make at least 5 or 10 years of payments to *O* or his heirs or devisees. In a similar vein, a married annuitant might buy a *joint and survivor annuity* that makes annuity payments until *O* and his wife both die.

Pension plans have long been subject to a complex overlay of federal regulation, most significantly the Employee Retirement Income Security Act of 1974 (ERISA). The question thus arises, does the federal regulation of pension plans preempt the applicability to them of the state subsidiary law of wills?

Egelhoff v. Egelhoff
Supreme Court of the United States, 2001
532 U.S. 141, 121 S. Ct. 1322, 149 L. Ed. 2d 264

THOMAS, J.   A Washington statute provides that the designation of a spouse as the beneficiary of a nonprobate asset is revoked automatically upon divorce. We are asked to decide whether the Employee Retirement Income Security Act of 1974 (ERISA), 29 U.S.C. §1001 et seq., pre-empts that statute to the extent it applies to ERISA plans. We hold that it does.

I

Petitioner Donna Rae Egelhoff was married to David A. Egelhoff. Mr. Egelhoff was employed by the Boeing Company, which provided him with a life insurance policy and a pension plan. Both plans were governed by ERISA, and Mr. Egelhoff designated his wife as the beneficiary under both. In April 1994, the Egelhoffs divorced. Just over two months later, Mr. Egelhoff died intestate following an automobile accident. At that time, Mrs. Egelhoff remained the listed beneficiary under both the life insurance policy and the pension plan. The life insurance proceeds, totaling $46,000, were paid to her.

Respondents Samantha and David Egelhoff, Mr. Egelhoff's children by a previous marriage, are his statutory heirs under state law. They sued petitioner in

Washington state court to recover the life insurance proceeds. Respondents relied on a Washington statute that provides:

> If a marriage is dissolved or invalidated, a provision made prior to that event that relates to the payment or transfer at death of the decedent's interest in a nonprobate asset in favor of or granting an interest or power to the decedent's former spouse is revoked. A provision affected by this section must be interpreted, and the nonprobate asset affected passes, as if the former spouse failed to survive the decedent, having died at the time of entry of the decree of dissolution or declaration of invalidity. Wash. Rev. Code §11.07.010(2)(a) (1994).

That statute applies to "all nonprobate assets, wherever situated, held at the time of entry by a superior court of this state of a decree of dissolution of marriage or a declaration of invalidity." §11.07.010(1). It defines "nonprobate asset" to include "a life insurance policy, employee benefit plan, annuity or similar contract, or individual retirement account." §11.07.010(5)(a).

Respondents argued that they were entitled to the life insurance proceeds because the Washington statute disqualified Mrs. Egelhoff as a beneficiary, and in the absence of a qualified named beneficiary, the proceeds would pass to them as Mr. Egelhoff's heirs. In a separate action, respondents also sued to recover the pension plan benefits. Respondents again argued that the Washington statute disqualified Mrs. Egelhoff as a beneficiary and they were thus entitled to the benefits under the plan. . . .

Courts have disagreed about whether statutes like that of Washington are pre-empted by ERISA. To resolve the conflict, we granted certiorari.

II

Petitioner argues that the Washington statute falls within the terms of ERISA's express pre-emption provision and that it is pre-empted by ERISA under traditional principles of conflict pre-emption. Because we conclude that the statute is expressly pre-empted by ERISA, we address only the first argument.

ERISA's pre-emption section, 29 U.S.C. §1144(a), states that ERISA "shall supersede any and all State laws insofar as they may now or hereafter relate to any employee benefit plan" covered by ERISA. We have observed repeatedly that this broadly worded provision is "clearly expansive." New York State Conference of Blue Cross & Blue Shield Plans v. Travelers Ins. Co., 514 U.S. 645, 655 (1995). But at the same time, we have recognized that the term "relate to" cannot be taken "to extend to the furthest stretch of its indeterminacy," or else "for all practical purposes pre-emption would never run its course." Ibid.

We have held that a state law relates to an ERISA plan "if it has a connection with or reference to such a plan." Shaw v. Delta Air Lines, Inc., 463 U.S. 85, 97 (1983). Petitioner focuses on the "connection with" part of this inquiry. Acknowledging that "connection with" is scarcely more restrictive than "relate to," we have cautioned against an "uncritical literalism" that would make preemption turn on "infinite connections." *Travelers*, supra, at 656. Instead, "to determine whether a state law has the forbidden connection, we look both to 'the objectives of the ERISA statute as a guide to the scope of the state law that Congress understood would survive,' as well as to the nature of the effect of the state law on ERISA plans." California Div. of Labor Standards Enforcement v. Dillingham Constr., N.A., Inc., 519 U.S. 316, 325 (1997), quoting *Travelers*, supra, at 656.

Applying this framework, petitioner argues that the Washington statute has an impermissible connection with ERISA plans. We agree. The statute binds ERISA plan administrators to a particular choice of rules for determining beneficiary status. The administrators must pay benefits to the beneficiaries chosen by state law, rather than to those identified in the plan documents. The statute thus implicates an area of core ERISA concern. In particular, it runs counter to ERISA's commands that a plan shall "specify the basis on which payments are made to and from the plan," §1102(b)(4), and that the fiduciary shall administer the plan "in accordance with the documents and instruments governing the plan," §1104(a)(1)(D), making payments to a "beneficiary" who is "designated by a participant, or by the terms of [the] plan." §1002(8). In other words, unlike generally applicable laws regulating "areas where ERISA has nothing to say," *Dillingham*, 519 U.S. at 330, which we have upheld notwithstanding their incidental effect on ERISA plans, this statute governs the payment of benefits, a central matter of plan administration.

The Washington statute also has a prohibited connection with ERISA plans because it interferes with nationally uniform plan administration. One of the principal goals of ERISA is to enable employers "to establish a uniform administrative scheme, which provides a set of standard procedures to guide processing of claims and disbursement of benefits." Fort Halifax Packing Co. v. Coyne, 482 U.S. 1, 9 (1987). Uniformity is impossible, however, if plans are subject to different legal obligations in different States.

The Washington statute at issue here poses precisely that threat. Plan administrators cannot make payments simply by identifying the beneficiary specified by the plan documents. Instead they must familiarize themselves with state statutes so that they can determine whether the named beneficiary's status has been "revoked" by operation of law. And in this context the burden is exacerbated by the choice-of-law problems that may confront an administrator when the employer is located in one State, the plan participant lives in another, and the participant's former spouse lives in a third. In such a situation, administrators might find that plan payments are subject to conflicting legal obligations.

To be sure, the Washington statute protects administrators from liability for making payments to the named beneficiary unless they have "actual knowledge of the dissolution or other invalidation of marriage," Wash. Rev. Code §11.07.010(3)(a) (1994), and it permits administrators to refuse to make payments until any dispute among putative beneficiaries is resolved, §11.07.010(3)(b). But if administrators do pay benefits, they will face the risk that a court might later find that they had "actual knowledge" of a divorce. If they instead decide to await the results of litigation before paying benefits, they will simply transfer to the beneficiaries the costs of delay and uncertainty. Requiring ERISA administrators to master the relevant laws of 50 States and to contend with litigation would undermine the congressional goal of "minimizing the administrative and financial burdens" on plan administrators — burdens ultimately borne by the beneficiaries. Ingersoll-Rand Co. v. McClendon, 498 U.S. 133, 142 (1990).

We recognize that all state laws create some potential for a lack of uniformity. But differing state regulations affecting an ERISA plan's "system for processing claims and paying benefits" impose "precisely the burden that ERISA pre-emption was intended to avoid." *Fort Halifax*, supra, at 10. And as we have noted, the statute at issue here directly conflicts with ERISA's requirements that plans be administered, and benefits be paid, in accordance with plan documents. We conclude that the Washington statute has a "connection with" ERISA plans and is therefore pre-empted.

III

Respondents suggest several reasons why ordinary ERISA pre-emption analysis should not apply here. . . .

[R]espondents emphasize that the Washington statute involves both family law and probate law, areas of traditional state regulation. There is indeed a presumption against pre-emption in areas of traditional state regulation such as family law. See, e.g., Hisquierdo v. Hisquierdo, 439 U.S. 572, 581 (1979). But that presumption can be overcome where, as here, Congress has made clear its desire for pre-emption. Accordingly, we have not hesitated to find state family law pre-empted when it conflicts with ERISA or relates to ERISA plans. See, e.g., Boggs v. Boggs, 520 U.S. 833 (1997) (holding that ERISA pre-empts a state community property law permitting the testamentary transfer of an interest in a spouse's pension plan benefits).

Finally, respondents argue that if ERISA pre-empts this statute, then it also must pre-empt the various state statutes providing that a murdering heir is not entitled to receive property as a result of the killing. See, e.g., Cal. Prob. Code Ann. §§250-259 (West 1991 and Supp. 2000); 755 Ill. Comp. Stat., ch. 755, §5/2-6 (1999). In the ERISA context, these "slayer" statutes could revoke the beneficiary status of someone who murdered a plan participant. Those statutes are not before us, so we do not decide the issue. We note, however, that the principle underlying the statutes — which have been adopted by nearly every State — is well established in the law and has a long historical pedigree predating ERISA. See, e.g., Riggs v. Palmer, 22 N.E. 188 (N.Y. 1889). And because the statutes are more or less uniform nationwide, their interference with the aims of ERISA is at least debatable. . . .

The judgment of the Supreme Court of Washington is reversed, and the case is remanded for further proceedings not inconsistent with this opinion.

It is so ordered.

BREYER, J., dissenting.   . . . The Court has previously made clear that the fact that state law "imposes some burden on the administration of ERISA plans" does not necessarily require pre-emption. De Buono v. NYSA-ILA Medical and Clinical Services Fund, 520 U.S. 806, 815 (1997). Precisely, what is it about this statute's requirement that distinguishes it from the "myriad state laws" that impose some kind of burden on ERISA plans? Ibid.

Indeed, if one looks beyond administrative burden, one finds that Washington's statute poses no obstacle, but furthers ERISA's ultimate objective — developing a fair system for protecting employee benefits. The Washington statute transfers an employee's pension assets at death to those individuals whom the worker would likely have wanted to receive them. As many jurisdictions have concluded, divorced workers more often prefer that a child, rather than a divorced spouse, receive those assets. Of course, an employee can secure this result by changing a beneficiary form; but doing so requires awareness, understanding, and time. That is why Washington and many other jurisdictions have created a statutory assumption that divorce works a revocation of a designation in favor of an ex-spouse. That assumption is embodied in the Uniform Probate Code; it is consistent with human experience; and those with expertise in the matter have concluded that it "more often" serves the cause of "justice." Langbein, The Nonprobate Revolution and the Future of the Law of Succession, 97 Harv. L. Rev. 1108, 1135 (1984).

In forbidding Washington to apply that assumption here, the Court permits a divorced wife, who already acquired, during the divorce proceeding, her fair share of the couple's community property, to receive in addition the benefits that the divorce court awarded to her former husband. To be more specific, Donna Egelhoff already received a business, an IRA account, and stock; David received, among other things, 100% of his pension benefits. David did not change the beneficiary designation in the pension plan or life insurance plan during the 6-month period between his divorce and his death. As a result, Donna will now receive a windfall of approximately $80,000 at the expense of David's children. The State of Washington enacted a statute to prevent precisely this kind of unfair result. But the Court, relying on an inconsequential administrative burden, concludes that Congress required it.

Finally, the logic of the Court's decision does not stop at divorce revocation laws. The Washington statute is virtually indistinguishable from other traditional state-law rules, for example, rules using presumptions to transfer assets in the case of simultaneous deaths, and rules that prohibit a husband who kills a wife from receiving benefits as a result of the wrongful death. It is particularly difficult to believe that Congress wanted to pre-empt the latter kind of statute. But how do these statutes differ from the one before us? Slayer statutes — like this statute — "govern the payment of benefits, a central matter of plan administration." And contrary to the Court's suggestion, ante, at 9-10, slayer statutes vary from State to State in their details just like divorce revocation statutes. Indeed, the "slayer" conflict would seem more serious, not less serious, than the conflict before us, for few, if any, slayer statutes permit plans to opt out of the state property law rule. . . .

For these reasons, I disagree with the Court's conclusion. And, consequently, I dissent.

NOTES AND QUESTIONS

1. In Estate of Morgan, 32 Emp. Ben. Cas. (BNA) 2722 (Wash. App. 2004), the Washington Court of Appeals dealt with a possible conflict between the Colorado simultaneous death statute, which imposes a 120-hour period of survivorship on pension assets (see pages 72-73), and ERISA, which has no such limitation. In *Morgan*, Tom shot his brother Casey and Casey's wife, Karen. While on the phone with a 911 operator, Tom noticed that his brother was still alive and shot him again. "Tom informed the operator he had to shoot his brother 'once more in the head' because he was still breathing." Because Casey probably survived Karen by a few minutes, does Casey's family take Karen's pension plan or is a 120-hour survivorship rule applied? In distributing the pension assets to Karen's family, the court held that (1) ERISA did *not* preempt the state simultaneous death statute, and (2) in any event, the plan administrator had discretion under the plan instrument to construe survivorship as precluding nearly simultaneous death.

2. After *Egelhoff*, it will be difficult for a state to unify its law of wills and will substitutes, something that is endorsed by the 1990 Uniform Probate Code, by

Restatement (Third) of Property: Wills and Other Donative Transfers §7.2 (2003), and by commentators such as Professor Langbein in his article cited by Justice Breyer.

One approach to establishing parallel rules for wills and pensions would be to amend ERISA to allow the state subsidiary law of wills to apply to testamentary pension dispositions. Or ERISA could be amended to adopt a federal rule for the distribution of pension assets on divorce, simultaneous death, slaying by a beneficiary, and other such matters. Or plan administrators could add language to their pension plans to address these issues. Or courts could develop a federal common law consistent with sound policy on these issues. See T.P. Gallanis, Reform of Qualified Retirement Plans: ERISA and the Law of Succession, 65 Ohio St. L.J. 185 (2004), endorsing the assimilation of the UPC and Restatement rules on these matters into federal pension law.

Metropolitan Life Ins. Co. v. Johnson, 297 F.3d 558 (7th Cir. 2002), represents a creative use of the federal common law approach. After divorce, *H* tried to replace his ex-spouse as his beneficiary under his pension plan, but on the beneficiary change form *H* checked the box for the wrong plan. Illinois law would treat the beneficiary change as effective under the substantial compliance doctrine, but in view of *Egelhoff*, the court held that ERISA preempts Illinois law. The court then held that the beneficiary change was effective by adopting substantial compliance as a federal common law gloss on ERISA.

In Ahmed v. Ahmed, 817 N.E.2d 424 (Ohio App. 2004), the court applied similar reasoning to the question of whether a slayer may take under an ERISA-regulated insurance policy. The court held that, even though ERISA preempts the Ohio slayer statute, as a matter of federal common law a slayer may not take under an ERISA plan. However, the court did not treat the slayer as having predeceased the victim, which is the usual state law approach, including that of the Ohio statute, but instead directed that the insurance proceeds would fall into the victim's probate estate.

Applying federal common law, at least one court has even reached the opposite result than in *Egelhoff*. In Keen v. Weaver, 121 S.W.3d 721 (Tex. 2003), the court held that ERISA preempted a state law that revoked pension interests on divorce. However, the court held that under federal common law, when waiver and assignment of pension assets in a divorce decree are specific enough, the pension plan may not pay the ex-spouse named as the pension beneficiary. See also Susan N. Gary, Applying Revocation-on-Divorce Statutes to Will Substitutes, 18 Quinnipiac Prob. L.J. 83 (2004).

3. Multiple-Party Bank and Brokerage Accounts

Multiple-party bank and brokerage accounts include a joint and survivor account, a P.O.D. account, an agency account, and a savings account (Totten) trust. With a joint and survivor bank or brokerage account owned by "*A* and *B*, as joint tenants with right of survivorship," both *A* and *B* have the power to draw on the account and the survivor owns the balance of the account, which will not pass through probate.

Sometimes, however, something other than a true joint tenancy account is intended. *A*, a bank depositor, may open a joint account with *B*, intending that *B* is not to have the power to draw on the account during life but is entitled to the balance upon *A*'s death—a P.O.D. account disguised as a joint account. Or *A* might intend that *B* is to have power to draw on the account during *A*'s life but is not entitled to the balance at *A*'s death — an agency account disguised as a joint account.

Because banks and brokerage houses often give their customers a joint tenancy form regardless of the customer's particular intention, courts are left with the problem of discerning which type of account is intended. If an agency account is intended, or if a P.O.D. account is intended in a state that does not allow them, the survivor is not entitled to the proceeds in the account, which belong instead to the depositor's estate.

FRANKLIN v. ANNA NATIONAL BANK OF ANNA, 488 N.E.2d 1117 (Ill. App. 1986): Frank Whitehead died on December 22, 1980. Enola Franklin, as the executor of his estate, sued to acquire the funds of a joint account at the Anna National Bank that had been in the name of Whitehead and Cora Goddard. Goddard, the sister of Whitehead's deceased wife Muriel, had moved in with him in early 1978 in part because his eyesight was failing.

> On April 17, 1978, Mrs. Goddard and decedent went to the bank, according to Mrs. Goddard to have his money put in both their names so she could get money when they needed it, "and he wanted me to have this money if I outlived him."
>
> A bank employee prepared a signature card for savings account No. 3816 and Mrs. Goddard signed it. A copy of this card was in evidence at trial. The signatures of decedent and Mrs. Goddard appear on both sides of the card. It appears that Muriel Whitehead's signature was "whited out" and Mrs. Goddard's signature added. The front of the card states that one signature is required for withdrawals. The back of the card states that all funds deposited are owned by the signatories as joint tenants with right of survivorship.
>
> Mrs. Goddard testified that she did not deposit any of the money in savings account No. 3816. She made no withdrawals, though she once took decedent to the bank so he could make a withdrawal. . . . Asked whether she ever had the passbook for savings account No. 3816 in her possession, Mrs. Goddard answered, "Only while I was at Frank's. It was there."

Enola Franklin then replaced Goddard as Whitehead's primary caretaker, which led to Whitehead's efforts to change his account, and the court's holding for Franklin, the executor.

> Later in 1978, Mrs. Franklin began to care for decedent. In January 1979, decedent telephoned the bank, then sent Mrs. Franklin to the bank to deliver a letter to Mrs. Kedron Boyer, a bank employee. The handwritten letter, dated January 13, 1979, and signed by decedent, stated: "I Frank Whitehead wish by [sic] Bank accounts be changed to Enola Stevens joint intendency [sic]. Nobody go in my lock box but me." According to Mrs. Franklin, Mrs. Boyer told her to tell decedent he would have to specify what type of account he was referring to. Decedent gave Mrs. Franklin a second letter which Mrs. Franklin delivered to Mrs. Carol Williams at the bank (Mrs. Boyer was absent). This handwritten letter, dated January 13, 1979, stated: "I Frank Whitehead want Enola Stevens and me only go in my lock box. Account type Saving and Checking. In case I can't see she is to take care of my bill or sick." According to Mrs. Franklin, Mrs. Williams said she would take care of it and give the letter to Mrs. Boyer. Mrs. Franklin testified that she signed the savings passbook in the presence of decedent and Mrs. Boyer. Mrs. Franklin took her present last name on May 8, 1979.
>
> . . . According to Mr. Mowery [the bank president], the bank would not remove a signature from a signature card based on a letter; the most recent signature card

the bank had for savings account No. 3816 was signed by decedent and Mrs. Goddard. . . .

The trial court found that Mrs. Goddard was the sole owner of the funds in savings account No. 3816 by right of survivorship as surviving joint tenant, and that no part of the funds became part of decedent's estate.

Mrs. Franklin argues that decedent did not intend to make a gift of savings account No. 3816 to Mrs. Goddard.

The instrument creating a joint tenancy account presumably speaks the whole truth. In order to go behind the terms of the agreement, the one claiming adversely thereto has the burden of establishing by clear and convincing evidence that a gift was not intended. . . .

There appears no serious doubt that in January of 1979, just nine months after adding Mrs. Goddard's name to savings account No. 3816, decedent attempted to remove Mrs. Goddard's name and substitute Mrs. Franklin's. The second of decedent's handwritten letters to the bank in January of 1979 indicates decedent's concern that he might lose his sight and be unable to transact his own banking business. These facts show that decedent made Mrs. Goddard (and later Mrs. Franklin) a signatory for his own convenience, in case he could not get his money, and not with intent to effect a present gift. . . .

In the case at bar, decedent's attempts to change the account show his consistent view of the account as his own. The surrounding circumstances show decedent's concern for his health and his relatively brief use of Mrs. Goddard (and later Mrs. Franklin) to assure his access to his funds. The money in account No. 3816 should have been found to be the property of the estate.

NOTES AND PROBLEMS

1. Why did not the bank offer Frank Whitehead his choice of three accounts: a true joint tenancy account, an agency account, or a P.O.D. account? If banks did this, much of the litigation over the depositor's intention would disappear.

A P.O.D. account is invalid in a few states for reasons given in the *Wilhoit* case, page 325. Professor Schoenblum lists 45 states and the District of Columbia as permitting P.O.D. bank accounts. Jeffrey A. Schoenblum, 2004 Multistate Guide to Estate Planning at Table 5.01.

To eliminate the extensive litigation over the depositor's intent in creating a joint bank account, several courts have held that a joint bank account *conclusively* establishes a right of survivorship; evidence to the contrary is not admissible. See, e.g., Robinson v. Delfino, 710 A.2d 154 (R.I. 1998).

2. *The savings account trust* (or *Totten trust*). One type of multiple-party bank account that functions as a P.O.D. account is the savings account trust (not usually available at banks for checking accounts). In the landmark case of In re Totten, 71 N.E. 748 (N.Y. 1904), *O* made deposits in a savings account in the name of "*O*, as trustee for *A*." *O* retained the right to revoke the trust by withdrawing the funds at any time during his life. Since *A* is entitled only to the amount on deposit at *O*'s death, in practical effect *A* is merely a P.O.D. beneficiary of a "trust" of a savings account. The court upheld this arrangement as not testamentary, declaring that a "tentative" revocable trust had been created at the time of the deposit. At *O*'s death, any funds in the account belong to *A*. Savings account trusts, often known at Totten trusts, have been accepted in almost all states. See Schoenblum, supra, at Table 5.01. See also Restatement (Third) of Trusts §26 (2003).

3. In 1969, the UPC authorized P.O.D. designations. In states adopting the UPC or otherwise permitting P.O.D. designations beyond those authorized by

federal law, brokerage houses allow P.O.D. designations on customers' stock port-
folios held in custodial accounts. Mutual funds — the immensely popular stock
market investment devices of the last few decades — permit P.O.D. designations.
The designation of a death beneficiary on these funds need not comply with the
Wills Act because they are governed by contract or trust principles. See E.F.
Hutton & Co. v. Wallace, 863 F.2d 472 (6th Cir. 1988).

In 1989, a Uniform Transfer on Death Security Registration Act was promulgated, permitting securities to be registered in a transfer-on-death (T.O.D.) form.
By 2004, such T.O.D. registrations were allowed in all states but Louisiana. See
Schoenblum, supra, at Table 5.01. Individual states have pushed the P.O.D. concept even further. For example, Kansas has enacted a statute permitting a death
beneficiary to be named in a deed of land; such designation, as is true of other
P.O.D.s, is revocable by the owner. Kan. Stat. Ann. §59-3501 (2004).

4.   The UPC provisions for multiple-party bank accounts are found in §§6-201
through 6-227. The UPC authorizes a joint tenancy account with the right of
survivorship, an agency account, and a P.O.D. account. Short forms for banks
to use in establishing each type of account are provided. The Totten trust is
abolished; it is treated as a P.O.D. account. Extrinsic evidence is admissible to
show that a joint account was opened solely for the convenience of the depositor.
UPC §§6-203, 6-204, 6-212, cmt. (1991).

Joint accounts belong to the parties during their joint lifetimes "in proportion to
the net contribution of each to the sums on deposit, unless there is clear and
convincing evidence of a different intent." UPC §6-211(b) (1990). The beneficiary
of a P.O.D. account has no rights to sums on deposit during the lifetime of the
depositor.

A requirement of survivorship is imposed on beneficiaries of P.O.D. bank
accounts (UPC §6-212), as well as on beneficiaries of securities in T.O.D. registration (UPC §6-307), but not, as discussed above, on beneficiaries of P.O.D. contracts
generally. However, the antilapse statute (UPC §2-706) substitutes in place of a
deceased beneficiary of a P.O.D. bank account the beneficiary's issue if the beneficiary was a close relative of the decedent (see page 397).

SECTION D. JOINT TENANCIES IN REALTY

A *joint tenancy* or a *tenancy by the entirety* in land is a common and popular method of
avoiding the cost and delay of probate. Perhaps most family homes in this country
are owned by husband and wife either in joint tenancy or tenancy by the entirety.
Upon the death of one joint tenant or tenant by the entirety, the survivor owns the
property absolutely, freed of any participation by the decedent. The common law
theory is that the decedent's interest vanishes at death, and therefore no probate is
necessary because no interest passes to the survivor at death. Joint tenancies and
tenancies by the entireties are ordinarily covered in first-year courses in property.
Only three features of joint tenancies need mention here.

First, the creation of a joint tenancy in land gives the joint tenants equal interests
upon creation. Unlike joint tenancies in personalty (for example, bank and brokerage accounts), joint tenancies in land require the agreement of all tenants to
take most important actions. A person who transfers land into a joint tenancy

cannot, during life, revoke the transfer and cancel the interest given the other joint tenant. In that sense, a joint tenancy in land is an imperfect will substitute (pure will substitutes are revocable gratuitous transfers that take effect at death).

Second, a joint tenant cannot devise her share by will. If a joint tenant wants someone other than the co-tenant to take her share at death, she must sever the joint tenancy during life, converting it into a tenancy in common. Why is a will ineffective to change survivorship rights in a joint tenancy? The first reason lies in the very nature of this reciprocal form of ownership: "The distinctive incident of the estate is the right of survivorship, sometimes referred to by its Latin name *jus accrescendi*, meaning that on the death of one joint tenant, that tenant's share accrues to the surviving tenant or tenants." John V. Orth, Joint Tenancy Law, 5 Green Bag 2d 173, 173-174 (2002). The second reason for not allowing joint tenancies to be conveyed by will, which is admittedly related to the first, is the vanishing theory of the common law. Since no property passes from the decedent joint tenant at death, there is no interest for the decedent's will to operate upon. Although both of these explanations might be seen as merely restating the definition of a joint tenancy, they are also thought to reflect the intent of those choosing this form of ownership. If two people do not want a truly joint form of ownership, one that carries with it a right of survivorship, then they should choose a form of ownership other than a joint tenancy.

This focus on the probable intent of the creators of a joint tenancy leads to another policy rationale: If a joint tenant could devise his share, the property would be subject to litigation to determine the validity of the will and, most importantly, whether the will made a disposition of the joint tenancy property. Does a residuary clause ("all the rest and residue of my property") dispose of *T*'s share of joint tenancy property? Is a specific reference required? How specific? If joint tenants could devise their share, the mere existence of the testamentary power would give them less assurance that the survivor would take, unentangled by will construction, probate costs, and claims of third parties, because of the possibilities of inadvertent exercise of the power. A large number of joint tenants select the tenancy precisely because of the high degree of assurance that there will be no entanglement with probate. To continue this assurance, the right of testamentary disposition must be denied, and the few attempts by ignorant testators to devise their part of joint tenancy property must fail.

The third feature of joint tenancy to be noted relates to creditors' rights. A creditor of a joint tenant must seize the joint tenant's interest during life. In almost all states, at death the joint tenant's interest vanishes and there is nothing for the creditor to reach; it is too late. See Jeffrey A. Schoenblum, 2004 Multistate Guide to Estate Planning at Table 9.04.

SECTION E. PLANNING FOR INCAPACITY

The topics in this section are not usually referred to as nonprobate transfers of property. Indeed, they do not necessarily involve transfers of property at all. Nonetheless, it is convenient to treat methods of dealing with incapacity here, in the same chapter as revocable trusts, because durable powers of attorney and health care directives as well as revocable trusts are among the tools available to the attorney planning for the possible incapacity of the client. And when the family looks for help on such matters, they often turn to their trusts and estates lawyer.

1. The Durable Power of Attorney

The durable power of attorney, like the revocable trust, is useful in planning for incapacity. An ordinary power of attorney creates an agency relationship whereby the agent, called an *attorney-in-fact* (though the agent need not be, and often is not, a lawyer), is given a written authorization to act on behalf of the principal. The power of attorney instrument solves one of the problems encountered by agents conducting business for their principals, namely, supplying sufficient evidence of the agent's authority to induce third parties to transact with the agent. However, a simple power of attorney is still limited by the traditional principle of agency law that the agent's authority terminates on the principal's incapacity. For this reason an ordinary power of attorney is of little use in planning for incapacity. Enter the *durable power of attorney*.

Unlike an ordinary power of attorney, a *durable* power continues throughout the incapacity of the principal until the principal dies. A durable power is permitted by UPC §§5-501 to 5-505 (1990) and by statutes in all states. Some specific language is usually required in the instrument creating the durable power expressing the intent of the principal that the power not terminate upon incapacity. Except for their durability into incompetence, durable powers are otherwise controlled by the common law of agency. The principal, if competent, can terminate the agency and durable power at any time, and the agent owes the principal the fiduciary duties of loyalty, care, and obedience. Durable powers must be created by a written instrument, and in some states witnessed or notarized. In some states, durable powers can be created by using a statutory short form, incorporating by reference statutory powers given the agent, or a durable power can be created by an instrument tailored to fit the wishes of a particular client.

The holder of a durable power is somewhat like a trustee, but there are important differences. First, a durable power ceases when the principal dies; the holder of the power can make no transfers after the principal's death. A durable power does not avoid probate. A trust continues after the settlor's death, transferring property without probate. Moreover, the trustee can be given authority to take action after the settlor's death to cure defects in the estate plan that surface for the first time when all the relevant facts are known. An agent cannot act after the death of the principal. Second, if an agent dies, the power terminates unless a successor agent is named by the principal. If a trustee dies, a successor trustee is appointed by a court. Third, a trustee has title to the trust assets and generally has all the powers an owner has. The trustee can sell and reinvest the trust property. The law of trustees' powers and duties is well developed and well known. In contrast, an agent does not own the property, and agency law sparingly implies powers and strictly construes express powers. Third parties readily deal with trustees but are cautious about dealing with agents. Some banks and other financial institutions, uncertain of an agent's authority and unfamiliar with a durable power, may refuse to accept a durable power of attorney (though they can be compelled by law to accept a statutory short form power of attorney). The upshot is that durable powers are useful for persons seeking a way of dealing with incompetency without creating a trust, but trusts are more flexible and satisfactory for most clients. Durable powers of attorney have, nonetheless, become an extremely popular device for dealing with incapacity among persons of modest means.

FRANZEN v. NORWEST BANK COLORADO, 955 P.2d 1018 (Colo. 1998): On February 4, 1992, James Franzen established a trust for the benefit of himself and his wife Frances, naming Norwest Bank as trustee. The corpus of the trust consisted of $74,251.19. Mr. Franzen died four months later.

Under the terms of the trust, Mrs. Franzen had the right within three months of James's death to terminate the trust and receive the proceeds. The trustee sent a letter to her at her nursing home informing her of this right. She responded by writing a "handwritten note at the bottom of the letter," which she signed and dated, stating that "I wish to leave the trust intact for my lifetime."

Then Mrs. Franzen's brother, James O'Brien, entered the picture:

> The bank, concerned about the disposition of the vacant house and other assets not included in the trust, contacted Mrs. Franzen's nephews, who were named as remaindermen of the trust. The two nephews were reluctant to assume responsibility for Mrs. Franzen's affairs, though, and Mrs. Franzen's brother, James O'Brien, intervened. O'Brien moved Mrs. Franzen to a nursing home in Kentucky, where he lived, and asked the bank to turn over Mrs. Franzen's assets to him.
>
> In the course of dealing with the bank, the nephews expressed concerns about O'Brien's motives. The bank declined to comply with O'Brien's request, and filed a Petition for Instruction and Advice in the Denver Probate Court. Before the hearing, O'Brien sent the bank a copy of a power of attorney purporting to authorize him to act in Mrs. Franzen's behalf and a letter attempting to revoke the trust and to remove the bank as trustee, citing Article 6.2 and Article 8 of the trust agreement.

Article 6.2 allowed Mrs. Franzen to remove the trustee without cause and Article 8 gave her the right to amend or revoke the trust.

> [T]he probate court ruled that the power of attorney had created a valid agency but that the trust had not been revoked and continued in existence. The probate court found that Mrs. Franzen needed protection, but a conservator was not available, so the court appointed the bank as "special fiduciary" with responsibility for both trust and non-trust assets. . . .
>
> On appeal, the court of appeals reversed, holding that the power of attorney authorized O'Brien to remove the bank as trustee and to revoke the trust. . . .

The case then moved to the Colorado Supreme Court, where the bank made two arguments. First, it argued that, under a Colorado statute taking effect in 1995, a power of attorney is ineffective to revoke a trust without a specific mention of the trust in the power of attorney. Second, it argued that this statute "merely restated the common law in effect prior to its adoption, so the same result should be reached even though the statute was not intended to be applied retroactively. The bank asserts that the common law would require the power of attorney to refer to the trust by name." The power of attorney in this case did not specifically reference the trust at issue by name. The court rejected the bank's arguments.

> [W]e are not persuaded that under the common law, an agency instrument must expressly refer to a particular trust by name in order to confer authority on the agent

to revoke it. . . . [T]he terms of the power of attorney need only evidence an intention to authorize the agent to make decisions concerning the principal's interests in trusts generally, not necessarily a particular trust.

Section 1(c) of the power of attorney executed by Mrs. Franzen expressly authorizes O'Brien "to manage . . . and in any manner deal with any real or personal property, tangible or intangible, or any interest therein . . . in my name and for my benefit, upon such terms as . . . [O'Brien] shall deem proper, including the funding, creation, and/or revocation of trusts or other investments."

We have little trouble concluding that the quoted language expressly authorizes O'Brien to revoke the Franzen trust, even though it does not mention the trust specifically by name. . . .

In conclusion, we hold that under the common law, a power of attorney that appears to give the agent sweeping powers to dispose of the principal's property is to be narrowly construed in light of the circumstances surrounding the execution of the agency instrument. However, the principal may confer authority to amend or revoke trusts on an agent without referring to the trusts by name in the power of attorney.

Accordingly, we affirm the judgment of the court of appeals.

PROBLEMS AND NOTES

1.   Suppose that O'Brien does not know the contents of Mrs. Franzen's will, which devises her home to him. Exercising his power of attorney, O'Brien sells the home and uses the proceeds to pay for Mrs. Franzen's care. Under the common law of ademption, when the devised property is not owned by the testator at death, the devise is adeemed and the devisee takes nothing. See Wasserman v. Cohen, 606 N.E.2d 901 (Mass. 1993), page 406. Upon Mrs. Franzen's death, what are O'Brien's rights under the common law? See In re Estate of Hegel, 668 N.E.2d 474 (Ohio 1996) (holding devise adeemed). Here is a paragraph from the dissent:

> Today's decision gives a dangerous power to all attorneys-in-fact to change a will once their charge becomes incompetent. There is now no protection against the greedy or unscrupulous attorneys-in-fact. At least in Hegel's case, Boettger [the agent] did what she believed was best for her charge, innocently depriving herself of her inheritance and providing an unintended windfall to the other heirs. But now, nothing prevents an attorney-in-fact from altering a will to his or her benefit. For example, a house, the main asset in the estate, may be left to Heir A. Heir B inherits the remaining cash. Heir B is appointed attorney-in-fact. The testator becomes incompetent. Heir B sells the house, claiming the cash is insufficient to pay debts. The bequest is adeemed; Heir B now inherits everything. Heir A is out in the cold. At least in a guardianship, a court can supervise an estate and prevent such injustice. Under this court's holding, there would be no recourse. [668 N.E.2d at 478.]

The hypothetical posited by the dissent in *Hegel* actually happened in Crosby v. Luehrs, 669 N.W.2d 635 (Neb. 2003). *B*, an attorney-in-fact under a power of attorney from *T*, converted *T*'s P.O.D. accounts, which would have favored *A*, to regular accounts in *T*'s name. This had the effect of increasing *B*'s share of *T*'s estate. However, the court in *Crosby* held that *B*'s closing of the P.O.D. accounts made out a prima facie case of constructive fraud and breached *B*'s fiduciary duties to *T*. Does this answer the dissent in *Hegel*?

2. A mother with two daughters has been giving each child $11,000 each year to take advantage of the annual exclusion of $11,000 gifts from the federal gift tax (see page 857). Mother grants the younger daughter a durable power of attorney. After mother becomes incompetent, the daughter, exercising the power of attorney, continues to make $11,000 annual gifts to herself and to her sister until her mother's death. Must the younger daughter return to her mother's estate the $11,000 gifts she made to herself exercising the durable power?

Under the federal estate tax, inter vivos transfers by the decedent over which the decedent retains the power to revoke are included in the decedent's taxable gross estate. In Townsend v. United States, 889 F. Supp. 369 (D. Neb. 1995), it was held that gifts made by an agent under a durable power were includible in the principal's gross estate because the power of attorney did not expressly authorize gifts. Without such authorization, the decedent could revoke the gifts. Accord, Estate of Casey v. Commissioner, 948 F.2d 895 (4th Cir. 1991). Drafting moral: Include in a durable power of attorney the power to make gifts if the donor so desires.

3. For comprehensive examinations of the durable power of attorney, see Karen E. Boxx, The Durable Power of Attorney's Place in the Family of Fiduciary Relationships, 36 Ga. L. Rev. 1 (2001); Carolyn L. Dessin, Acting as Agent under a Financial Durable Power of Attorney, 75 Neb. L. Rev. 574 (1996). Professor Dessin writes:

> Recently . . . concerns have been voiced that perhaps we have created an instrument of abuse rather than a useful tool. Sometimes the problems are as clear as wrongful misappropriation of the principal's property by the agent. Often, however, problems arise because the standards governing the behavior of agents under durable powers of attorney have never been clearly defined. In many instances, those standards have not even been considered. Legislatures, courts, and commentators have often simply assumed the application of various bodies of law without careful reflection. In light of the popularity of the financial durable power of attorney, it is surprising that there has been no in-depth consideration of the parameters of the agent's duty. There has been only the occasional sentence written, often merely noting the application of general fiduciary principles. . . .
>
> Once a financial durable power of attorney is validly executed, it can be an extremely powerful document, authorizing an agent to perform virtually any act with respect to the principal's property that the principal could perform. This breadth of power coupled with few required execution formalities creates a fear of overreaching by unscrupulous agents. [Id. at 575-576, 582.]

Professor Dessin's fears about the abuse of durable powers can be confirmed by searching under "durable powers of attorney" in Lexis or Westlaw, where a disturbing number of cases litigate misappropriation by the agent—usually a friend or relative of the principal. The very lack of oversight and ease of use that makes powers of attorney so attractive in planning for incapacity makes them especially easy to misuse.

4. If a lawyer drafts a durable power of attorney, the lawyer should carefully examine the use of the power in the particular client's estate plan. The power should be tailored to the client's needs and wishes.

If the client does not have a revocable trust, for instance, a durable power may authorize the holder of the power to create a revocable trust for the client upon the client's incompetency. For example, *O* may execute a durable power of attorney authorizing *A*, upon *O*'s incompetency, to execute, on behalf of *O*, a trust for *O*'s benefit, revocable by *O*, and also authorizing *A* to transfer *O*'s assets to the trustee of the trust. The revocable trust may be drafted at the same time the power is executed and attached to the power.

The holder of a durable power may be authorized to amend or revoke an existing trust or a P.O.D. designation, sever joint tenancies, or make lifetime gifts of the incompetent's property (useful for taking advantage of the $11,000 annual exclusion from gift taxes, see page 857). It is doubtful, however, whether the holder of the power can be authorized to make, amend, or revoke a will of the principal, as the Wills Act may be construed to require personal knowing action of the testator. On the other hand, if the holder of a durable power of attorney can be authorized to act with respect to a revocable inter vivos trust and contracts (which could include a contract to make a will), is there a practical or policy reason not to allow the agent also to make, amend, or revoke a will?

5. The Uniform Law Commission is now working on a Uniform Power of Attorney Act. This new act is designed to replace the 1979 Uniform Durable Power of Attorney Act. As of this writing, the current draft replaces the clumsy term *attorney-in-fact* with the simpler term *agent*. It also provides that (1) all powers-of-attorney are durable unless the instrument states otherwise (thus reversing the current default rule), and (2) the agent will not have the power to amend or revoke trusts or give away the principal's assets without express authorization to do so.

2. Directives Regarding Health Care and Disposition of the Body

a. Advance Directives: Living Wills, Health Care Proxies, and Hybrids

The Supreme Court has held that each person has a constitutional right to make health care decisions, including the right to refuse medical treatment. See Cruzan v. Director, Mo. Dept. of Health, 497 U.S. 261 (1990). If state law requirements are met, a person may state her wishes about terminating medical treatment or appointing an agent to make the decision for her. But where a person's wishes are not clearly expressed, the state may assert an interest in favor of preserving life and preventing the withdrawal of treatment.

In resolving a conflict over the wishes of an incompetent individual, the law relies on advance directives and default rules in the absence of such directives. Advance directives are of three basic types:

1. Instructional directives, such as a *living will* or a commonly used form known as a *Medical Directive*, which specify either generally or by way of hypothetical examples how one wants to be treated in end-of-life situations or in the event of incompetence;

2. Proxy directives, such as a *health care proxy* or *durable power of attorney for health care*, which designate an agent to make health care decisions for the patient (the power of the agent does not expire with the principal's incompetency); or

3. Hybrid or combined directives incorporating both of the first two approaches: directing treatment preferences *and* designating an agent to make substituted decisions.

Every state has statutes implementing the desire for advance direction of health care, but these vary in the particulars and often require specific forms. Thus, the lawyer advising a client to execute a directive should consult local law. See Bretton J. Hortter, A Survey of Living Will and Advanced Health Care Directives, 74 N.D.L. Rev. 233 (1998) (examining laws of each state).

The Uniform Health-Care Decisions Act, promulgated in 1993, takes a hybrid approach, including forms that create a durable power of attorney for health care and offer the person a chance to indicate how aggressively he would like to be treated. The agent must make decisions in accordance with the patient's wishes. The health care provider must follow the instructions except where contrary to the provider's conscience or contrary to generally accepted medical practice.

In 1991 Congress enacted the Patient Self-Determination Act (PSDA), 104 Stat. 1388 (codified in scattered sections of 42 U.S.C. (2004)). The PSDA requires that every patient admitted to a hospital receiving federal funds must be advised of the right to sign an advance directive indicating a desire to withdraw medical treatment in specified situations. For studies concluding that the PSDA has achieved only limited success in advancing its goals, see Edward J. Larson & Thomas A. Eaton, The Limits of Advance Directives: A History and Assessment of the Patient Self-Determination Act, 32 Wake Forest L. Rev. 249 (1997); Steven H. Miles, Robert Koepp & Eileen P. Weber, Advance End-of-Life Treatment Planning, 156 Archives Internal Med. 1062 (1996).

By permission of Chip Bok and Creators Syndicate, Inc.

Rebecca Dresser, Precommitment: A Misguided Strategy for
Securing Death with Dignity
81 Tex. L. Rev. 1823, 1823, 1825-1826, 1828-1831,
1833-1836, 1846-1847 (2003)

Scholars and researchers have analyzed advance directives for more than three decades. Their work exhibits two contradictory themes. First, precommitment remains an alluring strategy for many people worried about end-of-life care. People in this group cling to the notion that advance decisionmaking will deliver them a dignified and merciful death. Many philosophers, clinicians, judges, and legislators belong to this group. At the same time, a second body of work questions the wisdom of the first position. This work describes a host of ethical and practical problems with relying on precommitment to resolve decisions about life-sustaining treatment. . . .

The person completing an advance directive seeks to commit her future impaired self, and the family, physicians, and others confronting that self, to a particular treatment approach. She believes that she is in a better position now, than others will be in the future, to make decisions about the treatment she receives as an incompetent patient. . . .

Once writers introduced the advance directive concept, legal authorities moved quickly to incorporate it into policy. This move occurred without study of, or reflection on, the difficulties that might accompany putting advance directive theory into practice. With experience, however, came awareness of these problems. By 2002, empirical research revealed that the reality of advance directives did not conform to their creators' vision.

Studies of advance directives point to several practical problems. First, advance directives are rarely completed. Second, most of the directives that are completed fail to convey meaningful information. Third, people making directives often have a poor understanding of what they are deciding. In particular, they may not envision how they could experience their decisions in a future incapacitated state. . . .

Advance directives have been endorsed for more than thirty years, and [the federal Patient Self-Determination Act] has required since 1991 that hospitals and other health care organizations notify patients of their right to make a directive. Nevertheless, relatively few people complete directives. Researchers generally report that less than 25% of people have directives, though some studies have found higher completion levels among selected groups with serious illnesses. . . .

Most people completing directives do not attempt to issue detailed instructions for the variety of situations that could befall them. Instead, they supply only a general indication of how they would like to be treated. Such directives furnish little information to clinicians and families seeking to resolve actual treatment issues. . . .

To remedy the problem of imprecision, health professionals have created documents that elicit more specific information about treatment preferences. The most well-known of these is the Medical Directive, which sets forth six hypothetical clinical situations involving different physical and mental impairments and six categories of life-sustaining interventions. Even these documents may supply inadequate guidance, however. For example, the Medical Directive may not indicate how a person's wishes would apply in an actual treatment situation, because not all treatment situations fit neatly into one of thirty-six scenarios. . . .

Most people simply cannot predict all the medical conditions that the future might bring, much less understand what would be the possible harms and benefits of interventions targeting those conditions. . . .

A related problem is that a person's preferences regarding future life-sustaining treatment may change over time. Several studies have measured the stability of advance directive preferences over periods of up to two years. Most find what they label "moderate" stability. . . .

Advance directives are designed not to impose limits on an agent's future freedom of action, but to limit the treatment a person receives when agency is absent — when the person is vulnerable and reliant on others for care. The advance directive seeks to precommit physicians and others to certain behavior, to impose on them a responsibility to treat according to an individual's previous instructions. But this responsibility may conflict with a separate responsibility — the duty to protect incompetent patients from harm. . . .

Further work is needed to clarify when treatment is required because it would confer a material benefit and when it may be forgone because the benefit would be insufficient or outweighed by the harm treatment would impose.

In making health care decisions for an incompetent patient, an agent for health care decisions is held to a *substituted judgment* standard: what the patient has chosen or would have chosen in that situation. Some commentators have suggested that, instead of (or in addition to) this standard, the agent should act according to the best interests of the patient. In end-of-life situations, however, it is often unclear what the patient would have wanted or what is in the best interests of the patient.

In the absence of an advance directive designating an agent, responsibility for an incompetent patient's decisions regarding health care usually falls to the patient's spouse or next of kin, subject to the state's interest in preserving life. To give a clear order of priority among potential decision makers, many states have enacted a statutory hierarchy. For example, 755 Ill. Comp. Stat. §40/25(a) (2004), authorizes decisions to be made by surrogates in the following order:

(1)   the patient's guardian of the person;
(2)   the patient's spouse;
(3)   any adult son or daughter of the patient;
(4)   either parent of the patient;
(5)   any adult brother or sister of the patient;
(6)   any adult grandchild of the patient;
(7)   a close friend of the patient; and
(8)   the patient's guardian of the estate.

If there is more than one person in a class, the majority controls. Id. See generally Judith Areen, The Legal Status of Consent Obtained from Families of Adult Patients to Withhold or Withdraw Treatment, 258 JAMA 229 (1987).

Bush v. Schiavo

Supreme Court of Florida, 2004

885 So. 2d 321

PARIENTE, C.J.   The narrow issue in this case requires this Court to decide the constitutionality of a law passed by the Legislature that directly affected Theresa Schiavo, who has been in a persistent vegetative state since 1990. This Court . . . concludes that the law violates the fundamental constitutional tenet of separation of powers and is therefore unconstitutional both on its face and as applied to Theresa Schiavo. Accordingly, we affirm the trial court's order declaring the law unconstitutional.

FACTS AND PROCEDURAL HISTORY

. . . As set forth in the Second District's first opinion in this case, which upheld the guardianship court's final order,

> Theresa Marie Schindler was born on December 3, 1963, and lived with or near her parents in Pennsylvania until she married Michael Schiavo on November 10, 1984. Michael and Theresa moved to Florida in 1986. They were happily married and both were employed. They had no children.
>
> On February 25, 1990, their lives changed. Theresa, age 27, suffered a cardiac arrest as a result of a potassium imbalance. Michael called 911, and Theresa was rushed to the hospital. She never regained consciousness.
>
> Since 1990, Theresa has lived in nursing homes with constant care. She is fed and hydrated by tubes. The staff changes her diapers regularly. She has had numerous health problems, but none have been life threatening.[14]

In re Guardianship of Schiavo, 780 So. 2d 176, 177 (Fla. Dist. 2001) (Schiavo I).

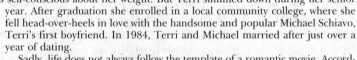

14. A devotee of romantic movies, Terri nonetheless avoided high school dances—including her prom—because she was self-conscious about her weight. But Terri slimmed down during her senior year. After graduation she enrolled in a local community college, where she fell head-over-heels in love with the handsome and popular Michael Schiavo, Terri's first boyfriend. In 1984, Terri and Michael married after just over a year of dating.

Sadly, life does not always follow the template of a romantic movie. According to Terri's high school friend Diane Meyer, Terri said that Michael warned her that "if she ever got fat like [high school] again he'd divorce her." CNN, Before Fight Over Death, Terri Schiavo Had a Life, Oct. 25, 2003, http://edition.cnn.com/2003/LAW/10/24/schiavo.profile.ap/.There are reports that "Mr. Schiavo was a penny pincher who kept track of the mileage on his wife's car and yelled at her for spending money on haircuts. . . . The couple worked opposite hours—she all day, he late into the night." With His Wife in Limbo, Husband Can't Move, N.Y. Times, Nov. 2, 2003, §1, at 18. According to Terri's brother, parents, and others, Terri was even contemplating a divorce in the year before her heart attack:

Terri Schiavo

The Schindlers say that on Feb. 25, 1990, Mrs. Schiavo told her brother that she and Mr. Schiavo had had a violent argument—a claim Mr. Schiavo denies. Mr. Schiavo has said his wife was asleep when he arrived home from work around 2 a.m. . . . [O]n "Larry King Live," he said that he awoke at 4:30 and heard a thud. It was his wife, whom he found on the floor, he said.

For the first three years after this tragedy, Michael and Theresa's parents, Robert and Mary Schindler, enjoyed an amicable relationship. However, that relationship ended in 1993 and the parties literally stopped speaking to each other. In May of 1998, eight years after Theresa lost consciousness, Michael petitioned the guardianship court to authorize the termination of life-prolonging procedures. By filing this petition, which the Schindlers opposed, Michael placed the difficult decision in the hands of the court.

After a trial, at which both Michael and the Schindlers presented evidence, the guardianship court issued an extensive written order authorizing the discontinuance of artificial life support. The trial court found by clear and convincing evidence that Theresa Schiavo was in a persistent vegetative state and that Theresa would elect to cease life-prolonging procedures if she were competent to make her own decision. This order was affirmed on direct appeal, see Schiavo I, 780 So. 2d at 177, and we denied review. See In re Guardianship of Schiavo, 789 So. 2d 348 (Fla. 2001). . . .

In affirming the trial court's order, the Second District concluded by stating:

> In the final analysis, the difficult question that faced the trial court was whether Theresa Marie Schindler Schiavo, not after a few weeks in a coma, but after ten years in a persistent vegetative state that has robbed her of most of her cerebrum and all but the most instinctive of neurological functions, with no hope of a medical cure but with sufficient money and strength of body to live indefinitely, would choose to continue the constant nursing care and the supporting tubes in hopes that a miracle would somehow recreate her missing brain tissue, or whether she would wish to permit a natural death process to take its course and for her family members and loved ones to be free to continue their lives. After due consideration, we conclude that the trial judge had clear and convincing evidence to answer this question as he did. . . .

[After two years of further litigation, which resulted in the original decision being upheld, "Theresa's nutrition and hydration tube was removed on

---

By the time paramedics arrived, Mrs. Schiavo's heart had not pumped for perhaps 10 minutes, doctors found. The prevailing theory is that she had an undiagnosed potassium deficiency, possibly due to extreme weight loss or even, her husband has said, bulimia. She had gone from over 200 pounds in high school to 110. . . .

Shortly after the legal battle began, Mr. Schiavo moved . . . with his girlfriend [Jodi Centonze and their child] into a middle-class neighborhood. Ms. Centonze, 38, often washes Mrs. Schiavo's clothes and accompanies Mr. Schiavo to visit her. . . .

For a long time, the Schindlers accused Mr. Schiavo of wanting his wife dead so he and Ms. Centonze could spend her settlement money [from a medical malpractice claim brought on Terri's behalf]. But Mr. Schiavo's lawyer, Mr. Felos, said all but $60,000 has been spent on medical care and legal fees, which have totaled more than $400,000, and that his client would not see a penny of what remains. [Id.]

Terri Schiavo did not leave an advance directive. Most experts, including an independent expert appointed by the trial court, determined that Terri was in a persistent vegetative state (PVS) and would not recover significantly. However, other experts disagreed, asserting that Terri was not in a PVS and perhaps could profit from therapy. See In re Schiavo, 851 So. 2d 182, 184-185 (Fla. App. 2003). — Eds.

October 15, 2003." Six days later the Florida legislature passed chapter 2003-418, which authorized the governor of Florida to stay the removal of nutrition and hydration on facts that matched the *Schiavo* case. Governor Jeb Bush immediately issued "executive order No. 03-201 to stay the continued withholding of nutrition and hydration from Theresa. The nutrition and hydration tube was reinserted pursuant to the Governor's executive order." After successful lower court challenges to the statute by Michael, the Florida Supreme Court issued this decision.]

ANALYSIS

We begin our discussion by emphasizing that our task in this case is to review the constitutionality of chapter 2003-418, not to reexamine the guardianship court's orders directing the removal of Theresa's nutrition and hydration tube, or to review the Second District's numerous decisions in the guardianship case. . . .

The language of chapter 2003-418 is clear. It states[:] . . .

(1) The Governor shall have the authority to issue a one-time stay to prevent the withholding of nutrition and hydration from a patient if, as of October 15, 2003:

(a) That patient has no written advance directive;
(b) The court has found that patient to be in a persistent vegetative state;
(c) That patient has had nutrition and hydration withheld; and
(d) A member of that patient's family has challenged the withholding of nutrition and hydration.

(2) The Governor's authority to issue the stay expires 15 days after the effective date of this act, and the expiration of the authority does not impact the validity or the effect of any stay issued pursuant to this act. The Governor may lift the stay authorized under this act at any time. A person may not be held civilly liable and is not subject to regulatory or disciplinary sanctions for taking any action to comply with a stay issued by the Governor pursuant to this act.

(3) Upon issuance of a stay, the chief judge of the circuit court shall appoint a guardian ad litem for the patient to make recommendations to the Governor and the court. . . .

ENCROACHMENT ON THE JUDICIAL BRANCH

. . . Under the express separation of powers provision in our state constitution, "the judiciary is a coequal branch of the Florida government vested with the sole authority to exercise the judicial power," and "the legislature cannot, short of constitutional amendment, reallocate the balance of power expressly delineated in the constitution among the three coequal branches." Children A, B, C, D, E, & F, 589 So. 2d 260, 268-69 (Fla. 1991).

As the United States Supreme Court has explained, the power of the judiciary is "not merely to rule on cases, but to decide them, subject to review only by superior courts" and "having achieved finality . . . a judicial decision becomes the last word of the judicial department with regard to a particular case or controversy." Plaut v. Spendthrift Farm, 514 U.S. 211, 218-19, 227 (1995). Moreover, "purely judicial acts . . . are not subject to review as to their accuracy by the Governor." In re Advisory Opinion to the Governor, 213 So. 2d 716, 720 (Fla. 1968). . . .

In this case, the undisputed facts show that the guardianship court authorized Michael to proceed with the discontinuance of Theresa's life support after the issue was fully litigated in a proceeding in which the Schindlers were afforded the opportunity to present evidence on all issues. This order as well as the order denying the Schindlers' motion for relief from judgment were affirmed on direct appeal. The Schindlers sought review in this Court, which was denied. Thereafter, the tube was removed. Subsequently, pursuant to the Governor's executive order, the nutrition and hydration tube was reinserted. Thus, the Act, as applied in this case, resulted in an executive order that effectively reversed a properly rendered final judgment and thereby constituted an unconstitutional encroachment on the power that has been reserved for the independent judiciary. . . .

When the prescribed procedures are followed according to our rules of court and the governing statutes, a final judgment is issued, and all post-judgment procedures are followed, it is without question an invasion of the authority of the judicial branch for the Legislature to pass a law that allows the executive branch to interfere with the final judicial determination in a case. That is precisely what occurred here and for that reason the Act is unconstitutional as applied to Theresa Schiavo.

DELEGATION OF LEGISLATIVE AUTHORITY

In addition to concluding that the Act is unconstitutional as applied in this case because it encroaches on the power of the judicial branch, we further conclude that the Act is unconstitutional on its face because it delegates legislative power to the Governor. . . .

In enacting chapter 2003-418, the Legislature failed to provide any standards by which the Governor should determine whether, in any given case, a stay should be issued and how long a stay should remain in effect. Further, the Legislature has failed to provide any criteria for lifting the stay. This absolute, unfettered discretion to decide whether to issue and then when to lift a stay makes the Governor's decision virtually unreviewable. . . .

CONCLUSION

. . . The continuing vitality of our system of separation of powers precludes the other two branches from nullifying the judicial branch's final orders. If the Legislature with the assent of the Governor can do what was attempted here, the judicial branch would be subordinated to the final directive of the other branches. Also subordinated would be the rights of individuals, including the well established privacy right to self determination. No court judgment could ever be considered truly final and no constitutional right truly secure, because the precedent of this case would hold to the contrary. Vested rights could be stripped away based on popular clamor. The essential core of what the Founding Fathers sought to change from their experience with English rule would be lost, especially their belief that our courts exist precisely to preserve the rights of individuals, even when doing so is contrary to popular will.

The trial court's decision regarding Theresa Schiavo was made in accordance with the procedures and protections set forth by the judicial branch and in accordance with the statutes passed by the Legislature in effect at that time. That decision is final and the Legislature's attempt to alter that final adjudication is unconstitutional as applied to Theresa Schiavo. Further, even if there had been no final judgment in this case, the Legislature provided the Governor constitutionally inadequate standards for the application of the legislative authority delegated in chapter 2003-418. Because chapter 2003-418 runs afoul of article II, section 3 of the Florida Constitution in both respects, we affirm the circuit court's final summary judgment.

NOTES

1. Governor Bush petitioned the U.S. Supreme Court for certiorari in Bush v. Schiavo, but his petition was denied in January 2005. At the time certiorari was denied, Terri was still alive but apparently unaware of her surroundings.

2. Michael's treatment choices took precedence over those of Terri's parents, the Schindlers, because Michael was appointed her guardian. Even without such an appointment, as her husband his directions would govern her care. In Florida, as in most states, spouses have priority over parents. Fla. Stat. §765.401(1) (2004).

James Lindgren, Death by Default
56 Law & Contemp. Probs. 185, 185-186, 227-230 (Summer 1993)

Every day, people are helped or allowed to die. Respirators are disconnected, life-saving operations are not performed, and doctors and nurses stand by doing nothing as patients in distress die under Do-Not-Resuscitate ("DNR") orders. These practices are routine in modern hospitals. Indeed, one study of all cardio-pulmonary arrests that occurred while in the hospital found that 75% of the patients were allowed to die because they were under a DNR order. Another study found that 39% of all deaths in intensive care units were preceded by DNR orders. Today you almost need someone else's permission to die.

Polls show that most Americans would not want to be kept alive if there were no hope of recovery. To meet the public's desire for an earlier death, states have rushed to enact right-to-die statutes and to put living wills, medical durable powers of attorney, and advance directives on a stronger legal footing. Although living wills and powers of attorney could theoretically be used to insist that all heroic efforts be made to preserve life, the assumption of the legislators who propose them, the hospitals that market them, and the patients who execute them is that they will facilitate death — an early death rather than the degraded life that the state or a hospital might impose on them.[15]

Even the right-to-die statutes typically operate only when the patient or some-one acting for the patient has spoken. Somewhat reluctantly and with much handwringing, most courts have been willing to enforce the wishes of terminally ill patients, as long as those wishes are sufficiently clearly expressed. But if they are not clearly expressed, some courts, especially recently, have mandated that the patients be kept alive. In other words, the default rule applied by many courts and

---

15. The living will statute of virtually every state contains a pregnancy exception: the provisions of a living will authorizing the discontinuation of heroic measures do not apply when the patient is pregnant. Is this a good idea? See Note, A Matter of Life and Death: Pregnancy Clauses in Living Will Statutes, 70 B.U.L. Rev. 867 (1990). — Eds.

medical ethicists is life aggressively pursued by medical treatment, even if ultimately treatment is usually withdrawn.

Yet if most people would not want to be kept alive with high technology, why do we require proof that they want what most people want? Why not require proof that they're different than most people, that they would want to be kept alive on life-support? If the patient's wishes are unknown, follow the course that most people would want for themselves in desperate end-of-life situations — a withdrawal of treatment to allow an earlier death. . . .

Thus, one must determine when most people would prefer to have at least some treatments withdrawn. According to national public opinion polls, it appears that there are at least eight such overlapping situations:

(1) patients on life support who have no hope of recovery;

(2) patients in a coma with no brain activity being kept alive by a feeding tube;

(3) patients who are terminally ill or in irreversible coma, supported by life support systems, including food and water;

(4) patients with an illness that makes them totally dependent on a family member or other person for all of their care (a situation in which they would not want their doctors "to do everything possible to save" life);

(5) patients with a disease with no hope of improvement suffering a great deal of physical pain;

(6) patients in a coma with no hope of recovery but no pain;

(7) hopelessly ill or comatose patients on life support if their families request the withdrawal of support; and

(8) permanently unconscious patients receiving food and water. . . .

Among the only contrary situations are resuscitation and hospitalization for AIDS patients[, who would want to be resuscitated in middle stages of the disease]. AIDS patients, however, seem to prefer not to be ventilated or resuscitated if the disease has progressed to severe memory loss and severe pneumonia. For other terminal illnesses, early treatments seem to be desired, but more extreme treatments are increasingly not desired.

How one should use all this information about patient preferences will depend on other views about decisionmaking for incompetent patients. Doctors advising a family can explain that most patients would want treatment withdrawn. . . . Families of patients in most end-of-life situations should be explicitly told, for example, that 73-85% of the adult population would prefer to have treatment withdrawn and that 86-93% of doctors would prefer no treatment for themselves. Because eventually most patients are allowed to die, making families aware of the preferences of most people should lessen anxiety and facilitate earlier resolution. Families who wish to follow the patient's wishes will have guidance and support. . . . [W]here families and patients disagree, the analysis becomes more complex. My analysis and the literature on patient preferences are inconclusive. Patients both want death and want their families to decide.

. . . Before doctors began to understand the etiology of disease in the late 1800s — when the chief medical treatments were bloodletting, cathartics, and blistering — common law courts developed a workable system for initiating and terminating treatment, the consent of the patient. Where it was difficult to know whether treatments would do any good, the wishes of the patient controlled. Ironically, the very proficiency of modern doctors and medical equipment has put us back in a situation much like that before the mid-1800s. Doctors can provide standard medical treatments to keep dying people alive, but it's unclear whether these treatments do any real good. Perhaps, like blistering, they do more harm than good. In this limbo, let patients decide. And where the patient would have chosen death rather than life, the default rule should be death.

NOTE

For a review of the psychological literature on euthanasia and assisted suicide, see Barry Rosenfeld, Methodological Issues in Assisted Suicide and Euthanasia Research, 6 Psych. Pub. Poly. & L. 559 (2000). In May 2004, the Ninth Circuit Court of Appeals upheld Oregon's "Death with Dignity Act," which allows doctor-assisted suicide. From the time that the law took effect in 1997 through early 2004, 171 people — most of them with terminal cancer — have made use of it. See Oregon v. Ashcroft, 368 F.3d 1118 (9th Cir. 2004). In February 2005, however, the U.S. Supreme Court granted certiorari under the name Gonzales v. Oregon, No. 04-623 (2005).

b. Disposition of the Body

Historically, a person other than a monarch has had little say about what is done to his body after death. The body was not considered to be property, so it was not disposable by will; nor was it owned by the decedent's estate or by his family. Until the twentieth century, burials were regarded as a matter of "sentiment and superstition" and were left to the jurisdiction of the church. With the rise of secularism, courts began to exercise a "benevolent discretion" to carry out the wishes of the deceased person, provided these wishes do not conflict unreasonably with the desires of the living. This power has been exercised in such a way that a person now has something more than a hope, but far less than an assurance, that his wishes will be carried out at death if the family objects.[16] In addition, if a person dies by violence or in suspicious circumstances, statutes in all states require an autopsy regardless of the wishes of the deceased person or next of kin. See Tanya K. Hernandez, The Property of Death, 60 U. Pitt. L. Rev. 971 (1999).

With the advent first of dissection, then of cadaver organ transplantation, the first principle of law, medicine, and ethics — saving human life — became a relevant consideration in the disposition of the dead. To increase the quantity of cadaver organs for transplantation, all states have enacted the Uniform Anatomical Gift Act, either verbatim or in some modified version. This act permits

---

16. In Holland v. Metalious, 198 A.2d 654 (N.H 1964), the will of Grace Metalious, author of the best-selling novel Peyton Place, forbade funeral services; the court refused to enjoin funeral services by the family.

In Meksrus Estate, 24 Pa. Fiduc. 249 (Orph. Ct. 1974), a testamentary direction to inter diamonds, jewelry, and paintings with the decedent's body was held to be against public policy and void. Such a provision, if enforced, the court thought, "is almost certain to tempt some people and invite others to overt action to procure the" buried treasure.

In March 1977, Sandra Ilene West of Beverly Hills died, devising her multimillion dollar estate to her brother-in-law upon the condition that he bury her in her 1964 baby-blue Ferrari dressed in a lace nightgown and with the seat slanted comfortably. Upon the brother-in-law's petition, the court ordered her buried, in the manner directed by her will, beside her husband in a cemetery in San Antonio, Texas. L.A. Times, May 20, 1977, pt. 1, at 3.

a person to give her body to any hospital, physician, medical school, or body bank for research or transplantation. It also permits a gift of a body, or parts thereof, to any specified individual for therapy or transplantation needed by the individual. Under the original Uniform Anatomical Gift Act of 1968, the gift can be made by a duly executed will or by a card carried on the person if the card is "signed by the donor in the presence of two witnesses who must sign the document in his presence." Id. §4(a). In 1987, a revised Uniform Anatomical Gift Act was promulgated. The witnessing requirement was eliminated; now only a signature on a card is required (§2(b)). In many states, additional legislation has been enacted providing for an organ donation form to be affixed to the back of a driver's license, which is also allowed under the Uniform Act (§2(c)). The Uniform Act provides that a surgeon who relies on the validity of the card or will "in good faith" is not civilly or criminally liable (§11(c)).

The Uniform Anatomical Gift Act itself has had little effect on easing the shortage of organs. There are a number of reasons for this: (1) the difficulty of imagining one's death and others' using one's organs; (2) the fear that physicians might hasten a person's death in order to obtain organs; (3) unwillingness to be cut open after death, sometimes because of religious belief; and (4) simply not thinking about the matter. Only in states with driver's license donation laws are there a substantial minority of persons who have elected to be organ donors (the best donors being healthy young persons who die from accidents). Yet organ shortages remain acute.

A number of commentators, and some entrepreneurs ready to buy and sell organs, have suggested that a market in human organs be established. A market, after all, is the traditional way of allocating scarce resources. In 1984, however, Congress forbade the sale of human organs. National Organ Transplant Act, 42 U.S.C. §274e (2004). The British Parliament outlawed sale of human organs in 1989, after a public outcry over the sale of a kidney to a Londoner for £2,000 by a Turkish peasant flown to London for the operation. N.Y. Times, Aug. 1, 1989, §B, at 5.

Suppose that the federal government gave a tax deduction to the estate of any cadaver organ donor. Should that be prohibited as a sale? Suppose that health insurance companies, as a result of collective bargaining or governmental requirement, offered lower premiums to persons who agreed to donate their organs at death. Would this be a sale? For arguments in favor of a futures market in cadaver organs, see Gregory S. Crespi, Overcoming the Legal Obstacles to the Creation of a Futures Market in Bodily Organs, 55 Ohio St. L.J. 1 (1994); Lloyd Cohen, Increasing the Supply of Transplant Organs: The Virtues of a Futures Market, 58 Geo. Wash. L. Rev. 1 (1989); Henry Hansmann, The Economics and Ethics of Markets for Human Organs, 14 J. Health Pol. Poly. & L. 57 (1989). See also Julia D. Mahoney, The Market for Human Tissue, 86 Va. L. Rev. 163 (2000).

Sensing that seeking the decedent's prior consent would not produce the necessary organs, the federal government in 1986 took another tack. Hospitals should put pressure on the next of kin to consent. A government report urged states to adopt statutes requiring hospitals to request from families of prospective donors at the time of death permission to remove organs for transplantation. And a federal regulation of the same year made this "routine request" a condition of hospital Medicare eligibility. See U.S. Dept. of Health & Human Services, Report of Task

Force on Organ Transplantation (Apr. 1986). Although most states have enacted "routine request" statutes, because of difficulties families have in facing such requests in time of shock and grief, the routine request approach has not been successful enough to relieve the shortage. A study in five states in 1988 and 1989 by the Center for Biomedical Ethics at the University of Minnesota found that less than one-third of families gave their consent to remove an organ from a family member who had died. Glenn Ruffenach, Trying to Cure Shortage of Organ Donors, Wall St. J., Mar. 13, 1991, at B1.

Others have favored establishing a nationwide system whereby every individual must answer the question: Do you give your organs for transplantation upon your death? The question could be required to be answered upon an application for a driver's license. This system is called "mandated choice."

A significant increase in the quantity of cadaver organs available for transplantation might result if the default rule were switched in favor of presuming that the deceased person has consented. Under such a system, usable organs would be routinely removed from cadavers unless, before the time of removal, an objection were entered, either by the deceased person during life or by the next-of-kin knowing of the decedent's objection immediately after the decedent's death. Such a switched default rule favors preserving life; the burden of objecting is put upon those who would deny life to another. See Jesse Dukeminier, Supplying Organs for Transplantation, 68 Mich. L. Rev. 811 (1970). Such opt-out systems are routinely in force in many states for corneas and pituitary glands (to extract human growth hormone). See Alexander Powhida, Comment, Forced Organ Donation: The Presumed Consent to Organ Donation Laws of the Various States and the United States Constitution, 9 Alb. L.J. Sci. & Tech. 349, 358 n.40 (1999).

In support of a presumption of donation, Professors Sunstein and Thaler argue that this would set the default rule closer to people's preferences:

> In many nations—Austria, Belgium, Denmark, Finland, France, Italy, Luxembourg, Norway, Singapore, Slovenia, and Spain—people are presumed to consent to allow their organs to be used, after death, for the benefit of others; but they are permitted to rebut the presumption, usually through an explicit notation to that effect on their drivers' licenses. In the United States, by contrast, those who want their organs to be available for others must affirmatively say so, also through an explicit notation on their drivers' licenses. The result is that in "presumed consent" nations over 90 percent of people consent to make their organs available for donation, whereas in the United States, where people have to take some action to make their organs available, only 28 percent elect to do so. We hypothesize that this dramatic difference is not a product of deep cultural differences, but of the massive effect of the default rule. Hence we would predict that a European-style opt-out rule in the United States would produce donation rates similar to those observed in the European countries that use this rule. Note in this regard that by one report, over 85 percent of Americans support organ donation—a statistic that suggests opt-outs would be relatively rare. [Cass R. Sunstein & Richard H. Thaler, Libertarian Paternalism Is Not an Oxymoron, 70 U. Chi. L. Rev. 1159, 1192 (2003).]

The median opt-out rate in countries with organ donation as the default is a staggeringly low 1 percent. In Belgium, organ donation increased 119 percent in the first three years after the implementation of the law. For a thorough evaluation of the presumed consent approach, see Committee Report, Ethical and Social Issues in Organ Procurement for Transplantation, 93 N.Y. St. J. Med., No. 1, at 30 (1993).

NOTE: ELDER LAW

A new field of law, called elder law, dealing with legal problems of the elderly, began to develop in the 1990s. Elder law deals with a wide range of issues facing the elderly, including health care, asset preservation, Medicaid eligibility, retirement, competency and guardianship, discrimination, elder abuse, and housing and institutionalization. Practitioners in this area deal with a number of personal health issues, such as nursing home care and continuing care retirement communities. On the property side, lawyers can help with pension plans and social security, estate planning, durable powers of attorney, conservatorships, and trusts to preserve assets if the elderly person is admitted into a state institution. For a taste of this field, see Lawrence A. Frolik & Alison McChystal Barnes, Elder Law (2d ed. 2003); John J. Regan, Rebecca C. Morgan & David M. English, Tax, Estate and Financial Planning for the Elderly (2003); A. Kimberley Dayton, Thomas P. Gallanis & Molly M. Wood, Elder Law: Readings, Cases, and Materials (2d ed. 2003); George P. Smith II, Legal and Healthcare Ethics for the Elderly (1996).

Representing an elderly client with diminishing capacity can be a special challenge. See A. Frank Johns, Older Clients with Diminishing Capacity and Their Advance Directives, 39 Real Prop., Prob. & Tr. J. 107 (2004). In 2002, the American Bar Association revised Model Rule of Prof. Conduct R. 1.14 (Client with Diminished Capacity) to give guidance to lawyers who deal with clients of any age with diminished capacity.

6

CONSTRUCTION OF WILLS

In speaking of the Sergeant of the Lawe, Chaucer, himself trained as a clerk in the Inns of Court, wrote:

> Therto he koude endite and make a thyng,
> Ther koude no wight pynche at his writyng.[1]

Most of the cases in this chapter — and in many of the following chapters too — raise an issue that should have been solved by appropriate drafting. One of the objectives of this book is to help you acquire the ability of Chaucer's Sergeant of the Lawe so that no one can fault your drafting. It is a skill that should stand you in good stead in drafting not only wills and trusts, but all kinds of instruments.

The goal in construing wills is to give effect to the testator's intent. In the words of Restatement (Third) of Property: Wills and Other Donative Transfers §10.1 (2003): "The controlling consideration in determining the meaning of a donative document is the donor's intention. The donor's intention is given effect to the maximum extent allowed by law." As we shall see, however, this is easier said than done.

SECTION A. MISTAKEN OR AMBIGUOUS LANGUAGE IN WILLS

1. The Traditional Approach: No Extrinsic Evidence, No Reformation

In construing wills, a majority of jurisdictions still follow (or purport to follow) two traditional rules that, operating in tandem, bar the admission of evidence to vary

---

1. Geoffrey Chaucer, Prologue to Canterbury Tales (line 325). Done into modern English by Frank E. Hill, The Canterbury Tales 9 (1946):

> And he could write, and pen a deed in law
> So in his writing none could pick a flaw.

the terms of the will. The first is called the *plain meaning* or *no extrinsic evidence* rule. Under the plain meaning rule, extrinsic evidence may be admitted to resolve some ambiguities, but the plain meaning of the words of the will cannot be disturbed by evidence that another meaning was intended.

The closely related second rule is the *no reformation* rule. Reformation is an equitable remedy that, if applied to a will, would correct a mistaken term in the will to reflect what the testator intended the will to say. The justification for refusing to reform wills is that the court is thereby compelled to interpret the words that the testator actually used, not to interpret the words that the testator is purported to have intended to use. Thus in 1922 the Supreme Judicial Court of Massachusetts said:

> Courts have no power to reform wills. Hypothetical or imaginary mistakes of testators can not be corrected. Omissions can not be supplied. Language cannot be modified to meet unforeseen changes in conditions. The only means for ascertaining the intent of the testator are the words written and the acts done by him. [Sanderson v. Norcross, 136 N.E. 170, 172 (Mass. 1922).]

Mahoney v. Grainger
Supreme Judicial Court of Massachusetts, 1933
283 Mass. 189, 186 N.E. 86

RUGG, C.J.   This is an appeal from a decree of a probate court denying a petition for distribution of a legacy under the will of Helen A. Sullivan among her first cousins who are contended to be her heirs at law. The residuary clause was as follows: "All the rest and residue of my estate, both real and personal property, I give, devise and bequeath to my heirs at law living at the time of my decease, absolutely; to be divided among them equally, share and share alike. . . ."

The trial judge made a report of the material facts in substance as follows: The sole heir at law of the testatrix at the time of her death was her maternal aunt, Frances Hawkes Greene, who is still living and who was named in the petition for probate of her will. The will was duly proved and allowed on October 8, 1931, and letters testamentary issued accordingly. The testatrix was a single woman about sixty-four years of age, and had been a school teacher. She always maintained her own home but her relations with her aunt who was her sole heir and with several first cousins were cordial and friendly. In her will she gave general legacies in considerable sums to two of her first cousins. About ten days before her death the testatrix sent for an attorney who found her sick but intelligent about the subjects of their conversation. She told the attorney she wanted to make a will. She gave him instructions as to general pecuniary legacies. In response to the questions "Whom do you want to leave the rest of your property to? Who are your nearest relations?" she replied "I've got about twenty-five first cousins . . . let them share it equally." The attorney then drafted the will and read it to the testatrix and it was executed by her.

The trial judge ruled that statements of the testatrix "were admissible only in so far as they tended to give evidence of the material circumstances surrounding the testatrix at the time of the execution of the will; that the words heirs at law were words in common use, susceptible of application to one or many; that when applied to the special circumstances of this case that the testatrix had but one heir, notwithstanding the added words 'to be divided among them equally, share and share alike,' there was no latent ambiguity or equivocation in the will itself which would permit the introduction of the statements of the testatrix to prove her testamentary intention." Certain first cousins have appealed from the decree dismissing the petition for distribution to them.

There is no doubt as to the meaning of the words "heirs at law living at the time of my decease" as used in the will. Confessedly they refer alone to the aunt of the testatrix and do not include her cousins.

A will duly executed and allowed by the court must under the statute of wills (G.L. [Ter. Ed.] c. 191, §1 et seq.) be accepted as the final expression of the intent of the person executing it. The fact that it was not in conformity to the instructions given to the draftsman who prepared it or that he made a mistake does not authorize a court to reform or alter it or remould it by amendments. The will must be construed as it came from the hands of the testatrix. Polsey v. Newton, 85 N.E. 574 (Mass. 1908). Mistakes in the drafting of the will may be of significance in some circumstances in a trial as to the due execution and allowance of the alleged testamentary instrument. Richardson v. Richards, 115 N.E. 307 (Mass. 1917). Proof that the legatee actually designated was not the particular person intended by the one executing the will cannot be received to aid in the interpretation of a will. Tucker v. Seaman's Aid Society, 7 Metc. 188, 210 (Mass. 1843). When the instrument has been proved and allowed as a will oral testimony as to the meaning and purpose of a testator in using language must be rigidly excluded. Sibley v. Maxwell, 89 N.E. 232 (Mass. 1909); Saucier v. Saucier, 152 N.E. 95 (Mass. 1926); Calder v. Bryant, 184 N.E. 440 (Mass. 1933).

It is only where testamentary language is not clear in its application to facts that evidence may be introduced as to the circumstances under which the testator used that language in order to throw light upon its meaning. Where no doubt exists as to the property bequeathed or the identity of the beneficiary there is no room for extrinsic evidence; the will must stand as written. Barker v. Comins, 110 Mass. 477, 488 (1872); Best v. Berry, 75 N.E. 743 (Mass. 1905).

In the case at bar there is no doubt as to the heirs at law of the testatrix. The aunt alone falls within that description. The cousins are excluded. The circumstance that the plural word "heirs" was used does not prevent one individual from taking the entire gift. Calder v. Bryant, 184 N.E. 440 (Mass. 1933).

Decree affirmed.[2]

---

2. Chief Justice Rugg was not a man plagued by doubts about the law, nor was he much interested in equal rights for women. In Commonwealth v. Welosky, 177 N.E. 656 (Mass. 1931), the question was whether, after women acquired the right to vote by the Nineteenth Amendment, women could serve on juries, a right conferred on "a person qualified to vote" by a Massachusetts statute enacted prior to the Nineteenth Amendment. In denying women this right, Rugg, C.J., reasoned, "The change in the legal status of women wrought by the Nineteenth Amendment was radical, drastic and unprecedented. While it is to be given full effect in its field, it is not to be extended by implication. It is unthinkable that those who first framed and selected the words for the statute [stating qualifications for jury service] had any design that it should ever include women within its scope." Massachusetts did not change its statute, permitting women to serve as jurors, until 1949. In 1950 Harvard Law School followed suit and admitted women as students.

Is Chief Justice Rugg's application of the plain meaning rule to wills consistent with his interpretation of statutes? — Eds.

NOTES AND QUESTIONS

1. In Gustafson v. Svenson, 366 N.E.2d 761 (Mass. 1977), the Massachusetts court reaffirmed Mahoney v. Grainger. The will devised property to Enoch Anderson or "his heirs per stirpes." Enoch predeceased the testator, leaving a wife but no issue. Under Massachusetts law, Enoch's widow was his heir. The court held that testimony of the drafting attorney that the testator did not intend Enoch's devise to go to his widow was inadmissible since the court was of the opinion that the phrase "heirs per stirpes" was not ambiguous. Hence Enoch's widow took the devise.

In 2000, the Massachusetts court went further, explicitly rejecting reformation of wills other than to obtain tax advantages. See Flannery v. McNamara, 738 N.E.2d 739 (Mass. 2000).

2. In Estate of Smith, 555 N.E.2d 1111 (Ill. App. 1990), the testator left a bequest to "PERRY MANOR, INC., Pinckneyville, Illinois." At the time the will was executed, Perry Manor, Inc., a Nevada corporation, operated a nursing home called Perry Manor in Pinckneyville. Before the testator died, Perry Manor, Inc., sold the nursing home to Lifecare Center of Pinckneyville, Inc. Lifecare continued to operate the nursing home and continued to call it Perry Manor. The court held the bequest went to the Nevada corporation, which alone fit exactly the description of the legatee: "PERRY MANOR, INC." The words, "Pinckneyville, Illinois," which were not capitalized, merely described the location of the named legatee at the time of execution. Hence there was no ambiguity, and extrinsic evidence of the testator's intent was inadmissible. To consider such evidence, the court said, "would have the same effect as rewriting the will."

Suppose that the legatee had been described as PERRY MANOR, without the INC. What result?

The *Smith* case is reminiscent of National Socy. for the Prevention of Cruelty to Children v. Scottish Natl. Socy. for the Prevention of Cruelty to Children, [1915] A.C. 207. In this case, a Scotsman, who had always lived in Scotland and was interested in Scottish charities, leaving a number of bequests to them by will, bequeathed £500 to "The National Society for the Prevention of Cruelty to Children," which was the charter name of a society in London, of which the testator had never heard. Near his home was a branch office of the *Scottish National Society for the Prevention of Cruelty to Children,* whose activities he knew. Which charity should get the £500? The House of Lords held the remote charity in London should get the money because "he had by name designated it." For criticism of this case, in a classic article on the meaning of words, see Zechariah Chaffee, Jr., The Disorderly Conduct of Words, 41 Colum. L. Rev. 381, 385 (1941).

3. *Personal usage exception.* If the extrinsic evidence shows that the testator always referred to a person in an idiosyncratic manner, the evidence is admissible to show that the testator meant someone other than the person with the legal name of the legatee. Thus in Moseley v. Goodman, 195 S.W. 590 (Tenn. 1917), the testator, in a list of bequests, left $20,000 to "Mrs. Moseley." Mrs. Lenore Moseley, the wife of the cigar store owner where the testator traded, but whom the testator had never met, claimed the bequest. The court, however, held that the bequest went to Mrs. Lillian Trimble, whom the testator called Mrs. Moseley.

Trimble's husband was a salesman in Moseley's cigar store and was called "Moseley" by the testator; his wife — dubbed Mrs. Moseley by the testator — managed the apartment house where the testator lived and did kind things for him.

4. *Patent ambiguities*. A patent ambiguity is an ambiguity that appears on the face of the will. For example, in Succession of Neff, 716 So. 2d 410 (La. App. 1998), one clause in *T*'s will left the "disposable portion of my estate" to *T*'s daughter *A*, while the very next clause left "my entire estate" to *T*'s daughters *A* and *B*. In some states, extrinsic evidence is not admissible to clarify even a patent ambiguity, and the will or the devise fails. Increasingly, however, as in *Neff*, extrinsic evidence is allowed to aid in interpreting a patent ambiguity. See Andrea W. Cornelison, Dead Man Talking: Are Courts Ready to Listen? The Erosion of the Plain Meaning Rule, 35 Real Prop., Prob. & Tr. J. 811 (2001). Another approach is to construe the language of the will without the aid of extrinsic evidence in a manner that saves the devise. For example, in Estate of Akeley, 215 P.2d 921 (Cal. 1950), the testator, purporting to devise her entire estate, gave 25 percent to each of three charities. The court construed the clause to give one-third shares to each charity on the theory that the testator intended to devise her entire estate.[3] And in Smith v. Burt, 57 N.E.2d 493 (Ill. 1944), the testator, a distinguished judge, devised to *A* 80 acres out of the Station Street Farm and to *B* the remaining 140 acres of the same farm. The patent ambiguity is: Which 80 acres? The court held that *A* had no right of selection, which other courts might have given *A*, but that *A* and *B* were intended to be tenants in common in fractional shares in the farm. See also Stephenson v. Rowe, 338 S.E.2d 301 (N.C. 1986) (holding devisee has power to select 30 acres out of 164 and discussing other alternative constructions and cases from many states); Annot., 35 A.L.R.4th 788 (1985, rev. 1993).

5. *Latent ambiguities*. A latent ambiguity is an ambiguity that does not appear on the face of the will but manifests itself when the terms of the will are applied to the testator's property or designated beneficiaries. Oral declarations of intent to the scrivener are admitted in most jurisdictions in cases of latent ambiguity.

"Generally, there are two types of latent ambiguity. The first type occurs when a will clearly describes a person or thing, and two or more persons or things exactly fit that description. The second type of latent ambiguity exists when no person or thing exactly fits the description, but two or more persons or things partially fit." Phipps v. Barbera, 498 N.E.2d 411, 412 n.3 (Mass. App. 1986).

The first type of latent ambiguity is called *equivocation*. Admission of extrinsic evidence to clarify a latent ambiguity first began in such cases, where a description fits two or more people or things equally well (e.g., a devise "to my niece Alicia," when in fact the testator has two nieces named Alicia). The courts reasoned that the extrinsic evidence did not add anything to the will, which would

---

3. Devises of fractional shares that total less or more than one remind us of the old brainteaser about a man whose will specified that his 11 horses be divided so that his eldest son would get 1/2, his middle son would get 1/4, and his youngest son would get 1/6. When he died, his executor could not figure out how to carry out these instructions. After all, horses are of little value when sliced into fractional parts. The executor went to a lawyer for advice. The lawyer solved the problem. How? The lawyer lent the executor his horse. The 12 animals were then easily divided according to the formula in the will, the eldest son getting six, the middle son three, and the youngest two. One horse was then left over, which was returned to the lawyer. That's horse sense for you!

be forbidden; the evidence merely made the terms of the will more specific. See Succession of Bacot, 502 So. 2d 1118 (La. App. 1987) (will left "all to Danny"; court chose one of three homosexual lovers, all named Danny, who extrinsic evidence showed had the closest relationship to testator). Where there is an equivocation, direct expressions of the testator's intent are admissible in evidence.

The second type of latent ambiguity, where the description in the will does not exactly fit any person or thing, is more common. For example, in Ihl v. Oetting, 682 S.W.2d 865 (Mo. App. 1984), the testator devised his home to "Mr. and Mrs. Wendell Richard Hess, or the survivor of them, presently residing at No. 17 Barbara Circle." When the will was executed in 1979, Wendell Hess and his wife Glenda resided at No. 17 Barbara Circle. Soon thereafter Wendell divorced Glenda, they sold No. 17 Barbara Circle, and Wendell married Verna. At the testator's death in 1983, Verna, relying on the rule that a will speaks as of the testator's death, claimed the "Mrs. Hess" share of the devise. She argued that no extrinsic evidence should be admitted since there was no ambiguity in the will — she alone met the description of "Mrs. Wendell Richard Hess." The court, however, found that a latent ambiguity arose from the description of the beneficiaries as "residing at No. 17 Barbara Circle." (Why was not this struck out as a misdescription? See page 373.) Verna Hess met the description of Mrs. Wendell Richard Hess at the time of the testator's death but she never resided at No. 17 Barbara Circle. Glenda met the description of the Mrs. Hess residing at No. 17 Barbara Circle when the will was executed but she no longer met that description at the time of the testator's death. The court admitted extrinsic evidence that, the court decided, showed an intent that Glenda — who shared a common interest in antiques with the testator — take.

6. Whether an ambiguity is patent or latent may depend on who the reader is. In Estate of Black, 27 Cal. Rptr. 418 (App. 1962), the testator, a resident of northern California, left her estate "to the University of Southern California known as The U.C.L.A." The trial court ruled there was no ambiguity and construed the gift to be "to the university in Southern California known as The U.C.L.A." The appellate court reversed, holding the devise to be ambiguous. However, the ambiguity was deemed latent not patent, and extrinsic evidence could be admitted to resolve it. Why not a patent ambiguity?

> The provision in question is not, on its face, susceptible to one of two constructions. The language is clear, intelligible and suggests a single meaning. A reader unacquainted with the fact that there are two universities in Southern California, one known as the University of Southern California, and another commonly referred to by the initials U.C.L.A., would readily attribute to said provision the meaning that it refers to an institution named "University of Southern California," which is known by the initials U.C.L.A. [27 Cal. Rptr. at 424.]

Suppose the devise had been "to Harvard University known as M.I.T." Or "to New York Law School known as N.Y.U." Patent or latent ambiguity?

7. The plain meaning or no extrinsic evidence rule has been criticized as fundamentally misdirected.[4] Professor Wigmore, the great authority on evidence,

---

4. Another view of the plain meaning rule was expressed by A.P. Herbert's Lord Mildew: "If Parliament does not mean what it says it must say so." A.P. Herbert, Uncommon Law 313 (2d ed. 1936).

vigorously attacked the rule, saying, "The fallacy consists in assuming that there is or ever can be *some one real* or absolute meaning. In truth there can be only *some person's* meaning: and that person, whose meaning the law is seeking, is the writer of the document. . . . [T]he 'plain meaning' is simply the meaning of the people who did *not* write the document." 9 John H. Wigmore, Evidence §2462, at 198 (James H. Chadbourn rev. 1981) (emphasis in original). The plain meaning rule reflects a dream, a hope, of

> that lawyer's Paradise, where all words have a fixed, precisely ascertained meaning, and where, if the writer has been careful, a lawyer having a document referred to him may sit in his chair, inspect the text, and answer all questions without raising his eyes. . . . But the fatal necessity of looking outside the text in order to identify persons and things, tends steadily to destroy such illusions and to reveal the essential imperfection of language, whether spoken or written. [James B. Thayer, A Preliminary Treatise on Evidence 428 (1898).]

Compare the view of Justice Holmes, who insisted that the proper standard was not what the writer meant to say but the public meaning of the words in the writer's specific circumstances:

> [W]e ask, not what this man meant, but what those words would mean in the mouth of a normal speaker of English, using them in the circumstances in which they were used, and it is to the end of answering this last question that we let in evidence as to what the circumstances were. . . . But the normal speaker of English is merely a special variety, a literary form, so to speak, of our old friend the prudent man. He is external to the particular writer, and a reference to him as the criterion is simply another instance of the externality of the law. [Oliver Wendell Holmes, The Theory of Legal Interpretation, 12 Harv. L. Rev. 417, 417-418 (1899).]

See also Jane B. Baron, Intention, Interpretation, and Stories, 42 Duke L.J. 630 (1992); Mary L. Fellows, In Search of Donative Intent, 73 Iowa L. Rev. 611 (1988).

8.   For a thorough discussion of the problem of resolving ambiguities in donative instruments, see Restatement (Third) of Property: Wills and Other Donative Transfers §§11.1-11.3 (2003).

2.   *Slouching Toward Reformation: Correcting Mistakes Without the Power to Reform Wills*

To the extent that the traditional hostility toward reforming wills rests on the premise that mischief will ensue if the courts are allowed to reject the seemingly clear words of the will, the question then arises, how do we explain the doctrines of undue influence, testamentary capacity (including insane delusions), duress, and fraud? In a case involving any of these doctrines, the court looks at evidence of the circumstances surrounding the will's execution in order to ascertain whether the will in fact reflects the wishes of the testator. On this view, the rule against reformation — that is, the rule against correcting an innocent mistake in the terms of a will — is at odds with routine practice in other areas of the law of wills. Thus:

The Causes and Effects of Will Defects

	Effect: Lack of Volition	Effect: Mistaken Terms
Cause: Intentional Wrongdoing	**Undue Influence, Duress** (relief granted)	**Fraud** (relief granted)
Cause: Innocent Acts	**Lack of Capacity, Insane Delusion** (relief granted)	**Mistake** (no relief)

If intentional wrongdoing causes a mistaken term in a will (*fraud*), that term can be struck or its effect undone. If a lack of volition has an innocent cause (*lack of capacity*), the will is not given effect. And if a particularly bizarre mistaken belief about a member of the testator's family influences the testator's dispositive scheme, the courts sometimes remedy this mistake by calling it an *insane delusion*. Yet if a mistaken term has an innocent cause (*mistake*), then no relief is available to correct the error.

The rule against reformation is an even greater outlier than this chart implies. Under traditional law, courts remedy mistaken revocation of wills under the doctrine of dependent relative revocation (see page 259). If a testator fails to provide for a living child solely because he mistakenly believes the child to be dead, under Uniform Probate Code §2-302(c) (1990) the child receives an intestate share in the testator's estate (see page 155). And if a testator forgets to update his will after a major life event such as a divorce or the birth of a child, statutes in many states partially or completely revoke or otherwise modify the testator's will accordingly (see pages 269-270).

In this light, consider again the rules on patent and latent ambiguity (including equivocation) and the personal usage exception that are discussed in the notes after Mahoney v. Grainger, supra. Under the guise of resolving ambiguity, are not the courts in effect correcting mistakes by reference to extrinsic evidence? For example, in Moseley v. Goodman, supra, the court read "Mrs. Moseley" to mean "Mrs. Trimble." Is this not a reformation of a mistake — that is, a correction of the instrument to reflect what the testator meant to say?

A careful review of the cases reveals an unmistakable trend toward admitting extrinsic evidence not merely to resolve ambiguities, but also to correct mistakes in view of the actual intent of the testator.

Arnheiter v. Arnheiter

Superior Court of New Jersey, Chancery Division, 1956
42 N.J. Super. 71, 125 A.2d 914

SULLIVAN, J.   Burnette K. Guterl died on December 31, 1953, leaving a last will and testament which has been admitted to probate by the Surrogate of Essex

County. By paragraph 2 of said will her executrix was directed "to sell my undivided one-half interest of premises known as No. 304 Harrison Avenue, Harrison, New Jersey," and use the proceeds of sale to establish trusts for each of decedent's two nieces.

This suit comes about because the decedent did not own or have any interest in 304 Harrison Avenue either at her death or at the time her will was executed. At the hearing it was established that the decedent, at the time her will was executed and also at the time of her death, owned an undivided one-half interest in 317 Harrison Avenue, Harrison, New Jersey, and that this was the only property on Harrison Avenue that she had any interest in.

Plaintiff-executrix has applied to this court to correct an obvious mistake and to change the street number in paragraph "2" of the will to read "No. 317 Harrison Avenue" instead of "No. 304 Harrison Avenue." Relief cannot be granted to the plaintiff in the precise manner sought. It matters not that an obvious mistake in the form of a misdescription is proved. A court has no power to correct or reform a will or change any of the language therein by substituting or adding words. The will of a decedent executed pursuant to statute is what it is and no court can add to it.

Plaintiff, however, is not without recourse. In the construction of wills and other instruments there is a principle *"falsa demonstratio non nocet"* (mere erroneous description does not vitiate), which applies directly to the difficulty at hand.

> Where a description of a thing or person consists of several particulars and all of them do not fit any one person or thing, less essential particulars may be rejected provided the remainder of the description clearly fits. This is known as the doctrine of *falsa demonstratio non nocet.* Clapp, 5 N.J. Practice, §114, at 274. . . .

Turning to the problem at hand and to the description of the property as set forth in paragraph 2 of the will, we find the street number "304" to be erroneous because decedent did not own that property. If we disregard or reject that item of description, the will then directs the executrix "to sell my undivided one-half interest of premises known as Harrison Avenue, Harrison, New Jersey." Since it has been established that the decedent, at the time of her death and also when she executed her will, had an interest in only one piece of property on Harrison Avenue, Harrison, New Jersey; that her interest was an undivided one-half interest; that the property in question is 317 Harrison Avenue; and that decedent made no other specific provision in her will relating to 317 Harrison Avenue, we are led inevitably to the conclusion that even without a street number, the rest of the description in paragraph 2 of the will is sufficient to identify the property passing thereunder as 317 Harrison Avenue.

Judgment will be entered construing decedent's will as aforesaid.

QUESTIONS

What is the difference between reformation and the principle that "mere erroneous description does not vitiate"? Do not both doctrines give testamentary effect to extrinsic evidence of what the testator *meant* to say instead of what the testator *actually* said?

ESTATE OF GIBBS, 111 N.W.2d 413 (Wis. 1961): George and Lena Adele Gibbs both died in 1960. In their respective wills they each made the following bequest:

> To Robert J. Krause, now of 4708 North 46th Street, Milwaukee, Wisconsin, if he survives me, one per cent (1%).

The Robert J. Krause who lived at 4708 North 46th Street in Milwaukee was quite happy to claim part of George and Lena's estates, but neither George nor Lena knew him. Their friend for three decades was Robert *W.* Krause, who lived at a different address. After the cases were consolidated, the trial court awarded both bequests to Robert *W.* Krause.

On appeal, the Wisconsin Supreme Court acknowledged the traditional rule against reformation. "It is traditional doctrine that wills must not be reformed even in the case of demonstrable mistake." The court also observed that, "Under rules as to construction of a will, unless there is ambiguity in the text of the will read in the light of surrounding circumstances, extrinsic evidence is inadmissible for the purpose of determining intent." In this case, "The terms of the bequest exactly fit appellant [Robert *J.* Krause] and no one else. There is no ambiguity."

Despite disavowing the power of reformation, and finding no ambiguity that would have justified recourse to extrinsic evidence, the court nonetheless corrected the mistake:

> Although the courts subscribe to an inflexible rule against reformation of a will, it seems that they have often strained a point in matters of identification of property or beneficiaries in order to reach a desired result by way of construction. . . .
>
> We conclude that details of identification, particularly such matters as middle initials, street addresses, and the like, which are highly susceptible to mistake, particularly in metropolitan areas, should not be accorded such sanctity as to frustrate an otherwise clearly demonstrable intent. Where such details of identification are involved, courts should receive evidence tending to show that a mistake has been made and should disregard the details when the proof establishes to the highest degree of certainty that a mistake was, in fact, made.
>
> We therefore consider that the county court properly disregarded the middle initial and street address, and determined that respondent was the Robert Krause whom testators had in mind.

QUESTION

Does the question of who takes the property under a will raise a mere detail of identification?

3.   *Openly Reforming Wills for Mistake*

Erickson v. Erickson
Supreme Court of Connecticut, 1998
246 Conn. 359, 716 A.2d 92

BORDEN, J.   The dispositive issue in this appeal is whether, pursuant to General Statutes (Rev. to 1995) §45a-257 (a), the trial court should have admitted extrinsic evidence regarding the decedent's intent that his will would not be revoked automatically by his subsequent marriage.[5] The named plaintiff, Alicia Erickson,[6] who is the daughter of the decedent, Ronald K. Erickson, appeals from the judgment of the trial court in favor of the defendant, Dorothy Erickson,[7] the executrix of the estate of the decedent, dismissing the plaintiff's appeal from the decree of the Probate Court for the district of Madison. The Probate Court had admitted the will of the decedent to probate. The trial court ruled that the decedent's will, which had been executed shortly before his marriage to the defendant, provided for the contingency of marriage.

The plaintiff claims on her appeal that the trial court improperly concluded that the decedent's will provided for the contingency of marriage. The defendant claims on her cross appeal that the trial court improperly excluded certain extrinsic evidence regarding the decedent's intent. We conclude that the trial court should have permitted the defendant to introduce extrinsic evidence of the decedent's intent. Accordingly, we reverse the judgment of the trial court and order a new trial.

Certain facts in this appeal are undisputed. On September 1, 1988, the decedent executed a will. At that time, he had three daughters and was unmarried. Two days later, on September 3, 1988, he married the defendant. He died on February 22, 1996.

The six articles of his will provide as follows. The first article provides for the payment of funeral expenses and debts by the estate. The second article states that the residue of the estate will pass to the defendant. The third article provides that if the defendant predeceases the decedent, one half of the residuary estate will pass in equal parts to the decedent's three daughters, Laura Erickson Kusy, Ellen Erickson Cates and Alicia Erickson, and one half of the residuary estate will pass in equal parts to Thomas Mehring, Christopher Mehring, Maureen Mehring and Kathleen Mehring, the children of the defendant. The fourth article appoints the defendant as the executrix of the will, with Attorney Robert O'Brien as the contingent executor in the event that the defendant is unable to or refuses to serve as executrix. The fifth article gives the executrix or executor the power to dispose of property of the estate as necessary. The sixth article appoints the defendant as the guardian of any of the decedent's children who have not reached the age of eighteen at the time of his death.

The Probate Court admitted the decedent's will to probate. The plaintiff appealed from the Probate Court's judgment. Prior to trial, the plaintiff filed a motion in limine to exclude extrinsic evidence of the decedent's intent. The plaintiff argued that "§45a-257 makes the Court's inquiry very simple: to determine whether the will was revoked, the Court need examine only [the decedent's] will, his marriage certificate to [the defendant], and his death certificate. Extrinsic evidence regarding [the decedent's] intentions is inadmissible because the language of [the decedent's] will is unambiguous, and therefore under . . . §45a-257 the operation of the marriage to revoke the will is automatic and mandatory."

---

5. General Statutes (Rev. to 1995) §45a-257 (a) provides: "If, after the making of a will, the testator marries . . . and no provision has been made in such will for such contingency, such marriage . . . shall operate as a revocation of such will. . . ."

6. The decedent's other two daughters, Laura Erickson Kusy and Ellen Erickson Cates, did not appeal from the judgment of the trial court. Hereafter, we refer to Alicia Erickson as the plaintiff.

7. The defendant's name before her marriage to the decedent was Dorothy A. Mehring.

The defendant, in opposition to the plaintiff's motion, made a detailed offer of proof to show the contrary intent of the decedent.[8]

The admission of certain evidence was undisputed, namely, the will, the marriage certificate of the decedent and the defendant, and the decedent's death certificate. The trial . . . granted the motion in limine, however, with respect to any other evidence regarding the decedent's intent.

With respect to the other issue at trial, namely, whether the decedent's will provided for the contingency of his marriage to the defendant, the trial court, in a de novo proceeding, concluded that the Probate Court properly had admitted the will to probate because the will provided for the contingency of marriage. The trial court reasoned that "[the decedent's] will bequeathed all of his estate to the woman he was licensed to marry and did marry two days later. In his will, he named her executrix and designated her the guardian of his daughters, whose mother had previously died. The nature of these provisions, coupled with the extreme closeness in time of the marriage constitutes clear and convincing evidence of provision for the contingency of marriage. It would be preposterous to assume that [the decedent] was instead executing a will to make provisions that were to be revoked two days later." Accordingly, the trial court rendered judgment affirming the Probate Court's judgment admitting the will, and denied the plaintiff's appeal. This appeal followed. . . .

8. The defendant's offer of proof provided in part: "May it please the court, if [O'Brien and the defendant] were permitted to testify they would testify as follows. [O'Brien] would testify that he is an attorney before the Hartford [bar], that he was for many years prior to the marriage in 1988 the attorney for [the decedent].

"In addition to being his attorney on a variety of business and personal matters, he was also a close friend of [the decedent]. He was aware that [the decedent] was courting [the defendant] who became [his wife] and he was invited to their wedding which was scheduled for September 3, 1988.

"About one week prior to that time he received a call from [the decedent] saying he and [the defendant] immediately after the wedding were going to go to New York and then take a Concorde flight to Ireland and they wanted to arrange, as many of us do prior to events like that, for their wills to be drafted prior to the marriage ceremony.

"He gave him instructions that the wills would be identical, that is, that all of his estate was to go to [the defendant]. If [the defendant] should predecease him it should go to, half should go to his children, half to [the defendant's] children. That [the defendant] should be the executrix of the will and that she would be appointed guardian of his children, and that [her] will be exactly the same.

"On Thursday, September 1, two days before the wedding, the two of them went to Hartford and executed the wills. I would offer [the defendant's] will as a piece of evidence. And I represent to the court that it is a mirror image of [the decedent's] will that you have admitted as an exhibit. She, like [the decedent], leaves everything to him. If he should predecease her half of her estate goes to his children, half to her children. He appoints her guardian of his children and appoints [her] executor of his estate.

"During the course of the execution of the wills there was no conversation whatsoever about the fact that the Saturday marriage would revoke the will that had been drafted on Thursday. The wedding to take place two days later would revoke the will that had been drafted on Thursday, although there was considerable discussion about the marriage itself and the festivities and the guests and things like that.

"[O'Brien] would testify that the reason that he did not place in the will any specific mention of the marriage or talk about it at all with [the defendant] or [the decedent] was because in his view when a man executes a will two days before his marriage in which he leaves everything to the woman that he's about to marry, makes her guardian of his children, makes her executrix of the estate, and if she should predecease him, leaves half of his estate to her kids, . . . [it] clearly makes provision in the will for not just a contingency, but the imminent [inevitability] of the marriage that's going to take place two days later. So he didn't think there was any necessity that he had to put in words when it was so clear that it was making [provision for his imminent marriage.] . . .

[The lawyer O'Brien would also testify that he visited the testator while he was suffering from terminal cancer. Twice O'Brien reviewed the will with the decedent and assured the decedent that his property was going to his wife. At the second such meeting, the decedent asked O'Brien to set up a corporation and distribute stock in it to his daughters, which O'Brien did. The widow would also testify to similar facts.]

We conclude that the will, in and of itself, did not provide for the contingency of the subsequent marriage of the decedent and, therefore, under existing case law, properly would have been revoked by that marriage pursuant to §45a-257(a). We also conclude, however, that under the circumstances of this case, the trial court improperly excluded evidence of a mistake by the scrivener that, if believed, would permit a finding that the will provided for the contingency of marriage. We therefore reverse the judgment of the trial court and order a new trial in which such evidence may be considered by the trial court.

On the basis of existing case law, the question of whether a will provides for the contingency of a subsequent marriage must be determined: (1) from the language of the will itself; and (2) without resort to extrinsic evidence of the testator's intent. Fulton Trust Co. v. Trowbridge, 11 A.2d 393 (Conn. 1940). . . . Applying this standard, we conclude that the trial court should not have admitted the will because, notwithstanding the inferences that the trial court drew from the dates of the marriage license and the will, and from the identity of certain of the named beneficiaries in the will, there was no language in the will providing for the contingency of the subsequent marriage of the decedent. . . .

This conclusion does not, however, end our inquiry in this case. In Connecticut Junior Republic v. Sharon Hospital, 448 A.2d 190 (Conn. 1982),[9] this court considered the issue of "whether extrinsic evidence of a mistake by a scrivener of a testamentary instrument is admissible in a proceeding to determine the validity of the testamentary instrument." In a three to two decision, this court held that such evidence is not admissible. Upon further consideration, we now conclude that the reasons given by the dissent in that case are persuasive and apply to the facts of the present case. We, therefore, overrule *Connecticut Junior Republic*, and hold that if a scrivener's error has misled the testator into executing a will on the belief that it will be valid notwithstanding the testator's subsequent marriage, extrinsic evidence of that error is admissible to establish the intent of the testator that his or her will be valid notwithstanding the subsequent marriage. Furthermore, if those two facts, namely, the scrivener's error and its effect on the testator's intent, are established by clear and convincing evidence, they will be sufficient to establish that "provision has been made in such will for such contingency," within the meaning of §45a-257(a).

In Connecticut Junior Republic v. Sharon Hospital, supra, this court reasserted the familiar rule that, although extrinsic evidence is not admissible to prove an intention not expressed in the will itself or to prove a devise or bequest not

9. In Connecticut Junior Republic v. Sharon Hospital, the testator, Richard Emerson, executed a will on May 19, 1960, which created trusts for a designated person for life, remainder to seven named charities (the 1960 charities). In 1969, Emerson executed a codicil to his will deleting six of the seven 1960 charities as remaindermen and substituting for the six 11 different charities (the 1969 charities). Soon after the 1969 codicil was executed, the Internal Revenue Code was amended to deny the charitable deduction to bequests of remainders unless they were made in the form of a unitrust or annuity trust (see pages 917-918); the remainders in Emerson's 1969 codicil did not qualify. The executor and trustee of Emerson's will, Sager McDonald, called this point to the attention of Emerson in 1975, and Emerson instructed his attorney, Paul Doherty, to amend the will and codicil in such a manner as to qualify the trusts as charitable bequests under the Tax Reform Act of 1969. The attorney then drafted a second codicil, making the requested changes but also mistakenly reinstating the 1960 charities as remaindermen and deleting the 1969 charities. Emerson, who had never requested or authorized this change, signed the second codicil in 1975. Upon Emerson's death in 1979, the probate court admitted the second codicil to probate, refusing to permit introduction of extrinsic evidence as to the scrivener's mistake. The supreme court affirmed. — Eds.

Justice Ellen A. Peters
Her dissent in Connecticut
Junior Republic becomes law.

contained in the will, such evidence is admissible to identify a named devisee or legatee, to identify property described in the will, to clarify ambiguous language in the will, and to prove fraud, incapacity or undue influence. . . .

The dissent in that case by Justice Peters and joined by Justice Shea, concluded that it "would permit extrinsic evidence of a scrivener's error to be introduced in litigation concerned with the admissibility of a disputed will to probate." Id., 22. The dissent gave three principal reasons for its conclusion, each of which we consider to be persuasive and each of which applies to this case.

First, given that extrinsic evidence is admissible to prove that a will was executed by the testator "in reliance on erroneous beliefs induced by fraud, duress, or undue influence," there is no discernible policy difference between that case and a case in which "a will is executed in reliance on erroneous beliefs induced by the innocent error, by the innocent misrepresentation, of the scrivener of a will." Id., 23. In each instance, "the testamentary process is distorted by the interference of a third person who misleads the testator into making a testamentary disposition that would not otherwise have occurred." Id., 22-23. "In each instance, extrinsic evidence is required to demonstrate that a will, despite its formally proper execution, substantially misrepresents the true intent of the testator." Id., 23.

Similarly, in the present case, there is no discernible policy difference between extrinsic evidence offered to show fraud, duress or undue influence, and extrinsic evidence offered to show that a scrivener's error induced the decedent to execute a will that he believed would survive his subsequent marriage. In both instances, the testamentary process was distorted by the interference of a third person who misled the testator into executing a will that would not otherwise have been executed — in the present case, a will that would be revoked upon his marriage because it did not contain language providing for the contingency of marriage. Thus, as in the case of fraud, duress or undue influence, extrinsic evidence is required to demonstrate that the will that the testator executed did not substantially state his true intention.[10]

Second, the dissent recognized that, based on the policy of the statute of wills, the "risk of subversion of the intent of a testator, who cannot personally defend his testamentary bequest, is without doubt a serious concern." Id., 24. The dissent, however, persuasively underscored the counterbalancing "risk of blindly enforcing

---

10. We acknowledge that permitting extrinsic evidence of a scrivener's error will lead to the introduction of extrinsic evidence of intent, which, as we noted previously, is not permitted. For the reasons discussed herein, this common-law exception is no different, however, from the extrinsic evidence of intent permitted in cases alleging fraud, undue influence and duress.

a testamentary disposition that substantially misstates the testator's true intent." Id. Again drawing on the analogy to the case of fraud, duress or undue influence, the dissent stated that "had the decedent's lawyer deliberately and fraudulently altered the second codicil, the relevant extrinsic evidence would unquestionably have been admitted." Id., 25. The dissent contended that "innocent misrepresentation is treated as generally equivalent to fraud in terms of its legal consequences." Id. Therefore, the dissent asserted, the "statute of wills does not compel enforcement of testamentary dispositions that a testator never intended to make." Id.

Similarly, in the present case, had the decedent's attorney deliberately and fraudulently, rather than innocently but mistakenly, misrepresented to the decedent that his will would be valid despite his subsequent marriage, it is at least arguable that the beneficiaries of that fraudulent conduct, namely, the heirs-at-law of the decedent who would inherit in the event of his intestacy, would not be permitted to take advantage of that fraud, and that a court of equity could impress a constructive trust on their inheritance. We conclude that, analogously, in this case, the extrinsic evidence should be admissible to establish the decedent's true intent.

Third, the dissent examined and rejected the two main objections to the admission of extrinsic evidence of a scrivener's error. One objection was "that whatever error the scrivener may have made was validated and ratified by the testator's act in signing his will." Id., 26. The dissent responded, correctly in our view, that, although "signing [a] will creates a strong presumption that the will accurately represents the intentions of the testator, that presumption is a rebuttable one." Id. Similarly, in the present case, although the fact that the decedent signed the will may create a rebuttable presumption that he did not intend it to survive his subsequent marriage, that presumption should be rebuttable by persuasive extrinsic evidence to the contrary.

The other objection was "that allowing extrinsic evidence of mistake will give rise to a proliferation of groundless will contests." Id. The dissent presented a two part response, with which we also agree. First, it noted that, "in the law of contracts, where the parol evidence rule has undergone considerable erosion, this risk has not been found to have been unmanageable. In the law of wills, the risk is limited by the narrowness of the exception that this case would warrant . . . [namely, to] permit the opponent of a will to introduce extrinsic evidence of the error of a scrivener, and [to] require proof of such an extrinsic error to be established by clear and convincing evidence." Id., 26-27.

Similarly, in the present case, the admissibility of such extrinsic evidence, in our view, will not prove to be any less manageable than in cases of parol evidence in contract disputes. Furthermore, we would impose the same elevated burden of proof on the proponent of the will in a case such as this. The proponent would have to establish the scrivener's error by clear and convincing evidence.

. . . The dissent in *Connecticut Junior Republic* phrased the issue in that case as follows: "Must the true intent of the testator be thwarted when, because of the mistake of a scrivener, he has formally subscribed to a written bequest that substantially misstates his testamentary intention?" Id., 22. That is precisely the issue in the present case. The dissent in *Connecticut Junior Republic* answered that question in the negative, recognizing that evidence of a scrivener's mistake should be admissible where offered to establish that a written bequest should not be admitted to probate because its execution was the product of a mistake of the scrivener and, therefore, did not embody the disposition intended by the testator. Likewise, in the present case, evidence of a scrivener's mistake should be admissible to establish that a written bequest should be admitted to probate because the disposition provided by the bequest would have obtained, in accordance with the decedent's intent, but for the scrivener's mistake. . . .

Applying these principles to the facts of the present case, we conclude that the extrinsic evidence offered, if believed, could prove clearly and convincingly that there was a scrivener's error that induced the decedent to execute a will that he intended to be valid despite his subsequent marriage. The offer of proof indicates that the evidence would be susceptible to an inference by the fact finder that there had been an implied assertion by the scrivener that the will would be valid despite the decedent's subsequent marriage. This inference could have been bolstered, moreover, by the evidence of the conversations between the decedent and the scrivener shortly before the decedent's death.

The judgment is reversed and the case is remanded for a new trial.

Restatement (Third) of Property: Wills and Other Donative Transfers (2003)

§12.1 REFORMING DONATIVE DOCUMENTS TO CORRECT MISTAKES

A donative document, though unambiguous, may be reformed to conform the text to the donor's intention if the following are established by clear and convincing evidence:

(1) that a mistake of fact or law, whether in expression or inducement, affected specific terms of the document; and

(2) what the donor's intention was.

Direct evidence of intention contradicting the plain meaning of the text as well as other evidence of intention may be considered in determining whether elements (1) and (2) have been established by clear and convincing evidence.

John H. Langbein, Curing Execution Errors and Mistaken Terms in Wills
18 Prob. & Prop. 28, 28-31 (Jan./Feb. 2004)

In recent years a remarkable change has been emerging in the way American courts treat cases involving errors in the execution or mistakes in the content of wills. When some innocuous blunder occurred in complying with the Wills Act formalities, such as when one attesting witness went to the washroom before the other had finished signing, the courts used to apply a rule of strict compliance and hold the will invalid. Likewise, in cases of mistaken terms, for example, when the typist dropped a paragraph from the will or the drafter misrendered names or other attributes of a devise, the courts applied a no reformation rule; the will could not be corrected no matter how conclusively the mistake was shown.

Ironically, these intent-defeating results were reached in the name of legal requirements that were meant to be intent-serving. . . . The formalities [for executing wills] are not difficult to comply with, and cases of breach mostly arise when the testator does not use counsel. . . . Cases involving omitted or mistaken terms raise a similar issue — whether to restore to a will language that was to have been included within the will but was accidentally omitted or misrendered before the will was signed and attested.

THE TREND AWAY FROM FORMALISM

Leading modern authority in a number of American states has now reversed the strict compliance and no reformation rules. Both by judicial decision and by legislation, the courts have been empowered to excuse harmless execution errors and to reform mistaken terms. . . .

MISTAKEN TERMS

Section 12.1 of the [Restatement (Third) of Property: Wills and Other Donative Transfers] authorizes courts to reform mistaken terms in a will. The measure is based upon an extensive body of supporting case law, which the Restatement canvasses in its Reporter's Notes. Section 12.1 provides that a court may reform any donative document, including a will, to "conform the text to the donor's intention if it is established by clear and convincing evidence (1) that a mistake of fact or law, whether in expression or inducement, affected specific terms of the document; and (2) what the donor's intention was."

The Restatement also endorses the movement to allow courts to reform wills, trusts, and other donative documents quite apart from instances of mistake, in situations in which reformation would achieve a tax objective that the donor would have wished. Restatement §12.2 (extensive case law is reviewed in the Reporter's Notes).[11]

WHY THE CHANGE?

The reorientation toward a more intent-serving approach to the Wills Act formalities is the product of many influences. The scholarly literature that has accompanied the change has drawn attention to four main factors:

(1)   the rise of the nonprobate system;
(2)   experience in other jurisdictions;
(3)   growing embarrassment that failure to cure well-proved mistakes inflicts unjust enrichment; and
(4)   concern to spare lawyers from needless malpractice liability.

UNIFYING THE LAW OF PROBATE AND NONPROBATE TRANSFERS

Since World War II the use of nonprobate modes of transfer on death has burgeoned. Far more wealth now flows through the main will substitutes (inter vivos

---

11. We take up reformation of trusts for mistake, modification to achieve tax savings, and modifications made desirable in view of changed circumstances in Chapter 8 at pages 572-587. — Eds.

trusts, beneficiary designations in pension accounts, life insurance policies, and POD/TOD accounts with banks, mutual funds, and brokerage houses) than passes through probate. A dominant theme of law revision activity during this period has been to unify the constructional principles across the field of probate and non-probate transfers. . . . The harmless error and reformation rules now being applied to mistakes in wills are part of this process of unification, because they are the rules that have long applied in the nonprobate system. Courts of equity have for centuries exercised the power to reform (to "rectify" in English law) mistakes in trusts, deeds of gift, and beneficiary designations. Likewise, there is a well-developed doctrine of excusing defective compliance with the contractually required formalities for change-of-beneficiary designations in the nonprobate system for life insurance policies and joint-and-survivor accounts. . . .

The ostensibly new rules being recognized by the courts and endorsed in the Restatement turn out, therefore, to be quite old; what is new is applying them to wills as well as to will substitutes. The principle being recognized in the Restatement is that wills and will substitutes entail a ommon issue, ascertaining the intention of a deceased transferor. The lesson of the nonprobate system, now being absorbed as the probate rule, is that in cases of mistake in execution or mistaken terms, the purposes of the formal requirements can be served by allowing the proponent of the instrument to prove by clear-and-convincing evidence that the testator intended the transfer. . . .

PREVENTING UNJUST ENRICHMENT

When an innocuous execution error defeats a will, or when a scrivener's mistake defeats a devise, the failure to implement the testator's intent not only frustrates the testator's wishes, but it also works unjust enrichment. The devisee or distributee who takes is unjustly enriched at the expense of the intended beneficiary. Preventing unjust enrichment is the central policy value of the law of restitution. The field of restitution emerged only in the twentieth century as a result of the fusion of law and equity, which allowed the common principle of preventing unjust enrichment to be generalized from the older law of quasicontract and constructive trust. The modern understanding of the importance of avoiding unjust enrichment has been an important stimulus to the development of the rules curing harmless execution errors and reforming mistaken terms.

MALPRACTICE LIABILITY

Although most execution blunders occur when laypersons attempt testation without the help of counsel, cases (such as *Snide*, [see page 223]) do occur in which counsel's negligence causes or contributes to the error. By contrast, cases of mistaken terms more often involve a lawyer-drafter, who has misrendered instructions or omitted intended terms. In these cases in which the lawyer might be liable to the intended beneficiaries for malpractice, it can be argued that making available a remedy to correct the mistake is unnecessary, because the curative doctrines benefit the lawyer, who would otherwise bear the malpractice liability. There are, however, many objections to this line of reasoning. Malpractice liability does nothing about the cases in which lawyers are not involved or not culpable. When there is a lawyer to sue, he or she may be wholly or partially judgment-proof—for example, when the lawyer is uninsured or underinsured. For devises of unique property, such as the family home or the family Bible, relief in damages cannot be adequate. Most importantly, what is wrong with the malpractice solution is that, by transforming the mistake claim into tort, it neglects the unjust enrichment intrinsic to mistake cases. Whereas most forms of malpractice cause deadweight loss that can only be remedied by compensation, in the testamentary mistake cases a benefit is transferred from the intended devisee to the mistaken devisee (or intestate taker). Because the mistaken devisee has no claim of entitlement, he or she is unjustly enriched. The malpractice solution leaves the unjust enrichment unremedied and instead creates a needless loss to be charged against the drafter. The mistake remedies (harmless error, reformation) respond to the simple truth that preventing loss is better than compensating loss.

NEW VISTAS FOR THE PROBATE LAWYER

... The older conventions of the strict compliance rule and the no reformation rule are now open to challenge everywhere. Lawyers processing probate matters need to be alert to the opportunity they now have to raise issues that used to be foreclosed. Sad cases of defeated intent that used to be beyond hope are now remediable, an innocuous formal defect can be excused, mistaken terms can be reformed, but only if counsel sees the issue and brings it forward.

QUESTIONS AND NOTES

1. In some cases, courts have remedied mistakes by the scrivener. In Estate of Lord, 795 A.2d 700 (Me. 2002), the residuary clause was mistakenly drafted to refer to a "trust" and a "trustee" that never came into existence, but the court interpreted these words to mean "estate" and "personal representative" instead. In Estate of Getman, 15 Quinnipiac Prob. L.J. 257 (Conn. Prob. 2000), the court corrected language in a will that identified an inter vivos trust as "created this date" to "created May 9, 1999." In Estate of Ikuta, 639 P.2d 400 (Haw. 1981), the court substituted the word "youngest" for the word "oldst [oldest]" where extrinsic evidence showed that "oldst" did not make sense and was a scrivener's mistake.

Where there has been an accidental omission by the scrivener or typist, courts have sometimes inserted the missing words when convinced from the face of the will and extrinsic evidence what missing words were intended. In Estate of Herceg, 747 N.Y.S.2d 901 (Sur. 2002), the last lines of the residuary clause were left off so that there was no indication who was to take the residue. In three prior wills, the testator had left the residue to his nephew or, if his nephew predeceased him, to his nephew's wife. The attorney-scrivener testified that the omission of the rest of the residuary clause was caused by a computer error, that no change in beneficiaries was intended by the testator. Endorsing Restatement (Third) of Property §12.1, supra, the court held that the omission of the nephew's wife was unintentional and awarded her the residue of the estate. In Wilson v. First Fla. Bank, 498 So. 2d 1289 (Fla. App. 1986), a will disposed of personal items, made pecuniary gifts, and then said, "To the University of Georgia" for a scholarship fund, but did not say what was given the university.

The court admitted extrinsic evidence, including the embarrassed draftsman's testimony, and held that the will gave the residue to the university.

There is also a growing number of cases reforming testamentary trusts in order to obtain a tax advantage. See pages 578-579.

2. Professor Langbein argues that it is better to remedy lawyers' drafting mistakes by correcting them. Do you agree? Would it be preferable to hold the lawyer liable for malpractice? If drafting mistakes in will substitutes, such as revocable trusts, can be corrected after the settlor's death, why not in wills? See In re Estate of Robinson, 720 So. 2d 540 (Fla. App. 1998); Martin L. Fried, The Disappointed Heir: Going Beyond the Probate Process to Remedy Wrongdoing or Rectify Mistake, 39 Real Prop., Prob. & Tr. J. 357 (2004); John H. Langbein & Lawrence W. Waggoner, Reformation of Wills on the Ground of Mistake: Change of Direction in American Law?, 30 U. Pa. L. Rev. 521, 588-590 (1982).

When a lawyer has drafted an ambiguous will, should the lawyer be liable in malpractice for any costs and loss from litigation to construe the will? In Ventura County Humane Socy. v. Holloway, 115 Cal. Rptr. 464 (App. 1974), the court held that although an attorney is liable to testamentary beneficiaries if the beneficiaries clearly designated by the testator lose their legacy as a direct result of the attorney's negligence, the attorney is not liable for drafting an ambiguous document. "[T]he task of proving whether the claimed ambiguity was the result of negligence of the drafting attorney or whether it was the deliberate choice of the testator, would impose an insurmountable burden on the parties. . . . The duty thus created would amount to a requirement to draft litigation-proof legal documents . . . [and would be an] almost intolerable burden on the legal profession." But see Angela M. Vallario, Shape Up or Ship Out: Accountability to Third Parties for Patent Ambiguities in Testamentary Documents, 26 Whittier L. Rev. 59 (2004) (arguing that drafting a will with patent ambiguity should be prima facie evidence of negligence).

3. *Gifts by implication.* One of the recurring oversights in drafting is to leave a gap in the dispositive provisions, that is, a particular contingency (which occurs) is not provided for. To fill gaps in wills, New Jersey has developed a *doctrine of probable intent.* If a contingency for which no provision is made in the will occurs, the court studies the family circumstances and the plan of testamentary disposition set forth in the will. Then the court places itself in the position of the testator and decides how the testator probably would have responded to the contingency had he envisioned its occurrence. Engle v. Siegel, 377 A.2d 892 (N.J. 1977). See also In re Bieley, 695 N.E.2d 1119 (N.Y. 1998) (implying a gift to fill an omission, where testator's dominant purpose and design to distribute her estate completely was apparent from the face of the will; extrinsic evidence of testator's intent not admissible).

Gifts filling a gap in a will may also be implied by the process of construction. For example, in Estate of Kime, 193 Cal. Rptr. 718 (App. 1983), the testator, using a printed form, filled in blanks as italicized here ("I appoint *Betty J. Hyde* as Execu*tris* of this Will"), but she failed to name a beneficiary. The court ordered the admission of evidence, including oral declarations, tending to show that the testator believed the printed word "appoint" designated a beneficiary and the word "executris" meant one to receive her estate.

4. Although much is gained by allowing corrections of mistakes in wills, what is lost? Once the courts move away from the words on the face of the will, testators potentially lose the safe harbor of a written will. How can a testator be certain that

her wishes will be followed after her death if the courts feel free to rewrite her will (albeit ostensibly to make it more consistent with her intentions)? See Pamela R. Champine, My Will Be Done: Accommodating the Erring and the Atypical Testator, 80 Neb. L. Rev. 387 (2001) (arguing that testators should have to "opt-in" in order to have their wills governed by a rule allowing reformation for mistake).

As an example of how aggressive courts can be in rewriting wills, consider the case of Diana, Princess of Wales. When Princess Diana was killed in a car crash on August 31, 1997, she left a six-page will, awkwardly drafted to an American eye, devising her estate in trust for her two children, William and Henry. Her estate totaled £21,468,352, with a tax bill of £8,502,330 (most or all of which could have been avoided by better planning). The will was reformed under a court "variation order" into a much longer, more elaborate document than the original. The reformed will not only changed the payout schedule for William and Henry, but also added charitable gifts, an executor, new trusts to deal with intellectual property, a £50,000 devise to Diana's butler Paul Burrell, and gifts of personal items to each of Diana's 17 godchildren. Post-death revisions to reduce or eliminate the tax bill might also have been possible, but whether for political reasons or otherwise, the will was not so revised. Whose wishes were being followed in these revisions, Diana's or those of her executors? On reformation (rectification) in Britain and Hong Kong, see Christopher Sherrin, Rectification: Correcting Mistakes in Wills, 30 Hong Kong L.J. 223 (2000).

5.   Not everyone is enamored with the trend toward reforming wills and the admission of extrinsic evidence. In 2000, the Supreme Judicial Court of Massachusetts, which is a leader in allowing reformation to obtain tax advantages (see pages 366-368), rejected reformation of wills for other purposes:

> [T]he reformation of a will, which would dispose of estate property based on unattested testamentary language, would violate the Statute of Wills. Strong policy reasons also militate against the requested reformation. To allow for reformation in this case would open the floodgates of litigation and lead to untold confusion in the probate of wills. It would essentially invite disgruntled individuals excluded from a will to demonstrate extrinsic evidence of the decedent's "intent" to include them. The number of groundless will contests could soar. We disagree that employing "full, clear and decisive proof" as the standard for reformation of wills would suffice to remedy such problems. Judicial resources are simply too scarce to squander on such consequences. Finally, we are not persuaded by the decisions of other jurisdictions. Therefore, we decline to join the minority and decline to follow the Restatement. [Flannery v. McNamara, 738 N.E.2d 739, 746 (Mass. 2000).]

See also San Antonio Area Found. v. Lang, 35 S.W.3d 636 (Tex. 2000) (extrinsic evidence was inadmissible because the words "real estate" were not ambiguous); Burnett v. First Commercial Trust Co., 939 S.W.2d 827 (Ark. 1997) (extrinsic evidence was inadmissible to fill an omission even though the evidence showed the omission was by clerical error). Accordingly, if given the chance to decide Mahoney v. Grainger, supra, once again, the Massachusetts court would almost certainly reach the same result. Would you? On the other hand, as demonstrated by the next case, not even the Massachusetts court resists extrinsic evidence to vary the plain meaning of a will in *all* cases.

FLEMING v. MORRISON, 72 N.E. 499 (Mass. 1904): Francis Butterfield wanted to sleep with Mary Fleming. In order to induce her to do so, Butterfield had his lawyer, Sidney Goodridge, draft a will leaving Butterfield's entire estate to Fleming. After Butterfield signed the will and Goodridge signed as the first witness (but before the last two of the necessary three witnesses had signed), Butterfield told Goodridge "that this was a 'fake' will, made for a purpose." Butterfield then took the will to two more witnesses, acknowledged his signature to them, whereupon they both signed as witnesses. Butterfield did not disclose to these other witnesses that he intended the will to be nothing more than a ploy to trick Fleming into sleeping with him.

On the basis of extrinsic evidence, the Massachusetts Supreme Judicial Court held the will invalid:

> [The contestants argue that] the proponent of the will has failed to prove the necessary animus testandi. We are of the opinion that this contention must prevail.
>
> The finding that, before Butterfield and Goodridge "parted," Butterfield told Goodridge that the instrument which had been signed by Butterfield as and for his last will and testament, and declared by him to be such in the presence of Goodridge, and attested and subscribed by Goodridge as a witness, "was a 'fake' will, made for a purpose," is fatal to the proponent's case. This must be taken to mean that what had been done was a sham. . . . The whole finding, taken together, amounts to a finding that Butterfield had not intended the transaction which had just taken place to be in fact what it imported to be, that is to say, a finding that when Butterfield signed the instrument, and asked Goodridge to attest and subscribe it as his will, he did not, in fact, then intend it to be his last will and testament, but intended to have Mary Fleming think that he had made a will in her favor to induce her to let him sleep with her.
>
> We are of opinion that it is competent to contradict by parol the solemn statements contained in an instrument that it is a will; that it has been signed as such by the person named as the testator, and attested and subscribed by persons signing as witnesses. . . .
>
> [T]he animus testandi must exist when [the will] is signed or acknowledged before, and attested and subscribed by, each of the necessary three witnesses. If this is not done, the statutory requirements have not been complied with.

Because Goodridge knew that Butterfield had not intended the instrument to be his will—a fact that, to repeat, was established by extrinsic evidence—the will lacked the necessary three witnesses to Butterfield's testamentary intent in executing the document.

QUESTIONS

1. If the drafting attorney can introduce evidence to show that a will, which recites that it is the testator's will, is not intended as such, thus contradicting the words of the instrument, why cannot the attorney testify that the "plain meaning" of the words of the will was not the meaning intended by the testator?

2. Assume that, after executing the will litigated in Fleming v. Morrison, Francis Butterfield showed Mary Fleming the will, and, relying upon its validity, Mary slept with Francis. Does Mary have any remedy against Francis's estate? Contract to devise? Sexual intercourse (battery) by fraud in the inducement? Civil action for rape? Or was Mary essentially trading sex for money?

What do you think of the ethics of the lawyer Sidney Goodridge? Should Goodridge's testimony, which contradicts the attestation clause, be "viewed with suspicion and received with caution"? See Estate of Wright, page 141. Should Goodridge be estopped to testify the will was a sham?

Does Mary have any cause of action against Goodridge? Tortious interference with her expectancy (see page 194)? Did Goodridge have a duty to warn Mary under Tarasoff v. Regents of Univ. of Cal., 551 P.2d 334 (Cal. 1976) (psychotherapist has a common law duty "to use reasonable care to protect the intended victim" of a patient who "presents a serious danger of violence")?

SECTION B.   DEATH OF BENEFICIARY BEFORE DEATH OF TESTATOR

1.   Introduction

If a devisee does not survive the testator, the devise *lapses* (that is, it fails). All gifts made by will are subject to a requirement that the devisee survive the testator, unless the testator specifies otherwise. In nearly all states, however, *antilapse statutes* have been enacted that, under certain specified circumstances, substitute another beneficiary for the predeceased devisee.

Before examining antilapse statutes, it is important to get a firm hold on the common law rules regarding lapsed devises. These are the default rules that apply if the will does not provide what happens when a devisee predeceases the testator.

(1) *Specific or general devise.* If a specific or general devise lapses, the devise falls into the residue. Thus:

> Case 1. *T*'s will bequeaths her watch (a specific bequest) to *A* and $10,000 (a general bequest) to *B*. The residuary devisee is *C. A* and *B* predecease *T*. The watch and the $10,000 go to *C*.

(2) *Residuary devise.* If the devise of the entire residue lapses, because the sole residuary devisee or all the residuary devisees predecease the testator, the heirs of the testator take by intestacy. If a share of the residue lapses, such as when one of two residuary devisees predeceases the testator, at common law the lapsed residuary share passes by intestacy to the testator's heirs rather than to the remaining residuary devisees. This rule (called the *no-residue-of-a-residue* rule) is followed in Estate of Russell, infra.

> Case 2. After making several specific and general devises to a number of persons, *T* devises the residue of her estate one-half to *B* and one-half to *C. B* predeceases *T. B*'s one-half share goes to *T*'s heirs, not to *C*.

The no-residue-of-a-residue rule, probably laid down by English courts to protect the interests of the primogenitary heir, does not carry out the average testator's intent in this country and has been roundly criticized by courts and commentators alike. In a majority of states, this rule has been overturned by statute or judicial decision, and it is clearly on its way out. See UPC §2-604(b) (1990); Restatement (Third) of Property: Wills and Other Donative Transfers §5.5, cmt. o (1999).

(3) *Class gift.* If the devise is to a class of persons, and one member of the class predeceases the testator, the surviving members of the class divide the gift. Thus:

> *Case 3.* T bequeaths $10,000 to the children of A (a class gift). One child of A, named B, predeceases T. At T's death, T is survived by another child of A, named C. Because this is a class gift, C takes B's share, or the entire $10,000.

(4) *Void devise.* Where a devisee is dead at the time the will is executed, or the devisee is a dog or cat or some other ineligible taker, the devise is void. The same general default rules govern the disposition of void devises as govern lapsed devises.

Estate of Russell

Supreme Court of California, 1968
69 Cal. 2d 200, 444 P.2d 353, 70 Cal. Rptr. 561

SULLIVAN, J.   Georgia Nan Russell Hembree appeals from a judgment (Prob. Code, §1240[12]) entered in proceedings for the determination of heirship decreeing inter alia that under the terms of the will of Thelma L. Russell, deceased, all of the residue of her estate should be distributed to Chester H. Quinn.

Thelma L. Russell died testate on September 8, 1965, leaving a validly executed holographic will written on a small card. The front of the card reads:

> Turn
> the card   March 18-1957
> I leave everything
> I own Real &
> Personal to Chester
> H. Quinn & Roxy Russell
> Thelma L. Russell

The reverse side reads:

> My ($10.) Ten dollar gold
> Piece & diamonds I leave
> to Georgia Nan Russell.
> Alverata, Geogia [sic]

Chester H. Quinn was a close friend and companion of testatrix, who for over 25 years prior to her death had resided in one of the living units on her property and had stood in a relation of personal trust and confidence toward her. Roxy Russell was testatrix' pet dog which was alive on the date of the execution of testatrix' will but predeceased her.[13] Plaintiff is testatrix' niece and her only heir-at-law.

---

12. Hereafter unless otherwise indicated all section references are to the Probate Code.
13. Actually, the record indicates the existence of two Roxy Russells. The original Roxy was an Airedale dog which testatrix owned at the time she made her will, but which, according to Quinn,

In her petition for determination of heirship plaintiff alleges, inter alia, that "Roxy Russell is an Airedale dog";[14] that section 27 enumerates those entitled to take by will; that "Dogs are not included among those listed in . . . Section 27. Not even Airedale dogs"; that the gift of one-half of the residue of testatrix' estate to Roxy Russell is invalid and void; and that plaintiff was entitled to such one-half as testatrix' sole heir-at-law.

At the hearing on the petition, plaintiff introduced without objection extrinsic evidence establishing that Roxy Russell was testatrix' Airedale dog which died on June 9, 1958. To this end plaintiff, in addition to an independent witness, called defendant pursuant to former Code of Civil Procedure section 2055 (now Evid. Code, §776). Upon redirect examination, counsel for Quinn then sought to introduce evidence of the latter's relationship with testatrix "in the event that your Honor feels that there is any necessity for further ascertainment of the intent above and beyond the document." Plaintiff's objections on the ground that it was inadmissible under the statute of wills and the parol evidence rule "because there is no ambiguity" and that it was inadmissible under section 105, were overruled. Over plaintiff's objection, counsel for Quinn also introduced certain documentary evidence consisting of testatrix' address book and a certain quitclaim deed "for the purpose of demonstrating the intention on the part of the deceased that she not die intestate." Of all this extrinsic evidence only the following infinitesimal portion of Quinn's testimony relates to care of the dog: "Q [Counsel for Quinn] Prior to the first Roxy's death did you ever discuss with Miss Russell taking care of Roxy if anything should ever happen to her? A Yes." Plaintiff carefully preserved an objection running to all of the above line of testimony and at the conclusion of the hearing moved to strike such evidence. Her motion was denied.

The trial court found, so far as is here material, that it was the intention of testatrix "that Chester H. Quinn was to receive her entire estate, excepting the gold coin and diamonds bequeathed to" plaintiff and that Quinn "was to care for the dog, Roxy Russell, in the event of Testatrix's death. The language contained in the Will, concerning the dog, Roxy Russell, was precatory in nature only, and merely indicative of the wish, desire and concern of Testatrix that Chester H. Quinn was to care for the dog, Roxy Russell, subsequent to Testatrix's death."[15]

---

died after having had a fox tail removed from its nose, and which, according to the testimony of one Arthur Turner, owner of a pet cemetery, was buried on June 9, 1958. Roxy was replaced with another dog (breed not indicated in the record before us) which, although it answered to the name Roxy, was according to the record, in fact registered with the American Kennel Club as "Russel's [sic] Royal Kick Roxy."

14. In his "Petition for Probate of Holographic Will and for Letters of Administration with the Will Annexed," Quinn included under the names, ages and residences of the devisees and legatees of testatrix the following: "Roxy Russell, A 9 year old Airedale dog, [residing at] 4422 Palm Avenue, La Mesa, Calif." [Is this correct? Since the will was executed when the first Roxy was alive, isn't the second Roxy a pretermitted Airedale? — Eds.]

15. The memorandum decision elaborates on this point, stating in part: "The obvious concern of the human who loves her pet is to see that it is properly cared for by someone who may be trusted to honor that concern and through resources the person may make available in the will to carry out this entreaty, desire, wish, recommendation or prayer. This, in other words, is a most logical example of a precatory provision. It is the only logical conclusion one can come to which would not do violence to the apparent intent of Mrs. Russell."

The trial court found further: "Testatrix intended that Georgia Nan Russell Hembree was not to have any other real or personal property belonging to Testatrix, other than the gold coin and diamonds." This finding also was elaborated on in the memorandum decision: "In making the will it is apparent she had Georgia on her mind. While there is other evidence in the case about Thelma Russell's frame of mind concerning her real property and her niece, which was admitted by the Court, over counsel's

Thelma Russell's property at 4422 Palm Avenue (1999)

The court concluded that testatrix intended to and did make an absolute and outright gift to Mr. Quinn of all the residue of her estate, adding: "There occurred no lapse as to any portion of the residuary gift to Chester H. Quinn by reason of the language contained in the Will concerning the dog, Roxy Russell, such language not having the effect of being an attempted outright gift or gift in trust to the dog. The effect of such language is merely to indicate the intention of Testatrix that Chester H. Quinn was to take the entire residuary estate and to use whatever portion thereof as might be necessary to care for and maintain the dog, Roxy Russell." Judgment was entered accordingly. This appeal followed.

Plaintiff's position before us may be summarized thusly: That the gift of one-half of the residue of the estate to testatrix' dog was clear and unambiguous; that such gift was void and the property subject thereof passed to plaintiff under the laws of intestate succession; and that the court erred in admitting the extrinsic evidence offered by Quinn but that in any event the uncontradicted evidence in the record did not cure the invalidity of the gift.

. . . [W]e think it is self-evident that in the interpretation of a will, a court cannot determine whether the terms of the will are clear and definite in the first place until it considers the circumstances under which the will was made so that the judge may be placed in the position of the testator whose language he is interpreting. . . . Failure to enter upon such an inquiry is failure to recognize that the "ordinary standard or 'plain meaning,' is simply the meaning of the people who did *not* write the document." (9 Wigmore on Evidence §2462 (3d ed. 1940).)

. . . [E]xtrinsic evidence of the circumstances under which a will is made (except evidence expressly excluded by statute) may be considered by the court in ascertaining what the testator meant by the words used in the will. If in the light of such extrinsic evidence, the provisions of the will are reasonably susceptible of two or

---

vigorous objection, because it concerned testatrix' frame of mind, a condition relevant to the material issue of intent, nevertheless this additional evidence was not necessary to this Court in reaching its conclusion." The additional evidence referred to included an address book of testatrix upon which she had written: "Chester, Don't let Augusta and Georgia have one penny of my place if it takes it all to fight it in Court. Thelma."

more meanings claimed to have been intended by the testator, "an uncertainty arises upon the face of a will" (§105) and extrinsic evidence relevant to prove any of such meanings is admissible. . . . If, on the other hand, in the light of such extrinsic evidence, the provisions of the will are not reasonably susceptible of two or more meanings, there is no uncertainty arising upon the face of the will . . . and any proffered evidence attempting to show an intention *different* from that expressed by the words therein, giving them the only meaning to which they are reasonably susceptible, is inadmissible. . . .

Examining testatrix' will in the light of the foregoing rules, we arrive at the following conclusions: Extrinsic evidence offered by plaintiff was admitted without objection and indeed would have been properly admitted over objection to raise and resolve the latent ambiguity as to Roxy Russell and ultimately to establish that Roxy Russell was a dog. Extrinsic evidence of the surrounding circumstances was properly considered in order to ascertain what testatrix meant by the words of the will, including the words: "I leave everything I own Real & Personal to Chester H. Quinn & Roxy Russell" or as those words can now be read "to Chester H. Quinn and my dog Roxy Russell."

However, viewing the will in the light of the surrounding circumstances as are disclosed by the record, we conclude that the will cannot reasonably be construed as urged by Quinn and determined by the trial court as providing that testatrix intended to make an absolute and outright gift of the entire residue of her estate to Quinn who was "to use whatever portion thereof as might be necessary to care for and maintain the dog." No words of the will give the entire residuum to Quinn, much less indicate that the provision for the dog is merely precatory in nature. Such an interpretation is not consistent with a disposition which by its language leaves the residuum in equal shares to Quinn and the dog.[16] A disposition in equal shares to two beneficiaries cannot be equated with a disposition of the whole to one of them who may use "whatever portion thereof as might be necessary" on behalf of the other. . . .

Accordingly, since in the light of the extrinsic evidence introduced below, the terms of the will are not reasonably susceptible of the meaning claimed by Quinn to have been intended by testatrix, the extrinsic evidence offered to show such an intention should have been excluded by the trial court. Upon an independent examination of the will we conclude that the trial court's interpretation of the terms thereof was erroneous. Interpreting the provisions relating to testatrix' residuary estate in accordance with the only meaning to which they are reasonably susceptible, we conclude that testatrix intended to make a disposition of all of the residue of the estate to Quinn and the dog in equal shares; therefore, as tenants in common. As a dog cannot be the beneficiary under a will the attempted gift to Roxy Russell is void.[17]

There remains only the necessity of determining the effect of the void gift to the dog upon the disposition of the residuary estate. That portion of any residuary estate that is the subject of a lapsed gift to one of the residuary beneficiaries

---

16. This is slippery work in paraphrasing. Thelma Russell did not write "in equal shares." — Eds.

17. As a consequence, the fact that Roxy Russell predeceased the testatrix is of no legal import. As appears, we have disposed of the issue raised by plaintiff's frontal attack on the eligibility of the dog to take a testamentary gift and therefore need not concern ourselves with the novel question as to whether the death of the dog during the lifetime of the testatrix resulted in a lapsed gift. (§92.)

remains undisposed of by the will and passes to the heirs-at-law. (§§92, 220.) The rule is equally applicable with respect to a void gift to one of the residuary beneficiaries. (§220.) Therefore, notwithstanding testatrix' expressed intention to limit the extent of her gift by will to plaintiff one-half of the residuary estate passes to plaintiff as testatrix' only heir-at-law (§225). We conclude that the residue of testatrix' estate should be distributed in equal shares to Chester H. Quinn and Georgia Nan Russell Hembree, testatrix' niece.

The judgment is reversed. . . .

QUESTIONS AND NOTE

1. The no-residue-of-a-residue rule, which was not attacked by Chester's counsel or questioned by the court, necessitated the court's elaborate discussion of the admission of extrinsic evidence. But is the rule sound? If *T* devises her entire estate to *A* and *B*, but *B* predeceases *T*, what result is more likely to be consistent with *T*'s probable intent: that *A* receive *T*'s entire estate, or that *A* receive one-half of *T*'s estate with the other half passing by intestacy? The no-residue-of-the-residue rule assumes the latter. In rejecting the rule, modern authorities such as UPC §2-604(b) (1990) assume the former, and well-drafted wills almost invariably reallocate shares in the residue to the other residuary takers.

2. On trusts for the benefit of pet animals, and the phenomenon of gifts to pets more generally, see pages 522-527.

2. Antilapse Statutes

Now let us turn to the effect of an antilapse statute upon a lapsed gift. In a sense, antilapse statutes are misnamed. They do not prevent a lapse; they merely substitute other beneficiaries (usually issue) for the dead beneficiary if certain requirements are met. A typical antilapse statute provides that if a devisee is of a specified relationship to the testator and is survived by issue who survive the testator, the issue are substituted for the predeceased devisee. The statute changes the common law so as to give the predeceased devisee's gift to his issue.

An antilapse statute applies to a lapsed devise *only* if the devisee bears the particular relationship to the testator specified in the statute. Some statutes apply only to descendants of the testator. Others are broader, applying to descendants of the testator's grandparents, or to all kindred of the testator, or occasionally to kindred of the testator's spouse. In a few states, the statute applies to all devisees, whether a relative of the testator or not. The antilapse statute in the UPC applies only to devises to a grandparent or a lineal descendant of a grandparent. (In 1990, the statute was amended to include a devise to a stepchild.) Thus:

> *Case 4.* *T* devises her home to her niece, *A*, and the residue of her estate to *B*. *A* predeceases *T*, leaving a child *C* who survives *T*. Under the UPC antilapse statute, *C* takes *T*'s home because *A* is a descendant of *T*'s grandparent and hence comes within the required relationship. If the antilapse statute applies only to *T*'s descendants, *C* does not take *T*'s home. The devise lapses and falls into the residue given to *B*.

In requiring a close blood relationship to the testator in order to substitute the devisee's children for the dead devisee, experience has shown that most antilapse statutes are too narrowly drawn. There appears to be no empirical evidence to support limiting antilapse statutes to close relatives even though most legislatures do so. What do you think? Would the average testator want issue to be substituted for a dead devisee in every case? Why substitute issue only? Why not substitute heirs, including a spouse?

The antilapse statute, which supersedes the common law where applicable, is also a default rule. It applies unless the testator indicates that it not apply. If the testator manifests an intent that the antilapse statute not apply, and he does not include an alternative gift when a devisee predeceases the testator, the common law default rules apply.

For penetrating examinations of the merits and demerits of antilapse statutes, see Susan F. French, Antilapse Statutes Are Blunt Instruments: A Blueprint for Reform, 37 Hastings L.J. 335 (1985); Patricia G. Roberts, Lapse Statutes: Recurring Construction Problems, 37 Emory L.J. 323 (1988).

UPC §2-605 (1969) is a typical antilapse statute.

Uniform Probate Code (1969)

§2-605.   Antilapse; Deceased Devisee; Class Gifts

If a devisee who is a grandparent or a lineal descendant of a grandparent of the testator is dead at the time of execution of the will, fails to survive the testator, or is treated as if he predeceased the testator, the issue of the deceased devisee who survive the testator by 120 hours take in place of the deceased devisee and if they are all of the same degree of kinship to the devisee they take equally, but if of unequal degree then those of more remote degree take by representation. One who would have been a devisee under a class gift if he had survived the testator is treated as a devisee for purposes of this section whether his death occurred before or after the execution of the will.

Allen v. Talley
Texas Court of Appeals, Eleventh District, 1997
949 S.W.2d 59

WRIGHT, J.   This is a will construction case. The question presented is whether the decedent's will contains words of survivorship which preclude application of the anti-lapse statute.[18] The trial court held that it did and granted summary judgment accordingly. We affirm.

18. Tex. Prob. Code Ann. §68 (Vernon Supp. 1997) provides in relevant part:

(a) If a devisee who is a descendant of the testator or a descendant of a testator's parent is deceased at the time of the execution of the will, fails to survive the testator, or is treated as if the devisee predeceased the testator by Section 47 of this code or otherwise, the descendants of the

The facts are not disputed. The controversy results from the will of Mary B. Boase Shoults, deceased, which provides in relevant part:

> I give, devise and bequeath unto my living brothers and sisters: John Allen, Claude Allen, Lewis Allen, Lera Talley, and Juanita Jordan, to share and share alike, all of the property, real, personal and mixed, of which I may die seized and possessed or be entitled to at my death.

At the time she executed her will, Mary had 3 brothers and 2 sisters who were alive. However, by the time that Mary died, all of her brothers and sisters had predeceased her except for her brother, Claude Allen, and her sister, Lera Talley. Each of the siblings who predeceased Mary left surviving children. Lewis Eugene Allen, Jr. is a surviving child of Lewis Allen, Sr. He filed an application to probate Mary's will. He also asked for the issuance of letters of administration and opposed Lera's request that letters of administration be issued to her. The court admitted the will to probate, but the order did not appoint an administrator.

Both Lewis, Jr. and Lera filed petitions for declaratory judgment. Lera argued that Mary intended that her estate pass to her brothers and sisters who were living at the time of her death and that the phrase "I give, devise and bequeath unto my living brothers and sisters: [naming them], to share and share alike" operates as words of survivorship precluding the application of the anti-lapse statute. On the other hand, Lewis, Jr. maintained that those words are not words of survivorship, that they do not create a class gift, and that the anti-lapse statute applies. If Lera is correct, then she and her brother, Claude, Mary's only living siblings as of the date of Mary's death, will share the entire estate. If Lewis, Jr.'s position is correct, then three-fifths of the estate will be shared by the survivors of Mary's deceased siblings because of the anti-lapse statute. Under Lewis, Jr.'s theory of the case, the remaining two-fifths would be shared equally by Claude and Lera. Both Lewis, Jr. and Lera filed motions for summary judgment. The trial court agreed with the position taken by Lera and granted her motion for summary judgment. In two points of error, Lewis, Jr. argues that the trial court erred in granting Lera's motion for summary judgment and in denying his motion for summary judgment.

The primary concern of the court in the construction of a will is to determine the testator's intent. *Henderson v. Parker*, 728 S.W.2d 768, 770 (Tex. 1987). The intent of the testator must be ascertained by reviewing the will in its entirety.

Neither party argues that the will is ambiguous, although both parties offer differing constructions of the will based on the same language. In the absence of ambiguity, we must construe the will based on the express language used.

---

devisee who survived the testator by 120 hours take the devised property in place of the devisee. The property shall be divided into as many shares as there are surviving descendants in the nearest degree of kinship to the devisee and deceased persons in the same degree whose descendants survived the testator. Each surviving descendant in the nearest degree receives one share, and the share of each deceased person in the same degree is divided among his descendants by representation. For purposes of this section, a person who would have been a devisee under a class gift if the person had survived the testator is treated as a devisee unless the person died before the date the will was executed. [Representation is defined here to mean the modern per stirpes system. See pages 74-75.—Eds.] . . .

(e) This section applies unless the testator's last will and testament provides otherwise. For example, a devise or bequest in the testator's will such as "to my surviving children" or "to such of my children as shall survive me" prevents the application of Subsection (a) of this section.

Henderson v. Parker, supra. We must determine what Mary meant by what she actually said, and not by what she should have said, giving the words used in the will their common and ordinary meaning absent a contrary expression in the will. White v. Taylor, 286 S.W.2d 925 (Tex. 1956). If the court can give a "certain or definite legal meaning or interpretation" to the words of an instrument, the instrument is unambiguous; and the court may construe it as a matter of law. Coker v. Coker, 650 S.W.2d 391, 393 (Tex. 1983). . . .

Here, Mary's will contained one general provision devising her entire estate to her "living brothers and sisters." There were no other specific provisions. Logically, Mary would not have devised any property owned at her death to any brothers or sisters who were deceased at the time the will was executed. Moreover, when the phrase "living brothers and sisters" is construed in light of the entire sentence, it is clear that Mary intended that it was her brothers and sisters who were living at the time of her death who were to participate in the ownership of her estate. Otherwise, the phrase "share and share alike," followed by no specific provisions to the contrary, would add nothing to the meaning of the will. We construe "living brothers and sisters," as used in the entire context of Mary's will, to be words of survivorship. Therefore, neither those who did not survive Mary nor their heirs are entitled to take under Mary's will. As Mary's only surviving siblings, Lera Talley and Claude Allen are entitled to share equally in the entire estate. Appellant's points of error are overruled.

The judgment of the trial court is affirmed.

PROBLEMS AND NOTES

1. Suppose *T* devises the residue of his estate to "*A, B,* and *C,* share and share alike." *A* and *B* predecease *T,* with *A* leaving a surviving son. Does the antilapse statute apply to give *A*'s son a share, or does all the residue go to *C* instead? See Estate of Kuruzovich, 78 S.W.3d 226 (Mo. 2002).

Suppose a clause in *T*'s will makes several specific devises to *A, B,* and *C* and then conveys to *T*'s children all the residue, "including all lapsed legacies and devises, or other gifts made by this will which fail for any reason." Is this language clear enough to preclude application of the antilapse statute? See Colombo v. Stevenson, 563 S.E.2d 591 (N.C. App. 2002), aff'd mem., 579 S.E.2d 269 (N.C. 2003) (yes).

2. Since an antilapse statute is a default rule, applying only when the testator fails to evidence a "contrary intention," in many cases it is necessary to determine whether the language of the will indicates that the testator has a contrary intention and does not want issue of the deceased devisee substituted by the antilapse statute. Suppose that *T*'s will devises Blackacre "to my son Sidney if he survives me" and devises the residue of this estate to his wife Wilma. Sidney dies in his father's lifetime, leaving a daughter Debby. *T* is survived by Wilma and Debby. Who takes Blackacre, Wilma or Debby?

The issue is whether the words "if he survives me" evidence an intention that Sidney's child not be substituted for Sidney. The majority of cases hold that an express requirement of survivorship states an intent that the antilapse statute not apply and that Debby not be substituted for her father.

The 1990 UPC revised the 1969 UPC antilapse statute (§2-605, reproduced above). The revisers reversed the majority rule and provided in the revised anti-lapse statute that "words of survivorship, such as in a devise to an individual 'if he survives me,' or in a devise to 'my surviving children,' are not, in the absence of additional evidence, a sufficient indication of an intent contrary to the application of this section." UPC §2-603(b)(3) (1990, rev. 1993). The official comment suggests the rationale for discarding the rule that words of survivorship establish a contrary intention:

> The argument is that attaching words of survivorship indicates that the testator thought about the matter and intentionally did not provide a substitute gift to the devisee's descendants. At best, this is an inference only, which may or may not accurately reflect the testator's actual intention. An equally plausible inference is that the words of survivorship are in the testator's will merely because the testator's lawyer used a will form with words of survivorship.

This provision of UPC §2-603 (1990, rev. 1993) has come under sharp criticism from commentators. Professor Ascher writes:

> Apparently, the revisers believe their own antilapse provisions are likely to reflect any particular testator's intent more faithfully than *the testator's own will*. This conclusion is not only pretentious, it disputes what should be obvious — that most testators expect *their wills* to dispose of their property *completely* — without interference from a statute of which they have never heard. Instead of allowing "if he survives me" to mean what almost everyone would expect it to mean, the revisers have translated it into, "if he survives me, and, if he does not survive me, to his issue who survive me." For those unfamiliar with estate planning esoterica, therefore, it has become yet more difficult to figure out what the words in a will actually mean. [Mark L. Ascher, The 1990 Uniform Probate Code: Older and Better, or More Like the Internal Revenue Code?, 77 Minn. L. Rev. 639, 652-655 (1993).]

See also Martin D. Begleiter, Article II of the Uniform Probate Code and the Malpractice Revolution, 59 Tenn. L. Rev. 101, 126-130 (1991) (warning of malpractice risks for lawyers using their old forms in states adopting the 1990 UPC antilapse statute).

The revisers defend their work in Edward C. Halbach, Jr. & Lawrence W. Waggoner, The UPC's New Survivorship and Antilapse Provisions, 55 Alb. L. Rev. 1091 (1992); Mary L. Fellows, Traveling the Road of Probate Reform: Finding the Way to Your Will (A Response to Professor Ascher), 77 Minn. L. Rev. 659 (1993).

3. *Drafting advice.* In any jurisdiction, you should not rely upon presumptions. You should make the client's intent clear by providing what happens if the intended devisee does not survive the testator. If there is a gift over to another devisee, you should provide what happens if the second devisee predeceases the testator. Thus, for example, "to *A* if *A* survives me, but if *A* does not survive me, to *B* if *B* survives me, and if both *A* and *B* do not survive me, to be added to the residue of my estate." See John L. Garvey, Drafting Wills and Trusts: Anticipating the Birth and Death of Possible Beneficiaries, 71 Or. L. Rev. 47, 49-54 (1992).

Disregarding survivorship language such as "if he survives me" has been defended on the ground that such language is more likely to reflect rote inclusion of boilerplate rather than the testator's intent. See Halbach & Waggoner, supra, at 1109–1115. Yet the drafters of the 1990 UPC antilapse statute failed to reckon with the insight that rules designed to change results after the fact also have an effect on behavior before the fact. Thus, in response to the 1990 UPC antilapse statute, some firms have added a clause to their standard will forms stating that "No lapse or antilapse statute shall apply to any disposition of property under this will." Like an antibiotic-resistant strain of bacteria, boilerplate is exceedingly difficult to stamp out.

4.   After reversing the rule that words of survivorship state an intent that the antilapse statute not apply, the 1990 UPC revisers went further and replaced the straightforward 1969 antilapse statute (see page 393), which has been adopted in many jurisdictions, with an intricately complicated antilapse statute, §2-603 of the 1990 Code. The labyrinthine language of UPC §2-603 (1990, rev. 1993), occupying two and one-half printed pages and setting forth a complex system of priorities for primary and secondary substitute gifts, requires considerable time to penetrate. Inasmuch as §2-603 has been adopted only in about a dozen states, it is not reproduced here. Some version of the 1969 UPC antilapse statute remains the model followed in most states. (You may, if you wish, find UPC §2-603 in the Uniform Laws Annotated database in Westlaw or through the Uniform Law Commission's web page.)

5.   *Nonprobate transfers.* Under the law of wills, a beneficiary is required to survive the testator in order to take. If a beneficiary does not survive, an antilapse statute may be applicable if its terms are met. Should the survival requirement and the antilapse statute be applied to nonprobate transfers? Case authority on these matters is slim.

(a) *Payable-on-death (P.O.D.) designations.* Under the law of contracts, third party beneficiaries of contracts are not required to survive the benefactor or the time of performance and may pass their contract rights to their heirs or devisees. The 1990 UPC changes this rule in at least two circumstances. Beneficiaries of both payable-on-death bank accounts and transfer-on-death brokerage accounts must survive the depositor. UPC §§6-212, 6-307 (1990). In practice, however, most contracts with death beneficiaries provide that the funds are payable on the contractor's death "to *A* if she is living." By contract, survivorship is required.

Should the antilapse statute apply to payable-on-death beneficiaries who predecease the contractor? UPC §2-706 (1990) provides an antilapse statute for beneficiaries of insurance policies, bank accounts in P.O.D. form, contracts with a P.O.D. beneficiary, pension plans, and the like. The terms of this statute parallel §2-603, and thus a designation of a beneficiary "if she survives me" does not prevent the application of the antilapse statute.

(b) *Revocable trusts.* Inter vivos trusts ordinarily create vested or contingent remainders in the beneficiaries. The law of future interests thus comes into play, and this law is quite different from the law of wills. Traditionally, no requirement of survivorship is implied when a remainder is created. See page 637.

Statutes in a few states require the beneficiary of a revocable trust to survive the transferor and apply an antilapse statute if the beneficiary predeceases the transferor. See Cal. Prob. Code §§21109, 21110 (2004); UPC §2-707 (1990), discussed at pages 643-648.

(c) *Joint tenancies*. A joint tenant who predeceases the other joint tenant loses her interest in the property. Under common law theory, it vanishes. No antilapse statute applies to joint tenancies.

JACKSON v. SCHULTZ, 151 A.2d 284 (Del. Ch. 1959): Leonard Bullock, who had no children of his own, married Bessie Bullock in 1918. Bessie had three children from a prior marriage. Leonard cared for Bessie's children, his stepchildren, until they were adults. Leonard died on September 8, 1958, about five years after Bessie's death, leaving a will executed in 1937. The disputed clause of Leonard's will provided as follows:

> I give, bequeath and devise unto my beloved wife, Bessie H. Bullock, all my property real, personal and mixed wheresoever situate and of whatever nature and kind, to her and her heirs and assigns forever.

Because the applicable Delaware antilapse statute covered only devises and bequests to lineal descendants or brothers and sisters of the testator, the gift to Bessie lapsed.[19] Accordingly, unless the phrase "and her heirs and assigns forever" created a substitute gift in Bessie's heirs, the property would pass by intestacy, where it would escheat to the state because Leonard had no heirs.

Believing that there was a valid substitute gift to them, Bessie's children sold their interest in the property to a third party. This litigation ensued, between Bessie's children and the third party, to determine whether the children indeed held marketable title to the property.

As a general rule, in a devise by *T* "to *A and* her heirs and assigns," the phrase "to *A*" is read as *words of purchase*, indicating to whom the property is devised, and the phrase "and her heirs and assigns" is read as *words of limitation*, indicating what property rights are devised (here a fee simple). On the other hand, a devise by *T* "to *A or* her heirs" can be read to include only words of purchase, indicating that *A* is the primary devisee and that *A*'s heirs are the substitute takers if *A* predeceases *T*. The question thus arose, could the "and" in Leonard's devise to Bessie be read as an "or"? To avoid a lapse, and thus an escheat to the state, the Vice-Chancellor answered Yes.

> It has . . . been held that the words "or" and "and" may be substituted for each other in arriving at a proper construction of a will, "and" having been read as "or" for the purpose of carrying out an obvious testamentary purpose in the cases of Kerrigan v. Tabb, 39 A. 701 (N.J. Ch. 1898), and Huntress v. Place, 137 Mass. 409 (1884). . . .
>
> [Leonard's] wife having predeceased him and there being no known next of kin of the testator at the time of his death, [Leonard's] will should be read not only so as to carry out his intent but construed, if possible, so as to avoid not merely intestacy but a total escheat. . . .
>
> There being a recognized rule of construction permitting "and" to be read as "or" when so to do will carry out the testator's intent in will construction cases such as this,

---

19. In 1974, Delaware adopted §2-605 of the 1969 UPC, page 393, which applies to devises to the testator's grandparents and lineal descendants of grandparents. Del. Code Ann. tit. 12, §2313 (2004).

Should the antilapse statute be broadened to apply to devises to the testator's spouse? In a handful of states, the antilapse statute applies to spouses. The California antilapse statute (Cal. Prob. Code §21110(c) (2004)) applies to devises to kindred of the testator's spouse but not to devises to the spouse.

I adopt such rule of construction in the light of the facts in the record before me. The language used by the draftsman of the will namely, ". . . to her and her heirs . . ." adapts readily to the rule which permits such a substitution. . . . [T]his is a case in which the total testamentary background calls for a finding of intent that a substitutionary gift over to the testator's stepchildren be made in the event of his wife's death prior to his own.

NOTE AND PROBLEM

1. Hofing v. Willis, 201 N.E.2d 852, 856-857 (Ill. 1964):

While there is some support for the proposition that the phrase "and to their heirs" could be considered as words of purchase by reading the word "and" as "or," the presence of the words "and assigns" makes such a construction unacceptable. If the word "and" is read "or," the language creates a substitutionary gift in favor of the "heirs and assigns" of George's sisters, who would take as purchasers. That a deceased sister's heirs should take as purchasers by way of substitution would be quite reasonable. But it is hardly reasonable to suppose that the grantor would create a substitutionary gift and at the same time designate the assigns of the named takers to take by way of substitution.

2. *T* devises his estate "to *A* and her heirs." *A* predeceases *T*, leaving her husband *B* as her sole heir. *T* dies. Citing Jackson v. Schultz, *B* argues that he should take *A*'s share. Citing Hofing v. Willis, *T*'s heirs argue that they should take *A*'s share. What result? See Estate of Straube, 990 S.W.2d 40 (Mo. App. 1999).

3. Class Gifts

Under the common law of lapse, a class gift is treated differently from a gift to individuals. If a class member predeceases the testator, the surviving members of the class divide the total gift, including the deceased member's share. Thus the crucial question is: What is a class? The test is often said to be whether the testator is "group minded." The testator is thought to be group minded if he uses a class label in describing the beneficiaries, such as "to *A*'s children" or "to my nephews and nieces." Beneficiaries described by their individual names, but forming a natural class, may be deemed a class gift if the court decides, after admitting extrinsic evidence, that the testator would want the survivors to divide the property.

Restatement (Third) of Property: Wills and Other Donative Transfers
(T.D. No. 4, 2004)

§13.1 CLASS GIFT DEFINED — HOW CREATED

(a) A class gift is a disposition to beneficiaries who are described by a group label and are intended to take as a group. Taking as a group means that:
   (1) the membership of the class is typically not static, but is subject to fluctuation by increase or decrease until the time when a class member is entitled to distribution; and

(2) upon distribution, the property is divided among the then-entitled class members on a fractional basis.

(b) If the terms of the disposition identify the beneficiaries only by a group label, the disposition creates a class gift, unless the language or circumstances indicate that the transferor intended the beneficiaries to take as individuals.

§13.2   CLASS GIFT DISTINGUISHED FROM DISPOSITION TO BENEFICIARIES
        TAKING AS INDIVIDUALS — HOW CREATED

. . . (b) If the terms of the disposition identify the beneficiaries only by name, without any reference to a group label, the disposition does not create a class gift, but is to the beneficiaries taking as individuals.

(c) If the terms of the disposition identify the beneficiaries (i) by a group label and (ii) either by name or by the number of beneficiaries who then fit the group label, the disposition is presumed not to create a class gift, but is to the beneficiaries taking as individuals. The presumption is rebutted if the language or circumstances indicate that the transferor intended the beneficiaries to take as a group.

Dawson v. Yucus
Illinois Appellate Court, 1968
97 Ill. App. 2d 101, 239 N.E.2d 305

[Nelle G. Stewart, who died on May 29, 1965, devised her interest in her late husband's family farm to two nephews on her husband's side of the family. The second clause of her will provided:

> Through the Will of my late husband, Dr. Frank A. Stewart, I received an undivided one-fifth (1/5) interest in two hundred sixty-one and thirty-eight hundredths (261.38) acres of farm lands located in . . . Sangamon County, Illinois, and believing as I do that those farm lands should go back to my late husband's side of the house, I therefore give, devise and bequeath my one-fifth (1/5) interest in said farm lands as follows: One-half (1/2) of my interest therein to Stewart Wilson, a nephew, now living in Birmingham, Michigan and One-half (1/2) of my interest to Gene Burtle, a nephew, now living in Mission, Kansas.

Gene Burtle, one of the nephews, predeceased the testator. The residue was divided between Ina Mae Yucus and Hazel Degelow. At issue was whether the gift to the nephews Wilson and Burtle was a class gift, in which case the surviving nephew, Wilson, would take Burtle's share. If it was not a class gift, then Burtle's share would lapse, and so would pass to Yucus and Degelow as the residuary devisees. To strengthen the moral claim for finding a class, Wilson conveyed his interest in Burtle's share to Burtle's surviving children, who were substituted as plaintiffs. The court held that a class gift was not intended.]

JONES, J.   . . . At the trial the court found that the death of Gene Burtle prior to that of the testatrix created a latent ambiguity and admitted extrinsic evidence relating to testatrix' intentions. . . . [Of the] relatives of Dr. Stewart, only Gene Burtle and Stewart Wilson had a close personal relationship with the testatrix. Gene Burtle died on May 15, 1963, and the testatrix knew of his death but made no changes in her previously executed will. There was evidence from four witnesses that in conversations had with testatrix she stated she wanted the one-fifth interest in the farm to go either to her husband's side of the house, or to Gene Burtle and Stewart Wilson because she felt especially close to them and none other of Dr. Stewart's relatives had any contact with her.

The trial court held, we think correctly, that clause two of testatrix' will did not create a class gift and that the gift in that clause to Gene Burtle lapsed and, pursuant to the Illinois Lapse Statute, Chapt. 3, Sec. 49, I.R.S. 1965, passed into the residue of her estate.

The definition of class gifts and pertinent rules of construction as followed by Illinois courts are set forth in the case of Strohm v. McMullen, 89 N.E.2d 383 (Ill. 1949):

> The definition of a class gift adopted by this court, as laid down by Mr. Jarman in his work on Wills, Vol. I, p. 534, 5th Am. Ed., is:
>
> "A gift to a class is defined . . . as a gift of an aggregate sum to a body of persons uncertain in number at the time of the gift, to be ascertained at a future time, and who are all to take in equal or in some other definite proportions, the share of each being dependent for its amount upon the ultimate number of persons."
>
> "A class, in its ordinary acceptation, is a number or body of persons with common characteristics or in like circumstances, or having some common attribute, and, as applied to a devise, it is generally understood to mean a number of persons who stand in the same relation to each other or to the testator." Blackstone v. Althouse, 116 N.E. 154 (Ill. 1917). And it has been definitely decided in this State that in determining whether a devise is to a class or to individuals depends upon the language of the will. If from such language it appears that the amounts of their shares are uncertain until the devise or bequest takes effect, the beneficiaries will generally be held to take as a class; but where at the time of making the gifts the number of beneficiaries is certain, and the share each is to receive is also certain, and in no way dependent for its amount upon the number who shall survive, it is not a gift to a class, but to the individuals.
>
> There is an exception to the rule that naming the individual prevents the gift from becoming a class gift, stated in Strauss v. Strauss, 2 N.E.2d 699 (Ill. 1936), holding that the mere fact that the testator mentions by name the individuals who make up the class is not conclusive, and that if the intention to give a right of survivorship is collected from the remaining provisions of the will, as applied to the existing facts, such an intention must prevail.

Admittedly the gift in clause two is not made with the usual generic class description such as "children," "brothers," "nephews," "cousins," "issue," "descendants," or "family" but is in fact to two named individuals, conditions which militate against construction of the clause as a class gift. However, plaintiffs argue that because of the death of Gene Burtle prior to that of the testatrix a latent ambiguity exists and extrinsic evidence was properly received to show the true intention of the testatrix in clause two of her will, and that the phrase in clause two, "and believing as I do that these farm lands should go back to my husband's side of the house," together with the extrinsic evidence, clearly requires class gift construction. . . .

In this case the testatrix named the individuals, Stewart Wilson and Gene Burtle, and gave them each a one-half portion of her interest in the farm, thus making certain the number of beneficiaries and the share each is to receive. The shares in no way depend upon the number who shall survive the death of the testatrix. There is nothing in the language of the will that indicates the testatrix intended to create a class or survivorship gift. The only other provision of the will, also contained in clause two, that has any bearing on the question is the statement, ". . . believing as I do that those farm lands should go back to my late husband's side of the house . . . ." While it is true that this language recites testatrix' desire that the one-fifth interest in the farm go back to her husband's side of the house, it does not indicate a survivorship gift was intended. Her intention to return the farm to her husband's side of the house was fulfilled when she named Stewart Wilson and Gene Burtle as the donees of the interest. . . .

Further emphasis for the result we have reached is supplied by other factors found in the will and extrinsic evidence. First, the testatrix created a survivorship gift of the residue of her estate in the ninth clause of her will, thus indicating she knew how to manifest an intent to create a class or survivorship gift; hence, the language of clause two, phrased differently, was intended to create a gift to individuals distributively. . . . Secondly, the common characteristic of the alleged class described by plaintiffs is that of relation to Dr. Stewart, or, in the words of clause two, the class is of "my late husband's side of the house." However, this characteristic is also shared by three other heirs of Dr. Stewart of the same degree of relationship to him as Stewart Wilson and Gene Burtle. It thus appears that Gene Burtle and Stewart Wilson do not constitute the alleged class but are individuals named from the class. . . .

The devise in clause two was not to persons who come within the designation of a class but was to individuals distributively. It was not so made or limited to prevent the operation of the Illinois Lapse Statute which must be given its intended effect. The court below correctly held that upon the death of Gene Burtle prior to that of the testatrix the devise to him lapsed and passed under the residuary clause of the will. The Decree will be affirmed.

Affirmed.

NOTE

In Sullivan v. Sullivan, 529 N.E.2d 890 (Mass. App. 1988), the testator devised her property "to my nephews Marshall John McDonough, and David Condon McDonough, and to my niece Martha McDonough Sullivan, in equal shares, that is one-third each." She omitted mention of two nieces from whom she was estranged. One mentioned nephew (Marshall) predeceased the testator without issue. To avoid intestacy, the court held the residuary devise was to a class and that the property was to be divided equally between the survivors David and Martha.

It has been held that a gift "to Bessie and Louise," who happened to be the testator's close friends, is a class gift, where the court admitted extrinsic evidence of the surrounding circumstances and concluded that the testator would not want Bessie's share to pass by intestacy. Iozapavichus v. Fournier, 308 A.2d 573 (Me. 1973).

IN RE MOSS, [1899] 2 Ch. 314, aff'd, [1901] A.C. 187 (H.L.): The testator owned a minority share in the Daily Telegraph newspaper,[20] which at the time had

20. The Daily Telegraph was organized as a partnership in 1855 by J.M. Levy. The Levy family held all but a one-eighth interest, which was sold to George Moss for £500. Moss (nicknamed "Pubby") is variously reported to have been the superintendent of Levy's printing plant or the owner of a public house nearby where the printers repaired for ale. The newspaper was an immediate success, selling for a

the world's leading circulation. The testator devised his interest in the newspaper to his wife and his niece E.J. Fowler as trustees, to pay the income to the wife for life, and on her death "upon trust for the said E.J. Fowler and the child or children of my sister Emily Walter who shall attain the age of twenty-one years equally to be divided between them as tenants in common."

At issue was whether the share of E.J. Fowler, who had predeceased the testator, lapsed and so fell into the residue of the estate, or whether instead the remainder in the newspaper stock was a class gift with Fowler and the children of Emily as the class members. If the latter, then Fowler's share would be reallocated to Emily's children.

On the one hand, all the beneficiaries of the purported class shared the characteristic of being nephews and nieces of the testator, and they were each given equal shares. On the other hand, Fowler was separately identified by name.

Concluding that the testator intended a class gift, Lord Lindley noted that "the authorities do not help one much, because they are in inextricable confusion." Lord Lindley continued:

> Who are the persons now entitled to the share of the testator in the Daily Telegraph newspaper? There are several rival views. One view is, and that is the one adopted by the learned judge below, that the share which Elizabeth Jane Fowler would have taken if she were alive — that is, one-sixth, as I understand it — has lapsed and has fallen into the residuary estate, so that, according to that view, one-sixth of that share has gone to persons who were certainly never intended to take it. That is obvious. That may be the legal result of the gift, but it is obvious it was never dreamt of by the testator. What he intended was that his share should go amongst the persons he has named and to no one else.
>
> Now the difficulty lies in this. We hear about classes, and gifts to classes, and definitions of classes. You may define a class in a thousand ways: anybody may make any number of things or persons a class by setting out an attribute more or less common to them all and making that the definition of the class. . . . Now what is to be done with the share of this lady who has died? . . . It seems to me that it is to go to such of them as shall be living. That is the obvious intention. The alternative view takes the share away where it was never intended to go. . . .

In reaching this conclusion, Lord Lindley was persuaded by his colleague, Lord Romer, who emphasized the equality of the shares:

> In the absence of any context negativing this view, I think that, when a testator gives property X to A and a class of persons — say the children of B — in equal shares, he intends that the whole of X shall pass by his gift if any one of the children of B survive him, even although A does not. . . . I think that, in such a gift as I have mentioned, what the testator really means is that the property is to be shared equally by a body

---

penny a copy, featuring brilliant young writers on politics, and factually reporting titillating court proceedings involving divorce, crime, and sex (a practice continuing to this day in most London newspapers). Levy invented the classified ad with a box number return in which persons could advertise for matrimonial or sexual partners. The Daily Telegraph, together with the New York Herald, sent Stanley to the rescue of Livingstone. On finding Livingstone near the shores of Lake Tanganyika, Stanley inquired, "Dr. Livingstone, I presume?" By the end of the 1800s the Daily Telegraph had the largest circulation in the world.

Moss's investment of £500 proved extremely profitable, soon returning £15,500 annually on Moss's capital investment. Walter Moss, the testator in the principal case, was the son of George Moss.

The Daily Telegraph remains today a leading London newspaper. See Edward F. Burnham, Peterborough Court: The Story of the Daily Telegraph 1-3 (1955).

constituted of such of the following as should be existing at the date of the testator's death, that is to say, *A* and the children of *B*. . . . In my opinion it is correct to say that a gift by will to a class properly so called and a named individual such as *A* equally, so that the testator contemplates *A* taking the same share that each member of the class will take, is prima facie a gift to a class.[21]

5 AMERICAN LAW OF PROPERTY §22.13 (1952): "The prevailing view seems to be that a gift 'to *A* and the children of *B*' is a gift to an individual and a class in the absence of additional factors. Thus, if *A* dies before the testator, his share lapses and does not pass to the children of *B*. Likewise, if all the children of *B* die, their share lapses. Also the revocation of the share of *A* or of the share given the children of *B* should result in a lapse as to the revoked share.

"Such a view appears to be sound. The inferences deducible from a gift to an entity are such that the finding of a gift to an entity should be made only when the beneficiaries are drawn together, either by language or by circumstances, so that the identity of the individuals is submerged. The language of the cases under discussion does not justify the assumption that *A* is to lose his identity in a group composed of himself and the children of another. Thus, the construction preference should be, as it is, for a gift to an individual and a class."

Compare Restatement of Property §284 (1940), which states that the presumption is that the named individual and the group form one class. The authorities are, as Lord Lindley said in *Moss*, "in inextricable confusion."

Application of antilapse statutes to class gifts. Almost all states apply their antilapse statutes to class gifts and most statutes expressly so provide. See UPC §2-605 (1969); Restatement (Third) of Property: Wills and Other Donative Transfers §5.5, statutory note (1999). In states where the statute is unclear, courts reason that the antilapse statutes are designed to carry out the average testator's intent and that the average testator would prefer for the deceased beneficiary's share to go to the beneficiary's descendants rather than to the surviving members of the class. However, in some states, antilapse statutes do not apply to dispositions to class members who die before execution of the will. See, e.g., Tex. Prob. Code Ann. §68(a) (1997) (page 393, n.18). In these states it is assumed that the testator did not have the dead class member in mind and did not want him to take. Thus:

> *Case 5.* *T*, a widow, dies leaving a will devising Blackacre "to my sisters," and devising her residuary estate to her stepson, *S*. When *T* executed the will, *T* had two sisters living, *A* and *B*. One sister, *C*, died before the will was executed, leaving children who survived *T*. *A* died during *T*'s lifetime leaving two children. *T* is survived by *B*, *A*'s children, *C*'s children, and *S*. Who takes Blackacre? Assuming the antilapse statute

---

21. Lord Romer was a professor of mathematics before he took up the study of law, and it shows in his argument. A crucial premise of his theory is that the testator intended E.J. Fowler to take a one-sixth share (or a share equal to that of the other nephews and nieces). His theory wouldn't work if E.J. Fowler was intended to take one-half and the children of Emily the other one-half. Some courts, particularly courts following the English classic per stirpes construction calling for distribution down family lines, would construe the bequest to be one-half to E.J. Fowler and one-half to the children of Emily. Even under this latter construction, however, shouldn't this bequest of Daily Telegraph stock be held to be a class gift? — Eds.

applies to devises to sisters, in most states *B* takes a one-third share, *A*'s children a one-third share, and *C*'s children a one-third share. In a minority of states, *C*'s children do not share because *C* was dead when the will was executed, and Blackacre goes one-half to *B* and one-half to *A*'s children. If the antilapse statute did not apply to class gifts, *B*, as the sole surviving member of the class, would take Blackacre.

SECTION C.   CHANGES IN PROPERTY AFTER EXECUTION OF WILL

1. *Ademption by Extinction*

What happens if a will includes a specific devise of an item of property, but the testator sells or gives the item away before death? Specific devises of real and personal property are subject to the doctrine of *ademption by extinction*. Thus:

> *Case 6. T's* will devises Blackacre to her son, John, and the residuary estate to her daughter, Mary. Some years later, the testator sells Blackacre and uses the sale proceeds to purchase Whiteacre, then dies without having changed her will. The gift of Blackacre is adeemed (from the Latin *adimere:* to take away). Since Blackacre is not owned by the testator at her death, the devise fails. John has no claim to Whiteacre, for the will does not devise Whiteacre to him.

Ademption applies only to specific devises. Generally speaking, a *specific* devise is a disposition of a specific item of the testator's property. Gifts of Blackacre or of "my three-carat diamond ring given to me by my Aunt Jane" are examples. Ademption does not apply to *general, demonstrative*, or *residuary* devises. A devise is *general* when the testator intends to confer a general benefit and not give a particular asset — for example, a legacy of $100,000 to *A*. If there is not $100,000 in cash in the testator's estate at death, the legacy is not adeemed; other assets must be sold to satisfy *A*'s general legacy. A *demonstrative* devise is a hybrid: a general devise, yet payable from a specific source. Suppose that the testator's will gives *B* "the sum of $100,000 to be paid from the proceeds of sale of my General Motors stock." Most courts would hold this to be a demonstrative devise. If the testator owns sufficient GM stock at death, in raising the $100,000 the executor must comply with the testamentary direction to sell the stock. But if the testator does not own any GM stock at death, the devise is not adeemed. Other assets must be sold in order to raise the $100,000. A *residuary* devise conveys that portion of the testator's estate not otherwise effectively devised by other parts of the will, such as a devise to A of "all the rest, residue, and remainder of my property and estate."[22]

---

22. Restatement (Third) of Property: Wills and Other Donative Transfers §5.1 (1999) defines specific, general, demonstrative, and residuary devises as follows (we have included examples from the official comments in brackets):

> (1) A *specific devise* is a testamentary disposition of a specifically identified asset. [Examples: "my desk," "my Buick," "the house I own and am residing in at my death."]

Under the traditional *identity theory* of ademption, if a specifically devised item is not in the testator's estate, the gift is extinguished (subject to limited exceptions noted below). Under the *intent theory* of ademption, if the specifically devised item is not in the testator's estate, the beneficiary may nonetheless be entitled to the cash value of the item, depending on whether the beneficiary can show that this is what the testator would have wanted.

Wasserman v. Cohen

Supreme Judicial Court of Massachusetts, 1993
414 Mass. 172, 606 N.E.2d 901

LYNCH, J. This appeal raises the question whether the doctrine of ademption by extinction applies to a specific gift of real estate contained in a revocable inter vivos trust. The plaintiff, Elaine Wasserman, brought an action for declaratory judgment in the Middlesex Division of the Probate and Family Court against the defendant, David E. Cohen (trustee), as he is the surviving trustee of a trust established by Frieda M. Drapkin (Drapkin). In her complaint the plaintiff requested that the trustee be ordered to pay her the proceeds of the sale of an apartment building which, under the trust, would have been conveyed to the plaintiff had it not been sold by Drapkin prior to her death. Pursuant to the trustee's motion to dismiss under Mass. R. Civ. P. 12(b)(6), 365 Mass. 754 (1974), the probate judge dismissed the action. The plaintiff appealed. We granted the plaintiff's application for direct appellate review and now affirm.

1. [Frieda Drapkin created a revocable inter vivos trust in December, 1982.] . . . On her death, the trustee was directed to distribute the property as set out in the trust. The trustee was ordered to convey to the plaintiff "12-14 Newton Street, Waltham, Massachusetts, Apartment Building, (consisting of approximately 11,296 square feet)."

When she executed the trust, Drapkin held record title to the property at 12-14 Newton Street in Waltham, as trustee of Z.P.Q. Realty Trust. However, she sold the property on September 29, 1988, for $575,000, and had never conveyed her interest in the property to the trust.[23]

Drapkin died on March 28, 1989. Her will, dated December 26, 1982, devised all property in her residuary estate to the trust to be disposed of in accordance with the trust's provisions.

2. The plaintiff first contends that the probate judge erred in failing to consider Drapkin's intent in regard to the gift when she sold the property. We disagree.

---

(2) A *general devise* is a testamentary disposition, usually of a specified amount of money or quantity of property, that is payable from the general assets of the estate. [Examples: "$100,000," "1,000 shares of X-Y-Z Corporation."]

(3) A *demonstrative devise* is a testamentary disposition, usually of a specified amount of money or quantity of property, that is primarily payable from a designated source, but is secondarily payable from the general assets of the estate to the extent that the primary source is insufficient. [Examples: "$5,000 out of my bank account," "$10,000 from the proceeds of the sale of my X-Y-Z bonds."]

(4) A *residuary devise* is a testamentary disposition of property of the testator's net probate estate not disposed by a specific, general, or demonstrative devise. [Example: "all the rest, residue, and remainder of my estate."]

23. Drapkin amended the trust by instruments dated December 16, 1982, and February 8, 1989. The amendments did not reference the gift to the plaintiff.

We have long adhered to the rule that, when a testator disposes, during his lifetime, of the subject of a specific legacy or devise in his will, that legacy or devise is held to be adeemed, "whatever may have been the intent or motive of the testator in doing so." Walsh v. Gillespie, 154 N.E.2d 906 (Mass. 1959), quoting Richards v. Humphreys, 15 Pick. 133, 135 (Mass. 1833). The focus is on the actual existence or nonexistence of the bequeathed property, and not on the intent of the testator with respect to it. Bostwick v. Hurstel, 304 N.E.2d 186 (Mass. 1973). To be effective, a specific legacy or devise must be in existence and owned by the testator at the time of his death. Moffatt v. Heon, 136 N.E. 123 (Mass. 1922).

The plaintiff asks us to abandon the doctrine of ademption. She contends that, because the doctrine ignores the testator's intent, it produces harsh and inequitable results and thus fosters litigation that the rule was intended to preclude. See Note, Ademption and the Testator's Intent, 74 Harv. L. Rev. 741 (1961). This rule has been followed in this Commonwealth for nearly 160 years. See Richards v. Humphreys, supra. Whatever else may be said about it, it is easily understood and applied by draftsmen, testators, and fiduciaries. The doctrine seeks to give effect to a testator's probable intent by presuming he intended to extinguish a specific gift of property when he disposed of that property prior to his death. As with any rule, exceptions have emerged.[24] These limited exceptions do not lead us to the abandonment of the rule. Its so-called harsh results can be easily avoided by careful draftsmanship and its existence must be recognized by any competent practitioner. When we consider the myriad of instruments drafted in reliance on its application, we conclude that stability in the field of trusts and estates requires that we continue the doctrine.

3. The plaintiff also argues that deciding ademption questions based on a determination that a devise is general or specific is overly formalistic and fails to serve the testator's likely intent. She maintains that the court in Bostwick v. Hurstel, supra, moved away from making such classifications. In *Bostwick*, the court held that a gift of stock was not adeemed where the stock had been sold and repurchased prior to the death of the testatrix, and where it had been subject to two stock splits. However, the court confined the holding specifically to its facts.[25] See Bostwick v. Hurstel, supra, 304 N.E. at 193-194. In addition, the court stated: "Our holding does not indicate that we have abandoned the classification of bequests as general or specific for all purposes. We have no occasion at this time to express any opinion on the continuing validity of such distinctions in those cases where abatement or ademption of the legacy is at issue. . . ." Id. at 192.[26] We now have such an occasion,

24. This court has created two exceptions to the "identity" theory. In Walsh v. Gillespie, 154 N.E.2d 906 (Mass. 1959), a conservator appointed for the testatrix five years after her will was executed sold shares of stock that were the subject of a specific legacy. The court held that the sale did not operate as an ademption as to the unexpended balance remaining in the hands of the conservator at the death of the testatrix. Id. at 910. In Bostwick v. Hurstel, 304 N.E.2d 186 (Mass. 1973), a conservator had sold, then repurchased, stock that was the subject of a specific legacy and that had been split twice, before the death of the testatrix. The court held that the bequest of stock was not adeemed but emphasized, "we do not violate our rule that 'identity' and not 'intent' governs ademption cases." Id. at 194. See Baybank Harvard Trust Co. v. Grant, 504 N.E.2d 1072 (Mass. App. 1987).

25. "This conclusion is not based upon our present rejection of the general versus specific legacy distinction for resolving questions concerning stock splits; rather, we think that the concept of ademption in and of itself need not and should not be interpreted to include within its scope the circumstances present in this case." Bostwick v. Hurstel, supra, 304 N.E.2d at 193.

26. We recognize that some courts criticize the process of first classifying legacies before determining whether they are adeemed. See Note, Ademption and the Testator's Intent, 74 Harv. L. Rev. 741, 743-745 (1961). See also Baybank Harvard Trust Co. v. Grant, supra, 504 N.E.2d at 1074 n.4.

and we hold that, at least in regard to the conveyance of real estate at issue here, the practice of determining whether a devise is general or specific is the proper first step in deciding questions of ademption.

4. We have held that a trust, particularly when executed as part of a comprehensive estate plan, should be construed according to the same rules traditionally applied to wills. In Clymer v. Mayo, 473 N.E.2d 1084 (Mass. 1985), we reasoned that "[t]reating the components of the decedent's estate plan separately, and not as parts of an interrelated whole, brings about inconsistent results." We also quoted one commentator who wrote, "The subsidiary rules [of wills] are the product of centuries of legal experience in attempting to discern transferors' wishes and suppress litigation. These rules should be treated as presumptively correct for will substitutes as well as for wills." Id. at 1093, quoting Langbein, The Nonprobate Revolution and the Future of the Law of Succession, 97 Harv. L. Rev. 1108, 1136-1137 (1984). We agree with this reasoning. As discussed above, the doctrine of ademption has a "long established recognition" in Massachusetts. See Second Bank-State St. Trust Co. v. Pinion, 170 N.E.2d 350, 354 (Mass. 1960). Furthermore, Drapkin created the trust along with her will as part of a comprehensive estate plan. Under the residuary clause of her will, Drapkin gave the majority of her estate to the trustee, who was then to dispose of the property on her death according to the terms of the trust. We see no reason to apply a different rule because she conveyed the property under the terms of the trust, rather than her will. Thus, we conclude that the doctrine of ademption, as traditionally applied to wills, should also apply to the trust in the instant case.

5. Conclusion. Since the plaintiff does not contest that the devise of 12-14 Newton Street was a specific devise,[27] it follows that the devise was adeemed by the act of Drapkin.

So ordered.

PROBLEMS AND NOTES

1. Suppose *T* contracts to sell certain real estate to *B*, but dies before the closing. In her will, *T* leaves the real estate to *A*. After *T*'s death, the executor closes on the deal, as he is required to do. Does the gift of the real estate to *A* adeem? See Kelley v. Neilson, 745 N.E.2d 952 (Mass. 2001) (holding that the devise to *A* adeems, deviating from Massachusetts' usual identity theory approach, and using an intent theory instead).

Suppose *T* bequeaths "my bank account in First National Bank" to *A*. After executing her will, *T* closes the account at First National and purchases certificates of deposit to obtain a higher rate of interest. At *T*'s death is *A* entitled to the certificate of deposit? Is the change only a change in form? See Mayberry v. Mayberry, 886 S.W.2d 627 (Ark. 1994) (adeemed); Church v. Morgan, 685 N.E.2d 809 (Ohio App. 1996) (adeemed).

27. "A specific legacy is one which separates and distinguishes the property bequeathed from the other property of the testator, so that it can be identified. It can only be satisfied by the thing bequeathed; if that has no existence, when the bequest would otherwise become operative, the legacy has no effect." Moffatt v. Heon, 136 N.E. 123, 123 (1922), quoting Tomlinson v. Bury, 14 N.E. 137, 140 (1887).

Suppose *T* devises "187 acres of land to each of my three children." After executing her will, to reduce estate taxes *T* conveys the land to a corporation in return for stock. At *T*'s death are *T*'s children entitled to the stock? Is the transfer only a change in form? See Redditt v. Redditt, 820 So. 2d 782 (Miss. App. 2002) (change in form, not adeemed).

2.   *T* devises his house, which is encumbered by a mortgage, to his niece *A*. *T* faithfully makes all the payments on the mortgage until a few months before his death, when he falls ill. The bank quickly forecloses just before *T* dies. Does *A* take the surplus proceeds from the foreclosure sale of the house? Or does the devise adeem, in which event the surplus proceeds would go to the residuary taker? What result under the identity theory? What result under the intent theory? See In re Estate of Hume v. Klank, 984 S.W.2d 602 (Tenn. 1999) ("We conclude that the testator's intent is irrelevant in deciding the question of whether a specific bequest has been adeemed by extinction. We further conclude that a foreclosure sale so alters the form of the specific bequest of a house that an ademption by extinction results regardless of whether identifiable proceeds remain from the foreclosure sale.").

3.   In jurisdictions following the identity theory, courts have developed several escape routes to avoid ademption.

(a) *Classify the devise as general or demonstrative rather than specific.* If *T* bequeaths "100 shares of Tigertail Corporation" to *A*, and *T* owns no shares of Tigertail at death, the court will probably declare this to be a general devise if Tigertail Corporation has widely held stock traded on a major exchange. *A* is entitled to the value of 100 shares of Tigertail at *T*'s death. On the other hand, if testator had said "*my* 100 shares of Tigertail," the court will almost surely hold it a specific devise and adeemed to the extent the shares are missing at death. A gift that looks specific might also be declared to be demonstrative and not adeemed. Thus a bequest "of $10,000, more or less, entered on my bank book" has been held demonstrative. Kenaday v. Sinnott, 179 U.S. 606 (1900).

(b) *Classify the inter vivos disposition as a change in form, not substance.* Suppose that after *T* executes her will giving "my 100 shares of Tigertail Corporation" to *A*, Tigertail Corporation merges into Lion Corporation, which retires the Tigertail stock and issues in its place 85 shares of Lion stock for every 100 shares of Tigertail. Does *A* take the 85 shares of Lion stock? Most courts hold that corporate merger or reorganization is only a change in form, not substance, and *A* takes the Lion stock. UPC §2-605(a)(2) (1990) agrees.

(c) *Construe the meaning of the will as of the time of death rather than as of the time of execution.* By this technique a bequest of "my Lincoln automobile" passed a 1989 Lincoln owned by testator at her death, though at the time the will was executed testator owned a 1984 Lincoln. McIntyre v. Kilbourn, 885 S.W.2d 54 (Mo. App. 1994). This approach is most viable when the language of the will is broad enough to cover the new item and the new item was purchased not to change the estate plan, but rather as a matter of ordinary living. Such cases fall under the doctrine of *acts of independent significance* (see pages 285-286). But see Estate of Morris, 169 N.Y.S.2d 881 (Sur. 1957), where the bequest failed when testator sold a diamond-studded watch referred to in the will and bought another diamond-studded watch worth approximately five times as much.

(d) *Create exceptions.* If the conservator of an incompetent or insane person transfers the item, most cases have held the legacy not adeemed on the theory that ademption requires a voluntary act of the testator. See Wasserman v. Cohen, supra, at n.24; Annot., 84 A.L.R.4th 462 (1991, rev. 2003).

4. The 1969 UPC followed the traditional identity theory used in solving ademption problems, but it provided for five exceptions often followed by courts when the specific property is not in the testator's estate. These include giving the specific devisee

(1) any remaining balance on the purchase price of the specific property sold,
(2) any unpaid amount of condemnation award for the property,
(3) any unpaid fire or casualty insurance proceeds after the property has been destroyed,
(4) any property owned by the testator as a result of foreclosing a mortgage devised to the specific devisee, and
(5) the sale price of specifically devised property sold by a conservator.

See UPC §2-608(a) & (b) (1969, rev. 1987).

5. The 1990 UPC abandons the identity theory and adopts the intent theory, but as amended in 1997 creates a presumption in favor of ademption. The party opposing ademption, that is, the party claiming the cash value of a specifically devised item that is not in the testator's estate, has the burden of proving that ademption is inconsistent with the testator's intent. UPC §2-606(a)(6) (1990, rev. 1997). The 1990 Code continues the application of the exceptions provisions in the 1969 Code to circumstances falling within them. UPC §2-606(a)(1)-(4) & (b). The 1990 UPC also added an additional exception for replacement property in §2-606(a)(5). The 1999 Restatement (Third) of Property likewise adopts the intent theory.

Uniform Probate Code (1990, as amended 1997)

§2-606. Nonademption of Specific Devises; Unpaid Proceeds of Sale, Condemnation, or Insurance; Sale by Conservator or Agent

(a) A specific devisee has a right to the specifically devised property in the testator's estate at death and:

(1) any balance of the purchase price, together with any security agreement, owing from a purchaser to the testator at death by reason of sale of the property;

(2) any amount of a condemnation award for the taking of the property unpaid at death;

(3) any proceeds unpaid at death on fire or casualty insurance or on other recovery for injury to the property;

(4) property owned by the testator at death and acquired as a result of foreclosure, or obtained in lieu of foreclosure, of the security interest for a specifically devised obligation;

(5) real or tangible personal property owned by the testator at death which the testator acquired as a replacement for specifically devised real or tangible personal property; and

(6) if not covered by paragraphs (1) through (5), a pecuniary devise equal to the value as of its date of disposition of other specifically devised property disposed of during the testator's lifetime but only to the extent it is established

that ademption would be inconsistent with the testator's manifested plan of distribution or that at the time the will was made, the date of disposition or otherwise, the testator did not intend that the devise adeem.

(b) If specifically devised property is sold or mortgaged by a conservator or by an agent acting within the authority of a durable power of attorney for an incapacitated principal, or if a condemnation award, insurance proceeds, or recovery for injury to the property are paid to a conservator or to an agent acting within the authority of a durable power of attorney for an incapacitated principal, the specific devisee has the right to a general pecuniary devise equal to the net sale price, the amount of the unpaid loan, the condemnation award, the insurance proceeds, or the recovery.

(c) The right of a specific devisee under subsection (b) is reduced by any right the devisee has under subsection (a). . . .

PROBLEMS AND NOTE

1.   Under UPC §2-606(a)(5) (1990) dealing with replacement property, if *T* executes a will bequeathing "my Ford car" to *A* and later sells the Ford and buys a Rolls-Royce, is *A* entitled to the Rolls? Suppose *T* sold the Ford and bought two cars, a Honda and a Rolls-Royce. What result? Suppose *T* sold the Ford and bought a motorcycle. What result?

If *T* devises Blackacre to *A* and sells it and buys Whiteacre with the proceeds, is *A* entitled to Whiteacre?

2.   Aunt Fanny Fox has a collection of Chinese snuff bottles. Snuff bottles were first made in China around 1650 when the First Manchu emperor, Kangzi, began to inhale snuff (powdered tobacco) brought by European traders. Sniffing snuff quickly became popular, and thousands upon thousands of small snuff bottles, each with a tiny spoon, were made to carry around in a pocket. Some snuff bottles were carved from jade, agate, and semi-precious stones; others were made of

Two of Aunt Fanny's snuff bottles

amber, ivory, and glass, sometimes with a scene painted inside. Ordinary Chinese snuff bottles of the eighteenth and nineteenth centuries can be found today for $800 or so, very good ones for perhaps $3,000; exceptional bottles may fetch $50,000 or more. Since each bottle is unique, each is individually priced in accordance with its quality of workmanship, rarity, and particular appeal to collectors' tastes.

Aunt Fanny bought her bottles from the 1950s through the 1970s, one at a time, as she ran across one catching her eye. She kept no records as to costs, and the bottles were not insured.

Aunt Fanny's will bequeaths her snuff bottles to Wendy Brown. At Aunt Fanny's death, the snuff bottles are not found in her house. No one knows how many bottles there were. Zoë Preston thinks there were 60 or more; Aunt Fanny displayed only part of her collection at any one time. Wendy recalls seeing "about 20" in Aunt Fanny's display cabinet. Aunt Fanny might have given the bottles away, or sold them, or her nurses may have taken them during her long illness. No one knows for sure.

What are Wendy's rights under the common law identity theory? Under UPC §2-606(a)(6)?

3. UPC §2-606(a)(6) (1990) has been criticized for abandoning the identity theory, on the grounds that the intent theory will increase litigation and that the UPC changes the meaning of a bequest of "my diamond ring" to "my diamond ring or its equivalent value," muddying up clear language and inserting a devise the testator did not make. See Mark L. Ascher, The 1990 Uniform Probate Code: Older and Better or More Like the Internal Revenue Code?, 77 Minn. L. Rev. 639 (1993). For contrary arguments, approving UPC §2-606(a)(6), see Gregory S. Alexander, Ademption and the Domain of Formality in Wills Law, 55 Alb. L. Rev. 1067 (1992); Mary L. Fellows, Traveling the Road of Probate Reform: Finding the Way to Your Will (A Response to Professor Ascher), 77 Minn. L. Rev. 659 (1993). See also Mary K. Lundwall, The Case Against the Ademption by Extinction Rule: A Proposal for Reform, 29 Gonz. L. Rev. 105 (1994).

UPC §2-606(a)(6), adopting the intent theory, has been enacted in a handful of states.

2. Stock Splits and the Problem of Increase

Suppose that T executes a will devising 100 shares of stock of Tigertail Corporation to A. Subsequently Tigertail Corporation splits its stock three-for-one. At T's death, T owns 300 shares of Tigertail stock. Does A take 100 shares or 300 shares? The old-fashioned approach was to ask whether the bequest was specific or general. If the court found T intended to separate out and bequeath particular shares in T's possession, the bequest was termed specific and A received the specified shares (100) as well as any accretions in a stock split (200). On the other hand, if the court found T did not have in mind particular property of his own but only desired to confer a general benefit, A received only 100 shares of stock.

This mechanical approach misconceives the basic nature of a stock split, which is a change in form, not substance. The shares held after the split represent the same proportional ownership of the corporation as the number of shares held before the split. The market value of 300 shares of Tigertail after the split should be approximately the same as 100 shares before the split. Therefore, many modern courts have discarded the old approach in the case of stock splits and have held that, absent a contrary showing of intent, a devisee of stock is entitled to additional shares received by the testator as a result of a stock split.

Stock dividends are treated differently from stock splits by some courts. They analogize a stock dividend to a cash dividend and conclude that the devisee cannot logically be awarded the former when he is denied the latter. However, this analogy ignores the fact of corporate finance that after a stock dividend, as after a stock split, the testator's percentage of ownership remains the same.

Under both the UPC and the Restatement (Third) of Property, stock dividends are treated the same as stock splits: the beneficiary gets them along with the other shares. See UPC §2-605 (1990); Restatement (Third) of Property: Wills and Other Donative Transfers §5.3 (1999).

3. Satisfaction of General Pecuniary Bequests

The doctrine of *satisfaction* (sometimes known as *ademption by satisfaction*) applies when the testator makes a transfer to a devisee after executing the will. If the testator is a parent of the beneficiary (or stands in loco parentis) and after execution of the will transfers to the beneficiary property of a similar nature to that given by the will, there is a rebuttable presumption that the gift is in satisfaction of the gift made by the will. Thus:

> *Case 7.* T's will bequeaths $50,000 to her son, S, and her residuary estate to her daughter, D. After executing the will, T gives S $30,000. There is a presumption that the gift was in partial satisfaction of the legacy, so that S will take only $20,000 at T's death.

This doctrine, which is akin to the doctrine of advancements under intestacy law (see page 114), applies to general pecuniary bequests but not to specific bequests. When specific property (such as a painting or the family Bible) is devised by the terms of the will to a beneficiary, but is given to that beneficiary during the testator's life, the gift is adeemed by extinction, not by satisfaction. Satisfaction may also apply to residuary gifts and to demonstrative gifts, but the cases are not uniform in their holdings. In all states satisfaction depends upon the intention of the testator.

Because the intent of the testator is frequently difficult to ascertain, some states have enacted statutes requiring that the intention of a testator to adeem by satisfaction must be shown in writing. UPC §2-609 (1990) so provides, paralleling its rule on advancements (§2-109, page 115). Under such a statute, there is no presumption of satisfaction by a gift to a child. See also Restatement (Third) of Property: Wills and Other Donative Transfers §5.4 (1999) (requiring a writing to evidence satisfaction).

4. Exoneration of Liens

When a will makes a specific devise of land, on which there is a mortgage, the question may arise whether the land devised passes free of the mortgage. Suppose that *T*'s will devises Blackacre to her daughter *A*. At *T*'s death, Blackacre is subject to a mortgage that secures a note on which *T* was personally liable. Does *A* take Blackacre subject to the mortgage, or is she entitled to have the note paid out of residuary assets so that the title will pass to *A* free of the lien? In some states, *A* takes Blackacre free of the mortgage. These jurisdictions apply the common law doctrine of *exoneration of liens*. Under this doctrine, when a will makes a specific disposition of real or personal property that is subject to a mortgage to secure a note on which the testator is personally liable, it is presumed, absent contrary language in the will, that the testator wanted the debt, like other debts, to be paid out of the residuary estate. It is unclear, however, whether this presumption accords with the probable intent of the average testator, and the risk is that the residue will be depleted by exonerating the lien. See Robert Whitman, Exoneration Clauses in Wills and Trust Instruments, 4 Hofstra Prop. L.J. 123 (1992).

Dissatisfaction with the exoneration doctrine has led to the enactment, in a number of states, of statutes reversing the common law rule, as does UPC §2-607 (1990): "A specific devise passes subject to any mortgage interest existing at the date of death, without right of exoneration, regardless of a general directive in the will to pay debts."

5. *Abatement*

Abatement, like ademption, often turns on the classification of a devise as specific, general, or residuary. The problem of abatement arises when the estate has insufficient assets to pay debts as well as all the devises; some devises must be abated or reduced. By divvying up a limited pie among claimants of different priorities, abatement operates like bankruptcy. In the absence of any indication in the will as to how devises should abate or be reduced, devises ordinarily abate in the following order: (1) residuary devises are reduced first, (2) general devises are reduced second, and (3) specific and demonstrative devises are the last to abate and are reduced pro rata. This plan is believed to follow the testator's intent that specific devises be given effect before general devises, and both be given effect before a residuary devise. But the residuary devisee is often the most important devisee of the testator. Thus:

> *Case 8. T* executes a will in which he devises $300,000 to charity *B*, $100,000 to charity *C*, and the residue of his estate to his son *A*. At the time of the will's execution, *T* has $800,000 in assets. *T* then becomes ill and undergoes an experimental treatment costing $500,000. The treatment fails, and *T* dies. Under traditional abatement rules, *A* takes nothing, *B* takes $225,000, and *C* takes $75,000.

Is it likely that *T* would have wanted *B* and *C* to take to the exclusion of his son *A*? UPC §3-902 (1990) provides that, "if the testamentary plan . . . would be defeated by" the usual order of abatement, "the shares of the distributees abate as may be necessary to give effect to the intention of the testator." Under §3-902, what result in Case 8 above? See In re Estate of Tateo, 768 A.2d 243 (N.J. App. Div. 2001), holding that a specific devise to *T*'s son would not be given priority over general devises to *T*'s daughter and grandchildren.

It is of course preferable to avoid the problem through better drafting. For example, in Case 8, if *T* had devised one-half of the residue of his estate to the charities and the other half to his son *A*, then all three gifts would have adjusted automatically in accord with the size of *T*'s estate. For this reason, it is often wise to make substantial devises in the form of shares of the residue.

7

RESTRICTIONS ON THE POWER OF DISPOSITION: PROTECTION OF THE SPOUSE AND CHILDREN

SECTION A. RIGHTS OF THE SURVIVING SPOUSE

1. Introduction to Marital Property Systems

In the United States, two basic marital property systems exist—the system of *separate property*, originating in the common law of England, and the system of *community property*, originating on the continent of Europe and brought to this country by French and Spanish settlers. The fundamental difference between these systems is that under the common law husband and wife own separately all property each acquires (except those items one spouse has agreed to put into joint ownership with the other), whereas under community property husband and wife own all acquisitions from earnings after marriage in equal undivided shares. There are, to be sure, many variations among the states adhering to one or another of these systems, and community property ideas have made noticeable inroads into the separate property system within the last 50 years. Nonetheless, separate property and community property are quite different ways of thinking about marital property ownership. The former stresses the individual's autonomy over his or her earnings, the latter stresses sharing of earnings between husband and wife.

Community property developed throughout the continent of Europe, allegedly spread by Germanic tribes after the fall of Rome. From these western countries it was taken by European settlers to Central and South America, Mexico, and states along the southern and western borders of the United States. It is odd, then, that in England—separated from the continent by only a 21-mile-wide channel of water—there arose a separate property system, based on the husband's autonomy and the effacement of the wife. Why the English resisted so powerful an idea as the sharing principle of community property has intrigued scholars for generations. The most plausible explanations connect the separate property system with the highly centralized English feudal system, dominated by a powerful king, which

417

required succession of power (land) from father to son and fealty between a (male) lord and a (male) tenant. Women were supported by their husbands, but they were denied an ownership share of, or power over, their husbands' acquests. Whatever the reason for its existence, the English separate property system became well entrenched by the fourteenth century and was taken by the English settlers to the eastern seaboard of the United States, whence it spread westward.

Under the separate property system, whatever the worker earns is his — or hers. There is no sharing of earnings. If one spouse is the wage earner while the other spouse works in the home, the wage-earning spouse will own all the property acquired during marriage (other than gifts or inheritances from relatives or gifts by the wage earner to the homemaker). Thus, a crucial issue under a separate property system is what protection against disinheritance should be given the surviving spouse who works in the home or works at a lower-paying job? All but one of the separate property states answer this question by giving the surviving spouse, by statute, an *elective share* (or *forced share*) in the estate of the deceased spouse. The elective share is not, however, limited to a share of property acquired with earnings. It is enforceable against all property owned by the decedent spouse at death.

In eight states (Arizona, California, Idaho, Louisiana, Nevada, New Mexico, Texas, and Washington), a community property system has long existed. The fundamental principle of community property is that all earnings of the spouses and property acquired from earnings are community property. Each spouse is the owner of an undivided one-half interest in the community property. The death of one spouse dissolves the community. The deceased spouse owns and has testamentary power over only his or her one-half community share.

A simple illustration shows the difference between the principles underlying the separate property and the community property systems:

> *Case 1.* *H* works outside the home, earning $50,000 a year. *W* works in the home, earning no wages. At the end of 20 years, *H* has through savings of his salary bought a house in his name, a life insurance policy payable to his daughter, and $100,000 worth of stocks in his name. Under a separate property regime, during life *W* owns none of that property. At *H*'s death, *W* has an elective share (usually one-third) of the house and the stocks but usually not the insurance policy because it is not in *H*'s probate estate. In a community property state, *W* owns half of *H*'s earnings during life, and thus at *H*'s death *W* owns one-half of the acquisitions from earnings (the house, the insurance proceeds, and the stocks). If *W* dies first, *W* can dispose of her half of the community property by will. In a separate property state, if *W* dies first, she has no property to convey.

Community property is based on the idea that husband and wife are a marital partnership, that they decide together how to allocate the time of each to earning income, homemaking, leisure, and so forth to maximize their joint happiness. On this view, they should share the earnings of each equally. Property acquired before marriage and property acquired during marriage by gift, devise, or descent is the acquiring spouse's separate property (as long as it is kept separate).

In the late twentieth century, many academics came to favor community property. In 1983, the National Conference of Commissioners on Uniform State Laws promulgated a Uniform Marital Property Act. The act adopts community property principles, though the phrase *community property* is avoided and *marital property* is used instead. See Kathy T. Graham, The Uniform Marital Property Act: A Solution for Common Law Property Systems?, 48 S.D.L. Rev. 455 (2003). Wisconsin is the only state to have adopted the act; hence, Wisconsin must now be reckoned a community property state. Wis. Stat. Ann. §§766.001-766.097 (2004).

In 1998, Alaska enacted a statute permitting married couples to elect to hold their property as community property. Alaska Stat. §§34.77.010-34.77.160 (2004). This seems a good idea, worthy of consideration in all separate property states. It gives couples choices of marital property systems. It provides a test of which system married couples prefer, which has never been done.

In examining the surviving spouse's rights, we turn first to rights of the surviving spouse to *support*, which (except for dower) are generally the same in both separate property and community property states. We next turn to the central topic — the right of the surviving spouse to a *share* in the decedent spouse's property or in the marital property. We examine this matter first in the separate property states and then in the community property states. For further examination of recent developments on the topics covered in this chapter, see Ralph C. Brashier, Inheritance Law and the Evolving Family (2004).

2. Rights of Surviving Spouse to Support

a. Social Security

In the 1930s, Congress established the social security system, under which retirement benefits are paid to a worker and his or her surviving spouse. In 2004, workers paid 6.2 percent of their earnings up to $87,900 into the system, matched by 6.2 percent paid by employers. Self-employed workers paid the entire 12.4 percent themselves. In addition, there is a 2.9 percent Medicare tax split between employer and employee.

Where does the money go? According to the Social Security Administration, this

tax money is used to pay benefits to:

- People who already have retired;
- People who are disabled;
- Survivors of workers who have died; and
- Dependents of beneficiaries.

The money you pay in taxes is not held in a personal account for you to use when you get benefits. Your taxes are being used right now to pay people who now are getting benefits. Any unused money goes to the Social Security trust funds, not a personal account with your name on it. [Understanding The Benefits, SSA Publication No. 05-10024 (March 2004), at 4.]

Eligibility for full benefits depends on the year you were born. People born before 1938 are entitled to full benefits at 65; people born between 1943 and 1954 are entitled to full benefits at 66; and people born after 1960 are entitled to full benefits at 67. People born in the gaps are entitled to benefits at the age given plus some number of months depending on the year of birth. If you elect to receive benefits before full eligibility, you get reduced monthly payments.

If a worker dies, his or her surviving spouse receives the worker's whole monthly Social Security benefits. The worker has no power to transfer this spousal right to benefits to any other person. A divorced ex-spouse of the worker has a right to benefits if the marriage lasted for 10 years or longer.

The current Social Security regime raises issues of gender equity. For example, "Divorce is common, and because two-thirds of all divorces occur within ten years of the wedding, a majority of divorcees are not entitled to retirement or disability based on their former husbands' work records." Lawrence A. Frolik & Alison McChystal Barnes, Elder Law 197 (3d ed. 2003). Even more serious is the differential treatment of families where one spouse worked in comparison to families in which both spouses worked. Suppose that *H1* works for a bank and makes $80,000 a year, while his wife *W1* stays home and raises the children. *H1* retires at age 66, starts receiving Social Security benefits, and then dies in a boating accident with his next-door neighbor, *H2*. Under the current system, *W1* receives *H1*'s full monthly retirement benefits until she dies. Now assume that the next-door neighbors, *H2* and *W2*, both work at the same bank, making $40,000 each. Both *H2* and *W2* retire and both receive Social Security benefits. Then *H2* dies in the boating accident. *W2* gets only her own Social Security benefit, or her deceased husband's, whichever is larger — not both. Hence *W2*'s benefits will be smaller than *W1*'s even though both marital partnerships generated equal incomes and paid equal amounts into the system. If Social Security fully reflected the partnership model of marriage, both *W1* and *W2* should receive the same amount of benefits upon the deaths of *H1* and *H2*.

How large are social security benefits? They are computed by a formula that takes into account the amount of quarters worked (it takes 40 quarters — ten years — to be fully insured), the amount of earnings taxed, and the age of retirement. A large majority of all persons aged 65 or older receive social security benefits, with an average monthly benefit of $922 for retired workers and $1,523 for retired couples in 2004. The average monthly benefit for nondisabled surviving spouses was $888. See Understanding the Benefits, supra.

b. Private Pension Plans

Private pension plans funded by employers or jointly funded by employer and employee contributions mushroomed in the twentieth century. As of 2002, roughly $10 trillion was held in private pension funds. Most of these plans are governed by the federal Employee Retirement Income Security Act of 1974 (ERISA), 29 U.S.C. §§1001 et seq. (2004). On the role of pension accounts in effecting nonprobate transfers, see pages 333-336. Most private pension plans are of two types. The first is a *defined contribution plan*, which is typically funded by contributions from both the employer and the employee. At retirement, the employee is entitled to the assets in the fund held in her name, including any investment returns that have accrued over the years. The second is a *defined benefit plan*, which is typically funded by the employer. At retirement, the employee is entitled to a defined benefit — for example, 40 percent of the average of the employee's three highest years of annual income.

ERISA, as amended by the Retirement Equity Act in 1984, requires that the spouse of an employee must have survivorship rights if the employee predeceases the spouse. Its purpose is to insure a stream of income to surviving spouses. For many plans, if the employee spouse survives to retirement age, the pension must be paid as a joint and survivor annuity to the employee and his or her spouse, unless the nonemployee spouse consents to some other form of payment of the retirement benefit, such as a lump sum. If the employee dies before retirement and the pension is vested, the surviving spouse is entitled to a preretirement survivor annuity. ERISA thus increases the amount of income payable to workers' surviving spouses. For a summary of spousal rights in pensions, see John H. Langbein & Bruce A. Wolk, Pension and Employee Benefit Law 577-587 (3d ed. 2000).

ERISA preempts inconsistent state law. See Egelhoff v. Egelhoff, page 336. Accordingly, not state law but ERISA governs spouse's rights in pension plans. In Boggs v. Boggs, 520 U.S. 833 (1997), a first wife had a community property share in her husband's pension, which, under community property law, she could devise to whom she pleased. She devised this to her husband for life and then to her three sons. The husband married again after his first wife's death. Upon his death, the Supreme Court held that his pension benefits must be used to support his second wife in order to carry out ERISA's object of insuring support for surviving spouses. ERISA preempted state community property law to the extent state law allowed the first wife to make a testamentary transfer of her interest in her husband's pension and make it unavailable to a second wife.

Waiver. A spouse may waive her rights to benefits under the employee's pension plan, but ERISA discourages waivers by strict rules regarding their validity. For example, waiver requires the written consent of the spouse—and one who is not yet a spouse cannot so consent. Hence premarital agreements cannot waive ERISA-covered pension rights. In addition, workers under the age of 35 cannot effectuate a waiver of spousal benefits. See Hurwitz v. Sher, 982 F.2d 778 (2d Cir. 1992); Langbein & Wolk, supra, at 581-582.

PROBLEM

W designates *H* as the death beneficiary of her employer's pension plan. Subsequently *W* divorces *H*. Upon *W*'s death before retirement, is *H* entitled to the death benefits? See Egelhoff v. Egelhoff, page 336, and note 2, page 340. What result if *W* had remarried? If *W* had changed the death beneficiary to her sister *S* after the divorce?

c. Homestead

Nearly all states have homestead laws designed to secure the family home to the surviving spouse and minor children, free of the claims of creditors. Such a homestead is frequently called a *probate homestead*. Although the homestead laws vary in many details, generally the surviving spouse has the right to occupy the family home (or maybe the family farm) for his or her lifetime. In some states, the homestead must be established by the decedent during life, usually by filing a declaration of homestead in some public office; in other states, the probate court has power to set aside real property as a homestead. The amount of the homestead exemption is ridiculously small in some states and provides little protection to the surviving spouse. Uniform Probate Code (UPC) §2-402 (1990) recommends $15,000. But in several states the homestead exemption is substantial and may even exempt the family home regardless of its value. The decedent has no power to dispose of a homestead so as to deprive the surviving spouse of statutory rights therein. The right to occupy the homestead is given in addition to any other rights the surviving spouse has in the decedent's estate. See Carolyn S. Bratt, Family Protection Under Kentucky's Inheritance Laws: Is the Family Really Protected?, 76 Ky. L.J. 387 (1988) (criticizing homestead, personal property exemptions, and family allowances as being wholly inadequate to protect a decedent's family from hardship).

d. Personal Property Set-Aside

Related to homestead is the right of the surviving spouse (and sometimes of minor children) to have set aside certain tangible personal property of the decedent up to a certain value. UPC §2-403 (1990) sets the limit at $10,000. These items, which are also exempt from creditors' claims, usually include household furniture and clothing, but may also include a car and farm animals. The set-aside is usually subject to several conditions and limitations, but, if these are met, the decedent usually has no power to deprive the surviving spouse of the exempt items.

e. Family Allowance

Every state has a statute authorizing the probate court to award a family allowance for maintenance and support of the surviving spouse (and often of dependent children). The allowance may be limited by the statute to a fixed period (typically one year), or it may continue thereafter while the will is being contested or for the entire period of administration. The allowance, as with the homestead and personal property set-aside, is in addition to whatever other interests pass to the surviving spouse.

In some states, the maximum allowance that can be awarded is fixed by statute. In other states, a reasonable allowance tied to the spouse's standard of living is permitted. UPC §2-404 (1990) allows a reasonable allowance, which cannot continue beyond one year if the estate is inadequate to pay creditors. Maintenance of the decedent's spouse and dependent children is not allowed after the estate is closed.

Later in this chapter (see page 468), we examine proposals to import to the United States the broader system of family maintenance that is used in England, Australia, New Zealand, and most Canadian provinces. These jurisdictions grant the court discretion to override the terms of the decedent's will and to distribute some or all of the estate to the decedent's family and other dependents if the court determines that they deserve a larger share.

f. Dower and Curtesy

At common law, a widow had *dower* in all land of which her deceased husband had been seised during marriage and which was inheritable by the issue of husband

and wife. Dower entitles the widow to a life estate in one-third of her husband's qualifying land. Thus:

> *Case 2.* *H*, married to *W*, buys Blackacre, taking title in himself in fee simple. *H* subsequently dies. *W* is entitled to a life estate in one-third of Blackacre. (If *W* had predeceased *H*, her dower interest would be extinguished.)

In feudal times, when land was the chief form of wealth, dower provided generous support to the widow of a propertied man. But today, when many people rent their homes and by far the greater part of wealth is in the form of intangible personal property (such as stocks and bonds) and human capital (arising from education and training), dower may give the surviving spouse no protection at all.

The right of dower attaches the moment the husband acquires title to land or upon marriage, whichever is later. Dower remains inchoate until the husband's death, when it becomes possessory. Once inchoate dower has attached, the husband cannot sell the land free and clear of the wife's dower interest. In Case 2, if *H*, after buying Blackacre, had conveyed it to *A*, *A* would take title subject to *W*'s dower, and if and when *W* survived *H*, *W* would be entitled to a life estate in one-third of Blackacre (now owned by *A*). No purchaser, bona fide or not, can cut off the wife's dower without her consent. Dower functions today primarily to make the signatures of both spouses a practical requirement to the sale of one spouse's land.

At common law, a husband had a support interest in his wife's lands, called *curtesy*. It was comparable to dower except (1) the husband did not acquire curtesy unless children were born of the marriage, and (2) the husband was given a life estate in the entire parcel, not merely in one-third. Curtesy survives today in a handful of states, but in most of these it is only a label given to the support interest of the husband, which in fact has been made identical with the wife's support interest.

Dower has been abolished in the great majority of states. In only four jurisdictions does dower as it was known to the common law exist. See Ark. Code Ann. §28-11-301 (2004); Ky. Rev. Stat. Ann. §392.020 (2004); Mich. Comp. Laws §558.1 (2004); Ohio Rev. Code Ann. §2103.02 (2004). In all of these except Michigan, dower has been extended to the husband as well as the wife. The Michigan statute, providing dower for a wife but not for a husband, is of doubtful constitutionality. Similar statutes were found to violate the Equal Protection Clause in Stokes v. Stokes, 613 S.W.2d 372 (Ark. 1981), and Boan v. Watson, 316 S.E.2d 401 (S.C. 1984). In Ohio and Michigan, the surviving spouse must elect to take dower, or to take a statutory share of the decedent's estate, or to take a share under the decedent's will. As the statutory elective share is almost always greater than dower, dower is rarely elected.

PROBLEM

W, a real estate developer, wants to be able to buy land and sell it without the consent or interference of her husband. The jurisdiction has common law dower for husbands and wives. *W* consults you. What do you recommend?

"Now read me the part again where I disinherit everybody."

Drawing by Peter Arno.
© The New Yorker Collection 1940 Peter Arno from cartoonbank.com.
All Rights Reserved.

3.   *Rights of Surviving Spouse to a Share of Decedent's Property*

a.   **The Elective Share and Its Rationale**

All but one[1] of the separate property states give the surviving spouse, in addition to any support rights mentioned above, an *elective share* (sometimes called a *forced share*) of the decedent's property. Traditional statutes provide the surviving spouse with an election: (1) The spouse can take under the decedent's will, or (2) the spouse can renounce the will and take a fractional share of the decedent's estate.

The primary policy justification for the elective share is that the surviving spouse contributed to the decedent's acquisition of wealth and deserves to have a portion of it. On this account, the elective share implements the partnership model of marriage. A second but more narrow policy justification is to provide the surviving spouse with adequate support.

Although both the *partnership* and *support* theories justify the existence of *an* elective share, they are often in tension when it comes to designing *the* elective share that is to be implemented in practice. For example, the partnership theory militates toward awarding the surviving spouse one-half of the decedent's property acquired during the marriage, whereas in many cases the support theory justifies a smaller share but would apply it to all the decedent's property.

Another example: Suppose *H* dies leaving a will that excludes *W*. Then, before *W* exercises her right of election, but before the period for doing so runs out, *W* dies. Should *W*'s personal representative be allowed to renounce *H*'s will and take a forced share? If the answer is Yes, then *W*'s elective share of *H*'s property will pass to *W*'s heirs or devisees. If the answer is No, then it will pass to *H*'s devisees. Under the support theory, the answer should be No; after her death *W* no longer needs support. Under the partnership theory, however, the answer should be Yes; *W* is entitled to direct the disposition of her share of the property accumulated in the marital partnership. In most states, and under the UPC, the answer is No.

Yet another example: Can the elective share be satisfied with a life interest in property held in trust? Under the support theory, the answer should be Yes. Under the partnership theory, the answer should be No. As we shall see, the law is trending toward answering No in this situation, but for many years the answer was Yes, and in some jurisdictions the answer is still Yes (see pages 445-447).

The tension between the partnership and support theories of the elective share is a theme that will recur throughout the materials that follow.

Caution. There is no subject in this book on which there is more statutory variation than the surviving spouse's elective share. For an overview, see Jeffrey A.

---

1. Georgia is the only separate property state without an elective share statute, though it does mandate at least one year of support for the spouse. Professor Chaffin, a leading authority on Georgia wills law, approves of this on the ground that the vast majority of husbands do support their wives after death and the elective share permits the surviving spouse to wreck a sound estate plan. Verner F. Chaffin, A Reappraisal of the Wealth Transmission Process: The Surviving Spouse, Year's Support and Intestate Succession, 10 Ga. L. Rev. 447, 464-470 (1976). Not all his students are convinced, however. In Note, Preventing Spousal Disinheritance in Georgia, 19 Ga. L. Rev. 427 (1985), the author argues for equitable distribution of a portion of the decedent's property to the surviving spouse. Observing that the Georgia Supreme Court adopted equitable distribution upon divorce on its own after the Georgia legislature failed to act, the note suggests that the court should atone for a supine legislature by extending equitable distribution to termination of marriage by death.

Schoenblum, 2004 Multistate Guide to Estate Planning at Table 6. Even most of the states adopting the 1969 or 1990 UPC provisions, which had the purpose of bringing uniformity, made important substantive changes in the elective share provisions. There are many reasons for this: different opinions about how much the surviving spouse (read *widow*) deserves under various circumstances, including length of marriage, existence of children, and her own wealth; differences about what property of the decedent should be subject to the elective share; and the inability of legislators to decide definitively what is the purpose of the elective share and to carry this purpose through to its logical ends.

Uniform Probate Code (1990)

ARTICLE II, PART 2
ELECTIVE SHARE OF SURVIVING SPOUSE

GENERAL COMMENT
THE PARTNERSHIP THEORY OF MARRIAGE

The partnership theory of marriage, sometimes also called the marital-sharing theory, is stated in various ways. Sometimes it is thought of "as an expression of the presumed intent of husbands and wives to pool their fortunes on an equal basis, share and share alike." M. Glendon, The Transformation of Family Law 131 (1989). Under this approach, the economic rights of each spouse are seen as deriving from an unspoken marital bargain under which the partners agree that each is to enjoy a half interest in the fruits of the marriage, i.e., in the property nominally acquired by and titled in the sole name of either partner during the marriage (other than in property acquired by gift or inheritance). A decedent who disinherits his or her surviving spouse is seen as having reneged on the bargain. Sometimes the theory is expressed in restitutionary terms, a return-of-contribution notion. Under this approach, the law grants each spouse an entitlement to compensation for non-monetary contributions to the marital enterprise, as "a recognition of the activity of one spouse in the home and to compensate not only for this activity but for opportunities lost." Id.

No matter how the rationale is expressed, it is sometimes thought that the community-property system, including that version of community law promulgated in the Uniform Marital Property Act, recognizes the partnership theory, but that the common-law system denies it. In the ongoing marriage, it is true that the basic principle in the common-law (title-based) states is that marital status does not affect the ownership of property. The regime is one of separate property. Each spouse owns all that he or she earns. By contrast, in the community-property states, each spouse acquires an ownership interest in half the property the other earns during the marriage. By granting each spouse *upon acquisition* an immediate half interest in the earnings of the other, the community-property regimes directly recognize that the couple's enterprise is in essence collaborative.

The common-law states, however, also give effect or purport to give effect to the partnership theory when a marriage is dissolved by divorce. If the marriage ends in divorce, a spouse who sacrificed his or her financial-earning opportunities to contribute so-called domestic services to the marital enterprise (such as child-rearing and homemaking) stands to be recompensed . . . [under] the equitable-distribution system.

The other situation in which spousal property rights figure prominently is disinheritance at death. . . .

Elective-share law in the common-law states, however, has not caught up to the partnership theory of marriage. Under typical American elective-share law, including the elective share provided by the pre-1990 Uniform Probate Code, a surviving spouse may claim a one-third share of the decedent's estate — not the 50 percent share of the couple's combined assets that the partnership theory would imply.

To the extent that the primary contemporary policy underlying the elective share is to reward the surviving spouse's contribution to the economic partnership that is the marriage, in most states the elective share only roughly implements that policy. The traditional elective share gives the surviving spouse a fixed fractional share (often one-third) of the decedent's estate regardless of the length of marriage. The marriage may have lasted one hour[2] or 50 years; the elective share fraction is the same.

The 1990 UPC changes this result by giving the surviving spouse a sliding-scale percentage of the elective share amount, based upon the duration of the marriage (3 percent after one year, growing to 50 percent after 15 years of marriage). UPC §2-202(a) (1990, as amended 1993). The 1990 UPC revisers believe that the accrual system will approximate the results reached in most community property marriages, where the amount of acquisitions from earnings (community property) ordinarily increases with the duration of the marriage. A sliding-scale, or accrual, elective share also deals more equitably with second marriages among the elderly.

Although we speak of a surviving *spouse's* elective share, in the vast majority of cases it is in actuality a *widow's* share. As a matter of historical fact, men have earned more than women, but women tend to outlive men. Hence the prototype situation to which the elective share is applicable is a propertied dead husband and poorer widow. Accordingly, the real test of whether an elective share system implements the partnership theory of marriage comes when the wife predeceases her husband. If the wife dies before her husband, she cannot dispose of any of the "partnership property" titled in her husband's name. Suppose, for example, that *H* owns $500,000 in acquisitions from his earnings and *W* owns $100,000 from her earnings. If *W* dies first, *W* can dispose of only her $100,000 (and *H* may even have an elective share in that). If the couple had community property, *W* would own half of it, or $300,000, and could dispose of her half by will. As you study the elective

---

2. Or less. In Estate of Neiderhiser, 2 Pa. D. & C.3d 202 (1977), the groom dropped dead during the marriage ceremony, after he and the bride had each said "I will" (equal in other marriage ceremonies to "I do"). The court held that marriage is a contract that becomes binding upon the exchange of vows, and the bride was entitled to an elective share in the groom's estate.

In 2004 a woman in France was permitted to marry her deceased fiancé. The marriage was retroactive to the night before the groom's death. See Craig S. Smith, A Love That Transcends Death Is Blessed by the State, N.Y. Times, Feb. 19, 2004, at A4.

share system, you should look for other features that deny the concept of an equal marital partnership.

For further discussion of the dependency role assigned to women by the elective share, the federal estate tax marital deduction, and estate planning practices, see Mary L. Fellows, Wills and Trusts: "The Kingdom of the Fathers," 10 J.L. & Inequality 137 (1991). See also Mary M. Wenig, The Marital Property Law of Connecticut: Past, Present and Future, 1990 Wis. L. Rev. 807, 877 (criticizing UPC elective share as "a nod in the direction of the contribution rationale for the forced share . . . [while] actually resting their device only on the support or need rationale, tempered by a kind of deservedness based on the length of marriage").

NOTE: THE ESTATE TAX MARITAL DEDUCTION AND THE DEPENDENCY OF WOMEN

In the 1940s, with a steep increase in federal income tax rates to finance World War II, the income tax advantages of community property became very clear. The earnings of the husband were taxable one-half to the husband and one-half to the wife (who owned one-half). Because of the graduated step-up in brackets, the total tax on earnings split between husband and wife could be considerably less than the one tax on the husband's earnings in separate property states. Similarly, federal estate taxes in community property states were lower because only the husband's half of the community property was taxable at his death whereas all the husband's earned property was taxable at his death in separate property states.

To reap these federal tax advantages, Michigan, Nebraska, Oklahoma, Oregon, and Pennsylvania adopted community property in the 1940s. Several more states had community property bills in the legislative hoppers. But this revolution in marital property was not to be. In 1948, Congress—a virtually all-male club[3]—intervened. Congress amended the Internal Revenue Code to eliminate the tax advantages of community property. It permitted married couples to split their earned income equally between them by filing a joint return.[4] The five states that had switched to community property repealed or abrogated their statutes. See Carolyn Jones, Split Income and Separate Spheres: Tax Law and Gender Roles in the 1940s, 6 Law & Hist. Rev. 259 (1988).

Our concern here is not the federal income tax, but the federal estate tax, which also offered tax advantages in community property states. In 1948, Congress undertook to eliminate them and equalize the estate tax consequences between couples residing in community property states and couples residing in common law property states. The essential problem was how to put the common law property wife, who had acquired no or little property from her earnings, into an estate

---

3. In the 80th Congress beginning in January 1948, there were 96 senators (all men) and 435 Representatives (6 women). Congress remains a mostly male club. In the 108th Congress, which ended in January 2005, only 14 percent of the House and Senate members were women (though Nancy Pelosi, a woman, was the House Minority Leader).

4. Congress did not eliminate all the income tax advantages of community property, however. Community property still has an income tax advantage in that upon the death of the first spouse to die all of the community property gets a stepped-up basis (eliminating any income tax on past capital gain in the property), even though only one-half is included in the decedent spouse's estate tax return. With separate property, only the property included in the decedent spouse's estate receives a stepped-up basis. See page 460.

tax position comparable with the community property wife, who owns half the acquisitions from her husband's earnings. Congress solved the problem by giving the husband an estate tax marital deduction, up to 50 percent of the value of his estate, for property left to his surviving wife in a form comparable to the outright ownership the community property wife had. The word "comparable" is the rub. To equate the position of the separate property wife exactly with the community property wife, the former must end up with *outright ownership* of one-half her husband's earnings. Yet, for Congress to provide a powerful tax incentive for a husband to devise his widow outright ownership of half of his property was highly objectionable to (mostly male) estate planners and trust companies in New York and other rich separate property states; they thought the husband should have the right to put the widow's share in trust for her without suffering a tax disadvantage. The objection was that a housewife, without business experience, might be incapable of managing her inherited wealth. (Never mind that widows in California, Texas, and other community property states had long been legally entrusted with managing their property after their husbands' deaths, with no noticeable adverse consequences to them.[5]) Congress effected a compromise: If a husband gave his wife a *life estate* (support) with the *power to appoint* the property to anyone she wished at her death (equivalent to complete ownership at her death), this arrangement would be deemed comparable to a fee simple and would qualify for the marital deduction.

In 1982, the federal estate tax marital deduction was changed to incorporate a completely new principle: Interspousal transfers will not be taxed at all, provided the donor spouse gives the donee spouse at least a life estate in the property. A gift of a fee simple or its alleged equivalent (a life estate coupled with a general power of appointment) is no longer required for the marital deduction. The marital deduction is unlimited in amount. Internal Revenue Code of 1986, §2056.

The 1948 version of the marital deduction provided a tax incentive to the donor spouse to give the surviving spouse support and an ownership share of the decedent spouse's property (even though complete control of that share could be postponed until the surviving spouse's death). The current marital deduction requires only that the donor spouse create a trust giving his surviving spouse support for life to avoid transfer taxation (called a QTIP trust). Thus, viewed through the precise eye of the marital deduction provisions only, the homemaker (or the spouse with lower earnings) appears further now than before from being treated as well as her counterpart in community property states — as deserving a share of outright ownership in recognition of her contribution to the economic gains of a marriage.

The QTIP trust is fundamentally inconsistent with the partnership theory of marriage. For the rich, who must pay estate taxes, Professor Mary Moers Wenig put it crisply: "With QTIP, the new federal law of dower was born." Mary M. Wenig, "Taxing Marriage," 6 S. Cal. Rev. L. & Women's Stud. 561 (1997). See the debate between Professors Gerzog, Zelenak, and Dodge: Wendy C. Gerzog, The Marital Deduction QTIP Provisions: Illogical and Degrading to Women, 5 UCLA Women's L.J. 301 (1995); Lawrence Zelenak: Taking Critical Tax Theory Seriously, 76 N.C.L. Rev. 1521 (1998); Wendy C. Gerzog, The Illogical and Sexist QTIP Provisions: I Just Can't Say It Ain't So, 76 N.C.L. Rev. 1597 (1998); Joseph M.

---

5. But cf. the "widow's election," page 457.

Dodge, A Feminist Perspective on the QTIP Trust and the Unlimited Marital Deduction, 76 N.C.L. Rev. 1729 (1998).

The end result of these changes in the federal estate tax law is that today the following transfers qualify for the marital deduction:

(a) *H* transfers property outright or in fee simple to *W*;

(b) *H* creates a trust giving *W* income for life and a power to appoint the trust principal at death to whomever she pleases (a life estate coupled with a general power of appointment);

(c) *H* creates a trust giving *W* income for life (a QTIP trust).

For further discussion of the marital deduction, see pages 900-905.

In re Estate of Cross

Supreme Court of Ohio, 1996
75 Ohio St. 3d 530, 664 N.E.2d 905

On August 23, 1992, Carroll R. Cross died testate leaving his entire estate to his son, Ray G. Cross, who was not a child of the surviving spouse. At the time of his death, Beulah Cross, the surviving spouse, was apparently close to eighty years old, was suffering from Alzheimer's disease, and was living in a nursing home paid by Medicaid. Due to Mrs. Cross's incompetency, she was unable to make an election under R.C. 2106.01 as to whether she should take against her husband's will. Therefore, pursuant to R.C. 2106.08, the probate court appointed a commissioner, who investigated the matter and determined that the court elect for Mrs. Cross to take her intestate share under R.C. 2105.06 and against the will. As a result of this election, Mrs. Cross would receive twenty-five thousand dollars in spousal allowance and one-half of the net estate, which was approximately nine thousand dollars. Following a hearing before a referee, Judge John E. Corrigan of the probate court elected for Mrs. Cross to take against decedent's will.

Decedent's son appealed the probate court's decision. While the appeal was pending, Mrs. Cross died. The court of appeals, with one judge dissenting, reversed, finding that the election to take against the will was against Mrs. Cross's best interest and was not necessary to provide her adequate support, since the cost of her nursing home care was already covered by Medicaid. Rosemary D. Durkin, Administrator of the Estate of Beulah Cross, filed a notice of appeal to this court, as did intervenor, Cuyahoga County Board of Commissioners.

SWEENEY, J. At issue in this case is whether Judge Corrigan abused his discretion in electing for decedent Carroll Cross's surviving spouse, who depended solely upon Medicaid benefits for her support and care, to take against the will and under R.C. 2105.06. For the following reasons, we uphold the election made by Judge Corrigan for Mrs. Cross, and reverse the decision of the court of appeals.

Where a surviving spouse is under a legal disability, the probate court is given the authority under R.C. 2106.08 to appoint a suitable person to ascertain the surviving spouse's adequate support needs and to compare the value of the surviving spouse's rights under the will with the value of her rights under the statute of descent and distribution. R.C. 2106.08 further provides that the court may elect for the surviving spouse to take against the will and under R.C. 2105.06 "only if it finds, after taking into consideration the other available resources and the age, probable life expectancy, physical and mental condition, and present and reasonably anticipated future needs of the surviving spouse, that the election to take under 2105.06 of the Revised Code is necessary to provide adequate support for the surviving spouse during his life expectancy."

Prior to the amendment of former R.C. 2107.45 (now renumbered R.C. 2106.08), effective December 17, 1986, the probate court made its determination of whether to elect to take under the will or against the will based upon which provision was "better for such spouse." In essence, the court based its decision on which provision was more mathematically advantageous to the surviving spouse. See In re Estate of Cook, 249 N.E.2d 799, 802 (Ohio 1969). However, in passing R.C. 2106.08, the General Assembly moved away from a simple mathematical calculation, taking into consideration such factors as other available resources, age, life expectancy, physical and mental condition, and the surviving spouse's present and future needs. In either case, the probate court must ascertain what the surviving spouse would have done for her financial benefit had she been competent to make the decision herself. See In re Estate of Hinklin, 586 N.E.2d 130, 132 (Ohio App. 1989).

In this case, the court of appeals . . . , in striking down the election made by Judge Corrigan for Mrs. Cross to take against the will, . . . ignored Medicaid eligibility requirements.

. . . [E]ligibility for Medicaid benefits is dependent upon a recipient's income or available resources. Ohio Adm. Code 5101:1-39-05. The term "resources" includes "property owned separately by the person, his share of family property, and property devised to him from a parent or spouse." Ohio Adm. Code 5101:1-39-05(A)(4). This also encompasses "those resources in which an applicant/recipient has a legal interest and the legal ability to use or dispose of . . . ." Ohio Adm. Code 5101:1-39-05(A)(8).

Mrs. Cross clearly had a legal interest in and the ability to use or dispose of her intestate share under her right to take against the will. Thus, she had available to her a potential resource for Medicaid eligibility purposes. This is critical to the facts presented, since the Medicaid rules specifically state that the nonutilization of available income renders a Medicaid applicant or recipient ineligible for benefits. According to Ohio Adm. Code 5101:1-39-08(A)(2), "A basic tenet of public assistance is that all income must be considered in determining the need of an individual for public assistance. Potential income must be explored prior to approving medicaid. An individual who does not avail himself of a potential income is presumed to fail to do so in order to make himself eligible for public assistance. Such nonutilization of income available upon request constitutes ineligibility. . . ."

As applied to this case, in order to maintain Mrs. Cross's Medicaid eligibility and to continue to have her nursing home expenses provided for by public assistance, Judge Corrigan was required to elect for Mrs. Cross to take against the will and to receive her intestate share. Otherwise, if the election was to take under the will, Mrs. Cross would receive no income and would be deemed ineligible for benefits for failing to avail herself of a potential income. Thus, the election to take against the will was necessary for Mrs. Cook's future support and met the requirements of R.C. 2106.08. We find that the probate court, by appointing a commissioner to investigate the matter and by electing for Mrs. Cross to take against the will, was correct in its actions. Through his decision, Judge Corrigan acted in the best interests of this surviving spouse and protected the interests of all litigants coming before him. Consequently, Judge Corrigan did not abuse his discretion in electing for Mrs. Cross to take against the will.

Accordingly, we reverse the judgment of the court of appeals and reinstate the judgment of the probate court.

NOTES AND QUESTIONS

1. In Estate of Faller, 66 P.3d 114 (Colo. App. 2002), *W* petitioned to take her elective share in *H*'s estate in trust in order to preserve her Medicaid eligibility. Under the terms of the trust, *W* was barred from receiving any payment that would disqualify her from Medicaid coverage. The court held that this restriction violated Colorado statutes and that the assets must be taken into account in determining benefits.

Suppose that *W* had not asked the probate court to place her elective share in trust, but rather she opted not to elect against *H*'s will, and the will established a testamentary trust that barred the use of income or principal for *W*'s benefit if doing so would jeopardize her Medicaid eligibility. Since *W* could have elected to receive her elective share outright, would *W* still qualify for Medicaid? See Estate of DeMartino v. Division of Med. Assistance & Health Servs., 861 A.2d 138 (N.J. Super. 2004). For more on the use of trusts to preserve eligibility for governmental benefits, see pages 569-572.

How do these cases square with the majority rule that the right to an elective share is personal to the surviving spouse and that creditors of the surviving spouse cannot force her to elect her elective share (so held in Aragon v. Snyder, 715 A.2d 1045 (N.J. Super. 1998))?

2. If the surviving spouse is incompetent, a guardian of the spouse can elect against the decedent's will if it is in the "best interests" of the spouse, with approval of the probate court. A minority of states hold that the guardian should elect to take against the will if it is to the surviving spouse's economic benefit, calculated mathematically. A majority of states hold, as did the court in Estate of Cross, that all the surrounding facts and circumstances should be taken into consideration by the probate court. The majority view allows the guardian to take into account the preservation of the decedent's estate plan and whether the surviving spouse would have wanted to abide by her dead spouse's will. See Foman v. Moss, 681 N.E.2d 1113 (Ind. App. 1997).

The 1969 UPC took another view. Section 2-203 provided that the probate court, acting for an incompetent, could order election against the spouse's will only "after finding that exercise is necessary to provide adequate support for the protected person during his probable life expectancy." This implements the view that the elective share is for the support of the surviving spouse, not a partnership share of economic gains from marriage.

The 1990 UPC continued the view that the elective share is for support when the spouse is incompetent, but it implemented the view in a different way. UPC §2-212 (1990, as amended 1993) provides that if a conservator or guardian elects the elective share, the portion of the elective share that exceeds what the decedent spouse provided for the survivor must be placed in a *custodial trust* for the benefit of the surviving spouse. The trustee of such a trust, appointed by a court, has the power to expend income and principal for the surviving spouse's support, and upon the spouse's death the trustee must transfer the trust property to the residuary devisees under the will of the predeceased spouse against whom the elective share was taken or to the predeceased spouse's heirs. Thus, the husband can prevent the wife's conservator from upsetting his estate plan. The official comment to UPC §2-212 says the purpose of these changes is "to assure that that part of the elective share is devoted to the personal economic benefit and needs of the surviving spouse, but not to the economic benefit of the surviving spouse's heirs or devisees."

Why does a surviving spouse who happens to be incompetent at the decedent's death deserve, in recognition of her contribution to the marriage, only support and not an ownership share that will pass to her heirs? Why should a surviving spouse lose the fractional share of ownership rights that she has acquired in her husband's property (the "partnership property") if she becomes incompetent?

3. In Estate of Bilse, 746 A.2d 1090 (N.J. Super. 1999), *W* predeceased *H*, who then died while in the process of claiming his forced share in *W*'s estate. The court held that, since *H*'s own assets were sufficient to pay his expenses before death, *H*'s estate could not collect *H*'s forced share. Is this an application of the support theory? Can the result be justified on simultaneous death principles?

4. In some states the elective share is denied to a spouse who has abandoned or refused to support the other spouse. See, e.g., N.Y. Est. Trusts & Powers Law §5-1.2 (2004). The difficulty of proving abandonment is illustrated by In re Riefberg's Estate, 446 N.E.2d 424 (N.Y. 1983), where the wife, who had excluded her husband from the marital home and lived separately, was held not to have abandoned her husband. In most states, the spouse who abandons the other spouse is entitled to an elective share.

If the rationale for the elective share is sharing the economic fruits of marriage, should one spouse lose his or her share upon leaving the other? Or should the elective share apply only to property the abandoned spouse owned on the date of abandonment?

In most community property states, if the couple separates, the earnings of both spouses continue to be community property until divorce. In California, earnings acquired after separation are not community property.

5. The failure of a lawyer to warn the client about the elective share, which would dismantle the client's estate plan, can be grounds for a malpractice action. See Johnson v. Sandler, 958 S.W.2d 42 (Mo. App. 1997).

Thus far we have been speaking of the elective share rights of surviving spouses. What of partners in a relationship that approximates marriage?

In re Estate of Cooper

New York Supreme Court,
Appellate Division, Second Department, 1993
187 A.D.2d 128, 592 N.Y.S.2d 797

MANGANO, P.J.　The question to be resolved on this appeal is whether the survivor of a homosexual relationship, alleged to be a "spousal relationship," is entitled to a right of election against the decedent's will, pursuant to EPTL 5-1.1. In our view, the question must be answered in the negative.

I

William Thomas Cooper died on February 19, 1988. The decedent died testate, leaving everything to the petitioner [Ernest Chin] as a specific and residuary legatee, with the exception of certain real estate, allegedly constituting over 80% of the value of the estate, which was left to a former homosexual lover of the decedent.

In support of this proceeding to determine that he is entitled to exercise a right of election against the decedent's will, the petitioner alleged, inter alia, as follows:

> I met William Cooper in 1984. From approximately the middle of 1984 until his sudden death from a congenital heart condition in February 1988, I lived with him in Apartment 1, 183 Wyckoff Street, Brooklyn, New York in a spousal-type situation. Except for the fact that we were of the same sex, our lives were identical to that of a husband and wife. We kept a common home; we shared expenses; our friends recognized us as spouses; we had a physical relationship. Of course, we could not obtain a marriage license because no marriage license clerk in New York will issue such a document to two people of the same sex. . . .
>
> The only reason Mr. Cooper and I were not legally married is because marriage license clerks in New York State will not issue licenses to persons of the same sex. . . .
>
> However unconstitutional the denial of the right to a marriage license to Mr. Cooper and myself may have been, the Court cannot undo that now that Mr. Cooper is deceased. Since the Court, however, also is an instrument of the State . . . it cannot compound this unconstitutionality by saying that because we could not obtain a State-issued marriage license, I cannot be recognized as a spouse by a State Court for the purpose of claiming spousal rights. . . .
>
> I ask this Court simply to declare that if I can establish that Mr. Cooper and I, at the time of his death, were living in a spousal-type relationship, I am entitled to spousal rights, and the State-imposed unconstitutional impediment of making it impossible for two people of the same sex to obtain a marriage license does not alter this.

Upon submission of opposing papers and an application to dismiss the petition by the executrix of Cooper's estate, Acting Surrogate Pizzuto held that a survivor of a homosexual relationship, alleged to be a "spousal relationship," was not entitled to a right of election against the decedent's will pursuant to EPTL 5-1.1, stating, inter alia: "This court holds that persons of the same sex have no constitutional rights to enter into a marriage with each other. Neither due process nor equal protection of law provisions are violated by prohibiting such marriages. Nor does Mr. Chin have any right or standing to elect against decedent's will."

II

The right of election by a "surviving spouse," insofar as is relevant to the facts at bar, is contained in EPTL 5-1.1(c)(1)(B), as follows:

> (c) Election by surviving spouse against wills executed and testamentary provisions made after August thirty-first, nineteen hundred sixty-six . . . :
> (1) Where, after August thirty-first, nineteen hundred sixty-six, a testator executes a will disposing of his entire estate, and is survived by a spouse, a personal

right of election is given to the surviving spouse to take a share of the decedent's estate, subject to the following:

(B) The elective share . . . is one-third of the net estate if the decedent is survived by one or more issue and, in all other cases, one-half of such net estate.

We reject the petitioner's argument that he must be considered a "surviving spouse" within the meaning of the statute. "Generally, in the construction of statutes, the intention of the Legislature is first to be sought from a literal reading of the act itself or of all the statutes relating to the same general subject matter" (McKinney's Cons. Laws of N.Y., Book 1, Statutes §92, at 182). The Legislature has expressly defined a "surviving spouse" in EPTL 5-1.2, as follows: "§5-1.2 Disqualifications as surviving spouse. (a) A husband or wife is a surviving spouse within the meaning, and for the purposes of . . . 5-1.1."

Indeed, even in the absence of any express definition of the term "surviving spouse," an interpretation of the statute to the same effect would be warranted. It is well settled that "the language of a statute is generally construed according to its natural and most obvious sense . . . in accordance with its ordinary and accepted meaning, unless the Legislature by definition or from the rest of the context of the statute provides a special meaning" (McKinney's Cons. Laws of N.Y., Book 1, Statutes §94, at 191-193). An illustration of this latter approach may be ascertained from the reasoning of the Supreme Court of Minnesota in Baker v. Nelson, 191 N.W.2d 185 (Minn. 1971). In that case, the court rejected an argument that the absence of an express statutory prohibition against same-sex marriages evinced a legislative intent to authorize such marriages. The Supreme Court of Minnesota held in this regard (Baker v. Nelson, supra, 191 N.W.2d at 185-186): "[The statute], which governs 'marriage,' employs that term as one of common usage, meaning the state of union between persons of the opposite sex. It is unrealistic to think that the original draftsmen of our marriage statutes, which date from territorial days, would have used the term in any different sense."

We reject, as meritless, the contention of both the petitioner and the amicus curiae that, based on the Court of Appeals decision in Braschi v. Stahl Assocs. Co., 543 N.E.2d 49 (N.Y. 1989), the traditional definition of the term "surviving spouse" must be rejected, and replaced with a broader definition which would include the petitioner. In Braschi v. Stahl Assocs. Co., the Court of Appeals held that same-sex partners were "family members" for purposes of the rent control regulations at issue therein, prohibiting the eviction of "family members" upon the death of the tenant of record. Specifically, the Court of Appeals stated[:] "The intended protection against sudden eviction should not rest on fictitious legal distinctions or genetic history, but instead should find its foundation in the reality of family life. In the context of eviction, a more realistic, and certainly equally valid, view of a family includes two adult lifetime partners whose relationship is long term and characterized by an emotional and financial commitment and interdependence. This view comports both with our society's traditional concept of 'family' and with the expectations of individuals who live in such nuclear units."

However, in Matter of Alison D. v. Virginia M., 552 N.Y.S.2d 321 (App. Div. 1990), aff'd, 572 N.E.2d 27 (N.Y. 1991), this court held, in an opinion and order subsequently affirmed by the Court of Appeals, that a lesbian partner was not a "parent" under Domestic Relations Law §70 and rejected, as "totally misplaced," the argument that the holding in Braschi v. Stahl Assocs. Co. compelled a different result.

Accordingly, the term "surviving spouse," as used in EPTL 5-1.1, cannot be interpreted to include homosexual life partners.

III

The petitioner and the amicus curiae argue that such a narrow definition of the term "surviving spouse" is unconstitutional as it violates the equal protection clause of the State Constitution. Specifically, they argue that this unconstitutional definition directly derives from, and compounds, the State's unconstitutional conduct in interpreting the relevant provisions of the Domestic Relations Law as prohibiting members of the same sex from obtaining marriage licenses (see, e.g., Francis B. v. Mark B., 355 N.Y.S.2d 712 (Sup. Ct. 1974); Anonymous v. Anonymous, 325 N.Y.S.2d 499 (Sup. Ct. 1971)).

It is to this argument that we now turn.

It is well settled that there are three standards that may be applied in reviewing equal protection challenges: strict scrutiny, heightened scrutiny, and rational basis review (City of Cleburne, Tex. v. Cleburne Living Center, 473 U.S. 432, 440-441 (1985)).

We note that Acting Surrogate Pizzuto correctly held that any equal protection analysis in the instant factual scenario is to be measured by the rational basis standard, i.e., the legislation (or government action) "is presumed to be valid and will be sustained if the classification drawn . . . is rationally related to a legitimate state interest" (City of Cleburne, Tex. v. Cleburne Living Center, supra, at 440), and not by the more stringent standards of heightened scrutiny or strict scrutiny.

In Baker v. Nelson, 191 N.W.2d 185, supra, the petitioners, both adult males, made application to the clerk of the County District Court for a marriage license pursuant to the relevant Minnesota statute. The clerk declined to issue the license on the sole ground that the petitioners were of the same sex, "it being undisputed that there were otherwise no statutory impediments to a heterosexual marriage by either petitioner" (Baker v. Nelson, supra, at 185).

The Supreme Court of Minnesota rejected the petitioners' argument that a prohibition on same sex marriages denied them equal protection of the laws, holding (Baker v. Nelson, supra, at 186-187):

> These constitutional challenges have in common the assertion that the right to marry without regard to the sex of the parties is a fundamental right of all persons and that restricting marriage to only couples of the opposite sex is irrational and invidiously discriminatory. We are not independently persuaded by these contentions and do not find support for them in any decisions of the United States Supreme Court.
>
> The institution of marriage as a union of man and woman, uniquely involving the procreation and rearing of children within a family, is as old as the book of Genesis. Skinner v. Oklahoma ex rel. Williamson, 316 U.S. 535, 541 (1942), which invalidated Oklahoma's Habitual Criminal Sterilization Act on equal protection grounds, stated in part: "Marriage and procreation are fundamental to the very existence and survival of the race." This historic institution manifestly is more deeply founded than the asserted contemporary concept of marriage and societal interests for which petitioners contend. The due process clause of the Fourteenth Amendment is not a charter for restructuring it by judicial legislation. . . .
>
> The equal protection clause of the Fourteenth Amendment, like the due process clause, is not offended by the state's classification of persons authorized to marry.

There is no irrational or invidious discrimination. Petitioners note that the state does not impose upon heterosexual married couples a condition that they have a proved capacity or declared willingness to procreate, posing a rhetorical demand that this court must read such condition into the statute if same-sex marriages are to be prohibited. Even assuming that such a condition would be neither unrealistic nor offensive under the *Griswold* rationale, the classification is no more than theoretically imperfect. We are reminded, however, that "abstract symmetry" is not demanded by the Fourteenth Amendment.

The appeal from the Minnesota Supreme Court to the United States Supreme Court was dismissed for want of a substantial Federal question (Baker v. Nelson, 409 U.S. 810), and, as Acting Surrogate Pizzuto accurately noted (Matter of Cooper, 564 N.Y.S.2d 684, 686 (Sur. Ct. 1990)): "Such a dismissal is a holding that the constitutional challenge was considered and rejected (Hicks v. Miranda, 422 U.S. 332 (1975))."

The rational basis standard has been also applied in other similar instances where equal protection challenges have been raised to classifications based on sexual orientation (see, High Tech Gays v. Defense Industrial Security Clearance Office, 895 F.2d 563 (9th Cir. 1990), in which the court, relying on the Supreme Court's ruling in Bowers v. Hardwick, 478 U.S. 186 (1986), that homosexual activity is not a fundamental right, applied the rational basis standard, and rejected an equal protection challenge to a Defense Department policy of conducting expanded investigations into backgrounds of all gay and lesbian applicants for secret and top secret security clearance; see also, Adams v. Howerton, 673 F.2d 1036 (9th Cir. 1982), in which the court held that a citizen's "spouse" within the meaning of section 201[b] of the Immigration and Nationality Act of 1952, as amended, 8 U.S.C. §1151[b], must be an individual of the opposite sex and that, in accordance with the rational basis standard, such a bar against an alleged homosexual "spouse" was not unconstitutional).

Based on these authorities, we agree with Acting Surrogate Pizzuto's conclusion that "purported [homosexual] marriages do not give rise to any rights . . . pursuant to . . . EPTL 5-1.1 [and that] [n]o constitutional rights have been abrogated or violated in so holding" (Matter of Cooper, supra, 149 Misc. 2d at 288, 564 N.Y.S.2d 684).

Accordingly, the order and decree is affirmed insofar as appealed from.

Ordered that the order and decree is affirmed insofar as appealed from, *with costs payable by the appellant personally* [emphasis added].

NOTES AND PROBLEM

1. The *Cooper* case was appealed, but the appeal was dismissed by the New York Court of Appeals on the ground that no substantial constitutional question was directly involved. In re Cooper, 624 N.E.2d 696 (N.Y. 1993).

2. Marriage brings a number of legal and economic consequences, mostly beneficial, to a surviving spouse. A married partner is entitled to social security benefits based on the other partner's earnings, to pension rights from the other partner's job, to an elective share of the other partner's estate, and to the federal estate tax marital deduction (eliminating all estate taxes on property one married partner transfers to the other at death). Unmarried surviving partners have none of these benefits.

In 1996, Congress enacted the Defense of Marriage Act, 1 U.S.C. §7 (2004). Section 2 of the act provides that no state shall be required under the Full Faith and Credit Clause of the Constitution to give effect to a same-sex marriage contracted in another state. Section 3 provides that for all purposes of federal law "the word 'marriage' means only a legal union between one man and one woman as husband and wife, and the word 'spouse' refers only to a person of the opposite sex who is a husband or a wife." The latter section thus deprives same-sex married couples (assuming they are recognized by a state) of the social security, tax, and welfare benefits of federal law. See Patricia McCain, Tax and Financial Planning for Same-Sex Couples, 8 Law & Sexuality 613 (1998). Most states have passed similar statutes, and some have revised their state constitutions to bar same-sex marriages.

However, as we noted in connection with the recognition of inheritance rights for domestic partners (see page 65), change is afoot. Since 1996, three states have enacted legislation granting same-sex couples inheritance *and elective share* rights: (1) Hawaii for "reciprocal beneficiaries" in 1997, (2) Vermont for "civil unions" in 2000, and (3) California for "domestic partners" in 2000. See Haw. Rev. Stat. Ann. §§560:2-102, 2-201 to 2-214 (2004); Vt. Stat. Ann. tit. 15, §§1201-1207 (2004); Cal. Fam. Code Ann. §297 (2004). In addition, same-sex marriages have been authorized for Massachusetts residents by Goodridge v. Department of Pub. Health, 798 N.E.2d 941 (Mass. 2003) and Opinion of the Justices to the Senate, 802 N.E.2d 565 (Mass. 2004). On the other hand, the Massachusetts legislature has proposed an amendment to the Massachusetts constitution that would authorize civil unions, not marriages, for same-sex couples. See T.P. Gallanis, Inheritance Rights for Domestic Partners, 79 Tul. L. Rev. 55, 72-73 (2004).

In May 1999, the Supreme Court of Canada struck down a heterosexual definition of the word *spouse* in Ontario's Family Law, in part because the law had "the effect of perpetuating or promoting the view that the individual is less capable or worthy of recognition or value as a human being or as a member of Canadian society." The Atty. Gen. for Ont. v. M. & H., 1999 Can. Sup. Ct. Lexis 28.

For further discussion of recent developments in this area, see Gallanis, supra, and the Note on Domestic Partners and Intestate Succession in Chapter 2 at page 65.

b. Property Subject to the Elective Share

The original elective share statutes gave the surviving spouse a fractional share (now usually one-third) of the decedent's estate, which implicitly meant the *probate estate*. With the proliferation of nonprobate transfers (see Chapter 5), should the elective share be extended to some or all nonprobate transfers? Consider the following case study:

> *Case 3. W*, a fabulously successful lawyer, wants to leave the bulk of her fortune to her daughter, *D*, rather than to her tedious husband, *H*, even though she amassed this fortune during the marriage. Knowing of *H*'s right of election against her probate estate, *W* transfers $2.9 million to *X* in trust to pay income to *W* for life and the principal to *D* on *W*'s death. *W* retains the right to revoke the trust. *W* then dies without having done so. *W*'s will leaves her entire probate estate, worth $100,000,

to *H*. Can *H* elect to take against the $2.9 million that, under the terms of the trust, will pass outside of probate to *D*?

In Case 3, unless *H*'s forced share reaches *W*'s nonprobate transfers, it is possible for *W* to achieve a near disinheritance of *H* while still leaving him all of her probate estate. Note also that, if nonprobate transfers are reachable by the elective share, then *H* (the surviving spouse) is protected from disinheritance by nonprobate transfers not only if *W* leaves a will, but also if *W* dies intestate. Which is going to be larger, an intestate share of the probate estate or an elective share over both the probate estate and nonprobate transfers? The answer depends both on the relative sizes of the decedent's probate estate and nonprobate transfers, and on the relative sizes of the surviving spouse's elective share and intestate share percentages.

We shall first treat (1) the judicial responses to whether nonprobate transfers may be reached by the elective share, then (2) some nonuniform legislative responses, and then (3) the approaches of the 1969 and 1990 Uniform Probate Codes.

(1) JUDICIAL RESPONSES

Sullivan v. Burkin

Supreme Judicial Court of Massachusetts, 1984
390 Mass. 864, 460 N.E.2d 571

WILKINS, J.[6] Mary A. Sullivan, the widow of Ernest G. Sullivan, has exercised her right, under G.L. c. 191, §15, to take a share of her husband's estate. By this action, she seeks a determination that assets held in an inter vivos trust created by her husband during the marriage should be considered as part of the estate in determining that share. A judge of the Probate Court for the county of Suffolk rejected the widow's claim and entered judgment dismissing the complaint. The widow appealed, and, on July 12, 1983, a panel of the Appeals Court reported the case to this court.

In September, 1973, Ernest G. Sullivan executed a deed of trust under which he transferred real estate to himself as sole trustee. The net income of the trust was payable to him during his life and the trustee was instructed to pay to him all or such part of the principal of the trust estate as he might request in writing from time to time. He retained the right to revoke the trust at any time. On his death, the successor trustee is directed to pay the principal and any undistributed income equally to the defendants, George F. Cronin, Sr., and Harold J. Cronin, if they should survive him, which they did. There were no witnesses to the execution of the deed of trust, but the husband acknowledged his signatures before a notary public, separately, as donor and as trustee.

The husband died on April 27, 1981, while still trustee of the inter vivos trust. He left a will in which he stated that he "intentionally neglected to make any provision for my wife, Mary A. Sullivan and my grandson, Mark Sullivan." He

---

6. Justice Herbert Wilkins, who was one of the intellectual leaders of the Massachusetts court in recent decades, made a specialty of trust cases. He wrote the opinions in Sullivan v. Burkin; Dewire v. Haveles, page 649; Beals v. State Str. Bank & Tr. Co., page 613; and Loring v. Marshall, page 618. From 1996 through 1999, Justice Wilkins was Chief Justice, a position once held by his father. — Eds.

directed that, after the payment of debts, expenses, and all estate taxes levied by reason of his death, the residue of his estate should be paid over to the trustee of the inter vivos trust. The defendants George F. Cronin, Sr., and Harold J. Cronin were named coexecutors of the will. The defendant Burkin is successor trustee of the inter vivos trust. On October 21, 1981, the wife filed a claim, pursuant to G.L. c. 191, §15, for a portion of the estate.[7]

Although it does not appear in the record, the parties state in their briefs that Ernest G. Sullivan and Mary A. Sullivan had been separated for many years. We do know that in 1962 the wife obtained a court order providing for her temporary support. No final action was taken in that proceeding. The record provides no information about the value of any property owned by the husband at his death or about the value of any assets held in the inter vivos trust. At oral argument, we were advised that the husband owned personal property worth approximately $15,000 at his death and that the only asset in the trust was a house in Boston which was sold after the husband's death for approximately $85,000.

As presented in the complaint, and perhaps as presented to the motion judge, the wife's claim was simply that the inter vivos trust was an invalid testamentary disposition and that the trust assets "constitute assets of the estate" of Ernest G. Sullivan. There is no suggestion that the wife argued initially that, even if the trust were not testamentary, she had a special claim as a widow asserting her rights under G.L. c. 191, §15. If the wife is correct that the trust was an ineffective testamentary disposition, the trust assets would be part of the husband's probate estate. In that event, we would not have to consider any special consequences of the wife's election under G.L. c. 191, §15, or, in the words of the Appeals Court, "the present vitality" of Kerwin v. Donaghy, 59 N.E.2d 299 (Mass. 1945).

We conclude, however, that the trust was not testamentary in character and that the husband effectively created a valid inter vivos trust. . . . A trust with remainder interests given to others on the settlor's death is not invalid as a testamentary disposition simply because the settlor retained a broad power to modify or revoke the trust, the right to receive income, and the right to invade principal during his life. . . . We believe that the law of the Commonwealth is correctly represented by the statement in Restatement (Second) of Trusts §57, Comment h (1959), that a trust is "not testamentary and invalid for failure to comply with the requirements of the Statute of Wills merely because the settlor-trustee reserves a beneficial life interest and power to revoke and modify the trust. The fact that as trustee he controls the administration of the trust does not invalidate it."[8]

We come then to the question whether, even if the trust was not testamentary on general principles, the widow has special interests which should be recognized.

7. As relevant to this case, G.L. c. 191, §15, provides:

> The surviving husband or wife of a deceased person . . . within six months after the probate of the will of such deceased, may file in the registry of probate a writing signed by him or by her . . . claiming such portion of the estate of the deceased as he or she is given the right to claim under this section, and if the deceased left issue, he or she shall thereupon take one third of the personal and one third of the real property . . . except that . . . if he or she would thus take real and personal property to an amount exceeding twenty-five thousand dollars in value, he or she shall receive, in addition to that amount, only the income during his or her life of the excess of his or her share of such estate above that amount, the personal property to be held in trust and the real property vested in him or her for life, from the death of the deceased. . . .

8. Thus the Massachusetts court, like other courts, agrees with Farkas v. Williams, 125 N.E.2d 600 (Ill. 1955), page 299, that a revocable trust is valid. — Eds.

Courts in this country have differed considerably in their reasoning and in their conclusions in passing on this question. . . .

The rule of Kerwin v. Donaghy, 59 N.E.2d 299 (Mass. 1945), is that

> [t]he right of a wife to waive her husband's will, and take, with certain limitations, "the same portion of the property of the deceased, real and personal, that . . . she would have taken if the deceased had died intestate" (G.L. [Ter. Ed.] c. 191, §15), does not extend to personal property that has been conveyed by the husband in his lifetime and does not form part of his estate at his death. Fiske v. Fiske, 53 N.E. 916 (Mass. 1899). Shelton v. Sears, 73 N.E. 666 (Mass. 1905). In this Commonwealth a husband has an absolute right to dispose of any or all of his personal property in his lifetime, without the knowledge or consent of his wife, with the result that it will not form part of his estate for her to share under the statute of distributions (G.L. [Ter. Ed.] c. 190, §§1, 2), under his will, or by virtue of a waiver of his will. That is true even though his sole purpose was to disinherit her.

In the *Kerwin* case, we applied the rule to deny a surviving spouse the right to reach assets the deceased spouse had placed in an inter vivos trust of which the settlor's daughter by a previous marriage was trustee and over whose assets he had a general power of appointment. The rule of Kerwin v. Donaghy has been adhered to in this Commonwealth for almost forty years and was adumbrated even earlier.[9] The bar has been entitled reasonably to rely on that rule in advising clients. In the area of property law, the retroactive invalidation of an established principle is to be undertaken with great caution. We conclude that, whether or not Ernest G. Sullivan established the inter vivos trust in order to defeat his wife's right to take her statutory share in the assets placed in the trust and even though he had a general power of appointment over the trust assets, Mary A. Sullivan obtained no right to share in the assets of that trust when she made her election under G.L. c. 191, §15.

We announce for the future that, as to any inter vivos trust created or amended after the date of this opinion, we shall no longer follow the rule announced in Kerwin v. Donaghy. There have been significant changes since 1945 in public policy considerations bearing on the right of one spouse to treat his or her property as he or she wishes during marriage. The interests of one spouse in the property of the other have been substantially increased upon the dissolution of a marriage by divorce. We believe that, when a marriage is terminated by the death of one spouse, the rights of the surviving spouse should not be so restricted as they are by the rule in Kerwin v. Donaghy. It is neither equitable nor logical to extend to a divorced spouse greater rights in the assets of an inter vivos trust created and controlled by the other spouse than are extended to a spouse who remains married until the death of his or her spouse.

The rule we now favor would treat as part of "the estate of the deceased" for the purposes of G.L. c. 191, §15, assets of an inter vivos trust created during the

---

9. In early opinions, this court considered an intent to deny inheritance rights to be a ground for invalidating an inter vivos transfer, but in the first part of this century it abandoned that position. . . .

Opinions in this Commonwealth, and generally elsewhere, considering the rights of a surviving spouse to a share in assets transferred by the deceased spouse to an inter vivos trust have analyzed the question on grounds of public policy, as if establishing common law principles. These opinions have not relied in any degree on what the Legislature may have intended by granting a surviving spouse certain rights in the "estate" of a deceased spouse.

marriage by the deceased spouse over which he or she alone had a general power of appointment, exercisable by deed or by will. This objective test would involve no consideration of the motive or intention of the spouse in creating the trust. We would not need to engage in a determination of "whether the [spouse] has in good faith divested himself [or herself] of ownership of his [or her] property or has made an illusory transfer" (Newman v. Dore, 9 N.E.2d 966 (N.Y. 1937)) or with the factual question whether the spouse "intended to surrender complete dominion over the property" (Staples v. King, 433 A.2d 407, 411 (Me. 1981)). Nor would we have to participate in the rather unsatisfactory process of determining whether the inter vivos trust was, on some standard, "colorable," "fraudulent," or "illusory."

What we have announced as a rule for the future hardly resolves all the problems that may arise. . . .

The question of the rights of a surviving spouse in the estate of a deceased spouse, using the word "estate" in its broad sense, is one that can best be handled by legislation. See Uniform Probate Code, §§2-201, 2-202, 8 U.L.A. 74-75 (1983). See also Uniform Marital Property Act, §18 (1983), which adopts the concept of community property as to "marital property." But, until it is, the answers to these problems will "be determined in the usual way through the decisional process." Tucker v. Badoian, 384 N.E.2d 1195, 1201 (Mass. 1978) (Kaplan, J., concurring).

We affirm the judgment of the Probate Court dismissing the plaintiff's complaint.

So ordered.

BONGAARDS v. MILLEN, 793 N.E.2d 335 (Mass. 2003): In 2003, the Supreme Judicial Court of Massachusetts faced some of the questions left open by its decision in *Sullivan*. Jean Bongaards was the life tenant of a trust established by her mother. Under the terms of the trust, Jean had a limited power of appointment over the remainder, and during her life she could have terminated the trust, whereupon the entire corpus would have been paid to her. Jean never exercised her right to terminate. Instead, ten days before her death, Jean appointed the trust remainder to her sister Nina. Having been left out of Jean's will,[10] her husband George claimed an elective share against her estate. Inasmuch as the trust corpus (which included the $1.4 million apartment building in which they lived[11]) would have been treated as marital property subject to equitable division on divorce, George argued that it should be included within her estate for purposes of calculating his elective share.

10. Jean Bongaards explicitly disinherited her husband: "My failure to provide in this will for my husband, George Bongaards, is intentional, and not due to accident or mistake, and is not a reflection of any lack of regard or appreciation on my part." SJC Case Challenges Antiquated Inheritance Law, Boston Globe, Feb. 9, 2003, at B1.

11. George did receive a summer house on Cape Cod because he and Jean had owned it in joint tenancy. But he received nothing from Jean's estate, not even her furniture or the apartment building in which they had lived for 30 years, which passed instead to Jean's sister Nina and Nina's children.

The trust at issue was created by Jean's mother, Josephine D'Amore, an Italian immigrant and single mother. Although Josephine spoke English, she could not read it. But Josephine could cook — she owned a successful restaurant in the North End of Boston, which enabled her to buy substantial buildings and put them in separate trusts for each of her six children.

After George and Jean moved into the first floor of Jean's building in 1965, George paid rent to Jean's mother Josephine, and after Josephine's death, to his wife Jean. The lawyer for Jean's sister Nina told the Boston Globe that the property was always meant to stay in Josephine's family: "George Bongaards knew that his whole life. He admitted it repeatedly in his depositions, yet when his wife died, he ignored that and decided to try and get a piece of the building." Boston Globe, Feb. 9, 2003, supra.

Rejecting George's claim, the court held that "the trust property at issue here is . . . not subject to the plaintiff's elective share for the simple reason that the trust was created by a third party, [Jean's mother], and not by Jean. The rule announced in *Sullivan* applies only to assets of a trust 'created during the marriage by the deceased spouse.'" The court continued:

> Indeed, there does not appear to be any ambiguity in the Legislature's use of the term "estate of the deceased" in G.L. c. 191, §15. In context, "estate of the deceased" refers to the decedent's probate estate — the will being waived by the surviving spouse would ordinarily be the operative instrument that would divide the decedent's probate estate, and a spouse dissatisfied with the will's provisions for that division could instead opt for the statutory division of that same "estate." Absent any ambiguity in the term "estate of the deceased" . . . , there would be no basis to interpret that term to mean anything other than the decedent's probate estate.
>
> Regardless whether changing times and the modern array of possible will substitutes may make it advisable to expand the term beyond the mere probate estate, we are not at liberty to update statutes merely because, in our view, they no longer suffice to serve their intended purpose. This is particularly true when the Legislature itself has recently considered numerous proposals to modernize the elective share statute, with differing approaches regarding how the elective share should be harmonized with contemporary concepts of marriage and property, and has yet to adopt any of them. See Note, Marital Property Reform in Massachusetts: A Choice for the New Millennium, 34 New Eng. L. Rev. 261, 270-271, 337-338 (1999) (outlining various proposals to reform elective share statute submitted to Legislature between 1991 and 1999). That the current version of the statute is woefully inadequate to satisfy modern notions of a decedent spouse's obligation to support the surviving spouse or modern notions of marital property does not authorize us to tinker with the statute's provisions in order to remedy those inadequacies. It is up to the Legislature to choose between the complex — and apparently controversial — options for modernizing this outdated scheme, not up to us to modernize it piecemeal according to our views of what remedies should be made available to a disinherited spouse.
>
> It could be argued that *Sullivan* already represents such a tinkering with the definition of "estate" for purposes of G.L. c. 191, §15, and that ordinary principles of statutory construction should therefore not prevent us from continuing the process begun in *Sullivan*. However, that justification for a significant expansion of the term "estate" in G.L. c. 191, §15, ignores the fact that *Sullivan* merely closed a loophole through which spouses had been able to evade §15. As articulated in *Sullivan*, what was to remain part of the "estate" subject to the elective share was property that previously belonged to the deceased spouse. But for the spouse's artificially distancing the property from that "estate" by the creation of a trust while still, for all practical purposes, retaining absolute control over and use of the property, the property would have been part of the deceased spouse's probate, and hence the elective share, "estate." In other words, *Sullivan* kept in the elective share "estate" property that would ordinarily have been in that "estate," refusing to give effect to a spouse's attempt to remove that property from the elective share "estate" but still retain access to it by means of a "trust."
>
> It is one thing for this court to plug loopholes to prevent a spouse's evasion of the elective share statute. It is quite another to expand the reach of the elective share statute itself and, by so doing, frustrate the intent of a third party who is a stranger to the marriage. The recognition in *Sullivan* that property in a trust created by a third party presents "a different situation" from property in a trust "created during the marriage by the deceased spouse," was not some hypertechnical distinction. A third

party has no obligation to support someone else's spouse, and property owned by a third party has never been part of someone else's spouse's elective share "estate." Thus, when a third party places that property in a trust, the property is not being removed — artificially or otherwise — from that elective share "estate." The property was never in that "estate" in the first place . . . . The proposed revision of the definition of "estate" to include trust property that was never, prior to the trust's creation, the property of either spouse is not designed merely to prevent evasion of the elective share statute. Rather, it would represent a judicially created expansion of the reach of the statute. It goes far beyond the modest prophylactic measure announced in *Sullivan* and cannot be justified as a mere "extension" of *Sullivan*.

NOTES AND PROBLEMS

1. In Sullivan v. Burkin, the court rejected several tests applied in various states to determine what nonprobate transfers are subject to the surviving spouse's election. The first, and most famous, is the *illusory transfer* test laid down by Newman v. Dore, 9 N.E.2d 966 (N.Y. 1937) (now superseded by statute in New York). In *Newman,* the court upheld a widow's claim that a revocable inter vivos trust established by her husband during their marriage is "illusory" and invalid.[12] After some years of uncertainty and confusion about the holding in *Newman,* courts following *Newman* held that an "illusory" revocable trust is not invalid, but it does count as part of the decedent's assets subject to the elective share; the trustee may have to contribute some of the trust assets to make up the elective share. The illusory transfer test is the most widely adopted of the judicial tests for subjecting nonprobate property to the elective share. See Pezza v. Pezza, 690 A.2d 345 (R.I. 1997) (adopting illusory transfer test and holding that an irrevocable trust created during marriage by husband, who retained some income interests, was not illusory). The illusory transfer test has been adopted by the South Carolina legislature. S.C. Code Ann. §62-7-112 (2004).

What kind of ownership rights retained by the decedent make a transfer illusory was left unclear in *Newman* and was little clarified in later cases. The key is said to be the amount of control retained by the decedent spouse. But how much is too much? Are any of the following nonprobate transfers illusory? Would it matter if these property arrangements were made before or after marriage?

(a) *H* owns an insurance policy naming his two daughters as beneficiaries. *H* has the rights to cash in the policy and to change the beneficiaries.

(b) *H* has an account with a stock brokerage house, which holds all his stocks as custodian. *H* has named his daughters as payable-on-death beneficiaries of the account.

(c) *H* has two bank accounts: one naming his daughters as payable-on-death beneficiaries, and a second a joint account with his daughters.

(d) *H* bought Blackacre and took title with his daughters in joint tenancy.

---

12. The facts of Newman v. Dore are unusual. The husband was 80 and his wife in her 30s when they married. After four years of marriage, the wife sued for separation, claiming her husband's perverted sexual habits made it impossible to live with him. The record does not make clear what the octogenarian's alleged perversions were, though he did receive monkey glands by surgical transplant. Indignant over his wife's charges, the husband instructed his lawyer to disinherit her. The separation action was still pending at his death. See Elias Clark, Louis Lusky, Arthur W. Murphy, Mark L. Ascher & Grayson M.P. McCouch, Gratuitous Transfers 128 (4th ed. 1999).

2. Some states found the illusory transfer test itself illusory and adopted instead an *intent to defraud* test. In determining whether the decedent intended to defraud his surviving spouse of her elective share, some look for subjective intent. Others look for objective evidence of intent: the control retained by the transferor, the amount of time between the transfer and death, the degree to which the surviving spouse is left without an interest in the decedent's property or other means of support. See In re Estate of Froman, 803 S.W.2d 176 (Mo. App. 1991) (subjective intent, codified as Mo. Rev. Stat. §474.150(1) (2004)); Hanke v. Hanke, 459 A.2d 246 (N.H. 1983) (objective intent).

Another test, slightly different from the intent-to-defraud test, is whether the decedent had a *present donative intent* to transfer a present interest in the property. This test focuses not on what the transferor retained, but on whether the transferor intended to make a present gift. Factors similar to those weighed in the objective intent-to-defraud test appear to be used in applying this test. See In re Estate of Defilippis, 683 N.E.2d 453 (Ill. App. 1997). Under all of these tests, which do not spell out the criteria specifically, the cases tend to be resolved by examining closely the circumstances of the particular case. In jurisdictions following one of these tests, lawyers must advise clients to exercise extreme caution in making nonprobate transfers without the other spouse's consent that might have the effect of diminishing the other spouse's elective share.

3. In some states, such as Connecticut and Ohio, revocable trusts and other nonprobate transfers are not subject to the elective share. The surviving spouse's elective share is only in the decedent's probate estate. See Jeffrey A. Schoenblum, 2004 Multistate Guide to Estate Planning at Table 6.03.

4. *H* and *W*, both 65 years of age, live in State Red. In State Red, a surviving spouse can include a revocable inter vivos trust created by the decedent in the decedent's assets subject to her elective share. In State Blue, a revocable inter vivos trust is not reachable by the surviving spouse. *H* takes a trip to State Blue and sets up a revocable inter vivos trust there, naming a State Blue bank as trustee. The trust instrument provides that the law of State Blue shall govern the trust. *H* transfers almost all his assets to the State Blue trustee. *H* dies domiciled in State Red. Can *W* reach the assets in the inter vivos trust in State Blue? Compare National Shawmut Bank v. Cumming, 91 N.E.2d 337 (Mass. 1950) (applying law of trustee's domicile to defeat elective share claim of spouse domiciled out of state), with In re Clark, 236 N.E.2d 152 (N.Y. 1968) (applying law of state where couple were domiciled, deeming it to have paramount interest).

UPC §2-202(d) (1990) provides that the law of the decedent's domicile shall govern the right to take an elective share of property located in another state. But not all states agree. In Estate of Pericles, 641 N.E.2d 10 (Ill. App. 1994), the court applied the standard conflict of laws rule that the law of the state where real property is located governs the elective share in such real property. See generally 1 Jeffrey A. Schoenblum, Multistate and Multinational Estate Planning §§10.02, 10.04-10.05 (2d ed. 1999).

(2) Statutory Schemes

Dissatisfied with vague tests laid down by courts, many state legislatures have enacted statutes providing objective criteria for determining what nonprobate transfers are subject to the elective share. These statutes eschew the judicially crafted illusory transfer and other like tests, favoring instead a clear list of non-probate transfers that are added to the probate estate to constitute a *net estate* or an *elective estate* against which the surviving spouse may elect to take his or her statutory share. We treat here the representative New York and the interesting Delaware approaches, both of which may be contrasted with the schemes set forth in the 1969 and 1990 Uniform Probate Codes discussed in the next section.

(a) New York

In 1965 New York became the first state to enact a net estate type approach, replacing the illusory transfer test developed by the courts with a statutory scheme for subjecting some nonprobate transfers to the elective share. After subsequent amendments, the New York statute now gives the surviving spouse $50,000 or one-third of the decedent's net estate, whichever is greater, plus a personal property set-aside (page 422). N.Y. Est. Powers & Trusts Law §5-1.1-A (2004).

In New York, the decedent's estate that is subject to the elective share includes the probate estate and the following nonprobate transfers:

(1)   gifts causa mortis (gifts of tangible personal property contingent on death);
(2)   gifts made within one year before death, except gifts not exceeding $11,000 per person;
(3)   savings account (Totten) trusts;
(4)   joint bank accounts, to the extent of the decedent's contribution;
(5)   joint tenancies and tenancies by the entireties, to the extent of the decedent's contribution;
(6)   property payable on death to a person other than the decedent;
(7)   lifetime transfers in which the decedent retained possession or life income or a power to revoke or a power to consume, invade, or dispose of the principal;
(8)   pension plans or the like; and
(9)   any property over which the decedent had a general power of appointment enabling him to appoint the property to whomever he pleases.

The amount of the elective share is reduced by deducting the value of any interest, other than a life estate, which passes from the decedent to the surviving spouse by intestacy, by will, or by will substitute. See N.Y. Est. Powers & Trusts Law §5-1.1-A(a)(4)(A) (2004).

(b) Delaware

Delaware takes a different but more elegant approach. It defines the property subject to the elective share as all property includible in the decedent's gross estate under the federal estate tax, whether or not the decedent files an estate tax return. If a nonprobate transfer is taxable at death (as are revocable trusts, P.O.D. contracts, and joint tenancies), the surviving spouse — as well as Uncle Sam — can reach it. Del. Code Ann. tit. 12, §902 (2004). Driven by budgetary exigencies to maximize revenue, federal tax authorities pay little attention to the distinction between probate and nonprobate transfers, focusing instead on the underlying question whether an economic benefit is transferred from the decedent to another person. The Delaware approach thus has the advantage of incorporating into elective share law the well-defined standards of federal estate tax law, which have evolved out of long experience in dealing with decedents trying to avoid estate tax by lifetime transfers.

For a detailed examination and approval of using the federal estate tax laws to govern the elective share, see Susan N. Gary, Marital Partnership Theory and the Elective Share: Federal Estate Tax Law Provides a Solution, 49 U. Miami L. Rev. 567 (1995) (limiting the elective share to the part of the federal gross estate that is marital property acquired during marriage); Sidney Kwestel & Rena C. Seplowitz, Testamentary Substitutes: Retained Interests, Custodial Accounts and Contractual Transactions—A New Approach, 38 Am. U.L. Rev. 1 (1988). For discussion of what nonprobate transfers are subject to federal estate taxation, see pages 872-891.

(3)   THE UNIFORM PROBATE CODE

(a) 1969 Uniform Probate Code

Inspired by New York's innovations, the 1969 UPC introduced the concept of the *augmented estate* (the probate estate augmented with certain nonprobate transfers). UPC §2-202 (1969). The surviving spouse is entitled to an elective share of one-third of the augmented estate. The augmented estate includes the probate estate and the following nonprobate and inter vivos transfers made without consideration at any time *during the marriage*:

(1)   any transfer under which the decedent retains the right to possession or income from the property;

(2)   any transfer which the decedent can revoke or invade or dispose of the principal for his own benefit;

(3)   any transfer in joint tenancy with someone other than the spouse;

(4)   any transfer made within two years before death exceeding $3,000 per donee per year ($3,000 was, at the time, the maximum amount exempt from the federal gift tax under the annual exclusion; it is now $11,000);

(5)   property given to the surviving spouse during life, including a life estate in a trust, and property received by the spouse at death derived from the decedent, such as life insurance and pensions.

The purpose of augmenting the probate estate with items (1) through (4) above was, in the words of the official comment: "to prevent the owner of wealth from making arrangements which transmit his property to others by means other than probate deliberately to defeat the right of the surviving spouse to a share." The augmented estate expressly excluded life insurance payable to a person other than the surviving spouse on the questionable ground that "it is not ordinarily purchased as a way of depleting the probate estate and avoiding the elective share of the spouse."

Observe that the 1969 UPC includes in the augmented estate property given to the surviving spouse by the decedent during life (item 5 listed above). The purpose of this innovation is to prevent a spouse who has been well provided for by lifetime or nonprobate transfers from electing against the will and claiming more than a fair share. Thus:

> *Case 4. H*, married to *W*, owns the family home in joint tenancy with *W* (the house is worth $80,000 at *H*'s death). *H* owns insurance on his own life in the amount of $100,000, payable to *W*. During life *H* transfers $200,000 to a trust to pay *H* the income for life, then to pay *W* the income for life, then to pay the principal to *H*'s

children. *H* dies, leaving a probate estate of $100,000, which he devises to his children. In a majority of states the elective share system does not take into account the property given *W*. *W* can elect to take a fractional share of *H*'s probate estate regardless of how much she has received from *H* by nonprobate routes.

To be equitable, the 1969 UPC includes gifts to the spouse in the decedent's augmented estate, gifts that are credited against the elective share to which the surviving spouse is entitled.

The 1969 UPC augmented estate approach was adopted and remains in effect in a number of states. In addition, the concept of augmenting the probate estate with transfers *during marriage* that the decedent continued to control influenced other states in revising their elective share systems, even though they did not adopt the UPC.

(b) 1990 Uniform Probate Code

The 1990 UPC completely redesigned the elective share and the augmented estate so that it achieves results closer to those of a community property system, which the revisers took to be the desideratum. The central idea of the 1990 UPC elective share is to add up all the property of both spouses and split it according to a percentage based on the length of the marriage. The revisers believe that this will result in treating spouses in common law property jurisdictions in pretty much the same way they are treated in community property jurisdictions (assuming that the spouses have only community property and each spouse owns half of their community property assets).

The 1990 UPC also changed the policy of the 1969 UPC elective share of including in the augmented estate only transfers made during marriage. The 1990 UPC includes in the augmented estate many transfers made before marriage, as well as transfers during marriage, where the decedent retained substantial control of the property. It also includes property or powers received from others. In this respect, the 1990 UPC resembles the Internal Revenue Code, which subjects to estate taxation property transferred by the decedent during life over which the decedent retained substantial control as well as property subject to a general power of appointment given the decedent by others. The purpose of the augmented estate is no longer to protect against "fraud on the widow's share." According to the official general comment, it is instead to implement the partnership theory of the elective share by increasing "the entitlement of a surviving spouse in a long-term marriage in cases in which the marital assets were disproportionately titled in the decedent's name."

Because the 1990 UPC elective share is rather complex, we do not reproduce its provisions here, though you can retrieve them from the Uniform Laws Annotated database on Westlaw or from the web page of the Uniform Law Commission. Instead, we give here a bare bones outline of how it works, beginning with Professor Waggoner's explanation of how the augmented estate is computed (Waggoner was the reporter for the 1990 UPC revisions):

> *Step one: determine the "elective-share percentage."* That percentage is determined under the schedule set forth in section 2-202(a) [see page 427]. Under that schedule, the elective-share percentages range from a low of zero percent for a marriage of less than a year to a high of fifty percent for a marriage of fifteen years or more.

Step two: determine the value of the "augmented estate." Under section 2-203, the value of the augmented estate is determined by adding up the value of four components, as described in sections 2-204 through 2-207. Those components are:

- the value of the decedent's net probate estate (section 2-204);
- the value of the decedent's nonprobate transfers to others, consisting of will-substitute-type inter vivos transfers made by the decedent to others than the surviving spouse (section 2-205);
- the value of the decedent's nonprobate transfers to the surviving spouse, consisting of will-substitute-type inter vivos transfers made by the decedent to the surviving spouse (section 2-206); and
- the value of the surviving spouse's net assets at the decedent's death, plus the surviving spouse's nonprobate transfers to others (section 2-207).

Step three: determine the "elective-share amount." The elective-share amount is the amount to which the surviving spouse is entitled. The elective-share amount is calculated by multiplying the augmented estate by the elective-share percentage. [Lawrence W. Waggoner, The Uniform Probate Code's Elective Share: Time for a Reassessment, 37 U. Mich J.L. Ref. 1, 7-8 (2003).]

In funding the elective share amount, the 1990 UPC credits the surviving spouse with nonprobate transfers to the surviving spouse and marital assets that are already owned by the surviving spouse. Thus:

Case 5. H and W have been married for 25 years, so under §2-202, W is entitled to an elective share of 50 percent. H's augmented estate consists of:

(a)	$100,000	probate estate, devised to A
(b)	$150,000	nonprobate transfers to others than W
(c)	$ 25,000	life insurance payable to W
(d)	$ 50,000	H's half interest in joint tenancy held with W
(e)	$ 75,000	W's property
(f)	$ 50,000	W's half interest in the joint tenancy
	$450,000	

W has an elective share of 50 percent of the whole, or $225,000. Since W owns $75,000 in her own name, this amount is credited against her elective share, reducing it to $150,000. Also credited against the elective share are $25,000 in life insurance received by W, $50,000 for H's half of the joint tenancy, and $50,000 for W's half of the joint tenancy. Thus, the amount of W's elective share payable out of H's probate estate and nonprobate transfers is $25,000.

Although the revisers wanted the elective share to resemble the results of a community property system, some differences remain. The 1990 UPC augmented estate includes all property of both spouses, and not only property acquired from earnings. Community property, owned equally by the spouses, includes only earnings and acquisitions from earnings. It does not apply to property brought to the marriage or acquired by gift or inheritance, which is the separate property of the acquiring spouse. The decedent spouse can dispose of his separate property any way he likes; the surviving spouse has no claim to it.

The revisers justify including all property of the spouses in the redesigned elective share on the ground that it avoids problems of classifying property as community (earned) or separate, particularly when the couple has mixed their property. On the other hand, by including all property of the spouses in the elective share, the 1990 UPC makes it impossible for one spouse to keep his or her property acquired before marriage or by inheritance free from the elective share of the other spouse without the consent of the other spouse.

The 1990 UPC elective share provisions have been adopted in only eight states, mainly in the Great Plains. See Jeffrey A. Schoenblum, 2004 Multistate Guide to Estate Planning at Table 6.03.

NOTES, PROBLEM, AND QUESTIONS

1. In 2003 Professor Waggoner proposed another revision of the UPC, this time simplifying the structure of the augmented estate and extending the phase-in period of the spouse's share from 15 to 25 years. The purposes of these changes are two: (1) to deal better with the possibility of second marriages, and (2) to reflect the view that the accumulation of marital wealth is perhaps slower than that is supposed by 1990 UPC §2-202. See Lawrence W. Waggoner, The Uniform Probate Code's Elective Share: Time for a Reassessment, 37 U. Mich J.L. Ref. 1 (2003).

2. Before his second marriage, *H* creates an irrevocable trust, reserving the right to income for life, remainder to his daughter *A*. The trustee, a bank, has the power to dip into principal if necessary for *H*'s support. At *H*'s death thereafter, is his second wife entitled to reach the trust to satisfy her elective share under UPC §2-205? Suppose that *H* had made the transfer after marrying his second wife. What result? See Rena C. Seplowitz, Transfers Prior to Marriage and the Uniform Probate Code's Redesigned Elective Share: Why the Partnership Is Not Yet Complete, 26 Ind. L. Rev. 1 (1991) (arguing that premarital transfers under which the decedent retained substantial rights should be included in the augmented estate).

3. Should *life insurance* owned by the decedent be subject to the elective share? The 1969 UPC exempted it. The 1990 UPC included it. The life insurance industry has fought this, just as it has fought allowing the policy beneficiary to be changed by will. What is the reason for the opposition?

In the chapter on federal estate taxation at pages 875-876, you will see that the life insurance industry has been successful in obtaining favorable treatment from Congress in taxing life insurance.

4. For further analysis and discussion of the UPC augmented estate, see Alan Newman, Incorporating the Partnership Theory of Marriage into Elective-Share Law: The Approximation System of the Uniform Probate Code and the Deferred-Community-Property Alternative, 49 Emory L.J. 487 (2000); Patricia G. Roberts, The 1990 Uniform Probate Code's Elective Share Provisions—West Virginia's Enactment Paves the Way, 95 W. Va. L. Rev. 55 (1992); Lawrence W. Waggoner, The Multiple-Marriage Society and Spousal Rights Under the Revised Uniform Probate Code, 76 Iowa L. Rev. 223 (1991); Charles H. Whitebread, The Uniform Probate Code's Nod to the Partnership Theory of Marriage: The 1990 Elective Share Revisions, 11 Prob. L.J. 125 (1992).

NOTE: MUST THE SURVIVING SPOUSE
ACCEPT A LIFE ESTATE?

Once the amount of the elective share has been determined, when the surviving spouse elects against the will, she is usually credited (or, in legal language, *charged*) with the value of all interests given her by the will. If the amount of the bequests to the surviving spouse does not satisfy the elective share, the difference must be made up either by pro rata contributions from all the other beneficiaries (the majority and UPC rule) or from the residuary estate.

Suppose that the decedent has left the surviving spouse a life estate in a certain amount of property. Must the surviving spouse accept the life estate or its value in partial satisfaction of her elective share? Under the original 1969 UPC and the law of most states, if the surviving spouse renounces the life estate and elects to take her share in fee simple, she is not charged for the value of the life estate. In 1975, the 1969 UPC was amended to provide that a life estate given the spouse by will is charged to the surviving spouse. Under the 1969 UPC, as amended, the surviving spouse who rejects the life estate is charged an amount equal to one-half the total value of the property subject to the life estate. Charging the surviving spouse with the value of the life estate was carried over into the 1990 UPC. The practical effect of so charging the surviving spouse forced the surviving spouse to take the life estate given her by the decedent's will. The object of the UPC revisers was to cause as little distortion in the decedent's estate plan as possible, but charging the widow with a life estate forces the widow to bend to her husband's will and take only lifetime support rather than a share of outright ownership. Under heavy criticism from commentators, in 1993 the UPC was amended to provide that a life estate renounced by the surviving spouse is not charged against her elective share. UPC §2-209 (1990, amended 1993). See Ira M. Bloom, The Treatment of Trust and Other Partial Interests of the Surviving Spouse Under the Redesigned Elective-Share System: Some Concerns and Suggestions, 55 Alb. L. Rev. 941 (1992).

Two states offer *only* a life estate as the elective share. See Conn. Gen. Stat. §45a-436 (2004) (one-third life estate in probate property); R.I. Gen. Laws §33-25-2 (2004) (life estate in all real estate). Under these schemes, a surviving spouse can take under the will or elect to take a life estate as the forced share.

c. Waiver

The right of election allows the surviving spouse to take his or her statutory share in spite of the decedent spouse's will. The question thus arises, can the spouses agree to waive the survivor's elective share? The prototypical waiver occurs in a premarital agreement.

Before the 1970s, premarital agreements were strongly disfavored by the courts as contrary to public policy. However, with the seminal decisions of Posner v. Posner, 233 So. 2d 381 (Fla. 1970), and In re Marriage of Dawley, 551 P.2d 323 (Cal. 1976), judicial hostility to prenuptial agreements began to wane. In 1983, the Uniform Premarital Agreement Act (UPAA) recognized the enforceability of premarital agreements. Today the UPAA has been enacted in just over half the states, and it has been influential even in states that have not adopted it. Every separate property state recognizes the validity of premarital agreements, enforcing waiver of the right of election.

Although the courts regularly enforce premarital agreements, there remains concern that these agreements may not reflect an arm's-length bargain. Visualize the prenuptial agreement thrust upon the poorer spouse the night before the wedding. Accordingly, in many states enforcement of premarital agreements is conditioned on full and fair disclosure, particularly of finances. See Jeffrey A. Schoenblum, 2004 Multistate Guide to Estate Planning at Table 6.04. In addition, it is often sensible for each spouse to have independent counsel. For a discussion of when husband and wife need separate lawyers and when it is ethical for one lawyer to represent both, see ABA Special Comm. Report, Husband and Wife, 28 Real Prop., Prob. & Tr. J. 762 (1994).

Uniform Probate Code (1990, as amended 1993)

§2-213. WAIVER OF RIGHT TO ELECT AND OF OTHER RIGHTS

(a) The right of election of a surviving spouse and the rights of the surviving spouse to homestead allowance, exempt property, and family allowance, or any of them, may be waived, wholly or partially, before or after marriage, by a written contract, agreement, or waiver signed by the surviving spouse.

(b) A surviving spouse's waiver is not enforceable if the surviving spouse proves that:

(1) he [or she] did not execute the waiver voluntarily; or

(2) the waiver was unconscionable when it was executed and, before execution of the waiver, he [or she]:

(i) was not provided a fair and reasonable disclosure of the property or financial obligations of the decedent;

(ii) did not voluntarily and expressly waive, in writing, any right to disclosure of the property or financial obligations of the decedent beyond the disclosure provided; and

(iii) did not have, or reasonably could not have had, an adequate knowledge of the property or financial obligations of the decedent.

(c) An issue of unconscionability of a waiver is for decision by the court as a matter of law.

(d) Unless it provides to the contrary, a waiver of "all rights," or equivalent language, in the property or estate of a present or prospective spouse or a complete property settlement entered into after or in anticipation of separation or divorce is a waiver of all rights of elective share, homestead allowance, exempt property, and family allowance by each spouse in the property of the other and a renunciation by each of all benefits that would otherwise pass to him [or her] from the other by intestate succession or by virtue of any will executed before the waiver or property settlement.

UPC §2-213 incorporates the standards by which the validity of a premarital agreement is determined under Uniform Premarital Agreement Act §6. For discussion, see Gail F. Brod, Premarital Agreements and Gender Justice, 6 Yale J.L. & Feminism 229 (1994); Note, Planning for Love: The Politics of Prenuptial Agreements, 49 Stan. L. Rev. 887 (1997) (arguing that abuse of these agreements is best handled by requiring both parties to consult independent counsel). See also Note, Developments in the Law: Marriage as Contract and Marriage as Partnership: The Future of Antenuptial Agreement Law, 116 Harv. L. Rev. 2075 (2003).

In re Estate of Garbade
Supreme Court, Appellate Division, New York, 1995
221 A.D.2d 844, 633 N.Y.S.2d 878

MERCURE, J.   Respondent and J. Robert Garbade (hereinafter decedent) were married on February 2, 1990. Each had been previously married and divorced. Decedent was a wealthy executive who owned his own construction company and had interests in other enterprises; respondent was unemployed and brought no assets to the marriage. Prior to the wedding, respondent and decedent executed a prenuptial agreement, under the terms of which each waived any right to, inter alia, maintenance, equitable distribution or community property rights with regard to assets titled in the name of the other or, of primary relevance here, an elective share of the other's estate. However, the agreement required decedent to maintain a $100,000 policy of insurance on his life for respondent's benefit.

In July 1992, decedent died unexpectedly at the age of 52, survived by respondent and petitioners, his two sons. Petitioners thereafter qualified as personal representatives of decedent's estate. Notwithstanding her waiver and the fact that she received assets totaling approximately $340,000 by virtue of decedent's death, respondent filed notice of her election to take her share of decedent's estate pursuant to EPTL 5-1.1. Surrogate's Court granted petitioners' motion [for summary judgment] and authorized the entry of judgment setting aside respondent's notice of election. Respondent now appeals.

We affirm. Fundamentally, "a duly executed antenuptial agreement is given the same presumption of legality as any other contract, commercial or otherwise. It is presumed to be valid in the absence of fraud" (Matter of Sunshine, 381 N.Y.S.2d 260 (App. Div.), aff'd 357 N.E.2d 999 (N.Y. 1976)). Moreover, the party attacking the validity of the agreement has the burden of coming forward with evidence of fraud, which, in the absence of facts from which concealment may reasonably be inferred, will not be presumed. In light of that standard, even crediting every factual allegation advanced by respondent and drawing the most favorable inferences therefrom, we agree with Surrogate's Court that respondent has raised no legitimate triable issue as to whether the prenuptial agreement and, more to the point, respondent's waiver of her right to elect against decedent's estate was the product of fraud, misrepresentation, duress, imposition or undue influence.

Respondent presented evidence establishing at most that (1) it was decedent, and not she, who first raised the issue of a prenuptial agreement and requested that one be executed prior to the wedding, (2) the agreement was prepared by decedent's attorneys, at his request and in accordance with his direction, (3) the prenuptial agreement was executed only a few hours prior to the parties' wedding, (4) respondent did not seek or obtain independent legal counsel and the agreement was not read by her or to her before she signed it, (5) respondent was not specifically advised that the agreement provided for a waiver of her right to elect against decedent's will, and (6) respondent was not furnished with a copy of the agreement.

At the same time, it is uncontroverted that (1) respondent readily acceded to decedent's request that they enter into a prenuptial agreement and willingly signed the instrument because she did not want any of decedent's money or property, she only wanted to be his wife, (2) respondent was advised to obtain the services of independent counsel, (3) respondent was given an adequate opportunity to read the instrument before she signed it, and (4) prior to executing the prenuptial agreement, respondent was provided with detailed disclosure of decedent's $2.5 million net worth.

In our view, respondent has established nothing more than her own dereliction in failing to acquaint herself with the provisions of the agreement and to obtain the benefit of independent legal counsel. Although this dereliction may have caused her to be ignorant of the precise terms of the agreement, the fact remains that, absent fraud or other misconduct, parties are bound by their signatures. Further, the absence of independent counsel will not of itself warrant setting aside the agreement. There being no competent evidence of fraud, respondent has merely resorted to reliance upon a number of innocuous circumstances (such as the fact that the wedding date was changed from February 14 to February 2, 1990 to accommodate a Florida trip, that decedent's attorney did not finish drafting the agreement until shortly prior to the wedding and, incredibly, that the parties went out to lunch before going to sign the agreement) to fuel speculation that fraud was practiced upon her. . . .

Ordered that the order and judgment are affirmed, with costs.

IN RE GRIEFF, 703 N.E.2d 752 (N.Y. 1998): In a prenuptial agreement between a man, 77, and a woman, 65, the parties waived the statutory right of election as against the estate of the other. Three months after the marriage, the husband died, leaving a will devising his entire estate to his children from a prior marriage. The wife filed a petition for a statutory elective share. The surrogate invalidated the prenuptial agreement on the ground that the husband "was in a position of great influence and advantage" in his relationship with his wife-to-be. The surrogate found the husband exercised bad faith and overreaching, particularly noting the husband "selected and paid for" the wife's attorney.

The appellate division reversed on the law, simply declaring that the wife had failed to establish that her execution of the prenuptial agreement was procured by her then-fiancé's fraud or overreaching. The court of appeals reversed the appellate division. The court of appeals held that the contestant of a prenuptial agreement must "establish a fact-based, particularized inequality before a proponent of a prenuptial agreement suffers a shift in the burden to disprove fraud or overreaching." Inasmuch as the appellate division did not undertake to determine whether, based on all the relevant evidence, the nature of the relationship at the time the agreement was signed was such as to shift the burden of proof to the husband's children, the court of appeals remanded the case to the appellate division to make that determination.

The court of appeals held that "a particularized and exceptional scrutiny" must be given to prenuptial agreements, inasmuch as the relationship between prospective spouses is "by its nature permeated with trust, confidence, honesty and reliance."

NOTE

Grieff notwithstanding, the courts are increasingly willing to enforce one-sided agreements if disclosure was adequate. See In re Estate of Lutz, 620 N.W.2d 589 (N.D. 2000) (agreement not unconscionable; *W* "clearly understood" that property was "supposed to be reserved for [*H*]'s children and grandchildren as a condition of the marriage. [*W*] voluntarily entered into the agreement, and has received exactly what she agreed to receive"); Waton v. Waton, 887 So. 2d 419 (Fla. App. 2004) ("even though an agreement is one-sided and unfair, that alone does not make it the result of overreaching"; wife gets nothing from $3 million estate on divorce because she had independent counsel and disclosure was adequate). But the courts will not imply broader waivers than are stated in the agreement. See Estate of Jakopovic, 622 N.W.2d 651 (Neb. 2001) (allowing *H* to take an elective share in *W*'s savings bonds that were not listed in the antenuptial agreement).

4. *Rights of Surviving Spouse in Community Property*

a. Basic Information

Eight states — containing more than one-fourth of the population of the United States — have a system of community property. These community property states, sweeping around the southwest border of the country from the Mississippi River to Canada, are Louisiana, Texas, New Mexico, Arizona, California, Nevada, Washington, and Idaho. In addition, Wisconsin must now be considered a community property state since it has adopted the Uniform Marital Property Act (providing for community property under the name of "marital property"). And Alaska permits spouses to elect community property rather than separate property, if they so choose.

Community property in the United States is a community of acquests: Husband and wife own the earnings and acquisitions from earnings of both spouses during marriage in undivided equal shares. Whatever is bought with earnings is community property. All property that is not community property is the separate property of one spouse or the other or, in the case of a tenancy in common or joint tenancy, of both. Separate property includes property acquired before marriage and property acquired during marriage by gift or inheritance. In Idaho, Louisiana, and Texas, income from separate property is community property. In the other community property states, income from separate property retains its separate character. Where the characterization of the property is doubtful, there is a strong presumption that the property is community property.

Where property has been commingled by the spouse, or acquired from both separate and community funds, states often have a rule about how to characterize the property in a particular situation. For example, if a husband uses his earnings after marriage to pay premiums on a life insurance policy acquired before marriage, some states, applying the inception-of-title rule, hold the policy remains the husband's separate property and the community is entitled only to a return of premiums paid with interest. Other states apply a pro rata share rule to insurance policies, dividing the policy proceeds between separate and community property according to the proportion of payments paid.

To avoid tracing problems, couples can make agreements regarding the character of their property. By agreement they may change separate property into community property, or they may change community property into a joint tenancy, a tenancy in common, or sole ownership of one spouse. Texas has a peculiar rule. Spouses can convert community property into separate property, but they cannot convert separate property into community property.

Couples may agree that all their property is held as community property to achieve favorable income tax treatment given community property. Upon the death of one spouse, the entire value of community property receives a stepped-up basis for determining capital gains when the property is sold thereafter. Any appreciation in value between acquisition and the date of the spouse's death is never taxed as capital gain. If the property is owned as separate property by the decedent spouse, either alone, in joint tenancy, or in tenancy in common, only the decedent's interest in the property receives a stepped-up basis.[13]

Upon the death of one spouse, the deceased spouse can dispose of his or her half of the community assets. The surviving spouse owns the other half, which is not, of course, subject to testamentary disposition by the deceased spouse. The one-half of the community property belonging to the deceased spouse may be devised to whomever the decedent pleases, the same as separate property.

Because community property belongs to both even when title appears on its face to be in the name of one spouse, problems arise over which spouse can manage the property and deal with third persons respecting the property. These problems may concern sale, leasing, or mortgaging the property or subjecting the property to creditors. Each community property state has statutes on this matter. Although these statutes differ in many details, we can indicate broadly the management roles. In Texas, the wife has sole management power over her earnings kept separate and the husband sole power over his. If the earnings are commingled, they are subject to the joint management of the spouses. In California and most other community property states, either the husband or wife, acting alone, has the power to manage community property. Statutes, however, ordinarily require both spouses to join in transfers or mortgages of community real property.

13. *The Alaska Community Property Trust.* Couples not domiciled in Alaska can transfer their personal property into an Alaska Community Property Trust and provide in the trust agreement that the property is community property. Alaska Stat. §34.75.060(b) (2004). This trust, appointing as trustee a bank in Alaska (thus ensuring a local payoff), will be governed by Alaska law if the settlors so intend. A major advantage of an Alaska Community Property Trust is that it apparently enables residents of noncommunity property states to take advantage of Internal Revenue Code §1014(b)(6), which provides that, upon the death of one spouse the entire community property is given a stepped-up basis (the value of the property on the date of the spouse's death). The surviving spouse will thus have to pay no tax on capital gain incurred before the decedent's death if she sells the property. No ruling by the Internal Revenue Service has yet been made, however, as to whether property in an Alaska Community Property Trust created by nonresidents is community property under I.R.C. §1014(b)(6). See Ira Mark Bloom, How Federal Transfer Taxes Affect the Development of Property Law, 48 Clev. St. L. Rev. 661, 671–672 (2000).

In exercising management power, one spouse may sell community property to a purchaser for a valuable consideration, but a spouse cannot freely give away community property. States give various remedies to the nondonor spouse in case of a gift to a third party. Thus:

> *Case 6.* *H*, married to *W*, purchases a life insurance policy on his life with his earnings. The policy is community property. *H* names *A* as beneficiary. Upon *H*'s death, what are *W*'s rights in the policy proceeds? In California, *W* is entitled, after *H* dies, to set aside the gift to the extent of one-half. (During *H*'s life, *W* is entitled to set aside an entire gift and reclaim the property for the community, but, after *H* dies, a gift by *H* during life of community property is treated as if it were a devise by *H* of his half share.) In Texas, the manager of community property (*H* in this instance) can make reasonable gifts to others, but excessive gifts are deemed in fraud of the other spouse's rights. If the court finds the gift to have been in fraud of *W*'s rights, *W* is entitled to half the policy proceeds. See Givens v. Girard Life Ins. Co., 480 S.W.2d 421 (Tex. App. 1972). The other community property states divide between the California and Texas views, sometimes with variations.

Almost all community property states follow the theory that husband and wife own equal shares in each item of community property at death. They do not own equal undivided shares in the aggregate of community property. Thus, if *H* and *W* own Blackacre (worth $50,000) and Whiteacre (worth $50,000), each owns a half share in each tract. *W*'s will cannot devise Blackacre to *H* and Whiteacre to *D*, her daughter by a previous marriage, even though *H* would end up receiving property equal to the value of his community share. (Divorce is different. In most community property states, the divorce court may award Blackacre to *H* and Whiteacre to *W*; it may award specific items of community property to one spouse or the other, provided each spouse ends up with a share of the aggregate value of community property.)

In jurisdictions applying a reasonable gifts rule to lifetime transfers and an item theory to death transfers, should nonprobate transfers to a person other than the spouse be treated as inter vivos transfers or death transfers? If they are death transfers, the surviving spouse is entitled to one-half of each. If they are inter vivos transfers, the surviving spouse may set aside only those transfers deemed unreasonable.

b. Putting the Survivor to an Election

An estate planning device, known as the *widow's election*, developed in community property states in the days when the husband was the manager of community property and the wife was seen as a housewife without business experience, whatever the realities. Even after statutes gave the wife equal management power, after many wives went into business, and after gender-neutral terms were widely adopted, the name "widow's election" is still used to describe this election plan, which may be applicable to widowers as well as to widows. In explaining the widow's election, we shall assume the husband dies first, which is true in most cases.

A widow's election involves a will executed by the husband devising *all* the community property in trust to pay the income to his wife for life, with remainder to others on the wife's death, and requiring the wife to elect between surrendering her half of the community property and taking under the husband's will. If the widow wants to share in her husband's trust, she must surrender her community property. The object of the widow's election is to create, at the death of the husband, one trust of all the community property—both the husband's half and the wife's half—paying the widow all the income for her life. To do this, the widow must consent to the transfer of her share of the community property by electing to take under the will. If the widow so elects, the situation is treated as though the widow transferred her one-half community interest to the trust in exchange for receiving a life estate in her husband's one-half community interest. If, instead, the widow elects against the will, she takes the one-half interest in community property to which she is entitled by law, but she forfeits the life estate in the husband's half of the community property devised to her by her husband's will.

The widow's election may have estate and gift tax advantages, which flow from the fact that the widow has made an exchange for consideration, receiving a life estate in her husband's half of the community property in exchange for transferring a remainder interest in her half of the community property. However, the possible income tax disadvantage is such that most estate planners do not recommend a forced widow's election plan. See John R. Price, Contemporary Estate Planning §§9.23-9.39 (2d ed. 2000).

An alternative to a forced widow's election is a plan by husband and wife to transfer all the community property into a revocable trust, paying income to husband and wife for their joint lives and for the life of the survivor, remainder to their children or to others. The revocable trust becomes irrevocable upon the death of one spouse. This has none of the possible estate and gift tax benefits of a forced widow's election because it is not an exchange of the widow's property for consideration. But it does not have an income tax disadvantage. The joint revocable trust plan may be attractive to couples who want unified trust management of the community property after the death of one of the spouses and assurances that the trust corpus will pass to their issue upon the death of the surviving spouse. See Melinda S. Merk, Joint Revocable Trusts for Married Couples Domiciled in Common-Law Property States, 32 Real Prop., Prob. & Tr. J. 345 (1997).

5. *Migrating Couples and Multistate Property Holdings*

The classic conflict of laws rules used to determine which state law governs marital property are these:

(1) The law of the situs controls problems related to land.

(2) The law of the marital domicile at the time that personal property is acquired controls the characterization of the property (that is, as separate or community).

(3) The law of the marital domicile at the death of one spouse controls the survivor's marital rights.

The application of these rules is briefly examined in this subsection. For a thorough discussion, see 1 Jeffrey A. Schoenblum, Multistate and Multinational Estate Planning §10.21 (2d ed. 1999).

It should be noted that although the state of the situs has the power to control its land, it may choose to apply the law of the marital domicile. UPC §2-202(d), for example, provides that the rights of a spouse to an elective share in land located in the state shall be governed by the law of the decedent's domicile at death.

a. Moving from a Separate Property State to a Community Property State

If a couple acquires property in a separate property state and moves to a community property state, serious problems of fairness to the surviving spouse may arise. The ownership of movable property is determined by the laws of the state where the couple is domiciled when the property is acquired. Thus, if the husband is the wage earner, all of the property is the husband's in a separate property state. The wife is protected by the elective share scheme. When the couple moves to a community property state, the property remains the husband's and is now characterized as the husband's separate property. If the couple remains domiciled in the community property state until the husband dies, the law of the state of domicile at date of death governs the disposition of movable property. If neither spouse works in the community property state, there may be no community property for the surviving spouse. Hence, as a result of the move, the wife loses protection of the elective share system provided by the state where the movable property was acquired and is not protected by the system of community property (which she would have if the couple had been domiciled in the community property state when the husband was working).

Several community property states give a remedy to the surviving spouse in this situation. These states have a concept of *quasi-community property*. Quasi-community property is property owned by the husband or the wife acquired while domiciled elsewhere, which would have been characterized as community property if the couple had been domiciled in the community property state when the property was acquired.[14] Real property situated outside the state is not treated as quasi-community property because the spouse retains in it any forced share or dower given by the law of the situs.[15] During the continuance of the marriage, quasi-community property is treated for most purposes as the separate property of the acquiring spouse. However, upon the death of the acquiring spouse, one-half of the quasi-community property belongs to the surviving spouse; generally the other half is subject to testamentary disposition by the decedent.[16] Quasi-community property is analogous to an elective share in the deceased spouse's property acquired from earnings while domiciled in another state. See Cal. Prob.

---

14. Arizona, New Mexico, and Texas have adopted the quasi-community property concept for purposes of equitable division upon divorce. Quasi-community property is treated the same as community property in that situation. Ariz. Rev. Stat. §25-318 (2004); N.M. Stat. Ann. §40-3-8 (2004); Tex. Fam. Code §7.002 (2004). These states do not apply the quasi-community concept to dissolution of the marriage by death.

15. The surviving spouse of a couple domiciled in a separate property state who buy land in a community property state may have the same elective share in the land as she would have in land in the domiciliary state. See Cal. Prob. Code §120 (2004).

16. If the nonacquiring spouse dies first, the quasi-community property belongs absolutely to the acquiring spouse; the nonacquiring spouse has no testamentary power over it.

Code §§66, 101 (2004); Idaho Code §15-2-201 (2004); La. Civ. Code Ann. art. 3526 (2004); Wash. Rev. Code Ann. §§26.16.220-230 (2004).

> *Case 7.* H and W are domiciled in Illinois. H saves $500,000 from his earnings, which he invests in stocks and bonds. In Illinois this is his separate property. H and W then retire to California. The stocks and bonds become quasi-community property in California. Upon H's death, W owns one-half of the stocks and bonds. If W dies first, she cannot dispose of any part of this wealth by will; H owns it all. If, instead, H and W had moved to Texas, on H's death W would have no interest in the assets brought from Illinois.

To prevent a spouse from attempting to defeat the survivor's quasi-community property rights by inter vivos transfers, the surviving spouse may have the right to reach one-half of any nonprobate transfer of quasi-community property where the decedent retained possession or enjoyment, or the right to income, or the power to revoke or consume, or a right of survivorship. See Cal. Prob. Code §102 (2004). Cf. Idaho Code §15-2-202 (2004).

b. Moving from a Community Property State to a Separate Property State

Suppose that a husband and wife who have acquired community personal property move to a separate property state. What is the effect of this move on the community property? Generally, a change in domicile from a community property state to a separate property state does not change the preexisting property rights of the husband or wife. Community property continues to be community property when the couple and the property move to a separate property state. The Uniform Disposition of Community Property Rights at Death Act (1971), enacted in 14 separate property states, provides that community property brought into the state (and all property — including land in the state — traceable to community property) remains community property for purposes of testamentary disposition, unless the spouses have agreed to convert it into separate property. Each spouse has the right to dispose of one-half of the community property by will. Under the Uniform Act, community property brought into the state is not subject to the elective share. See Stanley M. Johanson, The Migrating Client: Estate Planning for the Couple from a Community Property State, 9 U. Miami Inst. Est. Plan. ¶¶800 et seq. (1975).

Any couple moving community property into a separate property state should be careful to preserve its community nature, if doing so is desirable. If the community property is sold and the proceeds used to purchase other assets, title to the new property should be taken in the name of husband and wife as community property. If resistance from transfer agents, bankers, or title companies — who may know little about community property — is met, the husband and wife should take title in the name of both spouses, at the same time executing a written agreement reciting their intention to retain the asset as community property. Or the spouses may preserve the community property character of their property by creating a revocable trust of the community property and stating in the trust instrument that all property of the trust is community property.

Because lawyers in separate property states sometimes lack understanding of the community property system, lawyers may recommend to couples who are bringing community property into a separate property state that they change the title to joint tenancy or some other separate property form. If this is done, with the intent of changing community property into a common law concurrent interest, the income tax advantage of community property is lost and the lawyer could be liable for malpractice. An example:

> *Case 8.* H and W, domiciled in Texas, buy property for $100,000. Since the property is paid for out of H and W's earnings, it is community property. At H's death several years later, the property is worth $300,000. Under the federal estate tax law, one-half the value of the community property ($150,000) is subject to estate tax at H's death (but it qualifies for the marital deduction if devised to W, thus incurring no estate taxation). *Note, however, the income tax consequences.* At the death of one spouse, the *entire* value of community property acquires a stepped-up basis for income tax purposes, that is, its value at H's death ($300,000). Internal Revenue Code of 1986, §§1014(a) and 1014(b)(6). If W sells the property after H's death for $325,000, she will pay income tax only on $25,000 capital gain.
>
> Suppose that before H dies, H and W move to Massachusetts. A Massachusetts lawyer advises them to change the title to the property to H and W as joint tenants. H and W do this. Then H dies, and the property is worth $300,000. The estate tax consequences of joint tenancy are the same as if the property had remained community property, but the income tax consequences are very different. Only one-half the value of joint tenancy property receives a stepped-up basis at H's death. Rev. Rul. 68-80, 1968-1 C.B. 348. W's new basis is $50,000 (her half of the old basis) plus $150,000 (stepped-up basis on H's half) or $200,000. If W sells the property for $325,000, she will pay an income tax on $125,000 capital gain. Income tax on $100,000, which could have been avoided, is the result of advice by a lawyer unknowledgeable about community property.

A new form of community property has been proposed and adopted in several community property states — community property with a right of survivorship (as in a joint tenancy). Under this form, the decedent spouse cannot dispose of his share of the community property by will; it passes under a right of survivorship to the surviving spouse. This form of community property is now an option in Arizona, Idaho, Nevada, New Mexico, Texas, Washington, and Wisconsin (called survivorship marital property). The purpose of this is to avoid probate costs on the passage of the decedent's half of community property to the surviving spouse — in effect making community property with right of survivorship nonprobate property. California took another route to solve the probate cost problem. Cal. Prob. Code §13500 (2004) provides that when property passes at death to the decedent's spouse, no administration is necessary unless the surviving spouse elects administration. California declined to permit community property with right of survivorship because of the fear that it would be treated by the Internal Revenue Service as joint tenancy property, not qualifying for the stepped-up basis, and because it was called community property would mislead couples into thinking it would so qualify. See James R. Ratner, Community Property, Right of Survivorship, and Separate Property Contributions to Marital Assets: An

Interplay, 41 Ariz. L. Rev. 993 (1999); Arthur W. Andrews, Community Property with Right of Survivorship: Uneasy Lies the Head that Wears a Crown of Surviving Spouse for Federal Income Tax Basis Purposes, 17 Va. Tax Rev. 577 (1998). See also Robert T. Danforth, The Role of Federalism in Administering a National System of Taxation, 57 Tax Law. 625, 634-635, 655-658 (2004).

6. *Spouse Omitted from Premarital Will*

Estate of Shannon

California Court of Appeal, Fourth District, 1990
224 Cal. App. 3d 1148, 274 Cal. Rptr. 338

HUFFMAN, P.J. Gilbert A. Brown, executor of the will of Lila Demos Shannon (also known as Lila King Demos), appeals on behalf of Lila's estate from an order of the probate court denying her petition for determination of heirship as an omitted spouse under Probate Code[17] section 6560 in the estate of Russell Donovan Shannon. We reverse.

FACTUAL AND PROCEDURAL BACKGROUND

On January 25, 1974, Russell, an unmarried widower, executed his last will and testament, naming his daughter, Beatrice Marie Saleski, executrix and sole beneficiary. The will also provided his grandson, Donald Saleski, would inherit his estate in the event Beatrice did not survive him for "thirty (30) days" and contained a disinheritance clause which provided as follows:

> SEVENTH: I have intentionally omitted all other living persons and relatives. If any devises, legatee, beneficiary under this Will, or any legal heir of mine, person or persons claiming under any of them, or other person or persons shall contest this Will or attack or seek to impair or invalidate any of its provisions or conspire with or voluntarily assist anyone attempting to do any of those things mentioned, in that event, I specifically disinherit such person or persons.
>
> If any Court finds that such person or persons are lawful heirs and entitled to participate in my estate, then in that event I bequeath each of them the sum of one ($1.00) dollar and no more.

On April 27, 1986, Russell married Lila. On February 22, 1988, Russell died. He did not make any changes in his will after his marriage to Lila and before his death. His 1974 will was admitted to probate May 9, 1988, and Beatrice was named executrix of his estate.

On September 27, 1988, Lila filed a petition for family allowance, to set apart probate homestead and for determination of entitlement to estate distribution as an omitted surviving spouse. The court denied the petition for family allowance and Lila withdrew her petition to set apart probate homestead. The remaining

---

17. All statutory references are to the Probate Code unless otherwise specified. When referring to statutory subparts we omit repetition of the word "subdivision."

issue of Lila's entitlement to share in Russell's estate was heard December 14, 1988, and taken under submission.

On March 24, 1989, the probate court issued its order denying Lila's petition to determine heirship. She timely appealed only from this latter order.

During the pendency of this appeal, Lila died and her son Brown was named executor of her estate and substituted in her place as appellant.[18] He has objected to the distribution of Russell's estate until after this appeal is decided.

DISCUSSION

On appeal, Lila contends she was a pretermitted spouse within the meaning of section 6560 and does not fall under any of the exceptions under section 6561 which would preclude her from sharing in Russell's estate as an omitted spouse. We agree and reverse.

Section 6560 . . . states:

> Except as provided in Section 6561, if a testator fails to provide by will for his or her surviving spouse who married the testator after the execution of the will, the omitted spouse shall receive a share in the estate consisting of the following property in the estate:
>
> (a) The one-half of the community property that belongs to the testator. . . .
>
> (b) The one-half of the quasi-community property that belongs to the testator. . . .
>
> (c) A share of the separate property of the testator equal in value to that which the spouse would have received if the testator had died intestate, but in no event is the share to be more than one-half the value of the separate property in the estate.

Section 6561 states:

> The spouse does not receive a share of the estate under Section 6560 if any of the following is established:
>
> (a) The testator's failure to provide for the spouse in the will was intentional and that intention appears from the will.
>
> (b) The testator provided for the spouse by transfer outside the will and the intention that the transfer be in lieu of a testamentary provision is shown by statements of the testator or from the amount of the transfer or by other evidence.
>
> (c) The spouse made a valid agreement waiving the right to share in the testator's estate.

It is well established section 6560 reflects a strong statutory presumption of revocation of the will as to the omitted spouse based upon public policy. Such presumption is rebutted only if circumstances are such as to fall within the literal terms of one of the exceptions listed in section 6561. The burden of proving the presumption is rebutted is on the proponents of the will.

Here, Russell failed to provide for Lila in his will. Under the language of section 6560, she is thus an omitted spouse and the crucial inquiry becomes whether Beatrice met the burden of rebutting this presumption. Specifically, the issues are whether the will shows a specific intent to exclude Lila pursuant to section

---

18. In this opinion, we refer to Lila's estate as Lila.

6561(a) and whether Beatrice presented sufficient evidence to show Russell had intended to otherwise provide for Lila outside of his will in lieu of her taking under it pursuant to section 6561(b), or to show Lila waived her rights to share in his estate under section 6561(c).

The will on its face does not evidence an intent on Russell's part to disinherit Lila. As the presumption under section 6560 is only rebutted by a clear manifestation of such intent on the face of the will, "regardless of what may have been the wishes of the [decedent]" (Estate of Basore, 96 Cal. Rptr. 874, 876 (App. 1971)), the section 6561(a) exception has not been established.

. . . Estate of Axcelrod, 147 P.2d 1 (Cal. 1944) . . . held a general provision in a will that the testator "intentionally omitted all of my heirs who are not specifically mentioned herein, intending thereby to disinherit them," may not be construed as mentioning a subsequently acquired spouse in such a way as to show an intention not to make provision for the spouse, where the testator at the time the will was executed had no spouse who could become "an heir." (147 P.2d at 11-12.)

Case law has also held exclusionary clauses in wills which fail to indicate the testator contemplated the possibility of a future marriage are insufficient to avoid the statutory presumption. Even testamentary clauses specifically disinheriting a named individual whom the testator planned to marry and a clause stating "any other person not specifically mentioned in this Will, whether related by marriage or not" have been held insufficient to disclose the explicit intention of a testator to omit provision for another woman the testator married after executing the will either as a member of the designated disinherited class or as a contemplated spouse. (Estate of Green, 174 Cal. Rptr. 654 (App. 1981).) As there is no mention of Lila or the fact of a future marriage in the disinheritance clause of the will, it does not manifest Russell's intent to specifically disinherit Lila as his surviving spouse.

Nor have the circumstances of section 6561(b) or (c) been established. Beatrice asserts a retired California Highway Patrolmen Widow's and Orphan's Fund from which $2,000 was paid to Lila as Russell's beneficiary, coupled with a declaration of Russell's attorney "[t]hat in the twelve months immediately preceding [Russell's death, he] informed this declarant that he had remarried and that his wife was independently wealthy and that she had more than he had and that he wanted his daughter to have his estate upon his death . . . ," evidence Russell's intent to provide for Lila outside the will in lieu of a testamentary provision and satisfy the requirements of section 6561(b). In support of this argument she cites a New Mexico case, Matter of Taggart, 619 P.2d 562 (N.M. 1980), which held the omission of an after-acquired spouse in a will can be shown to be intentional by a transfer outside the will such as life insurance or other joint arrangement based on evidence of the testator's statements, the amount of the transaction, or other evidence. She claims Russell's intent she take his entire estate is paramount and the presumption under section 6560 must yield to that intent.

. . . [S]uch [evidence] was insufficient to rebut the presumption of section 6560 because it does not show Russell provided the trust fund benefits for Lila in lieu of sharing in his estate.

Moreover, the facts presented at the probate hearing that Russell and Lila kept their property separate during the course of their marriage is not sufficient to show "a valid agreement waiving the right to share" in each other's estate pursuant to section 6561(c). (See Estate of Butler, 252 Cal. Rptr. 210, 213-214 (App. 1988).)

Beatrice has simply not met her burden of proving Russell's intent to disinherit Lila and rebut the presumption of revocation under section 6560. The probate court therefore erred in denying Lila's petition to determine heirship.

DISPOSITION

The order denying Lila's petition for heirship is reversed and remanded for further proceedings consistent with this opinion.

Uniform Probate Code (1990, as amended 1993)

§2-301. ENTITLEMENT OF SPOUSE; PREMARITAL WILL

(a) If a testator's surviving spouse married the testator after the testator executed his [or her] will, the surviving spouse is entitled to receive, as an intestate share, no less than the value of the share of the estate he [or she] would have received if the testator had died intestate as to that portion of the testator's estate, if any, that is neither devised to a child of the testator who was born before the testator married the surviving spouse and who is not a child of the surviving spouse nor devised to a descendant of such a child or passes under sections 2-603 or 2-604 to such a child or to a descendant of such a child, unless:

(1) it appears from the will or other evidence that the will was made in contemplation of the testator's marriage to the surviving spouse;

(2) the will expresses the intention that it is to be effective notwithstanding any subsequent marriage; or

(3) the testator provided for the spouse by transfer outside the will and the intent that the transfer be in lieu of a testamentary provision is shown by the testator's statements or is reasonably inferred from the amount of the transfer or other evidence.

(b) In satisfying the share provided by this section, devises made by the will to the testator's surviving spouse, if any, are applied first, and other devises, other than a devise to a child of the testator who was born before the testator married the surviving spouse and who is not a child of the surviving spouse or a devise or substitute gift under sections 2-603 or 2-604 to a descendant of such a child, abate as provided in section 3-902.

QUESTIONS AND NOTES

1. If H marries W some years after making his will leaving everything to his daughter by a previous marriage, under UPC §2-301 W is not entitled to an intestate share in H's estate. She must elect to take against the will, where her share may be less than an intestate share. Mongold v. Mayle, 452 S.E.2d 444 (W. Va. 1994) (interpreting UPC). On the other hand, if H had left his property by will to his alma mater, W would take an intestate share. What is the reason for this?

2. When a surviving spouse elects against a will, in many states the spouse is entitled to include nonprobate assets as part of the decedent's estate (called the "augmented estate" by the UPC). A spouse omitted from a will made before marriage is not able to reach nonprobate assets; her share is solely of the probate estate. See Estate of Allen, 16 Cal. Rptr. 2d 352 (App. 1993). Why is this? Why did the UPC revisers treat the situations differently?

If the surviving spouse is richer than the decedent spouse, the surviving spouse has no forced share under the 1990 UPC (see pages 448-450). But a richer surviving spouse omitted from a premarital will can take an intestate share. Why are the situations treated differently?

3. The failure of a lawyer to advise a client to execute a new will if the client wants to disinherit a recently married spouse has given rise to malpractice actions. In Heyer v. Flaig, 449 P.2d 161 (Cal. 1969), the client told her lawyer that she was planning to marry a man named Glen and she wished her estate to pass to her two daughters by a previous marriage. The lawyer drafted a will, which the client executed, leaving her estate to the daughters and not mentioning Glen. Subsequently she married Glen; then she died, and Glen claimed his intestate share as an omitted spouse. The daughters sued the lawyer for malpractice, claiming damages in the amount of Glen's intestate share. Upon demurrer, the court held the daughters stated a cause of action. "The intended beneficiary . . . suffers a great and irrevocable loss: he has nowhere to turn but to the attorney for compensation. Indeed, . . . unless the beneficiary can recover from the attorney the beneficiary suffers a wrong without a compensating remedy." Would reforming the will in *Heyer* to indicate that Glen was omitted intentionally be a better solution? Compare Erickson v. Erickson, excerpted at page 374.

Suppose that when the lawyer draws the will, the client has no plans to marry Glen and does not mention him to the lawyer. Four months after executing the will, the lawyer receives an invitation to the wedding of the client and Glen. Does the lawyer have a duty to advise the client of the effect of the marriage upon the client's will? See ABA, Model Code of Prof. Responsibility DR 2-104(A)(1) (1981), referring to ABA Op. 210 (1941): "It is our opinion that where the lawyer has no reason to believe that he has been supplanted by another lawyer, it is not only his right but it might even be his duty to advise his client of any change of fact or law which might defeat the client's testamentary purpose as expressed in the will."

SECTION B.   RIGHTS OF ISSUE OMITTED FROM THE WILL

1. Protection from Intentional Omission

a.   The Domestic Approach

In all states except Louisiana, a child or other descendant has no statutory protection against intentional disinheritance by a parent. There is no requirement that a testator leave any property to a child, not even the proverbial one dollar.[19]

19. At common law, a child omitted from his parent's will had no remedy. It may have been thought that it was necessary to leave the heir a shilling to disinherit him effectively, but Blackstone says that this

*"Everything I have, son, I have because your grandfather left
it to me. I see now that that was a bad thing."*

Indeed, it is extremely common for married testators to leave their entire estate to their surviving spouse, with their minor children receiving property only if the testator's spouse predeceases the testator.

Even though a parent has the power to disinherit children, unless the parent does so in favor of a surviving spouse, the parent should think twice or, better, three times, before exercising the power. The law does not favor cutting children out of the parent's estate when there is no surviving spouse. To this end, a number of doctrines have been flexibly used to protect children, with the consequence that disinheritance is almost always a risky affair. A will disinheriting a child virtually invites a will contest. As we saw in Chapter 3, "lack of testamentary capacity," "undue influence," and "fraud" are subtle and elastic concepts that judges and juries can use to rewrite the testator's distributive plan in order to

---

was an error. 2 William Blackstone, Commentaries *502. Blackstone says "cutting the heir off with a shilling" is traceable to a Roman law notion that the testator had lost his memory or mind unless he gave some legacy to each child.

"do justice." In contests by disinherited children, judges and juries are frequently influenced by their sympathies for the children. This is well known to practicing lawyers, who will often advise the devisees to agree to an out-of-court settlement with a disinherited child.

QUESTIONS AND NOTES

1. Would a forced share for children reduce the number of will contests? Professor Langbein suggests that "the American rule, by allowing liberal disinheritance of children, creates the type of plaintiff who is most prone to bring these actions." John H. Langbein, Book Review: Will Contests, 103 Yale L.J. 2039, 2042 (1994). Even so, he prefers "the American position of liberal testamentary freedom to disinherit children who turn out to be . . . disappointing and unsavory." Id. Do you?

2. *Louisiana*. The Louisiana forced share for children, which is derived from French law, is called a *legitime*. It protects against the disinheritance of children under 23, the mentally infirm, and the disabled. Prior to a constitutional amendment in 1995, the forced share extended to all children. See Katherine S. Spaht, Forced Heirship Changes: The Regrettable Revolution Completed, 57 La. L. Rev. 55 (1996); Forced Heirship Symposium, 43 Loy. L. Rev. 1 (1997). For an explication of how the Louisiana forced share is calculated, see 1 Max Nathan, Jr. & Carole Cukell Neff, Louisiana Estate Planning §13.2 (2002).

The Louisiana forced share for children is not absolute, however; it makes provision for disinheriting a child for "just cause," including:

> (1) The child has raised his hand to strike a parent, or has actually struck a parent; but a mere threat is not sufficient.
> (2) The child has been guilty, towards a parent, of cruel treatment, crime, or grievous injury. . . .
> (6) The child, being a minor, has married without the consent of the parent. . . .
> (8) The child, after attaining the age of majority and knowing how to contact the parent, has failed to communicate with the parent without just cause for a period of two years . . . . [La. Civ. Code Ann. §1621(A) (2004).]

The cause for disinheriting the child must have existed at the time of the will's execution. Id. at §1621(B).

b. A Look Abroad: Family Maintenance Statutes

Another way of providing support to both children and spouses is a discretionary system in which courts have the power to order distributions from the estate to the decedent's dependents based on their need and prevailing societal views of the morality of the decedent's estate plan. In 1900 New Zealand pioneered such an approach. England, Australia, and most Canadian provinces now have similar legislation.

Under the English law, which is representative, the decedent's property may be used to support those who were dependent upon the decedent during lifetime. Eligible dependents include the decedent's spouse, former spouse who has not remarried, children, and any other person who was being maintained by the decedent. See United Kingdom Inheritance (Provisions for Family and Dependants) Act 1975, §1(1). Note, then, that the rules examined in this subsection apply not only to children but to spouses as well. The decedent's spouse is entitled to a financial provision "as would be reasonable in all the circumstances for a husband or wife to receive, whether or not that provision is required for his or her maintenance." Id. §1(2)(a). Other eligible dependents such as children are entitled to receive such financial provision "as it would be reasonable in all the circumstances of the case for the applicant to receive for his maintenance." Id. §1(2)(b).

Accordingly, in England and the other Commonwealth jurisdictions, surviving spouses do not have a right to an elective share of their spouse's property. Instead, the surviving spouse, along with surviving children and other dependents, have a right to maintenance in an amount determined within the discretion of the court.

Lambeff v. Farmers Co-operative Executors & Trustees Ltd.

Supreme Court of South Australia, 1991
56 S.A.S.R. 323, 1991 WL 1121294

MATHESON, J. The plaintiff is the only daughter of George Lambeff who died at Ceduna on 23 March 1989, aged 63. She claims provision from his estate pursuant to the provisions of the Inheritance (Family Provision) Act 1972.

The last will and testament of the deceased was made on 14 March 1988 and probate was granted to the defendants on 15 November 1989. They were the executors named in the will. The second and third defendants were the only sons of the deceased. The will directed that upon payment of debts and funeral expenses the whole estate should be held upon trust for the two sons in equal shares absolutely. As at the date of swearing of the first affidavit of the trust manager of the first defendant, namely, 28 February 1990, the estimated value of the assets in the estate was $220,058.87. As at 24 December 1990, he deposed that the value of the net estate was $209,522.76. The major assets were a home unit at 15/17 MacFarlane Street, Glenelg North, valued at approximately $50,000, in which the deceased's former de facto wife, Barbara Lambeff, the mother of his two sons, lived, and a leasehold property at Ceduna, upon which there was an old stable, 18 powered caravan sites and a sand mine, and valued at $144,500. In addition, the deceased was the joint owner of a property at 13 Park Terrace, Ceduna with Barbara Lambeff, the capital value of which, according to the Valuer-General, was $120,000. The deceased lived with Barbara Lambeff from about 1956 to 1980 with several separations. She is not a party to these proceedings.

The deceased married the plaintiff's mother in Czechoslovakia on 28 June 1945 and the plaintiff was born there on 21 June 1946. The deceased, the plaintiff's mother and the plaintiff moved to Perth in the State of Western Australia in July 1950. The deceased and his wife separated in 1956, and in or about that year he commenced an association with Barbara Lambeff and moved to Ceduna where the deceased lived until his death. On 3 October 1957, the second defendant, Nicholas George Lambeff, was born and on 5 April 1961 the third defendant, Christopher Jordan Lambeff, was born. The deceased worked in Perth as a builder and continued so to work at Ceduna after setting up house there.

The plaintiff attended high school until the end of second year and then did a secretarial course at a technical college in Perth. Her mother married Leons Romanovskis in Perth on 29 December 1965. The plaintiff remained with her mother until October 1966, and then moved to Melbourne where she has lived and worked ever since. Her mother and her stepfather moved to Adelaide in about November 1974. At the time of her father's death, the plaintiff was employed by Scottish Amicable Life Assurance Society. Since the merger of that company with Colonial Mutual Life Assurance Society Ltd, the plaintiff has been working as a marketing officer. She proofreads marketing literature, assists with advertising and performs a variety of tasks within the marketing department. Her gross salary is $33,000. She has purchased a flat at 13 Hawkesburn Road, South Yarra. It cost $78,000 and the mortgage was $66,000. It will be repaid when she is 60. It was valued in January 1990 at $120,000. Her only other assets are clothes, furniture and jewellery. She is unmarried and has had no children.

It is convenient here to quote from the plaintiff's affidavit . . . :

> When I overcame my distress at being abandoned by my father in 1960, I wrote to him on three occasions, the first being in 1967, endeavouring to re-establish contact with him. I received no acknowledgment of the letters and interpreted this behaviour to be his total rejection of me. My letters were written at about five-yearly intervals. I believe the lack of response from my father at the time was due to the animosity he harboured towards my mother and/or the influence held over him by his de facto wife, Barbara.

. . . The defendant, Nicholas Lambeff, is 33 years of age. He has a wife and two children. They are expecting their third child. Nicholas Lambeff left school after attempting second year high school twice. He has four restricted building licences. He said that from about the age of 10 he worked for the deceased, helping him establish the caravan park, the largest asset of the estate. He said that any remuneration he received for his services was inadequate when compared with the number of hours he worked. He stated that he continued to help the deceased until his death because he had told him on many occasions that one day the caravan park would belong to him. He and his family have lived in the caravan park for about the last 15 years. He says that he and his wife have managed it since 1980, and for their livelihood they rely on the income earned from it and from some irregular contract work. His wife has no formal qualifications, but has assisted with the running of the caravan park and has worked as an assistant in a local chemist shop on a casual basis. They do not own any real estate. Their assets are worth approximately $27,500.

The defendant, Christopher Lambeff, is 30 years of age. He has a de facto wife and two children. He left school after failing fourth year high school, and has no qualifications. He also worked for his father from an early age in the caravan park. He has had various labouring jobs. His de facto wife has been a governess and a teacher's aide, but has not worked since the birth of their first child. They have no real estate. Their assets are worth approximately $30,350. They have been living at 13 Park Terrace, Ceduna, rent free, in the house now registered in the name of Barbara Lambeff. . . .

Section 7 of the Inheritance (Family Provision) Act states:

> (1) Where —
>   (a) a person has died domiciled in the State or owning real or personal property in the State; and
>   (b) by reason of his testamentary dispositions or the operation of the laws of intestacy or both, a person entitled to claim the benefit of this Act is left without adequate provision for his proper maintenance, education or advancement in life,
> the Court may in its discretion, upon application by or on behalf of a person so entitled, order that such provision as the Court thinks fit be made out of the estate of the deceased person for the maintenance, education or advancement of the person so entitled. . . .
>   (3) The Court may refuse to make an order in favour of any person on the ground that his character or conduct is such as, in the opinion of the Court, to disentitle him to the benefit of this Act, or for any other reason that the Court thinks sufficient. . . .

The plaintiff's case is that she was left without adequate provision for her proper advancement in life.

I was referred to the judgment of King, C.J., in Estate of Puckridge (1978) 20 S.A.S.R. 72. His Honour said (at 77):

> The words "advancement in life" have a wide meaning and application and there is nothing to confine the operation of the provision to an early period of life in the members of the family. In McCosker v. McCosker (1957), 97 C.L.R. 566, the expression was held to be wide enough to embrace the provision of capital for the poultry farming business of a claimant. The word "proper" is of considerable importance and means proper in all the circumstances of the case. The circumstances include the size of the estate, the needs of the applicants, the nearness or remoteness of the applicants' blood and personal relationship to the deceased, any special claims which the applicants may have on the bounty of the deceased, and competing claims of others.

In Bosch v. Perpetual Trustee Co. Ltd., [1938] A.C. 463 at 478-479, their Lordships said:

> . . . that in every case the court must place itself in the position of the testator and consider what he ought to have done in all the circumstances of the case, treating the testator for that purpose as a wise and just, rather than a fond and foolish, husband or father.

As Dixon, C.J., said in Blore v. Lang (1960), 104 C.L.R. 124 at 128: "Some moral claim to which a wise and just testator might be expected to respond must exist, but it may rise out of relationship." . . .

I agree . . . that there are now two totally separate family units. I also agree that upon the evidence the plaintiff has a secure, well-paid job, that she has a substantial equity in her flat and that she has no dependants. She has good prospects of benefiting from the estates of her mother and stepfather, although the poor health of her stepfather raises a question mark over that. The deceased's sons, on the other hand, have little in the way of assets and they have families to support. The estate is by no means large. They are, however, both young and fit.

It may well be that the plaintiff has established that she has a special claim upon the estate within the meaning of some of the earlier cases. I do not need to find one, because I do not think it is necessary to show such a claim on a statute worded as is the South Australian statute. . . .

The plaintiff was abandoned by the deceased at the age of 10, and had no support from him thereafter. She later made efforts to befriend her father. She has done nothing to disentitle herself. It is true that she has acquitted herself reasonably well in life without her father's support, but I think she would have done better with proper support for her advancement in life. I think her claim succeeds, but in all the circumstances the provision should be modest. I order that the defendants pay her a legacy of $20,000 out of the estate.

NOTES AND PROBLEM

1.   Professor Foster summarizes the debate over extending the family maintenance model of the English Commonwealth to the United States:

> Proponents laud the model's flexibility, which they claim allows estate distribution to be "tailored to individual need" and "evolving lifestyles." They also cite the "strong ethical appeal" of the family maintenance model. They praise this approach for exalting the moral principle that familial responsibility does not terminate at death. They stress that the model addresses ethical issues on an individual level as well. The family maintenance model authorizes courts to evaluate on a case-by-case basis the morality of both the decedent's dispositive scheme and the claims of survivors. Proponents argue that by promoting private support of dependents the model not only provides moral guidance but also performs a vital social welfare function. They conclude that the family maintenance model offers the optimal mechanism to secure meaningful protection of family members with the least intrusion on freedom of testation. Unlike the alternative foreign and U.S. entitlement-based systems, they argue, the family maintenance scheme "does not apply automatically" but rather comes into play only upon petition by qualifying "aggrieved claimants."
>
> For critics of the family maintenance model, judicial discretion is a "terrible price" to pay for improved support of dependents. They view the model as fundamentally unsuited to the U.S. environment. They claim adoption of its discretionary scheme would be ill-advised, even "frightening" given the peculiarities of the U.S. probate system—a system, they argue, that is comprised of multiple, local probate courts, staffed often by lay judges chosen on the basis of politics rather than merit. For opponents, the costs of a discretionary redistribution scheme are also unacceptable. They contend it would "promote litigation," increase "information and administrative costs," and "deplete estates." Critics also argue that the family maintenance model would introduce such complexity and unpredictability into the U.S. probate process that it would undermine estate planning and obstruct simple, orderly transfer of property rights. For some opponents, the model could even pose a threat to family harmony and privacy. It would encourage claimants to air "an enormous amount of a family's dirty laundry" to persuade a judge that the decedent's will disposition is unjust. Critics reject the model on theoretical as well as practical grounds. Despite proponents' claims to the contrary, critics conclude that the model's equitable redistribution scheme runs contrary to cherished American notions of testamentary freedom. Freedom of testation, they warn, "withers under the system of testator's family maintenance." [Frances Foster, Linking Support and Inheritance: A New Model from China, 1999 Wis. L. Rev. 1199, 1213-1215.]

What do you think?

2. For a thorough examination of the English system, comparing it with the UPC elective share and concluding that the UPC needs more flexibility in dealing with the needy surviving spouse, see Helene S. Shapo, "A Tale of Two Systems": Anglo-American Problems in the Modernization of Inheritance Legislation, 60 Tenn. L. Rev. 707 (1993). See also Ralph C. Brashier, Inheritance Law and the Evolving Family, 23-27, 108-109 (2004).

3. The American rule allowing testators to disinherit their children has been disapproved by several commentators. Some scholars recommend forced shares for children, such as Louisiana provides in some circumstances, while others suggest discretionary family maintenance systems, such as the English Commonwealth jurisdictions have chosen. Compare Deborah A. Batts, I Didn't Ask to Be Born: The American System of Disinheritance and a Proposal for Change in a System of Protected Inheritance, 41 Hastings L.J. 1197 (1990) (recommending forced share legislation for children), with Ronald Chester, Should American Children Be Protected Against Disinheritance?, 32 Real Prop., Prob. & Tr. J. 405 (1997) (recommending a Commonwealth family maintenance system). See also John H. Langbein & Lawrence W. Waggoner, Redesigning the Spouse's Forced Share, 22 Real Prop., Prob. & Tr. J. 303, 304-314 (1987); Mary Ann Glendon, Fixed Rules and Discretion in Contemporary Family Law and Succession Law, 60 Tul. L. Rev. 1165 (1986).

4. Suppose you are a lawyer in South Australia. *T*, a married man with assets worth $2 million, comes to your office and wants to leave half of his estate to charity, a quarter to his second wife *W2*, and the remaining quarter split between his two children from his first marriage. *T* explains that *W2* already has substantial assets and that his children both have good jobs and solid finances. *T* has heard about the family maintenance statute and wants you to provide an estate plan that will be hard for any of his dependents to challenge successfully. What do you advise?

2. Protection from Unintentional Omission

We turn now to pretermission statutes, designed to prevent the *unintentional* disinheritance of descendants. It was such a statute that induced Calvin Coolidge, noted for economy of language,[20] to add an opening phrase to his will—the

---

20. Many stories are told about Coolidge, who regularly slept 11 hours a day, including a 2- to 4-hour nap almost every afternoon. H.L. Mencken said that Coolidge's "chief feat" was "to sleep more and say less" than any other president. See Paul F. Boller, Jr., Presidential Anecdotes 234, 243-244 (rev. ed. 1986). Here are some of our favorite stories about "Silent Cal":

1. Once a society woman was seated next to President Coolidge at a formal dinner. She playfully opened her conversation by saying, "You must talk to me, Mr. Coolidge. I made a bet today that I could get more than two words out of you." Coolidge replied, "You lose." And she did.
2. "When Coolidge was Vice-President, his successor as Governor of Massachusetts, Channing Cox, paid him a visit. Cox asked how Coolidge had been able to see so many visitors a day when he was Governor, but always leave the office at 5:00 P.M., while Cox himself found he often left as late as 9:00 P.M. 'Why the difference?' he asked. 'You talk back,' said Coolidge."
3. Coolidge once explained to his successor, Herbert Hoover, how to deal with "long-winded visitors": "If you keep dead still they will run down in three or four minutes."
4. In 1933 when Dorothy Parker, *New Yorker* writer and Algonquin Roundtable regular, heard the news that President Coolidge had died suddenly, she quipped, "How can they tell?" [Id. at 235, 239-241.]

shortest will of any president of the United States. Coolidge's will read in its entirety:

"The White House"
Washington
Will of Calvin Coolidge of Northampton,
Hampshire County, Massachusetts

Not unmindful of my son John, I give all my estate both real and personal to my wife Grace Coolidge, in fee simple — Home at Washington, District of Columbia this twentieth day December, A.D. nineteen hundred and twenty six.

_____
                                        /s/ Calvin Coolidge

Signed by me on the date above in the presence of the testator and of each other as witnesses to said will and the signature thereof.

_____
                                        /s/ Everett Sanders

_____
                                        /s/ Edward T. Clark

_____
                                        /s/ Erwin C. Geisser

President Calvin Coolidge exercising
in the gym of the House of
Representatives, 1923

In an October 2000 survey of 78 prominent historians, law professors, and political scientists, Calvin Coolidge ranked 25th among American presidents, one place below Bill Clinton. Coolidge was among the more controversial presidents, with a substantial minority of scholars listing him as underrated. See James Lindgren & Steven G. Calabresi, Rating the Presidents of the United States, 1789-2000: A Survey of Scholars in Political Science, History, and Law, 18 Const. Comment. 583 (2001).

Azcunce v. Estate of Azcunce

Florida Court of Appeal,
Third District, 1991
586 So. 2d 1216

HUBBART, J.   The central issue presented by this appeal is whether a child who is born after the execution of her father's will but before the execution of a codicil to the said will is entitled to take a statutory share of her father's estate under Florida's pretermitted child statute — when the will and codicils fail to provide for such child and all the other statutory requirements for pretermitted-child status are otherwise satisfied. We hold that where inter alia the subject codicil expressly republishes the original will, as here, the testator's child who is living at the time the codicil is executed is not a pretermitted child within the meaning of the statute. We, accordingly, affirm the final order under review which denies the child herein a statutory share of her father's estate as a pretermitted child.

I

The facts of this case are entirely undisputed. On May 4, 1983, the testator René R. Azcunce executed a will which established a trust for the benefit of his surviving spouse and his then-born children: Lisette, Natalie, and Gabriel; the will contained no provision for after-born children. On August 8, 1983, and June 25, 1986, the testator executed two codicils which did not alter in any way this testamentary disposition and also made no provision for after-born children.

On March 14, 1984, the testator's daughter Patricia Azcunce was born — after the first codicil was executed, but before the second codicil was executed. The first codicil expressly republished all the terms of the original will; the second codicil expressly republished all the terms of the original will and first codicil.

On December 30, 1986, the testator, who was thirty-eight (38) years old, unexpectedly died of a heart attack — four months after executing the second codicil. After the will and codicils were admitted to probate, Patricia filed a petition seeking a statutory share of her father's estate as a pretermitted child; the trial court denied this petition. Patricia appeals.

II

The statute on which Patricia relies for a share of her father's estate provides:

> When a testator omits to provide in his will for any of his children *born or adopted after making the will* and the child has not received a part of the testator's property equivalent to a child's part by way of advancement, the child shall receive a share of the estate equal in value to that he would have received if the testator had died intestate, unless:
> (1) It appears from the will that the omission was intentional; or
> (2) The testator had one or more children when the will was executed and devised substantially all his estate to the other parent of the pretermitted child. . . . Section 732.302, Florida Statutes (1985) (emphasis added).

Without dispute, Patricia was a pretermitted child both at the time the testator's will and the first codicil thereto were executed, as, in each instance, the testator "omit[ted] to provide in his will [or codicil] for [Patricia who was] born . . . after . . . the will [or codicil was executed]"; moreover, Patricia at no time received a part of the testator's property by way of advancement, the will and first codicil do not expressly disinherit Patricia, and the testator did not substantially devise all of his estate to Patricia's mother. The question in this case is whether the testator's execution of the *second* codicil to the will *after* Patricia had been born destroyed her prior statutory status as a pretermitted child.

It is well settled in Florida that, as a general rule, the execution of a codicil to a will has the effect of republishing the prior will as of the date of the codicil. Waterbury v. Munn, 32 So. 2d 603 (Fla. 1947).[21] Although this is not an inflexible rule and must at times give way to a contrary intent of the testator, . . . it always applies where, as here, the codicil expressly adopts the terms of the prior will; this is so for the obvious reason that such a result comports with the express intent of the testator. See T. Atkinson, Law of Wills ch. 10 §91 (2d ed. 1953); 2 W. Bowe & D. Parker, Page on Wills §23.18 (1960); Evans, Testamentary Republication, 40 Harv. L. Rev. 71, 100-04 (1926).

III

Turning to the instant case, it is clear that the testator's second codicil republished the original will and first codicil because the second codicil expressly so states. This being so, Patricia's prior status as a pretermitted child was destroyed inasmuch as Patricia was alive when the second codicil was executed and was not, as required by Florida's pretermitted child statute, born after such codicil was made. Presumably, if the testator had wished to provide for Patricia, he would have done so in the second codicil as she had been born by that time; because he did not, Patricia was, in effect, disinherited, which the testator clearly had the power to do. Indeed, the result we reach herein is in full accord with the results reached by courts throughout the country based on identical circumstances. Young v. Williams, 116 S.E.2d 778 (N.C. 1960); Laborde v. First State Bank & Trust Co., 101 S.W.2d 389 (Tex. Civ. App. 1936); Gooch v. Gooch, 113 S.E. 873 (Va. 1922); Francis v. Marsh, 46 S.E. 573 (W. Va. 1904).

To avoid this inevitable result, Patricia argues that the will and two codicils are somehow ambiguous and that, accordingly, the court should have accepted the parol evidence adduced below that the testator intended to provide for Patricia; Patricia also urges that the will should have been voided because the draftsman made a "mistake" in failing to provide for Patricia in the second codicil. These arguments are unavailing. First, there is utterly no ambiguity in the subject will and codicils which would authorize the taking of parol evidence herein, and the trial court was entirely correct in rejecting same. Barnett First Nat'l Bank of Jacksonville v. Cobden, 393 So. 2d 78 (Fla. 5th DCA 1981). Second, the mistake of which Patricia complains amounts, at best, to the draftsman's alleged professional negligence in failing to apprise the testator of the need to expressly provide for Patricia in the second codicil; this is not the type of mistake which voids a will under Section 732.5165, Florida Statutes (1987). In re Mullins' Estate, 128 So. 2d 617 (Fla. 2d DCA 1961).

---

21. Although it is true that Waterbury v. Munn says, "The execution of a codicil has the effect of republishing the prior will as of the date of the codicil," it goes on to qualify that statement by adding that republication is "subject, of course, to the cardinal rule applicable to the construction of testamentary instruments, that the intention of the testator, if ascertainable, must prevail." 32 So. 2d at 606. See also Restatement (Third) of Property: Wills and Other Donative Transfers §3.4 (1999) (emphasis added): "A will is treated as if it were executed when its most recent codicil was executed, whether or not the codicil expressly republishes the prior will, *unless the effect of so treating it would be inconsistent with the testator's intent.*" — Eds.

For the above-stated reasons, the final order under review is, in all respects, Affirmed.

NOTES, QUESTIONS, AND PROBLEMS

1.   *Aftermath*. After the decision in *Azcunce*, Marta (Azcunce) Espinosa—on behalf of Patricia (the omitted child) and René's estate—brought a malpractice suit against the law firm that had prepared René's will and codicils. In the course of that litigation, the question arose whether either Patricia or the estate had standing to sue, which was eventually resolved by the Florida Supreme Court:

> An attorney's liability for negligence in the performance of his or her professional duties is limited to clients with whom the attorney shares privity of contract. In a legal context, the term "privity" is a word of art derived from the common law of contracts and used to describe the relationship of persons who are parties to a contract. To bring a legal malpractice action, the plaintiff must either be in privity with the attorney, wherein one party has a direct obligation to another, or, alternatively, the plaintiff must be an intended third-party beneficiary. In the instant case, Patricia Azcunce does not fit into either category of proper plaintiffs.
>
> In the area of will drafting, a limited exception to the strict privity requirement has been allowed where it can be demonstrated that the apparent intent of the client in engaging the services of the lawyer was to benefit a third party. Because the client is no longer alive and is unable to testify, the task of identifying those persons who are intended third-party beneficiaries causes an evidentiary problem closely akin to the problem of determining the client's general testamentary intent. To minimize such evidentiary problems, the will was designed as a legal document that affords people a clear opportunity to express the way in which they desire to have their property distributed upon death. To the greatest extent possible, courts and personal representatives are obligated to honor the testator's intent in conformity with the contents of the will.
>
> If extrinsic evidence is admitted to explain testamentary intent, as recommended by the petitioners, the risk of misinterpreting the testator's intent increases dramatically. Furthermore, admitting extrinsic evidence heightens the tendency to manufacture false evidence that cannot be rebutted due to the unavailability of the testator. For these reasons, we adhere to the rule that standing in legal malpractice actions is limited to those who can show that the testator's intent as expressed in the will is frustrated by the negligence of the testator's attorney. . . . Because Patricia cannot be described as one in privity with the attorney or as an intended third-party beneficiary, a lawsuit alleging professional malpractice cannot be brought on her behalf.
>
> René's estate, however, stands in the shoes of the testator and clearly satisfies the privity requirement. Therefore, we agree with the district court's decision that the estate may maintain a legal malpractice action against Roskin for any acts of professional negligence committed by him during his representation of René. [Espinosa v. Sparber, Shevin, Shapo, Rosen & Heilbronner, 612 So. 2d 1378, 1379-1380 (Fla. 1993).]

A few states adhere to the old rule barring malpractice suits unless there is privity between the plaintiff and the lawyer. Most states allow any person who was an intended beneficiary of the lawyer-client contract to sue. See Simpson v. Calivas, page 49. In the states that have repudiated the privity rule, the question arises, who qualifies as an intended beneficiary? In most the answer is anyone who can show by competent evidence that he or she was an intended beneficiary of the testator. In a minority of states that includes Florida, however, the plaintiff's status as an intended beneficiary must be clear from the face of the will. As the court in *Simpson* explained, under this approach "a beneficiary whose interest violated the rule against perpetuities would have a cause of action against the drafting attorney, but a beneficiary whose interest was omitted by a drafting error would not." Thus, because Patricia was omitted from the will, she lacked standing to sue her father's lawyer.

The testator's personal representative typically has standing to sue because the estate is the successor in interest to the testator; there is no privity problem. But there is a problem in proving damages to the testator's estate. Although the Florida Supreme Court did not reach this issue, the district court of appeals had determined that, even if the estate proved malpractice, its damages were at most the fees that René paid the defendant law firm for drafting his will and codicils and the attorney's fees and expenses that the estate incurred in defending against Patricia's unsuccessful suit as a pretermitted child. The real pecuniary injury was suffered by Patricia, who is not allowed to maintain a suit.

Sparber, Shevin, Shapo, Rosen & Heilbronner, the law firm that had represented René Azcunce and was the defendant in the malpractice suit, was dissolved in 1988.

2.   In the district court of appeal in the *Azcunce* and *Espinosa* cases, Judge Levy concurred in the result, which he felt was compelled by Florida law. Nonetheless, he thought Patricia was done a terrible injustice. In his opinion in the *Espinosa* case, he wrote:

> Clearly, in the instant case, the testator's intent is not "expressed in the will." That is exactly the problem! The very essence of Patricia's complaint, as carried forward in the action filed on her behalf against the draftsman of the second codicil, is that the testator's intent was not reflected in the face of the will and, knowing that, the draftsman of the second codicil, acting as the testator's attorney, allowed the testator to sign the second codicil knowing that it specifically republished the testator's original will and first codicil, thereby eliminating Patricia's chances to be protected as a pretermitted child as provided for in Section 732.302, Florida Statutes (1985).
>
> Accordingly, Patricia is relegated to the never-never land of the ultimate in circuitous reasoning. Namely, Patricia would appear to have a colorable claim against the draftsman of the second codicil for not either advising her father of the legal consequences of signing the second codicil (to-wit: that Patricia would lose her status as a pretermitted child) or providing for her in the second codicil, or some other such document, so as to give life and vitality to her father's (the testator's) wishes. However, according to Florida law, she cannot sue the draftsman of the second codicil for leaving her name out of the second codicil because, wonder of wonders, her name is not mentioned in the second codicil. . . .
>
> In view of the foregoing, one must wonder as to who will have the unenviable task of trying to convince Patricia that, according to the case law of the State of Florida, the Constitution of this State requires that there be a remedy for every wrong. If there ever was a case where a person was wronged, but allowed to fall through a crack in the legal system, this is the case. However, in this case it was not a crack, but rather, a monumental abyss. [Espinosa v. Sparber, Shevin, Shapo, Rosen & Heilbronner, 586 So. 2d 1221, 1227-1228 (Fla. App. 1991) (Levy J., concurring).]

The Florida Supreme Court in *Espinosa* assumed that the lawyer's client is the father of the family, René. Why is not the client the whole family? See Teresa S. Collett, The Ethics of Intergenerational Representation, 62 Fordham L. Rev. 1453 (1994).

Besides suing for a pretermitted child's share and for malpractice, what other remedy might Patricia have? Does she have a claim against her father's lawyer for tortious interference with her expectancy (page 194)? If Patricia sues the executor of René's estate as a pretermitted child, and the executor settles her claim for 75 cents on the dollar, can the executor recover this amount as damages from the lawyer?

Is Patricia entitled to have a constructive trust imposed on the will devisees to prevent unjust enrichment by the negligent act of the lawyer? In Pope v. Garrett, 211 S.W.2d 559 (Tex. 1948), page 193, the court imposed a constructive trust on innocent heirs when the testator was forcefully prevented by some wrongdoing heirs from executing a will leaving his property to the plaintiff. Can a constructive trust be imposed on innocent parties who profit by the negligence of a lawyer? Compare In re Estate of Tolin, 622 So. 2d 988 (Fla. 1993), page 258, where the court imposed a constructive trust when the testator tore up a photocopy of his will, believing, on the mistaken advice of a retired lawyer, that the act revoked his will.

3.   *Guardians ad litem.* In the probate court litigation, Patricia's mother and adult sibling consented to Patricia's receiving a share as a pretermitted child. Because her other siblings were minors, however, the court appointed a guardian ad litem to protect their interests, and the guardian opposed Patricia's petition. In a footnote in the malpractice litigation, the Florida Supreme Court had this to say about that decision:

> We are not privy to the factors that the guardian ad litem considered in deciding not to consent to Patricia's classification as a pretermitted child, a decision that deprived Patricia of a share in the estate and ultimately led to costly litigation. We hope, however, that a guardian evaluating the facts of this case would not focus strictly on the financial consequences for the child, but would also consider such important factors as family harmony and stability. [Espinosa v. Sparber, Shevin, Shapo, Rosen & Heilbronner, 612 So. 2d 1378, 1379 n.1 (Fla. 1993).]

Why was the guardian ad litem unwilling to consider the interests of the entire family? By focusing narrowly on the financial consequences for the other children, did the guardian in fact act in their best interests? See generally Martin D. Begleiter, The Guardian ad Litem in Estate Proceedings, 20 Willamette L. Rev. 643 (1984).

4.   In McAbee v. Edwards, 340 So. 2d 1167 (Fla. App. 1976), the court held the lawyer liable for malpractice on the following facts: Testator made a will leaving everything to her daughter and then subsequently remarried. After remarriage, she consulted a lawyer to make sure that her daughter remained the sole beneficiary of her estate. The lawyer assured the testator that no change in her will was necessary to effect this intention. Upon the testator's death, her second husband claimed and was awarded an intestate share as an omitted spouse. The court held the lawyer liable to the daughter for malpractice.

Is the *Espinosa* case consistent with McAbee v. Edwards?

Uniform Probate Code (1990, as amended 1993)

§2-302.   Omitted Children

(a) Except as provided in subsection (b), if a testator fails to provide in his [or her] will for any of his [or her] children born or adopted after the execution of the will, the omitted after-born or after-adopted child receives a share in the estate as follows:

(1) If the testator had no child living when he [or she] executed the will, an omitted after-born or after-adopted child receives a share in the estate equal in value to that which the child would have received had the testator died intestate,

unless the will devised all or substantially all of the estate to the other parent of the omitted child and that other parent survives the testator and is entitled to take under the will.

(2) If the testator had one or more children living when he [or she] executed the will, and the will devised property or an interest in property to one or more of the then-living children, an omitted after-born or after-adopted child is entitled to share in the testator's estate as follows:

(i) The portion of the testator's estate in which the omitted after-born or after-adopted child is entitled to share is limited to devises made to the testator's then-living children under the will.

(ii) The omitted after-born or after-adopted child is entitled to receive the share of the testator's estate, as limited in subparagraph (i), that the child would have received had the testator included all omitted after-born and after-adopted children with the children to whom devises were made under the will and had given an equal share of the estate to each child.

(iii) To the extent feasible, the interest granted an omitted after-born or after-adopted child under this section must be of the same character, whether equitable or legal, present or future, as that devised to the testator's then-living children under the will.

(iv) In satisfying a share provided by this paragraph, devises to the testator's children who were living when the will was executed abate ratably. In abating the devises of the then-living children, the court shall preserve to the maximum extent possible the character of the testamentary plan adopted by the testator.

(b) Neither subsection (a)(1) nor subsection (a)(2) applies if:

(1) it appears from the will that the omission was intentional; or

(2) the testator provided for the omitted after-born or after-adopted child by transfer outside the will and the intent that the transfer be in lieu of a testamentary provision is shown by the testator's statements or is reasonably inferred from the amount of the transfer or other evidence.

(c) If at the time of execution of the will the testator fails to provide in his [or her] will for a living child solely because he [or she] believes the child to be dead, the child is entitled to share in the estate as if the child were an omitted after-born or after-adopted child.

(d) In satisfying a share provided by subsection (a)(1), devises made by the will abate under Section 3-902.

NOTES, PROBLEMS, AND QUESTIONS

1. Pretermitted child statutes, which have been enacted in almost all states, follow one of two patterns. Some statutes protect only children born (or adopted) after execution of the will. See UPC §2-302, supra. Other statutes operate in favor of children alive when the will was executed as well as afterborns. Under these latter statutes, the failure to name all of the testator's living children in the will invites a challenge under the pretermitted child statute.

Pretermitted heir statutes can also be classified as "Missouri" type or "Massachusetts" type. Under a Missouri-type statute, the statute usually is drawn to benefit children "not named or provided for" in the will. Hence, it must appear from the will itself that omission of the child or other heir was intentional. Extrinsic evidence of intent is not admissible. Under a Massachusetts-type statute, the child takes "unless it appears that such omission was intentional and not occasioned by any mistake." Extrinsic evidence is admitted to show both the presence or absence of intent to disinherit. See Annot., 88 A.L.R.2d 616 (1963, rev. 2002).

UPC §2-302 does not permit extrinsic evidence to show that the omission was intentional; such intent must be shown by the will itself. However, if a testator made nonprobate transfers to the omitted child, the testator's intent that these transfers bar the child from claiming a pretermitted share can be shown by the testator's statements or other extrinsic evidence.

2.   In Azcunce v. Estate of Azcunce, if René had not made the second codicil to his will and Patricia had been pretermitted, Patricia would have taken her intestate share. What would be her share under UPC §2-302 (1990)? On the distortions pretermission statutes can cause in estate plans, see Jan E. Rein, A More Rational System for the Protection of Family Members Against Disinheritance, 15 Gonz. L. Rev. 11 (1979).

3.   When T executes her will, she has two living children, A and B. Her will devises $7,500 to each child. After T executes her will she has another child, C. T dies. To what amount is C entitled under UPC §2-302 (1990)? The official comment says C is entitled to $5,000 taken one-half from A's devise (reducing it to $5,000) and one-half from B's. Suppose that T had devised $10,000 to A and $5,000 to B. What would C take and where would it come from?

4.   In a jurisdiction where the pretermission statute includes children born before the execution of the will, what provision would you recommend including in a will so as to cut out a child born out of wedlock without mentioning the child by name or suggesting his existence? Courts have been sticklers in requiring the testator to indicate clearly an intention to disinherit such a child, either by express words or by necessary implication. For example, in Estate of Robbins, 756 A.2d 602 (N.H. 2000), the will provided: "Except as otherwise expressly provided by this will, I intentionally make no provisions for the benefit of any other heir of mine." The court held that this language did not disinherit a natural and an adopted child. See also Estate of Torregano, 352 P.2d 505 (Cal. 1960), holding a bequest of $1 to any person asserting any claim "by virtue of relationship or otherwise" insufficient to bar an omitted child.

Would a person who wants to disinherit a child born out of wedlock be wise to transfer his assets into a revocable inter vivos trust that does not provide for, or mention, the child?

In re Estate of Laura
Supreme Court of New Hampshire, 1997
141 N.H. 628, 690 A.2d 1011

THAYER, J.   The testator, Edward R. Laura, Sr., died on August 23, 1990. The petitioners, two generations of the testator's heirs who were excluded from his will, appeal a decision of the Rockingham County Probate Court (Maher, J.), approving the order of the Master (Gerald Taube, Esq.), that barred them from inheriting any portion of the testator's estate. On appeal, the petitioners argue that the probate court erred in . . . ruling that the testator's great-grandchildren were not pretermitted heirs under RSA 551:10 (1974). . . . We affirm. . . .

The record reveals the following facts. The testator had three children. Two children, Edward R. Laura, Jr. and Shirley Chicoine, survived him. Shirley and Edward each have three children. The testator's third child, Jo Ann Laura, died in 1974. She was survived by two children, Richard Chicoine and Neil F. Chicoine, Jr. Neil died in 1988 and is survived by two children, Cecilia Chicoine and Neil F. Chicoine, III, the testator's great-grandchildren. Richard, acting on behalf of himself and the testator's great-grandchildren, and Edward are the petitioners here.

Sometime prior to September 17, 1984, the testator hired an attorney to draft his will. The will was executed on September 26, 1984. It provided that the testator's estate would pass to his daughter, Shirley, who was also designated as the executrix of his estate. In addition, the will named the testator's deceased daughter, Jo Ann, and explicitly named his son, Edward, and his grandchildren, Richard and Neil, in a paragraph designed to disinherit them. Paragraph seven of the will provided:

> I have intentionally omitted to provide in this Will for any heirs at law, next of kin, or relatives of mine, by blood, marriage or adoption, specifically but not limited to my son, Edward and my grandchildren, Richard and Neil, except as aforesaid, and such omissions are not occasioned by accident or mistake.

The will did not mention the testator's two great-grandchildren. Cecilia Chicoine was born one day before the will was executed; Neil F. Chicoine, III was not born until two years after the will was executed.

In 1990, the testator attempted to execute a codicil to his will. The codicil would have altered the disposition of his estate, giving three equal shares to Edward, Shirley, and Richard, and equal shares to Shirley's and Edward's respective children. The parties agree, however, that the codicil was not properly witnessed and therefore did not become effective.

Following the testator's death, his 1984 will was presented to the probate court. The will was proved and allowed, and Shirley was appointed executrix on September 30, 1990. In 1991, Richard, on behalf of himself and the testator's great-grandchildren, and Edward petitioned the probate court to reexamine the 1984 will. They challenged the will on [the ground that] . . . the testator's great-grandchildren were entitled to an intestate share of his estate because they qualified as pretermitted heirs under RSA 551:10.

. . . The master . . . ruled that the testator's great-grandchildren were not pretermitted heirs under RSA 551:10. . . . The probate court adopted each of the master's findings. . . .

RSA 551:10 protects a testator's heirs against unintentional omission from the testator's will. It provides:

> Every child born after the decease of the testator, and every child or issue of a child of the deceased not named or referred to in his will, and who is not a devisee or legatee, shall be entitled to the same portion of the estate, real and personal, as he would be if the deceased were intestate.

The statute creates a rule of law that the omission of a child or issue of a child from a will is accidental "unless there is evidence in the will itself that the omission was intentional." In re Estate of MacKay, 433 A.2d 1289, 1290 (N.H. 1981). "The statute . . . is not a limitation on the power to make testamentary dispositions but rather is an attempt to effectuate a testator's presumed intent. It prevents forgetfulness, not disinheritance." Royce v. Estate of Denby, 379 A.2d 1256, 1258 (N.H. 1977).

Relying on the statute, the petitioners argue that the testator's great-grandchildren were not named or referred to in the testator's will and therefore are entitled to an intestate share of his estate. They contend that the testator's decision to specifically name Neil F. Chicoine, Jr., the father of the petitioning great-grandchildren, in paragraph seven of the will was irrelevant in determining whether they are pretermitted heirs under RSA 551:10. According to the petitioners, testators must name or refer to their children (or in this case, grandchildren) as well as the issue of their children (or in this case, great-grandchildren) in their wills; otherwise any issue not named or referred to is pretermitted. We disagree.

We hold that a testator who specifically names one heir in an effort to disinherit him has "referred to" the issue of that heir for purposes of the statute. If a testator has a predeceased child who is neither named, referred to, nor a devisee or legatee under the testator's will, then the naming of the next degree of issue in the line of descent will successfully preclude issue more removed from the testator from invoking the statute. On the other hand, where an issue of a child is named, referred to, or a devisee or legatee, but the testator's child is neither named, referred to, nor a devisee or legatee, then the testator's child is pretermitted, provided the child has not predeceased the testator. See Gage v. Gage, 29 N.H. 533, 543 (1854). Our holding is supported by our case law, in which we have acknowledged that a testator's reference to an heir "need not be direct" to exclude the heir under RSA 551:10.

Here, the testator specifically named Neil Chicoine, Jr., the father of the great-grandchildren, in paragraph seven of his will. As a result, the testator "referred to" the descendant great-grandchildren for purposes of the pretermitted heir statute.

Furthermore, the testator named his daughter, Jo Ann—the grandmother of petitioners Cecilia and Neil—in his will. When a testator's child has been named, referred to, or is a devisee or legatee under the will, the child's issue cannot invoke the statute even if the issue are neither named, referred to, nor devisees or legatees under the will. Accordingly, the testator's great-grandchildren were not pretermitted heirs under RSA 551:10 and were not entitled to collect an intestate share of his estate.

ESTATE OF TRELOAR, 859 A.2d 1162 (N.H. 2004): Josiah James Treloar's grandchildren, Andrew and Peter Merrill, sought a share of Treloar's estate as pretermitted heirs. Treloar's 1998 will made no mention of James or Peter. Nor did the 1998 will make direct mention of their mother Evelyn, who was Treloar's daughter. Treloar's earlier 1986 will had provided for Evelyn, but when she predeceased Treloar in 1998, he revised his will and had her removed.

Trealor's 1998 will did mention Andrew and Peter's father: "I hereby nominate and so far as I legally may appoint as Executor of this will, my son-in-law, Leon Merrill of Concord, New Hampshire." Disputing Andrew and Peter's claim to be pretermitted heirs, William Hall, the court-appointed executor of Trealor's estate, argued that Evelyn was thus mentioned indirectly. The main question before the court was whether, under Estate of Laura, supra, this indirect reference to Evelyn in the 1998 will was sufficient to preclude Andrew and Peter's claim as pretermitted heirs:

> The petitioner . . . argues that the reference to Leon as the testator's "son-in-law" showed that he had Evelyn in mind when he drafted the 1998 will. The petitioner likens this case to Boucher v. Lizotte, 161 A. 213, 213 (N.H. 1932). We find *Boucher* factually distinguishable. In *Boucher*, the testatrix died leaving three children. She bequeathed $500 to "Marianna Lizotte, wife of my son Alphonse Lizotte." We held that the use of the son's name in defining a gift to his family was a sufficient reference to the son to disinherit him. By contrast, in this case, the testator did not use his daughter's name. Nor did he use the phrase "son-in-law" in a bequest. Rather, he used the phrase "son-in-law" to identify the individual he wished to appoint as his executor.

Having found that neither Evelyn nor her children, Peter and Andrew Merrill, were mentioned in Treloar's 1998 will, the court held that Andrew and Peter were pretermitted grandchildren and thus were entitled to a share of Treloar's estate.

QUESTION AND NOTE

1. With Estate of Treloar, contrast Estate of Laura and Boucher v. Lizotte (discussed in *Treloar*). In *Treloar*, the testator omitted two grandchildren but named their father, the testator's son-in-law, as executor. The court held that this indirect reference to their mother was insufficient to preclude application of the pretermission statute to the grandchildren. In *Boucher*, on the other hand, the testator made a bequest to "Marianna Lizotte, wife of my son Alphonse Lizotte." The court held that this reference to the son was sufficient to preclude application of the pretermitted child statute to the testator's grandchildren. While the mention in *Treloar* is indeed less specific than in *Boucher*, is this distinction meaningful for determining whether the testators' failure to provide shares for their grandchildren was a mistake? Is not rectifying a mistaken omission the purpose of the pretermission statutes? Does it matter that in *Laura* there was a clause that explicitly disinherited the ancestor of the claimant?

2. Suppose you are in a state like New Hampshire, which has a broad pretermission statute that covers not just children but also the issue of children. Must you rewrite your will every time a new grandchild or great-grandchild is born? The answer is No. In most states, pretermission can be avoided by providing for contingent shares for issue with representation. None of your descendants would be pretermitted if you devise the residue of your estate "to my husband, *H*, if he survives me by 90 days, or if not, to such of my issue as survive me by 90 days, per stirpes."[22] You need not mention your descendants by name; you simply make them contingent takers *if* their parents should predecease you.

---

22. *Caution:* You would still need additional language here or elsewhere in the will to preclude the application of an antilapse statute (page 392) and to define which version of per stirpes is intended (pages 653-655) to ensure that the testator's wishes are followed.

8

TRUSTS: CREATION AND CHARACTERISTICS

> Of all the exploits of Equity the largest and the most
> important is the invention and development of the Trust. . . .
> This perhaps forms the most distinctive achievement of
> English lawyers. It seems to us almost essential to civilization,
> and yet there is nothing quite like it in foreign law.

> FREDERIC W. MAITLAND
> *Equity: A Course of Lectures* 23
> (*John Brunyate* 2d ed. 1936)

SECTION A. INTRODUCTION

1. Background

A trust is, generally speaking, a device whereby a trustee manages property as a fiduciary for one or more beneficiaries. The trustee holds legal title to the property and, in the usual trust, can sell the trust property and replace it with property thought more desirable. The beneficiaries hold equitable title and, in the usual trust, are entitled to payments from the trust income and sometimes from the trust corpus too.

The trust developed out of the historical circumstance that England had separate courts of law and equity. The ancestor of the modern trust is the medieval *use* (from a corruption of the Latin word *opus*, meaning benefit). Legal historians have traced the use back to the middle of the thirteenth century when the Franciscan friars came to England. Because the friars were forbidden to own any sort of property, pious benefactors conveyed land to suitable persons in the neighborhood to hold to the use of the friars. Thus *O*, owner of Blackacre, would enfeoff *A* and his heirs to hold Blackacre *to the use of* the friars. By this transfer, the legal fee simple passed to the *feoffee to uses, A*, who held it for the benefit of the *cestui que use*, the mendicant order. The cestui que use went into possession of Blackacre, with the legal title being held by *A*.

Although there is some evidence that ecclesiastical courts enforced early uses, in the beginning uses were not enforceable in the civil courts. Since no common law form of action existed whereby the cestui could bring an action against the feoffee, the law courts — paralyzed by the rigidity of their procedures — offered no relief. In time, this state of affairs appeared to be unconscionable to the chancellor, the "keeper of the king's conscience," and early in the fifteenth century the chancellor began to compel feoffees to uses to perform as they had promised. Once the chancellor enforced uses, thus removing the risk of faithless feoffees, uses grew rapidly. Landowners found that all sorts of benefits could be accomplished by putting legal title in a feoffee to uses. For example, prior to the Statute of Wills in 1540, land could not be devised by will; it descended to the eldest son. Landowners seeking relief from forced primogeniture turned to the use and found the desired flexibility there. *O* could enfeoff *A* and his heirs to the use of *O* during *O*'s lifetime and then to the use of such persons as *O* might appoint by will. The chancellor enforced the use in favor of *O*'s devisees. Particularly because of its success in evading feudal death taxes (known as feudal incidents), the use became universally popular. It was the use of the use to avoid taxes that brought on the Statute of Uses.

Searching for a way to restore his feudal incidents and replenish his treasury, Henry VIII determined to abolish the use. Henry interested himself personally in a lawsuit in the courts, which resulted in a decision putting into doubt the legality of the use generally. Fearing that uses might become unenforceable, with drastic consequences for the cestuis, Parliament, on Henry's urging, reluctantly enacted the Statute of Uses in 1535, which became effective in 1536. By this statute, uses were not made illegal. On the contrary, legal title was taken away from the feoffee to uses and given to the cestui que use. In the words of the time, the use was executed, that is, converted into a legal interest. The former cestuis — now clothed with legal title — could breathe easy, but they had to pay the king his due upon death.

Although the purpose of the Statute of Uses was to abolish uses, imaginative lawyers and judges found holes in the statute. Courts held that the statute did not operate if the feoffee to uses (trustee in modern language) was given *active duties* to perform. An active trust — imposing a duty on the trustee to deal with the property in a special manner — was regarded as quite different from the old use, where the feoffee merely held legal title and allowed the cestui que use himself to take the profits from the land. This reading of the statute permitted chancery to reassert its jurisdiction over uses under the name of trust and to develop the modern trust, wherein the trustee has legal title and the responsibilities of management and the beneficiaries have equitable title and the benefits flowing from the trustee's management.[1]

The trust has thus evolved into a flexible tool that can be used for purposes "as unlimited as the imagination of lawyers." Austin W. Scott, Trusts §1, at 2 (William F. Fratcher 4th ed. 1987). These diverse purposes range from a simple estate plan to provide for a surviving spouse and children in accordance with their respective needs (here the trust is a vehicle for gratuitous wealth transfer), to commercial enterprises such as mutual funds, pensions, and various structured finance

---

1. For the history of the development of the trust, see Frederic W. Maitland, Equity: A Course of Lectures (John Brunyate 2d ed. 1936). See also Gregory S. Alexander, The Transformation of Trusts as a Legal Category, 1800-1914, 5 Law & Hist. Rev. 303 (1987); John H. Langbein, The Contractarian Basis of the Law of Trusts, 105 Yale L.J. 625 (1995).

Austin Wakeman Scott
Professor, Harvard Law School,
1909-1961

Professor Scott, together with Professor George G. Bogert of the University of Chicago, molded the modern law of trusts in this country. Their influential treatises on the law of trusts, constantly cited by courts, are the starting point for the analysis of questions of trust law.

transactions (here the trust is a form of business organization). Because of its extraordinary flexibility, in the practice of law you will find many uses for the trust, particularly in situations where there are many beneficiaries or owners and it is desirable to avoid fragmented management of the property. The crucial point is that the trust provides managerial intermediation. Because the trustee manages the property on behalf of the beneficiary, the trust "separate[s] the benefits of ownership from the burdens of ownership." Id.

Although the *business trust* has considerable transactional and capital markets importance, our present focus — and the primary focus of the remainder of this book — is on the *private express trust* created *gratuitously* for the benefit of individual beneficiaries. We do, however, say a few words about the commercial uses of the trust at pages 496-498. Trusts for *charitable purposes* are the subject of Chapter 12.

The private express trust can be used to effect numerous forms of gratuitous wealth transfer. We introduce you here to five common uses of trusts in estate planning:

Case 1. Revocable trust. O declares herself trustee of property to pay the income to O for life, then on O's death to pay the principal to O's children. O retains the power to revoke the trust. A revocable trust avoids the delays, costs, and publicity of probate. The revocable trust has other advantages discussed at pages 316-322.

Case 2. Testamentary marital trust. The federal estate tax law permits a marital deduction for property given to the surviving spouse. The deduction is allowed for a life estate given to the spouse (see pages 902-905). To get the deduction, H devises property to X in trust to pay the income to W for her life, and on her death to pay the principal to H's children. This trust qualifies for the marital deduction. No estate taxes are payable at H's death; they are postponed until W's death. This trust may be particularly useful when W needs professional money management or is the stepparent of H's children and might not bequeath the property to them if left to her outright.

Case 3. Trust for incompetent person. O's son A is mentally or physically impaired and is unable to manage his property. O transfers property to X in trust to pay the income to *A* for life, remainder to *A*'s issue, and if *A* dies without issue to his sister *B*.

Case 4. Trust for minor. The federal gift tax law allows a tax-free gift of $11,000 per year to a donee. A gift to a minor creates special problems inasmuch as the minor is legally unable to manage her property. To permit annual tax-free gifts of $11,000 to his minor daughter *A*, *O* creates a trust to use the income and principal for the benefit of *A* before she reaches 21, and to pay *A* the principal when she reaches 21. Every year *O* can make a tax-free gift of $11,000 to the trustee for *A* (see page 858).

Case 5. Discretionary trust. *T* devises property to *X* in trust. The trust provides that the trustee in its sole and absolute discretion may pay the income or principal to *A*, or for *A*'s benefit, as the trustee may see fit. Or the trustee may be given discretion to pay income to any one or more of a class of persons, such as *A* and her issue. Discretionary trusts are useful in lessening the tax burden on family wealth by distributing income to the members of the family in the lowest tax brackets. Discretionary trusts are also useful in preventing creditors of the beneficiary — including ex-spouses with alimony or child support judgments, Uncle Sam with an unpaid tax bill, and Medicaid authorities deciding whether the trust is a resource of the trust beneficiary — from reaching the income or principal of the trust.

These skeletal examples barely scratch the surface of the myriad donative and estate planning uses to which trusts are amenable.

NOTE: FOREIGN TRUST LAW

In the epigraph that opens this chapter, the great scholar of the common law Frederic W. Maitland asserts that "there is nothing quite like [the trust] in foreign law." This refrain, that the trust is uniquely a creature of the common law, is often repeated. Given the trust's manifest usefulness in commercial transactions and gratuitous transfers, however, one should approach the claim of uniqueness with some skepticism. If the trust is so useful, would not other legal systems have developed something similar? The answer is Yes. A trust-like device — the *fideicommissum* — existed in Roman law. The English judges who developed the trust were influenced by the German *treuhand*. In Hindu law, one finds a trust-like device called *benami.* In Islamic law one finds the *waqf.* A useful summary, plus references to apposite scholarly discussion, may be found in 1 Austin W. Scott, Trusts §1.9 (William F. Fratcher 4th ed. 1987). See also David Johnston, The Roman Law of Trusts (1988); Itinera Fiduciae: Trust and Treuhand in Historical Perspective (Richard Helmholz & Richard Zimmermann eds., 1998); Gilbert Paul Verbit, The Origins of the Trust (2002).

Today there is a Japanese trust law, and trusts or trust-like devices are found in a host of other countries — including some that follow the civil law tradition. See Makoto Arai, The Law of Trusts and the Development of Trust Business in Japan, *in* Modern International Developments in Trust Law 63 (David Hayton ed., 1999); Maurizio Lupoi, Trusts: A Comparative Study (Simon Dix trans., 2000). In a similar vein, the 1985 Hague Convention on the Law Applicable to Trusts and on Their Recognition was established to provide guidance on the recognition of, and choice of law for, trusts in jurisdictions that lack a native trust law. See Emmanuel Gaillard & Donald T. Trautman, Trusts in Non-Trust

Countries: Conflicts of Laws and the Hague Convention on Trusts, 35 Am. J. Comp. L. 307 (1987).

2. The Parties to a Trust

A trust ordinarily involves at least three parties: the settlor, the trustee, and one or more beneficiaries. But three different persons are not necessary for a trust. One person can wear two, or even all three, hats.

a. The Settlor

The person who creates a trust is the *settlor* (the word comes from our ancestors, who said the person makes a settlement in trust) or *trustor*. The trust may be created during the settlor's life, in which case it is an *inter vivos* trust. Or it may be created by will, in which case it is a *testamentary* trust. An inter vivos trust may be created either by a *declaration of trust* (in which the settlor declares that he holds certain property in trust) or by a *deed of trust* (in which the settlor transfers property to another person as trustee).

Case 1, above, is an illustration of a declaration of trust. As we have seen in Chapter 5, the declaration of trust is often used as a will substitute. Under a declaration of trust, the settlor is the trustee. Unlike an outright gift of property, however, which requires that the donor deliver the property or execute a deed of gift, a declaration of trust of personal property requires neither delivery nor a deed of gift. All that is necessary is that the donor manifest an intention to hold the property in trust. Although a declaration of trust of personal property may be oral, if the trust is to be funded with real property, the Statute of Frauds requires a written declaration of trust. See Restatement (Third) of Trusts §20 (2003).

The settlor of the trust may be both a trustee and a beneficiary. Thus:

> *Case 6. O* executes a written declaration of trust declaring herself trustee of Whiteacre, to pay the income therefrom to herself for life, and upon her death Whiteacre is to pass to *A*. This is a valid trust. *Note:* In order to have a valid trust, the trustee must owe equitable duties to someone other than herself. Thus, if *O* were the sole trustee and also the sole beneficiary, the equitable and legal titles would merge, leaving *O* with absolute legal title. This rarely happens, however, because most trusts have different beneficiaries at some point in the life of the trust. In this case *O* owes equitable duties to *A*.

If the settlor is not the trustee of an inter vivos trust, a deed of trust is necessary. In order to bring the trust into being, the deed of trust or the trust property must be delivered to the trustee. Thus, in Case 6, if *O* wanted to make her lawyer, *C*, trustee, *O* would have to deliver a deed of trust to *C*.

If the trust is created by will, the settlor cannot, of course, be the trustee. The trustee will necessarily be someone other than the settlor. Although our focus in

Chapter 5 was on the declaration of trust used as a will substitute, our focus now shifts to the trust managed by a trustee other than the settlor.

b. The Trustee

There may be one trustee or several trustees. The trustee may be an individual or a corporation. Almost every large bank has a trust department set up to manage trusts and carry out the duties expected and required of a trustee.

The trustee may be the settlor or a third party, or the trustee may be a beneficiary. Thus:

> *Case 7.* By will, *H* devises property to *W* in trust to pay the income to *W* for life, and upon *W*'s death the property is to pass to *H*'s children free of trust. This is a valid trust. Although *W* is both trustee and beneficiary, *W* is not the sole beneficiary. *H*'s children have a remainder interest and can bring an action against *W* to enforce her duties as trustee. This trust arrangement has many advantages over a legal life estate in *W*, remainder in *H*'s children. *W* as trustee must keep the trust property separate from her own property and has broader powers of management, sale, and reinvestment than has a legal life tenant (see pages 494-496).

If the settlor intends to create a trust but fails to name a trustee, a court will appoint a trustee to carry out the trust. See Restatement (Third) of Trusts §§31, 34 (2003). This rule is sometimes stated: *A trust will not fail for want of a trustee.* Thus:

> *Case 8.* *T* dies leaving a will that devises his residuary estate in trust, to pay the income to *A* for life, and on *A*'s death to distribute the trust property to *B*. However, the will does not name anyone as trustee. Since *T*'s will clearly manifests an intention to create a trust, the court will appoint a suitable person — often the executor if one is named — as trustee to carry out *T*'s trust purposes. (If the trust is created by a deed of trust and no trustee is named, the trust may fail for want of a transferee or for want of delivery.)

If *T*'s will names someone as trustee but the named person refuses the appointment or dies while serving as trustee, and the will does not make provision for a successor trustee, the court will appoint a successor trustee.[2]

The trustee holds legal title to the trust property; the beneficiaries have the equitable, beneficial interests. To safeguard the beneficiary against mismanagement or misappropriation by the trustee, the trustee is held to a *fiduciary* standard of conduct. The fiduciary obligation in trust law comprises duties of *loyalty,*

---

2. This rule does not apply if the court finds (or if the trust instrument specifies) that the trust powers were *personal to the named trustee.* If it is determined that the settlor intended the trust to continue only as long as the person designated as trustee continues to serve in that capacity, the trust terminates when the named person ceases to serve as trustee. This exception is rarely invoked, however. In the usual case, the court will determine that the primary purpose of the settlor was to have the trust continue for the indicated purposes and not that the particular person, and only that person, serve as trustee. See 2 Scott, supra, §101.1.

prudence, and a host of *subsidiary rules* that reinforce the duties of loyalty and prudence. Under the duty of loyalty, the trustee must administer the trust solely in the interest of the beneficiaries; self-dealing (wherein the trustee acts in the same transaction both in its fiduciary capacity and in an individual capacity) is sharply limited and often prohibited altogether. Under the duty of prudence, the trustee is held to an objective standard care. Important subsidiary rules include: (1) the duty of impartiality between classes of beneficiaries such as the income beneficiaries (who are interested in income and high yields) and the remaindermen (who are concerned about preservation of principal and appreciation in values), (2) the duty to keep the trust property separate from the trustee's own property, and (3) the duty to inform and account to the beneficiaries. If the trustee improperly manages the trust estate, the trustee may be denied compensation, subjected to personal liability, and removed as trustee by a court. In Chapter 13, we give extended consideration to important problems in trust administration and to the distinctive nature of the fiduciary office.

In order to have a trust, it is necessary for the trustee to have some duties to perform. If the trustee has no duties at all, there is no reason to have, or to recognize, a trust. The trust is then said to be "passive," or "dry," and the trust fails. When a trust fails because the trustee has no active duties, the beneficiaries acquire legal title to the trust property. See Restatement (Third) of Trusts §6 (2003).

Because a trustee has onerous duties and is thus exposed to significant potential liability, the law does not impose upon a person the office of trustee unless the person accepts. At common law, once a person accepts the office of trustee, the person can be released from liability only with consent of the beneficiaries or by a court order. However, Uniform Trust Code §705 (2000) modifies this rule to allow for resignation by the trustee with 30 days notice to all interested parties. Well drafted trusts often contain a clause to a similar effect.

PROBLEM, QUESTION, AND NOTE

1. In January, *O* executes a written instrument creating an irrevocable trust and naming *X* as trustee. The trust instrument provides that the income from the trust is to be paid to *A* for life, and upon *A*'s death the corpus is to be distributed to *B*. Shortly thereafter, *O* delivers a copy of the trust instrument and $100,000 in cash to *X* and tells *X* that this money is to be held by *X* under the trust. *X* immediately puts the money in his safe-deposit box.

O dies the following February. In November, *X*, saying that he does not want to be trustee, divides the money between *D* and *E*, the residuary legatees of *O*'s estate, paying $50,000 to each. Has a trust been established? See 1 Scott, *supra*, §35. Is *X* liable for $100,000? See 2 id. §102.2. Can *A* and *B* recover the $100,000 from *D* and *E*? See 4 id. §292. See also Restatement (Third) of Trusts §35 (2003); Uniform Trust Code (UTC) §701 (2000).

2. Given the potential for substantial fiduciary liability, why would you agree to serve as a trustee? There are two common scenarios. One is the amateur trustee, a trusted friend or relative of the settlor. This person serves out of sense of friendship, duty, or familial obligation, not in order to receive trustee's fees (though this person may be paid). The advantage of choosing an amateur trustee is that the

amateur usually costs less and, perhaps more importantly, is likely to have a personal connection to the settlor and so a strong sense of the settlor's wishes. The disadvantages of the amateur — and of individual trustees generally — is that the individual may become too elderly or incompetent to do a good job, may be inexperienced in portfolio management, or may die before the end of the trust's term, in which case trustee succession becomes an issue.

The other and more recent scenario is the fee-paid institutional trustee such as a bank or trust company. Institutional trustees offer expertise in portfolio management and trust administration. These institutions also have deep pockets, which means that in the case of breach, the beneficiary has a good chance of actually recovering on an award of damages. Moreover, the existence of the inevitable institutional bureaucracy provides the beneficiary with additional safeguards, as do federal and state banking regulations. See 12 C.F.R. §9 (2004). The cost of expertise and deep pockets, however, is that an institutional trustee is likely to demand a sizeable commission. Moreover, some believe that trust companies are unresponsive to the beneficiaries and in general are highly inflexible, a point to which we will return at the end of this chapter in connection with the law of trustee removal.

In some states, the trustee's default commission is set by statute at a specified percentage of the trust corpus. See, e.g., N.Y. Surr. Ct. Proc. Act §2309 (2004). More recently there has been a trend toward a "reasonable compensation" standard as the default rule. See Cal. Prob. Code §15681 (2004); Restatement (Third) of Trusts §38 (2003); UTC §708 (2000). Of course, as default rules these terms are subject to displacement by contrary agreement, and indeed corporate fiduciaries typically insist upon adoption of their own fee schedules as a condition precedent to accepting an appointment as trustee.[3]

As of 2003, trust companies and other corporate fiduciaries that are required to make regular reports to federal banking authorities held roughly $1 trillion in noncommercial — that is, donative and charitable — trust assets. See Robert H. Sitkoff & Max Schanzenbach, Jurisdictional Competition for Trust Funds: An Empirical Analysis of Perpetuities and Taxes, 115 Yale L.J. (forthcoming 2005). Professional trusteeship is big business indeed!

3.   When advising clients on the choice of trustee, it might be helpful to consider more specifically what exactly it is that a trustee does.

> Trusteeship entails three relatively distinct functions: investment, administration, and distribution. *Investment* includes not only the initial selection of securities or other assets, but also the tasks of monitoring the investments for continuing suitability, investing new funds, and voting the shares. *Administration* includes the range of accounting, reporting, and tax filing. The responsibility for taking custody of securities is another branch of trust administration. Unusual trust assets may require other administrative work — maintaining and leasing real estate, insuring and safe-keeping the Picasso and the diamond tiara, and so forth. *Distribution* is sometimes mechanical, but trust investments often bestow upon trustees the discretion to spray, sprinkle, invade, accumulate, terminate, and so forth. Distribution, therefore,

---

3. The June 2004 fee schedule for Chicago-based Northern Trust Company was as follows: a minimum annual fee of $12,500 for any size trust up to $1 million, plus 0.80 percent for the next $2 million; 0.70 percent for the next $2 million; 0.50 percent for the next $5 million; 0.45 percent for the next $5 million; 0.45 percent for the next $15 million; and 0.40 percent for the next $25 million. Under this schedule, the annual fee for a $3 million trust would be $28,500 and for a $10 million trust would be $67,500.

requires interpreting and applying the sometimes complex language of the trust instrument; and it commonly involves contact with the current beneficiaries, in order to keep abreast of their needs and circumstances. [John H. Langbein, The Uniform Prudent Investor Act and the Future of Trust Investing, 81 Iowa L. Rev. 641, 665 (1996).]

For discussion of considerations relevant to the choice of trustee, see Jonathan R. Price, Price on Contemporary Estate Planning §10.43 (2d ed. 2000).

c. The Beneficiaries

The beneficiaries hold equitable interests. Generally speaking, this means that the beneficiaries have interests that originated in chancery and have different characteristics from legal interests. Of special importance are the remedies available to the beneficiaries for breach of trust. The beneficiaries have a personal claim against the trustee for breach of trust. However, this personal claim has no higher priority than the claim of other creditors of the trustee and thus might not protect the beneficiaries if it were their only remedy. But equity gives the beneficiaries additional remedies relating to the trust property itself. Personal creditors of the trustee, other than the trust beneficiaries, cannot reach the trust property. If the trustee wrongfully disposes of the trust property, the beneficiaries can recover the trust property unless it has come into the hands of a bona fide purchaser for value. If the trustee disposes of trust property and acquires other property with the proceeds of sale, the beneficiaries can enforce the trust on the newly acquired property.

Private trusts almost always create successive beneficial interests. Typically, trust income is payable to the beneficiary (or class of beneficiaries) for life, perhaps to be followed by life interests in another class of beneficiaries, with the trustee to distribute the trust corpus to yet another class of beneficiaries upon termination of the trust. Thus the creation of a trust involves the creation of one or more equitable future interests as well as a present interest in the income.

> *Case 9.* O transfers securities worth $100,000 to X in trust, to pay the income to A for life and then to B for life. On the death of the survivor of A and B, the trustee is to distribute the trust principal to B's issue then living. X has legal title to the trust assets and has a fiduciary duty to manage and invest the assets for the benefit of the indicated beneficiaries. A has an equitable life estate. B has an equitable remainder for life. B's issue have an equitable contingent remainder in fee simple. O has an equitable reversion (often called a resulting trust). If on the death of the survivor of A and B there are no issue of B then living, the trust property will revert to O (or to O's successors if O has died in the meantime).

Today, most life estates and future interests are equitable rather than legal interests; they are created in trusts. Legal life estates and future interests in tangible or intangible personal property are rare and almost always inadvisable. Legal life estates and future interests in land are sometimes encountered. These too are almost always inadvisable. A trust with equitable interests is a much more flexible and useful means of giving property than a disposition that creates legal interests.

3. *A Trust Compared with a Legal Life Estate*

A person who wants to give another a life estate may give the donee either a legal life estate or create a trust with the donee as life beneficiary. A legal life tenant has possession and control of the property, whereas a trustee has legal title to the trust property. Let us compare a legal life estate ("to *A* for life, remainder to *A*'s children") with an equitable life estate ("to *X* in trust for *A* for life, remainder to *A*'s children"). Is a legal life estate more or less desirable than a trust? This question is best answered by looking at problems that may arise during the legal life tenant's life and how proper drafting might solve them.

(1) *Sale*. The legal life tenant has no power to sell a fee simple unless such a power is granted in the instrument creating the life estate. Otherwise, to sell a fee simple it is necessary that the life tenant and *all* the remaindermen and reversioners agree to the sale or that the life tenant obtains judicial approval.

(2) *Reinvestment of proceeds of sale*. If the property is sold under a power of sale, what is to be done with the proceeds? If the life tenant is given a power of sale under which the proceeds go to the life tenant, the power of sale is in effect a general power of appointment, which has serious estate tax disadvantages.[4] To get around this problem, the instrument could provide that the proceeds are to be held in trust (with the life tenant as trustee), but this requires invoking trust law in the original conveyance.

(3) *Borrowing money*. During the life tenant's lifetime, the real estate cannot be mortgaged by the life tenant. No banker is so foolish as to lend money with only a life estate as security. To put up the fee simple as security for a loan, it is necessary that the life tenant and *all* the remaindermen and reversioners sign the mortgage. It may be impossible to procure these signatures if the future takers are unascertained. Moreover, if the life tenant is given the power to mortgage real estate and can appropriate the loan to herself, the power to mortgage is in effect a general power of appointment that may lead to tax problems in the life tenant's estate.

(4) *Leasing*. If rental property is involved, someone should be given the power to lease the property for a period extending beyond the life tenant's death. Otherwise it may be impossible to rent the premises. However, if the life tenant is given this power and can accept a lump-sum payment in advance for the rent, the life tenant has the power to appropriate part of the remainder to herself. To the extent the life tenant can appoint the remainder to herself, the life tenant has a general power of appointment.

(5) *Waste*. The life tenant may want to take oil out of the land, cut timber, or take down a still usable building. Each of these actions constitutes waste, and the remaindermen may be entitled to an injunction or damages. If the life tenant is given the power to drill for oil, open mines, or commit waste with impunity, the life tenant may be held to have a general power of appointment for tax purposes.

(6) *Expenses*. If land is involved, someone must pay taxes and maintain the property. The general rule is that the life tenant has the duty to pay taxes and keep the property in repair, but only to the extent the income from the property is adequate to cover those charges. The life tenant also has the duty to pay interest on, but not the principal of, the mortgage.

---

4. A general power of appointment is a power given to the donee (holder) of the power that authorizes the donee to appoint the property to the donee herself, the donee's estate, the creditors of the donee, or the creditors of the donee's estate. Property over which a person holds a general power of appointment is included in the person's taxable gross estate at death, on which a federal estate tax may be payable. See page 892. Property subject to a nongeneral or special power of appointment is not subject to estate taxation at the death of the holder of the power. See page 892. We examine powers of appointment generally in Chapter 9.

(7) *Creditors.* If the life tenant gets into debt, the creditor can seize the life estate and sell it. Of course, very little may be realized upon sale. Likely the creditor will buy it on judicial sale for a small amount, and if the life tenant lives a long time the creditor reaps a windfall. If the debtor is a remainderman, the creditor may be able to seize the remainder and sell it. As with the life estate, the remainder may sell for very little, and the creditor usually will be the purchaser.

(8) *Personalty versus realty.* Life estates in personal property pose special problems. Personal property often requires expert management (think of stocks, bonds, and other financial assets) and, in some cases, is perishable or easily transportable. The application of the law of waste to life estates in personal property is uncertain and thus insufficient to protect the remainderman from misappropriation or mismanagement by the life tenant.[5]

(9) *Miscellaneous.* Many other problems may arise. Trespassers may damage the property; the government may exercise eminent domain; a third party may be injured on the premises. The respective rights of the life tenant and the remaindermen must be covered in the testator's will unless the law regarding the rights of a legal life tenant is clear and certain and satisfactory, and we can assure you that it isn't. If these problems are not covered in the testator's will, they may end up being decided in expensive court proceedings.

When we consider all the problems that may arise in the future, we find that a trust is almost always preferable to a legal life estate. If an independent trustee is not selected, the life tenant should be made a trustee rather than being given a legal life estate. Most of the above problems are administrative problems, and the law of trust administration is well established and extensive. If the trustee's powers are not spelled out in the trust instrument, modern law will supply a charter of administration. Trust administration law is for the most part quite rational; in any case, it is simpler and far more rational than the law respecting legal life estates and remainders. Let us look at the problems above once again.

(1) Standard administrative provisions from any form book, and the default law of trustees' powers, almost always give the trustee a power of sale (for sample language, see pages 124-125). Even if the settlor creates an array of exotic beneficial interests such as a life tenant, multiple remainderpersons, and executory interests, when those present and future interests are created in trust rather than as legal interests, third parties need deal only with the trustee. See Thomas W. Merrill & Henry E. Smith, The Property/Contract Interface, 101 Colum. L. Rev. 773, 847-849 (2001).

(2) If the property is sold by a legal life tenant and the proceeds are to be put in trust, a trust must be created for the proceeds. This trust should be spelled out in the will, so the lawyer will not be saving words by creating a legal life estate. Why not have a trust from the beginning?

(3, 4, 5, and 6) As powers of sale are routinely put in any trust instrument and are often included in the statutory default powers of the trustee, so are powers to mortgage, to lease, to give oil leases, and to pay taxes, insurance, and current charges.

(7) A major difference between legal estates and equitable estates is that the latter can be put out of the reach of creditors (see Section D at page 543).

---

5. Pennsylvania has abolished life estates in personalty, converting the life tenant into a trustee. See 20 Pa. Consol. Stat. Ann. §6113 (2004). Statutes in a handful of other states require the life tenant to account like a trustee, and in some states the courts may require the life tenant to give security. The Pennsylvania approach was endorsed by the late Professor A. James Casner in his classic treatise on property law. See American Law of Property §2.27, at 172 (1952).

(8 and 9) Trust law supplies a law of fiduciary administration that spells out the trustee's duties in managing trust property and in balancing the interests of life and remainder beneficiaries.

QUESTION AND NOTE

1. In view of the disadvantages of a legal life estate, why is not a legal life estate converted into a trust by statute? What purposes are served in having two bodies of law, one applicable to legal life estates and one applicable to life estates in trust?

2. By the English Law of Property Act of 1925, the legal life estate was abolished. Since that date only two kinds of legal estates can exist in England: the fee simple absolute in possession and the leasehold. Apart from leaseholds, all life estates and future interests of every kind (remainders, executory interests, reversions, possibilities of reverter, rights of entry) are equitable interests. The holder of the fee simple absolute in possession holds the property in trust for the other interested parties. The purpose of this legislation is to make land marketable by ensuring that a fee simple absolute owner is always available to sell the land. The result is to turn all family property settlements into trusts. See C. Dent Bostick, Loosening the Grip of the Dead Hand: Shall We Abolish Legal Future Interests in Land, 32 Vand. L. Rev. 1061 (1979); Ronald H. Maudsley, Escaping the Tyranny of Common Law Estates, 42 Mo. L. Rev. 355 (1977).

4. Commercial Uses of the Trust

Although this book is focused on the use of trusts in gratuitous wealth transfers, it is worth pausing for a moment to consider the extraordinary role of the trust in business transactions. In the late 1800s and early 1900s, before the corporate form had matured, large-scale business enterprise regularly organized in trust form — the common law *business trust*. Thus in Nathan Isaacs, Trusteeship in Modern Business, 42 Harv. L. Rev. 1048 (1929), the author observed that "modern business has become honey-combed with trusteeship. Next to contract, the universal tool, and incorporation, the standard instrument of organization, it takes place wherever the relations to be established are too delicate or too novel for these coarser devices." Id. at 1060. John D. Rockefeller's infamous Standard Oil Company was organized as a trust, not a corporation, and the salience in 1890 of the trust as a mode of business organization is why today we have antitrust law, not competition or monopoly law, as it is known abroad.

The primary explanation for the historical success of the business trust is that, like the corporation, the trust allows for the pooling of passive investment with professional managers. Unlike the corporate law of the late 1800s and early 1900s, however, the common law business trust was not subject to an intrusive regulatory overlay. Entrepreneurs thus used the business trust to escape this regulation. In fact, the use of the business trust for this purpose was so pronounced in Massachusetts, which forbade corporate ownership of real estate, that the term *Massachusetts trust* became synonymous with business trust.

Over the course of the twentieth century, with the emergence of permissive and enabling corporate law, the corporation came to dominate trust as the entity of choice for the organization of operating business enterprises. Even so, the trust remains a vital cog in the modern economy. Among other purposes, the trust today is a preferred form of organization for mutual funds and for structured finance transactions such as asset securitization, and federal law imposes a mandatory trust form on employee pension funds. See John H. Langbein, The Secret Life of the Trust: The Trust as an Instrument of Commerce, 107 Yale L.J. 165 (1997). Thus:

> *Case 10. Mutual fund. T*, an investment professional, approaches *A, B, C*, and others like them and agrees to pool certain of their assets in a common fund to be managed by *T. A, B, C*, and the other investors each receive tradable shares of the fund in an amount proportional to their investment. By structuring their collective investment in this way, *A, B, C*, and the others are able to take advantage of economies of scale, hire a professional investment advisor, *T*, and obtain a more diversified portfolio than each could have individually. In managing the portfolio, *T* is subject to a fiduciary obligation to *A, B, C*, and the other investors in the fund. *Note*: Mutual funds are subject to regulation under the Investment Company Act of 1940 and other federal securities laws.
>
> *Case 11. Asset securitization. O*, a bank, regularly makes loans both to individuals and to businesses. The individual loans are secured by mortgages on the individuals' homes. The business loans are unsecured. The business loans are therefore riskier because if the business goes bankrupt, *O* may not be able to recover on the debt. Thus *O* sells all its rights to payments under its entire portfolio of individual loans to *T* as trustee of an asset securitization trust. To pay for those rights, *T* sells passive equitable ownership shares in the trust to sophisticated investors such as *A, B*, and *C*. By this process, the rights to repayment under the secured individual loans are segregated in the trust. Accordingly, *A, B*, and *C* need not consider the risk attending to *O*'s business loans when making their investment in the asset securitization trust. In this way, *O* is able to realize the full value of its portfolio of individual loans notwithstanding its risk on the business loans. Once the transaction is complete, *T* manages the portfolio of individual loans subject to a fiduciary obligation to *A, B*, and *C*. Often *T* will hire *O*, the bank that originated the loans, to undertake the day-to-day management of those loans.[6]
>
> *Case 12. Pension fund. C* hires *A* to work for *C* in *C*'s business. Under the terms of the employment contract, *C* agrees to pay a weekly wage to *A* and to contribute an amount representing 10 percent of *A*'s weekly wage to a pension trust for the benefit of *A*, payable to *A* upon her retirement. Until *A*'s retirement, the pension trust is managed by a professional trustee who is subject to a fiduciary obligation to *A*. *Note*: Most employee pension trusts are subject to the federal Employee Retirement Income Security Act of 1974 (ERISA).

Pension funds hold over $10 trillion; mutual funds hold over $7 trillion; and there is at least $1 trillion in asset securitization trusts. Thus, from the perspective of aggregate volume, the commercial uses of the trust appear to dwarf the use of the trust for gratuitous wealth transfer. Reliable data is hard to come by, but our research suggests that the aggregate wealth held in donative trusts is probably on the order of $1 trillion.

Interestingly, twenty-nine states have codified the common law business trust, thereby creating the *statutory business trust*. See Robert H. Sitkoff, Trust as

---

6. See Claire A. Hill, Securitization: A Low-Cost Sweetener for Lemons, 74 Wash. U.L.Q. 1061 (1996); Steven L. Schwartz, The Alchemy of Asset Securitization, 1 Stan. J.L. Bus. & Fin. 133 (1994).

Uncorporation: A Research Agenda, 2005 U. Ill. L. Rev. (forthcoming). Today, most structured finance transactions and mutual funds that make use of the business trust employ a statutory trust rather than one arising under the common law. The leading business trust statute is the Delaware Statutory Trust Act of 1988, Del. Code Ann. tit. 12, §§3801-3862 (2004). Since 1998, hoping to compete with Delaware or at least to stem the loss of further business to Delaware, several other states have copied the Delaware statute. In 2003, the Uniform Law Commission formed a committee to draft a Uniform Business Trust Act.

For further examination of the trust as a mode of business organization, see Langbein, supra; Henry Hansmann & Ugo Mattei, The Functions of Trust Law: A Comparative Legal and Economic Analysis, 73 N.Y.U.L. Rev. 434, 466-469, 472-478 (1998); Steven L. Schwarcz, Commercial Trusts as Business Organizations: Unraveling the Mystery, 58 Bus. Law. 559 (2003); Sitkoff, supra.

SECTION B.   CREATION OF A TRUST

1. *Intent to Create a Trust*

No particular form of words is necessary to create a trust. The words *trust* or *trustee* need not be used. The sole question is whether the grantor manifested an intention to create a trust relationship. See Restatement (Third) of Trusts §13 (2003); Uniform Trust Code §402(a)(2) (2000).

Where the grantor conveys property to a grantee to hold "for the use and benefit" of another, this is a sufficient manifestation of an intention to create a trust. See Restatement, supra, illus. 1. Thus, in Fox v. Faulkner, 1 S.W.2d 1079 (Ky. 1927), the grantor conveyed land "to Mary Pursiful for the use and benefit of Moses A. Cottrell, during his natural life—if said Moses A. Cottrell should leave children in lawful wedlock it shall go to them." The court held that a trust was created, saying:

> Though Mary Pursiful was designated as party of the second part in the deed, and the qualifying word "trustee" was not added after her name to indicate that she took merely in that capacity, the language of the granting clause is such as to exclude the conclusion that she took under it in any capacity other than as trustee for Moses A. Cottrell. The case is on a par with the celebrated bear case (Prewitt v. Clayton, 5 T.B. Mon. 5), where it was said: "A bear well painted and drawn to the life is yet a picture of a bear, although the painter may omit to write over it, 'This is the bear.'" [Id. at 1080.]

LUX v. LUX, 288 A.2d 701 (R.I. 1972): In 1968, Philomena Lux died testate. Litigation ensued over whether she devised certain property to her grandchildren outright or in trust. The pertinent provisions of her will were as follows:

> 2. All the rest, residue and remainder of my estate, real and personal, of whatsoever kind and nature, and wherever situated, of which I shall die seized and possessed, or over which I may have power of appointment, or to which I may be in any manner entitled at my death, I give, devise and bequeath to my grandchildren, share and share alike.

3. Any real estate included in said residue shall be maintained for the benefit of said grandchildren and shall not be sold until the youngest of said grandchildren has reached twenty-one years of age.

4. Should it become necessary to sell any of said real estate to pay my debts, costs of administration, or to make distribution of my estate or for any other lawful reason, then, in that event, it is my express desire that said real estate be sold to a member of my family. . . .

Based on this language, the court concluded that "Philomena intended that her real estate be held in trust for the benefit of her grandchildren." The court explained:

In reaching this conclusion, we must emphasize that there is no fixed formula as to when a testamentary disposition should be classified as an outright gift or a trust. The result reached depends on the circumstances of each particular case.

We are not unmindful of the formal requirements necessary for the creation of a testamentary trust. It is an elementary proposition of law that a trust is created when legal title to property is held by one person for the benefit of another. . . . However, no particular words are required to create a testamentary trust. The absence of such words as "trust" or "trustee" is immaterial where the requisite intent of the testator can be found. . . . A trust never fails for lack of a trustee. . . .

When the residuary clause in the instant case is viewed in its entirety, it is clear that Philomena did not give her grandchildren a fee simple title to the realty. It appears that she, realizing the nature of this bequest and the age of the beneficiaries, intended that someone would hold and manage the property until they were of sufficient age to do so themselves. The property is income-producing and apparently she felt that the ultimate interest of her grandchildren would be protected if the realty was left intact until the designated time for distribution. The use of the terms "shall be maintained" and "shall not be sold" is a strong indication of Philomena's intent that the property was to be retained and managed by some person for some considerable time in the future for the benefit of her son's children. This is a duty usually associated with a trustee. We therefore hold that Philomena's will does create a trust on her real estate.

Having found the trust, the question of who shall serve as trustee is easily answered. The general rule is that, unless a contrary intention appears in the will or such an appointment is deemed improper or undesirable, the executor would be named to the position of trustee.

Jimenez v. Lee

Supreme Court of Oregon, 1976
274 Or. 457, 547 P.2d 126

O'CONNELL, C.J.   This is a suit brought by plaintiff against her father[7] to compel him to account for assets which she alleges were held by defendant as trustee for her. Plaintiff appeals from a decree dismissing her complaint.

7. Jason Lee, the defendant in Jimenez v. Lee, was elected to the Oregon Court of Appeals in 1974, unseating an incumbent judge. As a result of the bitter campaign, a newspaper reporter sued the state bar under Oregon's open records law to reveal its disciplinary records on Jason Lee. In 1975, Lee filed for the Oregon Supreme Court seat of Chief Justice O'Connell, who was retiring in 1976. The decision in Jimenez v. Lee, written by Chief Justice O'Connell, was handed down on March 18, 1976. The next day, March 19, Jason Lee withdrew from the Supreme Court race. In June 1976, the Supreme Court decided the reporter's lawsuit and ordered the Jason Lee disciplinary records opened to the public.

Plaintiff's claim against her father is based upon the theory that a trust arose in her favor when two separate gifts were made for her benefit. The first of these gifts was made in 1945, shortly after plaintiff's birth, when her paternal grandmother purchased a $1,000 face value U.S. Savings Bond which was registered in the names of defendant "and/or" plaintiff "and/or" Dorothy Lee, plaintiff's mother. It is uncontradicted that the bond was purchased to provide funds to be used for plaintiff's educational needs. A second gift in the amount of $500 was made in 1956 by Mrs. Adolph Diercks, one of defendant's clients. At the same time Mrs. Diercks made identical gifts for the benefit of defendant's two other children. The $1,500 was deposited by the donor in a savings account in the names of defendant and his three children.

In 1960 defendant cashed the savings bond and invested the proceeds in common stock of the Commercial Bank of Salem, Oregon. Ownership of the shares was registered as "Jason Lee, Custodian under the Laws of Oregon for Betsy Lee [plaintiff]." At the same time, the joint savings account containing the client's gifts to defendant's children was closed and $1,000 of the proceeds invested in Commercial Bank stock.[8] Defendant also took title to this stock as "custodian" for his children.

The trial court found that defendant did not hold either the savings bond or the savings account in trust for the benefit of plaintiff and that defendant held the shares of the Commercial Bank stock as custodian for plaintiff under the Uniform Gift to Minors Act.[9] Plaintiff contends that the gifts for her educational needs created trusts in each instance and that the trusts survived defendant's investment of the trust assets in the Commercial Bank stock.

It is undisputed that the gifts were made for the educational needs of plaintiff. The respective donors did not expressly direct defendant to hold the subject matter of the gift "in trust" but this is not essential to create a trust relationship. It is enough if the transfer of the property is made with the intent to vest the beneficial ownership in a third person. That was clearly shown in the present case. Even defendant's own testimony establishes such intent. When he was asked whether there was a stated purpose for the gift, he replied: "Mother said that she felt that the children should all be treated equally and that she was going to supply a bond to help with Elizabeth's educational needs and that she was naming me and Dorothy, the ex-wife and mother of Elizabeth, to use the funds as may be most conducive to the educational needs of Elizabeth." Defendant also admitted that the gift from Mrs. Diercks was "for the educational needs of the children."

Lee's files weighed 15 pounds and revealed many complaints. A public letter of reprimand, for ambulance chasing and for directing his secretary as a notary to execute false acknowledgments, had been issued to Lee in 1965.

Judge Jason Lee did not resign from the Court of Appeals. Still sitting on that court, Lee died of a heart attack in 1980. Lee's will left all his property to his second wife, Merie. If Merie predeceased him (she didn't), his will devised his property in trust for his grandchildren: "I leave nothing but my love to my children."

The information in this footnote was furnished to the editors by Professor Valerie Vollmar of Willamette University College of Law. — Eds.

8. The specific disposition of the balance of this account is not revealed in the record. Defendant testified that the portion of the gift not invested in the stock "was used for other unusual needs of the children." Defendant could not recall exactly how the money was used but thought some of it was spent for family vacations to Victoria, British Columbia, and to satisfy his children's expensive taste in clothing.

9. The Uniform Transfers to Minors Act, which is the successor to the Uniform Gifts to Minors Act, is examined at pages 118-119. — Eds.

There was nothing about either of the gifts which would suggest that the beneficial ownership of the subject matter of the gift was to vest in defendant to use as he pleased with an obligation only to pay out of his own funds a similar amount for plaintiff's educational needs.

Defendant himself demonstrated that he knew that the savings bond was held by him in trust. In a letter to his mother, the donor, he wrote: "Dave and Bitsie [plaintiff] & Dorothy are aware of the fact that I hold $1,000 each for Dave & Bitsie in trust for them on account of your E-Bond gifts." It is fair to indulge in the presumption that defendant, as a lawyer, used the word "trust" in the ordinary legal sense of that term. . . .

Having decided that a trust was created for the benefit of plaintiff, it follows that defendant's purchase of the Commercial Bank stock as "custodian" for plaintiff under the Uniform Gift to Minors Act was ineffectual to expand defendant's powers over the trust property from that of trustee to that of custodian.[10]

Defendant's attempt to broaden his powers over the trust estate by investing the trust funds as custodian violated his duty to the beneficiary "to administer the trust solely in the interest of the beneficiary." Restatement (Second) of Trusts §170, p. 364 (1959). . . .

The decree of the trial court is reversed and the cause is remanded for further proceedings consistent with this opinion.

NOTES

1. *Precatory language.* In a surprisingly large number of cases, the testator expresses a "wish," "hope," or "recommendation" that the property devised should be disposed of by the devisee in some particular manner, but this language does not clearly indicate whether the testator intends to create a trust (with a legal duty so to dispose of the property) or merely a moral obligation unenforceable in court. If the language indicates the latter, it is called precatory language. And sometimes courts speak of *precatory trusts,* meaning unenforceable dispositions of this sort. Typical language raising this issue is a bequest "to A with the hope that A will care for B" or a devise of land "to C and it is my wish and desire that D should be able to live on the land during her life."

In Colton v. Colton, 127 U.S. 300 (1888), the testator devised his entire estate to his wife and then continued, "I recommend to her the care and protection of my mother and sister, and request her to make such gift and provision for them as in her judgment will be best." The question thus arose, did the testator's wife take the entire estate absolutely, or did she take it subject to a trust for benefit of the testator's mother and sister?

---

10. If defendant were "custodian" of the gifts, he would have the power under the Uniform Gift to Minors Act (O.R.S. 126.820) to use the property "as he may deem advisable for the support, maintenance, education and general use and benefit of the minor, in such manner, at such time or times, and to such extent as the custodian in his absolute discretion may deem advisable and proper, without court order or without regard to the duty of any person to support the minor, and without regard to any other funds which may be applicable or available for the purpose." As custodian defendant would not be required to account for his stewardship of the funds unless a petition for accounting were filed in circuit court no later than two years after the end of plaintiff's minority. O.R.S. 126.875. As the trustee of an educational trust, however, defendant has the power to use the trust funds for educational purposes only and has the duty to render clear and accurate accounts showing the funds have been used for trust purposes. See O.R.S. 128.010; Restatement (Second) of Trusts §172 (1959).

On the one hand, the words may be merely those of suggestion, counsel, or advice, intended only to influence, and not to take away, the discretion of the legatee growing out of his right to use and dispose of the property given as his own. On the other hand, the language employed may be imperative in fact though not in form, conveying the intention of the testator in terms equivalent to a command, and leaving to the legatee no discretion to defeat his wishes, although there may be a discretion to accomplish them by a choice of methods, or even to define and limit the extent of the interest conferred upon his beneficiary. [Id. at 312-313.]

After parsing the language of the will and the context in which the will was drafted, the Court concluded that the testator intended to create an enforceable trust.

As illustrated by the *Colton* case, to fathom the testator's intent, each will must be construed in accordance with the language used in each particular case in light of all the circumstances. The result: much litigation. See County of Suffolk v. Greater N.Y. Councils, Boy Scouts of Am., 413 N.E.2d 363 (N.Y. 1980) ("my wish," precatory); Levin v. Fisch, 404 S.W.2d 889 (Tex. 1966) ("my desire," mandatory under the circumstances); McKinsey v. Cullingsworth, 9 S.E.2d 315 (Va. 1940) ("take care of Lula the best you can," nonbinding). See also Restatement (Third) of Trusts §13, cmt. d (2003). The lesson: Do not put recitals in testamentary instruments or, if you must, be clear in your drafting. "I wish, but do not legally require, that *C* permit *D* to live on the land."

2. *Equitable charge.* Another distinction needs mention here: the difference between a trust and an equitable charge. If a testator devises property to a person, subject to the payment of a certain sum of money to a third person, the testator creates an equitable charge, not a trust. An equitable charge creates a security

interest in the transferred property; there is no fiduciary relationship. The relationship between the holder of the charge and the beneficiary is more in the nature of a debtor and secured creditor. See 1 George G. Bogert & George T. Bogert, The Law of Trusts and Trustees §31, at 393 (2d rev. ed. 1984). See also Restatement, supra, §5, cmt. h.

3. The stakes in disputes over a transferor's intent to create a trust usually boil down to the applicability of the fiduciary obligation. If the transferor intended only a moral obligation or is found to have created an equitable charge, then there is no trust—and hence no fiduciary relationship. Consider again Jimenez v. Lee. In the portion of the opinion excerpted above, the court determined that the father held the property in trust.

Professor George G. Bogert
Chicago's great authority on trust law

The court then continued:

> The money from the savings bond and savings account are clearly traceable into the bank stock. Therefore, plaintiff was entitled to impose a constructive trust or an equitable lien upon the stock so acquired. Plaintiff is also entitled to be credited for any dividends or increment in the value of that part of the stock representing plaintiff's proportional interest. Whether or not the assets of plaintiff's trust are traceable into a product, defendant is personally liable for that amount which would have accrued to plaintiff had there been no breach of trust. Defendant is, of course, entitled to deduct the amount which he expended out of the trust estate for plaintiff's educational needs. However, before he is entitled to be credited for such expenditures, he has the duty as trustee to identify them specifically and prove that they were made for trust purposes. A trustee's duty to maintain and render accurate accounts is a strict one. . . .
>
> Defendant did not keep separate records of trust income and trust expenditures. He introduced into evidence a summary of various expenditures which he claimed were made for the benefit of plaintiff. It appears that the summary was prepared for the most part from cancelled checks gathered together for the purpose of defending the present suit. This obviously did not meet the requirement that a trustee "maintain records of his transactions so complete and accurate that he can show by them his faithfulness to his trust." . . .
>
> Defendant contends that even if a trust is found to exist and that the value of the trust assets is the amount claimed by plaintiff there is sufficient evidence to prove that the trust estate was exhausted by expenditures for legitimate trust purposes. Considering the character of the evidence presented by defendant, it is difficult to understand how such a result could be reached. As we noted above, the trust was for the educational needs of plaintiff. Some of the expenditures made by defendant would seem to fall clearly within the purposes of the trust. These would include the cost of ballet lessons, the cost of subscribing to a ballet magazine, and other items of expenditure related to plaintiff's education. But many of the items defendant lists as trust expenditures are either questionable or clearly outside the purpose of an educational trust. For instance, defendant seeks credit against the trust for tickets to ballet performances on three different occasions while plaintiff was in high school. The cost of plaintiff's ticket to a ballet performance might be regarded as a part of plaintiff's educational program in learning the art of ballet, but defendant claims credit for expenditures made to purchase ballet tickets for himself and other members of the family, disbursements clearly beyond the purposes of the trust. . . .
>
> The case must, therefore, be remanded for an accounting to be predicated upon a trustee's duty to account, and the trustee's burden to prove that the expenditures were made for trust purposes. . . . In determining whether defendant has met this strict burden of proof, the trial court must adhere to the rule that all doubts are resolved against a trustee who maintains an inadequate accounting system.

We examine the law of fiduciary administration in Chapter 13.[11]

To make an outright gift of personal property, as compared to a gift in trust, the donor must deliver the property to the donee, and the donee must accept the gift. See Restatement (Third) of Property: Wills and Other Donative Transfers §6.1 (2003). But courts infer acceptance from the absence of refusal or disclaimer, and

---

11. Even without having studied Chapter 13, you are now in a position to evaluate the following Ann Landers exchange of May 23, 2002, which bears a striking similarity to Jimenez v. Lee:

delivery need not be physical—a constructive or symbolic delivery will do. A *constructive delivery* gives the donee the means of obtaining the property such as a key. A *symbolic delivery* gives the donee something symbolic of the object. The most common example of a symbolic delivery is a written instrument handed over when manual delivery is impractical. See Restatement of Property, supra, §6.2 cmt. g. These rules concerning gifts collide with the law of trust formation when the donor fails to perfect a gift to the donee. In such a case the question arises, can the failed gift be saved by recharacterizing it as a declaration of trust? A declaration of trust, unlike an absolute gift, does not require delivery since the settlor is also the trustee and thus already has possession. In addition, a declaration of trust can be made orally (subject to the statute of frauds). All that is necessary is that the donor manifest an intention to hold the property in trust.

The Hebrew University Association v. Nye

Supreme Court of Connecticut, 1961
148 Conn. 223, 169 A.2d 641

KING, J. The plaintiff obtained a judgment declaring that it is the rightful owner of the library of Abraham S. Yahuda, a distinguished Hebrew scholar who died in 1951. The library included rare books and manuscripts, mostly relating to the Bible, which Professor Yahuda, with the assistance of his wife, Ethel S. Yahuda, had collected during his lifetime. Some of the library was inventoried in Professor Yahuda's estate and was purchased from the estate by his wife. There is no dispute that all of the library had become the property of Ethel before 1953 and was her property when she died on March 6, 1955, unless by her dealings with the plaintiff between January, 1953, and the time of her death she transferred ownership to the plaintiff. While the defendants in this action are the executors under the will of Ethel, the controversy as to ownership of the library is, in effect, a contest between two Hebrew charitable institutions, the plaintiff and a charitable trust or foundation to which Ethel bequeathed the bulk of her estate.

Dear Ann Landers: I am a 15-year-old girl. When my sister and I were born, my parents set up college accounts with our parents named as trustees. My parents divorced seven years ago, and my mother discovered that Dad had gone into those accounts and withdrawn half the balances. He opened new savings accounts for my sister and me, listing himself as the sole trustee.

My sister recently discovered that her account has no money in it. When I asked Dad to see my balance statement, he was evasive and said I was "too young to understand." He would not let me withdraw any money from the account. I'm pretty sure he has spent all of it. My mother cannot possibly afford to pay for all our college expenses. How can I approach Dad about what's going on without hurting his feelings? Is there any way I can get the money back?

Ann Landers   —Loving Daughter in North Carolina

Dear Daughter: Don't be so worried about hurting Dad's feelings. He should be honest with you about the money so you can prepare for your future.

If the funds are gone, there is no way you can get them back. Ask your father point-blank if there is money left in the account and how much. Tell him you need to know so you can start saving for college as soon as possible. Meanwhile, be prepared to check out student loans and scholarships at state universities. Lack of money is no reason to miss out on a college education.

If Ann Landers had asked you what advice she should give Loving Daughter, what would you have said?

The pertinent facts recited in the finding may be summarized as follows: Before his death, Professor Yahuda forwarded certain of the books in his library to a warehouse in New Haven with instructions that they be packed for overseas shipment. The books remained in his name, no consignee was ever specified, and no shipment was made. Although it is not entirely clear, these books were apparently the ones which Ethel purchased from her husband's estate. Professor Yahuda and his wife had indicated to their friends their interest in creating a scholarship research center in Israel which would serve as a memorial to them. In January, 1953, Ethel went to Israel and had several talks with officers of the plaintiff, a university in Jerusalem. One of the departments of the plaintiff is an Institute of Oriental Studies, of outstanding reputation. The library would be very useful to the plaintiff, especially in connection with the work of this institute. On January 28, 1953, a large luncheon was given by the plaintiff in Ethel's honor and was attended by many notables, including officials of the plaintiff and the president of Israel. At this luncheon, Ethel described the library and announced its gift to the plaintiff. The next day, the plaintiff submitted to Ethel a proposed newspaper release which indicated that she had made a gift of the library to the plaintiff. Ethel signed the release as approved by her. From time to time thereafter she stated orally, and in letters to the plaintiff and friends, that she "had given" the library to the plaintiff. She refused offers of purchase and explained to others that she could not sell the library because it did not belong to her but to the plaintiff. On one occasion, when it was suggested that she give a certain item in the library to a friend, she stated that she could not, since it did not belong to her but to the plaintiff.

Early in 1954, Ethel began the task of arranging and cataloguing the material in the library for crating and shipment to Israel. These activities continued until about the time of her death. She sent some items, which she had finished cataloguing, to a warehouse for crating for overseas shipment. No consignee was named, and they remained in her name until her death. In October, 1954, when she was at the office of the American Friends of the Hebrew University, a fund-raising arm of the plaintiff in New York, she stated that she had crated most of the miscellaneous items, was continuously working on cataloguing the balance, and hoped to have the entire library in Israel before the end of the year. Until almost the time of her death, she corresponded with the plaintiff about making delivery to it of the library. In September, 1954, she wrote the president of the plaintiff that she had decided to ship the library and collection, but that it was not to be unpacked unless she was present, so that her husband's ex libris could be affixed to the books, and that she hoped "to adjust" the matter of her Beth Yahuda and her relations to the plaintiff. A "beth" is a building or portion of a building dedicated to a particular purpose.

The complaint alleged that the plaintiff was the rightful owner of the library and was entitled to possession. It contained no clue, however, to the theory on which ownership was claimed. The prayers for relief sought a declaratory judgment determining which one of the parties owned the library and an injunction restraining the defendants from disposing of it. The answer amounted to a general denial. The only real issues raised in the pleadings were the ownership and the right to possession of the library. As to these issues, the plaintiff had the burden of proof. The judgment found the "issues" for the plaintiff, and further recited that "a trust [in relation to the library] was created by a declaration of trust made by Ethel S. Yahuda, indicating her intention to create such a trust, made public by her."

We construe this language, in the light of the finding, as a determination that, at the luncheon in Jerusalem, Ethel orally constituted herself a trustee of the library for future delivery to the plaintiff. The difficulty with the trust theory adopted in the judgment is that the finding contains no facts even intimating that Ethel ever regarded herself as trustee of any trust whatsoever, or as having assumed any enforceable duties with respect to the property. The facts in the finding, in so far as they tend to support the judgment for the plaintiff at all, indicate that Ethel intended to make, and perhaps attempted to make, not a mere promise to give, but an executed, present, legal gift inter vivos of the library to the plaintiff without any delivery whatsoever.

Obviously, if an intended or attempted legal gift inter vivos of personal property fails as such because there was neither actual nor constructive delivery, and the intent to give can nevertheless be carried into effect in equity under the fiction that the donor is presumed to have intended to constitute himself a trustee to make the necessary delivery, then as a practical matter the requirement of delivery is abrogated in any and all cases of intended inter-vivos gifts. Of course this is not the law. A gift which is imperfect for lack of a delivery will not be turned into a declaration of trust for no better reason than that it is imperfect for lack of a delivery. Courts do not supply conveyances where there are none. This is true, even though the intended donee is a charity. The rule is approved in 1 Scott, Trusts §31.

It is true that one can orally constitute himself a trustee of personal property for the benefit of another and thereby create a trust enforceable in equity, even though without consideration and without delivery. 1 Scott, op. cit. §28; §32.2, p. 251. But he must in effect constitute himself a trustee. There must be an express trust, even though oral. It is not sufficient that he declare himself a donor. 1 Scott, op. cit. §31, p. 239; 4 id. §462.1. While he need not use the term "trustee," nor even manifest an understanding of its technical meaning or the technical meaning of the term "trust," he must manifest an intention to impose upon himself enforceable duties of a trust nature. Cullen v. Chappell, 116 F.2d 1017 (2d Cir. 1941); Restatement (Second), 1 Trusts §§23, 25; 1 Scott, op. cit., pp. 180, 181. There are no subordinate facts in the finding to indicate that Ethel ever intended to, or did, impose upon herself any enforceable duties of a trust nature with respect to this library. The most that could be said is that the subordinate facts in the finding might perhaps have supported a conclusion that at the luncheon she had the requisite donative intent so that, had she subsequently made a delivery of the property while that intent persisted, there would have been a valid, legal gift inter vivos. . . . The judgment, however, is not based on the theory of a legal gift inter vivos but on that of a declaration of trust. Since the subordinate facts give no support for a judgment on that basis, it cannot stand.

[The court remanded the case for a new trial at which the plaintiff could present its case on other theories than a declaration of trust.]

The Hebrew University Association v. Nye

Superior Court of Connecticut, 1966
26 Conn. Supp. 342, 223 A.2d 397

PARSKEY, J.   Most of the facts in this case are recited in Hebrew University Assn. v. Nye, 148 Conn. 223. Additionally, it should be noted that at the time of the announcement of the gift of the "Yahuda Library" the decedent gave to the plaintiff a memorandum containing a list of most of the contents of the library and of all of the important books, documents and incunabula. . . .

The plaintiff claims a gift inter vivos based on a constructive or symbolic delivery. . . . For a constructive delivery, the donor must do that which, under the circumstances, will in reason be equivalent to an actual delivery. It must be as nearly perfect and complete as the nature of the property and the circumstances will permit. The gift may be perfected when the donor places in the hands of the donee the means of obtaining possession of the contemplated gift, accompanied with acts and declarations clearly showing an intention to give and to divert himself of all dominion over the property. It is not necessary that the method adopted be the only possible one. It is sufficient if manual delivery is impractical or inconvenient. Constructive delivery has been found to exist in a variety of factual situations: delivery of keys to safe deposit box; pointing out hiding places where money is hidden; informal memorandum.

Examining the present case in the light of the foregoing, the court finds that the delivery of the memorandum coupled with the decedent's acts and declarations, which clearly show an intention to give and to divest herself of any ownership of the library, was sufficient to complete the gift. If the itemized memorandum which the decedent transmitted had been incorporated in a formal document, no one would question the validity of the gift. But formalism is not an end in itself. "Whatever the value of the notion of forms, the only use of the forms is to present their contents." Holmes in Justice Oliver Wendell Holmes — His Book Notices and Uncollected Letters and Papers, p. 167 (Shriver Ed.). This is not to suggest that forms and formalities do not serve a useful and sometimes an essential purpose. But where the purpose of formalities is being served, an excessive regard for formalism should not be allowed to defeat the ends of justice. The circumstances under which this gift was made — a public announcement at a luncheon attended by a head of state, accompanied by a document which identified in itemized form what was being given — are a sufficient substitute for a formal instrument purporting to pass title. . . .

The court recognizes, in arriving at this result, that it is abrogating in some respects the requirement of delivery in a case involving an intended gift inter vivos. Obviously, it would be neither desirable nor wise to abrogate the requirement of delivery in any and all cases of intended inter-vivos gifts, for to do so, even under the guise of enforcing equitable rights, might open the door to fraudulent claims. But neither does it mean that the present delivery requirement must remain inviolate. "Equity is not crippled . . . by an inexorable formula." Marr v. Tumulty, 256 N.Y. 15, 21 (1931). If it be argued that hard cases make bad law, the short response is, not while this court sits. . . .

Rules of law must, in the last analysis, serve the ends of justice or they are worthless. For a court of equity to permit the decedent's wishes to be doubly frustrated for no better reason than that the rules so provide makes no sense whatsoever. "The plastic remedies of the chancery are moulded to the needs of justice."

Accordingly, judgment may enter declaring that the plaintiff is the legal and equitable owner of the "Yahuda Library" and has a right to the immediate possession of its contents.

NOTES AND QUESTION

1. Not all courts are as strict as the Connecticut Supreme Court in requiring evidence that the donor considers herself a trustee. "The law will delineate a trust where, in view of a sufficiently manifested purpose or intent, that is the appropriate instrumentality, even though its creator calls it something else, or doesn't call it anything." Elyachar v. Gerel Corp., 583 F. Supp. 907, 922 (S.D.N.Y. 1984) (enforcing oral trust where father noted transfers of stock on his books but kept possession of the stock in order to maintain voting control of small corporations). See also In re Smith's Estate, 22 A. 916 (Pa. 1891) (bonds found in decedent's safe-deposit box with note indicating that they were "held for" another indicated a trust relationship).

Professor Scott disapproved of cases where the intention to make a gift seems plain and the gift fails for lack of delivery but courts "torture" the gift into a declaration of trust in order to save it. 1 Austin W. Scott, Trusts §31 (William F. Fratcher 4th ed. 1987) (intimating no objection to liberalizing the requirement of delivery for gifts). But see Sarajane Love, Imperfect Gifts as Declarations of Trust: An Unapologetic Anomaly, 67 Ky. L.J. 309 (1979), taking the opposite view.

2. Restatement (Third) of Trusts §16(2) (2003) provides: "If a property owner intends to make an outright gift inter vivos but fails to make the transfer that is required in order to do so, the gift intention will not be given effect by treating it as a declaration of trust." But Comment d goes on to fuzz up the picture considerably:

> If the manifestations of intention provide reliable, objective evidence of a deceased property owner's intended purpose and there is no indication that this purpose has been abandoned, the conduct and words ordinarily are interpreted as intending a type of transaction that would be effective to accomplish this purpose under the circumstances. That is, the preferred interpretation in marginal cases of this type is not that the property owner was merely expressing an intention to make a gift in the future but rather that the owner intended a declaration of trust. (If tenable under the circumstances, it is also possible that marginal acts that might or might not constitute delivery would be treated as a delivery based on a finding that they were in fact undertaken with the intention of making a present, outright gift.)

With admirable candor and greater clarity, Restatement (Third) of Property: Wills and Other Donative Transfers §6.2, cmt. yy (2003), analogizes the problem to that of excusing noncompliance with will execution formalities (see pages 225-235). Accordingly, it provides that "a gift of personal property can be perfected on the basis of donative intent alone if the donor's intent to make a gift is established by clear and convincing evidence." The underlying policy question is whether noncompliance with the formality of delivery should be excused in the face of clear and convincing evidence of donative intent. What do you think?

2. *Necessity of Trust Property*

The usual definition of a trust includes three elements: a trustee, a beneficiary, and trust property. Since a trust is a method of disposing of, or managing, property, it is said that a trust cannot exist without trust property, often called the *res*.[12] When the meaning of property is examined, however, we find that it may refer to something other than a piece of land or a hefty chunk of money. The trust res may be one dollar or one cent or it may be any interest in property that can be transferred. See Restatement (Third) of Trusts §40 (2003). Contingent remainders, leasehold interests, choses in action, royalties, life insurance policies — anything that is called property — may be put in trust. The critical question is whether a court will call the particular claim property. When one ventures beyond what are historically conceded to be property interests, the circumstances that lead a court to classify a claim as property require a careful analysis of many variables.

Unthank v. Rippstein
Supreme Court of Texas, 1964
386 S.W.2d 134

STEAKLEY, J. Three days before his death C.P. Craft penned a lengthy personal letter to Mrs. Iva Rippstein. The letter was not written in terms of his anticipated early death; in fact, Craft spoke in the letter of his plans to go to the Mayo Clinic at a later date. The portion of the letter at issue reads as follows:

> Used most of yesterday and day before to "round up" my financial affairs, and to be sure I knew just where I stood before I made the statement that I would send you $200.00 cash the first week of each month for the next 5 years, provided I live that long, also to send you $200.00 cash for Sept. 1960 and thereafter send that amount in cash the first week of the following months of 1960, October, November and December. [opposite which in the margin there was written:]
> I have stricken out the words "provided I live that long" and hereby and herewith bind my estate to make the $200.00 monthly payments provided for on this Page One of this letter of 9-17-60.

Mrs. Rippstein, Respondent here, first sought, unsuccessfully, to probate the writing as a [holographic] codicil to the will of Craft. The Court of Civil Appeals held that the writing was not a testamentary instrument which was subject to probate. In re Craft Estate, 358 S.W.2d 732 (Tex. App. 1962). We refused the application of Mrs. Rippstein for writ of error with the notation "no reversible error." See Rule 483, Texas Rules of Civil Procedure.

The present suit was filed by Mrs. Rippstein against the executors of the estate of Craft, Petitioners here, for judgment in the amount of the monthly installments which had matured, and for declaratory judgment adjudicating the liability of the executors to pay future installments as they mature. The trial court granted the motion of the executors for summary judgment. The Court of Civil Appeals reversed and rendered judgment for Mrs. Rippstein, holding that the writing in question established a voluntary trust under which Craft bound his property to the extent of the promised payments; and that upon his death his legal heirs held the legal title for the benefit of Mrs. Rippstein to that portion of the estate required to make the promised monthly payments.

---

12. *Note:* As we saw in Chapter 5, under the Uniform Testamentary Additions to Trusts Act, no res is required for an inter vivos trust if the settlor executes a pour-over will (page 310).

In her reply to the application for writ of error Mrs. Rippstein states that the sole question before us is whether the marginal notation constitutes "a declaration of trust whereby [Craft] agrees to thenceforth hold his estate in trust for the explicit purpose of making the payments." She argues that Craft imposed the obligation for the payment of the monies upon all of his property as if he had said "I henceforth hold my estate in trust for [such] purpose." She recognizes that under her position Craft became subject to the Texas Trust Act in the management of his property. Collaterally, however, Mrs. Rippstein takes the position that it being determinable by mathematical computation that less than ten per cent of the property owned by Craft at the time he wrote the letter would be required to discharge the monthly payments, the "remaining ninety per cent remained in Mr. Craft to do with as he would." Her theory is that that portion of Craft's property not exhausted in meeting his declared purpose would revert to him by way of a resulting trust eo instante with the legal and equitable title to such surplus merging in him.

These arguments in behalf of Mrs. Rippstein are indeed ingenious and resourceful, but in our opinion there is not sufficient certainty in the language of the marginal notation upon the basis of which a court of equity can declare a trust to exist which is subject to enforcement in such manner. The uncertainties with respect to the intention of Craft and with respect to the subject of the trust are apparent. The language of the notation cannot be expanded to show an intention on the part of Craft to place his property in trust with the result that his exercise of further dominion thereover would be wrongful except in a fiduciary capacity as trustee, and under which Craft would be subject to suit for conversion at the hands of Mrs. Rippstein if he spent or disposed of his property in a manner which would defeat his statement in the notation that a monthly payment of $200.00 in cash would be sent her the first week of each month. It is manifest that Craft did not expressly declare that all of his property, or any specific portion of the assets which he owned at such time, would constitute the corpus or res of a trust for the benefit of Mrs. Rippstein; and inferences may not be drawn from the language used sufficient for a holding to such effect to rest in implication. The conclusion is compelled that the most that Craft did was to express an intention to make monthly gifts to Mrs. Rippstein accompanied by an ineffectual attempt to bind his estate in futuro; the writing was no more than a promise to make similar gifts in the future and as such is unenforceable. The promise to give cannot be tortured into a trust declaration under which Craft while living, and as trustee, and his estate after his death, were under a legally enforceable obligation to pay Mrs. Rippstein the sum of $200.00 monthly for the five-year period. . . .

The judgment of the Court of Civil Appeals is reversed and that of the trial court is affirmed.

QUESTIONS AND NOTES

1. What policies are served by refusing to give effect to C.P. Craft's written intent? Where there is a written instrument making a gratuitous promise, which shows clearly that the donor intended to be legally bound, should the court give it effect as a declaration of trust? What would be the trust res? See Jane B. Baron, The Trust Res and Donative Intent, 61 Tul. L. Rev. 45 (1986) (arguing that the trust res requirement, supported by unconvincing rationales, defeats donative intent).

Recall that under the Uniform Testamentary Additions to Trusts Act, no res is required for an inter vivos trust if the settlor executes a pour-over will (see page 310). If a trust res can be dispensed with by exercising a pour-over will, why cannot it be dispensed with in the *Unthank* case?

The letter in *Unthank* was refused probate as a holographic will on the ground that it was not a "testamentary instrument." In view of In re Estate of Kuralt, page 244, would the result change in a Montana court under Uniform Probate Code §2-502(b)-(c) (1990)?

2.   *Trusts distinguished from debts.* The requirement of an identifiable trust res distinguishes a trust from a debt. A trust involves a duty to deal with some specific property, kept separate from the trustee's own funds. A debt involves an obligation to pay a sum of money to another. The crucial factor in distinguishing between a trust relationship and an ordinary debt is whether the recipient of the funds is entitled to use them as his own and commingle them with his own monies.

Money deposited in a bank ordinarily creates a debt, for the money is not segregated from the bank's general funds. However, the chose in action against the bank can serve as a res if the depositor transfers it in trust to another. What legal consequences might turn on the characterization of a relationship as a trust rather than a debt? See Restatement (Third) of Trusts §5, cmt. k (2003); 1 Austin W. Scott, Trusts §12 (William F. Fratcher 4th ed. 1987).

3.   *Resulting trusts.* In *Unthank*, Iva Rippstein argued that Craft, after transferring all his property into trust, had a resulting trust in the amount of his property not required to meet the payments to her. A resulting trust is an *equitable reversionary interest* that arises by operation of law in two situations: (1) where an express trust fails or makes an incomplete disposition (see Restatement, supra, §8) or (2) where one person pays the purchase price for property and causes title to the property to be taken in the name of another person who is not a natural object of the bounty of the purchaser (see Restatement, supra, §9). Thus:

> *Case 13. O* devises property to *X* in trust to pay the income to *A* for life and upon *A*'s death to distribute the property to *A*'s descendants. *A* dies without descendants. The remainder to *A*'s descendants fails. *X* holds the remainder on resulting trust for *O*'s heirs or devisees.
>
> *Case 14. B* purchases Blackacre with money supplied by *A*. Unless *B* can show that *A* intended to make a gift to *B*, *B* holds title to Blackacre on resulting trust for *A*, often called a *purchase money resulting trust.*

In both settings the transferee is not entitled to the beneficial interest, so the interest "is said 'to result' (that is, it reverts) to the transferor or to the transferor's estate or other successor(s) in interest." Restatement, supra, §7. Once a resulting trust is found, the trustee must reconvey the property to the beneficial owner upon demand.

BRAINARD v. COMMISSIONER, 91 F.2d 880 (7th Cir. 1937): In December 1927, Brainard orally stated, before his wife and mother, that he declared a trust of his expected profits from stock trading during 1928 for the benefit of his wife, mother, and two minor children, ages one and three. However, Brainard "agreed to assume personally any losses resulting from the venture." In 1928, Brainard traded in stock and turned a profit. After deducting his compensation as trustee, which he paid himself and declared as income on his income tax return, the remaining profits were divided into equal shares and credited on Brainard's books to the trusts of the four beneficiaries. Following the tax law then applicable to valid trusts, the beneficiaries reported the profits credited to their trusts on their respective 1928 income tax returns.

The question presented was whether the taxpayer's 1927 declaration created a valid trust over the future 1928 profits. If the trust did not arise until after Brainard credited the 1928 profits on his books to the four beneficiaries, then those profits accrued to the taxpayer before the transfer in trust; hence, under the applicable tax law those profits were taxable in 1928 to Brainard. If, however, the trust arose in December 1927 when the oral declaration was made, then the profits were taxable in 1928 to the beneficiaries.

The court held that the trust did not arise until after the profits were credited on the taxpayer's books on the ground that there was no res at the time of the declaration of trust (December 1927). "It is clear that the taxpayer, at the time of his declaration, had no property interest in 'profits in stock trading in 1928, if any,' because there were none in existence at that time. . . . It is obvious that the respective profits came into existence when and if such stocks were sold at a profit in 1928." Where there is no res at the time of a declaration of trust, the settlor must manifest anew his intent to create a trust when the res comes into being. During "such intervening time . . . the taxpayer must be considered as the sole owner of the profits and they were properly taxed to him as a part of his income."

Speelman v. Pascal

Court of Appeals of New York, 1961
10 N.Y.2d 313, 178 N.E.2d 723, 222 N.Y.S.2d 324

DESMOND, C.J. Gabriel Pascal, defendant's intestate who died in 1954, had been for many years a theatrical producer. In 1952 an English corporation named Gabriel Pascal Enterprises, Ltd., of whose 100 shares Gabriel Pascal owned 98, made an agreement with the English Public Trustee who represented the estate of George Bernard Shaw. This agreement granted to Gabriel Pascal Enterprises, Ltd., the exclusive world rights to prepare and produce a musical play to be based on Shaw's play "Pygmalion" and a motion picture version of the musical play. The agreement recited, as was the fact, that the licensee owned a film scenario written by Pascal and based on "Pygmalion." In fact Pascal had, some time previously, produced a nonmusical movie version of "Pygmalion" under rights obtained by Pascal from George Bernard Shaw during the latter's lifetime. The 1952 agreement required the licensee corporation to pay the Shaw estate an initial advance and thereafter to pay the Shaw estate 3% of the gross receipts of the musical play and musical movie with a provision that the license was to terminate if within certain fixed periods the licensee did not arrange with Lerner[13] and

---

13. Alan Jay Lerner, dying in 1986, left what might be called a delicious bequest:

Third: I give and bequeath to Benjamin Welles, if he survives me, and Sydney Gruson, if he survives me, the sum of $1,000.00 each. The purpose of this modest remembrance is to defray the cost of one evening's merriment to be devoted to cheerful recollections of their departed friend.

The abstemious Bernard Shaw, vegetarian and teetotaller, who scathingly denounced the "artificial happiness, artificial courage, and artificial gaiety" provided by alcohol, would not have been amused. — Eds.

Loewe or other similarly well-known composers to write the musical play and arrange to produce it. Before Pascal's death in July, 1954, he had made a number of unsuccessful efforts to get the musical written and produced and it was not until after his death that arrangements were made, through a New York bank as temporary administrator of his estate, for the writing and production of the highly successful "My Fair Lady." Meanwhile, on February 22, 1954, at a time when the license from the Shaw estate still had two years to run, Gabriel Pascal, who died four and a half months later, wrote, signed and delivered to plaintiff a document as follows:

Dear Miss Kingman

This is to confirm to you our understanding that I give you from my shares of profits of the Pygmalion Musical stage version five per cent (5%) in England, and two per cent (2%) of my shares of profits in the United States. From the film version, five per cent (5%) from my profit shares all over the world.

As soon as the contracts are signed, I will send a copy of this letter to my lawyer, Edwin Davies, in London, and he will confirm to you this arrangement in a legal form.

This participation in my shares of profits is a present to you in recognition for your loyal work for me as my Executive Secretary.[14]

> Very sincerely yours,
>
> *Gabriel Pascal*

The question in this lawsuit is: Did the delivery of this paper constitute a valid, complete, present gift to plaintiff by way of assignment of a share in future royalties when and if collected from the exhibition of the musical stage version and film version of "Pygmalion"? A consideration was, of course, unnecessary (Personal Property Law, §33, subd. 4). . . .

The only real question is as to whether the 1954 letter above quoted operated to transfer to plaintiff an enforcible right to the described percentages of the royalties to accrue to Pascal on the production of a stage or film version of a musical play based on "Pygmalion." We see no reason why this letter does not have that effect. It is true that at the time of the delivery of the letter there was no musical stage or film play in existence but Pascal, who owned and was conducting negotiations to realize on the stage and film rights, could grant to another a share of the moneys to accrue from the use of those rights by others. There are many instances of courts enforcing assignments of rights to sums which were expected thereafter to become due to the assignor. A typical case is Field v. Mayor of New York (6 N.Y. 179 (1852)). One Bell, who had done much printing and similar work for the City of New York but had no present contract to do any more such work, gave an

---

14. Pascal's loyal "Executive Secretary" is portrayed somewhat differently by Pascal's widow, Valerie, in her book, The Disciple and His Devil (1970). Marianne Speelman, also known as Zaya Kingman, was half Chinese and half Irish and the exotically beautiful widow of a Dutch banker who had made a fortune in China. She invited Gabriel Pascal to dinner in March of 1953 and that same night began a torrid love affair (id. at 252). As a result of her herb teas and food prepared with "life elixir," Pascal experienced "prodigious sexual powers" and felt as if he were flying. Marianne wrote that anybody who had ever made love to her could never again be satisfied with any other woman (id. at 255). Valerie states that soon after delivering the document in this case (id. at 297), Pascal attempted to break off his volcanic affair and, under the influence of an Indian mystic, renounced his fleshly desires forever (id. at 299). Spent, Pascal died some four months later. — Eds.

Marianne Speelman (Zaya Kingman)

assignment in the amount of $1,500 of any moneys that might thereafter become due to Bell for such work. Bell did obtain such contracts or orders from the city and money became due to him therefor. This court held that while there was not at the time of the assignment any presently enforcible or even existing chose in action but merely a possibility that there would be such a chose of action, nevertheless there was a possibility of such which the parties expected to ripen into reality and which did afterwards ripen into reality and that, therefore, the assignment created an equitable title which the courts would enforce. A case similar to the present one in general outline is Central Trust Co. v. West India Improvement Co. (169 N.Y. 314 (1901)) where the assignor had a right or concession from the Colony of Jamaica to build a railroad on that island and the courts upheld a mortgage given by the concession owner on any property that would be acquired by the concession owner in consideration of building the railroad if and when the railroad should be built. The Court of Appeals pointed out in *Central Trust Co.*, at page 323, that the property as to which the mortgage was given had not yet come into existence at the time of the giving of the mortgage but that there was an expectation that such property, consisting of securities, would come into existence and accrue to the concession holder when and if the latter performed the underlying contract. This court held that the assignment would be recognized and enforced in equity. The cases cited by appellant (Young v. Young, 80 N.Y. 422 (1880); Vincent v. Rix, 248 N.Y. 76 (1928); Farmers' Loan & Trust Co. v. Winthrop, 207 App. Div. 356, mod. 238 N.Y. 477 (1924)) are not to the contrary. In each of those instances the attempted gifts failed because there had not been such a completed and irrevocable delivery of the subject matter of the gift as to put the gift beyond cancellation by the donor. In every such case the question must be as to whether there was a completed delivery of a kind appropriate to the subject property. Ordinarily, if the property consists of existing stock certificates or corporate bonds, as in the *Young* and *Vincent* cases (supra), there must be a completed physical transfer of the stock certificates or bonds. In Farmers' Loan & Trust Co. v. Winthrop (supra) the dispute was as to the effect of a power of attorney but the maker of the power had used language which could not be construed as effectuating a present gift of the property which the donor expected to receive in the future from another estate.[15] The *Farmers' Loan & Trust Co.* case does not hold that property to be the subject of a valid gift must be in present physical existence and in the possession of the donor but it does hold that the language used in the particular document was not sufficient to show an irrevocable present intention to turn over to the donee securities which would come to the donor on the settlement of another estate. At page 485 of 238 New York this court held that all that need be established is "an intention that the title of the donor shall be presently divested and presently transferred" but that in the particular document under scrutiny in the *Farmer's Loan & Trust Co.* case there was lacking any language to show an irrevocable intent of a gift to become operative at once. In our present case there was nothing left for Pascal to do in order to make an irrevocable transfer to plaintiff of part of Pascal's right to receive royalties from the productions. . . .

Judgment affirmed.

NOTES, PROBLEMS, AND QUESTIONS

1.   Restatement (Third) of Trusts §41 (2003) provides: "An expectation or hope of receiving property in the future, or an interest that has not come into existence or has ceased to exist, cannot be held in trust." What doctrinal, factual, or other distinction justifies the different results reached in the *Brainard* case and the *Speelman* case? In terms of ritual and evidentiary policies, are the cases consistent?

---

15.   In Farmers' Loan & Trust Co. v. Winthrop, the settlor executed an inter vivos trust with Farmers' Loan as trustee of $5,000 "and all other property hereafter delivered." On the same day she gave a power of attorney to Farmers' Loan authorizing it to collect the assets she was entitled to receive from the estate of Jabez Bostwick "and to transfer such securities and property to yourself as trustee." Before the executor of the Bostwick estate delivered the property to Farmers' Loan, the settlor died. The court held that the attempted transfer failed. — Eds.

2. In which of the following cases has there been an effective transfer? Compare them with what happened in *Brainard* and *Speelman*.

(a) *O* orally declares to *A*: "I give you 5 percent of the profits of a musical play based upon Shaw's Pygmalion, if I produce it and if there are any profits."

(b) *O* orally declares himself trustee for one year of all stocks he owns, with any profits from stock trading to go to *A*. See Barnette v. McNulty, 516 P.2d 583 (Ariz. App. 1973).

(c) In a notarized writing *O* declares himself trustee for the benefit of *A* of any profits *O* makes from stock trading during the next calendar year.

(d) *O* orally declares himself trustee for the benefit of *A* of five percent of the profits, if there are any, of a musical play that *O* is writing, based upon Shaw's Pygmalion. See 1A Austin W. Scott, Trusts §86.2 (William F. Fratcher 4th ed. 1987).

3. The prevailing view is that a person can assign future earnings from an existing contract. The theory is that the future yield of an existing property right can be transferred even though property to be acquired in the future cannot be. In the *Speelman* case, Pascal had exclusive rights (a license) from the Shaw estate to make a musical version of Pygmalion. But the contract with Lerner and Loewe to write the musical version was not made by Pascal's administrator until nearly a year after Pascal's death. Was the license enough to give Pascal an assignable right to profits or did the right to profits arise only after Pascal's death when the contract was signed? Or, did it matter at all to the court that Pascal had a license? Should it matter? See E. Allan Farnsworth, Changing Your Mind 143-147 (1998).

NOTE: TAXATION OF GRANTOR TRUSTS

In Brainard v. Commissioner, page 511, the settlor of the trust sought to obtain an income tax advantage by creating a trust of his future profits from stock trading. If a valid trust were created, these profits would be taxable to the trust beneficiaries, at a lower bracket, and not to the settlor. This kind of transfer, avoiding income tax to the settlor on future income, is not available to a taxpayer today.

In Helvering v. Clifford, 309 U.S. 331 (1940), the Supreme Court held that where a taxpayer declared a trust of securities for five years with income payable to another for the five-year term but with the settlor retaining complete control over the principal and reversion of the corpus at the end of five years, the taxpayer could be treated as owner, and taxed on the income, by the federal taxing authorities. Subsequently, the Treasury Department issued regulations spelling out in detail the circumstances under which the settlor of a trust would be taxable on the trust income on the ground of retained dominion and control (the "Clifford regulations"). These were in turn supplanted by amendments to the Internal Revenue Code itself. Sections 671-677 of the Code now govern the circumstances when the settlor is taxable on trust income because of retained dominion and control. Where the settlor wants to avoid being taxed on the trust income, care must be taken to avoid these sections.

Sections 671-677 define what are called *grantor trusts* — trusts in which the income is taxable to the settlor (grantor) because the settlor has retained substantial control and is deemed by the Code still to be the owner of the trust assets. We have noted earlier, at page 317, that trust income of a revocable trust is taxable to the settlor. A revocable trust is an example of a grantor trust. I.R.C. §676. Now we attend to grantor trusts where the settlor retains not a right to revoke the trust but some lesser power.

Under these sections of the Code, there is a spousal attribution rule: A settlor is treated as holding any power or interest that is held by the settlor's spouse if the spouse is living with the settlor at the time the property is transferred into trust.

Where the grantor has a *reversionary interest,* either in the corpus or in the income, and the reversionary interest at the inception of the trust exceeds 5 percent of the value of the corpus or the income, the trust is a grantor trust. The income from the trust is taxable to the settlor. I.R.C. §673. There is one important exception. The settlor is exempt from this rule if she creates a trust for a minor lineal descendant, who has the entire present interest, and the settlor retains a reversionary interest that will take effect only upon the death of the lineal descendant under the age of 21. I.R.C. §673(b). The drafting moral here is clear: Except in the one case mentioned, when drafting an irrevocable trust for shifting income taxes on assets, do not leave a reversionary interest of any value in the settlor.

Where the *settlor* or a *nonadverse party* — either as trustee or in any individual capacity — is given discretionary power over income or principal exercisable without the consent of an adverse party, the trust is a grantor trust. The income is taxable to the settlor. I.R.C. §674. Thus:

> *Case 15.* O creates a trust, with herself and the First National Bank as co-trustees, to pay the income to O's two children in such amounts as the trustees shall determine or to accumulate it and, upon the death of O's two children, to distribute the principal to O's grandchildren then living. The trustees earn $70,000 income the first year, which the trustees distribute equally to O's two children. The $70,000 income is taxable to O, the settlor of a grantor trust, *and* O has made a gift to each child of $35,000. Each gift qualifies for a $11,000 annual gift tax exclusion, so O has made a taxable gift to each child of $24,000. (On the gift tax exclusion, see page 857.) The amount received by O's children is not income to them because it is a gift from O.

There are two major exceptions to §674. The first is that a discretionary power to distribute, apportion, or accumulate income or to pay out corpus can be given to an *independent* trustee without adverse tax consequences to the settlor. I.R.C. §674(c). If in Case 15 the First National Bank had been named sole trustee, the income would not be taxable to O. It is important to distinguish between an independent trustee and a nonadverse party. An independent trustee is one who is not related or subordinate to the settlor nor subservient to her wishes, whereas a nonadverse party is a person who lacks a substantial beneficial interest that would be adversely affected by the exercise or nonexercise of the power.

The second major exception to §674 permits (a) a power to be given the settlor or any trustee to distribute *corpus* pursuant to a "reasonably definite standard which is set forth in the trust instrument" or (b) a power to be given any trustee other than the settlor or the settlor's spouse to distribute *income* pursuant to a "reasonably definite external standard which is set forth in the trust instrument." I.R.C. §674(b)(5)(A), (d).

Another type of grantor trust is one where certain administrative powers can be exercised for the benefit of the settlor rather than for the beneficiaries of the trust. Generally, the settlor will be subject to tax on the income if there is a power exercisable by the settlor or a nonadverse party (1) to purchase trust assets for less than an adequate consideration, (2) to borrow trust assets without adequate security, (3) to vote or acquire stock in a corporation in which the settlor has a significant voting interest, or (4) to reacquire the trust corpus. Any of these indicia of dominion and control may be sufficient to tax the settlor on the trust income. See I.R.C. §675.

The category of grantor trusts also includes a trust where the settlor, a nonadverse party, or an independent trustee has the power to distribute trust income to the settlor or the settlor's spouse. I.R.C. §677(a). Under §677, income is not taxable to the settlor merely because the trustee may distribute it for the support of a beneficiary (other than the settlor's spouse) whom the settlor is legally obligated to support. If the trust property is in fact used to discharge the settlor's legal obligation, however, the settlor is taxable on the income to the extent income is actually so used. I.R.C. §677(b). Thus:

> *Case 16. O* transfers property to the First National Bank in trust to pay the income in its discretion for the support of *O*'s children. Even though the trustee has discretion to use the income for the support of *O*'s minor children (thereby discharging *O*'s legal obligation of support), *O* is taxable on the income only to the extent it is actually so applied. If the income used for the support of *O*'s children is in excess of the amount *O* is legally obligated to provide, the excess income is not taxable to *O*.

In Case 16, a provision could be inserted in the trust instrument providing that any distributions by the trustee would not discharge the settlor's legal obligation of support. Such a provision would prevent taxation of the income to the settlor and would not, as a practical matter, interfere with any trust distribution by the trustee.

Any lawyer creating an inter vivos trust should pay close attention to §§671-677 of the Internal Revenue Code and the relevant regulations if the settlor desires to escape taxation on the income. Also, it should be kept in mind that although the income tax and the estate and gift taxes are not exactly parallel, if the settlor is treated as owner and taxable on the income of the trust assets, there is a good chance that the trust assets will be subject to estate taxation at the settlor's death. See discussion of I.R.C. §§2036 and 2038 at pages 876, 887. For a client who wants to avoid income and estate taxation, the lawyer will want to draft a trust that skirts the reach of both the income and estate tax sections of the Code and leaves the client in a safe harbor.

3. Necessity of Trust Beneficiaries

It is said that a trust must have one or more ascertainable beneficiaries. See Restatement (Third) of Trusts §44 (2003); Uniform Trust Code §402(a)(3) (2000). The reason: There must be someone to whom the trustee owes fiduciary duties, someone who can call the trustee to account. Underpinning the beneficiary principle is the policy that a private trust must be for the benefit of its beneficiaries.

See generally John H. Langbein, Mandatory Rules in the Law of Trusts, 98 Nw. U.L. Rev. 1105 (2004).

There are exceptions, however, to this rule. Unlike a private trust, a charitable trust need not have an ascertainable beneficiary to be valid (we take up charitable trusts in Chapter 12). Moreover, the beneficiaries of a private trust may be unborn or unascertained when the trust is created. Thus a trust created by O, who is childless, for the benefit of her future children would be valid. The courts would protect the interests of the unborn children from improper acts of the trustee. See Restatement, supra, §44, cmts. b-c. On the other hand, if at the time the trust becomes effective the beneficiaries are too indefinite to be ascertained, the attempted trust may fail for want of ascertainable beneficiaries.

Clark v. Campbell
Supreme Court of New Hampshire, 1926
82 N.H. 281, 133 A. 166

Snow, J.   The ninth clause of the will of deceased reads:

> My estate will comprise so many and such a variety of articles of personal property such as books, photographic albums, pictures, statuary, bronzes, bric-a-brac, hunting and fishing equipment, antiques, rugs, scrapbooks, canes and masonic jewels, that probably I shall not distribute all, and perhaps no great part thereof, during my life by gift among my friends. Each of my trustees is competent by reason of familiarity with the property, my wishes and friendships, to wisely distribute some portion at least of said property. I therefore give and bequeath to my trustees all my property embraced within the classification aforesaid in trust to make disposal by the way of a memento from myself, of such articles to such of my friends as they, my trustees, shall select. All of said property, not so disposed of by them, my trustees are directed to sell and the proceeds of such sale or sales to become and be disposed of as a part of the residue of my estate.

The question here reserved is whether . . . the bequest for the benefit of the testator's "friends" must fail for the want of certainty of the beneficiaries.

By the common law there cannot be a valid bequest to an indefinite person. There must be a beneficiary or a class of beneficiaries indicated in the will capable of coming into court and claiming the benefit of the bequest. This principle applies to private but not to public trusts and charities. The basis assigned for this distinction is the difference in the enforceability of the two classes of trusts. In the former there being no definite cestui que trust to assert his right, there is no one who can compel performance, with the consequent unjust enrichment of the trustee; while in the case of the latter, performance is considered to be sufficiently secured by the authority of the attorney-general to invoke the power of the courts. . . .

That the foregoing is the established doctrine seems to be conceded, but it is contended in argument that it was not the intention of the testator by the ninth clause to create a trust, at least as respects the selected articles, but to make an absolute gift thereof to the trustees individually. . . . It is a sufficient answer to this contention that the language of the ninth clause does not warrant the assumed construction. . . . When the clause is elided of unnecessary verbiage the testator is made to say: "I give to my trustees my property (of the described class) in trust to make disposal of to such of my friends as they shall select." It is difficult to conceive of language more clearly disclosing an intention to create a trust.

It is further sought to sustain the bequest as a power. The distinction apparently relied upon is that a power, unlike a trust, is not imperative and leaves the act to be done at the will of the donee of the power. But the ninth clause by its terms imposes upon the trustees the imperative duty to dispose of the selected articles among the testator's friends. If, therefore, the authority bestowed by the testator by the use of a loose terminology may be called a power, it is not an optional power but a power coupled with a trust to which the principles incident to a trust so far as here involved clearly apply. . . .

We must, therefore, conclude that this clause presents the case of an attempt to create a private trust. . . .

The question presented, therefore, is whether or not the ninth clause provides for definite and ascertainable beneficiaries so that the bequest therein can be sustained as a private trust. . . .

Like the direct legatees in a will, the beneficiaries under a trust may be designated by class. But in such case the class must be capable of delimitation, as "brothers and sisters," "children," "issue," "nephews and nieces." A bequest giving the executor authority to distribute his property "among his relatives and for benevolent objects in such sums as in their judgment shall be for the best" was sustained upon evidence within the will that by "relatives" the testator intended such of his relatives within the statute of distributions as were needy, and thus brought the bequest within the line of charitable gifts and excluded all others as individuals. Goodale v. Mooney, 60 N.H. 528, 536 (1881). Where a testator bequeathed his stocks to be apportioned to his "relations" according to the discretion of the trustee, to be enjoyed by them after his decease, it was held to be a power to appoint amongst his relations who were next of kin under the statute of distribution. . . .

In the case now under consideration the cestuis que trustent are designated as the "friends" of the testator. The word "friends" unlike "relations" has no accepted statutory or other controlling limitations, and in fact has no precise sense at all. Friendship is a word of broad and varied application. It is commonly used to describe the undefinable relationships which exist not only between those connected by ties of kinship or marriage, but as well between strangers in blood, and which vary in degree from the greatest intimacy to an acquaintance more or less casual. . . . There is no express evidence that the word is used in any restricted sense. The only implied limitation of the class is that fixed by the boundaries of the familiarity of the testator's trustees with his friendships. If such familiarity could be held to constitute such a line of demarcation as to define an ascertainable group, it is to be noted that the gift is not to such group as a class, the members of which are to take in some definite proportion (1 Jarman, Wills, 534; 1 Schouler, Wills, s. 1011) or according to their needs, but the disposition is to "such of my friends as they, my trustees, may select." No sufficient criterion is furnished to govern the selection of the individuals from the class. The assertion of the testator's confidence in the competency of his trustees "to wisely distribute some portion" of the enumerated articles "by reason of familiarity with the property, my wishes and friendships," does not furnish such a criterion. . . . Where an executor was given direction to distribute in a manner calculated to carry out "wishes which

I have expressed to him or may express to him" and such wishes had been orally communicated to the executor by the testator, the devise could not be given effect as against the next of kin. Olliffe v. Wells, 130 Mass. 221, 224, 225 (1881). Much less can effect be given to the uncommunicated wishes of the testator here.

It was the evident purpose of the testator to invest his trustees with the power after his death to make disposition of the enumerated articles among an undefined class with practically the same freedom and irresponsibility that he himself would have exercised if living; that is, to substitute for the will of the testator the will and discretion of the trustees. Such a purpose is in contravention of the policy of the statute which provides that "no will shall be effectual to pass any real or personal estate . . . unless made by a person . . . in writing, signed by the testator or by some one in his presence and by his direction, and attested and subscribed in his presence by three or more credible witnesses." P.L., c. 297, §2.

Where a gift is impressed with a trust ineffectively declared and incapable of taking effect because of the indefiniteness of the cestui que trust, the donee will hold the property in trust for the next taker under the will, or for the next of kin by way of a resulting trust. . . . The trustees therefore hold title to the property enumerated in the paragraph under consideration, to be disposed of as a part of the residue, and the trustees are so advised. . . .

Case discharged.

NOTE AND QUESTIONS

1.   Professor Scott argued that where there is a transfer in trust for members of an indefinite class of persons, no enforceable trust is created, but the transferee has a discretionary power to convey the property to such members of the class as he may select. 2 Austin W. Scott, Trusts §122 (William F. Fratcher 4th ed. 1987). In other words, the transferee has a power of appointment. Restatement (Third) of Trusts §46(2) (2003), adopts Scott's position.

A valid power of appointment may have a definite class of beneficiaries (for example, "my issue") or it may not (for example, "anyone except the donee or her creditors or her estate"). The test of validity is: If the class of beneficiaries is so described that some person might reasonably be said to answer the description, the power is valid. An appointment is invalid, however, if it cannot be determined whether the appointee answers the description.

In trusts today, beneficiaries are often given powers of appointment, that is, powers to choose among a designated class of persons the next taker under the trust. For example, *T* may devise his residuary estate in trust "for my wife *W* for life, and then to distribute the trust assets to such of my issue as my wife appoints." The power of appointment is discretionary; it is a nonfiduciary power. If *W* fails to exercise the power, the trust property passes to *T*'s heirs upon *W*'s death. Powers of appointment are treated in Chapter 9.

In Clark v. Campbell, the court says it cannot treat the will as creating a power of appointment because it is given to *trustees*. They hold it in a fiduciary capacity (unlike a nonfiduciary power given a beneficiary). It is not an optional power but a "power coupled with a trust." Therefore, trust principles apply. If the power of selection had been given "to my sister Polly and my friend Herbert" and not "to

Polly and Herbert, *trustees* (or *executors*)" it would be a valid nonfiduciary power of appointment. (What is the drafting moral here?)

2.   The will of Marilyn Monroe, the actress and celebrity icon whose death in 1962 was ruled a probable suicide, contained the following clause: "I give and bequeath all of my personal effects and clothing to Lee Strasberg,[16] or if he should predecease me, then to my Executor hereinafter named, it being my desire that he distribute these, in his sole discretion, among my friends, colleagues and those to whom I am devoted." Did Monroe intend to create a trust? If so, did Monroe designate an ascertainable beneficiary? Cf. Strasberg v. Odyssey Group, Inc., 59 Cal. Rptr. 2d 474 (App. 1996).

In re Searight's Estate
Ohio Court of Appeals, Ninth District, 1950
87 Ohio App. 417, 95 N.E.2d 779

HUNSICKER, J.   George P. Searight, a resident of Wayne county, Ohio, died testate on November 27, 1948. Item "third" of his will provided:

> I give and bequeath my dog, Trixie, to Florence Hand of Wooster, Ohio, and I direct my executor to deposit in the Peoples Federal Savings and Loan Association, Wooster, Ohio, the sum of $1000.00 to be used by him to pay Florence Hand at the rate of 75 cents per day for the keep and care of my dog as long as it shall live. If my dog shall die before the said $1000.00 and the interest accruing therefrom shall have been used up, I give and bequeath whatever remains of said $1000.00 to be divided equally among those of the following persons who are living at that time, to wit: Bessie Immler, Florence Hand, Reed Searight, Fern Olson and Willis Horn.

At the time of his death, all of the persons, and his dog, Trixie, named in such item third, were living.

Florence Hand accepted the bequest of Trixie, and the executor paid to her from the $1000 fund, 75 cents a day for the keep and care of the dog. The value of Trixie was agreed to be $5.

The Probate Court [held item third valid]. . . . The questions presented by this appeal on questions of law are:

1.   Is the testamentary bequest for the care of Trixie (a dog) valid in Ohio—
     (a) as a proper subject of a so-called "honorary trust"?
     (b) as not being in violation of the rule against perpetuities? . . .

1(a). . . . We do not have, in the instant case, the question of a trust established for the care of dogs in general or of an indefinite number of dogs, but we are here considering the validity of a testamentary bequest for the benefit of a specific dog.

16. Before his death in 1982, Lee Strasberg achieved considerable notoriety in his own right as an actor and acting coach in the method acting tradition. In 1952 he was named the artistic director of the prestigious Actor's Studio, a position that he held until his death. In addition to Monroe, Strasberg's students included James Dean, Robert DeNiro, Jane Fonda, Dustin Hoffman, Paul Newman, and Al Pacino. The Actor's Studio is perhaps best known today as the home of James Lipton, the sycophantic host of the Bravo cable network's Inside the Actor's Studio, in which Lipton conducts astonishingly obsequious celebrity interviews that are at times weirdly riveting.—Eds.

This is not a charitable trust, nor is it a gift of money to the Ohio Humane Society or a county humane society, which societies are vested with broad statutory authority, Section 10062, General Code, for the care of animals.

Text writers on the subject of trusts and many law professors designate a bequest for the care of a specific animal as an "honorary trust"; that is, one binding the conscience of the trustee, since there is no beneficiary capable of enforcing the trust.

The rule in Ohio, that the absence of a beneficiary having a legal standing in court and capable of demanding an accounting of the trustee is fatal and the trust fails, was first announced in Mannix, Assignee v. Purcell, 19 N.E. 572 (Ohio 1888). . . .

In 1 Scott on the Law of Trusts, Section 124, the author says:

> There are certain classes of cases similar to those discussed in the preceding section in that there is no one who as beneficiary can enforce the purpose of the testator, but different in one respect, namely, that the purpose is definite. Such, for example, are bequests for the erection or maintenance of tombstones or monuments or for the care of graves, and bequests for the support of specific animals. It has been held in a number of cases that such bequests as these do not necessarily fail. It is true that the legatee cannot be compelled to carry out the intended purpose, since there is no one to whom he owes a duty to carry out the purpose.
>
> Even though the legatee cannot be compelled to apply the property to the designated purpose, the courts have very generally held that he can properly do so, and that no resulting trust arises so long as he is ready and willing to carry it out. The legatee will not, however, be permitted to retain the property for his own benefit; and if he refuses or neglects to carry out the purpose, a resulting trust will arise in favor of the testator's residuary legatee or next of kin. . . .

The object and purpose sought to be accomplished by the testator in the instant case is not capricious or illegal. He sought to effect a worthy purpose — the care of his pet dog.

Whether we designate the gift in this case as an "honorary trust" or a gift with a power which is valid when exercised is not important, for we do know that the one to whom the dog was given accepted the gift and indicated her willingness to care for such dog, and the executor proceeded to carry out the wishes of the testator.

> Where the owner of property transfers it upon an intended trust for a specific non-charitable purpose and there is no definite or definitely ascertainable beneficiary designated, no trust is created; but the transferee has power to apply the property to the designated purpose, unless he is authorized by the terms of the intended trust so to apply the property beyond the period of the rule against perpetuities, or the purpose is capricious. I Restatement of the Law of Trusts, Section 124.

To call this bequest for the care of the dog, Trixie, a trust in the accepted sense in which that term is defined is, we know, an unjustified conclusion. The modern authorities, as shown by the cases cited earlier in this discussion, however, uphold the validity of a gift for the purpose designated in the instant case, where the person to whom the power is given is willing to carry out the testator's wishes. Whether called an "honorary trust" or whatever terminology is used, we conclude that the bequest for the care of the dog, Trixie, is not in and of itself unlawful.

1(b). In Ohio, by statute, Section 10512-8, General Code, the rule against perpetuities is specifically defined, and such statute further says: "It is the intention by the adoption of this section to make effective in Ohio what is generally known as the common law rule against perpetuities."

It is to be noted, in every situation where the so-called "honorary trust" is established for specific animals, that, unless the instrument creating such trust limits the duration of the trust — that is, the time during which the power is to be exercised — to human lives, we will have "honorary trusts" established for animals of great longevity, such as crocodiles, elephants and sea turtles. . . .

If we then examine item third of testator's will, we discover that, although the bequest for his dog is for "as long as it shall live," the money given for this purpose is $1000 payable at the rate of 75¢ a day. By simple mathematical computation, this sum of money, expended at the rate determined by the testator, will be fully exhausted in three years and 238 1/3 days. If we assume that this $1000 is deposited in a bank so that interest at the high rate of 6% per annum were earned thereon, the time needed to consume both principal and interest thereon (based on semiannual computation of such interest on the average unused balance during such six month period) would be four years, 57 1/2 days.

It is thus very apparent that the testator provided a time limit for the exercise of the power given his executor, and that such time limit is much less than the maximum period allowed under the rule against perpetuities.

We therefore conclude that the bequest in the instant case for the care of the dog, Trixie, does not, by the terms of the creating instrument, violate the rule against perpetuities. . . .

The judgment of the Probate Court is affirmed.

NOTES AND QUESTIONS

1. In *Searight's Estate* the Department of Taxation of Ohio argued that an inheritance tax was levied on the amount used for the care of Trixie. Ohio General Code §5332 levied a tax on all property passing to a "person, institution or corporation." In an omitted portion of the opinion, the court decided that a dog was none of these, and no inheritance tax was levied on the amount used for Trixie's care. A tax was levied, however, on the contingent amount passing to the five persons on the death of Trixie.

In the probate court proceedings, the Department also argued that a dog is personal property and a thing of value and should have been taxed as an inheritance of Florence Hand. The executor of the estate of George P. Searight testified:

If the Court please: I am an innocent bystander of this situation and am not personally interested one way or the other except to be right. Let me say this to the Court, — I wrote this provision in the Will, and frankly, the question as to whether the dog was taxable or not was never considered. I had no idea we would have such a problem. When the time came to make the Will George was concerned that when something happened to him that the dog was not to go to the dog pound. In fact he had as much affection for his dog as for his relatives. He lived with the dog and lived down there like a recluse.

So far as the tax matter is concerned, let me take Mr. Annat's last contention, so far as taxing the dog as a thing of value. The dog may have a value of two, three or five dollars. It has no value other than that of a mongrel fox-terrier dog. Frankly I would say it could be argued that the fair market value of the dog was zero. If Florence tried to sell the dog I don't think she could give it away. On the contention of whether or not it is a thing of value I am not disposed to argue. Whether it can be sold, I don't know. I do know this, — George had it and I know there was some question about Florence taking it, and only because he made that instruction in the Will she took it.

The parties settled the matter by agreeing that the dog had a value of $5 and Florence Hand owed a tax on that.

The executor's final accounting reported that $255.75 was distributed to Florence Hand for the care of Trixie, who died on October 30, 1949, after being struck by a car. The balance of the $1,000 was divided among the five legatees.

2.   In Gerry W. Beyer, Pet Animals: What Happens When Their Humans Die?, 40 Santa Clara L. Rev. 617 (2000), the author states:

Over two-thirds of pet owners treat their animals as members of their families. . . . Pet owners are extremely devoted to their animal companions with 80% bragging about their pets to others, 79% allowing their pets to sleep in bed with them, 37% carrying pictures of their pets in their wallets, and 31% taking time off from work to be with their sick pets. . . .

An owner's love for his pet transcends death, as documented by studies revealing that between 12% and 27% of pet owners include pets in their wills. The popular media frequently reports cases involving pet owners who provide for the care of their beloved companions after death. For example, singer Dusty Springfield's will made extensive provisions for her cat, Nicholas. The will instructed that Nicholas' bed be lined with Dusty's nightgown, Dusty's recordings be played each night at Nicholas' bedtime, and that Nicholas be fed imported baby food. Doris Duke, the sole heir to tobacco baron "Buck" Duke, who founded Duke University and started the American Tobacco Company, left $100,000 in trust for the benefit of her dog. . . . The wills of well-known individuals who are still alive may also contain pet provisions. For example, Oprah Winfrey's will purportedly mandates that her dog live out his life in luxury.[17] [Id. at 617-619.]

17. To this litany we add two of our favorites:

1. The high cost of a dog's life in Beverly Hills. Sidney Altman did not want his cocker spaniel Samantha (age 15), described as "my loving companion," to suffer a major change in her life at his death in 1998. His will left $350,000 for Samantha's upkeep in his Beverly Hills home, plus $60,000 a year tax-free to his girlfriend of six years, Marie Dana, to take care of Samantha, plus an additional one-time $50,000 payment to Dana so that she could redecorate the house and go "on a massive shopping spree at Polo." Altman also left $150,000 to his business partner to check on Samantha every three months, to make sure that Samantha was being treated well. On Samantha's death, the remainder of Altman's $6 million fortune was to be shared by two animal rights charities. Dana sued for half of Altman's estate, claiming that Altman had promised to support her for her life, not for a dog's life. "I was shocked and deeply disappointed when I learned that at Samantha's death I would be homeless and without support," Dana told a reporter for the Los Angeles Times. Ann W. O'Neill, Girlfriend Sues as Samantha the Dog Inherits Man's Millions, L.A. Times, Sept. 23, 1998, at B1.

Samantha and Marie Dana
Los Angeles Times
Photo by Anacleto Rapping

See also Lynn Asinof, Pet-Estate Plans Gain Respect, Wall St. J., Apr. 5, 2002, at B1, reporting that "[e]state planning lawyers with pet-estate planning expertise are also gaining respectability." At least one national law firm with a large trusts and estates practice has a partner who is known as "the pet guy." Id.

3.   The main doctrinal impediments to providing at death for one's pet or other domestic animal are two. First, as illustrated by Estate of Russell, 444 P.2d 353 (Cal. 1968), excerpted at page 388, pets are themselves property and hence ineligible to take under a will. An outright bequest to a pet animal is void. Second, pets do not qualify as a beneficiary whose existence can validate a trust. To repeat, for a valid trust there must be some person to whom the trustee owes fiduciary duties, someone who can call the trustee to account—and the law regards pets as property, not persons with capacity to sue. The lack of an ascertainable beneficiary scotches not only trusts for pets, *but also trusts for any specific, noncharitable purpose*. There are, however, at least two ways around this problem.

(a) *Honorary trusts.* Following the lead of §124 of the First and Second Restatements of Trusts, some courts allow pet benefactors to create what has come to be known as an *honorary trust.* See also Restatement (Third) of Trusts §47 (2003) (setting forth a similar adapted trust regime). This approach was followed in *Searight's Estate.* Not limited to trusts for the care of pet animals, an honorary trust may be for any specific, designated purpose that is not capricious. Although the transferee is not under a legal obligation to carry out the purpose (hence the qualifier honorary), if she declines she is then said to hold the property upon a resulting trust and the property must be returned to the settlor or the settlor's successors. On resulting trusts, which are equitable reversionary interests, see page 511. In addition to benefiting pets, other common applications are trusts for the care of a cemetery plot and the saying of masses. See Restatement (Second) of Trusts §124 cmt. d (1959).

Suppose, however, that an honorary trust was funded with far more money than its purpose could reasonably need. Would such a trust fail as capricious? See Restatement (Second), supra, at cmt. g. What about a trust for the payment of criminal fines or to pay judgments for intentional torts?

Tinker

2. *Stray cat goes from rags to riches.* Margaret Layne, an elderly, childless widow who lived in London, took in a stray cat named Tinker. Soon Tinker became accustomed to life in his English manor, and Layne took measures to ensure that Tinker could continue in this life of luxury after her death in 2003. Under Layne's will, Tinker was given the run of her house, worth £350,000, plus a trust fund of £100,000. The trustees make a daily delivery of food and milk. "The sliding door to the green house—where Tinker likes to go 'for a bit of a lie-down'—is left open to save the indignity of him squeezing through a cat flap." Emma Hartley, Lucky Black Cat Strays Across the Path of a Pounds 1/2M Fortune, The Times (London), May 6, 2003. Layne did put one condition on Tinker's bounty: "If Tinker abandons the property permanently the trustees shall at their discretion be entitled to bring the trust to an end." At last report Tinker was still living in the house, along with Lucy and Stardust, two other cats who had since befriended him, doubtless for his personality and not his money.

—Eds.

In drafting an honorary trust, care must be taken not to offend the Rule against Perpetuities. In a state that has retained the common law Rule, an honorary trust to support a pet animal is void if it can last beyond all relevant lives in being at the creation of the trust plus twenty-one years — and the pet itself is *not* a relevant measuring life. See Restatement (Second), supra, at cmt. f; 2 Austin W. Scott, Trusts §124.1 (William F. Fratcher 4th ed. 1987). Inasmuch as cockatoos can live to be 80, and tortoises have been known to live for over 150 years, this poses drafting challenges. For a thoughtful examination of trusts for purposes and the Rule against Perpetuities, see Adam J. Hirsch, Trusts for Purposes: Policy, Ambiguity, and Anomaly in the Uniform Laws, 26 Fla. St. U.L. Rev. 913, 930-950 (1999).

After you study the Rule against Perpetuities in Chapter 11, consider whether the court's assumption of a 6 percent interest rate in *Searight's Estate* is consistent with the orthodox understanding of the Rule. Related, in deciding the perpetuities question, why did the court not take into account the fact that Trixie had died before the court's decision was rendered?

(b) *Statutory reform.* Several states have enacted statutes that permit a trust for a specific, noncharitable purpose to endure for a given amount of time. For example, Cal. Prob. Code §15212 (2004) provides that a trust for care of a designated pet animal may be performed by the trustee for the life of the animal, and Wis. Stat. Ann. §701.11(2) (2004) authorizes trusts for the perpetual care of a cemetery plot. See also 760 Ill. Comp. Stat. §15/2 (effective January 1, 2005) (validating trusts for pet animals).

Uniform Probate Code §2-907 (1993) provides that a trust for the care of a pet animal is valid for the life of the animal. Other noncharitable purpose trusts are valid for 21 years. In both cases, §2-907 authorizes the court to "reduce the amount of the property transferred" if it determines that the "amount substantially exceeds the amount required for the intended use." To resolve the problems of enforcement that arise when the trustee does not owe duties to a person who can call the trustee to account, the Code takes its cue from trusts for the benefit of minors and other incompetents. "The intended use of the [trust fund] can be enforced by an individual designated for that purpose in the trust instrument or, if none, by an individual appointed by [the] court." At least seven states — Alaska, Arizona, Colorado, Michigan, Montana, New Mexico, and Utah — have enacted some form of UPC §2-907. In addition, North Carolina and New York have enacted statutes that appear to borrow key provisions from §2-907. See N.C. Gen. Stat. §36A-147 (2004); N.Y. Est. Powers & Trusts Law §7-8.1 (2004).

Uniform Trust Code §§408-409 (2000) set forth provisions for trusts for the care of animals and for other noncharitable purposes that are similar to those of UPC §2-907. As of this writing, the UTC had been adopted in Kansas, Maine, Missouri, Nebraska, New Hampshire, New Mexico, Tennessee, Utah, Wyoming, and the District of Columbia.

4.   For an illuminating examination of the policies underlying the law governing noncharitable purpose trusts, see Adam J. Hirsch, Bequests for Purposes: A Unified Theory, 56 Wash. & Lee L. Rev. 33 (1999). Professor Hirsch points out that the law divides bequests for purposes into three categories — (1) charitable; (2) not charitable but not harmful, and (3) antisocial — and treats each category differently. He argues that, apart from a tiny number of bequests for harmful

purposes (such as the payment of criminal fines, as in Thrupp v. Collett, 53 Eng. Rep. 844 (M.R. 1858)), bequests for all sorts of purposes, whether deemed charitable or not, merit facilitation because they provide either social utility or personal utility to the settlor. The challenging issue under Hirsch's approach is to distinguish the merely capricious, which he would allow, from the harmful, which he would not. See Hirsch, supra, at 69-84.

5. We address charitable purposes and the formation of charitable trusts in Chapter 12 at pages 729-737.

4. Necessity of a Written Instrument

As we have seen, an inter vivos oral declaration of trust of personal property is enforceable. On the other hand, the Statute of Frauds requires any inter vivos trust of land to be in writing. And, of course, the Statute of Wills requires that a testamentary trust be created by a will. Nonetheless, under certain circumstances a court will enforce an inter vivos oral trust of land or an oral trust arising at death. It is to these circumstances that we now turn.

a. Oral Inter Vivos Trusts of Land

Where *O* conveys land to *X* upon an oral trust to pay the income to *A* for life and upon *A*'s death to convey the land to *B*, the Statute of Frauds prevents enforcement of the express trust. Is *X* permitted to keep the land? The cases split between permitting *X* to retain the land, on the ground that the Statute of Frauds forbids proof of the oral trust, and imposing a constructive trust on *X* to prevent his unjust enrichment. See discussion and collection of cases in 1 Austin W. Scott, Trusts §45 (William F. Fratcher 4th ed. 1987); Restatement (Third) of Trusts §24, cmts. h-j (2003). Most decisions have permitted *X* to retain the land, but this view appears to be losing ground. In any event, a constructive trust for the beneficiaries will be imposed where the transfer was wrongfully obtained by fraud or duress, where the transferee, *X*, was in a confidential relationship with the transferor, or where the transfer was made in anticipation of the transferor's death. And most of the cases involve one of these situations.

More common than an oral trust for a third party is an oral trust for the benefit of the transferor. Indeed, judging by the cases, a surprising number of persons put title to land in another, relying upon the transferee's oral promise to reconvey. Some of the transferors are attempting to avoid their creditors or spouses or to achieve some tax benefit. Of course, any lawyer knows these transferors are asking for trouble, and, human nature being what it is, usually they, like King Lear, get it. See, e.g., Evicted Couple Leave Pictures of Son Who Threw Them Out, L.A. Times, Dec. 10, 1977, at 24 (*H* and *W* convey title to their home to their son *A*; *A* then evicts *H* and *W*).

HIEBLE v. HIEBLE, 316 A.2d 777 (Conn. 1972): In 1959 plaintiff transferred title to certain real property from herself alone to herself in joint tenancy with her son, the defendant, and her daughter. The plaintiff was fearful of a return of cancer, for which she had previously undergone surgery, and apparently wanted to avoid probate.

She and the grantees orally agreed that the transfer would be a temporary arrangement; that she would remain in control of the property and pay all expenses and taxes; that once the danger of recrudescence had passed, the defendant and his sister would reconvey the property to the plaintiff on request. After the transfer, the plaintiff continued to reside on the property with her aged mother, whom she supported, her daughter and the defendant. In 1960, after the plaintiff expressed displeasure over the daughter's marriage, the daughter agreed to relinquish her interest in the property.

In 1964 plaintiff requested her son to reconvey his interest. He refused, assuring plaintiff he would continue to live with her. In 1967 the son married and moved out of the house. After the son refused to reconvey his interest to plaintiff, she brought suit in 1969 seeking a reconveyance.

Under the Statute of Frauds, oral agreements concerning real property are unenforceable. Since the oral agreement could not be enforced, the case presented "one of the most vexatious problems facing a court of equity in the area of constructive trusts, namely, whether equity should impose a constructive trust where a donee who by deed has received realty under an oral promise to hold and reconvey to the grantor has refused to perform his promise." The court concluded that a constructive trust should be decreed on the basis of the oral agreement and the confidential relationship of the parties.

> We grant that the bond between parent and child is not per se a fiduciary one; it does generate, however, a natural inclination to repose great confidence and trust. Coupled with the plaintiff's condition of weakness, her recent surgery, her anticipation of terminal illness, and the defendant's implicit reassurances of his faithfulness, this relationship becomes a classic example of the confidentiality to which equity will fasten consequences.

There being no evidence that the plaintiff intended to defraud creditors, the court concluded that the case was governed by Restatement (Second) of Trusts §44 (1959):

> Where the owner of an interest in land transfers it inter vivos to another in trust for the transferor, but no memorandum properly evidencing the intention to create a trust is signed, as required by the Statute of Frauds, and the transferee refuses to perform the trust, the transferee holds the interest upon a constructive trust for the transferor, if . . . the transferee at the time of the transfer was in a confidential relation to the transferor.

The trial court's order for the son to reconvey the property to his mother was affirmed.

NOTES AND QUESTION

1.   The law applied in Hieble v. Hieble is approved in Restatement (Third) of Trusts §24 (2003).

2.   In Pappas v. Pappas, 320 A.2d 809 (Conn. 1973), Andrew Pappas, age 67, married a 23-year-old woman while on a visit to Greece. On their return, marital difficulties arose, and just prior to the wife's suing for divorce, Andrew conveyed certain real estate to his son, George. George agreed to transfer the property back

to Andrew once his marital difficulties were over. In the divorce action, Andrew testified that he made the conveyance for consideration in satisfaction of certain financial and other obligations. Immediately after the divorce action was concluded, with a lump-sum alimony award to the wife of $25,000, Andrew demanded a reconveyance from George. George refused. The court held that a constructive trust could not be imposed upon George because Andrew, in misrepresenting the nature of the transfer in the divorce action, had perpetrated a fraud on the court and therefore did not have "clean hands."

Suppose Andrew Pappas, before the divorce suit, had consulted you. Would it be ethical to recommend that he transfer real estate to his son with a secret agreement by the son to convey it back after the divorce? See Jan E. Rein, Clients with Destructive and Socially Harmful Choices—What's an Attorney to Do? Within and Beyond the Competency Construct, 62 Fordham L. Rev. 1101 (1994).

b. Oral Trusts for Disposition at Death

Olliffe v. Wells

Supreme Judicial Court of Massachusetts, 1881
130 Mass. 221

[Ellen Donovan died in 1877 leaving a will devising her residuary estate to the Rev. Eleazer M.P. Wells "to distribute the same in such manner as in his discretion shall appear best calculated to carry out wishes which I have expressed to him or may express to him." Wells was named executor. Ellen's heirs brought suit, claiming the residue should be distributed to them. In his answer, Wells stated that Ellen Donovan, before and after the execution of the will, had orally expressed to him her wish that her estate be used for charitable purposes, and especially for the poor, aged, infirm, and needy under the care of Saint Stephen's Mission of Boston.[18] Wells further stated that he desired and intended to distribute the residue for

---

18. Eleazer Mather Porter Wells, born in 1783, entered Brown University at the age of 22 but was dismissed as a result of a practical joke played on a professor by his roommates. (O tempora! O mores!)

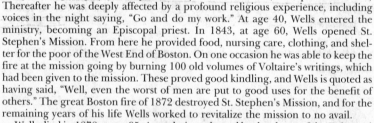

Thereafter he was deeply affected by a profound religious experience, including voices in the night saying, "Go and do my work." At age 40, Wells entered the ministry, becoming an Episcopal priest. In 1843, at age 60, Wells opened St. Stephen's Mission. From here he provided food, nursing care, clothing, and shelter for the poor of the West End of Boston. On one occasion he was able to keep the fire at the mission going by burning 100 old volumes of Voltaire's writings, which had been given to the mission. These proved good kindling, and Wells is quoted as having said, "Well, even the worst of men are put to good uses for the benefit of others." The great Boston fire of 1872 destroyed St. Stephen's Mission, and for the remaining years of his life Wells worked to revitalize the mission to no avail.

Wells died in 1878 at age 95. A resolution adopted by the clergy of the Episcopal Diocese of Massachusetts paid tribute to Wells as

The Rev. Wells

[a] clergyman of stainless reputation and incorruptible integrity; an enthusiast in his sacred calling, especially in his self-selected mission to the destitute and afflicted, the outcast and the erring. . . . The work of Dr. Wells, continued so long a period at St. Stephen's Mission in Boston, and as the trusted almoner of very many of his fellow citizens, and withal his pure and consistent life as a man of God and of unremitting prayer, furnish a splendid commendation of religion.

these purposes. The parties agreed that the facts alleged in the answer should be taken as true.]

GRAY, C.J. Upon the face of this will the residuary bequest to the defendant gives him no beneficial interest. It expressly requires him to distribute all the property bequeathed to him, giving him no discretion upon the question whether he shall or shall not distribute it, or shall or shall not carry out the intentions of the testatrix, but allowing him a discretionary authority as to the manner only in which the property shall be distributed pursuant to her intentions. The will declares a trust too indefinite to be carried out, and the next of kin of the testatrix must take by way of resulting trust, unless the facts agreed show such a trust for the benefit of others as the court can execute. Nichols v. Allen, 130 Mass. 211. . . .

It has been held in England and in other States, although the question has never arisen in this Commonwealth, that, if a person procures an absolute devise or bequest to himself by orally promising the testator that he will convey the property to or hold it for the benefit of third persons, and afterwards refused to perform his promise, a trust arises out of the confidence reposed in him by the testator and of his own fraud, which a court of equity, upon clear and satisfactory proof of the facts, will enforce against him at the suit of such third persons. . . .

Upon like grounds, it has been held in England that, if a testator devises or bequeaths property to his executors upon trusts not defined in the will, but which, as he states in the will, he has communicated to them before its execution, such trusts, if for lawful purposes, may be proved by the admission of the executors, or by oral evidence, and enforced against them. . . . And in two or three comparatively recent cases it has been held that such trusts may be enforced against the heirs or next of kin of the testator, as well as against the devisee. . . . But these cases appear to us to have overlooked or disregarded a fundamental distinction.

Where a trust not declared in the will is established by a court of chancery against the devisee, it is by reason of the obligation resting upon the conscience of the devisee, and not as a valid testamentary disposition by the deceased. Cullen v. Attorney General, L.R. 1 H.L. 190. Where the bequest is outright upon its face, the setting up of a trust, while it diminishes the right of the devisee, does not impair any right of the heirs or next of kin, in any aspect of the case; for if the trust were not set up, the whole property would go to the devisee by force of the devise; if the trust setup is a lawful one, it enures to the benefit of the cestuis que trust; and if the trust setup is unlawful, the heirs or next of kin take by way of resulting trust.

Where the bequest is declared upon its face to be upon such trusts as the testator has otherwise signified to the devisee, it is equally clear that the devisee takes no beneficial interest; and, as between him and the beneficiaries intended, there is as much ground for establishing the trust as if the bequest to him were absolute on its face. But as between the devisee and the heirs or next of kin, the case stands differently. They are not excluded by the will itself. The will upon its face showing

---

Information supplied by Mark J. Duffy, Archivist of the Episcopal Diocese of Massachusetts, in a letter to Jesse Dukeminier dated April 13, 1982.

To what extent, if any, does the court's decision in Olliffe v. Wells turn on the facts that St. Stephen's Mission had been destroyed and the "trusted almoner" had died before the case reached the Supreme Judicial Court?

that the devisee takes the legal title only and not the beneficial interest, and the trust not being sufficiently defined by the will to take effect, the equitable interest goes, by way of resulting trust, to the heirs or next of kin, as property of the deceased, not disposed of by his will. Sears v. Hardy, 120 Mass. 524, 541, 542. They cannot be deprived of that equitable interest, which accrues to them directly from the deceased, by any conduct of the devisee; nor by any intention of the deceased, unless signified in those forms which the law makes essential to every testamentary disposition. A trust not sufficiently declared on the face of the will cannot therefore be set up by extrinsic evidence to defeat the rights of the heirs at law or next of kin. . . .

Decree for the plaintiffs.

NOTES AND PROBLEMS

1. Olliffe v. Wells is the origin of the distinction between a *secret* and a *semisecret* trust followed in a considerable number of states in this country, although it is rejected in England and several states. The distinction is this: If Ellen Donovan had left a legacy to the Reverend Wells absolute on its face, without anything in the will indicating an intent to create a trust, a promise by the Reverend Wells to Ellen Donovan to use the legacy for St. Stephen's Mission would be enforceable by a constructive trust imposed upon Wells. This is called a secret trust because the will indicates no trust. Courts admit evidence of the promise for the purpose of preventing the Reverend Wells from unjustly enriching himself by pocketing the legacy. Having admitted proof of the promise, they proceed to enforce the promise by imposing a constructive trust on Wells for the benefit of St. Stephen's Mission.

On the other hand, if the will indicates that the Reverend Wells is to hold the legacy in trust but does not identify the beneficiary (as was true in Olliffe v. Wells), a semisecret trust is created. Since the will shows on its face an intent not to benefit Wells personally, it is not necessary to admit evidence of Wells' promise in order to prevent his unjust enrichment. Such evidence is excluded, and the legacy to Wells fails.

Restatement (Second) of Trusts §55, cmt. h (1959), takes the view that a con-structive trust should be imposed in favor of the intended beneficiary in the semisecret, as well as secret, trust situation. Restatement (Third) of Trusts §18, cmt. c (2003), agrees, but the reporter's notes admit that enforcing a semisecret trust by imposing a constructive trust "probably does not reflect the current weight of authority," which follows Olliffe v. Wells.

2. Suppose Charles Kuralt is your client (see pages 244-249). Kuralt has a long-time lover, named Shannon, who lives out of town and whom he sees when he travels. Kuralt wishes to leave Shannon $10,000 at his death, without advertising the matter. Would you recommend that Kuralt leave $10,000 in his will to his good friend Walter and obtain a secret promise from Walter that Walter will give Shannon the $10,000? Would this accomplish his objective of a secret gift? Would you recommend that Walter make the promise in a signed writing, which Kuralt is to keep in his safe-deposit box? See Pfahl v. Pfahl, 225 N.E.2d

305 (Ohio Prob. 1967). Would you recommend that Kuralt leave the money to you and you promise to give it to Shannon?

SECTION C.   RIGHTS OF THE BENEFICIARIES TO DISTRIBUTIONS FROM THE TRUST

Trusts can be divided into mandatory trusts and discretionary trusts. In a *mandatory trust*, the trustee must distribute all the income. Thus:

> *Case 17. O* transfers property to *X* in trust to distribute all the income to *A*. This is a mandatory trust. The trustee has no discretion to choose either the persons who will receive the income or the amount to be distributed.

In a *discretionary trust*, the trustee has discretion over payment of either the income or the principal or both. Discretionary powers of a trustee may be drafted in limitless variety. The following hypothetical case illustrates discretionary powers over income:

> *Case 18. O* transfers property to *X* in trust to distribute all the income to one or more members of a group consisting of *A, A*'s spouse, and *A*'s children in such amounts as the trustee determines. This is a kind of discretionary trust known as a spray trust. The trustee must distribute all the income currently, but has discretion to determine who gets it and in what amount. If desired, the trustee could be given discretionary power to accumulate income and add it to principal.

The trustee's discretion may be limited by an ascertainable support standard ("such amounts as are necessary to support my children in the style of living to which they are accustomed"), or the trustee may be given wide discretion. The former is sometimes called a *support trust*, to distinguish it from a purely discretionary trust in which the payouts are not governed by a stated support standard. Still another permutation is the *discretionary support trust*, which combines an explicit statement of discretion with a stated support standard ("such amounts as the trustee shall, in his uncontrolled discretion, deem necessary to support my children in the style of living to which they are accustomed"). See Evelyn Ginsberg Abravanel, Discretionary Support Trusts, 68 Iowa L. Rev. 273 (1983).

As compared to mandatory trusts, discretionary trusts provide greater flexibility, which is often desirable because the settlor cannot foresee all of the problems or opportunities that her family might face after the trust is created. On the other hand, with discretion comes the need for a mechanism to police the trustee's exercise of that discretion. In modern trust practice, the primary mechanism for safeguarding the beneficiary against abuse of discretion by the trustee is the fiduciary obligation. Although we defer systematic examination of fiduciary administration until Chapter 13, we include here a case that examines the beneficiary's rights to the trust fund in a discretionary support trust. The trust at issue contained an ascertainable standard ("comfortable support and maintenance") as well as a broad grant of discretion ("sole and uncontrolled").

Marsman v. Nasca

Massachusetts Appeals Court, 1991
30 Mass. App. 789, 573 N.E.2d 1025

DREBEN, J.   This appeal raises the following questions: Does a trustee, holding a discretionary power to pay principal for the "comfortable support and maintenance" of a beneficiary, have a duty to inquire into the financial resources of that beneficiary so as to recognize his needs? If so, what is the remedy for such failure? . . .

1. *Facts.* We take our facts from the findings of the Probate Court judge, supplemented on occasion by uncontroverted evidence. . . .

Sara Wirt Marsman died in September, 1971, survived by her second husband, T. Frederik Marsman (Cappy), and her daughter by her first marriage, Sally Marsman Marlette. Mr. James F. Farr, her lawyer for many years, drew her will and was the trustee thereunder.[19]

. . . Sara's will provided in relevant part:

It is my desire that my husband, T. Fred Marsman, be provided with reasonable maintenance, comfort and support after my death. Accordingly, if my said husband is living at the time of my death, I give to my trustees, who shall set the same aside as a separate trust fund, one-third (1/3) of the rest, residue and remainder of my estate . . . ; they shall pay the net income therefrom to my said husband at least quarterly during his life; and after having considered the various available sources of support for him, my trustees shall, if they deem it necessary or desirable from time to time, in their sole and uncontrolled discretion, pay over to him, or use, apply and/ or expend for his direct or indirect benefit such amount or amounts of the principal thereof as they shall deem advisable for his comfortable support and maintenance.

[The remainder interest was given to Sara's daughter Sally, who was Cappy's stepdaughter, and to Sally's family.]

The will also contained the following exculpatory clause: "No trustee hereunder shall ever be liable except for his own willful neglect or default."

During their marriage, Sara and Cappy lived well and entertained frequently. Cappy's main interest in life centered around horses. An expert horseman, he was riding director and instructor at the Dana Hall School in Wellesley until he was retired due to age in 1972. Sally, who was also a skilled rider, viewed Cappy as her mentor, and each had great affection for the other. Sara, wealthy from her prior marriage, managed the couple's financial affairs. She treated Cappy as "Lord of the Manor" and gave him money for his personal expenses, including an extensive wardrobe from one of the finest men's stores in Wellesley.

In 1956, Sara and Cappy purchased, as tenants by the entirety, the property in Wellesley which is the subject of this litigation. Although title to the property

19. The will provided for two trustees; however, one resigned in April, 1972, and thereafter Farr acted as sole trustee. [James F. Farr, who died in 1993, was a prominent trusts and estates lawyer in Boston and the author of a leading practitioner's handbook, James F. Farr & Jackson W. Wright, Jr., An Estate Planner's Handbook (4th ed. 1979). He was also the author of the sixth edition of Augustus Peabody Loring's Trustee's Handbook, first published in 1898 and the Bible of Boston trustees for several generations, referred to by the court in footnote 21, below. — Eds.]

passed to Cappy by operation of law on Sara's death, Sara's will also indicated an intent to convey her interest in the property to Cappy. In the will, Cappy was also given a life estate in the household furnishings with remainder to Sally.

After Sara's death in 1971, Farr met with Cappy and Sally and held what he termed his "usual family conference" going over the provisions of the will. At the time of Sara's death, the Wellesley property was appraised at $29,000, and the principal of Cappy's trust was about $65,600.

Cappy continued to live in the Wellesley house but was forced by Sara's death and his loss of employment in 1972 to reduce his standard of living substantially. He married Margaret in March, 1972, and, shortly before their marriage, asked her to read Sara's will, but they never discussed it. In 1972, Cappy took out a mortgage for $4,000, the proceeds of which were used to pay bills. Farr was aware of the transaction, as he replied to an inquiry of the mortgagee bank concerning the appraised value of the Wellesley property and the income Cappy expected to receive from Sara's trust.

In 1973, Cappy retained Farr in connection with a new will. The latter drew what he described as a simple will which left most of Cappy's property, including the house, to Margaret. The will was executed on November 7, 1973.

In February, 1974, Cappy informed [Farr] that business was at a standstill and that he really needed some funds, if possible. Farr replied in a letter in which he set forth the relevant portion of the will and wrote that he thought the language was "broad enough to permit a distribution of principal." Farr enclosed a check of $300. He asked Cappy to explain in writing the need for some support and why the need had arisen. The judge found that Farr, by his actions, discouraged Cappy from making any requests for principal.

Indeed, Cappy did not reduce his request to writing and never again requested principal. Farr made no investigation whatsoever of Cappy's needs or his "available sources of support" from the date of Sara's death until Cappy's admission to a nursing home in 1983 and, other than the $300 payment, made no additional distributions of principal until Cappy entered the nursing home.

By the fall of 1974, Cappy's difficulty in meeting expenses intensified.[20] Several of his checks were returned for insufficient funds, and in October, 1974, in order that he might remain in the house, Sally and he agreed that she would take over the mortgage payments, the real estate taxes, insurance, and major repairs. In return, she would get the house upon Cappy's death.

Cappy and Sally went to Farr to draw up a deed. Farr was the only lawyer involved, and he billed Sally for the work. He wrote to Sally, stating his understanding of the proposed transaction, and asking, among other things, whether Margaret would have a right to live in the house if Cappy should predecease her. The answer was no. No copy of the letter to Sally was sent to Cappy. A deed was executed by Cappy on November 7, 1974, transferring the property to Sally and

20. After Sara's death, Cappy's income was limited, particularly considering the station he had enjoyed while married to Sara. In 1973, including the income from Sara's trust of $2,116, his income was $3,441; in 1974 it was $3,549, including trust income of $2,254; in 1975, $6,624, including trust income of $2,490 and social security income of $2,576. Margaret's income was also minimal; $499 in 1974, $4,084 in 1975, including social security income of $1,686. Cappy's income in 1976 was $8,464; in 1977, $8,955; in 1978, $9,681; in 1979, $10,851; in 1980, $11,261; in 1981, $12,651; in 1982, $13,870; in 1983, $12,711; in 1984, $12,500; in 1985, $12,567; in 1986, $12,558. The largest portion from 1975 on came from social security benefits.

her husband Richard T. Marlette (Marlette) as tenants by the entirety, reserving a life estate to Cappy. No writing set forth Sally's obligations to Cappy.

The judge found that there was no indication that Cappy did not understand the transaction, although, in response to a request for certain papers by Farr, Cappy sent a collection of irrelevant documents. The judge also found that Cappy clearly understood that he was preserving no rights for Margaret, and that neither Sally nor Richard nor Farr ever made any representation to Margaret that she would be able to stay in the house after Cappy's death. . . .

Sally and Marlette complied with their obligations under the agreement. Sally died in 1983, and Marlette became the sole owner of the property subject to Cappy's life estate. Although Margaret knew before Cappy's death that she did not have any interest in the Wellesley property, she believed that Sally would have allowed her to live in the house because of their friendship. After Cappy's death in 1987, Marlette inquired as to Margaret's plans, and, subsequently, through Farr, sent Margaret a notice to vacate the premises. Margaret brought this action in the Probate Court.

After a two-day trial, the judge held that [Farr] was in breach of his duty to Cappy when he neglected to inquire as to the latter's finances. She concluded that, had Farr fulfilled his fiduciary duties, Cappy would not have conveyed the residence owned by him to Sally and Marlette. The judge ordered Marlette to convey the house to Margaret and also ordered Farr to reimburse Marlette from the remaining portion of Cappy's trust for the expenses paid by him and Sally for the upkeep of the property. If Cappy's trust proved insufficient to make such payments, Farr was to be personally liable for such expenses. Both Farr and Marlette appealed from the judgment, from the denial of their motions to amend the findings, and from their motions for a new trial. Margaret appealed from the denial of her motion for attorney's fees. . . . [W]e agree with the judge that Sara's will imposed a duty of inquiry on the trustee, but we disagree with the remedy and, therefore, remand for further proceedings.

2. *Breach of trust by the trustee.* Contrary to Farr's contention that it was not incumbent upon him to become familiar with Cappy's finances, . . . Sara's will clearly placed such a duty upon him. In his brief, Farr claims that the will gave Cappy the right to request principal "in extraordinary circumstances" and that the trustee, "was charged by Sara to be wary should Cappy request money beyond that which he quarterly received." Nothing in the will or the record supports this narrow construction. To the contrary, the direction to the trustees was to pay Cappy such amounts "as they shall deem advisable for his comfortable support and maintenance." This language has been interpreted to set an ascertainable standard, namely to maintain the life beneficiary "in accordance with the standard of living which was normal for him before he became a beneficiary of the trust." Woodberry v. Bunker, 268 N.E.2d 841 (Mass. 1971).

Even where the only direction to the trustee is that he shall "in his discretion" pay such portion of the principal as he shall "deem advisable," the discretion is not absolute. "Prudence and reasonableness, not caprice or careless good nature, much less a desire on the part of the trustee to be relieved from trouble . . . furnish the standard of conduct." Boyden v. Stevens, 188 N.E. 741 (Mass. 1934).

That there is a duty of inquiry into the needs of the beneficiary follows from the requirement that the trustee's power "must be exercised with that soundness of judgment which follows from a due appreciation of trust responsibility." Id. In Old

Colony Trust Co. v. Rodd, 254 N.E.2d 886 (Mass. 1970), the trustee sent a questionnaire to each potential beneficiary to determine which of them required assistance but failed to make further inquiry in cases where the answers were incomplete. The court agreed with the trial judge that the method employed by the trustee in determining the amount of assistance required in each case to attain "comfortable support and maintenance" was inadequate. There, as here, the trustee attempted to argue that it was appropriate to save for the beneficiaries' future medical needs. The court held that the "prospect of illness in old age does not warrant a persistent policy of niggardliness toward individuals for whose comfortable support in life the trust has been established. The payments made to the respondent and several other beneficiaries, viewed in light of their assets and needs, when measured against the assets of the trust show that little consideration has been given to the 'comfortable support' of the beneficiaries."

Farr, in our view, did not meet his responsibilities either of inquiry or of distribution under the trust. The conclusion of the trial judge that, had he exercised "sound judgment," he would have made such payments to Cappy "as to allow him to continue to live in the home he had occupied for many years with the settlor" was warranted.

3. *Remedy against Marlette*. [The trial judge ordered Marlette to convey the house to Margaret on the ground that, had Farr not been in breach of trust, Cappy would have died owning the house and thus would have been able to devise it to Margaret. This court vacated that order. The conveyance to Sally and Marlette was supported by consideration, and Sally and Marlette did not have notice of Farr's breach of trust. Sally and Marlette were thus bona fide purchasers without notice.]

4. *Remainder of Cappy's trust*. The amounts that should have been expended for Cappy's benefit are, however, in a different category. More than $80,000 remained in the trust for Cappy at the time of his death. As we have indicated, the trial judge properly concluded that payments of principal should have been made to Cappy from that fund in sufficient amount to enable him to keep the Wellesley property. . . . The remedy in such circumstances is to impress a constructive trust on the amounts which should have been distributed to Cappy but were not because of the error of the trustee. Even in cases where beneficiaries have already been paid funds by mistake, the amounts may be collected from them unless the recipients were bona fide purchasers or unless they, without notice of the improper payments, had so changed their position that it would be inequitable to make them repay. Here, the remainder of Cappy's trust has not yet been distributed, and there is no reason to depart from the usual rule of impressing a constructive trust in favor of Cappy's estate on the amounts wrongfully withheld. . . .

That Cappy assented to the accounts is also no bar to recovery by his estate. The judge found that he was in the dark as to his rights to receive principal for the upkeep of the home. An assent may be withdrawn by a judge "if it is deemed improvident or not conducive to justice." Swift v. Hiscock, 183 N.E.2d 875, 877 (Mass. 1962). [In addition, the accounts had not been approved by the court.][21] . . .

The amounts to be paid to Cappy's estate have not been determined. On remand, the Probate Court judge is to hold such hearings as are necessary to determine the

---

21. . . . In Loring, A Trustee's Handbook §62 (Farr rev. 1962) the author states: "[P]reparing annual accounts, signed by the adult beneficiaries and allowing them to continue without adjudication is an unsafe procedure for the trustee."

amounts which should have been paid to Cappy to enable him to retain possession of the house.

5. *Personal liability of the trustee.* . . . The . . . difficult question is the effect of the exculpatory clause. As indicated in part 3 of this opinion, we consider the order to Marlette to reconvey the property an inappropriate remedy. In view of the judge's finding that, but for the trustee's breach, Cappy would have retained ownership of the house, the liability of the trustee could be considerable.

Although exculpatory clauses are not looked upon with favor and are strictly construed, such "provisions inserted in the trust instrument without any over-reaching or abuse by the trustee of any fiduciary or confidential relationship to the settlor are generally held effective except as to breaches of trust 'committed in bad faith or intentionally or with reckless indifference to the interest of the beneficiary.'" New England Trust Co. v. Paine, 59 N.E.2d 263 (Mass. 1945). The actions of Farr were not of this ilk and also do not fall within the meaning of the term used in the will, "willful neglect or default."

Farr testified that he discussed the exculpatory clause with Sara and that she wanted it included. Nevertheless, the judge, without finding that there was an overreaching or abuse of Farr's fiduciary relation with Sara, held the clause ineffective. Relying on the fact that Farr was Sara's attorney, she stated: "One cannot know at this point in time whether or not Farr specifically called this provision to Sara's attention. Given the total failure of Farr to use his judgment as to [C]appy's needs, it would be unjust and unreasonable to hold him harmless by reason of the exculpatory provisions he himself drafted and inserted in this instrument."

Assuming that the judge disbelieved Farr's testimony that he and Sara discussed the clause, although such disbelief on her part is by no means clear, the conclusion that it "would be unjust and unreasonable to hold [Farr] harmless" is not sufficient to find the overreaching or abuse of a fiduciary relation which is required to hold the provision ineffective. See Restatement (Second) of Trusts §222, Comment d (1959). We note that the judge found that Sara managed all the finances of the couple, and from all that appears, was competent in financial matters.

There was no evidence about the preparation and execution of Sara's will except for the questions concerning the exculpatory clause addressed to Farr by his own counsel. No claim was made that the clause was the result of an abuse of confidence.

The fact that the trustee drew the instrument and suggested the insertion of the exculpatory clause does not necessarily make the provision ineffective. Restatement (Second) of Trusts §222, Comment d. No rule of law requires that an exculpatory clause drawn by a prospective trustee be held ineffective unless the client is advised independently.

The judge used an incorrect legal standard in invalidating the clause. While recognizing the sensitivity of such clauses, we hold that, since there was no evidence that the insertion of the clause was an abuse of Farr's fiduciary relationship with Sara at the time of the drawing of her will, the clause is effective. . . .

The judgment is vacated, and the matter is remanded to the Probate Court for further proceedings to determine the amounts which, if paid, would have enabled Cappy to retain ownership of the residence. Such amounts shall be paid to Cappy's estate from the trust for his benefit prior to distributing the balance thereof to the [remainder beneficiaries].

So ordered.

NOTES AND QUESTIONS

1. Would Margaret's elective share apply to the Wellesley house under Massachusetts law as explicated in Sullivan v. Burkin, page 439, and Bongaards v. Millen, page 442?

2. Why is there a natural tendency for trustees to favor the remaindermen over the life tenant, to be conservative in paying out income or principal? See Robert H. Sitkoff, An Agency Costs Theory of Trust Law, 89 Cornell L. Rev. 621, 676 (2004).

3. *Duty to inquire*. Because the trust in Marsman v. Nasca entitled Cappy to so much of the trust principal as the trustees "deem advisable for his comfortable support and maintenance," the court held that, as trustee, Farr was under a duty to inquire into Cappy's needs and circumstances. This is a standard interpretation. For example, in Kolodney v. Kolodney, 503 A.2d 625 (Conn. App. 1986), after concluding "that the [trustee] was obligated to pay the [beneficiary] whatever sum was necessary for her comfortable maintenance, support and education," the court held that the trustee "had a duty to inquire as to what sums were necessary to maintain that standard of living. His failure to do so constituted an abuse of discretion." Id. at 628. See also 3 Austin W. Scott, Trusts §187.3 (William F. Fratcher 4th ed. 1988). Why did Farr's request that Cappy explain his need for funds in writing not satisfy this duty?

For discussion of the meaning of common standards—including support, maintenance, comfort, health, best interests, welfare, and accustomed manner of living—see Restatement (Third) of Trusts §50, cmt. d (2003).

4. *The beneficiary's other resources*. A troublesome source of litigation is whether a trustee, in exercising a discretionary power to spend income or principal for the beneficiary's support, may consider the other resources of the beneficiary. In Marsman v. Nasca, this matter was covered by the trust instrument: "after having considered the various available sources of support for [Cappy], my trustees shall . . . ." If Cappy had been independently wealthy, the trustees would not have had to support him.

Where not dealt with in the trust instrument, the issue may wind up in court because it is a question of interpretation of the trust instrument. According to Professor Scott, the presumption is that the settlor intended the beneficiary to receive his support from the trust estate regardless of the beneficiary's other financial resources, but this presumption can be rebutted by the special circumstances of the case.

> It is a question of interpretation whether the beneficiary is entitled to support out of the trust fund even though he has other resources. Where the trustee is directed to pay to the beneficiary or to apply for him so much as is necessary for his maintenance or support, the inference is that the settlor intended that he should receive his support from the trust estate, even though he might have other resources. The settlor may, however, manifest an intention that the trust property should be applied to his support only if and to the extent that he is in actual need, in which case he is not entitled to support out of the trust fund if he has other and sufficient resources. [2 Austin W. Scott, Trusts §128.4, at 353-357 (William F. Fratcher 4th ed. 1987).]

The cases are highly fact dependent. Compare Godfrey v. Chandley, 811 P.2d 1248 (Kan. 1991) (surviving wife's personal income should not be considered by trustee), with In re Estate of Winston, 613 N.Y.S.2d 461 (App. Div. 1994) (trustee should consider the beneficiary's other sources of support).

In a regrettable bit of fuzzy drafting, Restatement, supra, §50, cmt. e, offers little in the way of illumination: "[T]he presumption is that the trustee is to take the beneficiary's other resources into account in determining whether and in what amounts distributions are to be made, except insofar as, in the trustee's discretionary judgment, the settlor's intended treatment of the beneficiary or the purposes of the trust will in some respect be better accomplished by not doing so."

5. *The ethical dilemmas of James F. Farr*. In Marsman v. Nasca, James F. Farr was a lawyer for Sara, Cappy, Sally, and Marlette, all more or less at the same time. Do you have any problems with this? To whom does Farr owe a duty of loyalty? Is it ethical to represent "the family"? Compare Thomas L. Shaffer, The Legal Ethics of Radical Individualism, 65 Tex. L. Rev. 963, 982 (1987), with Teresa S. Collett, And the Two Shall Become as One . . . Until the Lawyers Are Done, 7 Notre Dame J.L. Ethics & Pub. Poly. 101 (1993); Russell G. Pearce, Family Values and Legal Ethics: Competing Approaches to Conflicts in Representing Spouses, 62 Fordham L. Rev. 1253 (1994). See also ACTEC, Commentaries on the Model Rules of Professional Conduct (3d ed. 1999) (commentary on Rule 1.7).

NOTE: EXTENDED DISCRETION

If the trustee has simple discretion unqualified by adjectives such as *sole, absolute, uncontrolled*, or the like, the courts will not substitute their judgment for that of the trustee so long as the trustee "acts not only in good faith and from proper motives, but also within the bounds of a reasonable judgment." 3 Austin W. Scott, Trusts §187, at 14 (William F. Fratcher 4th ed. 1988). When the instrument purports to free the trustee from some or all of these limitations, however, problems in construction arise. At one extreme are instruments that purport to give unlimited discretionary power to the trustee. But a discretionary power to be exercised "in the trustee's absolute and uncontrolled discretion" is not in fact absolute or uncontrolled. As Judge Learned Hand remarked:

> [N]o language, however strong, will entirely remove any power held in trust from the reach of a court of equity. After allowance has been made for every possible factor which could rationally enter into the trustee's decision, if it appears that he has utterly disregarded the interests of the beneficiary, the Court will intervene. Indeed were that not true, the power would not be held in trust at all; the language would be no more than a precatory admonition. [Stix v. Commissioner, 152 F.2d 562, 563 (2d Cir. 1945).]

What, then, are the limitations on the trustee's freedom when the trustee has "absolute and uncontrolled discretion"? Professor Scott argued for a subjective standard, emphasizing the trustee's "good faith" and proper motives and dispensing with the requirement of reasonableness. He suggested, and the Restatement for which he was the reporter adopted, a standard of whether the trustee has acted "in that state of mind in which it was contemplated by the settlor that he should act." Scott, supra, at 16; Restatement (Second) of Trusts §187, cmt. j (1959). Some courts, relying on the Restatement's good faith standard, declare that the trustee must not act arbitrarily or capriciously, seemingly bringing in a reasonableness test under the guise of other words. Other courts apply a reasonableness test even when the discretion is "absolute."

Under Uniform Trust Code §814 (2000), "Notwithstanding the breadth of discretion granted to a trustee in the terms of the trust, including such terms as 'absolute,' 'sole,' or 'uncontrolled,' the trustee shall exercise a discretionary power in good faith and in accordance with the terms and purposes of the trust and the interests of the beneficiaries." Likewise, Restatement (Third) of Trusts §50, cmt. c (2003), provides that "words such as 'absolute' or 'unlimited' or 'sole and uncontrolled' are not interpreted literally. Even under the broadest grant of fiduciary discretion, a trustee must act honestly and in a state of mind contemplated by the settlor. Thus, the court will not permit the trustee to act in bad faith or for some purpose or motive other than to accomplish the purposes of the discretionary power."

In the final analysis, it appears that the difference between simple discretion and "absolute" discretion is one of degree and that the trustee's action must not only be in good faith but also to some extent reasonable, with more elasticity in the concept of reasonableness the greater the discretion given.

NOTE: EXCULPATORY CLAUSES

In Marsman v. Nasca, the testamentary trust Farr drafted for Sara Marsman included an *exculpatory clause* (sometimes called an *exoneration clause*), excusing the trustees (and so Farr himself!) from liability except for "willful neglect or default." The court upheld this clause because there was no evidence that it was inserted as a result of an abuse of confidence reposed by the client in the lawyer. Margaret did not meet her burden of proof.

Do you think it is ethical to include an exculpatory clause like this in a will you draft naming yourself trustee? Is this a freely and knowingly bargained agreement between lawyer and client? Who should have the burden of showing this? See generally Paula A. Monopoli, Fiduciary Duty: A New Ethical Paradigm for Lawyer/Fiduciaries, 67 Mo. L. Rev. 309 (2002). To borrow an idea from the literature of contract law, if the settlor's lawyer is also named trustee, does the danger of overreaching in the insertion of an exculpatory clause call for a penalty default rule whereby the burden is shifted to the lawyer to prove an absence of abuse? Professors Ayres and Gertner explain the concept:

> Penalty defaults are designed to give at least one party to the contract an incentive to contract around the default rule and therefore to choose affirmatively the contract provision they prefer. In contrast to the received wisdom, penalty defaults are purposefully set at what [one or both] parties would not want — in order to encourage the parties to reveal information to each other. [Ian Ayres & Robert Gertner, Filling Gaps in Incomplete Contracts: An Economic Theory of Default Rules, 99 Yale L.J. 87 (1989).]

This is the strategy taken by Uniform Trust Code §1008(b) (2000):

> An exculpatory term drafted or caused to be drafted by the trustee is invalid as an abuse of a fiduciary or confidential relationship unless the trustee proves that the

exculpatory term is fair under the circumstances and that its existence and contents were adequately communicated to the settlor.

By placing the burden on a trustee who was also the settlor's lawyer to show that the settlor had affirmative knowledge of the clause and its meaning, the UTC helps to ensure that the clause was not unwittingly embraced by the settlor. See Robert H. Sitkoff, An Agency Costs Theory of Trust Law, 89 Cornell L. Rev. 621, 645 (2004).

In spite of Marsman v. Nasca, there is precedent for the UTC approach. For example, in Rutanen v. Ballard, 678 N.E.2d 133 (Mass. 1997), the court refused to enforce an exculpatory provision on the ground that the draftsman/trustee had not adequately advised the settlor about the clause. See also Scott, supra, §222.4, at 394, stating that where the trustee "was the settlor's attorney, and where he inserted the provision without calling the settlor's attention to it and knowing that the settlor did not realize the effect of it, it is ineffective to protect the trustee."

In assessing whether an exculpatory clause should be voided on the ground that it was inserted in an abuse of a fiduciary relationship, what considerations should be relevant? See official comment to UTC §1008; Restatement (Second) of Trusts §222 cmt. d (1959).

Thus far we have been supposing that the settlor's lawyer both drafted the trust instrument and is named as trustee. Now suppose instead a bank or trust company insists upon using its own form as a condition precedent to its accepting appointment as trustee. If the form contains an exculpatory clause, is not that an exculpatory clause drafted by the trustee? The answer is Yes, and so the same rules apply, but with a critical difference in the facts. Now the settlor's lawyer is not interested in the clause (is this true if the lawyer has a long-term relationship with the bank?), which means that the settlor might be protected by her lawyer. The official comment to UTC §1008 would make this a safe harbor: "The requirements of subsection (b) are satisfied if the settlor was represented by independent counsel."

Suppose an exculpatory clause was not inserted as a result of abuse by the trustee. Should the law impose an outer limit on the permissible scope of such a clause? In McNeil v. McNeil, 798 A.2d 503, 509 (Del. 2002), the trust at issue provided that the trustees' decisions were "not subject to review by any court." Observing, nonetheless, that courts "flatly refuse to enforce provisions relieving a trustee of all liability," the court reviewed the trustees' actions. The reason: "A trust in which there is no legally binding obligation on a trustee is a trust in name only and more in the nature of an absolute estate or fee simple grant of property." Id. See also George G. Bogert & George T. Bogert, The Law of Trusts and Trustees §542, at 188-189 (rev. 2d ed. 1993).

Generally speaking, the line is drawn at bad faith, reckless indifference, and intentional or willful neglect. An exculpatory clause that purports to immunize the trustee for any such conduct will not be enforced. See Bogert & Bogert, supra, at 208-209; Scott, supra, §222.3, at 391-392. See also UTC §§1008(a)(1), 105(b)(2); Restatement (Second) of Trusts §222(2) (1959). In New York, by statute, an attempted grant to a testamentary trustee of immunity from liability for failure to exercise *reasonable* care is deemed contrary to public policy and void. N.Y. Est. Powers & Trusts Law §11-1.7 (2004).

For recent commentary on exculpatory clauses, see David M. English, The Uniform Trust Code (2000): Significant Provisions and Policy Issues, 67 Mo. L.

Rev. 143, 206-207 (2002); John H. Langbein, Mandatory Rules in the Law of Trusts, 98 Nw. U.L. Rev. 1105, 1123-1125 (2004); Sitkoff, supra.

NOTE: MANDATORY ARBITRATION CLAUSES

Suppose the trust instrument provides that all disputes between the trustee and the beneficiary must be resolved by arbitration. Does this clause prevent a beneficiary from bringing suit against the trustee in court? In Schoneberger v. Oelze, 96 P.3d 1078 (Ariz. App. 2004), the court held No.

> We can see why a trustor . . . might wish to require arbitration of disputes involving the trust. "The primary attraction of arbitration is an expeditious and inexpensive method of dispute resolution." Rancho Pescado, Inc. v. Northwestern Mutual Life Ins. Co., 680 P.2d 1235, 1243-44 (Ariz. App. 1984). A trustor's right to reserve power over trust administration matters is not, however, absolute and a trustor of an inter vivos trust may not unilaterally strip trust beneficiaries of their right to access the courts absent their agreement. [Id. at 1083-1084].

Given that an exculpatory clause is enforceable (unless it authorizes bad faith or reckless indifference), why is a mandatory arbitration clause not enforceable? Many lawyers and legal scholars believe that arbitration is a simpler and quicker means of resolving disputes than litigation. On this view, arbitration is a mode of enforcing the trust, not a mode of defeating enforcement. In view of the growing support for arbitration, it seems unlikely that *Schoneberger* will be the last word on this question.

SECTION D.   RIGHTS OF THE BENEFICIARY'S CREDITORS

> The law, in its majestic equality, forbids the rich as well as
> the poor to sleep under bridges, to beg in the streets,
> and to steal bread.
>
> ANATOLE FRANCE
> *Le Lys Rouge, ch. 7 (1894)*

The rich have—at least in Anglo-American history—continually sought ways to secure their property to their children and grandchildren so that it remains in the family safe from the accidents of fortune and bad management. The fee tail and later the strict settlement were the standard devices used in England to keep land in the family. The fee tail was early abolished in this country, and the strict settlement never took hold here. The spendthrift trust, an American invention not recognized in England, and the discretionary trust, which is recognized throughout the common law world, are their ideological descendants. Both provide a means of making property available to the beneficiary, but not the beneficiary's creditors. In this section, we explore the asset-protection features of trust law by examining the rights of the beneficiary's creditors to the trust fund in (1) a *discretionary trust*, (2) the uniquely American *spendthrift trust*, and (3) the *self-settled asset protection trust* — that is, a trust in which the settlor is also a beneficiary but against which the settlor's creditors have no recourse.

1. Discretionary Trusts

Suppose that a discretionary trust beneficiary is in default to a creditor, and the terms of the trust do not supply an ascertainable support standard. In such a case, does the beneficiary's creditor have any rights to the trust fund? The traditional answer is No. The creditor cannot, by judicial order, compel the trustee of a discretionary trust to pay him. The theory is that, because the beneficiary has no right to a payment, neither does the beneficiary's creditor. See United States v. O'Shaughnessy, 517 N.W.2d 574 (Minn. 1994); Restatement (Second) of Trusts §155 (1959). In some states this rule has been codified by statute. See, e.g., Ariz. Rev. Stat. §14-7704(A) (2004); Cal. Prob. Code §15303(a) (2004); Mont. Code Ann. §72-33-304(1) (2004). Professor Scott summarizes the traditional understanding:

> Where by the terms of the trust a beneficiary is entitled only to so much of the income or principal as the trustee in his uncontrolled discretion shall see fit to give him, he cannot compel the trustee to pay to him or to apply for his use any part of the trust property. In such a case, an assignee of the interest of the beneficiary cannot compel the trustee to pay any part of the trust property, nor can creditors of the beneficiary reach any part of the trust property. This is true even in jurisdictions where spend-thrift trusts are not permitted. If the beneficiary himself cannot compel the trustee to pay over any part of the trust fund, his assignee and his creditors are in no better position. It is the character of the beneficiary's interest, rather than the settlor's intention to impose a restraint on its alienation, which prevents its being reached. [2A Austin W. Scott, Trusts §155 (William F. Fratcher 4th ed. 1987).]

In some states, the creditor may be entitled to an order directing the trustee to pay the creditor before paying the beneficiary. The trustee need not pay any part of the trust fund to the beneficiary, but if the trustee determines to do so, the trustee must pay the creditors who now stand in the beneficiary's shoes. By this procedure, a creditor can deprive the beneficiary of trust income even though the creditor will not necessarily be paid.

The foregoing cutting-off-income procedure was approved in the leading case of Hamilton v. Drogo, 150 N.E. 496 (N.Y. 1926), which involved a discretionary trust established by the will of the dowager Duchess of Manchester to provide her spendthrift son, the ninth duke,[22] freedom from the travails of penury. Andrews, J., explained how the rule worked:

> We may not interfere with the discretion which the testatrix has vested in the trustee any more than her son may do so. Its judgment is final. But at least annually

---

22. William Angus Drogo Montagu, ninth Duke of Manchester, "had been kept so short of cash as a boy, with pocket money of one penny a day, that he grew up with no real sense of its value. On an allowance of £400 a year at Cambridge, he ran up debts totalling £2,000. He spent much time in America, Africa, and India, avoiding creditors, looking for a rich wife, and sponging off his friends." David Cannadine, The Decline and Fall of the British Aristocracy 403 (1990).

this judgment must be exercised. And if it is exercised in favor of the duke [the beneficiary], then there is due him the whole or such part of the income as the trustee may allot to him. After such allotment, he may compel its payment. At least for some appreciable time, however brief, the award must precede the delivery of the income he is to receive, and during that time the lien of the execution attaches. [Id. at 497.]

Since the trustee is said to exercise discretion to pay the beneficiary at a moment in time before the property is transferred to the beneficiary, during which period the lien attaches, it is important to know what acts constitute an exercise of discretion. Crediting the beneficiary's account on the trustee's books or an oral or written declaration to the beneficiary may be a sufficient act to indicate the power has been exercised. After such exercise by the trustee, the creditor may seize the property awarded to the beneficiary while it remains in the hands of the trustee.

QUESTIONS

1. Why is the cutting-off-income procedure sanctioned in Hamilton v. Drogo of use to a creditor if the trustee can simply decline to make a payment?

2. Can the Hamilton v. Drogo cutting-off-income procedure be circumvented by a provision in the trust instrument that permits the trustee, in its discretion, not only to pay the beneficiary directly but also to pay third parties for the support of the beneficiary? See Wilcox v. Gentry, 867 P.2d 281 (Kan. 1994); Restatement (Second) of Trusts §155, cmt. i (1959). See also Restatement (Third) of Trusts §60, cmt. c (2003).

———

Thus far we have assumed a discretionary trust not governed by an ascertainable standard. Now suppose that a trust beneficiary is in default to a creditor, but the terms of the trust *do* supply an ascertainable support standard — that is, suppose a support trust that requires the trustee to make payments of income (or, if so specified, of principal too) to the beneficiary in an amount necessary for the education or support of the beneficiary. The traditional view is that the beneficiary of a support trust cannot alienate her interest. Nor can creditors of the beneficiary reach the beneficiary's interest, except suppliers of necessaries may recover through the beneficiary's right to support. See Restatement (Second) of Trusts, supra, §154.

Unlike the case of a pure discretionary trust, however, there is authority which holds that the beneficiary's children and spouse may enforce claims for child support and alimony against the beneficiary's interest in a support trust. See Scott, supra, §157.1 (collecting cases).

———

After the ninth duke's death, the Manchester family fortunes continued in an irreversible decline set in motion by three spendthrift dukes in a row (the seventh, eighth, and ninth). All the family land was sold off to support high living. The tenth duke moved to Kenya seeking a new fortune, but Kenyan independence sank that venture. The eleventh duke became an alligator hunter in Australia, but after a while he moved back to England where he became a business consultant in Bedford.

Drawing a distinction between a pure discretionary trust and a support trust is a dubious exercise. Also dubious is the idea that, in a pure discretionary trust, the beneficiary has no right to a payout. Even when the trustee is vested with absolute, sole, uncontrolled, or some other form of extended discretion, the beneficiary may nonetheless ask the court to review the trustee's exercise of that discretion for abuse or bad faith. See page 540. Likewise, an exculpatory clause purporting to insulate the trustee from judicial review altogether is unenforceable. See page 541. Given that a trust beneficiary can always obtain *some* form of judicial review of the trustee's exercise of discretion, would you allow the creditors of a discretionary trust beneficiary to stand in the beneficiary's shoes and bring suit against the trustee for so much of the trust fund as the beneficiary could have reached?

Both the Restatement (Third) of Trusts and the Uniform Trust Code reject the distinction between support and discretionary trusts, unifying the rules regarding creditors' rights for all trusts that had fit within either of the former categories — but they state different rules. Restatement (Third) of Trusts §60 (2003) provides that "if the terms of a trust provide for a beneficiary to receive distributions in the trustee's discretion, a transferee or creditor of the beneficiary is entitled to receive or attach any distributions the trustee makes or is required to make in the exercise of that discretion." Hence the Restatement allows the beneficiary's creditors to stand in the beneficiary's shoes and compel a distribution. UTC §504, excerpted below, takes the opposite view.

Uniform Trust Code (2000, as amended 2004)

§504. Discretionary Trusts; Effect of Standard

(a) In this section, "child" includes any person for whom an order or judgment for child support has been entered in this or another State.

(b) Except as otherwise provided in subsection (c), whether or not a trust contains a spendthrift provision, a creditor of a beneficiary may not compel a distribution that is subject to the trustee's discretion, even if:

(1) the discretion is expressed in the form of a standard of distribution; or

(2) the trustee has abused the discretion.

(c) To the extent a trustee has not complied with a standard of distribution or has abused a discretion:

(1) a distribution may be ordered by the court to satisfy a judgment or court order against the beneficiary for support or maintenance of the beneficiary's child, spouse, or former spouse; and

(2) the court shall direct the trustee to pay to the child, spouse, or former spouse such amount as is equitable under the circumstances but not more than the amount the trustee would have been required to distribute to or for the benefit of the beneficiary had the trustee complied with the standard or not abused the discretion.

(d) This section does not limit the right of a beneficiary to maintain a judicial proceeding against a trustee for an abuse of discretion or failure to comply with a standard for distribution.

(e) The provisions of this section apply even if the beneficiary is the co-trustee of the trust.

PROBLEM AND NOTE

1. *T* devises property to *X* in trust to pay so much of the income and principal to *A* as *X* determines is necessary for *A*'s support. *A* is insolvent. As trustee, *X* refuses to make a payment to *A*. *B*, a creditor of *A*, sues *X* on the ground that, since *A* is insolvent, it would be an abuse of *X*'s discretion as trustee not to make a payment to *A*, and thus *B* is entitled to stand in *A*'s shoes and receive that payment. What result under Restatement (Third) of Trusts §60? See id. at cmt. e. What result under UTC §504? See generally Alan Newman, The Rights of Creditors of Beneficiaries Under the Uniform Trust Code: An Examination of the Compromise, 69 Tenn. L. Rev. 771, 803-816 (2002).

2. *Protective trusts*. Suppose that you have a client who wants the beneficiary to have a mandatory right to regular payments out of the trust fund, but who also wants the asset protection features of a discretionary trust. Particularly if you are in a jurisdiction that does not recognize spendthrift trusts, for this client you might consider a mandatory trust subject to a protective provision. In a *protective trust*, the trustee is directed to pay income to *A*, but if *A*'s creditors attach *A*'s interest, *A*'s mandatory income interest ceases, whereupon a discretionary trust automatically arises. The trustee then has discretion to apply the income for *A*'s benefit, and the creditors of *A* cannot demand any part of it. See Restatement (Third) of Trusts §57 (2003).

In England, which does not enforce spendthrift provisions, protective trusts are so common that, under §33 of the Trustee Act of 1925, 15 & 16 Geo. 5, ch. 19, the court will insert a protective provision into any trust for which the settlor manifested an intent to create a protective trust. See Paul Todd & Sarah Wilson, Textbook on Trusts §2.6 (6th ed. 2003). Professor Hayton explains: "Discretionary trusts thus have the advantage of protecting beneficiaries from themselves besides the obvious advantage of flexibility. However, there is the corresponding disadvantage that such trusts create uncertainty since [the beneficiary] has no fixed entitlement.... To tackle this disadvantage there arose the protective trust." David J. Hayton, Hayton and Marshall Commentary and Cases on the Law of Trusts and Equitable Remedies 280-281 (11th ed. 2001).

2.   Spendthrift Trusts

The Anglo-American jurisprudential tradition abhors restraints on the alienation of property. Consistent with this policy, the beneficiary's interest in a trust is ordinarily freely transferable, both voluntarily by sale and involuntarily to satisfy a judgment against the beneficiary.

On first glance, the spendthrift trust is a stark exception to this general policy. A beneficiary of a spendthrift trust cannot voluntarily alienate her interest. Nor can her creditors reach her interest in the trust. This is true even if the trust provides for mandatory payments to the beneficiary. A spendthrift trust is created by imposing a disabling restraint upon the beneficiaries and their creditors. See Restatement (Third) of Trusts §58 (2003). Thus:

> *Case 19. T* devises property to *X* in trust to pay the income to *A* for life and upon *A*'s death to distribute the property to *A*'s children. A clause in the trust provides that *A*

may not transfer her life estate, and it may not be reached by *A*'s creditors (see the spendthrift clauses in Scheffel v. Krueger and Shelley v. Shelly, both of which are excerpted below). By this trust *A* is given a stream of income that *A* cannot alienate and her creditors cannot reach.

In most jurisdictions, trusts are not spendthrift unless the settlor expressly inserts a spendthrift clause, but spendthrift provisions are routinely included in professionally drafted trusts, if only by rote inclusion of formbook boilerplate. In New York, all trusts are spendthrift as to income unless the settlor expressly makes the beneficiary's interest transferable. N.Y. Est. Powers & Trusts Law §7-1.5 (2004).

The two decisions largely responsible for the spendthrift trust doctrine are Nichols v. Eaton, 91 U.S. 716 (1875), and Broadway Natl. Bank v. Adams, 133 Mass. 170 (1882). In Nichols v. Eaton, Justice Miller inserted an elaborate dictum upholding spendthrift trusts: "Why a parent, or one who loves another, and wishes to use his own property in securing the object of his affection, as far as property can do it, from the ills of life, the vicissitudes of fortune, and even his own improvidence, or incapacity for self-protection, should not be permitted to do so, is not readily perceived." 91 U.S. at 727. In Broadway Natl. Bank v. Adams, the Massachusetts court upheld the spendthrift trust.

On this account, the spendthrift trust does comport with policy in favor of free transferability; the restraint on the beneficiary's right to alienate arises from the settlor's right to condition the terms of her transfer. Accordingly, the underlying policy issues are whether to allow the reach of the dead hand, and if so, how far. Consider the following two case studies:

> *Case 20.* X, a successful businessman, enjoys good health and is now entering his eightieth year. Spoiled by the luxury afforded to him during his youth, *X*'s son, *A*, runs up a host of debts and has no job. Because *X* is still alive and in possession of his fortune, he is able to provide *A* with a comfortable style of living despite *A*'s debts. *A*'s creditors have no recourse against *X*'s assets.
>
> *Case 21.* Y, a successful businessman, died at an early age, survived by his son, *B*. Spoiled by his early life of luxury and damaged by the tragic early loss of his father, *B* has run up a host of debts and has no job. Because *Y* died intestate, *B* inherited a large share of *Y*'s fortune. However, these funds have either been lost through *B*'s mismanagement or have been attached by *B*'s creditors.

As articulated by Justice Miller, the argument in favor of recognizing spendthrift trusts is that, with respect to protecting their children from improvidence, a spendthrift trust would put *Y* in the same position as *X*.

Not surprisingly, the spendthrift trust — and its strong endorsement of the dead hand's reach — has been sharply criticized. John Chipman Gray, the great oracular property teacher at Harvard, was so outraged at the introduction of spendthrift trusts that he was moved to write his Restraints on the Alienation of Property, first published in 1883, in refutation of Nichols v. Eaton. He said, "The general introduction of spendthrift trusts would be to form a privileged class, who could indulge in every speculation, could practice every fraud, and, provided they kept on the safe side of the criminal law, could yet roll in wealth." John C. Gray, Restraints on the Alienation of Property 262 (1883). In spite of Gray's strictures, by the time the second edition of his book was published, the battle was lost. "State after State has given in its adhesion to the new doctrine . . . and yet I cannot recant." Id. (2d ed. 1885) at iv-v. The spendthrift trust is today recognized throughout the United States.

Scheffel v. Krueger
Supreme Court of New Hampshire, 2001
146 N.H. 669, 782 A.2d 410

DUGGAN, J.   In 1998, the [plaintiff, Lorie Scheffel, individually and as mother of Cory C.,] filed suit in superior court asserting tort claims against the defendant, Kyle Krueger. In her suit, the plaintiff alleged that the defendant sexually assaulted her minor child, videotaped the act and later broadcasted the videotape over the Internet. The same conduct that the plaintiff alleged in the tort claims also formed the basis for criminal charges against the defendant.[23] The court entered a default judgment against the defendant and ordered him to pay $551,286.25 in damages. To satisfy the judgment against the defendant, the plaintiff sought an attachment of the defendant's beneficial interest in the Kyle Krueger Irrevocable Trust (trust).

The defendant's grandmother established the trust in 1985 for the defendant's benefit. Its terms direct the trustee to pay all of the net income from the trust to the beneficiary, at least quarterly, or more frequently if the beneficiary in writing so requests. The trustee is further authorized to pay any of the principal to the beneficiary if in the trustee's sole discretion the funds are necessary for the maintenance, support and education of the beneficiary. The beneficiary may not invade the principal until he reaches the age of fifty, which will not occur until April 6, 2016.

The beneficiary is prohibited from making any voluntary or involuntary transfers of his interest in the trust. Article VII of the trust instrument specifically provides:

> No principal or income payable or to become payable under any of the trusts created by this instrument shall be subject to anticipation or assignment by any beneficiary thereof, or to the interference or control of any creditors of such beneficiary or to be taken or reached by any legal or equitable process in satisfaction of any debt or liability of such beneficiary prior to its receipt by the beneficiary.

Asserting that this so-called spendthrift provision barred the plaintiff's claim against the trust, the trustee defendant moved to [dismiss the plaintiff's claim]. The trial court ruled that under RSA 564:23 (1997), this spendthrift provision is enforceable against the plaintiff's claim and dismissed [the plaintiff's claim]. . . .

We first address the plaintiff's argument that the legislature did not intend RSA 564:23 to shield the trust assets from tort creditors, especially when the beneficiary's conduct constituted a criminal act. . . . "We interpret legislative intent from the statute as written, and therefore, we will not consider what the legislature might have said or add words that the legislature did not include." Rye Beach Country Club v. Town of Rye, 719 A.2d 623 (N.H. 1998).

---

23. Having been turned in by his wife, who found the incriminating videotape among Krueger's belongings in their bedroom, Krueger was convicted of "eighty counts of aggravated felonious sexual assault, seven counts of attempted aggravated felonious sexual assault, two counts of felonious sexual assault, and one count of simple assault." State v. Krueger, 776 A.2d 720 (N.H. 2001).—Eds.

We begin by examining the language found in the statute. RSA 564:23, I, provides:

> In the event the governing instrument so provides, a beneficiary of a trust shall not be able to transfer his or her right to future payments of income and principal, and a creditor of a beneficiary shall not be able to subject the beneficiary's interest to the payment of its claim.

The statute provides two exceptions to the enforceability of spendthrift provisions. The provisions "shall not apply to a beneficiary's interest in a trust to the extent that the beneficiary is the settlor and the trust is not a special needs trust established for a person with disabilities," RSA 564:23, II, and "shall not be construed to prevent the application of RSA 545-A or a similar law of another state [regarding fraudulent transfers]," RSA 564:23, III. Thus, under the plain language of the statute, a spendthrift provision is enforceable unless the beneficiary is also the settlor or the assets were fraudulently transferred to the trust. The plaintiff does not argue that either exception applies.

Faced with this language, the plaintiff argues that the legislature did not intend for the statute to shield the trust assets from tort creditors. The statute, however, plainly states that "a creditor of a beneficiary shall not be able to subject the beneficiary's interest to the payment of its claim." RSA 564:23, I. Nothing in this language suggests that the legislature intended that a tort creditor should be exempted from a spendthrift provision. Two exemptions are enumerated in sections II and III. Where the legislature has made specific exemptions, we must presume no others were intended. "If this is an omission, the courts cannot supply it. That is for the Legislature to do." Brahmey v. Rollins, 179 A. 186 (N.H. 1935).

The plaintiff argues public policy requires us to create a tort creditor exception to the statute. The cases the plaintiff relies upon, however, both involve judicially created spendthrift law. See Sligh v. First Nat. Bank of Holmes County, 704 So. 2d 1020, 1024 (Miss. 1997); Elec. Workers v. IBEW-NECA Holiday Trust, 583 S.W.2d 154, 162 (Mo. 1979). In this State, the legislature has enacted a statute repudiating the public policy exception sought by the plaintiff. Compare RSA 564:23, I, with Athorne v. Athorne, 128 A.2d 910 (N.H. 1957). This statutory enactment cannot be overruled, because "[i]t is axiomatic that courts do not question the wisdom or expediency of a statute." Brahmey, 179 A. 186, 192-93. Therefore, "[n]o rule of public policy is available to overcome [this] statutory rule." Id. . . .

Finally, the plaintiff asserts that the trial court erred in denying her request that the trust be terminated because the purpose of the trust can no longer be satisfied. The plaintiff argues that the trust's purpose to provide for the defendant's support, maintenance and education can no longer be fulfilled because the defendant will likely remain incarcerated for a period of years. The trial court, however, found that the trust's purpose "may still be fulfilled while the defendant is incarcerated and after he is released." The record before us supports this finding.

Affirmed.

SHELLEY v. SHELLEY, 354 P.2d 282 (Or. 1960): *T*'s will left his residuary estate in trust for his son Grant. The income was to be paid to Grant for life. In addition, the trustee was to begin distributing corpus to Grant after he reached age 30 in amounts that the trustee and other named persons deemed Grant capable of investing properly. The trustee was also given discretion to distribute corpus to

Grant or his children in case of an emergency where unusual and extraordinary expenses were incurred for their support and care. Finally, Grant's interest in the trust was made inalienable by a spendthrift clause:

> Each beneficiary hereunder is hereby restrained from alienating, anticipating, encumbering, or in any manner assigning his or her interest or estate, either in principal or income, and is without power so to do, nor shall such interest or estate be subject to his or her liabilities or obligations nor to judgment or other legal process, bankruptcy proceedings or claims of creditors or others.

Grant married twice and divorced twice, leaving two children by each marriage. Both divorce decrees obligated Grant to make child support payments, and the second decree also called for alimony payments. Grant subsequently disappeared, and the trustee bank filed an interpleader in response to claims made against the trust by Grant's children and former wives for satisfaction of his support and alimony obligations.

> The question on this appeal is whether the spendthrift provision will be given effect to bar the claims of the beneficiary's children for support and the plaintiff's claim for alimony. In Cogswell v. Cogswell, 167 P.2d 324, 335 (Or. 1946), we held that the spendthrift provision of a trust is not effective against the claims of the beneficiary's former wife for alimony and for support of the beneficiary's child. . . .
>
> The defendant bank concedes that the *Cogswell* case is controlling in the case at bar, but asks us to overrule it on the ground that it is inconsistent with our own cases recognizing the testator's privilege to dispose of his property as he pleases and, further, that it is inconsistent with various Oregon statutes expressing the same policy of free alienation. If we should accept the premise urged by the defendant bank, that a testator has an inviolable right to dispose of his property as he pleases subject only to legislative restriction, the conclusion is inevitable that the testator may create in a beneficiary an interest free from all claims, including those for support and alimony.
>
> But the premise is not sound. The privilege of disposing of property is not absolute; it is hedged with various restrictions where there are policy considerations warranting the limitation. . . . Not all of these restrictions are imposed by statute. The rule against perpetuities, the rule against restraints on alienation, the refusal to recognize trusts for capricious purposes or for illegal purposes, or for any purpose contrary to public policy, are all instances of judge-made rules limiting the privilege of alienation. Many others could be recited. It is within the court's power to impose upon the privilege of disposing of property such restrictions as are consistent with its view of sound public policy, unless, of course, the legislature has expressed a contrary view. Our own statutes do not purport to deal with the specific question before us, that is as to whether there should be limitations on the owner's privilege to create a spendthrift trust. . . .

Having concluded that it had the power to make exceptions to the general rule that a spendthrift clause bars the claims of the beneficiary's creditors, the court turned to the specific claims presented in this case.

> The question is whether a person should be entitled to enjoy the benefits of a trust and at the same time refuse to pay the obligations arising out of his marriage.
>
> We have no hesitation in declaring that public policy requires that the interest of the beneficiary of a trust should be subject to the claims for support of his children. . . . Certainly the defendant will accept the societal postulate that parents

have the obligation to support their children. If we give effect to the spendthrift provision to bar the claims for support, we have the spectacle of a man enjoying the benefits of a trust immune from claims which are justly due, while the community pays for the support of his children. We do not believe that it is sound policy to use the welfare funds of this state in support of the beneficiary's children, while he stands behind the shield of immunity created by a spendthrift trust provision. To endorse such a policy and to permit the spectacle which we have described above would be to invite disrespect for the administration of justice. . . .

The justification for permitting a claim for alimony is, perhaps, not as clear. The adjustment of the economic interests of the parties to a divorce may depend upon a variety of factors, including the respective fault of the parties, the ability of the wife to support herself, the duration of the marriage, and other considerations. Whether alimony is to be granted and its amount are questions which are determined in light of these various interests. It is probably fair to say that the duties created by the marriage relation, at least as they are evaluated upon the termination of the marriage, are conceived of as more qualified than those arising out of the paternal relationship. On the theory that divorce terminates the husband's duty to support his former wife and that she stands in no better position than other creditors, some courts have held that the spendthrift provision insulates the beneficiary's interest in the trust from her claim. Recognizing the difference in marital and parental duties suggested above, it has been held that a spendthrift trust is subject to the claims for the support of children but free from the claims of the former wife. . . . A majority of the cases, however, hold that a spendthrift provision will not bar a claim for alimony. . . .

The duty of the husband to support his former wife should override the restriction called for by the spendthrift provision. The same reason advanced above for requiring the support of the beneficiary's children will, in many cases, be applicable to the claim of a divorced wife; if the beneficiary's interest cannot be reached, the state may be called upon to support her.

The court thus held that Grant's interest in the trust income was subject to the claims of his children and former wives.

With respect to the trust corpus, the analysis was different because Grant's interest was discretionary.

> The question of the claimants' rights to reach the corpus of the trust involves other considerations. For the reasons heretofore stated, the beneficiary's interest in the corpus is not made immune from these claims. But, by the terms of the trust, the disbursement of the corpus is within the discretion of the trustee (or, in some instances subject to the approval of others), and, therefore, Grant Shelley's right to receive any part of the corpus does not arise until the trustee has exercised his discretion and has decided to invade the corpus.

Accordingly, the court held that Grant's former wives could not reach the trust corpus. Grant's children likewise could not enforce their claim against their father's rights to the trust corpus. The trust also named Grant's children as beneficiaries, however, so they could seek payment from the trust, not as Grant's creditors, but as beneficiaries themselves.

> The trust directed and authorized the trustee, in the exercise of its sole discretion . . . , to make disbursements for the use and benefit not only of Grant Shelley, but also for his children. The disbursements were to be made "in case of any

emergency arising whereby unusual and extraordinary expenses are necessary for the proper support and care of my said son, or said children." Here the children are named as beneficiaries of the trust and need not claim derivatively through their father. However, they are entitled to a share of the corpus only if, in the trustee's discretion, it is determined that an emergency exists. The defendant bank contends that the expenses of supporting Grant Shelley's children claimed in this case were for the usual and ordinary costs of support and do not, therefore, constitute "unusual and extraordinary expenses" within the meaning of the trust provision. . . . We disagree with defendant's interpretation. We construe the clause to include the circumstances involved here, i.e., where the children are deserted by their father and are in need of support. We think that the testator intended to provide that in the event that the income from the trust was not sufficient to cover disbursements for the support and care of either the son or his children an "emergency" had arisen and the corpus could then be invaded.

Uniform Trust Code (2000)

§502.   SPENDTHRIFT PROVISION

(a) A spendthrift provision is valid only if it restrains both voluntary and involuntary transfer of a beneficiary's interest.

(b) A term of a trust providing that the interest of a beneficiary is held subject to a "spendthrift trust," or words of similar import, is sufficient to restrain both voluntary and involuntary transfer of the beneficiary's interest.

(c) A beneficiary may not transfer an interest in a trust in violation of a valid spendthrift provision and, except as otherwise provided in this [article], a creditor or assignee of the beneficiary may not reach the interest or a distribution by the trustee before its receipt by the beneficiary.

§503.   EXCEPTIONS TO SPENDTHRIFT PROVISION

(a) In this section, "child" includes any person for whom an order or judgment for child support has been entered in this or another State.

(b) Even if a trust contains a spendthrift provision, a beneficiary's child, spouse, or former spouse who has a judgment or court order against the beneficiary for support or maintenance, or a judgment creditor who has provided services for the protection of a beneficiary's interest in the trust, may obtain from a court an order attaching present or future distributions to or for the benefit of the beneficiary.

(c) A spendthrift provision is unenforceable against a claim of this State or the United States to the extent a statute of this State or federal law so provides.

NOTES AND QUESTIONS

1.   The court in Shelley v. Shelley held that the trust established for Grant Shelley was subject to the claims of his children and former wives. The court in Scheffel v. Krueger held that the trust established for Kyle Krueger was not subject to the claims of the child whom Krueger had sexually assaulted. Can these results be reconciled? Is there a moral, ethical, or other principled

distinction between the claims of the beneficiary's children and former spouses, and the claims of tort victims? Should the law recognize a distinction between ordinary contract creditors (such as lenders) and involuntary creditors (such as tort victims and children)?

> In many of the cases in which it has been held that by the terms of the trust the interest of a beneficiary may be put beyond the reach of his creditors, the courts have laid some stress on the fact that the creditors had only themselves to blame for extending credit to a person whose interest under the trust had been put beyond their reach. The courts have said that before extending credit they could have ascertained the extent and character of the debtor's resources. Certainly, the situation of a tort creditor is quite different from that of a contract creditor. A man who is about to be knocked down by an automobile has no opportunity to investigate the credit of the driver of the automobile and has no opportunity to avoid being injured no matter what the resources of the driver may be. [2A Austin W. Scott, Trusts §157.5 (William F. Fratcher 4th ed. 1987).]

If spendthrift trust law were to recognize a distinction between voluntary and involuntary creditors, on which side of the line would spouses fall?

Would the result in either *Shelley* or *Krueger* change under UTC §§502-503? For an analysis of the relevant UTC provisions, see Alan Newman, The Rights of Creditors of Beneficiaries Under the Uniform Trust Code: An Examination of the Compromise, 69 Tenn. L. Rev. 771, 782-803 (2002).

The court in *Shelley* held that the beneficiary's children and former spouses could not reach his discretionary interest in the trust. UTC §504(c), excerpted above at page 546, would change this result if the trustee has abused her discretion. Is this a sensible reform? Does your answer depend on whether the state recognizes an exception in spendthrift trusts for children, spouses, and former spouses?

2. On the rise of the spendthrift trust in the United States, see Mary Louise Fellows, Spendthrift Trusts: Roots and Relevance for Twenty-First Century Planning, 50 Rec. Assn. B. City N.Y. 140 (1995). For reflective analysis of the issues underlying spendthrift trusts, compare Anne S. Emanuel, Spendthrift Trusts: It's Time to Codify the Compromise, 72 Neb. L. Rev. 179 (1993), with Adam Hirsch, Spendthrift Trusts and Public Policy: Economic and Cognitive Perspectives, 73 Wash. U.L.Q. 1 (1995).

3. *England.* In contrast with the American states, England and the rest of the common law world are less solicitous of the dead hand. Neither England nor the other common law jurisdictions recognize the spendthrift trust. The leading case is Brandon v. Robinson, 34 Eng. Rep. 379 (Ch. 1811). This is not to say, however, that creditors of English trust beneficiaries necessarily fare better than creditors of American trust beneficiaries. English law does not allow creditors to recover against a discretionary trust beneficiary's interest, and through use of a protective trust, the beneficiary's interest can be made mandatory unless the beneficiary's creditors attach the beneficiary's interest, whereupon a discretionary trust automatically arises. Which would you prefer as a creditor? As a settlor? As a beneficiary?

Why do all the common law jurisdictions tolerate some form of shielding of the trust fund from the beneficiary's creditors, albeit through different means? In Robert H. Sitkoff, An Agency Costs Theory of Trust Law, 89 Cornell L. Rev. 621, 676-677 (2004), the author answers that, "Without the option of at least one enforceable protective measure, settlors who are concerned about a beneficiary's future insolvency would be channeled toward informal arrangements such as outright transfers to trusted kin or friends with a wink and a nod that the transferee will take care of the would-be beneficiary. The potential . . . costs to the beneficiaries and the settlor of this approach, which would hardly benefit the beneficiaries' creditors, are manifest." For further analysis in this vein, see Hirsch, supra, at 70-71.

4. The rights of tort creditors (Scheffel v. Krueger) and of spouses and children (Shelley v. Shelley) are only two of the many vexing issues in spendthrift trust law.

(a) *Child support and alimony.* Judgments for child or spousal support can be enforced against the debtor's interest in spendthrift trusts in the majority of states, as in Shelley v. Shelley, and under UTC §503(b) (2000) and Restatement (Third) of Trusts §59(a) (2003). In a minority, a spouse or child cannot reach a spendthrift trust to satisfy judgments for support. In some states, the power to permit courts to order child and spousal support payments from spendthrift or discretionary trusts is provided by statute. See Jeffrey A. Schoenblum, 2004 Multistate Guide to Estate Planning at Table 9.05. For an illuminating examination of this issue, see Carolyn L. Dessin, Feed a Trust and Starve a Child: The Effectiveness of Trust Protective Techniques Against Claims for Support and Alimony, 10 Ga. St. U.L. Rev. 691 (1994).

(b) *Tort creditors.* Whether a spendthrift clause prevents tort victims of a trust beneficiary from reaching the beneficiary's interest in the trust is not entirely settled. See Schoenblum, supra. In Scheffel v. Krueger, the court held the spendthrift clause effective against a tort creditor. So too did the court in the even more recent case of Duvall v. McGee, 826 A.2d 416 (Md. 2003). On the other hand, in Sligh v. Sligh, 704 So. 2d 1020 (Miss. 1997), the court held that a tort creditor could enforce a judgment against the tortfeasor's interest in a spendthrift trust or in a discretionary trust, but the very next year the Mississippi legislature enacted the Family Trust Preservation Act, which reversed *Sligh* and exempted spendthrift trusts from tort creditors. Miss. Code Ann. §91-9-503 (2004). In Georgia, tort victims are entitled to enforce a judgment against the tortfeasor's interest in a spendthrift trust. Ga. Code Ann. §53-12-28(c) (2004).

UTC §503 does not recognize an exception for tort creditors, and the official comment makes clear that this omission was deliberate. Alas, the position of the Restatement (Third) of Trusts is fuzzier. Although §59 does not recognize an exception for tort creditors, Comment a(2) to that section contemplates that "evolving policy" might "justify recognition of other exceptions." Comment a(2) then continues: "The nature or a pattern of tortious conduct by a beneficiary . . . may on policy grounds justify a court's refusal to allow spendthrift immunity to protect the trust interest and the lifestyle of that beneficiary, especially one whose willful or fraudulent conduct or persistently reckless behavior causes serious harm to others."

(c) *Furnishing necessary support.* The traditional rule is that a person who has furnished necessary services or support can reach the beneficiary's interest in a spendthrift trust (the paradigmatic examples are physicians and grocers). See 2A Austin W. Scott, Trusts §157.2 (William F. Fratcher 4th ed. 1987) (collecting cases). This view is carried forward in Restatement (Third) of Trusts §59(b). It is rejected, however, by UTC §503. The official comment to §503 explains: "Most of these cases involve claims by governmental entities, which the drafters concluded are better handled by the enactment of special legislation as authorized by subsection (c)." For a thoughtful examination of this policy decision, see Alan Newman, The Rights of Creditors of Beneficiaries Under the Uniform Trust Code: An Examination of the Compromise, 69 Tenn. L. Rev. 771, 791-798 (2002).

(d) *Federal tax lien.* The United States can reach the beneficiary's interest to satisfy a tax claim against the beneficiary. Federal tax law trumps state spendthrift trust rules. See La Salle Natl. Bank v. United States, 636 F. Supp. 874 (N.D. Ill. 1986); United States v. Riggs Natl. Bank, 636 F. Supp. 172 (D.D.C. 1986). See generally Scott, supra, §157.4. Whether a state can reach the beneficiary's interest to satisfy a state tax claim depends on the applicable state statute. UTC §503(c) and Restatement (Third) of Trusts §59, cmt. a, are in accord with respect to both federal and state tax claims.

(e) *Excess over amount needed for support.* In New York, the beneficiary's creditors can reach that part of spendthrift trust income in excess of the amount needed for the support and education of the beneficiary. N.Y. Est. Powers & Trusts Law §7-3.4 (2004). Several states have copied this statute. In determining what is necessary for the support of the beneficiary and what is excess (reachable by creditors), courts developed a *station-in-life rule.* Creditors can reach only the amount in excess of what is needed to maintain the beneficiary in his station in life. The station-in-life rule rendered these excess-income statutes relatively useless to creditors. Spendthrift trusts are often created by persons of considerable wealth who have raised their children in substantial luxury. The accustomed manner of living of such a beneficiary is likely to require the full income from the trust.[24]

(f) *Percentage levy, spendthrift caps.* In a few states a creditor is permitted to reach a certain percentage (usually between 10 and 30 percent) of the income of the spendthrift trust beneficiary in a garnishment proceeding ordinarily applicable to wage earners. See, e.g., Cal Prob. Code §15306.5 (2004) (25 percent). In addition, a handful of states cap the amount of income or principal that can be shielded by a spendthrift provision. See, e.g., Okla. Stat. Ann. tit. 60, §175.25 (2004) (providing that trust income due to the beneficiary in excess of $25,000 per year is subject to garnishment by creditors).

5. *Pension trusts.* The federal Employee Retirement Income Security Act (ERISA), 29 U.S.C. §1056(d)(1) (2004), requires that "Each pension plan [covered by the act] shall provide that benefits provided under the plan may not be assigned or alienated." ERISA also provides that such benefits may be reached for child

---

24. John Chipman Gray was even more scornful of the New York scheme than of spendthrift trusts generally.

> It may be said that, if the Courts have been wrong in tolerating spendthrift trusts, a remedy is to be found in the legislatures. If the remedy is like that applied in New York, it is, if not worse, more disgusting than the disease. . . . The Statutes of New York, as interpreted by the Courts, provide that the surplus of income given in trust beyond what is necessary for the education and support of the beneficiary shall be liable for his debts. . . . The Court takes into account that the debtor is "a gentleman of high social standing, whose associations are chiefly with men of leisure, and who is connected with a number of clubs," and that his income is not more than sufficient to maintain his position according to his education, habits, and associations.
>
> To say that whatever money is given to a man cannot be taken by his creditors is bad enough; at any rate, however, it is law for rich and poor alike; but to say that from a sum which creditors can reach one man, who has lived simply and plainly, can deduct but a small sum, while a large sum may be deducted by another man because he is "of high social standing" . . . is to descend to a depth of as shameless snobbishness as any into which the justice of a country was ever plunged. [John C. Gray, Restraints on the Alienation of Property x-xi (2d ed. 1895).]

support, alimony, or marital property rights. Id. at §1056(d)(3). The principle underlying ERISA is that the employee's future retirement security should be protected even at the expense of current creditors. See Guidry v. Sheet Metal Workers Natl. Pension Fund, 493 U.S. 365 (1990); John H. Langbein & Bruce A. Wolk, Pension and Employee Benefit Law 574-577 (3d ed. 2000). For further examination of creditor rights to pensions and other retirement accounts, see Patricia J. Dilley, Hidden in Plain View: The Pension Shield Against Creditors, 74 Ind. L.J. 355 (1999). See also John K. Eason, Retirement Security Through Asset Protection: The Evolution of Wealth, Privilege, and Policy, 61 Wash. & Lee L. Rev. 159 (2004).

As detailed below, *self-settled spendthrift trusts* are not recognized under traditional principles. Does protection from creditors of earned wealth located in pension plans compensate for limiting spendthrift trusts to inherited wealth?

6. *Bankruptcy*. A beneficial interest in a spendthrift trust cannot be reached by creditors in bankruptcy. The Bankruptcy Code provides that an interest in trust that is not alienable under local law does not pass to the trustee in bankruptcy. 11 U.S.C. §541(c)(2) (2004). The Code also excludes from the bankrupt's estate any interest in a pension trust covered by ERISA, inasmuch as such interests are made nonassignable by ERISA. Patterson v. Shumate, 504 U.S. 753 (1992). See Langbein & Wolk, supra, at 639-643 (discussing exemption of IRAs, Keogh plans, and 401(k) and 403(b) plans).

3. Self-Settled Asset Protection Trusts

A longstanding principle of trust law holds that you cannot shield your assets from creditors by placing them in a trust for your own benefit. Your creditors always have recourse against your entire interest in a self-settled trust, even if the trust is discretionary, spendthrift, or both. Creditors can reach the maximum amount that the trustee could pay the settlor or apply for the settlor's benefit. Thus:

> *Case 22. O*, a surgeon, transfers property to *X* in trust to pay so much of the income and principal to *O* as *X* determines in *X*'s sole and absolute discretion. Five years later, *O* botches a routine surgery, causing grievous injury to the patient, *A. A* may enforce an award of damages against the entire corpus of the trust, because *X* could, in *X*'s discretion, pay the entire corpus to *O*. This is true even if the trust instrument provides that *O*'s interest may not be reached by *O*'s creditors (a spendthrift clause). Nor does it matter that *O*'s right to the trust assets is subject to *X*'s discretion.

These rules are carried forward in UTC §505 (2000) and Restatement (Third) of Trusts §§58(2) & 60, cmt. f (2003).

The question thus arises, why is protection from creditors available only to recipients of *inherited* wealth and not also to persons who *earn* wealth and then create a self-settled trust? The traditional answer is that the protective justification for allowing a donor to insulate a gift from the claims of the donee's creditors collapses when the donor and the donee are one in the same. "[A]lthough courts and legislatures have had some sympathy for property owners seeking to protect their imprudent or profligate children, the notion that property owners ought to be able to protect themselves against their own profligacy, at the expense of their creditors, has been much harder to swallow." Stewart E. Sterk, Asset Protection

Trusts: Trust Law's Race to the Bottom?, 85 Cornell L. Rev. 1035, 1043-1044 (2000). See also Robert T. Danforth, Rethinking the Law of Creditors' Rights in Trusts, 53 Hastings L.J. 287 (2002) (reexamining the asset protection features of modern trust law).

Suppose, however, that a state were to authorize a self-settled trust that insulated the trust fund from the settlor's creditors. Would not such an innovation attract trust funds to the state? Believing that the answer is Yes, a number of jurisdictions—both offshore and now a handful of domestic states too—have enacted statutes that validate self-settled asset protection trusts. Such trusts can be created in these jurisdictions by people who live elsewhere, but to ensure the desired choice of law, settlors are typically advised to appoint as trustee a bank or trust company located in the state whose law is being invoked. Not coincidentally, these statutes have been enacted largely at the behest of local banks and lawyers. Both stand to benefit from an influx of trust assets.

A similar dynamic is at work in the race to abolish the Rule against Perpetuities, a development discussed at pages 711-723. See also Robert H. Sitkoff & Max Schanzenbach, Jurisdictional Competition for Trust Funds: An Empirical Analysis of Perpetuities and Taxes, 115 Yale L.J. (forthcoming 2005). But where the race to abolish the Rule against Perpetuities is driven by the generation-skipping transfer tax, the fear of ruinous liability drives the competition over self-settled asset protection trusts. For example, there is anecdotal evidence that, in the face of rising premiums, some doctors have opted to drop their malpractice insurance altogether in favor of moving their assets into a self-settled asset protection trust (this is the motivation for Case 22 above). See Rachel Emma Silverman, Litigation Boom Spurs Efforts to Shield Assets, Wall St. J., Oct. 14, 2003, at D1. On this account, the self-settled asset protection trust might be reckoned as the revenge of the trust lawyers against the tort lawyers. Some have even defended the self-settled asset protection trust on the ground that "our tort systems were out of control." Roundtable Discussion, 32 Vand. J. Transnatl. L. 779, 793-794 (1999).

"OK, you're going to feel a little prick, followed by a burning desire to sue me."

The story of the recognition of self-settled asset protection trusts begins in the sunny Caribbean, South Pacific, and other exotic locales. In the 1980s, a host of offshore jurisdictions — including Antigua, Bahamas, Barbados, Belize, Bermuda, Cayman Islands, Cook Islands, Cyprus, Gibraltar, Grenada, Isle of Man, Jersey, Liechtenstein, Mauritius, Nevis, Samoa, St. Lucia, and Tuks and Caicos — amended their trust laws to allow the creation of a self-settled trust against which the settlor's creditors have no recourse. See Denis Kleinfeld, Choosing an Offshore Jurisdiction, *in* Asset Protection Strategies: Planning with Domestic and Offshore Entities 73 (Alexander A. Bove, Jr., ed., 2002).

The Cook Islands' International Trusts Act of 1984, which is representative, validates *self-settled spendthrift trusts*, provided that the settlor is not a resident of the Cook Islands. As Professor Sterk has observed, this qualification is "a sure sign that the purpose of the statute was to attract foreign capital." Sterk, supra, at 1048. The Cook Islands law also provides that no judgment rendered by a foreign court against a Cook Islands trust, or against the settlor, trustee, or beneficiary of a Cook Islands trust, will be enforced by a Cook Islands court. See id. at 1050.

In 1997 the self-settled asset protection trust migrated to Alaska. Under the Alaska statute, the settlor's creditors have no recourse against the settlor's interest in a *self-settled discretionary trust* so long as the initial transfer was not fraudulent. Alaska Stat. §34.40.110 (2004). To ensure a local payoff, Alaska law provides that, if an Alaska resident or banking institution is designated as trustee and some of the trust assets are deposited in an Alaska institution, both jurisdiction in Alaska courts and the applicability of Alaska law will be ensured. Alaska Stat. §13.36.035 (2004). As to already existing trusts, a subsequently enacted provision authorizes the settlor to move the trust to Alaska. Alaska Stat. §13.36.043 (2004). According to the web page for the Alaska Trust Company, the Alaska statute had its genesis in a fishing trip by Douglas Blattmachr, now the president and CEO of the company, his brother "Jonathan Blattmachr, a noted [New York] estate planning attorney, and Richard Thwaites, an estate planning attorney and life-long Alaskan." The Genesis of Alaska Trust Company, http://www.alaskatrust.com/www/thegen.html.

Not to be outdone by Alaska, Delaware validated a similar self-settled asset protection trust in 1997. See Del. Code Ann. tit. 12, §§3570-3576 (2004). The official synopsis of the Delaware Act states that it "is similar to legislation recently enacted in Alaska. It is intended to maintain Delaware's role as the most favored domestic jurisdiction for the establishment of trusts." 71 Del. Laws ch. 159 (1997). However, the Delaware statute carves out an exception for support claims by children and former spouses and for claims arising from death, personal injury, or property damage that occurred before the trust was settled. Del. Code Ann. tit. 12, §3573 (2004). See also Richard W. Nenno & John E. Sullivan III, Delaware Asset Protection Trusts, 32 Est. Plan. 22 (2005).

Nevada, Oklahoma, Rhode Island, and Utah have since passed statutes authorizing some form of self-settled asset protection trust, bringing the domestic count to at least six.[25] See Nev. Rev. Stat. §166.040(1)(b) (2004); Okla. Stat. Ann. tit. 31,

---

25. Some commentators have read an older statute in Colorado to authorize self-settled asset protection trusts as to future creditors, see Colo. Rev. Stat. §38-10-111 (2004), but in dicta the Colorado Supreme Court has rejected that interpretation. See In re Cohen, 8 P.3d 429, 432-434 (Colo. 1999). In 1986, Missouri amended its statutory rules on spendthrift trusts in a manner that could be read to

§§10-18 (2004); R.I. Gen. Laws §§18-9.2-1–18-9.2-5 (2004); Utah Code Ann. §25-6-14 (2004). Oklahoma's statute limits settlors to a single asset protection trust, and the permissible initial funding is capped at $1 million.

The crucial question thus arises, will the courts in fact bar recovery by the settlor's creditors against the settlor's interest in a self-settled asset protection trust?

Federal Trade Commission v. Affordable Media, LLC

United States Court of Appeals, Ninth Circuit, 1999
179 F.3d 1228

WIGGINS, Circuit Judge.   A husband and wife, Denyse and Michael Anderson, were involved in a telemarketing venture that offered investors the chance to participate in a project that sold such modern marvels as talking pet tags and water-filled barbells by means of late-night television. Although the promoters promised that an investment in the project would return 50 per cent in a mere 60 to 90 days, the venture in fact was a Ponzi scheme,[26] which eventually unraveled and left thousands of investors with tremendous losses. . . .

While the investors' money was lost in the fraudulent scheme, the Andersons' profits from their commissions remained safely tucked away across the sea in a Cook Islands trust. When the [Federal Trade] Commission brought a civil action to recover as much money as possible for the defrauded investors, the Andersons . . . claimed that they were unable to repatriate the assets in the Cook Islands trust because they had willingly relinquished all control over the millions of dollars of commissions in order to place this money overseas in the benevolent hands of unaccountable overseers, just on the off chance that a law suit might

---

authorize self-settled asset protection trusts, but there is some contrary case law and the literature tends not to regard Missouri as a self-settled asset protection trust jurisdiction. See Markmueller v. Case, 51 F.3d 775 (8th Cir. 1995); John K. Eason, Retirement Security Through Asset Protection: The Evolution of Wealth, Privilege, and Policy, 61 Wash. & Lee L. Rev. 159, 174 n.54 (2004). The language of the 1986 amendment has been carried forward into the Missouri enactment of UTC §505. See 2004 Mo. HB 1511; Mo. Rev. Stat. §456.080 (superseded statute).

26. The expression *Ponzi scheme* derives from Charles Ponzi's infamous swindle in the early 1920s. Ponzi hatched his scheme upon discovering that, under the Universal Postal Convention then in effect, it was possible to buy a stamp in Europe that was worth a few cents more in the United States than it cost in Europe. Claiming that he would exploit this opportunity for postal arbitrage, Ponzi solicited investors with promises of returns on the order of 50 percent in 45 days. Investors were given tradable notes on which, for a time, Ponzi made good. But he did so by paying off the earlier investors with the proceeds raised from later investors. Ponzi did not actually undertake substantial postal arbitrage, and in view of the transaction costs, no wonder. Having taken in a reported $15 million from investors, it would have required a phalanx of workers to process, and an armada of vessels to transport, the billions of stamps necessary to achieve his promised returns. Ultimately, as in the case of all Ponzi schemes, the bubble of Ponzi's scheme burst. Investors recovered only twelve cents on the dollar, and Ponzi wound up serving a stint in prison—neither his first nor his last. Today the term *Ponzi scheme* is used to describe any scam in which subsequent receipts are used to make good on promises to earlier investors. Doing so gives the scam the appearance of genuine returns and the con artist a measure of credibility. For a vivid portrayal of Ponzi and the original Ponzi scheme, see Francis Russell, Bubble, Bubble—No Toil, No Trouble, 24 Am. Heritage 74 (Feb. 1973).—Eds.

result from their business activities. The learned district court was skeptical . . . and choose to grant the Commission its requested preliminary relief.

An old adage warns that a fool and his money are easily parted. This case shows that the same is not true of a district court judge and his common sense. After the Andersons refused to comply with the preliminary injunction by refusing to return their illicit proceeds, the district court found the Andersons in civil contempt of court. The Andersons appealed. . . .

I

Sometime after April 1997, Denyse and Michael Anderson became involved with The Sterling Group ("Sterling"). Sterling sold such imaginative products as the "Aquabell," a water-filled dumbbell, the "Talking Pet Tag," and a plastic wrap dispenser known as "KenKut" by means of late-night television com-mercials broadcast between the hours of 11:00 P.M. and 4:00 A.M. The Andersons formed Financial Growth Consultants, LLC ("Financial") to serve as the primary telemarketer of media units, an investment that afforded purchasers the opportunity to receive a portion of the profits gen-erated from the sales of Sterling's outlandish products. Financial's tele-marketers thereupon set about lo-cating prospective investors in the media unit scheme.

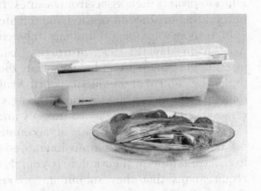

KenKut plastic wrap dispenser and a wrapped plate of strawberries

The media units sold for $5,000. Each media unit entitled the investor to participate in the sale of Sterling's products from 201 of the late-night commer-cials. Each product sold for $20.00. The investor would receive $7.50 for each product sold during his 201 commercials, up to a maximum of five products per commercial. According to Financial's telemarketers, the investors would likely receive $37.50 per commercial (from five products sold during each com-mercial) for a total of $7,537.50—an astronomical fifty percent return in sixty to ninety days. Financial, for its part, would receive forty-five percent of the inves-tor's $5,000.00 investment, an amount that the Andersons assert is the industry standard.

It appears that Financial's telemarketers were especially skilled at marketing the media units. Financial may have raised at least $13,000,000 from investors in the media-unit scheme, retaining an estimated $6,300,000 in commissions for itself. Perhaps unsurprisingly to those not involved in the media-unit project, it turned out that Sterling could not sell enough Talking Pet Tags and Aquabells to return the promised yields to the media-unit investors. Instead, it appears that Sterling used later investors' investments to pay the promised yields to earlier investors — a classic Ponzi scheme.

On April 23, 1998, the Federal Trade Commission (the "Commission") filed a complaint in the United States District Court for the District of Nevada, charging the Andersons, Financial, and others with violations of the Federal Trade Commission Act (the "Act") and the Telemarketing Sales Rule for their participation in a scheme to telemarket fraudulent investments to consumers. Upon motion by the Commission, the district court issued an ex parte temporary restraining order against the defendants. After hearings on April 30 and May 8, 1998, the district court entered a preliminary injunction against the defendants, which incorporated the provisions of the temporary restraining order. Both the temporary restraining order and the preliminary injunction required the Andersons to repatriate any assets held for their benefit outside of the United States.

In July, 1995, the Andersons had created an irrevocable trust under the law of the Cook Islands. The Andersons were named as co-trustees of the trust, together with AsiaCiti Trust Limited ("AsiaCiti"), a company licensed to conduct trustee services under Cook Islands law. Apparently, the Andersons created the trust in an effort to protect their assets from business risks and liabilities by placing the assets beyond the jurisdiction of the United States courts. . . .

In response to the preliminary injunction, the Andersons faxed a letter to AsiaCiti on May 12, 1998, instructing AsiaCiti to provide an accounting of the assets held in the trust and to repatriate the assets to the United States to be held under the control of the district court. AsiaCiti thereupon notified the Andersons that the temporary restraining order was an event of duress under the trust, removed the Andersons as co-trustees under the trust because of the event of duress, and refused to provide an accounting or repatriation of the assets.[27] . . .

On May 7, 1998, the Commission moved the district court to find the Andersons in civil contempt for their failure to comply with the temporary restraining order's requirements that they submit an accounting of their foreign assets to the Commission and to repatriate all assets located abroad. At a hearing on June 4, 1998, the district court found the Andersons in civil contempt of court for failing to repatriate the trust assets to the United States and failing to provide an accounting of the trust's assets. The district court, however, continued the hearing until June 9, then until June 11, and finally until June 17, in an effort to allow the Andersons to purge themselves of their contempt. In attempting to purge themselves of their contempt, the Andersons attempted to appoint their children as trustees of the trust, but AsiaCiti removed them from acting as trustees because the event of duress was continuing. At the June 17 hearing, the district court indicated that it believed that the Andersons remained in control of the trust and rejected their assertion that compliance with the repatriation provisions of the trust was impossible. At the close of the June 17 hearing, the district judge ordered the Andersons taken into custody because they had not purged themselves of their contempt. The Andersons timely appealed the district court's issuance of the preliminary injunction and finding them in contempt. We affirm the district court.

---

27. The Andersons' trust created the circumstances in which a foreign trustee would refuse to repatriate assets to the United States by means of so-called duress provisions. Under the trust agreement, an event of duress includes "[t]he issuance of any order, decree or judgment of any court or tribunal in any part of the world which in the opinion of the protector will or may directly or indirectly, expropriate, sequester, levy, lien or in any way control, restrict or prevent the free disposal by a trustee of any monies, investments or property which may from time to time be included in or form part of this trust and any distributions therefrom." Upon the happening of an event of duress, the trust agreement provides that the Andersons would be terminated as co-trustees, so that control over the trust assets would appear to be exclusively in the hands of a foreign trustee, beyond the jurisdiction of a United States court. . . . [Footnote relocated. — Eds.]

II

[The court upheld the preliminary injunction.]

III

The next issue on appeal is the district court's finding the Andersons in contempt for refusing to repatriate the assets in their Cook Islands trust. . . . Based on the record before us, we find that the district court did not abuse its discretion in holding the Andersons in contempt. . . .

The temporary restraining order required the Andersons, in relevant part, to "transfer to the territory of the United States all funds, documents and assets in foreign countries held either: (1) by them; (2) for their benefit; or (3) under their direct or indirect control, jointly or singly." These provisions were continued in the preliminary injunction. It is undisputed that the Andersons are beneficiaries of an irrevocable trust established under the laws of the Cook Islands. The Andersons do not dispute that the trust assets have not been repatriated to the United States. Instead, the Andersons claim that compliance with the temporary restraining order is impossible because the trustee, in accordance with the terms of the trust, will not repatriate the trust assets to the United States.

A party's inability to comply with a judicial order constitutes a defense to a charge of civil contempt. The Andersons claim that the refusal of the foreign trustee to repatriate the trust assets to the United States, which apparently was the goal of the trust, makes their compliance with the preliminary injunction impossible.

Although the Andersons assert that their "inability to comply with a judicial decree is a complete defense to a charge of civil contempt, *regardless of whether the inability to comply is self-induced*" (emphasis added), we are not certain that the Andersons' inability to comply in this case would be a defense to a finding of contempt. It is readily apparent that the Andersons' inability to comply with the district court's repatriation order is the intended result of their own conduct— their inability to comply and the foreign trustee's refusal to comply appears to be the precise goal of the Andersons' trust. The Andersons claim that they created their trust as part of an "asset protection plan." These "[s]o-called asset protection trusts are designed to shield wealth by moving it to a foreign jurisdiction that does not recognize U.S. judgments or other legal processes, such as asset freezes." Debra Baker, Island Castaway, ABA Journal, October 1998, at 55. The "asset protection" aspect of these foreign trusts arises from the ability of people, such as the Andersons, to frustrate and impede the United States courts by moving their assets beyond those courts' jurisdictions:

> Perhaps most importantly, situs courts typically ignore United States courts' demands to repatriate trust assets to the United States. A situs court will not enforce a United States order from a state court compelling the turnover of trust assets to a creditor that was defrauded under United States law, or assets that were placed into a self-settled spendthrift trust.

James T. Lorenzetti, The Offshore Trust: A Contemporary Asset Protection Scheme, 102 Com. L.J. 138, 143-144 (1997).

Because these asset protection trusts move the trust assets beyond the jurisdiction of domestic courts, often times all that remains within the jurisdiction is the physical person of the defendant. Because the physical person of the defendant remains subject to domestic courts' jurisdictions, courts could normally utilize their contempt powers to force a defendant to return the assets to their jurisdictions. Recognizing this risk, asset protection trusts typically are designed so that a defendant can assert that compliance with a court's order to repatriate the trust assets is impossible:

> Another common issue is whether the client may someday be in the awkward position of either having to repatriate assets or else be held in contempt of court. A well-drafted [asset protection trust] would, under such a circumstance, make it impossible for the client to repatriate assets held by the trust. Impossibility of performance is a complete defense to a civil contempt charge.

Barry S. Engel, Using Foreign Situs Trusts for Asset Protection Planning, 20 Est. Plan. 212, 218 (1993).

Given that these offshore trusts operate by means of frustrating domestic courts' jurisdiction, we are unsure that we would find that the Andersons' inability to comply with the district court's order is a defense to a civil contempt charge. We leave for another day the resolution of this more difficult question because we find that the Andersons have not satisfied their burden of proving that compliance with the district court's repatriation order was impossible. It is well established that a party petitioning for an adjudication that another party is in civil contempt does not have the burden of showing that the other party has the capacity to comply with the court's order. Instead, the party asserting the impossibility defense must show "categorically and in detail" why he is unable to comply.

In the asset protection trust context, moreover, the burden on the party asserting an impossibility defense will be particularly high because of the likelihood that any attempted compliance with the court's orders will be merely a charade rather than a good faith effort to comply. Foreign trusts are often designed to assist the settlor in avoiding being held in contempt of a domestic court while only feigning compliance with the court's orders. . . .

With foreign laws designed to frustrate the operation of domestic courts and foreign trustees acting in concert with domestic persons to thwart the United States courts, the domestic courts will have to be especially chary of accepting a defendant's assertions that repatriation or other compliance with a court's order concerning a foreign trust is impossible. Consequently, the burden on the defendant of proving impossibility as a defense to a contempt charge will be especially high. . . .

The Andersons claim that they have "demonstrated to the district court 'categorically and in detail' that they can not comply with the repatriation section of the preliminary injunction." The district court was not convinced and neither are we. While it is possible that a rational person would send millions of dollars overseas and retain absolutely no control over the assets, we share the district court's skepticism. The district court found, notwithstanding the Andersons' protestations, that

> As I look at the totality of the scheme of what I see before me at this time, I have no doubt that the Andersons can if they wish to correct this problem and provide the means of putting these funds in a position that they can be accountable if the final

determination of the Court is that the funds should be returned to those who made these payments.

We cannot say that this finding was clearly erroneous. The Andersons had previously been able to obtain in excess of $1 million from the trust in order to pay their taxes. Given their ability to obtain, with ease, such large sums from the trust, we share the district court's skepticism regarding the Andersons' claim that they cannot make the trust assets subject to the court's jurisdiction.

Moreover, beyond this general skepticism concerning the Andersons' lack of control over their trust, the specifics of the Andersons' trust indicate that they retained control over the trust assets. These offshore trusts allow settlors, such as the Andersons, significant control over the trust assets by allowing the settlor to act as a cotrustee or "protector" of the trust.[28] When the settlors retain this type of control, however, they can jeopardize the asset protection scheme because they will be subject to a U.S. court's personal jurisdiction and be forced to exercise their control to repatriate the assets.

The district court's finding that the Andersons were in control of their trust is well supported by the record given that the Andersons were the protectors of their trust. A protector has significant powers to control an offshore trust. A protector can be compelled to exercise control over a trust to repatriate assets if the protector's powers are not drafted solely as the negative powers to veto trustee decisions or if the protector's powers are not subject to the anti-duress provisions of the trust.[29] The Andersons' trust gives them affirmative powers to appoint new trustees and makes the anti-duress provisions subject to the protectors' powers, therefore, they can force the foreign trustee to repatriate the trust assets to the United States.

Perhaps the most telling evidence of the Andersons' control over the trust was their conduct after the district court issued its temporary restraining order ordering the repatriation of the trust funds.... After the Andersons claimed that compliance with the repatriation provisions of the temporary restraining order was impossible, the Commission revealed to the court that the Andersons were the protectors of the trust. The Andersons immediately attempted to resign as protectors of the trust. This attempted resignation indicates that the Andersons knew

---

28. The office of the trust protector is a creature of the trust instrument. Its purpose is to provide flexibility and a check on the trustee. Thus the protector is often vested with special powers such as removing and replacing the trustee or making modifications to the trust in light of changed circumstances. For more on trust protectors, see page 579. — Eds.

29. ... In provisions of the trust agreement that the Andersons conveniently fail to reference, the trust agreement makes clear that the Andersons, as protectors, have the power to determine whether or not an event of duress has occurred: "For the purpose of determining whether an Event of Duress has occurred pursuant to paragraph (c) and paragraph (d) of this clause (1)(a)(vi) of this Deed, *the written certificate of the Protector to that effect shall be conclusive.*" Trust Agreement (emphasis added). Moreover, the very definition of an event of duress that the Andersons assert has occurred makes clear that whether or not an event of duress has occurred depends upon the opinion of the protector: "The issuance of any order, decree or judgement of any court or tribunal in any part of the world *which in the opinion of the Protector* will or may directly or indirectly, expropriate." Trust Agreement (emphasis added). Therefore, notwithstanding the provisions of the trust agreement that the Andersons point to, it is clear that the Andersons could have ordered the trust assets repatriated simply by certifying to the foreign trustee that in their opinion, as protectors, no event of duress had occurred .... [Footnote relocated. — Eds.]

that, as the protectors of the trust, they remained in control of the trust and could force the foreign trustee to repatriate the assets.

Because we see no clear error in the district court's finding that the Andersons remain in control of their trust and could repatriate the trust assets, the district court did not abuse its discretion in holding them in contempt. We, therefore, affirm the district court's finding the Andersons in contempt. Given the nature of the Andersons' so-called "asset protection" trust, which was designed to frustrate the power of United States' courts to enforce judgments, there may be little else that a district court judge can do besides exercise its contempt powers to coerce people like the Andersons into removing the obstacles they placed in the way of a court. Given that the Andersons' trust is operating precisely as they intended, we are not overly sympathetic to their claims and would be hesitant to overly-restrict the district court's discretion, and thus legitimize what the Andersons have done.

Affirmed.

IN RE LAWRENCE, 279 F.3d 1294 (11th Cir. 2002): Two months after he created and funded an offshore asset protection trust in Mauritius with $7 million, Stephan Jay Lawrence lost a securities law arbitration proceeding, which resulted in a $20.4 million judgment against him. Lawrence then filed for bankruptcy. The bankruptcy court ordered Lawrence to turn over to the bankruptcy trustee the assets held in the offshore trust. Lawrence did not comply, and so on October 5, 1999, the court held Lawrence in contempt and jailed him pending compliance with the turnover order.

On appeal, Lawrence argued that, because he had no control over the offshore trust fund, compliance with the turnover order was impossible and hence he should be released. Lawrence stressed that he had been removed as a beneficiary under a duress provision in the trust that extinguished his interest in the event of bankruptcy. The court rejected this argument on the ground that, under the terms of the trust, Lawrence retained the authority to appoint trustees, and these trustees would have the discretion to reinstate Lawrence as a beneficiary. Once restored as a beneficiary, the new trustees could distribute the entire trust fund to Lawrence. The court was therefore unimpressed with the duress provision. "The sole purpose of this provision appears to be an aid to the settlor to evade contempt while merely feigning compliance with the court's order. . . . [W]here the person charged with contempt is responsible for the inability to comply, impossibility is not a defense to the contempt proceedings."

NOTES AND QUESTIONS

1. *Epilogue.* Over the Christmas holiday in 1998, less than a month before the Ninth Circuit heard oral argument in *Affordable Media*, the district court purged the Andersons of their contempt, freeing them after serving six months in jail. In September 1999, two months after the Ninth Circuit rendered its decision and almost a year after the Andersons were freed, the FTC brought suit in the Cook Islands against AsiaTrust Limited, the trustee of the Andersons' offshore trust. The parties settled the Cook Islands litigation in 2002 for $1.2 million, the equivalent of six cents on the dollar; the FTC had sought $20 million. The settlement proceeds went to a fund for defrauded customers.

As of this writing, Stephan Jay Lawrence, 59, a graduate of M.I.T., once a hot-shot options trader on Wall Street, remains incarcerated in the Miami Federal Detention Center, where he is known as inmate number 49061-004.

2.   Does the validation of the contempt power in FTC v. Affordable Media and In re Lawrence signal the end of the offshore asset protection trust?

> Civil contempt sanctions . . . do not appear to offer a stable long-term solution . . . . First, when the Andersons created their Cook Islands trust, they retained broad powers over the trust funds as trust protectors. . . . The Ninth Circuit seized upon these powers, which settlors typically do not include in offshore trusts, as evidence that the Andersons had power to arrange repatriation of trust assets. . . . [I]t remains to be seen how often, and in what circumstances courts will be willing to impose contempt sanctions on settlors who retain fewer powers.
>
> Second, *Affordable Media* fails to answer one critical question: For how long will a court be willing to incarcerate an offshore trust settlor for civil contempt? . . . Penalties for civil contempt are designed to coerce the contemnor into compliance with the court's order. If incarceration will not induce compliance, the foundation for imprisonment collapses. [Stewart E. Sterk, Asset Protection Trusts: Trust Law's Race to the Bottom?, 85 Cornell L. Rev. 1035, 1102-1104 (2000).]

Does the asset protection afforded by these trusts need to be complete for them to be worthwhile to the settlor? Perhaps not. To the extent that the existence of a self-settled asset protection trust gives the settlor additional negotiating leverage, it might be valuable even if its asset protection is imperfect. As Eric Henzy, who represented the plaintiff in In re Brooks, 217 B.R. 98 (Bankr. D. Conn. 1998), explained, "In *Brooks* we got a judgment essentially voiding this offshore trust. We then settled for approximately fifty cents on the dollar, because the enforcement problems were so significant." Roundtable Discussion, 32 Vand. J. Transnatl. L. 779, 786 (1999).

3.   Among lawyers who specialize in asset protection, *Affordable Media* and *Lawrence* are viewed as cautionary tales on how not to draft an offshore asset protection trust.

> One of the riskiest situations occurs when a [trust] protector is given broad powers and is a U.S. person or organization subject to jurisdiction of U.S. Courts. For asset protection purposes, this could be disastrous, because a U.S. Court could treat the protector as the debtor/settlor's agent and order the protector to act, subjecting the protector to contempt proceedings if he refuses to comply with the order. [Alexander A. Bove, Jr., Drafting Offshore Trusts, Tr. & Est., July 2004, at 45-46.]

See also Barry S. Engel, Eric D. Sanderson, & Edward D. Brown, Asset Protection Planning and Contempt of Court, *in* Asset Protection Strategies: Planning with Domestic and Offshore Entities 347 (Alexander A. Bove, Jr., ed., 2002).

One of the Andersons' blunders was naming themselves as trust protectors. Doubtless they did so because they were chary about turning over their fortune to an offshore trustee without assurance that the trustee would do as they wished. But giving authority over the trust fund to a domestic person gives domestic courts an opening to assert jurisdiction. There is, in other words, a tradeoff between control and the potency of the trust's asset protection shielding. In this light, consider Professor Danforth's review of the more common features of offshore asset protection trusts:

> First, if the APT is properly established in a foreign country, in most cases a court in the United States will lack personal jurisdiction over the trustee. . . . Second, many offshore jurisdictions recognize the role of a trust "protector," a person granted special non-fiduciary powers to control the administration of the trust, with respect to such matters as removal and replacement of trustees, control over discretionary actions of the trustees, etc. By use of the trust protector mechanism, a settlor is able to vest in some trusted person substantial control over trust administration, while at the same [time] being able to resist the claim that the settlor himself or herself (whose actions will be subject to the authority of a United States court) retains such control. . . . Third, many offshore APTs include a so-called duress clause, under which the trustee is directed to ignore any directions received from a settlor or trust protector who is under duress[, which is defined to include] . . . a United States court's order. Finally, most offshore APTs also include a "flight" clause, under which the trustee is authorized to change the situs of the trust, change the applicable law, and move the trust assets to a new jurisdiction, if a claim against the trust threatens to be successful. [Robert T. Danforth, Rethinking the Law of Creditors' Rights in Trusts, 53 Hastings L.J. 287, 309-310 (2002).]

4.   Should the law draw a distinction between self-settled asset protection trusts established before any claims against the settlor are pending, threatened, or expected and those that are established after that time? Under traditional *fraudulent conveyance* law, codified in the widely adopted Uniform Fraudulent Transfer Act (1984), a transfer made with the intent to hinder, delay, or defraud creditors is actual fraud. A creditor is defined to include persons holding a claim, and a claim is defined to include even contingent, disputed, and unmatured rights to payment. Is it ethical for an attorney to assist in the creation of such a trust once claims against the settlor are pending, threatened, or expected? See generally Henry J. Lischer, Jr., Professional Responsibility Issues Associated with Asset Protection Trusts, 39 Real Prop., Prob. & Tr. J. 561 (2004).

5.   Most states privilege claims by *spouses* and *children* against ordinary spendthrift trusts. Suppose there is a claim by a spouse or child against a self-settled asset protection trust. Not all of the domestic self-settled asset protection trust statutes explicitly carve out claims by spouses and children. What result under one of the statutes without such an exception? Speaking of a self-settled asset protection trust located in the Bahamas, the court in Breitenstine v. Breitenstine, 62 P.3d 587, 593 n.1 (Wyo. 2003), stated in dicta that "the use of such trusts to avoid alimony, child support, and a fair division of marital property upon divorce is reprehensible to us." The court did not reach the issue of whether to recognize an exception for claims by spouses and children, because it found that the underlying transfer to the trust was a fraudulent conveyance under Wyoming law.

6.   There is considerable awareness among sophisticated practitioners of the domestic asset protection alternative to offshore trusts. See, e.g., David G. Shaftel, Domestic Asset Protection Trusts: Key Issues and Answers, 30 ACTEC J. 10 (2004). Given that local lawyers and banks appear to be the principal interest groups that lobby in favor of domestic asset protection trusts, this is hardly surprising.

For a comparison of domestic and offshore asset protection trusts, see Barry S. Engel & David L. Lockwood, Domestic Asset Protection Trusts Contrasted with

Foreign Trusts, 29 Est. Plan. 288 (2002). See also Asset Protection Strategies: Planning with Domestic and Offshore Entities (Alexander A. Bove, Jr., ed., 2002) (published by the American Bar Association); Duncan E. Osborne & Elizabeth Morgan Schurig, Asset Protection: Domestic and International Law and Tactics (2004) (four volume loose-leaf published by Thomson West).

For an illuminating and entertaining roundtable discussion of leading practitioners on this and related issues, moderated by Professor Jeffrey Schoenblum, this country's leading choice-of-law scholar in estate planning matters, see Roundtable Discussion, 32 Vand. J. Transnatl. L. 779 (1999).

7. It remains to be seen how domestic courts will react to self-settled asset protection trusts from out of state. There is, however, a cautionary scholarly literature that explores bankruptcy law, fraudulent conveyance law, choice of law principles, federal constitutional principles (such as the Contract and the Full Faith and Credit Clauses), and other doctrinal bases for refusing enforcement. In addition to Sterk, supra, 85 Cornell L. Rev. 1035, see Karen E. Boxx, Gray's Ghost — A Conversation about the Onshore Trust, 85 Iowa L. Rev. 1195 (2000); John K. Eason, Developing the Asset Protection Dynamic: A Legacy of Federal Concern, 31 Hofstra L. Rev. 23 (2002); Henry J. Lischer, Jr., Domestic Asset Protection Trusts: Pallbearers to Liability, 35 Real Prop., Prob. & Tr. J. 479 (2000); Randall J. Gingiss, Putting a Stop to "Asset Protection" Trusts, 51 Baylor L. Rev. 987 (1999). See also Eric Henzy, Offshore and "Other" Shore Asset Protection Trusts, 32 Vand. J. Transnatl. L. 739 (1999); John E. Sullivan III, Gutting the Rule Against Self-Settled Trusts: How the New Delaware Trust Law Competes with Offshore Trusts, 23 Del. J. Corp. L. 423 (1998).

For a discussion of related tax considerations, see John K. Eason, Home from the Islands: Domestic Asset Protection Trust Alternatives Impact Traditional Estate and Gift Planning Considerations, 52 Fla. L. Rev. 41 (2000).

8. The crucial development that underpins the jurisdictional competition for self-settled asset protection trusts is that financial assets have eclipsed land as the primary mode of wealth accumulation. This simplifies the task of moving one's wealth to a more favorable jurisdiction. Professor LoPucki explains:

> The essence of the offshore asset-protection trust problem is that the world recognizes the right of an owner of liquid wealth to move it to any nation that offers a better deal. A significant number of nations now offer to protect that wealth against liability. Unless the world community overrules those nations by imposing some sort of sanctions, they will continue to provide strategists with the means to defeat liability in individual cases, demoralize nonstrategists, and thereby contribute to the ultimate demise of liability itself. [Lynn M. LoPucki, The Death of Liability, 106 Yale L.J. 1, 38 (1996).]

NOTE: TRUSTS FOR THE STATE-SUPPORTED

An individual qualifies for Medicaid and public support benefits only if the individual has financial resources less than a few thousand dollars. The question arises whether trusts benefiting the individual can be counted as resources available for the support of the individual. Federal law draws a distinction between *self-settled trusts* and *trusts created by third parties* for the benefit of the individual. The paradigmatic case of the former arises when an individual seeks to guard against the consumption of the individual's assets by health care and other related expenses that otherwise would be covered by a government benefit program. The paradigmatic case of the latter arises when an individual seeks to provide resources for the supplemental needs of a child or other loved one who is otherwise eligible for government benefits without undermining the beneficiary's eligibility for those benefits. For a sympathetic exposition of relevant considerations in establishing a *supplemental needs trust* for a disabled child penned by a law student whose son has autism, see Gail C. Eichstadt, Using Trusts to Provide for the Needs of an Adult Child with a Disability: An Introduction for Family Concerns for Lawyers and a Primer on Trusts for Parents, 45 S.D.L. Rev. 622 (2000).

Let us look first at *self-settled trusts*. For Medicaid purposes, a trust is created by the individual applicant "if assets of the individual were used to form all or part of the corpus of the trust" and the trust was established by the individual, by the individual's spouse, or by a person or court with legal authority to act on behalf of, or on request of, the individual or the individual's spouse. 42 U.S.C. §1396p(d) (2004). If the trust is revocable by the individual, the corpus and all income of the trust are considered resources available to the individual. If the trust is irrevocable, any income or corpus that *under any circumstances* could be paid to or applied for the benefit of the individual are considered resources of the individual. Hence, in the case of a discretionary trust, the Medicaid applicant will be deemed to have resources in the maximum amount that could be distributed to him, assuming full exercise of discretion by the trustee in his favor. See Masterson v. Department of Soc. Servs., 969 S.W.2d 746 (Mo. 1998). If the individual transfers assets into a self-settled trust, the period of ineligibility for Medicaid benefits may last up to 60 months. See Note, Long-Term Care Financing Crisis — Recent Federal and State Efforts to Deter Asset Transfers as a Means to Gain Medicaid Eligibility, 74 N.D.L. Rev. 383 (1998). Compare Canter v. Commissioner of Pub. Welfare, 668 N.E.2d 783 (Mass. 1996).

There are two important exceptions. First, a discretionary trust created by the *will* of one spouse for the benefit of the surviving spouse is not deemed a resource available to the surviving spouse. 42 U.S.C. §1396p(d)(2)(A) (2004). This makes it possible for one spouse to create a wholly discretionary trust for the benefit of the surviving spouse, who may qualify for Medicaid if the survivor's other resources are below the eligibility amount. Second, a trust will not be considered a resource available to the Medicaid recipient if it is established for a disabled individual from the individual's property, by a parent, grandparent, or guardian of the individual or by a court, and the trust provides that the state will receive upon the individual's death all amounts remaining in the trust up to the amount equal to the total medical assistance paid by the state, 42 U.S.C. §1396p(d)(4)(A) (2004). This makes it possible to settle the proceeds of a tort recovery, after an accident in which an individual is disabled, in a trust to provide supplemental care for the individual above what the state provides, if the trust reimburses the state out of the trust assets at the individual's death.

With respect to trusts *established by a third person* for the benefit of a Medicaid applicant, the rules are different. Medicaid regulations provide that trust income or principal is "considered available both when actually available and when the applicant or recipient has a legal interest in a liquidated sum and has the legal ability to make such sum available for support and maintenance." 45 C.F.R.

§233.20(a)(3)(ii)(D) (2004). Thus, if a mandatory or support trust is created, wherein the beneficiary has the legal right to income, such income is treated as a resource available to the beneficiary. But if a discretionary trust is created, giving the individual no legal right to trust income or principal, the trust is not considered a resource available to the individual in applying for Medicaid unless it was intended to be used for the applicant's support. See generally Medicare & Medicaid Guide (CCH, regularly updated loose-leaf).

Reimbursement for state-supported trust beneficiaries. In most states, persons institutionalized in state hospitals are responsible for the cost of their care. In seeking to reach self-settled trusts, courts have permitted states to recover the maximum amount that could be paid to the settlor (generally the same amount as is deemed an available resource under the Medicaid eligibility rules). The courts follow the common law rule applicable to creditors of settlors of self-settled trusts. See State v. Hawes, 564 N.Y.S.2d 637 (App. Div. 1991).

If a trust has been set up by a third party for the institutionalized beneficiary, the courts have generally followed the common law rules applicable to creditors of beneficiaries of mandatory, support, and discretionary trusts. If the beneficiary has a right to trust income or principal, the state can reach it. At common law, a spendthrift clause is unenforceable against the state because the state is furnishing necessaries to the institutionalized beneficiary. In a similar vein, although Uniform Trust Code §503 (2000) does not recognize an exception for those who provide the beneficiary with necessary support, its drafters contemplated that the exception under §503(c) for claims by the state would address cases in which the state provided necessary support. See David M. English, The Uniform Trust Code (2000): Significant Provisions and Policy Issues, 67 Mo. L. Rev. 143, 183-184 (2002). See also Alan Newman, The Rights of Creditors of Beneficiaries Under the Uniform Trust Code: An Examination of the Compromise, 69 Tenn. L. Rev. 771, 791-798 (2002).

Most of the litigation concerns discretionary trusts. Generally, the state cannot reach discretionary trusts. Many discretionary trusts are hybrids, however, combining the purpose of support with discretion in the trustee ("to provide for the comfort and support of my daughter in the trustee's sole and absolute discretion"). If a beneficiary of a discretionary trust can, under some conceivable circumstances, obtain a court order requiring payment to the beneficiary, because the trustee has an obligation to exercise discretion consistent with the purpose of the trust, it is possible that the trust assets may be reached by the state. See Estate of Rosenberg v. Department of Pub. Welfare, 679 A.2d 767 (Pa. 1996). On the other hand, if the settlor intended to provide only benefits that the state is unable or unwilling to provide, a so-called *supplemental needs trust*, the state cannot reach the trust assets. See Miller v. Department of Mental Health, 442 N.W.2d 617 (Mich. 1989); Minn. Stat. Ann. §501B.89 (2004); N.Y. Est. Powers & Trusts Law §7-1.12 (2004). For an examination of the history behind, and current regulation of, supplemental needs trusts, see Joseph A. Rosenberg, Supplemental Needs Trusts for People with Disabilities: The Development of a Private Trust in the Public Interest, 10 B.U. Pub. Int. L.J. 91 (2004). See also Scott Gardner, Comment, Supplemental Needs Trusts: A Means to Conserve Family Assets and Provide Increased Quality of Life for the Disabled Family Member, 32 Duq. L. Rev. 555 (1994).

Because this is an evolving area of the law involving unsettled questions of public policy at both state and federal levels, increasing pressures on the public purse, and not-very-predictable judicial interpretations of trust language, practitioners must use great caution in advising clients who want to create a trust for a disabled child that the state cannot reach. For further discussion, see Clifton B. Kruse, Jr., Third-Party and Self-Created Trusts: Planning for the Elderly and Disabled Client (3d ed. 2002).

PROBLEMS

1. Barbara is a developmentally disabled person. Her mother, Edith, neglected Barbara and failed to provide her with social security benefits that Edith had received on behalf of Barbara. Upon suit by Barbara's aunt, her guardian, a consent decree was entered ordering Edith to fund a trust for the benefit of Barbara with $150,000 Edith had inherited from her sisters. Edith complied by creating a discretionary trust for Barbara with a spendthrift provision. The trust agreement named Edith as settlor. It directed the trustee to terminate the trust immediately should any agency providing support for Barbara attempt to reach it. Can the trust assets be reached by the state to provide for Barbara's care? Hertsberg Trust v. Department of Mental Health, 578 N.W.2d 289 (Mich. 1998).

2. Wendy and Howard Brown's elder daughter, Sarah, has been injured in an automobile accident that left her unable to care for herself or manage her affairs. Sarah has been placed in a nursing home. The cost of the nursing home is $40,000 a year. Sarah received $200,000 in insurance proceeds. Howard, as Sarah's conservator, has applied for Medicaid. (For more on the Brown family, see pages 40-48.)

Howard and Wendy want your advice as to (1) what to do with the $200,000 and (2) what provisions they should make in their wills to provide more comfortable support for Sarah than the minimum provided by Medicaid. Advise them. See Stell v. Boulder County Dept. of Soc. Serv., 92 P.3d 910 (Colo. 2004); Gold v. United Health Serv. Hosp., Inc., 746 N.E.2d 172 (N.Y. 2001); Cricchio v. Pennisi, 683 N.E.2d 301 (N.Y. 1997).

SECTION E. MODIFICATION AND TERMINATION OF TRUSTS

1. Introduction

If the *settlor* and *all the beneficiaries* consent, an irrevocable trust may be modified or terminated. No one else has any beneficial interest in the trust. The trustee has no beneficial interest and cannot object. Such a right exists even if the trust contains a spendthrift clause.

If, however, the settlor is dead or does not consent to the modification or termination of the trust, the question arises whether the beneficiaries can modify or terminate the trust if they all agree. Let us look first at the law in England. In Saunders v. Vautier, 49 Eng. Rep. 282 (1841), the English court held that a trust can be terminated at any time if all the beneficiaries are adult and sui juris and all consent. In the 1950s, at the behest of trust beneficiaries who urgently sought to modify trusts to escape serious tax disadvantages, Parliament enacted the English Variation of Trusts Act of 1958, 6 & 7 Eliz. 2, ch. 53, §1, which greatly expanded the power of courts to modify or terminate trusts. The act provides that a court may consent to modification or termination of a trust on behalf of incompetent, minor, or unborn beneficiaries whenever the court finds it beneficial to these beneficiaries. See Graham Moffat, Trusts Law 248-273 (3d ed. 1999). Similar statutes have been enacted in Canada and Australia.

What has happened in England and some of the Commonwealth countries is that, after the settlor's death, the trust is regarded as the beneficiaries' property, not as the settlor's property—and the dead hand continues to rule only by the sufferance of the beneficiaries. As Mummery, L.J., explained, "The principle recognises the rights of beneficiaries . . . to overbear and defeat the intention of a testator or settlor." Goulding v. James, 2 All E.R. 239, 247 (C.A. 1997). Concurring in the same case, Sir Ralph Gibson added, "it is not clear to me why evidence of the intention of the testator can be of any relevance whatever. . . . The fact that a testator would not have approved or would have disapproved very strongly does not alter the fact that the beneficiaries are entitled in law to do it." Id. at 252.

Do you see a connection between the law of variation and termination and the law of spendthrift trusts? Both touch on the underlying tension of whose preferences should be paramount—those of the beneficiary or those of the settlor. In rejecting spendthrift trusts, the English courts made the beneficiary's interest alienable regardless of the settlor's intent (though the beneficiary's interest can still be shielded against creditors through a well-drafted discretionary or protective trust). The same hostility to the dead hand explains the English law of variation and termination. "The court [in Saunders v. Vautier] explicitly connected the question of a beneficiary's power to compel termination in anticipation of the time prescribed by the trustor with the question of the beneficiary's power to alienate his equitable interest. Since no valid restraint could be imposed upon an equitable fee, a provision postponing possession of the trust estate could not be given effect." Gregory Alexander, The Dead Hand and the Law of Trusts in the Nineteenth Century, 37 Stan. L. Rev. 1189, 1201 (1985).

Modification and termination of trusts in England is strikingly different from the practice in this country. In the United States, the great weight of authority holds that a trust cannot be terminated or modified prior to the time fixed for termination, even if all the beneficiaries consent, *if termination or modification would be contrary to a material purpose of the settlor*. The leading case establishing this rule is Claflin v. Claflin, 20 N.E. 454 (Mass. 1889), and the rule, which was preserved in Restatement (Second) of Trusts §337 (1959), is often referred to as the *Claflin doctrine*. In that case, a trust was established for testator's son, with principal to be paid to the son at age 30. After age 21 the son sued to terminate the trust, pointing out that he was the sole beneficiary. Echoing Justice Miller's elaborate dictum upholding spendthrift trusts in Nichols v. Eaton, discussed at page 548, the court refused to permit termination as this would violate the intent of the testator.

[A] testator has a right to dispose of his own property with such restrictions and limitations, not repugnant to law, as he sees fit, and . . . his intentions ought to be carried out, unless they contravene some positive rule of law, or are against public policy. . . . It cannot be said that these restrictions upon the plaintiff's possession and control of the property are altogether useless, for there is not the same danger that he will spend the property while it is in the hands of the trustees as there would be if it were in his own. [20 N.E. at 456.]

Accordingly, American irrevocable trusts have proved difficult to amend or terminate without the settlor's consent, something that is, of course, hard to obtain from the settlor of a testamentary trust.

2. Modification

In re Trust of Stuchell
Oregon Court of Appeals, 1990
104 Or. App. 332, 801 P.2d 852

BUTTLER, J.   Petitioner appeals from the trial court's dismissal of her petition for approval of an agreement to modify a trust. The stated purpose of the proposed modification is to protect a retarded remainder beneficiary. We affirm.

Petitioner is one of two surviving life-income beneficiaries of a testamentary trust established by her grandfather, J. W. Stuchell, in his 1947 will. The trust will terminate on the death of the last income beneficiary, at which time the remainder is to be distributed equally to petitioner's children or their lineal descendants, per stirpes. One of petitioner's four children, John Harrell (Harrell), is a mentally retarded 25 year old who is unable to live independently without assistance. His condition is not expected to improve, and he will probably require care and supervision for the rest of his life. No guardian or conservator has been appointed for him. The Oregon Mental Health Division currently provides his basic care in the Eastern Oregon Training Center, a residential facility for mentally and physically disabled persons. He receives Medicaid and Social Security benefits, both of which have income and resource limitations for participants.

In December, 1989, petitioner requested the court to approve, on behalf of Harrell, an agreement, which had been approved by the other income beneficiary and remaindermen, to modify the trust. If the trust is not modified, Harrell's remainder will be distributed directly to him if he survives the two life-income beneficiaries. If and when that happens, his ability to qualify for public assistance will be severely limited. The proposed modification provides for the continuation of the trust, if Harrell survives the two life-income beneficiaries, and contains elaborate provisions that are designed to avoid his becoming disqualified, in whole or in part, for any public assistance programs. The stated purpose is to ensure that the trust funds be used only as a secondary source of funds to supplement, rather than to replace, his current income and benefits from public assistance.

Petitioner relies on . . . the common law. She contends that Closset v. Burtchaell, 230 P. 554 (Or. 1924), is authority for allowing a court to approve her proposed modification. That case holds that a trust may be terminated, if (1) all of the beneficiaries agree, (2) none of the beneficiaries is under a legal disability and (3) the trust's purposes would not be frustrated by doing so. 230

P. 554. The court said: "It is a well-established rule that where the purposes for which a trust has been created have been accomplished and all of the beneficiaries are sui juris, a court will, on the application of all of the beneficiaries or of one possessing the entire beneficial interest declare a termination of the trust[.]" Restatement (Second) Trusts §337 (1959) follows that rule. By its terms, that rule applies only to the termination of a trust under very limited circumstances. Petitioner, relying on Restatement (Second) Trusts §167(1) (1959), urges us to extend the rule to permit modification. That section provides:

> The court will direct or permit the trustee to deviate from a term of the trust if owing to circumstances not known to the settlor and not anticipated by him compliance would defeat or substantially impair the accomplishment of the purposes of the trust; and in such case, if necessary to carry out the purposes of the trust, the court may direct or permit the trustee to do acts which are not authorized or are forbidden by the terms of the trust.

Comment b to that section states:

> The court will not permit or direct the trustee to deviate from the terms of the trust merely because such deviation would be more advantageous to the beneficiaries than a compliance with such direction.

See In re Traung's Estate, 24 Cal. Rptr. 872 (App. 1962), and Dyer v. Paddock, 70 N.E.2d 49 (Ill. 1946), which apply the rule as stated in that comment. Even assuming that the Restatement rule were to be adopted as the law in Oregon, it is clear that the limitation imposed by the comment would preclude permitting the proposed amendment, the only purpose of which is to make the trust more advantageous to the beneficiaries. The most obvious advantage would be to the three remaindermen who have consented to the amendment.

There being no statutory or common law authority for a court to approve the proposed agreement modifying the trust, the trial court did not err in dismissing the petition.[30]

Affirmed.

NOTES AND QUESTIONS

1.   Do you think that the testator, who did not anticipate Harrell's special needs, would have objected to the proposed modification once those needs became apparent? Why did the court not regard this as the relevant question?

2.   A recurring fact pattern in modification cases involves a widow who cannot live comfortably on the income from a trust created by her husband and asks a court to permit invasion of principal for support. Unless all the remainder beneficiaries consent (which usually is not possible because the remainder may ultimately vest in persons now unascertained or unborn), relief is often denied unless the trust is

---

30. We express no opinion as to whether the proposed modification would survive a challenge by state or federal agencies that are providing assistance to Harrell. [On trusts for the state-supported and so-called special needs trusts, see page 569. — Eds.]

construed to contain a power to invade, express or implied. See Estate of Van Deusen, 182 P.2d 565 (Cal. 1947); Staley v. Ligon, 210 A.2d 384 (Md. 1965).

Do you think it likely that, by denying the widow's petition in such cases, the court is giving effect to the settlor's probable intent? In other words, do you think that the settlor's failure to authorize the invasion of principal was considered, or was it more likely the result of a failure accurately to anticipate the widow's needs?

In some states, the problem of the impecunious widow has been ameliorated by statute. See N.Y. Est. Powers & Trusts Law §7-1.6(b) (2004) (giving court discretion to make allowance from principal to provide sufficient support for income beneficiary, if court is satisfied that such invasion effectuates the intention of the settlor). See also Wis. Stat. Ann. §701.13(2) (2004); 2A Austin W. Scott, Trusts §168, at 306-309 (William F. Fratcher 4th ed. 1987) (discussing other statutes).

3. *Drafting advice.* Many unforeseen problems may arise during long-term trusts: turnover in the named beneficiaries; changes in the named beneficiaries' needs and abilities; changes in the tax laws and in different types of investment opportunities; inflation and changes in the purchasing power of the dollar. When you are drafting a trust that is to last into the unforeseeable future, you should consider giving a beneficiary — either the life tenant or a remainderman — or an independent third party (sometimes called a *trust protector*, on which see page 579) the power to modify or terminate the trust. See Jeffrey N. Pennell, Wealth Transfer Planning and Drafting ch. 4, at 2-6 (2005).

If the petitioner in *Stuchell*, the life beneficiary, had been given a special power to amend the trust, she could have changed Harrell's interest to a discretionary trust to supplement his government support, saving the remainder for other family members. Ditto for a trust protector. The lawyer left the testator's family in a straitjacket.

4. *Administrative deviation and changed circumstances.* Courts have been much more liberal in permitting trustees to deviate from administrative directions in the trust, because of change of circumstances, than they have been in permitting modification of distributive provisions. For example, in 1911 Joseph Pulitzer's will created a trust for the benefit of his descendants. Pulitzer bequeathed to the trustees shares of stock in a corporation publishing the World newspapers (including one of the major papers of the day, the New York World), and his will provided that the sale of these shares was not authorized under any circumstances. After several years of large and increasing losses from the publication of the World, the trustees in 1931 petitioned the court to approve sale of the shares. The court held that, even though sale was prohibited by Pulitzer, it had power to authorize sale in circumstances where the trust estate was in jeopardy, and it approved the sale. In re Pulitzer, 249 N.Y.S. 87 (Sur. Ct. 1931), aff'd mem., 260 N.Y.S. 975 (App. Div. 1932). The court explained: "The dominant purpose of Mr. Pulitzer must have been the maintenance of a fair income for his children and the ultimate reception of an unimpaired corpus by the remaindermen." 249 N.Y.S. at 94.

Extending the facts in *Pulitzer*, Professor Langbein removes the unanticipated circumstances, positing the following hypothetical:

Suppose . . . that the settlor in *Pulitzer* had foreseen and recited in the trust instrument the danger that the newspaper might become unprofitable, and he directed the trustees to continue operating it anyhow. In the actual case, the court refused to consider the possibility that a settlor of such "sagacity and business ability" could have intended "from mere vanity" to keep the newspaper operating at the expense of the trust. But suppose he had. Suppose the settlor spelled out that he foresaw the possibility that the paper would cease to be economically viable, but he wanted it maintained regardless of the impairment of the interests of the beneficiaries. [John H. Langbein, Mandatory Rules in the Law of Trusts, 98 Nw. U.L. Rev. 1105, 1118-1119 (2004).]

In such a case, should the court nonetheless authorize the sale of the newspaper stock? For Langbein's views, see id. See also Uniform Trust Code §412(b) (2000), reproduced below. Should the trustee have an affirmative duty to petition the court for a modification when the trust's administrative terms are rendered unwise by changed circumstances? See Restatement (Third) of Trusts §66(2) (2003).

A broader question raised by Langbein's hypothetical is whether the settlor should be permitted to make the trust's terms immutable, that is, to opt out of the law of modification and termination. Under UTC §105(b)(4), the answer is No. What do you think? Consider Judge Posner's musings:

> [S]ince no one can foresee the future, a rational donor knows that his intentions might eventually be thwarted by unpredictable circumstances and may therefore be presumed to accept implicitly a rule permitting modification of the terms of the bequest in the event that an unforeseen change frustrates his original intention. The presumption is not absolute. Some rational donors, mistrustful of judicial capacity intelligently to alter the terms of the bequests in light of changed conditions, might prefer to assume the risks involved in rigid adherence to the original terms. Should their desire be honored? Notice that doing so would make wills more rigid than constitutions, which can be amended, though with difficulty. [Richard A. Posner, Economic Analysis of Law §18.3, at 520 (6th ed. 2003).]

5. *Equitable deviation of dispositive terms and changed circumstances.* Should changes in circumstances justify a modification to, or deviation from, a distributive provision? Cal. Prob. Code §15409 (2004), which was enacted in 1990, authorizes the court to "modify the administrative or dispositive provisions of the trust or terminate the trust if, owing to circumstances not known to the settlor and not anticipated by the settlor, the continuation of the trust under its terms would defeat or substantially impair the accomplishment of the purposes of the trust." See also Alaska Stat. §13.36.345 (2004) (similar); Fla. Stat. §737.4041(1) (2004) (similar). These statutes confirm the applicability of equitable deviation to administrative terms and extend it to the trust's dispositive terms. Would the result in *Stuchell* be different under these statutes?

The California statute has had a strong influence on the UTC and Restatement (Third) of Trusts.

Uniform Trust Code (2000)

§412.   Modification or Termination Because of Unanticipated Circumstances or Inability to Administer Trust Effectively

(a) The court may modify the administrative or dispositive terms of a trust or terminate the trust if, because of circumstances not anticipated by the settlor, modification or termination will further the purposes of the trust. To the extent practicable, the modification must be made in accordance with the settlor's probable intention.

(b) The court may modify the administrative terms of a trust if continuation of the trust on its existing terms would be impracticable or wasteful or impair the trust's administration.

(c) Upon termination of a trust under this section, the trustee shall distribute the trust property in a manner consistent with the purposes of the trust.

QUESTIONS AND NOTE

1.   By making modification easier for the beneficiary to obtain, will the extension of equitable deviation to distributive provisions dissuade potential settlors from establishing a trust in the first place? Does your analysis depend on whether the court's power to modify is limited to effecting the settlor's probable intent in view of changed circumstances? See Robert H. Sitkoff, An Agency Costs Theory of Trust Law, 89 Cornell L. Rev. 621, 661-662 (2004). Although modification of an administrative or dispositive term under UTC §412(a) must accord with the settlor's probable intent, administrative deviation under §412(b) is not so limited. On the other hand, is it not sensible to authorize administrative deviation when the settlor's instruction has become "wasteful"? Compare the statement of *cy pres* for charitable trusts in UTC §413, discussed at page 741, which allows distributive deviation in charitable trusts on the ground of wastefulness.

2.   For further examination of recent trends in trust law reform regarding modification and termination of private trusts, see Ronald Chester, Modification and Termination of Trusts in the 21st Century: The Uniform Trust Code Leads a Quiet Revolution, 35 Real Prop., Prob. & Tr. J. 697 (2001) (note that the relevant UTC sections have been renumbered plus one since Chester penned his article); David M. English, The Uniform Trust Code (2000): Significant Provisions and Policy Issues, 67 Mo. L. Rev. 143, 169-176 (2002); Edward C. Halbach, Jr., Uniform Acts, Restatements, and Trends in American Trust Law at Century's End, 88 Cal. L. Rev. 1877, 1901 (2000); Sitkoff, supra, 89 Cornell L. Rev. at 658-663.

NOTE: REFORMATION AND MODIFICATION FOR TAX ADVANTAGES

In recent years, courts in several states have reformed or modified a trust so as to obtain income or estate tax advantages. See Dassori v. Patterson, 802 N.E.2d 553 (Mass. 2004); Walker v. Walker, 744 N.E.2d 60 (Mass. 2001); In re Estate of Branigan, 609 A.2d 431 (N.J. 1992); 2A Austin W. Scott, Trusts §167, at 331-332 (William F. Fratcher 4th ed. 1987 & Supp. 2003 by Mark L. Ascher) (discussing numerous cases from New York Surrogate's Courts modifying trusts to minimize taxes). See also Pond v. Pond, 678 N.E.2d 1321 (Mass. 1997), excerpted at pages 912-914. But see Fifth Third Bank v. Simpson, 730 N.E.2d 406 (Ohio App. 1999) (2-1 opinion refusing modification).

Sometimes the courts have corrected a lawyer's error in drafting the instrument; in other cases the courts have modified the trust because of changed circumstances.

The former is an application of *reformation*, an equitable remedy that conforms the instrument to what the settlor actually intended at the time of its execution. The innovation here, as explored in Chapter 6, is the application of the reformation concept to testamentary trusts. See UTC §415 (2000); Restatement (Third) of Property: Wills and Other Donative Transfers §12.1 (2003).

In contrast, modification to achieve the settlor's probable intent in light of changed circumstances is an application of *equitable deviation*, which is extended in Restatement (Third) of Trusts §66 (2003) and UTC §412 to distributive provisions. The application of equitable deviation to achieve tax savings is also specifically endorsed by UTC §416: "To achieve the settlor's tax objectives, the court may modify the terms of a trust in a manner that is not contrary to the settlor's probably intention. The court may provide that the modification has retroactive effect." Accord, Restatement (Third) of Property: Wills and Other Donative Transfers §12.2: "A donative document may be modified, in a manner that does not violate the donor's probable intention, to achieve the donor's tax objectives."

The distinction between reformation and modification bears repeating. Reformation is an equitable remedy that conforms an instrument to what it was intended to say. Modification under equitable deviation principles changes the terms of the instrument to reflect not what the settlor meant to say, but what the court believes the settlor would have said had the settlor anticipated the changed circumstances.

NOTE: TRUST PROTECTORS

Having gained prominence as a check on local trustees in offshore trusts, the appointment of a trust protector is becoming more common in domestic trusts as a response to the reality that the donor of a gift cannot foresee all of the problems or opportunities that her family might face after the gift is made. Thus:

> *Case 23.* T devises property to X, a bank, in trust to pay the income to A for life and upon A's death to distribute the property to A's children. T also names her trusted friend P, who lacks the skills to serve as the trustee herself, as the trust protector. T authorizes P, as trust protector, (1) to replace X with another corporate fiduciary, (2) to approve modifications to the trust's administrative and dispositive provisions (including increases to A's lifetime share), (3) to terminate the trust, and (4) to select a successor trust protector.

Like powers of appointment, which are the subject of Chapter 9, naming a trust protector and arming that person with broad powers builds flexibility into what might otherwise be a rigid trust. In Case 23, if A's needs change or a different arrangement becomes more tax efficient, P can modify the trust accordingly. Likewise, if X proves to be lackadaisical in responding to A's needs or if X poorly manages the trust portfolio, P can fire X and replace it with another bank or trust company that promises to be more responsive.

The office of the trust protector, which is created by the underlying trust instrument, has been codified in a handful of states. See Alaska Stat. §13.36.370 (2004); S.D. Codified Laws §55-1B-6 (2004). See also Del. Code Ann. tit. 20, §3313 (2004) (trust advisors). The use of trust protectors is ratified by UTC §808(b)-(d) (2000).

NOTES

1. Alaska Stat. §13.36.370(d) (2004) establishes as a default rule that the protector is not subject to a fiduciary obligation. In states without such a statutory provision, there is uncertainty on this question. See Alexander A. Bove, Jr., The Trust Protector: Trust(y) Watchdog or Expensive Exotic Pet?, 30 Est. Plan. 390 (2003); Restatement (Third) of Trusts §64, reporter's notes to cmts. b-d (2003).

2. For more on trust protectors, see David Hayton, English Fiduciary Standards and Trust Law, 32 Vand. J. Transnatl. L. 555, 579-590 (1999); James L. Dam, More Estate Planners Are Using "Trust Protectors," Law. Wkly. U.S.A., Oct. 29, 2001, at 14. See also Robert H. Sitkoff, An Agency Costs Theory of Trust Law, 89 Cornell L. Rev. 621, 670-671 (2004).

3. Termination

Although the Claflin doctrine is easy to state, there is considerable disagreement as to the circumstances under which *termination* would be contrary to the purpose of the settlor. Generally, a trust cannot be terminated if it is a spendthrift trust, if the beneficiary is not to receive the principal until attaining a specified age (that is, enjoyment is postponed), if it is a discretionary trust, or if it is a trust for support of the beneficiary. Such provisions are usually deemed to state a material purpose of the settlor. The cases are collected in George G. Bogert & George T. Bogert, Trusts and Trustees §§1007-1008 (rev. 2d ed. 1983); 4 Austin W. Scott, Trusts §§337-337.8 (William F. Fratcher 4th ed. 1989).

In re Estate of Brown
Supreme Court of Vermont, 1987
148 Vt. 94, 528 A.2d 752

GIBSON, J. The trustee of a testamentary trust appeals an order of the Washington Superior Court granting the petition of the lifetime and residual beneficiaries of the trust to terminate it and to distribute the proceeds to the life tenants. We reverse.

The primary issue raised on appeal is whether any material purpose of the trust remains to be accomplished, thus barring its termination. The appellant/trustee also raises the closely related issue of whether all beneficiaries are before the court, i.e., whether the class of beneficiaries has closed.

Andrew J. Brown died in 1977, settling his entire estate in a trust, all of which is held by the trustee under terms and conditions that are the subject of this appeal. The relevant portion of the trust instrument provides:

> (3) The . . . trust . . . shall be used to provide an education, particularly a college education, for the children of my nephew, Woolson S. Brown. My Trustee is hereby directed to use the income from said trust and such part of the principal as may be necessary to accomplish this purpose. Said trust to continue for said purpose until the last child has received his or her education and the Trustee, in its discretion, has determined that the purpose hereof has been accomplished.

At such time as this purpose has been accomplished and the Trustee has so determined, *the income from said trust and such part of the principal as may be necessary shall be
used by said Trustee for the care, maintenance and welfare of my nephew, Woolson S. Brown
and his wife, Rosemary Brown, so that they may live in the style and manner to which they are
accustomed, for and during the remainder of their natural lives.* Upon their demise, any
remainder of said trust, together with any accumulation thereon, shall be paid to their
then living children in equal shares, share and share alike. (Emphasis added.)

The trustee complied with the terms of the trust by using the proceeds to pay for
the education of the children of Woolson and Rosemary Brown. After he determined that the education of these children was completed, the trustee began
distribution of trust income to the lifetime beneficiaries, Woolson and Rosemary.

On June 17, 1983, the lifetime beneficiaries petitioned the probate court
for termination of the trust, arguing that the sole remaining purpose of the
trust was to maintain their lifestyle and that distribution of the remaining assets
was necessary to accomplish this purpose. The remaindermen, the children of
the lifetime beneficiaries, filed consents to the proposed termination. The probate
court denied the petition to terminate, and the petitioners appealed to the
Washington Superior Court. The superior court reversed, concluding that continuation of the trust was no longer necessary because the only material purpose, the
education of the children, had been accomplished. This appeal by the trustee
followed.

Ordinarily, a trial court's conclusions will be upheld where they are supported
by its findings. Dartmouth Savings Bank v. F.O.S. Associates, 486 A.2d 623, 625
(Vt. 1984). Here, the superior court's conclusion that the trust could be terminated
because the material purpose of the trust had been accomplished has an insufficient basis in its findings, and this conclusion cannot stand.

An active trust may not be terminated, even with the consent of all the beneficiaries, if a material purpose of the settlor remains to be accomplished. Restatement (Second) of Trusts §337 (1959). This Court has invoked a corollary of this
rule in a case where partial termination of a trust was at issue. In re Bayley Trust,
250 A.2d 516, 519 (Vt. 1969).

As a threshold matter, we reject the trustee's argument that the trust cannot be
terminated because it is both a support trust and a spendthrift trust. It is true that,
were either of these forms of trust involved, termination could not be compelled by
the beneficiaries because a material purpose of the settlor would remain unsatis-
fied. See Restatement (Second) of Trusts §337.

The trust at issue does not qualify as a support trust. A support trust is created
where the trustee is directed to use trust income or principal for the benefit of an
individual, but only to the extent necessary to support the individual. 2 A. Scott,
Scott on Trusts §154, at 1176; G. Bogert, Trusts and Trustees §229, at 519 (2d ed.
rev. 1979). Here, the terms of the trust provide that, when the educational purpose
of the trust has been accomplished and the trustee, in his discretion, has so determined, "the income . . . and such part of the principal as may be necessary shall
be used by said Trustee for the care, maintenance and welfare of . . . [Rosemary
and Woolson Brown] so that they may live in the style and manner to which they
are accustomed. . . ." The trustee has, in fact, made the determination that the
educational purpose has been accomplished and has begun to transfer the income
of the trust to the lifetime beneficiaries. Because the trustee must, at the very least,

pay all of the trust income to beneficiaries Rosemary and Woolson Brown, the trust cannot be characterized as a support trust.

Nor is this a spendthrift trust. "A trust in which by the terms of the trust or by statute a *valid restraint on the voluntary and involuntary transfer of the interest* of the beneficiary is imposed is a spendthrift trust." Restatement (Second) of Trusts §152(2). (Emphasis added.) While no specific language is needed to create a spendthrift trust, id. at Comment c, here the terms of the trust instrument do not manifest Andrew J. Brown's intention to create such a trust. . . .

Although the issue as to whether a material purpose of the trust remains cannot be answered through resort to the foregoing formal categories traditionally imposed upon trust instruments, we hold that termination cannot be compelled here because a material purpose of the settlor remains unaccomplished. In the interpretation of trusts, the intent of the settlor, as revealed by the language of the instrument, is determinative. In re Jones, 415 A.2d 202, 205 (Vt. 1980).

We find that the trust instrument at hand has two purposes. First, the trust provides for the education of the children of Woolson and Rosemary Brown. The Washington Superior Court found that Rosemary Brown was incapable of having more children and that the chance of Woolson Brown fathering more children was remote; on this basis, the court concluded that the educational purpose of the trust had been achieved.

The settlor also intended a second purpose, however: the assurance of a lifelong income for the beneficiaries through the management and discretion of the trustee. We recognize that, had the trust merely provided for successive beneficiaries, no inference could be drawn that the settlor intended to deprive the beneficiaries of the right to manage the trust property during the period of the trust. Estate of Weeks, 402 A.2d 657, 658 (Pa. 1979) (quoting Restatement (Second) of Trusts §337 Comment f). Here, however, the language of the instrument does more than create successive gifts. The settlor provided that the trustee must provide for the "care, maintenance and welfare" of the lifetime beneficiaries "so that they may live in the style and manner to which they are accustomed, *for and during the remainder of their natural lives*." (Emphasis added.) The trustee must use all of the income and such part of the principal as is necessary for this purpose. We believe that the settlor's intention to assure a life-long income to Woolson and Rosemary Brown would be defeated if termination of the trust were allowed. See 4 Scott, Scott on Trusts §337.1, at 2261-64; see also Will of Hamburger, 201 N.W. 267, 271 (Wis. 1924) (court refused to terminate trust since testator desired it to continue during life of his wife).

Because of our holding regarding the second and continuing material purpose of the trust, we do not reach the question of whether the trial court erred in holding that the educational purpose of the trust has been accomplished.

Reversed; judgment for petitioners vacated and judgment for appellant entered.

NOTES AND QUESTIONS

1. To the extent that all trusts interpose a trustee between the beneficiary and the trust fund, would not the early termination of any trust offend the settlor's material purpose under the reasoning in *Brown*? If not, what precisely is the

material purpose that would have been offended by early termination in *Brown*? Observe that, because the trust did not contain a spendthrift limitation, Woolson and Rosemary could have sold their interests in the trust to another in return for a lump-sum payment. Likewise, Woolson and Rosemary could have assigned their interests to their children. If they had done so, could the children have terminated the trust? See generally Gail B. Bird, Trust Termination: Unborn, Living, and Dead Hands—Too Many Fingers in the Trust Pie, 36 Hastings L.J. 563 (1985).

2.   The application of the material purpose standard to a proposed modification is not necessarily identical to its application to a proposed termination. See Restatement (Third) of Trusts §65, cmt. f (2003). Modification cases commonly pit the beneficiary's desires against those of the settlor. Termination cases typically raise not only this tension, but also pit the current against the remainder beneficiaries. *Brown* is an interesting counterexample because the living remainder beneficiaries consented to the early termination. Given the court's assumption that neither Woolson nor Rosemary were likely to have more children, the class of remainder beneficiaries was not likely to increase.

3.   It may be possible to terminate a testamentary trust by a compromise agreement ending a will contest. In most states, courts will approve compromise agreements that deliberately eliminate trusts, even spendthrift trusts. In Budin v. Levy, 180 N.E.2d 74 (Mass. 1962), the court decided that a compromise agreement was effective without regard to whether a material purpose of the testator was defeated thereby. This approach is approved by Restatement (Third) of Trusts §65, cmt. h (2003), provided that there is a bona fide underlying dispute. See also Uniform Probate Code §3-1101 (1990).

Some courts, however, refuse to approve a will compromise where the compromise destroys a trust that is essential to a material purpose of the settlor. See Adams v. Link, 145 A.2d 753 (Conn. 1958). See also Annot., 29 A.L.R.3d 8 (1970, rev. 2003).

4.   As in the case of trust modification, the UTC and Restatement (Third) of Trusts advance several liberalizations in the law of trust termination. Among the more important are the following:

(a) *Spendthrift trusts and material purpose*. Contrary to existing case law, as originally drafted UTC §411(c) provided that the existence of a spendthrift clause "is not presumed to constitute a material purpose of the trust." Accord, Restatement, supra, §65, cmt. e. On this approach, the existence of a spendthrift clause is merely a relevant consideration in assessing whether an early termination would offend a material purpose of the settlor. The drafters of the UTC and Restatement justified this reform on the ground that spendthrift clauses often reflect rote duplication of formbook language, not a considered judgment by the settlor. In 2004, however, the Uniform Law Commissioners deleted §411(c) on the ground that several enacting jurisdictions had done so and at least one had reversed the provision so that a spendthrift clause was presumed to be a material purpose.

(b) *Change in circumstances*. As detailed in the notes that follow In re Trust of Stuchell, supra, UTC §412(a) allows for termination in light of "circumstances not anticipated by the settlor" if "termination will further the purposes of the trust." In addition to those states that have adopted the UTC, several others have statutes to similar effect. See, e.g., Cal. Prob. Code §15409 (2004); 20 Pa. Consol. Stat. Ann. §6102 (2004). Accord, Restatement, supra, §66.

(c) *Uneconomic trusts; combination and division*. UTC §414 provides a mechanism for modifying or terminating small trusts in which the "value of the trust property is insufficient to justify the cost of administration." UTC §417 authorizes the combination or division of trusts if doing so does not adversely affect any beneficiary or the purposes of the trust. Accord, Restatement, supra, §68.

(d) *Unanimity of the beneficiaries.* UTC §411(e) provides a mechanism for obtaining a modification or termination even without the consent of all the beneficiaries, provided that "the interests of a beneficiary who does not consent will be adequately protected." See also Restatement, supra, §65, cmt. b (discussing the issue).

(e) *Continuing viability of the material purpose standard.* Restatement, supra, §65 authorizes modification without a showing of unanticipated circumstances and without the settlor's consent if all the beneficiaries consent and the beneficiaries can show that the rationale for the modification outweighs the settlor's material purpose. In contrast, UTC §411(b) hews closer to the traditional Claflin doctrine, allowing such a modification only if it is not inconsistent with a material purpose of the trust.

In the introduction to this section, we suggested that the English law of modification and termination of trusts is very different from the law in this country. If the foregoing liberalizations take hold—in particular, the balancing test of Restatement, supra, §65 and the availability of relief without unanimous consent by the beneficiaries under UTC §411(e)—will this remain true? See generally Ronald Chester, Modification and Termination of Trusts in the 21st Century: The Uniform Trust Code Leads a Quiet Revolution, 35 Real Prop., Prob. & Tr. J. 697 (2001); Robert H. Sitkoff, An Agency Costs Theory of Trust Law, 89 Cornell L. Rev. 621, 660-663 (2004).

5.   In states that have not abolished it, the Rule against Perpetuities indirectly limits the duration of trusts because at the end of the perpetuities period the beneficiaries can terminate the trust. The settlor cannot prevent this. See Restatement (Second) of Property: Donative Transfers §2.1 (1981). Inasmuch as forever is a long time, making unforeseen contingencies likely to arise, will the fall of the Rule against Perpetuities boomerang into a liberalization of the rules of trust termination and modification? See Jesse Dukeminier & James E. Krier, The Rise of the Perpetual Trust, 50 UCLA L. Rev. 1303, 1327-1335 (2003). See also David M. English, The Uniform Trust Code (2000): Significant Provisions and Policy Issues, 67 Mo. L. Rev. 143, 169 (2002) (defending liberalization of modification and termination in light of the "increasing use in recent years of long-term trusts").

NOTE: REVOCABLE VERSUS IRREVOCABLE TRUSTS

In most states a trust created by a written instrument is irrevocable unless there is an express or implied provision that the settlor reserves the power to revoke.[31] In a handful of states, however, including California, Iowa, Montana, Oklahoma, and Texas, the opposite presumption holds. A trust is revocable unless declared to be irrevocable. UTC §602(a) (2000) adopts the minority rule: "Unless the terms of a trust expressly provide that the trust is irrevocable, the settlor may revoke or

---

31. For bank account (Totten) trusts, the presumption is reversed: Revocability is presumed. See page 343.

amend the trust." According to Professor Langbein, the Code's approach will better satisfy expectations:

> This change will be of no practical importance in the world of professionally drafted trust instruments, because no competent drafter ever leaves that question to default law. Rather, a well-drafted trust spells out that the trust is revocable or irrevocable. Accordingly, the change made by the Code will be of importance primarily for "kitchen table trusts," that is, for instruments drafted by non-lawyers (or dreadful lawyers). In such cases, the Code's intuition is that the settlor's intention is mostly to use the trust as a will substitute, and that, accordingly, the trust was meant to be revocable. [John H. Langbein, The Uniform Trust Code: Codification of the Law of Trusts in the United States, 15 Tr. L. Intl. 66, 70 (2001).]

See also David M. English, The Uniform Trust Code (2000): Significant Provisions and Policy Issues, 67 Mo. L. Rev. 143, 186-193 (2002); Restatement (Third) of Trusts §63, cmt. c (2003).

A related question is whether a revocable trust, particularly when used as a will substitute, can be revoked by will. Unless the terms of the trust so provide, the traditional answer is No. The UTC reverses this rule on that ground that doing so better comports with expectations. In cases where "the terms of the trust do not provide a method or the method provided in the terms is not expressly made exclusive," UTC §602(c)(2)(A) allows for revocation by "a later will or codicil that expressly refers to the trust or specifically devises property that would otherwise have passed according to the terms of the trust." Accord, Restatement (Third) of Property: Wills and Other Donative Transfers §7.2, cmt. e (2003).

4. *Trustee Removal*

As a doctrinal matter, removal of the trustee is a remedy for breach of trust, not a modification of the trust terms. See, e.g., Dennis v. Rhode Island Hosp. Tr. Co., 744 F.2d 893 (1st Cir. 1984), excerpted at pages 821-826. We nonetheless take up the issue here rather than with our examination of the fiduciary obligation in Chapter 13 because trustee removal involves a similar tension between the interests of the settlor and the interests of the beneficiary to that of trust termination and modification. The task is to set the threshold for trustee removal high enough so that the trustee can carry out the settlor's wishes (including the protection of future beneficiaries) in the teeth of a contrary preference of the current beneficiary without setting it so high as in effect to sanction shirking or mismanagement by the trustee. See Robert H. Sitkoff, An Agency Costs Theory of Trust Law, 89 Cornell L. Rev. 621, 663-664 (2004).

The traditional balance struck by the law is this: Courts are authorized to remove a trustee who is dishonest or who has engaged in a serious breach of trust, but may not remove a trustee for a breach that is not serious or for a simple disagreement with the beneficiary. Trustees who were chosen by the settlor, as compared to those named by a court, are even less readily removed — there is something of a thumb on the scale for them. Moreover, if the settlor was aware of an asserted ground for removal at the time of naming the trustee, that ground will not serve as a basis for the later removal of the trustee unless the trustee is entirely unfit to serve.

See id.; 2 Austin W. Scott, Trusts §§107-107.3 (William F. Fratcher 4th ed. 1987); Restatement (Second) of Trusts §107 (1959).

Accordingly, even if the beneficiary is dissatisfied with the performance of the trustee or is dissatisfied with the fees charged, the court will not remove the trustee and appoint a new one unless the trustee has been guilty of breach of trust or has shown unfitness. Some have argued that the inability of beneficiaries to change trustees lessens competition among trust companies and contributes to higher trustees' fees. Should this rule be changed?

In answering this question, consider the erosion of personal traditional fiduciary relationships in recent years. Bank trust accounts experience turnover in their management, particularly after a bank merger or acquisition, which suggests a weakened personal link between settlor and trustee. See In re Fleet Natl. Bank's Appeal from Prob., 837 A.2d 785 (Conn. 2004) (noting that Connecticut's statutory liberalization of trustee removal was prompted in part by mergers and acquisitions in the banking industry). Should the beneficiaries now be offered the opportunity to change trustees if they are disadvantaged by these transactions? There is an old saw in the banking industry: "How do you get a small fortune? Give a bank trust department a large one." Dissatisfaction with institutional trustees has led to the creation of a beneficiaries' interest group, Heirs, Inc., which claims to be "the first group of 'unhappy' beneficiaries in the country dedicated to reforming the administration of trusts/estates." http://www.heirs.net. See also Kathy Kristof, An Heir of Confidence, Chi. Trib., May 21, 1996, at C7.

Consider also that modern prudent investor standards grant the trustee greater discretion in portfolio management. Hence fiduciary law has replaced limited trustees' powers as the primary means of safeguarding the beneficiary from mismanagement and misappropriation by the trustee. Do these changes argue for a liberalization of removal standards? Perhaps another relevant consideration is that well-drafted trusts typically allow for the removal of the named trustee provided that the replacement is independent. The power to remove and replace the trustee can be given to the settlor (subject to tax considerations), to the beneficiary, or to a third party (sometimes called a trust protector, on which see page 579). Should the default law of trustee removal, which applies to trusts drafted by the unsophisticated, be reformed to match the terms that are regularly included in professionally drafted trusts? Consider UTC §706.

Uniform Trust Code (2000)

§706. REMOVAL OF TRUSTEE

(a) The settlor, a cotrustee, or a beneficiary may request the court to remove a trustee, or a trustee may be removed by the court on its own initiative.

(b) The court may remove a trustee if:

(1) the trustee has committed a serious breach of trust;

(2) lack of cooperation among cotrustees substantially impairs the administration of the trust;

(3) because of unfitness, unwillingness, or persistent failure of the trustee to administer the trust effectively, the court determines that removal of the trustee best serves the interests of the beneficiaries; or

(4) there has been a substantial change of circumstances or removal is requested by all of the qualified beneficiaries, the court finds that removal of the trustee best serves the interests of all of the beneficiaries and is not inconsistent with a material purpose of the trust, and a suitable cotrustee or successor trustee is available.

(c) Pending a final decision on a request to remove a trustee, or in lieu of or in addition to removing a trustee, the court may order such appropriate relief under Section 1001(b) as may be necessary to protect the trust property or the interests of the beneficiaries.

NOTES AND QUESTIONS

1.   In granting the settlor standing to seek the trustee's removal and expanding the grounds for removal, UTC §706 relaxes the traditional law. The official comment states that "a long-term pattern of mediocre performance, such as consistently poor investment results when compared to comparable trusts," might qualify as a "persistent failure to administer the trust effectively" warranting removal under §706(b)(3). Professor Langbein defends this reform on the ground that it responds "to the concern that under traditional law beneficiaries have had little recourse when trustee performance has been indifferent, but not so egregious as to be in breach of trust." John H. Langbein, The Uniform Trust Code: Codification of the Law of Trusts in the United States, 15 Tr. L. Int. 66, 76 (2001). Are you persuaded? If not, does this reform tip the balance too far away from the settlor and to the beneficiary? What about §706(b)(4), which allows removal on the basis of changed circumstances? See David M. English, The Uniform Trust Code (2000): Significant Provisions and Policy Issues, 67 Mo. L. Rev. 143, 199 (2002).

2.   For a thoughtful examination of contemporary issues in trustee removal, see Ronald Chester & Sarah Reid Ziomek, Removal of Corporate Trustees Under the Uniform Trust Code and Other Current Law: Does a Contractual Lense Help Clarify the Rights of Beneficiaries?, 67 Mo. L. Rev. 241 (2002). See also Restatement (Third) of Trusts §37, cmt. e (2003); Sitkoff, supra, 89 Cornell L. Rev. at 663-666.

9

BUILDING FLEXIBILITY INTO TRUSTS: POWERS OF APPOINTMENT

SECTION A.   INTRODUCTION

1. Types of Powers

The settlor of a trust cannot foresee all of the problems or opportunities that her family might face after the trust is created. Accordingly, trusts often contain *powers of appointment* in trust beneficiaries, powers that give the beneficiaries the ability to choose who next will take the beneficial interest in the property subject to the power. Tax considerations aside (we will turn to tax considerations in just a few pages), powers of appointment are routinely found in well-drafted trusts because through them the settlor is able to *postpone* and *delegate* decisions about who should receive a future interest in the trust. Powers of appointment thus allow the settlor to leave it to the beneficiaries to deal flexibly with changing circumstances in the future—with births, deaths, and marriages in the family; with the ability of children to manage property; with changes in the economy and investment returns; and with changes in the law.

In studying the law of powers, you must first get the terminology and relationships straight. The person who creates the power of appointment is the *donor* of the power; the person who holds the power is the *donee*. The persons in whose favor the power may be exercised are the *objects* of the power. When a power is exercised in favor of a person, such person becomes an *appointee*. The instrument creating the power may provide for *takers in default of appointment* if the donee fails to exercise the power.

All powers can be divided into general powers and special powers. A *general power* is, in the language of the Internal Revenue Code, "a power which is exercisable in favor of the decedent [donee], his estate, his creditors, or the creditors of his estate."[1] Under the federal estate and gift tax laws, any power that is

---

1. Int. Rev. Code of 1986, §2041(b) (estate tax). The comparable definition under the federal gift tax is in §2514(c). The Code goes on to exclude from the definition of a general power a power to

not a general power is classified as a special power. Thus, a *special power* is a power not exercisable in favor of the donee, his estate, his creditors, or the creditors of his estate. Prevailing professional usage of these terms is in accord with their meanings under the tax code.[2]

A general power of appointment may permit the donee to do most of the things that an owner of the fee simple could do. This is true of a general power presently exercisable. Thus:

> *Case 1.* T devises property to X in trust to pay the income to A for life, or until such time as A appoints, and to distribute the principal to such person or persons as A shall appoint either by deed during A's lifetime or by will; if A does not exercise the power of appointment, at A's death X is to distribute the principal to B. T is the donor. A is the donee of a general power of appointment exercisable by deed or will. B is the taker in default of appointment.

In Case 1, A is very close to being absolute owner of the property: the only thing that stands between A and absolute ownership is a piece of paper A can sign at any time. To acquire title, A has merely to write, "I hereby appoint to myself." Even though A can acquire absolute ownership at any time, however, A does not have ownership until the power is exercised in A's favor. If A does not exercise the power, the property will pass to the taker in default, B, and not to A's heirs. If the creating instrument does not name a taker in default, the property passes back to the donor or the donor's estate if the power is not exercised.

The most common kind of special power is the power to appoint among the issue of the donee. Thus:

> *Case 2.* T devises property to X in trust to pay the income to A for life, and on A's death to distribute the principal to such one or more of A's issue as A shall appoint by will; if A does not exercise the power of appointment, at A's death X is to distribute the principal to A's then living issue, such issue to take per stirpes.

There is a profound difference between the general power presently exercisable in Case 1 and the special power in Case 2. In Case 2, A occupies a position similar to that of T's agent. A can exercise the power to benefit A's issue, but A cannot appoint the property in such a way as to benefit A or A's estate.[3]

---

consume principal "limited by an ascertainable standard relating to the health, education, support, or maintenance" of the donee, a power held with an adverse party, and certain powers created prior to 1942. §§2041(b)(1)(A)-(C) and 2514(c)(1)-(3). See pages 891-893.

2. Restatement (Second) of Property: Donative Transfers §11.4 (1984) prefers the term *non-general* to *special*. The special power is sometimes also called a *limited* power.

3. The existence of the power can, of course, benefit A by assuring filial devotion.

> It doubtless occurred to the testator that by restraining a disposition of his property except by will, which is in its nature revocable, [his widow] would, to the end of her life, retain the influence over, and secure the respect of, the several objects of his bounty, which he intended her to have — a result less likely to be accomplished if power were given her to dispose of the property by deed or other irrevocable act to take effect in her lifetime. [Hood v. Haden, 82 Va. 588, 591 (1886).]

As someone once said, a special power to appoint $100,000 never hurt an old lady — or an old man.

Although it is sometimes said that the objects of a general power of appointment are necessarily broader than the objects of a special power, this is not always true. Thus:

> *Case 3.* T devises property to X in trust to distribute the income and principal to such of the creditors of A's estate as A shall appoint by will. Because A can appoint to the creditors of her estate, this is a general power of appointment.
>
> *Case 4.* T devises property to X in trust to pay the income and principal to any person whom A appoints by deed or by will except that A may not appoint to herself, her estate, her creditors, or the creditors of her estate. Because A cannot appoint to herself, her creditors, her estate, or the creditors of her estate, this is a special power of appointment.

Case 3 involves a general power even though there are usually only a few creditors of an estate. And even though the objects of the power in Case 4 number in the billions, it is a special power.

Powers of appointment may be created so as to be exercisable either by deed or by will as in Case 1, by deed alone, or by will alone as in Case 2. When exercisable only by will, the power is called a *testamentary* power; when exercisable during life, the power is called a *lifetime* power.

To be absolutely accurate, we should point out that a power of appointment may be created in a trustee, a beneficiary of a trust, a person with a legal interest not held in trust, or in a person who has no other interest in the property. In other words, a power may be created in anyone. Almost all powers of appointment are created in trustees or in beneficiaries of trusts, however. A trustee who has discretion to pay income or principal to a named beneficiary, or discretion to spray income among a group of beneficiaries, has a special power of appointment. Special powers in trustees were treated in the section on discretionary trusts in Chapter 8. In this chapter, we are primarily concerned with powers of appointment given to beneficiaries of trusts.

2. Does the Appointive Property Belong to the Donor or the Donee?

At common law, property subject to a power of appointment was viewed as belonging to the donor, and the power was conceived as merely the authority of the donee to do an act for the donor. Viewed in this manner, the donee merely has the power to fill in a blank in the donor's will, and the appointee receives the property from the donor, not the donee. This is known as the *relation-back doctrine*. Though the doctrine accurately enough describes the law's treatment of special powers of appointment, where the donee can reap no personal pecuniary benefit, its underlying principle has never been consistently applied to general powers of appointment. See Melanie B. Leslie, Note, The Case Against Applying the Relation-Back Doctrine to the Exercise of General Powers of Appointment, 14 Cardozo L. Rev. 219 (1992).

In some situations, the donee of a general power of appointment is treated as owner of the property. The primary example is under the federal tax laws. The donee of a general power is treated as owner of the appointive property for income, estate, and gift tax purposes. Disregarding the technicalities of property law, Congress made taxation turn upon the fact that the donee, if she chooses, can receive an economic benefit by exercising the power.

The question thus arises, what rights, if any, do creditors of the donee of a general power have with respect to the appointive property?

Irwin Union Bank & Trust Co. v. Long
Indiana Court of Appeals, 1974
160 Ind. App. 509, 312 N.E.2d 908

LOWDERMILK, J. On February 3, 1957, Victoria Long, appellee herein, obtained a judgment in the amount of $15,000 against Philip W. Long, which judgment emanated from a divorce decree. This action is the result of the filing by appellee of a petition in proceedings supplemental to execution on the prior judgment. Appellee sought satisfaction of that judgment by pursuing funds allegedly owed to Philip W. Long as a result of a trust set up by Laura Long, his mother.

Appellee alleged that the Irwin Union Bank and Trust Company (Union Bank) was indebted to Philip W. Long as the result of its position as trustee of the trust created by Laura Long. On April 24, 1969, the trial court ordered that any income, property, or profits, which were owed to Philip Long and not exempt from execution should be applied to the divorce judgment. Thereafter, on February 13, 1973, the trial court ordered that four percent (4%) of the trust corpus of the trust created by Laura Long which benefited Philip Long was not exempt from execution and could be levied upon by appellee and ordered a writ of execution. . . .

The pertinent portion of the trust created by Laura Long is as follows, to-wit:

ITEM V C

Withdrawal of Principal
When Philip W. Long, Jr. has attained the age of twenty-one (21) years and is not a full-time student at an educational institution as a candidate for a Bachelor of Arts or Bachelor of Sciences degree, Philip W. Long shall have the right to withdraw from principal once in any calendar year upon thirty (30) days written notice to the Trustee up to four percent (4%) of the market value of the entire trust principal on the date of such notice, which right shall not be cumulative.

The primary issue raised on this appeal is whether the trial court erred in allowing execution on the 4% of the trust corpus.

Appellant contends that Philip Long's right to withdraw 4% of the trust corpus is, in fact, a general power of appointment. Union Bank further contends that since Philip Long has never exercised his right of withdrawal, pursuant to the provisions of the trust instrument, no creditors of Philip Long can reach the trust corpus. Appellant points out that if the power of appointment is unexercised, the creditors cannot force the exercise of said power and cannot reach the trust corpus in this case. . . .

Appellee argues that Philip has absolute control and use of the 4% of the corpus and that the bank does not have control over that portion of the corpus if Philip decides to exercise his right of withdrawal. Appellee argues that the intention of Laura Long was to give Philip not only an income interest in the trust but a fixed amount of corpus which he could use as he saw fit. Thus, Philip Long would have a right to the present enjoyment of 4% of the trust corpus. A summation of appellee's argument, as stated in her brief, is as follows: "So it is with Philip — he can get it if he desires it, so why cannot Victoria get it even if Philip does not desire it?"

We have had no Indiana authority directly in point cited to us by either of the parties and a thorough research of this issue does not reveal any Indiana authority on point. Thus, this issue so far as we can determine is one of first impression in Indiana. . . .

The leading case on this issue is Gilman v. Bell (1881), 99 Ill. 144, 150, 151, wherein the Illinois Supreme Court discussed powers of appointment and vesting as follows:

> No title or interest in the thing vests in the donee of the power until he exercises the power. It is virtually an offer to him of the estate or fund, that he may receive or reject at will, and like any other offer to donate property to a person, no title can vest until he accepts the offer, nor can a court of equity compel him to accept the property or fund against his will, even for the benefit of creditors. If it should, it would be to convert the property of the person offering to make the donation to the payment of the debts of another person. Until accepted, the person to whom the offer is made has not, nor can he have, the slightest interest or title to the property. So the donee of the power only receives the naked power to make the property or fund his own. And when he exercises the power, he thereby consents to receive it, and the title thereby vests in him, although it may pass out of him *eo instanti*, to the appointee.

Contrary to the contention of appellee, it is our opinion that Philip Long has no control over the trust corpus until he exercises his power of appointment and gives notice to the trustee that he wishes to receive his 4% of the trust corpus. Until such an exercise is made, the trustee has the absolute control and benefit of the trust corpus within the terms of the trust instrument.

. . . The trust as a whole is set up to give the grandchildren of Laura Long the substantial portion of the assets involved. We note with interest that the percentage of corpus which Philip Long may receive is carefully limited to a percentage less than that which would be includable in the gross estate of Philip Long should he die within a year in which he had allowed his power of appointment to lapse.[4]

. . . The trust created in the will of Laura Long, in our opinion, has the legal effect of creating a [general] power of appointment in Philip Long under Item V C of the trust.

Philip Long has never exercised his power of appointment under the trust. Such a situation is discussed in II Scott on Trusts, §147.3 as follows:

> Where the power is a special power, a power to appoint only among a group of persons, the power is not beneficial to the donee and cannot, of course, be reached by his creditors. Where the power is a general power, that is, a power to appoint to anyone including the donee himself or his estate, the power is beneficial to the donee. If the donee exercises the power by appointing to a volunteer, the property appointed can be reached by his creditors if his other assets are insufficient for the payment of his debts. But where the donee of a general power created by some person other than himself fails to exercise the power, his creditors cannot acquire the power or compel

---

4. Philip's interest would have been includable in his gross estate if the value of the lapsed power exceeded the greater of $5,000 or 5 percent of the value of the appointive property. I.R.C. §2041(b)(2). This rule is discussed at pages 893. — Eds.

its exercise, nor can they reach the property covered by the power, unless it is otherwise provided by statute.

Indiana has no statute which would authorize a creditor to reach property covered by a power of appointment which is unexercised.

In Gilman v. Bell, supra, the court analyzed the situation where a general power of appointment was unexercised and discussed the position of creditors of the donee of the power as follows:

> But it is insisted, that, conceding it to be a mere naked power of appointment in favor of himself, in favor of creditors he should be compelled by a court of equity to so appoint, or be treated as the owner, and the property subjected to the payment of his debts. The doctrine has been long established in the English courts, that the courts of equity will not aid creditors in case there is a non-execution of the power.

Appellee concedes that if we find that Philip Long had merely an unexercised power of appointment then creditors are in no position to either force the exercise of the power or to reach the trust corpus. Thus, it is clear that the trial court erred. . . .

Reversed and remanded.

NOTES AND QUESTIONS

1. *Creditors of a donee of a general power.* The decision in *Long* is in accord with the traditional view that the donee of a general power has no property interest in the appointive property unless the donee exercises that power, and that the right to do so is personal to the donee. As Lord Justice Fry once said: "The power of a person to appoint an estate to himself is, in my judgment, no more his 'property' than the power to write a book or to sing a song." In re Armstrong, 17 Q.B.D. 521, 531 (1886). This approach was carried forward in Restatement (Second) of Property: Donative Transfers §13.2 (1986). However, if the donee of a presently exercisable general power may reach the property simply by asking for it, one might reasonably ask, dogmatic formalism aside, should not the donee's creditors be able to reach it? As a functional matter, is there any difference between the appointive property and money in the donee's checking account?

By statute, a number of states have abrogated the traditional rule, as does Uniform Trust Code (UTC) §505(b) (2000) and Restatement (Third) of Trusts §56, cmt. b (2003). Under this approach, creditors of a donee of a general power presently exercisable are permitted to reach the appointive property, albeit sometimes with the qualification that the creditors must first exhaust the donee's own assets before resorting to the appointive property. See Cal. Prob. Code §682 (2004); Mich. Comp. Laws §556.123 (2004); Wis. Stat. Ann. §702.17 (2004). These statutes and the Restatement (Third) of Trusts—but not the UTC, which is deliberately silent—provide that the creditors of the donee of a general testamentary power can also reach the appointive property, but only at the donee's death. In New York, creditors of a general power presently exercisable can reach the appointive property, but creditors of a donee of a general testamentary power cannot. N.Y. Est. Powers & Trusts Law §§10-7.2, 10-7.4 (2004). Likewise, under federal bankruptcy law, a general power presently exercisable passes to the donee's trustee in bankruptcy, but a special power and a general testamentary power do not. 11 U.S.C. §541(b)(1) (2004).

If the donee of a general power is also the donor of the power, creditors may reach the appointive assets. Restatement (Second) of Property, supra, §13.3. This principle is analogous to the traditional rule against self-settled asset protection trusts (see page 557).

2. *Surviving spouse of the donee.* If the surviving spouse of the donee seeks to reach the appointive property at the donee's death under elective share statutes, the donee of a general power, as well as the donee of a special power, is not, in most states, treated as owning the property. Under traditional principles, the surviving spouse has a claim against the donee's *probate* estate, and since the appointive assets are not in the donee's probate estate, the spouse may not reach them. See Margaret M. Mahoney, Elective Share Statutes: The Right to Elect Against Property Subject to a General Power of Appointment in the Decedent, 55 Notre Dame Law 99 (1979). Uniform Probate Code §2-205(1)(i) (1990), page 449, changes this rule and includes in the augmented estate subject to the elective share any property over which the decedent had a general power of appointment. New York Est. Powers & Trusts Law §5-1.1-A(b)(1)(H) (2004), is to the same effect.

3. *Creditors of a donee of a special power.* The rule that the creditors of a donee of a special power cannot reach the property subject to the power is more easily explained: The donee can reap no personal pecuniary benefit. However, it has been held that where the life beneficiary of a trust has a special inter vivos power to appoint trust principal to his descendants, children of the donee who have a support order may reach the trust principal even though the trust contains a spendthrift clause. In re Marriage of Chapman, 697 N.E.2d 365 (Ill. App. 1998). Could the donee's children with a support order reach trust principal that is subject to a general inter vivos power in the donee? Compare the ability of children to reach the income interest of their parent in a spendthrift trust, page 555.

NOTE: TAX CONSIDERATIONS FOR POWERS

Powers of appointment are extensively employed in trusts not only to provide flexibility or to give the donee control over the trust property, but also to obtain tax benefits. Thus, although we defer most tax matters until Chapter 14, some discussion of the tax considerations for powers of appointment is appropriate here.

The federal tax laws provide that the holder of a general power of appointment is treated as the owner of the property. The income from the property is taxable to the donee (Internal Revenue Code of 1986, §678). If the donee exercises the power during life, the property transferred to others by exercise is subject to gift taxation (I.R.C. §2514; see page 892). If the donee dies holding a general power, the property is included in the donee's federal gross estate and is subject to estate taxation (I.R.C. §2041; pages 891-893). On the other hand, *property subject to a special power of appointment is not treated as owned by the donee.* To avoid estate taxation at the death of the donee, while giving the donee significant control over the trust property, you should create a special power of appointment and not a general power.

Estate tax advantages of special powers. By carefully tailoring the powers given a donee to fit the Internal Revenue Code, a donee can be given power to do almost anything an owner of property can do while not being treated as owner for federal tax purposes. Suppose that *T* wishes to pass property to her daughter, *A*, for *A*'s life and then to *A*'s children. At the same time, *T* wishes to give *A* as much power over the property as possible without causing *A* to be treated as owner for estate tax purposes. Although *T* cannot escape taxation at *her own* death, *T* wishes to avoid estate taxation on *A*'s death. To accomplish this, *T* might do the following:

(1)   *T*'s will transfers the legal title to the property to *A* as trustee. *As trustee, A* can manage the property, deciding when to sell and in what to reinvest. If the trustee's powers are broadly drafted, *A* can manage the property almost as if she owned it herself.

(2)   *T*'s will gives to *A, not as trustee but as a beneficiary*:
      (a)   the right to receive all the income;
      (b)   a special power of appointment exercisable by deed or will to appoint the trust property to anyone *A* desires except herself, her creditors, her estate, or the creditors of her estate;
      (c)   a power to consume the trust property measured "by an ascertainable standard relating to the health, education, support or maintenance"[5] of *A*; and
      (d)   a power to withdraw each year $5,000 or 5 percent of the corpus, whichever is greater.[6]

(3)   If *T* desires to make sure that *A* will be able to use the entire property if she needs it, *T* can appoint an independent co-trustee and give this co-trustee the power to pay *A* the entire principal or to terminate the trust.

None of the above powers given *A*, individually or collectively, causes *A* to be treated as owner of the trust fund under the federal estate tax. Yet these powers give *A* almost as much control over the trust fund as she would have had if she had been bequeathed the property outright.

Prior to the Tax Reform Act of 1986, federal estate taxes could be avoided over several generations through the creation of successive life estates. To give the desired flexibility to cope with changing events, each successive life tenant could be given special powers of appointment as indicated above. This tax avoidance device has now been curtailed by the imposition of a tax on certain generation-skipping transfers.

Generation-skipping transfer tax advantages of special powers. In 1986, Congress enacted a generation-skipping transfer (GST) tax to deal with estate tax avoidance resulting from the exemption of life estates from estate taxation. I.R.C. §§2601-2663, discussed at pages 919-928. A GST tax is imposed on the death of a life tenant of a younger generation than the settlor's (on *A*'s death in the above example). It is

---

5. Powers measured by an ascertainable standard are not treated as general powers under the Code. See pages 891-896.

6. Under a "$5,000 or 5 percent" power, $5,000 or 5 percent of the corpus (whichever is greater) will be included in the estate of the donee to the extent the power is not exercised in the year of the donee's death. I.R.C. §2041(b)(2), discussed at pages 892-893. This is a small price to pay for the flexibility gained thereby. This is the type of power involved in Irwin Union Bank & Trust Co. v. Long, supra.

now Congress's policy to exact a wealth transfer tax at every generation, either an estate tax or a GST tax.

Nonetheless, special powers of appointment continue to be useful in avoiding the GST tax. First, the GST tax does not apply to trusts established before 1986. If the beneficiaries of these trusts have special powers of appointment, as many do, these trusts may be kept going — transfer tax free — for about a hundred years from the date of their creation (which is, roughly speaking, the perpetuities period) by creating new special powers in each succeeding generation.

Second, each transferor has a $2 million exemption from GST tax.[7] Each transferor can transfer up to $2 million in a trust, often called a *dynasty trust*, which will be exempt from GST tax for the duration of the trust. Hence in the above example, *T* could create a trust of $2 million for her daughter *A* and her descendants, giving each generation special powers as outlined above, with the trust to endure until 21 years after the death of all *T*'s living descendants or other named persons living at *T*'s death (the perpetuities period). In some states, a trust for generation after generation can endure in perpetuity, a subject we take up at page 711. No GST tax is payable so long as the trust endures. If *T* is married, she and her husband (using his $2 million exemption) can transfer $4 million in such a GST-tax-exempt dynasty trust. See page 927.

Third, a trust beneficiary may not have sufficient assets of his own to use up his GST exemption amount. Giving the beneficiary a special power of appointment allows the beneficiary to choose between paying the GST tax or the estate tax. I.R.C. §2041(a)(3). (This option involves both the Rule against Perpetuities and the tax code and hence is deferred until the chapter on perpetuities. See pages 694-696.)

Although general powers should not be created if the donor is seeking favorable tax treatment, there are exceptions. First, property that passes to the surviving spouse in such a manner as to qualify for the *marital deduction* is not taxable under the estate tax. A life estate coupled with a general testamentary power in the surviving spouse qualifies for the marital deduction (I.R.C. §2056(b)(5), discussed at page 903) and is a common estate planning tool. Thus:

> *Case 5. H* devises property to *X* in trust to pay the income to *W* and on *W*'s death to distribute the principal to such person or persons as *W* by her will appoints. *H*'s devise qualifies for the marital deduction; no federal estate taxes are payable on the property at *H*'s death. However, since *W* has a general power, the property is subject to estate taxation on *W*'s death. In effect, the marital deduction permits taxation to be postponed until the death of the surviving spouse.

Second, the donor is entitled to exclude $11,000 of gifts to a donee each year as long as the gift qualifies as a present interest. I.R.C. §2503(b). If the donor transfers property into trust, the gift will be treated as a present interest if the donee has a general power of appointment. See page 858. In this situation, the donee's general power is usually limited to the amount that will qualify for the gift tax annual exclusion.

---

7. The GST exemption amount is now equal to the estate tax exemption amount. This amount is $1.5 million in 2004 and 2005, $2 million in 2006 through 2008, and $3.5 million in 2009.

SECTION B.   CREATION OF A POWER
OF APPOINTMENT

1. Intent to Create a Power

To create a power of appointment, the donor must manifest an intent to do so, either expressly or by implication. No particular form of words is necessary. It is not necessary that the words *power of appointment* or *appoint* be used. A power of appointment confers discretion on the donee, who may choose to exercise the power or not, and is to be distinguished from a direct nondiscretionary disposition by the donor. Thus:

> *Case 6.* Aunt Fanny executes a will in 2001 bequeathing her tangible personal property "to my niece Wendy Brown, to dispose of in accordance with a letter addressed to Wendy dated January 4, 2000, which is in my safe-deposit box." Aunt Fanny has incorporated the letter by reference and the tangible personal property must be distributed in accordance therewith. Wendy does not have a power of appointment.

Words that merely express a wish or desire (*precatory words*) do not create a power of appointment in the absence of other circumstances indicating a contrary intent. If in Case 6 Aunt Fanny had left her tangible personal property to Wendy "with the request that she give some of the property to my other relatives," Wendy would take a fee simple; the precatory words would not create a power of appointment.

For further discussion and helpful illustrations, see Restatement (Second) of Property: Donative Transfers §12.1 (1986).

2. Powers to Consume

One of the most frequently litigated problems in regard to creation of powers is whether a power to consume principal has been created and, if so, what standard governs the exercise of the power. Much of this litigation stems from homemade wills, but some litigation, alas, results from inadequate drafting by lawyers.

Sterner v. Nelson
Supreme Court of Nebraska, 1982
210 Neb. 358, 314 N.W.2d 263

KRIVOSHA, C.J.   The instant case involves the construction of the last will and testament of Oscar Wurtele, deceased. The appellants appeal from a summary judgment entered by the District Court for Otoe County, Nebraska, finding that the nature of the devise and bequest made by Oscar Wurtele to his wife, Mary Viola Wurtele, by his last will and testament was a fee simple absolute. We believe the trial court was correct and affirm the judgment.

As noted, the appeal herein arises out of the last will and testament of Oscar Wurtele, executed on August 4, 1939. While the will is simple and to the point, it is not a model for estate planners. It reads in total as follows:

I, the undersigned, Oscar Wurtele do hereby make, publish and declare the following as and for my Last Will and Testament:

I hereby give, devise and bequeath all of my property of every kind and nature to my wife Mary Viola Wurtele to be her property *absolutely with full power in her to make such disposition of said property as she may desire;* conditioned, however, that if any of said property is remaining upon the death of said Mary Viola Wurtele, or in the event that she predeceases me then and in such event such of said property as remains shall vest in my foster daughter Gladys Pauline Sterner and her children.

I hereby nominate and appoint my said wife, Mary Viola Wurtele, of Nebraska City, Nebraska, as executrix of this My Last Will and Testament.

Dated at Nebraska City, Nebraska, this 4th day of August, 1939. Oscar Wurtele. [Emphasis supplied.]

Following Oscar Wurtele's death in 1955 his will was admitted to probate in the county court of Otoe County, Nebraska, and all of the property which Oscar Wurtele owned at the time of his death was devised and bequeathed to his wife, Mary Viola Wurtele, to be hers absolutely. Certain of the property, including two commercial buildings, a farm, and a residence, were held in joint tenancy and passed to Mary Viola Wurtele by action of law and are not in any manner involved in this case. Two other commercial buildings, however, did pass to Mary Viola Wurtele by reason of the will of her husband, Oscar Wurtele, as well as certain personal property having an estimated value of $19,000. Mary Viola Wurtele thereafter married one Aaron Rose with whom she lived until her death on March 7, 1978. Mary Viola Rose died testate leaving her property to various individuals, including her husband, Aaron, and certain other nieces and nephews, but leaving no property to the appellants herein who are the foster daughter and her children referred to in the last will and testament of Oscar Wurtele. Aaron Rose died on June 24, 1979.

The evidence further discloses that in 1963 Mary Viola Rose sold the four commercial buildings for a total sale price of $70,000. No division of the sale price was made between the joint tenancy property and the property received under the will of her former husband. It is, however, clear from the evidence that none of the original property devised and bequeathed to Mary Viola Wurtele remained at the time of her death, though she did die owning property, some of which may have been purchased from the proceeds of either the personal property or the sale of the real estate. Following a hearing, the trial court found that the will of Oscar Wurtele devised and bequeathed all of his property to his wife, Mary Viola Wurtele, in fee simple absolute, and granted the personal representative's motion for summary judgment. The trial court's opinion provides in part as follows: "The Court is of the opinion that the language in the Oscar Wurtele will is so precise as to create a fee simple title in the wife, Mary Viola Wurtele."

Appellants have raised a number of errors, but the principal issue which needs to be addressed is whether the devise and bequest by Oscar Wurtele to Mary Viola Wurtele was a fee simple absolute or merely a life estate with authority to dispose of so much of the property as she chose during her lifetime. For, obviously, if we conclude, as the trial court did, that the devise and bequest was a fee simple absolute, then Mary Viola Rose was entitled to do whatever she wished with her property, both during her lifetime and upon her death, and Gladys Pauline

Sterner and her children would not be entitled to any portions of the property remaining at the death of Mary Viola Rose. . . .

The general and majority rule is as expressed in 28 Am. Jur. 2d Estates §94 at 198-99 (1966), wherein it provides in part:

> It is a well-settled, general rule that where there is a grant, devise, or bequest to one in general terms only, expressing neither fee nor life estate, and there is a subsequent limitation over of what remains at the first taker's death, if there is also given to the first taker an unlimited and unrestricted power of absolute disposal, express or implied, the grant, devise, or bequest to the first taker is construed to pass a fee. The attempted limitation over, following a gift which is in fee with full power of disposition and alienation, is void, . . . the purported gift over merely being an invalid repugnancy.

The American Jurisprudence annotation cited above then goes on to note that the general rule is consistently applied even in cases involving wills of slightly different but substantial tenor, a number of which are similar to the language of the Wurtele will.

One may likewise find cases in Nebraska and other jurisdictions to support the general view expressed in the American Jurisprudence citation. In the case of Moffitt v. Williams, 219 N.W. 138, 139 (Neb. 1928), we said: . . . "'The settled rule of law is that, if a deed or will conveys an absolute title in fee simple, an inconsistent clause in the instrument attempting merely to limit that title or convey to the same person a limited title in the same land will be disregarded.'"

Cases may likewise be found in a majority of the jurisdictions which support the general rule. In the case of Moran v. Moran, 106 N.W. 206 (Mich. 1906), the Michigan Supreme Court was presented a will which provided in part as follows: "'I give and bequeath to my beloved wife . . . all my property real and personal, of every name, nature and description to be hers absolutely, providing however, that if at her death any of the said property be still hers, then the residue still hers shall go to my, not her, nearest heir or heirs.'" The court held that such language created a fee simple absolute in the wife and the provision for the property remaining was void and unenforceable. . . . [Numerous citations from other states omitted.]

In the instant case it is not possible to reconcile the devise given by Oscar Wurtele to his wife, on the one hand, and the expression of desire concerning his foster daughter, on the other.

The grant to Mary Viola Wurtele was clear and unambiguous. She was to have the property to "be her property absolutely with full power in her to make such disposition of said property as she may desire." That intent is clear. By having the property as hers "absolutely" and with "full power" to "dispose" of the property as she may desire, she had not only the right to sell or give away the property during her lifetime but the right to will the property upon her death as well. Anything less would not have granted her the property "absolutely" with "full power in her to make such disposition" as she desired. The authority given was not limited to sale or disposition during her lifetime, but rather was to be *absolute*. . . .

No reason is given to us nor are we able to find any on our own as to why the majority rule following the common law should not be the rule in this jurisdiction. . . . If the testator does not desire for the devisee to have a fee simple, it is easy enough to say so. But having once granted the devise or bequest in language which standing alone constitutes an absolute conveyance, the balance of the limitations should be disregarded, regardless of the intent of the testator, on the basis that the intent is in conflict with the first grant. Either a devisee has received the property absolutely or the devisee has not received the property absolutely. Like honesty, morality, and pregnancy, an absolute devise cannot be qualified. . . .

We, therefore, now adopt the majority rule to the effect that where there is a grant, devise, or bequest to one in general terms only, expressing neither fee nor life estate, and there is a subsequent limitation over of what remains at the first taker's death, if there is also given to the first taker an unlimited and unrestricted power of absolute disposal, express or implied, the grant, devise, or bequest to the first taker is construed to pass a fee. The attempted limitation over, following a gift which is in fee with full power of disposition and alienation, is void.

. . . The judgment of the trial court, therefore, is affirmed.

NOTES AND QUESTIONS

1. Oscar Wurtele's will appears to have been drafted by a lawyer. Should the lawyer be liable to Gladys for malpractice? For discussion of successful ways to make a gift over to Gladys of whatever is left on Mary Viola's death, see William F. Fratcher, Bequests of Orts, 48 Mo. L. Rev. 475 (1983).

2. In Sterner v. Nelson, the court says, "No reason is given to us nor are we able to find any on our own as to why the majority rule following the common law should not be the rule in this jurisdiction." If counsel and court had dug a bit deeper, they would have unearthed an extended, critical treatment of the rule of repugnancy in Lewis M. Simes & Allan F. Smith, The Law of Future Interests §§1481-1491 (2d ed. 1956), or the summary of criticisms, originating with Professor Gray, in 6 American Law of Property §26.43 (1952). For more criticism of this senseless rule, see the dissenting opinion of Chief Justice Vanderbilt in Fox v. Snow, 76 A.2d 877 (N.J. 1950). The rule of repugnancy is not followed in Caldwell v. Walraven, 490 S.E.2d 384 (Ga. 1997).

One thing can be said in favor of the rule of repugnancy applied in Sterner v. Nelson. It enables the court to avoid hard questions. If the devise over to Gladys were valid, could Mary Viola use the devised property to support her second husband, to take a round-the-world cruise, to spend the winter in Florida, to build a room on her house? Could she give away the property? Does Mary Viola have to give a bond to protect Gladys's interest in the personal property valued at $19,000? These questions often arise where the life tenant is given a power to consume, and litigation over ambiguous language is extensive. See Annots., 31 A.L.R.3d 6 (1970) (158 pages); id. at 169 (129 pages); id. at 309 (61 pages). Compare the rights of the survivor whose property is bound by a contract not to revoke a will at page 294.

A good attorney will never create a *legal* fee simple with the power to consume because of the danger of running afoul of the rule of repugnancy. Nor will a good attorney create a *legal* life estate at all; a trust with a life beneficiary is preferable in almost all situations (see page 493 for reasons why). If the life beneficiary of a trust is to have rights to consume the principal, the attorney drafting a will or trust should make clear under what circumstances the life tenant can reach the principal.

3.   *Taxation of powers to consume*. Property subject to a general power of appointment is in the donee's federal gross estate at death and subject to estate taxation. And if a power to consume permits the donee to appoint the property to herself during life, then it is a general power of appointment. However, there is an important exception under I.R.C. §2041(b)(1)(A): "A power to consume, invade, or appropriate property for the benefit of the decedent which is limited by an ascertainable standard relating to the health, education, support, or maintenance of the decedent shall not be deemed a general power of appointment." Hence, the tax question respecting each power to consume is this: Is the power at hand limited by an ascertainable standard relating to the health, education, support, or maintenance of the decedent? If it is not so limited, the property subject to the power is included in the donee's gross estate. Thus the lawyer drafting a power to consume must carefully track the words of §2041(b)(1)(A) or the regulations. Consider that a power to consume for the donee's "comfort, welfare, or happiness" is not limited by the requisite standard, but a power to consume "to maintain the standard of living to which the donee is accustomed" is regarded as limited by the requisite standard. See Estate of Vissering v. Commissioner, 990 F.2d 578 (10th Cir. 1993), page 894, citing numerous cases involving this question.

The lawyer drafting a trust instrument may decide that, rather than give the beneficiary a power to consume, it is safer to give a trustee who is not the beneficiary a discretionary power to use corpus to maintain the beneficiary in the style of living to which she is accustomed.

SECTION C.   RELEASE OF A POWER OF APPOINTMENT

The donor of a life estate coupled with a testamentary power usually intends to protect the donee from an indiscreet or unwise exercise of the power during life: that the power is testamentary ensures that the donee is free to exercise discretion up until the moment of death. Hence, the donee of a testamentary power of appointment cannot enter into an enforceable *contract* to make an appointment in the future. The promisee may, however, obtain restitution of the value that the promisee gave the donee in consideration for the donee's (unenforceable) promise. In such a case, restitution is based on the donee's unjust enrichment. If the law afforded specific performance or damages for breaches of such contracts, the donee of a testamentary power could in effect exercise the power during life by contracting to exercise it. The courts have not allowed the donor's intent to be defeated in this manner.

On the other hand, if the donee promises to exercise a testamentary power in a certain way, and the donee's will exercises the power as promised, the exercise is not rendered invalid because the donee could not have been compelled to exercise the power in that way. See Benjamin v. Morgan Guar. Tr. Co., 609 N.Y.S.2d 276 (App. Div. 1994).

Although a contract to exercise a testamentary power is not enforceable, a similar result can sometimes be obtained by *releasing* the power of appointment.

If a power is released, the uncertainty it creates as to the ultimate takers is removed. Thus:

> Case 7. T devises property in trust for A for life, then as A by will appoints, and in default of appointment, to A's children equally. A releases her power of appointment. A's children now have an indefeasibly vested remainder. A could not make an enforceable *contract* to appoint to her children, but she may achieve her objective by a *release*.

All powers of appointment except powers in trust or imperative powers have been made releasable in all jurisdictions either by judicial decision or by statute. A releasable power may be released with respect to the whole or any part of the appointive property and may also be released in such manner as to reduce or limit the permissible appointees. See Restatement (Second) of Property: Donative Transfers §§14.1, 14.2 (1986), including statutory notes and reporter's notes.

Seidel v. Werner

New York Supreme Court, Special Term, New York County, 1975
81 Misc. 2d 220, 364 N.Y.S.2d 963,
aff'd on opinion below, 50 A.D.2d 743, 376 N.Y.S.2d 139

SILVERMAN, J.   Plaintiffs, trustees of a trust established in 1919 by Abraham L. Werner, sue for a declaratory judgment to determine who is entitled to one-half of the principal of the trust fund—the share in which Steven L. Werner, decedent (hereinafter "Steven"), was the life beneficiary and over which he had a testamentary power of appointment. The dispute concerns the manner in which Steven exercised his power of appointment and is between Steven's second wife, Harriet G. Werner (hereinafter "Harriet"), along with their children, Anna G. and Frank S. Werner (hereinafter "Anna" and "Frank") and Steven's third wife, Edith Fisch Werner (hereinafter "Edith").

Anna and Frank claim Steven's entire share of the trust remainder on the basis of a Mexican consent judgment of divorce,[8] obtained by Steven against Harriet on

---

8. Before the liberalization of American divorce law and the spread of the no-fault divorce in the 1970s, couples wanting to end their marriage often found it necessary to travel to another state or even to another country in order to escape their home state's hostility to divorce. Nevada emerged as the domestic leader in this jurisdictional competition for divorces, so much so that "'Going to Reno' became almost a synonym for getting a divorce." Lawrence M. Friedman, A Dead Language: Divorce Law and Practice Before No-Fault, 86 Va. L. Rev. 1497, 1504-1505 (2000). Mexico was among the more popular international destinations: The number of Mexican divorces granted to couples in which at least one of the spouses was born in the United States increased from 230 in 1926 to over 4,300 in 1955. The latter figure accounts for roughly one-third of all divorces in Mexico that year. Paul H. Jacobson, American Marriage and Divorce 108-109 (1959). For those not inclined, or wealthy enough, to travel and establish a temporary residency elsewhere, New York's especially severe statute, under which evidence of adultery was necessary for a divorce decree, prompted what has come to be called "soft-core adultery." Professor Friedman explains:

> This involved a little drama performed in a hotel. The cast of characters included the husband, a woman (generally a blonde who was hired for the occasion), and a photographer, of course. An article in the *New York Sunday Mirror* magazine section, published in 1934, had the intriguing title: "I was the Unknown Blonde in 100 New York Divorces." The "unknown blonde" usually charged $50 for her work. She was in fact a woman named Dorothy Jarvis, who (according to the

December 9, 1963, which incorporated by reference and approved a separation agreement, entered into between Steven and Harriet on December 1, 1963. That agreement included the following provision:

> 10. The Husband shall make, and hereby promises not to revoke, a will in which he shall exercise his testamentary power of appointment over his share in a trust known as "Abraham L. Werner Trust No. 1" by establishing with respect to said share a trust for the benefit of the aforesaid Children, for the same purposes and under the same terms and conditions, as the trust provided for in Paragraph "9" of this Agreement, insofar as said terms and conditions are applicable thereto.

Paragraph 9 in relevant part provides for the wife to receive the income of the trust, upon the death of the husband, for the support and maintenance of the children, until they reach twenty-one years of age, at which time they are to receive the principal in equal shares.

On March 20, 1964, less than four months after entry of the divorce judgment, Steven executed a will in which, instead of exercising his testamentary power of appointment in favor of Anna and Frank, he left everything to his third wife, Edith:

> First, I give, devise and bequeath all of my property . . . including . . . all property over which I have a power of testamentary disposition, to my wife, Edith Fisch Werner.

Steven died in April 1971 and his Will was admitted to probate by the Surrogate's Court of New York County on July 11, 1973.

(1) Paragraph 10 of the Separation Agreement is a contract to exercise a testamentary power of appointment not presently exercisable (EPTL 10-3.3) and as such is invalid under EPTL 10-5.3, which provides as follows:

> (a) The donee of a power of appointment which is not presently exercisable or of a postponed power which has not become exercisable, cannot contract to make an appointment. Such a contract, if made, cannot be the basis of an action for specific performance or damages, but the promisee can obtain restitution of the value given by him for the promise unless the donee has exercised the power pursuant to the contract.

This is a testamentary power of appointment. The original trust instrument provided in relevant part that: ". . . Upon the death of such child [Steven] the

---

Mirror) had "retired as a professional co-respondent in view of her forthcoming marriage to a man she met while performing her role."

Whatever sins the blonde may have committed in her young life, sex with the men who paid her was not among them. She simply played a part in a sordid little drama. She went to a hotel room with the man. There would be a certain amount of undressing. At some point, they would hear a knock on the door — a maid with towels, or the bellboy bringing a telegram. This too was a charade of course. When the door opened, the photographer would burst into the room and take pictures. A study of about 500 cases in the 1930s revealed the following fascinating facts: In 23 cases the man was totally nude; in 2 he was wrapped in a towel; in 8, he wore a nightgown; in 119, he was in his "B.V.D. or underwear"; bathrobe or dressing gown accounted for another 101; pajamas, 227 cases; in 4 he was wearing a "kimono." The woman was nude no less than 55 times (twice she only wore a brassiere); she was in a "negligee" 67 times; underwear 26 times; "chemise," 24 times; nightgown, 126; pajamas, 73; bathrobe or dressing gown, 32; "kimono," 68. [Friedman, supra, at 1511-1513.]

—Eds.

principal of such share shall be disposed of as such child shall by its last will direct, and in default of such testamentary disposition then the same shall go to the issue of such child then surviving per stirpes. . . ." It is not disputed that New York law is determinative of the validity of Paragraph 10 of the Separation Agreement; the Separation Agreement itself provides that New York law shall govern.

The reasoning underlying the refusal to enforce a contract to exercise a testamentary power was stated by Justice Cardozo in the case of Farmers' Loan & Trust Co. v. Mortimer, 114 N.E. 389, 390 (N.Y. 1916):

> The exercise of the power was to represent the final judgment, the last will, of the donee. Up to the last moment of his life he was to have the power to deal with the share as he thought best. . . . To permit him to bargain that right away would be to defeat the purpose of the donor. Her command was that her property should go to her son's issue unless at the end of his life it remained his will that it go elsewhere. It has not remained his will that it go elsewhere; and his earlier contract cannot nullify the expression of his final purpose.

See also In re Estate of Brown, 306 N.E.2d 781 (N.Y. 1973).

(2) The question then is whether entry of the Mexican divorce decree, incorporating the Separation Agreement, alters this result; I do not think it does. . . .

[The court held that the Mexican divorce decree was not controlling, because, first, it did not direct Steven to exercise his power of appointment but merely approved the separation agreement as fair and reasonable, and, second, the Mexican court did not pass on or consider rules of New York property law.]

(3) As indicated, the statute makes a promise to exercise a testamentary power in a particular way unenforceable. However, EPTL 10-5.3(b) permits a donee of a power to release the power, and that release, if in conformity with EPTL 10-9.2, prevents the donee from then exercising the power thereafter.

Under the terms of the trust instrument, if Steven fails to exercise his power of appointment, Anna and Frank (along with the children of Steven's first marriage) take the remainder, i.e., the property which is the subject of Steven's power of appointment. Therefore, Harriet, Anna and Frank argue that at a minimum Steven's agreement should be construed as a release of his power of appointment, and that Anna and Frank should be permitted to take as on default of appointment.

There is respectable authority — by no means unanimous authority, and none binding on this Court — to the effect that a promise to appoint a given sum to persons who would take in default of appointment should, *to that extent*, be deemed a release of the power of appointment. See Restatement of Property §336 (1940); Simes & Smith, The Law of Future Interests §1016 (1956).

This argument has the appeal that it seems to be consistent with the exception that the release statute (EPTL 10-5.3(b)) carves out of EPTL 10-5.3(a); and is also consistent with the intentions and reasonable expectation of the parties at the time they entered into the agreement to appoint, here in the separation agreement; and that therefore perhaps in these circumstances the difference between what the parties agreed to and a release of the power of appointment is merely one of form. Whatever may be the possible validity or applicability of this argument to other circumstances and situations, I think it is inapplicable to this situation because:

(a) It is clear that the parties did not intend a release of the power of appointment. Cf. Matter of Haskell, 300 N.Y.S.2d 711 (Sup. Ct. 1969). Indeed, the agreement—unlike a release of a power of appointment—expressly contemplates that something will be done by the donee of the power in the future, and that that something will be an exercise of the power of appointment. Thus, the agreement, in the very language said to be a release of the power of appointment, says (Par. 10): "the Husband *shall* make . . . a will in which he *shall exercise* his testamentary power of appointment. . . ." (emphasis added).

(b) Nor is the substantial effect of the promised exercise of the power the same as would follow from release of, or failure to exercise, the power.

(i) Under the separation agreement, the power is to be exercised so that the entire appointive property shall be for the benefit of Anna and Frank; under the trust instrument, on default of exercise of the power, the property goes to all of Steven's children (Anna, Frank and two children of Steven's first marriage). Thus the agreement provides for appointment of a greater principal to Anna and Frank than they would get in default of appointment.[9]

(ii) Under the trust instrument, on default of exercise of the power, the property goes to the four children absolutely and in fee. The separation agreement provides that Steven shall create a *trust*, with *income* payable to *Harriet as trustee*, for the support of Anna and Frank until they both reach the age of 21, at which time the principal shall be paid to them or the survivor; and if both fail to attain the age of 21, then the principal shall revert to Steven's estate. Thus, Anna and Frank's interest in the principal would be a defeasible interest if they did not live to be 21; and indeed at Steven's death they were both still under 21 so that their interest was defeasible.

(iii) Finally, under the separation agreement, as just noted, if Anna and Frank failed to qualify to take the principal, either because they both died before Steven or before reaching the age of twenty-one, then the principal would go to Steven's estate. Under the trust instrument, on the other hand, on default of appointment and an inability of Anna and Frank to take, Steven's share of the principal would not go to Steven's estate, but to his other children, if living, and if not, to the settlor's next of kin.

In these circumstances, I think it is too strained and tortuous to construe the separation agreement provision as the equivalent of a release of the power of appointment. If this is a release then the exception of EPTL 10-5.3(b) has swallowed and destroyed the principal rule of EPTL 10-5.3(a). . . .

Accordingly, I hold that the separation agreement is not the equivalent of a total or partial release of the power of appointment.

(4) Anna and Frank also seek restitution out of the trust fund of the value given by them in exchange for Steven's unfulfilled promise. EPTL 10-5.3(a) provides that although the contract to make an appointment cannot be the basis for an action for specific performance or damages, "the promisee can obtain restitution of the value given by him for the promise unless the donee has exercised the power pursuant to contract."

Anna and Frank's remedy is limited, however, to the claim for restitution that they have (and apparently have asserted) against Steven's estate. They may not seek restitution out of the trust fund, even if their allegation that the estate lacks

9. In 1977, two years after this case, the legislature amended N.Y. Est. Powers & Trusts Law §10-5(3)(b) to provide that a release was valid "except that where the donor designated persons or a class to take in default of the donee's exercise of the power, a release with respect to the appointive property must serve to benefit all those so designated as provided by the donor." — Eds.

sufficient assets to meet this claim were factually supported, because the trust fund was not the property of Steven, except to the extent of his life estate, so as to be subject to the equitable remedy of restitution, but was the property of the donor of the power of appointment until it vested in someone else. Farmers' Loan & Trust Co. v. Mortimer, 114 N.E. 389, 390 (N.Y. 1916); see Matter of Rosenthal, 127 N.Y.S.2d 778, 780 (App. Div. 1954); see also EPTL §§10-7.1 and 10-7.4.

(5) Finally, Edith moves for summary judgment that she is entitled to receive Steven's share of the trust fund on the ground that Steven exercised his testamentary power in her favor in his will of March 20, 1964, in the provision quoted at the beginning of this decision.

Since there are no factual questions raised as to Steven's exercise of his testamentary power of appointment in Edith's favor in that will provision, and since each of the other defendants' conflicting claims to the share of trust principal has been dismissed, Edith's motion for summary judgment is granted.

(6) Accordingly, on the motions for summary judgment I direct judgment declaring that defendant Edith Fisch Werner is entitled to the one-half share of Steven L. Werner in the principal of the Abraham L. Werner trust; to the extent that the counterclaims and cross-claims asserted by Harriet, Anna and Frank seek relief other than a declaratory judgment, they are dismissed.

QUESTION

Steven Ludwig Werner was a lawyer and, at the time of his death, a professor of labor relations at Cornell. If Steven had known, when he agreed to the divorce settlement, that the contract to appoint the trust fund was unenforceable, was his conduct unethical? If you think so, what would be the remedy?

SECTION D.   EXERCISE OF A POWER OF APPOINTMENT

1.   *Exercise by Residuary Clause in Donee's Will*

Beals v. State Street Bank & Trust Co.
Supreme Judicial Court of Massachusetts, 1975
367 Mass. 318, 326 N.E.2d 896

WILKINS, J.   The trustees under the will of Arthur Hunnewell filed this petition for instructions, seeking a determination of the proper distribution to be made of a portion of the trust created under the residuary clause of his will. A judge of the Probate Court reserved decision and reported the case to the Appeals Court on the pleadings and a stipulation of facts. We transferred the case here.

Arthur Hunnewell died, a resident of Wellesley,[10] in 1904, leaving his wife and four daughters. His will placed the residue of his property in a trust, the income of

---

10. The town of Wellesley, and the college, are named after Isabella Welles Hunnewell, Arthur's mother. — Eds.

which was to be paid to his wife during her life. At the death of his wife the trust was to be divided in portions, one for each then surviving daughter and one for the then surviving issue of any deceased daughter. Mrs. Hunnewell died in 1930. One of the four daughters predeceased her mother, leaving no issue. The trust was divided, therefore, in three portions at the death of Mrs. Hunnewell. The will directed that the income of each portion held for a surviving daughter should be paid to her during her life and on her death the principal of such portion should "be paid and disposed of as she may direct and appoint by her last Will and Testament duly probated." In default of appointment, the will directed that a daughter's share should be distributed to "the persons who would be entitled to such estate under the laws then governing the distribution of intestate estates."

This petition concerns the distribution of the trust portion held for the testator's daughter Isabella H. Hunnewell, later Isabella H. Dexter (Isabella). Following the death of her mother, Isabella requested the trustees to exercise their discretionary power to make principal payments by transferring substantially all of her trust share "to the Dexter family office in Boston, there to be managed in the first instance by her husband, Mr. Gordon Dexter." This request was granted, and cash and securities were transferred to her account at the Dexter office. The Hunnewell trustees, however, retained in Isabella's share a relatively small cash balance, an undivided one-third interest in a mortgage and undivided one-third interest in various parcels of real estate in the Commonwealth, which Isabella did not want in kind and which the trustees could not sell at a reasonable price at the time. Thereafter, the trustees received payments on the mortgage and proceeds from occasional sales of portions of the real estate. From her one-third share of these receipts, the trustees made further distributions to her of $1,900 in 1937, $22,000 in 1952, and $5,000 in 1953.

In February, 1944, Isabella, who was then a resident of New York, executed and caused to be filed in the Registry of Probate for Norfolk County an instrument which partially released her general power of appointment under the will of her father. See G.L. c. 204, §§27-36, inserted by St. 1943, c. 152. Isabella released her power of appointment "to the extent that such power empowers me to appoint to any one other than one or more of the . . . descendants [surviving me] of Arthur Hunnewell."[11]

On December 14, 1968, Isabella, who survived her husband, died without issue, still a resident of New York, leaving a will dated May 21, 1965.[12] Her share in the

---

11. Isabella did this to avoid federal estate taxes. In 1942 the Internal Revenue Code was changed to provide that property subject to a general power created before 1942 was includible in the donee's federal taxable estate if the power was exercised. However, Congress permitted powers created before 1942 to be released partially (converting them into special powers) without adverse tax consequences, if the conversion took place before 1951. Thus, by this partial release Isabella kept limited control over the property and avoided estate taxes. — Eds.

12. N.Y. Times, Sept. 28, 1894, at 5:

HARRIMAN — HUNNEWELL

BOSTON, Mass., Sept. 27. — The beautiful country seat of Mr. and Mrs. Arthur Hunnewell, at Wellesley, was a scene of joy and festivity yesterday, when their daughter, Miss Isabella, was married to Herbert M. Harriman of New-York. The ceremony was performed by the Rev. Leighton Parks, pastor of the Emanuel Church. There were no bridesmaids. The groom's brother, Joseph, was best man.

The ushers were Lawrence Kip of New-York, Belmont Tiffany of New-York, Edgar Scott of Philadelphia, Columbus Baldwin of New-York, Gordon Dexter, and W. S. Patten. Of the bridegroom's kinsfolk there were present: His mother, Mr. and Mrs. Border Harriman, and Mr. and Mrs. Oliver Harriman.

trust under her father's will then consisted of an interest in a contract to sell real estate, cash, notes and a certificate of deposit, and was valued at approximately $88,000. Isabella did not expressly exercise her power of appointment under her father's will. The residuary clause of her will provided in effect for the distribution of all "the rest, residue and remainder of my property" to the issue per stirpes of her sister Margaret Blake, who had predeceased Isabella.[13] The Blake issue would take one-half of Isabella's trust share, as takers in default of appointment, in all events. If, however, Isabella's will should be treated as effectively exercising her power of appointment under her father's will, the Blake issue would take the entire trust share, and the executors of the will of Isabella's sister Jane (who survived Isabella and has since died) would not receive that one-half of the trust share which would go to Jane in default of appointment.

In support of their argument that Isabella's will did not exercise the power of appointment under her father's will, the executors of Jane's estate contend that (1) Massachusetts substantive law governs all questions relating to the power of appointment, including the interpretation of Isabella's will; (2) the power should be treated as a special power of appointment because of its partial release by Isabella; and (3) because Isabella's will neither expresses nor implies any intention to exercise the power, the applicable rule of construction in this Commonwealth is that a general residuary clause does not exercise a special power of appointment. The Blake issue, in support of their argument that the power was exercised, contend that (1) Isabella's will manifests an intention to exercise the power and that no rule of construction need be applied; (2) the law of New York should govern the question whether Isabella's will exercised the power and, if it does, by statute New York has adopted a rule that a special power of appointment is exercised by a testamentary disposition of all of the donee's property; and (3) if Massachusetts law does apply, and the will is silent on the subject of the exercise of the power, the principles underlying our rule of construction that a residuary clause exercises a general power of appointment are applicable in these circumstances.

The wedding breakfast was spread beneath the grand old trees which dot the lawn before the mansion. At the expiration of a short wedding trip Mr. and Mrs. Harriman will reside in New-York.

Twelve years later, Isabella Hunnewell and Herbert Harriman were divorced. N.Y. Times, Dec. 16, 1968, at 47:

MRS. GORDON DEXTER

Mrs. Isabella Hunnewell Dexter, widow of Gordon Dexter, a Boston businessman, clubman and yachtsman, died Saturday in her home at 680 Madison Avenue. Her age was 97.

Mrs. Dexter's previous marriages, to Herbert M. Harriman and J. Searlo Barclay, ended in divorce.

— Eds.

13. The significant portion of the residuary clause reads as follows:

All the rest, residue and remainder of my property of whatever kind and wherever situated (including any property not effectively disposed of by the preceding provisions of this my will and all property over which I have or may have the power of appointment under or by virtue of the last will and testament dated November 27, 1933 and codicils thereto dated January 7, 1935 and January 8, 1935 of my husband, the late Gordon Dexter) . . . I give, devise, bequeath and appoint in equal shares to such of my said nephew George Baty Blake and my said nieces Margaret Cabot and Julia O. Beals as shall survive me and the issue who shall survive me of any of my said nephew or nieces who may predecease me, such issue to take per stirpes.

1. We turn first to a consideration of the question whether Isabella's will should be construed according to the law of this Commonwealth or the law of New York.[14] There are strong, logical reasons for turning to the law of the donee's domicil at the time of death to determine whether a donee's will has exercised a testamentary power of appointment over movables. See Restatement 2d: Conflict of Laws, §275, Comment c (1971); Scott, Trusts, §642, p.4065 (3d ed. 1967); Scoles, Goodrich's Conflict of Laws, §§175-177, p.346 (4th ed. 1964). Most courts in this country which have considered the question, however, interpret the donee's will under the law governing the administration of the trust, which is usually the law of the donor's domicil. . . . This has long been the rule in Massachusetts. . . . Fiduciary Trust Co. v. First Natl. Bank, 181 N.E.2d 6 (Mass. 1962) (inter vivos trust).[15]

If the question were before us now for the first time, we might well adopt a choice of law rule which would turn to the substantive law of the donee's domicil, for the purpose of determining whether the donee's will exercised a power of appointment. However, in a field where much depends on certainty and consistency as to the applicable rules of law, we think that we should adhere to our well established rule. Thus, in interpreting the will of a donee to determine whether a power of appointment was exercised, we apply the substantive law of the jurisdiction whose law governs the administration of the trust.

2. Considering the arguments of the parties, we conclude that there is no indication in Isabella's will of an intention to exercise or not to exercise the power of appointment given to her under her father's will. A detailed analysis of the various competing contentions would not add to our jurisprudence.[16] In the absence of an intention disclosed by her will construed in light of circumstances known to her when she executed it, we must adopt some Massachusetts rule of construction to resolve the issue before us. The question is what rule of construction. We are unaware of any decided case which, in this context, has dealt with a testamentary general power, reduced to a special power by action of the donee.

3. We conclude that the residuary clause of Isabella's will should be presumed to have exercised the power of appointment. We reach this result by a consideration of the reasons underlying the canons of construction applicable to general and

14. The applicable rules of construction where a donee's intention is not clear from his will differ between the two States. In the absence of a requirement by the donor that the donee refer to the power in order to exercise it, New York provides by statute that a residuary clause in a will exercises not only a general power of appointment but also a special power of appointment, unless the will expressly or by necessary implication shows the contrary. 17B McKinney's Consol. Laws of N.Y. Anno., E.P.T.L., c. 17-b, §10-6.1 (1967). See Matter of Hopkins, 259 N.Y.S.2d 565 (Surr. Ct. 1964). "'Necessary implication'" exists only where the will permits no other construction. Matter of Deane, 151 N.E.2d 184 (N.Y. 1958). In Massachusetts, unless the donor has provided that the donee of the power can exercise it only by explicit reference to the power, a general residuary clause in a will exercises a general power of appointment unless there is a clear indication of a contrary intent. . . . However, in Fiduciary Trust Co. v. First Natl. Bank, 181 N.E.2d 6 (Mass. 1962), we held that a general residuary clause did not exercise a special testamentary power of appointment in the circumstances of that case.

15. Of course, the law of the donee's domicile would be applied if the donor expressed such an intention. . . .

16. Isabella's residuary clause disposed of her "property." Because the trustees had agreed to distribute her trust portion to her and had largely done so and because, in a sense, she had exercised dominion over the trust assets by executing the partial release, a reasonable argument might be made that she regarded the assets in her portion of the trust as her "property." However, a conclusion that she intended by implication to include assets over which she had a special power of appointment within the word "property" is not justifiable because her residuary clause refers expressly to other property over which she had a special power of appointment under the will of her husband.

special testamentary powers of appointment. Considered in this way, we believe that a presumption of exercise is more appropriate in the circumstances of this case than a presumption of nonexercise.

When this court first decided not to extend to a special power of appointment the rule of construction that a general residuary clause executes a general testamentary power (unless a contrary intent is shown by the will), we noted significant distinctions between a general power and a special power. Fiduciary Trust Co. v. First Natl. Bank, supra. A general power was said to be a close approximation to a property interest, a "virtually unlimited power of disposition," while a special power of appointment lacked this quality. We observed that a layman having a general testamentary power over property might not be expected to distinguish between the appointive property and that which he owns outright, and thus "he can reasonably be presumed to regard this appointive property as his own." On the other hand, the donee of a special power would not reasonably regard such appointive property as his own: "[h]e would more likely consider himself to be, as the donor of the power intended, merely the person chosen by the donor to decide who of the possible appointees should share in the property (if the power is exclusive), and the respective shares of the appointees."

Considering the power of appointment given to Isabella and her treatment of that power during her life, the rationale for the canon of construction applicable to general powers of appointment should be applied in this case. This power was a general testamentary power at its inception. During her life, as a result of her request, Isabella had the use and enjoyment of the major portion of the property initially placed in her trust share. Prior use and enjoyment of the appointive property is a factor properly considered as weighing in favor of the exercise of a power of appointment by a will. Fiduciary Trust Co. v. First Natl. Bank, supra. Isabella voluntarily limited the power by selecting the possible appointees. In thus relinquishing the right to add the trust assets to her estate, she was treating the property as her own. Moreover, the gift under her residuary clause was consistent with the terms of the reduced power which she retained. In these circumstances, the partial release of a general power does not obviate the application of that rule of construction which presumes that a general residuary clause exercises a general power of appointment.

4. A decree shall be entered determining that Isabella H. Dexter did exercise the power of appointment, partially released by an instrument dated February 25, 1944, given to her by art. Fourth of the will of Arthur Hunnewell and directing that the trustees under the will of Arthur Hunnewell pay over the portion of the trust held under art. Fourth of his will for the benefit of Isabella H. Dexter, as follows: one-third each to George Baty Blake and Julia O. Beals; and one-sixth each to Margaret B. Elwell and to the estate of George B. Cabot. The parties shall be allowed their costs and counsel fees in the discretion of the probate court.

So ordered.

NOTES

1. *Choice of law*. When the appointive asset is land, the choice of law for interpreting a power of appointment is straightforward: The law of the jurisdiction where the land is located governs. But when the appointive asset is personal

property and the donor and donee live in different jurisdictions, choice of law is more complex. In *Beals*, despite the "strong, logical reasons" for applying the law of the donee's domicile in determining whether the donee properly exercised a testamentary power of appointment, the court looked instead to the law of the donor's domicile. Accord, N.Y. Est. Powers & Trusts Law §3-5.1(g)(2)(A) (2004). However, in White v. United States, 680 F.2d 1156 (7th Cir. 1982), the court held that the law of the donee's domicile governs issues concerning the donee's intention to exercise a power of appointment by will. The court said: "We recognize the special need for certainty and consistency in laws affecting trusts [citing *Beals*], but fail to see how that end is promoted by perpetuation of a legal fiction that confuses lawyers and laymen alike." Id. at 1160. See also Estate of McMullin, 417 A.2d 152 (Pa. 1980); Restatement (Second) of Conflict of Laws §275 (1971).

The lawyer drafting an instrument creating a power should consider whether it is wise to avoid possible conflict of laws problems by specifying in the trust instrument that the law of a particular state governs any question presented in connection with a power of appointment. If the power is created by an inter vivos trust, the donor may select the law of the domicile of the donor or the donee or of the state where the trust is administered. If the power is created by a testamentary trust, the states are split. Some states permit the donor's intention to control. Other states apply the law of the donor's domicile to a testamentary trust and do not permit the donor's intention to control.

For a meticulous examination of choice of law issues regarding powers of appointment, see 1 Jeffrey A. Schoenblum, Multistate and Multinational Estate Planning §17.08 (2d ed. 1999).

2. *Residuary clauses and testamentary powers of appointment*. Considerable disagreement exists over whether a residuary clause should presumptively exercise a general or special power of appointment. The large majority of jurisdictions takes the position that a residuary clause does *not* exercise a power of appointment held by the testator. States adhering to the majority rule differ on whether the search for a contrary intent is limited to the face of the will or may be aided by extrinsic evidence. Restatement (Second) of Property: Donative Transfers §17.3 (1986) presumes that a residuary clause does not exercise a power because "the donee does not own the property subject to the power" but permits use of a wide variety of extrinsic evidence to show a contrary intent.

In a minority of jurisdictions, a residuary clause exercises a general power of appointment unless a contrary intent affirmatively appears. In a few jurisdictions — New York is the leading example — a residuary clause exercises a special power of appointment if the residuary devisees are objects of the power. See Will of Block, 598 N.Y.S.2d 668 (Sur. 1993).

At the time of the *Beals* case, Massachusetts adhered to the minority rule, but, in 1978, Massachusetts changed to the majority rule. See Mass. Gen. Laws Ann. ch. 191, §1A(4) (2004). A number of other states that formerly adhered to the minority rule have in the recent past enacted statutes adopting the majority rule.

The positions of the various states are analyzed in detail in Susan F. French, Exercise of Powers of Appointment: Should Intent to Exercise Be Inferred from a General Disposition of Property?, 1979 Duke L.J. 749. See also Sheldon F. Kurtz, Powers of Appointment Under the 1990 Uniform Probate Code: What Was Done — What Remains to Be Done, 55 Alb. L. Rev. 1151, 1162-1172 (1992).

Uniform Probate Code (1990)

§2-608.   EXERCISE OF POWER OF APPOINTMENT

In the absence of a requirement that a power of appointment be exercised by a reference, or by an express or specific reference, to the power, a general residuary clause in a will, or a will making general disposition of all of the testator's property, expresses an intention to exercise a power of appointment held by the testator only if (i) the power is a general power and the creating instrument does not contain a gift if the power is not exercised or (ii) the testator's will manifests an intention to include the property subject to the power.

§2-704.   POWER OF APPOINTMENT; MEANING OF SPECIFIC
REFERENCE REQUIREMENT

If a governing instrument creating a power of appointment expressly requires that the power be exercised by a reference, an express reference, or a specific reference, to the power or its source, it is presumed that the donor's intention, in requiring that the donee exercise the power by making reference to the particular power or to the creating instrument, was to prevent an inadvertent exercise of the power.

NOTE AND PROBLEM

1.   To prevent an unintentional exercise of a power of appointment, the donor may provide that the power can be exercised only by an instrument, executed after the date of the creating instrument, that refers specifically to the power. Courts have been rather strict in requiring a "specific reference" to the creating document. Thus, where a wife was given a power of appointment by her husband's will executed in 1982, and her will specifically exercised a power given her in a similar will executed by her husband in 1966, since revoked, the court held the wife had not exercised the power created by her husband's 1982 will. Estate of Hamilton, 593 N.Y.S.2d 372 (App. Div. 1993).

Blending clauses. Suppose that the donee's residuary clause gives all her property "and all property over which I have a power of appointment" to *A*. Does this exercise the power under a specific reference requirement? The official comment to UPC §2-704 says that, under the section, the mere use of a blending clause (also called a "blanket-exercise clause") as in the above example is ineffective to exercise the power because it does not make a specific reference. However, if it could be shown by extrinsic evidence that the donee intended to exercise the power by a blending clause, the power would be exercised.

2.   *Lapse: Appointee dies before donee dies.* In the *Beals* case, the court held that the donee, Isabella, exercised her power in favor of the issue of her sister, Margaret Blake, who had predeceased Isabella. Suppose that Isabella's will had been executed during Margaret's lifetime, and Isabella had exercised the power by appointing to Margaret. If Margaret had predeceased Isabella, would Margaret's issue take the appointive property under the antilapse statute? See Thompson v. Pew, 102 N.E. 122 (Mass. 1913); Susan F. French, Application of Antilapse Statutes to Appointments Made by Will, 53 Wash. L. Rev. 405, 421-428 (1978).

Suppose that Isabella had a special power to appoint among her nephews and nieces and that she exercised the power by appointing to the issue of a niece who had predeceased her. What result? See French, supra, at 428-431. If Isabella could have appointed to the niece, with the issue of the niece taking the appointive property under the antilapse statute, why not permit Isabella to appoint directly to the issue? See Restatement (Second) of Property: Donative Transfers §18.6 (1986), providing that takers substituted by an antilapse statute are regarded as objects of the power.

Suppose that Isabella had a general testamentary power created by her husband's will and had appointed to her husband's nephew, who predeceased Isabella, leaving issue. Would the issue of the nephew take under the antilapse statute? See French, supra, at 417-421; Restatement (Second) of Property, supra, §18.6, cmt. b.

2. *Limitations on Exercise of a Special Power*

In almost all jurisdictions, a donee of a *general* power of appointment can appoint outright or in further trust and can create new powers of appointment. Because the donee of a general power could first appoint to himself or to his estate and then, by a second instrument or a second clause in his will, appoint in further trust, it would make little sense to forbid the donee to appoint in further trust when he uses only one piece of paper or one clause in his will.

With respect to a *special* power of appointment, the donee's authority is more limited. The donee of a special power may not be able to appoint in further trust, meaning that the donee would have to appoint the property outright to the objects of the power, unless the creating instrument expressly permits appointment to a trust for the benefit of the objects of the power. In some older cases, courts — influenced by the idea that the donee of a special power was a limited agent of the donor — read the donee's power narrowly. Without authorization, the donee could only select the persons among the designated class and determine the proportion each should take. These cases may still be viable in a few jurisdictions. See Loring v. Karri-Davies, 357 N.E.2d 11 (Mass. 1976), changing the rule prospectively to allow donees of special powers created after the date of the opinion to appoint in further trust.

A similar question is whether the donee can create a new power of appointment. For example, suppose T gives A a power to appoint among A's issue. Can A exercise the power by creating in his daughter B a life estate plus a special power to appoint among B's children (who are, of course, objects of the original power)? The answer clearly should be Yes; since A could appoint outright to B, there is no persuasive reason for refusing to permit A to appoint to B something less than absolute ownership. Yet the older cases are divided on this point. Some of them hold that the creation of a new power is an impermissible delegation of the special power. See 5 American Law of Property §23.49 (1952).

Restatement (Second) of Property: Donative Transfers §19.4 (1986) takes the position that the donee of a special power can create a general power in an object of the special power or create a special power in any person to appoint to an object of the original special power. The latter situation includes an appointment in further trust, giving the trustee discretionary power to appoint to the objects.

A special power may be exclusive or nonexclusive. If it is *exclusive*, the donee can exclude entirely one or more objects of the power. The donee can appoint all the property to one member of the class of permissible appointees, excluding the rest. If the power is *nonexclusive*, the donee must appoint some amount to each permissible object. Thus, suppose that *T* bequeaths a fund in trust for *A* for life, remainder as *A* shall appoint by will among his children. *A* has three children, *B*, *C*, and *D*. If the power is exclusive, *A* can appoint all the property to *C*. If the power is nonexclusive, *A* must give some amount each to *B*, *C*, and *D* if *A* exercises the power. You must readily see the great difficulty with nonexclusive powers: How much must the donee give each member of the class? Can *A* appoint $1 each to *B* and *D* and the remainder of the fund to *C*? Apparently, in a few states, the amount cannot be too small because of the "illusory appointment" rule requiring that each permissible appointee receive a "substantial" sum; in most states the illusory appointment rule has been repudiated. See 5 American Law of Property, supra, §23.58.

Whether a power is exclusive or nonexclusive depends upon the intention of the donor as revealed by the creating instrument. A power to appoint to *"any one or more of A's issue* in such amount or amounts and for such estates and interests and upon such conditions and limitations as *A* shall designate" would create an exclusive power. If the creating instrument does not reveal the donor's intent, classification will turn upon the presumption adhered to in the jurisdiction. Restatement (Second) of Property, supra, §21.1, provides that, in the absence of a contrary intent, special powers of appointment are presumptively exclusive. The problem, as well as the other possible limitations on the scope of the power mentioned above, can and should be avoided by proper drafting.

3.   Fraud on a Special Power

An appointment in favor of a person who is not an object of the power is invalid. An appointment to an object for the purpose of circumventing the limitation on the power is a "fraud on the power" and is void to the extent it is motivated by such purpose. See Restatement (Second) of Property: Donative Transfers §20.2 (1986).

PROBLEM

Elsa Milliken held a special testamentary power to appoint among her "kindred," and in default of appointment the property was to pass to Elsa's descendants or, if none, to the donor's heirs. Elsa, who had no issue, wanted to appoint $100,000 to her husband. She approached her cousin Paul Curtis and told him that she was going to leave him $150,000 and an additional $100,000, which she would like him to give to her husband. Paul said he would be happy to sign a paper to that effect. Elsa's attorney prepared a letter, directed to her and signed by Paul, which read: "I am informed that by your last will and testament you have given me and bequeathed to me the sum of Two Hundred and Fifty Thousand Dollars ($250,000). In the event that you should predecease me and I should receive the bequest before mentioned, I hereby promise and agree, in consideration of the said bequest, that I will pay to your husband, Foster Milliken, Jr., the sum of One Hundred Thousand Dollars ($100,000) out of the said bequest which you have given to me by your said will." Elsa died leaving a will appointing $250,000 to Paul. Is Paul entitled to $250,000, $150,000, or zero? See *In re Carroll's Will*, 8 N.E.2d 864 (N.Y. 1937).

4. Ineffective Exercise of a Power

When the donee intends to exercise a power of appointment, but the exercise is ineffective for some reason, it may be possible to carry out the donee's intent through the doctrines of allocation and of capture.

a. Allocation of Assets

The doctrine of *allocation* (also known as marshaling) applies when *appointive assets* and *assets owned by the donee* are disposed of under a common dispositive instrument (usually the donee's will). Its purpose is to try to allocate these assets to different provisions under the donee's will to give effect to the donee's intent when the appointive assets cannot go where the donee intended. Typical cases applying allocation involve an ineffective appointment to a nonobject of a power or an appointment that violates the Rule against Perpetuities. It is important to realize that, where assets are allocated by a court, the donee could have provided for the allocation in specific language and the court is merely doing what the donee would have done but for the ineptness of the donee's lawyer.

The doctrine of allocation is: If the donee *blends* both the appointive property and the donee's own property in a common disposition, the blended property is allocated to the various interests in such a way as to increase the effectiveness of the disposition. Restatement (Second) of Property: Donative Transfers §§22.1, 22.2 (1986). Thus:

> *Case 8.* A holds a special testamentary power created by her father to appoint trust property among A's issue. The trust assets are worth $100,000. A also owns outright $350,000. A's will provides:
>
> > I give all my property, including any property over which I have a power of appointment, as follows:
> >
> > 1. I give $100,000 to my daughter-in-law, B, widow of my deceased son, S.
> > 2. I give all the rest to my daughter, D.
>
> Since B is not an object of the special power, the trust assets cannot be allocated to her. They will be allocated to D, and $100,000 of A's owned assets will be allocated to B.

If, in Case 8, A had owned assets of only $50,000, B would receive only $50,000 because the trust assets cannot be allocated to B. Hence, to satisfy completely the ineffective appointment, allocation requires that the donee have property of her own sufficient to substitute for the appointive property.

The blending requirement of the doctrine of allocation is met in Case 8 by the introductory clause of *A*'s will. The blending requirement may also be met by a residuary clause disposing of both appointive property and owned property. Suppose that, in Case 8, there had been no introductory clause, and *A* had bequeathed the appointive property to *B* and her own property to *D*. Since *A* did not blend the property but specifically bequeathed the appointive property to *B*, the appointment would fail, and none of *A*'s owned assets would be allocated to *B*. See Restatement (Second) of Property, supra, §22.1, cmt. g.

b. Capture

If the donee of a power makes an ineffective appointment, and the donee's intent cannot be given effect through allocation of assets, to whom does the appointive property pass? The general rule is that the property passes in default of appointment or, if there is no gift in default, to the donor's estate. To this rule is one important exception: the doctrine of *capture*, which captures the property for the donee's estate.

Capture occurs when the donee of a *general* power "manifests an intent to assume control of the appointive property for all purposes and not merely for the limited purpose of giving effect to the expressed appointment." Restatement (Second) of Property, supra, §23.2. The doctrine of capture rests upon the conception that, inasmuch as the donee of a general power could appoint to her estate, the appointive property will pass to her estate if she would prefer that in case of an ineffective appointment. Ineffective appointments raising the issue of whether capture applies usually involve lapse of an appointment to a dead appointee, or a violation of the Rule against Perpetuities, or failure of the donee to comply with some prescribed formality in exercising the power.

The intent of the donee to assume control of the appointive property for all purposes is most commonly manifested by provisions in the donee's will that *blend* the owned property of the donee with the appointive property. As with the doctrine of allocation, the requisite blending can occur in a residuary clause disposing of both the appointive property and the donee's own assets or in an introductory clause stating that the donee intends the appointive property to be treated as her own property. Thus:

> *Case 9.* *A* is donee of a general power. *A*'s will provides:
>
> I give all my property and any property over which I have a power of appointment as follows:
>
> 1. $10,000 to my friend *B* [who predeceases *A*, and no antilapse statute applies].
> 2. $15,000 in trust for my dog Trixie [which violates the Rule against Perpetuities and fails also for lack of an ascertainable beneficiary (dogs are not valid beneficiaries)].
> 3. All the rest to *C*.
>
> *A* has captured the appointive property by blending it with her own. *C* takes everything, including the appointive property.

Capture applies only to general powers and only when the attempted exercise of the general power is ineffective or incomplete.

SECTION E. FAILURE TO EXERCISE A POWER OF APPOINTMENT

If the donee of a *general* power fails to exercise it, the appointive property passes in default of appointment. If there is no gift in default of appointment, the property reverts to the donor's estate. If the donee of a *special* power fails to exercise it, and there is no gift in default of appointment, the appointive property may — if the objects are a defined limited class — pass to the objects of the power.

Loring v. Marshall

Supreme Judicial Court of Massachusetts, 1985
396 Mass. 166, 484 N.E.2d 1315

WILKINS, J.   This complaint, here on a reservation and report by a single justice of this court, seeks instructions as to the disposition of the remainder of a trust created under the will of Marian Hovey. In Massachusetts Inst. of Technology v. Loring, 99 N.E.2d 854 (Mass. 1951), this court held that the President and Fellows of Harvard College, the Boston Museum of Fine Arts, and Massachusetts Institute of Technology (the charities) would not be entitled to the remainder of the trust on its termination. The court, however, did not decide, as we now must, what ultimate disposition should be made of the trust principal.

Marian Hovey died in 1898, survived by a brother, Henry S. Hovey, a sister, Fanny H. Morse, and two nephews, John Torrey Morse, Third, and Cabot Jackson Morse. By her will, Marian Hovey left the residue of her estate in trust, the income payable in equal shares to her brother and sister during their lives. Upon her brother's death in 1900, his share of the income passed to her sister, and, upon her sister's death in 1922, the income was paid in equal shares to her two nephews. John Torrey Morse, Third, died in 1928, unmarried and without issue. His share of the income then passed to his brother, Cabot Jackson Morse, who remained the sole income beneficiary until his death in 1946.

At that point, the death of the last surviving income beneficiary, Marian Hovey's will provided for the treatment of the trust assets in the following language:

> At the death of the last survivor of my said brother and sister and my two said nephews, or at my death, if none of them be then living, the trustees shall divide the trust fund in their hands into two equal parts, and shall transfer and pay over one of such parts to the use of the wife and issue of each of my said nephews as he may by will have appointed; provided, that if his wife was living at my death he shall appoint to her no larger interest in the property possessed by me than a right to the income during her life, and if she was living at the death of my father, he shall appoint to her no larger interest in the property over which I have a power of disposition under the will of my father than a right to the income during her life; and the same limitations shall apply to the appointment of income as aforesaid. If either of my said nephews shall leave no such appointees then living, the whole of the trust fund shall be paid to the appointees of his said brother as aforesaid. If neither of my said nephews leave such appointees then living the whole trust fund shall be paid over and transferred in equal shares to the Boston Museum of Fine Arts, the Massachusetts Institute of Technology, and the President and Fellows of Harvard College for the benefit of

the Medical School; provided, that if the said Medical School shall not then admit women to instruction on an equal footing with men, the said President and Fellows shall not receive any part of the trust property, but it shall be divided equally between the Boston Museum of Fine Arts and the Massachusetts Institute of Technology.[17]

The will thus gave Cabot Jackson Morse, the surviving nephew, a special power to appoint the trust principal to his "wife and issue" with the limitation that only income could be appointed to a widow who was living at Marian Hovey's death.[18] Cabot Jackson Morse was survived by his wife, Anna Braden Morse, who was living at Marian Hovey's death, and by his only child, Cabot Jackson Morse, Jr., a child of an earlier marriage, who died in 1948, two years after his father. Cabot Jackson Morse left a will which contained the following provisions:

> *Second:* I give to my son, Cabot Jackson Morse, Jr., the sum of one dollar ($1.00), as he is otherwise amply provided for.
>
> *Third:* The power of appointment which I have under the wills of my aunt, Marian Hovey, and my uncle, Henry S. Hovey, both late of Gloucester, Massachusetts, I exercise as follows: I appoint to my wife, Anna Braden Morse, the right to the income during her lifetime of all of the property to which my power of appointment applies under the will of Marian Hovey, and I appoint to my wife the right during her widowhood to the income to which I would be entitled under the will of Henry S. Hovey if I were living.
>
> *Fourth:* All the rest, residue and remainder of my estate, wherever situated, real or personal, in trust or otherwise, I leave outright and in fee simple to my wife, Anna Braden Morse.

In Welch v. Morse, 81 N.E.2d 361 (Mass. 1948), we held that the appointment of a life interest to Anna Braden Morse was valid, notwithstanding Cabot Jackson Morse's failure fully to exercise the power by appointing the trust principal. Consequently, the trust income following Cabot Jackson Morse's death was paid to Anna Braden Morse until her death in 1983, when the principal became distributable. The trustees thereupon brought this complaint for instructions.

The complaint alleges that the trustees

> are uncertain as to who is entitled to the remainder of the Marian Hovey Trust now that the trust is distributable and specifically whether the trust principal should be paid in any one of the following manners: (a) to the estate of Cabot Jackson Morse, Jr. as the only permissible appointee of the remainder of the trust living at the death of Cabot Jackson Morse; (b) in equal shares to the estates of Cabot Jackson Morse, Jr. and Anna Braden Morse as the only permissible appointees living at the death of Cabot Jackson Morse; (c) to the estate of Anna Braden Morse as the only actual appointee living at the death of Cabot Jackson Morse; (d) to the intestate takers of Marian

---

17. The parties have stipulated that at the relevant time the Harvard Medical School admitted women to instruction on an equal footing with men. [Women were permitted to attend Harvard Medical School beginning on September 26, 1944. N.Y. Times, Sept. 26, 1944, at 20. This amounts to something of a posthumous triumph for Marian Hovey, who in 1878 had offered Harvard a $10,000 endowment on the condition that it admit women to the medical school. Harvard demurred. — Eds.]

18. We are concerned here only with "property possessed" by the testatrix at her death and not property over which she had "a power of disposition under the will of [her] father." That property was given outright to his widow under the residuary clause of the will of Cabot Jackson Morse.

Hovey's estate on the basis that Marian Hovey failed to make a complete disposition of her property by her will; (e) to Massachusetts Institute of Technology, Museum of Fine Arts and the President and Fellows of Harvard College in equal shares as remaindermen of the trust; or (f) some other disposition.

Before us each named potential taker claims to be entitled to trust principal.

In our 1951 opinion, Massachusetts Inst. of Technology v. Loring, 99 N.E.2d 854, we explained why in the circumstances the charities had no interest in the trust:

> The rights of the petitioning charities as remaindermen depend upon the proposition that Cabot J. Morse, Senior, did not leave an "appointee" although he appointed his wife Anna Braden Morse to receive the income during her life. The time when, if at all, the "whole trust fund" was to be paid over and transferred to the petitioning charities is the time of the death of Cabot J. Morse, Senior. At that time the whole trust fund could not be paid over and transferred to the petitioning charities, because Anna Braden Morse still retained the income for her life. We think that the phrase no "such appointees then living" is not the equivalent of an express gift in default of appointment, a phrase used by the testatrix in the preceding paragraph.

In Frye v. Loring, 113 N.E.2d 595 (Mass. 1953), the court reiterated that the charities had no interest in the trust fund.

It is apparent that Marian Hovey knew how to refer to a disposition in default of appointment from her use of the terms elsewhere in her will. She did not use those words in describing the potential gift to the charities. A fair reading of the will's crucial language may rightly be that the charities were not to take the principal unless no class member who could receive principal was then living (i.e., if no possible appointee of principal was living at the death of the surviving donee). Regardless of how the words "no such appointees then living" are construed, the express circumstances under which the charities were to take did not occur. The question is what disposition should be made of the principal in the absence of any explicit direction in the will.

Although in its 1951 opinion this court disavowed making a determination of the "ultimate destination of the trust fund," the opinion cited the Restatement of Property §367(2) (1940), and 1 A. Scott, Trusts §27.1 (1st ed. 1939) to the effect that, when a special power of appointment is not exercised and absent specific language indicating an express gift in default of appointment, the property not appointed goes in equal shares to the members of the class to whom the property could have been appointed. . . . [S]ee 5 American Law of Property §23.63, at 645 (A.J. Casner ed. 1952 & Supp. 1962) ("The fact that the donee has failed to apportion the property within the class should not defeat the donor's intent to benefit the class").

Applying this rule of law, we find no specific language in the will which indicates a gift in default of appointment in the event Cabot Jackson Morse should fail to appoint the principal. The charities argue that the will's reference to them suggests that in default of appointment Marian Hovey intended them to take. On the other hand, in Welch v. Morse, 81 N.E.2d 361, we commented that Marian Hovey's "will discloses an intent to keep her property in the family." The interests Marian Hovey gave to her sister and brother were life interests, as were the interests given to her nephews. The share of any nephew who died unmarried and without issue, as did one, was added to the share of the other nephew. Each nephew was limited to exercising his power of appointment only in favor of his issue and his widow.[19] We think the apparent intent to keep the assets within the family is sufficiently strong to overcome any claim that Marian Hovey's will "expressly" or "in specific language" provides for a gift to the charities in default of appointment.[20] . . .

[The charities argued that the principle of res judicata was not applicable because the attorney general, the supervisor of public charities, was not a party to Massachusetts Inst. of Technology v. Loring, 99 N.E.2d 854 (Mass. 1951). The court rejected this argument and held that "the public interest in protecting the charities' rights was fully accommodated by the Justices of this court in its prior decision."]

What we have said disposes of the claim that the trust principal should pass to Marian Hovey's heirs as intestate property, a result generally disfavored in the interpretation of testamentary dispositions. . . . The claim of the executors of the estate of Anna Braden Morse that her estate should take as the class, or at least as a member of the class, must fail because Marian Hovey's will specifically limits such a widow's potential stake to a life interest.

A judgment shall be entered instructing the trustees under the will of Marian Hovey to distribute the trust principal to the executors of the estate of Cabot Jackson Morse, Jr. The allowance of counsel fees, costs, and expenses from the principal of the trust is to be in the discretion of the single justice.

So ordered.

PROBLEM AND NOTE

1.   The theory of the court in Loring v. Marshall was that there was an implied gift in default of appointment to the potential appointees. This theory is adopted by Restatement (Second) of Property: Donative Transfers §24.2 (1986).

Another way of solving the problem in the case is to say that Cabot Jackson Morse had an *imperative* special power of appointment. A special power is imperative when the creating instrument manifests an intent that the permissible appointees be benefited even if the donee fails to exercise the power. If a special power is imperative, the donee must exercise it or the court will divide the assets equally among the potential appointees. The term *imperative power* is used in Cal. Prob. Code §613 (2004) and N.Y. Est. Powers & Trusts Law §10-3.4 (2004).

In most cases it is not likely to make any difference whether a court adopts an implied gift in default theory or an imperative power theory. The same result is ordinarily reached under both because both are based on the inferred intent of the

---

19. The gift to any widow was to be a life interest if she were living at Marian Hovey's death.

20. The nominal distribution made to his son in the donee's will provides no proper guide to the resolution of the issues in this case. We are concerned here with the intention of Marian Hovey, the donor of the special power of appointment. The intentions of the donee of the power of appointment are irrelevant in constructing the donor's intent. Similarly, those who rely on language in Frye v. Loring, 113 N.E.2d 595 (Mass. 1953), as instructive in resolving questions in this case miss the point that Cabot Jackson Morse's intention with regard to his exercise of the power of appointment is irrelevant in determining his aunt's intention concerning the consequences of his partial failure to exercise that power.

donor. But in a few situations, the theory followed may make a difference. Consider Bridgewater v. Turner, 29 S.W.2d 659 (Tenn. 1930). The testator's will provided:

> I bequeath to Eliza V. Seay during her life that portion of the old home tract and household furniture etc., which lies between the Trousdale Ferry turnpike road and the creek of Round Lick and Jennings Fork, and, at her death I desire it to go to one of my nephews and I leave it with her to decide which one it shall be. . . . It is my desire that the above described tract shall remain in the hands of the family as long as possible, for here sleeps my wife, my father and mother.

At the testator's death, he had four nephews, W.S., John C., W.R., and Richard. Richard died before the life tenant, Eliza, leaving as his heirs two children, Elizabeth and Carr. Eliza died without exercising her power of appointment. Who owns the old home tract? Cf. Waterman v. New York Life Ins. & Tr. Co., 142 N.E. 668 (N.Y. 1923). If Elizabeth and Carr now share in ownership, could Eliza have appointed the old home tract to Elizabeth?

2.   Suppose that the failure to exercise a testamentary power of appointment is the result of inadvertence or sloppy drafting. Should courts correct such mistakes? In 1982, Evelyn Anderson executed a will that exercised a testamentary power of appointment over a trust created by her deceased husband. In 1993, Evelyn executed a second will that expressly revoked all prior wills and that inadvertently failed to exercise the power of appointment. Extrinsic evidence showed that if the power of appointment were not exercised, Evelyn's estate plan would not be carried out. The court held that the doctrine of dependent relative revocation could be used to probate the 1993 will and the portion of the 1982 will exercising the power of appointment. Estate of Anderson, 65 Cal. Rptr. 2d 307 (App. 1997). See also In re Strobel, 717 P.2d 892 (Ariz. 1986).

10

CONSTRUCTION OF TRUSTS: FUTURE INTERESTS

SECTION A. INTRODUCTION

Today future interests arise primarily in the context of trust settlements. Whenever a life estate is given, a future interest is also created: Someone is going to take the property upon the termination of the life estate. Hence, the attorney drafting trusts must be familiar with the types of future interests that can be employed and with constructional and other problems with their use.

The basic conceptual idea underlying the law of future interests is that future interests are thought of as "things."[1] In your course in property, you were introduced to the reification of abstractions, particularly the fee simple. Now, when you think of a fee simple, your mind's eye undoubtedly sees it as a thing, and you probably speak of a fee simple as a *bundle* of rights. Indeed, once you have been introduced to property law, it is hard not to think of a fee simple in any way but as a thing: The owner may transfer *it*, creditors may seize *it*, *it* passes on death, and so forth. Future interests are reified in the same manner.

So now we take a look at the law of future interests, for they are the stuff of which the dispositive provisions of trusts are made. We seek to help you gain an understanding of how future interests can be created and precisely tailored to the settlor's intent with respect to future events. You must be able to identify, so that you can avoid, intent-defeating technical rules of future interests law still with us, as well as commonly encountered examples of ambiguous language.

It is written in Psalms 39:6: "Surely every man walketh in a vain shew: . . . he heapeth up riches and knoweth not who shall gather them." When you are admitted to the bar, let not these words of David be said of your clients.

---

1. Compare the White King speaking to Alice about the two Messengers:

"... And I haven't sent the two Messengers, either. They're both gone to the town. Just look along the road and tell me if you see either of them."

"I see nobody on the road," said Alice.

"I only wish *I* had such eyes," the King remarked in a fretful tone. "To be able to see Nobody! And at that distance too! Why, it's as much as *I* can do to see real people, by this light!" [Lewis Carroll, Through the Looking-Glass, ch. 7.]

SECTION B.   CLASSIFICATION OF FUTURE INTERESTS

1.   *Types of Future Interests*

Future interests recognized by our legal system are:

1. Interests in the transferor known as:
   a. Reversion
   b. Possibility of reverter
   c. Right of entry (also known as power of termination)
2. Interests in a transferee known as:
   a. Vested remainder
   b. Contingent remainder
   c. Executory interest

All future interests in property must be placed in one of the above categories. For a stimulating argument in favor of eliminating this mandatory taxonomy, and a proposed Uniform Future Interests Act that would do so, see T.P. Gallanis, The Future of Future Interests, 60 Wash. & Lee L. Rev. 513 (2003).

These interests are called *future interests* because the person who holds one of them is not entitled to present possession or enjoyment of the property but may or will become entitled to possession in the future. However, future interests are presently existing interests. A person who has a future interest has present rights and liabilities. Take this case: *O* conveys "to *A* for life, then to *B*." *B* has a remainder, which *B* can sell or give away. *B*'s creditors can reach it. *B* can enjoin *A* from committing waste or doing other acts that impair the value of *B*'s right to future possession. If *B* dies before *A*, the value of *B*'s remainder is subject to federal estate taxation. But because *B* does not have perhaps the most important right in the bundle — the right to present possession — we call *B*'s interest a "future interest."

Any estate that may be created in possession, such as a fee simple or a life estate, may be created as a future interest. Hence, *O* may convey "to *A* for life, then to *B* for life, then to *C*." *B* has a remainder for life, and *C* has a remainder in fee simple. By saying that *C* has a remainder in fee simple, we mean that when *C*'s remainder becomes possessory it will be a fee simple.

2.   *Future Interests in the Transferor*

a.   **Reversion**

There are three types of future interests that may be retained by the transferor: reversion, possibility of reverter, and right of entry for condition broken. By far the most important of these is the *reversion*. "A reversion is the interest remaining in the grantor, or in the successor in interest of a testator, who transfers a vested estate of a lesser quantum than that of the vested estate which he has." 1 American Law of Property §4.16 (1952). A reversion is never created; it is a retained interest that arises by operation of law when the transferor has conveyed away a lesser estate than the transferor had. If a reversion is retained in an inter vivos conveyance, it is retained by the grantor. If a reversion is retained by a will, it is retained in the testator's heirs who are substituted by law for the dead transferor.

A reversion cannot be created in a transferee. If by deed or will a future interest is created in a transferee, the future interest must be given one of the labels that we give to future interests in transferees: It is either a remainder or an executory interest.

PROBLEM

T's will devises Blackacre to *A* for life, and the residue of *T*'s property to *B*. What interest does *B* have in Blackacre?

Reversions are thought of as part of the transferor's old estate: what the transferor retained when he conveyed away less than he had. Hence, all reversions are *vested* interests. The fact that all reversions are vested does not mean, however, that all reversions will become possessory. A reversion following a contingent remainder, for instance, may not become possessory. Thus:

> *Case 1. O* conveys property in trust "for *A* for life, then to *A*'s children who survive *A*." *A*'s children have a contingent remainder. *O* has a *vested reversion*, which will be divested if *A* leaves surviving children. (*Warning:* Do not call *O*'s interest a contingent reversion or a possibility of reversion as there are no such interests known to law. If you use the latter term, you may end up confusing a reversion with a *possibility of reverter*, an entirely different interest. Call the interest by its correct name.)

Case 1 illustrates that the concept of a future interest *vested in interest* — so important in future interests law — has nothing to do with whether the future interest will necessarily become possessory. The reversion in Case 1, vested in interest, may not become possessory. Future interests are deemed vested or not by arbitrary rules of the common law, not by the certainty or uncertainty of future possession.

b. Possibility of Reverter; Right of Entry

A *possibility of reverter* is the future interest that remains in the grantor who conveys a fee simple determinable. For example, *O* conveys "to School Board so long as used for a school." The School Board has a fee simple determinable; *O* has a possibility of reverter, which becomes possessory automatically upon expiration of the determinable fee.

A *right of entry* for condition broken is the future interest that is retained by the grantor who conveys a fee simple subject to a condition subsequent. For example, *O* conveys "to School Board, but if the land ceases to be used for school purposes, *O* has a right to reenter." The School Board has a fee simple subject to condition subsequent; *O* has a right of entry, which *O* has the option to exercise or not.

Possibilities of reverter and rights of entry are almost never encountered in a trust. They are typically retained to control the use of land and are covered in the basic course in property.

3. *Future Interests in Transferees*

There are three types of future interests in transferees: vested remainders, contingent remainders, and executory interests.

a.   **Remainders**

A *remainder* is a future interest in a transferee that will become possessory, if at all, upon the expiration of all prior interests simultaneously created. A remainderman waits patiently until the preceding estates expire, and then, if the remainder is not contingent, the remainderman is entitled to possession. To be a remainder, it must only be possible, not necessarily certain, that the future interest will become possessory upon the termination of the preceding estates. Thus:

> *Case 2.* O conveys a fund in trust "for A for life, then to B." B has a remainder which will certainly become possessory upon the expiration of A's life estate. Because it is certain to become possessory, we call it an *indefeasibly vested remainder*. If B dies during A's life, B's remainder, like B's other property, passes under B's will or by intestacy to B's heirs. If B leaves neither a will nor heirs, the remainder escheats to the state, and the state is entitled to the property upon A's death.
>
> *Case 3.* O conveys a fund in trust "for A for life, then to B if B survives A." B has a remainder, for it is possible (but not certain) that B will take the property upon A's death. If B is then alive, B will take, and if B is then dead, the property will revert to O. B has a *contingent remainder*.

Remainders are either vested or contingent. A remainder is vested if (1) it is given to a presently ascertained person and (2) it is not subject to a condition precedent (other than the termination of the preceding estates). A remainder is contingent if (1) it is not given to a presently ascertained person or (2) it is subject to a condition precedent. In Case 3, B's remainder is contingent because it is subject to the condition precedent of surviving A.

Suppose a remainder is given to a class of persons, some but not all of whom are ascertained, and the remainder is not subject to a condition precedent. This remainder is vested in the present members of the class subject to partial divestment by additional persons coming into the class. Thus:

> *Case 4.* O conveys a fund in trust "for A for life, then to A's children." If A has no children at the time of the conveyance, the remainder is contingent because the takers are unascertained. On the other hand, if A has a child (let's call her B), B has a *vested remainder subject to partial divestment* (sometimes called a *vested remainder subject to open*). If A has any more children, B's share will be diminished. The amount of B's share will depend on how many children, if any, are subsequently born to A. If A has another child born (let's call her C), B is partially divested, that is, divested of C's share. The class gift will remain subject to partial divestment (or open) until A's death.

A class gift is not vested subject to partial divestment if it is subject to a condition precedent. In Case 4, if the conveyance had been "to *A* for life, then to *A*'s children who survive *A*," the remainder would be contingent even though *A* had one or more children alive.

Where a remainder is given to a class of persons described as "the heirs of *A* (a living person)," the takers are not ascertained until *A*'s death.

PROBLEMS

1. *O* conveys a fund in trust "for *A* for life, and on *A*'s death to *A*'s children in equal shares." At the time of the conveyance, *A* has two children, *B* and *C*. Two years later, *D* is born to *A*. A year after that, *B* dies intestate and then *A* dies. To whom should the trust assets be distributed? See In re DiBiasio, 705 A.2d 972 (R.I. 1997); Coleman v. Coleman, 500 S.E.2d 507 (Va. 1998).

2. In 1999 *O* conveys property in trust "for *A* for life, and on *A*'s death to the heirs of *B*." At the time of the conveyance, *A* and *B* are both alive and *B* has two children, *C* and *D*. If *B* were to die intestate immediately after the conveyance, *C* and *D* would be *B*'s heirs. In 2000, *D* dies, leaving a minor son, *E*, and a will devising all his property to his wife, *W*. In 2002, *B* dies, leaving a will that devises *B*'s entire estate to the American Red Cross. *A* dies in 2004; *A* is survived by *C*, *E*, and *W*. To whom should the trust assets be distributed? What would be the result if *B* had died before *D*?

Now we must speak of the difference between a *remainder vested subject to divestment* and a *contingent remainder*. This is a fundamental distinction in the law of future interests. A remainder vested subject to divestment is a remainder given to an ascertained person, with a proviso that the remainder will be divested if a *condition subsequent* happens. It is not subject to a condition precedent. Whether a remainder is contingent or vested subject to divestment depends solely upon the language of the instrument. And, with few exceptions, it depends upon *the sequence of words in the instrument*. Interests are classified in sequence as they are written in the instrument. If a condition is incorporated into the gift of the remainder — if it comes, so to speak, between the commas setting apart the remainder — the condition is a condition precedent. But if the remainder is given, and then words of divestment are added, the condition is subsequent. This distinction is best seen by examples.

> *Case 5.* *O* conveys a fund in trust "for *A* for life, then to *B* if *B* survives *A*, and if *B* does not survive *A*, to *C*." *B* has a contingent remainder because the words "if *B* survives *A*" are incorporated into *B*'s gift; they come between the commas. (Of course, if the commas were not there, you would have to decide where the court would mentally insert the commas. The essential idea to grasp is that the words "if *B* survives *A*" are part of the gift to *B*.) *C* has an alternative contingent remainder.
>
> *Case 6.* *O* conveys a fund in trust "for *A* for life, then to *B*, but if *B* does not survive *A*, to *C*." *B* has a vested remainder subject to divestment by *C*'s executory interest. Between the commas setting off *B*'s gift there are no words of condition. There is a condition subsequent to *B*'s gift introducing the divesting gift over to *C*.

As Cases 5 and 6 illustrate, you must look very carefully at the exact language used and classify the interests in sequence. *O*'s intent may be identical in those two cases, but it has been expressed in different ways, resulting in different interests being created. As you can see, much turns on careful drafting.

Let us now return briefly to the subject of reversions, so that you may see how reversions interrelate with vested remainders and contingent remainders. To determine when a transferor has a reversion, you can save yourself much trouble if you will memorize this simple Rule of Reversions:

> *O*, owner of a fee simple, will not have a reversion in fee simple if *O* transfers a possessory fee simple or a vested remainder in fee simple; in all other cases where *O* transfers a present possessory interest, *O* will have a reversion in fee simple.

Hence, whenever *O* transfers a life estate, not followed by a vested remainder in fee, *O* has a reversion. If *O* transfers a life estate followed by 100 contingent remainders in fee, but no vested remainder in fee, *O* retains a reversion.

You will see why this rule operates if you consider a reversion a shorthand way of saying that when a vested estate of the same duration is not transferred, "there is either a certainty or a possibility that the right to possession will return to the grantor." Thus when the owner of a fee simple carves out a lesser estate and does not add a vested remainder in fee simple, there is a possibility that the property will be his again.

PROBLEMS

1. *O* conveys Blackacre "to *A* for life, then to *B* if *B* survives *A*, and if *B* does not survive *A*, to *C*." Does *O* have a reversion? Yes. But how is it possible for Blackacre to return to *O*? At common law, the answer was easy: A life estate could terminate prior to the death of the life tenant if the life tenant were convicted of a felony or committed a tortious feoffment. But in the United States, forfeiture on these grounds has been abolished. Can you think of any way for Blackacre to return to *O*? See Jesse Dukeminier, Perpetuities: The Measuring Lives, 85 Colum. L. Rev. 1648, 1690-1692 (1985).

2. *O* conveys property in trust "for *A* for life, then to *B*, but if *B* dies before *A* without issue surviving *B*, then to *C* at *A*'s death." Does *O* have a reversion? Suppose that *B* dies leaving a surviving child, *D; B*'s will devises all her property to her husband, *H*. Then *D* dies. Then *A* dies. To whom should the trust property be distributed?

3. *O* conveys Blackacre in trust "for *A* for life, then to *B* or her heirs." Subsequently *B* dies, devising her property to *C. B*'s heir is *D*. Upon *A*'s death, who owns Blackacre? See Rowett v. McFarland, 394 N.W.2d 298 (S.D. 1986).

b. Executory Interests

An executory interest differs from a remainder in that it is a *divesting* interest. A remainder never divests a preceding estate prior to its expiration; that is the job of an executory interest. An executory interest that may divest another *transferee* if a specified event happens is called a *shifting* executory interest because, if the event happens, the executory interest will shift the property from one transferee to another transferee. In Case 6 above, *C* has a shifting executory interest. An executory interest that may divest the *transferor* in the future if a specified event happens is called a *springing* executory interest because, if the event happens, the property will spring out from the transferor to the transferee. An old example of a springing executory interest at early common law was a marriage arrangement whereby the father of the bride would convey land "to my daughter *A* when she marries *B*." Springing executory interests are rare today.

Executory interests are future interests that would have been enforced by the court of chancery, but not by the law courts, before the Statute of Uses in 1536. The Statute of Uses converted these interests, previously valid only in equity, into legal interests. For an extended treatment of the history of executory interests, see Jesse Dukeminier & James E. Krier, Property 278-286 (5th ed. 2002).

Executory interests are almost always created in one of two basic forms. These are illustrated by Cases 7 and 8.

> *Case 7. Executory interest divesting a possessory fee simple upon an uncertain event. O* conveys Blackacre "to *A*, but if *A* dies at any time without issue surviving her, to *B*." *A* has a fee simple subject to divestment by *B*'s shifting executory interest. *B*'s executory interest is subject to a condition precedent (*A*'s death without surviving issue) and is not certain to become possessory.

Another example of an executory interest divesting a possessory fee simple is a conveyance by *O* "to *B* if *B* returns from Rome." This gives *B* a springing executory interest divesting the transferor, *O*, rather than a transferee.

More common than Case 7 is Case 8:

> *Case 8. Executory interest divesting a vested remainder. O* conveys a fund in trust "for *A* for life, and on *A*'s death to *B*, but if *B* is not then living, to *C*." *B* has a vested remainder in fee simple subject to divestment by *C*'s shifting executory interest. *C*'s executory interest is subject to a condition precedent (*B* dying before *A* dies) and is not certain to become possessory.

The executory interests in Cases 7 and 8 are analogous to contingent remainders. They are not called contingent remainders because they are divesting interests. However, in almost all situations today, executory interests are treated the same as contingent remainders.

PROBLEMS AND NOTE

1. (a) *O* conveys a fund in trust "for *A* for life, then to *A*'s children, but if at *A*'s death *A* is not survived by any children, then to *B*." At the time the trust is created, *A* has no children. What interests are created?

(b) Consider the same facts as in Problem 1(a). A few years later, two children, *C* and *D*, are born to *A*. *C* dies, devising his property to his wife, *W*. *A* dies. To whom should the trust assets be distributed?

2. *O* conveys a fund in trust "for *A* for life, then to such of *A*'s children as survive *A*, but if none of *A*'s children survive *A*, then to *B*." At the time the trust is created,

A has two children, *C* and *D*. Then *C* dies, devising his property to his wife, *W*. *A* dies. To whom should the trust assets be distributed?

3. *T* devises Blackacre to *A* for life, then to *A*'s children who survive her. The residuary clause of *T*'s will devises to *B* "all the rest and residue of my property, including any of the foregoing gifts in this will which for any reason fail to take effect." What is the state of the title to Blackacre? See Wythe Holt, The Testator Who Gave Away Less Than All He or She Had: Perversions in the Law of Future Interests, 32 Ala. L. Rev. 69 (1980).

4. *Remainders in default of appointment.* Exercise of a power of appointment is viewed as operating as a condition subsequent on the remainder in default of appointment. If the donee exercises the power, the remainderman is deprived of his interest. Thus, suppose that *T* devises property in trust "for *A* for life, then to such persons as *A* by will appoints, and in default of appointment, to *A*'s children." Because the power is treated as a condition subsequent, this devise is read as if it were "for *A* for life, then to *A*'s children, but if *A* otherwise appoints by will, to such appointees." Assume *A* has one child, *B*. *B* has a vested remainder subject to partial divestment by the birth of other children and also subject to complete divestment by *A*'s exercise of the power of appointment. If *A* has no children, the remainder is contingent because the takers are not ascertained.

SECTION C. CONSTRUCTION OF TRUST INSTRUMENTS

The title of this section is a play on words. A court construes an instrument in order to construct an estate plan. In the process, rules of construction are developed. These rules of construction must be heeded by lawyers in constructing their clients' estate plans.

This section has two purposes. One is to teach the techniques and rules courts have developed in construing instruments. The second, and more important, is to explore the ambiguities lying hidden in common provisions in wills and trusts. The second is more important because only by training in spotting ambiguities, and in foreseeing everything that may happen to the people involved, can you develop the ability to draft an air-tight instrument.

For an analytical examination of construction problems along a lineal time progression, see Raymond C. O'Brien, Analytical Principle: A Guide for Lapse, Survivorship, Death Without Issue, and the Rule, 10 Geo. Mason U.L. Rev. 383 (1988).

1. Preference for Vested Interests

The common law had a strong preference for construing ambiguous instruments as creating a vested rather than a contingent remainder. As Sir Edward Coke said, "the law always delights in vesting of estates, and contingencies are odious in the law, and are the causes of troubles, and vesting and settling of estates, the cause of repose and certainty." Roberts v. Roberts, 80 Eng. Rep. 1002, 1009 (K.B. 1613). This preference arose in feudal England at a time when contingent interests were barely recognized as interests, and it continued to modern times because of the allegedly desirable consequences of a vested construction. These consequences were:

1. A vested remainder was not subject to the doctrine of *destructibility of contingent remainders* that defeated the grantor's intent. This doctrine provided that a *legal* contingent remainder in *land* was destroyed if it did not vest at or before the termination of the preceding freehold estate. The doctrine is a "feudal relic" that, except possibly in Florida, Mississippi, Missouri, and New Mexico, is no longer good law. T.P. Gallanis, The Future of Future Interests, 60 Wash. & Lee L. Rev. 513, 530-534 (2003) (collecting authority).

2. A vested remainder *accelerated* into possession upon termination of the life estate, solving vexing problems of possession and undisposed income (see below).

3. A vested remainder was *transferable inter vivos*, making land more alienable (see page 636).

4. A vested remainder was not subject to the *Rule against Perpetuities*, a rule that defeats the grantor's intent (see Chapter 11).

In addition to the different consequences at common law attendant upon a vested or contingent classification, a new problem has arisen in modern times. In many states, *upon divorce*, a court makes an equitable distribution of a couple's "property" including inherited property. The question thus arises, is a vested remainder or a contingent remainder in a trust created by the husband's mother property of the husband that is subject to equitable division? The courts appear to agree that an indefeasibly vested remainder is the husband's property and can be valued in accordance with life expectancy tables (see page 637). On the other hand, a vested remainder subject to divestment if the husband does not survive the life tenant or a remainder contingent upon surviving the life tenant is not the husband's property for purposes of equitable distribution. If the divesting event or contingency is something other than surviving the life tenant, the courts appear to struggle with the vested-contingent dichotomy with varying results. See In re Balanson, 25 P.3d 28 (Colo. 2001); In re Marriage of Beadle, 268 P.2d 698 (Mont. 1998).

If your client wants to set up a trust with a remainder in a child, you should draft a remainder contingent upon surviving to the time of possession if your client wishes to insulate the remainder from the claims of the child's spouse upon divorce.

a. Acceleration into Possession

Under the common law, a vested remainder accelerates into possession whenever and however the preceding estate ends. A contingent remainder, on the other hand, does not accelerate because the remaindermen are not entitled to possession until they are all ascertained and any condition precedent has occurred. Thus:

Case 9. *T* devises property in trust for *W* for life, remainder to *T*'s children (who survive *W*). *W* disclaims the life estate. If the language in parentheses is not included in the instrument, the children of *T* have a vested remainder that accelerates into possession. If the language in parentheses is included, the children of *T* have a contingent remainder that will not accelerate into possession. What is then done with the income during *W*'s life?

When a life tenant disclaimed a life estate, the rule that contingent remainders do not accelerate did not always appear to carry out the testator's intent, who might, as in Case 9, have postponed the gift to his children merely to give his spouse life income. If the spouse rejected life income, the testator would not want the trust to continue. Accordingly, courts began to disregard the technical classification of the remainder and to decide disclaimer cases based on what the testator probably would have intended had he anticipated disclaimer. See Ohio Natl. Bank of Columbus v. Adair, 374 N.E.2d 415 (Ohio 1978). Because this approach meant that almost every case of disclaimer had to be litigated, legislatures passed disclaimer statutes, such as the Uniform Disclaimer of Property Interests Act (UDPIA) (1999, last amended 2002).[2] Under these statutes, the disclaimant is treated as having predeceased the testator (see page 635), and remainders take effect or fail proceeding on this assumption. See Patricia G. Roberts, The Acceleration of Remainders: Manipulating the Identity of the Remaindermen, 42 S.C.L. Rev. 295 (1991).

In re Estate of Gilbert
New York Surrogate's Court, New York County, 1992
156 Misc. 2d 379, 592 N.Y.S.2d 224

ROTH, S.   The executor of the estate of Peter Gilbert asks the court to declare null and void a renunciation by Mr. Gilbert's son, Lester, of his interest in two

Surrogate Renee R. Roth

wholly discretionary trusts under decedent's will.

Mr. Gilbert died on March 26, 1989, leaving an estate of over $40,000,000.[3] He was survived by his wife and four children. Under his will, testator, after making certain pre-residuary legacies, created an elective share trust for the life income benefit of his wife. The amount of decedent's generation-skipping transfer (GST) tax exemption was divided into four discretionary trusts, one for the primary benefit of each of his children. The residue of Mr. Gilbert's estate was similarly divided. Upon the death of the widow, the remainder of her trust is to be added in equal shares to the residuary trusts for decedent's children. The trusts are wholly discretionary. Decedent's son, Lester, is therefore a discretionary

2. In 2002, the UDPIA was incorporated into the Uniform Probate Code as Article 2, Part 11 (§§2-1101–2-1107), replacing former §2-801.

3. Peter Gilbert, born in Austria, fled the Nazis with his family at age seven. Gilbert became a pioneer of cable television and the owner of the Colorado Rockies of the National Hockey League, now the New Jersey Devils. — Eds.

income beneficiary of two testamentary trusts, one of which will be augmented at the widow's death. Decedent's issue, including Lester's sisters, nieces and nephews as well as Lester's issue (should he have any), are also discretionary beneficiaries of both of Lester's trusts.

Lester, who has no issue, timely served on the executor a notice of renunciation of his "dispositive share in the estate of Peter Gilbert."

The executor, supported by the guardian ad litem for decedent's minor grand-children, takes the position that Lester's renunciation should be declared invalid. First, he states that permitting the renunciation would violate the testator's inten-tion to provide for Lester. Second, the executor argues that Lester possesses no current property interest and therefore has nothing to renounce. The executor maintains that Lester's renunciation is premature and may be made only if, and at such time as, the trustees exercise their discretion to distribute income or principal to him.

The executor explains decedent's intention as follows:

> Lester, who is approximately 32 years of age, . . . has left the religion of his birth and has for some time lived in Virginia with a small group of people who share a similar religious doctrine. Some months ago he phoned your petitioner and announced that he planned to renounce whatever bequest was left for him. When asked what he planned to do if he were ever taken seriously ill and needed expensive medical care, he responded "Jesus will provide for me."
>
> The fact that Lester had chosen to alienate himself from his family did not stop the decedent from loving his son or worrying about his future needs. . . . [T]he decedent wanted to know that funds would be available if the Trustees, acting in the manner that they thought the decedent would have acted had he then been living, should ever decide, for example, to pay a medical bill for Lester.

In effect, the executor argues that if the beneficiary of a wholly discretionary trust is permitted to renounce his or her interest, then no trust can ever be created to protect someone who is now disdainful of financial assistance but may in the future be in dire need, or simply have a change of heart.

However, under these circumstances, decedent's intention is not controlling. With respect to every renunciation, the intent to make a transfer is thwarted by the beneficiary who refuses to accept it. But clearly, "the law does not compel a man to accept an estate, either beneficial or in trust, against his will" (Burritt v. Silliman, 13 N.Y. 93, 96 (1855).

The executor suggests in his memorandum that he might be forced "to inquire into the mental capacity of Lester, since there is no rational reason which explains Lester's conduct." However, the desire to renounce wealth is not necessarily irra-tional. Presumably, the executor would not argue that a nun who takes a vow of poverty is mentally incompetent. Here, the acceptance of a monetary benefit apparently conflicts with Lester's religious beliefs. It would not be appropriate for the court to determine the validity of those beliefs, even if requested to do so. Furthermore, even if Lester's renunciation were purely whimsical, this would not in itself be sufficient reason either to reject the renunciation (Matter of Suter, supra) or to find him incompetent. In any event, the question of Lester's mental capacity has not been raised. There is no allegation in the petition or in any affidavit that Lester is a person under disability. The court must therefore proceed on the assumption that Lester is competent to make an effective renunciation.

The executor's second argument is that Lester has no current property interest which he can renounce. Rather, the executor maintains that Lester must wait until the trustees exercise their discretion to distribute income or principal to him, at which time, the executor asserts, Lester can renounce the property subject to such exercise of discretion. [The executor analogized these facts to the cases in which the beneficiary's creditors try to reach the beneficiary's interest in a discretionary trust. In those cases, courts usually hold that the creditor cannot reach the trust property until a distribution is made. See page 544. The court rejected this argument, reasoning that the better analogy is to the cases in which a trust beneficiary seeks to compel a distribution by the trustee even though the trustee is vested with "absolute," "sole," or some other form of extended discretion. In those cases, courts order a distribution to the beneficiary if the trustee's failure to make one was an abuse of the trustee's discretion. See page 540. Thus, because "Lester may have the right to compel the trustees to distribute trust property to him under certain circumstances," the court concluded that he "has a current interest which could be deemed 'property' for the purpose of an effective renunciation."]

Lester's renunciation also applies to his remainder interest in the elective share trust, which is contingent upon his surviving the widow. As discussed above, any interest, whether or not contingent, is within the scope of the statute. Even if the executor's interpretation is correct and a renunciation must relate to an interest in property, a contingent remainder has historically been recognized as a property interest.

Finally, the guardian ad litem argues that if Lester's renunciation is allowed, the remainder interests in his trusts should not be accelerated. The remainder of Lester's trusts would be payable to his issue. As mentioned earlier, Lester has no issue. If the interests are accelerated, Lester's unborn issue would be cut off and decedent's living grandchildren would lose certain present interests in these trusts. It is noted that acceleration of the trust remainders would have no direct tax consequences and any indirect effects would be relatively minor.

The question is whether under EPTL 2-1.11(d) this court has any discretion to suspend acceleration. Such statute, in relevant part, provides that:

> Unless the creator of the disposition has otherwise provided, the filing of a renunciation, as provided in this section, has the same effect with respect to the renounced interest as though the renouncing person had predeceased the creator or the decedent . . . and shall have the effect of accelerating the possession and enjoyment of subsequent interests.

Thus, it appears that under the language of the statute, the remainder interests in Lester's trusts will be accelerated unless the decedent has "otherwise provided." There is no explicit "otherwise provision" in testator's will, but the guardian ad litem argues that the court should infer an "otherwise provision" from the general language of the will and the circumstances surrounding its execution. . . .

When EPTL 2-1.11 was enacted in 1977, the language regarding acceleration was added to resolve the dispute reflected in a number of conflicting decisions. Those cases looked to testator's intent as the appropriate guideline and determined acceleration on a case-by-case basis, with unpredictable results. It is clear the addition of this language was intended to provide uniformity (see, e.g., Memorandum in Support of Amended Bill, New York State Assembly, L. 1977, ch. 861, Governor's Bill Jacket). To engage in the type of analysis suggested by the guardian ad litem would mean a return to the approach rejected by the Legislature.

Based upon the foregoing, it is concluded that Lester's renunciation is valid as to any and all interests in his father's estate. Lester is thus to be treated as if he predeceased his father without issue.

NOTE, QUESTIONS, AND PROBLEM

1.   Under most state disclaimer statutes, the donee of a contingent or defeasibly vested interest may wait until nine months after the interest becomes indefeasibly vested to disclaim, and under the Uniform Disclaimer of Property Interests Act (1999, last amended 2002) (UDPIA), there is no time limit.[4] Both approaches therefore allow the contingent remainderman to decide at the life tenant's death whether to accept the property or not. Thus:

> *Case 10.* *T* devises property in trust "for my daughter *A* for life, then to my granddaughter *B* [now age 21] if *B* survives *A*, and if *B* does not survive *A*, to *B*'s issue." At *A*'s death, *B* can decide whether to disclaim and let the property pass to *B*'s issue.[5]
>
> *Case 11.* *T* devises property in trust "for my daughter *A* for life, then to *A*'s issue." At *T*'s death, *A* can decide whether to disclaim and let the property pass to *A*'s issue.

Observe that in Case 10 *B*'s disclaimer cuts out *B*'s afterborn issue, and in Case 11 *A*'s disclaimer cuts out *A*'s afterborn issue. The question thus arises, is this consistent with *T*'s probable intent? In Case 10, if *B* had not disclaimed, then she would have received the property outright, and hence subsequently she could convey any, all, or none of the property to some, all, or none of her issue. Viewed in this manner, it seems likely that *B*'s decision to disclaim at *T*'s death would not frustrate

---

4. *Caution*: Under federal tax law, a disclaimer is treated as a gift by the disclaimant to the persons who take as a result of the disclaimer, *unless the disclaimer occurs within nine months after the interest is created* or nine months after the donee reaches 21, whichever is later. I.R.C. §2518(b)(2). Thus, if in Case 10 *B* does not disclaim within nine months after *T* dies, for federal tax purposes *B* is the owner of the remainder, and if *B* disclaims the remainder at *A*'s death, *B* makes a taxable gift to *B*'s issue of the value of the trust assets at *A*'s death.

5. *Disclaimers and the generation-skipping transfer tax.* The federal government imposes a generation-skipping transfer (GST) tax upon any transfer to a grandchild or other person two or more generations removed from the transferor. I.R.C. §§2601-2663, pages 919-928. In Case 10, for example, an estate tax is payable at *T*'s death and a GST tax is payable at *A*'s death, when possession of the property is transferred to *T*'s granddaughter. In Case 10, suppose that *A* disclaims her life estate at *T*'s death. The effect of the disclaimer is that a GST tax is payable at *T*'s death, when *B* (the settlor's grandchild) takes possession, rather than at *A*'s death. The GST tax is in addition to the estate tax levied on *T*'s estate. This last point is sometimes difficult for students to understand because it looks, at first glance, like double taxation. But remember the tax policy: a transfer tax imposed on each living generation. Therefore, where a transfer is made to a grandchild, an estate tax is imposed on *T*'s transfer of his estate, and, because the first generation below *T* has been skipped over and an estate tax at the death of that generation avoided, a GST tax is also imposed on the transfer to the second generation below *T*. Were this not so, a person could avoid estate taxes in a child's estate by transferring property directly to a grandchild. Congress has closed this loophole.

The tax effect of *A*'s disclaimer in Case 10 would be that a GST tax becomes payable earlier — at *T*'s death rather than at *A*'s death. You can see why, with the enactment of the GST tax in 1986, disclaimers became decidedly less popular. For further discussion, see Joan B. Ellsworth, On Disclaimers: Let's Renounce I.R.C. Section 2518, 38 Vill. L. Rev. 693 (1993) (arguing that I.R.C. §2518 should be repealed now that the GST tax has greatly reduced the tax incentives for using disclaimers).

T's intent. In Case 11, however, if *A* had not disclaimed, then *A*'s issue born after *T*'s death would have been entitled to a share of the property. Hence *A*'s disclaimer and its consequent acceleration of the remainder in *A*'s issue might well frustrate *T*'s intent. This was the executor's argument in *Gilbert*. Because Lester's disclaimer accelerated the remainder in his issue, but at the time Lester had no issue, in effect Lester disclaimed any interest in his father's trust that his future issue otherwise might have had. The court's answer was that the statute was enacted for the purpose of avoiding litigation over the testator's probable intent. Could this result have been avoided with better drafting?

2.   *T*'s will devises property in separate trusts, one "for my son *A* for life, then to the issue of *A* and *B*," and the other "for my son *B* for life, then to the issue of *A* and *B*." If, when *T* dies, *A* has issue but *B* does not, by disclaiming does *A* cut off *B*'s afterborn issue from the first trust, thereby ensuring that it will pass entirely to *A*'s issue? See Pate v. Ford, 376 S.E.2d 775 (S.C. 1989). But compare Linkous v. Candler, 508 S.E.2d 657 (Ga. 1998).

3.   For further study of the intersection between disclaimer and acceleration, the impact of the UDPIA, and analysis of the potential for manipulation of the identity of the remainder beneficiaries through strategic disclaimers, see T.P. Gallanis, The Future of Future Interests, 60 Wash. & Lee L. Rev. 513, 523-529 (2003); Adam J. Hirsch, Revisions in Need of Revising: The Uniform Disclaimer of Property Interests Act, 29 Fla. St. U.L. Rev. 109, 170-175 (2001); William P. LaPiana, Some Property Law Issues in the Law of Disclaimers, 38 Real Prop., Prob. & Tr. J. 207, 220-225 (2003). See also Patricia G. Roberts, The Acceleration of Remainders: Manipulating the Identity of the Remaindermen, 42 S.C.L. Rev. 295 (1991).

b. Transferability

At common law, vested remainders, including defeasibly vested ones, were transferable inter vivos. A contingent remainder and an executory interest, on the other hand, were not transferable because in early law they were thought of not as interests but as mere chances of ownership. There were a few exceptions to this rule of inalienability. Today, however, only nine states retain some version of the common law rule of inalienability for contingent interests; the rest have repudiated the rule by statute or by judicial decision. T.P. Gallanis, The Future of Future Interests, 60 Wash. & Lee L. Rev. 513, 516-519 (2003) (collecting authority). Future interests in trust, however, may still be made inalienable by a spendthrift clause.

Reversions, remainders, and executory interests are descendible and devisable at death in the same manner as possessory interests. The future interest passes to the heirs or devisees of its owner. Thus:

> *Case 12. O* conveys property in trust "for *A* for life, then to *B*." *B* dies during *A*'s lifetime. *B*'s remainder passes to *B*'s devisees if *B* leaves a will or to *B*'s heirs if *B* dies intestate.

A future interest contingent upon surviving to the time of possession is not transferable at death. Thus, if in Case 12 *O* had conveyed a remainder "to *B* if *B* survives *A*," *B* could not transmit the remainder to another person if *B* died during *A*'s lifetime.

The federal government subjects to estate taxation the transfer of any property interest. I.R.C. §2033. A future interest, like a possessory estate, is an interest in property and hence is subject to federal estate taxation. If in Case 12 *B* dies during *A*'s lifetime, the value of *B*'s remainder is subject to estate taxation because it is *transmissible* at death. ("Transmissible" is a term of lawyers' art meaning the interest passes at death by intestacy to the remainderman's heirs or by will to the remainderman's devisees.) Federal estate taxation turns upon whether a future interest is transmissible, not upon whether it is vested or contingent. If it is transmissible, it is subject to taxation.

PROBLEM AND NOTES

1. *T*'s will devises property in trust "for *A* for life, then to *B*, and if *B* does not survive *A*, to *C*." If *B* dies during *A*'s lifetime, is the value of *B*'s remainder includible in *B*'s taxable gross estate under the federal estate tax? If *C* dies before *A* and *B*, is the value of *C*'s future interest includible in *C*'s taxable gross estate?[6]

2. *Valuation of a future interest.* If a future interest is subject to estate taxation, the value of the future interest depends upon the life tenant's life expectancy and the market rate of interest. The federal government publishes life expectancy tables and valuation tables for future interests that must be used. See I.R.C. §7520. For an explanation of how future interests are valued, see Jesse Dukeminier & James E. Krier, Property 229-230 (5th ed. 2002).

When a future interest cannot be valued by resort to mortality tables, as where, for example, it may be destroyed by the trustee using principal to support the life tenant, the interest is valued with reference to all relevant facts, including the likelihood of the contingent events happening.

3. *Drafting advice.* You can give a remainderman the power to transfer his remainder at death without the remainder being subject to the estate tax. How is this done? Give the remainderman a remainder contingent upon surviving to the time of possession (thereby escaping the estate tax) *and a special power of appointment* (thereby giving the remainderman power to decide who takes the remainder). Property subject to a special power (unlike owned property) is not subject to estate taxation (see page 595). Here is an example:

> Case 13. *T* devises his residuary estate in trust "for *A* for life, then to *B* if *B* survives *A*, and if *B* does not survive *A*, then to such of *B*'s spouse or one or more of *B*'s issue as *B* appoints by will." *B* has a contingent nontransmissible remainder and a special power of appointment. If *B* dies during *A*'s life, *B*'s remainder disappears and is not taxable in *B*'s estate. In this event, the property passes on *A*'s death to persons to whom *B* appoints or, if *B* fails to appoint, to *T*'s heirs.

---

6. *Caution*: As pointed out in the prior footnote, a federal generation-skipping transfer tax is levied upon a transfer from a trust settlor to the settlor's grandchild. The GST tax is levied at the highest rate of the estate tax. If *B* is *T*'s child and *C* is *B*'s child, a GST tax will be levied on the trust at *A*'s death if *B* predeceases *A*. At that point in time, there will be a transfer from the settlor to the settlor's grandchild. Therefore, avoiding an estate tax at *B*'s death at the cost of paying a GST tax at *A*'s later death is not necessarily a good idea. We shall return later to the taxation of remainders. If you don't quite have a grasp on the estate tax and the GST tax, you will find it easier to understand them in the context of actual family trusts. See pages 919-922.

If *A* is the spouse of *T* and *B* is *T*'s child and *B* dies before *A*, the special power of appointment in *B* also enables *B* to choose to pay an estate tax on the value of the remainder at *B*'s death rather than a GST tax on the value of the trust principal at *A*'s death, when the principal is distributed to *T*'s grandchildren, if the estate tax would be lower than the GST tax (see page 694). Case 13 is an example of skilled estate planning.

c.   Requiring Survival to Time of Possession

As a general rule, there is no requirement that a remainderman live to the time of possession; the usual common law rule of construction, which reflects the traditional preference for vesting, holds that survival is not an implied condition of the gift. Thus, if the remainderman dies before the life tenant, the remainder passes to the remainderman's estate. Of course, because this is a rule of construction, not a rule of law, the testator may expressly require survival; and in a few specialized situations, hereafter noted, courts will imply a requirement of survival.

If a vested remainder subject to divestment is created, courts ordinarily read the divesting language strictly as written and do not expand it to cause divestment in events other than those stated.

FIRST NATIONAL BANK OF BAR HARBOR v. ANTHONY, 557 A.2d 957 (Me. 1989): In 1975 Franklin Anthony created a revocable inter vivos trust, with income payable to the settlor for life, then to his wife Ethel for life, and upon the death of the settlor and his wife Ethel, the trust corpus was to be divided in equal shares among the settlor's children: John, Peter, and Dencie. The settlor's wife Ethel died in 1982. In 1983 John died, leaving three children, Deborah, Christopher, and Paul. In 1984 the settlor, Franklin, died. His will devised two-thirds of his estate to his son Peter and one-third to his daughter Dencie. The children of John were excluded from his will.

John's children claimed John's one-third interest in the corpus of the trust. Peter and Dencie opposed them. The lower court held that the gift to John in the trust "lapsed because his interest did not vest until the death of the survivor of the settlor and his wife," but the antilapse statute did not apply to revocable trusts, only to wills, so John's children could not take. On the basis of orthodox future interests doctrine, the Supreme Judicial Court reversed, holding that "the remainder interest of John M. Anthony was a present, vested interest at the time of the creation of the inter vivos trust." The court explained:

> We note the following: (1) the settlor explicitly retained the right to change his beneficiaries if he wanted to alter the trust's disposition; (2) the settlor imposed no restrictions on what his children could do with their respective shares; (3) aside from his power to revoke or amend the trust, the settlor specifically limited his own benefit to income during his lifetime and payment of certain expenses associated with his death; (4) the settlor made survival an explicit condition of any benefit to his wife, but did not include such language in the case of his children. The unexercised right to make a change in beneficiaries, the absence of any control over how the children might dispose of their shares, and the overall assignment of economic benefits lead us to conclude that this plan of disposition effectively eliminated any further interest of the settlor in the trust principal unless he affirmatively chose to intervene.

His failure to change the plan coupled with the omission of a survival requirement in the case of the children's's shares, suggests a disposition to a predeceased child's estate rather than a reversion to the settlor's estate. As a result of this construction of the instrument, it may be said that [John's, Peter's, and Dencie's] interests were vested, subject to defeasance or divestment if the settlor chose to amend or revoke the trust or change his beneficiaries. . . .

The trust instrument before us contains no requirement that the remainder beneficiaries survive the life tenants and we see no reason to imply a requirement of survival. Only the settlor's subsequent revocation or substitution would divest the remainder interest.

Since John had a vested remainder subject to divestment by the settlor exercising his power of revocation, his interest in the trust passed to his children when he died. The settlor could have taken this interest away from them by revoking the trust, but he did not. Therefore, upon the settlor's death, John's children took possession of John's one-third share of the trust. The court did not reach the question of whether the Maine antilapse statute should be applied to an inter vivos trust.

NOTES, QUESTIONS, AND PROBLEM

1.   The position of the court in *Anthony* is the orthodox one: A vested remainder in a trust passes to the estate of the remainderman at his death unless the instrument provides expressly that the remainder is divested by his death. A typical antilapse statute, by its terms, applies only to a devise by *will* where the devisee predeceases the *testator*; it provides that the issue of a predeceased devisee will take the devisee's share (see page 392). Inasmuch as a remainder in a trust may be transmissible at death to the remainderman's estate by the rules of future interests law, there is no need to bring the antilapse statute into the picture to pass the remainder on to the remainderman's children. See Baldwin v. Branch, 888 So. 2d 482 (Ala. 2004). Nonetheless, because a revocable trust is a will substitute, a couple of courts have confused the situation by holding that an antilapse statute applies to a transmissible remainder created in a revocable trust where the remainderman predeceased the settlor. See Dollar Sav. & Trust Co. v. Turner, 529 N.E.2d 1261 (Ohio 1988) (reversed by Ohio Rev. Code Ann. §2107.01 (2004)); In re Estate of Button, 490 P.2d 731 (Wash. 1971).

In the *Anthony* case, the application of the rule that remainders not expressly conditioned on survivorship are transmissible at the remainderman's death and the application of the antilapse statute would bring the same result. John's remainder would pass to John's children (his heirs) under either theory. But in the following cases, the two theories would produce different results:

(a) Suppose John dies intestate, survived by a wife and children. Under the transmissible remainder theory, in many states both wife and children share in John's remainder interest as John's heirs, while in many others (and under Uniform Probate Code §2-102 (1990)), John's wife takes to the exclusion of the children, provided that all the children were hers and John's. Under an antilapse statute, only John's children take.

(b) Now suppose that John leaves a will devising all his property to his wife. Under the transmissible remainder theory, his wife takes the remainder. Under an antilapse statute, only John's children take the remainder.

(c) Now suppose that John is not survived by issue and that by will he devises his property to his wife (or a friend). Under the transmissible remainder theory, John's wife (or other devisee) takes the remainder. Under the antilapse statute, the result is unclear. There are no issue to substitute for John. Does this mean that the remainder then fails? If so, does applying the antilapse statute result in all remainders in revocable trusts being turned into remainders contingent upon surviving the settlor (just as devises are contingent upon surviving the testator)?

The transmissible remainder theory gives the remainderman considerably more control over the remainder at death than does an antilapse statute. Like a power of appointment, introducing this sort of flexibility into a trust is desirable because the settlor cannot foresee the future and determine who will be deserving or needy upon the termination of the trust.

2. *Taxation of remainders*. A transmissible remainder, like any transferable interest, is subject to federal estate taxation upon the death of the remainderman (see page 637). Thus John Anthony's remainder in the revocable trust created by his father would be subject to estate taxation at his death. However, no taxes would be payable because John's remainder could be destroyed unconditionally by his father; it has a value of zero. Thus we observe that, even though a transmissible remainder is subject to estate taxation, under the circumstances of a given case, no taxes may be payable.

Before 1986, there was a clear tax advantage in creating remainders contingent upon survival to the time of possession. If the remainderman died before the life tenant, no estate tax was payable on the value of the remainder. This tax advantage was neutralized by the enactment of the generation-skipping transfer tax in 1986 (page 919). A GST tax, levied at the highest estate tax rate, is payable on the life tenant's death if the trust principal is then payable to the settlor's grandchildren or any other person two or more generations below the settlor. If, in the *Anthony* case, John M. Anthony had held a remainder contingent upon his survival to the time of possession, no estate tax would be payable upon his death, but *on the settlor-life tenant's death a GST tax would be levied on the value of the property received by John's children* (the settlor's grandchildren).

Since the enactment of the GST tax, no clear general taxpayer advantage results from creating a remainder contingent upon survival rather than a remainder transferable at death. Tax advantage turns on the individual case — available exemptions from estate and GST taxes, marital deduction for estate tax, stepped-up basis for assets subject to estate tax, the life tenant's life expectancy, and so on. As noted earlier (page 637), the skilled drafter of a trust with remainders to the settlor's children will create a special power of appointment either in the life tenant or in the remaindermen to let the donee (or donees) determine which tax does the least damage to the family and pay that one.

3. *Single- and multigenerational classes*. Although courts do not imply survival requirements in gifts to single-generational classes, such as "children" or "brothers and sisters," they do imply survival requirements in gifts to multigenerational classes, such as "issue" or "descendants." See Restatement (Third) of Property: Wills and Other Donative Transfers §§15.3-15.4 (T.D. No. 4, 2004); Edward C. Halbach, Jr., Future Interests: Express and Implied Conditions of Survival, 49 Cal. L. Rev. 297, 314-315 (1961).

Thus, suppose that *T*'s will devises property "to *A* for life, then to *A*'s issue." *A* has a son, *B*, and a daughter, *C*. *B* predeceases *A*, devising all his property to his wife. *B* is also survived by a daughter, *D*. Because a requirement of survival is imposed on *A*'s issue, *B*, who dies during *A*'s life, cannot devise his share to his wife. Instead, *D*, *B*'s child, takes from *T* the share *B* would have taken had *B* survived. Similarly, where there is a gift to the "heirs" of *A*, a survival requirement to the death of *A* is implied.

4. When the testator inserts the word "surviving" in a trust instrument, the word is ambiguous unless an additional word or words tell us *at what time* the donee must be surviving. The requirement of survival may relate to surviving the testator, the life tenant, or a preceding remainderman. Take this example: *T* devises property in trust "for *A* for life, then to *B*, but if *B* dies before *A* to *B*'s surviving children." *B* has two children, *C* and *D*. Then *B* dies. Then *D* dies intestate, survived by a child, *E*. *A* dies. Does *E* share? It depends upon whether "surviving" means "surviving *A*," in which case *E* would not share because *D* did not survive *A*, or "surviving *B*," in which case *E* would share because *D* survived *B*. The majority of cases appear to favor the view that "surviving" means surviving to the time of possession, thus excluding *E*. See 5 American Law of Property §21.15 (1952).

Sometimes, in an effort to specify at what time the donee must be surviving, ambiguity is created if the instrument is drafted poorly. Suppose *T* conveys property in trust for *T* for life, and then "upon the death of *T*, the trustee shall pay over whatever remains of the trust estate, discharged of trust, to *T*'s son *A* if he shall then be living. If *T*'s son *A* shall then be deceased, to *T*'s then living issue." *T* dies. Then, before the trustee could distribute the trust property to *A*, *A* dies. *C* and *D*, the surviving children of *A*'s brother *B*, who predeceased both *A* and *T*, argue that "then living" refers to the time of distribution, not *T*'s death, and hence that they are entitled to the trust property. *E*, the beneficiary of *A*'s will, who is unrelated to *T*, argues that "then living" refers to the time of *T*'s death, and hence that he is entitled to the trust property. What result? See Chavin v. PNC Bank, 816 A.2d 781 (Del. 2003).

5. *T* bequeaths a fund in trust "for *A* for life, then to *B*, but if *B* dies without issue surviving her, to *C*." Does *T* intend *C* to take only if *B* dies *before A* without issue? Or does *T* intend *C* to take if *B* dies *at any time* without issue? The majority of courts favors the first construction, which permits the trust to terminate on *A*'s death. Accordingly, if *B* survives *A*, the trust property is distributed to *B* and *C* can never take. See 5 American Law of Property §21.53 (1952).

Observe also that under orthodox construction there is no requirement that *C* live to the time of possession. If *B* dies before *A*, and then *C* dies during *A*'s life, *C*'s interest passes to *C*'s heirs or devisees. In a couple of states a different rule is followed. If a future interest is contingent upon an event other than survival to the time of possession (such as "if *B* dies without issue"), the future interest is also contingent on surviving to the time of possession. See Rushing v. Mann, 910 S.W.2d 672 (Ark. 1995); Lawson v. Lawson, 148 S.E.2d 546 (N.C. 1966). The rule may be limited to class gifts. This minority rule is criticized in Patricia G. Roberts, Class Gifts in North Carolina — When Do We "Call the Roll"? 21 Wake Forest L. Rev. 1 (1985).

Clobberie's Case

Court of Chancery, England, 1677
2 Vent. 342, 86 Eng. Rep. 476

In one Clobberie's case it was held, that where one bequeathed a sum of money to a woman, at her age of twenty-one years, or day of marriage, to be paid unto her with interest, and she died before either, that the money should go to her executor; and was so decreed by my Lord Chancellor Finch [who was later titled Lord Nottingham and became famous for getting the Rule against Perpetuities started in the Duke of Norfolk's Case, page 672].

But he said, if money were bequeathed to one at his age of twenty-one years, if he dies before that age, the money is lost.

On the other side, if money be given to one, to be paid at the age of twenty-one years; there, if the party dies before, it shall go to the executors.

NOTES AND PROBLEM

1.   The first and third rules of construction laid down in Clobberie's Case are widely followed today. They apply to immediate gifts as well as to remainders, and to a gift to a class as well as to a gift to an individual.

Under the first rule in Clobberie's Case, a gift of the *entire income* to a person (or to a class), with principal to be paid at a designated age, indicates survival to the time of possession is not required. The reason for this rule is that all interests in the property — both income and principal — are given to the same person or persons, with only possession of the principal postponed. When the beneficiary dies before reaching the stated age, there is no point in delaying payment of the principal to the beneficiary's estate. See 5 American Law of Property §21.20 (1952). Under the third rule in Clobberie's Case, a gift "payable" at a designated age indicates that survival to the time of possession is not required. If the beneficiary dies under that age, the principal will be paid at the beneficiary's death to the beneficiary's estate, unless someone would be harmed by such payment. If the income is payable to another, for example, the principal cannot be paid to the principal beneficiary's estate until the income beneficiary dies. See id. §21.18.

The American cases are split over whether to follow the second rule, which states that a gift "at" a designated age implies a requirement of survivorship to that age. See id. §21.17. The distinction between a legacy "at 21" (survivorship to 21 required) and a legacy "to be paid at 21" (survivorship to 21 is not required) has been criticized by most commentators as a distinction without a difference.

2.   *T* bequeaths $10,000 "to *A* when *A* attains 21." *A* is age 15 at *T*'s death. Who is entitled to income from the $10,000 before *A* reaches 21? If *A* dies at age 16, does the legacy fail or is *A*'s administrator entitled to demand payment of $10,000 at *A*'s death or when *A* would have reached 21 had *A* lived? See Edward C. Halbach, Jr., Future Interests: Express and Implied Conditions of Survival, 49 Cal. L. Rev. 297, 299-302 (1961).

3.   *T* bequeaths a fund in trust "for *A* for life, then after *A*'s death to *A*'s children, each share payable as each child respectively reaches the age of 30, if he or she has not reached age 30 before *A* dies." The gift to each child of *A* is vested upon birth, with possession postponed until *A* dies or the child reaches 30, whichever later

happens. If a child of *A* dies at age 10 during *A*'s life, the child's administrator can demand payment of the child's share at *A*'s death. There is no requirement that the child survive to the time designated for possession.

4. *T* bequeathed a fund in trust for the benefit of her child Benjamin "until my child attains age twenty-five (25), at which time the income and principal shall be distributed and paid over to him and the trust shall terminate." *T*'s will did not name a trust beneficiary if Benjamin died under 25. Benjamin died at 20 in 1994. Benjamin's heir is his father, who was divorced from Ben's mother in 1983. The court, following the rules in Clobberie's Case, held that the remainder vested in Benjamin upon creation and passed on his death to his father. Summers v. Summers, 699 N.E.2d 958 (Ohio App. 1997).

5. A recent decision extended the first rule in Clobberie's Case to a trust in which the beneficiary was entitled to only a fractional share of the income. In Goldenberg v. Golden, 769 So. 2d 1144 (Fla. App. 2000), the testator bequeathed a fund in trust for the benefit of his daughter, who was to receive three-fourths of the income, and his two grandchildren, who were to share one-fourth of the income divided equally. Upon his daughter's death, the principal was to be divided equally between his two grandchildren, half when each turned 25 and the remainder when each turned 30. At age 44, while the testator's daughter was still alive, one of the grandchildren died intestate, leaving his wife as his only heir. The testator's other grandchild and the deceased grandchild's wife both argued that each was the successor to the deceased grandchild's interest in the trust. Quoting a Florida Supreme Court decision that embraced the first rule in Clobberie's Case, the court held that the deceased grandchild's interest was vested and hence passed to his wife. The court did not discuss the fact that the deceased grandchild had been entitled to only one-eighth of the trust income rather than the entire income from the share of the principal that he would have received upon his mother's death.

NOTE: UNIFORM PROBATE CODE §2-707 — A NEW SYSTEM OF FUTURE INTERESTS FOR TRUSTS

In 1990, the revisers of the Uniform Probate Code made a revolutionary change in the law of future interests that, if adopted, will change the rules previously studied in this chapter. Under UPC §2-707 (1990), unless the instrument provides otherwise, the following rules apply:

1. All future interests in trust are contingent on the beneficiary's surviving to the date of distribution.
2. If a remainderman does not survive to the distribution date, UPC §2-707 creates a substitute gift in the remainderman's descendants who survive to the date of distribution (that is, the antilapse idea from the law of wills is extended to all future interests in trust and to include all beneficiaries, not just those closely related to the donor).
3. If a remainderman dies before distribution and leaves no descendants, the remainder fails, and, if there is no alternative remainder that takes effect, the trust property passes to the settlor's residuary devisees or the settlor's heirs.

As proposed law reform, UPC §2-707 can be justified only (1) if it better carries out the settlor's intent, or better serves other relevant public policies, than does the common law rule of transmissible remainders, and (2) if it does so without introducing administrative complexity and other costs disproportionate to its benefits. See Jesse Dukeminier, The Uniform Probate Code Upends the Law of Remainders, 94 Mich. L. Rev. 148, 149 (1995).

In assaying the merits of §2-707, the point of departure is to ask whether the typical settlor would prefer the flexibility of the transmissible remainder rule, which permits the beneficiary to devise the remainder to whomever he pleases, or the rigid substitution of the beneficiary's descendants that is provided by the antilapse statute, which allows the beneficiary to do with the remainder as he pleases only if he survives to possession. Consider the following case study:

> *Case 14.* T devises property in trust "for A for life, then to A's daughter B." Under present law, if B dies during the life of A, B can devise her remainder to her spouse, to her issue, to charity, or to anyone she pleases, outright or in further trust, perhaps setting up a discretionary trust for a disabled child whose disability manifested after T's death but before B died. Under UPC §2-707, B's remainder is made contingent upon B's surviving A. If B dies during A's life leaving issue, B's issue are substituted for B. B has no power to transfer the remainder to others. This may trigger an expensive guardianship for B's children and may leave B's surviving husband without sufficient assets to care for B's children. If B is not survived by issue, the gift fails, and the property reverts to T's residuary devisee or T's heirs on A's death. Yet if B survives A by 120 hours, then B takes possession and is free to devise the property not only to her issue, the result under §2-707 if B had not survived A, but also to her spouse, to charity, or to anyone she pleases.

In Chapter 9, you studied powers of appointment, which should be considered for every well-drafted trust. Powers of appointment permit beneficiaries to name the future takers of a trust as circumstances may indicate desirable. As Case 14 illustrates, *the transmissible remainder rule gives the remainderman the equivalent of a general testamentary power of appointment over the remainder.* Spouses are likely to be the persons most disadvantaged by UPC §2-707 because only issue, and not spouses, are substituted for the deceased remainderman. The broader point is that no statute can pick the substitute takers as well as living persons. The transmissible remainder rule affords the remainder beneficiary the opportunity to devise the remainder, outright or in further trust, as changed circumstances warrant, regardless of whether he survives to the time of distribution.

Professor Waggoner advocates the new system of future interests that he helped introduce into §2-707. See Lawrence W. Waggoner, The Uniform Probate Code Extends Antilapse-Type Protection to Poorly Drafted Trusts, 94 Mich. L. Rev. 2309 (1996). Waggoner contends that where an instrument is ambiguous and a default rule is required, the default rule should provide a solution that a skilled estate planner would have provided. Few would disagree with that proposition. Waggoner then continues: "Standard practice gives the power of appointment to the life tenant, not the remainder beneficiary. A capable estate planner, wishing to insert flexibility into a trust, never uses transmissible future interests and seldom thinks of giving a power of appointment to a remainder beneficiary." Id. at 2334. But this observation, even if correct,[7] begs the question. The issue here is what to do when the life tenant has not been given a power of appointment, and the settlor chose a remainder beneficiary, perhaps because the life tenant was incompetent or had an adverse relationship with the remainderman. In such a case, if the remainder beneficiary does not survive the life tenant, would a well-drafted estate plan provide for the remainderman's share to be distributed to his issue, regardless of age or capabilities, or would a skilled estate planner instead give the remainderman the power to choose his successor? We suggest the latter. Indeed, even when the life tenant is given a special power of appointment, an expert might well give the remainderman who dies before the life tenant a special power exercisable if the life tenant does not exercise her power or cannot exercise her power because of incompetence.

Giving a contingent remainderman a special power of appointment was first recommended, so far as we can tell, by that master of will drafting, W. Barton Leach, Story Professor of Law at Harvard, in his article, Planning and Drafting a Will, 27 B.U.L. Rev. 157 (1947). This article described his wills course at Harvard, which emphasized intelligent drafting. Implementing his recommendation, Leach created special powers of appointment in remaindermen who predecease the life tenant in Paragraph VII, Clauses (f)(1) & (3) of his model will (id. at 182, 184). Leach later used this model will, with special powers in remaindermen, in his Cases and Text on the Law of Wills 260-264 (2d ed. 1951) (Paragraph VII, Clauses (f)(1) & (3)). Throughout his long and influential career at Harvard, Leach continued to advocate giving remaindermen special powers of appointment when appropriate in the family situation. In his 1961 casebook on estate planning, in discussing a trust created by a testator for his wife for life, remainder to his two sons, Leach asked how the will should be drafted to take care of the situation if one of the sons predeceased the life tenant. His answer: "*Obviously*, provide that if a son predeceases his mother he shall have a special power of appointment over half the principal." W. Barton Leach & James K. Logan, Cases and Text on Future Interests and Estate Planning 329 (1961) (emphasis added). See also Paragraph VII(2)(e)(3) of Leach & Logan's model will creating a special power of appointment in the remainderman (id. at 970-972).

In a comprehensive examination of the matter some years ago, before the UPC revisers acted, Professor Susan French compared the current rule of transmissible remainders with a proposal to make remainders contingent on survival and impose an antilapse statute on them (in essence, UPC §2-707's solution). French concluded that imposing a requirement of survival on remaindermen was justified only if they were given, by statute, a broad special power of appointment permitting the remainderman maximum flexibility to adapt to changes after the creation of the trust — in other words, providing a default scheme by statute that mirrored what Leach had recommended. Susan F. French, Imposing a General Survival Requirement on Beneficiaries of Future Interests: Solving the Problems Caused by the Death of a Beneficiary Before the Time Set for Distribution, 27 Ariz. L. Rev. 801 (1985).[8]

---

7. Interestingly, Example 5 to UPC §2-707 concerns a power of appointment given to a remainder beneficiary: "G created an irrevocable trust, income to A for life, remainder in corpus to B, but if B predeceases A, to the person B appoints by will."

8. Since the enactment of the generation-skipping transfer tax in 1986, French's sensible proposal has become even more attractive. It gives the remainderman a special power of appointment, which the remainderman can choose to exercise so as to put her remainder in her taxable gross estate, paying an estate tax on the remainder and avoiding a higher GST tax on the trust principal at the life tenant's death.

The Official Comment to UPC §2-707 states that its rationale is "to prevent cumbersome and costly distributions to and through the estates of deceased beneficiaries of future interests who may have died long before the distribution date." This is a curious basis for excluding remainders in trust from the remainderman's estate, since other nonpossessory interests — such as copyright royalties, an option to purchase, a landlord's reversion, or a legal future interest — are routinely included. Future interests in trust are certainly no more "cumbersome and costly" to administer, or to value, than other nonpossessory interests.

To be sure, it is possible that the remainderman's personal representative might overlook the remainder and thus not include it as an asset of the remainderman's probate estate. But it does not follow automatically that the remainderman's probate estate would have to be reopened and a new administrator appointed when the life tenant dies in order to pass title to the remainderman's heir or devisees. In many states, the order for final distribution of a probate estate contains an omnibus clause distributing "hereafter discovered" property to specified persons, in which case no subsequent administration is necessary. Even without an omnibus clause, no good reason appears why the trustee should not be able to distribute the trust principal upon termination of the trust directly to the residuary beneficiaries or heirs if they have been determined in the probate decree. Several cases so hold. See Security Trust Co. v. Irvine, 93 A.2d 528, 383 (Del. Ch. 1953); Cooling v. Security Trust Co., 76 A.2d 1, 5 (Del. Ch. 1950). See also Estate of Waller, 559 S.W.2d 312, 317 (Mo. App. 1977), quoting 4 Almon H. Maus, Probate Law and Practice §1523, at 644 (1960). As Professor Cunningham has explained, as compared to §2-707, "a far less drastic solution would be a statute authorizing a trustee to distribute the interest of a deceased remainder beneficiary directly to the persons entitled to the interest under the beneficiary's will, or to her heirs if she died without a will." Laura E. Cunningham, The Hazards of Tinkering with the Common Law of Future Interests: The California Experience, 48 Hastings L.J. 667, 699 (1997).

Because of the necessity of dealing with two or more alternative future interests, for which substitute gifts are created, and providing for tie-breakers where two groups of substitute takers appear to have equal claims, UPC §2-707 turns out to be devilishly complex. It invents a whole new vocabulary of future interests. The drafters themselves call the statute "elaborate and intricate" and admit that it will require "a few hours" of intense study. Edward C. Halbach, Jr. & Lawrence W. Waggoner, The UPC's New Survivorship and Antilapse Provisions, 55 Alb. L. Rev. 1091, 1148 (1992).

UPC §2-707 changes many rules that lawyers have relied on for centuries. For example, §2-707 provides that words of survivorship attached to a future interest do *not* state an intent that descendants not be substituted for the deceased remainderman. This rule of construction is likely to trip up the average or the experienced lawyer. Thus:

> *Case 15.* T devises a fund in trust "for A for life, then to B if B survives A." Under §2-707, the words "if B survives A" do not indicate that the transferor does not want B's descendants substituted for B if B predeceases A. If B predeceases A, leaving descendants, the descendants take, in spite of this language.

This rule of construction, which is taken from the 1990 UPC antilapse statute applicable to wills (§2-603), has been sharply criticized by commentators as changing the ordinary meaning of words into something unexpected (see page 396).

Yet another lurking surprise is that UPC §2-707 abrogates the Rule of Reversions, page 628, with respect to inter vivos trusts. Suppose that the settlor creates an irrevocable inter vivos trust for *A* for life, remainder to *B*, similar to Case 15 above. UPC §2-707 converts the remainder to *B* to a remainder "to *B* if *B* survives *A*, and if *B* does not survive *A* to *B*'s issue who survive *A*." If *B* predeceases *A* without issue, at common law the property would revert to the settlor on *A*'s death. Section 2-707 does not permit reversion to the settlor, however. On *A*'s death, even though the settlor is alive, the settlor is treated as dead. On *A*'s death, the property goes to the settlor's heirs ascertained as if the settlor had died the moment before *A*. UPC §§2-707(d), 2-711. The settlor's heirs may be remote cousins in whom the settlor has no interest, but the settlor has lost the property to them. Worse, if the settlor survives *A* but has no known heirs at *A*'s death, applying the principle that the settlor is treated as having predeceased *A*, the property escheats to the state.[9] Escheat will surely come as a shocker to the settlor, the lawyer who drafted the trust, and the lawyer's malpractice insurance carrier!

In David M. Becker, Uniform Probate Code §2-707 and The Experienced Estate Planner: Unexpected Disasters and How to Avoid Them, 47 UCLA L. Rev. 339 (1999), the author undertakes an in-depth analysis of the complexities of UPC §2-707 and its effect upon the drafting of documents by skilled estate planners.[10] Professor Becker suggests that, because it is beset with invisible boomerangs, experienced lawyers will likely block its application by inserting a clause that it is not to apply to instruments they draft:

> Skilled and conscientious lawyers do have a way to overcome §2-707 and thereby protect themselves and the integrity of the dispositive provisions they design and draft. . . . [T]hey will in all probability insulate their trusts from outside forces such as the overlay of §2-707. This is their ultimate solution, and they can readily accomplish it with a general provision that totally disclaims the rules of construction embodied by §2-707.
>
> Within a short time, such a provision should find its way into in-house forms that experienced estate planners create and regularly use, and not long thereafter, such a disclaimer should become a standard feature of published forms available to all lawyers. Finally, once published, it should soon emerge in the trust forms that every lawyer uses — including those who are inexperienced. Once this happens, §2-707 will be emasculated for all, and its curative effect will be lost as to the very group of lawyers whose work product it was intended to improve. The bottom line is that §2-707 will either be a disaster waiting to happen for experienced estate planners or

9. The Official Comment says: "Note also that the meaning of the back-stop gift [the "back-stop gift" is what the UPC calls the reversion at common law] is governed by Section 2-711 [reproduced in this book at page 660], under which the gift is to the transferor's heirs determined as if the transferor died when *A* died. Thus there will always be a set of substitute takers, even if it turns out to be the State." The settlor is excluded as a substitute taker.

10. "In preparation for writing this Article, I spent *many* hours studying §2-707, as did my student research assistants before critiquing my early drafts. We are an intelligent group of people. We think that we have mastered §2-707 after *many* hours of collective work. But then again, we are not certain." Becker, supra, at 347 n.35.

in time it will become an exercise in futility. In either case, §2-707 is not a good idea. [Id. at 408-409.]

To the extent that the drafters of §2-707 (and §2-603) sought to overcome boilerplate survivorship language, they failed to reckon with the insight that rules designed to change results after the fact (ex post) also affect behavior before the fact (ex ante). The result of §2-707 might be limited to the emergence of new boilerplate such as: "No lapse or antilapse statute (including, but not limited to, any statute based on Uniform Probate Code §§2-603 or 2-707 (1990)) shall apply to any disposition of property hereunder."

UPC §2-707 has been adopted only in Alaska, Arizona (modified version), Colorado, Hawaii, Michigan (modified version), Montana, New Mexico, North Dakota, South Dakota (modified version), and Utah (modified version), and a related provision has been enacted in Iowa. With the exception of Hawaii's statute, which is expressly prospective, these enactments are silent as to whether they are intended to be applied to already existing trusts. On the one hand, retrospective application might be unconstitutional as a taking of property from the current owners of the transmissible remainders. See Lake of the Woods Assn. v. McHugh, 380 S.E.2d 872 (Va. 1989) (holding unconstitutional retroactive application of wait-and-see perpetuities statute to previously vested interests). On the other hand, if these statutes, like Hawaii's, are applied prospectively only, then in those states two systems of future interests are in effect. The common law of future interests continues to apply to legal future interests in land and personal property, as well as to trusts created prior to the enactment of the state's version of §2-707, but the new rules apply to future interests in trusts created after the statutes were enacted.

Students usually find the common law of future interests tough going. To require them also to learn the different and more complicated UPC system of future interests, unless it has been adopted in their state, seems questionable. Because of the length and complexities of UPC §2-707, it is not reproduced here. You may, if you wish, find §2-707 in the Uniform Laws Annotated database in Westlaw or on the web page of the Uniform Law Commission.

2. *Gifts to Classes*

As you may recall from Chapter 6 (see page 399), a *class gift* arises when the donor is "group minded." The donor is thought to be group minded if she uses a class label in describing the beneficiaries, such as "to *A*'s children" or "to my nephews and nieces." But a class label is not necessary for a class gift. Beneficiaries described by their individual names, but forming a natural class, may be deemed a class gift if the court decides, after admitting extrinsic evidence, that the testator would want the survivors to divide the property. See Restatement (Third) of Property: Wills and Other Donative Transfers §§13.1-13.2, excerpted at page 399.

Gifts to classes raise a host of interpretive and constructional problems. We examine here some of the recurring problems under this heading.

a.   Gifts of Income

Dewire v. Haveles

Supreme Judicial Court of Massachusetts, 1989
404 Mass. 274, 534 N.E.2d 782

WILKINS, J.   This petition for a declaration of rights seeks answers to questions arising from an artlessly drafted will that, among its many inadequacies, includes a blatant violation of the rule against perpetuities. . . .

Thomas A. Dewire died in January, 1941, survived by his widow, his son Thomas, Jr., and three grandchildren (Thomas, III, Paula, and Deborah, all children of Thomas, Jr.). His will placed substantially all his estate in a residuary trust. The income of the trust was payable to his widow for life and, on her death, the income was payable to his son Thomas, Jr., the widow of Thomas, Jr., and Thomas Jr.'s children.[11] After the testator's death, Thomas, Jr., had three more children by a second wife. Thomas, Jr., died on May 28, 1978, a widower, survived by all six of his children. Thomas, III, who had served as trustee since 1978, died on March 19, 1987, leaving a widow and one child, Jennifer. Among the questions presented, and the most important one for present purposes, is to whom the one-sixth share of the trust income, once payable to Thomas, III, is now payable.

In his will, the testator stated: "It is my will, except as hereinabove provided, that my grandchildren, under guidance and discretion of my Trustee, shall share equally in the net income of my said estate." At another point, he referred to the trust income being "divided equally amongst my grandchildren." The rule against perpetuities violation occurred because the will provided for the trust's termination "twenty-one years after the death of the last surviving child of my said son, Thomas A. Dewire, Jr., when the property of the trust shall be equally divided amongst the lineal descendants of my grandchildren."[12]

There is no explicit provision in the will concerning the distribution of income on the death of a grandchild while the gift of income to grandchildren continues, nor is there any statement as to what the trustee should do with trust income between the death of the last grandchild and the date assigned for termination of the trust twenty-one years later.

Our task is to discern the testator's intention concerning the distribution of a grandchild's share of the trust income on his death. As a practical matter, in cases

11. The language of the will directing this distribution appears in article third of the will and reads as follows:

> Third: To my wife, Mabel G. Dewire, I give, devise and bequeath all the rest, residue and remainder of all the estate of which I shall die seized, for and during the term of her natural life, and upon her decease to my son, Thomas A. Dewire, Jr., and his heirs and assigns, but in trust nevertheless upon the following trusts and for the following purposes:
>
> A. To hold, direct, manage and conserve the trust estate, so given, for the benefit of himself, his wife and children in the manner following, that is to say:
>
> To expend out of the net income so much as may be necessary for the proper care, maintenance of himself and wife conformable to their station in life, and for the care, maintenance and education of his children born to him in his lifetime, in such manner as in his judgment and discretion shall seem proper, and his judgment and discretion shall be final.

12. As we shall explain, the possibility that Thomas, Jr., would have a child born after the testator's death was sufficient to cause the violation of the rule against perpetuities. The fact that Thomas, Jr., had children born after the testator's death makes possible a violation of the rule in actual fact.

of this sort, where there is no express intention, we must resort to reasonable inferences in the particular circumstances which on occasion shade into rules of construction that are applied when no intention at all can be inferred on the issue. In this case, the reasonable inference as to the testator's intention is that Jennifer should take her father's share in the income.

Certain points are not in serious controversy and are relatively easy to resolve. The gift of net income to the testator's grandchildren, divided equally or to be shared equally, is a class gift. . . . The class includes all six grandchildren, three of whom were born before and three of whom were born after the testator's death. . . . Because there is a gift over at the end of the class gift, the testator intended the class gift to his grandchildren only to be a gift of a life interest in the income of the trust. . . . The general rule is that, in the absence of a contrary intent expressed in the will or a controlling statute stating otherwise, members of a class are joint tenants with rights of survivorship. Old Colony Trust Co. v. Treadwell, 43 N.E.2d 777, 779 (Mass. 1942). Meserve v. Haak, 77 N.E. 377, 379 (Mass. 1906). See G.L. c. 191, §22 (1986 ed.) (antilapse statute).

This last stated principle becomes important in deciding whether Jennifer, the child of the deceased grandson, takes her deceased father's share in the trust income or whether the remaining class members, the other five grandchildren, take that income share equally by right of survivorship. Jennifer argues, under the general rule, that the will manifests an intent contrary to a class gift with rights of survivorship. We agree with this conclusion. Thus we need not decide, as Jennifer further argues, whether the rule of construction presuming a right of survivorship in class members should be rejected in the circumstances and replaced by a rule based on principles similar to those expressed in the antilapse statute.[13]

Before we explain why the will expresses an intention that, during the term of the class gift, Jennifer, while living, should take her father's share in the income, we discuss the rule against perpetuities problem.[14] The prospect that interests under this will may vest beyond the permissible limit of the rule against perpetuities is not only theoretically possible, it is actuarially likely. The interests of the grandchildren in the trust income vested at their father's death (if not sooner) and, because he was a life in being at the testator's death, those interests vested within

13. The Massachusetts antilapse statute applies only to testamentary gifts to a child or other relation of a testator who predeceased the testator leaving issue surviving the testator and to class gifts to children or other relations where one or more class member predeceased the testator (even if the class member had died before the will was executed). G.L. c. 191, §22. The rule of construction of §22 is that the issue of a deceased relation take his share by right of representation "unless a different disposition is made or required by the will."

In this case, no class member predeceased the testator, and, therefore, §22 does not explicitly aid Jennifer. The policy underlying §22 might fairly be seen as supporting, as a rule of construction (absent a contrary intent), the substitution of a class member's surviving issue for a deceased class member if the class is made up of children or other relations of the testator. See Bigelow v. Clap, 43 N.E. 1037, 1038 (Mass. 1896). It has been suggested that "[t]he policy of [antilapse] statutes [dealing with the death of a class member after the testator's death] commends itself to decisional law." Restatement (Second) of Property, Donative Transfers §27.3 Comment i (Tent. Draft No. 9, 1986). If the antilapse statute protects the interests of the issue of a relation who predeceases a testator, there is a good reason why we should adopt, as a rule of construction, the same principle as to a relation of a testator who survives the testator but dies before an interest comes into possession. In the case of a class gift of income from a trust, the interest could be viewed as coming into possession of each income distribution date.

14. In its classic formulation, the rule against perpetuities declares that: "No interest is good unless it must vest, if at all, not later than twenty-one years after some life in being at the creation of the interest." J.C. Gray, The Rule Against Perpetuities §201, at 191 (4th ed. 1942). See Eastman Marble Co. v. Vermont Marble Co., 128 N.E. 177, 182 (Mass. 1920).

the period of the rule. The gift over at the end of the class gift of income to the grandchildren, however, might not vest seasonably because another grandchild could have been born after the testator's death and could be the surviving grandchild. In this case, in fact, the three youngest grandchildren were born after the death of the testator but they are measuring lives for the term of the class gift. The parties agree that the purported gift of the remainder to the lineal descendants of the testator's grandchildren "twenty-one years after the death of the last surviving" grandchild violates the rule against perpetuities in its traditional form and would be void. See Second Bank-State St. Trust Co. v. Second Bank-State St. Trust Co., 140 N.E.2d 201, 205-206 (Mass. 1957). There is no need at this time to decide the question of the proper distribution of trust income or assets at the death of the last grandchild. The question will be acute at the death of the last grandchild, when the class gift of income from the trust will terminate.

The rule against perpetuities problem need not be resolved at this time. It has some bearing, however, on what should be done during the term of the class gift with the one-sixth share of the trust income that is in dispute. We reject the argument that, because of the violation of the rule against perpetuities, the income interests should be treated as being more than life interests. There is no authority for such a proposition. Although the gift over violates the rule against perpetuities in its traditional form and in time may prove to violate it in actual fact, the language providing for such a distribution may properly be considered in determining a testator's intention with respect to other aspects of his will. . . .

We are now in a position to discuss the question whether the class gift of income to grandchildren calls for the payment of income equally to those grandchildren living from time to time (as joint tenants with rights of survivorship) or whether the issue of any deceased grandchild succeeds by right of representation to his income interest. The latter result better conforms with the testator's intentions.

The testator provided that the trust should terminate twenty-one years after the death of his last grandchild. It is unlikely that the testator intended that trust income should be accumulated for twenty-one years, and we would tend to avoid such a construction. See Meserve v. Haak, 77 N.E. 377, 378-379 (Mass. 1906). Certainly, we should not presume that he intended an intestacy as to that twenty-one year period. See Anderson v. Harris, 67 N.E.2d 670, 672-673 (Mass. 1946). He must have expected that someone would receive distributions of income during those years. The only logical recipients of that income would be the issue (by right of representation) of deceased grandchildren, the same group of people who would take the trust assets on termination of the trust (assuming no violation of the rule against perpetuities).[15] If these people were intended to receive income during the last twenty-one years of the trust as well as the trust assets on its termination, it is logical that they should also receive income during the term of the class gift if their ancestor (one of the grandchildren) should die. Such a pattern treats each grandchild and his issue equally throughout the intended term of the trust. Where, among other things, every other provision in the will concerning the distribution of trust income and principal (after the death of the testator and his wife) points to equal treatment of the testator's issue per stirpes,

---

15. "[T]he property of the trust shall be equally divided amongst the lineal descendants of my grandchildren." "Equally," referring to a multigenerational class, normally means per stirpes. New England Trust Co. v. McAleer, 181 N.E.2d 569, 572 (Mass. 1962).

there is a sufficient contrary intent shown to overcome the rule of construction that the class gift of income to grandchildren is given to them as joint tenants with the right of survivorship.

Judgment shall be entered declaring that (1) Jennifer Ann Dewire in her lifetime is entitled to one-sixth of the net income of the trust during the period of the class gift of income, that is, until the death of the last grandchild (and a proportionate share of the income of any grandchild who dies leaving no issue), [and] (2) no declaration shall be made at this time concerning the disposition of trust income or principal on the death of the last grandchild of Thomas A. Dewire. . . .

So ordered.

PROBLEM AND NOTE

1.   *T* bequeaths a fund in trust to pay the income "to each of my children Gertrude, Charlotte, and John in equal amounts during their lives, and upon the death of the last survivor, to distribute the principal to their issue per stirpes then living." Gertrude dies. What distribution of income is made? If Charlotte and John receive Gertrude's share, Gertrude's spouse and children are cut off from any benefits they have been receiving from Gertrude's share and the surviving children get richer. Cf. Svenson v. First Natl. Bank of Boston, 363 N.E.2d 1129 (Mass. App. 1977) (devise of income substantially identical except made to testator's servants rather than her children; court held gift of income was a class gift, to be divided by surviving servants); Westervelt v. First Interstate Bank, 551 N.E.2d 1180 (Ind. App. 1990) (holding income goes to surviving child on theory that each child has an implied cross remainder in the other child's share).

Under the traditional approach, which was followed in *Svenson* and *Westervelt*, Thomas III's share in *Dewire* would have been paid to the surviving grandchildren, not to his issue. Of course, the rules of construction that lead to this result can be overcome by contrary intent, and *Dewire* is a rare — but sensible — example of a court finding a contrary intent. Restatement (Third) of Trusts §49, cmt. c(3) (2003), not only approves of this result, but it also modifies the applicable rules of construction so that it would be more common. Under the Restatement approach, in cases "in which the remainder is to pass to the descendants of the income beneficiaries upon the survivor's death," and one of the income beneficiaries dies, "the normal inference is that the settlor intended the income share to be paid to the issue (if any) of the deceased income beneficiary." Id. Accord, Restatement (Third) of Property: Wills and Other Donative Transfers §14.1, cmt. g(4) (T.D. No. 4, 2004).

2.   *Drafting advice*. When you give income to a class of persons, do not dispose of the principal upon the death of the survivor, which leaves open the question litigated in *Dewire*. Instead, say "upon the death of each life tenant," and go on to provide what is to be done with the individual life tenant's share. See John L. Garvey, Drafting Wills and Trusts: Anticipating the Birth and Death of Possible Beneficiaries, 71 Or. L. Rev. 47 (1992).

b.   Gifts to Children, Issue, or Descendants

The law presumes that the word *children* means only the immediate offspring of the parent and does not include grandchildren. Sometimes the testator's probable intent is not carried out by this presumption. Here is a case that happens all too frequently:

> *Case 16.* T bequeaths a fund in trust "for my daughter, *A*, for life, then to *A*'s surviving children." At *T*'s death, *A* has two children, *B* and *C*. Subsequently *C* dies, leaving a child, *D*. Then *A* dies survived by *B* and *D*. If *children* means what it says, *B* takes all the trust fund and *D* does not share. So held in In re Gustafson, 547 N.E.2d 1152 (N.Y. 1989), denying *A*'s grandchild a share, over a strong dissent.

In cases like Case 16, one has a nagging suspicion that the drafter carelessly chose the word *children* when the word *issue* or *descendants*, incorporating the principle of representation so prominent in the law of inheritance, would have fit the client's intent better. This suspicion has given rise to numerous cases, often involving home-made wills, litigating the question of whether the testator (drafter?) meant by *children* persons other than immediate offspring. Sometimes courts have held that other language in the will or extrinsic circumstances indicate that the testator in fact meant *descendants*. See also Restatement (Third) of Property: Wills and Other Donative Transfers §14.1, cmt. g (T.D. No. 4, 2004), which provides that a gift to *children* usually excludes grandchildren and more remote descendants, but may mean *issue* if coupled with language of representation or other reasons for interpreting so.

Where *T* makes a gift in trust "to the issue of *A*," the question arises whether the issue take *per capita* or *per stirpes*. If the issue take *per capita*, all issue who are born before the period of distribution take an equal share. Descendants with living parents share equally with their parents. Thus if *A* has three surviving children and one of these children has two surviving children, the property is divided into five shares. If, on the other hand, the issue take *per stirpes* or *by right of representation* (the terms are synonymous in most states), the children of a child of the designated ancestor take nothing if their parent is alive, and if the parent is dead, the children take by representation. Thus if *A* has three children and one of these three predeceases *A*, leaving two children surviving *A*, the property is divided into three shares and the children of the predeceased child divide that child's one-third share.

Most jurisdictions start with a presumption that a gift to "issue" or "descendants" implies some form of representation (not a per capita distribution), but courts vary on what language is sufficient to overcome the presumption. For example, suppose *T* devises property in trust with the remainder to the descendants of *A*, "share and share alike." Is the remainder distributed per capita (with all descendants of *A*, including those with living parents, sharing in the estate equally), or is the property distributed per stirpes (with descendants of *A* taking only if their ancestors have predeceased)? Compare Estate of Goodwin, 739 N.Y.S.2d 239 (Sur. 2002) (remainder to "descendants, share and share alike" distributed to all descendants per capita), with First Illini Bank v. Pritchard, 595 N.E.2d 728 (Ill. App. 1992) (remainder to "descendants, share and share alike" distributed to descendants per stirpes).

Where a will or trust explicitly uses the phrase *per stirpes* or *by right of representation*, which version of representation is intended: (1) English per stirpes, (2) modern per stirpes, or (3) per capita with representation?

(1) *English per stirpes.* In England the intestacy statute divides the decedent's property into as many shares as there are children of the decedent alive or

dead but leaving issue surviving the decedent. The issue of any deceased child succeeds to that child's share. See page 74. The English courts interpret the words *per stirpes* in a will or trust to call for a similar distribution. Thus the distribution of a bequest to the "issue per stirpes" of a named person mirrors intestate distribution to the issue of that person.

(2) *Modern per stirpes.* In this country, the intestacy statutes of nearly half the states provide for a per stirpes distribution dividing the property into shares at the first generational level where a descendant is alive, called the *modern per stirpes* system (see page 74). In a trust distribution to the settlor's issue, if the settlor died leaving grandchildren, but no surviving children, then the first division would be into as many shares as there are surviving grandchildren (and deceased grandchildren with surviving issue). In many states the words *per stirpes* in a will or trust, by reference to the intestacy law, call for this modern per stirpes distribution.

(3) *Per capita at each generation.* The Uniform Probate Code's intestacy law, §2-106, gives a new meaning to representation, defining it to mean *per capita at each generation.* Under this more complicated system, which is described at pages 75-76, shares passing to more remote generations are pooled together before being divided among the takers at the next generation. Thus, all surviving children would take equal shares, and all grandchildren with a deceased parent would take shares equal to the shares of all the other grandchildren who take.

The first Restatement of Property §303 (1940) took the position — as do the English courts — that the phrase *per stirpes* or *by right of representation*, used in a will or trust, is to be given the same meaning as representation has under the local intestacy statute. On this approach, the intent of a testator making a gift to issue is presumed to be the same as that of the average person dying without a will. The First Restatement's position appears to accord with that taken by a majority of domestic courts. Thus, since the intestacy statutes of nearly half the states provide for a per stirpes distribution dividing the property into shares at the first generational level where a descendant is alive, the *modern per stirpes* system, most trust distributions to the settlor's issue will be interpreted likewise.

A second approach is to treat gifts to "issue" or "issue by representation" in the same way as the first approach (that is, according to the local intestacy law's system of representation), but to distribute gifts to "issue per stirpes" according to the English per stirpes system regardless of the system of representation stated in the local intestacy law. The rationale for this approach is to reflect what is thought to be the probable expectations of drafters who use the phrase *per stirpes*, many of whom might have had the traditional English per stirpes system in mind rather than their state's intestacy statute. Taking this second approach are UPC §§2-708 and 2-709 (1990, revised 1993) and Restatement (Third) of Property: Wills and Other Donative Transfers §14.4 (T.D. No. 4, 2004).

Another question that has sometimes vexed the courts is whether adopted individuals are to be included in a gift to "children," "issue," or "descendants." Today almost all states presumptively include adopted individuals (and children born out of wedlock) in gifts to these classes. But problems can still arise with adult adoptions and with older wills and trusts drafted before the presumption of equal treatment for adopted children evolved. On the question of adult adoption, see Minary v. Citizens Fidelity Bank & Trust Co., 419 S.W.2d 340 (Ky. 1967), excerpted at page 89. The new forms of parentage stemming from advances in medical science have the potential to cause still further interpretive difficulties. For example, should a posthumously conceived child be included in a trust distribution to "children," "issue," or "descendants"? See Note 5 at page 111, and the Note later in this chapter at page 664, citing the views of Professor Kristine S. Knaplund and the 2004 tentative draft of the Restatement (Third) of Property.

Because of the close connection between these questions and the interpretation of intestate succession statutes, for further discussion see Chapter 2, in which we have flagged these problems throughout.

Drafting note: In view of the unsettled state of the law, we recommend that, in instruments you draft, you define *issue, descendants, per stirpes*, and other such terms.[16]

c.   Gifts to Heirs

Estate of Woodworth

California Court of Appeal, Fifth District, 1993
18 Cal. App. 4th 936, 22 Cal. Rptr. 2d 676

DiBIASO, J.   The Regents of the University of California (Regents) appeal from an order of the probate court which rejected their claim to the remainder of a testamentary trust. We will reverse. We will apply the common law preference for early vesting and hold that, absent evidence of the testator's intent to the contrary, the identity of "heirs" entitled to trust assets must be determined at the date of death of the named ancestor who predeceased the life tenant, not at the date of death of the life tenant.

---

16. Here are some definitions concerning systems of representation:

Reference to intestacy law: When a distribution is directed to be made to any person's issue or issue per stirpes, distribution shall be made to such issue in such shares as they would receive under the (state) law of intestate succession if such person had died intestate on the date of the final ascertainment of the membership in the class, owning the subject matter of the gift.

English per stirpes: When a distribution is directed to be made to any person's issue or issue per stirpes, the property shall be divided into as many equal shares as there are (1) living children of the person, if any, and (2) deceased children who leave issue then living. Each living child of the person shall be allocated one share, and the share of each deceased child who leaves issue then living shall be divided in the same manner.

Modern per stirpes: When a distribution is directed to be made to any person's issue or issue per stirpes, the property shall be divided into as many equal shares as there are (1) living members of the nearest generation of issue then living and (2) deceased members of that generation who leave issue then living. Each living member of the nearest generation of issue then living shall be allocated one share, and the share of each deceased member of that generation who leaves issue then living shall be divided among his or her then living issue in the same manner.

Per capita at each generation: When a distribution is directed to be made to any person's issue or issue per stirpes, the property shall be divided into as many equal shares as there are (1) living members of the nearest generation of issue then living and (2) deceased members of that generation who leave issue then living. Each living member of the nearest generation then living shall be allocated one share, and the remaining shares, if any, shall be combined and then divided among the living issue of the deceased members of that generation as if the issue already allocated a share and their descendants were then dead.

Harold Evans Woodworth died testate in 1971. His will was thereafter admitted to probate; in 1974 a decree of distribution was entered. According to this decree,[17] a portion of the estate was distributed outright to the testator's surviving spouse, Mamie Barlow Woodworth. The balance of the estate was distributed to Mamie Barlow Woodworth and the Bank of America, to be held, administered and distributed in accord with the terms of a testamentary trust established by the will of Harold Evans Woodworth. The life tenant of the trust was Mamie Barlow Woodworth. Among the trust provisions was the following:

> This trust shall terminate upon the death of MAMIE BARLOW WOODWORTH. Upon the termination of this trust, my trustee shall pay, deliver and convey all of the trust estate then remaining, including all accrued and/or undistributed income thereunto appertaining, to MRS. RAY B. PLASS, also known as Elizabeth Woodworth Plass [Elizabeth Plass], whose present address is 90 Woodland Way, Piedmont, California, if she then survives, and if not then to her heirs at law.

Elizabeth Plass was the testator's sister; he also had two brothers who predeceased him. One died without issue. The other was survived by two children, Elizabeth Woodworth Holden, a natural daughter, and James V. Woodworth, an adopted son.

Elizabeth Plass died in 1980; she was survived by her husband, Raymond Plass. Raymond Plass died testate in 1988. In relevant part, he left the residue of his estate to the Regents for use on the University's Berkeley campus.

Mamie Woodworth, the life tenant, died in 1991. Thereafter, Wells Fargo Bank, as successor trustee of the Woodworth trust, petitioned the probate court pursuant to Probate Code section 17200 to determine those persons entitled to distribution of the trust estate. The petition alleged that "The petitioner [was] uncertain as to whether Elizabeth Plass' 'heirs at law' under [the decree] should be determined as of February 14, 1980, the date of her death, or August 13, 1991, the date of Mamie [Barlow] Woodworth's death."

It is undisputed that (1) as of February 14, 1980, Elizabeth Plass' heirs at law were her husband, Raymond Plass, her niece, Elizabeth Woodworth Holden, and her nephew, James V. Woodworth; and (2) as of August 13, 1991, Elizabeth Plass' heirs at law were Elizabeth Woodworth Holden and James V. Woodworth (the Woodworth heirs).

... [T]he probate court concluded that the identity of the heirs entitled to the trust assets must be determined as of the date of death of the life tenant. The probate court therefore ordered the trustee to deliver the remaining trust assets in equal shares to the Woodworth heirs.

DISCUSSION ...

2. ISSUES

The Regents contend the probate court erroneously failed to apply the general rule of construction which requires that the identity of "heirs" entitled to take a

---

17. The decedent's will was not introduced in the probate court proceedings. A decree of distribution is a conclusive determination of the terms of a testamentary trust and the rights of all parties claiming any interest under it. (Estate of Easter, 148 P.2d 601 (Cal. 1944)).

remainder interest be determined as of the date of death of the denominated ancestor, in the absence of any contrary intent expressed by the testator. (See Estate of Stanford, 315 P.2d 681 (Cal. 1957); Estate of Liddle, 328 P.2d 35 (Cal. App. 1958); and Estate of Newman, 229 P. 898 (Cal. App. 1924).) Had the probate court construed the decree in accord with this principle, the Regents would have been entitled to share in the trust assets as a residuary legatee of Raymond Plass, an heir at law of Elizabeth Plass at the time of her death in 1980.

The Woodworth heirs respond by asserting the probate court's decision is consistent with an exception to the general rule which requires that the determination be made at the date of death of the life tenant. (See Wells Fargo Bank v. Title Ins. & Trust Co., 99 Cal. Rptr. 464 (App. 1971); and Estate of McKenzie, 54 Cal. Rptr. 888 (App. 1966).) Under this principle, the Regents have no interest in the trust assets, because Raymond Plass predeceased Mamie Barlow Woodworth.[18]

3. THE EARLY VESTING RULE

Estate of Liddle, supra, 328 P.2d 35, reflects the common law preference for vested rather than contingent remainders. Thus, unless a particular instrument disclosed a different intent on the part of the testator, a remainder to a class of persons, such as children, became vested in the class when one or more of its members came into existence and could be ascertained, even though the class was subject to open for future additional members. (Estate of Stanford, supra, 315 P.2d 681.) Furthermore, the fact that takers of a postponed gift were described by a class designation did not, under the common law rule, give rise to any implied condition of survival.

The circumstances involved in *Liddle* are substantially indistinguishable from those of the present case. In *Liddle*, the remainder of a testamentary trust was to be distributed to the testatrix's attorney or, in the event of his death, the attorney's heirs-at-law. Although the attorney survived the testatrix, he predeceased the life tenant. [His wife was his heir.] The wife's heirs and the administrator of her estate clashed with certain remote cousins of the attorney over the ownership of the trust assets.

The appellate court ruled in favor of the wife's estate. Relying upon statutes, treatises, and case law expressing common law notions, including Estate of Stanford, supra, 315 P.2d 681, the court construed the phrase "heirs at law" according to its technical meaning, that is, the person or persons who are entitled to succeed to the property of an intestate decedent. The *Liddle* court then held the members of this class must be determined as of the death of the named ancestor. The rule was summarized as follows:

> Normally, when a gift has been made to the "heirs" or "next of kin" of a named individual, the donor has said in effect that he wants the property distributed as the law would distribute it if the named person died intestate. Accordingly, the normal time for applying the statute of descent or distribution is at the death of the named individual. This is, however, merely a rule of construction, and if the testator or

---

18. It is undisputed that had the testator in this case died on or after January 1, 1985, the Regents would have no claim to the trust assets. Under Probate Code sections 6150 and 6151 which have been in effect since 1985, a devise of a future interest to a class, such as heirs, includes only those who fit the class description at the time the legacy is to take effect in enjoyment.

grantor manifests an intention that the statute be applied either at an earlier or a later time, such intention will be given effect. (*Liddle*, supra.)

The designated ancestor in *Liddle* was the attorney. Because his wife was his intestate heir at the time he died, the court found she was the proper recipient of the trust estate.

4. THE CONTINGENT SUBSTITUTIONAL GIFT EXCEPTION

On the other hand, *Wells Fargo Bank*, supra, 99 Cal. Rptr. 464, reflects the application of an exception to the early vesting principle. In *Wells Fargo Bank*, a woman had conveyed, by a grant deed, a life estate in certain real property to her daughter, with remainders to the grantor's two other children. If the life tenant died without issue and the two other children died without issue before the grantor's death, the instrument provided that the remainder interest in the property would belong to the grantor's "heirs." The trial court determined the heirs should be ascertained as of the date of the grantor's death.

The court of appeal reversed, . . . [relying on] Simes & Smith, The Law of Future Interests (2nd ed.) §735, p. 210. . . . [U]nder consideration at the cited portion of this treatise is the situation where "a testator devises a life estate or defeasible fee to *a person who is one of his heirs*, followed by a remainder or executory interest to the testator's heirs." (Simes & Smith, supra, §735, p. 206; emphasis added.) As Simes and Smith point out, in such circumstances, some courts have rejected the general rule that the members of the class are to be determined at the death of the ancestor (i.e., the testator), and instead have applied an exception which identifies the heirs who will take the remainder as those in being upon the death of the holder of the life estate or defeasible fee. The rationale for these decisions is an assumption the testator did not intend to give both a present and a future interest to the same person. (See Simes & Smith, supra, §735, at pp. 206-210.)

Wells Fargo Bank involved a bequest of the same type as that which is the subject of section 735 of the Simes and Smith treatise. In *Wells Fargo Bank*, the estate of the life tenant would have been entitled to receive a portion of the remainder if the identity of the grantor's heirs was determined at the time of the grantor's death rather than at the date of the life tenant's death. The *Wells Fargo Bank* court essentially adopted the analysis in section 735 of Simes and Smith that: "[I]f the general rule is applied, an incongruous result would be reached by taking the property away from [the holder of the possessory interest] because he died without issue and giving it back to him because of the same reason." (*Wells Fargo Bank*, supra.) . . .

By contrast, in the instant case we do not have a contingent, substituted gift to a class of recipients which includes the deceased interim beneficiary. As in *Liddle*, the class of contingent, substituted heirs does not encompass any prior contingent interim beneficiary. . . .

Thus, we believe the exception to the general rule of early vesting, as implemented in *Wells Fargo Bank*, should not be applied to the remainder interest contained in the decree of distribution here.

5. OTHER CONSIDERATIONS

For the reasons which follow, we find no other justification for departing from *Liddle*. First, there is nothing in the language of the other provisions of the decree of distribution before us which reveals the testator's intent or desire. Since the record does not include Harold Evans Woodworth's will, we cannot resort to it to attempt to divine his wishes.

Second, the fact that the University, an entity, is not a relative of Elizabeth Plass or one of her heirs at law is not material. Unlike the *Wells Fargo Bank* court, we are unwilling to say that application of the general rule "would result in thwarting the expressed intention of the Grantor by distributing the corpus of the trust to persons or entities other than [Elizabeth Plass'] heirs." (*Wells Fargo Bank*, supra) Had the instrument in *Wells Fargo Bank* satisfactorily disclosed the grantor's intentions regarding the distribution of the remainder interest in the property, there would have been no need for the court to have even considered the competing rules of construction in order to decide the case.

It would be pure speculation for us to conclude that Harold Evans Woodworth would not have wanted Raymond Plass to inherit a portion of the trust assets. It appears from the record that Raymond Plass and Elizabeth Plass were married at the time the testator executed his will. It has long been the law in California that a husband is an heir of his deceased wife. Nothing in the decree forecloses the possibility the testator took into account the fact that Elizabeth Plass might predecease, and Raymond Plass might outlive, Mamie Barlow Woodworth, resulting in Raymond Plass' succession to a portion of the trust remainder.

Third, the rule of construction which favors descent according to blood in cases of ambiguity in testamentary dispositions should likewise not determine the result in this case. The general rule favoring early vesting was well-established long before the testator died. We do not think it should be abandoned in order to carry out some purportedly perceived, but entirely speculative, notion about the intent of the testator based upon events which occurred well after the testator's death. (See Estate of McKenzie, supra, 54 Cal. Rptr. 888.) As we noted earlier, it is perfectly conceivable that Harold Evans Woodworth took into account in making his will the possibility that his property would pass to Raymond Plass and thereafter be transferred to strangers to the Woodworth line.

. . . In the absence of any firm indication of testamentary intent, the rules of construction must be implemented in order to insure uniformity and predictability in the law, rather than disregarded in order to carry out a court's ad hoc sense of what is, with perfect hindsight, acceptable in a particular set of circumstances. . . .

Last, none of the other exceptions identified in *Wells Fargo Bank* to the early vesting rule apply under the circumstances of this case. This is not a situation where the "life tenant is the sole heir, but the will devises the remainder to the testator's 'heirs.'" (*Wells Fargo Bank*, supra; Estate of Wilson, 193 P. 581 (Cal. 1920).)

In addition, the language of the decree does not contain any "expression of futurity in the description of the ancestor's heirs" (*Wells Fargo Bank*, supra), such as "my then living heirs-at-law" (Estate of Layton, 19 P.2d 793 (Cal. 1933)). When, as here, "the gift is in terms 'then to the heirs' of a designated person, the word 'then' merely indicates the time of enjoyment and has no significance in relation to the rule [of early vesting]." (Estate of Miner, 29 Cal. Rptr. 601, 606-607 (App. 1963).) . . .

Finally, and contrary to the contention of the Woodworth heirs, we do not find the words "pay to" contained in the instant decree to be equivalent to the word "vest" or otherwise constitute an "expression of futurity" for purposes of determining the identity of the relevant heirs. Rather, the instruction pertains to the time when the recipients of the assets are entitled to have them.

DISPOSITION

Accordingly, we must reverse the probate court's ruling that the Regents have no claim to the assets of the testamentary trust.

The judgment (order) appealed from is reversed.

NOTE

Because a transmissible remainder is subject to the federal estate tax, estate planners in several states have successfully urged legislatures to enact a statute providing that where a remainder is given to a person's heirs, the heirs will not be ascertained until the remainder becomes possessory. See also Restatement (Third) of Property: Wills and Other Donative Transfers §16.1 (T.D. No. 4, 2004). Under such a statute, no remainderman has a transmissible interest because if he dies before the remainder becomes possessory, he will not be alive when heirs are ascertained and, therefore, cannot be an heir. Cal. Prob. Code §6151, referred to in footnote 18 in the *Woodworth* case and now renumbered §21114, is such a statute. So is UPC §2-711.

Uniform Probate Code (1990, amended in 1993)

§2-711.   FUTURE INTERESTS IN "HEIRS" AND LIKE

If an applicable statute or a governing instrument calls for a present or future distribution to or creates a present or future interest in a designated individual's "heirs," "heirs at law," "next of kin," "relatives," or "family," or language of similar import, the property passes to those persons, including the state, and in such shares as would succeed to the designated individual's intestate estate under the intestate succession law of the designated individual's domicile if the designated individual died when the disposition is to take effect in possession or enjoyment. If the designated individual's surviving spouse is living but is remarried at the time the disposition is to take effect in possession or enjoyment, the surviving spouse is not an heir of the designated individual.

NOTE: THE DOCTRINE OF WORTHIER TITLE

Under the doctrine of worthier title, when a settlor transfers property in trust, with a life estate in the settlor or in another, and purports to create a remainder in the *settlor's heirs*, it was conclusively presumed that the settlor intended to retain a reversion in himself and not create a remainder in his heirs. The rationale for this rule of law, which as such did not yield to a showing of contrary intent, is obscure, but probably it was to ensure that property passed to descendants by descent rather than by purchase (that is, other than by inheritance). Property acquired by inheritance was deemed "worthier" and, perhaps more importantly, feudal lords exacted dues on inheritance but not other forms of transfer.

In England, Parliament abolished this remnant of feudal times in 1833. Inheritance Act, 3 & 4 Wm. IV, c. 106, §3 (1833). In the United States, however, the doctrine was roused from a sleep of several centuries by Judge Cardozo in

Doctor v. Hughes, 122 N.E. 221 (N.Y. 1919), and recast as a *rule of construction* in order to do equity on some particular facts. This revitalized the doctrine as a rule of presumed intent, which can be rebutted by evidence that the settlor did intend to create a remainder in his heirs. Thus:

> *Case 17. O* transfers property to *X* in trust "to pay the income to *O* for life, then to distribute the principal to *A* if *A* is living, and if *A* is not living, to distribute the principal to *O*'s heirs." The presumption is that *O* has a reversion and *O*'s heirs do not have a remainder. *O* may convey the reversion by will to whomever *O* chooses.

The states that followed Cardozo's lead and adopted the doctrine as a rule of construction found that it produced a passel of lawsuits involving speculative evidence about whether the settlor intended to create a remainder rather than retain a reversion. As a result, a majority of states have jettisoned the doctrine by statute or by judicial decision, both as a rule of law and as a rule of construction. T.P. Gallanis, The Future of Future Interests, 60 Wash. & Lee L. Rev. 513, 543-548 (2003) (collecting authority). Restatement (Third) of Property: Wills and Other Donative Transfers §16.3 (T.D. No. 4, 2004), Restatement (Third) of Trusts §49, cmt. a(1) (2003), and UPC §2-710 (1990) are in accord.

Although rejection of the doctrine of worthier title seems sound, it does leave us with the problem of securing consent of the unascertained heirs of a living settlor to modification or termination of a trust. In Case 17, for example, if *O* and *A* want to terminate the trust, they must secure the consent of *O*'s unknown heirs. Statutes in some states abolishing worthier title have dealt with this problem by providing that a trust may be revoked by the settlor and other ascertained beneficiaries when the only other interested persons are the settlor's heirs. See, e.g., N.Y. Est. Powers & Trusts Law §7-1.9(b) (2004).

NOTE: THE RULE IN SHELLEY'S CASE

At common law, if land were conveyed to a grantee for life, then to the *grantee's heirs*, the attempted creation of a contingent remainder in the heirs was not recognized. Instead, the grantee took the remainder. The life estate then merged into the remainder, giving the grantee a possessory fee simple absolute.

Here is a simplified statement of the rule: If

(1)   one instrument (deed, will, or trust)
(2)   creates a life estate in land in *A*, and
(3)   purports to create a remainder in *A*'s heirs (or the heirs of *A*'s body), and
(4)   the estates are both legal or both equitable,

the remainder becomes a remainder in fee simple (or fee tail) in *A*. If there is no intervening estate, the life estate merges into the remainder, giving *A* a fee simple (or fee tail). The rule in Shelley's Case is not a rule of construction. It is a rule of law, and thus it applies regardless of the intent of the transferor. Here is an example:

> *Case 18. O* conveys land in trust "for *A* for life, and then to *A*'s heirs." Under the rule in Shelley's Case, *A* (and not *A*'s heirs) has the remainder, which then merges with *A*'s life

estate, giving *A* all the equitable interest in the trust. *A* may by will dispose of the land as *A* chooses.

The rule in Shelley's Case has been abolished in practically all states and the District of Columbia, as well as in England.[19] Restatement (Third) of Property: Wills and Other Donative Transfers §16.2, reporter's note (T.D. No. 4, 2004). See also Restatement (Third) of Trusts §49, cmt. a(1) (2003). In some states, however, the abolition by statute is fairly recent and does not apply retroactively. In these states, cases involving the rule may still crop up from time to time.

For an engaging discussion of the "mystery" in Shelley's Case — "not what it is or why it came to be, but why it stayed so long" — see John V. Orth, The Mystery of the Rule in Shelley's Case, 7 Green Bag 2d 45 (2003).

d. The Class-Closing Rule

(1) Introduction

A central characteristic of a gift to a class of persons, such as "to the children of *B*," is that if *B* is alive and capable of having more children, the persons to whom the class description applies can increase in number. The problem we now deal with is: How long can the class increase in membership? In a gift "to *B* for life, then to *B*'s children," all of *B*'s children will be alive (or in gestation) when the class is physiologically closed at *B*'s death.[20] No difficulties will be encountered on distributing the property upon *B*'s death among all *B*'s children or their estates. But suppose the disposition is "to *A* for life, then to *B*'s children." Here we may have a different kettle of fish. If *A* dies during *B*'s lifetime, what should be done with the property, inasmuch as *B* may have more children?

There are several alternative solutions possible when the class is not closed physiologically, but one or more members of the class stand ready to take their shares. Distribution could be postponed until all possible class members are on the

---

19. Brian Simpson, a distinguished English legal historian who is now a law professor at the University of Michigan, had this to say about the place of the rule in Shelley's Case in contemporary England and America:

> [W]hen I studied property law in Oxford in 1952 we still had to know what it was, since otherwise, it was argued with perverse but yet compelling logic, we could not understand what precisely had been abolished. And the rule could and indeed still can apply to legal instruments executed before 1 January 1926.
>
> Elsewhere in the common law world the rule in *Shelley's Case* still enjoys a curious twilight existence. In legal education it flourishes in the American law schools; its archaic nature and sheer incomprehensibility positively attracts some students of property law, who are fascinated by the absurd, whilst utterly repelling others. Those who teach property law can always establish their dominance by teaching the rule, since a high proportion of their class can be relied upon to misunderstand it, and their confusion can always be enhanced by teaching the doctrine of worthier title, another Gothic relic, at the same time. Outside the classroom its status resembles that of the Big Foot, the Yeti, or the Tasmanian Tiger; sightings are still possible. . . . Although American courts cheerfully invent new constitutional and common law doctrines, and abrogate old ones, as the whim takes them, they shrink with a sort of superstitious awe from disrespectful treatment of the sacred rule in *Shelley's Case*. [A.W. Brian Simpson, Leading Cases in the Common Law 41 (1995).]

20. We attend to the possibility of posthumous conception and its effect on the class closing rules at page 664.

scene. Or a partial distribution could be made to *B*'s present children and a "reasonable" portion withheld (until *B*'s death) for possible future distribution to later-born children. Or full distribution could be made to the children now at hand, subject to a requirement that they rebate a portion of each share as *B* has more children. Or the class could be "closed" at *A*'s death, with full distribution to the present children and the exclusion of all children later born to *B*.

The practical problems that would be raised by postponing distribution, or by making a partial or defeasible distribution to existing class members, have led the courts to adopt the last alternative. This is called the *class-closing rule* or the *rule of convenience*. It is a rule of construction, giving way to sufficient evidence of the testator's contrary intent, but it is adhered to more closely than any other rule of construction — so closely, in fact, that it has sometimes been referred to erroneously as a rule of law. See Re Wernher's Settlement Trusts, [1961] 1 All E.R. 184.

Under the class-closing rule, *a class will close whenever any member of the class is entitled to possession and enjoyment of his or her share*. The key point in time is when one member is *entitled* to demand payment. The fact that actual payment may be delayed because of administrative problems does not keep the class open; it closes when the right to payment arises. For discussion and illustrations of the class-closing rule, see Restatement (Third) of Property: Wills and Other Donative Transfers §15.1 (T.D. No. 4, 2004).

When a class is open, persons not yet born can come into the class. When a class is closed, no more members can be added to the class. Note well that this is all we mean when we say that a class is closed: *No person born hereafter can share in the property*.[21] The fact that a class is closed does not mean that all members of the class will share in the property. No additional members can come in, but present class members can drop out by failing to meet some condition precedent.

(2) Immediate gifts

The class-closing rule can best be understood by examining a series of illustrative cases. In all these cases involving gifts to the children of *B*, it is assumed that *B* is alive at the testator's death. Otherwise the class would be physiologically closed.

Where there is an immediate gift to a class, the class closes as soon as any member can demand possession, either at the testator's death or later. Thus:

> *Case 19. T* bequeaths $10,000 "to the children of *B*." *B* is alive and has two children, *C* and *D*. *C* and *D* can demand immediate possession of their shares. The class closes. *C* is paid $5,000 and *D* is paid $5,000. A year later, *E* is born to *B*. *E* does not share in the bequest.

---

21. More accurately, we would say that no person conceived after this date can share, for here, as elsewhere in property law, a child is treated as in being from the time of conception if later born alive. We speak of birth, but we mean conception.

Even more accurately, when children are adopted, the time of adoption, not birth, is controlling. Estate of Markowitz, 312 A.2d 901, 903 (N.J. Super. 1973); In re Silberman's Will, 243 N.E.2d 736 (N.Y. 1968). The adopted child must be adopted into the class before the class closes. A child in being when the class closes, but subsequently adopted, does not share. Do you see the reason for this? See Samuel M. Fetters, The Determination of Maximum Membership in Class Gifts in Relation to Adopted Children: In re Silberman's Will Examined, 21 Syracuse L. Rev. 1 (1969).

There is an exception to this rule if no members of the class have been born before the testator's death. Since the testator must have known there were no class members alive at his death, it is assumed the testator intended all class members, whenever born, to share. Hence, in this case, the class does not close until the death of the designated ancestor of the class. In Case 19, if *B* had no children born before the testator's death, the class would not close until *B*'s death. See Restatement (Third) of Property: Wills and Other Donative Transfers §15.1, cmt. k (T.D. No. 4, 2004).

> *Case 20.* *T* bequeaths $10,000 "to the children of *B* who reach 21." *B* has children alive, but no child is 21 at *T*'s death. The class will close when a child of *B* reaches 21.
>
> *Case 21.* *T* bequeaths $10,000 "to the children of *B*, to be paid to them in equal shares as they respectively reach 21." *B* has children alive, but all are under 21. The gift is vested with payment postponed. The class will close when the eldest child of *B* reaches 21 or, if the eldest child dies under that age, when the eldest child would have reached 21 had he lived. See Restatement (Third) of Property, supra, cmt. m.

PROBLEMS

1. *T* bequeaths $15,000 "to the children of *B* who reach 21." At *T*'s death, *B* has two children, *C* (age 7) and *D* (age 4). Three years later, *E* is born to *B*. Thereafter *C* reaches 21. What distribution is made to *C*? One year thereafter *F* is born to *B*. *D* dies at age 20. Is any distribution made? *E* then reaches 21. Is any distribution made? *F* then reaches 21. Is any distribution made?

2. A devise of property "to *B* and her children" is obviously ambiguous. Does *B* take a life estate and the children a remainder? Or do *B* and her children take equal shares as tenants in common? Under the rule in Wild's Case, decided in 1599, if *B* has children at the time of the devise, *B* and her children take as tenants in common. Some states continue to follow this rule. Others follow a life estate and remainder construction. See David M. Becker, Debunking the Sanctity of Precedent, 76 Wash. U.L.Q. 853, 861-886 (1998). The rule in Wild's Case is repudiated by Restatement (Third) of Property, supra, §14.2, cmt. f. In a jurisdiction that follows the rule in Wild's Case, what effect does the rule of convenience have on *B*'s children conceived after the testator's death?

NOTE: CLASS-CLOSING RULES AND POSTHUMOUSLY CONCEIVED CHILDREN

With the emergence of posthumously conceived children, see Woodward v. Commissioner of Social Security, page 102, a new question arises: Are posthumously conceived children cut out of participation in class gifts that would otherwise have closed before their conception? We are not aware of any cases that answer this question — yet. For useful analysis applying the traditional rule of convenience, see Kristine S. Knaplund, Postmortem Conception and a Father's Last Will, 46 Ariz. L. Rev. 91, 108-114 (2004). See also Restatement (Third) of Property, supra, at §15.1, cmt. j, which proposes the following approach:

In cases in which the distribution date is the deceased parent's death, a child produced posthumously by assisted reproduction is treated as in being at the decedent's death, for purposes of the class-closing rules, if the child was born within a reasonable time after the decedent's death. Determining whether birth occurred within a reasonable time after the decedent's death requires a balancing of the interest in final settlement of trusts and estates and allowing the surviving spouse or domestic partner time to grieve before making a decision whether to go forward with an assisted-reproduction procedure, and how soon after death an attempt was made to produce a pregnancy through assisted reproduction, whether successful or not.

In cases in which the distribution date arises after the deceased parent's death, a child produced posthumously by assisted reproduction is in being on the date of conception for purposes of the class-closing rules, just as is any other child.

In Woodward v. Commissioner, which involved the intestate succession rights of posthumously conceived twins, the court balanced the reproductive rights of the decedent, the best interests of the child, and the state's interest in finality. Are those factors equally relevant in interpreting donative instruments? What about the intent of the donor? An important difference between intestacy and the interpretation of donative instruments is that the former effects a generalized, average intent whereas the goal in the latter is to give effect to a specific decedent's intent.

A related interpretive issue is whether in assaying the validity of a contingent interest under the Rule against Perpetuities, the possibility of posthumously conceived children should be considered. See page 680.

(3) Postponed gifts

If the gift is postponed in possession until a life tenant dies, the class will not close under the class-closing rule until the time for taking possession. Thus a gift to a class of remaindermen will not close until the life tenant is dead, and it will not then close under the rule of convenience unless one remainderman is entitled to possession.

> *Case 22.* *T* bequeaths $10,000 "to *A* for life, then to the children of my daughter *B*." The class will not close in any event, under the rule of convenience, until the death of *A*. Suppose that *B* survives *A*. The class will close at *A*'s death if (a) a child of *B* is then alive, (b) a child of *B* predeceased *T* and the gift did not lapse but went to such child's issue under an antilapse statute, or (c) a child of *B* was alive at *T*'s death or was born after *T*'s death and such child predeceased *A*. In each of those cases, a child or the child's representative can demand payment at *A*'s death.

Suppose that in Case 22, at the death of *A*, *B* has not yet had any children born to her. Will the class be left open until the death of *B*, as in the case of an immediate gift to a class where no one has yet been born at the time of taking possession? Restatement (Third) of Property, supra, §15.1, cmt. k, states that the answer is Yes, but there are few cases on the matter. The Restatement goes on to state, however, that "if the circumstances indicate that it is improbable that there will be any after-conceived or after-adopted class members because of the age or physical condition of the prospective parent," it would be preferable for the gift to fail. Id.

The class-closing rule described above applies only to gifts of principal, not to gifts of income. In a trust to pay income to the children of *B*, the class closes for the payment of income periodically as the income is accrued.

PROBLEMS

1.   *T* bequeaths a fund in trust "to pay the income to *A* for life, then to distribute the principal to the children of *B* who reach 21, and in the meantime the children of *B* who are eligible to receive, but have not yet received, a share of the principal are to receive the income." At *A*'s death, *B* is alive and has one child, *C* (age 5). After *A* dies, the following events occur: *D* is born to *B*; *C* reaches 21; one year later, *E* is born to *B*; *D* and, later, *E* reach 21.

(a)   After *A*'s death, who is entitled to the income?
(b)   When is the first distribution of principal made, to whom, and how much?
(c)   How is the principal ultimately divided?

2.   *T* bequeaths a fund in trust "to divide the fund among the children of *B*, payable to each at age 21, and in the meantime they are to receive the income." At *T*'s death, *B* is alive and has one child, *C* (age 5). One year later, *C* dies. Is *C*'s administrator entitled to demand immediate distribution of *C*'s share? Would your answer be different if *B* predeceased *T*?

Lux v. Lux

Supreme Court of Rhode Island, 1972
109 R.I. 592, 288 A.2d 701

KELLEHER, J.   The artless efforts of a draftsman have precipitated this suit which seeks the construction of and instructions relating to the will of Philomena Lux who died a resident of Cumberland on August 15, 1968. We hasten to add that the will was drawn by someone other than counsel of record. . . .

Philomena Lux executed her will on May 9, 1966. She left her residuary estate to her husband, Anthony John Lux, and nominated him as the executor. Anthony predeceased his wife. His death triggered the following pertinent provisions of Philomena's will:

> Fourth: In the event that my said husband, Anthony John Lux, shall predecease me, then I make the following disposition of my estate:
> 1. . . .
> 2. All the rest, residue and remainder of my estate, real and personal, of whatsoever kind and nature, and wherever situated, of which I shall die seized and possessed, or over which I may have power of appointment, or to which I may be in any manner entitled at my death, I give, devise and bequeath to my grandchildren, share and share alike.
> 3. Any real estate included in said residue shall be maintained for the benefit of said grandchildren and shall not be sold until the youngest of said grandchildren has reached twenty-one years of age.

4. Should it become necessary to sell any of said real estate to pay my debts, costs of administration, or to make distribution of my estate or for any other lawful reason, then, in that event, it is my express desire that said real estate be sold to a member of my family.

Philomena was survived by one son, Anthony John Lux, Jr., and five grandchildren whose ages range from two to eight. All the grandchildren were children of Anthony. The youngest grandchild was born after the execution of the will but before Philomena's death. The son is named in the will as the alternate executor. He informed the trial court that he and his wife plan to have more children. At the time of the hearing, Anthony was 30. The Superior Court appointed a guardian ad litem to represent the interests of the grandchildren. It also designated an attorney to represent the rights of the individuals who may have an interest under the will but who are at this time unknown, unascertained or not in being. . . .

At the time of her death, the testatrix owned real estate valued at approximately $35,000 and tangible and intangible personal property, including bank accounts, that totaled some $7,400. The real estate, which consists of two large tenement houses, is located in Cumberland.

[The court first addressed the issue of whether Philomena made an absolute gift to the grandchildren or if instead the devise was in trust for their benefit. For the reasons detailed at page 666, the court concluded] that Philomena intended that her real estate be held in trust for the benefit of her grandchildren. [Since no trustee was named in the will, the court appointed the executor to the position of trustee. The court then turned to the constructional issue.] . . .

The ascertainment of time within which a person who answers a class description such as "children" or "grandchildren" must be born in order to be entitled to share in a testator's bounty is not an easy matter. In seeking a solution, the court must seek to effectuate the testator's intent. . . .

The rationale for permitting a class to increase in size until the time for distribution stems from a judicial recognition that generally, when a testator describes the beneficiaries of his bounty by some group designation, he has in mind all those persons whenever born who come within the definition of the term used to describe the group. Normally, if he had in mind the individual members of the designated group, he would have described them by name. This recognition is tempered by the presumption that testators usually would not intend to keep the class open at the expense of an indefinite delay in the distribution of the estate. Since there is no good reason to exclude any person who is born before the period of distribution, all such persons are, in the absence of a contrary testamentary intent, deemed to be members of the class. Casner, Class Gifts to Others than to "Heirs" or "Next of Kin": Increase in the Class Membership, 51 Harv. L. Rev. 254 (1938); 5 American Law of Property §§22.40, 22.41 (1952); see concurring opinion, Frost and Roberts, JJ., Rhode Island Hospital Trust Co. v. Bateman, 172 A.2d 84 (R.I. 1961).

Despite our invocation of the rule requiring the class to remain open until the corpus is distributed, we still must determine what Philomena intended when she said that the corpus has to be preserved until the "youngest grandchild" becomes twenty-one.

There are four possible distribution dates depending on the meaning of "youngest." Distribution might be made when the youngest member of the class in being when the will was executed attains twenty-one; or when the youngest in being when the will takes effect becomes twenty-one; or when the youngest of all living class members in being at any one time attains twenty-one even though it is physically possible for others to be born; or when the youngest whenever it is born attains twenty-one. This last alternative poses a question. Should we delay distribution here and keep the class open until the possibility that Philomena's son can become a father becomes extinct? We think not.

We are conscious of the presumption in the law that a man or a woman is capable of having children so long as life lasts. A construction suit, however, has for its ultimate goal the ascertainment of the average testator's probable intent if he was aware of the problems that lead to this type of litigation. Manufacturers National Bank v. McCoy, 212 A.2d 53 (R.I. 1965). It is our belief that the average testator, when faced with the problem presented by the record before us, would endorse the view expressed in 3 Restatement, Property §295, Comment k at 1594 (1940), where in urging the adoption of the rule that calls for the closing of the class when the youngest living member reaches the age when distribution could be made, states:

> When all existent members of the class have attained the stated age, considerations of convenience . . . require that distribution shall then be made and that the property shall not be further kept from full utilization to await the uncertain and often highly improbable conception of further members of the group. The infrequency with which a parent has further children after all of his living children have attained maturity, makes this application of the rule of convenience justifiable and causes it to frustrate the unexpressed desires of a conveyor in few, if any, cases.

We hold, therefore, that distribution of the trust corpus shall be made at any time when the youngest of the then living grandchildren has attained the age of twenty-one. When this milestone is reached, there is no longer any necessity to maintain the trust to await the possible conception of additional members of the class.

Although Philomena declared that the real estate was not to be sold until the youngest grandchildren became twenty-one, her later statements about the necessity of its sale amounted to her awareness that future circumstances might require the liquidation of her real estate sometime prior to the time her youngest grandchild becomes twenty-one. The Superior Court was informed and documentary evidence was introduced which showed such a precipitous drop in the rental income as would warrant a trustee to seek a better investment.

Section 18-4-2(b) provides that, in the absence of any provision to the contrary, every trust shall be deemed to have conferred upon the trustee a discretionary power to sell the trust estate, be it real or personal property. Section 18-4-10 specifically authorizes a trustee, whenever he believes it desirable to sell trust property, to seek the Superior Court's approval for such a transaction.

When the real estate is sold, the proceeds from such sale shall, because of the doctrine of the substitute res, replace the realty as the trust corpus. Industrial National Bank v. Colt, 233 A.2d 112 (R.I. 1957); Dresser v. Booker, 69 A.2d 45 (R.I. 1949).

The impending sale brings into focus the testatrix's "express *desire* that said real estate be sold to a member of my family" (emphasis added). The words "express desire" are purely precatory. We have said that precatory language will be construed as words of command only if it is clear that the testator intended to impose on the individual concerned a legal obligation to make the desired disposition. Young v. Exum, 179 A.2d 107 (R.I. 1962). We think it clear that since Philomena's primary goal was to benefit her grandchildren, we see nothing in the record that would justify a conclusion that she intended that the potential purchasers of her real estate be limited to the members of her family.

Finally, we come to the allocation of income. The will is silent as to this item. Over a half-century ago, we said that if the will shows no intention on the part of the testator that income be accumulated, income is payable to the beneficiary as it accrues. Butler v. Butler, 101 A. 115 (R.I. 1917). This rule has been reaffirmed on many occasions. Should Philomena's son's hope for additional progeny become a reality, the quantum of each share of income received by a grandchild would be reduced as each new member of the class joins his brothers and sisters.

The parties may present to this court for approval a form of judgment in accordance with this opinion, which will be entered in the Superior Court.

(4) Gifts of specific sums

If a specific sum is given to each member of the class, the class closes at the death of the testator regardless of whether any members of the class are then alive. Thus:

> *Case 23.* T bequeaths £500 apiece to each child of A. A has no children living at T's death. The class closes at T's death, and no child of A ever takes anything. Rogers v. Mutch, 10 Ch. Div. 25 ([Eng.] 1878).

> Life looked rosy to *A* as he sat
> By the crepe-draped casket of *T*.
> Five hundred pounds for each child he begat
> Would soon make him wealthy mused he.
> So he married at once, and began procreating
> At five hundred per, he supposed;
> But you know and I know (what hardly needs stating)
> That the class had already closed.
> Mistakes of this sort are bound to arise
> When a client takes actions like these
> Without seeing his lawyer as soon as *T* dies,
> And paying the usual fees.
>   FRANK L. DEWEY[22]

What is the reason for closing the class at the death of the testator when the gift is of a fixed sum to each member of a class?

Gifts of specific sums to each member of a class are sometimes called "per capita" gifts.

---

22. Reproduced from W. Barton Leach, Langdell Lyrics of 1938 (1938).

11

TRUST DURATION AND THE RULE AGAINST PERPETUITIES

SECTION A. INTRODUCTION

1. *Development of the Rule Against Perpetuities*

The classic statement of the Rule against Perpetuities, formulated with Delphic simplicity by John Chipman Gray, reads:

> No interest [in real or personal property] is good unless it must vest, if at all, not later than twenty-one years after some life in being at the creation of the interest. [John C. Gray, The Rule Against Perpetuities §201, at 191 (4th ed. 1942).]

By virtue of his erudition, his rigorous logic, his magisterial style, and his position as a celebrated teacher of property law at Harvard, Gray became established in the late nineteenth century as not just a leading authority on the Rule but as *the* authority.[1] Because of the deference paid to Gray's work by the courts, the Rule has sometimes been treated as if it were laid down at one time by this one man. In fact, the Rule had a long and involved evolution over several centuries. The origins of the Rule against Perpetuities are somewhat obscure because of the ambiguous nature of the concept *perpetuity*. The political and social evils attending on perpetual entails, permitted by the Statute de Donis (1285), led judges to become suspicious of allowing any limitation tying up land in perpetuity.

From the sixteenth until the nineteenth century, judges struggled against perpetuities, without ever defining exactly what a perpetuity was. There were several unrefined notions and ambiguous doctrines that might be called rules against perpetuities. It fell the lot of Lord Chancellor Nottingham[2] to clarify

---

1. On the role of Gray, see Stephen A. Siegel, John Chipman Gray, Legal Formalism, and the Transformation of Perpetuities Law, 36 U. Miami L. Rev. 439 (1982).

2. Lord Nottingham, born Heneage Finch, was one of the greatest of English Chancellors and called the "Father of Equity" by Justice Story. He was equally devoted to the law and to his family. When he lost

these ancient contradictory decisions and point the way for the modern development of the Rule.

The Rule against Perpetuities as we know it began with the Duke of Norfolk's Case, 22 Eng. Rep. 931 (Ch. 1682). The Earl of Arundel had eight sons. Thomas, the eldest son and heir apparent, was weak in mind and body, and not expected to have children. Hence, the earl assumed that after his own death and the death of Thomas, the earldom and the estates accompanying it would likely descend to his second son, Henry, and Henry's issue. If Henry did inherit the earldom at Thomas's death, the earl wanted the barony of Grostock, which he planned to give initially to Henry, to shift to his fourth son, Charles. The earl went to an experienced estate planner (known as a conveyancer in those days when land was the chief form of wealth), Sir Orlando Bridgeman. This outstanding member of the bar, who later became Lord Keeper, drew up a set of highly complicated documents that cannot easily be summarized. It is enough to say that the limitation that brought on the Duke of Norfolk's Case boiled down to this: The barony of Grostock was given to Henry, but a shifting executory limitation was created, providing that if the eldest son, Thomas, should die without issue in the lifetime of Henry, so that Henry inherited the earldom, then the barony would go to Charles.

In 1652, the Earl of Arundel died, and the earldom descended to the mentally defective son, Thomas. Henry then moved into action. He assumed full control of the properties accompanying the title, and he sent Thomas to Padua in Italy where he was incarcerated until his death. Henry also engineered the restoration of the title, "Duke of Norfolk," to the family. In 1572, Queen Elizabeth I had beheaded the fourth duke for intrigues involving Mary, Queen of Scots, and by attainder all his lands and titles were forfeited.[3] In 1660, Parliament, with the consent of Charles II, restored the dukedom of Norfolk, and the incompetent Thomas became the premier duke of England. When Thomas died without issue in 1677, Henry became the sixth Duke of Norfolk.

---

his wife, mother of his 14 children, he comforted himself by taking the Great Seal to bed with him. 4 John Lord Campbell, Lives of the Lord Chancellors 273 (1857).

3. The turbulence of the times is reflected in the history of the title of Duke of Norfolk, who is the premier duke, ranking just below the blood royal. The title goes back to the first Earl of Norfolk, one of the Breton followers of William the Conqueror. After several attainders and lapses of the earldom, the dukedom was created anew by Richard II in 1397 and given to his chief supporter Thomas Mowbray, perhaps best remembered for his quarrel with Henry Bolingbroke, Duke of Hereford (afterward Henry IV), which forms Act I of Shakespeare's Richard II and which resulted in Mowbray's banishment. After four Mowbray dukes, the title lapsed.

In 1483, after the murder of the princes in the Tower, Richard III conferred the dukedom on Sir John Howard, an heir of the Mowbray estates and the first of the Howard dukes. Two years later, "Jack of Norfolk" died fighting for Richard at Bosworth; the title and the estates were forfeited to the victorious Henry Tudor, who ascended the throne as Henry VII. The first duke's son regained royal favor by commanding, in his 70th year, the army that defeated the Scots at Flodden, and in 1514 Henry VIII restored the title. Two nieces of the third duke, Anne Boleyn and Catherine Howard, were wives of Henry VIII, both beheaded for infidelity. Subsequently, the Howard family fell from grace; the third duke's son was executed on a charge of treason, and the duke himself was arrested, stripped of his title, and ordered to be beheaded. During the night before the morning set for execution, Henry VIII died and the duke was spared. Seven years later, Queen Mary released him from prison and restored the dukedom to him. The third duke was succeeded by his grandson, who in turn was executed by Elizabeth I for plotting with Mary Stuart. His son Philip, through inheritance from Philip's mother, became the Earl of Arundel. His grandson, the third Earl of Arundel, made the disposition at issue in the Duke of Norfolk's Case.

Since the fourteenth century, the Duke of Norfolk has been the hereditary earl marshal of England. The highest ranking Catholic lord of the realm, the duke attends the sovereign upon the opening of Parliament, walking at his or her right hand, and arranges state ceremonies such as coronations, royal marriages, and funerals.

**The Sixth Duke of Norfolk
by Gerard Soest, ca. 1677
Tate Gallery, London**

Reproduced by permission of the Tate Gallery.

His greed brought on the case
that originated the Rule
against Perpetuities.

**The First Earl of Nottingham, Lord
Chancellor after Godfrey Kneller, 1680
National Portrait Gallery, London**

*Reproduced by permission of the
National Portrait Gallery.*

His decision gave the rich the power
to secure family wealth
for another generation.

After succeeding to the dukedom and its properties, greedy Henry did not want to give up the barony of Grostock. Charles brought a bill in chancery to enforce his interest. Henry resisted, claiming the gift to Charles was in the nature of a perpetuity and hence void. Sympathetic to the rational estate planning of a landowner with an incompetent eldest son, Lord Chancellor Nottingham was of the opinion that Charles's interest would "wear itself out" in a single lifetime (Thomas's) and should not be regarded as a perpetuity. The sole matter of concern, ruled Nottingham, is the time at which a future interest will vest, and if a future interest must vest, if at all, during or at the end of a life in being, it is good. Upon appeal to the House of Lords, after two days of argument in a crowded house with King James II present, the Lords voted overwhelmingly to affirm Nottingham's decision.

In the Duke of Norfolk's Case, Lord Nottingham indicated that a rule against perpetuities should be concerned solely with the time of vesting in the future, but he did not attempt a definitive statement of how long dead-hand rule would be allowed. When asked, "Where will you stop?" he replied, "I will tell you where I will stop: I will stop wherever any visible Inconvenience doth appear." From this beginning — judicial acceptance of tying up land for a single life in being — the judges gradually extended the permissible period of dead-hand rule until, 150 years later, they finally fixed it at lives in being plus 21 years. In Scatterwood v. Edge, 91 Eng. Rep. 203 (K.B. 1699), it was held sufficient if an interest would vest within a considerable number of lives in being, not merely one or two, "For let the lives be never so many, there must be a survivor, and so it is but the length of that life; for Twisden used to say, the candles were all lighted at once." In Thellusson v. Woodford, 32 Eng. Rep. 1030 (Ch. 1805), it was held that any number of lives reasonably capable of being traced could be used to measure the applicable perpetuities period. Concurrently with the expansion of lives in being from one or two to a considerable number, the courts were adding, first, a minority period and, subsequently, a period of 21 years in gross. Finally, in Cadell v. Palmer, 6 Eng. Rep. 956 (H.L. 1832, 1833), the period allowed by the Rule was settled: any reasonable number of lives in being plus 21 years thereafter plus any actual periods of gestation.

The classic introduction to the Rule for students is Professor W. Barton Leach's famous article, Perpetuities in a Nutshell, 51 Harv. L. Rev. 638 (1938), updated by Leach in Perpetuities: The Nutshell Revisited, 78 Harv. L. Rev. 973 (1965). This lucid article, written in a lively, piquant style by the modern master of the Rule, for four generations now has introduced students into the magic garden of perpetuities. For a more recent synopsis of the Rule dealing with developments such as wait-and-see reforms as well as the traditional Rule, see Jesse Dukeminier, A Modern Guide to Perpetuities, 74 Cal. L. Rev. 1867 (1986). For a more extensive analysis of the methodology for solving perpetuities problems, see David M. Becker, Perpetuities and Estate Planning (1993). For a critique of the legal academy's failure to develop a satisfying account of the Rule's development and durability, see Peter A. Appel, The Embarrassing Rule Against Perpetuities, 54 J. Legal Educ. 264 (2004).

2. Summary of the Rule

a. Introduction

(1) The rule and its policies

The Rule against Perpetuities is a restriction on the remote vesting of interests, in trust or otherwise, but it does not apply to charitable trusts, which are privileged with an exemption from the Rule. The fundamental policy assumption of the Rule is that vested interests are not objectionable, but contingent interests are. As you may recall from Chapter 10, executory interests are always contingent, but remainders may be vested or contingent. A remainder is vested if (1) it is given to a presently ascertained person and (2) it is not subject to a condition precedent (other than the termination of the preceding estates). A remainder is contingent if (1) it is not given to a presently ascertained person or (2) it is subject to a condition precedent. Thus, if *O* conveys a fund in trust "for *A* for life, then to *B*," *B* has a vested remainder, but if *O* conveys a fund in trust "for *A* for life, then to *B* if *B* survives *A*," then *B* has a contingent remainder. *The Rule against Perpetuities limits the time during which property can be made subject to contingent interests to "lives in being plus 21 years."*

The assumption that only *contingent* future interests are objectionable is questionable. The Rule is said to have two basic purposes: (1) to keep property marketable and available for productive development in accordance with market demands, and (2) to limit "dead hand" control over the property, which prevents the current owners from using the property to respond to present needs. The first purpose is implemented by preventing the indefinite fracturing of ownership in property (the perils of which are illustrated by the facts in Hodel v. Irving, excerpted at page 3). The second purpose is implemented by curbing future interests that, after a period of time and change in circumstances, tie up the family in disadvantageous and undesirable arrangements, leaving the living members unable to meet current exigencies.

Whenever future interests exist, regardless of whether they are vested or contingent, these objectives can be compromised. It is therefore arguable that the Rule against Perpetuities should prohibit all future interests, and not merely contingent interests, that exist beyond the perpetuities period. But history has settled the question differently. The Rule prohibits only those interests that may remain contingent beyond the perpetuities period. On the other hand, the creation of contingent interests *in trust*, as compared to contingent *legal* future interests, does not inhibit the marketability of the underlying property if the trustee, who holds legal title to the trust property, has the power to sell and then reinvest the proceeds. Measured against its twin aims, the Rule is thus both too broad and too narrow. Even so, it does, by and large, effectively prevent tying up property for an inordinate length of time.

Although the Rule began as a device to curb tying up land for an undue length of time, it was eventually extended to personal property. Today, because almost all life estates and future interests are *equitable* rather than *legal* interests, and because financial assets have eclipsed land as the primary mode of wealth accumulation, the Rule's primary application is to personal property held in trust.

All legal and equitable contingent future interests created in *transferees* are subject to the Rule against Perpetuities. Hence, all contingent remainders and executory interests come within the ambit of the Rule. Future interests retained by the *transferor* — reversions, possibilities of reverter, and rights of entry — are not subject to the Rule against Perpetuities. Should interests retained by the transferor be subject to a durational limit, after which the possessory fee would become absolute? By statute a number of states have answered Yes. See Cal. Civ. Code §885.030 (2004); Mass. Gen. Laws ch. 184A, §7 (2004); N.Y. Real Prop. Law §345 (2004); N.C. Gen. Stat. §41-32 (2004).

(2) Why lives in being are used to measure the period

At the time of the formulation of the Rule against Perpetuities, heads of families — the fathers — were much concerned about securing the family land, perhaps acquired only a couple of generations earlier, from incompetent sons. In the Duke of Norfolk's Case, Lord Chancellor Nottingham recognized this concern as legitimate, and he and his successor judges developed an appropriate period during which the father's judgment could prevail. The father could realistically and perhaps wisely assess the capabilities of *living* members of his family, and so, with respect to them, the father's informed judgment, solemnly inscribed in an instrument, was given effect. But the head of the family could know nothing of unborn persons. Hence, the father was permitted control only as long as his judgment was informed with an understanding of the capabilities and needs of persons alive when the judgment was made.

Lord Hobhouse put it this way in his lectures on the dead hand:

> A clear, obvious, natural line is drawn for us between those persons and events which the Settlor knows and sees, and those which he cannot know or see. Within the former province we may trust his natural affections and his capacity of judgment to make better dispositions than any external Law is likely to make for him. Within the latter, natural affection does not extend, and the wisest judgment is constantly baffled by the course of events. I submit, then, that the proper limit of Perpetuity is that of lives in being at the time when the settlement takes effect. [Arthur Hobhouse, The Dead Hand 188 (1880).]

Professor Leach observed that the balance struck by the courts permitted "a man of property . . . [to] provide for all of those in his family whom he personally knew and the first generation after them upon attaining majority." 6 American Law of Property §24.16 (1952). To give testators this maneuvering room, it was not necessary that the actual minority period first tacked onto lives in being be converted into a 21-year period in gross, but so it evolved. In any case, the 21-year period in gross proved fortunate when the rule was extended to commercial interests such as options. See The Symphony Space, Inc. v. Pergola Properties, Inc., 669 N.E.2d 799 (N.Y. 1996).

(3) The rule is a rule of proof

The essential thing to grasp about the Rule against Perpetuities is that *it is a rule of logical proof.* A contingent future interest is void from the outset, if it is not certain that the interest will either *vest or fail* — that one or the other *must* happen — within 21 years after the death of "some life in being at the creation of the interest." The phrase "some life in being" has always puzzled students. Who is the "life in being"? The answer is the life in being can be *any* person if you can prove that the interest will vest or fail within that life or within 21 years after its expiration.

Case 1 shows how to make the necessary proof that an interest will vest or fail within the relevant lives.

> *Case 1. O* transfers a fund in trust "to pay the income to *A* for life, then to *A*'s children for their lives, then to pay the principal to *B*." *A* has no children. *A*'s life estate is vested in possession *upon creation*. The remainder to *A*'s children for their lives will vest in possession or, if there are no children, fail *upon A's death*. *B*'s remainder is vested in interest *upon creation*. Thus, all interests created by the transfer are valid.

As Case 1 shows, the crucial inquiry under the Rule is: When will the interest vest? An interest that is vested upon creation is not subject to the Rule. A contingent interest satisfies the Rule if it will necessarily vest, if at all, either *in possession* or *in interest* within the relevant lives in being plus 21 years. Observe that in Case 1, *B*'s remainder is valid because it vests in interest upon creation. It is valid despite the fact that it may vest in possession at the death of *A*'s children, which could be well beyond the relevant lives in being plus 21 years if *A* has children born after the transfer. Observe also that Case 1 contains a trust that may endure for the lives of *A*'s children born after the date of the transfer. So the trust might last longer than lives in being at the date of the transfer plus 21 years. Nonetheless, the trust is not void. *The Rule against Perpetuities does not directly limit trust duration. It is concerned only with the time when interests vest. Hence the Rule against Perpetuities indirectly limits the duration of a trust.* By requiring that equitable interests must vest or fail within the perpetuities period, the identity of all persons with a claim to the property will be ascertained within the period. These ascertained beneficiaries can terminate the trust when the perpetuities period expires. The settlor cannot prevent this. See Restatement (Second) of Property: Donative Transfers §2.1 (1981); 1A Austin W. Scott, Trusts §62.10 (William F. Fratcher 4th ed. 1987). If they do not terminate the trust, the trust principal will be distributed to the principal beneficiaries when the preceding life estates expire. In Case 1, all interests in the trust either are presently vested or will vest, if at all, within the period allotted by the Rule. Therefore, the trust is valid in its entirety. If an interest in trust violates the Rule, only to that extent is a trust void.[4]

Here are other illustrations of contingent interests that can be proven valid because they will vest or fail within the perpetuities period:

> *Case 2. T* bequeaths $10,000 "to *A*, when she marries" and $5,000 "to *A*'s first child." *A* is unmarried and without children. The bequest to *A* will vest during *A*'s *life*, if at all; it is valid. The bequest to *A*'s first child also will vest during *A*'s *life*, if at all; it is valid.
>
> *Case 3. O*, a teacher, declares a trust of her first edition of Charles Dickens's Bleak House "for the first student in *O*'s current wills class to be sworn in as a judge." The gift will vest or fail within the *lives of the students* in the class. The condition precedent will necessarily be met, if it is ever met, before the last surviving student dies.
>
> *Case 4. O* transfers a fund in trust "to pay the income to *A* for life, then to pay the principal to *A*'s children who reach 21." The remainder is valid because it will vest, at the latest, *21 years after A's death*, for all *A*'s children must reach 21 within 21 years after *A* dies (plus a period of gestation).

The period of the Rule includes any actual periods of gestation involved. The Rule thus follows the general principle of property law that a person is in being from the time of conception, if later born alive. (We defer questions concerning the treatment under the Rule of posthumous conception until page 687.)

Because the Rule against Perpetuities is a rule of logical proof, you must look for a life that works in making the proof required. This person, if found, is sometimes known as the *measuring life*, but we prefer the more accurate term, *validating life*.

PROBLEMS AND NOTE

1. *T* bequeaths a fund in trust "for *A* for life, then to the first child of *A* to be admitted to the bar." Is the latter gift valid? If so, who is the validating life?

2. Compare the following bequests:

(a) To *A* for life, then to *B* if *B* goes to the planet Saturn.

(b) To *A* for life, then to *B* if any person goes to the planet Saturn.

(c) To *A* for life, then to *B* for life if any person goes to the planet Saturn.

Is *B*'s remainder good in each bequest? Who is the validating life?

---

4. This statement must be qualified to allow for the case in which the invalid interest is essential to the coherence of the transferor's dispositive scheme. Under the doctrine of *infectious invalidity*, the court may invalidate the entire transfer if doing so will better approximate the transferor's intentions than invalidating only the offending interest. See Lewis M. Simes & Allan F. Smith, The Law of Future Interests §1262 (2d ed. 1956, with supplements); 6 American Law of Property §24.47-24.52 (1952).

3.   The validating lives do not have to have any connection with the family involved. The sole issue is whether these lives permit you to prove that the gift will vest or fail within 21 years after their expiration. In this imaginative and famous passage, Professor Leach explains:

> The settled inclusion of twenty-one years in gross and the admission of extraneous lives bring it about that a testator or settlor, when motivated by vanity, is able to tie up his property, regardless of lives and deaths in his own family, for an unconscionable period — viz., twenty-one years after the deaths of a dozen or so healthy babies chosen from families noted for longevity, a term which, in the ordinary course of events, will add up to about a century. [6 American Law of Property §24.16, at 52 (1952).]

A trust to pay the income to the testator's issue per stirpes, who are living when each income payment is made, until 21 years after the death of the survivor of 12 named healthy babies born last week in local hospitals, then to distribute the principal to the testator's issue per stirpes then living, is valid.

b.   When the Lives in Being Are Ascertained

Although Gray said the life in being must be a person alive "at the creation of the interest," it is more accurate to say that the validating life or lives must be in being *when the perpetuities period starts to run*. Generally, the perpetuities period begins when the instrument takes effect. If an interest is created by *will*, the validating life or lives must be in being at the testator's death. If the interest is created by *deed* or *irrevocable trust*, the validating life or lives must be persons in being when the deed or trust takes effect.

Different rules for determining validating lives govern revocable trusts and interests created by the exercise of a power of appointment. If the interest is created by an *inter vivos trust revocable by the settlor alone*, the validating life or lives must be persons in being when the power to revoke terminates. If the power to revoke terminates at the settlor's death, as is usually the case, the validating lives must be persons alive at the settlor's death. The perpetuities period begins when the power to revoke terminates because, so long as one person has the power to revoke the trust and receive absolute title to the trust assets, the property is not tied up. We take up interests created by the exercise of a power of appointment in Section D.

SECTION B.   THE REQUIREMENT OF NO POSSIBILITY OF REMOTE VESTING

The poet Marianne Moore once wrote of an imaginary garden with real toads in it. Because *any* possibility that an interest might vest too remotely invalidates the interest, the Rule against Perpetuities is much like Marianne Moore's garden. Developed by the active imagination of lawyers, the Rule is the abode of such fantastical characters as the *fertile octogenarian*, the *unborn widow*, and other imaginary beings with power to bring the Rule down hard on the head of any trespasser. No matter how fantastic or ridiculous or improbable the scenario, an interest that might not vest or fail within the perpetuities period is void. In states retaining the common law Rule, courts apply it ruthlessly and without mercy.

1. The Fertile Octogenarian

The first of the fantastical characters we meet is the *fertile octogenarian*. The fertile octogenarian usually appears in a two-generation trust such as the following.

> *Case 5. T* bequeaths a fund in trust for her sister "*A* (age 80) for life, then for *A*'s children for their lives, then to distribute the trust assets to *A*'s issue then living." The law *conclusively presumes* that *A* is capable of having more children. Because of this assumption, the remainder to *A*'s children for their lives may include an afterborn child of *A*, and the remainder to *A*'s issue might vest on the death of this afterborn child, which is too remote. The remainder to *A*'s issue is void.

The conclusive presumption of fertility was laid down in the old case of Jee v. Audley, 29 Eng. Rep. 1186 (Ch. 1787). In this case, the Master of the Rolls, Lord Kenyon, said: "I am desired to do in this case something which I do not feel myself at liberty to do, namely, to suppose it impossible for persons in so advanced an age as John and Elizabeth Jee [both septuagenarians] to have children; but if this can be done in one case it may in another, and it is a very dangerous experiment, and introductive of the greatest inconvenience to give a latitude to such sort of conjecture."

PROBLEMS, QUESTIONS, AND NOTES

1. *T* bequeaths a fund in trust "for *A* for life, then to such of *A*'s nephews and nieces as live to attain the age of 21." At the time of *T*'s death, *A* is living and has a sister, *B*, and four nephews and nieces (the children of *B*), all of whom are under age 21. Is the interest given to *A*'s nephews and nieces valid under the Rule against Perpetuities? (A clue: The answer is, "It depends.")

2. Could the remainder to *A*'s issue in Case 5 be saved by construing "*A*'s children" to refer to *A*'s children living at *T*'s death? Should the court do this?

3. Keeping in mind the conclusive presumption of fertility, which of the following bequests would be valid? *T* devises Blackacre to Mary Hall, but if the Brooklyn Bridge ever falls—

(a) to the children of Elizabeth Jee now living.

(b) to the children of Elizabeth Jee then living.

(c) to the children of Elizabeth Jee now living who are then living.

4. If you think the conclusive presumption of fertility is absurd, at what age would you presume women could not bear children?[5] Men? Now that adoption

---

5. Consider this report of a fertile sexagenarian female from England:

   The oldest woman to give birth in Britain believes she conceived after celebrating becoming a pensioner, a friend disclosed last night.

   Elizabeth Buttle, who will be 61 next month, went into hiding yesterday with her son Joe, now two months old, and boyfriend, Peter Rawstron . . . .

has become widely accepted, is it not theoretically possible that *any* living person could have a child regardless of age and fertility?

In an engaging and thoughtful study of the litigation in, and the aftermath of, Jee v. Audley, Professor Simpson examines the argument "that 'there was no real possibility of John and Elizabeth Jee having children, they being then 70 years old.'" A.W. Brian Simpson, Leading Cases in the Common Law 91 (1995). According to Simpson, "in 1787 knowledge about the fertility of the old was not what it now is; it was widely believed, for example, that Old Thomas Parr . . . had fathered a bastard child at the age of 105. There was clear Biblical warrant for late childbirth in women; Sarah bore Isaac at the age of 90." Id. at 91-92.

To be sure, we have a better understanding of the science of fertility today. But modern medical science perhaps makes this problem even less tractable because it has wrought new technological possibilities. For example, what about sperm or ova that are stored in sperm banks? Professor Leach argued that such sperm or ova should count as lives in being. W. Barton Leach, Perpetuities in the Atomic Age: The Sperm Bank and the Fertile Decedent, 48 A.B.A.J. 942 (1962). Do you see any problems with this proposal? See Celia Hall, Baby Boy Born from Sperm Frozen for 21 Years, Daily Telegraph (London), May 25, 2004, at 01.

What about the possibility of posthumous conception? As we have seen (Woodward v. Commissioner of Social Security, page 102), the birth of children conceived after death — children *en ventre sa frigidaire* — is now a reality. The question thus arises, how should the possibility of posthumous parentage be assimilated, if at all, into the application of the Rule against Perpetuities? Perhaps because myriad contingent future interests in children or descendants would be rendered void by considering the possibility of posthumous parentage (do you see why?), like the proverbial ostrich with its head in the sand, the courts thus far have ignored the issue.[6] For further discussion and a proposal for reform, see Sharona

---

Mrs Buttle told the friend she believed she might have conceived on the night of her 60th birthday. Mrs Buttle and Mr Rawstron celebrated the occasion with dinner. The friend said: She's not sure of her exact dates but says it is very likely to have been on her birthday."

The whitewashed cottage two miles outside the town of Lampeter in west Wales, where Mrs Buttle lives with her partner and a herd of goats, was deserted yesterday after the family left with a police escort, spurning offers of riches from tabloid newspapers.

They are believed to have gone to another farm which she owns in the Carmarthenshire countryside. Her eldest grandson, Nick Pleavin, 19, who lives in a caravan behind the house, said: "My gran is amazing. She's just taken this in her stride, although I don't think she is planning any more. She has always been very fit, working on the farm all her life.

"When my mother told me there would be a new baby in the family I thought she meant her not my gran. My mum is in her late thirties and I thought that was a bit late to have another, but for my gran to have one is fantastic." Mr Rawstron's wife, Vera, 56, the mother of his other four children, was less delighted. . . .

Mrs Rawstron says she was upset at what she described at the "scandal" of her husband having a baby by a mistress of 60.

"Most babies are a cause for celebration but this one is not. It is not a happy event. We have four grownup children to consider who have been very upset. This is a small, close-knit community and this trouble could badly affect the family and our business. Peter promised me this would all be kept very hush-hush. Like a lot of wives, I've been left to pick up the pieces."

The Rawstrons' home is at Llangybi, five miles from the village of Cwmann where Mrs Buttle lives. The love affair began while he was delivering food for her goats.

Simon de Bruxelles, Baby Conceived After 60th Birthday Celebration, The (London) Times, Jan. 16, 1998.

6. Section 1(d) of the Uniform Statutory Rule Against Perpetuities, reprinted at page 703, provides that "the possibility that a child will be born to an individual after the individual's death is disregarded."

Hoffman & Andrew P. Morriss, Birth After Death: Perpetuities and the New Reproductive Technologies, 38 Ga. L. Rev. 575 (2004).

5.   The underlying policy question presented by the fertile octogenarian and the other fantastical characters who inhabit perpetuities land is: Should a highly unlikely possibility of a remote vesting be enough to void an interest under the Rule? With respect to the fertile octogenarian, Illinois and New York have limited the presumption of fertility in perpetuities cases to likely childbearing years (say, between 13 and 65) and permit the introduction of evidence of infertility. See 765 Ill. Comp. Stat. §305/4(c)(3) (2004); N.Y. Est. Powers & Trusts Law §9-1.3(e) (2004). The Illinois and New York statutes also provide that the possibility that a person may adopt a child is disregarded. Is this a sensible reform?

6.   *The precocious toddler*. What is the youngest age of procreation presumed by the law?[7] This has never been established. Only one known case has dealt with the issue. In re Gaite's Will Trusts, 1 All E.R. 459 (Ch. 1949), the court had before it a bequest that would be void only if it were assumed that a person under the age of five could have a child. The court validated the gift, not on the ground of physical impossibility of a person becoming a parent at an age under five, but on the ground that a child born to so young a person would necessarily be born out of wedlock and hence excluded as a child. Under modern law, however, it is usually presumed in construing trusts and related instruments that references to children and other relatives of a person include children born out of wedlock. Hence the constructional escape from the Rule used by the court in In re Gaite's Will Trusts is probably no longer available.

2.   The Unborn Widow

Dickerson v. Union National Bank of Little Rock

Supreme Court of Arkansas, 1980
268 Ark. 292, 595 S.W.2d 677

SMITH, J.   The principal question on this appeal is whether a trust created by the holographic will of Nina Martin Dickerson, who died on June 21, 1967, is void under the rule against perpetuities, because it is possible that the interest of the various beneficiaries may not vest within the period allowed by that rule. Cecil H. Dickerson, Jr., one of the testatrix's two sons, attacks the validity of the trust. The chancellor rejected Cecil's attack on two grounds: First, Cecil should have raised the question of the validity of the trust in the probate court in connection with the

---

7. The youngest mother on record is Lina Medina of Lima, Peru. On May 14, 1939, at the age of 5, she was delivered of a 6 1/2-pound boy by Caesarean section. An investigation revealed that she had been raped by a mentally retarded teenage stepbrother. In a story in the New York Times, April 3, 1963, at 70, one of Lina's obstetricians, Dr. Rolando Colareta, recalled that he and his colleagues were astounded to discover that "although Lina had every aspect of a five-year-old infant, her sexual development corresponded to that of a young lady over 15 years old. . . . Surprising though it seems, we confirmed that Lina had menstrual periods since she was one-month old." Dr. Colareta went on to point out that cases of 12- and 13-year-old mothers were common in the Andes, where Lina came from. "As a matter of fact," he said, "I delivered a child to a 9-year-old girl here last week and it didn't even make the newspapers." The New York Times reported that Lina, then 28 and still unmarried, was working as a secretary. Her son Gerardo, then 23, was living with Lina's parents and studying accounting. For a photograph of the pregnant Lina, age 5, see 8 The Bloodless Phlebotomist, No. 6, p. 2 (1940).

probate of the will and the administration of the estate. His failure to do so makes the issue res judicata. Second, on the merits, the trust does not violate the rule against perpetuities. We disagree with the chancellor on both grounds.

The facts are not in dispute. The testatrix was survived by her two children. Cecil, 50, was single, and Martin 45, was married. At that time the two sons had a total of seven children, who of course were the testatrix's grandchildren.

The testatrix named the appellee bank as executor and directed that at the close of the administration proceedings the bank transfer to itself as trustee all the assets of the estate. The terms of the trust are quite long, but we may summarize them as follows.

The trust is to continue until the death of both sons and of Martin's widow, *who is not otherwise identified*. The income is to be divided equally between the two sons during their lives, except that Cecil's share is to be used in part to provide for a four-year college education for his two minor children, who are named, and for the support and education of any bodily heirs by a later marriage. When the two named minor children finish college, their share of the income is to revert to Cecil. Upon Martin's death his share of the income is to be paid monthly to his widow and children living in the home, but the share of each child terminates and passes to the widow when that child marries or becomes self-supporting. The trustee is given discretionary power to make advance payments of principal in certain cases of emergency or illness. If either son and his wife and all his bodily heirs die before the final distribution of the trust assets, that son's share in the estate and in the income passes to the other son and then to his bodily heirs.

As far as the rule against perpetuities is concerned, the important part of the will is paragraph VIII, from which we quote:

> VIII. This Trust shall continue until the death of both my sons and my son Martin's widow and until the youngest child of either son has reached the age of twenty-five years, then at that time, the Trust shall terminate and the Union National Bank Trustee shall distribute and pay over the entire balance of the Trust Fund in their hands to the bodily heirs of my son, Cecil H. Dickerson, and the bodily heirs of my son, William Martin Dickerson, in the same manner and in the same proportions as provided for by the general inheritance laws of Arkansas.

Upon the death of the testatrix in 1967, her will was presented to the Faulkner Probate Court by her son Cecil, who lived in Conway, Arkansas. (The other son, Martin, was living in Indiana.) The probate court entered a routine order reciting that the will had been properly executed, admitting the instrument to probate, and appointing the bank as executor, without bond. On May 31, 1968, the probate court entered another routine order approving the executor's first and final accounting, allowing fees to the executor and its attorneys, discharging the executor, and closing the administration of the estate. That order made no reference to the validity of the trust or to the manner in which the assets of the estate were to be distributed.

In fact, the assets of the estate, except for $18,000 set aside for administration expenses and estate taxes, had already been transferred by the bank to itself as trustee. On August 11, 1967, about a month after the probate of the will, the bank filed in the Faulkner Chancery Court an ex parte "Declaration of Trust," in which the bank expressed its desire to perform the trust and asked the court to find and decree that it held the property in trust for the beneficiaries of the testamentary trust. . . .

Nothing further appears to have taken place in the case until 1977, when Cecil Dickerson filed . . . the present complaint against the bank and its trust officer. The complaint, after reciting the background facts, asserts that the trust is void under the rule against perpetuities. The complaint charges the trust officer with violations of his fiduciary duties in failing to deliver all the assets of the estate to the heirs of the testatrix and in failing to ask the probate court to construe the will with respect to violations of the rule against perpetuities. The complaint charges that the trust officer concealed the trust's defects from the court and from the testatrix's two sons. The prayer is for an order restraining the trustee from making further transfers or distributions of the trust funds, for recovery of Cecil's half interest in the estate, for compensatory and punitive damages, and for other proper relief. The charges of negligence and wrongdoing on the part of the bank were later dismissed without prejudice. The other matters were heard upon stipulated facts, culminating in the decree dismissing Cecil's complaint. . . .

First, there is no merit in the argument that Cecil's failure to challenge the validity of the trust in the probate proceedings precludes him from raising that issue now.

. . . The complications that may be presented by the rule against perpetuities are so numerous and difficult that even experienced lawyers and judges must usually consult the authorities to be certain about its application to a given set of facts. There was not the slightest reason for Cecil or Martin Dickerson to suspect a possible invalidity in their mother's testamentary trust, nor any duty on their part to raise such a question. To deprive them of their property on the basis of res judicata would actually be to deny them their day in court.

Indeed, if there was any duty on anyone to raise the issue, that duty rested on the bank. It was a fiduciary, both as executor and as trustee. It owed a duty of good faith and loyalty to all the beneficiaries of the estate and of the trust and a duty to act impartially as between successive beneficiaries. Restatement of Trusts (2d), §§170 and 232 (1959), and Arkansas Annotations (1939) to those sections. We do not imply any wrongdoing on the part of this appellee, but it is certainly not in a position to ignore the possible invalidity of the trust both in the probate court and in the ex parte chancery court case and then take advantage, to its own pecuniary benefit, of the beneficiaries' similar course of conduct. A contrary rule would compel the beneficiaries of an estate or trust to hire a lawyer to watch the executor or trustee, when the law actually permits them to rely upon the fiduciary.

Second, the trust is void because there is a possibility that the estate will not vest within a period measured by a life or lives in being at the testatrix's death, plus 21 years. A bare possibility is enough. "The interest *must* vest within the time allowed by the rule. If there is any possibility that the contingent event may happen beyond the limits of the rule, the transaction is void." Comstock v. Smith, 501 S.W.2d 617 (Ark. 1973).

The terms of this trust present an instance of the "unborn widow," a pitfall that is familiar to every student of the rule against perpetuities. This trust is not to terminate until the deaths of Cecil, Martin, and Martin's widow, but the identity of Martin's widow cannot be known until his death. Martin might marry an 18-year-old woman twenty years after his mother's death, have additional children by her, and then die. Cecil also might die. Martin's young widow, however, might live for another 40 or 50 years, after which the interests would finally vest. But since Cecil and Martin would have been the last measuring lives in being at the death of the testatrix, the trust property would not vest until many years past the maximum time allowed by the rule. The rule was formulated to prevent just such a possibility—uncertainty about the title to real or personal property for an unreasonably long time in the future.

The violation of the rule, except for the interposition of a trust, is actually so clear that the appellee does not argue the point. Instead, it insists that the property would vest in Cecil and Martin's bodily heirs at their deaths, with only the right of possession of the property being deferred until the termination of the trust.

This argument overlooks the fact that the words "bodily heirs" were used in the decisive paragraph VIII of the will not as words of limitation, to specify the duration of an estate granted to Cecil and Martin, but as words of purchase, to specify the persons who would take at the termination of the trust. Obviously the identity of those persons cannot be determined until the death of Martin's widow; so the ownership would not vest until that time. . . .

Here the testatrix directed that at the termination of the trust the property be distributed as provided by the general inheritance laws of Arkansas. At the time of the deaths of Cecil and Martin it would be utterly impossible to say who would take, in the case we have supposed, at the death of Martin's young widow 50 years later. Under our law the surviving descendants would then take per capita if they were related to Cecil and Martin in equal degree, but per stirpes if in unequal degree. Ark. Stat. Ann. §§61-134 and -135 (Repl. 1971). If there were no surviving descendants of one brother, the entire property would go to the surviving descendants of the other. If there were no surviving descendants of either, the property would revert to the testatrix's estate and go to her collateral heirs. Thus it is really too plain for argument that the interest of every descendant (or "bodily heir") of Cecil or Martin would be contingent upon his surviving the death of Martin's widow, at which time—and only at which time—the title would finally vest. . . .

Reversed and remanded for further proceedings.

PROBLEMS AND NOTES

1. Why did not the gift to Cecil's and Martin's bodily heirs vest at their deaths? See Note 3 at page 640. If the gift had been to Cecil's and Martin's heirs, would the remainder be valid?

2. *T* bequeaths a fund in trust to pay the income "to my son for life, then to my son's widow, if any, for life; then to pay the principal to my son's children, but if no child of my son is alive at the death of the survivor of my son and his widow, then to pay the principal to the American Red Cross." Is any gift invalid? See John H. Morris & W. Barton Leach, The Rule Against Perpetuities 44 (2d ed. 1962).

Any interest that violates the Rule against Perpetuities is struck out and the valid interests are left standing (subject to the doctrine of *infectious invalidity*, on which see footnote 4 at page 677). What is the result of an invalid gift in this trust?

3. Once again the question arises, should a highly unlikely possibility of a remote vesting be enough to void an interest under the Rule? N.Y. Est. Powers & Trusts Law §9-1.3(c) (2004) provides: "Where an estate would, except for this paragraph, be invalid because of the possibility that the person to whom it is given or limited may be a person not in being at the time of the creation of the estate, and such person is referred to in the instrument creating such estate as the spouse of another

without other identification, it shall be presumed that such reference is to a person in being on the effective date of the instrument." 765 Ill. Comp. Stat. §365/4(c)(1)(C) (2004) is similar.

Why did not the court in *Dickerson* construe the word *widow* to refer to a person in being when the testator died?

4. *Alternative contingencies.* Under the alternative contingencies doctrine, if the testator makes gifts on alternative contingencies, one of which offends the Rule against Perpetuities and the other of which does not, the gifts are judged separately. The invalid gift fails; the valid gift takes effect if the event happens upon which it is limited. See First Portland Natl. Bank v. Rodrique, 172 A.2d 107 (Me. 1961); 6 American Law of Property §24.54 (1952).

To illustrate this, suppose that *T* bequeaths a fund in trust "to my son *A* for life, then to *A*'s widow for life, then upon the widow's death *or* upon *A*'s death if *A* leaves no widow, to *A*'s issue." *T* has split the contingencies, making a gift on the widow's death and a separate gift on the death of *A* leaving no widow. The gift on the death of the widow is void. The gift to *A*'s issue on *A*'s death is valid if *A* actually leaves no widow. However, the testator must expressly separate the contingencies. The court will not do it for him. Thus, if the words "or upon *A*'s death if *A* leaves no widow" are omitted by the drafter, the gift to *A*'s issue is wholly void, even though this second contingency is implicit in the will as drafted.

3. The Slothful Executor

Another unusual possibility, occasionally overlooked by the drafter, is that a will may not be probated, or an estate distributed, for many years after the testator's death. Distribution of an estate ordinarily is completed within a few years of the testator's death, but in a few cases the estate has been tied up for many years in litigation or the will has been found many years after the testator dies. See, e.g., Estate of Garrett, 94 A.2d 357 (Pa. 1953) (estate closed after 23 years); Richards v. Tolbert, 208 S.E.2d 486 (Ga. 1974) (will found and probated 57 years after the testator's death).

The possibility of remote distribution gives rise to what are known as the *slothful executor* cases. Thus:

> *Case 6.* *T* devises property "to *T*'s issue living upon distribution of *T*'s estate." *T*'s purpose is to avoid extra administrative costs and possible taxation in the estates of any of *T*'s issue who die before *T*'s estate is distributed. Yet, because *T*'s estate may not be distributed for many years, perhaps after all *T*'s surviving issue are dead, the gift to *T*'s issue living at distribution may be held void.

There are at least two arguments that can be made to save the gift in Case 6. First, it can be argued that distribution of the estate will not be delayed beyond a reasonable time, which necessarily is less than 21 years. This argument was accepted in Belfield v. Booth, 27 A. 585 (Conn. 1893). Second, it can be argued that, inasmuch as the testator did not intend the executor to have the power to select recipients by delaying distribution, the class of issue will close at the time distribution reasonably should be made. See Estate of Taylor, 428 P.2d 301 (Cal. 1967).

The administrative contingency involved in Case 6 is a true condition precedent: *T*'s will requires *T*'s issue to survive distribution in order to take. Some administrative contingency cases, however, involve language that ought not to be construed to create a condition precedent to vesting. Examples include "to *A* upon distribution of my estate," "to my issue when my debts are paid," and "to *A* upon probate of this will." Language of this sort, not requiring survival, should be construed as merely postponing possession and not imposing a condition precedent. See Deiss v. Deiss, 536 N.E.2d 120 (Ill. App. 1989).

4.   The Magic Gravel Pit and Other Marvels

Here are some other extraordinary occurrences in the magic garden of perpetuities:

> *Case 7. The Magic Gravel Pit. T* devises his gravel pits to his trustees to work them until the pits are exhausted and then to sell them and divide the proceeds among *T*'s issue then living. Since the gravel pits might produce gravel for hundreds of years, the gift to *T*'s issue is void. So held in In re Wood, [1894] 3 Ch. 381, even though the pits were in fact exhausted in six years.
>
> *Case 8. The War That Never Ends.* During World War II, *T*, whose husband was a German immigrant, devised $20,000 to her husband's family in Germany who should survive the war. The devise was held void in Brownell v. Edmunds, 209 F.2d 349 (4th Cir. 1953), on the ground that World War II might not have ended within lives in being plus 21 years.
>
> *Case 9. The Birthday Present That Blows Up. T* devises a fund in trust for *A* for life, then to such of *A*'s children as reach their respective twenty-first birthdays. Under the common law, a person reaches 21 at the first moment of the day before his birthday; the theory is that a person is in existence on the day of his birth, and that on the day before his first birthday he has completed one year. His birthday is the first day of the second year. See Annot. 5 A.L.R.2d 1143 (1949, rev. 2003). In effect, then, this remainder is to such of *A*'s children as shall be living one day after they reach the age of 21. It is thus arguable that this gift exceeds by one day the Rule against Perpetuities. See W. Barton Leach, The Careful Draftsman: Watch Out!, 47 A.B.A.J. 259 (1961).

The foregoing scenarios do not exhaust the extravagant possibilities that can be dreamed up to invalidate gifts. But together with the previous cases, they should suffice to show that the most remote possibilities can lead to invalidating an interest. It is these cases that have brought the Rule (but not its underlying policy against remote vesting) into disrepute.

SECTION C.   APPLICATION OF THE RULE TO CLASS GIFTS

1.   The Basic Rule: All-or-Nothing

Under the Rule against Perpetuities, a class gift cannot be partially valid and partially void. It must be valid for all members of the class, or it is valid for none. If the interest of any member possibly can vest too remotely, the entire class gift is bad. This rule was established in Leake v. Robinson, 35 Eng. Rep. 979 (Ch. 1817).

The *all-or-nothing* rule requires that (a) the class must close and (b) all conditions precedent for every member of the class must be satisfied, if at all, within the perpetuities period. Case 10 illustrates a common class gift that is void according to these principles.

> *Case 10.* T bequeaths property in trust "for A for life, then for A's children for life, and then to distribute the property to A's grandchildren." The remainder to A's grandchildren is void because every member of the class will not be ascertained until the death of A's children, some of whom might not be in being at T's death. If at T's death A has a grandchild, G, alive, G's gift is vested in interest subject to open for after-born grandchildren, but it is not vested for purposes of the Rule, and it is therefore void. *Repeat: A remainder that is vested subject to open is not vested for purposes of applying the Rule against Perpetuities.* The class must be *closed* before a remainder in a class is vested under the Rule.

Some gifts to a class may be saved through the operation of the *rule of convenience*, which may close the class prior to the time it closes physiologically. Under the rule of convenience, the class will close when any member of the class is entitled to immediate possession and enjoyment. See page 663. Thus:

> *Case 11.* O transfers property in an irrevocable trust "for my daughter A for life, then to distribute the principal to my grandchildren." At the time of the transfer O has one grandchild, G, alive. Under the rule of convenience, G or her administrator is entitled to demand possession of her share at A's death, closing the class and forcing distribution among the grandchildren then living and the estates of grandchildren then dead.[8] The gift thus is valid. If O had no grandchild alive at the date of the transfer, the gift to grandchildren would be void.

QUESTION

If the instrument in Case 11 were a will or a revocable trust rather than an irrevocable trust, the gift to the transferor's grandchildren would be valid regardless of whether a grandchild were alive when the instrument became effective. Do you see why?

It does not necessarily follow from the closing of the class within the perpetuities period that the gift is valid. Every member of the class may be ascertained, but every member may not have satisfied some condition precedent, and this too is required. For a gift of a fee simple to vest, the ultimate number of takers in the class must be fixed so that it neither increases nor decreases. Thus:

> *Case 12.* T bequeaths property in trust "for A for life, then to distribute the property to such of A's children as attain the age of 25." The class will close physiologically at A's

---

8. Suppose that G is living in Argentina, doesn't learn of A's death until several years after A dies, and therefore doesn't appear at A's death to demand payment. Will the class nevertheless close at A's death? Yes. The class will close whenever a class member has the *right* to demand possession. Were this not so, the rule of convenience could never save a class gift because it is possible that the qualified class member would not actually demand possession at the time the right to possession arises.

death (a life in being), but the exact share each child of *A* will take cannot be determined until all of *A*'s children have passed 25 or have died under that age. Here is what might happen: Suppose, at *T*'s death, *A* has one child, *C*, age 10. After *T*'s death *A* might have another child, *D*. Before *D* reaches age 4, *A* and *C* might die. Since *D* might meet the condition precedent more than 21 years after the expiration of any relevant life in being at *T*'s death, the remainder fails.

QUESTION AND PROBLEMS

1. Suppose that in Case 12 a child of *A* is age 25 at *T*'s death. Is the gift good? If you say Yes, you have not mastered the principle illustrated by this case.

2. *T* devises Blackacre "to such of the grandchildren of *A* as shall attain the age of 25." Unless otherwise stated, assume that no grandchild of *A* has reached age 25. Is the gift valid if at *T*'s death:

(a) *A* is dead?

(b) *A* and all of *A*'s children are dead?

(c) *A* is alive and one grandchild of *A* is 25?

(d) *A* is dead and one grandchild of *A* is 25?

(e) *A* is dead and the eldest grandchild of *A* is 4?

3. *T* bequeaths a fund in trust "to pay the income to *A* for life, and then in further trust for the grandchildren of *B*, their shares to be payable at their respective ages of 25." Is the gift valid if *T* is survived by *A* and *B* and:

(a) the eldest grandchild of *B* is 25 at *T*'s death?

(b) the eldest grandchild of *B* is 10 at *T*'s death?

(c) the eldest grandchild of *B* is 2 at *T*'s death?

Suppose that *B* survives *T*, but *A* predeceases *T*, and the eldest grandchild of *B* is 2 at *T*'s death. Is the gift valid?

Suppose that *A* survives *T*, but *B* predeceases *T*, and the eldest grandchild of *B* is 2 at *T*'s death. Is the gift valid?

2. Exceptions to the Class Gift Rule

We now turn to two exceptions to the all-or-nothing rule of class gifts: (a) gifts to subclasses and (b) gifts of specific sums to each member of a class. These exceptions are discussed in 6 American Law of Property §§24.29, 24.28 (1952).

a. Gifts to Subclasses

AMERICAN SECURITY & TRUST CO. v. CRAMER, 175 F. Supp. 367 (D.D.C. 1959): Abraham Hazen bequeathed property in trust for his wife for life, then to his "adopted daughter" Hannah for life, then to Hannah's children for their lives. "Upon the death of each [child] the share of the one so dying shall go absolutely to the persons who shall then be her or his heirs at law" under the District of Columbia law of intestate succession.

Abraham died in 1901. At his death Hannah had two children, Mary and Hugh. After Abraham's death, Hannah had two more children, Depue and Horace. Hannah died in 1915; Abraham's widow died in 1916. Depue died in 1954. This action was commenced to determine the validity of the remainder following his life estate. While the case was pending, Horace died. A supplemental bill was filed to determine also the validity of the interest following his life estate.

Because the will makes a gift to each child's heirs upon the death of *each* child, and not a gift to the next generation upon the death of *all* of Hannah's children, the court applied the "gifts to subclasses" exception to the class gift rule. The gifts over following the life estates in Depue and Horace were void since neither was alive at Abraham's death. However, the gifts over following the life estates in Mary and Hugh were valid. These "remainders are not affected by the two invalid remainders, since the four remainders are to subclasses and stand (or fall) separately." Under a long line of cases beginning with Cattlin v. Brown, 68 Eng. Rep. 1318 (Ch. 1853), "if the ultimate takers are not described as a single class but rather as a group of subclasses, and if the share to which each separate subclass is entitled will finally be determined within the period of the rule, the gifts to the different subclasses are separable for the purpose of the rule." The remainders following the life estates in Depue and Horace being void, this left a reversion in Abraham's estate, which passes to his heirs.

NOTE

Estate of Coates, 652 A.2d 331 (Pa. Super. 1994), held that where there is a trust for *A* for life, then to *A*'s children for their lives, then "to *A*'s grandchildren per stirpes," the subclass doctrine applies even though possession by the grandchildren was postponed until the death of all *A*'s children. The shares of the grandchildren are fixed at the death of each child.

b. Specific Sum to Each Class Member

The other important exception to the all-or-nothing class gift rule applies where there is a gift of a specific sum to each member of a class. In Storrs v. Benbow, 43 Eng. Rep. 153 (Ch. 1853), the testator bequeathed £500 apiece to each grandchild of his brothers, to be paid at age 21. The testator had two brothers living at his death. The court held that, as a matter of construction, applying the ordinary class closing rule applicable to specific sum gifts (see page 669), the gift benefited only grandchildren living at the testator's death. The court went on to say, however, in a dictum that has been treated as law ever since, that if the testator meant to include grandchildren born after his death, the bequest would be valid for all children born to the brothers' children living at his death and invalid for all children of the brothers' afterborn children. The amount intended to be received by each member of the class is ascertainable without reference to the number of persons in the class, and hence each gift is tested separately under the Rule. Thus:

> *Case 13.* *T* bequeaths "$1,000 apiece to my nephews and nieces, whether born before or after my death." *T* is survived by his parents, his sister *A*, and *A*'s daughter

B. After *T*'s death, a child, *C*, is born to *T*'s parents, and *A* has another child, *D*. Twenty years later, *C* marries and has a child, *E*. *B* is entitled to receive $1,000 because her gift vests at *T*'s death. *D* is entitled to receive $1,000 because, viewed at *T*'s death, her gift will necessarily vest during the life of *A*, a person in being at *T*'s death. *E* is not entitled to receive $1,000 because her gift will not necessarily vest during the life of a person in being. The validity of each gift is judged separately since the amount each nephew or niece takes is fixed at $1,000 and cannot increase or decrease by any fluctuation in the number of recipients.

SECTION D. APPLICATION OF THE RULE TO POWERS OF APPOINTMENT

In applying the Rule against Perpetuities to powers of appointment, it is necessary to separate powers into (1) general powers presently exercisable and (2) general testamentary powers and all special powers. The former are rarely created, except in the form of a power to revoke a trust. Hence, our main concern is with testamentary and special powers.

1. *General Powers Presently Exercisable*

a. Validity of Power

General powers presently exercisable are treated as absolute ownership for purposes of the Rule. Nothing stands between the donee and absolute ownership except a piece of paper that can be signed at any time; hence, the property is not tied up. To be a valid power, a general inter vivos power must *become exercisable*, or fail, within the perpetuities period. Once the power becomes exercisable, the property becomes marketable, and the policies that underpin the Rule are not offended. See Restatement (Second) of Property: Donative Transfers §1.2, cmt. h (1983). For example, *T* devises property "to *A* for life, then to *A*'s children for their lives, with a general power in each child, exercisable by deed, to appoint a proportionate share of the corpus." Each child's power is valid because the power in each child will become exercisable at *A*'s death or, if a child is then a minor, within 21 years thereafter.

b. Validity of Exercise

Since the donee of a general power presently exercisable is treated as owner of the property, the validity of an interest created by exercise of the power is determined on the same basis as if the donee owned the property in fee. The perpetuities period begins to run when the power is exercised.

An unconditional power to revoke in one person is treated the same as a general power presently exercisable if the holder can exercise the power to revoke for his or her own exclusive benefit. The perpetuities period does not begin to run until the termination of the power. See Restatement (Second) of Property, supra, §1.2.

PROBLEM

O creates a revocable trust "to pay the income to *O* for life, then to pay the income to *O*'s children for their lives, then to distribute the principal to *O*'s grand-children." Does the gift to grandchildren violate the Rule against Perpetuities? Would it if the trust were irrevocable?

2. General Testamentary Powers and Special Powers

General testamentary powers and all special powers are treated differently from a general power presently exercisable. A person holding one of these powers does not have an absolute and unlimited present right to alienate the property, and consequently the donee is not treated as owner. The donor is treated as still controlling the property through the exercise of the power. In applying the Rule to these powers, two questions arise: (a) Is the power itself valid? (b) Are the interests created by the exercise of the power valid?

a. Validity of Power

For a general testamentary power or a special power to be valid, it must not be possible for the power to be exercised beyond the perpetuities period. If it can possibly be exercised beyond the period, it is void ab initio. A testamentary or special power cannot be given to an afterborn person unless its exercise is limited to the perpetuities period.

> *Case 14.* *T* bequeaths a fund in trust "to pay the income to *A* for life, then to *A*'s children for their lives, and, as each child of *A* dies, to pay his or her proportionate part of the principal as such child shall appoint by will." At the time of *T*'s death, *A* has one child, *B*. Another child, *C*, is born a year later. The gift to subclasses doctrine applies to the testamentary powers given *A*'s children since each child has a power exercisable only over his or her portion of the principal at death. The testamentary power given to *B* is valid because *B* was in being at *T*'s death. The testamentary power given to *C*, born after *T*'s death, is void.

A discretionary power of distribution in a trustee is the equivalent of a special power of appointment.

> *Case 15.* *T* bequeaths a fund in trust "to pay the income to *A* for life, then in the trustee's *discretion* to pay the income to *A*'s children during their lives or to accumulate the income and add it to principal." *A* has no children at *T*'s death. The discretionary power in the trustee to pay or accumulate income is either partially or totally void (see below).

Gray took the position that a discretionary trust did not create one power that was either entirely valid or entirely void, but a succession of annual powers that were exercisable with respect to each year's income. Thus, a discretionary power in a trustee exercisable during lives not in being, as during the lives of *A*'s children in Case 15, could be exercised for 21 years after *A*'s death but no longer. See John C. Gray, The Rule Against Perpetuities §§410.1-410.5 (4th ed. 1942). However, in the few cases in which this issue has been directly before the court, the discretionary power has been held void in its entirety if it is capable of being exercised in favor of persons not in being. See Arrowsmith v. Mercantile-Safe Deposit & Trust Co., 545 A.2d 674 (Md. 1988); Bundy v. United States Trust Co., 153 N.E. 337 (Mass. 1926).

b. Validity of Exercise

(1) Perpetuities period runs from creation of power

General testamentary powers are treated like special powers in determining the validity of the appointment. The donee of a testamentary power or a special power is regarded as an agent of the donor, not as the beneficial owner of the property. The appointments under testamentary and special powers are read back into the instrument creating the power. The perpetuities period applicable to the appointed interests runs from the creation of the power.

Although it is now well settled in most of the states that general testamentary powers are to be treated like special powers under the Rule, in a few states general testamentary powers are treated the same way as general inter vivos powers. The perpetuities period on the appointed interests runs from the exercise of a general testamentary power. See Del. Code Ann. tit. 25, §501 (2004); Mo. Rev. Stat. §442.557 (2004). See also S.D. Codified Laws §43-5-5 (2004) (suspension of the power of alienation); Wis. Stat. Ann. §700.16(1)(c) (2004) (same). See generally Robert L. Fletcher, Perpetuities: Basic Clarity, Muddled Reform, 63 Wash. L. Rev. 791, 815-818 (1988).

(2) The second-look doctrine

Any interest created by exercise of a testamentary or special power is void unless it must vest, if at all, *within 21 years after the death of some life in being at the date the power was created*. The exercise of the power is read back into the original instrument—but facts existing on the date of exercise are taken into account. This is known as the *second-look doctrine*. This means we wait and see how the donee actually appoints the property, and then we determine on the basis of facts existing at the date of the appointment whether the appointive interests will vest within the period (computed from the date of creation of the power). Thus:

> *Case 16. T* devises property "to *A* for life, remainder to such persons as *A* appoints by will, outright or in further trust." *A* appoints in further trust "to my children for life, remainder to my grandchildren in fee." We now read *A*'s appointment into the will that created the power; the disposition is treated as though *T*'s will read "to *A* for life, then to *A*'s children for life, then to *A*'s grandchildren in fee." However, under the second-look doctrine we are allowed to take into account facts existing at the time of

A's appointment. If, at *A*'s death, all of *A*'s surviving children were born in *T*'s lifetime, the remainder to the grandchildren is valid because it will vest, if at all, at the death of persons in being at *T*'s death. Otherwise the remainder is void.

SECOND NATIONAL BANK OF NEW HAVEN v. HARRIS TRUST & SAVINGS BANK, 283 A.2d 226 (Conn. Supp. 1971): In 1922 Caroline Trowbridge created an irrevocable inter vivos trust that gave her daughter Margaret a life income interest and a general testamentary power of appointment over one-half of the corpus. "The remaining one-half, as well as the half subject to the power in default of its exercise, would be distributed to" Margaret's issue per stirpes or, if none, to another daughter of the settlor. Caroline reserved the right to "revoke, modify, or alter" the trust "respecting the payment of income." In 1929 Mary was born to Margaret. In 1941 Caroline died. In 1969 Margaret died, leaving a will purporting to exercise the power by creating another trust to pay the income to Margaret's daughter Mary for 30 years, and then to distribute the principal to Mary, but if Mary dies during the 30-year period, to distribute the principal to Mary's issue per stirpes. The issue presented was whether the interests created under Margaret's will were valid under the Rule against Perpetuities.

The court first determined that the perpetuities period commenced from the date the trust was created in 1922, not from Caroline's death in 1941, because the trust was revocable only as to the income interest. That is, Caroline's power to revoke did not reach the principal, and therefore it was not equivalent to absolute ownership. Accordingly, the court held that the Rule "would bar any future interest which might not vest within twenty-one years after the life of some person in being [in 1922,] the date the trust was established. Since Mary was not born until . . . 1929, she was not in being at the creation of the trust and her life cannot be taken as a measuring life."

The court then turned to the various interests. Reading the appointment back into the trust, but taking the facts as they exited when Margaret died into account (the second look), at issue was a trust to pay the income to Margaret for life, then to pay the income to (unborn) Mary for 30 years, then to pay the principal to Mary, but if she dies during the 30-year period, to pay the principal to Mary's issue per stirpes. The court held that the 30-year income interest was valid because it vested in possession on the death of Margaret, a life in being. Likewise, the remainder limited to Mary at the end of 30 years was valid because, at Margaret's death, it was vested subject to total divestment. The gift-over to Mary's issue was held void, however, because it might not vest until more than 21 years after the death of Margaret. The issue must survive to the time of possession, which might occur 29 years after Margaret's death. The second-look doctrine was of no help. Taking into account facts existing at Margaret's death did not save the gift because Mary was not alive at the settlor's death, and so Mary cannot be used as a life in being.

The divesting gift to Mary's issue being void, it was stricken. Quoting Gray's classic treatise, the court explained: "If future interests created by any instrument are avoided by the Rule against Perpetuities, the prior interests become what they would have been had the limitation of the future estate been omitted from the instrument." Mary was therefore left with an indefeasibly vested remainder in the corpus of the trust. If Mary were to live for 30 years, she would take the principal. If not, the principal would pass to her estate.

NOTE AND QUESTIONS

1. If Mary had been alive in 1922, Margaret's appointment would be entirely valid. The interest in Mary's issue would vest, if at all, at Mary's death.

Do you see how, as lawyer for Margaret Trowbridge Marsh, you could have almost certainly carried out her wishes by a further appointment using extraneous persons born before 1922 and living when her will was executed to measure the duration of the trust?

2. If a donee makes an invalid appointment, what are the consequences? The property passes in default of appointment to the takers in default or, if none, to the donor or the donor's estate unless the doctrine of capture applies. On capture, see page 617.

NOTE: THE "DELAWARE TAX TRAP" OR HOW THE DONEE CAN CHOOSE BETWEEN PAYING AN ESTATE TAX OR A GENERATION-SKIPPING TRANSFER TAX

In Delaware a statute provides that all interests created by the exercise of *all* powers, *special as well as general*, must vest within 21 years of the death of some life in being at the time the power is *exercised*, not some life in being at the date of creation of the power. Del. Code Ann. tit. 25, §501 (2004). Under the Delaware statute, a new perpetuities period begins each time a special power is exercised. Thus, it is possible to create a private trust that can last forever. *T* can set up a trust giving her child *A* the income for life and a special testamentary power to appoint outright or in further trust among *A*'s descendants. *A* can exercise the power by appointing in further trust for her child *B* for life, giving *B* a special testamentary power in favor of *B*'s descendants. *B* can exercise the power by appointing in further trust for her child — and so on down the generations.

Under the federal estate tax, neither a life estate nor property subject to a special power of appointment is taxable at the death of the life tenant or donee of the power. Although the property escapes estate taxation at that time, it will become subject to estate taxation within a generation or two thereafter because the common law Rule against Perpetuities ultimately calls a halt to successive life estates. In Delaware, however, life estates can be created in indefinite succession through the exercise of successive special powers of appointment.

Out of concern for estate tax avoidance through the use of Delaware trusts, Congress enacted §2041(a)(3) of the Internal Revenue Code. As amended, this statute taxes the appointive assets in the donee's estate if the donee exercises a special power "by creating another power of appointment which under the applicable local law can be validly exercised so as to postpone the vesting of any estate or interest in such property, . . . for a period ascertainable without regard to the date of the creation of the first power."

This provision plugs the tax loophole that would otherwise exist for Delaware trusts — but the general language of the statute creates a tax trap for residents of all states. In any jurisdiction, *if a donee by will exercises a special power in such a manner as to create a general inter vivos power, the property subject to the special power will be includible in the donee's gross estate taxable under the estate tax*. Reread the quoted statutory provision, and you will see that this is so.

Although it was once sound advice never to exercise a special power by creating a general inter vivos power, which would throw the trust assets into the donee's taxable gross estate, such advice is no longer necessarily sound. In 1986, Congress enacted the generation-skipping transfer (GST) tax, which imposes a GST tax on a transfer to a person two generations below the transferor. In the trust above, where the transferor's child *A* is given a life estate and a special power of appointment, a GST tax will be levied at *A*'s death if the trust assets pass to the next generation, *unless the trust assets are subject to an estate tax levied on A's estate.* By exercising her special power so as to create a general inter vivos power in her child, *B*, *A* can subject the trust assets to the estate tax and, thus, avoid a GST tax. Whether to pay the estate tax or the GST tax depends on the availability of estate and GST exemptions as well as the current tax rates. Hence, the Delaware Tax Trap has turned out to be useful in sophisticated estate planning. See Jonathan G. Blattmachr & Jeffrey N. Pennell, Adventures in Generation-Skipping, or How We Learned to Love the "Delaware Tax Trap," 24 Real Prop., Prob. & Tr. J. 75 (1989).

Similarly, giving a remainderman a special power of appointment may permit the remainderman to choose which tax to pay. Take this case:

> *Case 17. T* bequeaths a fund in trust to his wife *W* for life, then to his daughter *A* if *A* survives *W*. If *A* dies before *W*, *A* is given a special power to appoint the distribution of the trust assets at *W*'s death, and in default of appointment to *A*'s children. If *A* dies before *W*, the trust assets will not be included in *A*'s federal gross estate, but a GST tax on the value of the trust principal will be payable on *W*'s death when the trust principal passes to *T*'s grandchildren. If an estate tax would do less damage to the family, *A* can exercise her power of appointment by creating general inter vivos powers in *A*'s children, thus falling into the Delaware Tax Trap. In that case, an estate tax would be payable at *A*'s death on the value of the remainder rather than a GST tax payable at *W*'s death on the value of the trust principal.

SECTION E.   SAVING CLAUSES

Because of the ease with which even experienced attorneys can overlook some remote possibility of untimely vesting, experienced estate planners today always incorporate in trusts they draft a perpetuities *saving clause* to take care of any possible violation. The perpetuities saving clause[9] is not actually intended to govern the duration of the trust, except in the event some overlooked violation of the Rule unexpectedly extends the trust too long. The perpetuities saving clause's purpose is simply to make sure the Rule is not violated.

Here is an example of a saving clause:

> Notwithstanding any other provisions in this instrument, any trust created hereunder shall terminate, if it has not previously terminated, 21 years after the death of the survivor of the beneficiaries of the trust living at the date this instrument becomes

---

9. Not savings clause, which is grammatically incorrect. As an adjective, *saving* — without the *s* — has the sense of "rescuing." See William Safire, On Language, N.Y. Times Mag., Apr. 2, 1995, at 22, explaining that *savings* is the sum of separate acts of saving, as in a savings account.

effective. In case of such termination, the then remaining principal and undistributed income of the trust shall be distributed to the then income beneficiaries in the same proportions as they were, at the time of termination, entitled to receive the income. The term "beneficiaries" includes persons originally named as beneficiaries in this instrument as well as persons, living at the date this instrument becomes effective, subsequently named as beneficiaries by a donee of a power of appointment over the trust assets exercising such power.

Observe that, under this saving clause, the trust terminates 21 years after the death of all beneficiaries, originally or subsequently named as such, who were in being when the trust became effective. The principal is then distributed as provided in the saving clause. Because the trust ends within or at the end of the perpetuities period, at which time the trust assets are distributed, no interest in the trust assets can violate the Rule against Perpetuities.

The last sentence of the saving clause is important. It makes clear that the donee of a power of appointment can change the measuring lives for the trust, provided the donee does not select someone not alive when the trust was created. There may be substantial estate tax or generation-skipping transfer tax advantages in keeping the trust going for the maximum perpetuities period by each generation exercising special powers of appointment prolonging the trust. If the trust is a family dynasty trust and the settlor's issue alive at the creation of the trust have all expired, or are about to expire, the donee of a special power can continue the trust for the lives of 12 healthy persons who were born before the trust was created, plus 21 years, by giving these persons a small beneficial interest in the trust (hence making them beneficiaries). If this is done, the trust can endure for 100 years or so.[10]

For a thorough discussion of saving clauses, see David M. Becker, Perpetuities and Estate Planning 133-184 (1993).

NOTE: ATTORNEY LIABILITY FOR VIOLATING THE RULE

In most states, attorneys are liable to the intended beneficiaries of negligently drafted instruments. See page 52. On the authority of Lucas v. Hamm, 364 P.2d 685 (Cal. 1961), it is sometimes said that it is not malpractice to draft an instrument that violates the Rule against Perpetuities. In *Lucas*, the court held the attorney who violated the Rule was not negligent on the specific facts of the case (involving an administrative contingency). Given the ease with which compliance can be assured through use of a saving clause, however, *Lucas* is a shaky precedent. Indeed, for precisely this reason a lower California court has warned that *Lucas* is of doubtful validity today. Wright v. Williams, 121 Cal. Rptr. 194, 199 n.2 (App. 1975). See also Robert E. Megarry, Note, 81 L.Q. Rev. 465, 478-481 (1965), in which Vice-Chancellor Megarry criticizes *Lucas* as an embarrassment to the profession.

---

10. The English have long used a saving clause in the form of a *royal lives clause*. The trust is to continue until 21 years after the death of all the descendants of Queen Victoria (or of George V or of some other British monarch) living at the creation of the trust. The lives thus selected have no connection with the intended beneficiaries, but, because of their prominence, their deaths can usually be ascertained, though sometimes with difficulty, using such sources as Debrett's Peerage and Baronetage (Charles Kidd ed., 2003) (published every few years). By using all these royal lives, the trust can last well over 100 years.

In sum, it is almost certainly malpractice to violate the Rule against Perpetuities by failing to include a perpetuities saving clause.

SECTION F.   PERPETUITIES REFORM

The Rule against Perpetuities has never been popular with lawyers. In the last half of the twentieth century and continuing into the present, extensive debate erupted over whether the Rule should be reformed or abolished. The reformers' ideas and judicial and legislative changes in the law can be sorted into three basic kinds: (1) the cy pres doctrine, (2) the wait-and-see doctrine, and (3) abolition of the Rule.

1.   *The Cy Pres or Reformation Doctrine*

Under the cy pres doctrine, a court reforms a trust that violates the Rule against Perpetuities so as to carry out the testator's intent within the perpetuities period. This doctrine has been adopted in a few states. In exercising the cy pres power (meaning "as near as possible"), a court might insert a saving clause adapted to the particular possibility that causes the gift to be invalid and, in this manner, interfere with the testator's expressed wishes as little as possible. In Case 12, page 687, for example, the saving clause might read: "If any child of A is under the age of 4 at the death of A, the age contingency shall be reduced to the age reached by adding 21 to the age of A's youngest child living at A's death." If no child were under 4 at A's death, no reduction in the age contingency would occur. If the youngest child were age 2 at A's death, the age contingency would be reduced to 23. For illustrations of how a cy pres saving clause works, see Jesse Dukeminier, A Modern Guide to Perpetuities, 74 Cal. L. Rev. 1867, 1898-1901 (1986). See also In re Estate of Anderson, 541 So. 2d 423 (Miss. 1989); Abrams v. Templeton, 465 S.E.2d 117 (S.C. App. 1995).

Judicial reformation of an invalid interest at the time the instrument becomes effective is authorized by Mo. Rev. Stat. §442.555 (2004); Okla. Stat. tit. 60, §75 (2004); Tex. Prop. Code Ann. §5.043 (2004).

NOTE

Illinois and New York have adopted by statute specific correctives for the most frequent violations of the Rule. Age contingencies in excess of 21 that cause a gift to fail are reduced to 21 as to all persons subject to such contingency, and administrative contingencies are presumed to be intended to occur within 21 years. Recall also that in these states the unborn widow is dealt with by a presumption that a gift to a spouse is a gift to a person in being, and the fertile octogenarian is dealt with by a presumption that a woman is incapable of bearing children after a specified age and by the admission of extrinsic evidence of infertility (see pages 681 and 679). 765 Ill. Comp. Stat. §305/4(c) (2004); N.Y. Est., Powers & Trusts Law

§§9-1.2 & 9-1.3 (2004). The assumption that underpins these statutes is that the transferor intended the interest to be valid, and thus instruments of transfer are to be construed to avoid the Rule. Do you think that these statutes go too far? Not far enough?

2. The Wait-and-See Doctrine

In 1947, the Pennsylvania legislature decided to eliminate the requirement of the Rule that there be no possibility that an interest might vest too remotely. Pa. Stat. Ann. tit. 20, §6104(b) (2004) provides:

> Upon the expiration of the period allowed by the common law rule against perpetuities as measured by actual rather than possible events any interest not then vested and any interest in members of a class the membership of which is then subject to increase shall be void.

In 1952 Professor W. Barton Leach of Harvard began his attack upon the Rule against Perpetuities in its orthodox form. Dubbing the Pennsylvania approach "wait-and-see," Leach strongly approved it in a seminal article, Perpetuities in Perspective: Ending the Rule's Reign of Terror, 65 Harv. L. Rev. 721 (1952). The essence of the wait-and-see doctrine is that *we wait and see what actually happens*; we do not invalidate an interest because of what might happen.

Professor Leach, writing with eloquence and wit, and sensing a general unhappiness with the Rule's remote possibilities test, fired up a movement to adopt the wait-and-see doctrine. After Leach first promoted the wait-and-see doctrine, a flood of articles appeared, some in favor of wait-and-see, some against. The primary arguments against wait-and-see were three: (1) inconveniences would arise from not knowing whether an interest was valid or void; (2) wait-and-see was a long step in extending the control of the dead hand; and (3) some critics believed the common law did not provide any measuring lives for a wait-and-see period. Professor Leach replied to his critics in an entertaining article, Perpetuities Legislation, Hail Pennsylvania!, 108 U. Pa. L. Rev. 1124 (1960). For a listing of articles on wait-and-see, see 10 Richard R. Powell, Powell on Real Property §75A.07 (Michael Allan Wolf ed., 2000).

When Professor James Casner, Leach's colleague at Harvard, was appointed Reporter for the second Restatement of Property, he proposed adding wait-and-see to the new Restatement. This prompted

Professor W. Barton Leach

Professor Richard R. Powell, who had been the Reporter for the prior Restatement and who by this point was eighty-eight years old, to come out of retirement to speak against Casner's proposal. Two annual meetings of the American Law Institute were given to the battle. Casner prevailed, however, and wait-and-see was written into the new Restatement. Casner's main argument for wait-and-see was that the traditional what-might-happen test penalizes persons who do not consult skilled lawyers, who avoid the rule by saving clauses or other drafting devices. "The adoption of the wait-and-see approach in this Restatement is largely motivated by the equality of treatment that is produced by placing the validity of all nonvested interests on the same plane, whether the interest is created by a skilled draftsman or one not so skilled." Restatement (Second) of Property: Donative Transfers §13, introductory note (1983).

QUESTIONS

1. The justification offered by the Restatement (Second) of Property for wait-and-see can have far-reaching applications. Think back over the wills and trust cases you have read where the drafter failed to include a special power of appointment (which a skilled drafter almost surely would have included), cut out a child negligently, used ambiguous language, or failed to avoid unnecessary taxation. Can the substantive law be changed, in these cases, to give the advantage of skilled drafting to persons who consult the unskilled? How?

2. As compared to cy pres, what are the advantages and disadvantages of wait-and-see?

The adoption of wait-and-see by the Restatement (Second) provided a renewed stimulus for the wait-and-see movement. Wait-and-see has now been adopted in a majority of states, either by statute or judicial decision. The states divide between those waiting during the common law perpetuities period and those waiting for 90 years, as provided by the Uniform Statutory Rule Against Perpetuities.

a.   Wait-and-See for the Common Law Perpetuities Period

Professor Leach believed that the common law provided an inherent wait-and-see period: the lives relevant to vesting of the interest plus 21 years. The leading English authorities, Vice-Chancellor Megarry and Professor Wade, saw it the same way:

> [T]he only lives in being which are significant under the rule at common law are those which in some way restrict the time within which the gift can vest, and which are expressly or impliedly connected with the gift by the donor's directions. The available perpetuity period must always be ascertained before it can be said whether the gift succeeds or fails. The conditions governing the vesting of the gift, and the lives implicated in those conditions, necessarily remain the same, whether or not the conditions are ultimately satisfied. [Robert Megarry & H.W.R. Wade, The Law of Real Property 254 (5th ed. 1984).]

See also David J. Hayton, The Law of Trusts 106-107 (4th ed. 2003).

Under this view, the lives that can affect vesting fix the common law perpetuities period applicable to the particular interest. These lives are sometimes said to be "causally related to vesting." See Jesse Dukeminier, Perpetuities: The Measuring Lives, 85 Colum. L. Rev. 1648 (1985); Jesse Dukeminier, Wait-and-See: The Causal Relationship Principle, 102 L.Q. Rev. 250 (1986).

States adopting wait-and-see for the common law perpetuities period measured by the relevant common law lives include Kentucky, Mississippi, Ohio, Pennsylvania, and Vermont. Iowa waits out a list of lives closely resembling the relevant common law lives. Maine and Maryland wait out the lives of the preceding life tenants. Illinois applies wait-and-see to trusts for the lives of the trust beneficiaries before determining the validity of a remainder. Many of these states provide that, at the end of the waiting period, if an interest has not vested, it shall be reformed by a court to carry out the intention of the testator as far as possible within the perpetuities period. (In Illinois, Maine, Maryland, and Ohio, however, recent statutes have authorized perpetual trusts, and thus made the wait-and-see statutes inapplicable to most trusts. See page 719).

Here's how wait-and-see works for the common law perpetuities period:

> *Case 18. The Fertile Octogenarian.* T bequeaths a fund in trust "for A for life, then for A's children for their lives, then to A's issue then living." At common law, the remainder in fee simple is void because A is conclusively presumed to be capable of having another child. Under wait-and-see, *the lives relevant to vesting are A and all of A's issue living at T's death.* A and A's children are relevant on two scores: They are preceding life tenants, and they can, by procreating, affect the identity of the remainder beneficiaries. A's grandchildren and great-grandchildren in being at T's death are relevant because they are beneficiaries and also, by procreating or dying, they can affect the identity of the class of issue who take the remainder.
>
> *Case 19. Age Contingency.* T bequeaths a fund in trust "for A for life, then to A's children who reach 25." This is void at common law because A can leave, at his death, an afterborn child under the age of 4. The class members will not necessarily take fixed shares within 21 years after A's death. *The wait-and-see lives are A and all of A's children living at T's death.* A qualifies as a measuring life on two counts: A is the preceding life tenant, and A, by begetting a child who shares in the remainder, can affect the identity of the beneficiaries. The children of A in being at T's death who are under 25 can, by dying under 25, affect the identity of the class members. Those children over 25 at T's death are identified beneficiaries in whom the gift vests.

From these examples you should be able to discern the relevant measuring lives for wait-and-see in all cases you can think of, but if you cannot, see Dukeminier, 85 Colum. L. Rev. 1648, supra, where the measuring lives for all of the standard cases arising under the Rule against Perpetuities are set forth.

b. The Uniform Statutory Rule Against Perpetuities

The drafters of the Uniform Statutory Rule Against Perpetuities (USRAP) adopted wait-and-see, but they rejected using causally related measuring lives. They took the view that the only relevant lives at common law were those that validated the gift. Therefore, lives that might cause vesting, but did not validate the gift, did not implicitly provide a perpetuities period for the particular interest.[11] Thus, they thought, it was necessary to provide an artificial wait-and-see period. They chose a wait-and-see period of 90 years. Why 90 years?

Professor Lawrence W. Waggoner, the principal drafter of the uniform rule, says that the drafters endeavored

> to fix a period of time that approximates the average period of time that would traditionally be allowed by the wait-and-see doctrine. . . . Using four hypothetical families deemed to be representative of actual families, the framers determined that, on average, the transferor's youngest descendant in being at the transferor's death — assuming the transferor's death to occur between ages 60 and 90, which is when 73 percent of the population die — is about 6 years old. The remaining life expectancy of a 6-year-old is about 69 years. The 69 years, plus the 21-year tack-on period, gives an allowable waiting period of 90 years. Although this method may not be scientifically accurate to the nth degree, the Drafting Committee considered it reliable enough to support a waiting period of 90 years. [Lawrence W. Waggoner, The Uniform Statutory Rule Against Perpetuities: The Rationale of the 90-Year Waiting Period, 73 Cornell L. Rev. 157, 162, 166-168 (1988).]

Professor Jesse Dukeminier was not convinced. "Not a scrap of hard data — not a single bit of empirical information about the actual ages of the parties in Rule-violating trusts — is offered for this inherently implausible assumption." Jesse Dukeminier, The Uniform Statutory Rule Against Perpetuities: Ninety Years in Limbo, 34 UCLA L. Rev. 1023, 1033 (1987). Worse still, Dukeminier argued, the Rule would not "survive 90 years in desuetude. . . . . If the Rule cannot strike down any interest for 90 years, I predict it will not be taught and knowledge of it will be lost to lawyers. It will become a piece of history." Id. at 1026.

With ink as their weapon of choice, an epic battle thereupon broke out between Dukeminier and Waggoner, albeit one fought on the pages of the law reviews. See Lawrence W. Waggoner, Perpetuity Reform, 81 Mich. L. Rev. 1718 (1983); Pages 1648 through 1747, inclusive, of Volume 85 of the Columbia Law Review (1985) (comprising five(!) articles); Dukeminier, supra, 34 UCLA L. Rev. 1023; Waggoner, supra, 73 Cornell L. Rev. 157. There is no precise count of the trees sacrificed to this struggle.

Another possible explanation for USRAP's 90-year period is that 90 years is a fair, if somewhat shorter, approximation of the period produced by using Leach's "dozen or so healthy babies" plus 21 years (page 678), which a skilled lawyer might use as a saving clause. See Dukeminier, supra, 34 UCLA L. Rev. at 1034. This approach could be justified on the rationale of the Restatement (Second): "placing the validity of all nonvested interests on the same plane, whether the interest is created by a skilled draftsman or one not so skilled" (page 699).[12]

---

11. This view has been most forcefully presented in David E. Allen, Perpetuities: Who Are the Lives in Being?, 81 L.Q. Rev. 106 (1965), and Ronald H. Maudsley, The Modern Law of Perpetuities 94-100 (1979). For a more recent presentation of this view, see Lawrence W. Waggoner, Perpetuities: A Perspective on Wait-and-See, 85 Colum. L. Rev. 1714 (1985).

12. A similar rationale underpins the English Law Commission's recent recommendation of a 125-year period for vesting, with complete abolition of the common law Rule. English Law Commission, The Rules Against Perpetuities and Excessive Accumulations, Report No. 251 (1998), discussed at page 723. The Commission recommended adopting for wait-and-see a fixed number of years equal to the maximum time a skilled lawyer could obtain using a royal lives clause (see footnote 10, page 696).

At any rate, under USRAP,[13] the common law Rule against Perpetuities is put in abeyance for 90 years. All interests are valid for 90 years after creation. At the end of 90 years, any interest that has not vested is reformed by a court so as to best carry out the intention of the long-dead testator.

USRAP has been supported by state bar associations. After all, it is easier to tick off the 90-year wait-and-see period than to determine and keep track of the lives causally related to vesting, and a 90-year wait-and-see period effectively eliminates malpractice liability for violating the Rule for a lawyer's entire career at the bar. As of this writing, USRAP was in force in Arizona, California, Colorado, Connecticut, the District of Columbia, Georgia, Hawaii, Indiana, Kansas, Massachusetts, Michigan, Minnesota, Montana, Nebraska, Nevada, New Mexico, North Carolina, North Dakota, Oregon, South Carolina, Tennessee, Virginia, and West Virginia. (Note, however, that Arizona, Colorado, Nebraska, and Virginia also authorize perpetual trusts. Similarly, although Florida and Utah have enacted much of the language of USRAP, each has extended the time period applicable to trusts to 360 and 1,000 years respectively. See page 719).

For further analyses and assessments of USRAP by persons other than Dukeminier and Waggoner, see Ira M. Bloom, Perpetuities Refinement: There Is an Alternative, 62 Wash. L. Rev. 23 (1987); Mary L. Fellows, Testing Perpetuity Reforms: A Study of Perpetuity Cases 1984-89, 25 Real Prop., Prob. & Tr. J. 597 (1990); Amy M. Hess, Freeing Property Owners from the RAP Trap: Tennessee Adopts the Uniform Statutory Rule Against Perpetuities, 62 Tenn. L. Rev. 267 (1995); Ronald C. Link & Kimberly A. Licata, Perpetuities Reform in North Carolina: The Uniform Statutory Rule Against Perpetuities, Nondonative Transfers, and Honorary Trusts, 74 N.C.L. Rev. 1783 (1996).

Uniform Statutory Rule Against Perpetuities
(1986, as amended 1990)

§1. STATUTORY RULE AGAINST PERPETUITIES

(a) [*Validity of Nonvested Property Interest.*] A nonvested property interest is invalid unless:

(1) when the interest is created, it is certain to vest or terminate no later than 21 years after the death of an individual then alive; or

(2) the interest either vests or terminates within 90 years after its creation.

(b) [*Validity of General Power of Appointment Subject to a Condition Precedent.*] A general power of appointment not presently exercisable because of a condition precedent is invalid unless:

(1) when the power is created, the condition precedent is certain to be satisfied or becomes impossible to satisfy no later than 21 years after the death of an individual then alive; or

---

13. Professor Link finds one aspect of USRAP "puzzling — its pronunciation. Both 'use-rap' and 'us-rap' seem acceptable to its drafter and advocates." Ronald C. Link & Kimberly A. Licata, Perpetuities Reform in North Carolina: The Uniform Statutory Rule Against Perpetuities, Nondonative Transfers, and Honorary Trusts, 74 N.C.L. Rev. 1783, 1789 n.28 (1996).

(2) the condition precedent either is satisfied or becomes impossible to satisfy within 90 years after its creation.

(c) [*Validity of Nongeneral or Testamentary Power of Appointment.*] A nongeneral power of appointment or a general testamentary power of appointment is invalid unless:

(1) when the power is created, it is certain to be irrevocably exercised or otherwise to terminate no later than 21 years after the death of an individual then alive; or

(2) the power is irrevocably exercised or otherwise terminates within 90 years after its creation.

(d) [*Possibility of Post-death Child Disregarded.*] In determining whether a nonvested property interest or a power of appointment is valid under subsection (a)(1), (b)(1), or (c)(1), the possibility that a child will be born to an individual after the individual's death is disregarded.

(e) [*Effect of Certain "Later-of" Type Language.*] If, in measuring a period from the creation of a trust or other property arrangement, language in a governing instrument (i) seeks to disallow the vesting or termination of any interest or trust beyond, (ii) seeks to postpone the vesting or termination of any interest or trust until, or (iii) seeks to operate in effect in any similar fashion upon, the later of (a) the expiration of a period of time not exceeding 21 years after the death of the survivor of specified lives in being at the creation of the trust or other property arrangement or (b) the expiration of a period of time that exceeds or might exceed 21 years after the death of the survivor of lives in being at the creation of the trust or other property arrangement, that language is inoperative to the extent it produces a period of time that exceeds 21 years after the death of the survivor of the specified lives.

§2. WHEN NONVESTED PROPERTY INTEREST OR POWER OF APPOINTMENT CREATED

(a) Except as provided in subsections (b) and (c) and in Section 5(a), the time of creation of a nonvested property interest or a power of appointment is determined under general principles of property law.

(b) For purposes of this [Act], if there is a person who alone can exercise a power created by a governing instrument to become the unqualified beneficial owner of (i) a nonvested property interest or (ii) a property interest subject to a power of appointment described in Section 1(b) or 1(c), the nonvested property interest or power of appointment is created when the power to become the unqualified beneficial owner terminates. [For purposes of this [Act], a joint power with respect to community property or to marital property under the Uniform Marital Property Act held by individuals married to each other is a power exercisable by one person alone.]

(c) For purposes of this [Act], a nonvested property interest or a power of appointment arising from a transfer of property to a previously funded trust or other existing property arrangement is created when the nonvested property interest or power of appointment in the original contribution was created.

§3. REFORMATION

Upon the petition of an interested person, a court shall reform a disposition in the manner that most closely approximates the transferor's manifested plan of distribution and is within the 90 years allowed by Section 1(a)(2), 1(b)(2), or 1(c)(2) if:

(1) a nonvested property interest or a power of appointment becomes invalid under Section 1 (statutory rule against perpetuities);

(2) a class gift is not but might become invalid under Section 1 (statutory rule against perpetuities) and the time has arrived when the share of any class member is to take effect in possession or enjoyment; or

(3) a nonvested property interest that is not validated by Section 1(a)(1) can vest but not within 90 years after its creation.

§4. Exclusions from Statutory Rule Against Perpetuities

Section 1 (statutory rule against perpetuities) does not apply to:

(1) a nonvested property interest or a power of appointment arising out of a nondonative transfer. . . . [Other exclusions omitted.]

§5. Prospective Application

(a) Except as extended by subsection (b), this [Act] applies to a nonvested property interest or a power of appointment that is created on or after the effective date of this [Act]. For purposes of this section, a nonvested property interest or a power of appointment created by the exercise of a power of appointment is created when the power is irrevocably exercised or when a revocable exercise becomes irrevocable.

(b) If a nonvested property interest or a power of appointment was created before the effective date of this [Act] and is determined in a judicial proceeding, commenced on or after the effective date of this [Act], to violate this State's rule against perpetuities as that rule existed before the effective date of this [Act], a court upon the petition of an interested person may reform the disposition in the manner that most closely approximates the transferor's manifested plan of distribution and is within the limits of the rule against perpetuities applicable when the nonvested property interest or power of appointment was created.

In re Trust of Wold
Superior Court of New Jersey, Chancery Division, Middlesex County, 1998
310 N.J. Super. 382, 708 A.2d 787

HAMLIN, P.J. This written decision amplifies an earlier oral bench opinion rendered on plaintiff's petition for interpretation and direction regarding the application of the "New Jersey Uniform Statutory Rule Against Perpetuities." N.J.S.A. 46.2F-1-8, to a proposed exercise by the beneficiary of her power of appointment under the terms of this 1944 Trust. It is an issue of first impression requiring the court to determine if the ninety year period of N.J.S.A. 46.2F-8 enacted on July 3, 1991, may be invoked by the beneficiary in regard to the exercise of that power of appointment vested in her by the 1944 Trust. The issue arises following inquiry by Elaine Johnson Wold, the life beneficiary of the Trust, to the trustees. More specifically she advised the trustees that she wishes to create a testamentary Trust appointing the proceeds of the 1944 Trust in further trust for the benefit of her spouse and surviving issue. The proposed testamentary trust would create non-vested property interests in one or more issue. By way of illustration the proposed exercise of the power in a new testamentary trust created by Mrs. Wold would permit property held for one of her children, upon the death of that child, to continue in trust for the benefit of that child's own issue. Thus, the trust interest of that child would be considered non-vested since it would pass to the next generation upon the occurrence of a specific event, i.e. the death of the child.

The proposed exercise of Mrs. Wold's power of appointment under the 1944 Trust through the creation of her own testamentary trust would permit such generational structure to continue for the full period permitted under the Rule Against Perpetuities. In delineating the maximum term of the trust she would create for her spouse and issue, Mrs. Wold has expressed to the trustees her intention to rely on the ninety year "wait and see" perpetuities period as codified in the 1991 legislation.

In order to ensure the validity of her long term estate planning and to make certain that the trustees will be permitted to make distributions of the trust estate in accordance with her expressed intentions Mrs. Wold, through the trustees, asks this court to determine the applicability and construction of the New Jersey Rule Against Perpetuities Act as it applies to the exercise of her special power of appointment. In the absence of clear and binding precedent or other authority, neither Mrs. Wold nor the trustees can be assured that the intended disposition will not be later found to violate the applicable rule against perpetuities. Without a present determination, there exists the possibility that the testamentary trust created by Mrs. Wold might, after her death, be voided or reformed in a manner that is inconsistent with her expressed intention. In addition, the trustees seek direction from the court regarding the proposed testamentary exercise of Mrs. Wold's power of appointment under the terms of the 1944 instrument. They assert that they are in doubt as to whether the power granted Mrs. Wold to dispose of the trust res includes the power to appoint the trust assets by a successive testamentary trust. The trustees seek to invoke the traditional equitable power of the Chancery court to resolve their concerns about the exercise of their fiduciary duty as governed by the provision of the original trust which states:

> Upon the death of Elaine Johnson (Wold), the Trustees are directed to divide, transfer and pay over absolutely, outright and forever, the trust property as follows: to the surviving spouse and issue of Elaine Johnson (Wold) or any of them in such shares as she may direct by her Last Will and Testament duly admitted to probate. . . .

All persons having an interest in the issue presented have been served and have chosen not to take a position on the application.

CREATION OF THE 1944 TRUST

J. Seward Johnson (hereinafter Seward) created this trust on October 20, 1944 to benefit his daughter Elaine Johnson Wold.[14] It was one of several trusts

---

14. For more on Seward Johnson and his family, see pages 176-183. Elaine Johnson was unmarried and had no children in 1944 when the trust was created. She married Keith Wold in 1949. — Eds.

he created contemporaneously for each of his children. Each was identical in language with the exception of the named beneficiaries. Subsequently the settlor created at least two additional charitable lead trusts to further benefit his issue. The trust plan was neither haphazard nor one dimensional. The trusts were initially funded by substantial shares of the health care corporate giant, Johnson and Johnson (J&J). Seward and his brother, Robert Wood Johnson were the principal heirs of the controlling stock of J&J, which was already a major national corporation at that time. Robert Wood Johnson succeeded to the leadership of the company. Through his efforts and subsequent astute business management, J&J has become a major international diversified business presence. Thus, the original 15,000 shares of J&J stock which initially funded the trust have multiplied in value so that they now constitute one of the most significant family fortunes in America. Since J&J has been headquartered in New Brunswick, New Jersey for over a century and the trusts were created here, the Middlesex County Courts and more specifically the Chancery Division of this venue, have had long interaction with the construction and administration of the various trusts created by Seward. Many accountings have been presented over the years. Specific previous applications by trustees have been the subject of decisions and unpublished opinions. Likewise there has been significant litigation involving the trusts, their creation and purpose, which resulted in published opinions that are helpful to our overall understanding of the trust scheme established by Seward with the assistance of sophisticated estate planning counsel. See Hill v. Estate of Mary Lea Johnson-Richards, 667 A.2d 695 (N.J. 1995); Wiedenmayer v. Johnson, 254 A.2d 534 (N.J. App. Div. 1969), aff'd 55 N.J. 81 (1970); Barbara P. Johnson v. Seward Johnson, Jr., 515 A.2d 255 (N.J. Ch. Div. 1986); and Burke v. Director, Division of Taxation, 11 N.J. Tax 29 (1990).

The trust instrument itself is comprehensive and clearly designed to accomplish several salutory ends. Foremost is the provision for support and income to the beneficiary and such of her heirs as she may select. Such income was maximized to the fullest by utilizing tax saving devices permitted by law.

Under the terms of the Trust, the trustees were directed during the lifetime of Elaine Johnson Wold to collect and receive the income and profits from the trust property and, after deducting those expenses of "the trust" which are payable out of the income, to accumulate the net income and add it at the end of each calendar year to the trust property. Once Elaine Johnson Wold attained the age of twenty-one (21) years, the trust agreement authorized the trustees to pay to her so much of the net income in any year as the trustees in their absolute and uncontrolled discretion deemed to be for her best interest. The trust instrument further permits the trustees to transfer and pay over to the life beneficiary ". . . any or all of the Trust property."

Upon the death of Elaine Johnson Wold, the trust agreement directs the trustees to divide, transfer and pay over absolutely, outright and forever, the trust property as follows:

a. To the surviving spouse and issue of Elaine Johnson (Wold) or any of them in such shares as she may direct by her last Will and Testament duly admitted to probate, or failing such testamentary direction, then,

b. To her issue in equal shares per stirpes. . . .

Does the Trust Prohibit the Proposed Exercise?

At the threshold this court notes that the trust instrument, by its very language, vested in the trustees the broadest possible discretion that may be found in any trust instrument. They are to be guided solely by their evaluation of the beneficiary's best interest. Clearly the settlor intended to repose in the trustees maximum flexibility in addressing the needs of the beneficiaries. By way of illustration it is clear that had the trustees distributed the entire income and corpus to Mrs. Wold during her lifetime, leaving nothing to be appointed to subsequent heirs, it would have been permissible absent claim of corruption, intentional misconduct or gross negligence. In regard to the instant matter this court is mindful that the sole inference from the unambiguous language of the trust instrument was the desire of the settlor to create a flexible instrument to meet the developing needs of his children both at the time of the creation of the trust and for unforeseen events that would occur. It is an expansive rather than a restrictive instrument.

The law of trusts lends support to Mrs. Wold's position that she should be able to exercise the special power of appointment created by her father, Seward, in a testamentary trust by her for the benefit of her granddaughters. The Restatement (Second) of Trusts §17 provides that "[a] trust may be created by (d) an appointment of one person having a power of appointment to another person as trustee for the donee of the power or for a third person."

The comments to the section explain that "if a person has a special power of appointment . . . he can effectively appoint interests to trustees for the benefit of objects of the power unless the donor manifested a contrary intent." Restatement (Second) of Trusts, §17 cmt. f. Further, it is clear that one can infer that the donor of a special power intended the donee to have the same discretion in making an appointment that he had in the disposition of his own property, so far as the extent and nature of the interests which he might give to the members of the class are concerned. Id; see also Restatement (Second) of Property §19.3 (1984).

It has long been accepted that a person holding powers of appointment may appoint to the fullest extent of the authority or to such lesser estate or interest as he may see fit in the absence of an express prohibition by the settlor in the trust instrument. . . .

While the trust instrument speaks in terms of appointment including distribution of the corpus in fee simple, if the beneficiary saw fit, it should not be construed as a form of limitation. The hallmark of this trust, as the others, is the flexibility of the trustees, and implicitly the donee of the power, to be permitted maximum discretion.

The court is not unmindful of the clear purpose of the settlor to protect the trust from tax burdens to the fullest extent permitted by law. There can be no question that the proposed testamentary trust exercise of the power will effect significant tax savings. As this court observed in a matter involving another long term trust created by Seward, one of the significant purposes of the Trust scheme was ". . . that the Grantor was able to shelter the fund and its appreciation in value from his estate for estate tax purposes and to incorporate then permissible generation skipping features." Such a purpose, as evidenced by the sophisticated estate planning devices used by Seward, are to be given effect in the exercise of the power of appointment rather than restricted. The proposed creation of the testamentary trust as described by Mrs. Wold is well within the contemplation and intent of the trust instrument. The trustees may honor the proposed exercise of the power of appointment at the appropriate time and make a consistent distribution of the trust assets.

THE APPLICATION OF N.J.S.A. 46:2A-1-5

New Jersey adopted the Uniform Statutory Rule Against Perpetuities on July 3, 1991. In so doing it adopted the "wait and see" approach long advocated by reformers of the common law rule against perpetuities so painfully committed to memory by generations of law students. The statute may well sound the death knell for Leach's "Perpetuities In A Nut Shell."

Under the common law approach, if an interest was not certain to vest within the specified period, then the disposition was considered invalid. Under the Act, an interest that would have been invalid at common law is nevertheless valid if it does in fact vest within ninety years of its creation, and becomes invalid only if it remains in existence and does not ultimately vest within that time period. Under the statutory provision, "a non-vested property interest is invalid unless (1) When the interest is created, it is certain to vest or terminate no later than 21 years after the death of an individual then alive, or (2) the interest either vests or terminates within 90 years after its creation."

The Statute, in a specific and distinguishable fact pattern, was applied prospectively. In Juliano & Sons Enterprises, Inc. v. Chevron U.S.A., Inc., 593 A.2d 814 (N.J. App. Div. 1991), which is the only reported New Jersey decision that has addressed the new statute, the court held that the statutory rule was not retroactive and intended to apply only to property interests created on or after the effective date of the statute. See also U.L.A. Perpetuities 5 (1990). Thus, an interest created under a trust established in 1944 would arguably not fall under the new legislation.

However, while the statute may not apply retroactively as a general matter, for purposes of determining the applicability of the new statutory period the law specifically provides that an interest created pursuant to a power of appointment is deemed to be created upon the exercise of the power. N.J.S.A. 46:2F-5(a). Therefore, even if created under a pre-existing power of appointment, the New Jersey Uniform Statutory Rule Against Perpetuities would apply to an interest created under that power, whether general or specific, if exercised after July 3, 1991.

This interpretation is supported by the clear language of the statute as well as by the comments to the Uniform Laws Annotated. "All provisions of the [Uniform] Act except section 5(b) apply to a non-vested property interest (or power of appointment) created by a donee's exercise of a power of appointment where the donee's exercise, whether revocable or irrevocable, occurs on or after the effective date of [the] Act." (Section 5(b) allows reformation of non-vested interests created before the new law.) The U.L.A. comment also makes clear that the special rule bringing a non-vested interest created under a power of appointment within the scope of the new law "applies to the exercise of all types of powers of appointment—presently exercisable general powers, general testamentary powers, and non-general powers."

Consistent with the language of the statute as well as the persuasive analysis of secondary authority this court concludes that the statutory period applies to the non-vested interest that would be created pursuant to the exercise of the power and measured from the creation of the 1944 Trust.

NOTES AND QUESTIONS

1. In the *Wold* case, the trust created by Seward Johnson in 1944 was grand-fathered in and not subject to the generation-skipping transfer tax enacted in 1986, which was not retroactive. Quite naturally, the donee of the special power of appointment, Elaine Johnson Wold, wanted to prolong this tax-exempt trust as long as possible.

Elaine Johnson Wold wanted to appoint in further trust for 90 years from 1944, benefitting her spouse and descendants. The trust would last until 2034. Why did the donee not want to appoint in further trust using artificial measuring lives (for example, 12 persons from long-lived families who were infants in 1944) plus 21 years? The statistical probabilities are that this would produce a period longer than one ending in 2034.

Suppose that Elaine Johnson Wold appointed in further trust until 2034 giving her descendants special inter vivos powers of appointment. When the 90-year period is approaching expiration, can the donees exercise the powers, switching the trust duration over to the common law perpetuities period, using lives in being in 1944? USRAP §1(e) does not prohibit switching to the common law perpetuities period at the end of 90 years.

2. In this case it is highly unlikely that the Seward Johnson trust contained a saving clause. Saving clauses came into general use in the 1960s. Suppose, however, that the Seward Johnson trust had contained a saving clause providing that the trust would terminate 21 years after the death of the survivor of Seward's issue living when the trust was created. Could Elaine Johnson Wold change the duration of the trust to 90 years? If not, what does this suggest about the drafting of a perpetuities saving clause?

3. The wave of state legislation permitting perpetual trusts has reached New Jersey (see page 719), which in 1999 repealed USRAP and replaced it with a rule permitting a perpetual trust if the trustee has power to sell, either expressed or implied, or if there is an unlimited power to terminate the trust in one or more living persons. N.J. Stat. Ann. §§46:2F-9–46:2F-10 (2004).

USRAP and the Generation-Skipping Transfer (GST) Tax. When USRAP was drafted, its drafters ignored the interaction of USRAP with the GST tax. The GST tax, you will recall, is payable on a transfer to a person two or more generations removed from the transferor, such as a grandchild. Trusts created before 1986 were grandfathered in. Under Treasury regulations at the time USRAP was drafted, pre-1986 trusts are not subject to the GST tax unless a special power of appointment over the pre-1986 trust is exercised in a manner that postpones vesting of an interest beyond lives in being at the creation of the trust plus 21 years. The purpose of the regulation is to prevent tax exemption from enduring longer than the perpetuities period beginning at the creation of the trust.

After USRAP was promulgated, it was discovered that USRAP contained an unexpected tax trap: In a USRAP jurisdiction, a grandfathered trust loses its

GST tax exemption if the donee of a special power of appointment exercises the power so as to violate the common law Rule against Perpetuities, thus bringing into play the 90-year wait-and-see period, which may extend the trust beyond lives in being at the creation of the trust plus 21 years.

When the USRAP tax trap was brought to the attention of the USRAP drafting committee in 1990, the committee negotiated a solution for the problem with the Treasury Department. Treasury accepted the 90-year perpetuities period as the functional equivalent of the common law perpetuities period. Treasury was unwilling, however, to extend a tax exemption to a trust that could continue for either the common law perpetuities period or for 90 years, whichever period turned out to be longer. This could result in an even more substantial extension of the tax exemption as well as give an unfair advantage to longer-of-two-perpetuities-periods trusts available in USRAP states but not in states adhering to the common law. To satisfy Treasury's demand that a clause terminating a trust on the later of the two perpetuities periods be prohibited, USRAP was amended in 1990 by adding §1(e).

Although §1(e) may seem hard to follow upon first reading, it provides that when a gift is made on two alternative contingencies, one of which (A) will necessarily vest, if at all, within the common law perpetuities period, and the second of which (B) might vest beyond that period, the language of (B) is rendered inoperative to the extent it produces a period in excess of 21 years after the specified lives in being. When a clause terminates a trust at the conclusion of either the common law perpetuities period or a 90-year period, whichever is later, §1(e) gives effect only to the common law perpetuities period termination date.

After USRAP was amended to add §1(e), Treasury issued a regulation stating that if a special power of appointment in a grandfathered trust were "directly or indirectly" exercised in a manner that attempts to obtain the longer of the two perpetuities periods available under USRAP, the GST tax exemption is lost. Treas. Reg. §26.2601-1(b)(1)(v)(B)(2) & (D), examples 6 & 7 (1997).

Here is how §1(e) works:

> *Case 20*. Seward Johnson creates an irrevocable trust in 1944 to pay the income to his daughter Elaine for life, then as Elaine appoints by will among her spouse and issue and issue of spouses, and in default to her issue per stirpes. Elaine dies in 2000 appointing the income of the trust property to her descendants until the death of the survivor of 12 persons who were infants in 1944 or until 2034, whichever is longer, and then to distribute the principal to her issue per stirpes. This appointment creates two gifts on alternative contingencies, whichever happens last: (A) at the end of lives in being in 1944 plus 21 years or (B) at the end of 90 years from 1944. The appointment is entirely valid under the alternative contingencies doctrine in a USRAP jurisdiction. The gift on event (A) is valid under the common law Rule (USRAP §1(a)(1)); the gift on event (B) is valid under the 90-year wait-and-see period of USRAP §1(a)(2). This appointment would forfeit the GST tax exemption of the trust but for USRAP §1(e). Section 1(e) voids the gift on event (B), leaving only a gift on the death of persons in being in 1944 plus 21 years.

Although the Treasury regulation forbids the exercise of the power in an attempt to obtain the longer of the two USRAP perpetuities periods, it permits the donee to appoint in further trust for 90 years or less. Hence, a grandfathered trust initially governed by the common law perpetuities period may be turned into a 90-year trust by the exercise of a special power of appointment, provided, of course, that the special power may be so exercised under the instrument. This is what Elaine Johnson Wold wanted to do in the *Wold* case, which the court approved.

USRAP §1(e) has not been enacted in some states that adopted USRAP before it was amended in 1990. In these states, when a special power in a grandfathered trust is exercised so as to terminate the trust at the end of the common law perpetuities period or 90 years, whichever is later, such as in Case 20, creating alternative contingencies, the first of which is valid at common law and the second valid under USRAP, the trust may lose its GST tax exemption. See Jesse Dukeminier, The Uniform Statutory Rule Against Perpetuities and the GST Tax: New Perils for Practitioners and New Opportunities, 30 Real Prop., Prob. & Tr. J. 185, 198-199 (1995).

Lawyers in USRAP states who are dealing with grandfathered trusts should take special care not to violate the common law Rule against Perpetuities if they decide not to extend the trust for 90 years. If the common law Rule is violated, bringing into play the 90-year wait-and-see period as an alternative trust termination date, this may result in the longer of the two perpetuities periods applying and the loss of GST tax exemption. Id. at 199-202.

As you can see, the interaction of USRAP and the GST tax is a complicated matter, which you will have to unravel if you are advising the donee of a special power in a grandfathered trust. USRAP may save the lawyer from malpractice liability for violating the Rule when the GST tax is not involved. But it does not save the lawyer from possible liability for negligently losing the GST tax exemption.

PROBLEMS AND QUESTIONS

1. Apply USRAP, as amended by §1(e), to the following devise: "To my issue, two years after the death of my widow or 40 years after my death, whichever is later." Here, we have alternative contingencies, one valid and one void at common law. Under USRAP §1(e), the "language is inoperative to the extent it produces a period of time that exceeds 21 years after the death of" the widow. Why does not the gift get the benefit of the 90-year wait-and-see period, inasmuch as the gift will undoubtedly vest within 90 years? Has the tax tail wagged the dog?

2. Apply USRAP to the following devise: "In trust to pay income to my descendants from time to time living, per stirpes, for as long as the law allows, then to pay principal to my descendants then living." Is the trust valid for the lives of the testator's descendants living at his death plus 21 years, or for 90 years, or for whichever is longer? Suppose that the jurisdiction has enacted USRAP but has not adopted §1(e). Is the trust valid for whichever of these two periods turns out to be longer? If so construed, would the trust be disqualified for the federal GST tax exemptions?

3. Abolition of the Rule Against Perpetuities

The Rule against Perpetuities no longer commands universal respect or fear. Its storied absurdities seem remnants of a bygone age. There is no longer a consensus on how long the dead hand should be permitted to govern. The question thus arises: Should the Rule against Perpetuities be abolished altogether?

Jesse Dukeminier & James E. Krier, The Rise of the Perpetual Trust
50 UCLA L. Rev. 1303, 1311-1319, 1321-1328, 1335, 1338-1339, 1343 (2003)

The two reforms traced above—the wait-and-see doctrine, and then, especially, USRAP—might have weakened the Rule against Perpetuities, but they honored its purpose. Neither reform embodied any intention to free the dead hand of age-old restrictions; to the contrary, both shared that central policy of the Rule. But they, as much as the old Rule, are being undermined by the recent wave of state legislation permitting perpetual trusts. To account for that legislation, we have to begin with the federal estate tax.

1. The Generation-Skipping Transfer Tax

The federal estate tax, first enacted in 1916, levies a tax on any property interest transferred by will, intestacy, or survivorship to another person, except for transfers to spouses and charities. The tax can be avoided, however, by the use of life estates. At the death of a life tenant, the tenancy ends, leaving no transfer to be taxed. For seventy years, lawyers took advantage of this loophole by creating trusts with successive life estates, which could continue without any estate taxes being levied against succeeding generations until after the termination of the trust. And the trusts themselves could continue until the Rule against Perpetuities, in one or another variant, called a halt. Here is an example:

> *Case [21]. T* devises property in trust to pay the income to his daughter *A* for life, then to pay the income to *A*'s children for their lives, then to distribute the principal to *A*'s grandchildren (with a saving clause or other wording to avoid a perpetuities violation). At *T*'s death an estate tax is levied on the property, but no estate tax is levied at the death of *A* or at the death of *A*'s children because these persons do not have interests transferable on death. An estate tax will not be levied again until the death of *A*'s grandchildren, perhaps more than a hundred years after *T*'s death.

In 1986 Congress closed this loophole in the tax laws, deciding that a transfer tax is due at the expiration of each generation. After 1986, if a transferor creates a life estate in a child that avoids ("skips") the federal estate tax at the child's death, as in *Case [21]*, a generation-skipping transfer (GST) tax is due at the child's death if the property passes to the next generation. The GST tax is levied at the highest rate of the estate tax.... In *Case [21]*, no federal estate tax is payable at *A*'s death because *A* does not have a transmissible interest. However, at *A*'s death, a generation-skipping transfer occurs, from *T* to his grandchildren. And so, at *A*'s death, the GST tax is levied on the value of the nonexempt corpus of the trust. Upon the death of *A*'s children, another generation-skipping transfer tax is levied.

At the same time it amended the federal transfer tax laws by adding the GST tax, Congress lightened the taxpayer burden by providing a $1 million exemption from the GST tax for each transferor (doubled in the case of married couples).

An inflation adjustment in 2002 increased the amount to $1.1 million; it will increase again to $1.5 million in 2004 and ultimately, in gradual steps, to $3.5 million in 2009. The exemption can be allotted to direct gifts to grandchildren or to a trust producing one or more generation-skipping transfers. The estate tax law itself places no limitation on the duration of such trusts. A transferor can create a trust, with $1.1 million ($3.5 million after 2008) as principal, for his children for life, with successive life estates in succeeding generations, for as long as state perpetuities law allows. Thanks to the exemption, no estate tax or GST tax is due until the trust terminates. In states following the Rule against Perpetuities, these tax-exempt dynasty trusts can endure for lives-in-being at the creation of the trust, plus twenty-one years; in USRAP states they can last for that period or for ninety years.

2. State Legislation

When Congress enacted the GST tax, it probably assumed that most states would continue to adhere to the Rule against Perpetuities in one or another variation, but this has proved unfounded. Before 1986, only three states . . . had abolished the Rule and adopted a prohibition against suspension of the power of alienation. Perpetual trusts have thus been permitted in these states for some time, provided there is some person, such as a trustee with a power of sale, who can transfer title to (alienate) the trust property. But since 1986, at least seventeen more states have enacted legislation permitting perpetual, or almost perpetual, trusts . . . .

The [number of states permitting perpetual trusts] will almost certainly grow. . . . The reason has little if anything to do with some wish on the part of wealthy people to control the lives of their unknown descendants; rather, it has to do with their interest in saving on federal transfer taxes imposed at the descendants' deaths, and on competition among the states to cater to that interest. . . . [P]erpetual trusts have long been permitted in Idaho, South Dakota, and Wisconsin, but they were seldom created before the appearance of the GST tax in 1986. Once the GST tax was enacted, however, perpetual trusts became much more attractive, and suddenly the three perpetual-trust states had a comparative advantage in attracting trust business and capital.

This did not go unnoticed. Delaware, the first state to permit perpetual trusts after 1986, did so explicitly to remain competitive in the trust market. One state after another followed suit, and, so far as one can tell, all for that same reason. New Jersey, for example, repealed its USRAP "to permit banks and trust companies to offer 'dynasty trusts' to their customers, such as those that are being offered by banks and trust companies located in other states," like Delaware and South Dakota. In Connecticut, where perpetual trust legislation is being considered, local banks and lawyers have argued that "people who want to set up dynastic trusts for their grandchildren, great-grandchildren and down the line of genera- tions, are doing them in other states." Of course, Connecticut lawyers can, even without state legislation, draft trusts to be set up elsewhere, but when they do they usually work in consultation with lawyers in the other states; this increases legal fees and "sometimes causes the client to simply hire out-of-state counsel in the first place."

The Rule Against Perpetuities: If You Repeal It, They Will Come

It is difficult to get hard data on the popularity of perpetual trusts among consumers, but there appears to be enough interest among the relatively wealthy to create a tidy market. South Dakota, for example, has enjoyed a substantial increase in trust business since 1986, most of it on behalf of nonresident clients. . . . One New York City lawyer guesses, based on his own experience, that the number of perpetual trusts created nationwide now runs into the thousands per year; his firm "alone probably does 100 or more annually." His brother works for an Alaska trust company that has done "700 or so I would guess. South Dakota and Delaware institutions probably have more."

Marketing is part of the picture; people involved in the trust business have not been shy in their efforts to attract trust customers. . . .

. . . Passage of the GST tax, coupled with competition for highly mobile trust capital and trust business, has spurred state after state to abolish the Rule in one manner or another, and the trend shows no signs of abating.[15] . . . [The] absence of interest in perpetual trusts prior to the GST tax gives rise to the troubling likelihood that the Rule against Perpetuities is being abolished with little if any reflection upon the merits of the Rule *on its own*, without regard to tax considerations. . . .

II. PROBLEMS AND PALLIATIVES

The wisdom of abolishing the Rule against Perpetuities in the case of perpetual trusts has to turn on the merits of the Rule's underlying policies. The

---

15. As John Langbein has nicely remarked to us, the GST tax proved to be "a natural predator" for the Rule against Perpetuities.

policy analysis has to be done in context, because an argument that supports restrictions on perpetuities in general might carry little weight with respect to perpetual trusts. Let us begin with a sketch of what a typical perpetual dynasty trust might look like.

Here is an outline: *O* transfers $1.1 million to a trust that will pay the income to *O*'s daughter, *A*, for life, then the trust principal is divided into separate shares for each of *A*'s children. Each child allocated a trust share is given a life estate in that share, and upon the child's death, his or her trust share is further divided per stirpes to be held in trust for that child's issue. This process of dividing and subdividing on a stirpital basis continues down through the succeeding generations until one line runs out of issue, at which time the assets will be shifted to other branches of the family. To provide flexibility to deal with changing circumstances, *A* is given a special (or limited) power to appoint the trust principal during life or by will, outright or in further trust, to any one or more of a class of persons consisting of *A*'s spouse, the descendants of *O*, and spouses of those descendants. This power permits *A* to modify or terminate the trust at any time during her life or at death by distributing the trust principal among her family. Each successive income beneficiary is given a special power of appointment over the share of the principal from which the beneficiary is receiving the income. The special power enables the beneficiaries, in succession, to modify or terminate their shares of the trust in any way that does not benefit the donees of the special powers. In addition, or in the alternative, the settlor may create as a dynasty trust a discretionary trust with discretionary powers in the trustee.

We are now in a position to consider the policies underlying the Rule against Perpetuities — in the context of perpetual trusts. There are essentially three concerns, each of which can be stated in terms of a problem arising from a persistent dead hand. The first, the problem of inalienability, is of little importance in our context because it can be avoided by any well-drafted trust. The second, which we shall call the problem of first-generation monopoly, is contentious; we shall satisfy ourselves simply with describing the competing outlooks. The third, the problem of duration, is a catch-all for a host of difficulties that can arise as an uncertain future unwinds . . . .

A. THE PROBLEM OF INALIENABILITY

Transferability (or "alienability") of property promotes efficiency; it allows the movement of resources from lower to higher valued uses through voluntary transactions between buyers and sellers that leave both sides of the bargain better off. So it is unsurprising that free alienability is one of the enduring principles of English, and subsequently American, property law. . . .

In the United States today, the assets of the wealthy consist largely of personal property, not land. Transfers of personal property, and of land as well, for the benefit of succeeding generations are almost always in trust, and trustees almost always have a power to sell the trust property and invest in other assets. In almost all states permitting perpetual trusts, trustees must be given this power by the instrument if it is not granted by statute. A well-drafted trust will grant the power in any event. Hence, perpetual trusts do not give rise to a problem of inalienability; the trust assets are freely marketable.

B. THE PROBLEM OF FIRST-GENERATION MONOPOLY

. . . [In 1955 Professor Lewis Simes described] what we call the problem of first-generation monopoly, meaning by "first generation" the generation of the settlor who sets up a perpetual trust. Simes wrote:

> [I]t is good public policy to allow each person to dispose of his property as he pleases. The policy extends not only to the present generation but to future generations. If we are to permit the present generation to tie up all existing capital for an indefinitely long period of time, then future generations will have nothing to dispose of by will except what they have saved from their own income; and the property which each generation enjoys will already have been disposed of by ancestors long dead. The rule against perpetuities would appear to strike a balance between the unlimited disposition of property by the members of the present generation and its unlimited disposition by members of future generations.[16]

This is an old and appealing sentiment. . . . [Indeed, Simes] thought that the force of the argument against first-generation monopoly "can scarcely be denied." And yet it can. Professor Thomas Gallanis notes . . . that sentiments about the dead hand rest on dubious assumptions about what people actually want.[17] . . . Consider, for example, the likely preferences of the mentally incompetent; of minor children; of bad money managers who lack the discipline to lash themselves to the mast; of people (maybe those same people!) hounded by creditors and vulnerable to bankruptcy; of people, supported by the state, who are beneficiaries of discretionary trusts, which the state cannot touch; of people contemplating divorce and interested in having their property out of reach of the other half; of people who reap nice tax advantages from trusts, including spouses who benefit from the marital deduction, and beneficiaries of tax-exempt dynasty trusts, among others. . . .

Beyond that, one should consider goals other than satisfaction of preferences. A goal of equality, for example, might support placing restraints on the ability of one generation to limit the opportunities of the next; a goal of donative freedom, on the other hand, would cut in the opposite direction. . . .

[E]quality of opportunity is not provided by income alone. As Professors Blum and Kalven pointed out years ago, the gravest source of inequality of opportunity is inequality of human capital, the knowledge and education embodied in individuals.[18] Human capital is created by family cultural influence on children, as well as by education. The knowledge and education of parents and more remote ancestors are passed along from generation to generation. Judge Posner puts the point in another way: "The inheritance of a large amount of money may seem to confer an unfair advantage, but why more unfair than inheriting brains and energy?"

. . . [T]here is an argument that trusts concentrate economic power in the rich or, more accurately, in the trustees for the rich. In the case of trusts, the trustees, not the beneficiaries, have the power of investment. They decide where the trust capital is to be invested. . . . [But] the wealth invested by trustees is only a small fraction of the total amount of risk capital made available by other investors. . . .

---

16. Lewis M. Simes, Is the Rule Against Perpetuities Doomed? The "Wait and See" Doctrine, 52 Mich. L. Rev. 179, 191-192 (1953). — Eds.

17. Thomas P. Gallanis, The Rule Against Perpetuities and the Law Commission's Flawed Philosophy, 59 Cambridge L.J. 284, 287-290 (2000).

18. An excerpt from the Blum and Kalven article appears at page 18. — Eds.

Consider finally the argument that the certainty of receiving trust income makes beneficiaries lazy and unproductive. . . . When the Republic was established, England had a "leisure class," composed of nobles and country gentlemen who lived off their land rents and inheritances and refrained from something as low as work. . . . But this country has never had a leisure class like England's. We have no sense of inherited hierarchy. Our work ethic, deeply imbedded from the times of the Puritans, has spared us a class of great drones. . . .

. . . [Our] work ethic is paired with another ethic: The rich should share their wealth with the less fortunate. From the time when great fortunes were accumulated at the end of the nineteenth century to the present, the American rich, to justify their moral instinct, have given great sums to philanthropic enterprises. . . . This tradition of giving, reflecting conceptions about how society should be organized and what benefits the public, continues to this day. . . . [C]haritable support has given us in the United States universities and hospitals and cultural institutions that are the envy of the world. The diversity of privately supported philanthropic enterprises is enormous, far greater than in Western European countries where the charitable agenda is largely set and supported by the government.

. . . Perhaps the objection is to the creation of family dynasties, which receive trust income generation after generation.[19] The answer is this: The Rule against Perpetuities has not prevented the creation of family dynasties. Witness the Rockefellers (now in their fifth generation), the Du Ponts of high dynastic numbering (whose fortune dates from the War of 1812), and the Mellons (with a fortune predating the Civil War). These are extreme cases, but the fact is that smaller fortunes have supported many other families over several generations. Dozens of the lesser rich families have entrenched themselves from generation to generation in communities across the United States. The same is true in England . . . . If family dynasties are to be prevented, only the federal government, through income and death taxes, can do it. As Susan French has noted, the power of the dead hand is always at the sufferance of the living, who are perfectly free to change the laws that created the power in the first place.[20]

C. THE PROBLEM OF DURATION

The longer trusts endure, the more troublesome they become, thanks largely to uncertainty. . . .

1. *Change in Circumstances*

No one can foresee the future. After some years pass, events never anticipated by trust settlors and their lawyers are likely to occur — for example, changes in the number, needs, and abilities of beneficiaries; changes in tax law and trust doctrine; changes in investment opportunities, in the rate of inflation and the value of the

---

19. Recall the quotation attributed to Tocqueville in the excerpt from Oliver, Shapiro & Press, page 11: "What is the most important for democracy is not that great fortunes should not exist, but that great fortunes should not remain in the same hands. In that way there are rich men, but they do not form a class." — Eds.

20. See Susan F. French, Perpetuities: Three Essays in Honor of My Father, 65 Wash. L. Rev. 323, 350-352 (1990).

dollar; changes in trustees and the quality of their performance. The welfare of beneficiaries might be reduced in consequence, or economic waste might result. The Rule against Perpetuities mitigates the difficulty by finally terminating trusts and forcing distribution of assets. Absent the Rule, termination or modification after a change in circumstances must be dealt with in other ways. . . .

2.   *Trustees*

Any number of problems can arise with trustees, and the longer a trust lasts, the greater the burden of these. . . . When settlors choose a trustee, they cannot know the course of future events. This might well lead them to choose a corporate trustee instead of a trusted friend, if for no other reason than that friends eventually die. But then, so too do corporate trustees, in a sense. Their employees pass on, or away; the corporate trustee itself may merge with another company. . . . Beneficiaries, especially beneficiaries of long-term and perpetual trusts, may end up with a trustee of a sort the settlor would never have wished to choose — such as a bank the beneficiaries find to be distant, cold, and unresponsive to their needs. . . .

3.   *Multiplication of Beneficiaries*

When a trust is limited to one hundred years or so, the number of beneficiaries will usually stay a manageable size, even though administrative costs may rise as the class of beneficiaries increases. In a perpetual trust, the number of beneficiaries can multiply relentlessly from generation to generation. If a trust is set up for two children of the settlor and their descendants, and each child has two children — which is pretty close to the statistical average — and each grandchild has two children, and so on down the generations, and each generation is measured by twenty-five years, there will be sixteen beneficiaries of the trust after one hundred years and 256 after two hundred years. Eventually the trust might become unmanageable. But the problem can be avoided if separate trusts can be created for the various beneficiaries. . . . The Uniform Trust Code grants just such a power to trustees, letting them divide a trust into two or more separate trusts without court approval, so long as notice is given to the beneficiaries.

Multiplication of beneficiaries is not such a bad thing, provided it does not result in burdensome and costly trust administration. It tends to dilute the concentration of wealth — unless family wealth increases as fast as the family itself. . . .

IV.   THE FUTURE OF PERPETUAL TRUSTS

. . . The short of it is that Congress has come to be in charge of trust duration. The future of perpetual trusts is in its hands, to be dealt with through the tax system. The role of the states is to develop affordable means for modifying and terminating trusts when that is in the best interests of the beneficiaries. We have reached a great turning point in the law of trusts.

NOTES AND QUESTIONS

1. As of this writing, perpetual trusts appear to be authorized in Alaska, Arizona, Colorado, Delaware, Idaho, Illinois, Maine, Maryland, Missouri, Nebraska, New Hampshire, New Jersey, Ohio, Rhode Island, South Dakota, Virginia, and Wisconsin (we say appear because the language of several of the statutes is opaque). In addition, Florida, Utah, and Wyoming have established lengthy perpetuity periods (360 years for Florida and 1,000 years for Utah and Wyoming). As such, they are often included in counts of perpetual trust states.

In several of these states, the Rule against Perpetuities has experienced an odd transmogrification rather than outright repudiation: Colorado, Illinois, Maine, Maryland, Missouri, Nebraska, New Hampshire, Ohio, Virginia, and Wyoming have reduced the Rule to a default out of which the settlor may, if she wishes, opt out. Classically understood, however, the Rule was designed to curtail the dead hand by frustrating the settlor's intent. Gray expressed this view in stronger language:

> The Rule against Perpetuities is not a rule of construction, but a peremptory command of law. It is not, like a rule of construction, a test, more or less artificial, to determine intention. Its object is to defeat intention. Therefore every provision in a will or settlement is to be construed as if the Rule did not exist, and then to the provision so construed the Rule is to be remorselessly applied. [John C. Gray, The Rule Against Perpetuities §629 (4th ed. 1942).]

Reconfiguring the Rule as a default to be applied only if the settlor does not express a contrary intent strips it of its mandatory, intention-defeating character and hence its ability to curtail the reach of the dead hand. Of course, that is

Perpetual Trust States (2004)

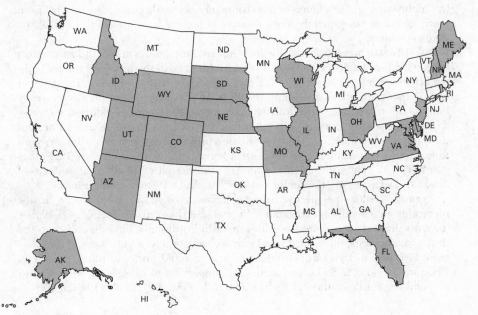

precisely the objective of the perpetual trust legislation. Still, in a jurisdiction in which the Rule is retained only as a default rule, interesting questions abound: Is it malpractice to use a standard saving clause instead of opt-out language? If a trust is drafted with opt-out language, should it contain a saving clause for the possibility that another state might assert jurisdiction and apply its Rule against Perpetuities? Should a generation-skipping transfer (GST) tax exempt perpetual trust contain language that permits its termination if the federal government were to reset the GST tax to a federal perpetuities period?

The race to validate perpetual trusts has brought into focus yet another interesting variant in the Rule from one state to another. The Rule is enshrined in the constitutions of Arkansas and Nevada. Hence, before those states can jump on the perpetual trust bandwagon, their constitutions will have to be amended. In Nevada such an amendment was rejected in the 2002 general election by a margin of 60 percent to 40 percent. Election 2002, Reno Gazette-Journal, Nov. 8, 2002, at 3C. Why would the Nevada population reject such an amendment? The amendment had the strong support of local lawyers, two of whom were so confident that before the vote they wrote of the amendment's "expected voter approval." Steven J. Oshins & Judith K. Ruud, Dynasty Trusts in Nevada: Countdown to 12/01/02, 9 Nev. Law. 18 (2001).

2. As we have seen with the self-settled spendthrift trust (see page 557), the statutory business trust (see page 497), and the Alaska Community Property Trust (see page 456), state lawmakers sometimes compete to attract business or people to their states by providing a regulatory environment that is favorable to the firms or people being wooed. This phenomenon is known as *regulatory competition* or *jurisdictional competition*. To the list of doctrines affected by jurisdictional competition in trust law we may now add the Rule against Perpetuities. Thus it is worth asking, what is the payoff to the state from abrogating the Rule as applied to interests in trust? Professor Sterk answers:

> Trust business is good for a state's economy. If banks and trust companies expand within the state, or if new banks or trust companies set up shop, the state benefits from more jobs, and consequently more disposable income to stimulate the rest of the state's economy.
>
> . . . [I]f a state were to abolish the Rule Against Perpetuities in order to attract trust business, out-of-staters could not easily take advantage of the new legal regime without actually using the facilities of the state's banks or trust companies. It is true, of course, that the statutes abolishing the Rule Against Perpetuities do not expressly limit abolition to trusts created with a local trustee. But if an out-of-state settlor creates a trust using a trust company in her home state as trustee, that state's courts are not likely to apply [another state's] law to validate a provision that violates the home state's Rule Against Perpetuities, even if the trust agreement expressly chooses [that other state's] law. . . . Thus, if the settlor wants to avail herself of all of the advantages of Alaska or Delaware law, the settlor must use Alaska or Delaware institutions.
>
> From the settlor's perspective, using a Delaware or Alaska institution as trustee represents an insignificant constraint. Capital is extraordinarily mobile, so whether the trust property constitutes securities or cash, it will make little difference to the settlor whether legal title is held by a Delaware bank or a New York bank. If the law is more favorable in Delaware, an informed settlor would prefer to transfer assets to Delaware. [Stewart E. Sterk, Jurisdictional Competition to Abolish the Rule Against Perpetuities: R.I.P. for the R.A.P., 24 Cardozo L. Rev. 2097, 2103-2104 (2003).]

Sterk's explanation is consistent with Dukeminier and Krier's concern that in the race to authorize perpetual trusts, there has been "little if any reflection upon the merits of the Rule *on its own*." Dukeminier and Krier, supra, at 1317. It appears that the stimulus for the race to abolish the Rule was the enactment of the GST tax.

3.   Based on reports to federal banking authorities, it has been estimated that, through 2003, a state's abolition of the Rule increased its trust assets held by institutional trustees by $6 billion (a 20% increase on average) and increased its average trust account size by $200,000. These estimates indicate that roughly $100 billion in trust funds have moved to take advantage of the abolition of the Rule. This amounts to perhaps as much as $1 billion in annual fees to local banks and trust companies. See Robert H. Sitkoff & Max Schanzenbach, Jurisdictional Competition for Trust Funds: An Empirical Analysis of Perpetuities and Taxes, 115 Yale L.J. (forthcoming 2005).

4.   Has the role of the Rule against Perpetuities in the course of history played out? The Rule has two main functions: (1) ensuring that property is freely alienable and (2) curtailing the dead hand, so that property is controlled by the living. As for the first function, property in trust is almost always alienable because the trustee typically has a power of sale. But what about curtailing the dead hand?

5.   What American state legislators giveth to the dead hand in the form of perpetual trusts, American state court judges can taketh away in the form of a liberalized law of trust modification and termination. (For current American law on trust modification and termination, which makes trust termination and modification difficult, see page 572.) It seems likely that, in the not-so-distant future, the courts will be confronted by clauses in perpetual trusts that no longer make sense in light of changed circumstances. The question thus arises, will abrogation of the Rule against Perpetuities boomerang into a more liberal law of modification and termination? "[S]ince no one can foresee the future, a rational donor knows that his intentions might eventually be thwarted by unpredictable circumstances and may therefore be presumed to accept implicitly a rule permitting modification of the terms of the bequest in the event that an unforeseen change frustrates his original intention." Richard A. Posner, Economic Analysis of Law §18.4, at 520 (6th ed. 2003).

The Uniform Trust Code (and its parallel provisions in the Restatement (Third) of Trusts) states a somewhat more liberal standard for trust modification and termination than was traditionally recognized by the common law. Ironically, however, its enactment could stymie the further judicial evolution of modification and termination law by freezing into place the standard stated in the code. In a similar vein, it is worth pondering whether perpetual trusts might also stimulate new developments in the law of trustee removal (see page 585).

If you were asked to draft a statute on trust modification or termination for a state in which perpetual trusts were authorized, how would you proceed? In 1983, the Canadian province of Manitoba abolished the Rule against Perpetuities, and at the same time transformed legal future interests into trust interests and gave courts broad power to alter or terminate any trust if this will benefit the beneficiaries. 1982-1983 Man. Rev. Stat. chs. 38, 43. Termination of a trust with court approval requires a lawsuit, however, perhaps a costly one, whereas the Rule against Perpetuities brings about the termination of a trust by force of law, without a lawsuit.

For further discussion, see Dukeminier & Krier, supra, at 1327-1342 (exploring the problem of, and palliatives for, the problem of changed circumstances in perpetual trusts); Joshua C. Tate, Perpetual Trusts and the Settlor's Intent, 53 U. Kan. L. Rev. (forthcoming 2005) (criticizing Dukeminier & Krier's proposals). On trust modification, termination, trustee removal, and the tension between the preferences of the settlor and the beneficiaries, see Robert H. Sitkoff, An Agency Costs Theory of Trust Law, 89 Cornell L. Rev. 621, 658-666 (2004).

6. The erosion of the Rule against Perpetuities, and the drive toward perpetual trusts that are exempt from the GST tax, has been the subject of a burgeoning literature. In addition to Dukeminier & Krier, supra; Sitkoff & Schanzenbach, supra; Sterk, supra; and Tate, supra, see Ira Mark Bloom, The GST Tax Tail Is Killing The Rule Against Perpetuities, 87 Tax Notes 569 (2000); Verner F. Chaffin, Georgia's Proposed Dynasty Trust: Giving the Dead Too Much Control, 35 G.L. Rev. 1 (2000); Joel C. Dobris, The Death of the Rule Against Perpetuities, or the RAP Has No Friends—An Essay, 35 Real Prop., Prob. & Tr. J. 601 (2000); Stephen E. Greer, The Alaska Dynasty Trust, 18 Alaska L. Rev. 253 (2001); Garrett Moritz, Note, Dynasty Trusts and the Rule Against Perpetuities, 116 Harv. L. Rev. 2588 (2003); Angela M. Vallario, Death by a Thousand Cuts: The Rule Against Perpetuities, 25 J. Legis. 141 (1999). See also Eric Rakowski, The Future Reach of the Disembodied Will, 4 Pol., Phil. & Econ. 91 (2005).

On the intersection of federal transfer tax policy and state perpetuities policy more generally, see Bloom, supra; John G. Shively, Note, The Death of the Life in Being—The Required Federal Response to State Abolition of the Rule Against Perpetuities, 78 Wash. U.L.Q. 371 (2000). See also Ira Mark Bloom, How Federal Transfer Taxes Affect the Development of Property Law, 48 Clev. St. L. Rev. 661 (2000); Robert T. Danforth, The Role of Federalism in Administering a National System of Taxation, 57 Tax Law. 625 (2004).

7. In January 2000, the National Conference of Commissioners on Uniform State Laws issued a press release regarding perpetual, GST tax-exempt trusts:

> This movement is ill-advised, says Lawrence W. Waggoner, Director of Research of the Joint Editorial Board for the Uniform Probate Code, because Congress is not likely to allow this loophole to continue indefinitely. In addition, he says, the creation of such trusts is problematic. Over time, the administration of such trusts is likely to become unwieldy and very costly.
>
> Government statistics indicate that the average married couple has 2.1 children. Under this assumption, the average settlor will have more than 100 descendants (who are beneficiaries of the trust) 150 years after the trust is created, around 2,500 beneficiaries 250 years after the trust is created, and 45,000 beneficiaries 350 years after the trust is created. Five hundred years after the trust is created, the number of living beneficiaries could rise to an astounding 3.4 million. [NCCUSL, Uniform Statutory Rule Against Perpetuities Is Law in 26 States: Move of a Few States to Abolish the Rule in Order to Facilitate Perpetual (Dynasty) Trusts Is Ill-Advised.]

Dukeminier and Krier suggest that the problem of multiplying beneficiaries can be avoided with a clause in the trust instrument or a statute that authorizes the trustee to divide the trust into two or more separate trusts. See Dukeminier & Krier, supra, at 1339. According to the reporter's notes to Restatement (Third) of Property: Wills and Other Donative Transfers §12.2 (2003), 17 states have legislation to this effect. See also UTC §417 (2000); Restatement (Third) of Trusts

§68 (2003). On the other hand, if the theoretical possibility of exponential growth in the number of beneficiaries were actually to occur with any frequency, then the power to *terminate* small trusts might prove more important than the power to *divide* the trust into two or more separate trusts. It seems unlikely that the growth in the trust corpus could match an exponential growth in the number of beneficiaries, especially if the current beneficiaries are entitled to the trust income.

8.   *England.* In 1964 England adopted a variant on wait-and-see whereby an interest is good until "it becomes absolutely certain that it must vest in interest, if at all, outside the perpetuity period of 21 years from the death of statutory lives in being or of a period not exceeding 80 years." D.J. Hayton, The Law of Trusts 106 (4th ed. 2003).

In the 1990s, England revisited the perpetuities question, and in 1998 the English Law Commission released its report on whether the Rule should be reformed further or abolished. See English Law Commission, The Rules against Perpetuities and Excessive Accumulations, Report No. 251 (1998). Although a "distinguished minority" of experts consulted urged abolition, the Law Commission concluded that some rule was needed to "plac[e] some restrictions on how far settlors could tie up property for the future." Hence, it recommended abolishing the common law Rule against Perpetuities and replacing it with a rule that any contingent interest that did not actually vest within 125 years would be void. It fixed on 125 years because this is probably the longest period that can be obtained under present law by using a royal lives clause (comparable in this country to a dozen-healthy-babies clause). Thus far, Parliament has not acted on the Law Commission's report.

For a somewhat similar proposal in this country to abolish the application of the Rule against Perpetuities to trusts and to terminate trusts after 120 years, see Paul G. Haskell, A Proposal for a Simple and Socially Effective Rule Against Perpetuities, 66 N.C.L. Rev. 545 (1988). For a critique of the Law Commission's focus on intergenerational fairness instead of the Rule's economic consequences, see T.P. Gallanis, The Rule Against Perpetuities and the Law Commission's Flawed Philosophy, 59 Cambridge L.J. 284 (2000).

SECTION G.   OTHER DURATIONAL LIMITS

1.   *The Rule Against Suspension of the Power of Alienation*

Although since the time of Gray it has been settled that the rule against remote vesting is *the* common law Rule against Perpetuities, it was not clear before Gray whether there was also a common law *rule against suspension of the power of alienation*. The power of alienation is the power to convey title. A suspension of the power of alienation over specified property occurs when no living person, or living persons joined together, can convey an absolute fee. The rule prohibiting suspension of the power of alienation is easily distinguished from the rule against remote vesting. The rule against remote vesting (the common law Rule against Perpetuities) is directed against contingent interests that may remain contingent beyond lives in being plus 21 years. The policy underlying it is that all contingent interests, assignable and nonassignable, impair marketability. The rule against suspension of the power of alienation is directed against interests that make the property inalienable. If there is any possibility that the power of alienation will be suspended longer than lives in being plus 21 years, the interests causing such invalid suspension are void ab initio.

Gray insisted that there was no common law rule against suspension of the power of alienation apart from the rule against remote vesting (that is, the Rule against Perpetuities), and his view ultimately prevailed in the cases. However, in 1830, before the question was settled in the cases, New York enacted legislation forbidding suspension of the power of alienation for more than a specified period. Several other states copied or were influenced by New York's position.

Today there are two views of when the power of alienation is suspended by the creation of a trust. Under one view, the Wisconsin view, the power of alienation is not suspended if the trustee has the power to sell the trust assets, making them alienable, or if a living person has an unlimited power to terminate the trust. Wis. Stat. §700.16 (2004). This view is taken in many of the states that have authorized perpetual trusts — the *quid pro quo* for the trust's exemption from the Rule against Perpetuities.

The other view, held in New York, is different. In New York, if a transfer is made in trust, the power of alienation is suspended if *either* the legal fee simple to the specific property held in trust cannot be transferred *or* the owners of all the equitable interests cannot convey an equitable fee simple. In other words, under the New York view the creation of a trust suspends the power of alienation *unless* the trustee is given the power to sell the specific assets *and* the beneficiaries of the trust can convey their interests.[21] However, since all vested and contingent future interests are assignable or releasable if (1) the holders thereof are ascertainable and (2) there is no express restraint upon alienation, the only interests that suspend the power of alienation in a New York trust in which the trustee has the power to sell the trust property are (a) those subject to an express restraint upon alienation such as a spendthrift clause or (b) those given to unborn or unascertained persons.

The impact of category (a), interests subject to an express restraint upon alienation such as a spendthrift clause, is magnified by New York's statutory presumption that an income beneficiary's interest in trust is inalienable (that is, subject to a spendthrift constraint) unless the settlor expressly provides otherwise. N.Y. Est., Powers & Trusts Law §7-1.5 (2004). If the income beneficiaries' interests are inalienable, the trust suspends the power of alienation during the income beneficiaries' lives. *Hence, the duration of a spendthrift trust in New York is limited to the perpetuities period.* Such a trust is partially or wholly invalid if it can exceed the perpetuities period in duration. Therein lies the most important difference today between the common law Rule against Perpetuities (which does not directly restrict

---

21. Hence, the New York policy in favor of alienability is directed *both* at the specific assets in the trust *and* at the beneficial interests in the trust. N.Y. Est., Powers & Trusts Law §9-1.1(a) (2004) provides:

(1) The absolute power of alienation is suspended when there are no persons in being by whom an absolute fee or estate in possession can be conveyed or transferred.
(2) Every present or future estate shall be void in its creation which shall suspend the absolute power of alienation by any limitation or condition for a longer period than lives in being at the creation of the estate and a term of not more than twenty-one years. . . .

The rule against remoteness of vesting is also part of New York law. N.Y. Est., Powers & Trusts Law §9-1.1(b) (2004). New York thus has *both* the common law Rule against Perpetuities *and* the rule against suspension of the power of alienation.

the duration of trusts) and the New York rule against suspension of the power of alienation. Thus:

> *Case 22. T*, domiciled in New York, dies in 2005. She bequeaths a fund in a spend-thrift trust "to pay the income to *A* for life, then to pay the income to *A*'s children for their lives, and then to pay the principal to New York University." The gift does not violate the Rule against Perpetuities. However, the income interests in *A* and *A*'s children are inalienable. Since the power of alienation might be suspended during the lifetime of afterborn persons (*A*'s children born after *T*'s death), the life income interests in *A*'s children are void. The remainder in New York University will be accelerated (unless the court determines that the stricken interests are so crucial to *T*'s dispositive scheme that invalidating the entire bequest would better approximate *T*'s intent[22]).

If, in Case 22, *T* had by her will expressly provided that *A*'s children could alienate their interests, the trust would be wholly valid. The power of alienation would be suspended only during *A*'s lifetime, a life in being. At *A*'s death, all of *A*'s children are in being, and, together with New York University, they can convey a fee simple absolute.

On the suspension rule in New York, and other aspects of New York perpetuities law, see 10 Powell on Real Property ch. 74 (Michael Allan Wolf ed., 2000).

2.   *The Rule Against Accumulations of Income*

Originating in the decision of the House of Lords in Thellusson v. Woodford, 32 Eng. Rep. 1030 (Ch. 1805), there appears to exist a common law doctrine — *the rule against accumulations of income* — that limits the period during which the settlor may direct the trustee to accumulate and retain income in trust.

At issue in the *Thellusson* case was the will of Peter Thellusson, which provided that his considerable estate, plus all of the accrued income thereon during the lives of nine named people then in being, should be accumulated for the ultimate benefit of his eldest male descendant at the end of that period. The House of Lords, speaking through Lord Eldon, concluded that there was no violation of the Rule against Perpetuities. The interest in Thellusson's eldest male descendant would vest at the end of the nine measuring lives. Lord Eldon then turned to the question of whether the bequest violated a separate rule against accumulations of income:

> [A]nother question arises out of this Will; which is a pure question of equity: whether a testator can direct the rents and profits to be accumulated for that period, during which he may direct, that the title shall not vest, and the property shall remain unalienable; and, that he can do so, is most clear law. [Id. at 1043.]

Thus the House of Lords held that, under the common law, a direction to accumulate income during the period of the Rule against Perpetuities is good.

---

22. This would be an application of the doctrine of *infectious invalidity*, described in footnote 4 at page 677.

Although sanctioned by the House of Lords in 1805, Thellusson's accumulation plan was so unpopular — with fantastic scenarios of the compounding of interest in mind, Lord Loughborough called it "unkind and illiberal" — that even before the House of Lords issued its ruling Parliament enacted the Thellusson Act, 39 & 40 Geo. III c. 98 (1800). The Act required that accumulations of income must be limited to (1) the life the settlor, (2) twenty-one years from the death of the settlor, (3) the minority of any person living (or in gestation) at the time of the settlor's death, or (4) the minority of any person who, upon majority, would be entitled to the income being accumulated. With only minor modifications, this statutory rule against accumulations remains good law in England. See D.J. Hayton, The Law of Trusts 107-108 (4th ed. 2003).

Just as the fear of compounding interest and geometrically growing fortunes tied up in trust inflamed passions about the dead hand in England, Thellusson's plan likewise met with hostility in several American states. One judge worried that such a trust might "draw into its vortex all the property in the state." Hillyard v. Miller, 10 Pa. 326, 336 (1849). Hence several states adopted statutes similar to the Thellusson Act or, in the case of New York, an even more restrictive one. See Restatement (Second) of Property: Donative Transfers §2.2, statutory note (1983); Lewis M. Simes, Public Policy and the Dead Hand 86-88 (1955); 5 William J. Bowe & Douglas H. Parker, Page on the Law of Wills §42.14 (rev. ed. 1962).

This fear was unfounded. When Benjamin Franklin died in 1790, he left two charitable trusts of £1,000 each that were directed to accumulate income with no payouts for 100 years, then to spend most of the principal for the benefit of public purposes in Boston and Philadelphia, and then to accumulate again for another 100 years. Both trusts performed relatively poorly, with the Boston trust drawing less than $5 million into its vortex by 1990 and the Philadelphia trust sucking in less than half that amount. See Clark DeLeon, Divvying up Ben: Let's Try for 200 More, Phila. Inq., Feb. 7, 1993, at B3. As Professor Hayton put it: "The economic and social fears of accumulation have proved groundless." Hayton, supra, at 108.

In the twentieth century, "the tide turned in this country against the strict type of legislation for which the Thellusson Act was a model." Simes, supra, at 88. In states with a statutory rule against the accumulation of income in private trusts today, the accumulation period is typically the same as the period for the rule against the suspension of the power of alienation or the Rule against Perpetuities. See, e.g., Cal. Civ. Code Ann. §724 (2004) (keyed to the "time permitted for the vesting of future interests"); Minn. Stat. Ann. §500.17(2) (2004) (keyed to suspension of the power of alienation); N.Y. Est., Powers & Trusts Law §9-2.1(b) (2004) (keyed to Rule against Perpetuities); Pa. Cons. Stat. Ann. §6106(b) (2004) (keyed to Rule against Perpetuities). Under these statutes Thellusson's will would be upheld.

In part because the English courts never had occasion to develop their common law rule against accumulations of income, until the mid-twentieth century there remained ambiguity as to whether the American states that had not enacted a statutory rule against accumulations would recognize a common law version, and if so, for what duration accumulations would be permitted. This ambiguity was resolved by Gertman v. Burdick, 123 F.2d 924 (D.C. Cir. 1941). At issue in *Gertman* was a bequest in trust to accumulate income during the lives of two named people and then for 21 years after the death of the survivor of them. In a learned opinion by Judge Fred Vinson, who would later become Chief Justice of the United States, the court upheld the bequest, and in so doing stated that "a rule permitting accumulations for as long as the period of the rule against perpetuities . . . has been the common law of this country and of this jurisdiction." Id. at 930-931. The rule against accumulations was therefore recognized as an independent doctrine from the Rule against Perpetuities, though its durational limit was that of the permissible perpetuities period. Thus:

> *Case 23. O* bequeaths a fund in trust to *T* "to pay so much of the income to *A* during *A*'s life as *T* may determine, then to pay so much of the income to *A*'s children for their lives as *T* may determine, then to pay the remainder to *B.*" At *O*'s death, *A* has no children. *A*'s life estate is vested in possession upon *O*'s death. The life estate in *A*'s children will vest in possession or, if there are no children, fail, upon *A*'s death. *B*'s remainder is vested in interest upon *O*'s death. Thus, all interests created by the transfer are valid under the Rule against Perpetuities. However, *T* has the discretion to accumulate income in the trust after the perpetuities period for this trust, which is 21 years after the death of the survivor of *A* and *B*. This could happen, for example, if *A* has a child *C* who survives *A* and *B* by more than 21 years. In some states, the accumulation is void as to the excess; in others, the direction to accumulate is void in its entirety. See Restatement (Second) of Property: Donative Transfers §2.2, reporter's note (1983).

With the recent proliferation of legislation that abrogates or alters the common law Rule against Perpetuities, a new question now arises: How does perpetuities reform relate to the rule against accumulations? Delaware, Illinois, and South Dakota, which are among the most aggressive of the perpetual trust states, have dealt with this question with an explicit abrogation of the rule against accumulations (Delaware), by providing that the accumulations rule does not apply to trusts when the settlor opts out of the rule against perpetuities (Illinois), or by repealing its statutory rule against accumulations (South Dakota). See Del. Code Ann. tit. 25, §506 (2004); 765 Ill. Comp. Stat. §315/1 (2004); 1998 S.D. Laws ch. 282, §27. In states without legislative action, the law is less clear. Since the rule against accumulations is measured by the period of the Rule against Perpetuities, it follows that if the applicable perpetuities period is modified by legislation, then the accumulations rule would likewise be modified. In 10 Powell on Real Property 76-22 (Michael Allan Wolf ed., 2000), it is predicted that the cases will so hold.

In White v. Fleet Bank of Me., 739 A.2d 373 (Me. 1999), however, the Supreme Court of Maine came out the other way. At issue in *White* was a holographic will that contained a bequest in trust from which three-fourths of the income would be paid to the testator's lineal descendants and the other one-fourth would be "reinvested annually for the increase of funds in the Trust." The trust was to continue, "following the lines of direct descent, as long as the Trust may be made to endure." As to the Rule against Perpetuities, the court held that the quoted language was a saving clause such that, under applicable wait-and-see legislation, the bequest was valid. It was possible that all future income interests would vest within 21 years of the death of the last life in being.

As to the rule against the accumulation of income, the court held that, because the reinvestment of income clause did not reference any life in being, its permissible duration was limited to the traditional common law perpetuities period of 21 years in gross. The court specifically rejected the argument that, by modifying the common law Rule against Perpetuities, Maine's wait-and-see statute likewise modified the rule against accumulations. Accordingly, because the reinvestment clause was not limited to 21 years, the court held that it violated the rule against accumulations and, there being no provision for distribution of the trust corpus or accumulated income, the court ordered the property subject to the reinvestment clause be disbursed to the testator's intestate heirs on resulting trust.

It remains to be seen whether the *White* decision will be followed in a state that has abolished the Rule against Perpetuities in order to permit perpetual trusts. For further discussion of the rule against accumulations, *White*, and the rise of the perpetual trust, see Robert H. Sitkoff, The Lurking Rule Against Accumulations of Income, 100 Nw. U.L. Rev. (forthcoming 2006); Karen J. Sneddon, Comment, The Sleeper Has Awakened: The Rule Against Accumulations and Perpetual Trusts, 76 Tulane L. Rev. 189 (2001).

CHARITABLE TRUSTS

SECTION A.   NATURE OF CHARITABLE PURPOSES

Unlike a private trust, a charitable trust need not have an ascertainable beneficiary
to be valid. However, to qualify as a charitable trust, the trust must have a valid
charitable purpose.

Shenandoah Valley National Bank v. Taylor

Supreme Court of Appeals of Virginia, 1951
192 Va. 135, 63 S.E.2d 786

MILLER, J.   Charles B. Henry,[1] a resident of Winchester, Virginia, died testate
on the 23rd day of April, 1949. His will dated April 21, 1949, was duly admitted to
probate and the Shenandoah Valley National Bank of Winchester, the designated
executor and trustee, qualified thereunder.

1. The testator, Charles B. Henry, operated a fruit and vegetable stand until shortly before his death.
In earlier years, in addition to the stand, he hawked fruits and vegetables through the town from a
horse-drawn wagon.

> A number of years before his death he lost his only child, a very pretty little daughter. This, so
> I am told, profoundly affected him, causing him to become more and more a recluse and this
> became even more pronounced after the death of his wife, who predeceased him by some years.
> Along with this increasing withdrawal from general social intercourse, there seems to have de-
> veloped an increasing tendency to become miserly. This was indicated by such things as
> avoidance of use of electric lights except when absolutely necessary and making the produce
> which was no longer salable a substantial part of his diet.
> Nonetheless, perhaps because of memory of his own deceased child, he seems to have main-
> tained a strong affection for children generally. As a fruit vendor, he was widely known among
> the older generation of local citizens.
> He saved and hoarded his money and made some investments, and I recollected being told by
> someone, possibly an official of the Shenandoah Valley Bank that when the Great Depression
> struck, he was frantic to the point of unnatural frenzy at the depreciation of his investments.
> My firm received the case as a result of the complainant being the babysitter for my partner's
> sister and brother-in-law and was the second or third cousin to Charlie Henry. For some time she
> had been helping to look after him and bringing him food, undoubtedly with that expectation so
> often disappointed that he would remember her in his will; in fact, I recollect that she claimed
> that he had flatly promised to do so or by artful insinuation had convinced her that he would. Her

729

Subject to two inconsequential provisions not material to this litigation, the testator's entire estate valued at $86,000, was left as follows:

> Second: All the rest, residue and remainder of my estate, real, personal, intangible and mixed, of whatsoever kind and wherever situate, . . . I give, bequeath and devise to the Shenandoah Valley National Bank of Winchester, Virginia, in trust, to be known as the "Charles B. Henry and Fannie Belle Henry Fund," for the following uses and purposes:
>
> (a) My Trustee shall invest and reinvest my trust estate, shall collect the income therefrom and shall pay the net income as follows:
>
> (1) On the last school day of each calendar year before Easter my Trustee shall divide the net income into as many equal parts as there are children in the first, second and third grades of the John Kerr School of the City of Winchester, and shall pay one of such equal parts to each child in such grades, to be used by such child in the furtherance of his or her obtainment of an education.
>
> (2) On the last school day of each calendar year before Christmas my trustee shall divide the net income into as many equal parts as there are children in the first, second and third grades of the John Kerr School of the City of Winchester, and shall pay one of such equal parts to each child in such grades, to be used by such child in the furtherance of his or her obtainment of an education.

By paragraphs (3) and (4) it is provided that the names of the children in the three grades shall be determined each year from the school records, and payment of the income to them "shall be as nearly equal in amounts as it is practicable" to arrange.

Paragraph (5) provides that if the John Kerr School is ever discontinued for any reason the payments shall be made to the children of the same grades of the school or schools that take its place, and the School Board of Winchester is to determine what school or schools are substituted for it.

Under clause "Third" the trustee is given authority, power, and discretion to retain or from time to time sell and invest and reinvest the estate, or any part thereof, as it shall deem to be the best interest of the trust.

The John Kerr School is a public school used by the local school board for primary grades and had an enrollment of 458 boys and girls so there will be that number of pupils or thereabouts who would share in the distribution of the income.

The testator left no children or near relatives. Those who would be his heirs and distributees in case of intestacy were first cousins and others more remotely related. One of these next of kin filed a suit against the executor and trustee, and others challenging the validity of the provisions of the will which undertook to create a charitable trust. . . .

The sole question presented is: does the will create a valid charitable trust?

Construction of the challenged provisions is required and in this undertaking the testator's intent as disclosed by the words used in the will must be ascertained. If his dominant intent as expressed was charitable, the trust should be accorded efficacy and sustained.

---

disappointment and resulting ire prompted her to seek counsel. [Letter to the editors, dated July 7, 1975, from the Hon. Robert K. Waltz, winning counsel in the *Taylor* case and later circuit court judge in Virginia.]

— Eds.

But on the other hand, if the testator's intent as expressed is merely benevolent, though the disposition of his property be meritorious and evince traits of generosity, the trust must nevertheless be declared invalid because it violates the rule against perpetuities. . . .

Authoritative definitions of charitable trusts may be found in 4 Pomeroy's Equity Jurisprudence, 5th Ed., sec. 1020, and Restatement of the Law of Trusts, sec. 368, p.1140. The latter gives a comprehensive classification definition. It is:

> Charitable purposes include:
>
> (a)   the relief of poverty;
> (b)   the advancement of education;
> (c)   the advancement of religion;
> (d)   the promotion of health;
> (e)   governmental or municipal purposes; and
> (f)   other purposes the accomplishment of which is beneficial to the community.[2]

In the recent decision of Allaun v. First National Bank, 56 S.E.2d 83 (Va. 1949), the definition that appears in 3 M.J., Charitable Trust, sec. 2, p.872, was approved and adopted. It reads:

> "A charity," in a legal sense, may be described as a gift to be applied, consistently with existing laws, for the benefit of an indefinite number of persons, either by bringing their hearts under the influence of education or religion, by relieving their bodies from disease, suffering or constraint, by assisting them to establish themselves for life, or by erecting or maintaining public building or works, or otherwise lessening the burdens of government. It is immaterial whether the purpose is called charitable in the gift itself, if it is so described as to show that it is charitable. Generally speaking, any gift not inconsistent with existing laws which is promotive of science or tends to the education, enlightening, benefit or amelioration of the condition of mankind or the diffusion of useful knowledge, or is for the public convenience is a charity. It is essential that a charity be for the benefit of an indefinite number of persons; for if all the beneficiaries are personally designated, the trust lacks the essential element of indefiniteness, which is one characteristic of a legal charity. (190 Va. p.108.) . . .

In the law of trusts there is a real and fundamental distinction between a charitable trust and one that is devoted to mere benevolence. The former is public in nature and valid; the latter is private and if it offends the rule against perpetuities, it is void. "It is quite clear that trusts which are devoted to mere benevolence or liberality, or generosity, cannot be upheld as charities. Benevolent objects include acts dictated by mere kindness, good will, or a disposition to do good. . . . Charity in a legal sense must be distinguished from acts of liberality or benevolence. To

---

2. Taken literally, "other purposes" that are "beneficial to the community" is an open-ended category. But the courts have glossed this language to require a purpose "of a character sufficiently beneficial to the community to justify permitting property to be devoted for an indefinite time to their accomplishment." 4A Austin W. Scott, Trusts §374 (William F. Fratcher 4th ed. 1989). Thus only a limited set of purposes has been found to fall within this heading. For examples, see id. at §§374.1-374.12.

With only cosmetic changes, the First Restatement's list of charitable purposes, which derives from the Statute of Charitable Uses, 43 Eliz. I, c. 4 (1601), is carried forward in Restatement (Third) of Trusts §28 (2003) and Uniform Trust Code §405(a) (2000). — Eds.

constitute a charity the use must be public in its nature." Zollman on Charities, sec. 398, p.268.

We are, however, reminded that charitable trusts are favored creatures of the law enjoying the especial solicitude of courts of equity and a liberal interpretation is employed to uphold them. Zollman on Charities, sec. 570, p.391; 2 Bogert on Trusts, sec. 369, p.1129. . . .

Appellant contends that the gift . . . not only meets the requirements of a charitable trust as defined in Restatement of the Law of Trusts, supra, but specifically fits two of those classifications, viz.:

> (b) trusts for the advancement of education;
> (f) other purposes the accomplishment of which is beneficial to the community.

We now turn to the language of the will for from its context the testator's intent is to be derived. Sheridan v. Krause, 172 S.E. 508 (Va. 1934). Its interpretation must be free from and uninfluenced by the unyielding rule against perpetuities. Yet, when the testator's intent is ascertained, if it is found to be in contravention of the rule, the will, in that particular, must be declared invalid. . . .

In paragraphs (1) and (2), respectively, of clause "Second" in clear and definite language the discretion, power and authority of the trustee in its disposition and application of the income are specified and limited. Yearly on the last school day before Easter and Christmas each youthful beneficiary of the testator's generosity is to be paid an equal share of the income. In mandatory language the duty and the duty alone to make cash payments to each individual child just before Easter and Christmas is enjoined upon the trustee by the certain and explicit words that it "shall divide the net income . . . and shall pay one of such equal shares to each child in such grades."

Without more, that language, and the occasions specified for payment of the funds to the children being when their minds and interests would be far removed from studies or other school activities definitely indicate that no educational purpose was in the testator's mind. It is manifest that there was no intent or belief that the funds would be put to any use other than such as youthful impulse and desire might dictate. But in each instance immediately following the above-quoted language the sentence concludes with the words or phrase "to be used by such child in the furtherance of his or her obtainment of an education." It is significant that by this latter phrase the trustee is given no power, control or discretion over the funds so received by the child. Full and complete execution of the mandate and trust imposed upon the trustee accomplishes no educational purpose. Nothing toward the advancement of education is attained by the ultimate performance by the trustee of its full duty. It merely places the income irretrievably and forever beyond the range of the trust.

Appellant says that the latter phrase, "to be used by such child in furtherance of his or her obtainment of an education," evinces the testator's dominant purpose and intent. Yet it is not denied that the preceding provision "shall divide the net income into as many equal parts . . . and shall pay one of each equal parts to such child" is at odds with the phrase it relies upon. The appended qualification, it says, however, discloses a controlling intent that the 450 or more shares are to be used in the furtherance of education, and it was not really intended that a share be paid to each child so that he or she could during the Christmas and Easter holidays, or at any other time, use it "without let or hindrance, encumbrance or care." With that construction we cannot agree. In our opinion, the words of the will import an intent to have the trustee pay to each child his allotted share. If that be true, — and it is directed to be done in no uncertain language — we know that the admonition to the children would be wholly impotent and of no avail.

In construing wills, we may not forget or disregard the experiences of life and the realities of the occasion. Nor may we assume or indulge in the belief that the testator by his injunction to the donees intended or thought that he could change childhood nature and set at naught childhood impulses and desires.

Appellant asserts that literal performance of the duty imposed upon it — pay to each child his share — would be impracticable and should not be done. Its position in that respect is stated thus: "We do not understand that under the law of Virginia a court would pay money for education into the hands of children who are incapable of handling it." It then says that the funds could be administered by a guardian or under sec. 8-751, Code, 1950 (where the amounts are under $500), a court could direct payment to be made to the recipient's parents.

With these statements, we agree. But because the funds could be administered under applicable statutes has no bearing upon nor may that device be resorted to as an aid to prove or establish the testator's intent. We are of opinion that the testator's dominant intent appears from and is expressed in his unequivocal direction to the trustee to divide the income into as many equal parts as there are children beneficiaries and pay one share to each. This expressed purpose and intent is inconsistent with the appended direction to each child as to the use of his respective share and the latter phrase is thus ineffectual to create an educational trust. The testator's purpose and intent were, we think, to bestow upon the children gifts that would bring to them happiness on the two holidays, but that falls short of an educational trust.

If it be determined that the will fails to create a charitable trust for *educational purposes* (and our conclusion is that it is inoperative to create such a trust), it is earnestly insisted that the trust provided for is nevertheless charitable and valid. In this respect it is claimed that the two yearly payments to be made to the children just before Christmas and Easter produce "a desirable social effect" and are "promotive of public convenience and needs, and happiness and contentment" and thus the fund set up in the will constitutes a charitable trust. 2 Bogert on Trusts, sec. 361, p.1090, and 3 Scott on Trusts, sec. 368, p.1972. . . .

Numerous cases that deal with and construe specific provisions of wills or other instruments are cited by appellant to uphold the contention that the provisions of this will, without reference to and deleting the phrase "to be used by such child in the furtherance of his or her obtainment of an education" meet the requirements of a charitable trust.

Upon examination of these decisions, it will be found that where a gift results in mere financial enrichment, a trust was sustained only when the court found and concluded from the entire context of the will that the ultimate intended recipients were poor or in necessitous circumstances.

A trust from which the income is to be paid at stated intervals to each member of a designated segment of the public, without regard to whether or not the recipients are poor or in need, is not for the relief of poverty, nor is it a social benefit to the community. It is a mere benevolence — a private trust — and may not be upheld as a charitable trust. Restatement of the Law of Trusts, sec. 374, p.1156: ". . . if a large sum of money is given in trust to apply the income each year in paying a certain sum to every inhabitant of a city, whether rich or poor, the trust is not charitable, since although each inhabitant may receive a benefit, the social interest of the community as such is not thereby promoted."

In 2 Bogert on Trusts, sec. 380, we find:

> As previously stated, gifts which are mere exhibitions of liberality and generosity, without regard to their effect upon the donees, are not charitable. There must be an amelioration of the condition of the donees as a result of the gift, and this improvement must be of a mental, physical, or spiritual nature and not merely financial. Thus, trusts to provide gifts to children, regardless of their need, or to make Christmas gifts to members of a certain class, without consideration of need or effect, are not charitable. . . . (p. 1218.)
>
> Gifts which are made out of mere sentiment, and will have no practical result except the satisfying of a whim of the donor, are obviously lacking in the widespread social effect necessary to a charity. (p. 1219.)

Nor do we find any language in this will that permits the trustee to limit the recipients of the donations to the school children in the designated grades who are in necessitous circumstances, and thus bring the trust under the influence of the case styled Appeal of Eliot, 51 A. 558 (Conn. 1902).

The conclusion there reached was that where a trust is set up and a class is designated as beneficiary which generally contains needy persons, the testator will be presumed to have intended as recipients those members of the class who are in necessitous circumstances.

Payment to the children of their cash bequests on the two occasions specified would bring to them pleasure and happiness and no doubt cause them to remember or think of their benefactor with gratitude and thanksgiving. That was, we think, Charles B. Henry's intent. Laudable, generous and praiseworthy though it may be, it is not for the relief of the poor or needy, nor does it otherwise so benefit or advance the social interest of the community as to justify its continuance in perpetuity as a charitable trust. . . .

No error is found in the decrees appealed from and they are affirmed.

NOTES AND QUESTIONS

1. Charitable trusts may endure forever; they are privileged with an exemption from the Rule against Perpetuities. This exemption is not given to a trust for a noncharitable purpose. At common law, such a trust is void ab initio if it can last longer than the perpetuities period. This is the rule that the Henry Trust, called the "candy trust" in the newspapers of the day, ran afoul of.

In Marsh v. The Frost Natl. Bank, 129 S.W.3d 174 (Tex. App. 2004), the court held that a bequest "to provide a million dollar trust fund for every American 18 years or older" by accumulating income for 346 years on the proceeds from the sale of certain property was not charitable and hence violated the Rule against Perpetuities. The testator had wanted the trust "to be called the James Madison Fund to honor our fourth president, James Madison, the Father of the Constitution" and for the president, vice president, and the speaker of the House of Representatives to be the "permanent Trustees of the Fund."

During the latter part of the twentieth century, and continuing into the present, a majority of states modified the common law Rule against Perpetuities by adopting a form of wait-and-see such as that provided by the Uniform Statutory Rule Against Perpetuities, or have abrogated the rule altogether with respect to trusts for which the trustee has the power of alienation (see Chapter 11). How would these reforms alter the result, if at all, in *Taylor?* For careful, indeed fastidious, analysis, see Adam J. Hirsch, Trusts for Purposes: Policy, Ambiguity, and Anomaly in the Uniform Laws, 26 Fla. St. U.L. Rev. 913, 930-950 (1999).

2. In the heyday of the Rule against Perpetuities, there was considerable pressure on the *charitable purpose* trigger, as the consequence of finding a charitable purpose was that the trust could continue indefinitely. To be classified as charitable, a trust must be for the relief of poverty or for the advancement of education, religion, health, or other charitable purpose. A trust is not charitable merely because it is for the benefit of a class of persons. Thus, a trust for the benefit of sick or needy employees is charitable, but a trust for the general benefit of employees is not. Likewise, a trust to pay the salary of a law professor is charitable because it promotes education, but a trust for the general benefit of lawyers is not. See 4A Austin W. Scott, Trusts §375 (William F. Fratcher 4th ed. 1989). There is authority in the cases for liberal constructions that favor charitable bequests. See McDonald & Co. Secs. v. Alzheimer's Assn., 747 N.E.2d 843, 849 (Ohio App. 2000).

A trust may be a valid charitable trust although the persons who directly benefit are limited in number. For example, a trust awarding scholarships or prizes for educational achievement is charitable, even if only one or two students will receive the scholarships or prizes, provided that the class of eligible recipients is broad. Thus, a trust to educate a particular person or named persons is not charitable. So also a trust to educate the descendants of the settlor is not charitable. Restatement (Third) of Trusts §28, cmt. a(1) (2003); In re Estate of Keenan, 519 N.W.2d 373 (Iowa 1994). On the other hand, a trust for education of young people has been held charitable even if in selecting beneficiaries the trustee must give preference to the descendants of the settlor's grandparents. 4A Scott, supra, §375.3. And a trust to send a young person through medical school upon her promise that she will return to the testator's hometown to practice has been held charitable. Estate of Carlson, 358 P.2d 669 (Kan. 1961).

A trust may also be a valid charitable trust although the settlor delegates the selection of charitable purpose to the trustee. Thus, *S* may convey a fund, in trust, to *T* "for such charitable purpose or purposes as *T* shall select." See Restatement (Third) of Trusts §28, cmt. a (2003).

For a comprehensive analysis of charitable gifts, and of the difficulties courts have had in defining *charitable*, see Mary Kay Lundwall, Inconsistency and Uncertainty in the Charitable Purposes Doctrine, 41 Wayne L. Rev. 1341 (1995). Lundwall agrees with Scott that what is a charitable gift should be broadly defined because charitable trusts can be used "to try many experiments to which it would be improper to devote the public funds, or that the public would be unwilling to support until convinced by proof of their success." 4A Scott, supra, §374.7.

3. *Noncharitable purpose trusts.* In a significant number of states, the rule that trusts for noncharitable purposes fail for want of an ascertainable beneficiary has been relaxed somewhat. First, many states have recognized so-called *honorary trusts*, where the trustee has the power, but not a duty, to perform. Second, quite a few states have enacted statutes that allow a trust for a specific purpose for 21 years or

longer, even if that purpose is not charitable and the trust lacks an ascertainable beneficiary, provided that the purpose is not capricious. Common applications are trusts for the care of a cemetery plot (for which many states have authorized perpetual purpose trusts), the care of an animal, and the saying of masses. For further discussion of trusts for purposes in connection with the requirement of an ascertainable beneficiary for private trusts, see pages 518-528.

4. *Trusts to benefit a political party.* It is against public policy to endow perpetually a political party; hence, a trust to promote the success of a particular political party is not charitable. However, a trust for the improvement of the structure and methods of government, in a manner advocated by a particular political party, is charitable. For example, a trust to advance "the principles of socialism and those causes related to socialism," including supporting candidates for public office espousing socialistic views, has been held charitable. In re Estate of Breeden, 256 Cal. Rptr. 813 (App. 1989).

A trust with the purpose of bringing about a change in the law may be charitable, provided the purpose is not to bring about changes in the law by illegal means, such as revolution or illegal lobbying. See Restatement (Third) of Trusts §28, cmt. l (2003).

5. In Estate of Kidd, 479 P.2d 697 (Ariz. 1971), James Kidd, a bachelor of frugal nature, wrote a holographic will in 1946 leaving his estate for "reserach [sic] or some scientific proof of a soul of the human body which leaves at death I think in time their [sic] can be a Photograph of soul leaving the human at death." Shortly thereafter, Kidd disappeared without a trace. In 1964, Kidd's will was discovered and offered for probate. His estate amounted to $175,000. More than a hundred claimants stepped forth. Some of the claimants argued that there was no intent to create a charitable trust but an outright bequest to any person who had scientific proof of a soul that leaves the body at death; one of these claimed to have seen her soul leave her body and another claimed that scientific proof included inductive logical arguments based upon the Bible. The court held, however, that a charitable trust was intended. Upon remand, the trial court awarded the bequest to the American Society for Psychical Research in New York City. 110 Tr. & Est. 1058 (1971). In 1975, the society filed a report in the Arizona probate court, stating that it had spent the money from the Kidd estate but had failed to prove the existence of the human soul. N.Y. Times, June 16, 1975, at 30.

6. *Drafting advice.* The lawyer drawing a will making a gift to charity should make sure (a) of the exact legal name of the charity, and (b) if the client wants an estate tax charitable deduction, which is usual, whether the charity is tax-exempt under the Internal Revenue Code. A purpose deemed charitable by a state court may not qualify for a federal estate tax charitable deduction; federal law denies the deduction to charities that indulge in certain prohibited activities (see page 917).

Trusts for *benevolent* or *philanthropic* purposes should be avoided. Some older cases held that these words are broader than *charitable*, and, if so, the trust may fail as a charitable trust because the income can be used for noncharitable purposes. Modern cases tend to construe these words as synonymous with charitable, and in a state that has adopted Uniform Trust Code §409 (2000) it is possible that the benevolent or philanthropic purpose might qualify as a valid trust for a noncharitable purpose, but out of caution these terms should be avoided nonetheless. See Wilson v. Flowers, 277 A.2d 199 (N.J. 1971).

7. *Mortmain statutes.* Most states once had statutes permitting spouses and children to set aside death-bed wills making gifts to charity (traceable to the medieval fear of overreaching by priests taking the last confession and will). Some of

these statutes restricted the share of an estate that could be left to charity even when the will was executed years before death. These statutes have all been either repealed or declared unconstitutional as a denial of equal protection of the law or on substantive due process grounds. See Restatement (Third) of Property: Wills and Other Donative Transfers §9.7 (2003).

NOTE: SHAW'S ALPHABET TRUSTS

George Bernard Shaw, winner of the 1925 Nobel Prize for Literature, was long interested in reforming the English alphabet so that letters, singly and in combination, would have only one pronunciation. He pointed out that fish could be spelled "ghoti" if the "gh" were pronounced like the "gh" in "enough," "o" like the "o" in "women," and "ti" like "ti" in "notion." (He did not note that Shaw could be spelled "pshaw.") Shaw devised the residue of his estate (fattened by royalties from My Fair Lady) to his executor, in trust for 21 years, to develop a new alphabet of 40 letters and to propagandize for its adoption. Upon the termination of the alphabet trusts "or if and so far as such trusts shall fail through judicial decision," the principal was to be distributed one-third to the British Museum "in acknowledgment of the incalculable value to me of my daily resort to the reading room of that institution at the beginning of my career," one-third to the National Gallery of Ireland, and one-third to the Royal Academy of Dramatic Art. The court held the alphabet trust was not for the advancement of education nor beneficial to the community, and therefore it was not a charitable trust. The court further held that the devise could not be treated as a private trust because it was not in favor of an ascertainable beneficiary. The court referred to the Restatement of Trusts §124, which approves treating the gift as a power, and stated that it was

> not at liberty to validate this trust by treating it as a power. . . . The result is that the alphabet trusts are, in my judgment, invalid, and must fail. It seems that their begetter suspected as much, hence his jibe about failure by judicial decision. I answer that it is not the fault of the law, but of the testator, who failed almost for the first time in his life to grasp the problem or to make up his mind what he wanted. [In re Shaw, 1 All E.R. 745, 759 (Ch. 1957).]

Who would have thought that the figure of Nemesis would appear to Shaw in the guise of an alphabet trust?

The case was appealed, but while the appeal was pending a compromise was effected by which a sum was set aside to employ a phonetic expert to develop a phonetic alphabet, transliterate Shaw's play Androcles and the Lion into the new alphabet, and publish the transliterated play. How would you have drafted Shaw's will to carry out his desires? See William F. Fratcher, Bequests for Purposes, 56 Iowa L. Rev. 773 (1971).

SECTION B.   MODIFICATION OF CHARITABLE TRUSTS: CY PRES

Under the *cy pres* doctrine, if the settlor's exact charitable purpose cannot be carried out, the court may direct the application of the trust property to another charitable purpose that approximates the settlor's intention. Cy pres is shorthand for the Norman French phrase *cy pres comme possible*, meaning "as nearly as possible."

In England there was a royal prerogative power of cy pres as well as a judicial doctrine of cy pres. Under the prerogative power, charitable gifts were expected to comply with public policy as established by the king. Any deviations were corrected by the crown, regardless of the testator's intent. For example, in Da Costa v. De Pas, 27 Eng. Rep. 150 (Ch. 1754), a Jewish testator left money in trust to form an assembly for the purpose of teaching Jewish law and religion. The trust encouraged a religion other than the state religion and was referred to the king by the chancellor for instructions. Applying prerogative cy pres, the king allotted the money to instruct foundlings in the Christian religion.

Largely as a reaction to the abuse of prerogative cy pres by the crown, disregarding entirely the probable wishes of the testator, courts in this country were reluctant to adopt judicial cy pres. It, too, could be abused. As the nineteenth century receded into history, however, various changes in circumstances made it difficult or impractical to administer charitable trusts as specifically intended by the donors. A nineteenth-century trust to care for old horses retired from pulling fire wagons and streetcars could not be administered for these purposes in the twentieth century. Hence, American courts finally came to accept a judicial doctrine of cy pres.

In re Neher
Court of Appeals of New York, 1939
279 N.Y. 370, 18 N.E.2d 625

LOUGHRAN, J. The will of Ella Neher was admitted to probate by the Surrogate's Court of Dutchess County December 22, 1930. Paragraph 7 thereof made these provisions:

> I give, devise and bequeath my home in Red Hook Village, on the east side of South Broadway, consisting of house, barn and lot of ground . . . to the incorporated Village of Red Hook, as a memorial to the memory of my beloved husband, Herbert Neher, with the direction to said Village that said property be used as a hospital to be known as "Herbert Neher Memorial Hospital." The trustees of the Village of Red Hook, consisting of the President and the Trustees, shall constitute the managing board with full power to manage and operate said hospital as they deem wise for the benefit of the people of Red Hook, and each succeeding Board of Trustees shall constitute the Board of Trustees for said hospital, so that any person duly elected and qualified or duly appointed and qualified as a President or Trustee of the said Village of Red Hook shall be a trustee of said hospital during such person's lawful term of office, and shall be succeeded as a trustee on the hospital board by his successor on the Village Board.

All her other estate Mrs. Neher gave to relatives and friends.

On September 1, 1931, the trustees of Red Hook (hereinafter called the village) resolved to "accept the real property devised and bequeathed by the Will of Ella Neher, deceased, according to the terms of the Will of said Ella Neher."

In March, 1937, the village presented to the Surrogate's Court its petition asserting that it was without the resources necessary to establish and maintain a

hospital on the property devised to it by the testatrix and that a modern hospital
theretofore recently established in the neighboring village of Rhinebeck adequately
served the needs of both communities. The prayer of this petition was for a decree
"construing and reforming paragraph Seven of the last Will and Testament of said
decedent directing and permitting your petitioner to receive said property and to
erect and maintain thereon a building for the administration purposes of said
Village to be known and designated as the Herbert Neher Memorial Hall, with
a suitable tablet placed thereon expressing such memorial."

This petition the Surrogate denied on the single ground "that to read into the
will a general intention to devote the property to charitable purposes instead of an
intention to limit the use of the property to the operation of a hospital, would do
violence to the expressed testamentary design of Mrs. Neher." The Appellate
Division has affirmed the Surrogate. The village brings the case here by our
leave. This gift was not a gift to a particular institution. There was to be no singular
object of the bounty. This gift was one to a whole community — "to the incorporated Village of Red Hook." The idea initially expressed by the testatrix was that
her home should be dedicated to the village in the name of her husband. The only
question is whether this first stated design of beneficence at large is necessarily to
be denied prime import, because of the words that immediately follow — "with the
direction to said Village that said property be used as a hospital to be known as
'Herbert Neher Memorial Hospital.'" This last phrase, it is to be noticed, gave no
hint in respect of a predilection for any certain type of the manifold varieties of
medical or surgical care. Nor did the will make any suggestion as to management
or control, save that the village trustees (as such) were designated as a governing
board. So great an absence of particularity is a strong circumstance against the
view that the instruction of the testatrix was of the substance of the gift.

When paragraph 7 of the will is taken as a whole, the true construction, we think,
is that the paramount intention was "to give the property in the first instance for
a general charitable purpose rather than a particular charitable purpose, and
to graft on to the general gift a direction as to the desires or intentions of the
testator as to the manner in which the general gift is to be carried into effect."
Parker, J., in Matter of Wilson, [1913] 1 Ch. 314, 321. Such a grafted direction may
be ignored when compliance is altogether impracticable and the gift may be
executed cy pres through a scheme to be framed by the court for carrying out
the general charitable purpose. See Real Property Law, Consol. Laws, ch. 50, §113,
subd. 2; Sherman v. Richmond Hose Co., 130 N.E. 613 (N.Y. 1921); Matter of
Gary's Estate, 288 N.Y.S. 382 (App. Div. 1936); In re Gary's Will, 5 N.E.2d 368
(N.Y. 1936); American Law Institute; Restatement of Law of Trusts, §399, comment at page 1211.

The order of the Appellate Division and the decree of the Surrogate's Court
should be reversed and the matter remitted to the Surrogate's Court for further
proceedings in accordance with this opinion, without costs.

NOTES, PROBLEM, AND QUESTIONS

1. "Cy pres may not be employed simply to promote what the court views as a
worthy charitable agenda; it is rather a power whose permissible use is confined to the
perpetuation and advancement, to the extent possible, of the particular dispositional

agenda prescribed in the dispositional instrument." Board of Trustees of the Museum of the Am. Indian, Heye Found. v. Board of Trustees of the Huntington Free Library and Reading Room, 610 N.Y.S.2d 488, 499 (App. Div. 1994).

Was permission to use the property in *Neher* "to erect and maintain . . . a building for the administration purposes of [the] Village" an approximation of the settlor's intention as nearly as possible?

2.   *T* devises property to *X* as trustee to pay the income to his niece *A* and, on *A*'s death, to pay the principal to the dental school that *T* had graduated from 50 years earlier. *T* dies. Two years later, while *A* is still alive, the dental school is closed and its resources are absorbed by the medical school and hospital of the same university. Eight years later, *A* dies, survived by a daughter, *B*. *B* argues that, because the dental school no longer exits, the gift fails and the trust property should revert to her on resulting trust as *T*'s successor. In response, the university asks the court to apply cy pres on the ground that, though it no longer offers the basic degree in dental medicine, it continues to offer dental treatment for patients and post-graduate education in dentistry through its medical school and hospital. What result? See Obermeyer v. Bank of Am., 140 S.W.3d 18 (Mo. 2004).

3.   Because it ultimately seeks to vindicate the settlor's generalized intent, cy pres has been justified as intent-implementing. Judge Posner explains:

> A policy of rigid adherence to the letter of the donative instrument is likely to frustrate both the donor's purposes and the efficient use of resources. . . . [Suppose that the settlor] had given the city a tuberculosis sanitarium. . . . As the incidence of tuberculosis declined and advances in medical science rendered the sanitarium method of treating tuberculosis obsolete, the value of the donated facilities in their intended use would have diminished. Eventually it would have become clear that the facilities would be more valuable in another use. . . . [E]nforcement would in all likelihood be contrary to the purposes of the donor, who intended by his gift to contribute to the cure of disease, not to perpetuate useless facilities.
>
> The foregoing discussion may seem tantamount to denying the competence of a donor to balance the value of a perpetual gift against the cost in efficiency that such gifts frequently impose. But since no one can foresee the future, a rational donor knows that his intentions might eventually be thwarted by unpredictable circumstances and may therefore be presumed to accept implicitly a rule permitting modification of the terms of the bequest in the event that an unforeseen change frustrates his original intention. . . .
>
> Where the continued enforcement of conditions in a charitable gift is no longer economically feasible, because of illegality . . . or opportunity costs (in the sanitarium example), the court, rather than declaring the gift void and transferring the property to the residuary legatees (if any can be identified), will authorize the administrators of the charitable trust to apply the assets to a related (cy pres) purpose within the general scope of the donor's intent. [Richard A. Posner, Economic Analysis of Law 519-520 (6th ed. 2003).]

See also Restatement (Third) of Trusts §67, cmt. a (2003), stating that the "doctrine's modern rationale rests primarily in the perpetual duration allowed charitable trust and in the resulting risk that designated charitable purposes may become obsolete as the needs and circumstances of society evolve over time."

4.   A number of commentators favor expanding the use of judicial cy pres to change charitable trust provisions to maximize community benefits as required by changing community needs. See Alex M. Johnson, Jr., Limiting Dead Hand Control

of Charitable Trusts: Expanding the Use of the Cy Pres Doctrine, 21 U. Haw. L. Rev. 353 (1999); Alex M. Johnson, Jr. & Ross D. Taylor, Revolutionizing Judicial Interpretation of Charitable Trusts: Applying Relational Contracts and Dynamic Interpretation to Cy Pres and America's Cup Litigation, 74 Iowa L. Rev. 545 (1989); Ronald Chester, Cy Pres: A Promise Unfulfilled, 54 Ind. L.J. 407 (1979).

Other commentators are less sanguine about the ability of courts to give effect to the settlor's general intention; these scholars are dubious about expanding cy pres. See Rob Atkinson, Reforming Cy Pres Reform, 44 Hastings L.J. 1112 (1993); Jonathan R. Macey, Private Trusts for the Provision of Private Goods, 37 Emory L.J. 295 (1988).

Professor Simes argued that after 30 years courts should have enlarged cy pres power to modify charitable trusts "not only if the original purpose was found impracticable but also if . . . the amount to be expended is out of all proportion to its value to society." Lewis M. Simes, Public Policy and the Dead Hand 139 (1955). Is this a good idea? See also Peter Luxton, Cy-Pres and the Ghost of Things That Might Have Been, 1983 Convey. 107, suggesting giving importance to the testator's intention in the early years of the trust but, at the end of the perpetuities period, treating the property as dedicated to charity. Should cy pres be applied more liberally after the period governed by the Rule against Perpetuities has expired? See Johnson, supra, 21 U. Haw. L. Rev. at 355-356 (arguing in the affirmative).

5. *Uniform Trust Code*. Section 413(a) of the Uniform Trust Code allows for cy pres if a particular charitable purpose becomes "unlawful, impracticable, impossible to achieve, or *wasteful*" (emphasis added). Restatement (Third) of Trusts §67 (2003) likewise includes wasteful as a basis for cy pres. The addition of wasteful reflects a deliberate effort to expand the range of circumstances under which the court might properly modify a charitable trust.

Another reform advanced by the UTC and Restatement (Third) of Trusts is a presumption of general charitable intent. The traditional rule is that, before a court can invoke cy pres to modify the specifics of the donor's charitable gift, there must be a showing that the donor had a general charitable intent. This was the main issue in *Neyer*. The UTC and Restatement shift the burden to the party opposing the application of cy pres to show that the donor did not have a general charitable intent. This reform also resolves a question that had existed in charitable trusts with a gift over. Some courts have taken the view that, in such a case, the settlor had a specific charitable intent and an alternative specific charitable intent, and thus the gift over precludes the application of cy pres to the primary gift. The better reasoned opinions view the presence of a gift over as only one factor to be weighed in ascertaining the settlor's intent. See Ronald Chester, Cy Pres or Gift Over? The Search for Coherence in Judicial Reform of Failed Charitable Trusts, 23 Suffolk U.L. Rev. 41 (1989). Given that, under traditional law, the settlor lacks standing to enforce the terms of a charitable gift, can you think of a strategic reason for a gift over, particularly a gift over to a sophisticated institution?

Speaking of gifts over, a further problem arises if the gift over is to a noncharitable beneficiary and there is a possibility of a remote vesting outside the period of the Rule against Perpetuities. UTC §413(b) addresses this problem by giving effect to a gift over upon the failure of the primary charitable purpose only if the trust property is to revert to the settlor or if the trust had been in existence for fewer than 21 years. See David M. English, The Uniform Trust Code (2000): Significant Provisions and Policy Issues, 67 Mo. L. Rev. 144, 179-180 (2002).

6.   Cy pres should be contrasted with *administrative deviation*. A court will permit deviation in the administrative terms of a trust when compliance would defeat or substantially impair the accomplishment of the purposes of the trust. See UTC §412(b), excerpted at page 578. It is not always clear what is an administrative term and what is a central purpose, however, and courts have been known to interpret "administrative" broadly on appealing facts. In Dartmouth College v. City of Quincy, 258 N.E.2d 745 (Mass. 1970), for example, the testator in 1870 established a trust to build and support the Woodward School for the education of females born in Quincy, Massachusetts. In 1968, the fund provided only $13,000 toward the school's total $53,000 operating costs, and to generate additional income the trustees proposed to admit non-Quincy-born girls, charging them a higher tuition than Quincy-born girls. The court held that it would permit deviation in the administrative terms of the trust and approved the trustees' plan. For an argument that deviation should be combined with cy pres, see Johnson, supra, 21 U. Haw. L. Rev. at 354.

NOTE: DISCRIMINATORY TRUSTS

Charitable trusts have been created to furnish benefits to one race, gender, or religion. Usually, benefits under these trusts are restricted to "whites" or to "men." Such trusts have been the subject of considerable litigation since the 1960s. See 4A Austin W. Scott, Trusts §399.4A (William F. Fratcher 4th ed. 1989). For example, after Amherst College refused a bequest to be used for scholarships for Protestant, gentile boys on account of the religious restriction, the court removed the clause. Howard Sav. Inst. v. Peep, 170 A.2d 39 (N.J. 1961). The court reasoned that the testator's primary charitable purpose was to benefit Amherst.

If the trustee of a racially restrictive trust is a governmental body (such as a public school granting scholarships to whites), courts have held that the administration of the trust in a racially discriminatory manner is discriminatory state action forbidden by the Equal Protection Clause of the Constitution. Courts have therefore ruled in most cases that the racial restriction is unenforceable. The question then becomes: Would the settlor prefer the trust to continue without the racial restriction or to terminate? Applying cy pres or the deviation doctrine, most courts have held that the testator would prefer the charitable trust to continue without the racial restriction. See Trammell v. Elliott, 199 S.E.2d 193 (Ga. 1973) (bequest to a public institution for the benefit of "poor white boys and girls" given effect minus the racial limitation).

A contrary example is provided by the infamous cases of Evans v. Newton, 382 U.S. 296 (1966), and Evans v. Abney, 396 U.S. 435 (1970). In the 1966 decision, the Supreme Court held that Senator Augustus O. Bacon's bequest of land to the City of Macon in trust for a park for white people was unconstitutional, regardless of whether it was administered by a governmental body or private trustees, because the park was a public institution. In the 1970 decision, however, the Court upheld the determination of the Georgia courts that the trust could not be modified, and so the property would pass on resulting trust to Bacon's heirs, on the ground that Bacon would have preferred the trust to fail rather than to allow it to operate free of the racial limitation.

Where the trustee is a private individual and not a public body, enforcing the racial restriction is usually not unconstitutional as discriminatory *state* action. See

In re Wilson, 452 N.E.2d 1228 (N.Y. 1983). For an interesting argument that racial and gender restrictions are unconstitutional even if the trustee is a private individual, see James W. Colliton, Race and Sex Discrimination in Charitable Trusts, 12 Cornell J.L. & Pub. Poly. 275 (2003).

Even if there is no constitutional difficulty, the trust may nonetheless run afoul of some federal or state statute forbidding racial discrimination. If so, the question arises whether the court should apply cy pres and strike the racial restriction. Most courts have done so. For example, in Home for Incurables of Baltimore City v. University of Md. Med. Sys. Corp., 797 A.2d 746 (Md. 2002), the court removed a racial restriction, illegal under state law, in a charitable bequest to the Home for Incurables of Baltimore City for the benefit of "white patients who need physical rehabilitation." The will also contained an alternative bequest to the University of Maryland in the event that the Home found the racial limitation "not acceptable." The alternative bequest was not subject to a racial limitation. The court held that the Home should take the bequest free from the racial limitation on the ground that, by ordering the proceeds be paid to the University, the court would be giving effect to the illegal racial discrimination.

Restricting the benefits of a private charitable trust to one gender is not unconstitutional, but it too may violate other federal or state law prohibiting gender discrimination. Again, courts in a number of cases have removed the gender restriction under the power of cy pres. See In re Certain Scholarship Funds, 676 A.2d 1325 (N.H. 1990) (invoking cy pres to remove gender and religious limitations to bring the trust in line with the state constitution).

A new question is now facing the courts: Is a charitable trust run by a public body giving scholarships exclusively to black persons constitutional? In Podberesky v. Kirwan, 38 F.3d 147 (4th Cir. 1994), the Fourth Circuit held that state university scholarships for blacks were invalid under the Equal Protection Clause unless they were justifiable to remedy present effects of past discrimination. In Grutter v. Bollinger, 539 U.S. 306 (2003), however, the Supreme Court upheld the University of Michigan Law School's race-conscious admissions policy on the ground that the school had a "compelling state interest" in obtaining a diverse student body. To the extent that achieving a racially diverse class requires not just admitting a diverse group of applicants, but also providing enough funding to nonwhite admittees to induce them to matriculate, does *Grutter* implicitly overrule *Podberesky*? This seems an issue that will likely be litigated. See B. Andrew Bednark, Note, Preferential Treatment: The Varying Constitutionality of Private Scholarship Preferences at Public Universities, 85 Minn. L. Rev. 1391 (2001); Amy Weir, Note, Should Higher Education Race-Based Financial Aid Be Distinguished from Race-Based Admissions?, 42 B.C.L. Rev. 967 (2001). See also Kirk A. Kennedy, Race-Exclusive Scholarships: Constitutional Vel Non, 30 Wake Forest L. Rev. 759 (1995).

SAN FRANCISCO CHRONICLE: THE BUCK TRUST

Beryl Buck, a childless widow, died in 1975 a resident of Marin County, California. Marin County, lying across the bay northward from San Francisco, at the north end of the Golden Gate Bridge, is the most affluent of the counties in the Bay Area. Known as the "hot-tub capital of the world," in per capita income Marin is one of the nation's wealthiest counties.

Mrs. Buck's will left the residue of her estate to the San Francisco Foundation, a community trust administering charitable funds in five counties in the San Francisco Bay Area (Alameda, Contra Costa, Marin, San Francisco, and San Mateo). Mrs. Buck's will directed that the residue of her estate, to be known and administered as the Leonard and Beryl Buck Foundation,

> shall always be held and used for exclusively non-profit charitable, religious, or educational purposes in providing care for the needy in Marin County, California, and for other non-profit charitable, religious, or educational purposes in that county.

At the time of Mrs. Buck's death, the largest asset in her estate consisted of a block of stock in Beldridge Oil Company, a privately held company with rich oil reserves in Southern California, founded by her father-in-law. In 1975, this stock was worth about $9 million, but soon thereafter, in 1979, Shell Oil won a bidding war and bought the stock in the Buck Trust for $260 million. This corpus increased to well over $300 million by 1984, all of which was directed by Mrs. Buck's will to be spent on 7 percent of the Bay Area's residents in rich Marin County — a sudden embarrassment of riches that seemed to threaten the integrity of the San Francisco Foundation in equitably administering charitable dollars in the Bay Area. In 1984 the Foundation brought suit seeking judicial authorization to spend some portion of Buck Trust income in the other four counties of the Bay Area.

The Foundation's petition for cy pres rested upon the following theory: The enormous increase in the value of principal was a posthumous "surprise," a change in circumstances raising substantial doubt whether Mrs. Buck, if she had anticipated such an event, would have limited her beneficence to Marin County. This "surprise" warranted inquiry into what Mrs. Buck would have done had she known of this bonanza. The Foundation argued that she would not have limited her beneficence to Marin County because (a) she selected as trustee a foundation administering funds for the benefit of five counties; (b) other philanthropists, as shown by the fifty largest American charitable foundations (with the sole exception of the Buck Trust), reach out beyond their parochial origins as their resources grow and seek to serve a more populous and diverse slice of humanity, following a principle of proportionality; and (c), in the face of such an increase in wealth, the donor would be less interested in a small geographical area and more interested in the efficiency of the charitable dollar. This, the Foundation argued, was the philanthropic standard followed by almost all the great philanthropists of wealth equal to Mrs. Buck's posthumous fortune. It was the way other extremely rich philanthropists behave.

The Foundation's action proved to be throwing fat into a fire. Marin County officials were outraged. One called the Foundation "grave-robbing bastards" and characterized the cy pres petition as a "criminal attack upon the sanctity of wills." Marin officials were joined by the Marin Council of Agencies (a consortium of Marin County nonprofit agencies) in opposing the petition. Forty-six individuals and charitable organizations in the other four counties (called "Objector-Beneficiaries") were allowed to intervene to object to the Marin-only limitation. The attorney general of California, as supervisor of charitable trusts, also intervened, arguing against cy pres and asking whether the Foundation was in violation of its fiduciary duties for bringing such a suit and ought to be removed as trustee.

The case caused an uproar in San Francisco, with the local newspaper columnists pulling out all the stops. At first, the commentators were incensed at all that money being spent in rich Marin, but then — on second thought — public opinion began to coalesce behind the idea that Mrs. Buck had the right to do with her property as she wished, and the San Francisco Foundation became an object of calumny.

Near the close of the respondent's case, after nearly six months of trial, the Foundation resigned as trustee, and the court dismissed its cy pres petition.

In the course of its opinion refusing to apply cy pres, not officially reported but reprinted in 21 U.S.F.L. Rev. 691 (1987), the trial court said:

> The Restatement (Second) of Trusts, section 399 at 297, describes the cy pres doctrine as follows: "If property is given in trust to be applied to a particular charitable purpose and *it is or becomes impossible or impracticable or illegal to carry out the particular purpose,* and if the settlor manifested a more general intention to devote the property to charitable purposes, the trust will not fail but the court will direct the application of the property to some charitable purpose which falls within the general charitable intention of the settlor. (Emphasis added). . . ."
>
> Ineffective philanthropy, inefficiency and relative inefficiency, that is, inefficiency of trust expenditures in one location given greater relative needs or benefits elsewhere, do not constitute impracticability. . . . Such situation is not the equivalent of impossibility; nor is there any threat that the operation of the trust will fail to fulfill the general charitable intention of the settlor.
>
> To the extent that concepts of effective philanthropy or efficiency relate to achieving the greatest benefit for the cost incurred they should not form the basis for modifying a donor's wishes. No law requires a testator to make a gift which the trustees deem efficient or to constitute effective philanthropy. Moreover, calculating "benefit" involves inherently subjective determinations; thus, what is "effective" or "efficient" will vary, depending on the interests and concerns of the person or persons making the determination. Cy pres does not authorize a court to vary the terms of the bequest merely because the variation will accommodate the desire of the trustee.
>
> To the extent that the term efficiency embraces the concept of relative need, it is not an appropriate basis for modifying the terms of a testamentary trust. If it were otherwise, all charitable gifts, and the fundamental basis of philanthropy would be threatened, as there may always be more compelling "needs" to fill than the gift chosen by the testator. Gifts to Harvard or Stanford University, for example, could fail simply because institutions elsewhere are more needy. Similarly, needs in the Bay Area cannot be equated with the grueling poverty of India or the soul-wrenching famine in Ethiopia. Moreover, a standard of relative need would interpose governmental regulation on philanthropy because courts would be required to consider questions of comparative equity, social utility, or benefit, perhaps even wisdom, and ultimately substitute their judgments or those of the trustees for those of the donors.
>
> The cy pres doctrine should not be so distorted by the adoption of subjective, relative, and nebulous standards such as "inefficiency" or "ineffective philanthropy" to the extent that it becomes a facile vehicle for charitable trustees to vary the terms of a trust simply because they believe that they can spend the trust income better or more wisely elsewhere, or as in this case, prefer to do so. There is no basis in law for the application of standards such as "efficiency" or "effectiveness" to modify a trust, nor is there any authority that would elevate these standards to the level of impracticability.

No appeal was taken from the superior court decision in *Buck.* The superior court ordered the creation of the Marin Community Foundation, which would replace the San Francisco Foundation in administering the Buck Trust.

The new foundation is governed by seven trustees, two appointed by the Marin County Board of Supervisors, one by the Marin Council of (Nonprofit) Agencies, one by the president of the University of California, one by the Interfaith Council of Marin, one by relatives of Mrs. Buck's husband, and one by the Marin Community Foundation board. The trial judge chose three Marin-based research institutes to divide a substantial portion of the income from the trust: The Buck Center on Aging, The Institute on Alcohol and Other Drug Problems, and The Marin Educational Institute.

Professor Simon is highly critical of the supervisory role assumed by the trial court over the Buck Trust at the end of the trial:

> The extraordinary command role the court reserved for itself over the decision-making process . . . violates the basic concept of private philanthropy and disregards the role assigned to charitable trustees in the nonprofit sector. . . .
>
> [I]t is not obvious that these programs would have been preferred by the donor over distributions to neighboring Bay Area counties served by the [San Francisco] Foundation. . . . [T]he fact that she picked a community foundation focused on the Bay Area as the instrument of her charity cannot be ignored when shaping a cy pres solution. [John G. Simon, American Philanthropy and the Buck Trust, 21 U.S.F.L. Rev. 641, 666-668 (1987).]

The Foundation Directory (2004) reports that the Marin Community Foundation, created out of the Buck Trust, had $1.2 billion in assets as of June 30, 2001. The San Francisco Foundation, without the Buck Trust, had assets of $664 million as of June 30, 2003.

NOTE AND QUESTION

1. For an analysis of community trusts generally, the Buck Trust in particular, and the relationship between cy pres and the *variance* power of community foundations and trusts to depart from their donors' specific instructions, see Mark Sidel, Law, Philanthropy and Social Class: Variance Power and the Battle for American Giving, 36 U.C. Davis L. Rev. 1145 (2003).

2. Recall that Uniform Trust Code §413(a) (2000) and Restatement (Third) of Trusts §67 (2003) allow for cy pres if a particular charitable purpose becomes wasteful. Would the *Buck* case be decided differently under these authorities? See David M. English, The Uniform Trust Code (2000): Significant Provisions and Policy Issues, 67 Mo. L. Rev. 144, 179 & n.164 (2002); Edward C. Halbach, Jr., Uniform Acts, Restatements, and Trends in American Trust Law at Century's End, 88 Cal. L. Rev. 1877, 1901-1902 (2000).

PHILADELPHIA STORY: THE BARNES FOUNDATION

The Barnes Foundation, in the Philadelphia suburb of Merion, was created by Dr. Albert Barnes, a chemist, who invented Argyrol, which became a leading treatment for colds, also prescribed as eyedrops for newborn babies to prevent blindness. Argyrol earned Dr. Barnes a great fortune, which he spent on buying art in the early years of the twentieth century. He descended on Paris, checkbook in hand, and, haunting the garrets and artists' studios in Montparnasse, bought dozens of paintings directly from artists. He amassed a collection of over 180

Renoirs, 100 Cezannes, 60 Matisses, 40 Picassos, and dozens of other artists. Today this collection, which has been characterized as perhaps "the greatest private art collection in American history," is valued in the billions of dollars. Jeffrey Toobin, Battle for the Barnes, The New Yorker, Jan. 21, 2002, at 34. Dr. Barnes hung his 2,000 pieces of art five or six atop each other in a gallery he built in Merion. "At first glance, the display . . . looks almost haphazard. Paintings are lined up next to and above one another, sometimes inches apart, and they are labeled with only a single word on their frames." Id.

Son of a butcher in South Philadelphia, Dr. Barnes was high-hatted by Philadelphia Main Line society and by art critics and scholars who panned his art. As a result, he would not permit them in to see the paintings after these artists became celebrated. He barred entry to all except "plain people, that is, men and women who gain their livelihood by daily toil in shops, factories, schools, and stores." Dr. Barnes admitted some scholars and literati on a selective basis. A few others were able to sneak in disguised as chauffeurs, miners, or workmen.

Dr. Barnes had unconventional theories about art education, developed with John Dewey. To further these theories, the Barnes Foundation was set up as an educational institution, not as an art gallery. The curriculum consisted solely of instruction in Barnes's aesthetic theories. Classes in Barnesian aesthetics were open to students for two hours in the afternoon. When Dr. Barnes died in 1951, the Barnes Foundation by-laws were set in stone. No painting was ever to be moved from where he hung it. No painting was to be sold or loaned. No painting could be added to the collection, and paintings from other galleries could not be exhibited there. The gallery was to be open to the general public only on Saturdays from September through June. Entrance fees were prohibited (remember: Dr. Barnes wanted only "plain people" to see his pictures). Also prohibited were "any society functions commonly designated receptions, teas, dinners, or banquets," public or private. The trustees were permitted to invest only in safe low-yield government bonds. Barnes mandated that the rules were "unamendable and shall never be amended in any manner whatsoever."

In 1961 the Pennsylvania attorney general brought a lawsuit, forcing the Barnes Gallery to open its doors to the general public two and one-half days a week in order to keep its charitable tax-exempt status. This suit was instigated by pressure from the Philadelphia Inquirer, which was then owned by Walter Annenberg, a noted art collector himself.

In 1988, upon the deaths of the last trustee appointed by Dr. Barnes, control of the Barnes Foundation passed to Lincoln University, a small historically black college in Chester County, Pennsylvania. (Justice Thurgood Marshall was a graduate.) During his life, Barnes had always admired and enjoyed African American culture and art, and so he gave Lincoln the power to nominate the trustees who would run his foundation after the death of his associates. The new trustees found the 1925 gallery in a sad state of repair. With an endowment of only $10 million, the income could pay for only half the guards needed. Thus, half the gallery was open for two hours, the public was then shooed out, and, after the guards moved to the other half, the public was readmitted to the latter half for two hours.

The new trustees looked around for ways of restoring the structure and generating income. In the 1990s, they brought a series of lawsuits asking the court to authorize deviation from Barnes's rigid rules. These petitions were opposed by a small group of former Barnes Foundation students, who adamantly opposed even

Barnes Foundation Gallery. **Top:** *Seurat, Models.* **Bottom:** *Cézanne,*
Card Players and Girl. **Upper left:** *Cézanne, The Drinker.* **Lower left:**
Cézanne, Still Life with Bottle. **Upper right:** *Corot, Woman in Gray.*
Lower right: *Cézanne, Leda and the Swan.*

the slightest deviation from what they regarded as Dr. Barnes's vision. The court authorized the trustees to open the gallery to the public three-and-a-half days a week during the whole year and to charge a $5 admission fee. The trustees were given greater discretion in investing the Barnes Foundation funds to produce a higher yield, and the trustees were permitted to hold fundraising events in the gallery, even though Dr. Barnes had forbidden this. The trustees also asked for the power to sell some pictures, but this brought a great outcry. The trustees then proposed, and the court approved, a world tour of 50 priceless masterworks from the collection to be shown in Washington, Paris, Toronto, Tokyo, Ft. Worth, and Philadelphia (which netted the Foundation about $17 million, of which $12 million were used to modernize the gallery). For those who could not see the paintings on the world tour, the trustees produced a CD-ROM, with photographs in color.

The world tour drew record crowds, more in Paris than had ever before lined up to see an art show. But the world tour brought protests from some Philadelphians, who were outraged that Dr. Barnes's intent had been violated in so many ways. The protestors—particularly the neighbors in Merion—were angry that the Barnes Foundation had been transformed from an educational institution serving a few into a museum drawing thousands of people in cars. Dr. Barnes, they said, must be spinning in his grave. But, maybe not. At the end of the tour, the paintings were rehung in the Barnes Gallery exactly as the eccentric Dr. Barnes had hung them—with some of the greatest works placed near the ceiling, difficult to see but hung according to his aesthetic theories.

The latest round in the "Battle for the Barnes" began in 2002. Explaining that the Foundation's financial condition had become so dire as to threaten its survival, the trustees again asked the court to authorize deviation from Barnes's rules, this time to permit moving the collection from the recently modernized Merion building to a new facility to be built in Philadelphia, close to the Philadelphia Museum of Art. The relocation plan was hatched as part of a deal between the trustees and the Pew Charitable Trusts and the Lenfest Foundation, both mainstays of Philadelphia philanthropy, whereby Pew and Lenfest would help the trustees raise $150 million for the construction of the new facility and to replenish the Barnes Foundation's depleted endowment. In the meantime, Pew and Lenfest provided the Foundation with $3.1 million in bridge financing and paid the costs associated with the litigation.

In January 2004 the court held that "the present location of the gallery is not sacrosanct, and relocation may be permitted *if necessary*." But the evidence before it did not make out a case of necessity. The court also had harsh words for the trustees over what it regarded as an unwillingness to consider selling some of the paintings that were not part of the public display. "[T]he possibility of selling some of these holdings has been dismissed by The Foundation as too little, too shortsighted, or unethical. The move to Philadelphia has been floated as the only lifeboat in the entire sea. Since the outside charities are footing The Foundation's legal bills in these hearings, we accept their single-option theory as the product of zealous advocacy." The court also had unkind words for the attorney general's office, which did little more than support the Foundation, "cheering on its witnesses. . . . The course chosen by the Office of the Attorney General prevented the court from seeing a balanced, objective presentation of the situation, and constituted an abdication of that office's responsibility."

Over the course of six days of hearings in late September 2004, which produced more than 1,200 pages of testimony, the trustees tried again — this time with more success. On December 13, 2004, the court held that the trustees had met their burden of proof and granted their petition. Although the plan calls for moving the art collection to Philadelphia, the Foundation will retain the Merion facility, which had undergone a $12 million renovation after the world tour. Said the court: "The irony of converting a state-of-the-art gallery into perhaps the most expensive administration building in the history of nonprofits is not lost to us. Looking to the future, it is of the utmost importance that the Board of Trustees steer The Foundation so that another such irony does not surface ten or fifteen years hence." And so the saga continues.

QUESTION AND NOTES

1. Would you, as a judge, have approved the trustees' deviations from Dr. Barnes's bylaws? See Bruce H. Mann, In the End, a Move Was Only Way Out, Phila. Inq., Dec. 15, 2004.

2. For a recent, book-length telling of the Barnes Foundation saga, see John Anderson, Art Held Hostage: The Story of the Barnes Collection (2003). See also Ilana H. Eisenstein, Comment, Keeping Charity in Charitable Trust Law: The Barnes Foundation and the Case for Consideration of Public Interest in Administration of Charitable Trusts, 151 U. Pa. L. Rev. 1747 (2003); Patty Gerstenblith, Acquisition and Deaquisition of Museum Collections and the Fiduciary Obligations of Museums to the Public, 11 Cardozo J. Intl. & Comp. L. 409 (2003). For a portrait of the irascible Dr. Barnes, see Howard Greenfield, The Devil and Dr. Barnes (1987).

3. For a similar dispute concerning the location and potential sale of artwork bequeathed to a Massachusetts community foundation called the White Fund with the purpose "to create and gratify a public taste for fine art, particularly among the people of the city of Lawrence," see Museum of Fine Arts v. Beland, 735 N.E.2d 1248 (Mass. 2000).

SECTION C. SUPERVISION OF CHARITABLE TRUSTS

Because charitable trusts lack an ascertainable beneficiary, the question arises, who ensures that the trustee acts in accord with the settlor's charitable purpose and refrains from abuse or breach of fiduciary obligation?

CARL J. HERZOG FOUNDATION, INC. v. UNIVERSITY OF BRIDGE-PORT, 699 A.2d 995 (Conn. 1997): In 1986, the Carl J. Herzog Foundation made a gift to the University of Bridgeport to provide scholarships to nursing students. In 1991, the University closed its nursing school and added the funds to its general endowment. The Herzog Foundation then brought suit for an injunction to re-establish the scholarships or to give the money to the Bridgeport Area Foundation, which was prepared to administer nursing scholarships.

The court held that the donor of a charitable gift has no standing to enforce the terms of the gift unless the donor "had expressly reserved the right to do so." The exclusive enforcement power is in the state attorney general, who alone has standing to enforce the terms of the gift. The court quoted Restatement (Second) of Trusts §391 (1959): "A suit can be maintained for the enforcement of a charitable trust by the Attorney General or other public officer, or by a co-trustee, or by a person who has a special interest in the enforcement of the charitable trust, but not by persons who have no special interest or by the settlor or his heirs, personal representatives or next of kin." In this case, because the donor had not expressly retained a reversionary interest, the court held that the Foundation lacked standing under the common law.

The court then considered the Foundation's argument that it had standing under the Uniform Management of Institutional Funds Act (1972), enacted in Connecticut and in over 40 other states. At issue was UMIFA §7, which supplements cy pres by providing that an institution may be released from a donative restriction with the donor's written consent or, if the donor is dead, disabled, or otherwise unavailable, with court approval. See Yale Univ. v. Blumenthal, 621 A.2d 1304 (Conn. 1993). The Foundation argued that this provision created an implicit private right of action for donors to enforce the terms of their gifts. In a 3-2 decision, the court rejected this argument. "The drafters of UMIFA expressly provided that the donor of a completed gift would not have standing to enforce the terms of the gift. 'The donor has no right to enforce the restriction, no interest in the fund and no power to change the eleemosynary beneficiary of the fund. He may only acquiesce in a lessening of a restriction already in effect.' UMIFA, §7, comment." Thus the majority held that Connecticut's enactment of UMIFA did not change the common law rule: The Herzog Foundation did not have standing as donor to challenge the University of Bridgeport's use of the donated funds.

Smithers v. St. Luke's-Roosevelt Hospital Center

Supreme Court, Appellate Division, New York, 2001
281 A.D.2d 127, 723 N.Y.S.2d 426

ELLERIN, J.   The issue before us is whether the estate of the donor of a charitable gift has standing to sue the donee to enforce the terms of the gift. We conclude that in the circumstances here present plaintiff estate does have the necessary standing. . . .

Plaintiff Adele Smithers is the widow of R. Brinkley Smithers, a recovered alcoholic who devoted the last 40 years of his life to the treatment and understanding of the disease of alcoholism.[3] In 1971 Smithers announced his intention to make a gift to defendant St. Luke's-Roosevelt Hospital Center (the "Hospital") of $10 million

---

3. From the age of 46 until his death at 86, Brink Smithers and the Christopher D. Smithers Foundation, which Brink Smithers and his mother, Mabel Brinkley Smithers, created and named after his father (an investment banker who helped finance the creation of IBM), donated over $40 million to the research and treatment of alcoholism. For example, in 1986, Smithers donated $6.7 million to Rutgers and Cornell Universities for the R. Brinkley Smithers Institute for Alcohol-Related Workplace Studies. He also helped fund the National Council on Alcoholism and Drug Dependence and then served at different times as its president, chairman, and treasurer. In 1970 Smithers played an important role in the enactment of the federal legislation that created the National Institute on Alcohol Abuse and Alcoholism. — Eds.

R. Brinkley Smithers

over time for the establishment of an alcoholism treatment center (the "Gift"). In his June 16, 1971 letter to the Hospital creating the Gift, Smithers stated, "Money from the $10 million grant will be supplied as needed. It is understood, however, that the detailed project plans and staff appointents must have my approval."

According to the complaint, the Hospital agreed to use the Gift to expand its treatment of alcoholism to include, following five days of detoxification in the hospital, "rehabilitation in a free-standing, controlled, uplifting and non-hospital environment," that is, a "therapeutic community" removed from the hospital setting. With $1 million from the first installment of the Gift, the Hospital purchased a building at 56 East 93rd Street in Manhattan to house the rehabilitation program, and in 1973 the Smithers Alcoholism Treatment and Training Center opened there.[4]

Smithers thereafter remained involved in the management and affairs of the Smithers Center. At times, according to the complaint, the Hospital sought to avoid its obligations under the terms of the Gift, and its relationship with Smithers was an uneasy one. On July 31, 1978, Smithers wrote that the Hospital had "not lived up to my letter of intent," and that "[u]nder the circumstances no funds or stock will be forthcoming from me." Only slightly more than half of the Gift had been made at that time.

In 1981 the president of the Hospital, Gary Gambuti, commenced discussions with Smithers in an effort to induce him to complete the Gift. . . .

Over the next two years, Gambuti repeatedly assured Smithers that the Hospital would strictly adhere to the terms of the Gift and carry out Smithers's intent in making it. Only when Smithers was completely satisfied of the Hospital's intentions did he agree to complete the Gift, which he accomplished in an October 24, 1983 letter, stating:

> . . . This final contribution is subject to the following restrictions . . . [I]t is my intention that my final contribution be set aside as an endowment fund, (the "Smithers

4. The 56 East 93rd Street "building" is a 55-room Upper East Side mansion that had previously served as the Algerian Embassy and had once been owned by Broadway impresario Billy Rose. Patients were assigned to dormitory-style rooms, except with vaulted ceilings and mahogany doors. Because of its celebrity patients, including novelists John Cheevers and Truman Capote and former New York Mets (and then New York Yankees) Dwight Gooden and Darryl Strawberry, the Center developed a reputation as the "alcoholism clinic to the stars." The Center treated approximately 4,000 patients annually, and its program served as the model for other treatment centers such as the Betty Ford Center in California. — Eds.

The Smithers Alcoholism Center, Rehabilitation Unit, 56 East 93rd Street

Endowment Fund"). The income is to be used exclusively for the support of the Smithers Center, to the extent necessary for current operations, and any unused income remaining at the end of each calendar year is to be accumulated and added to principal. Principal of the Smithers Endowment Fund is not to be expended for any purpose except for remodeling or rebuilding the administration section and out-patient floor at the Building on 58th Street, and for construction, repairs or improvements with respect to any other building space at any time used directly in connection with the Smithers Center. Such capital expenditures should be considered as secondary to the endowment function and should in no event exceed in the aggregate one half of the initial value of the Smithers Endowment Fund.

Beneath Smithers's signature is the following paragraph signed and dated by Gambuti:

> The contribution of the number of shares of IBM Stock referred to above by R. Brinkley Smithers is gratefully accepted, *subject to the restrictions set forth in this letter,* in full satisfaction of any outstanding pledge or other obligation. (Emphasis added.)

The existing rehabilitation services, which Smithers included in his definition of the Smithers Center and which the Hospital's acceptance of the Gift encompassed, were housed in the free-standing Smithers building and, according to the complaint, were intended always to be housed in *a* free-standing facility. . . .

From 1992 to March 1995, [Plaintiff] and, until his death in January 1994, Smithers successfully solicited millions of dollars' worth of donated goods and services for a total restoration of the building. . . . Then, in March 1995, just over a year after Smithers's death, the Hospital announced that it planned to move the Smithers Center into a hospital ward and sell the East 93rd Street building. The Hospital directed Mrs. Smithers, a month and a half before [a "Silver Anniversary Gala" was to be held in honor of her husband and herself], to cancel the event.

The Hospital's announced intentions aroused Mrs. Smithers's suspicions. . . . Mrs. Smithers notified the Hospital of her objections to the proposed relocation of the program and demanded an accounting of the Smithers Center's finances. . . .

[I]n May 1995 the Hospital disclosed that it had been misappropriating monies from the Endowment Fund since before Smithers's death, transferring such monies to its general fund where they were used for purposes unrelated to the Smithers Center. Mrs. Smithers notified the Attorney General, who investigated the Hospital's plan to sell the building and discovered that the Hospital had transferred restricted assets from the Smithers Endowment Fund to its general fund in what it called "loans." The Attorney General demanded the return of these assets and in August 1995 the Hospital returned nearly $5 million to the Smithers Endowment Fund, although it did not restore the income lost on those funds during the intervening years.

In the next three years, Mrs. Smithers tried to negotiate a resolution with the Hospital. The Attorney General participated in the negotiations, seeking . . . "to effectuate a settlement that would resolve the plaintiff's concerns and benefit the Smithers Alcoholism Program." . . . [These] negotiations proved unsuccessful . . . .

In July 1998, the Attorney General entered into an [agreement] with the Hospital. Under the terms of this [agreement] the Hospital agreed to make no more transfers or loans from Gift funds for any purpose other than the benefit of the Smithers Center and to return to the Gift fund $1 million from the proceeds of any sale of the building. The Attorney General did not require the Hospital to return the entire proceeds of such a sale, because he found that, contrary to Mrs. Smithers's contention, the terms of the Gift did not preclude the Hospital from selling the building.

Two months later, Mrs. Smithers commenced this suit to enforce the conditions of the Gift and to obtain an accounting by the Hospital of its handling of the Endowment Fund and property dedicated to the Smithers Center. The Hospital and the Attorney General were named, *inter alia,* as defendants. Mrs. Smithers had obtained Special Letters of Administration from the Nassau County Surrogate's Court appointing her the Special Administratrix of Smithers's estate for the purpose of pursuing claims by the estate against the Hospital in connection with its administration of the Smithers Center. . . .

The Hospital . . . moved to dismiss the complaint for lack of standing. The Attorney General also moved to dismiss for lack of standing and for failure to state a cause of action. [The Supreme Court, which in New York is a trial court, dismissed Mrs. Smithers's complaint, whereupon this appeal ensued].

On appeal, the Attorney General's office, having reevaluated the matter "under the direction of the newly elected Attorney General,"[5] reversed its position and urged this Court to remand for a hearing on the merits to determine whether or not the building was subject to gift restrictions. If it were, then all proceeds of the sale would be subject to the same restrictions and could not be used for the Hospital's general purposes. . . . [T]he Attorney General urged that the issue of Mrs. Smithers's standing to bring the suit need not, and should not, be reached in this action, since he certainly had standing and had joined with her in seeking reversal and remand. . . .

While this appeal was pending, the Attorney General and the Hospital reached another agreement. This agreement raised some issues for the first time, but it brought the position of the Attorney General and the Hospital on other issues into accord with Mrs. Smithers's position. For example, the Hospital agreed to allocate the entire net proceeds of the sale of the building to the restricted purposes of the Gift and to restore the income lost as a result of the transfer of Gift funds to its general fund. Reversing his position again, the Attorney General returned to his predecessor's contention that Mrs. Smithers has no standing to bring this suit, and asked this Court to modify the decision dismissing the complaint for lack of standing so as to hold only that plaintiff does not have standing as special administratrix of the donor's estate and affirm, as modified, on that narrow ground. . . .

The sole issue before us is whether Mrs. Smithers, on behalf of Smithers's estate, has standing to bring this action. The Attorney General maintains that, with a few exceptions inapplicable here, standing to enforce the terms of a charitable gift is limited to the Attorney General. Most recently, the Attorney General has urged that, pursuant to the above-mentioned proposed settlement stipulation between himself and the Hospital, he has achieved all the relief that is appropriate in this case.

We begin by acknowledging that, pursuant to Article 8 of the Estates, Powers & Trusts Law governing the disposition of property for charitable purposes, "[t]he Attorney General shall represent the beneficiaries of such dispositions for religious, charitable, educational or benevolent purposes and it shall be his duty to enforce the rights of such beneficiaries by appropriate proceedings in the courts" (EPTL 8-1.1[f]). . . .

The question of whether the donor who is living and can maintain his or her own action need rely on the protection of the Attorney General to enforce the terms of his gift . . . was addressed in Associate Alumni of the General Theological Seminary of the Protestant Episcopal Church in the United States of America v. The General Theological Seminary of the Protestant Episcopal Church in the United States, 57 N.E. 626 (N.Y. 1900). . . .

> The general rule is "If the trustees of a charity abuse the trust, misemploy the charity fund, or commit a breach of the trust, the property does not revert to the heir or legal

5. The new attorney general was Eliot Spitzer, who has since gained notoriety for his aggressive pursuit of alleged wrongdoing in the securities industry. See Nicholas Thompson, The Sword of Spitzer, Leg. Affairs, May/June 2004, at 50. Perhaps stung by the court's criticisms, the assistant attorney general who headed Spitzer's Charities Bureau published an article in the New York Law Journal discussing the case. See William Josephson, Guilding Practitioners and Fiduciaries on Charities, N.Y.L.J., Dec. 3, 2001, at 1. Josephson notes that, at the time of the *Smithers* decision, the attorney general had been supporting a bill in the New York State Senate that would have modified New York's enactment of UMIFA §7 to grant standing to donors of a charitable gift in the event that the recipient disregarded "a restriction imposed by the applicable gift instrument." N.Y. Sen. 7805-A (May 2, 2000). — Eds.

representative of the donor unless there is an express condition of the gift that it shall revert to the donor or his heirs, in case the trust is abused, but the redress is by bill or information by the attorney-general *or other person having the right to sue.*" . . .

[The *Associate Alumni* case] explicitly forecloses the conclusion that the Attorney General's standing in these actions is exclusive. . . .

Supreme Court incorrectly characterized Mrs. Smithers as one who "positions herself as the champion and representative of the possible beneficiaries of the Gift," with no tangible stake because she has no position or property to lose if the Hospital alters its administration of the Gift. Mrs. Smithers did not bring this action on her own behalf or on behalf of beneficiaries of the Smithers Center. She brought it as the court-appointed special administratrix of the estate of her late husband to enforce his rights under his agreement with the Hospital through specific performance of that agreement. Therefore, the general rule barring beneficiaries from suing charitable corporations has no application to Mrs. Smithers. Moreover, the desire to prevent vexatious litigation by "irresponsible parties who do not have a tangible stake in the matter and have not conducted appropriate investigations" has no application to Mrs. Smithers either. Without possibility of pecuniary gain for himself or herself, only a plaintiff with a genuine interest in enforcing the terms of a gift will trouble to investigate and bring this type of action. Indeed, it was Mrs. Smithers's accountants who discovered and informed the Attorney General of the Hospital's misdirection of Gift funds, and it was only after Mrs. Smithers brought her suit that the Attorney General acted to prevent the Hospital from diverting the entire proceeds of the sale of the building away from the Gift fund and into its general fund. The Attorney General, following his initial investigation of the Hospital's administration of the Gift, acquiesced in the Hospital's sale of the building, its diversion of the appreciation realized on the sale, and its relocation of the rehabilitation unit, even as he ostensibly was demanding that the Hospital continue to act "in accordance with the donor's gift." Absent Mrs. Smithers's vigilance, the Attorney General would have resolved the matter between himself and the Hospital in that manner and without seeking permission of any court.

The donor of a charitable gift is in a better position than the Attorney General to be vigilant and, if he or she is so inclined, to enforce his or her own intent. Smithers was the founding donor of the Smithers Center, which he established to carry out his vision of "first class alcoholism treatment and training." In his agreement with the Hospital he reserved to himself the right to veto the Hospital's project plans and staff appointments for the Smithers Center. He and Mrs. Smithers remained actively involved in the affairs of the Smithers Center until his death, and she thereafter. During his lifetime, when Smithers found that, as he wrote on July 31, 1978, "[c]ertain things that were definitely understood were not carried out" by the Hospital, he decided not to donate the balance of the Gift. It was only when the Hospital expressly agreed to the various restrictions imposed by Smithers that he completed the Gift. The Hospital's subsequent unauthorized deviation from the terms of the completed Gift commenced during Smithers's lifetime and was discovered shortly after he died. To hold that, in her capacity as her late husband's representative, Mrs. Smithers has no standing to institute an action to enforce the terms of the Gift is to contravene the well settled principle that a donor's expressed intent is entitled to protection and the longstanding recognition under New York law of standing for a donor such as Smithers. We have seen no New York case in which a donor attempting to enforce the terms of his charitable gift was denied standing to do so. Neither the donor nor his estate was before the court in any of the cases urged on us in opposition to donor standing. The courts in these cases were not addressing the situation in which the donor was still living or his estate still existed. Cf., Herzog Foundation v. University of Bridgeport, 699 A.2d 995 (Conn. 1997).

Moreover, the circumstances of this case demonstrate the need for co-existent standing for the Attorney General and the donor. The Attorney General's office was notified of the Hospital's misappropriation of funds by Mrs. Smithers, whose accountants performed the preliminary review of the Hospital's financial records, and it learned of the Hospital's closing of the detox unit — a breach, according to the Attorney General, of a specific representation — from Mrs. Smithers's papers in this action. Indeed, there is no substitute for a donor, who has a "special, personal interest in the enforcement of the gift restriction" (Note, Protecting the Charitable Investor: A Rationale for Donor Enforcement of Restricted Gifts, 8 B.U. Pub. Int. L.J. 361 (1999)). Mrs. Smithers herself, who the Supreme Court found had no position to lose if the Hospital altered its administration of the Gift, has her own special, personal interest in the enforcement of the Gift restrictions imposed by her husband, as is manifest from her own fundraising work on behalf of the Smithers Center and the fact that the gala that she organized and that the Hospital ultimately cancelled was to be in her honor as well as her husband's. In any event, the Attorney General's interest in enforcing gift terms is not necessarily congruent with that of the donor. The donor seeks to have his or her intent faithfully executed, which by definition will benefit the beneficiaries, and perhaps also to erect a tangible memorial to himself or herself. In the June 16, 1971 letter to the Hospital in which Smithers created the Gift, he wrote that it "is to be used to set up the Smithers Alcoholism Treatment and Training Center." . . . We conclude that the distinct but related interests of the donor and the Attorney General are best served by continuing to accord standing to donors to enforce the terms of their own gifts concurrent with the Attorney General's standing to enforce such gifts on behalf of the beneficiaries thereof.

Mrs. Smithers, appointed the Special Administratrix of Smithers's estate for the purpose of pursuing claims by the estate against the Hospital in connection with its administration of the Smithers Center, therefore has standing to sue the Hospital for enforcement of the Gift terms.

Since we hold that the common law of the State of New York permits Mrs. Smithers to bring this action, we need not reach the issue of whether N-PCL 522 authorizes it.[6] . . .

Order, Supreme Court, New York County, modified, on the law, to grant plaintiff's motion for a preliminary injunction to the extent of staying disbursement of the proceeds of the sale of the East 93rd Street building, to deny defendants' motion to dismiss the complaint and to reinstate the complaint, and otherwise affirmed, without costs.

6. N-PCL 522 is a reference to §522 of New York's Not-For-Profit Corporation Law, which was modeled on §7 of UMIFA (1972), the same section that was at issue in *Herzog*, and as to which at the time of this decision there was an amendment pending in the New York Senate that would have authorized donor standing. — Eds.

FRIEDMAN, J., dissenting. . . . [The issue on appeal] is whether Adele Smithers, as the representative of her husband's estate, has standing to bring this action seeking to enforce the terms of a charitable gift given by her husband, the funding of which was completed approximately 12 years before this action was commenced. Because I believe that plaintiff does not have standing, I respectfully dissent.

In considering the subject of standing, I begin with the observation that, when a charitable gift is made, without any provision for a reversion of the gift to the donor or his heirs, the interest of the donor and his heirs is permanently excluded. Accordingly, in the absence of a right of reverter, the right to seek enforcement of the terms of a charitable gift is restricted to the Attorney General. . . .

The New York general rule on standing is not only consistent with the common-law approach (see, Herzog Foundation v. University of Bridgeport, supra), but also with the approach taken by the Restatement (Second) of Trusts (see §§391[e] & [f]). . . .

In holding that standing is generally restricted to the Attorney General, our courts have pointed out that a limited standing rule is necessary to protect charitable institutions from "vexatious litigation" by parties who do not have a tangible stake in the outcome of the litigation. While the majority believes that this concern does not apply to Mrs. Smithers because her motives are altruistic (and I agree that they are), the limited standing rule enunciated by our Court of Appeals is a prophylactic one that does not permit a case-by-case inquiry into the subjective motivations of the party commencing the action. . . .

[I]t is uncontroverted that the estate was not the donor of the gift. Thus, even if pure donor standing were recognized (as the majority concludes), this could not be a basis for granting standing to Mr. Smithers's estate. Next, to the extent that Mr. Smithers may have had standing based upon his right to exercise discretionary control over the gift, i.e., via the right to appoint key staffing positions, that right was personal to him, abated upon his death, and did not devolve to his estate. Hence, as plaintiff concedes that the estate has no right to exercise control over the gift, this may not be a basis of standing. Finally, since it is uncontroverted that the estate does not have a right of reverter in the gift or, in fact, any right to control the gift by way of appointment to staff positions or otherwise, it follows that there is no retained interest that could support a claim of standing. In view of this, I fail to perceive the legal basis for the majority's grant of standing to plaintiff. . . .

Accordingly, I vote to affirm the order dismissing the complaint.

NOTES AND QUESTIONS

1. *Epilogues.* The nursing school at issue in *Herzog* was closed because the University of Bridgeport ran into severe financial trouble. In 1992, an affiliate of the Rev. Sun Myung Moon's Unification Church bailed out the University and took control of it. At about the same time, the law school of the

University of Bridgeport pulled up stakes and resettled itself at Quinnipiac College in Hamden, Connecticut.

The alcoholism center at issue in *Smithers* was renamed The Addiction Institute of New York as part of a settlement between the hospital, Mrs. Smithers, and the Smithers Foundation. Mrs. Smithers retained the exclusive right to use the Smithers name in connection with the treatment of alcoholism and substance abuse; the hospital agreed to return approximately $6 million for redirection by Mrs. Smithers and the Foundation to a new donee that would use the funds for a new, free-standing substance abuse facility; and the hospital promised to use any remaining proceeds from the 1999 sale of the 56 East 93rd Street building for the treatment of alcoholism (the building was purchased by the all-girls, Manhattan-based Spence School). The probate court with jurisdiction over Mr. Smithers's estate later held that Mrs. Smithers was entitled to be reimbursed for her legal fees even though, strictly speaking, the litigation did not result in a pecuniary benefit to Mr. Smithers's estate. Although "decedent's probate estate had no direct economic stake in the hospital proceedings," the court was satisfied that Mrs. Smithers "undertook this litigation with the best of motives, desiring nothing more than to vindicate her late husband's life's work that was allegedly being ignored by St. Luke's-Roosevelt Hospital." Estate of Smithers, 760 N.Y.S.2d 304, 307 (Sur. 2003).

Since Mr. Smithers's death, Mrs. Smithers, as the president of the Smithers Foundation, has continued her husband's efforts to fight alcoholism. For a profile of the indefatigable Mrs. Smithers, see Michael Unge, Making Her Pitch: Darryl Strawberry's Ongoing Battle with Substance Abuse Is Just One of the Causes Adele Smithers Has Made Her Own, Newsday, Aug. 15, 1999, at G16.

2. Although *Herzog* and *Smithers* involved charitable gifts, not charitable trusts, on most issues the law of charitable gifts is based on the law of charitable trusts. See 4A Austin W. Scott, Trusts §348.1 (William F. Fratcher 4th ed. 1989); Restatement (Second) of Trusts §348, cmt. f (1959). The common law rule has long been that the settlor does not have standing to enforce the terms of the trust—whether it is a private or a charitable trust—unless the settlor retains an interest in the trust property. Thus, for private trusts, in the absence of a reversionary interest in the settlor, only the beneficiary has standing to bring suit against the trustee. By definition, however, charitable trusts lack an ascertainable beneficiary. The question thus arises, if not the settlor, who enforces the terms of a charitable trust? Professor Brody strikes at the heart of the problem: "In the case of an entity having no owners and established for the benefit of indefinite beneficiaries, who is the principal on whom the law can rely to monitor the agents and enforce the charitable purposes?" Evelyn Brody, The Limits of Charity Fiduciary Law, 57 Md. L. Rev. 1400, 1429 (1998). The law has long answered this question by providing that the state attorney general, as *parens patriae*, is the exclusive party with standing to bring suit against the trustee of a charitable trust.

3. Is supervision by the attorney general sufficient to ensure that the trustees of charitable trusts act in accord with the settlor's charitable purpose and refrain from abuse or breach of fiduciary duty?

While the powers of the attorney general are substantial, the extent of the supervision the attorney general provides is limited. . . . In some states, several assistant attorneys general form a charitable division of the attorney general's office. . . . In other states, however, one assistant attorney general supervises the nonprofit sector as only one part of his or her assignment. Hawaii has reported 0.5 attorneys working with charities, and many states do not list any attorneys specifically assigned to charitable matters.

Those working in . . . New York, Connecticut and Massachusetts . . . report that inquiries or complaints from dissenting board members, employees, beneficiaries or other members of the public, including the press, are much more likely to trigger investigations than reviews of annual reports conducted in the attorney general's office. In determining which cases to pursue, the attorneys consider the amount involved, the size of the organization, the impact on the public, and the egregiousness of the conduct. The worst abuses receive attention, but many problems probably go undetected or unaddressed. The attorneys general perform an important supervisory role in the charitable sector, but other forms of supervision are both necessary and desirable. [Susan N. Gary, Regulating the Management of Charities: Trust Law, Corporate Law, and Tax Law, 21 U. Haw. L. Rev. 593, 622-624 (1999).]

As Professor Gary suggests, even though many states now require trustees of charitable trusts to register with the state attorneys general and to submit annual financial reports, enforcement of charitable trusts by the attorneys general has been sporadic. Unless newspaper publicity is given to some alleged irregularity, the attorneys general rarely investigate the internal workings of charitable foundations. "Political cynics believe that 'A.G.' stands not for 'attorney general' but for 'aspiring governor.'" Evelyn Brody, Whose Public? Parochialism and Paternalism in State Charity Law Enforcement, 79 Ind. L.J. 937, 946 (2004).

4. One possible response to the deficiencies in supervision by the attorneys general is an increased role for the federal government through more intensive regulation of charitable trusts by the Internal Revenue Service. We return to this possibility in connection with the Bishop Estate at page 763.

5. Why not allow donors to bring suit to enforce charitable trusts? Twenty years before *Smithers*, Professor Hansmann argued in favor of this approach:

[I]t makes sense to deny standing to [donors] only if the consequence would be large numbers of spite suits, strike suits, or suits filed through sheer idiocy—what are presumably what the courts and commentators have in mind when they raise the specter of "harassing" litigation—or of suits that, though based on a real grievance, are feebly litigated and thus do more harm than good. Yet it appears extraordinarily unlikely that suits of this nature would ever become a sufficiently significant problem to outweigh the benefits of enlisting [donors] into the enforcement effort. [Henry B. Hansmann, Reforming Nonprofit Corporation Law, 129 U. Pa. L. Rev. 497, 609 (1981).]

For a contrary analysis, see Rob Atkinson, Unsettled Standing: Who (Else) Should Enforce the Duties of Charitable Fiduciaries?, 23 J. Corp. L. 655 (1998).

The court in *Smithers* appears to have been persuaded by Hansmann's mode of reasoning. Moreover, though the decision in *Smithers* is a departure from traditional law, it is not alone in recognizing some form of donor standing. Uniform Trust Code §405(c) (2000) provides that "[t]he settlor of a charitable trust, among others, may maintain a proceeding to enforce the trust." In a similar vein, Wis. Stat. Ann. §701.10(3)(a)(3) (2004) grants standing to any "settlor or group of settlors who contributed half or more of the principal" of a charitable trust.

Note, however, that the UTC and Wisconsin provisions on donor standing are amenable to being read as creating only a personal right in the donor, one that does not survive the donor's death (there is no case authority either way). In contrast, the court in *Smithers* not only recognized the standing rights of the donor, but also the standing of the fiduciary of the donor's estate. Does it follow from *Smithers* that the donor's standing rights pass to the donor's heirs or successors? See Maria Newman, Princeton University Is Sued over Control of Foundation, N.Y. Times, July 18, 2002, at B5 (detailing litigation against Princeton brought by the heir of a donor who made a $35 million contribution, valued in 2002 at $550 million, for alleged breach of restrictions on the use and management of the funds). Suppose that, as in *Herzog*, the donor is an institution and hence capable of perpetual life. Under *Smithers*, would such an institution retain standing in perpetuity?

For an insightful and learned analysis of UTC §405(c) and *Smithers*, see Ronald Chester, Grantor Standing to Enforce Charitable Transfers Under Section 405(C) of the Uniform Trust Code and Related Law: How Important Is It and How Extensive Should It Be?, 37 Real Prop., Prob. & Tr. J. 611 (2003).

6.   In tension with the UTC, but consistent with the original 1972 promulgation of the Uniform Management of Institutional Funds Act, the latest draft of the revised Uniform Management of Institutional Funds Act does not provide for donor standing in the case of donations to charitable organizations. Nothing in the draft explains the discontinuity with the UTC. However, the draft comment to §6, which is the proposed successor to 1972 UMIFA §7, states that "a donor making a significant gift to an institution may include in the gift instrument a right to notice of any modification or a right to standing to enforce a gift." Such rights must be drafted carefully so as not to imperil the donor's charitable deduction under the tax code. See Richard L. Fox, Donor Control: Planning for Donor Control and Other Strings Attached to Charitable Contributions, 30 Est. Plan. 441 (2003). Given that the UTC recognizes settlor standing, why would the drafting committee for the revised UMIFA not follow suit?

7.   *Charitable trust monitors.* Professor Geoffrey Manne has put forward an intriguing variant on the foregoing: "the creation of private, for-profit monitoring companies" that would contract with charitable organizations "to monitor both the financial and charitable aspects of the nonprofit's operation. The monitoring companies would be granted, by contract, the right to sue in order to rectify perceived violations of a nonprofit's fiduciary duties or the terms of its charter." In Manne's view, reputation effects and the desire to attract business, which is to say a profit motive, would give the monitoring companies appropriate incentives to police charitable organizations. Geoffrey A. Manne, Agency Costs and the Oversight of Charitable Organizations, 1999 Wis. L. Rev. 227. See also Evelyn Brody, Agents Without Principals: The Economic Convergence of the Nonprofit and

For-Profit Organizational Forms, 40 N.Y.L. Sch. L. Rev. 457 (1996). With the recent emergence of monitoring organizations that offer accreditation to charities that meet certain minimum governance standards, see Rachel Emma Silverman, Charities Start to Grade Themselves, Wall St. J., Aug. 18, 2004, at D1, perhaps the charitable sector is warming to Manne's proposal.

8. *The English Charity Commission.* In contrast with the American approach, which vests state attorneys general with responsibility for overseeing charitable entities, in the United Kingdom the home secretary appoints three to five commissioners who comprise the Charity Commission for England and Wales. Initially established by the Charitable Trusts Act of 1853, today the Commission is authorized by the Charities Act of 1993 to intervene in the administration of charities to police misconduct or mismanagement. In addition, the Commission serves as the registrar of charities, offers advice to the trustees of charitable entities, and is granted limited judicial powers. See Peter Luxton, The Law of Charities 421-482 (2001).

9. For flavorful discussions of the oversight of charities with reference to the recent, high-profile dispute over the Hershey Trust (as in Hershey's chocolate), see Evelyn Brody, Whose Public? Parochialism and Paternalism in State Charity Law Enforcement, 79 Ind. L.J. 937, 985-999 (2004); Mark Sidel, The Struggle for Hershey: Community Accountability and the Law in Modern American Philanthropy, 65 U. Pitt. L. Rev. 1 (2003).

10. *Beneficiaries with special interests.* A person with a special interest as a beneficiary can enforce a charitable trust. The person must show that he or she is entitled to receive a benefit under the trust that is not available to the public at large or to an average beneficiary. Thus, for example, an elderly, indigent widow living in a charitable home for the aged has been held to have standing to sue the board of trustees who, because of the costs of operating an obsolete facility, propose to relocate the residents elsewhere. Hooker v. The Edes Home, 579 A.2d 608 (D.C. 1990). Similarly, a parishioner can sue to enforce a trust for the benefit of his church. Gray v. St. Matthews Cathedral, 544 S.W.2d 488 (Tex. App. 1976). But compare Fowler v. Bailey, 844 P.2d 141 (Okla. 1992), where members of a church brought suit against the pastor and board of trustees in order to examine the church financial records. They were immediately expelled from the church by other members at a hastily called business meeting after a Wednesday night prayer service. The court denied the plaintiffs standing on the ground that a civil court could not determine the validity of their expulsion, which was an ecclesiastical matter. Accord Williams v. Board of Trustees of Mt. Jezreel Baptist Church, 589 A.2d 901 (D.C. 1991).

In the last few decades, the courts have broadened the definition of what constitutes a special interest. A taxpayer has been permitted to sue to prevent the transfer of a library held in trust from the Peabody Institute in Baltimore to the Pratt Library in that city. Gordon v. City of Baltimore, 167 A.2d 98 (Md. 1970). A citizen has been permitted to sue to enjoin deviation where a gift of land was made to the University of Illinois for a park. Parsons v. Walker, 328 N.E.2d 920 (Ill. App. 1975). But taxpayers have no standing to challenge the tax-exempt status of a charitable institution on the grounds that it indulges in impermissible political activity. In re United States Catholic Conference, 885 F.2d 1020 (2d Cir. 1989).

Whether students have special standing to sue college trustees is not settled. See Miller v. Aderhold, 184 S.E.2d 172 (Ga. 1971) (denying standing); Jones v. Grant,

344 So. 2d 1210 (Ala. 1977) (granting standing); Charles R. Berry & Gerald J. Buchwald, Enforcement of College Trustees' Fiduciary Duties: Students and the Problems of Standing, 9 U.S.F.L. Rev. 1 (1974).

HAWAII JOURNAL: THE BISHOP ESTATE

For more than 100 years, the Bishop Estate has been a highly respected, almost untouchable force in Hawaii. The Bishop Estate, one of the world's wealthiest charities, was established in 1884 as a charitable trust under the will of Princess Bernice Pauahi Bishop, the last descendant of King Kamehameha I, Hawaii's first and most powerful king. The trust assets are estimated at $10 billion, which includes 8 percent of Hawaii's land mass, making it Hawaii's largest private landowner.

The princess's will directed that there be five trustees, appointed by the justices of the Supreme Court of Hawaii, which, in those days when Hawaii was a monarchy, also served as the probate court. The trustees were directed to erect two schools, one for boys and one for girls, and to expend the annual income of the trust on the maintenance of the schools. Two schools were built shortly after the princess's death, but many decades later they were combined in a single school for boys and girls known as the Kamehameha Schools. Although the will does not limit admission to native Hawaiians, with minor exceptions that has always been the policy.

A Bishop Estate trusteeship has long been a coveted position in Hawaii. During the 1990s, the trustees paid themselves annual fees of nearly $1 million each and contracted over trust business with friends and relatives. As the twentieth century was nearing its end, the Bishop Estate trustees, Hawaii supreme court justices, and leaders of the Hawaii legislature had what might charitably be described as a cozy relationship (others called it corrupt). To be appointed as a justice on the supreme court, a candidate had to be put on an approved list by the judicial selection commission, a majority of whose members were picked by the president of the senate, speaker of the house, chief justice of the supreme court, and the governor. Trustees selected by justices in recent years have included a president of the senate, speaker of the house, chief justice of the supreme court, and individuals with close ties to the governor.

In 1997, the trustees were Richard Wong, former state senate president; Henry Peters, a state house speaker who continued for years in that post while serving as a Bishop Estate trustee; Gerard Jervis, the governor's closest political ally and the sitting chairman of the judicial selection commission; Lokelani Lindsey, the governor's cousin and chairperson of his reelection committee on Maui (one of the Hawaiian islands); and Oswald Stender, former CEO of the Campbell Trust, Hawaii's second-largest private landowner. Known in Hawaii as "the accidental trustee," Stender was not even a candidate for the position until the justices reached a deadlock in their deliberations.

The trustees' gilt-edged world began to unravel when trustee Lokelani Lindsey intervened high-handedly in the day-to-day running of the schools. She soon was calling the teachers incompetent and countermanding decisions of the schools' president, Michael Chun, as well as the principals. She ordered that no Hawaiian words be taught — or even uttered on campus — unless the word existed in 1884, the year the princess died, and she commanded that nothing in writing leave the campus until it had been personally approved by her, creating a long backlog of important communications. An accrediting agency described the climate on campus under Lindsey as "oppressive, intimidating and fearful." When students protested her attacks on President Chun, she summoned the student body president to her downtown office for a two-hour, closed-door interrogation, asking him how he would feel if she wrote a letter to Princeton (where he had been offered a scholarship) denouncing him as a rabble-rouser. When trustee Lindsey wanted a particular child admitted to Kamehameha Schools, a red dot would appear in the applicant's file. Eventually, the Kamehameha ohana (community) revolted. Teachers and students were threatened with sanctions if they participated, but others marched, 1,000 strong, through downtown Honolulu, stopping at the Supreme Court building to ask that the justices do something about the situation.

Then came the spark that ignited the firestorm that was soon to engulf the trustees. On August 9, 1997, the Honolulu Star Bulletin published Broken Trust, a 6,500-word essay written by four prominent kupuna (elders) of the native Hawaiian community (a senior federal district judge; a retired state judge; a former principal of the Kamehameha Schools; and the head trustee of the Queen Liliuokalani Trust) and Professor Randall Roth of the University of Hawaii Law School. The essay began, "The time has come to say, 'no more.'" Reviewing the basics of trust law and judicial selection, the authors described how Bishop Estate trusteeships had become "political plums" that sullied the process for selecting justices, accused the Bishop Estate trustees of specific breaches of trust, and called for an investigation of trustee selection and performance. The article triggered a public outcry for reform. It also prompted the state attorney general, Margery Bronster, to launch an investigation into the trustees' actions.

A few months after the Broken Trust article appeared, a court-appointed master found numerous irregularities in the administration of the Bishop Estate. Investment decisions had been "ad hoc," based more on relationships than conventional financial analysis. There was no overall plan or apparent effort to diversify investments; more Estate money had been invested in complex oil and gas deals than in marketable securities. The trustees had taken out full-page ads claiming a 17 percent return on investment for the three years under review, but the master determined that the actual return had been −1 percent. The master discovered that the trustees had moved $350 million of income into corpus without noting it in their records or disclosing it in financial statements or annual reports to the court. He was also troubled that trustees created conflicts of interest by investing trust money in private deals in which they had a personal stake. Worse still, the master found that, for many years, the trustees never spent more than 1 percent of the trust assets on the trust's charitable purpose.

In addition to sloppy investment practices and the trustees' short-changing Kamehameha Schools, private benefits flowed to the trustees. Most of the trustees accepted free golf memberships from country clubs leasing Bishop Estate land. One pocketed substantial director fees and stock options from a company in which the Estate held a large block of stock. Another used Estate personnel to perform personal services and accepted trips to the Super Bowl and Olympics in private jets from persons doing business with the Estate. One trustee "recused" himself as trustee in order to negotiate a deal on behalf of an organization that was buying land from the Estate. And a highly-placed employee of the Estate (a powerful state senator) charged $28,000 to the Estate's credit card in casinos and sex clubs in Las Vegas and Honolulu. (When this was disclosed by newspaper investigations, the trustees gave the employee a retroactive bonus in the amount he needed to repay the Estate and to cover his taxes on the total bonus.)

Then, as in any good scandal, there was sex. A security guard caught trustee Jervis having sex with an Estate attorney in the toilet cubicle in a hotel men's room. The attorney, a married woman, killed herself the next day. One week later, the trustee reportedly took an overdose of sleeping pills, but survived.

Trustee Wong was indicted on charges that he received a $116,000 kickback in a real estate deal involving the trust and his brother-in-law. Wong's wife was also indicted. Trustee Peters was indicted for allegedly selling his condominium at an inflated price to a developer who was negotiating to buy a tract of land owned by the Bishop Estate.

The trustees fought back. They hired big-name lawyers, paying them millions in fees from Estate funds. According to a court-appointed master who later reviewed the legal invoices, "One can easily conclude, as this Master has, that a strategy was adopted to obstruct the legal process, to delay wherever possible, to object wherever possible, to utilize so many lawyers and so many arguments that the opposition would be overwhelmed and would choose to give up. . . . [M]illions of dollars of trust funds were wasted." Through their friends in the legislature, some of whom were on the Estate payroll, the trustees retaliated against Attorney General Bronster. In April 1999, the state senate refused to confirm her to a second term in office.

Enter the Internal Revenue Service. In 1995, the Internal Revenue Service began a full audit of the Estate. By the end of 1998, it had concluded that the Estate was not being operated primarily for charitable purposes; that it had gotten directly involved in local and national political campaigns; trustee fees were grossly in excess of the value of the trustees' services; and there had been numerous instances of private benefit of trust assets. The Service ceased communicating with the trustees because of their conflicts of interest. Concluding that the abuse had been serious and widespread, the Service also revoked the Estate's charitable tax exemption retroactively. However, the Service advised the probate court that it would restore the Estate's exemption if certain conditions were satisfied, including the immediate resignation or removal of the trustees. The probate court thereupon ordered the removal of trustees Peters, Lindsey, Jervis, and Wong, and trustee Stender resigned. See Todd S. Purdum, For $6 Billion Hawaii Legacy, a New Day, N.Y. Times, May 15, 1999, at A1.

Once out of office, the Service assessed roughly $5 million in sanctions against each of the former trustees for having taken excess compensation, and the attorney general sued them on behalf of the charity for more than $50 million in damages. Court-appointed masters recommended that the trustees be ordered to pay millions in surcharges and to reimburse the Estate for some of its legal fees. There was widespread speculation that the justices might be sued for negligence, or worse, in their selection of the Bishop Estate trustees. Although jurists normally enjoy judicial immunity for their judicial acts in deciding cases, this immunity usually does not extend to ministerial acts, let alone private ones. Here the justices had been careful to make clear that, in appointing the trustees, they were acting as individuals and not in their judicial capacities. Hence they might have been subject to liability on a negligent hiring theory.

Aftermath. In part to satisfy the Service's conditions, the probate court established a new selection process for trustees: a panel of seven committee members, chosen by the probate court, would screen applicants and provide a short list of candidates to the court, which would then make the selection. In addition, the court ordered the trustees to turn over day-to-day control of the Estate's operations to qualified professionals; capped the trustees' fees at $97,500 ($120,000 for the chair); prohibited politicians from serving as a trustee or even serving on the screening committee; and ordered the new trustees to adopt a strict conflict of interests policy, hire an internal auditor, follow generally accepted accounting principles, develop a strategic plan, adopt new investment policies and practices, and spend an average of 4 percent of the Estate's value each year on the charitable mission.

The new trustees agreed to pay a total of $85 million in back taxes. Shortly thereafter, the attorney general, the current and former trustees, and lawyers who had represented the former trustees entered into a "global settlement" that brought an end to the litigation between them. The settlement was financed not by the individuals involved, but by a payout on a $25 million insurance policy that the former trustees had acquired years earlier using Estate funds. Under the settlement, the former trustees did not return any of their (excessive) compensation or make good on the millions of dollars in surcharges that had been assessed against them. Similarly, the lawyers for the former trustees were allowed to keep all of their fees, including fees charged for research into ways to avoid state and federal oversight by moving the trust's situs to an Indian reservation in South Dakota. All criminal charges were dropped, except that trustee Lindsey was later indicted and convicted of bankruptcy fraud. Proponents of the settlement said that it would allow the healing process to begin. Critics said it would sweep under the rug evidence of further corruption.

The new trustees have increased dramatically the amount of money spent each year, not just on Kamehameha Schools, which now have three campuses and together represent the largest independent school in the country, but also on outreach efforts. These efforts include critically important support for public charter schools in areas heavily populated by native Hawaiians. Early indications are that these charter schools and other outreach activities are having a profoundly positive impact on a large number of Hawaiian children.

For a thorough and insightful scholarly review of the foregoing events, see Symposium, The Bishop Estate Controversy, 21 U. Haw. L. Rev. 353-714 (1999). For newspaper coverage, see http://starbulletin.com/specials/bishop.html.

QUESTIONS

1. Because taxpayers in effect subsidize charities by way of federal tax deductions, the federal government penalizes inefficiently run private foundations. I.R.C. §4942 imposes substantial tax penalties on private charitable foundations (but not on publicly supported charities) that do not distribute annually income in an amount equal to 5 percent of the value of the endowment. If a foundation has a return of less than 5 percent on its endowment, to avoid taxation it must distribute principal in an amount equal to the difference between the income distributed and 5 percent of the value of the foundation's assets.

Should administrative expenses, including board member salaries, count toward the 5 percent distribution requirement? Under current law, many such administrative expenses may be counted. A recent proposal to change that rule was defeated in part because of lobbying by nonprofit organizations. See Stephanie Strom, Foundations Resist Measure to Increase Charity Money, N.Y. Times, June 13, 2003, at A23. On the other hand, on August 10, 2004, the Internal Revenue Service announced "a new enforcement effort to identify and halt abuses by tax-exempt organizations that pay excessive compensation and benefits to their officers and other insiders." I.R.S. Press Release IR-2004-106.

On the intersection of federal and state regulation of charitable trusts, see Evelyn Brody, A Taxing Time for the Bishop Estate: What Is the I.R.S. Role in Charity Governance?, 21 U. Haw. L. Rev. 537 (1999). See also Evelyn Brody, Institutional Dissonance in the Nonprofit Sector, 41 Vill. L. Rev. 433 (1996).

2. Another idea sometimes discussed is to require charities to spend down all of their funds, thereby forcing them to appeal continually for new donations. Judge Posner explains:

> Even where no unforeseen contingencies occur, perpetual charitable gifts raise an economic issue that echoes the concern with the separation of ownership and control in the modern business corporation. A charitable foundation that enjoys a substantial income, in perpetuity, from its original endowment is an institution that does not compete in any product market or in the capital markets and that has no stockholders. Its board of trustees is self-perpetuating and is accountable to no one (except itself) for the performance of the enterprise. (Although state attorneys general have legal authority over the administration of charitable trusts, it is largely formal.) At the same time, neither the trustees nor the staff have the kind of property right in the foundation's assets or income that would generate a strong incentive for them to maximize value. Neither the carrot nor the stick is in play.
>
> The incentives to efficient management of foundation assets could be strengthened by a rule requiring charitable foundations to distribute every gift received, principal and interest, including the original endowment, within a specified period of years. The foundation would not be required to wind up its operations within the period; it could continue indefinitely. But it would have to receive new gifts from time to time in order to avoid exhausting all of its funds. Since donors are unlikely to give money to an enterprise known to be slack, the necessity of returning periodically to the market for charitable donations would give trustees and managers of charitable foundations an incentive they now lack to conduct a tight operation. Foundations — mostly religious and educational — that market their services or depend on continuing charitable support, and are therefore already subject to some competitive constraints, could be exempted from the exhaustion rule.
>
> The objections to the suggested rule are that it is unnecessary — donors are already free to limit the duration of their charitable bequests — and that it might therefore (why therefore?) reduce the incentives to make charitable gifts. A counterargument is that many perpetual foundations were established at a time when the foundation was a novel institution. A person creating one at that time may not have been able to foresee the problem of inefficient and unresponsive management that might plague a perpetual foundation as a result of the peculiar set of constraints (or rather lack of

constraints) under which they operate. [Richard A. Posner, Economic Analysis of Law §18.5, at 520-521 (6th ed. 2003).]

See also George P. Blumberg, Accountability: Spend It Now! Why Some Foundations Plan Their Demise, N.Y. Times, Nov. 17, 2003, at F18 (discussing the "tiny minority" of foundations that intentionally spend themselves out of existence).

3.   The rise of great charitable trusts in the United States came after industrial growth in the late nineteenth century produced enormous fortunes. Capital in charitable trusts continued to mushroom during the twentieth century, partly, or perhaps principally, because the federal government permits gifts to charity during life to be deducted from the donor's taxable income and gifts to charity at death to be deducted from the donor's taxable estate. Today, charities own property worth billions of dollars. The Foundation Directory ix-x (2004) reports that the 10,000 largest grant-making foundations in the United States have total assets in excess of $380 billion. Of these, 8,481 have assets of at least $1 million, and 6,358 have assets totaling $5 million or more. Twenty-one have assets exceeding $2 billion each. The top ten:

(Figures in billions of dollars)

Bill and Melinda Gates Foundation	24.0
Lilly Endowment Inc.	10.1
The Ford Foundation	9.3
J. Paul Getty Trust	8.6
The Robert Wood Johnson[7] Foundation	8.0
W.K. Kellogg Foundation	5.7
The William and Flora Hewlett Foundation	5.0
The David and Lucile Packard Foundation	4.8
John D. and Catherine T. MacArthur Foundation	3.8
The Pew Charitable Trusts	3.8

To put the increase in wealth held by charities in perspective, consider that, as reported in the prior edition of this book, as of 1998 only 12 foundations had assets exceeding $2 billion. The top position in the prior edition was held by the Ford Foundation, then with $8.1 billion.

The money held by charitable foundations is only part of the story, however. These figures do not include assets of universities, museums, libraries, churches, and other charitable institutions that are not "foundations" and do not make

---

7. Robert Wood Johnson was the brother of Seward Johnson, whose fortune did not go to charity. See page 176. Interestingly, in 2001 the Robert Wood Johnson Foundation gave only 3.3 percent of its assets to charity, but it did not violate the 5 percent rule because it had enough administrative expenses to make up the difference. See Stephanie Strom, Foundations Resist Measure to Increase Charity Money, N.Y. Times, June 13, 2003, at A23.

grants. For example, as of 2003, the ten largest university endowments were as follows:

(Figures in billions of dollars)

Harvard	18.8
Yale	11.0
Princeton	8.7
University of Texas	8.7
Stanford	8.6
Massachusetts Institute of Technology	5.1
University of California	4.4
Columbia	4.4
Emory	4.0
Texas A&M	3.8

National Association of College and University Business Officers, 2003 NACUBO Endowment Study. See generally Evelyn Brody, Charitable Endowments and the Democratization of Dynasty, 39 Ariz. L. Rev. 873 (1997) (examining the "hundreds of billions of dollars in endowments and other charity reserves").

13

TRUST ADMINISTRATION:
THE FIDUCIARY OBLIGATION

> [T]he normal private trust is essentially a gift, projected on
> the plane of time and so subjected to a management regime.
>
> BERNARD RUDDEN
> *in 44 Mod. L. Rev. 610 (1981) (book review)*

SECTION A.   INTRODUCTION

A donor cannot foresee all of the problems or opportunities that her family might face after a gift is made. And if the donor makes her gift outright, she cannot be certain that the beneficiary will use the property as the donor intended. The use of a trust ameliorates these problems by interposing a trustee between the beneficiary and the property. Perhaps the beneficiary is disabled or has special needs, or is very young, or is very old, or is a profligate spender, or is likely to amass debts, or lacks skills in property management. Or perhaps the settlor wants to ensure professional management of the family fortune given the possibility that a future beneficiary might be incapable of responsibly managing property (and note also that we have not yet mentioned the various tax reasons for using trusts). The crucial point, to borrow the words of Professor Scott, is that the trust makes it "possible to separate the benefits of ownership from the burdens of ownership." 1 Austin W. Scott, Trusts §1, at 2 (William F. Fratcher 4th ed. 1987).

This virtue, however, can also be a vice, for the beneficiary, not the trustee, bears the risk and receives the rewards of the trustee's bad or good management. If the trust property is invested wisely and produces handsome returns, the beneficiary, not the trustee, reaps most of the gains. If the trust property is invested poorly or is stolen by the trustee or others, the beneficiary, not the trustee, suffers the immediate consequences of the depletion in the trust fund. Putting aside reputational concerns and feelings of moral obligation (which is not to say that these considerations are unimportant), the problem is that trustee lacks a direct financial incentive to act with loyalty and care in managing the trust fund. The primary doctrinal answer to this problem, which is the focus of this chapter, is the *fiduciary obligation*. The fiduciary obligation in trust law comprises duties of *loyalty*, *prudence*, and a host of *subsidiary rules* that reinforce the duties of loyalty and prudence.

John H. Langbein, The Contractarian Basis of the Law of Trusts
105 Yale L.J. 625, 632-633, 637-638,
640-642, 655-657, 660-661 (1995)

Inserting a trustee between the beneficiary and the donative interest is manifestly clumsy and costly. The donor who structures a gift in this way expects compensating advantages. . . .

The trust developed at the end of the Middle Ages, an epoch in which real estate was the principal form of wealth. The primary purpose of the trust was to facilitate the transfer of freehold land within the family. The law governing the transmission of freehold land was deeply afflicted by feudal restrictions meant originally to concentrate landholdings for military and related advantages. Long after the feudal system lapsed, burdensome feudal landholding rules endured. Particularly resented were (1) the rule requiring that freehold land pass by descent rather than by will, hence that land was not devisable; (2) the rigid shares of primogeniture and dower; and (3) the bizarre fiscal exactions, called wardship and marriage, that functioned as penal transfer taxes on minors. . . .

Transferring land to trustees neatly defeated the feudal restrictions. Suppose the prototypical case, in which the settlor conveyed freehold land to trustees, who agreed to hold the land for the settlor for life and then to convey to selected family members as the remainder beneficiaries. Because the trustees were the nominal owners of the freehold, when the settlor died none of the feudal rules that turned on descent were triggered. The trustees continued to own the land, and they would then convey it to the remainder beneficiaries as they had undertaken.

The trustees of these early trusts were mere stakeholders, little more than nominees, with no serious powers or responsibilities of management. Commonly, the beneficiaries lived on the land and managed it. In the example I have given, the trustees' only significant duty was to hold until the settlor's death, and then to put themselves out of business by conveying the freehold to the remainder beneficiaries.

Long into the nineteenth century, the trust remained primarily a branch of the law of conveyancing. The trust was a means of transferring and holding title to real estate. . . . The modern law of fiduciary administration is simply not detectable [in the early treatises on trusts]. . . .

The feudal restrictions on the transfer of real property that gave rise to the conveyancing-type trust disappeared piecemeal from the late seventeenth to the early twentieth centuries. Although feudal land law no longer needs evading, the trust has endured because it has changed function. The trust has ceased to be a conveyancing device for holding freehold land and has become instead a management device for holding financial assets. . . .

Modern wealth takes the form of financial assets — for example, stocks, bonds, mutual fund shares, insurance and annuity contracts, pension plans, and bank deposits. The modern trust typically holds a portfolio of these complex financial assets, which are contract rights against the issuers. This portfolio requires active and specialized management, in contrast to the conveyancing trust that merely held ancestral land.

Modern forms of wealth allow the settlor to devolve more options on the trustee in the dispositive provisions of trusts, that is, in allocating and distributing beneficial interests. By comparison with the interests possible in a trust of ancestral land, the modern trust fund invites greater flexibility to accumulate, distribute, or spend trust funds on behalf of beneficiaries. . . .

The trust relationship of necessity puts the beneficiaries of a trust at the peril of the trustees' misbehavior — for example, if the trustees should misappropriate or mismanage the trust's assets. The central concern of modern trust law is to safeguard against those dangers.

The changed character of trust assets has brought about a significant change in the way trust law protects beneficiaries. An older scheme devoted to restricting trustees' powers has yielded to the surprisingly modern set of rules that trust lawyers call the law of fiduciary administration. . . . [T]he substitution of fiduciary law for law restricting the powers of the trustee is a central event in the development of modern trust law . . . .

In the first centuries of the trust, when trustees were mostly stakeholders for ancestral land, they were kept tightly in check by being disabled from doing much with the trust property. The default law supplied no trustees' powers. The trustees had only those powers that the trust instrument expressly granted, which were typically few, since the trustees' job was simply to hold and then to convey to the remainderpersons. Stakeholder trustees did not need to transact. Joseph Story summarized the law for Americans in his treatise on Equity Jurisprudence in 1836: "[T]he trustee has no right (unless express power is given) to change the nature of the estate, as by converting land into money, or money into land."

Indeed, the modern trustee still needs to look to the trust instrument or to remedial trustees' powers legislation for empowerment. "In the absence of legislation, a trustee has no power whatever by virtue of his office; his only powers are those expressly or impliedly conferred upon him by the terms of the trust."

The need for active administration of the modern trust portfolio of financial assets rendered obsolete this scheme of disempowering the trustee to transact with the trust property. The modern trustee conducts a program of investing and managing the assets that requires extensive discretion to respond to changing market forces.

A strategy of maximum empowerment displaced the former law, initially in professionally drafted trust instruments, and then in modern systems of default law such as the Uniform Trustees' Powers Act. These statutes empower trustees to engage in every conceivable transaction that might wrest market advantage or enhance the value of trust assets. . . .

Empowering the trustee to transact freely in the financial markets has shifted the locus of protection for beneficiaries from powers law to fiduciary law. Whereas disempowerment prevented the trustee from acting, modern trustees' powers law confers vast managerial discretion. Discretion entails the risk of harm as well as the opportunity to enhance the trust assets. To safeguard beneficiaries against abuse of this discretion, trust fiduciary law has developed as the functional replacement for the former scheme of trustee disability. Fiduciary law imposes two broad standards, loyalty and care, that regulate the exercise of the discretion that modern trustees' powers law bestows. . . .

The law of fiduciary administration . . . resolves into two great principles, the duties of loyalty and prudence. . . . The loyalty norm forbids the trustee from self-dealing with trust assets and from engaging in conflict-of-interest transactions adverse to the trust. . . . The duty of prudent administration is a reasonableness norm, comparable to the reasonable person rule of tort. . . . Subrules of fiduciary administration abound — for example, the duties to keep and render accounts, to furnish information, to invest or preserve trust assets and make them productive, to enforce and defend claims, to diversify investments, and to minimize costs. . . .

Trust fiduciary law regulates the trustee's exercise of discretion. Be it in trust law or in other fields of fiduciary obligation (for example, corporations, agency, or partnership), fiduciary duties are default norms imposed in juridical relations that feature "scope for the exercise of discretion." Fiduciary duties mean to "induce the fiduciary to use his power beneficently."

This combination of broad discretion in the trustee, coupled with fiduciary norms to protect the beneficiary against abuse of discretion, is a second-best solution to the problem of enforcing the trust deal. Ideally, as Cooter and Freedman observe, the deal between settlor and trustee would contain "specific rules that dictate how the fiduciary should manage the asset in the beneficiary's best interests." Alas, "the fiduciary's obligations are openended. Because asset management necessarily involves risk and uncertainty, the specific behavior of the fiduciary cannot be dictated in advance."[1] Easterbrook and Fischel observe in a similar vein that "the duty of loyalty is a response to the impossibility of writing contracts completely specifying the parties' obligations."[2]

Loyalty and prudence, the norms of trust fiduciary law, embody . . . criteria for regulating the trustee's behavior in these settings in which it is impractical to foresee precise circumstances and to specify more exact terms. . . .

I have emphasized that the modern trust is preeminently a management device for separating ownership and enjoyment; the trust deal sets the terms under which the trustee administers and applies the assets.

Unless modified or ousted, several blocks of trust default law define this relationship. Trustees' powers legislation authorizes transacting, fiduciary law regulates the purposes and standards of transacting. The default managerial regime also sets trustee compensation.

On all these matters the default regime impounds the experience of decades of trust practice, legislation, and case law. The transaction planner who invokes the default regime is spared the difficulty, uncertainty, and expense of attempting to design afresh a management regime capable of anticipating the imponderables that the future holds in store for the trust beneficiaries and the trust assets.

NOTE: AGENCY COSTS AND THE FIDUCIARY OBLIGATION

Safeguarding the beneficiary against mismanagement or misappropriation by the trustee presents what the law-and-economics literature calls a *principal-agent* or

---

1. Robert Cooter & Bradley J. Freedman, The Fiduciary Relationship: Its Economic Character and Legal Consequences, 66 N.Y.U.L. Rev. 1045 (1991). — Eds.
2. Frank H. Easterbrook & Daniel R. Fischel, Contract and Fiduciary Duty, 36 J.L. & Econ. 425 (1993). — Eds.

agency problem. Agency problems are not limited to relationships that are governed by the common law of agency. For example, suppose a real estate agent is working on a 5 percent commission. Such an agent will have no specific financial incentive (though, to be sure, she might have a reputational incentive or feel a moral obligation) to undertake even $10 of additional effort to increase the sale price by $100 because the payoff to the agent of doing so is only $5 (5 percent of $100). However, this $10 investment would have been worthwhile from the perspective of the homeowner because the payoff on the $10 investment is $100. See Frank H. Easterbrook & Daniel R. Fischel, The Economic Structure of Corporate Law 91 (1991). In this example, the property owner is the *principal*, the real estate agent is the *agent*, and the net loss is an *agency cost*.

Agency problems arise whenever the principal cannot spell out in advance what the agent should do in all possible future scenarios or, even if the agent's tasks can be spelled out with specificity, the principal cannot effectively monitor or supervise the agent. Agency problems are endemic in market economies because no one has the time and necessary skills to do everything for themselves.

The application of *agency theory* to law is perhaps most fully developed in the study of corporations. There the model is of shareholders as principals and managers as agents. On this account, much of the law of corporate governance can be understood as an attempt to minimize agency costs in the shareholder/manager relationship. Among the arsenal of agency-cost minimizing weapons in corporate law and practice are (1) the shareholders' right to vote on the composition of the board of directors, (2) the corporate fiduciary obligation, and (3) the corporate takeover market.

Agency costs are likewise a problem in trust governance. Both the condition of financial markets and the needs of the beneficiary will vary over time. It is therefore impractical for the settlor and the trustee to include in the trust instrument a detailed specification of precisely what the trustee should do in all possible future scenarios. Enter the fiduciary obligation:

> The fiduciary principle is an alternative to direct monitoring. It replaces prior supervision with deterrence, much as the criminal law uses penalties for bank robbery rather than pat-down searches of everyone entering banks. Acting as a standard-form penalty clause in every agency contract, the elastic contours of the fiduciary principle reflect the difficulty that contracting parties have in anticipating when and how their interests may diverge. [Frank H. Easterbrook & Daniel R. Fischel, Corporate Control Transactions, 91 Yale L.J. 698, 702 (1982).]

Because of the need for flexibility, modern trust law gives the trustee broad powers, leaving it instead to the fiduciary obligation to police the trustee's exercise of those powers through the threat of after-the-fact liability.

Unlike the corporate fiduciary obligation, however, the fiduciary obligation in trust law is not backstopped by the beneficiary's ability to replace the trustee easily (on trustee removal, see page 585) or by unfettered freedom to sell her beneficial interest (on spendthrift and other disabling restraints, see page 547). Hence the fiduciary obligation in trust law is the primary tool for minimizing agency costs in trust governance. Accordingly, courts often apply the fiduciary obligation in trust law with greater vigor than in corporate law. See Robert H. Sitkoff, Trust Law, Corporate Law, and Capital Market Efficiency, 28 J. Corp. L. 565 (2003) (comparing trust and corporate fiduciary law); Stegemeier v. Magness, 728 A.2d 557, 562-565 (Del. 1999) (noting "the stricter standards of trust law").

An important challenge in applying agency theory to trust law is ascertaining the identity of the principal. Thus far we have been speaking of the trustee's fiduciary obligation to the beneficiary. This is consistent with traditional doctrine. In an irrevocable trust, only the beneficiary has standing to bring suit against the trustee for breach of duty.[3] See Restatement (Second) of Trusts §200 (1959); 3 Austin W. Scott, Trusts §§200-200.1, at 207-212 (William F. Fratcher 4th ed. 1988). But the private trust created gratuitously for the benefit of one or more beneficiaries is a vehicle for effecting the settlor's donative intent. Thus, should not the settlor also be viewed as a principal? The answer is Yes. In many respects American trust law regards the settlor as the primary principal. Consider that the beneficiary cannot easily remove the trustee, modify or terminate the trust, or sell her beneficial interest. On each of those questions, American trust law respects the settlor's intent to subject the beneficiary's gift to the trust. See Robert H. Sitkoff, An Agency Costs Theory of Trust Law, 89 Cornell L. Rev. 621 (2004). As Professor Halbach has observed, the "theme" of modern trust law "is flexibility and efficiency in the pursuit of the best interests of the trust beneficiaries within the settlor's legally permissible objectives." Edward C. Halbach, Jr., Uniform Acts, Restatements, and Trends in American Trust Law at Century's End, 88 Cal. L. Rev. 1877, 1881 (2000).

For more on the application of agency theory to trust law, see also Jonathan R. Macey, Private Trusts for the Provision of Private Goods, 37 Emory L.J. 295 (1988); A.I. Ogus, The Trust as Governance Structure, 36 U. Toronto L.J. 186 (1986).

NOTES AND QUESTION

1. *What of morality?* Economics is hardly the only mode of analysis for throwing light on the nature and function of the fiduciary obligation. Even a fleeting examination of the cases reveals that they are rife with the language of morality and fairness — not economics. Perhaps the most famous example is the passage in Meinhard v. Salmon, 164 N.E. 545 (N.Y. 1928), in which Judge Cardozo wrote:

> Many forms of conduct permissible in a work-a-day world for those acting at arms length, are forbidden to those bound by fiduciary ties. A trustee is held to something stricter than the morals of the market place. Not honesty alone, but the punctilio of an honor the most sensitive, is then the standard of behavior. As to this there has developed a tradition that is unbending and inveterate. Uncompromising rigidity has been the attitude of courts of equity when petitioned to undermine the rule of undivided loyalty by the "disintegrating erosion" of particular exceptions. . . . Only thus has the level of conduct for fiduciaries been kept at a level higher than that trodden by the crowd. It will not consciously be lowered by any judgment of this court. [164 N.E. at 546.]

---

3. In recent years there has been mild erosion of this limitation in the context of donor standing to enforce charitable trusts (see Smithers v. St. Luke's-Roosevelt Hospital Center, page 760) and donor standing to seek removal of the trustee (see Uniform Trust Code §706, page 585).

Is this conception of the fiduciary obligation inconsistent with an agency theory of fiduciary duties?

2. There is a surfeit of scholarship that analyzes the fiduciary obligation from a variety of perspectives including, but not limited to, principles of morality and economics. For a sampling, see Gregory S. Alexander, A Cognitive Theory of Fiduciary Relationships, 85 Cornell L. Rev. 767 (2000); Henry N. Butler & Larry E. Ribstein, Opting Out of Fiduciary Duties: A Response to the Anti-Contractarians, 65 Wash. L. Rev. 1 (1990); Robert Cooter & Bradley J. Freedman, The Fiduciary Relationship: Its Economic Character and Legal Consequences, 68 N.Y.U.L. Rev. 1045 (1991); Deborah A. DeMott, Beyond Metaphor: An Analysis of Fiduciary Obligation, 1988 Duke L.J. 879; Frank H. Easterbrook & Daniel R. Fischel, Contract and Fiduciary Duty, 36 J.L. & Econ. 425 (1993); Tamar Frankel, Fiduciary Duties as Default Rules, 74 Or. L. Rev. 1209 (1995); Tamar Frankel, Fiduciary Law, 71 Cal. L. Rev. 795 (1983); L.S. Sealy, Fiduciary Relationships, 1962 Cambridge L.J. 69; J.C. Shepherd, Towards a Unified Concept of Fiduciary Relationships, 97 L.Q. Rev. 51 (1981); D. Gordon Smith, The Critical Resource Theory of Fiduciary Duty, 55 Vand. L. Rev. 1399 (2002); Ernest J. Weinrib, The Fiduciary Obligation, 25 U. Toronto L.J. 1 (1975).

3. For discussion of considerations relevant to choosing between an amateur trustee (such as a friend or relative) and a professional trustee (such as a bank or trust company), see page 491-493. That discussion also includes a summary of the law of trustee compensation and the three functions of modern trusteeship: *administration*, *distribution*, and *investment*.

NOTE: POWERS OF THE TRUSTEE

In the absence of legislation, the administrative powers of a trustee are derived exclusively from the instrument creating the trust. There are supposedly no "inherent" powers in a trustee; in this regard the trustee differs from the executor, who has inherent powers to collect the decedent's property, pay debts, and distribute the property to the beneficiaries. The task of a trustee is to carry out the settlor's intent, which varies from trust to trust.

Having in mind the uncertainty of trustees' powers, legislatures in a large majority of states enacted legislation to broaden trustees' powers. This legislation has usually taken one of two forms:

(a) An act that permits the settlor to *incorporate by express reference* in the trust instrument all or some enumerated statutory powers. This permits a trust drafter to omit a long and detailed list of trustee powers, incorporating the statutory powers instead.

(b) A broad trustees' powers act that *grants to trustees basic powers* set forth in the statute, as exemplified by the Uniform Trustees' Powers Act §3(c) (1964). Express incorporation of statutory powers in the trust instrument is unnecessary under this type of statute.

Uniform Trust Code (UTC) §815 (2000) takes the strategy of empowering the trustee to its logical conclusion. In addition to the "powers conferred by the terms of the trust," §815 authorizes the trustee to exercise "all powers over the trust property which an unmarried competent owner has over individually owned property" and "any other powers appropriate to achieve the proper investment, management, and distribution of the trust property." The official comment states that §815 "is intended to grant trustees the broadest possible powers."

QUESTIONS

1. UTC §816 enumerates more than two dozen specific transactional powers, including the power to "acquire or sell property," to "deposit trust money in an account in a regulated financial-service institution," to "pay or contest any claim," and to "sign and deliver contracts." In a jurisdiction that has adopted §815, is the detailed enumeration of powers in §816 an unnecessary redundancy? See UTC §816 cmt.

2. Regardless of the breadth of the local powers statute, it is almost always advisable to include a detailed schedule of powers when drafting a trust. For an illustration, see pages 124-125. Do you see why?

The common law required third persons dealing with a trustee to inquire into whether the trustee had authority to engage in the transaction. UTC §1012, which is based on §7 of the Uniform Trustees' Powers Act that it supercedes, eliminates this duty, replacing it with a duty to act in good faith. "A person . . . who in good faith deals with a trustee is not required to inquire into the extent of the trustee's powers or the propriety of their exercise." UTC §1012(b). The reason is to facilitate administrative efficiency in transferring trust property. For eliminating the duty of inquiry, UTPA §7, the predecessor to UTC §1012, is criticized in Peter T. Wendel, Examining the Mystery Behind the Unusually and Inexplicably Broad Provisions of Section Seven of the Uniform Trustees' Powers Act: A Call for Clarification, 56 Mo. L. Rev. 25 (1991). The newer language of UTC §1012, which makes explicit the requirement that the third party must be acting in good faith to fall within its protections, is defended in David M. English, The Uniform Trust Code (2000): Significant Provisions and Policy Issues, 67 Mo. L. Rev. 143, 208-211 (2002).

PROBLEMS

1. *T* devises Blackacre to *X* in trust with power to sell Blackacre if *X* decides that such sale is necessary to raise money for the support of *A*. *X* sells Blackacre to *B*, who has notice of the trust (*T*'s will is recorded) but believes that the sale is necessary for the support of *A*, although in fact it is not necessary. Does *B* take Blackacre free of trust? See Restatement (Second) of Trusts §297, illus. 4 (1959). Would the result be different if the trust were an inter vivos trust of which *B* had no notice?

2. *X*, as trustee, has no power to invest in non-income-producing property. *X* buys from *A* desert land, which produces no income. Must *A* refund the purchase price upon demand of the beneficiary? See 4 Austin W. Scott, Trusts §321.1 (William F. Fratcher 4th ed. 1988).

SECTION B.   THE DUTY OF LOYALTY

Although the modern trustee has broad powers, the exercise of those powers is regulated by the fiduciary obligation. The most fundamental principle of the fiduciary obligation is the duty of undivided *loyalty* to the beneficiaries: The trustee must administer the trust solely in the interest of the beneficiaries.

Hartman v. Hartle
New Jersey Court of Chancery, 1923
95 N.J. Eq. 123, 122 A. 615

FOSTER, V.C.   Mrs. Dorothea Geick died testate on April 8, 1921, leaving five children, one of them being the complainant. She named her two sons-in-law executors, and they qualified. Among other matters the will expressly directed her executors to sell her real estate and to divide the proceeds equally among her children.

On February 9, 1922, the executors sold part of the real estate known as the Farm, at public auction, for $3,900 to one of testatrix' sons, Lewis Geick, who actually bought the property for his sister, Josephine Dieker, who is the wife of one of the executors.

On April 11, 1922, Mrs. Dieker sold the property to the defendant Mike Contra (and another, who is not a party to the action) for $5,500, part cash and part on mortgage.

The executors settled their final accounts on April 21, 1922, and at or about that time complainant expressed to the deputy surrogate her dissatisfaction with the price realized from the sale of the farm. About March 21, 1923, she filed her bill in this cause charging the sale of the farm to have been improperly and fraudulently made by the executors to Mrs. Dieker, and further charging that Mrs. Dieker and the other heirs of the testatrix had agreed at sale, because of slow bidding and inadequate price, to have the farm bid in for the benefit of all the heirs.

At the hearing each and every one of these allegations were shown to be untrue by the great weight of the testimony; and this proof was so conclusive that it left complainant with but one contention to sustain her case, viz. that under the law the sale of the property by the executors and trustee to Mrs. Dieker, the wife of one of them, without previous authority from the court, was illegal and void, and that it should be set aside and the farm resold, or, if that be found impossible because of the sale made by Mrs. Dieker to Contra, an innocent purchaser, then that complainant should have paid to her one-fifth of the $1,600 profits realized by Mrs. Dieker from the sale of the property.

It is the settled law of this state that a trustee cannot purchase from himself at his own sale, and that his wife is subject to the same disability, unless leave so to do has been previously obtained under an order of the court. Scott v. Gamble, 9 N.J. Eq. 218 (1852). Bassett v. Shoemaker, 20 A. 52 (N.J. App. 1890); Bechtold v. Read, 22 A. 1085 (N.J. Ch. 1891). And under the circumstances of the case complainant cannot be charged with laches under the view expressed in Bechtold v. Read, supra.

In view of the fact that the property is now owned by innocent purchasers, a resale cannot be ordered, but, as an alternative, Mrs. Dieker and the executors will be held to account for complainant's one-fifth share of the profits made on the resale of the property under the authority of Marshall v. Carson, 38 N.J. Eq. 250 (1884), and a decree will be advised to that effect.

IN RE GLEESON'S WILL, 124 N.E.2d 624 (Ill. App. 1955): On March 1, 1950, Mary Gleeson leased 160 acres of farm land to Con Colbrook for one year. On March 1, 1951, Gleeson and Colbrook renewed the lease for another year. On February 14, 1952, just two weeks before the second lease was to expire, Gleeson died. In her will, Gleeson devised the land to Colbrook, as trustee, for the benefit of her three children. After Gleeson's death, with the expiration of the second lease imminent, Colbrook remained on the land for another year, until March 1, 1953, though he increased his rent payments from $6 per acre to $10 per acre plus a share of the crops. After the holdover year, he leased the land to another tenant. At issue was whether Colbrook breached his duty of loyalty by holding over from March 1, 1952, until March 1, 1953.

> The Courts of this state have consistently followed a general principle of equity that a trustee cannot deal in his individual capacity with the trust property. . . .
>
> Petitioner [Colbrook] recognizes the existence of this general rule, but argues that because of the existence of the peculiar circumstances under which the petitioner proceeded, the instant case must be taken to constitute one of the rare exceptions to such rule. The circumstances alluded to as peculiar are pointed out as being the facts that the death of Mrs. Gleeson occurred on February 14, 1952, only 15 days prior to the beginning of the 1952 farm year; that satisfactory farm tenants are not always available, especially on short notice; that the petitioner had in the preceding fall of 1951 sown part of the 160 acres in wheat to be harvested in 1952; that the holding over by the trustee and his partner was in the best interests of the trust; that the same was done in an open manner; that the petitioner was honest with the trust; and that it suffered no loss as a result of the transaction. . . .

The court was unimpressed with this argument:

> The good faith and honesty of the petitioner or the fact that the trust sustained no loss on account of his dealings therewith are all matters which can avail petitioner nothing so far as a justification of the course he chose to take in dealing with trust property is concerned.

Colbrook "should have . . . decided whether he chose to continue as a tenant or to act as trustee." The duty of loyalty proscribed his doing both. Accordingly, the court ordered Colbrook to account "for all monies received by him personally as a profit by virtue of his" holdover tenancy on the land "during the 1952 crop year, and to pay the amount of any such profit to the trust."

NOTES AND QUESTIONS

1. *Self-dealing.* If the trustee engages in self-dealing, good faith and fairness to the beneficiaries are not enough to save the trustee from liability. In such a case, *no*

further inquiry is made; the trustee's good faith and the reasonableness of the transaction are irrelevant. The beneficiaries can hold the trustee accountable for any profit made on the transaction, or, if the trustee has bought trust property, can compel the trustee to restore the property to the trust, or, if the trustee has sold his own property to the trust, can compel the trustee to repay the purchase price and take back the property. The only defenses the trustee has to self-dealing are that the settlor authorized the self-dealing transaction or that the beneficiaries consented to it after full disclosure. See Restatement (Second) of Trusts §§170(1) cmt. t, 216(1) (1959). Even then, the trustee must have acted in good faith and the self-dealing transaction must be objectively fair and reasonable. See id. §§170(2) cmt. t, 216(3). These rules are designed in part to channel the trustee toward seeking advance judicial approval for any self-dealing transaction. See id. §170(1) cmt. f.

2.   In Robert Cooter & Bradley J. Freedman, The Fiduciary Relationship: Its Economic Character and Legal Consequences, 68 N.Y.U.L. Rev. 1045 (1991), the authors make an economic analysis of the no-further-inquiry rule. Drawing on agency theory, they frame the problem as follows: "How can one party be induced to do what is best for another without specifying exactly what is to be done?" The no-further-inquiry rule, they contend, uses self-interest to compel the trustee to do what is best for the beneficiary. Because appropriation of the trust property is both very profitable for the fiduciary and often difficult for the beneficiary to detect, the authors believe that the law appropriately infers disloyalty from self-dealing. Cooter and Freedman would increase the sanction for self-dealing to include punitive damages to offset the reduced probability of detection.

But is it not possible that some self-dealing transactions would have been advantageous for the beneficiaries? If so, then the absolute nature of the no-further-inquiry rule prevents some desirable transactions. Professor Sitkoff replies that the no-further-inquiry rule may be justifiable nonetheless if, on balance, "these deals are so frequently undesirable that the costs of extirpating the entire class of transaction (a *rule*) are less than the costs of case-by-case adjudication (the fairness *standard*)." Robert H. Sitkoff, Trust Law, Corporate Law, and Capital Market Efficiency, 28 J. Corp. L. 565, 673-674 (2003). This mode of reasoning is not new. See George G. Bogert & George T. Bogert, The Law of Trusts and Trustees §543, at 228 (2d rev. ed. 1993): "[E]quity deems it better to . . . strike down all disloyal acts, rather than to attempt to separate the harmless and the harmful by permitting the trustee to justify his representation of two interests."

3.   *Categorical exceptions.* The sole benefit rule and its enforcement through the no-further-inquiry principle are no longer absolute. In the twentieth century, legislative and judicial exceptions developed. Many reflect the increasing frequency of institutional trusteeship. For example, statutes in most states allow a bank that serves as a trustee to deposit the trust assets with its own banking department. Likewise, statutes in most states allow an institutional trustee to invest the trust assets in a common trust fund or in a mutual fund that it operates. Both exceptions are designed to avoid the diseconomies that would result if the trustee were required to engage another entity in order to undertake the trust's banking and investing. In yet another exception, the trustee is entitled to reasonable compensation for serving as such even though, strictly speaking, by compensating herself the trustee

is engaged in self-dealing. For a codification of these exceptions, see UTC §802(f) & (h) (2000).

Taking note of the proliferation of categorical exceptions, and taking his cue from the application of the duty of loyalty in corporate and other fiduciary settings in which the duty is not absolute, in a provocative new article Professor Langbein suggests that the no-further-inquiry rule does more harm than good. See John H. Langbein, Questioning the Trust Law Duty of Loyalty: Sole Interest or Best Interest?, 114 Yale L.J. 929 (2005). Langbein argues that a transaction in which there has been conflict or overlap of interest should be sustained if the trustee can prove that the transaction was prudently undertaken in the best interest of the beneficiaries. Which is a better governance strategy, a best interests standard in all cases with the burden on the trustee, or a prohibition subject to a growing list of exceptions?

4.   The court in *Hartman* treated the trustee's sale of trust property to the trust-ee's spouse as self-dealing subject to the no-further-inquiry rule just as if the trustee had sold the property to himself. This is a common result in the cases. Should the same rule apply if the sale were to the trustee's lawyer or other agent? Some cases hold in the affirmative on the theory that the "attorney for a fiduciary has the same duty of undivided loyalty to the [beneficiary] as the fiduciary himself." In re Clarke's Estate, 188 N.E.2d 128, 130 (N.Y. 1962). See also Estate of Halas, 512 N.E.2d 1276, 1280 (Ill. App. 1987). For an interesting discussion from the practitioner's perspective of whether the trustee's lawyer owes the beneficiary the same fiduciary obligation as the trustee, see Marilyn G. Ordover & Charles F. Gibbs, Duty of Fiduciary's Attorney to Beneficiaries, N.Y.L.J., Feb. 28, 2000, at 3.

Although the common law duty of loyalty is largely codified in UTC §802 (2000), under subsection (c) a transaction by the trustee with a close relative or his lawyer is presumptively voidable, not absolutely forbidden. Under this provision, the trustee can escape from liability if he can show that the transaction was objectively fair and reasonable, and not affected by the conflict. For a thorough study of the duty of loyalty and the UTC, see Karen E. Boxx, Of Punctillios and Paybacks: The Duty of Loyalty under the Uniform Trust Code, 67 Mo. L. Rev. 279 (2002).

5.   *Trust pursuit rule.* One of the remedies afforded in equity for a breach of trust is known as the "trust pursuit rule." If the trustee, in wrongfully disposing of trust property, acquires other property, the beneficiary is entitled to enforce a constructive trust on the property so acquired, treating it as part of the trust assets. Restatement (Second) of Trusts §202 (1959). The trust pursuit rule also is applied where the property ends up in the hands of a third person, unless the third person is a bona fide purchaser for value and without notice of the breach of trust. Id. §284(1).

If the trustee in breach of trust transfers trust property to a person who takes with notice of the breach of trust, the transferee does not hold the property free of the trust, although he paid value for the transfer. Id. §288. Likewise, if the trustee in breach of trust transfers trust property and no value is given for the transfer, the transferee does not hold the property free of the trust, although he had no notice of the trust. Id. §289.

In re Rothko

Court of Appeals of New York, 1977
43 N.Y.2d 305, 372 N.E.2d 291, 401 N.Y.S.2d 449

COOKE, J. Mark Rothko, an abstract expressionist painter whose works through the years gained for him an international reputation of greatness, died testate on February 25, 1970. The principal asset of his estate consisted of 798 paintings of tremendous value, and the dispute underlying this appeal involves the conduct of his three executors in their disposition of these works of art.[4] In sum, that conduct as portrayed in the record and sketched in the opinions was manifestly wrongful and indeed shocking.

Rothko's will was admitted to probate on April 27, 1970 and letters testamentary were issued to Bernard J. Reis, Theodoros Stamos and Morton Levine.[5] Hastily and within a period of only about three weeks and by virtue of two contracts each dated May 21, 1970, the executors dealt with all 798 paintings.

By a contract of sale, the estate executors agreed to sell to Marlborough A.G., a Liechtenstein corporation (hereinafter MAG), 100 Rothko paintings as listed for $1,800,000, $200,000 to be paid on execution of the agreement and the balance of $1,600,000 in 12 equal interest-free installments over a 12-year period. Under the second agreement, the executors consigned to Marlborough Gallery, Inc., a domestic corporation (hereinafter MNY), "approximately 700 paintings listed on a Schedule to be prepared," the consignee to be responsible for costs covering items such as insurance, storage, restoration and promotion. By its provisos, MNY could sell up to 35 paintings a year from each of two groups, pre-1947 and post-1947, for 12 years at the best price obtainable but not less than the appraised estate value, and that it would receive a 50 percent commission on each painting sold, except for a commission of 40 percent on those sold to or through other dealers.

---

4. Personal representatives, executors, and administrators are held to the same fiduciary standards as trustees. See Uniform Probate Code §§3-703, 3-712 (1990). — Eds.

5. The executors were three of Rothko's most intimate companions during his last years. Bernard J. Reis, a certified public accountant who had graduated from law school but had not been licensed to practice law, had acted for years as Rothko's business and professional advisor and confidant. Reis drafted Rothko's will.

Theodoros Stamos was a fellow artist in whose family plot Rothko was buried. Stamos entered into a personal contract with Marlborough Gallery, Inc., on January 1, 1971, whereby Marlborough became Stamos's exclusive art dealer agent for four years at a commission of 50 percent. The Surrogate found "Executor Levine stated, and the court finds, that in a conversation in April, 1970, before the execution of the questioned agreements, executor Stamos related that Marlborough had evidenced interest in his paintings. The conversation led Levine to believe that Stamos was interested in entering into some contractual arrangement with Marlborough which indicated a conflict of interest on the part of Stamos. Levine testified that when he confronted Stamos with the impropriety of such motivation angry exchanges followed." In re Rothko, 379 N.Y.S.2d 923, 940 (Sur. 1975).

Morton Levine, professor of anthropology at Fordham University, was chosen by Rothko to act as guardian of his two children. Kate Rothko came of age soon after her father's death and, at her insistence, Levine was removed as guardian of Christopher Rothko. "It is recognized that Levine was neither an art expert nor an experienced fiduciary but he was an educated man who, despite his educational background and his position as a college professor, failed to exercise ordinary prudence in his performance of fiduciary obligations which he assumed. Levine's argument at best is a statement that he undertook a responsibility which he was unqualified to handle." Id. at 942.

On the Rothko litigation, see Lee Seldes, The Legacy of Mark Rothko (1979). — Eds.

Petitioner Kate Rothko, decedent's daughter and a person entitled to share in his estate by virtue of an election under EPTL §5-3.3,[6] instituted this proceeding to remove the executors, to enjoin MNY and MAG from disposing of the paintings, to rescind the aforesaid agreements between the executors and said corporations, for a return of the paintings still in possession of those corporations, and for damages. She was joined by the guardian of her brother Christopher Rothko, likewise interested in the estate, who answered by adopting the allegations of his sister's petition and by demanding the same relief. The Attorney General of the State, as the representative of the ultimate beneficiaries of the Mark Rothko Foundation, Inc., a charitable corporation and the residuary legatee under decedent's will, joined in requesting relief substantially similar to that prayed for by petitioner. . . .

Following a nonjury trial covering 89 days and in a thorough opinion, the Surrogate found: that Reis was a director, secretary and treasurer of MNY, the consignee art gallery, in addition to being a coexecutor of the estate; that the testator had a 1969 inter vivos contract with MNY to sell Rothko's work at a commission of only 10 percent and whether that agreement survived testator's death was a problem that a fiduciary in a dual position could not have impartially faced; that Reis was in a position of serious conflict of interest with respect to the contracts of May 21, 1970 and that his dual role and planned purpose benefited the Marlborough interests to the detriment of the estate; that it was to the advantage of coexecutor Stamos as a "not-too-successful artist, financially," to curry favor with Marlborough and that the contract made by him with MNY within months after signing the estate contracts placed him in a position where his personal interests conflicted with those of the estate, especially leading to lax contract enforcement efforts by Stamos; that Stamos acted negligently and improvidently in view of his own knowledge of the conflict of interest of Reis; that the third coexecutor, Levine, while not acting in self-interest or with bad faith, nonetheless failed to exercise ordinary prudence in the performance of his assumed fiduciary obligations since he was aware of Reis' divided loyalty, believed that Stamos was also seeking personal advantage, possessed personal opinions as to the value of the paintings and yet followed the leadership of his coexecutors without investigation of essential facts or consultation with competent and disinterested appraisers, and that the business transactions of the two Marlborough corporations were admittedly controlled and directed by Francis K. Lloyd. It was concluded that the acts and failures of the three executors were clearly improper to such a substantial extent as to mandate their removal . . . as estate fiduciaries. The Surrogate also found that MNY, MAG and Lloyd were guilty of contempt in shipping, disposing

---

6. Mark Rothko devised his residuary estate to the Mark Rothko Foundation, a charitable corporation, with Reis, Stamos, and Levine named as directors of the foundation. N.Y. Est., Powers & Trusts Law §5-3.3 (1967) provided that a child of a testator may set aside a testamentary disposition to charity to the extent it exceeds one-half of the testator's estate. Kate Rothko set aside the charitable gift in the amount permitted, with the result that one-half of the residuary gift passed to Rothko's heirs. Kate Rothko — who otherwise was left nothing by Mark Rothko's will — thus obtained an interest in her father's estate and had standing to attack the action of the executors.

N.Y. Est., Powers & Trusts Law §5-3.3 was repealed in 1981 (see Note 7 at page 736). Thus, if Rothko had died after 1981, under traditional principles only the Mark Rothko Foundation and the state attorney general, the overseer of charitable trusts, would have had standing to sue the executors. After Smithers v. St. Luke's-Roosevelt Hospital Center, page 751, however, it is an open question whether this is still true in New York. — Eds.

Mark Rothko
Number 22 (1969)
Collection, The Museum of Modern Art, New York

of and selling 57 paintings in violation of the temporary restraining order dated June 26, 1972 and of the injunction dated September 26, 1972; that the contracts for sale and consignment of paintings between the executors and MNY and MAG provided inadequate value to the estate, amounting to a lack of mutuality and fairness resulting from conflicts on the part of Reis and Stamos and improvidence on the part of all executors; that said contracts were voidable and were set aside by reason of violation of the duty of loyalty and improvidence of the executors, knowingly participated in and induced by MNY and MAG; that the fact that these agreements were voidable did not revive the 1969 inter vivos agreements since the parties by their conduct evinced an intent to abandon and abrogate these compacts. The Surrogate held that the present value at the time of trial of the paintings sold is the proper measure of damages as to MNY, MAG, Lloyd, Reis and Stamos. . . . It was held that Levine was liable for $6,464,880 in damages, as he was not in a dual position acting for his own interest and was thus liable only for the actual value of paintings sold MNY and MAG as of the dates of sale, and that Reis, Stamos, MNY and MAG, apart from being jointly and severally liable for the same damages as Levine for negligence, were liable for the greater sum of $9,252,000 "as appreciation damages less amounts previously paid to the estate with regard to sales of paintings." . . . The liabilities were held to be congruent so that payment of the highest sum would satisfy all lesser liabilities including the civil fines and the liabilities for damages were to be reduced by payment of the fine levied or by return of any of the 57 paintings disposed of, the new fiduciary to have the option in the first instance to specify which paintings the fiduciary would accept.

The Appellate Division, in an opinion by Justice Lane, modified to the extent of deleting the option given the new fiduciary to specify which paintings he would accept. Except for this modification, the majority affirmed on the opinion of Surrogate Midonick, with additional comments. Among others, it was stated that the entire court agreed that executors Reis and Stamos had a conflict of interest and divided loyalty in view of their nexus to MNY and that a majority were in agreement with the Surrogate's assessment of liability as to executor Levine and his findings of liability against MNY, MAG and Lloyd. The majority agreed with the Surrogate's analysis awarding "appreciation damages". . . . Justices Capozzoli and Nunez, in separate dissenting in part opinions, voted to modify and remit to determine the reasonable value of the paintings as of May 1970, when estate contracts with MNY and MAG had their inception in writing.

Since the Surrogate's findings of fact as to the conduct of Reis, Stamos, Levine, MNY, MAG and Lloyd and the value of the paintings at different junctures were affirmed by the Appellate Division, if there was evidence to support these findings they are not subject to question in this Court and the review here is confined to the legal issues raised. . . .

In seeking a reversal, it is urged that an improper legal standard was applied in voiding the estate contracts of May 1970, that the "no further inquiry" rule applies only to self-dealing and that in case of a conflict of interest, absent self-dealing, a challenged transaction must be shown to be unfair. The subject of fairness of the contracts is intertwined with the issue of whether Reis and Stamos were guilty of conflicts of interest. Scott is quoted to the effect that "[a] trustee does not necessarily incur liability merely because he has an individual interest in the transaction. . . . In Bullivant v. First National Bank, 246 Mass. 324, it was held that . . . the fact that the bank was also a creditor of the corporation did not make its assent invalid, *if it acted in good faith and the plan was fair . . .*" (emphasis added here) (II Scott on Trusts, §170.24, p.1384), and our attention has been called to the statement in Phelan v. Middle States Oil Corp. (220 F.2d 593) that Judge Learned Hand found "no decisions that have applied [the no further inquiry rule] inflexibly to every occasion in which the fiduciary has been shown to have had a personal interest that might in fact have conflicted with his loyalty" (p.603).

These contentions should be rejected. First, a review of the opinions of the Surrogate and the Appellate Division manifests that they did not rely solely on a "no further inquiry rule," and secondly, there is more than an adequate basis to conclude that the agreements between the Marlborough corporations and the estate were neither fair nor in the best interests of the estate. . . . The opinions under review demonstrate that neither the Surrogate nor the Appellate Division set aside the contracts by merely applying the no further inquiry rule without regard to fairness. Rather they determined, quite properly indeed, that these agreements were neither fair nor in the best interests of the estate.

To be sure, the assertions that there were no conflicts of interest on the part of Reis or Stamos indulge in sheer fantasy. Besides being a director and officer of MNY, for which there was financial remuneration, however slight, Reis, as noted by the Surrogate, had different inducements to favor the Marlborough interests, including his own aggrandizement of status and financial advantage through sales of almost one million dollars for items from his own and his family's extensive private art collection by the Marlborough interests. Similarly, Stamos benefited as an artist under contract with Marlborough and, interestingly, Marlborough purchased a Stamos painting from a third party for $4,000 during the week in May 1970 when the estate contract negotiations were pending. The conflicts are manifest. Further, as noted in Bogert, Trusts and Trustees (2d ed.), "The duty of loyalty imposed on the fiduciary prevents him from accepting employment from a third party who is entering into a business transaction with the trust" (§543[S], p.573). "While he [a trustee] is administering the trust he must refrain from placing himself in a position where his personal interest or that of a third person does or may conflict with the interest of the beneficiaries" (Bogert, Law of Trusts [Hornbook Series-5th ed.], p.343). Here, Reis was employed and Stamos benefited in a manner contemplated by Bogert (see also, Meinhard v. Salmon, 249 N.Y. 458, 464, 466-467). In short, one must strain the law rather than follow it to reach the result suggested on behalf of Reis and Stamos.

Levine contends that, having acted prudently and upon the advice of counsel, a complete defense was established.[7] Suffice it to say, an executor who knows that his coexecutor is committing breaches of trust and not only fails to exert efforts

---

7. The three executors sought advice from their legal counsel about entering into the contracts with MAG and MNY. Counsel advised the executors that Reis had a conflict of interest.

By the same letter, this law firm advised the executors that a petition for advance approval of any contracts for liquidation of the estate through Marlborough Galleries would not be entertained by a Surrogate. While it is true, as the law firm advised, that Surrogates do not usually give advance approval concerning matters of business judgment which are within the province of executors, no indication was given that the opposite rule governs when a fiduciary faces a conflict of interest. [In re Rothko, 379 N.Y.S.2d 923, 936 (Sur. 1975).]

Is the law firm liable to executor Levine for negligence? See Peter S. Cremer, Should the Fiduciary Trust His Lawyer?, 19 Real Prop., Prob. & Tr. J. 786 (1984). — Eds.

directed towards prevention but accedes to them is legally accountable even though he was acting on the advice of counsel (Matter of Westerfield, 32 App. Div. 324, 344; III Scott, Trusts [3d ed.], §201, p.1657). When confronted with the question of whether to enter into the Marlborough contracts, Levine was acting in a business capacity, not a legal one, in which he was required as an executor primarily to employ such diligence and prudence to the care and management of the estate assets and affairs as would prudent persons of discretion and intelligence, accented by "[n]ot honesty alone, but the punctilio of an honor the most sensitive" (Meinhard v. Salmon, 249 N.Y. 458, 464, supra). Alleged good faith on the part of a fiduciary forgetful of his duty is not enough. He could not close his eyes, remain passive or move with unconcern in the face of the obvious loss to be visited upon the estate by participation in those business arrangements and then shelter himself behind the claimed counsel of an attorney. . . .

Further, there is no merit to the argument that MNY and MAG lacked notice of the breach of trust. The record amply supports the determination that they are chargeable with notice of the executors' breach of duty.

The measure of damages was the issue that divided the Appellate Division. The contention of Reis, Stamos, MNY and MAG, that the award of appreciation damages was legally erroneous and impermissible, is based on a principle that an executor authorized to sell is not liable for an increase in value if the breach consists only in selling for a figure less than that for which the executor should have sold. For example, Scott states:

> The beneficiaries are not entitled to the value of the property at the time of the decree if it was not the duty of the trustee to retain the property in the trust and the breach of trust consisted *merely* in selling the property for too low a price (emphasis added) (III Scott, Trusts (3d ed.), §208.3, p.1687).
>
> If the trustee is guilty of a breach of trust in selling trust property for an inadequate price, he is liable for the difference between the amount he should have received and the amount which he did receive. He is not liable, however, for any subsequent rise in value of the property sold (Id., §208.6, pp.1689-1690).

A recitation of similar import appears in comment d under Restatement, Trusts, §205:

> d. Sale for less than value. If the trustee is authorized to sell trust property, but in breach of trust he sells it for less than he should receive, he is liable for the value of the property at the time of the sale less the amount which he received. If the breach of trust consists *only* in selling it for too little, he is not chargeable with the amount of any subsequent increase in value of the property under the rule stated in Clause (c), as he would be if he were not authorized to sell the property (see §208) (emphasis added).

However, employment of "merely" and "only" as limiting words suggests that where the breach consists of some misfeasance, other than solely for selling "for too low a price" or "for too little," appreciation damages may be appropriate. Under Scott (§208.3, pp.1686-1687) and the Restatement (§208), the trustee may be held liable for appreciation damages if it was his or her duty to retain the property, the theory being that the beneficiaries are entitled to be placed in the same position they would have been in had the breach not consisted of a sale of property that should have been retained. The same rule should apply where the breach of trust consists of a serious conflict of interest — which is more than merely selling for too little.

The reason for allowing appreciation damages, where there is a duty to retain, and only date of sale damages, where there is authorization to sell, is policy oriented. If a trustee authorized to sell were subjected to a greater measure of damages he might be reluctant to sell (in which event he might run a risk if depreciation ensued). On the other hand, if there is a duty to retain and the trustee sells there is no policy reason to protect the trustee; he has not simply acted imprudently, he has violated an integral condition of the trust.

"If a trustee in breach of trust transfers trust property to a person who takes with notice of the breach of trust, and the transferee has disposed of the property . . . [i]t seems proper to charge him with the value at the time of the decree, since if it had not been for the breach of trust the property would still have been a part of the trust estate" (IV Scott, Trusts [3d ed.], §291.2). This rule of law which applies to the transferees MNY and MAG also supports the imposition of appreciation damages against Reis and Stamos, since if the Marlborough corporations are liable for such damages either as purchasers or consignees with notice, from one in breach of trust, it is only logical to hold that said executors, as sellers and consignors, are liable also pro tanto.

. . . [S]ince the paintings cannot be returned, the estate is therefore entitled to their value at the time of the decree, i.e., appreciation damages. These are not punitive damages in a true sense, rather they are damages intended to make the estate whole. Of course, as to Reis, Stamos, MNY and MAG, these damages might be considered by some to be exemplary in a sense, in that they serve as a warning to others, but their true character is ascertained when viewed in the light of overriding policy considerations and in the realization that the sale and consignment were not merely sales below value but inherently wrongful transfers which should allow the owner to be made whole. . . .

The decree of the Surrogate imposed appreciation damages against Reis, Stamos, MNY and MAG in the amount of $7,339,464.72 — computed as $9,252,000 (86 works on canvas at $90,000 each and 54 works on paper at $28,000 each) less the aggregate amounts paid the estate under the two rescinded agreements and interest. Appellants chose not to offer evidence of "present value" and the only proof furnished on the subject was that of the expert Heller whose appraisal as of January 1974 (the month previous to that when trial commenced) on a painting-by-painting basis totaled $15,100,000. There was also testimony as to bona fide sales of other Rothkos between 1971 and 1974. Under the circumstances, it was impossible to appraise the value of the unreturned works of art with an absolute certainty and, so long as the figure arrived at had a reasonable basis of computation and was not merely speculative, possible or imaginary, the Surrogate had the right to resort to reasonable conjectures and probable estimates and to make the best approximation possible through the exercise of good judgment and common sense in arriving at that amount. . . . This is particularly so where the conduct of wrongdoers has rendered it difficult to ascertain the damages suffered with the precision otherwise possible. . . . Significantly, the Surrogate's factual finding as to the present value of these unreturned paintings was affirmed by the Appellate Division and, since that finding had support in the record and was not legally erroneous, it should not now be subjected to our disturbance. . . .

Accordingly, the order of the Appellate Division should be affirmed, with costs to the prevailing parties against appellants, and the question certified answered in the affirmative.

NOTES

1. *Epilogue.* Bernard Reis, Theodoros Stamos, and Morton Levine were removed as executors of Mark Rothko's will, and Kate Rothko was appointed sole administrator c.t.a. of Rothko's estate.[8] Kate Rothko was not agreeable to the bill for legal services presented by her counsel in the amount of $7.5 million and hired another lawyer to resist its collection out of the estate. In view of the fact that her lawyers had successfully recovered paintings then worth $40 million for the estate, the surrogate allowed the firm a fee of $2.6 million, which was about twice the hourly rate usually charged by the firm. In re Rothko, 414 N.Y.S.2d 444 (Sur. 1979).

Marlborough Gallery paid most of the $9.2 million assessed as damages in the principal case, but Reis, Stamos, and Levine were liable for the estate's legal fees and costs, and Bernard Reis filed for bankruptcy in 1978. N.Y. Times, Jan. 26, 1978, at C19. Stamos assigned his house to the Rothko estate, which permitted him to retain a life estate in it.

In 1977, Marlborough Gallery owner Frank Lloyd was indicted on charges of tampering with the evidence in the *Rothko* case by altering a gallery stock book containing the purchase and sale prices of Rothko works. Lloyd, a British subject, was outside the country when the indictment was handed up, and upon his return in 1982 he was tried and convicted on the charges. His sentence required him to set up a scholarship fund and art education programs at his gallery. N.Y. Times, Jan. 7, 1983, at 1.

In 1983, a painting by Rothko sold for $1.8 million at an auction at Sotheby's in New York. This price equalled the amount Marlborough A.G. was to pay for 100 paintings under its agreement with Rothko's executors. It was, at the time, the highest price ever paid for a modern work by an American artist. Twenty years later, in 2003, one of Rothko's paintings sold for $16.3 million.

For a retrospective view of the litigation, and the subsequent lives of the parties, see A Betrayal the Art World Can't Forget, N.Y. Times, Nov. 2, 1998, at B1.

2. The measure of damages applied in the *Rothko* case is sharply criticized in Richard V. Wellman, Punitive Surcharges Against Disloyal Fiduciaries — Is *Rothko* Right?, 77 Mich. L. Rev. 95 (1978). Professor Wellman would limit recovery against the two disloyal fiduciaries and the gallery to restitution (recovering all amounts received by the gallery for sales and resales of the paintings plus interest). Wellman's central point is that appreciation damages (a penalty) may be appropriate where a trustee sells an asset he has no authority to sell but are

---

8. *Administrator c.t.a.* is short for *administrator cum testamento annexo*, which means administrator with the will attached. Although the fiduciary for an estate is typically called an *executor* when there is a will and an *administrator* when the decedent dies intestate, this is not always so. When the testator fails to name an executor or the named executor (and any alternate) is disqualified, the court will appoint an administrator c.t.a.

inappropriate where a trustee has authority to sell (as did Rothko's executors) but is guilty of disloyalty or self-dealing. Wellman continues:

> [T]he wisdom of assessing any penalty can be questioned when a trustee has, or later may be said to have had, personal interests which conflict with his fiduciary duty. In such instances, it will usually be unclear whether the fiduciary has breached his duty of loyalty: liability is decided by hindsight and may arise in countless unforeseen ways. A penalty exceeding the liability of an insurer against controllable losses is simply an unjust remedy for conduct of only uncertain impropriety. Even in *Rothko,* the wrongfulness of the executors' conduct was not self-evident. For example, in 1969 Rothko sold a number of paintings to the gallery at prices comparable to those of the executors' 1970 sale and signed a long-term exclusive consignment contract with the gallery. Further, Rothko knew that Reis and Stamos had personal ties to the gallery. These facts suggest that Rothko wanted his executors to deal with the gallery. [Id. at 113.]

In a similar vein, Professor Langbein suggests that "[c]onflicts of interest are sometimes embedded in the very relationship that induces the settlor to ask the particular individual to serve as trustee." Thus, Langbein asks, "Did the two executors provoke a disloyal conflict, or did they pursue a course of action that Rothko tacitly authorized when he selected fiduciaries who came with an embedded conflict of interest? At this distance from the litigation, these questions that the court did not ventilate are hard to answer." John H. Langbein, The Contractarian Basis of the Law of Trusts, 105 Yale L.J. 625, 665-666 (1995).

Even if one were inclined to accept the argument that Rothko tacitly consented to Reis and Stamos's conflict, consider that the executors sold all of Rothko's paintings within three weeks of their appointment, without obtaining an independent expert appraisal, and on terms favorable to the gallery. Irrespective of the conflict-of-interest analysis, did the executors breach the duty of prudence? Although separate principles in theory, it is not uncommon in practice for a breach of one duty to be accompanied by a breach of the other.

NOTE: CO-TRUSTEES

The traditional rule is that if there is more than one trustee of a private, noncharitable trust, the trustees must act as a group and with unanimity, unless the trust instrument provides to the contrary. One of several trustees does not have the power alone to transfer or deal with the property. Since co-trustees must act jointly, a co-trustee is liable for the wrongful acts of a co-trustee to which he has consented or which, by his negligence through inactivity or wrongful delegation, he has enabled the co-trustee to commit. It is improper for one trustee to leave to the others the custody and control of the trust property.

The traditional rule of unanimity, however, is on the decline. Statutes in many states provide that a majority can act if there are three or more trustees. Both Uniform Trust Code §703 (2000) and Restatement (Third) of Trusts §39 (2003) are in accord with this trend, and the reporter's notes to the Restatement section trace the demise of the unanimity rule. Even if unanimity is not required, trustees remain under a duty to prevent a serious breach of trust by their co-trustees, if necessary by bringing suit.

In the realm of charitable trusts, the rule has long been that unanimity of action is not required of the trustees. Action by a majority is valid.

QUESTIONS

What would you, as counsel for Levine in the estate of Mark Rothko, have advised him to do when the conflict of interest of Reis became apparent? See 3 Austin W. Scott, Trusts §194 (William F. Fratcher 4th ed. 1988); UTC §703(g) (2000). Could Levine have resigned as executor and trustee? See Scott, supra, at §169; UTC §705.

Restatement (Second) of Trusts (1959)

§258.   CONTRIBUTION OR INDEMNITY FROM CO-TRUSTEE

(1) Except as stated in Subsection (2), where two trustees are liable to the beneficiary for a breach of trust, each of them is entitled to contribution from the other, except that

(a) if one of them is substantially more at fault than the other, he is not entitled to contribution from the other but the other is entitled to indemnity from him; or

(b) if one of them receives a benefit from the breach of trust, the other is entitled to indemnity from him to the extent of the benefit; and for any further liability, if neither is more at fault than the other, each is entitled to contribution.

(2) A trustee who commits a breach of trust in bad faith is not entitled to contribution or indemnity from his co-trustee.

SECTION C.   THE DUTY OF PRUDENCE

> October.
> This is one of the peculiarly dangerous months
> to speculate in stocks in.
> The others are July, January, September, April, November,
> May, March, June, December, August, and February.
> —*Pudd'nhead Wilson's Calendar*
>
> MARK TWAIN
> *The Tragedy of Pudd'nhead Wilson 166 (1st ed. 1900)*

After loyalty, the next great duty in trust fiduciary law is *prudence*. This duty imposes on the trustee an objective standard of care. Restatement (Second) of Trusts §174 (1959) gives the classic formulation: "The trustee is under a duty to the beneficiary in administering the trust to exercise such care and skill as a man of ordinary prudence would exercise in dealing with his own property." Uniform

Trust Code §804 (2000) updates this statement as follows: "A trustee shall administer the trust as a prudent person would, by considering the purposes, terms, distributional requirements, and other circumstances of the trust. In satisfying this standard, the trustee shall exercise reasonable care, skill, and caution."

With the ascendancy of financial assets over land as the primary mode of wealth accumulation, and the increasing use of the donative trust for intergenerational wealth management and transfer, the primary (but not exclusive) application of the duty of prudence in modern trust practice is in the law of trust investment.

1. The History of Trust-Investment Law

John H. Langbein & Richard A. Posner, Market Funds and
Trust-Investment Law
1976 Am. B. Found. Res. J. 1, 3-4

In 1719 the British Parliament authorized trustees to invest in the shares of the South Sea Company. The South Sea "Bubble" burst the next year, share prices fell by 90 percent, and "public confidence in joint stock companies and their securities was destroyed" for the rest of the eighteenth century.[9]

In the period of reaction to the Bubble the standard of prudence in trust investment acquired three notable characteristics. First, the Court of Chancery developed a "court-list" of presumptively proper investment. The courts "repeatedly decided" that "the trustee would be free from liability if he invested . . . in Government three per cent stock [i.e., bonds]." Some chancellors recognized "well-secured" first mortgages on realty as appropriate, although others questioned them well into the nineteenth century. Statutes extended the categories of presumptively proper investments. Lord St. Leonard's Act added East India stock to the court list and confirmed mortgage investments, "provided that such

---

9. The South Sea Company was granted a monopoly on British trade with the eastern coast of South America, where it was thought that the indigenous population would be willing to trade immense amounts of gold and silver for British manufactured goods. Unfortunately, Spain had control of the area and permitted only one Company ship a year to trade. Worse, this annual voyage occurred only once, in 1717, after which Spain prohibited further trade. Although the company had little or no actual profits, its stock sold briskly, especially after it agreed to take on the entire debt of England. Its stock price quickly rose from £130 before this ridiculous proposal to £310 when the proposal was accepted by Parliament. The company then issued huge amounts of new stock; over £1 million worth sold in just the first few hours after issue.

With outlandish schemes for making great fortunes, other "bubble companies" joined in the action. One company promised an annual 100 percent return on investments in a business that was not even disclosed; the prospectus described the venture simply as, "A company for carrying on an undertaking of great advantage, but nobody to know what it is." After collecting £2,000 on the first day of sales, the anonymous entrepreneur absconded to the Continent, never to be heard from again. Gullible investors bought stock in other imaginative businesses, including ventures for developing "a wheel for perpetual motion," for "extracting silver from lead," and for transmuting "quicksilver [mercury] into a malleable fine metal." Charles MacKay, 1 Extraordinary Popular Delusions and the Madness of Crowds 55-56, 61, 63 (2d ed. 1852).

By the summer of 1720, the South Sea Company's stock was trading at £1,000 per share. Then it became known that the Company's chairman and other insiders had sold their shares. The bubble burst, the stock price dropped 90 percent, and what money was left was eventually distributed to shareholders. Sir Isaac Newton, one of many disappointed investors, lamented, "I can calculate the motions of heavenly bodies, but not the madness of people." For the classic account of the South Sea Bubble and other speculative excesses, see id. at 46-88. — Eds.

Investment shall in other respects be reasonable and proper." Successive Parliaments added various local and colonial government issues, and in 1889 certain railway debentures and preferred stocks. Most American jurisdictions maintained similar statutory lists into the 1940s . . . .

Second, because investments not on the list were improper unless authorized in the trust instrument, England and many American jurisdictions forbade all trust investment in the securities of private enterprises until late in the nineteenth century, and greatly restricted such investments thereafter. . . .

Third, trust-investment law developed a preoccupation with the preservation of the corpus (principal) of the trust. In the words of a leading case, "the primary object to be attained by a trustee in the matter of investing the funds confided to his control is their safety." . . .

What emerged, in short, was an emphasis on "safe" investments, a category dominated in the mind of the judges and legislators by long-term fixed-return obligations such as mortgages and bonds. This approach to investment by trustees may have made sense in the eighteenth and nineteenth centuries in light of two facts which are not true today. First, the capital markets were relatively undeveloped and the opportunities to make passive, reasonably liquid investments in common stock were therefore limited. Second, there was relatively little inflation in the eighteenth and nineteenth centuries. Although the interest rate on a fixed-income security will include the anticipated rate of inflation, the investor bears the risk — which in an inflationary period is substantial for long-term instruments — that the actual rate of inflation will turn out to be higher than the anticipated rate.

Restatement (Third) of Trusts: Prudent Investor Rule (1992)

TOPIC 5. INVESTMENT OF TRUST FUNDS

INTRODUCTION

The foundation of trust investment law in the first and second Restatements has been the so-called "prudent man rule" of Harvard College v. Amory, 9 Pick. (26 Mass.) 446, 461 (1830). The opinion admonishes trustees "to observe how men of prudence, discretion and intelligence manage their own affairs, not in regard to speculation, but in regard to the permanent disposition of their funds, considering the probable income, as well as the probable safety of the capital to be invested." Thus, the rule of the Restatement, Second, of Trusts §227 (1959) directs trustees "to make such investments and only such investments as a prudent man would make of his own property having in view the preservation of the estate and the amount and regularity of the income to be derived." In generally similar language, influenced by the original Restatement, the prudent man rule has been adopted by decision or legislation in most American jurisdictions, often displacing the more restrictive, so-called "legal list" statutes.

Unfortunately, much of the apparent and initially intended generality and adaptability of the prudent man rule was lost as it was further elaborated in the courts and applied case by case. Decisions dealing with essentially factual issues were accompanied by generalizations understandably intended to offer guidance to other courts and trustees in like situations. These cases were subsequently treated as precedents establishing general rules governing trust investments. Specific case results and flexible principles often thereby became crystallized into specific subrules prescribing the types and characteristics of permissible investments for trustees.

Based on some degree of risk that was abstractly perceived as excessive, broad categories of investments and techniques often came to be classified as "speculative" and thus as imprudent per se. Accordingly, the exercise of care, skill, and caution would be no defense if the property acquired or retained by a trustee, or the strategy pursued for a trust, was characterized as impermissible.

Knowledge, practices, and experiences in the modern investment world have demonstrated that arbitrary restrictions on trust investments are unwarranted and often counterproductive. For example, understandable concern has existed that widely accepted theories and practices of investment management cannot properly be pursued by trustees under present judicial and treatise statements of the law. Prohibitions that developed under the traditional prudent man rule have been potential sources of unjustified liability for trustees generally and, more particularly, of inhibitions limiting the exercise of sound judgment by skilled trustees. This is particularly so for trustees whose fiduciary circumstances call for, or at least permit, investment programs that would include some high risk-and-return strategies (such as a venture capital program) or for the use of abstractly high-risk investments or techniques (such as futures or option trading) for the purpose of reducing the risk level of the portfolio as a whole.

These criticisms of the prudent man rule are supported by a large and growing body of literature that is in turn supported by empirical research, well documented and essentially compelling. Much but not all of this criticism is found in writings that have collectively and loosely come to be called modern portfolio theory.

NOTE: THE CONSTRAINED PRUDENT MAN RULE

Among the many problems with the constrained *prudent man rule*, in addition to its male chauvinism, was the prevalence of hindsight bias in its application by the courts. An egregious example is In re Chamberlain's Estate, 156 A. 42, 43 (N.J. Prerog. 1931): "It was common knowledge, not only amongst bankers and trust companies, but the general public as well, that the stock market condition [in August 1929] was an unhealthy one, that values were very much inflated, and that a crash was almost sure to occur." Common knowledge indeed! If most people know that the market will crash tomorrow, then most people will sell their stock today. If it had been common knowledge in August 1929 that a crash was looming, then the crash would have started in August, not October, because each person with such knowledge would have started selling in August, before prices collapsed when everyone else started selling. The court's opinion in Chamberlain's Estate defies logic and the teachings of modern financial theory.

During the latter part of the twentieth century, the constrained prudent man rule came under sustained attack from scholars. Drawing on the theory of efficient capital markets in general, and on modern portfolio theory in particular, this body of work made a compelling case for reform.[10] See Bevis Longstreth, Modern Investment Management and the Prudent Man Rule (1986); John H. Langbein & Richard A. Posner, Market Funds and Trust Investment Law, 1976 Am. B. Found. Res. J. 1; John H. Langbein & Richard A. Posner, Market Funds and Trust-Investment Law: II, 1977 Am. B. Found. Res. J. 1. See also Harvey E. Bines, Modern Portfolio Theory and Investment Management Law: Refinement of Legal Doctrine, 76 Colum. L. Rev. 721 (1976).

By deeming broad swaths of investments to be *safe* or *speculative*, the constrained prudent man rule ignored the reality that risk is correlated with return. In an efficient market, the tradeoff of risk and return is already reflected in a tradable security's price. As compared to less risky investments, higher risk investments must offer a higher return to compensate the

Nobel laureate Harry M. Markowitz, the father of modern portfolio theory

buyer for assuming the additional risk. There is no reason to suppose that in all cases the beneficiary will fare better with a trust portfolio that includes only investments with low risk/return tradeoffs.

Moreover, under the constrained prudent man rule, cautious trustees regularly invested heavily in government and corporate bonds. Although these types of investments have a relatively low risk of *default*, they expose the trust estate to significant *inflation* risk. If the rate of inflation exceeds the interest rate, in real value the trust estate will shrink. In contrast, a portfolio that includes stocks is more likely to experience a total return that exceeds the rate of inflation—and so does not shrink in real value—than a portfolio comprised exclusively of

---

10. This is not to say that the ideas advanced by these scholars were initially well received. One particularly amusing episode involved then-Professor Richard Posner:

> One snowy morning last January [1976], a law professor named Richard Posner gave a talk at a conference on pension-fund investing at New York's Plaza Hotel. Posner was far and away the least popular speaker at the conference. As the drift of his message began to get across to the audience, an angry buzz filled the Terrace Room; before he had finished speaking, many in the audience were no longer listening, but denouncing him to others at their tables. Subsequent speakers warmed themselves to the group by starting off with slighting references to Posner's remarks.

A.F. Ehrbar, Index Funds—An Idea Whose Time Is Coming, Fortune, June 1976, at 145.

government and corporate bonds. Consider the following descriptive statistics for average annual return from 1926 to 2002 on various investment vehicles:

Large company stocks	12.2%
Long-term corporate bonds	6.2%
Long-term government bonds	5.8%
Treasury bills	3.8%

During the same period, the average annual rate of inflation was 3.1%. Ibbotson Associates, Stocks, Bonds, Bills, and Inflation 2003 Yearbook 33, at Table 2.

Despite its many flaws, the constrained prudent man rule endured nonetheless into the 1990s. In Jeffrey N. Gordon, The Puzzling Persistence of the Constrained Prudent Man Rule, 62 N.Y.U.L. Rev. 52 (1987), the author examines the institutional features of the trust law reform process that allowed the prudent man rule to abide for so long in spite of its folly. Perhaps the most intriguing idea advanced by Professor Gordon is that the rule survived because it was merely a default. Those who knew of the rule's defects simply opted out of its application to their trusts. The ease with which the rule could be avoided dulled the incentive of those in the know to lobby for law reform. The unfortunate consequence of this was that, "for most of the [twentieth] century . . . the law has imposed the traditional standards largely on the beneficiaries of those trust settlors who failed to hire competent counsel." Langbein & Posner, supra, 1976 Am. B. Found. Res. J. at 5.

NOTE

For a lucid and accessible introduction to principles of modern finance written for the trusts and estates professional, see Jonathan R. Macey, An Introduction to Modern Financial Theory (2d ed. 1998). Professor Macey discusses both modern portfolio theory and the efficient capital markets hypothesis.[11]

2. *Modern Trust-Investment Law*

In the 1990s, the constrained *prudent man rule* was finally replaced with a modernized — and gender neutral — *prudent investor standard*. The deathblows to the old rule were two. First, in 1992, the American Law Institute published revisions to the trust-investment sections of the Restatement of Trusts. Second, in 1994, the Uniform Law Commission promulgated the Uniform Prudent Investor Act. The new Restatement and uniform act, both of which implement the teachings of

---

11. It should be noted that there is ongoing debate about the validity of the efficient capital markets hypothesis. See Donald C. Langevoort, Taming the Animal Spirits of the Stock Markets: A Behavioral Approach to Securities Regulation, 97 Nw. U.L. Rev. 135 (2002); Eugene Fama, Market Efficiency, Long-Term Returns and Behavioral Finance, 33 J. Fin. Econ. 3 (1998). See also James Lindgren, Telling Fortunes: Challenging the Efficient Markets Hypothesis by Prediction, S. Cal. Interdisc. L.J. 7 (1992). There is broad consensus, however, about modern portfolio theory and its application to trust-investment law.

modern portfolio theory, have been widely adopted.[12] Coincident with this domestic reform, the Trustee Act of 2000 likewise modernized the English law of trust investment. For an explication of the new Restatement and uniform act by their respective reporters, see Edward C. Halbach, Jr., Trust Investment Law in the Third Restatement, 77 Iowa L. Rev. 1151 (1992), and John H. Langbein, The Uniform Prudent Investor Act and the Future of Trust Investing, 81 Iowa L. Rev. 641 (1996). See also Joel C. Dobris, Speculations on the Idea of "Speculation" in Trust Investing: An Essay, 39 Real Prop., Prob. & Tr. J. 439 (2004).

The prudent investor standard of the new Restatement and uniform act implements three core reforms: (a) an increased sensitivity to the tradeoff between risk and return; (b) a diversification imperative; and (c) a reversal of the non-delegation rule.

a. Sensitivity to Risk and Return

Uniform Prudent Investor Act (1994)

§2.   STANDARD OF CARE; PORTFOLIO STRATEGY; RISK AND RETURN OBJECTIVES

(a) A trustee shall invest and manage trust assets as a prudent investor would, by considering the purposes, terms, distribution requirements, and other circumstances of the trust. In satisfying this standard, the trustee shall exercise reasonable care, skill, and caution.

(b) A trustee's investment and management decisions respecting individual assets must be evaluated not in isolation, but in the context of the trust portfolio as a whole and as a part of an overall investment strategy having risk and return objectives reasonably suited to the trust.

(c) Among circumstances that the trustee shall consider in investing and managing trust assets are such of the following as are relevant to the trust or its beneficiaries:

(1) general economic conditions;

(2) the possible effect of inflation or deflation;

(3) the expected tax consequences of investment decisions or strategies;

(4) the role that each investment or course of action plays within the overall trust portfolio, which may include financial assets, interests in closely held enterprises, tangible and intangible personal property, and real property;

(5) the expected total return from income and the appreciation of capital;

(6) other resources of the beneficiaries;

(7) needs for liquidity, regularity of income, and preservation or appreciation of capital; and

(8) an asset's special relationship or special value, if any, to the purposes of the trust or to one or more of the beneficiaries.

(d) A trustee shall take reasonable steps to verify facts relevant to the investment and management of trust assets.

---

12. Despite Judge Posner's role in the movement that toppled the traditional rule, it appears that he remains unaware of its demise. See Richard A. Posner, Economic Analysis of Law §15.6, at 454-455 (6th ed. 2003) (criticizing the older rules without mention of their having been supplanted).

(e) A trustee may invest in any kind of property or type of investment consistent with the standards of this [Act].

(f) A trustee who has special skills or expertise, or is named trustee in reliance upon the trustee's representation that the trustee has special skills or expertise, has a duty to use those special skills or expertise.

Estate of Collins
California Court of Appeal, Second District, 1977
72 Cal. App. 3d 663, 139 Cal. Rptr. 644

KAUS, J. Objectors ("plaintiffs") are beneficiaries under a testamentary trust established in the will of Ralph Collins, deceased. Carl Lamb and C.E. Millikan ("defendants") were, respectively, Collins' business partner and lawyer. They were named in Collins' will as trustees. In 1973 defendants filed a petition for an order approving and settling the first and final account and discharging the trustees. Plaintiffs objected on grounds that defendants had improperly invested $50,000 and requested that defendants be surcharged. After a hearing, the trial court ruled in favor of defendants, and approved the account, terminated the trust, and discharged the trustees. Plaintiff beneficiaries have appealed. . . .

The primary beneficiaries under the testamentary trust were Collins' wife and children; his mother and father were also named as beneficiaries. General support provisions were included; the will also specifically provided that the trustees pay his daughter $4,000 a year for five years for her undergraduate and graduate education.

The will authorized the trustees to purchase "every kind of property, real, personal or mixed, and every kind of investment, specifically including, but not by way of limitation, corporate obligations of every kind, and stocks, preferred or common, irrespective of whether said investments are in accordance with the laws then enforced in the State of California pertaining to the investment of trust funds by corporate trustees."

The will also provided:

> Unless specifically limited, all discretions conferred upon the Trustee shall be absolute, and their exercise conclusive on all persons interest[ed] in this trust. The enumeration of certain powers of the Trustee shall not limit its general powers, the Trustee, subject always to the discharge of its fiduciary obligations, being vested with and having all the rights, powers and privileges which an absolute owner of the same property would have.

Collins died in 1963 and his will was admitted to probate. In June 1965, the court ordered the estate to be distributed. After various other payments and distributions, defendant trustees received about $80,000 as the trust principal. After other distributions, such as the annual $4,000 payment for the education of Collins' daughter, the trustees had about $50,000 available for investment.

Defendant Millikan's clients included two real property developers, Downing and Ward. In March 1965, Millikan filed an action on behalf of Downing and Ward against a lender who refused to honor a commitment to carry certain construction loans. In June 1965, defendants learned that Downing and Ward wanted to borrow $50,000. Millikan knew that the builders wanted the loan because of their difficulties with the lender who had withdrawn its loan commitment.

The loan would be secured by a second trust deed to 9.38 acres of unimproved real property in San Bernardino County near Upland. This property was subject to a $90,000 first trust deed; the note which secured the first trust deed was payable in quarterly installments of interest only, and due in full in three years, that is, in July 1968. The $50,000 loan to be made by defendants would be payable in monthly installments of interest only, at ten percent interest with the full amount due in 30 months, that is, in January 1968.

Defendants knew that the property had been sold two years earlier in 1963 for $107,000. Defendants checked with two real estate brokers in the area, one of whom said that property in that area was selling for $18,000 to $20,000 an acre. They did not have the property appraised, they did not check with the county clerk or recorder in either Los Angeles or San Bernardino County to determine whether there were foreclosures or lawsuits pending against the construction company. In fact, when defendants made the loan in July 1965, there were six notices of default and three lawsuits pending against Downing and Ward.

Defendants obtained and reviewed an unaudited company financial statement. This statement indicated that the Downing and Ward Company had a net worth in excess of $2,000,000.

Downing and Ward told defendants that they were not in default on any of their loans, that they were not defendants in any pending litigation, and that there had never been any liens filed on any of their projects. Defendants phoned the bank with whom Downing and Ward had a line of credit and learned that the bank had a satisfactory relationship with the builders.

Based on this information, on July 23, 1965, defendants lent Downing and Ward $50,000 on the terms described above. In addition to the second trust deed, Downing and Ward pledged 20 percent of the stock in their company as security. However, defendants neither obtained possession of the stock, placed it in escrow, nor placed a legend on the stock certificates. Defendants also obtained the personal guarantees of Downing and Ward and their wives. However, defendants did not obtain financial statements from the guarantors.

When the loan was made in July 1965, construction in the Upland area was, as the trial court said, "enjoying boom times, although the bubble was to burst just a few months later." From July 1965 through September 1966, the builders made the monthly interest payments required by the note. In October 1966, Downing & Ward Construction Corporation was placed in involuntary bankruptcy and thereafter Mr. and Mrs. Ward and Mr. and Mrs. Downing declared personal bankruptcies. Defendants foreclosed their second trust deed in June 1967, and became the owners of the unimproved real property. They spent $10,000 in an unsuccessful effort to salvage the investment by forestalling foreclosure by the holder of the first trust deed. In September 1968, the holder of the first trust deed did foreclose. This extinguished the trustees' interest in the property and the entire investment. In short, about $60,000 of the trust fund was lost.

The trial court made findings of fact and drew conclusions of law. As relevant, the court found that defendant trustees "exercised the judgment and care, under the circumstances then prevailing, which men of prudence, discretion and intelligence exercised in the management of their own affairs, not in regard to speculation, but in regard to the disposition of their funds, considering the probable income, as well as the probable safety of their capital."[13] In making the loan, "the cotrustees used reasonable care, diligence and skill. The cotrustees did not act arbitrarily or in bad faith." . . .

The trial court's finding that defendants exercised the judgment and care "which men of prudence, discretion and intelligence exercised in the management of their own affairs," reflects the standard imposed upon trustees by Civil Code section 2261. (See also, Rest. 2d Trusts, §227 ["Restatement"].)

Plaintiffs contend, and we agree, that contrary to the trial court's findings and conclusions, defendants failed to follow the "prudent investor" standard, first, by investing two-thirds of the trust principal in a single investment, second, by investing in real property secured only by a second deed of trust, and third, by making that investment without adequate investigation of either the borrowers or the collateral.

Although California does not limit the trustee's authority to a list of authorized investments, relying instead on the prudent investor rule (see 7 Witkin, Summary of Cal. Law (8th ed.) Trusts, §63, p.5424), nevertheless, the prudent investor rule encompasses certain guidelines applicable to this case.

First, "the trustee is under a duty to the beneficiary to distribute the risk of loss by reasonable diversification of investments, unless under the circumstances it is prudent not to do so." (Rest., §228.) . . .

Second, ordinarily, "second or other junior mortgages are not proper trust investments," unless taking a second mortgage is a reasonable method of settling a claim or making possible the sale of property. (Rest., §227, p.533.) Stated more emphatically:

> While loans secured by second mortgages on land are sometimes allowed, they are almost always disapproved by courts of equity. The trustee should not place the trust funds in a position where they may be endangered by the foreclosure of a prior lien. . . . In rare cases equity will sanction an investment secured by a second mortgage, but only when the security is adequate and unusual circumstances justify the trustee in taking this form of investment. (Bogert, Trusts & Trustees (2d ed.) §675, p.274.)

Third, in "buying a mortgage for trust investment, the trustee should give careful attention to the valuation of the property, in order to make certain that his margin of security is adequate. He must use every reasonable endeavor to provide protection which will cover the risks of depreciation in the property and changes in price levels. And he must investigate the status of the property and of the mortgage, as well as the financial situation of the mortgagor." (Bogert, supra, §674, at p.267.) Similarly, the Restatement rule is that "the trustee cannot properly lend on a mortgage upon real property more than a reasonable proportion of the value of the mortgage property." (Sec. 229.)

---

13. This language is taken almost verbatim from Harvard College v. Amory, 26 Mass. (9 Pick.) 446, 461 (1830), which laid down the "prudent man" rule, referred to in this case as the "prudent investor" rule. Usually the latter term refers to the reformulated rule adopted by the 1992 Restatement (Third) and by the 1994 Uniform Prudent Investor Act. — Eds.

We think it apparent that defendants violated every applicable rule. First, they failed totally to diversify the investments in this relatively small trust fund. Second, defendants invested in a junior mortgage on unimproved real property, and left an inadequate margin of security. As noted, the land had most recently sold for $107,000, and was subject to a first trust deed of $90,000. Thus, unless the land was worth more than $140,000, there was no margin of security at all. Defendants did not have the land appraised; the only information they had was the opinion of a real estate broker that property in the area — not that particular parcel — was going for $18,000 to $20,000 an acre. Thus, any assumption that the property was worth about $185,000 — and therefore the $140,000 in loans were well-secured — would have been little more than a guess.

Third, the backup security obtained by defendants was no security at all. The builders pledged 20 percent of their stock, but defendants never obtained possession of the stock, placed it in escrow or even had it legended. They accepted the personal guarantees of the builders and their wives without investigating the financial status of these persons. They accepted at face value the claimed $2,000,000 value of the company shown in an unaudited statement. Defendant Millikan apparently ignored the fact that one lender had, for whatever reasons, reneged on a loan commitment to the builders.

Defendants contend that the evidence sustains the trial court's findings that they exercised the judgment and care under the circumstances then prevailing expected of men of prudence. They rely on the rule that the determination whether an investment was proper must be made in light of the circumstances existing at the time of the investment. (E.g., Witkin, supra, §63, p.5425.) That rule does not help defendants. Nothing that happened after the loan was made can change the fact that defendants invested two-thirds of the principal of the trust in a single second deed of trust on unappraised property, with no knowledge of the borrowers' true financial status, and without any other security. . . .

Defendants alternatively contend that the trust instrument conferred "absolute discretion" on them as trustees, and that the prudent-investor standard did not apply to their conduct. Rather, the only question is whether the trustee avoided arbitrary action and used his best judgment. (Coberly v. Superior Court 42 Cal. Rptr. 64 (App. 1965).)

We leave aside the question whether even a trustee with "absolute discretion" would be permitted to make this kind of investment, consistent with the rule that an absolute discretion does not permit a "trustee to neglect its trust or abdicate its judgment." (Coberly, supra, 42 Cal. Rptr. at p.67.) The instrument in this case conferred no such absolute discretion.

Defendants rely particularly on the rule that the prudent investor standard does not apply where the settlor himself specifies that the trustees of his trust are not limited by what the law provides are proper investments. (E.g., Stanton v. Wells Fargo Bank, etc. Co. 310 P.2d 1010 (Cal. App. 1957).) Their reliance on that rule is misplaced.

First, the provision in the trust instrument to purchase every kind of property and make every kind of investment "irrespective of whether said investments are in accordance with the laws then enforced in the State of California pertaining to the investment of trust funds by corporate trustees" does not authorize the trustees to make improper investments.

Neither Civil Code section 2261 nor any other authority which we can locate authorizes different types of investments for "corporate trustees" and for amateur trustees. The difference, rather, is that the corporate trustee is held to a greater standard of care based on his presumed expertise. . . . Thus, defendants might have been protected by that clause had they deviated in some respects from the general rules — for example, had they accepted a well-secured second trust deed, or possibly had they accepted a first trust deed without careful investigation. Here, however, defendants did nothing right. Second, the "absolute discretion" in the trust instrument is "specifically limited" by the requirement that the trustee is "subject always to the discharge of its fiduciary obligations. . . ."

In conclusion, the evidence does not support the trial court's conclusion that defendants acted properly in investing $50,000 in the property.

Reversed.

QUESTIONS AND NOTES

1.   Exactly what actions did the trustees take that violated or may have violated their duties? Inasmuch as one of the trustees, Millikan, had been Downing and Ward's lawyer (in a dispute with creditors to boot!), could not the case have been resolved on conflict-of-interest principles?

2.   The opinion in *Collins* exemplifies the old approach to evaluating the prudence of the trustee's investment decisions. How would the case be analyzed under modern prudent investor standards? The reasoning would change, to be sure. But would the result?

The Uniform Prudent Investor Act eliminates the old categoric restrictions on particular types of investments, such as the prohibition on junior mortgages. Section 2(e) of the Act provides: "A trustee may invest in any kind of property or type of investment consistent with the standards of this (Act)." . . . .

The drafters of the Uniform Prudent Investor Act reasoned that "trust beneficiaries are better protected by . . . emphasis on close attention to risk/return objectives . . . than in attempts to identify categories of investment that are per se prudent or imprudent." The heart of the Act, section 2(b), states that the "trustee's investment and management decisions" are required to "hav[e] risk and return objectives reasonably suited to the trust." The Act recognizes that investment returns correlate strongly with risk. However, as the official Comment explains, "tolerance for risk varies greatly with the financial and other circumstances of the investor, or in the case of a trust, with the purposes of the trust and the relevant circumstances of the beneficiaries." By way of illustration, the Comment observes that if the "main purpose" of the particular trust "is to support an elderly widow of modest means," that trust "will have a lower risk tolerance than a trust to accumulate for a young scion of great wealth."

Thus, the Act aspires to free trustees from the old preoccupation with avoiding speculation. Should we expect to see future trust portfolios stuffed with penny stocks, Polish zloty futures, and Czarist Russian bonds? The answer, of course, is no. For most trusts and trustees, the outer reaches of the risk/return distribution will be every bit as unsuitable as before. What has changed is that the trustee is now able to examine the risk tolerance of each particular trust and to tailor that trust's investment policy accordingly. [John H. Langbein, The Uniform Prudent Investor Act and the Future of Trust Investing, 81 Iowa L. Rev. 641, 649-650 (1996).]

In light of Downing and Ward's dodgy credit history, was investing $50,000 with them appropriately sensitive to the risk tolerance of the trust beneficiaries, the testator's surviving widow and child?

3. *Extended discretion.* The court rejected the trustees' argument that the "absolute discretion" language of the will absolved them from the prudence norm. On the contrary, "absolute discretion does not permit a 'trustee to neglect its trust or abdicate its judgment.'" The effect of absolute, sole, and uncontrolled discretionary clauses is discussed at page 540.

A related issue concerns the enforceability of *exculpatory* or *exoneration* clauses. These are provisions in the trust instrument that limit the trustee's liability to the beneficiary for breach of trust. We examine such clauses at page 541.

4. Under the modern law, instead of looking at individual investments in isolation, the prudence of the portfolio is evaluated as a whole. See Uniform Prudent Investor Act §2(b) (1994). The Introduction to the Restatement (Third) explains: "Caselaw and prior Restatements have condemned 'speculation' and excessive risk without definition, as if such risk could be recognized in the abstract without regard to portfolio context and objectives. The prudent investor rule recognizes that investments and courses of action are properly judged not in isolation but on the basis of the roles they are to play in specific trust portfolios and strategies." Thus the prudence of a particular investment cannot be ascertained without considering its relation to the trust portfolio as a whole.

This reform is strongly related to the duty to diversify, which we examine in the next subsection. After reviewing those materials, consider yet another ground under the modern law for resolving the case in *Collins*—the trustees placed nearly all of the trust assets in a single investment. As the court observed, the trustees "failed totally to diversify the investments in this relatively small trust fund."

5. How would you, as counsel for a trustee in a jurisdiction that has enacted the 1994 Uniform Prudent Investor Act or whose courts have embraced the 1992 Restatement (Third), advise your client to proceed in designing a prudent investment portfolio? See Restatement (Third) of Trusts: Prudent Investor Rule §227, cmts. h, k (1992).

NOTE: ERISA

The Employee Retirement Income Security Act of 1974 (ERISA) governs the investment of pension funds by the trustees managing the funds. ERISA applies to all pension funds except state and local pension funds exempt under 29 U.S.C. §1003(b) (2004). The standard governing investments is the prudent investor rule. The act provides that a fiduciary shall discharge his duties

with the care, skill, prudence, and diligence under the circumstances then prevailing that a prudent man acting in a like capacity and familiar with such matters would use in the conduct of an enterprise of a like character and with like aims; by diversifying the investments of the plan so as to minimize the risk of large losses unless under the circumstances it is clearly prudent not to do so. [29 U.S.C. §1104(a) (2004).]

Waiver of these limitations in the trust instrument is forbidden. 29 U.S.C. §1104(a)(1)(D) (2004). Thus the trustees of these funds are governed by standards of prudent investing similar to those that govern the trustees of private trusts. ERISA also provides that the trustee

shall discharge his duties with respect to a plan solely in the interest of the participants and the beneficiaries and . . . for the exclusive purpose of . . . providing benefits to participants and their beneficiaries. [29 U.S.C. §1104(a)(1)(A)(i) (2004).]

This is known as the exclusive benefit rule. The trust law analogue to the exclusive benefit rule is the trustee's duty of loyalty. For a critique of the exclusive benefit rule, see Daniel R. Fischel & John H. Langbein, ERISA's Fundamental Contradiction: The Exclusive Benefit Rule, 55 U. Chi. L. Rev. 1105 (1988).

Because the trustees of huge pension and employee benefit funds are subject to duties of loyalty and prudence that are analogous to the duties of loyalty and prudence in ordinary trust law, the law of private trusts is often at issue in ERISA litigation. For sharp criticism of the U.S. Supreme Court's applications of private trust law to ERISA disputes, see John H. Langbein, The Supreme Court Flunks Trusts, 1990 Sup. Ct. Rev. 20, and John H. Langbein, What ERISA Means by "Equitable": The Supreme Court's Trail of Error in Russell, Mertens, and Great-West, 103 Colum. L. Rev. 1317 (2003).

Just as private trust law has a profound influence on ERISA litigation, there is good reason to suppose that ERISA cases will likewise influence decisions involving private trusts.

NOTE: SOCIAL INVESTING

Can trustees invest the trust assets to accomplish social goals? For example, can trustees refuse to invest in the stock of a corporation that pollutes the atmosphere or publishes textbooks that teach the theory of evolution? Or can a labor union pension fund invest in projects that provide jobs to the union members (pension fund investment being subject to a similar standard of prudence)? Do such investments breach the duty of undivided loyalty to the fund beneficiaries? Are they prudent? See Ian D. Lanoff, The Social Investment of Private Pension Plan Assets: May It Be Done Lawfully under ERISA?, 31 Labor L.J. 387 (1980) (presenting the Department of Labor's conclusion that, under ERISA, the trustee must make investment decisions based on market returns and not in pursuit of a social or political cause).

For further discussion of social investing in trust law, compare John H. Langbein & Richard A. Posner, Social Investing and the Law of Trusts, 79 Mich. L. Rev. 72 (1980) (concluding that social investing is inconsistent with the duty of loyalty), with Joel C. Dobris, Arguments in Favor of Fiduciary Divestment of "South African" Securities, 65 Neb. L. Rev. 209 (1986) (presenting arguments in favor of social investing by trustees). See also Michael S. Knoll, Ethical Screening in Modern Financial Markets: The Conflicting Claims Underlying Socially Responsible Investment, 57 Bus. Law. 681 (2002).

b.   Diversification

Uniform Prudent Investor Act (1994)

§3.   DIVERSIFICATION

A trustee shall diversify the investments of the trust unless the trustee reasonably determines that, because of special circumstances, the purposes of the trust are better served without diversifying.

John H. Langbein, The Uniform Prudent Investor Act and the Future of Trust Investing
81 Iowa L. Rev. 641, 647–648 (1996)

[I]nsistence on diversifying investments responds to one of the central findings of Modern Portfolio Theory, that there are huge and essentially costless gains to diversifying the portfolio thoroughly. To understand why, begin with the obvious truth that some securities are riskier than others. Investors demand to be paid to bear the greater risk. For example, a start-up computer software company in Silicon Valley entails a far larger risk of disappointing returns or total failure than does a seasoned blue chip such as Mobil Oil or General Electric. If you are a Silicon Valley entrepreneur who wants me to invest in your start-up firm, you must offer me an expected return (that is, a combination of dividends and capital appreciation on the securities) that is higher than Mobil or GE will pay me in order to induce me to invest in your riskier venture. This calculation is called the risk/ return curve: The higher expected return on the investment compensates me for bearing the greater risk of the investment being disappointing.

Modern Portfolio Theory isolates three distinct components of the risk of owning any security: market risk, industry risk, and firm risk. Market risk is common to all securities; it reflects general economic and political conditions, interest rates, and so forth. Industry risk, by contrast, is specific to the firms in a particular industry or an industry grouping. Finally, firm risk refers to factors that touch the fortunes only of the individual firm. Thus, if we take the international oils for an example, we recall that all the producers suffered from the 1973 Arab oil embargo (industry risk), but only Exxon incurred the liabilities arising from the great Alaskan oil spill of March 1989 (firm risk).

. . . By definition, market risk cannot be eliminated through diversification, since market risk is common to all securities. But industry risk and firm risk can be reduced greatly through diversification. To continue with the example of the oil industry, contrast an investor who owned only international oil shares in 1973 with an investor whose portfolio was broadly diversified across many industries. The oil embargo damaged the international oils and the automobile and airline industries, but it triggered a boom in domestic oils, in coal stocks, in synthetic fuels, in the energy conservation firms, and in the oilfield equipment industry. We see, therefore, that industry risk is often negatively correlated. Owning stocks in these other industries would, in part, have offset the damage to the industries harmed by the embargo.

Likewise, within an industry, diversification reduces risk. Since I cannot predict the Alaskan oil spill, or any other firm-specific hazard, I can lower my exposure to such firm-specific risks by investing not only in Exxon, but also BP, Shell, Mobil,

Texaco, and the others. Indeed, it commonly happens that the performance of firms in the same industry is negatively correlated — the success of one firm comes at the expense of its competitors. Efficient market theory instructs us that it is impossible to outsmart the market by predicting which securities will do better or worse. Owning many securities enhances the chances of offsetting losers with winners.

In the literature of Modern Portfolio Theory, a telling expression has been coined to describe what is wrong with underdiversification: *uncompensated risk*. No one pays the investor for owning too few stocks. Recall that when I spoke of the difference between the Silicon Valley start-up and Mobil Oil, I said that the greater risk intrinsic to the start-up was reflected in its expected return. The investor faced with a choice between mature blue chips and an imperiled new venture will prefer the blue chips unless the new venture offers a superior return, a risk premium. Moving out on the risk/return curve in this way, we routinely observe that the investor who bears the greater risk is compensated for it. By contrast, no one compensates the investor for having a portfolio that neglects to hold securities in enough industries and firms to achieve effective diversification. Underdiversification entails needless risk, risk that can be avoided by constructing a sufficiently large and representative portfolio.

In re Estate of Janes
Court of Appeals of New York, 1997
90 N.Y.2d 41, 681 N.E.2d 332, 659 N.Y.S.2d 165

LEVINE, J.   Former State Senator and businessman Rodney B. Janes (testator) died on May 26, 1973, survived solely by his wife, Cynthia W. Janes, who was then 72 years of age. Testator's $3,500,000 estate consisted of a $2,500,000 stock portfolio, approximately 71% of which consisted of 13,232 shares of common stock of the Eastman Kodak Company.[14] The Kodak stock had a date-of-death value of $1,786,733, or approximately $135 per share.

Testator's 1963 will and a 1969 codicil bequeathed most of his estate to three trusts. First, the testator created a marital deduction trust consisting of approximately 50% of the estate's assets, the income of which was to be paid to Mrs. Janes for her life. In addition, it contained a generous provision for invasion of the principal for Mrs. Janes's benefit and gave her testamentary power of appointment over the remaining principal. The testator also established a charitable trust of approximately 25% of the estate's assets which directed annual distributions to selected charities. A third trust comprised the balance of the estate's assets and

14. Rodney Janes served in the New York State Senate from 1939 until 1946, representing the Rochester area, having been born in Rochester on October 21, 1892. At an early age Janes took on sales work, ultimately owning and operating a successful greeting card publishing business. During World War I, Janes served in the U.S. Navy. Inquiry by the editors revealed no clear explanation for Janes's high concentration of Kodak stock except for Kodak's being a Rochester company. — Eds.

Rodney B. Janes

directed that the income therefrom be paid to Mrs. Janes for her life, with the remainder pouring over into the charitable trust upon her death.

On June 6, 1973, the testator's will and codicil were admitted to probate. Letters testamentary issued to petitioner's predecessor, Lincoln Rochester Trust Company, and Mrs. Janes, as coexecutors, on July 3, 1973. Letters of trusteeship issued to petitioner alone. By early August 1973, petitioner's trust and estate officers, Ellison Patterson and Richard Young had ascertained the estate's assets and the amount of cash needed for taxes, commissions, attorneys' fees, and specific bequests.

In an August 9, 1973 memorandum, Patterson recommended raising the necessary cash for the foregoing administrative expenses by selling certain assets, including 800 shares of Kodak stock, and holding "the remaining issues . . . until the [t]rusts [were] funded." The memorandum did not otherwise address investment strategy in light of the evident primary objective of the testator to provide for his widow during her lifetime. In a September 5, 1973 meeting with Patterson and Young, Mrs. Janes, who had a high school education, no business training or experience, and who had never been employed, consented to the sale of some 1,200 additional shares of Kodak stock. Although Mrs. Janes was informed at the meeting that petitioner intended to retain the balance of the Kodak shares, none of the factors that would lead to an informed investment decision was discussed. At that time, the Kodak stock traded for about $139 per share; thus, the estate's 13,232 shares of the stock were worth almost $1,840,000. The September 5 meeting was the only occasion where retention of the Kodak stock or any other investment issues were taken up with Mrs. Janes.

By the end of 1973, the price of Kodak stock had fallen to about $109 per share. One year later, it had fallen to about $63 per share and, by the end of 1977, to about $51 per share. In March 1978, the price had dropped even further, to about $40 per share. When petitioner filed its initial accounting in February 1980, the remaining 11,320 shares were worth approximately $530,000, or about $47 per share. Most of the shares were used to fund the trusts in 1986 and 1987.

In addition to its initial accounting in 1980, petitioner filed a series of supplemental accountings that together covered the period from July 1973 through June 1994. In August 1981, petitioner sought judicial settlement of its account. Objections to the accounts were originally filed by Mrs. Janes in 1982, and subsequently by the Attorney-General on behalf of the charitable beneficiaries (collectively, "objectants"). In seeking to surcharge petitioner for losses incurred by the estate due to petitioner's imprudent retention of a high concentration of Kodak stock in the estate from July 1973 to February 1980, during which time the value of the stock had dropped to about one third of its date-of-death value, objectants asserted that petitioner's conduct violated EPTL 11-2.2(a)(1), the so-called "prudent person rule" of investment.[15] When Mrs. Janes died in 1986, the personal representative of her estate was substituted as an objectant.

---

15. Despite the use of "prudent person" language, the statute at issue was the predecessor to New York's current statute, which reflects the influence of the 1992 Restatement (Third) and 1994 Uniform Prudent Investor Act. The court observes this fact, and cites the new statute, in a later footnote that is reproduced below. — Eds.

Following a trial on the objections, the Surrogate found that petitioner, under the circumstances, had acted imprudently and should have divested the estate of the high concentration of Kodak stock by August 9, 1973. The court imposed a $6,080,269 surcharge against petitioner and ordered petitioner to forfeit its commissions and attorneys' fees. In calculating the amount of the surcharge, the court adopted a "lost profits" or "market index" measure of damages espoused by objectants' expert — what the proceeds of the Kodak stock would have yielded, up to the time of trial, had they been invested in petitioner's own diversified equity fund on August 9, 1973.

The Appellate Division modified solely as to damages, holding that "the Surrogate properly found [petitioner] liable for its negligent failure to diversify and for its inattentiveness, inaction, and lack of disclosure, but that the Surrogate adopted an improper measure of damages." In a comprehensive opinion by Presiding Justice M. Dolores Denman, the Court held that the Surrogate's finding of imprudence, as well as its selection of August 9, 1973 as the date by which petitioner should have divested the estate of its concentration of Kodak stock, were "well supported" by the record. The Court rejected the Surrogate's "lost profits" or "market index" measure of damages, however, holding that the proper measure of damages was "the value of the capital that was lost" — the difference between the value of the stock at the time it should have been sold and its value when ultimately sold. Applying this measure, the Court reduced the surcharge to $4,065,029. We granted petitioner and objectants leave to appeal, and now affirm.

I. Petitioner's Liability

Petitioner argues that New York law does not permit a fiduciary to be surcharged for imprudent management of a trust for failure to diversify in the absence of additional elements of hazard, and that it relied upon, and complied with, this rule in administering the estate. Relying on Matter of Balfe, 274 N.Y.S. 284, mod. 280 N.Y.S. 128 (App. Div. 1935), petitioner claims that elements of hazard can be capsulized into deficiencies in the following investment quality factors: "(i) the capital structure of the company; (ii) the competency of its management; (iii) whether the company is a seasoned issuer of stock with a history of profitability; (iv) whether the company has a history of paying dividends; (v) whether the company is an industry leader; (vi) the expected future direction of the company's business; and (vii) the opinion of investment bankers and analysts who follow the company's stock." Evaluated under these criteria, petitioner asserts, the concentration of Kodak stock at issue in this case, that is, of an acknowledged "blue chip" security popular with investment advisors and many mutual funds, cannot be found an imprudent investment on August 9, 1973 as a matter of law. In our view, a fiduciary's duty of investment prudence in holding a concentration of one security may not be so rigidly limited.

New York followed the prudent person rule of investment during the period of petitioner's administration of the instant estate. This rule provides that "[a] fiduciary holding funds for investment may invest the same in such securities as would be acquired by prudent [persons] of discretion and intelligence in such matters who are seeking a reasonable income and the preservation of their capital" (EPTL

11-2.2[a][1]).[16] Codified in 1970, the prudent person rule's New York common-law antecedents can be traced to King v. Talbot, 40 N.Y. 76 (1869), wherein this Court stated:

> [T]he trustee is bound to employ such diligence and such prudence in the care and management [of the trust], as in general, prudent men of discretion and intelligence in such matters, employ in their own like affairs.
>
> This necessarily excludes all speculation, all investments for an uncertain and doubtful rise in the market, and, of course, *everything that does not take into view the nature and object of the trust, and the consequences of a mistake in the selection of the investment to be made.* . . .
>
> *[T]he preservation of the fund, and the procurement of a just income therefrom, are primary objects* of the creation of the trust itself, and are to be primarily regarded (id., at 85-86 [emphasis supplied]).

No precise formula exists for determining whether the prudent person standard has been violated in a particular situation; rather, the determination depends on an examination of the facts and circumstances of each case. In undertaking this inquiry, the court should engage in "a balanced and perceptive analysis of [the fiduciary's] consideration and action in light of the history of each individual investment, viewed at the time of its action or its omission to act" (Matter of Donner, 626 N.E.2d 922 (N.Y. 1993)). And, while a court should not view each act or omission aided or enlightened by hindsight, a court may, nevertheless, examine the fiduciary's conduct over *the entire course of the investment* in determining whether it has acted prudently. Generally, whether a fiduciary has acted prudently is a factual determination to be made by the trial court.

As the foregoing demonstrates, the very nature of the prudent person standard dictates against any absolute rule that a fiduciary's failure to diversify, in and of itself, constitutes imprudence, as well as against a rule invariably immunizing a fiduciary from its failure to diversify in the absence of some selective list of elements of hazard, such as those identified by petitioner. Indeed, in various cases, courts have determined that a fiduciary's retention of a high concentration of one asset in a trust or estate was imprudent without reference to those elements of hazard (see, Matter of Donner, supra). The inquiry is simply whether, under all the facts and circumstances of the particular case, the fiduciary violated the prudent person standard in maintaining a concentration of a particular stock in the estate's portfolio of investments.

Moreover, no court has stated that the limited elements of hazard outlined by petitioner are the only factors that may be considered in determining whether a fiduciary has acted prudently in maintaining a concentrated portfolio. Again, as commentators have noted, one of the primary virtues of the prudent person rule "*lies in its lack of specificity*, as this permits the propriety of the trustee's investment decisions to be measured in light of the business and economic circumstances existing at the time they were made" (Laurino, Investment Responsibility

---

16. The recently enacted Prudent Investor Act requires a trustee "to diversify assets unless the trustee reasonably determines that it is in the interests of the beneficiaries not to diversify, taking into account the purposes and terms and provisions of the governing instrument" (EPTL 11-2.3[b][3][C]). The act applies to investments "made or held" by a trustee on or after January 1, 1995 and, thus, does not apply to the matter before us (EPTL 11-2.3[a]).

of Professional Trustees, 51 St. John's L. Rev. 717, 723 [1977] [emphasis supplied]).

Petitioner's restrictive list of hazards omits such additional factors to be considered under the prudent person rule by a trustee in weighing the propriety of any investment decision, as: "the amount of the trust estate, the situation of the beneficiaries, the trend of prices and of the cost of living, the prospect of inflation and of deflation" (Restatement [Second] of Trusts §227, comment e). Other pertinent factors are the marketability of the investment and possible tax consequences (id., comment o). The trustee must weigh all of these investment factors as they affect the principal objects of the testator's or settlor's bounty, as between income beneficiaries and remainder persons, including decisions regarding "whether to apportion the investments between high-yield or high-growth securities" (Turano and Radigan, New York Estate Administration ch. 14, §P, at 409 [1986]).

Moreover, and especially relevant to the instant case, the various factors affecting the prudence of any particular investment must be considered in the light of the "circumstances of the trust itself rather than [merely] the integrity of the particular investment" . . . .

Thus, the elements of hazard petitioner relies upon as demonstrating that, as a matter of law, it had no duty to diversify, suffer from two major deficiencies under the prudent person rule. First, petitioner's risk elements too narrowly and strictly define the scope of a fiduciary's responsibility in making any individual investment decision, and the factors a fiduciary must consider in determining the propriety of a given investment.

A second deficiency in petitioner's elements of hazard list is that all of the factors relied upon by petitioner go to the propriety of an individual investment "exclusively . . . as though it were in its own water-tight compartment," which would encourage a fiduciary to treat each investment as an isolated transaction rather than "in its relation to the whole of the trust estate." Thus, petitioner's criteria for elements of hazard would apply irrespective of the *concentration* of the investment security under consideration in the portfolio. That is, the existence of any of the elements of risk specified by petitioner in a given corporate security would militate against the investment even in a *diversified* portfolio, obviating any need to consider concentration as a reason to divest or refrain from investing. This ignores the market reality that, with respect to some investment vehicles, concentration itself may create or add to risk, and essentially takes lack of diversification out of the prudent person equation altogether. . . .

[I]n maintaining an investment portfolio in which Kodak represented 71% of the estate's stock holdings, and the balance was largely in other growth stocks, petitioner paid insufficient attention to the needs and interests of the testator's 72-year-old widow, the life beneficiary of three quarters of his estate, for whose comfort, support and anticipated increased medical expenses the testamentary trusts were evidently created. Testimony by petitioner's investment manager, and by the objectants' experts, disclosed that the annual yield on Kodak stock in 1973 was approximately 1.06%, and that the aggregate annual income from all estate stockholdings was $43,961, a scant 1.7% of the $2.5 million estate securities portfolio. Thus, retention of a high concentration of Kodak jeopardized the interests of the primary income beneficiary of the estate and led to the eventual need to substantially invade the principal of the marital testamentary trust.

Lastly, there was evidence in the record to support the findings below that, in managing the estate's investments, petitioner failed to exercise due care and the skill it held itself out as possessing as a corporate fiduciary. Notably, there was proof that petitioner (1) failed initially to undertake a formal analysis of the estate and establish an investment plan consistent with the testator's primary objectives; (2) failed to follow petitioner's own internal trustee review protocol during the administration of the estate, which advised special caution and attention in cases of portfolio concentration of as little as 20%; and (3) failed to conduct more than routine reviews of the Kodak holdings in this estate, without considering alternative investment choices, over a seven-year period of steady decline in the value of the stock.

Since, thus, there was evidence in the record to support the foregoing affirmed findings of imprudence on the part of petitioner, the determination of liability must be affirmed.

II. DATE OF DIVESTITURE

As we have noted, in determining whether a fiduciary has acted prudently, a court may examine a fiduciary's conduct throughout the entire period during which the investment at issue was held (see, Matter of Donner, supra). The court may then determine, within that period, the "reasonable time" within which divesture of the imprudently held investment should have occurred. What constitutes a reasonable time will vary from case to case and is not fixed or arbitrary. The test remains "the diligence and prudence of prudent and intelligent [persons] in the management of their own affairs." Thus, in *Donner*, we upheld both the Surrogate's examination of the fiduciary's conduct throughout the entire period during which the investment at issue was retained in finding liability, and the Surrogate's selection of the date of the testator's death as the time when the trustee should have divested the estate of its substantial holdings in high-risk securities.

Again, there is evidentiary support in the record for the trial court's finding, affirmed by the Appellate Division, that a prudent fiduciary would have divested the estate's stock portfolio of its high concentration of Kodak stock by August 9, 1973, thereby exhausting our review powers on this issue. Petitioner's own internal documents and correspondence, as well as the testimony of Patterson, Young, and objectants' experts, establish that by that date, petitioner had all the information a prudent investor would have needed to conclude that the percentage of Kodak stock in the estate's stock portfolio was excessive and should have been reduced significantly, particularly in light of the estate's over-all investment portfolio and the financial requirements of Mrs. Janes and the charitable beneficiaries.

III. DAMAGES

Finally, as to the calculation of the surcharge, we conclude that the Appellate Division correctly rejected the Surrogate's "lost profits" or "market index" measure of damages. Where, as here, a fiduciary's imprudence consists solely of negligent retention of assets it should have sold, the measure of damages is the value of the lost capital. Thus, the Surrogate's reliance on Matter of Rothko in imposing a "lost profit" measure of damages is inapposite, since in that case the fiduciary's misconduct consisted of deliberate self-dealing and faithless transfers of trust property.

In imposing liability upon a fiduciary on the basis of the capital lost, the court should determine the value of the stock on the date it should have been sold, and subtract from that figure the proceeds from the sale of the stock or, if the stock is still retained by the estate, the value of the stock at the time of the accounting. Whether interest is awarded, and at what rate, is a matter within the discretion of the trial court. Dividends and other income attributable to the retained assets should offset any interest awarded.

Here, uncontradicted expert testimony established that application of this measure of damages resulted in a figure of $4,065,029, which includes prejudgment interest at the legal rate, compounded from August 9, 1973 to October 1, 1994. The Appellate Division did not abuse its discretion in adding to that figure prejudgment interest from October 1, 1994 through August 17, 1995, $326,302.66 previously received by petitioner for commissions and attorneys' fees, plus post-judgment interest, costs, and disbursements.

Accordingly, the order of the Appellate Division should be affirmed, without costs.

NOTES AND QUESTIONS

1. The trustee in *Janes* defended its retention of the Kodak stock on the ground that Kodak was "an acknowledged 'blue chip' security popular with investment advisors and many mutual funds." In fact, by the middle of 1976, Kodak remained among the top five holdings of bank trust departments (the other four were IBM, Exxon, General Motors, and AT&T). Vartanig G. Vartan, Trust Portfolios Add Basic Stocks, N.Y. Times, Aug. 23, 1976, at 45. This raises the question of why investment professionals generally, and the bank trustee in this case specifically, remained loyal to Kodak's stock notwithstanding its precipitously declining price. Part of the answer is the so-called *nifty-fifty* phenomenon of the 1970s. Professor Malkiel explains:

> Nothing could be more prudent than to buy their shares and then relax on the golf course . . . .
>
> There were only four dozen or so of these premier growth stocks . . . . Their names were familiar — IBM, Xerox, Avon Products, Kodak, McDonald's, Polaroid, and Disney — and they were called the "Nifty Fifty." They were "big capitalization" stocks, which meant that an institution could buy a good-sized position without disturbing the market. And because most pros realized that picking the exact correct time to buy is difficult if not impossible, these stocks seemed to make a great deal of sense. So what if you paid a price that was temporarily too high? These stocks were proven growers, and sooner or later the price you paid would be justified. In addition, these were stocks that — like the family heirlooms — you would never sell. Hence they also were called "one decision" stocks. You made a decision to buy them, once, and your portfolio-management problems were over.
>
> These stocks provided security blankets for institutional investors in another way, too. They were so respectable. Your colleagues could never question your prudence in investing in IBM. True, you could lose money if IBM went down, but that was not considered a sign of imprudence . . . .

> The end was inevitable. The Nifty Fifty craze ended like all other speculative manias. . . . The stocks sank like stones into the ocean. . . . The real problem was never the particular needle that pricked each individual bubble. The problem was simply that the stocks were overpriced. Sooner or later the same money managers who had worshiped the Nifty Fifty decided to make a second decision and sell. In the debacle that followed, the premier growth stocks fell completely from favor. [Burton G. Malkiel, A Random Walk Down Wall Street 74-76 (rev. ed. 1999).]

What is the relevance, if any, of the nifty-fifty phenomenon when evaluating the prudence of the trustee's decision to retain the Kodak stock? In the trial court, the trustee argued that it had "made a conscious determination to retain the concentration of the stock of a 'great company' with a 'great track record' of 'financial strength,' 'growth' and 'business prospects.'" 630 N.Y.S.2d 472, 474 (Sur. 1995).

2.   In footnote 16, the court explained that, because the conduct by the trustee in *Janes* occurred before January 1, 1995, it was not subject to the new New York statutory requirement that the trustee "diversify assets unless the trustee reasonably determines that it is in the interests of the beneficiaries not to diversify." N.Y. Est. Powers & Trusts Law §11-2.3(b)(3)(C) (2004). Instead the case was to be decided under the prior rules. Do you accept this at face value? In Martin D. Begleiter, Does the Prudent Investor Need the Prudent Investor Act—An Empirical Study of Trust Investment Practices, 51 Me. L. Rev. 28, 70-72 (1999), the author suggests that the teachings of modern portfolio theory that animate the new statute influenced the court's reasoning.

Although a duty to diversify is detectable in the cases as early as the late 1800s, see Appeal of Dickinson, 25 N.E. 99 (Mass. 1890), the trustee's argument that, before January 1, 1995, New York law did not include a duty to diversify was not frivolous. At the time of the trustee's actions, this was a common belief. See Note, Trust Fund Investment in New York: The Prudent Man Rule and Diversification of Investments, 47 N.Y.U.L. Rev. 527, 533-536 (1972).

As in New York, prior to the enactment of its new statute Pennsylvania also lacked a clear duty to diversify. Unlike the New York statute, however, which governs the conduct of all trustees after its effective date, the Pennsylvania statute exempts from its duty to diversify any trust made irrevocable prior to the statute's effective date even if the action of the trustee occurs after that date. Pa. Cons. Stat. tit. 20, §7204(b) (2004). The rationale for exempting past conduct from a new law is clear: People ought to be able to rely on the law as it exists at the time of their actions. But if the duty to diversify reflects sound policy, why not apply it prospectively to all trusts?

3.   As a corporate fiduciary, the bank trustee was held to a higher standard than an ordinary trustee. Restatement (Third) of Trusts: Prudent Investor Rule §227, cmt. d (1992), explains: "[I]f a trustee, such as a corporate or professional fiduciary, procured appointment as trustee by expressly or impliedly representing that it possessed a greater skill than that of an individual of ordinary intelligence, or if the trustee has or represents that it has special facilities for investment management, the trustee is liable for a loss that results from failure to make reasonably diligent use of that skill or of those special facilities." See also UTC §806 (2000). Cf. Law v. Law, 753 A.2d 443, 448 (Del. 2000), holding the trustees to an ordinary standard of prudence "because they are not professional trustees or investors."

4. Although an undiversified portfolio normally incurs uncompensated risk, there are occasional exceptions to the duty to diversify. It may be imprudent to diversify when the tax or other costs of reorganizing the portfolio outweigh the benefits of diversification. See Malachowski v. Bank One, Indianapolis, 590 N.E.2d 559, 565 (Ind. 1992). An undiversified portfolio might be justifiable in the case of a trust that holds a family business, the family vacation home, the surviving spouse's residence, or other such investments. See Mazzola v. Myers, 296 N.E.2d 481, 488-489 (Mass. 1973). Diversification of the trust portfolio might not be necessary if the trust is but one component of a larger scheme such that the beneficiary's financial interests are diversified overall. See John H. Langbein, Mandatory Rules in the Law of Trusts, 98 Nw. U.L. Rev. 1105, 1114-1115 (2004). The trustee may invest the trust assets in a single entity that is itself diversified, such as a mutual fund, provided that the trustee exercises due care in choosing this single entity.

5. *Inception assets.* In assessing the prudence of the trustee's failure to diversify in *Janes*, what is the relevance, if any, of the fact that Kodak stock comprised over 70 percent of Janes's pre-death $2.5 million stock portfolio? Does this show, as one of the bank's account officers testified before the trial court, that Janes "loved Kodak"? If so, does this mean that Janes implicitly consented to the trustee's retention of the Kodak stock? The law does not give extra deference to a trustee who retains inception assets. See Uniform Prudent Investor Act §4 (1994): "Within a reasonable time after accepting a trusteeship or receiving trust assets, a trustee shall review the trust assets and make and implement decisions concerning the retention and disposition of assets, in order to bring the trust portfolio into compliance with the purposes, terms, distribution requirements, and other circumstances of the trust, and with the requirements of this [Act]." See also Restatement (Third) of Trusts: Prudent Investor Rule §229, cmt. a (1992), which is to a similar effect.

Suppose, however, that the trust instrument authorizes or even mandates the retention of the inception assets. What result then?

(a) *Retention authorized.* A number of older cases hold that, by express language in the trust instrument, the settlor can relieve the trustee of the duty to diversify so that the trustee may retain the trust's inception assets. See In re Clark's Will, 177 N.E. 397, 398 (N.Y. 1931); Warmack v. Crawford, 195 S.W.2d 919, 925 (Mo. App. 1946). See also Baldus v. Bank of Cal., 530 P.2d 1350, 1355-1357 (Wash. App. 1975). However, these authorities also recognize that, if the authorization to retain is discretionary or permissive, it may be an abuse of that discretion for the trustee to retain the inception assets. Thus, in Stevens v. National City Bank, 544 N.E.2d 612 (Ohio 1989), the court observed that "if by the terms of the trust the trustee is *authorized*, but not directed, to retain such investments, the trustee is not liable for retaining them unless under the circumstances it would be an abuse of discretion to retain them." Id. at 618.

No doubt influenced by the teaching of modern portfolio theory that the failure to diversify is almost always unwise, courts have increasingly given a narrow interpretation to provisions that purport to authorize undiversified trust portfolios. See, e.g., Rutanen v. Ballard, 678 N.E.2d 133, 139 (Mass. 1997) ("While the trust authorized the retention of property, it also authorized the sale of trust assets. . . . The trust instrument, on its face, manifests no clear preference for selling or retaining the properties."); Robertson v. Central Jersey Bank & Trust

Co., 47 F.3d 1268, 1275 (3d Cir. 1995) (holding that the trustees were subject to a "due diligence" standard in exercising a discretionary power to retain assets, and that "New Jersey has rejected the Bank's broad argument that the retention clause completely absolves it from any duty to diversify"); First Ala. Bank of Huntsville, N.A., 475 So. 2d 512, 515-516 (Ala. 1985) (finding imprudence in a trust "portfolio that contained an inordinate amount of the Bank's holding company stock, in violation of sound management practices," despite authorization in the trust instrument for the trustee to manage the trust portfolio "regardless of any lack diversification").

The Restatement (Third) endorses narrow constructions of clauses that permit the retention of inception assets: "[T]he fact that an investment is permitted does not relieve the trustee of the fundamental duty to act with prudence. The fiduciary must still exercise care, skill, and caution in making decisions to acquire or retain the investment. . . . Because permissive provisions do not abrogate the trustee's duty to act prudently and because diversification is fundamental to prudent risk management, trust provisions are strictly construed against dispensing with that requirement altogether." Restatement (Third) of Trusts §228, cmt. f (1992).

(b) *Retention required.* Instructions that the trustee must retain certain assets, irrespective of diversification, have proven more problematic. In Stevens v. National City Bank, supra, the court stated the traditional rule: "If by the terms of the trust a trustee is specifically *directed* to retain certain investments, such trustee is subject to liability if such investments are not retained (absent impossibility, illegality or a judicially determined change of circumstances)." 544 N.E.2d at 618.

The difficulty is that, as we have seen, underdiversification is almost never in the best interest of the beneficiary. Modern portfolio theory thus puts pressure on the exceptions; if an exception is found to apply, then the trustee is released from the requirement to retain the specified assets. As the most plastic of the exceptions, changed circumstances is the likeliest candidate, though in most cases court approval to deviate from the terms of the trust will be necessary. Restatement (Third) of Trusts: Prudent Investor Rule §228, cmt. e (1992), explains: The trustee is not "under a duty to comply with a term of the trust if a court order directs or authorizes non-compliance when, as a result of circumstances not known or anticipated by the settlor, compliance would defeat or substantially impair the accomplishment of the purposes of the trust. Indeed, under these circumstances, the trustee may have a duty to apply to the court for permission to deviate from the terms of the trust." In a similar vein, Restatement (Third) of Trusts §66, cmt. b (2003), states that a term "expressly directing or expressly forbidding the sale of certain properties or the acquisition of certain types of investments" is among the "terms of the trust that the court may modify, or from which the court may authorize deviation by the trustee."

Suppose that the settlor directs the trustee not to sell the trust's inception assets, in this case the stock of a company that the settlor founded. If the trustee can show that the company had become unprofitable, should the court authorize the trustee to sell the stock in that company? See Matter of Pulitzer, 249 N.Y.S. 87 (Sur. 1931), aff'd mem., 260 N.Y.S. 975 (App. Div. 1932).

Suppose that the settlor directs the trustee to invest only in first mortgages and government bonds and forbids investment in corporate stock. If the trustee can show that in an inflationary economy the value of the trust estate will seriously decline by investing in fixed-value obligations, should the court authorize the trustee to invest in common stock? See In re Trusteeship Agreement with Mayo, 105 N.W.2d 900 (Minn. 1960); Toledo Trust Co. v. Toledo Hosp., 187 N.E.2d 36 (Ohio 1962).

Suppose that, in either of the foregoing scenarios, the trustee refused to petition the court for modification of the trust's terms. In a subsequent suit against the trustee by the beneficiary, should the court hold the trustee liable to the beneficiary for this refusal? Compare Restatement (Third) of Trusts §66(2) (2003) (yes), with Uniform Trust Code §412 & cmt. (2000) (no).

The fundamental policy issue implicated by these questions is whether it is appropriate to disregard the settlor's mandated investment strategy. Professor Langbein argues in the affirmative:

> What is happening in [these cases] is that the settlor is imposing his supposed investment wisdom on the trust in circumstances in which the investment strategy is objectively stupid and imprudent. We now know that the advantages of diversifying a portfolio of securities are so great that it is folly not to do it. . . . [When] the trust assets are cash or cash-equivalent, in the sense that diversification can be achieved at little cost, I believe that the courts will come to view the advantages of diversification as so overwhelming that the settlor's interference with effective diversification will be found to be inconsistent with the requirement that a private trust must be for the benefit of the beneficiary. [John H. Langbein, The Uniform Prudent Investor Act and the Future of Trust Investing, 81 Iowa L. Rev. 641, 664-665 (1996).]

Analogizing settlor-mandated underdiversification to "directions to waste or destroy property," Langbein develops this benefit of the beneficiary argument further in John H. Langbein, Mandatory Rules in the Law of Trusts, 98 Nw. U.L. Rev. 1105, 1111-1117 (2004). The general issue of waste and destruction of property is discussed at page 28. The law of trust modification is treated at page 572 (see in particular *administrative deviation* at page 576).

6.   Thus far we have been speaking of authorization by the settlor to hold an undiversified portfolio. Suppose instead that the authorization comes from the beneficiary. That is, suppose that the beneficiary consents, in writing, to an undiversified portfolio and agrees not to seek to surcharge the trustee for losses stemming from a lack of diversification. Should such an agreement be enforced? See In re Saxton, 712 N.Y.S.2d 225 (App. Div. 2000).

7.   Diversification requires spreading the trust portfolio over a set of different investments. The question thus arises, how is diversification to be obtained in small trusts? The comment to Uniform Prudent Investor Act §3 (1994) explains:

> It is difficult for a small trust fund to diversify thoroughly by constructing its own portfolio of individually selected investments. Transaction costs such as the round-lot (100 share) trading economies make it relatively expensive for a small investor to assemble a broad enough portfolio to minimize uncompensated risk. For this reason, pooled investment vehicles have become the main mechanism for facilitating diversification for the investment needs of smaller trusts.
>
> Most states have legislation authorizing common trust funds . . . . As of 1992, 35 states and the District of Columbia had enacted the Uniform Common Trust Fund Act (UCTFA) (1938), overcoming the rule against commingling trust assets and expressly enabling banks and trust companies to establish common trust funds. The Prefatory

Note to the UCTFA explains: "The purposes of such a common or joint investment fund are to diversify the investment of the several trusts and thus spread the risk of loss, and to make it easy to invest any amount of trust funds quickly and with a small amount of trouble."

. . . Trusts can also achieve diversification by investing in mutual funds.

NOTE: CALCULATING DAMAGES FOR IMPRUDENT INVESTMENT

The core principle in trust remedy law is to put the beneficiary in at least the position that she would have been in but for the trustee's breach. This *make-whole* standard is implemented by a three-part remedial scheme: The beneficiary "can charge the trustee [1] with any loss that resulted from the breach of trust, or [2] with any profit made through the breach of trust, or [3] with any profit that would have accrued if there had been no breach of trust." 3 Austin W. Scott, Trusts §205, at 247 (William F. Fratcher 4th ed. 1988). The question thus arises, how is the make-whole policy applied in a case of imprudent investment?

In *Janes*, the trial court awarded *total return damages* of $6,080,269. In the trial court's view, this figure represented the amount "of the difference between what the estate actually received from the Kodak stock and what the estate would have received if the stock had been sold in August of 1973 and reinvested" in a prudent portfolio. For the model of what the performance of the Janes trust would have been had it been prudently managed, the trial court looked to the performance since August 9, 1973 of "the bank's own diversified equity fund,[17] the Lincoln First Income Development Trust." The choice of model portfolio is critical; other models produced measures of damages ranging between $4,065,029 and $7,530,547. In re Judicial Settlement of the Account of Lincoln First Bank, 630 N.Y.S.2d 472, 479-481 (Sur. 1995).

Suppose the trustee were an individual and not a bank with a common fund. In such a case, if multiple model portfolios would have been prudent, which should be used in computing damages? In Donovan v. Bierwirth, 754 F.2d 1049 (2d Cir. 1985), which is an ERISA case, the court held that "Where several alternative investment strategies were equally plausible, the court should presume that the funds would have been used in the most profitable of these. The burden of proving that the funds would have earned less than that amount is on the fiduciaries found to be in breach of their duty. Any doubt or ambiguity should be resolved against them." Id. at 1056-1057. The total return approach is endorsed by Restatement (Third) of Trusts §§205, 208-211 (1992). See also Estate of Wilde, 708 A.2d 273 (Me. 1998).

The Court of Appeals in *Janes* rejected the trial court's total return approach, awarding instead $4,065,029 as the measure of *capital lost plus interest*. This figure represents the value of the trust's Kodak stock on August 9, 1973, plus compound interest through October 1, 1994. Although the court indicated that the rate of interest, if any, should be set at the discretion of the trial court, it did not discuss what rate or rates were used in this case. Our review of the record on appeal indicates that the interest rate used was not constant, but rather varied from 6 to 9 percent from year to year.[18] The specific rate used in each year was the legal

---

17. It is interesting to note that Kodak stock composed less than 3 percent of this fund. — Eds.

18. We thank Professor Kenneth Joyce of the University of Buffalo Law School, State University of New York, for supplying us with the briefs and record on appeal. Professor Joyce was co-counsel on behalf of Mrs. Janes's estate before the New York Court of Appeals.

rate of interest, which is the statutory interest rate that is applied to money judgments, beginning on the date of entry, and ending on the date of satisfaction. At the time of this writing, that rate was 9 percent. N.Y. Civ. Prac. L. & R. §5004 (2004).

Like the choice of model portfolio in awarding total return damages, the choice of applicable interest rate is crucial in awarding capital lost plus interest, because there is wide variance in the interest calculation depending on the rate of interest used. Consider the following table, which shows the value of the trust's Kodak stock on August 9, 1973 ($1,687,647.30), plus interest through October 1, 1994, compounded yearly, at three different plausible rates:

Interest Rate	Value in 21 Years
3.1% (the historic average annual rate of inflation)	$ 3,218,579.15
5.8% (the historic average annual return on long-term government bonds)	$ 5,560,617.05
9% (the current New York legal rate)	$10,444,242.68

What considerations are relevant in choosing the rate of interest? Is the statutory legal rate of interest a good proxy for the rate of return that the trust portfolio would have experienced? Are there other policies, such as simplicity, in favor of using this rate?

For discussion of capital lost plus interest versus total return as measures of damages for imprudence, see Edward C. Halbach, Jr., Trust Investment Law in the Third Restatement, 77 Iowa L. Rev. 1151, 1181-1182 (1992); C. Boone Schwartzel, Is the Prudent Investor Rule Good for Texas, 54 Baylor L. Rev. 701, 810-817 (2002); Robert H. Sitkoff, Trust Law, Corporate Law, and Capital Market Efficiency, 28 J. Corp. L. 565, 585-586 (2003).

Coda: The Market-Index Measure. The *total return* measure of damages is related to a *market-index measure*, with which it sometimes overlaps. Usually with the assistance of expert testimony, the total return approach requires the finder of fact to assemble a hypothetical prudent portfolio and then to compare the actual performance of the imprudent portfolio against the performance that the hypothetical portfolio would have experienced during the same period of time (perhaps adjusting for taxes and other such expenses). The market-index approach compares the performance of the actual portfolio against the performance of a market index such as the S&P 500. In favor of this approach, like that of interest set at the legal rate, is simplicity; there is no need to consider alternative models of prudence. On the other hand, a market index such as the S&P 500 will not necessarily correspond with what would have been a prudent portfolio for the particular trust at issue. For further discussion of the use of market indexes in surcharge litigation, see Dominic J. Campisi & Patrick J. Collins, Index Returns as a Measure of Damages in Fiduciary Surcharge Cases, Tr. &. Est., June 2001, at 18.

c. Delegation

Restatement (Second) of Trusts §171 (1959) states the traditional nondelegation rule: "The trustee is under a duty to the beneficiary not to delegate to others the doing of acts which the trustee can reasonably be required personally to perform."

Comment h to that section sets forth its applicability to investment decisions: "A trustee cannot properly delegate to another power to select investments."

SHRINERS HOSPITALS FOR CRIPPLED CHILDREN v. GARDINER, 733 P.2d 1110 (Ariz. 1987): Laurabel Gardiner created a trust to pay income to her daughter, Mary Jane, and her two grandchildren, Charles and Robert, with the remainder to Shriners Hospitals. Laurabel appointed Mary Jane trustee, Charles first alternate trustee, and Robert second alternate trustee. Mary Jane was not an experienced investor, however, so she left all the investment decisions to Charles, an investment counselor and stockbroker. Sometime thereafter Charles embezzled $317,000 from the trust. Shriners brought a petition to surcharge Mary Jane for the $317,000 on the ground that she had improperly delegated investment authority to Charles.

The first issue was whether Mary Jane's delegation of investment power to Charles was a breach of her fiduciary duty. Mary Jane argued that her lack of investment experience justified delegating investment power to Charles.

> Mary Jane argues, and we agree, that a trustee lacking investment experience must seek out expert advice. Although a trustee must seek out expert advice, "he is not ordinarily justified in relying on such advice, but must exercise his own judgment." Mary Jane, though, did not evaluate Charles' advice and then make her own decisions. Charles managed the trust fund, not Mary Jane. A prudent investor would certainly participate, to some degree, in investment decisions.

In her second accounting Mary Jane stated, "All of said investments were made . . . by [Charles]," and her lawyer said that she turned over investment decisions to Charles, who "for all practical purposes really served as trustee."

> Together, the accounting and admissions establish that Charles was functioning as a surrogate trustee. Mary Jane was not exercising any control over the selection of investments. She clearly breached her duties to act prudently and to personally perform her duties as a trustee.
>
> It is of no import that Charles was named as alternate trustee. A trustee is not permitted to delegate his responsibilities to a co-trustee. Certainly, then, a trustee is subject to liability when she improperly delegates her investment responsibility to an alternate trustee.

The second issue was whether there was a causal connection between Mary Jane's "breach and the loss suffered by the trust."

> The very nature of the loss indicates that the breach was not causally connected to the loss. The accounting indicates that Charles embezzled the funds. Without the knowledge or consent of the Trustee, said person received from said investments, and diverted to his own use, a total believed by the Trustee to aggregate $317,234.36 ($116,695.55 on January 16, 1981 and $200,537.81 on March 4, 1981). The trustee did not learn of said diversions until long after they occurred. No part of the amount so diverted had been returned or paid to the Trustee or the Trust Estate. . . .
>
> If the trust had suffered because poor investments were made, the delegation of investment authority would unquestionably be the cause of the loss. Otherwise, a causal connection between Charles' diversion of funds and Mary Jane's breach is

absent unless the delegation of investment authority gave Charles control and dominion over the trust fund that permitted the defalcation.

A causal connection does not exist simply because "but for" Mary Jane's opening of the account at Dean Witter Reynolds, no loss would have occurred. A trustee is not personally liable for losses not resulting from a breach of trust. Mary Jane did not breach her duty by establishing an account at Dean Witter Reynolds, a major brokerage house. Charles was not only the type of person Mary Jane was obliged to seek out for investment advice, but he was a person whom Laurabel Gardiner indicated was trustworthy by naming him as second alternate trustee. Furthermore, the Dean Witter Reynolds account was apparently in Mary Jane's name. If Dean Witter Reynolds wrongfully allowed Charles access to the fund, Mary Jane is not personally liable.

The court remanded the case for further proceedings on the question of causation.

QUESTION AND NOTE

1.   Would Mary Jane have been in breach if, instead of delegating to Charles, she resigned as trustee knowing that, as the first alternate, Charles would succeed her?

2.   Suppose *T* conveys a fund to *X* in trust and names *Y* as the successor trustee. If *X* imprudently invests the trust assets or engages in self-dealing, and then resigns, can the beneficiary hold *Y* liable for the earlier breach of trust by *X*? The answer is No. A successor trustee is not personally liable to the beneficiary for the prior trustee's breach of trust unless the successor unreasonably fails to discover and rectify the prior breach. However, liability in this scenario arises out of the successor trustee's own breach in unreasonably failing to remedy the prior trustee's blunder. See Restatement (Second) of Trusts §223 (1959).

The nondelegation rule stated in the Second Restatement and applied in *Gardiner* has been abrogated by Restatement (Third) of Trusts: Prudent Investor Rule §171 (1992) and by Uniform Prudent Investor Act §9 (1994).

Uniform Prudent Investor Act (1994)

§9.   DELEGATION OF INVESTMENT AND MANAGEMENT FUNCTIONS

(a) A trustee may delegate investment and management functions that a prudent trustee of comparable skills could properly delegate under the circumstances. The trustee shall exercise reasonable care, skill, and caution in:

(1) selecting an agent;

(2) establishing the scope and terms of the delegation, consistent with the purposes and terms of the trust; and

(3) periodically reviewing the agent's actions in order to monitor the agent's performance and compliance with the terms of the delegation.

(b) In performing a delegated function, an agent owes a duty to the trust to exercise reasonable care to comply with the terms of the delegation.

(c) A trustee who complies with the requirements of subsection (a) is not liable to the beneficiaries or to the trust for the decisions or actions of the agent to whom the function was delegated. . . .

NOTES AND QUESTIONS

1.   Uniform Trust Code §807 (2000) extends the abrogation of the nondelega-tion rule to all aspects of trust administration with language that is otherwise verbatim to that of Uniform Prudent Investor Act §9. In abrogating the nondele-gation rule, the Restatement (Third), Uniform Prudent Investor Act, and UTC impose on the trustee duties of care, skill, and caution in selecting the agent, in setting the terms of the delegation, and in monitoring the agent through regular reviews of the agent's actions. Thus prohibition has been replaced by a duty of care in *selection, instruction*, and *monitoring*. A trustee who adheres to these three core principles in delegating authority is not liable to the beneficiary or to the trust for the subsequent actions of the agent.

2.   Return to the *Gardiner* case. Would Mary Jane's actions have been a breach of duty under Uniform Prudent Investor Act §9 (1994)?

3.   Suppose the trustee lacks investment or other skills such that under the circumstances a prudent person would normally obtain expert advice. Under the new rules, does the trustee have an affirmative *duty* to delegate in such a scenario? The answer is probably Yes. See Restatement (Third) of Trusts: Prudent Investor Rule §227, cmt. j (1992).

4.   Suppose the trustee exercises due care in selection, instruction, and moni-toring, but the trust suffers a loss as a result of the agent's negligence. In such a case, can an aggrieved beneficiary bring suit directly against the trustee's invest-ment advisor? Cf. City of Atascadero v. Merrill Lynch, Pierce, Fenner & Smith, Inc., 80 Cal. Rptr. 2d 329 (App. 1999).

SECTION D.   IMPARTIALITY AND THE PRINCIPAL AND INCOME PROBLEM

Perhaps the most frequently litigated of the fiduciary subrules is the duty of *impartiality*. The hallmark of the duty of impartiality is balance: The trustee must strike a fair balance between the beneficiaries, giving due regard to their respective interests.

Dennis v. Rhode Island Hospital Trust Co.
United States Court of Appeals, First Circuit, 1984
744 F.2d 893

BREYER, C.J.[19]   The plaintiffs are the great-grandchildren of Alice M. Sullivan and beneficiaries of a trust created under her will. They claimed in the district court that the Bank trustee had breached various fiduciary obligations owed them as beneficiaries of that trust. The trust came into existence in 1920. It will cease to exist in 1991 (twenty-one years after the 1970 death of Alice Sullivan's last surviv-ing child). The trust distributes all its income for the benefit of Alice Sullivan's living issue; the principal is to go to her issue surviving in 1991. Evidently, since the death of their mother, the two plaintiffs are the sole surviving issue,

---

19. In 1994 Circuit Judge Stephen Breyer was appointed to the U.S. Supreme Court. — Eds.

entitled to the trust's income until 1991, and then, as remaindermen, entitled to the principal.

The controversy arises out of the trustee's handling of the most important trust assets, undivided interests in three multistory commercial buildings in downtown Providence. The buildings (the Jones, Wheaton-Anthony, and Alice Buildings) were all constructed before the beginning of the century, in an area where the value of the property has declined markedly over the last thirty years. During the period that the trust held these interests the buildings were leased to a number of different tenants, including corporations which subsequently subleased the premises. Income distribution from the trust to the life tenants has averaged over $34,000 annually.

At the time of the creation of the trust in 1920, its interests in the three buildings were worth more than $300,000. The trustee was authorized by the will to sell real estate. When the trustee finally sold the buildings in 1945, 1970, and 1979, respectively, it did so at or near the lowest point of their value; the trust received a total of only $185,000 for its interests in them. These losses, in plaintiffs' view, reflect a serious mishandling of assets over the years.

The district court, while rejecting many of plaintiffs' arguments, nonetheless found that the trustee had failed to act impartially, as between the trust's income beneficiaries and the remaindermen; it had favored the former over the latter, and, in doing so, it had reduced the value of the trust assets. To avoid improper favoritism, the trustee should have sold the real estate interests, at least by 1950, and reinvested the proceeds elsewhere. By 1950 the trustee must have, or should have, known that the buildings' value to the remaindermen would be small; the character of downtown commercial Providence was beginning to change; retention of the buildings would work to the disadvantage of the remaindermen. The court ordered a surcharge of $365,000, apparently designed to restore the real value of the trust's principal to its 1950 level.

On appeal, plaintiffs and defendants attack different aspects of the district court's judgment. We have reviewed the record in light of their arguments. We will not overturn a district court's factual determination unless it is "clearly erroneous," Fed. R. Civ. P. 52(a). . . . [W]ith one minor exception, [we] affirm the district court's judgment. . . .

The trustee first argues that the district court's conclusions rest on "hindsight." It points out that Rhode Island law requires a trustee to be "prudent and vigilant and exercise sound judgment," Rhode Island Hospital Trust Co. v. Copeland, 98 A. 273, 279 (R.I. 1916), but "[n]either prophecy nor prescience is expected." Stark v. United States Trust Co. of New York, 445 F. Supp. 670, 678 (S.D.N.Y. 1978). It adds that a trustee can indulge a preference for keeping the trust's "inception assets," those placed in trust by the settlor and commended to the trustee for retention. See Peckham v. Newton, 4 A. 758, 760 (R.I. 1886); Rhode Island Hospital Trust Co. v. Copeland, supra. How then, the trustee asks, can the court have found that it should have sold these property interests in 1950?

The trustee's claim might be persuasive had the district court found that it had acted imprudently in 1950, in retaining the buildings. If that were the case, one might note that every 1950 sale involved both a pessimistic seller and an optimistic buyer; and one might ask how the court could expect the trustee to have known then (in 1950) whose prediction would turn out to be correct. The trustee's argument is less plausible, however, where, as here, the district court basically found

The Wheaton-Anthony Building, built in 1872, was the first building in Providence to have an elevator.

that in 1950 the trustee had acted not imprudently, but unfairly, between income beneficiaries and remaindermen.

Suppose, for example, that a trustee of farmland over a number of years over-plants the land, thereby increasing short run income, but ruining the soil and making the farm worthless in the long run. The trustee's duty to take corrective action would arise from the fact that he knows (or plainly ought to know) that his present course of action will injure the remaindermen; settled law requires him to act impartially, "with due regard" for the "respective interests" of both the life tenant and the remainderman. Restatement (Second) of Trusts §232 (1959). The district court here found that a sale in 1950 would have represented one way (perhaps the only practical way) to correct this type of favoritism. It held that instead of correcting the problem, the trustee continued to favor the life tenant to the "very real disadvantage" of the remainder interests, in violation of Rhode Island law. See Industrial Trust Co. v. Parks, 190 A. 32, 38 (R.I. 1937); Rhode Island Hospital Trust Co. v. Tucker, 160 A. 465, 466 (R.I. 1932).

To be more specific, in the court's view the problem arose out of the trustee's failure to keep up the buildings, to renovate them, to modernize them, or to take other reasonably obvious steps that might have given the remaindermen property roughly capable of continuing to produce a reasonable income. This failure allowed the trustee to make larger income payments during the life of the trust; but the size of those payments reflected the trustee's acquiescence in the gradual deterioration of the property. In a sense, the payments ate away the trust's capital.

The trustee correctly points out that it did take certain steps to keep up the buildings; and events beyond its control made it difficult to do more. In the 1920's, the trustee, with court approval, entered into very longterm leases on the Alice and Wheaton-Anthony buildings. The lessees and the subtenants were supposed to keep the buildings in good repair; some improvements were made. Moreover, the depression made it difficult during the 1930's to find tenants who would pay a high rent and keep up the buildings. After World War II the neighborhood enjoyed a brief renaissance; but, then, with the 1950's flight to the suburbs, it simply deteriorated.

Even if we accept these trustee claims, however, the record provides adequate support for the district court's conclusions. There is considerable evidence indicating that, at least by 1950, the trustee should have been aware of the way in which the buildings' high rents, the upkeep problem, the changing neighborhood, the buildings' age, the failure to modernize, all together were consuming the buildings' value. There is evidence that the trustee did not come to grips with the problem. Indeed, the trustee did not appraise the properties periodically, and it did not keep proper records. It made no formal or informal accounting in 55 years. There is no indication in the record that the trust's officers focused upon the problem or consulted real estate experts about it or made any further rehabilitation efforts. Rather, there is evidence that the trustee did little more than routinely agree to the requests of the trust's income beneficiaries that it manage the trust corpus to produce the largest possible income. The New Jersey courts have pointed out that an impartial trustee must view the overall picture as it is presented from all the facts, and not close its eyes to any relevant facts which might result in excessive burden to the one class in preference to the other. Pennsylvania Co. v. Gillmore, 43 A.2d 667, 672 (N.J. Eq. 1945). The record supports a conclusion of failure to satisfy that duty.

The district court also found that the trustee had at least one practical solution available. It might have sold the property in 1950 and reinvested the proceeds in other assets of roughly equivalent total value that did not create a "partiality" problem. The Restatement of Trusts foresees such a solution, for it says that the trustee is under a duty to the beneficiary who is ultimately entitled to the principal not to . . . retain property which is certain or likely to depreciate in value, although the property yields a large income, unless he makes adequate provision for amortizing the depreciation. Restatement (Second) of Trusts §232, Comment b. Rhode Island case law also allows the court considerable discretion, in cases of fiduciary breach, to fashion a remedy, including a remedy based on a hypothetical, earlier sale. In, for example, Industrial Trust Co. v. Parks, 190 A. at 42, the court apportioned payments between income and principal "in the same way as they would have been apportioned if [certain] rights had been sold by the trustees immediately after the death of the testator" for a specified hypothetical value, to which the court added hypothetical interest. In the absence of a showing that such a sale and reinvestment would have been impractical or that some equivalent or better curative steps might have been taken, the district court's use of a 1950 sale as a remedial measure of what the trustee ought to have done is within the scope of its lawful powers.

In reaching this conclusion, we have taken account of the trustee's argument that the buildings' values were especially high in 1950 (though not as high as in the late 1920's). As the trustee argues, this fact would make 1950 an unreasonable remedial choice, other things being equal. But the record indicates that other things were not equal. For one thing, the district court chose 1950, not because of then-existing property values, but because that date marks a reasonable outer bound of the time the trustee could plead ignorance of the serious fairness problem. And, this conclusion, as we have noted, has adequate record support. For another thing, the district court could properly understand plaintiffs' expert witness as stating that the suburban flight that led to mid-1950's downtown decline began before 1950; its causes (increased household income; more cars; more mobility) were apparent before 1950. Thus, the court might reasonably have felt that a brief (1948-52) downtown "renaissance" should not have appeared (to the expert eye) to have been permanent or longlasting; it did not relieve the trustee of its obligation to do something about the fairness problem, nor did it make simple "building retention" a plausible cure. Finally, another expert testified that the trustee should have asked for power to sell the property "sometime between 1947 and 1952" when institutional investors generally began to diversify portfolios. For these reasons, reading the record, as we must, simply to see if it contains adequate support for the district court's conclusion as to remedy (as to which its powers are broad), we find that its choice of 1950 as a remedial base year is lawful.

Contrary to the trustee's contention, the case law it cites does not give it an absolute right under Rhode Island law to keep the trust's "inception assets" in disregard of the likely effect of retention on classes of trust beneficiaries. Cf. Peckham v. Newton, supra (original holdings should be retained but only so long as there is no doubt as to their safety); Rhode Island Hospital Trust Co. v. Copeland, supra (court not sufficiently informed on safety of holding to order sale or retention). The district court's conclusion that the trustee should have sold the assets if necessary to prevent the trust corpus from being consumed by the income beneficiaries is reasonable and therefore lawful. Cf. Industrial Trust Co. v. Parks, supra (wasting assets); Rhode Island Hospital Trust v. Tucker, supra (similar). . . .

The trustee [also] challenges the district court's calculation of the surcharge. The court assumed, for purposes of making the trust principal whole, that the trustee had hypothetically sold the trust's interests in the Wheaton-Anthony and the Alice buildings in 1950, at their 1950 values (about $70,000 and $220,000, respectively). It subtracted, from that sum of about $290,000, the $130,000 the trust actually received when the buildings were in fact sold (about $40,000 for the Wheaton-Anthony interest in 1970 and about $90,000 for the Alice interest in 1979). The court considered the difference of $160,000 to be a loss in the value of the principal, suffered as a result of the trustee's failure to prevent the principal from eroding. The court then assumed that, had the trustee sold the buildings in 1950 and reinvested the proceeds, the trustee would have been able to preserve the real value of the principal. It therefore multiplied the $160,000 by 3.6 percent, the average annual increase in the consumer price index from 1950 to 1982, and multiplied again by 32, the number of full years since 1950. Finally, the court multiplied again by an annual 0.4 percent, designed to reflect an "allowance for appreciation." It added the result ($160,000 × 4 percent × 32), about $205,000, to the $160,000 loss and surcharged the trustee $365,000. . . . [The court approved the district court's calculation except for the additional 0.4 percent, designed to reflect "appreciation." The court found no reason to believe that the trustee would have outperformed inflation. The court therefore recalculated the surcharge, omitting the 0.4 percent, and reduced the surcharge from $365,781.67 to $345,246.56.]

[Finally, the] trustee objects to the court's having removed it as trustee. The removal of a trustee, however, is primarily a matter for the district court. A trustee can be removed even if "the charges of his misconduct" are "not made out." Petition of Slatter, 275 A.2d 272, 276 (R.I. 1971). The issue here is whether "ill feeling" might interfere with the administration of the trust. The district court concluded that the course of the litigation in this case itself demonstrated such ill feeling. Nothing in the record shows that the court abused its powers in reaching that conclusion. . . .

The judgment of the district court is modified and as modified affirmed.

NOTES AND QUESTIONS

1. In In re Mulligan, [1998] 1 N.Z.L.R. 481, the testator left property in trust in 1965 for his widow for life, then to his nephews and nieces. The widow and a trust company were named co-trustees. The trustees invested in fixed income securities paying a high rate of interest. The trust company officers tried to persuade the widow to invest in common stock to counter inflation, but she refused. At the widow's death in 1990, the real value of the trust capital was a small proportion of what it was in 1965 because of inflation. The remaindermen sued both the trust company and the widow's estate. The court held that the trustees were liable for not treating the income beneficiary and the remaindermen evenhandedly. The trustees were in breach of trust because they recognized the risk of inflation but did nothing to protect against it. The trust company officers had not acted forcefully enough to persuade the widow to invest in common stock; nor had they applied to the court for direction when she refused. They should not have deferred to her

wishes, particularly in view of her conflict of interest. In this case the duty of impartiality thus vindicated both loyalty and prudence principles.

2.   The court in *Dennis* decided the case under impartiality principles rather than prudence. If the case had been decided under modern principles of prudence, that is, under the modern law of trust investment, what result? Observe that the "most important trust assets" were three buildings in downtown Providence — real estate in one location.

3.   *Damages.* In setting damages, the court in *Dennis* supposed that the trust, if it had been properly invested, would have experienced a 3.6 percent gain each year. The court assumed that the trust's performance would have matched, but not exceeded, the average rate of inflation during the relevant period.

4.   *Trustee removal as a remedy.* The court in *Dennis* upheld the removal of the trustees. Although as a doctrinal matter trustee removal is a remedy for breach of trust, we address it in Chapter 8 in connection with trust modification and termination because it implicates many of the same policy questions. See page 585.

5.   In *Dennis*, the court found that the trustee favored the income beneficiaries by investing in property with high income return but depreciating capital value. Suppose it is the other way around: The trustee invests in unproductive assets (say, forest or open land producing no rental income) with high appreciation potential. What remedy is given the income beneficiaries? "When land held in trust appreciates in value to the point it becomes underproductive, and there are conflicting interests between income beneficiaries and remaindermen, the law will imply a duty to sell the land within a reasonable time, even in those instances where the testator authorized the trustee to retain the assets." In re Kuehn, 308 N.W.2d 398 (S.D. 1981). See also Rutanen v. Ballard, 678 N.E.2d 133 (Mass. 1997) (awarding damages against the trustees in the amount lost by failure to sell and awarding the income beneficiaries what they would have received had the proceeds of sale been invested in six-month U.S. Treasury bills). Similar problems obtain in allocating a surcharge for imprudent investment between the principal and income beneficiaries.

6.   Suppose that there is an ambiguity in the trust instrument that can be resolved in a manner favorable to either the income beneficiary or the principal beneficiary, but not both. In petitioning for a judicial construction, can the trustee argue in favor of one interpretation or the other? See Northern Trust Co. v. Heuer, 560 N.E.2d 961 (Ill. App. 1990).

NOTE: THE PRINCIPAL AND INCOME PROBLEM

The classic impartiality problem is presented by a trust with successive beneficiaries. Suppose *T* bequeaths a fund to *X* in trust to pay the income to *A* for life and then the principal to *B* on *A*'s death. Although the overall interests of *A* and *B* are grossly aligned on matters such as self-dealing or embezzlement by *X*, their specific interests in the day-to-day management of the trust fund will not necessarily be congruent. The problem is that under traditional fiduciary rules respecting allocation to income and principal, the particular *form* of the trust's investment return determines the beneficiary's return. Hence the income beneficiary, *A*, will prefer investments that produce returns that are classified as income while *B*, the principal beneficiary, will prefer investments that produce returns that are classified as principal.

For example, under traditional principles, cash dividends on common stock are classified as income, but appreciation in the stock price goes to principal.[20] Thus, if the trustee opts to invest in a stock that does not pay a dividend (in which case the stock's price will appreciate faster because profits will accumulate within the company), then the principal beneficiary is advantaged at the expense of the income beneficiary. Likewise, if the trustee opts to invest in a stock that does pay a dividend (in which case the stock's price will appreciate more slowly because profits will be distributed to the shareholders from time to time in the form of dividend checks), then the income beneficiary is advantaged at the expense of the principal beneficiary. As a matter of economic reality, however, the assignment of some forms of investment return to principal and other forms of return to income is fundamentally arbitrary. The consequence is that the income and principal beneficiaries are advantaged or disadvantaged by dint of the trustee's allocation of the trust fund between investments that produce income (as defined) versus appreciation of principal (as defined). As illustrated by the *Dennis* case, courts have traditionally adjudicated disputes over the trustee's allocations under the duty of impartiality.

The embrace of modern portfolio theory by the modern law of trust investment has brought into sharp relief the arbitrariness of allocating certain investment proceeds to income and others to principal based on the form of the proceeds in question. When the trust fund is invested for total return, that return might include cash dividends, stock dividends, capital gain, mineral royalties, derivatives (hedges, options, futures contracts, and the like), and a host of other potential receipts. Paying too much attention to the *form* of the investment will sometimes collide with the larger aim of maximizing the *value* of the total return. Just as a pound of lead weighs as much as a pound of feathers, tax considerations aside, a dollar of profit in one form is equal to a dollar of profit in another — a buck is a buck. It is better to invest for total return, and then allocate that return to the income and principal beneficiaries, than to allow the characterization of investment proceeds as income or principal to drive the trustee's investment decisions.

Accordingly, in 1997 the Uniform Law Commissioners promulgated a revised Uniform Principal and Income Act. The revised act, which has been widely adopted, is designed to address the tension between investing the trust portfolio for the highest total return and the need to allocate total return receipts between income and principal beneficiaries. The 1997 Act continues the traditional approach whereby the particular form of the return determines the beneficiary's return. But to free the trustee's hand in crafting a portfolio for total return, §104 of the Act gives the trustee the power to reallocate receipts to income or principal if the trustee concludes that wise investing leads, under the allocation rules, to unfair results. This power of *equitable adjustment* is a default rule, operational only if the settlor does not provide otherwise.

---

20. The 1962 Uniform Principal and Income Act is representative of the traditional approach. To income the 1962 Act allocates: (1) rent; (2) interest on loans and bonds; (3) cash dividends on stock; (4) net profits from a business or farming operation; (5) royalties from natural resources (except 27 1/2 percent allocated to principal); and (6) royalties from patents and copyrights (but not in excess of 5 percent per year of inventory value).

To principal, increasing the corpus of the trust, the 1962 Act allocates: (1) proceeds from sale of property; (2) proceeds of insurance on property; (3) stock splits and stock dividends; (4) corporate distributions from a merger or acquisition; (5) payment of bond principal; (6) royalties from natural resources (27 1/2 percent); and (7) royalties from patents and copyrights in excess of 5 percent of inventory value.

A different solution to the problem of fair allocation is the *unitrust*. The unitrust idea, which comes from the charitable remainder unitrust discussed at page 917, is that the settlor will set the percentage of the value of the trust principal that must be paid to the income beneficiary each year. The trust principal is revalued each year. Thus, if the income beneficiary is entitled to 5 percent of the value of the trust principal and the principal is worth $1 million, the income beneficiary receives $50,000. If the value of the trust principal increases in the next year to $1,200,000, the income beneficiary is entitled to $60,000. Both income and principal beneficiaries gain from capital appreciation. The unitrust lets the settlor determine the percentage of the total return that is to be paid to the income beneficiary, leaving it to the trustee to maximize the trust's total return irrespective of the form in which that return takes. The percentage need not be fixed; for example, the settlor might key the percentage to the rate of inflation or prevailing interest rates. Or the settlor might smooth the payouts by providing that the payout percentage should be multiplied by a three-year average value of the trust.

As means of ameliorating the tension between the arbitrary definitions of income and principal and total return investing under modern portfolio theory, neither the unitrust nor equitable adjustment is manifestly superior to the other.

> With equitable adjustment or a unitrust, the higher the total return, the better all the beneficiaries do. The unitrust does so with less discretion and so a reduced potential for agency costs. But it less perfectly aligns the interests of the income and principal beneficiaries, because a disproportionate share of the potential upside from higher risk investments will accrue to the principal beneficiaries. Equitable adjustment somewhat better aligns the beneficiaries' interests, but it increases the potential for agency costs . . . because it gives the trustee additional discretion. . . . Still, the exercise of this discretion is more transparent than the traditional approach of hiding the problem behind the portfolio's initial allocation between income-producing and capital-appreciating investments. [Robert H. Sitkoff, An Agency Costs Theory of Trust Law, 89 Cornell L. Rev. 621, 654 (2004).]

An interesting compromise approach is to give the trustee the power of equitable adjustment but to state a nonbinding guideline percentage.

This much is clear: Modern portfolio theory puts pressure on lawyers to discuss with clients the kind of income stream the client wants the income beneficiary to have. For already existing trusts, enactment of the 1997 Uniform Principal and Income Act will allow the trustee to embrace a total return investment strategy tempered by the power of equitable adjustment. See In re Jenkins, 97 S.W.3d 126, 131-132 (Tenn. App. 2002) (upholding prospective application of the statute to existing trusts).[21] In addition, some states have enacted legislation authorizing the conversion of an existing principal and income trust into a unitrust. See In re Ives, 745 N.Y.S.2d 904 (Sur. 2002) (first conversion case in New York).

Caution: A host of federal income, gift, and estate tax laws are keyed to definitions of income and principal. New treasury regulations effective January 2, 2004, validate the use of equitable adjustment or a unitrust percentage under these laws, provided that certain requirements are met, including in most cases the existence

---

21. Harold Jenkins, the testator in this case, was known professionally as Conway Twitty, the country music performer who had 55 number one albums, more than Elvis and the Beatles combined. See www.conwaytwitty.net.

of a validating state statute. For further discussion, see Robert B. Wolf & Stephan R. Leimberg, Total Return Trusts Approved by New Regs., but State Law Is Crucial, 31 Est. Plan. 179 (2004). See also Louis A. Del Cotto & Kenneth F. Joyce, Taxation of the Trust Annuity: The Unitrust Under the Constitution and the Internal Revenue Code, 23 Tax L. Rev. 257 (1968).

For further discussion of the new trust arrangements that will likely develop as a result of modern portfolio theory, and of the principal and income problem generally, see Robert B. Wolf, Estate Planning with Total Return Unitrusts: Meeting Human Needs and Investment Goals Through Modern Trust Design, 36 Real Prop., Prob. & Tr. J. 169 (2001); Jerold L. Horn, Prudent Investor Rule, Modern Portfolio Theory, and Private Trusts: Drafting and Administration Including the "Give-Me-Five" Unitrust, 33 Real Prop., Prob. & Tr. J. 1 (1998); Joel C. Dobris, Why Trustee Investors Often Prefer Dividends to Capital Gain and Debt Investments to Equity — A Daunting Principal and Income Problem, 32 Real Prop., Prob. & Tr. J. 255 (1997).

SECTION E.   SUBRULES RELATING TO THE TRUST PROPERTY

In the prior section, we examined the duty of impartiality, which is perhaps the most frequently litigated of the trust fiduciary law subrules. In this section, we continue our examination of the subsidiary rules of trust fiduciary law by looking at three that relate to the trustee's care of the trust property.

1.   Duty to Collect and Protect Trust Property

A trustee has the duty of obtaining possession of the trust assets without unnecessary delay. See Uniform Trust Code §809 (2000). What is unreasonable delay depends on the circumstances. When a testamentary trust is established, the trustee should collect the assets from the executor as promptly as circumstances permit. In addition, a testamentary trustee owes a duty to the beneficiaries to examine the property tendered by the executor to make sure it is what the trustee ought to receive. This means the trustee must look at the acts of the executor and require the executor to redress any breach of duty that diminished the assets intended for the trust. See In re First Natl. Bank of Mansfield, 307 N.E.2d 23 (Ohio 1974) (trustee is liable to beneficiaries for not objecting to executor's overpayment of inheritance tax). See also UTC §812 (2000).

Once having obtained the trust property, a trustee must act as a prudent person in its management.

2.   Duty to Earmark Trust Property

A trustee has a duty to *earmark* trust property. To earmark property is to designate it as trust property rather than the trustee's own. The reason: If the property is not earmarked, a trustee might later claim that the investments that proved profitable were the trustee's own investments and the investments that lost value were made for the trust. (Assets not subject to registration such as bearer bonds fall within an established exception to the earmarking requirement.)

Under the older view, where a trustee commits a breach of trust by failing to earmark a trust investment, the trustee is strictly liable for any loss resulting from the investment. Even if it clearly appears that the loss is not caused by the failure to earmark, a trustee is liable for the actual loss sustained by the trust. The more modern view, adopted by the Restatement (Second) of Trusts §179, cmt. d (1959), is that a trustee is liable only for such loss as results from the failure to earmark and is not liable for such loss as results from general economic conditions.

PROBLEMS

1. A trustee deposits money in Security Bank in the trustee's individual name. Security Bank fails. Is the trustee liable for the amount of the deposit? See 2A Austin W. Scott, Trusts §180 (William F. Fratcher 4th ed. 1987). Would it matter if the trustee were an officer or director of the bank and knew the bank was in difficulty? See Epworth Orphanage v. Long, 36 S.E.2d 37 (S.C. 1945).

2. A trustee invests in Baker Company stock, taking title to the certificates in the trustee's individual name. The trustee did this to facilitate later transfer since on subsequent sale the buyer might have to inquire into the terms of the trust if the buyer knew the shares were held in trust. Baker Company stock goes down in value. Is the trustee liable for the loss? Would it make any difference if the trustee had shown on the trustee's records that the stock was purchased for the trust? See White v. Sherman, 48 N.E. 128 (Ill. 1897); Miller v. Pender, 34 A.2d 663 (N.H. 1943). Would it make any difference if the trustee took title in the name of a nominee? See Potter v. Union & Peoples Natl. Bank, 105 F.2d 437 (6th Cir. 1939).

3. *Duty Not to Mingle Trust Funds with the Trustee's Own*

A trustee is guilty of a breach of trust if the trustee *commingles* the trust funds with his own, even if trustee does not use the trust funds for his own purposes. See UTC §810(b) (2000). The reason: Commingled trust funds become more difficult to trace and hence subject to the risk that personal creditors of the trustee can reach them. That the personal creditors of the trustee cannot normally reach the assets of the trust is a feature of trust law that has been stressed in a burgeoning literature on the nature and function of organizational forms. See Henry Hansmann & Reinier Kraakman, The Essential Role of Organizational Law, 110 Yale L.J. 387, 416 (2000); Henry Hansmann & Ugo Mattei, The Functions of Trust Law: A Comparative Legal and Economic Analysis, 73 N.Y.U.L. Rev. 434, 435 (1998). See also Robert H. Sitkoff, An Agency Costs Theory of Trust Law, 89 Cornell L. Rev. 621, 631-633, 641-643 (2004).

In recent years, however, the prohibition against commingling has been partially abrogated in almost all jurisdictions to permit a corporate fiduciary to hold and invest trust assets in a common trust fund. Building on this trend, UTC §810(d) allows all trustees to make a joint investment from separate trusts, provided that "the trustee maintains records clearly indicating the respective interests." The rationale for both reforms is to allow trustees to take advantage of economies of scale. Neither permit commingling with the trustee's own assets.

As with breach of the duty to earmark, there is a divergence of views regarding the extent of a trustee's liability for commingling. The older view is that a trustee is strictly liable, even though the loss would have occurred had there been no commingling. More recent authority holds a trustee liable only to the extent the commingling caused the loss.

PROBLEM

The trustee of a trust under the will of José Martinez places bearer bonds, bought for $10,000, in her individual safe-deposit box, in an envelope marked "Owned by José Martinez Trust." The trustee dies. The market value of the bonds is $9,500. Is the trustee's estate liable for the $500 loss? See Lavarelle's Estate, 13 Pa. D. & C. 703 (Orph. 1930), aff'd, 101 Pa. Super. 448 (1931):

> We freely concede that a trustee may illegally abstract assets from the box maintained in his own name, as trustee, quite as readily as he could by taking the securities from his individual box. On the other hand, either through accident or design, the envelope may become worn, dilapidated, or it may entirely disappear; the markings or writings on the envelope, in time, may fail to remain decipherable; the rubber bands surrounding the envelope may become hard and brittle and disintegrate, or the tape or string with which they are tied may break or disappear. In such event, the securities, unearmarked, may become commingled with those which the trustee may individually own. Should the trustee die under such circumstances, it may become impossible or difficult to segregate the trust securities from those of his own. Or should the trustee become insolvent, a contest with creditors may arise and jeopardize the trust assets. Furthermore, should a trustee keep assets in his individual box, *his* executor, on his death, may assume custody. Thus, securities come into possession of a stranger to the trust and without bond. Where, however, the box is in the name of the fiduciary as trustee, the appointment of a substituted trustee is requisite before access may be had to the box. This is an added protection to the trust estate. In our opinion, it is quite as reprehensible for a trustee to commingle trust (unregistered) securities with his own as it is to keep the cash of the estate in his own individual bank account. [13 Pa. D. & C. at 703.]

SECTION F. DUTY TO INFORM AND ACCOUNT TO THE BENEFICIARIES

Fletcher v. Fletcher
Supreme Court of Virginia, 1997
253 Va. 30, 480 S.E.2d 488

COMPTON, J.   In this chancery proceeding arising from a dispute over an inter vivos trust, we consider the extent of a trustee's duty to furnish information about the trust instrument and about other documents relating to the trust.

The facts are presented on appeal by a Rule 5:11 agreed statement of facts. During their lifetimes, J. North Fletcher and Elinor Leh Fletcher, his wife, residents of Fauquier County, accumulated substantial assets.

Following Mr. Fletcher's death in 1984, Mrs. Fletcher executed a revocable, inter vivos "Trust Agreement" in December 1985 in which she placed all her assets. The ten-page document, containing nine articles, named her as both "Grantor" and "Trustee." In August 1993, the Grantor modified the Trust Agreement by executing a "Trust Agreement Amendment." The five-page Amendment replaced Article Six of the Trust Agreement with a new Article Six.

The Trust Agreement as amended (the Trust Agreement) contains, among other things, specific provisions for the establishment of a number of trusts upon the Grantor's death, including three separate trusts for the respective benefit of appellee James N. Fletcher, Jr., an adult child of the Grantor, and his two children, Andrew N. Fletcher, born in 1972, and Emily E. Fletcher, born in 1976 (sometimes collectively, the beneficiaries). The three separate trusts were to be in the amount of $50,000 each. The Trust Agreement appointed appellant Henry L. Fletcher, another adult child of the Grantor, and appellant F & M Bank-Peoples Trust and Asset Management Group, formerly Peoples National Bank of Warrenton, as successor Trustees to act upon the Grantor's death.

Under the Trust Agreement, the Trustees are authorized, in their discretion, to expend for the benefit of James N. Fletcher, Jr., such amounts of the net income and principal of the $50,000 trust as may be necessary to provide him adequate medical insurance and medical care during his lifetime, or until such time as the trust is depleted. In the event the trust is still in existence at Fletcher's death, then the Trustees are required to transfer and pay over to his surviving children his or her proportionate share of the balance of the remaining principal and income.

Under the Trust Agreement, the Trustees also are authorized, in their discretion, to expend for the benefit of Fletcher's children such amounts of the income and principal of each of the $50,000 trusts as they deem advisable.

The Grantor died in June 1994. Upon her death, the Trust Agreement became irrevocable, and the successor Trustees assumed their duties. They established the three $50,000 trusts, and the beneficiaries have benefited from them.

In June 1995, beneficiary James N. Fletcher, Jr., instituted the present proceeding against the Trustees. In a bill of complaint, the plaintiff alleged that the December 1985 instrument recites that the Grantor "transferred, assigned and set over certain cash and securities which were . . . described in a schedule entitled 'A' attached to the trust agreement." The plaintiff further alleged that, upon his mother's death, he was advised that the assets had been transferred to "a new trust" with the defendants as Trustees.

The plaintiff also asserted that he "requested details from the defendants of both the December 3, 1985 trust and the trust created with the assets of that trust upon his mother's death," and that the Trustees have refused to comply with his request. He further asserted that he has been provided with only pages 1, 8 and 9 of the 1985 instrument and "two pages" from the Amendment. The plaintiff also asserted that "without a listing of the precise terms of both trust agreements or a complete listing of the assets of these trusts," he is "unable to determine whether or not the trust estate is being properly protected."

Plaintiff also alleged that Trustee Henry L. Fletcher "has repeatedly made a point of justifying his failure to disclose the requested information . . . by stating that it was his mother's request that the trust terms and dealings be kept confidential, even from the beneficiaries." Further, the plaintiff asserts that Trustee Fletcher "has failed to produce any written direction from [their mother] with respect to the confidentiality." This situation, along with other facts, according to the allegations, has resulted in "an extremely strained relationship between" the brothers.

Concluding, the plaintiff alleged that because he lacks the "relevant information" sought, "he is unable to determine whether or not either trustee is properly performing their duties as a trustee[ ] according to law." Thus, he asked the court to compel the Trustees "to provide full and complete copies of all trust instruments in their possession that relate to the two trusts referred to herein."

In a demurrer, the Trustees asserted that the bill of complaint failed to state a cause of action. In an answer, the Trustees denied that any "new trust" was created upon the Grantor's death, and asserted that the Trust Agreement remained in effect following the death. The Trustees asserted, however, that upon the death, "separate trusts were created under the express terms of the Trust Agreement," and that the plaintiff has been provided with "all provisions of the Trust Agreement relating to him and his children, along with regular accountings relating to his interest under the Trust Agreement." In sum, the Trustees denied the plaintiff is entitled to the information sought.

In October 1995, pursuant to an agreed order, the Trustees filed the Trust Agreement under seal with the court, to be examined only by the court.

Subsequently, the trial court heard argument on the demurrer and, during the hearing, ruled that the plaintiff was entitled to see all provisions of the Trust Agreement. The court noted that the plaintiff's "interests as a child of" the Grantor and as "a beneficiary of her trust outweighed the arguments advanced" by the Trustees.

Accordingly, in a January 1996 final order, the court said it was of opinion that the plaintiff "has an absolute right to complete copies of the Trust Agreement and all amendments referred to in the pleadings and associated documents." Thus, the court ordered the Trustees to provide the plaintiff with "full and complete copies of the Trust instruments that are referred to in the Bill of Complaint filed in this cause." The Trustees appeal.

The Trustees contend the trial court erred in finding that the plaintiff had an absolute right to review complete copies of the Trust Agreement and in ordering them to provide plaintiff with such copies. Emphasizing that the trust instrument established three separate trusts, the Trustees argue the trial court's order "ignores the fiduciary duty of confidentiality between the Trustees and other beneficiaries under the . . . Trust Agreement." Noting the use of revocable trusts in planning disposition of assets upon death, the Trustees say that following a grantor's death, "the trustees handle the trust assets for the various beneficiaries, in accordance with the grantor's instruction, in a manner appropriate for each beneficiary taking into account the unique circumstances applicable to each beneficiary."

Continuing, the Trustees observe that a grantor, as here, often "directs the trustee to segregate trust assets into separate trusts for the benefit of different beneficiaries." See Code §55-19.3 (trustee may divide a trust into two or more separate trusts). According to the Trustees, "Segregation of a trust into separate trusts for different beneficiaries not only segregates the assets, but also segregates the trustee's duties to the different beneficiaries." The Trustees say that a "trustee has a continuing duty to the grantor to fulfill the trustee's obligations under the trust agreement. The trustee also has a fiduciary duty to the beneficiaries of each trust established under the agreement. The trustee's duties to the beneficiaries of each separate trust do not overlap."

The Trustees point out the plaintiff has not alleged any wrongdoing on their part "nor has he alleged that he has any interest under the . . . Trust Agreement other than his interest in a separate trust established for his benefit." The Trustees state they have provided the plaintiff with copies of the portions of the Trust Agreement that pertain to the establishment and administration of the separate trusts, have submitted a copy of the Trust Agreement to the trial judge so the court may determine whether they have disclosed to the plaintiff all relevant information, and have provided regular accountings to the beneficiaries with respect to their separate trusts. The Trustees argue that the family relationship and the "specter" of disharmony, standing alone do not create a right in the plaintiff to compel disclosure. Finally, the Trustees argue "the trial court's Order compelling disclosure violates the public policy that permits individuals to ensure privacy of their affairs through the use of inter vivos trust agreements in lieu of wills."

We do not agree with the Trustees' contentions. They place too much emphasis upon the duties of trustees while neglecting the rights of beneficiaries.

This is a case of first impression in Virginia. The parties have not referred us to any cases elsewhere that are factually apposite, and we have found none. Nevertheless, text writers and the Restatement articulate settled principles that are applicable.

"The beneficiary is the equitable owner of trust property, in whole or in part. The trustee is a mere representative whose function is to attend to the safety of the trust property and to obtain its avails for the beneficiary in the manner provided by the trust instrument." Bogert, The Law of Trusts and Trustees §961, at 2 (Rev. 2nd ed. 1983). The fact that a grantor has created a trust and thus required the beneficiary to enjoy the property interest indirectly "does not imply that the beneficiary is to be kept in ignorance of the trust, the nature of the trust property and the details of its administration." Bogert, §961, at 2.

Therefore, "the trustee is under a duty to the beneficiary to give him upon his request at reasonable times complete and accurate information as to the nature and amount of the trust property, and to permit him or a person duly authorized by him to inspect the subject matter of the trust and the accounts and vouchers and other documents relating to the trust." Restatement (Second) of Trusts §173 (1959). Accord Bogert, §961, at 3-4; IIA Scott, The Law of Trusts §173, at 462 (4th ed. 1987). Indeed, "where a trust is created for several beneficiaries, each of them is entitled to information as to the trust." Scott, §173, at 464.

And, even though "the terms of the trust may regulate the amount of information which the trustee must give and the frequency with which it must be given, the beneficiary is always entitled to such information as is reasonably necessary to enable him to enforce his rights under the trust or to prevent or redress a breach of trust." Restatement §173 cmt. c. See In re Estate of Rosenblum, 328 A.2d 158, 164-165 (Pa. 1974).

Turning to the present facts, we observe that the appellate record fails to establish that the Grantor directed the Trustees not to disclose the terms of the entire Trust Agreement to the beneficiaries. The trust instrument, which we have examined, does not mention the subject. Although the Trustees assert the Grantor orally gave such instructions, the plaintiff questions this fact. And, there was no evidentiary hearing below to decide the matter. Thus, we express no opinion on what effect any directive of secrecy by the Grantor would have on the outcome of this case.

Recognizing the foregoing general principles of the law of trusts, the Trustees nevertheless seek to remove this case from the force of those rules by dwelling on the fact that three separate trusts were created. In essence, the Trustees treat this single integrated Trust Agreement as if there are three distinct trust documents, each entirely independent of the other, a circumstance that simply does not exist.

There is a single cohesive trust instrument based on a unitary corpus. The Trustees seek to avoid the beneficiary's scrutiny of eight pages of the Trust Agreement. They also seek to prevent review of Schedule "A," which lists the cash and securities the Grantor transferred to the trust corpus. This document was not even included in the sealed papers filed with the trial court.

The information not disclosed may have a material bearing on the administration of the Trust Agreement insofar as the beneficiary is concerned. For example, without access to the Trust Agreement (even though there are numerous separate trusts established), the beneficiary has no basis upon which he can intelligently scrutinize the Trustees' investment decisions made with respect to the assets revealed on Schedule "A." The beneficiary is unable to evaluate whether the Trustees are discharging their duty to use "reasonable care and skill to make the trust property productive." Sturgis v. Stinson, 404 S.E.2d 56, 58 (Va. 1991) (quoting Restatement (Second) of Trusts §181 (1959)). Also, the beneficiary is entitled to review the trust documents in their entirety in order to assure the Trustees are discharging their "duty to deal impartially" with all the beneficiaries within the restrictions and conditions imposed by the Trust Agreement. *Sturgis*, 404 S.E.2d at 58.

In sum, we hold that the trial court correctly required the Trustees to disclose the information sought. Thus, the judgment appealed from will be

Affirmed.

Uniform Trust Code (2000, as amended 2004)

§813. DUTY TO INFORM AND REPORT

(a) A trustee shall keep the qualified beneficiaries of the trust reasonably informed about the administration of the trust and of the material facts necessary for them to protect their interests. Unless unreasonable under the circumstances, a trustee shall promptly respond to a beneficiary's request for information related to the administration of the trust.

(b) A trustee:

(1) upon request of a beneficiary, shall promptly furnish to the beneficiary a copy of the trust instrument;

(2) within 60 days after accepting a trusteeship, shall notify the qualified beneficiaries of the acceptance and of the trustee's name, address, and telephone number;

(3) within 60 days after the date the trustee acquires knowledge of the creation of an irrevocable trust, or the date the trustee acquires knowledge that a formerly revocable trust has become irrevocable, whether by the death of the settlor or otherwise, shall notify the qualified beneficiaries of the trust's existence, of the identity of the settlor or settlors, of the right to request a copy of the trust

instrument, and of the right to a trustee's report as provided in subsection (c); and

(4) shall notify the qualified beneficiaries in advance of any change in the method or rate of the trustee's compensation.

(c) A trustee shall send to the distributees or permissible distributees of trust income or principal, and to other qualified or nonqualified beneficiaries who request it, at least annually and at the termination of the trust, a report of the trust property, liabilities, receipts, and disbursements, including the source and amount of the trustee's compensation, a listing of the trust assets and, if feasible, their respective market values. Upon a vacancy in a trusteeship, unless a cotrustee remains in office, a report must be sent to the qualified beneficiaries by the former trustee. A personal representative, [conservator], or [guardian] may send the qualified beneficiaries a report on behalf of a deceased or incapacitated trustee.

(d) A beneficiary may waive the right to a trustee's report or other information otherwise required to be furnished under this section. A beneficiary, with respect to future reports and other information, may withdraw a waiver previously given.

[Section 813(e) omitted]

NOTES AND QUESTIONS

1. If the settlor directs the trustee to disclose to a beneficiary only the provisions of the trust relating to that beneficiary, should it be upheld? Should the settlor be able to make, in effect, a secret will by using a revocable trust? See Taylor v. Nationsbank Corp., 481 S.E.2d 358 (N.C. App. 1997).

The Uniform Trust Code provides that, upon request, the trustee must "promptly furnish to the beneficiary a copy of the trust instrument." UTC §813(b)(1) (2000). However, this provision is omitted from the Code's schedule of mandatory rules in §105, so the settlor is free to provide otherwise in the trust instrument.

California Probate Code §16061.5 (2004) provides that when a revocable trust becomes irrevocable because of the death of the settlor, the trustee shall provide a complete copy of the terms of the irrevocable trust to any beneficiary *or heir* of the settlor who requests it. Why are heirs of the settlor entitled to see a trust document of which they are not beneficiaries? Should this requirement be extended to an irrevocable inter vivos trust?

2. Should the settlor be able to waive the beneficiary's information rights in their entirety? See Restatement (Second) of Trusts §173, cmt. c (1959). On the one hand, without rights to information, the beneficiary may not know of, or be able to enforce, his interest in the trust. As a check on the behavior of the trustee, the fiduciary obligation depends on the viability of the beneficiary's threat to bring suit. On the other hand, if the beneficiary's knowledge of a substantial trust fund will lead him to adopt a slothful, profligate, or wasteful existence, it might be in the beneficiary's best interest to conceal the existence of the trust. Should the ability of the settlor to conceal the trust's existence from the beneficiary be conditioned on the appointment of a third-party trust protector with the power to bring suit against the trustee for breach of trust (on protectors, see page 579)?

As originally drafted, under UTC §105(b)(9) the settlor could not waive the beneficiary's right under §813(a) to information reasonably related to the beneficiary's interest in the trust. Likewise, under §105(b)(8), the settlor could not waive the right under §813(b)(2)-(3) of a beneficiary who is at least 25 years of age to be notified by the trustee of the existence of the trust. See David M. English, The Uniform Trust Code (2000): Significant Provisions and Policy Issues, 67 Mo. L. Rev. 143, 202-203 (2002).

These mandatory provisions have been criticized by some practitioners, however, and Arizona, which enacted the UTC in 2003, repealed it in 2004 in part because of these provisions. See Rachel Emma Silverman, Trust Laws Get a Makeover, Wall St. J., July 29, 2004, at D1. In response, the Uniform Law Commissioners amended UTC §105 in the summer of 2004 to put §105(b)(8)-(9) in brackets. In a uniform law, brackets indicate that the provision is optional. Inasmuch as no state is required to adopt a uniform law, and that those that do are free to enact it in whole, in part, or with further amendments, does this revision reflect sound policy? If not, does it reflect sound politics? Would it have been better to condition the settlor's power to waive the beneficiary's information rights on the appointment of a trust protector with standing to enforce the trust?

3. *Major transactions.* Should the trustee have a duty to give beneficiaries advance notice of the sale of trust property that comprises a significant portion of the value of the trust property, or is otherwise difficult to value or replace? In Allard v. Pacific Natl. Bank, 663 P.2d 104 (Wash. 1983), the court surcharged the trustee for failing to give the beneficiaries advance notice of the proposed sale of real estate that was the sole asset of the trust. The court held that the trustee has a duty to inform the beneficiaries "of material facts in connection with a nonroutine transaction which significantly affects the trust estate and the interests of the beneficiaries prior to the transaction taking place." Id. at 110-111. See also In re Green Charitable Trust, 431 N.W.2d 492, 499-500 (Mich. App. 1988). The Comment to UTC §813 endorses *Allard* and reads its holding into §813(a).

4. *Trustee's agents.* Do agents of the trustee also have a duty to give information to the beneficiaries? The question is most commonly presented when the trustee's lawyer invokes the attorney-client privilege against a demand by the beneficiary for information concerning the attorney's representation of the trustee. The cases are sparse and contradictory. Compare Riggs Natl. Bank v. Zimmer, 355 A.2d 709 (Del. Ch. 1976) (allowing the beneficiaries to discover the attorney-trustee communications on the ground that the beneficiaries, not the trustee, are the "real" clients when a trustee, acting as such, hires a lawyer), with Wells Fargo Bank v. Superior Ct. (Boltwood), 990 P.2d 591 (Cal. 2000) (rejecting the analysis in *Riggs*). The prevailing view in ERISA litigation appears to be in favor of the beneficiaries. See United States v. Mett, 178 F.3d 1058, 1062-1064 (9th Cir. 1999).

The comment to UTC §813 states that, because of the wide divergence of opinion on this issue, the drafters left the question "open for further consideration by the courts." For further discussion, see Louis H. Hamel, Jr., Trustee's Privileged Counsel: A Rebuttal, 21 ACTEC Notes 156 (1995); Charles F. Gibbs & Cindy D. Hanson, The Fiduciary Exception to a Trustee's Attorney/Client Privilege, 21 ACTEC Notes 236 (1995). See also Jeffrey N. Pennell, Representations Involving Fiduciary Entities: Who Is the Client?, 62 Fordham L. Rev. 1319 (1994).

National Academy of Sciences v. Cambridge Trust Co.
Supreme Judicial Court of Massachusetts, 1976
370 Mass. 303, 346 N.E.2d 879

REARDON, J.   This matter is before us for further appellate review, the Appeals Court having promulgated an opinion.

The facts which give rise to the case are essentially as follows. Leonard T. Troland died a resident of Cambridge in 1932 survived by his widow, Florence R. Troland. By his will executed in April, 1931, he left all of his real and personal property to be held in trust by the Cambridge Trust Company (bank) with the net income of the trust, after expenses, "to be paid to, or deposited to the account of [his wife], Florence R. Troland" during her lifetime so long as she remained unmarried. He further provided that

> [k]nowing my wife, Florence's, generosity and unselfishness as I do, I wish to record it as my intention that she should not devote any major portion of her income under the provisions of this will, to the support or for the benefit of people other than herself. It is particularly contrary to my will that any part of the principal or income of my estate should revert to members of my wife's family, other than herself, and I instruct the trustees to bear this point definitely in mind in making decisions under any of the options of this will.

The testator went on to provide in part that on his wife's death or second marriage the bank would transfer the trusteeship to The National Research Council of Washington, D.C., which the petition alleged to be an agency of the National Academy of Sciences (academy), to constitute a trust to be known as the Troland Foundation for Research in Psychophysics. . . .

The will was allowed, the trust was established as provided by the testator, and the bank paid the income thereof to the widow until her death in 1967. During the period from 1932 to 1945 the widow provided eighteen different mailing addresses for income checks to be transmitted to her by the bank. On February 13, 1945, she married Edward D. Flynn in West Palm Beach, Florida, and failed to advise the bank of her remarriage. Following her remarriage she lived in Perth Amboy, New Jersey. Commencing on April 14, 1944, she directed the bank to forward all her monthly checks to her in care of Kenneth D. Custance, her brother-in-law through marriage to her sister. Over the years these checks were forwarded to two Boston addresses and were made payable to "Florence R. Troland." Custance in turn forwarded the checks to Florence R. Flynn who indorsed them in blank "Florence R. Troland" and returned them to Custance who also indorsed them prior to depositing them in bank accounts in his name maintained at the State Street Bank and Trust Company in Boston and the National Bank of Wareham, Massachusetts. After Florence R. Flynn's death on December 25, 1967, the bank for the first time learned of her remarriage.[22] Throughout her second marriage Florence R. Flynn lived with her husband who was able to provide support for her and who, although aware that she was receiving payments from the trust, was ignorant of the limitation on her rights to receive such payments. . . . The total of all checks collected by Florence R. Flynn following

---

22. A letter from Thomas Quarles, Jr., a lawyer in Manchester, New Hampshire, discloses some interesting information about the parties in this case. Quarles, who came upon this case while a law student using a prior edition of this book, writes:

her marriage in 1945 up to the date of her death is $106,013.41. The twelfth through thirty-third accounts of the bank covering that period between her remarriage and October 8, 1966, were presented to the Probate Court for Middlesex County in separate proceedings and allowed. The academy had formal notice prior to the presentation of the twelfth through fourteenth accounts and the eighteenth through thirty-third accounts, and with respect to the fifteenth through seventeenth accounts assented in writing to their allowance. The academy, unaware of the widow's remarriage, did not challenge any of the accounts and they were duly allowed.

The petition brought in the Probate Court by the academy seeks revocation of the seven decrees allowing the twelfth through thirty-third accounts of the bank, the excision from those accounts of "all entries purporting to evidence distributions to or for the benefit of 'Florence R. Troland' . . . subsequent to February 13, 1945," the restoration by the bank to the trust of the amounts of those distributions with interest at the rate of six percent, a final account reflecting the repayments and adjustments, [and] appointment of the academy as trustee. . . .

Following hearing a judge of the Probate Court revoked the seven decrees allowing the twelfth through thirty-third accounts, ordered restoration to the trust of $114,314.18, representing amounts erroneously distributed to Florence R. Flynn plus Massachusetts income taxes paid on those amounts from trust funds, together with interest thereon in the sum of $104,847.17 through March 31, 1973, and interest thereafter at the rate of six percent per annum to the date of restoration in full. . . .

The issues before us have to do with the power of the Probate Court judge to order the revocation of the decrees allowing the twelfth through thirty-third accounts, and the propriety of charging the bank for the amounts erroneously disbursed. . . .

The bank recited in the heading of each of the challenged accounts that the trust was "for the benefit of Florence R. Troland," and stated in schedule E of each

Leonard Troland

My father, Thomas Quarles, Sr., was the trust officer at the Cambridge Trust Company in charge of the Troland trust at the time of Florence Troland's death in 1967. Leonard Troland, the settlor of the trust, was apparently quite a colorful individual. A professor of psychology at Harvard for many years, he was also one of a group that developed the Technicolor motion picture film process. Proceeds from the sale of this invention formed part of the principal of the Troland trust. Mr. Troland apparently had a flair for the theatrical in his personal life as well. In 1932, he reportedly committed suicide by driving his car off the rim of the Grand Canyon at sunset.

Florence Troland was aware of the limitation in the trust that cut off her interest if she remarried. So was her brother-in-law, Kenneth Custance. Nevertheless, after her remarriage in 1945, he convinced her to keep quiet and to endorse her trust income check over to him. He told her that the money was needed to support a succession of spiritualist churches that he headed in the Onset, Massachusetts area. When Florence died in 1967, Kenneth apparently felt guilty about the years of fraud. At her funeral, he gave Florence's latest trust check to her surviving husband, who contacted the Cambridge Trust Company asking what he should do with it. It was only at that point that the Bank realized that through Mrs. Troland and Mr. Custance's fraud it had paid the wrong beneficiary for 22 years. Fortunately, my father kept his job. He had only been with the Bank for a few years and had only recently taken over the Troland trust. [Letter from Thomas Quarles, Jr., to Jesse Dukeminier, dated Dec. 1, 1986.]

— Eds.

account (in the first four accounts specifically as "Distributions to Beneficiary") that monthly payments of $225 or more were made to "Florence R. Troland." The Appeals Court held that these recitals and statements "constituted a continuing representation by the bank to the academy and to the court that the widow remained 'Florence R. Troland' despite her (then unknown) remarriage to Flynn, and that she remained the sole income beneficiary of the trust." . . . The court further held that those representations were technically fraudulent in that "[t]hey were made as of the bank's own knowledge when the bank had no such knowledge and had made absolutely no effort to obtain it." . . . With these views we find ourselves substantially in accord.

The doctrine of constructive or technical fraud in this Commonwealth is of venerable origin. As we pointed out in Powell v. Rasmussen, 243 N.E.2d 167 (Mass. 1969), the doctrine here was developed in two opinions by Chief Justice Shaw. In Hazard v. Irwin, 18 Pick. 95, 109 (1836), it was defined in the following terms: "[W]here the subject matter is one of fact, in respect to which a person can have precise and accurate knowledge, and . . . he speaks as of his own knowledge, and has no such knowledge, his affirmation is essentially false." This rule was reiterated by Chief Justice Shaw in Page v. Bent, 2 Met. 371, 374 (1841): "The principle is well settled, that if a person make[s] a representation of a fact, as of his own knowledge, in relation to a subject matter susceptible of knowledge, and such representation is not true; if the party to whom it is made relies and acts upon it, as true, and sustains damage by it, it is fraud and deceit, for which the party making it is responsible." In this case the marital status of Mrs. Troland/Flynn was a fact susceptible of precise knowledge, the bank made representations concerning this fact of its own knowledge when it had no such knowledge, and the academy to whom the representations were made relied on them to its detriment. While this standard of fraud in law has been developed primarily in the context of actions seeking rescission of contracts and of tort actions for deceit, we have indicated in past decisions that an analogous standard might be applicable to misrepresentations in the accounts of fiduciaries. See Greene v. Springfield Safe Deposit & Trust Co., 3 N.E.2d 254 (Mass. 1936); Welch v. Flory, 200 N.E. 900 (Mass. 1936); Brigham v. Morgan, 69 N.E. 418 (Mass. 1904). We hold today that "fraud" as used in G.L. c. 206, §24, contemplates this standard of constructive fraud at least to the extent that the fiduciary has made no reasonable efforts to ascertain the true state of the facts it has misrepresented in the accounts. This rule is not a strict liability standard, nor does it make a trustee an insurer against the active fraud of all parties dealing with the trust. Entries in the accounts honestly made, after reasonable efforts to determine the truth or falsity of the representations therein have failed through no fault of the trustee, will not be deemed fraudulent or provide grounds for reopening otherwise properly allowed accounts. However, in the instant case the probate judge found that the bank, through the twenty-two years covered by the disputed accounts, exerted "no effort at all . . . to ascertain if Florence R. Troland had remarried even to the extent of annually requesting a statement or certificate from her to that effect" and that "in administering the trust acted primarily in a ministerial manner and in disregard of its duties as a trustee to protect the terms of the trust." In these circumstances we have little trouble in concluding that the bank's representations as to the marital status of the testator's widow fully justified the reopening of the accounts.

Cases relied on by the bank in which this court refused to allow previously allowed accounts to be reopened are distinguishable in that either they did not involve representations of fact susceptible of precise knowledge but rather questions of judgment and discretion as to matters fully and frankly disclosed in the accounts . . . or that the alleged wrongful acts or mistakes of the trustee were discernible from an examination of the accounts, the trust documents and the law. . . . We adhere to our decisions that it is the duty of beneficiaries "to study the account presented to the Probate Court by the trustee, and to make their objections at the hearing." Greene v. Springfield Safe Deposit & Trust Co., supra, 3 N.E.2d at 257. However, in this case the fact of the widow's remarriage was not discernible from the most scrupulous examination of the accounts, the trust documents and the relevant law, and the bank cannot avoid responsibility here for its misrepresentations by alleging a breach of duty on the part of the academy.

As to the propriety of surcharging the bank for the amounts erroneously disbursed, when a trustee makes payment to a person other than the beneficiary entitled to receive the money, he is liable to the proper beneficiary to make restitution unless the payment was authorized by a proper court. . . . Since, as we have held the decrees allowing the twelfth through thirty-third accounts were revoked properly, the bank thus became liable to the academy to restore to the trust corpus the payments it made to Mrs. Troland/Flynn when she was not entitled to receive them. In addition to the amounts erroneously disbursed, the bank was also properly charged by the Probate Court judge with simple interest on those payments at the legal rate of six percent per annum. . . .

[T]he decree is affirmed.

NOTES AND PROBLEM

1. To avoid expensive accountings, provisions are often inserted in a trust instrument providing that judicial accountings should be dispensed with and accounts rendered periodically to the adult income beneficiaries of the trust. In the case of testamentary trusts, a few courts have indicated that a testator will not be permitted to dispense with statutorily required accountings. See In re Estates of Brush, 259 N.Y.S.2d 390 (Sur. 1965). In the case of inter vivos trusts, which are not placed under judicial supervision by statute, it would appear that a "no judicial accounting" provision does not contravene public policy. But here again, at least in New York, such a provision may run into trouble. In In re Crane, 34 N.Y.S.2d 9 (Sup. 1942), aff'd, 41 N.Y.S.2d 940 (App. Div. 1943), an irrevocable inter vivos trust provided: "The written acceptance of the beneficiary entitled to income of the correctness of any account rendered by the Trustee shall constitute a final and complete discharge to said Trustee in respect of the matters covered by such account." This clause was held not to divest the remaindermen of their right to question the actions of the trustee. The court said:

> It does not seem conscionable to me to hold that the life tenant, who enjoys merely the income and who does not own or directly control the principal, should be permitted to be placed in an immunized position where she might possibly squander, or indirectly control, principal, and thus not only cheat the remaindermen but flagrantly frustrate the settlor's intention. The possibilities for collusion are too obvious and manifold.

The opportunities for squeezing every penny of income from the principal so as to shrink the principal—by fair means or foul—to the serious detriment of the vested remaindermen, are so manifest that, unless compelled by mandatory language, the opportunities should not be sanctioned or emboldened. Rather, equity should, I think, barricade the door against the possibilities. [34 N.Y.S.2d at 14.]

This reasoning is criticized by David Westfall, Nonjudicial Settlement of Trustees' Accounts, 71 Harv. L. Rev. 40, 61 (1957). Professor Westfall argues that if the income beneficiaries can be given a power of appointment that diminishes or destroys the remainder, there is no reason to refuse to give effect to a clause permitting the income beneficiary to absolve the trustee from further accountability. Westfall also contends that public policy does not require the protection of remaindermen when the settlor has implicitly withheld protection.

In Briggs v. Crowley, 224 N.E.2d 417 (Mass. 1967), the court held that the clauses in an inter vivos trust instrument purporting to relieve the trustees of the duty to account to anyone were invalid as against public policy insofar as they purported to deprive a court of jurisdiction and the petitioner of standing to require the trustees to show that they had faithfully performed their duties.

2.   Uniform Trust Code §813 (2000, rev. 2004), excerpted at page 836, strikes an interesting balance. Section 813(c) requires the trustee to provide an annual "report" (the Code uses "report" and not "accounting" to indicate that the report need not adhere to a specific format or employ much formality), but the settlor may release the trustee from the requirement to "report" by the terms of the trust instrument since §813(c) is not included in the schedule of mandatory rules in §105. The beneficiaries may likewise waive their right to reports or other information. UTC §813(d). However, §813(d) does not appear to permit a beneficiary to make an irrevocable waiver of her right to reports and other information. Note also that the comment to §813 states that "a waiver of a trustee's report or other information does not relieve the trustee from accountability and potential liability for matters that the report or other information would have disclosed."

3.   *O* transfers property to *X* in trust to pay the income to *A* for life, remainder to *A*'s children. *A* is now 42 years old, is not married, and has no issue. To avoid expense, chargeable against the trust assets, *A* seeks to have the trustee account nonjudicially to her, agreeing to indemnify the trustee against any objections to its administration subsequently made by the remaindermen. Should the trustee agree to this? See UTC §§111, 1009 (2000).

14

WEALTH TRANSFER TAXATION: TAX PLANNING[1]

SECTION A.   INTRODUCTION

1.   A Brief History of Federal Wealth Transfer Taxation

Death duties have an ancient history and were known to the Greeks, Romans, and even to the Egyptians. In this country until World War I, federal death duties were levied only temporarily during times of urgent need for revenue. When relations with France deteriorated in 1797, Congress imposed stamp taxes on legacies; the taxes disappeared five years later when the revenue crisis had passed. During the Civil War, Congress levied an *inheritance tax*, which was promptly repealed after the war. Again in the 1890s, seeking revenue to finance our military encounters with Spain, Congress imposed an inheritance tax, which was discarded upon victory. In 1916, with military expenditures mounting, Congress turned again to death duties as an untapped source of revenue and enacted an *estate tax*. In general, an estate tax is imposed on the estate of a decedent, whereas an inheritance tax is imposed on the beneficiaries of an estate.

The 1916 estate tax was not repealed at the end of World War I because the tax had come to be seen also as a means of leveling great fortunes. Public hostility toward great wealth began to manifest itself in the late nineteenth century, soon after enormous fortunes had been amassed by John D. Rockefeller, Cornelius Vanderbilt, J.P. Morgan, and others during the "robber baron" era. Inheritance taxes were imposed by several states as a result of populist pressures, and soon after the turn of the century President Theodore Roosevelt proposed a steeply graduated inheritance tax on "swollen fortunes which it is certainly of no benefit to this country to perpetuate."[2] Thereafter the movement for an inheritance tax to

---

1. This chapter was revised for the Seventh Edition principally by Stephanie J. Willbanks, Professor of Law at Vermont Law School. For a more comprehensive treatment, see Stephanie J. Willbanks, Federal Taxation of Wealth Transfers: Cases and Problems (2004).

2. 17 Works of Theodore Roosevelt 434 (Memorial ed. 1925). Our historical summary of the estate tax draws heavily from Louis Eisenstein, The Rise and Decline of the Estate Tax, 11 Tax L. Rev. 223 (1956), which is well worth reading in its entirety.

break up hereditary accumulations gained many new supporters, even among conservatives. But Congress declined to act until the war required it to find new sources of revenue.

After World War I, Congress was subjected to conflicting pressures. Some groups wanted to retain the estate tax to reduce hereditary wealth; others wanted to repeal this "socialistic" tax on capital. Congress responded by leaving the tax in place but reducing rates. In 1931, beset by the need to increase revenues in the Great Depression, Congress again turned to the estate tax. With President Hoover's blessing (Hoover regarded the estate tax as a means of striking at "the evils of inherited economic power"), Congress doubled the rates of the estate tax, pushing the tax on any estate in excess of $10 million to 45 percent. At the same time, Congress imposed a gift tax to prevent avoidance of death taxes by inter vivos gifts.

With the Franklin D. Roosevelt administration, the estate tax entered a new phase. The leveling of great inherited fortunes was formally accepted as an objective of the estate tax. In a message to Congress, President Roosevelt declared:

> The desire to provide security for one's self and one's family is natural and whole-some, but it is adequately served by a reasonable inheritance. Great accumulations of wealth cannot be justified on the basis of personal and family security. In the last analysis such accumulations amount to the perpetuation of great and undesirable concentration of control in a relatively few individuals over the employment and welfare of many, many others. . . . [I]nherited economic power is as inconsistent with the ideals of this generation as inherited political power was inconsistent with the ideals of the generation which established our government. [H.R. Rep. No. 1681, 74th Cong., 1st Sess. 2 (1935), 1939-1 C.B. (part 2) 643.]

To level the fortunes of the rich and to raise money to finance World War II, Congress kept raising the rates every few years during the 1930s and 1940s. Finally, in 1954, the exemption from estate taxes was fixed at $60,000, and the rates went up to 77 percent on estates in excess of $10 million.

Though the rates were high, the loopholes in the 1954 Code were several. The term *loopholes* describes both ways of avoiding estate taxation intentionally provided by Congress and ways subsequently discovered by imaginative lawyers. The gift tax rates were set at 75 percent of estate tax rates, thus providing an incentive to make gifts before death. Both gift and estate taxes provided an unlimited deduction for transfers to charity. A taxpayer in the 77 percent bracket might well choose to leave huge sums to charity rather than pay 77 percent to the government. For example, like many other charitable foundations the Ford Foundation was established largely to avoid estate taxation. Other ways of avoiding the tax burden, intentionally provided by Congress, included devising property to the taxpayer's spouse (the marital deduction), buying life insurance (life insurance is not included in the gross estate unless the decedent possesses incidents of ownership over it), and creating a trust with successive life beneficiaries (the estate tax, imposed on transferable interests, does not apply on the death of a life tenant, who can transfer nothing).

This last loophole, continued from the earliest estate tax days, was the foundation of dynasty trusts set up to avoid estate taxes for future generations. A rich person, *O*, could create a trust for *A* for life, then in successive generations for *B* for life, then for *C* for life, and so on until the Rule against Perpetuities called a halt (approximately 100 years later). Although *O* had to pay either a gift or estate tax upon creating the trust, no estate tax would be levied at the death of *A*, *B*, *C*, or any succeeding life tenant. If *O* created the trust in 1935, the trust would still exist today, paying out income to successive life beneficiaries, without an estate tax ever having been levied since the creation of the trust.

The estate and gift tax scheme described above lasted about a generation. In 1976, Congress began tinkering with the Code, first with moderate revisions, later with a substantial restructuring that completely changed the life of estate planners. In the Tax Reform Act of 1976, the gift and estate taxes were unified. The same rate schedule was applied to both gifts and estates. The new rate schedule was applied to cumulative gifts and bequests; each taxable gift moved the taxpayer toward a higher bracket, and the estate tax bracket was determined by the sum of cumulative lifetime gifts plus the decedent's taxable estate at death, in effect making a bequest the final gift. Nonetheless, even though the gift and estate tax rates were unified, tax advantages in lifetime giving still remained (see page 852).

The 1976 change was only the beginning. During the presidency of Ronald Reagan, the federal estate and gift tax system was completely revised. The Economic Recovery Tax Act of 1981, enacted at the urging of President Reagan, provided considerable tax relief at both the lower and upper ends of the economic scale. The tax exemption (transformed into a credit) was increased to $600,000, thus eliminating estate tax worries for the vast majority of citizens. At the same time, the top rate was lowered to 55 percent, and an unlimited marital deduction was introduced. A husband or wife could now transfer unlimited amounts of property to his or her spouse tax free. Transfer taxes were not levied until the spouses' property was transferred outside the marital unit. With the unlimited marital deduction and the exemption of estates under $600,000, estate tax planning was necessary only for the rich. The middle class, which for more than 40 years had skewed its estate plans to avoid taxation on estates exceeding $60,000, was removed from the estate taxation system.

A second tax act of the Reagan administration, the Tax Reform Act of 1986, struck the rich a body blow. It closed the great loophole — the exemption of the life estate from estate taxation. History may record that this tax act did more damage to dynastic wealth in this country than any previous tax act. The Tax Reform Act of 1986 imposed a *generation-skipping transfer (GST) tax*, at the highest rate of the estate tax, upon any generation-skipping transfer (which is, generally speaking, a transfer that skips the estate tax for a generation). Hence, in the trust created by *O* above, a GST tax is payable at the death of *A*, at the death of *B*, and at the death of *C*. Because Congress decided that a wealth transfer tax must be exacted once every generation, the tax-saving possibilities of the dynasty trust have been severely curtailed.

The estate tax reform movement, side-tracked by the 1986 Act, regained momentum in the 1990s. Opponents of the *death tax* (as it was now characterized with less precision, as the term applies to both estate and inheritance taxes) claimed that family farms and businesses were being sacrificed to pay the tax, but there was almost no evidence to support this claim. Opponents of the estate tax also argued that, to avoid selling farms and businesses at death, individuals had to engage in expensive estate planning using funds that could have been put to more productive uses. Others asserted that the estate tax was widely evaded by both legal and illegal means, such as lifetime gifts to family members at falsely low valuations. Perhaps the most cogent rationale for reform was that the wealth of the middle class had increased so substantially that significant numbers of estates of middle class decedents dying in the next decade or two would begin to exceed the exemption amount of $600,000. Most law professors and policy analysts tended to favor retaining the estate tax, either in something like its traditional form or with the exemption raised to several million dollars so as to refocus its reach once again on the extremely wealthy. After further lobbying, Congress passed bills repealing the estate tax in 1999 and 2000, but President Clinton vetoed them both.

The 2000 election changed the political dynamic and brought estate tax repeal to reality. In 2001, President George W. Bush signed the Economic Growth and Tax Relief Reconciliation Act (EGTRRA), which phased in repeal by increasing the exemption amount, first to $1 million, and eventually to $3.5 million in 2009; and by decreasing the top tax rate, first to 50 percent, and eventually to 45 percent in 2007. Although touted as estate tax repeal, EGTRRA actually increased the estate tax burden for many because it phased out the credit for state death taxes. With decreasing rates, increasing exemption amounts, and disappearing credits, EGTRRA also complicated estate planning and made it more expensive — at least in the short run. Some attorneys and financial planners are even trying to patent their estate planning strategies! See Rachel Emma Silverman, The Patented Tax Shelter, Wall St. J., June 24, 2004, at D1. For an engaging discussion of EGTRRA and related tax issues, see Michael J. Graetz & Ian Shapiro, Death by a Thousand Cuts: The Fight over Taxing Inherited Wealth (2005).

Because of budget constraints and the exigencies of political compromise, the estate and GST taxes are actually repealed for only one year — 2010, and the gift tax remains in place to prevent avoidance of the income tax. Without further action, the 2001 amendments will sunset and all wealth transfer taxes will revert to their pre-2001 state on January 1, 2011. A ridiculous consequence of this state of affairs is that, for now, there is a strong financial incentive for the family of the wealthy but infirm to maintain their wealthy kin until 2010, in the hope that they will die before 2011. Attempts to make the repeal permanent or even to increase the exemption amount have failed. The future remains uncertain, but the structure of the transfer taxes as described in this chapter — (a) gift tax, (b) estate tax, and (c) generation-skipping transfer tax — remains essentially unchanged.

NOTE: ESTATE AND INHERITANCE
TAXES DISTINGUISHED

The federal government imposes an estate tax, whereas many of the states impose an inheritance tax. What is the difference? An *estate tax* is a tax upon the privilege of transfer and is levied upon the decedent's *gross estate,* a tax term invented to cover the probate estate, nonprobate transfers, and certain other property over which the decedent has powers. The tax is levied on the total amount transferred less certain deductions. An *inheritance tax* is a tax imposed upon each beneficiary for the privilege of receiving property from the dead. The amount each beneficiary pays in tax depends upon the size of the bequest received and the relationship of the beneficiary to the decedent (spouses and children pay lower rates than more remote kindred and friends). Under the federal estate tax, if a person dies leaving $2 million to ten children, the amount of tax is the same as if there were only one child. Under an inheritance tax with progressive rates for each beneficiary's share, the total amount of tax would be less for a decedent with ten children than it would be for a decedent with one child.

Whether an estate tax is preferable to an inheritance tax is debatable. An estate tax is generally thought to be easier to administer since it avoids valuing the share each beneficiary receives (especially where a discretionary trust or contingent future interest is involved). On the other hand, an inheritance tax might seem fairer because it is based on the amount each beneficiary receives (and not on the size of the donor's estate) and it is more generous to close relatives, who are usually subject to lower inheritance tax rates than more distant beneficiaries.

For academic proposals to restructure the wealth transfer taxes, see Karen C. Burke & Grayson M.P. McCouch, A Consumption Tax on Gifts and Bequests, 17 Va. Tax Rev. 657 (1998); Joseph M. Dodge, Comparing a Reformed Estate Tax with an Accessions Tax and an Income-Inclusion System, and Abandoning the Generation-Skipping Tax, 56 S.M.U.L. Rev. 551 (2003); Michael J. Graetz, To Praise the Estate Tax, Not to Bury It, 93 Yale L.J. 259 (1983); Edward J. McCaffery, The Uneasy Case for Wealth Transfer Taxation, 104 Yale L.J. 283 (1994); Colloquium on Wealth Transfer Taxation, 51 Tax L. Rev. 357 (1996) (articles discussing McCaffery's proposal to abolish the federal estate and gift tax by Anne L. Alstott, Joseph M. Dodge, Douglas Holtz-Eakin, and Eric Rakowski, with commentaries by others); James R. Repetti, Democracy, Taxes and Wealth, 76 N.Y.U.L. Rev. 825 (2001). See also the collection of papers in Rethinking Estate and Gift Taxation (William G. Gale, James R. Hines, Jr. & Joel Slemrod eds., 2001).

2. The Unified Federal Estate and Gift Taxes

One of the first things you need to do to understand the unified estate and gift tax system is to see how it works. If you understand the basic principles of the unified system, the details and modifications that come later will be easier to understand. In this brief introduction, we want to concentrate on how the cumulative unified credit works.

The Tax Reform Act of 1976 unified gift and estate taxes for estates of decedents dying after December 31, 1976, and for gifts made after that date. A single rate schedule applies to both gift and estate taxes. The rates are progressive on the basis of *cumulative* lifetime and death transfers. For lifetime gifts, the amount of the gift tax is determined by applying the rate schedule to cumulative gifts and then subtracting the gift taxes payable on gifts made in earlier tax periods. With each substantial gift, the taxpayer steps up into a higher bracket, until the top bracket is reached. The tentative estate tax is computed by applying the rate schedule to the aggregate of the decedent's taxable estate *plus* taxable gifts made after 1976. From this tentative tax are deducted gift taxes paid on the post-1976 gifts.[3]

The abridged tax rate schedule below sets forth the transfer tax rates.

Unified Transfer Tax Rate Schedule

If the Amount with Respect to Which the Tentative Tax to be Computed Is: . . .	*Then the Tentative Tax Is:*
over $100,000 but not over $150,000	$23,800 plus 30 percent of the excess of such amount over $100,000
over $150,000 but not over $250,000	$38,800 plus 32 percent of the excess of such amount over $150,000
over $250,000 but not over $500,000	$70,800 plus 34 percent of the excess of such amount over $250,000
over $500,000 but not over $750,000	$155,800 plus 37 percent of the excess of such amount over $500,000
over $750,000 but not over $1,000,000	$248,300 plus 39 percent of the excess of such amount over $750,000
over $1,000,000 but not over $1,250,000	$345,800 plus 41 percent of the excess of such amount over $1,000,000
over $1,250,000 but not over $1,500,000	$448,300 plus 43 percent of the excess of such amount over $1,250,000
over $1,500,000 but not over $2,000,000	$555,800 plus 45 percent of the excess of such amount over $1,500,000
over $2,000,000	$780,800 plus 47 percent [in 2005] of the excess of such amount over $2,000,000[4]

Congress has exempted a certain amount of property from transfer taxation. Prior to 1998, the exemption was $600,000. In 1998, Congress decided to increase the exemption in a series of steps until an exemption of $1 million was to be reached in 2006. In 2001, Congress again increased the exemption amount, but it also de-coupled the gift tax and estate tax exemption amounts. The gift tax exemption remains at $1 million, while the estate tax exemption amount increases as follows:

$1,000,000 in	2002 and 2003,
$1,500,000 in	2004 and 2005,
$2,000,000 in	2006, 2007, and 2008, and
$3,500,000 in	2009.

---

3. For a more detailed picture of how the tentative tax is figured, see page 869.

4. The Economic Growth and Tax Relief Reconciliation Act of 2001 decreased the top tax rate to 49 percent in 2003, 48 percent in 2004, 47 percent in 2005, 46 percent in 2006, and 45 percent in 2007, 2008, and 2009.

The exemption amount will revert to $1 million in 2011, but will be indexed for inflation in multiples of $10,000 — unless, of course, Congress acts again.

This exemption is given in the form of a tax credit, which is deducted from the tentative estate tax to determine the final estate tax. Although it would be simpler if Congress had merely exempted the first $1.5 million of taxable assets in estates in 2005, instead the Code first imposes a tentative tax on *all* the taxable assets and then provides a large tax credit. In 2005 the tax credit is $555,800, which cancels out the tentative tax on the first $1.5 million of taxable property in the estate, as you can see from looking at the rate schedule above. The amount of the credit is the amount of the tentative tax determined under the rate schedule for the amount of the exemption. If you examine the rate schedule, you will see that when the exemption was $1 million in 2003, the credit against the tentative tax was $345,800, and when the exemption is $2 million in 2006, the credit will be $780,800. (Yes, talking about credits rather than exemptions is more complicated, but we are stuck with what Congress has done.)

Case 1 illustrates how the tax applies to cumulative gifts and also illustrates the tax credit. To keep it simple, suppose that the gifts are made in 2006 and 2007, when the $2 million exemption takes effect.

Case 1. In 2006, *W*, a widow, gives Acme stock worth $261,000 to her daughter *D*. *W* is entitled to make a tax-free gift of up to $11,000 to any donee each year (see page 857); hence *W* is entitled to exclude $11,000 of this gift from taxable gifts. *W* makes no gifts of more than $11,000 to any other person in 2006. *W* has not made any taxable gifts in any earlier year. In 2006, *W* files a gift tax return showing:

$261,000	gift to *D* in 2006
−11,000	annual exclusion
$250,000	taxable gift in 2006
+0	taxable gifts in earlier years
$250,000	cumulative taxable gifts
$ 70,800	tentative gift tax
−70,800	unified gift tax credit used
$ 0	gift tax due

In 2007, *W* gives Beta stock worth $261,000 to *D*. *W* makes no gifts in excess of $11,000 to any other person in 2007. In 2007, *W* files a gift tax return showing:

$261,000	gift to *D* in 2007
−11,000	annual exclusion
$250,000	taxable gift in 2007
+250,000	taxable gifts in earlier years (Acme stock in 2006)[5]
$500,000	cumulative taxable gifts
155,800	tax on cumulative gifts
−70,800	tax on preceding gifts (2006)
$ 85,000	tentative gift tax
−85,000	unified gift tax credit used
$ 0	tax due

---

5. Taxable gifts in prior years are brought into the computation at their date-of-gift value. If Acme stock were worth $300,000 in 2007, it would still be included in the 2007 return at its previous taxable gift value ($250,000).

In Case 1, observe the effect of a rate schedule based on cumulative gifts. The tentative tax on the 2006 gift of Acme stock is at a marginal rate of 32 percent; the tentative tax on the 2007 gift of Beta stock of the same value is at a marginal rate of 34 percent. Under the cumulative transfer system, a donor does not start at the bottom rung of the rate schedule each year, but rather starts on the rung where prior gifts left the donor. Similarly, a decedent starts on the rung he was on when he made his last inter vivos gift. Observe also that in Case 1 *W* has used $155,800 of her gift tax credit of $345,800. If *W* dies in 2008, without making further gifts, *W* will have a credit of $625,000 to apply against the estate tax.[6]

QUESTION AND NOTE

1.   Apart from taking advantage of the annual exclusion of $11,000 per donee, is there any transfer tax advantage in *W*'s making inter vivos gifts to her daughter, as in Case 1? Suppose *W* has a choice of giving her daughter either $261,000 worth of large company stocks or a $261,000 corporate bond, paying current market interest rates, due in the year 2020. From the sole point of view of transfer taxes, which should she give? This bit of information might help you. From 1926-2002, large company stocks returned an average of 12.2 percent a year, while long-term corporate bonds returned 6.2 percent. Ibbotson Associates, Stocks, Bonds, Bills, and Inflation 2003 Yearbook 33, at Table 2. Ignoring income taxes, if *W* is 40 years old when she makes the gift, and the stocks appreciate at the historic rate of return, the gift will be worth $26 million after 40 years, while the bonds would be worth less than $3 million.

2.   One advantage of making a gift, which might not be obvious, results from the fact that the tax base for gifts is the value of the property transferred. If the transfer results in gift tax liability, the gift tax is not included in the gift tax base. By contrast, the estate tax is levied on the decedent's assets at death, which include the amount that will be transferred to Uncle Sam as estate taxes. To express this difference, sometimes it is said that the gift tax is *tax-exclusive*, whereas the estate tax is *tax-inclusive*.

To illustrate, suppose *O* aims to transfer $1 million to her daughter *A* and that this transfer is subject to a 50 percent rate. For *A* to receive by gift $1 million subject to a tax of $500,000, *O* must part with a total of $1.5 million. Hence, the tax rate on the amount parted with is really 33 1/3 percent. In contrast, for *O* to transfer $1 million to *A* at death, *O* must part with $2 million (subject to a 50 percent rate) to get $1 million in the hands of *A*. The tax preference for lifetime giving can be expressed as a rate reduction. If the maximum estate tax rate is 50 percent, the equivalent gift tax rate is 33 1/3 percent. To eliminate the tax preference for lifetime giving, the gift tax itself would have to be included in the gift tax base. As this example shows, the structure of the tax law rewards early transfers.

---

6. It is not technically accurate to say that *W* will have a credit of only $625,000 to apply against the estate tax. Since the taxable gifts of $500,000 made in 2006 and 2007 must be added to *W*'s gross estate to determine *W*'s estate tax, the entire credit of $780,800 is available to *W*'s estate. Our explanation, however, is a simple way of indicating how much credit (and how much exemption) *W* has left. Also remember that the gift tax credit is limited to $345,800 (the tax on $1 million) but the estate tax credit in 2008 is $780,800 (the tax on $2 million).

Liability for payment of taxes. The donor has the primary liability for paying the gift tax. If the donor does not pay, the donee is liable for any unpaid gift tax. The executor or administrator of a decedent's estate has personal liability for payment of the estate tax but is entitled to reimbursement out of the decedent's estate. If there is no administration of the decedent's estate, persons in possession of the decedent's property are liable for the tax due.

Although the executor or administrator must pay the entire estate tax due, the executor or administrator is entitled to be reimbursed from life insurance beneficiaries for the portion of the tax resulting from the inclusion of life insurance in the decedent's estate. I.R.C. §2206. Similarly, the executor is entitled to proportionate reimbursement from recipients of property over which the decedent had a general power of appointment. I.R.C. §2207. With these two exceptions, the Code does not generally provide for apportionment of estate taxes to the recipients but leaves the matter to state law. A large majority of states follows the rule that, unless the testator provides otherwise, federal estate taxes are apportioned and must be borne by each beneficiary pro rata. A minority of states follows the opposite default rule: The estate tax is paid out of the residuary estate unless the testator provides otherwise. The Uniform Estate Tax Apportionment Act (2003), which has been absorbed into the Uniform Probate Code as Part 9A of Article III, adopts the majority rule. See Douglas A. Kahn, The 2003 Revised Uniform Estate Tax Apportionment Act, 38 Real Prop., Prob. & Tr. J. 613 (2004).

SECTION B. THE FEDERAL GIFT TAX

1. *The Nature of a Taxable Gift*

Section 2501(a) of the Internal Revenue Code of 1986 imposes a gift tax on "the transfer of property by gift" during each calendar year by an individual. But nowhere in the Code is *gift* defined. The courts have decided that the question is not whether the donor has donative intent, but whether the donor gives up complete dominion and control. If the donor keeps dominion and control, the gift is not complete, and no taxable gift has been made. The creation of a revocable trust does not effect a taxable transfer. The transfer is not complete until the power of revocation ceases. If the power of revocation ceases at the donor's death, no gift tax is due, but the trust property is included in the donor's gross estate under the estate tax.

Holtz's Estate v. Commissioner
United States Tax Court, 1962
38 T.C. 37

DRENNAN, J. . . . The principal issue for decision is whether taxable gifts resulted from transfers to a trust established by [Leon Holtz, the decedent] by deed of trust dated June 12, 1953, wherein Leon was the settlor and Land Title Bank and Trust Company, now Provident Tradesmens Bank and Trust Company, was the sole trustee. The trust instrument provided that the trustee should distribute the net income therefrom and the principal thereof as follows. During the lifetime of settlor the income should be paid to him, and as much of the principal as the trustee "may from time to time think desirable for the welfare, comfort and support of Settlor, or for his hospitalization or other emergency needs," should be paid to him or for his benefit. Upon the death of the settlor, if his wife survived him, the income of the trust was to be paid to her during her lifetime, and a similar provision was made for invasion of principal for her benefit during her lifetime. The trust was to terminate at the death of the survivor of settlor and his wife and the "then-remaining principal" was payable to the estate of the survivor.

On June 12, 1953, Leon transferred property having a value of $384,117 to the trust, and on January 18, 1955, he transferred an additional $50,000 in cash to the trust. Respondent determined that, as a result of these transfers, Leon made taxable gifts in 1953 in the amount of $263,277.63, and in 1955 in the amount of $35,570, computing the value of the taxable gifts by reducing the value of the property transferred in each instance by the actuarial value of Leon's life estate and reversionary interest in each transfer. Petitioner claims the transfers were not completed gifts and that no part of the value thereof was subject to gift tax. . . .

The Internal Revenue Codes of 1939 and 1954 provide no guideposts for determining when a gift becomes complete for gift tax purposes beyond the direction that "the tax shall apply whether the transfer is in trust or otherwise, whether the gift is direct or indirect, and whether the property is real or personal, tangible or intangible." [I.R.C. §2511(a).] It is well settled in cases involving this issue, however, that the question whether a transfer in trust is a completed gift, and thus subject to gift tax, turns on whether the settlor has abandoned sufficient dominion and control over the property transferred to put it beyond recall. Burnet v. Guggenheim, 288 U.S. 280 (1933); Estate of Sanford v. Commissioner, 308 U.S. 39 (1939); Smith v. Shaughnessy, 318 U.S. 176 (1943).

Here we do not have a situation where the settlor either reserved the power in himself alone to modify, alter, or revoke the trust and thus revest the trust property in himself, as in Burnet v. Guggenheim, supra, or reserved the power to alter the disposition of the property or income therefrom in some way not beneficial to himself, as in Estate of Sanford v. Commissioner, supra, or reserved the power in conjunction with someone else to modify, alter, or revoke the trust, as in Camp v. Commissioner, 195 F.2d 999 (C.A. 1, 1952). Leon reserved no rights in himself to change the disposition of the income or principal of the trust as fixed in the trust agreement. However, the trust agreement itself gave the trustee power to pay directly to Leon or for his benefit as much of the principal of the trust as the trustee thought desirable for Leon's welfare, comfort, and support, or for his hospitalization or other emergency needs. The question is whether this discretionary power placed in the trustee by the settlor under the terms of the trust agreement made the gifts of the remainder interests incomplete for gift tax purposes.

A number of cases decided by this and other courts have held that the placing of discretionary power in the trustee to invade corpus makes the gift of corpus incomplete under certain circumstances. The rule of thumb generally accepted seems to be that if the trustee is free to exercise his unfettered discretion and there is nothing to impel or compel him to invade corpus, the settlor retains a mere expectancy which does not make the gift of corpus incomplete. But if the exercise of the trustee's discretion is governed by some external standard which a court may apply in compelling compliance with the conditions of the trust agreement, and the trustee's power to invade is unlimited, then the gift of corpus is incomplete, Commissioner v. Irving Trust Co., 147 F.2d 946 (C.A. 2, 1945), and this is true even though such words as "absolute" and "uncontrolled" are used in connection with the trustee's discretion, provided the external standards are clearly for the guidance of the trustee in exercising his discretion.

The theory behind this rule seems to be that by placing such standards for guidance of the trustee's discretion in the trust agreement itself, the settlor has not actually lost all dominion and control of the trust corpus or put it completely beyond recall because to ignore the implications and purpose for writing the standards into the invasion clause would be an abuse of discretion on the part of the trustee which the trustee would neither desire to do nor be likely to risk doing under State laws. . . .

The rule of thumb appears to be a reasonable application of the general rule established in the *Guggenheim, Sanford,* and *Shaughnessy* cases because where there is a reasonable possibility that the entire corpus might be repaid to the settlor there can be no assurance that anyone else will receive anything in the form of a gift, and if the corpus should happen to be kept intact until the settlor's death, even though the transfer in trust was not subjected to a gift tax, the corpus of the trust will in all likelihood be subjected to the estate tax in the settlor's estate.

Applying the above principles to the facts under consideration here, we conclude that no part of or interest in the property transferred to the trust constituted a completed gift for gift tax purposes when transferred to the trust.

The form of the trust agreement indicates that the principal beneficiary of the income, and the principal if it became desirable for his welfare, comfort, support, or emergency needs, was the settlor. The first instructions to the trustee, as shown by the part of the deed of trust quoted in our Findings of Fact, were to distribute net income and principal to the settlor during his lifetime. Only upon the death of the settlor, and if she survived him, was any provision made for payment of either income or principal to the settlor's wife. And only upon the death of the survivor of settlor and his wife was any provision made for distribution of the "then-remaining principal." The trustee had the unfettered power to use all of the corpus for the benefit of settlor, if it thought that it was desirable for the welfare, comfort, or needs of the settlor. The words used were broad enough to cover about anything Leon might want or need. It is reasonable to assume that the trustee would invade corpus and that it would be required to do so by a court if the welfare, comfort, or needs of the settlor made it seem desirable. Otherwise, there would not have been much reason for including the paragraph giving the trustee power to invade principal. It was entirely possible that the entire corpus might be distributed during the settlor's lifetime and no one other than the settlor would receive any portion thereof. As long as that possibility was present, by reason of the language employed by the settlor, the settlor had not abandoned sufficient dominion and control over the property transferred to make the gift consummate.

In addition to the trust agreement itself, the evidence indicates that the settlor, who was 80 years of age when the trust was established, expressed concern over whether he would have available sufficient funds to meet his needs. He asked the trust officer whether he would have enough money to buy an automobile and the trust officer reassured him by telling him that the trust agreement provided for the payment of all income to him and that he could also have money out of the principal, and that the trustee would be liberal in giving him money out of the principal. While the term "liberal" is not defined, the above conversation indicates the understanding of the parties was that the trustee recognized that principal should be distributed at any time the settlor's needs reasonably justified it. . . .

Decision will be entered for the petitioner.

NOTES AND PROBLEMS

1. *O* transfers property in trust to pay income to her son *A* for life and on *A*'s death to pay the principal to *A*'s daughter *B*. *O* retains the power to revoke the trust. Because *O* retains the power to revoke the trust, during *O*'s life the income from the trust property is taxed to *O* whether the income is paid to *O* or to *A*. See I.R.C. §§676, 677 (income tax). Suppose that the trustee earns $11,000 during the calendar year after the trust is created and the trustee pays the $11,000 to *A*. Who pays income tax on the $11,000? Has a taxable gift been made to *A*?

Suppose that *O* did not reserve the power to revoke the trust but reserved only the power to change the owner of the remainder interest from *B* to *A* at any time during *A*'s life. (At the time of transfer, *O*'s granddaughter *B* was in her teens and was a rather willful, indeed rebellious, young lady experimenting with drugs.) Has *O* made a taxable gift to *A*? To *B*? Suppose that after reaching majority during *A*'s life, *B* irrevocably assigns her interest to a Hindu mystic, under whose influence she has fallen. Has *B* made a taxable gift to the mystic?

If *O* cannot recover the transferred property, why should not *O* be treated as having made a completed gift? Has not *O*'s wealth been irrevocably depleted?

2. *O* establishes an irrevocable trust that is funded with securities worth $500,000. Trust income is to be paid to *O* for life, "and on her death the trustee shall distribute the trust corpus to such of the Settlor's issue as she shall appoint by will; and in default of such appointment the trustee shall distribute the corpus to the Settlor's issue then living, per stirpes." Has *O* made a taxable gift of a remainder? See Treas. Reg. §25.2511-2(b). Suppose that *O* releases the special power of appointment. Does the release result in a taxable gift of a remainder? If so, how is the remainder valued? See page 637.

3. If the donor can revoke a transfer only with the consent of an adverse party, a taxable gift has been made. Suppose that *O* transfers property in trust to pay the income to *A* for life, and on *A*'s death to distribute the principal to *B*. *O* retains the power to revoke or amend the trust instrument in whole or in part with the consent of *A*. Has a taxable gift been made? See Camp v. Commissioner, 195 F.2d 999 (1st Cir. 1952).

4. *Disclaimer*. Suppose that an heir or legatee disclaims his intestate share or the legacy. Has the heir or legatee made a taxable gift to the person who takes the disclaimed property? A disclaimer results in a taxable gift unless §2518 applies. Internal Revenue Code §2518(b) provides that no taxable gift is made if the refusal to take is a "qualified disclaimer." A disclaimer is "qualified" if:

> (a) the disclaimer is in writing, and made either within nine months after the interest is created or within nine months after the disclaimant reaches 21, whichever is later,
>
> (b) the disclaimant has accepted no interest in the property, and

(c) the transfer is to persons entitled under local law to disclaimed property and not to persons designated by the disclaimant.

Section 2518 applies only to disclaimers of an interest created by a transfer made after 1976. In the case of interests created earlier, a disclaimer is a gift unless it is made "within a reasonable time after knowledge of the existence of the transfer." Treas. Reg. §25.2511-1(c). See Grayson M.P. McCouch, Timely Disclaimers and Taxable Transfers, 47 U. Miami L. Rev. 1043 (1993).

NOTE: INCOME TAX BASIS

Under the Internal Revenue Code, income tax is levied on gain realized upon the sale of property. The amount of gain is the difference between the taxpayer's *basis* and the selling price. Generally speaking, if the taxpayer purchased the property, his basis is the purchase price. If *O* buys land for $50,000, and sells it for $75,000, the gain of $25,000 is subject to income taxation.

In the case of property acquired by *gift*, for purpose of computing gain on any subsequent sale by the donee, the donee takes the donor's basis. For the purpose of computing loss, the donee's basis is the value of the property on the date of the gift. I.R.C. §1015. If property is acquired from a *decedent*, the basis of the property for computing both gain and loss is the value of the asset on the decedent's death. Id. §1014. The *stepped-up basis* at death means that any capital gain on property held until death escapes income taxation.[7]

PROBLEM

O purchases 100 shares of IBM common stock for $50 per share. Over the years, the stock's value increases to $150 per share.

(a) If *O* sells the stock for $150 per share, what are the income tax consequences?

(b) If *O* gives the stock to her son *A* and then *A* sells the stock for $150 per share, what are the income tax consequences?

(c) If *O* dies leaving a will that bequeaths the stock to *A* and then *A* sells the stock for $150 per share, what are the income tax consequences?

2. The Annual Exclusion

Under §2503(b) of the Code, a taxpayer is permitted to exclude from taxable gifts the first $11,000[8] given to any person during the calendar year. The purpose of

---

7. Congress repealed §1014 effective in 2010 as part of the price paid for the repeal of the estate and GST taxes in EGTRRA. It also added a new §1022 that imposes a carryover basis similar to §1015 for transfers at death. Congress tried repealing §1014 once before—in the Tax Reform Act of 1976. Banks and other financial institutions serving as fiduciaries complained so loudly that the repeal was reversed before it became effective. It remains to be seen whether the 2001 repeal will suffer the same fate.

8. The annual exclusion was $5,000 from 1932 to 1939, $4,000 from 1939 to 1942, and $3,000 from 1943 to 1981. The Economic Recovery Tax Act of 1981 raised the annual exclusion to $10,000 beginning in 1982 and indexed it for inflation, but only in increments of $1,000. As a result, the amount of the annual exclusion did not rise to $11,000 until 2002. Rev. Proc. 2001-59, 2001-2 C.B. 623.

the exclusion "is to obviate the necessity of keeping an account of and reporting numerous small gifts, and . . . to fix the amount sufficiently large to cover in most cases wedding and Christmas gifts and occasionally gifts of relatively small amounts." H.R. Rep. No. 708, 72d Cong., 1st Sess. 29 (1932), 1939-1 C.B. (part 2) 457, 478. A donor must file a gift tax return only if gifts (other than marital deduction gifts) to any donee during the year exceed the annual exclusion and must report on the return only gifts in excess of $11,000 to any one person. Thus:

> *Case 2. A* gives $15,000 each to *B* and *C* and $5,000 to *D. A* must file a tax return reporting the gifts to *B* and *C*, from which two annual exclusions are deducted, leaving $8,000 in taxable gifts. The gift to *D* is not reported on the return because it is covered by the annual exclusion. If *A* gave only $11,000 each to *B* and *C*, no gift tax return need be filed.

In addition to the annual exclusion, §2503(e) of the Code allows an unlimited exclusion for *tuition payments* and *medical expenses* paid on behalf of any person. With the rising cost of education, the $11,000 annual exclusion might not cover college tuition and educational expenses of children who have reached majority. (A parent generally has no duty to support a child who has reached majority, which in most states is now age 18, and college tuition technically could be considered a gift.) Similarly, some taxpayers incur large medical expenses on behalf of an elderly relative, an adult child, or someone else. Congress has taken the view that such payments should be exempt from gift taxes without regard to the amounts paid for such purposes or to the relationship between the donor and the donee.

The §2503(e) exclusion applies only to payments made directly to the service provider and does not cover payments to reimburse expenses incurred by the donee. Also, the exclusion for educational expenses covers only "tuition [paid] to an educational institution" and does not include payments for related expenses such as dormitory bills, books, or living expenses.

Gifts of future interests. The annual exclusion is not available for gifts of future interests. The denial of an exclusion for a gift of a future interest rests upon the apprehended difficulty, in many instances, of determining the number of eventual donees and the value of their respective gifts.

> *Case 3. O* gives property worth $500,000 to *A* for life, remainder to *A*'s issue. Based upon *A*'s life expectancy, *A*'s life estate is worth $325,000; the value of the remainder is worth $175,000. *O* is entitled to a $11,000 exclusion for the gift to *A* of a possessory life estate, but *O* is not entitled to an exclusion for the remainder given to *A*'s issue.
>
> *Case 4. O* creates a trust to pay the income among *O*'s three children in such shares as the trustee in her uncontrolled discretion deems advisable. Even though all the net income must be distributed, since no beneficiary has a right to any ascertainable portion of the income, no beneficiary has a present interest. No exclusions are allowable with respect to the transfers in trust.

The denial of an exclusion for a gift of a future interest creates special problems when property is given to a minor. A child can be given possession of a doll or a toy; the doll or toy is not a future interest. But if the property is income-producing or requires management, ordinarily possession is not given the child. The child takes possession only upon reaching majority. Is, then, any gift of income-producing property to a child a gift of a future interest? The answer is No, with qualifications. If property is given outright to a minor, the gift qualifies for the exclusion. So too does a gift to a guardian of a minor. But guardianship is cumbersome, expensive, and not to the minor's advantage (see pages 117-118), and estate planners tend to avoid passing property to guardians. Property can be given in trust for a minor, but care must be taken to draft the trust so as to qualify for the annual exclusion. To permit flexible property management of a minor donee's property, Congress has provided in §2503(c) of the Code a way to avoid having a gift to a minor classified as a future interest.

SEC. 2503(c).   TRANSFER FOR THE BENEFIT OF MINOR

No part of a gift to an individual who has not attained the age of 21 years on the date of such transfer shall be considered a gift of a future interest in property for purposes of subsection (b) if the property and the income therefrom—

(1) may be expended by, or for the benefit of, the donee before his attaining the age of 21 years, and

(2) will to the extent not so expended—

(A) pass to the donee on his attaining the age of 21 years, and

(B) in the event the donee dies before attaining the age of 21 years, be payable to the estate of the donee or as he may appoint under a general power of appointment as defined in section 2514(c).

To create a §2503(c) trust for a minor qualifying for the annual exclusion, the donor must give the trustee power to expend *all* the income and principal on the donee before the donee reaches 21, and further provide that unexpended income and principal must pass to the donee at 21 or, if the donee dies under 21, to the donee's estate or as the donee appoints under a general power. No person other than the minor can have a beneficial interest in the property.

Section 2503(c) is not limited to transfers in trust. Any transfer that satisfies the statute's requirements qualifies for an exclusion. To provide a convenient form for making gifts to minors, every state has enacted the Uniform Transfers to Minors Act or its equivalent. Under the act, property can be transferred to a person (including the donor) as *custodian* for the benefit of a minor. The custodian's powers over income and principal, set forth in the act (see page 118), meet the requirements of §2503(c).

For discussion of gifts that qualify for the annual exclusion, see Jeffrey G. Sherman, 'Tis a Gift to Be Simple: The Need for a New Definition of "Future Interest" for Gift Tax Purposes, 55 U. Cin. L. Rev. 585 (1987); John G. Steinkamp, Common Sense and the Gift Tax Annual Exclusion, 72 Neb. L. Rev. 106 (1993).

PROBLEM

O creates a trust for a minor grandchild *A*. The trustees are directed to use income and principal for *A*'s support and education until *A* reaches 21, when *A* is to receive the principal. The trust also provides that if *A* dies under age 21, the trust assets are to be distributed among such of *O*'s descendants as *A* appoints by will and if *A* fails to exercise the power of appointment, to *A*'s heirs. Is

O entitled to the annual exclusion? See Ross v. Commissioner, 652 F.2d 1365 (9th Cir. 1981).

As you read the next case, keep this in the back of your mind: A person with a general power of appointment (that is, the power to appoint to himself) is treated under the Internal Revenue Code as owner of the property subject to the general power. I.R.C. §2041, page 891.

Estate of Cristofani v. Commissioner
United States Tax Court, 1991
97 T.C. 74

RUWE, J.   Respondent determined a deficiency in petitioner's Federal estate tax in the amount of $49,486. The sole issue for decision is whether transfers of property to a trust, where the beneficiaries possessed the right to withdraw an amount not in excess of the section 2503(b) exclusion within 15 days of such transfers, constitute gifts of a present interest in property within the meaning of section 2503(b).

FINDINGS OF FACT

Petitioner is the Estate of Maria Cristofani, deceased, Frank Cristofani, executor. Maria Cristofani (decedent) died testate on December 16, 1985. At the time of her death, decedent resided in the State of California. Petitioner's Federal estate tax return (Form 706) was timely filed with the Internal Revenue Service Center in Fresno, California, on September 16, 1986.

Decedent has two children, Frank Cristofani and Lillian Dawson. Decedent's children were both born on July 9, 1948. They were in good health during the years 1984 and 1985.

Decedent has five grandchildren. Two of decedent's five grandchildren are Frank Cristofani's children. They are Anthony Cristofani, born July 16, 1975,[9] and Loris Cristofani, born November 30, 1978. Decedent's three remaining grandchildren are Lillian Dawson's children. They are Justin Dawson, born December 1, 1972, Daniel Dawson, born August 9, 1974, and Luke Dawson, born November 14, 1981. During 1984 and 1985, the parents of decedent's grandchildren were the legal guardians of the person of their respective minor children. There were no independently appointed guardians of decedent's grandchildren's property.

---

9. In 1999, Anthony Cristofani, 23, and Emma Freeman, 18, students at the University of California in Santa Cruz, were arrested and charged with armed robbery of local shops. Emma Freeman said she did this so she wouldn't have to work while attending school; others said they did it for a thrill. The use of a gun in a robbery in California requires a prison sentence up to 20 years.

"Cristofani is described by friends as a flamboyant fellow, a philosophical merry prankster. He favored bright clothes, often donning orange shoes and silk shirts, and was known to jump atop a table in the cafeteria and dance, or bellow in Italian . . . . Several students said . . . [Cristofani and Freeman] were not reluctant to test dorm rules, showering together and pushing the limits of social conduct." L.A. Times, Feb.12, 1999, at A1.

Like grandmother, like grandson — pushing the limits of the rules? — Eds.

On June 11, 1984, decedent executed a durable power of attorney which named her two children, Frank Cristofani and Lillian Dawson, as her Attorneys in Fact. On that same day, decedent executed her will.

On June 12, 1984, decedent executed an irrevocable trust entitled the Maria Cristofani Children's Trust I (Children's Trust). Frank Cristofani and Lillian Dawson were named the trustees of the Children's Trust.

In general, Frank Cristofani and Lillian Dawson possessed the following rights and interests in the Children's Trust corpus and income. Under Article Twelfth, following a contribution to the Children's Trust, Frank Cristofani and Lillian Dawson could each withdraw an amount not to exceed the amount specified for the gift tax exclusion under section 2503(b). Such withdrawal period would begin on the date of the contribution and end on the 15th day following such contribution. Under Article Third, Frank Cristofani and Lillian Dawson were to receive equally the entire net income of the trust quarter-annually, or at more frequent intervals. After decedent's death, under Article Third, the Trust Estate was to be divided into as many equal shares as there were children of decedent then living or children of decedent then deceased but leaving issue. Both Frank Cristofani and Lillian Dawson survived decedent, and thus the Children's Trust was divided into two equal trusts. Under Article Third, if a child of decedent survived decedent by 120 days, that child's trust would be distributed to the child. Both Frank Cristofani and Lillian Dawson survived decedent by 120 days, and their respective trusts were distributed upon the expiration of the 120-day waiting period. During the waiting period, Frank Cristofani and Lillian Dawson received the entire net income of the separate trusts as provided for in Article Third.

In general, decedent's five grandchildren possessed the following rights and interests in the Children's Trust. Under Article Twelfth, during a 15-day period following a contribution to the Children's Trust, each of the grandchildren possessed the same right of withdrawal as described above regarding the withdrawal rights of Frank Cristofani and Lillian Dawson. Under Article Twelfth, the trustee of the Children's Trust was required to notify the beneficiaries of the trust each time a contribution was received. Under Article Third, had either Frank Cristofani or Lillian Dawson predeceased decedent or failed to survive decedent by 120 days, his or her equal portion of decedent's Children's Trust would have passed in trust to his or her children (decedent's grandchildren).

Under Article Third, the trustees, in their discretion, could apply as much of the principal of the Children's Trust as necessary for the proper support, health, maintenance and education of decedent's children. In exercising their discretion, the trustees were to take into account several factors, including "The Settlor's desire to consider the Settlor's children as primary beneficiaries and the other beneficiaries of secondary importance."

Decedent intended to fund the corpus of the Children's Trust with 100 percent ownership of improved real property, on which a warehouse was located, identified as the 2851 Spring Street, Redwood City, California, property (Spring Street property). Decedent intended that a one-third undivided interest in the Spring Street property be transferred to the Children's Trust during each of the 3 taxable years 1984, 1985, and 1986. The Spring Street property was unencumbered property at all times pertinent to this case.

Consistent with her intent, decedent transferred, on December 17, 1984, an undivided 33-percent interest in the Spring Street property to the Children's

Trust by a quitclaim deed. Similarly, in 1985, decedent transferred a second undivided 33-percent interest in the Spring Street property to the Children's Trust by a quitclaim deed which was recorded on November 27, 1985. Decedent intended to transfer her remaining undivided interest in the Spring Street property to the Children's Trust in 1986. However, decedent died prior to making the transfer, and her remaining interest in the Spring Street property remained in her estate.

The value of the 33-percent undivided interest in the Spring Street property that decedent transferred in 1984 was $70,000. The value of the 33-percent undivided interest in the Spring Street property that decedent transferred in 1985 also was $70,000.

Decedent did not report the two $70,000 transfers on Federal gift tax returns. Rather, decedent claimed seven annual exclusions of $10,000 each under section 2503(b) for each year 1984 and 1985. These annual exclusions were claimed with respect to decedent's two children and decedent's five grandchildren.

There was no agreement or understanding between decedent, the trustees, and the beneficiaries that decedent's grandchildren would not exercise their withdrawal rights following a contribution to the Children's Trust. None of decedent's five grandchildren exercised their rights to withdraw under Article Twelfth of the Children's Trust during either 1984 or 1985. None of decedent's five grandchildren received a distribution from the Children's Trust during either 1984 or 1985.

Respondent allowed petitioner to claim the annual exclusions with respect to decedent's two children. However, respondent disallowed the $10,000 annual exclusions claimed with respect to each of decedent's grandchildren claimed for the years 1984 and 1985. Respondent determined that the annual exclusions that decedent claimed with respect to her five grandchildren for the 1984 and 1985 transfers, of the Spring Street property, were not transfers of present interests in property. Accordingly, respondent increased petitioner's adjusted taxable gifts in the amount of $100,000.

OPINION

. . . Section 2503(b) provides that the first $10,000 of gifts to any person during a calendar year shall not be included in the total amount of gifts made during such year. A trust beneficiary is considered the donee of a gift in trust for purposes of the annual exclusion under section 2503(b). Sec. 25.2503-2(a), Gift Tax Regs. The section 2503(b) exclusion applies to gifts of present interests in property and does not apply to gifts of future interests in property. Sec. 2503(b); sec. 25.2503-3(a), Gift Tax Regs. The regulations define a future interest to include "reversions, remainders, and other interests or estates, whether vested or contingent, and whether or not supported by a particular interest or estate, which are limited to commence in use, possession or enjoyment at some future date or time." Sec. 25.2503-3(a), Gift Tax Regs. The regulations further provide that "An unrestricted right to the immediate use, possession, or enjoyment of property or the income from property (such as a life estate or term certain) is a present interest in property. An exclusion is allowable with respect to a gift of such an interest (but not in excess of the value of the interest)." Sec. 25.2503-3(b), Gift Tax Regs.

In the instant case, petitioner argues that the right of decedent's grandchildren to withdraw an amount equal to the annual exclusion within 15 days after decedent's contribution of property to the Children's Trust constitutes a gift of a present interest in property, thus qualifying for a $10,000 annual exclusion for each grandchild for the years 1984 and 1985. Petitioner relies upon Crummey v. Commissioner, 397 F.2d 82 (9th Cir. 1968), revg. on this issue T.C. Memo. 1966-144.

In Crummey v. Commissioner, T.C. Memo. 1966-144, affd. in part and revd. in part 397 F.2d 82 (9th Cir. 1968), the settlors created an irrevocable living trust for the benefit of their four children, some of whom were minors. The trustee was required to hold the property in equal shares for the beneficiaries. Under the terms of the trust, the trustee, in his discretion, could distribute trust income to each beneficiary until that beneficiary obtained the age of 21. When the beneficiary was age 21 and up until age 35, the trustee was required to distribute trust income to each beneficiary. When the beneficiary was age 35 and over, the trustee was authorized, in his discretion, to distribute trust income to the beneficiary or his or her issue. Upon the death of a beneficiary, his or her trust share was to be distributed to that beneficiary's surviving issue subject to certain age requirements. If a beneficiary died without issue, then his or her trust share was to be distributed equally to the trust shares of the surviving children of the grantors. In addition, each child was given an absolute power to withdraw up to $4,000 in cash of any additions to corpus in the calendar year of the addition, by making a written demand upon the trustee prior to the end of the calendar year.

Relying on these powers, the settlors claimed the section 2503(b) exclusion on transfers of property to the trust for each trust beneficiary.[10] Respondent permitted the settlors to claim the exclusions with respect to the gifts in trust to the beneficiaries who were adults during the years of the additions. However, respondent disallowed exclusions with respect to the gifts in trust to the beneficiaries who were minors during such years. Respondent disallowed the exclusions for the minor beneficiaries on the ground that the minors' powers were not gifts of present interests in property.

In deciding whether the minor beneficiaries received a present interest, the Ninth Circuit specifically rejected any test based upon the likelihood that the minor beneficiaries would actually receive present enjoyment of the property. Instead, the court focused on the legal right of the minor beneficiaries to demand payment from the trustee. The Ninth Circuit, relying on Perkins v. Commissioner, 27 T.C. 601 (1956), and Gilmore v. Commissioner, 213 F.2d 520 (6th Cir. 1954), stated:

> All exclusions should be allowed under the *Perkins* test or the "right to enjoy" test in *Gilmore*. Under *Perkins*, all that is necessary is to find that the demand could not be resisted. We interpret that to mean legally resisted and, going on that basis, we do not think the trustee would have any choice but to have a guardian appointed to take the property demanded. [Crummey v. Commissioner, 397 F.2d at 88.]

The court found that the minor beneficiaries had a legal right to make a demand upon the trustee, and allowed the settlors to claim annual exclusions, under section 2503(b), with respect to the minor trust beneficiaries. . . .

---

10. During the years in *Crummey*, 1962 and 1963, the sec. 2503(b) annual exclusion was $3,000.

Subsequent to the opinion in *Crummey*, respondent's revenue rulings have recognized that when a trust instrument gives a beneficiary the legal power to demand immediate possession of corpus, that power qualifies as a present interest in property. See Rev. Rul. 85-24, 1985-1 C.B. 329, 330 ("When a trust instrument gives a beneficiary the power to demand immediate possession of corpus, the beneficiary has received a present interest. Crummey v. Commissioner, 397 F.2d 82 (9th Cir. 1968)"); Rev. Rul. 81-7, 1981-1 C.B. 474 ("The courts have recognized that if a trust instrument gives a beneficiary the power to demand immediate possession and enjoyment of corpus or income, the beneficiary has a present interest. Crummey v. Commissioner, 397 F.2d 82 (9th Cir. . . . [1968]).").
While we recognize that revenue rulings do not constitute authority for deciding a case in this Court, . . . we mention them to show respondent's recognition that a trust beneficiary's legal right to demand immediate possession and enjoyment of trust corpus or income constitutes a present interest in property for purposes of the annual exclusion under section 2503(b). See Tele-Communications, Inc. v. Commissioner, 95 T.C. 495, 510 (1990). We also note that respondent allowed the annual exclusions with respect to decedent's two children who possessed the same right of withdrawal as decedent's grandchildren.

In the instant case, respondent has not argued that decedent's grandchildren did not possess a legal right to withdraw corpus from the Children's Trust within 15 days following any contribution, or that such demand could have been legally resisted by the trustees. In fact, the parties have stipulated that "following a contribution to the Children's Trust, each of the grandchildren possessed the *same right of withdrawal* as . . . the withdrawal rights of Frank Cristofani and Lillian Dawson." (Emphasis added.) The legal right of decedent's grandchildren to withdraw specified amounts from the trust corpus within 15 days following any contribution of property constitutes a gift of a present interest. Crummey v. Commissioner, supra.

On brief, respondent attempts to distinguish *Crummey* from the instant case. Respondent argues that in *Crummey* the trust beneficiaries not only possessed an immediate right of withdrawal, but also possessed "substantial, future economic benefits" in the trust corpus and income. Respondent emphasizes that the Children's Trust identified decedent's children as "primary beneficiaries," and that decedent's grandchildren were to be considered as "beneficiaries of secondary importance."

Generally, the beneficiaries of the trust in *Crummey* were entitled to distributions of income. Trust corpus was to be distributed to the issue of each beneficiary sometime following the beneficiary's death. See Crummey v. Commissioner, T.C. Memo. 1966-144. Aside from the discretionary actions of the trustee, the only way any beneficiary in *Crummey* could receive trust corpus was through the demand provision which allowed each beneficiary to demand up to $4,000 in the year in which a transfer to the trust was made. The Ninth Circuit observed:

> In our case . . . if no demand is made in any particular year, the additions are forever removed from the uncontrolled reach of the beneficiary since, with exception of the yearly demand provision, the only way the corpus can ever be tapped by a beneficiary, is through a distribution at the discretion of the trustee. [Crummey v. Commissioner, 397 F.2d at 88.]

In the instant case, the primary beneficiaries of the Children's Trust were decedent's children. Decedent's grandchildren held contingent remainder interests in the Children's Trust. Decedent's grandchildren's interests vested only in the event that their respective parent (decedent's child) predeceased decedent or failed to survive decedent by more than 120 days. We do not believe, however, that *Crummey* requires that the beneficiaries of a trust must have a vested present interest or vested remainder interest in the trust corpus or income, in order to qualify for the section 2503(b) exclusion.

As discussed in *Crummey*, the likelihood that the beneficiary will actually receive present enjoyment of the property is not the test for determining whether a present interest was received. Rather, we must examine the ability of the beneficiaries, in a legal sense, to exercise their right to withdraw trust corpus, and the trustee's right to legally resist a beneficiary's demand for payment. Crummey v. Commissioner, 397 F.2d at 88. Based upon the language of the trust instrument and stipulations of the parties, we believe that each grandchild possessed the legal right to withdraw trust corpus and that the trustees would be unable to legally resist a grandchild's withdrawal demand. We note that there was no agreement or understanding between decedent, the trustees, and the beneficiaries that the grandchildren would not exercise their withdrawal rights following a contribution to the Children's Trust.

Respondent also argues that since the grandchildren possessed only a contingent remainder interest in the Children's Trust, decedent never intended to benefit her grandchildren. Respondent contends that the only reason decedent gave her grandchildren the right to withdraw trust corpus was to obtain the benefit of the annual exclusion.

We disagree. Based upon the provisions of the Children's Trust, we believe that decedent intended to benefit her grandchildren. Their benefits, as remaindermen, were contingent upon a child of decedent's dying before decedent or failing to survive decedent by more than 120 days. We recognize that at the time decedent executed the Children's Trust, decedent's children were in good health, but this does not remove the possibility that decedent's children could have predeceased decedent.

In addition, decedent's grandchildren possessed the power to withdraw up to an amount equal to the amount allowable for the 2503(b) exclusion. Although decedent's grandchildren never exercised their respective withdrawal rights, this does not vitiate the fact that they had the legal right to do so, within 15 days following a contribution to the Children's Trust. Events might have occurred to prompt decedent's children and grandchildren (through their guardians) to exercise their withdrawal rights. For example, either or both of decedent's children and their respective families might have suddenly and unexpectedly been faced with economic hardship; or, in the event of the insolvency of one of decedent's children, the rights of the grandchildren might have been exercised to safeguard their interest in the trust assets from their parents' creditors. In light of the provisions in decedent's trust, we fail to see how respondent can argue that decedent did not intend to benefit her grandchildren.

Finally, the fact that the trust provisions were intended to obtain the benefit of the annual gift tax exclusion does not change the result. As we stated in Perkins v. Commissioner, supra, regardless of the petitioners' motives, or why they did what they in fact did, the legal rights in question were created by the trust instruments and could at any time thereafter be exercised. Petitioners having done what they purported to do, their tax-saving motive is irrelevant. [Perkins v. Commissioner, 27 T.C. at 606.]

Based upon the foregoing, we find that the grandchildren's right to withdraw an amount not to exceed the section 2503(b) exclusion, represents a present interest for purposes of section 2503(b). Accordingly, petitioner is entitled to claim annual exclusions with respect to decedent's grandchildren as a result of decedent's transfers of property to the Children's Trust in 1984 and 1985.

Decision will be entered for the petitioner.

NOTES AND PROBLEM

1.   The Internal Revenue Service has been not happy with the *Cristofani* decision. It has announced that it will challenge attempts to obtain annual exclusions where the substance of the transfer clearly indicates that the donor's purpose was to obtain the annual exclusion and not to benefit the recipient. If the persons with withdrawal rights have only discretionary income interests, remote contingent rights to the remainder, or no rights whatsoever in the income or remainder, the Service may challenge the annual exclusions. In these cases, the nonexercise of the withdrawal rights indicates, to the Service, some kind of prearranged understanding with the donor that the rights were not meant to be exercised. Tech. Adv. Mem. 96-28-004 (July 12, 1996). The Service does not contest gift tax exclusions for Crummey powers held by current income beneficiaries and persons with vested remainders on the theory that it is reasonable for them, with long-term economic interests in the trust, to decide not to exercise the withdrawal powers. See Marc A. Chorney, Transfer Tax Issues Raised by *Crummey* Powers, 33 Real Prop., Prob. & Tr. J. 755 (1999).

2.   Estate planners now have two basic options in drafting trusts for minors: (a) draft a §2503(c) trust, or (b) include a power in the minor, exercisable within a reasonably limited period, to withdraw the amount of the annual exclusion or less. See Richard B. Atkinson, Gifts to Minors: A Roadmap, 42 Ark. L. Rev. 567 (1989).

3.   *O* creates a trust to pay the income to her daughter *A* for life, remainder to *A*'s children. *A* is given the power to withdraw $5,000 out of the property *O* gives to the trust in any given year. If *A* does not exercise the power during a particular year, it lapses. *A* is 8 years old. No guardian has been appointed for *A*. *O* transfers $5,000 to the trust. Does this qualify for the annual exclusion?

So why would *O* transfer only $5,000 rather than $11,000, the amount of the gift tax annual exclusion? Surely *O* wants to transfer to *A* the maximum tax-free amount possible. The answer lies in the adverse gift tax consequences to *A*, the donee, when the power lapses, that is, when A fails to withdraw the amount subject to the general power. Section 2514(c) provides that a lapse of a general power in any calendar year is considered a gift by the donee of the power, *A*, to the extent that the property over which the power existed exceeds the greater of $5,000 or 5 percent of the value of the assets that could be appointed. (Lapse is also discussed with respect to §2041(b)(2), page 893.) If, for example, the donee of the power is the life beneficiary of the trust, the lapse of the power may result in a gift to the remaindermen. A gift of a remainder does not qualify for the annual exclusion and thus will use up a portion of *A*'s unified credit.

There are two ways of solving this dilemma so that *O* can transfer $11,000 a year for the benefit of *A* without running afoul of §2514(c). First, *O* can give *A*, the donee, a special power over the trust assets in addition to the general power to withdraw $11,000. If the general power lapses, the donee, *A*, has not made a gift because he has not given up all dominion and control over the trust property — he still has a special power. Second, *O* can transfer assets worth $220,000 or more into the trust. In this case, the lapse of the general power over $11,000 will not exceed 5 percent of the value of trust corpus, and *A* will not have made a gift.

4.   Suppose that, in Problem 3, *O* gives the trustee $5,000 each year to pay the premium on a life insurance policy on *O*'s life, which is owned by the trust. *O* gives *A* the right to withdraw $5,000 annually. Does this qualify for the annual exclusion? How much life insurance on the life of a 40-year-old woman (a nonsmoker in excellent health) can be purchased with an annual premium of $5,000? It might surprise you to learn it is $10 million for a 20-year term policy, which is quite a lot to transfer tax free to your child.

3.   *Gifts Between Spouses and from One Spouse to a Third Person*

Since 1981, the Code has permitted one spouse to take an *unlimited* marital deduction for gifts to the other spouse (see page 900). Any amount of property (except certain terminable interests) can now be transferred between the spouses, either during life or at death, without paying a gift or estate tax. The policy is this: Husband and wife are permitted to treat their property as assets of a marital unit, transferable between husband and wife without paying any transfer taxes. Only when the assets pass from one of the spouses to a third person is a transfer tax imposed.

The marital deduction is allowed only if a spouse makes transfers to the other spouse that would have been subject to taxation if the property had been transferred by the donee spouse to a third party. Inasmuch as a terminable interest (for example, a life estate) is not subject to transfer taxation when it terminates, a *terminable interest* does not qualify for the marital deduction, subject to certain exceptions. The two most important exceptions are set forth below as Cases 6 and 7. Because we give extended treatment to the marital deduction in connection with the estate tax (see page 900), we mention the nondeductible terminable interest rule here only in passing. It is enough to say — with an explanation to come later — that the following property interests qualify for the marital deduction under the gift tax and the estate tax:

> *Case 5. Fee simple or absolute ownership. W* gives *H* $2.5 million outright. No gift tax is payable by *W*. The $2.5 million will be included in *H*'s gross estate at death if *H* then owns it. If *H* gives the property to a third person, a gift tax will be payable.
>
> *Case 6. Power of appointment trust. W* transfers $2.5 million in trust to pay *H* the income for his life and upon *H*'s death to distribute the principal as *H* appoints by will. *H* has a terminable interest (a life estate), but it qualifies for the marital deduction because *H* has in addition a general power of appointment. No gift tax is payable by *W*. Because *H* has a general power, the value of the trust fund will be included in *H*'s gross estate at death.

Case 7. QTIP (qualified terminable interest property) trust. W transfers $2.5 million in trust to pay the income to *H* for life and upon *H*'s death to distribute the principal to *W*'s children. *W* may elect under §2523(f) of the Code to take a marital deduction for the terminable interest given *H*; as a result of this election, the value of the trust fund will be included in *H*'s gross estate at death even though *H* has only a life estate.

Observe that in all three transfers above, the gift by the wife qualifies for the marital deduction, but when the property is transferred by the husband to a (non-charitable) third party during life or at death, a gift or estate tax becomes payable. (If you want to know more about the marital deduction and cannot contain your curiosity, skip to page 900.)

When property is transferred by gift from one spouse to a third person, the transfer is subject to taxation. However, if the other spouse consents, §2513 of the Code permits the gift to be considered as made one-half by each spouse. Thus, if the wife transfers $200,000 to her daughter, this may be treated—with the husband's consent—as a transfer by the wife of $100,000 and a transfer by the husband of $100,000. One effect of §2513 is to double the available annual exclusion for the donor from $11,000 to $22,000, albeit at the cost of using the consenting spouse's exclusion.

PROBLEMS

1. *W* gives property worth $100,000 to *A*, and her husband *H* signifies his consent to splitting the gift by signing at the appropriate point on the gift tax return filed by the donor. Neither *W* nor *H* has made taxable gifts in any earlier year. What is the amount of taxable gift made by *W*? By *H*?

2. *H* and *W* have three children. They want to know (a) what is the maximum amount they can give to each child tax free each year without using any of their unified gift tax credits, and (b) what is the maximum amount they can give the children tax free in one year, using their annual exclusions and their unified gift tax credits. What will you tell them? Suppose that *H* dies after making these gifts, leaving all his property to *W*. Is any estate tax payable on *H*'s death?

SECTION C. THE FEDERAL ESTATE TAX

1. A Thumbnail Sketch of the Federal Estate Tax

The federal estate tax is imposed on the value of property owned or passing at death plus the value of property over which the decedent had substantial control. This is accomplished by imposing a graduated tax rate schedule on the aggregate of the decedent's *taxable estate* plus *adjusted taxable gifts*, against which various *credits* may be applied.

In determining the amount of the taxable estate, the first step is to compute the value of the decedent's *gross estate*. The federal estate tax attempts to subject to taxation all manner of transfers wherein an economic benefit is transferred from the decedent to another person at death. The Internal Revenue Code's definition of the gross estate encompasses three general categories of transfers: (a) transfers by will or intestacy, (b) certain lifetime transfers that, generally speaking, pass economic benefits at the death of the decedent, and (c) certain nonprobate transfers. The details of what transfers are included in the gross estate are spelled out in §§2033-2044 of the Code.

The gross estate includes all property owned at death (§2033). It thus includes all assets in the probate estate as well as assets passing outside probate by a payable-on-death (P.O.D.) designation. The gross estate also includes all lifetime transfers wherein the decedent retained a life estate or control of beneficial enjoyment (§2036), revocable transfers such as revocable trusts (§2038), and some gifts made within three years before death (§2035). It includes pension plan benefits passing to survivors (§2039), property held in joint tenancy or tenancy by the entirety (§2040), and life insurance policies over which the decedent had incidents of ownership (§2042). It also includes property over which the decedent had a general power of appointment (§2041) and QTIP property (§2044).

From the gross estate, certain *deductions* are authorized by the Code. These include deductions for expenses of administration, casualty losses, state death taxes,[11] and — of more importance in estate planning — deductions for transfers to a spouse (the marital deduction) and deductions for transfers to charity.

The gross estate minus deductions equals the *taxable estate*. To compute the estate tax, *adjusted taxable gifts* are added to the taxable estate. Adjusted taxable gifts are taxable gifts made after 1976 not otherwise includible in the gross estate. If the property was included in the gross estate under §§2033-2044 (such as a remainder in property in which the decedent retained a life estate, includible under §2036), the property is not also includible as an adjusted taxable gift, for that would result in double taxation. The taxable estate plus adjusted taxable gifts equals the *tentative estate tax base*, against which the tax rate schedule is applied to produce a *tentative estate tax*. From the tentative tax as thus computed are deducted gift taxes paid on taxable gifts made after 1976, which may be viewed as an advance payment of the estate tax, as well as various credits to which the estate may be entitled. These include a *credit for gift taxes on pre-1977 gifts* that are included in the gross estate under one of the lifetime transfer sections, a *credit for taxes on prior transfers* that were taxed in the estate of another decedent within the preceding ten years, and a *credit for foreign death taxes*. The most important credit is the *unified credit against the estate tax*, which is the equivalent of the applicable exemption. For the applicable exemption, see page 850.

Here follows an outline of the estate tax provisions of the Internal Revenue Code in table form:

§2033	Property owned at death
+ §2035	Transfers of life insurance policies and certain other interests within three years of death
+ §2036	Transfers with a retained life estate or with retained controls
+ §2037	Transfers taking effect at death

---

11. Before 2005, instead of a deduction, there was a credit for state death taxes. But the 2001 Act phased out this credit. If the 2001 Act amendments sunset as scheduled, the credit for state death taxes will reappear in 2011. See page 928.

+ §2038	Revocable transfers	
+ §2039	Annuities and employee benefits	
+ §2040	Property passing by right of survivorship (joint tenancy)	
+ §2041	General powers of appointment	
+ §2042	Life insurance	
+ §2043	Transfers for a partial consideration	
+ §2044	Certain property for which a marital deduction was previously allowed (QTIP property)	

= **Gross Estate**

−§2053	Deduction for administration expenses, debts, funeral expenses
−§2054	Deduction for casualty losses
−§2055	Charitable deduction
−§2056	Marital deduction
−§2058	Deduction for state death taxes

= **Taxable Estate**

+   *Adjusted taxable gifts* (taxable gifts made after 1976 other than gifts that are includible above in the decedent's gross estate)

= **Tentative Estate Tax Base**

× §2001   Estate tax rate schedule

= **Tentative Estate Tax**

−Gift taxes on gifts made after 1976	
−§2010	Unified estate tax credit
−§2012	Credit for pre-1977 gift taxes on property included in gross estate
−§2013	Credit for taxes on prior transfers
−§2014	Credit for foreign death taxes

= **Federal Estate Tax**

2. The Gross Estate: Property Passing by Will or Intestacy

a. Section 2033: Property Owned at Death

Section 2033 of the Internal Revenue Code provides: "The value of the gross estate shall include the value of property to the extent of the interest therein of the decedent at the time of his death." Section 2033 reaches all property owned at death that passes by will or intestacy. This includes real and tangible personal property; transmissible future interests; intangibles such as securities, patents, and copyrights; interests in an incorporated or unincorporated business; and undivided interests in property (such as the decedent's share of property held in a tenancy in common). In other words, the gross estate includes, under §2033, all items in the decedent's probate estate. Section 2033 also reaches property owned at death that passes under a payable-on-death (P.O.D.) provision of a contract (other than life insurance, annuities, or employee death benefits, which are governed by separate sections of the Code).

If the decedent owned a life estate created by another person,[12] nothing is includible in the decedent's gross estate under §2033. Since a life estate terminates at death, the decedent owns no interest that could pass by will or intestacy. This principle is of considerable importance in estate planning. It is possible to transfer property into a trust giving the beneficiary the income from the property for life without causing any *estate* tax to be levied on the life beneficiary's death. It is even possible to give the income beneficiary certain limited powers to invade the corpus of the trust for his or her benefit and a special power to appoint the remainder interest at death, all without estate tax cost (see page 892). However, if the income beneficiary is of a younger generation than the settlor, and the remainder is given to the life tenant's children, a *generation-skipping transfer tax* may be levied at the life tenant's death (see pages 919-928).

PROBLEM

Decedent is killed while piloting a plane containing several bales of marijuana weighing 662 pounds, which were subsequently confiscated. Is the value of the marijuana includible in the decedent's gross estate? In Tech. Adv. Mem. 92-07-004 (Feb. 14, 1992), the IRS ruled that the retail street value of the marijuana was includible in the gross estate because the decedent had possession and control over the drugs and was to receive the economic benefit from their disposition. It was not necessary to establish legal ownership. A deduction for its confiscation as a casualty loss was denied because to allow the deduction would violate the public policy against drug trafficking. Suppose that the decedent had survived the plane crash and had died after the marijuana was confiscated. What result?

b. Section 2034: Dower or Curtesy

As you may recall from Chapter 7, at common law spouses were traditionally given a right (called dower for women and curtesy for men) in some of the property of their deceased spouse. For estate tax purposes, property includible under §2033 includes assets passing to the surviving spouse by operation of law and over which the decedent did not have the power of disposition at death. Under §2034, "the value of the gross estate shall include the value of all property to the extent of any interest therein of the surviving spouse, existing at the time of the decedent's death as dower or curtesy, or by virtue of a statute creating an estate in lieu of dower or curtesy." Section 2034 does not apply to community property. In community property states, each spouse is the owner of an undivided one-half interest in community assets and has the power of testamentary disposition over only that one-half share. Only the value of the decedent's community half interest is includible as an owned interest under §2033.

---

12. If the decedent made an inter vivos transfer with a retained life estate, the value of the transferred property is includable in the decedent's gross estate under §2036. See page 876.

3. The Gross Estate: Nonprobate Property

a. Section 2040: Joint Tenancy

Although the decedent's interest in a joint tenancy is not taxed under §2033 because the decedent's interest terminates at death, joint tenancy interests are taxed under a different section, §2040. In discussing §2040, together with the gift tax rules applicable to the creation of joint tenancies, we must distinguish between (1) a joint tenancy between persons other than spouses and (2) a joint tenancy or tenancy by the entirety between husband and wife.

(1) Joint tenancy between persons other than husband and wife

(a) Gift tax. A joint tenancy (with right of survivorship) is treated differently under the gift tax from the way it is treated under the estate tax. Under the gift tax, a joint tenancy is treated the same as a tenancy in common on the theory that the donee co-tenant receives the same lifetime rights under both co-tenancies. The donee can sever the joint tenancy and turn it into a tenancy in common at any time. Case 8 illustrates the treatment of a tenancy in common created by the donor with the donee.

> *Case 8.* In 2006, *O* pays $40,000 for securities, taking title in the name of *O* and *A* as *tenants in common.* *O* and *A* each acquire an undivided one-half interest in the securities. *O* has made a gift of one-half the value of the property, or $20,000, to *A*. Deducting the $11,000 annual exclusion, *O* has made a taxable gift of $9,000. (No gift tax is actually payable unless *O* has already used up her unified credit.)

Since a joint tenant can sever the joint tenancy at any time, destroying the right of survivorship and converting the tenancy into a tenancy in common, the gift tax law assumes the donee joint tenant receives the same economic benefit as does a donee tenant in common. Thus:

> *Case 9.* In 2006, *O* pays $40,000 for securities, taking title in the name of *O* and *A* as *joint tenants with right of survivorship.* *O* has made a gift to *A* of one-half the value of the property, or $20,000. As in Case 8, deducting the $11,000 annual exclusion, *O* has made a taxable gift of $9,000. (No gift tax is actually payable unless *O* has already used up her unified credit.)

A joint and survivor bank account is treated somewhat differently. In such an account, either party can withdraw all funds on deposit, whereas a common law joint tenant can, by partition, only acquire title in severalty to his or her fractional share. Since a depositor in a joint and survivor account can withdraw the amount deposited (in effect, revoking the transfer), no gift occurs until the amount is withdrawn by the nondepositing party. Thus:

> *Case 10.* In 2006, *O* deposits $30,000 in a joint and survivor bank account; money in the account is payable to *O* or *A* or the survivor. Since *O* can withdraw the $30,000, the gift is incomplete (see page 853). If *A* withdraws funds from the account, a gift is then made from *O* to *A* of the amount withdrawn. Similarly, if *O* and *A* each deposit $15,000

in a joint account, no gift is made until either *O* or *A* withdraws more than the $15,000 each deposited. Treas. Reg. §25.2511-1(h)(4).

The rules applicable to a joint bank account also apply to a U.S. government bond registered in the name of "*O* or *A*." Under this "or" form of ownership, either *O* or *A* can present the bond for payment. Thus there is no gift unless *A* cashes in the bond.

(b) Estate tax. The decedent's share of a tenancy in common is included in his gross estate under §2033. If the decedent is one of two equal tenants in common, one-half the value of the property is included in the decedent's gross estate. Thus:

> *Case 8a.* Refer back to Case 8, involving the creation of a tenancy in common in 2006. *O* dies in 2008. *O* is survived by *A*. On *O*'s death, the securities are worth $60,000. The value of *O*'s one-half interest in the securities, or $30,000, is includible in *O*'s gross estate under §2033 as an interest owned at death. $9,000 is brought into the estate tax computation as an adjusted taxable gift.

A joint tenancy is not treated like a tenancy in common under the federal estate tax. With respect to a joint tenancy, the amount included in the decedent's gross estate is not the value of the decedent's fractional share of ownership. Where spouses are not involved, the portion included is based upon the percentage of the decedent's contribution to the total cost of the property. Section 2040(a) of the Code requires the inclusion of the entire value of the property held in joint tenancy, except such part of the entire value as is attributable to the amount of *consideration furnished* by the other joint tenant or was originally owned by the other joint tenant. This rule applies to property held in joint tenancy, joint bank accounts, and government bonds with survivorship provisions. Thus:

> *Case 9a.* Refer back to Case 9, involving the creation of a joint tenancy in 2006. *O* dies in 2008. At *O*'s death, the securities are worth $60,000. Under §2040, the full value of the securities, or $60,000, is includible in *O*'s gross estate. (There is no adjusted taxable gift inclusion because the property that was the subject of the gift is included in *O*'s gross estate under §2040.) If *O* paid a gift tax at the time the joint tenancy was created in 2006, there is no double taxation. Section 2001(b)(2) provides that the tentative estate tax is reduced by the amount of gift taxes paid on gifts made after 1976.

If, in Case 9a, *O* had contributed three-fourths of the purchase price of the securities ($30,000) and *A* one-quarter ($10,000), three-fourths of the value of the securities at the date of *O*'s death, or $45,000, would be included in *O*'s gross estate. The burden of showing the amount contributed by the survivor is on the decedent's personal representative. The value of the entire property will be included in the gross estate unless the amount contributed by the survivor is proved. When title is taken in joint tenancy form, it is important to keep records showing the source of the funds with which the property was acquired. Failure to do this may result in needless taxation if the decedent's personal representative cannot satisfactorily establish the amount of the contribution furnished by the survivor. With respect to joint bank owners, the decedent's personal representative must sustain the burden of showing the amount on deposit attributable to the survivor's contributions, or the full amount is included in the decedent's gross estate.

PROBLEM

O purchases Blackacre for $100,000 and takes title in the name of *O* and *A* as joint tenants with right of survivorship. *O* has used up her unified gift tax credit and therefore pays a gift tax on the $39,000 gift to *A* ($50,000 minus the $11,000 exclusion). A few years later *A* dies. Is *O* entitled to a return of the gift tax paid? Is *O*'s executor entitled to credit the gift tax paid against *O*'s estate tax when she dies? Suppose that *O* sells Blackacre before her death. Is *O*'s executor entitled to credit the gift tax paid against the estate tax?

(2) *Joint tenancy and tenancy by the entirety between husband and wife*

(a) Gift tax.   Internal Revenue Code §§2056 and 2523 provide for an unlimited marital deduction: Any amount of property may be transferred by one spouse to the other spouse as tenants in common, joint tenants, or tenants by the entirety tax free. Thus, if a wife buys property and takes title in the name of herself and her husband as joint tenants, a gift has been made to the husband of one-half the value of the property, as in Case 9, but the amount of the gift qualifies for the marital deduction and no gift tax is payable.

(b) Estate tax.   The who-furnished-the-consideration test applicable to joint tenancies between nonspouses does not apply to a "qualified joint interest" held between spouses. A qualified joint interest is a tenancy by the entirety or a joint tenancy with right of survivorship where the spouses are the only joint tenants. With respect to both of these forms of property holding, each spouse owns an undivided one-half interest in the property.

Section 2040(b) of the Code provides that with respect to property held by the decedent and the decedent's spouse as joint tenants with right of survivorship or as tenants by the entirety, one-half the value of the property is includible in the decedent's gross estate regardless of which spouse furnished the consideration for the property's acquisition. Hence, for both gift and estate tax purposes, a joint tenancy or tenancy by the entirety owned by husband and wife is treated as owned one-half by each. The one-half interest includible in the decedent's gross estate that passes to the surviving spouse qualifies for the unlimited marital deduction. Therefore, no estate taxes result from the inclusion of the decedent spouse's one-half interest.

b. Section 2039: Annuities and Employee Death Benefits

Generally, private pension plan benefits paid to a decedent's family are treated as part of her gross estate. Section 2039 of the Code provides that employee death benefits receivable by a beneficiary are includible in the gross estate of the decedent if the decedent "possessed the right to receive" any benefits during her lifetime. The type of right that usually causes §2039 to apply is the right of the decedent to an annuity or pension upon retirement. If the decedent has this right, and death benefits—usually in the form of an annuity or a lump sum payment— are payable to a surviving beneficiary, the value of the death benefits is includible in the decedent's gross estate. Individual Retirement Accounts (IRAs) and Keogh plans are included in the decedent's gross estate under §2039. Section 2039 is inapplicable to "insurance under policies on the life of the decedent," which is governed by §2042.

If the decedent has no power to select the beneficiary of his employee benefits because the death benefits are payable *by statute* to the decedent's spouse or children, the death benefits are not includable in the decedent's estate. Thus, for example, Social Security benefits are excludable.

Employee death benefits included in the decedent's estate and payable to the decedent's spouse ordinarily will qualify for the marital deduction.

Income tax treatment. When employee death benefits are received by a beneficiary after the death of the employee or of the owner of an income-tax-deferred plan (such as IRA or Keogh), the receipts are treated as "income in respect of a decedent" under §691(a) of the Code. This means the beneficiary stands in the income tax shoes of the decedent, with no step-up in basis. The beneficiary may deduct from her income tax return the estate tax attributable to the benefit. I.R.C. §691(c).

c. Section 2042: Life Insurance

Life insurance is sometimes included in a gross estate and sometimes not; with proper pre-death estate planning, it is often excludible. Section 2042(2) of the Code provides that the gross estate shall include the value of insurance proceeds on the life of the decedent (1) if the decedent possessed at death any of the *incidents of ownership* under the policies, or (2) if the policy proceeds were *payable to the insured's executor or estate*. The incidents of ownership include such policy rights as the right to change the beneficiary, to surrender, cancel, or assign the policy, or to borrow against the cash surrender value in the policy. Where a person takes out a policy on his own life and names some member of the family as beneficiary, the proceeds will be taxed in the insured's estate if he holds any incidents of ownership over the policy. This is true even of a term insurance policy that has no investment features and hence no cash surrender value, for the insured has the right to change the beneficiary designation and also the right to assign or cancel the policy. The retention of only one incident of ownership causes the full value of the insurance proceeds to be taxed under §2042.

If an insurance policy owned by a decedent spouse (and therefore includable in the decedent's gross estate) is payable to the surviving spouse in a lump sum, the policy proceeds qualify for the unlimited marital deduction. No taxes result from the inclusion of the policy in the decedent's gross estate. However, if the policy is payable to someone other than the surviving spouse, then to minimize estate taxes the beneficiary should, if possible, purchase and pay the premiums on the policy.

See generally Robert B. Smith, Reconsidering the Taxation of Life Insurance Proceeds Through the Lens of Current Estate Planning, 15 Va. Tax Rev. 283 (1995).

PROBLEMS

1. *H* is the insured under a $500,000 ordinary life insurance policy that names *W* as the owner of the policy and of all incidents of ownership therein. The policy was

issued in W's name as owner when it was taken out ten years ago, and all policy premiums have been paid out of W's funds. The policy names W as primary beneficiary and the couple's daughter, D, as contingent beneficiary. H dies, and the policy proceeds are paid to W. H leaves a will that devises his entire estate to W and D in equal shares. The will names W as executor. Are the policy proceeds includable in H's gross estate?

2.   Consider the same facts as in Problem 1 except that W predeceases H, leaving a will that devises "all my property" to H. On the date of W's death, the cash surrender value of the policy is $100,000. H dies a year later, and the $500,000 in policy proceeds are paid to the couple's daughter, D, as contingent beneficiary. What are the estate tax consequences in W's estate? In H's estate?

3.   If a donee of a special power of appointment can appoint trust property that includes a life insurance policy on the donee's life, the power to appoint is an incident of ownership, and the value of the insurance will be included in the donee's gross estate. In drafting special powers, you should take care to exclude such life insurance from the appointive property.

4.   The Gross Estate: Lifetime Transfers

The gross estate includes certain lifetime transfers made by the decedent. We take up the relevant sections here in the order that, we think, makes them easiest to understand — 2036, 2038, 2037, and 2035.

a.   Section 2036: Transfers with Life Estate or Control of Beneficial Rights Retained

When people transfer property, they often give it with strings attached. Section 2036(a) governs transfers with important rights retained by the donor:

> The value of the gross estate shall include the value of all property to the extent of any interest therein of which the decedent has at any time made a transfer (except in case of a bona fide sale for an adequate and full consideration in money or money's worth), by trust or otherwise, under which he has retained for his life or for any period which does not in fact end before his death —
>
>> (1) The possession or enjoyment of, or the right to the income from, the property, or
>>
>> (2) The right, either alone or in conjunction with any person, to designate the persons who shall possess or enjoy the property or the income therefrom.

Note that §2036 includes in the gross estate two types of lifetime transfers. Section 2036(a)(1) applies when the decedent retains a life estate in the transferred property. Although the life estate terminates at death, the transfer is subjected to estate taxation because the decedent retained the most important incident of property ownership: the right for life to possess and enjoy the property or to receive its income.

Section 2036(a)(2) reaches transfers in which the decedent retains the right to control beneficial enjoyment of the property, even though the right cannot be exercised in a manner that would benefit the transferor personally. To take an obvious case, when the transferor designates himself as a co-trustee and the trustees have a discretionary power to accumulate trust income or distribute it to the beneficiary, or a power to distribute the income among several beneficiaries in such shares as the trustees shall determine, the transfer is taxed under this section. The transfer is also taxed even though the power is exercisable only with the consent of a person having an interest that could be adversely affected by the exercise of the power.[13] To a considerable extent, as we shall see, §2036(a)(2) overlaps with §2038, which applies to lifetime transfers where the transferor possesses the power to alter, amend, or revoke.

PROBLEMS

1.   O transfers property to X in trust to pay the income to O for life and on O's death to distribute the trust assets to A. What are the gift and estate tax consequences of this transfer?

2.   O transfers property to X in trust. The trustee has unfettered discretion to pay the income to O or to accumulate it and to invade the corpus for O's benefit; on O's death, the trustee is to distribute the trust assets to A. What are the gift and estate tax consequences?

Estate of Maxwell v. Commissioner
United States Court of Appeals, Second Circuit, 1993
3 F.3d 591

LASKER, J.   This appeal presents challenges to the tax court's interpretation of section 2036(a) of the Internal Revenue Code, relating to "Transfers with retained life estate." The petitioner, the Estate of Lydia G. Maxwell, contends that the tax court erred in holding that the transaction at issue (a) was a transfer with retained life estate within the meaning of 26 U.S.C. §2036 and (b) was not a bona fide sale for adequate and full consideration under that statute.

The decision of the tax court is affirmed.

I

On March 14, 1984, Lydia G. Maxwell (the "decedent") conveyed her personal residence, which she had lived in since 1957, to her son Winslow Maxwell, her only

13. Sections 671-677 of the Internal Revenue Code spell out the circumstances under which the settlor of a trust is taxable on trust *income* on grounds of dominion and control. The income tax provisions are not entirely consistent with the estate tax provisions. A settlor may have succeeded in eliminating the trust income from his gross income but not the principal from his gross estate. For example, if the settlor has the power to control beneficial enjoyment of the income only with the consent of an *adverse party*, the income is not taxable to the settlor. I.R.C. §674(a). But the value of the principal is includable in the settlor's gross estate at death because §§2036 and 2038 do not distinguish between a power held with an adverse party and a power held with a nonadverse party. Likewise, if the settlor as trustee has only a discretionary power to pay income to, or accumulate it for, the life beneficiary, the settlor is not taxable on the income. Id. §674(b)(6). But the value of the trust property will be included in the settlor's gross estate. If your client wishes to create a trust and retain any power over income or principal, both income tax and estate tax sections must be explored if the settlor is successfully to eliminate the income from his gross income and the principal from his gross estate. See pages 516-518.

heir, and his wife Margaret Jane Maxwell (the "Maxwells"). Following the transfer, the decedent continued to reside in the house until her death on July 30, 1986. At the time of the transfer, she was eighty-two years old and was suffering from cancer.

The transaction was structured as follows:

1) The residence was sold by the decedent to the Maxwells for $270,000;[14]
2) Simultaneously with the sale, the decedent forgave $20,000 of the purchase price (which was equal in amount to the annual gift tax exclusion to which she was entitled);
3) The Maxwells executed a $250,000 mortgage note in favor of decedent;
4) The Maxwells leased the premises to her for five years at the monthly rental of $1,800; and
5) The Maxwells were obligated to pay and did pay certain expenses associated with the property following the transfer, including property taxes, insurance costs, and unspecified "other expenses."

While the decedent paid the Maxwells rent totalling $16,200 in 1984, $22,183 in 1985 and $12,600 in 1986, the Maxwells paid the decedent interest on the mortgage totalling $16,875 in 1984, $21,150 in 1985, and $11,475 in 1986. As can be observed, the rent paid by the decedent to the Maxwells came remarkably close to matching the mortgage interest which they paid to her. In 1984, she paid the Maxwells only $675 less than they paid her; in 1985, she paid them only $1,033 more than they paid her, and in 1986 she paid the Maxwells only $1,125 more than they paid her.

Not only did the rent functionally cancel out the interest payments made by the Maxwells, but the Maxwells were at no time called upon to pay any of the principal on the $250,000 mortgage debt; it was forgiven in its entirety. As petitioner's counsel admitted at oral argument, although the Maxwells had executed the mortgage note, "there was an intention by and large that it not be paid." Pursuant to this intention, in each of the following years preceding her death, the decedent forgave $20,000 of the mortgage principal, and, by a provision of her will executed on March 16, 1984 (that is, just two days after the transfer), she forgave the remaining indebtedness.

The decedent reported the sale of her residence on her 1984 federal income tax return but did not pay any tax on the sale because she elected to use the once-in-a-lifetime exclusion on the sale or exchange of a principal residence provided for by 26 U.S.C. §121.

She continued to occupy the house by herself until her death. At no time during her occupancy did the Maxwells attempt to sell the house to anyone else, but, on September 22, 1986, shortly after the decedent's death, they did sell the house for $550,000.

Under I.R.C. §2036(a), where property is disposed of by a decedent during her lifetime but the decedent retains "possession or enjoyment" of it until her death, that property is taxable as part of the decedent's gross estate, unless the

---

14. The parties have stipulated that the fair market value of the property on the date of the purported sale was $280,000.

transfer was a bona fide sale for an "adequate and full" consideration. 26 U.S.C. §2036.

On the decedent's estate tax return, the Estate reported only the $210,000 remaining on the mortgage debt (following the decedent's forgiveness of $20,000 in the two preceding years). The Commissioner found that the 1984 transaction constituted a transfer with retained life estate—rejecting the petitioners' arguments that the decedent did not retain "possession or enjoyment" of the property, and that the transaction was exempt from section 2036(a) because it was a bona fide sale for full and adequate consideration—, and assessed a deficiency against the Estate to adjust for the difference between the fair market value of the property at the time of decedent's death ($550,000) and the reported $210,000.

The Estate appealed to the tax court, which, after a trial on stipulated facts, affirmed the Commissioner's ruling, holding:

> On this record, bearing in mind petitioner's burden of proof, we hold that, notwithstanding its form, the substance of the transaction calls for the conclusion that decedent made a transfer to her son and daughter-in-law with the understanding, at least implied, that she would continue to reside in her home until her death, that the transfer was not a bona fide sale for an adequate and full consideration in money or money's worth, and that the lease represented nothing more than an attempt to add color to the characterization of the transaction as a bona fide sale.

There are two questions before us: Did the decedent retain possession or enjoyment of the property following the transfer? And if she did, was the transfer a bona fide sale for an adequate and full consideration in money or money's worth?

II

Section 2036(a) provides in pertinent part:

> The value of the gross estate shall include the value of all property to the extent of any interest therein of which the decedent has at any time made a transfer (except in case of a bona fide sale for an adequate and full consideration in money or money's worth), by trust or otherwise, under which he has retained for his life or for any period not ascertainable without reference to his death or for any period which does not in fact end before his death—(1) the possession or enjoyment of, or the right to the income from, the property, . . . 26 U.S.C. §2036(a).

In the case of real property, the terms "possession" and "enjoyment" have been interpreted to mean "the lifetime use of the property." United States v. Byrum, 408 U.S. 125, 147 (1972).

In numerous cases, the tax court has held, where an aged family member transferred her home to a relative and continued to reside there until her death, that the decedent-transferor had retained "possession or enjoyment" of the property within the meaning of §2036. As stated in Rapelje v. Commissioner, 73 T.C. 82 (1979): "Possession or enjoyment of gifted property is retained [by the transferor] when there is an express or implied understanding to that effect among the parties at the time of transfer." . . . As the *Rapelje* opinion indicates . . . courts have held that §2036(a) requires that the fair market value of such property be included in the decedent's estate if he retained the actual possession or enjoyment thereof, even though he may have had no enforceable right to do so. Estate of Honigman v. Commissioner, 66 T.C. 1080, 1082 (1976). In such cases, the burden is on the decedent's estate to disprove the existence of any adverse implied agreement or understanding and that burden is particularly onerous when intrafamily arrangements are involved. . . .

As indicated above, the tax court found as a fact that the decedent had transferred her home to the Maxwells "with the understanding, at least implied, that she would continue to reside in her home until her death." This finding was based upon the decedent's advanced age, her medical condition, and the overall result of the sale and lease. The lease was, in the tax court's words, "merely window dressing" — it had no substance.

The tax court's findings of fact are reversible only if clearly erroneous. We agree with the tax court's finding that the decedent transferred her home to the Maxwells "with the understanding, at least implied, that she would continue to reside in her home until her death," and certainly do not find it to be clearly erroneous. The decedent did, in fact, live at her residence until she died, and she had sole possession of the residence during the period between the day she sold her home to the Maxwells and the day she died. There is no evidence that the Maxwells ever intended to occupy the house themselves, or to sell or lease it to anyone else during the decedent's lifetime. Moreover, the Maxwells' failure to demand payment by the estate, as they were entitled to do under the lease, of the rent due for the months following decedent's death and preceding their sale of the property, also supports the tax court's finding.

The petitioner argues . . . that the decedent's tenancy alone does not justify inclusion of the residence in her estate, so it argues that the decedent's payment of rent sanctifies the transaction and renders it legitimate. Both arguments ignore the realities of the rent being offset by mortgage interest, the forgiveness of the entire mortgage debt either by gift or testamentary disposition, and the fact that the decedent was eighty-two at the time of the transfer and actually continued to live in the residence until her death which, at the time of the transfer, she had reason to believe would occur soon in view of her poor health.

The Estate relies primarily on Barlow v. Commissioner, 55 T.C. 666 (1971). In that case, the father transferred a farm to his children and simultaneously leased the right to continue to farm the property. The tax court held that the father did not retain "possession or enjoyment," stating that "one of the most valuable incidents of income-producing real estate is the rent which it yields. He who receives the rent in fact enjoys the property." *Barlow*, 55 T.C. at 671 (quoting McNichol's v. Commissioner, 265 F.2d 667, 671 (3d Cir. 1959)). However, *Barlow* is clearly distinguishable on its facts: In that case, there was evidence that the rent paid was fair and customary and, equally importantly, the rent paid was not offset by the decedent's receipt of interest from the family lessor.

. . . *Barlow* itself recognized that where a transferor "by agreement" "reserves the right of occupancy as an incident to the transfer," §2036(a) applies. *Barlow*, 55 T.C. at 670. . . .

For the reasons stated above, we conclude that the decedent did retain possession or enjoyment of the property for life and turn to the question of whether the transfer constituted "a bona fide sale for adequate and full consideration in money or money's worth."

III

Section 2036(a) provides that even if possession or enjoyment of transferred property is retained by the decedent until her death, if the transfer was a bona fide sale for adequate and full consideration in money or money's worth, the property is not includible in the estate. Petitioner contends that the Maxwells paid an "adequate and full consideration" for the decedent's residence, $270,000 total, consisting of the $250,000 mortgage note given by the Maxwells to the decedent, and the $20,000 the decedent forgave simultaneously with the conveyance.[15]

The tax court held that neither the Maxwells' mortgage note nor the decedent's $20,000 forgiveness constituted consideration within the meaning of the statute.

$250,000 MORTGAGE NOTE

As to the $250,000 mortgage note, the tax court held that:

> Regardless of whether the $250,000 mortgage note might otherwise qualify as "adequate and full consideration in money or money's worth" for a $270,000 or $280,000 house, the mortgage note here had no value at all if there was no intention that it would ever be paid. The conduct of decedent and the Maxwells strongly suggest that neither party intended the Maxwells to pay any part of the principal of either the original note or any successor note.

There is no question that the mortgage note here is a fully secured, legally enforceable obligation on its face. The question is whether it is actually what it purports to be—a bona fide instrument of indebtedness—or whether it is a facade. The petitioner argues not only that an allegedly unenforceable intention to forgive indebtedness does not deprive the indebtedness of its status as "consideration in money or money's worth" but also that "[t]his is true even if there was an implied agreement exactly as found by the Tax Court."

We agree with the tax court that where, as here, there is an implied agreement between the parties that the grantee would never be called upon to make any payment to the grantor, as, in fact, actually occurred, the note given by the grantee had "no value at all." We emphatically disagree with the petitioner's view of the law as it applies to the facts of this case. As the Supreme Court has remarked, the family relationship often makes it possible for one to shift tax incidence by surface changes of ownership without disturbing in the least his dominion and control over the subject of the gift or the purposes for which the income from the property is used. *Commissioner v. Culbertson,* 337 U.S. 733, 746 (1949). There can be no doubt that intent is a relevant inquiry in determining whether a transaction is "bona fide." As another panel of this Court held recently, construing a parallel provision of the Internal Revenue Code, in a case involving an intrafamily transfer:

> when the bona fides of promissory notes is at issue, the taxpayer must demonstrate affirmatively that "there existed at the time of the transaction a real expectation of repayment and an intent to enforce the collection of the indebtedness." *Estate of Van*

---

15. As noted above, the parties have stipulated that the fair market value of the property on the date of the purported sale was $280,000. The Estate contends that $270,000 was full and adequate consideration for the sale, with a broker, for a house appraised at $280,000. We assume this fact to be true for purposes of determining whether the transaction was one for "an adequate and full consideration in money or money's worth."

Anda v. Commissioner, 12 T.C. 1158, 1162 (1949), aff'd per curiam, 192 F.2d 391 (2d Cir. 1951).

In language strikingly apposite to the situation here, the court stated:

> it is appropriate to look beyond the form of the transactions and to determine, as the tax court did here, that the gifts and loans back to decedent were "component parts of single transactions." Id.

The tax court concluded that the evidence "viewed as a whole" left the "unmistakable impression" that regardless of how long decedent lived following the transfer of her house, the entire principal balance of the mortgage note would be forgiven, and the Maxwells would not be required to pay any of such principal.

... [T]he tax court found that, at the time the note was executed, there was "an understanding" between the Maxwells and the decedent that the note would be forgiven. In our judgment, the conduct of decedent and the Maxwells with respect to the principal balance of the note, when viewed in connection with the initial "forgiveness" of $20,000 of the purported purchase price, strongly suggests the existence of an understanding between decedent and the Maxwells that decedent would forgive $20,000 each year thereafter until her death, when the balance would be forgiven by decedent's will.

To conclude, we hold that the conveyance was not a bona fide sale for an adequate and full consideration in money or money's worth. The decision of the tax court is affirmed.

NOTES

1. In Wheeler v. United States, 116 F.3d 749 (5th Cir. 1997), the taxpayer, age 60, sold a remainder interest in his ranch to his two sons for the value of a remainder interest set forth in the actuarial tables of the Treasury regulations. The taxpayer reserved a life estate in the ranch and died at age 67. The court held the transfer was for full consideration, and thus the ranch was not part of the transferor's federal gross estate under §2036. Compare Gradow v. United States, 897 F.2d 516 (Fed. Cir. 1990).

2. Joseph Grace executes a trust instrument providing for payment of income to his wife, Janet, for her life, with payment to her of any part of the principal that a majority of the trustees think advisable. Mrs. Grace is given a special testamentary power of appointment over the trust estate. Named as trustees are Joseph, his nephew, and a third party. Shortly thereafter, Janet Grace, at Joseph's request, executes a virtually identical trust instrument naming Joseph as life beneficiary. Upon Joseph's death is the corpus of either of the trusts includable in Joseph's gross estate? See United States v. Estate of Grace, 395 U.S. 316 (1969).

In the *Grace* case, the Court held that, under the reciprocal trust doctrine, the value of the Janet Grace trust must be included in Joseph's estate. "[A]pplication of the reciprocal trust doctrine requires only that the trusts be interrelated, and that the arrangement, to the extent of mutual value, leaves the settlors in approximately the same economic position as they would have been in had they created trusts naming themselves as life beneficiaries." Id. at 324.

The reciprocal trust doctrine is rather vague, and, in applying the doctrine, the Internal Revenue Service has won some cases and lost some. It stands as a caution, however, to the lawyer who creates reciprocal trusts. See Elena Marty-Nelson, Taxing Reciprocal Trusts: Charting a Doctrine's Fall from Grace, 75 N.C.L. Rev. 1781 (1997).

Old Colony Trust Co. v. United States
United States Court of Appeals, First Circuit, 1970
423 F.2d 601

ALDRICH, J.   The sole question in this case is whether the estate of a settlor of an inter vivos trust, who was a trustee until the date of his death, is to be charged with the value of the principal he contributed by virtue of reserved powers in the trust. The executor paid the tax and sued for its recovery in the district court. All facts were stipulated. The court ruled for the government, 300 F. Supp. 1032, and the executor appeals.

The initial life beneficiary of the trust was the settlor's adult son. Eighty percent of the income was normally to be payable to him, and the balance added to principal. Subsequent beneficiaries were the son's widow and his issue. The powers upon which the government relies to cause the corpus to be includable in the settlor-trustee's estate are contained in two articles. . . .

Article 4 permitted the trustees to increase the percentage of income payable to the son beyond the eighty percent, "in their absolute discretion . . . when in their opinion such increase is needed in case of sickness, or desirable in view of changed circumstances." In addition, under Article 4 the trustees were given the discretion to cease paying income to the son, and add it all to principal, "during such period as the Trustees may decide that the stoppage of such payments is for his best interests."

Article 7 gave broad administrative or management powers to the trustees, with discretion to acquire investments not normally held by trustees, and the right to determine what was to be charged or credited to income or principal, including stock dividends or deductions for amortization. It further provided that all divisions and decisions made by the trustees in good faith should be conclusive on all parties, and in summary, stated that the trustees were empowered, "generally to do all things in relation to the Trust Fund which the Donor could do if living and this Trust had not been executed."

The government claims that each of these two articles meant that the settlor-trustee had "the right . . . to designate the persons who shall possess or enjoy the [trust] property or the income therefrom" within the meaning of section 2036(a)(2) of the Internal Revenue Code of 1954, 26 U.S.C. §2036(a)(2), and that the settlor-trustee at the date of his death possessed a power "to alter, amend, revoke, or terminate" within the meaning of section 2038(a)(1) (26 U.S.C. §2038(a)(1)).

If State Street Trust Co. v. United States, 1 Cir., 1959, 263 F.2d 635, was correctly decided in this aspect, the government must prevail because of the Article 7 powers. There this court, Chief Judge Magruder dissenting, held against the taxpayer because broad powers similar to those in Article 7 meant that the trustees "could very substantially shift the economic benefits of the trusts between the life tenants and the remaindermen," so that the settlor "as long as he lived, in substance and effect and in a very real sense . . . 'retained for his life . . . the right . . . to designate the persons who shall possess or enjoy the property or the income therefrom. . . .'" 263 F.2d at 639-640, quoting 26 U.S.C. §2036(a)(2). We accept the taxpayer's invitation to reconsider this ruling.

It is common ground that a settlor will not find the corpus of the trust included in his estate merely because he named himself a trustee. He must have reserved a power to himself[16] that is inconsistent with the full termination of ownership. The government's brief defines this as "sufficient dominion and control until his death." Trustee powers given for the administration or management of the trust must be equitably exercised, however, for the benefit of the trust as a whole. The court in *State Street* conceded that the powers at issue were all such powers, but reached the conclusion that, cumulatively, they gave the settlor dominion sufficiently unfettered to be in the nature of ownership. With all respect to the majority of the then court, we find it difficult to see how a power can be subject to control by the probate court, and exercisable only in what the trustee fairly concludes is in the interests of the trust and its beneficiaries as a whole, and at the same time be an ownership power.

The government's position, to be sound, must be that the trustee's powers are beyond the court's control. Under Massachusetts law, however, no amount of administrative discretion prevents judicial supervision of the trustee. Thus in Appeal of Davis, 1903, 67 N.E. 604 (Mass.), a trustee was given "full power to make purchases, investments and exchanges . . . in such manner as to them shall seem expedient; it being my intention to give my trustees . . . the same dominion and control over said trust property as I now have." In spite of this language, and in spite of their good faith, the court charged the trustees for failing sufficiently to diversify their investment portfolio. The Massachusetts court has never varied from this broad rule of accountability, and has twice criticized *State Street* for its seeming departure. Boston Safe Deposit & Trust Co. v. Stone, 1965, 348 Mass. 345, 351, n.8, 203 N.E.2d 547; Old Colony Trust Co. v. Silliman, 1967, 352 Mass. 6, 8-9, 223 N.E.2d 504. We make it a further observation, which the court in *State Street* failed to note, that the provision in that trust (as in the case at bar) that the trustees could "do all things in relation to the Trust Fund which I, the Donor, could do if . . . the Trust had not been executed," is almost precisely the provision which did not protect the trustees from accountability in Appeal of Davis, supra.

We do not believe that trustee powers are to be more broadly construed for tax purposes than the probate court would construe them for administrative purposes. More basically, we agree with Judge Magruder's observation that nothing is "gained by lumping them together." State Street Trust Co. v. United States, supra, 263 F.2d at 642. We hold that no aggregation of purely administrative powers can meet the government's amorphous test of "sufficient dominion and control" so as to be equated with ownership.

This does not resolve taxpayer's difficulties under Article 4. Quite different considerations apply to distribution powers. Under them the trustee can,

---

16. The number of other trustees who must join in the exercise of that power, unless the others have antagonistic interest of a substantial nature, is, of course, immaterial. Treas. Reg. §20.2036-1(a)(ii), (b)(3)(i) (1958); §20.2038-1(a) (1958).

expressly, prefer one beneficiary over another. Furthermore, his freedom of choice may vary greatly, depending upon the terms of the individual trust. If there is an ascertainable standard, the trustee can be compelled to follow it. If there is not, even though he is a fiduciary, it is not unreasonable to say that his retention of an unmeasurable freedom of choice is equivalent to retaining some of the incidents of ownership. Hence, under the cases, if there is an ascertainable standard the settlor-trustee's estate is not taxed, . . . but if there is not, it is taxed. . . .

The trust provision which is uniformly held to provide an ascertainable standard is one which, though variously expressed, authorizes such distributions as may be needed to continue the beneficiary's accustomed way of life. . . . On the other hand, if the trustee may go further, and has power to provide for the beneficiary's "happiness," Merchants Nat'l Bank v. Com'r of Internal Revenue, 1943, 320 U.S. 256, or "pleasure," Industrial Trust Co. v. Com'r of Internal Revenue, 1 Cir., 1945, 151 F.2d 592, or "use and benefit," Newton Trust Co. v. Com'r of Internal Revenue, 1 Cir., 1947, 160 F.2d 175, or "reasonable requirement[s]," State Street Bank & Trust Co. v. United States, 1 Cir., 1963, 313 F.2d 29, the standard is so loose that the trustee is in effect uncontrolled.

In the case at bar the trustees could increase the life tenant's income "in case of sickness, or [if] desirable in view of changed circumstances." Alternatively, they could reduce it "for his best interests." "Sickness" presents no problem. Conceivably, providing for "changed circumstances" is roughly equivalent to maintaining the son's present standard of living. . . . The unavoidable stumbling block is the trustees' right to accumulate income and add it to capital (which the son would never receive) when it is to the "best interests" of the son to do so. Additional payments to a beneficiary whenever in his "best interests" might seem to be too broad a standard in any event. In addition to the previous cases see Estate of Yawkey, 1949, 12 T.C. 1164, where the court said, at p.1170, "We can not regard the language involved ['best interest'] as limiting the usual scope of a trustee's discretion. It must always be anticipated that trustees will act for the best interests of a trust beneficiary, and an exhortation to act 'in the interests and for the welfare' of the beneficiary does not establish an external standard." Power, however, to decrease or cut off a beneficiary's income when in his "best interests," is even more troublesome. When the beneficiary is the son, and the trustee the father, a particular purpose comes to mind, parental control through holding the purse strings. The father decides what conduct is to the "best interests" of the son, and if the son does not agree, he loses his allowance. Such power has the plain indicia of ownership control. The alternative, that the son, because of other means, might not need this income, and would prefer to have it accumulate for his widow and children after his death, is no better. If the trustee has power to confer "happiness" on the son by generosity to someone else, this seems clearly an unascertainable standard.

The case of Hays' Estate v. Com'r of Internal Revenue, 5 Cir., 1950, 181 F.2d 169, is contrary to our decision. The opinion is unsupported by either reasoning or authority, and we will not follow it. With the present settlor-trustee free to determine the standard himself, a finding of ownership control was warranted. To put it another way, the cost of holding onto the strings may prove to be a rope burn. State Street Bank & Trust Co. v. United States, supra.

Affirmed.

NOTE AND QUESTION

1.   It might be thought that application of §2036(a)(2) to retained discretionary powers can be avoided by not naming the settlor as trustee or co-trustee. This alone, however, is not enough. If the named trustee has these powers, and if the settlor has the power to remove the trustee and appoint himself or a related or subordinate person as successor trustee, the settlor may be deemed to possess the powers, and estate taxation may result. The Internal Revenue Service gives some leeway, however, to trustee removal powers. It takes the position that, if the decedent possesses the power to remove the trustee and appoint an individual or corporate successor trustee that is not related or subordinate to the decedent, the decedent will not be deemed to retain a trustee's discretionary control over trust income. Rev. Rul. 95-58, 1995-2 CB. 191.

2.   Since the entire value of the property will be included in the donor's gross estate under §2036(a)(1), when the donor retains a life estate, why should the gift of a remainder be taxable as a gift? See W. Leslie Peat & Stephanie J. Willbanks, A Page of Logic Is Worth a Volume of History: The Treatment of Retained Interests Under the Federal Estate and Gift Tax Statutes, 3 Va. Tax Rev. 639 (1989).

NOTE: FAMILY LIMITED PARTNERSHIPS

Section 2036 brings into the gross estate lifetime transfers that are testamentary in nature. In Turner v. Commissioner, 382 F.3d 367 (3d Cir. 2004), the court held that a *family limited partnership* (FLP) was such a testamentary transfer on the ground that it was nothing more than "a vehicle for changing the form in which the decedent held his property—a recycling of value." Id. at 378. In an FLP, the decedent transfers assets (usually the majority of his assets) to the partnership in exchange for a limited partnership interest. The decedent's family likewise transfers assets (usually minimal assets, however) to the partnership in exchange for limited partnership interests. The general partner is a corporation owned by the decedent and his family. The reason for creating an FLP is that, when the decedent's limited partnership interests pass to his family, the value of those interests are discounted for estate tax purposes because of their lack of control rights and nonmarketability.

In *Turner*, the decedent transferred 95 percent of his assets to two FLPs—one organized with each of decedent's children—when he was 95 years old. After the transfers, the decedent did not have sufficient assets to support himself. Neither FLP engaged in any real business or commercial activity, and any profits earned by the FLPs passed through to the original owner of the underlying property. The court found that there was an implicit agreement that the decedent could obtain whatever resources he needed for support from the FLPs. In view of this finding, the court held that decedent had retained possession and enjoyment of his assets and hence that the transfer was not a bona fide sale for adequate consideration. The transfer, in other words, was motivated solely by estate tax savings. Accordingly, under §2036, the full value of the transferred assets, not the discounted value of the limited partnership interests, were included in the decedent's gross estate. See also Estate of Strangi v. Commissioner, 85 T.C.M. (CCH) 1331 (2003), on remand from 293 F.3d 279 (5th Cir. 2002), reaching the same conclusion where the decedent transferred 98 percent of his assets, including his residence, to the FLP, and the FLP paid his personal expenses and the expenses of his estate.

Not all FLPs run afoul of §2036, however. For example, in Estate of Stone v. Commissioner, 86 T.C.M. (CCH) 551 (2003), the court found that the transfers that underpinned the FLPs at issue were bona fide and for adequate consideration. Before the creation of the FLPs there were significant disputes within the family concerning the operation of the underlying businesses, and there had been substantial negotiation among the children and with decedent in the formation of the FLPs. The FLPs in this case involved ongoing business enterprises; they were not merely devices for holding decedent's passive investments.

In Kimbell v. United States, 371 F.3d 257 (5th Cir. 2004), the decedent created the FLP to manage her oil and gas interests. Although there were no intra-family squabbles, the court found sufficient business motives for the formation of the FLP in the decedent's desire to protect her assets from creditors; to avoid personal liability for environmental issues; to provide ongoing management; and to retain the business interests in a single, centralized entity rather than dispersing them through distributions to subsequent generations. Hence the court did not apply §2036.

b.   Section 2038: Revocable Transfers

Another Code section governs the inclusion in the gross estate of interests (usually in inter vivos trusts or other nonprobate transfers) that the decedent may alter, amend, or revoke. Section 2038(a) provides that the value of the gross estate shall include the value of all property:

> To the extent of any interest therein of which the decedent has at any time made a transfer (except in case of a bona fide sale for an adequate and full consideration in money or money's worth), by trust or otherwise, where the enjoyment thereof was subject at the date of his death to any change through the exercise of a power (in whatever capacity exercisable) by the decedent alone or by the decedent in conjunction with any other person (without regard to when or from what source the decedent acquired such power), to alter, amend, revoke or terminate, or when any such power is relinquished during the three-year period ending on the date of the decedent's death.

To a considerable extent, §2038 applies to the same transfers caught within §2036(a)(2). However, there are situations covered exclusively by §2038. Section 2036(a)(2) covers only a retained right to designate the *persons* who shall enjoy the property. Section 2038 is applicable if the transferor has the power to effect any change, including the *time* of enjoyment. Hence, §2038 alone applies where the settlor may terminate a trust and accelerate enjoyment by a beneficiary. Note also that §2038, like §2036(a)(2), is applicable even though the power is held in conjunction with an adverse party or is held by the settlor as trustee.

If the power to alter, amend, revoke, or terminate is given to some third person, the transfer is not taxed under §2038 even if the person given the power is a nonadverse party. It is for this reason that a trustee (or trust protector) who is not the settlor can be given broad discretionary powers, including the power to distribute a portion or all of the trust corpus (thereby terminating the trust), without adverse tax consequences. This last statement is subject to the same qualification that was made in the discussion of §2036. If a trustee has such a power, and if the transferor has the right to remove the trustee and appoint himself as trustee, the transferor is treated as having the power and §2038 is applicable. Treas. Reg. §20.2038-1(a)(3).

Although §2038 is generally referred to as the provision that includes in the gross estate revocable transfers, it reaches transfers over which the decedent held any one of the enumerated powers, even though the power cannot be exercised in such a way as to benefit the transferor. If *O* creates an irrevocable trust in which *O*, as co-trustee, has a discretionary power to accumulate or distribute trust income, or a discretionary power to distribute corpus to the income beneficiary, the property is included in *O*'s gross estate under §2038; *O*'s discretionary power is a power to alter or amend. (*O*'s reserved power would of course also cause inclusion under §2036(a)(2).)

PROBLEMS

1.   *O* transfers property to the First National Bank in trust to pay the income to *O*'s daughter, *A*, for life, and on *A*'s death to pay the trust principal to *O*'s granddaughter, *B*. The trust is irrevocable. *O* retains the power to invade corpus for the benefit of *B*. On *O*'s death, is any portion of the value of the trust corpus includable in *O*'s gross estate?

2.   What result if, on the facts in Problem 1, *O* has no power to invade corpus but retains the power to direct that all or a portion of trust income be accumulated and added to corpus?

3.   *O* transfers property to the Second National Bank in trust to pay the income to *O*'s daughter, *D*, until she reaches 25, and when *D* reaches 25 or, if *D* dies before reaching 25, when *D* would have reached 25 had she lived, to pay the trust principal to *D* or *D*'s estate. The trust is irrevocable. *O* retains the power to direct that all or a portion of the trust income be accumulated until *D* reaches 25 and also the power to invade the corpus for the benefit of *D*. *O* dies; *D* is 19 years old. Is any portion of the value of the trust corpus includable in *O*'s gross estate? See Lober v. United States, 346 U.S. 335 (1953).

4.   Under the Uniform Transfers to Minors Act, page 859, if the donor names himself as custodian and dies while serving in that capacity, the value of the custodial property is included in the donor's gross estate for federal estate tax purposes. Because the donor-custodian's discretionary power to distribute the custodial property to the minor is a retained power to alter the time of enjoyment, the value of the custodial property is included in the donor's estate under §2038. If a parent wants to make a gift of income-producing assets to a minor child and be either the trustee or the custodian, is a trust or a custodianship preferable if estate taxes are a concern?

c.   Section 2037: Transfers with Reversionary Interest Retained

In keeping nonprobate assets out of your gross estate, you need to be careful if you retain even a right to some types of reversions should the nonprobate transfer terminate or fail. Under §2037 of the Code, the value of property transferred during life is includable in the transferor's gross estate if

> (1) possession or enjoyment of the property can . . . be obtained only by surviving the decedent, and
> (2) the decedent has retained a reversionary interest in the property . . . , and the value of such reversionary interest immediately before the death of the decedent exceeds five percent of the value of the property.

Both of the above conditions must be present for §2037 to apply. Thus:

> *Case 11.* H conveys $500,000 to X in trust, to pay income to W for life, then to distribute the trust principal to H if H is then living or, if H is not then living, to his daughter A or her issue. Condition (1) above is met. A cannot obtain possession or enjoyment without surviving H. Therefore if the value of H's reversionary interest exceeded 5 percent of the value of the property, the value of the trust assets, less W's life estate, will be includable in H's gross estate if H predeceases W. (The value of H's reversionary interest would be measured by the actuarial probability of H outliving W.)

If no beneficiary's enjoyment of the property depends upon surviving the decedent, §2037 is inapplicable. Thus, in Case 11 if there were no gift over to A, §2037 would not apply. Only the value of H's reversionary interest would be included under §2033.

Since instruments are seldom drawn that meet both conditions of §2037, this section is of little concern to the practitioner. For the attorney drafting an irrevocable inter vivos trust, §2037 can be avoided by eliminating any possibility that the trust property will revert to the settlor or the settlor's estate. This can be accomplished by making sure that some person other than the settlor or the settlor's estate will take the property regardless of what contingencies occur. The attorney may include an end-limitation to charity to take effect if all of the designated beneficiaries die before they become entitled to their interests.

d.   Section 2035: Transfers Within Three Years of Death

What about gifts before death? Why couldn't someone on her deathbed give away her assets to remove them from her taxable estate? Not surprisingly, death taxes cannot be evaded so easily. Gift taxes would have to be paid. In addition, §2035 brings into the decedent's gross estate certain inter vivos transfers made within three years prior to death, but not all deathbed gifts.

The purpose of §2035 is to close some tax avoidance opportunities that would otherwise exist in the few years prior to death. Section 2035 has undergone numerous alterations since 1916, when its predecessor section was first enacted. In 1916 the section taxed transfers "in contemplation of death," with Congress first creating a rebuttable presumption that a transfer within two years of death was in contemplation of death. After ten years, Congress changed the section to create a conclusive presumption, but after another six years, the presumption again became rebuttable. Later, Congress lengthened the presumptive period to three years. Because the question whether a transfer was in contemplation of death turned on the subjective state of mind of the transferor, much litigation resulted. In 1976 Congress eliminated the contemplation of death language and made the test objective. It reworded §2035 to require that all gifts made within three years of death be included in the gross estate. Upon reflection, this did not seem necessary inasmuch as the gift and estate taxes were unified in 1976, and any gift made within three years of death would be taxed at the same rate as a bequest. In 1981, the Economic Recovery Tax Act changed §2035 again, this time to eliminate its application to all gifts except those, generally speaking, that have a lower valuation as a gift than they have at death.

Under §2035, any of the following transfers made within three years of death are included in the decedent's gross estate:

(1) Any gift tax paid by the decedent or his estate on gifts made within three years of death. [The purpose of this subsection is to prevent a person from giving property away immediately prior to death and removing the amount of gift tax from the gross estate.]

(2) Any transfer or release of an interest in property if, had such interest been retained, the property would have been included in the decedent's gross estate under any of the following sections of the Internal Revenue Code: §2036 (transfers with retained life estate); §2037 (transfers taking effect at death); §2038 (revocable transfers); or §2042 (life insurance). The gross estate includes the value of any property which would have been included had such transfer or release not been made. [The purpose of this subsection is to prevent persons from avoiding taxes by making gifts soon before death of property that balloons in value at death.]

Unless an inter vivos transfer is referred to above, it is not includable in the decedent's gross estate even though made within three years of death. Hence, if *O* gives Blackacre to *A* two months before *O*'s death, a taxable gift is made at the time of transfer, and Blackacre is not included in *O*'s gross estate at death. (The amount of gift tax paid is, however, included in *O*'s gross estate.)

It is apparent that Congress's major purpose is to deter taxpayers, in the few years before death, from giving away property that greatly increases in value by reason of the person's death. A gift of a life insurance policy will illustrate this.

Case 12. O owns a life insurance policy on her life with a face value of $500,000. The cash surrender value is $231,000. *O* gives the policy to her son *A*, paying a gift tax on $220,000 ($231,000 minus the annual exclusion of $11,000). *O* dies one year later, and $500,000 is payable to *A*. If the policy proceeds were not included in *O*'s gross estate, *O* could transfer this asset to *A* at a low gift tax valuation immediately prior to death. Section 2035 requires the inclusion of the policy proceeds in *O*'s gross estate.

Without §2035, the owner of a life insurance policy on the owner's life would have a strong tax incentive to give the policy away prior to death, perhaps on her deathbed. A holder of a life estate would also have a strong tax incentive to release the life estate when death appeared imminent. Thus:

Case 13. In 1998, *O* creates an irrevocable trust of securities worth $300,000, retaining a life estate, with remainder to *O*'s son *A*. This results in a taxable gift to *A* of the value of the remainder in assets worth $300,000. In 2005, the trust assets are worth $500,000, and *O*, ill with cancer, releases her life estate. The release is a taxable gift to *A* of the value of *O*'s life estate in $500,000. *O* dies in 2006. If there were no

§2035, *O*'s 2005 release would have eliminated transfer tax on the value of a remainder in $200,000 worth of assets. But §2035 prevents *O* from doing this by requiring the inclusion of the entire $500,000 worth of assets in *O*'s gross estate. (The gift tax paid in 1998 is credited against estate taxes payable at *O*'s death.)

PROBLEMS

1. Suppose your client, a 72-year-old widow with a $5 million estate, has been diagnosed as having terminal cancer. Her present will leaves her entire estate to her two children in equal shares. The client has a daughter, a son, two in-laws, and five grandchildren. What advice would you give her?

2. The same client's will includes a bequest of $50,000 to her alma mater. Is there any advantage in the client's making the $50,000 gift to the alma mater during life in lieu of the testamentary gift?

3. *H*, a widower, is the insured under a $500,000 life insurance policy that names his daughter *D* as a primary beneficiary. In 2004, *H* irrevocably assigned the policy and all of its incidents of ownership to *D*. At the time of the transfer, the cash surrender value of the property was $200,000. *H*'s other assets are large enough that his estate is taxable. What are the estate tax consequences of the life insurance to *H*'s estate (a) if *H* dies in 2006 or (b) if *H* dies in 2008?

4. Suppose that *A* wants to purchase a life insurance policy and wants his daughter *B* to be the beneficiary. If *A* purchases the policy, is named as owner, and thereafter assigns the policy to *B*, *A* has made a gift of insurance proceeds that will be included in *A*'s gross estate if *A* dies within three years. On the other hand, if *B* is named as owner of the policy as well as beneficiary from the beginning, the proceeds of the policy are not includable in *A*'s gross estate if he dies within three years because *A* never had any incidents of ownership over the policy. It does not matter that *A* pays the premiums. Estate of Headrick v. Commissioner, 918 F.2d 1263 (6th Cir. 1990); Estate of Perry v. Commissioner, 931 F.2d 1044 (5th Cir. 1992).

Suppose that *B* is a minor, age 12. How do you advise *A* to arrange for the purchase of life insurance for which *A* is to pay the premiums?

5. *A* enters an airport preparing to take a trip on an airplane. At a machine selling insurance, *A* buys a life insurance policy for the trip payable to *B*. The insurance application asks the applicant to check one of two boxes: ☐ insured is owner, or ☐ beneficiary is owner. Which box should *A* check?

6. See generally Jon J. Gallo, The Use of Life Insurance in Estate Planning and Drafting — Part I, 33 Real Prop., Prob. & Tr. J. 685 (1999), Part II, 34 Real Prop., Prob. & Tr. J. 55 (1999).

5. The Gross Estate: Powers of Appointment (§2041)

Sections 2036 and 2038 deal with lifetime transfers by the decedent where the decedent retained benefits or controls. By contrast, §2041 deals with powers of appointment that the decedent received from someone else. As you may recall from Chapter 9, the donor of a power of appointment gives the donee of a power (here the decedent) the right to appoint assets to other people or institutions.

Powers of appointment, used primarily in trusts, postpone a decision about who takes property and delegate that decision to someone other than the donor of the power.

Under §2041, the gross estate includes the value of property over which the decedent at the time of his death held a general power of appointment. A *general* power of appointment is defined as a power exercisable in favor of any one or more of the following: the decedent, his creditors, his estate, or the creditors of his estate. The assets subject to the general power are taxed in the decedent's estate regardless of whether the power was exercisable during lifetime or by will and (if the power was created after October 21, 1942)[17] whether the decedent actually exercised the power.

> *Case 14.* *H*'s will creates a testamentary trust providing for the payment of trust income to *H*'s wife *W* for life and on her death "to pay the trust principal to such person or persons as *W* appoints by her will." On *W*'s subsequent death, the value of the trust corpus is includable in her gross estate regardless of whether *W* exercised the power of appointment by her will. Although *W* was restricted to the income from the trust, and she could not exercise the power of appointment in such a way as to benefit herself or her creditors during her lifetime, at death she held a power of appointment that was exercisable in favor of her estate or the creditors of her estate.

The donee of a general power of appointment is treated, under the Code, as owner of the property subject to the power. If a donee exercises or releases a general power of appointment, the donee makes a taxable gift. If a donee exercises or releases the power under circumstances that would have resulted in taxability if the property had been the donee's own (such as releasing a general power and reserving a life estate), estate tax liability results. A donee of a general power of appointment is treated as owner under the generation-skipping transfer tax (see page 925).

Powers of appointment other than general ones are termed *special* powers of appointment. A special power of appointment is a power to appoint among a class of persons or institutions that cannot include any of the following: the decedent, his creditors, his estate, or the creditors of his estate. If the decedent held a special power of appointment, the property subject to the power is not taxed under §2041.[18]

> *Case 15.* *H*'s will creates a testamentary trust providing for the payment of trust income to *H*'s wife *W* for life and on her death "to pay the trust principal to such one or more of her descendants or spouses of descendants as she shall appoint by her will." On *W*'s subsequent death, the trust corpus is not subject to taxation in her estate. Since *W*'s life estate terminated at her death, nothing is taxed under §2033. Since *W*'s power of appointment was not a general power, nothing is taxed under §2041.

As Case 15 demonstrates, it is possible to give a beneficiary a life income interest in property and also a limited power to control devolution of the property at death

---

17. Property subject to a general power created on or before October 21, 1942, is taxed in the estate of the holder of the power only if the power is exercised. I.R.C. §2041(a)(1).

18. Treas. Reg. §20.2041-1(c)(1) (1958). There is one important, and very useful, exception to this general rule. See the "Delaware Tax Trap," page 694.

without subjecting the property to estate taxation in the beneficiary's estate. It is also possible to give the beneficiary certain limited powers to appoint property to himself during his lifetime without adverse estate tax consequences. Under §2041(b)(1)(A), "[a] power to consume, invade, or appropriate property for the benefit of the decedent which is limited by an ascertainable standard relating to the health, education, support, or maintenance of the decedent shall not be deemed a general power of appointment." Hence a power in the donee to appoint to the donee limited by the quoted standard is not a general power of appointment.

In addition to a power limited by a standard, a donee may be given a "$5,000 or 5 percent" power (known as a *5 and 5 power*) with little tax cost. Section 2041(b)(2) provides that, if the decedent held a power to consume or invade that was limited to the greater of $5,000 or 5 percent of corpus each year, the maximum amount includable in the donee's gross estate is $5,000 or 5 percent of the corpus. If the donee has fully exercised the power in the year of death, withdrawing $5,000 or 5 percent from the trust, nothing is included in the donee's estate.

Under §2041(b)(2), a lapse of a power in any calendar year is considered a release (with resulting gift tax liability) to the extent that the property over which the power existed exceeded the greater of $5,000 or 5 percent of the value of the assets that could be appointed. Thus:

> *Case 16.* In 2003, *T* bequeaths $500,000 in trust to pay income to *A* for life. *A* is given a power to withdraw $5,000 or 5 percent of the corpus of the trust in any given year. The right is noncumulative, so that *A* can never withdraw more than $25,000 in any one year, even if *A* fails to withdraw the full amount in a preceding year. In 2004, *A* does not exercise the power. The power lapses, but no taxable gift results. In 2005, *A* withdraws $25,000. In 2006, *A* dies, after withdrawing $10,000 in that year. The amount still subject to *A*'s power of withdrawal at death — $15,000 — is included in *A*'s gross estate.

Special powers of appointment and limited invasion powers (measured by a standard of "$5,000 or 5 percent"), and also discretionary powers given to a trustee, can be employed to create a flexible estate plan that allows for unforeseen circumstances. Contrast such a flexible plan with an old-fashioned settlement of property "to my wife for life, and on her death remainder to my descendants per stirpes." At the time the transfer is made, the income from the property may appear to ensure that the wife's support and other needs will be met. But if the wife (or one of the couple's children) should encounter unusual medical or other expenses, or if inflation erodes the real value of the income interest, the income from the property may be insufficient to meet the wife's needs. If, on the other hand, the trustee is given a discretionary power to distribute corpus to the wife whenever it is needed to supplement the trust's income, and if the wife is given an "ascertainable standard" or "$5,000 or 5 percent" invasion power, the corpus of the trust can be used to satisfy the wife's support and other needs whenever trust income proves insufficient.

Under §2041, all of these powers can be given to the income beneficiary and trustee with little or no estate tax cost. See John G. Steinkamp, Estate and Gift Taxation of Powers of Appointment Limited by Ascertainable Standards, 79 Marq. L. Rev. 195 (1995).

Estate of Vissering v. Commissioner
United States Court of Appeals, Tenth Circuit, 1993
990 F.2d 578

LOGAN, C.J.   The estate of decedent Norman H. Vissering appeals from a judgment of the Tax Court determining that he held at his death a general power of appointment as defined by I.R.C. §2041, and requiring that the assets of a trust of which he was cotrustee be included in his gross estate for federal estate tax purposes. The appeal turns on whether decedent held powers permitting him to invade the principal of the trust for his own benefit unrestrained by an ascertainable standard relating to health, education, support, or maintenance. The trust was created by decedent's mother in Florida and specifies that Florida law controls in the interpretation and administration of its provisions.

The estate argues that decedent was not a trustee at the time of his death because a New Mexico court's adjudication that he was incapacitated two months before his death divested him of those powers. Decedent was not formally removed as trustee; if he ceased to serve it was by operation of Florida law. However, we assume for purposes of this opinion that decedent continued as trustee until his death and that his powers are to be adjudged as if he were fully competent to exercise them at the time of his death.

The trust at issue was created by decedent's mother, and became irrevocable on her death in 1965. Decedent and a bank served as cotrustees. Under the dispositive provisions decedent received all the income from the trust after his mother's death. On decedent's death (his wife, a contingent beneficiary, predeceased him), remaining trust assets were to be divided into equal parts and passed to decedent's two children or were held for their benefit. Decedent developed Alzheimer's disease and entered into a nursing home in 1984, but he tendered no resignation as trustee, nor did his guardian or conservator do so on his behalf after he was found to be incapacitated.

The Tax Court's decision, based entirely upon stipulated facts, resolved only questions of law, and consequently our review is de novo.

Under I.R.C. §2041 a decedent has a general power of appointment includable in his estate if he possesses at the time of his death a power over assets that permits him to benefit himself, his estate, his creditors, or creditors of his estate. A power vested in a trustee, even with a cotrustee who has no interest adverse to the exercise of the power, to invade principal of the trust for his own benefit is sufficient to find the decedent trustee to have a general power of appointment, unless the power to invade is limited by an ascertainable standard relating to health, education, support, or maintenance. Treas. Reg. §20.2041-1(c), -3(c)(2). See, e.g., Estate of Sowell v. Commissioner, 708 F.2d 1564, 1568 (10th Cir. 1983) (invasion of trust corpus in case of emergency or illness is an ascertainable standard under §2041(b)(1)(A)); see also Merchants Nat'l Bank v. Commissioner, 320 U.S. 256, 261 (1943) (invasion of trust corpus for "the comfort, support, maintenance and/or happiness of my wife" is not a fixed standard for purposes of charitable deductions); Ithaca Trust Co. v. United States, 279 U.S. 151, 154 (1929) (invasion of trust corpus for any amount "that may be necessary to suitably maintain [decedent's wife] in as much comfort as she now enjoys" is a fixed standard for purposes of charitable deduction).

The relevant provisions of the instant trust agreement are as follows:

> During the term of [this trust], the Trustees shall further be authorized to pay over or to use or expend for the direct or indirect benefit of any of the aforesaid beneficiaries, whatever amount or amounts of the principal of this Trust as may, in the discretion of the Trustees, be required for the continued comfort, support, maintenance, or education of said beneficiary.

The Internal Revenue Service (IRS) and the Tax Court focused on portions of the invasion provision providing that the trust principal could be expended for the "comfort" of decedent, declaring that this statement rendered the power of invasion incapable of limitation by the courts.

We look to state law (here Florida's) to determine the legal interests and rights created by a trust instrument, but federal law determines the tax consequences of those interests and rights. . . .

Despite the decision in Barritt v. Tomlinson, 129 F. Supp. 642 (S.D. Fla. 1955), which involved a power of invasion broader than the one before us, we believe the Florida Supreme Court would hold that a trust document permitting invasion of principal for "comfort," without further qualifying language, creates a general power of appointment. Treas. Reg. §20.2041-1(c). See First Virginia Bank v. United States, 490 F.2d 532, 533 (4th Cir. 1974) (under Virginia law, right of invasion for beneficiary's "comfort and care as she may see fit" not limited by an ascertainable standard); Lehman v. United States, 448 F.2d 1318, 1320 (5th Cir. 1971) (under Texas law, power to invade corpus for "support, maintenance, comfort, and welfare" not limited by ascertainable standard); Miller v. United States, 387 F.2d 866, 869 (3d Cir. 1968) (under Pennsylvania law, power to make disbursements from principal in amounts "necessary or expedient for [beneficiary's] proper maintenance, support, medical care, hospitalization, or other expenses incidental to her comfort and well-being" not limited by ascertainable standard); Estate of Schlotterer v. United States, 421 F. Supp. 85, 91 (W.D. Pa. 1976) (power of consumption "to the extent deemed by [beneficiary] to be desirable not only for her support and maintenance but also for her comfort and pleasure" not limited by ascertainable standard); Doyle v. United States, 358 F. Supp. 300, 309-310 (E.D. Pa. 1973) (under Pennsylvania law, trustees' "uncontrolled discretion" to pay beneficiary "such part or parts of the principal of said trust fund as may be necessary for her comfort, maintenance and support" not limited by ascertainable standard); Stafford v. United States, 236 F. Supp. 132, 134 (E.D. Wisc. 1964) (under Wisconsin law, trust permitting husband "for his use, benefit and enjoyment during his lifetime," unlimited power of disposition thereof "without permission of any court, and with the right to use and enjoy the principal, as well as the income, if he shall have need thereof for his care, comfort or enjoyment" not limited by ascertainable standard).

However, there is modifying language in the trust before us that we believe would lead the Florida courts to hold that "comfort," in context, does not permit an unlimited power of invasion. The instant language states that invasion of principal is permitted to the extent "required for the continued comfort" of the decedent, and is part of a clause referencing the support, maintenance and education of the beneficiary. Invasion of the corpus is not permitted to the extent "determined" or "desired" for the beneficiary's comfort but only to the extent that it is "required." Furthermore, the invasion must be for the beneficiary's "continued" comfort, implying, we believe, more than the minimum necessary for survival, but nevertheless reasonably necessary to maintain the beneficiary in his accustomed manner of living. These words in context state a standard essentially no different from the examples in the Treasury Regulation, in which phrases such as "support in reasonable comfort," "maintenance in health and reasonable comfort," and "support in his accustomed manner of living" are deemed to be limited by an ascertainable standard. Treas. Reg. §20.2041-1(c)(2). See, e.g., United States v. Powell, 307 F.2d 821, 828 (10th Cir. 1962) (under Kansas law, invasion of the corpus if "it is necessary or advisable . . . for the maintenance, welfare, comfort or happiness" of beneficiaries, and only if the need justifies the reduction in principal, is subject to ascertainable standard); Hunter v. United States, 597 F. Supp. 1293, 1295 (W.D. Pa. 1984) (power to invade for "comfortable support and maintenance" of beneficiaries is subject to ascertainable standard).

We believe that had decedent, during his life, sought to use the assets of the trust to increase significantly his standard of living beyond that which he had previously enjoyed, his cotrustee would have been obligated to refuse to consent, and the remainder beneficiaries of the trust could have successfully petitioned the court to disallow such expenditures as inconsistent with the intent of the trust instrument. The Tax Court erred in ruling that this power was a general power of appointment includable in decedent's estate.

Reversed and remanded.

QUESTION AND NOTE

1.   After the death of his mother, Norman Vissering consults you regarding her will (which you did not draw). You spot the drafting error, the use of the word *comfort*. To avoid litigation and the possible inclusion of his mother's trust in his federal gross estate, would you recommend that he decline to serve as trustee? That he disclaim the power to go into principal for "comfort"?

Treas. Reg. §25.2518-3(a)(2) takes the position that

> all interests in the corpus of a trust are treated as a single interest [and] in order to have a qualified disclaimer of an interest in corpus the disclaimant must disclaim all such interests, either totally or as to an undivided portion. Thus, if a disclaimant has a testamentary power of appointment over the trust corpus coupled with either an inter vivos power to invade corpus or an interest as discretionary appointee, a disclaimer by that person can constitute a qualified disclaimer only if both such interests are disclaimed.

Given this regulation, what would you recommend?

2.   In Kinney v. Shinholser, 663 So. 2d 643 (Fla. App. 1995), the court held a lawyer was liable to the estate of the life tenant who was given a general testamentary power for not explaining the tax consequences of not disclaiming the power of appointment within nine months of the transferor's death. Because the power was not disclaimed, the life tenant's estate was obliged to pay estate taxes of $320,000 on the trust property.

Estate of Kurz v. Commissioner
United States Court of Appeals, Seventh Circuit, 1995
68 F.3d 1027

EASTERBROOK, J.   Between her husband's death, in 1971, and her own, in
1986, Ethel H. Kurz was the beneficiary of two trusts. Kurz received the
income from each. She was entitled to
as much of the principal of one (which
we call the Marital Trust) as she
wanted; all she had to do was notify
the trustee in writing. She could take
only 5 percent of the other (which we
call the Family Trust) in any year, and
then only if the Marital Trust was
exhausted. When Kurz died, the
Marital Trust contained assets worth
some $3.5 million, and the Family
Trust was worth about $3.4 million.
The estate tax return included in the
gross estate the whole value of the
Marital Trust and none of the value
of the Family Trust. The Tax Court
held that Kurz held a general power
of appointment over 5 percent of the

Judge Frank H. Easterbrook

Family Trust, requiring the inclusion of another $170,000 under 26 U.S.C.
§2041(a)(2). 101 T.C. 44 (1993); see also T.C. Memo 1994-221 (computing a tax
due of approximately $31,000).

Section 2041(b)(1) defines a general power of appointment as "a power which is
exercisable in favor of the decedent, his estate, his creditors, or the creditors of his
estate." Kurz had the power to consume or appoint the corpus of the Marital Trust
to anyone she pleased whenever she wanted, and the Estate therefore concedes
that it belongs in the gross estate. For her part, the Commissioner of Internal
Revenue concedes that the 95 percent of the Family Trust that was beyond Kurz's
reach even if the Marital Trust had been empty was not subject to a general power
of appointment. What of the other 5 percent? None of the Family Trust could be
reached while the Marital Trust contained 1¢, and the Estate submits that, until the
exhaustion condition was satisfied (which it never was), the power to appoint
5 percent in a given year was not "exercisable," keeping the Family Trust outside
the gross estate. To this the Commissioner replies that a power is "exercisable" if a
beneficiary has the ability to remove the blocking condition. Suppose, for example, that the Family Trust could not have been touched until Ethel Kurz said
"Boo!". Her power to utter the magic word would have been no different from
her power, under the Marital Trust, to send written instructions to the trustee.

The Tax Court was troubled by an implication of the Commissioner's argument.
Suppose the Family Trust had provided that Kurz could reach 5 percent of the
principal if and only if she lost 20 pounds, or achieved a chess rating of 1600, or
survived all of her children. She could have gone on a crash diet, or studied the

games of Gary Kasparov, or even murdered her children. These are not financial decisions, however, and it would be absurd to have taxes measured by one's ability to lose weight, or lack of moral scruples. Imagine the trial, five years after a person's death, at which friends and relatives troop to the stand to debate whether the decedent was ruthless enough to kill her children, had enough willpower to lay off chocolates, or was smart enough to succeed at chess. The Tax Court accordingly rejected the Commissioner's principal argument, ruling that raw ability to satisfy a condition is insufficient to make a power of appointment "exercisable."

If not the Commissioner's position, then what? The Estate's position, 180° opposed, is that the condition must be actually satisfied before a power can be deemed "exercisable." The Tax Court came down in the middle, writing that a condition may be disregarded when it is "illusory" and lacks any "significant non-tax consequence independent of the decedent's ability to exercise the power." Of course, illusions are in the eye of the beholder, and we are hesitant to adopt a legal rule that incorporates a standard well suited to stage magicians (though some legal drafters can give prestidigitators a run for their money). No one doubts that the Kurz family had good, non-tax reasons for the structure of the trust funds. The only question we need resolve is whether a sequence of withdrawal rights prevents a power of appointment from being "exercisable." Despite the large number of trusts in the United States, many of them arranged as the Kurz trusts were, this appears to be an unresolved issue. Neither side could find another case dealing with stacked trusts, and we came up empty handed after independent research.

For a question of first principles, this one seems remarkably simple. Section 2041 is designed to include in the taxable estate all assets that the decedent possessed or effectively controlled. If only a lever must be pulled to dispense money, then the power is exercisable. The funds are effectively under the control of the beneficiary, which is enough to put them into the gross estate. Whether the lever is a single-clutch or double-clutch mechanism can't matter. Imagine a trust divided into 1,000 equal funds numbered 1 to 1,000, Fund 1 of which may be invaded at any time, and Fund n of which may be reached if and only if Fund n-1 has been exhausted. Suppose the beneficiary depletes Funds 1 through 9 and dies when $10 remains in Fund 10. Under the Kurz Estate's view, only $10 is included in the gross estate, because Funds 11 through 1,000 could not have been touched until that $10 had been withdrawn. But that would be a ridiculously artificial way of looking at things. Tax often is all about form, see Howell v. United States, 775 F.2d 887 (7th Cir. 1985), but §2041 is an anti-formal rule. It looks through the trust to ask how much wealth the decedent actually controlled at death. The decedent's real wealth in our hypothetical is $10 plus the balance of Funds 11 through 1,000; the decedent could have withdrawn and spent the entire amount in a trice. Whether this series of trusts has spendthrift features (as the Kurz trusts did) or is invested in illiquid instruments (as the Kurz trusts were) would not matter. The Estate does not deny that Kurz had a general power of appointment over the entire Marital Trust, despite these features. If the costs of removing wealth from the trust do not prevent including in the gross estate the entire corpus of the first trust in a sequence (they don't), then the rest of the sequence also is includable.

Wait!, the Estate exclaims. How did first principles get into a tax case? After consulting the statute, a court turns next to the regulations. 26 C.F.R. §20.2041-3(b) provides:

> For purposes of section 2041(a)(2), a power of appointment is considered to exist on the date of a decedent's death even though the exercise of the power is subject to the precedent giving of notice, or even though the exercise of the power takes effect only on the expiration of a stated period after its exercise, whether or not on or before the decedent's death notice has been given or the power has been exercised. However, a power which by its terms is exercisable only upon the occurrence during the decedent's lifetime of an event or a contingency which did not in fact take place or occur during such time is not a power in existence on the date of the decedent's death. For example, if a decedent was given a general power of appointment exercisable only after he reached a certain age, only if he survived another person, or only if he died without descendants, the power would not be in existence on the date of the decedent's death if the condition precedent to its exercise had not occurred.

The Kurz Estate takes heart from the provision that "a power which by its terms is exercisable only upon the occurrence during the decedent's lifetime of an event or a contingency which did not in fact take place or occur during such time is not a power in existence on the date of the decedent's death." Like the Tax Court, however, we do not find in this language the strict sequencing principle the Estate needs.

This is the Commissioner's language, and the Commissioner thinks that it refers only to conditions that could not have been satisfied. Regulation-writers have substantial leeway in their interpretation, because the delegation of the power to make substantive regulations is the delegation of a law-creation power, and interpretation is a vital part of the law-creation process. A reading must of course be reasonable — must be an interpretation — else the rulemaker is revising the law without the requisite notice and opportunity for comment. The Commissioner's understanding of the regulation tracks its third sentence, which is designed to illustrate the second. It says: "For example, if a decedent was given a general power of appointment exercisable only after he reached a certain age, only if he survived another person, or only if he died without descendants, the power would not be in existence on the date of the decedent's death if the condition precedent to its exercise had not occurred." All three examples in the third sentence deal with conditions the decedent could not have controlled, at least not in the short run, or lawfully. The rate of chronological aging is outside anyone's control, whether one person survives another does not present an option that may be exercised lawfully, and whether a person has descendants on the date of death is something that depends on the course of an entire life, rather than a single choice made in the administration of one's wealth.

By contrast, the sequence in which a beneficiary withdraws the principal of a series of trusts barely comes within the common understanding of "event or . . . contingency." No one could say of a single account: "You cannot withdraw the second dollar from this account until you have withdrawn the first." The existence of this sequence is tautological, but a check for $2 removes that sum without satisfying a contingency in ordinary, or legal, parlance. Zeno's paradox does not apply to financial transactions. Breaking one account into two or more does not make the sequence of withdrawal more of a "contingency" — at least not in the sense that §20.2041-3(b) uses that term.

No matter how the second sentence of §20.2041-3(b) should be applied to a contingency like losing 20 pounds or achieving a chess rating of 1,600, the regulation does not permit the beneficiary of multiple trusts to exclude all but the first from the estate by the expedient of arranging the trusts in a sequence. No matter how long the sequence, the beneficiary exercises economic dominion over all funds that can be withdrawn at any given moment. The estate tax is a wealth tax, and dominion over property is wealth. Until her death, Ethel Kurz could have withdrawn all of the Marital Trust and 5 percent of the Family Trust by notifying the Trustee of her wish to do so. This case is nicely covered by the first sentence of §20.2041-3(b), the notice provision, and the judgment of the Tax Court is therefore

Affirmed.

6. The Marital Deduction

a. Introduction

Section 2056 allows a marital deduction for certain dispositions of property to a decedent's spouse. Before 1982, the primary purpose of the marital deduction was to equalize the tax treatment of couples residing in separate property and community property states. The marital deduction enabled spouses to split their gifts and estates for transfer tax purposes, in effect having them taxed the same as community property is taxed. See pages 428-429. Generally speaking, if the couple's wills were properly drafted, one-half of the couple's total property would be taxable at the husband's death and one-half at the wife's death.

The marital deduction provisions of the Economic Recovery Tax Act of 1981 were based on an altogether different policy: Interspousal transfers should not be subject to taxation. The act adopted an unlimited marital deduction rule under both the estate tax and the gift tax. Thus, unlimited amounts of property (other than certain "terminable interests") now can be transferred between spouses without the imposition of either a gift tax or an estate tax.

For many couples, the changes made by the 1981 act eliminated any concerns about transfer taxes in the estate of either spouse. Because of the unlimited marital deduction, a husband or wife can leave his or her entire estate to the other spouse without the imposition of an estate tax. Taxes in the estate of the surviving spouse are not a concern unless the projected value of the survivor's estate is greater than $1.5 million in the year 2005, $2 million in 2006-2008, or $3.5 million in the year 2009.[19]

PROBLEM

Suppose *H* has an estate worth $4 million. *H* is married to *W*, and the couple has three adult children. *W* has little property of her own. *H* presently has a will that devises his entire estate outright to *W*, with an alternate gift to the couple's children. What will be the estate taxes (a) in *H*'s estate and (b) in *W*'s estate if *H* dies in 2006 and *W* dies one year later? Assume that there are no deductions for

---

19. If the 2001 Tax Act amendments sunset as scheduled, the exemption amount will revert to $1 million in 2011.

administration expenses, debts, and funeral expenses allowable in *H*'s estate, that the value of the property passing from *H* to *W* neither increases nor decreases in value from *H*'s death to *W*'s death, and that there are no deductions.

b.   Interests that Qualify for the Deduction

(1) The nondeductible terminable interest rule

For an interest to qualify for the marital deduction, five requirements must be met.

(1)   The decedent must have been survived by his or her spouse.

(2)   The surviving spouse must be a citizen of the United States or the property must pass to a *qualified domestic trust* (see page 915).

(3)   The value of the interest deducted must be includable in the decedent's gross estate.

(4)   The interest must pass from the decedent to the surviving spouse.

(5)   The interest must be a deductible interest. More precisely, it must not be a "nondeductible terminable interest" within the meaning of §2056(b).

The first and third requirements are straightforward. As for the "passing" requirement, this is defined rather broadly in §2056(c) to include interests passing by will, by inheritance, by trust, by right of survivorship, by dower or elective share, by the exercise or nonexercise of a power of appointment held by the decedent, pursuant to a life insurance beneficiary designation, or by other transfer.

The fifth requirement is the most important and the most productive of litigation. In general, to qualify for the marital deduction the interest passing to the surviving spouse must be such that it is subject to taxation in the spouse's estate (to the extent not consumed or disposed of by the spouse during his or her lifetime). The marital deduction permits deferral of estate taxation until the surviving spouse's death. In effect, Congress has said: "We won't tax your property in your estate, so long as you leave it to your spouse in a form that exposes it to taxation in your spouse's estate on his or her death." The clearest example of an interest that qualifies for the deduction is an outright (or "fee simple") gift of property to the spouse.

From this it does not follow that any interest that will be taxed in the surviving spouse's estate qualifies for the deduction. To qualify, the interest must not run afoul of the *nondeductible terminable interest rule*:

> Where, on the lapse of time, on the occurrence of an event or contingency, or on the failure of an event or contingency to occur, an interest passing to the surviving spouse will terminate or fail, no deduction shall be allowed under this section with respect to such interest—
>
> (A) if an interest in such property passes or has passed (for less than an adequate and full consideration in money or money's worth) from the decedent to any person other than such surviving spouse (or the estate of such spouse); and
>
> (B) if by reason of such passing such person (or his heirs or assigns) may possess or enjoy any part of such property after such termination or failure of such interest so passing to the surviving spouse. [I.R.C. §2056(b)(1).]

14. *Wealth Transfer Taxation: Tax Planning*

Absent special exception, the clearest example of a terminable interest is a life estate given to a surviving spouse, with the remainder to pass to other persons on the spouse's death. On the occurrence of an event or contingency—the spouse's death—the interest will terminate or fail. Upon such termination, an interest in the property—the remainder interest—will pass from the decedent to persons other than the surviving spouse or her estate. By reason of such passing, the remaindermen may possess or enjoy the property on the termination of the spouse's life estate.

PROBLEM

H has a pension plan providing for payments to himself for life and then to his wife *W* for life if *W* survives *H*. On the death of *H* and *W*, all payments will cease. *H* dies, and the value of the annuity (that is, the discounted value of the remaining annuity payments to which *W* is entitled) is included in *H*'s gross estate under §2039. Does the value of this interest qualify for the marital deduction? See Treas. Reg. §20.2056(b)-1(g), ex. (3).

(2) *Exceptions to the terminable interest rule*

In determining whether an interest passing to a spouse is, or is not, deductible in computing the taxable estate, one needs to know the four important exceptions to the nondeductible terminable interest rule.

(a) Estate trust exception. The *estate trust* exception to the nondeductible terminable interest rule is included within the statement of the rule. An interest is a nondeductible terminable interest only if, on termination of the spouse's interest, the property passes *to someone other than the surviving spouse or the spouse's estate.* Consequently, a disposition of property "to my husband for life, and on his death to his estate," whether in the form of a legal life estate or in a trust settlement, qualifies for the marital deduction.

The estate trust is seldom used as a means of qualifying for the deduction because of its relative inflexibility. Also, an estate trust causes the assets to be subject to creditors' claims and administration expenses in the spouse's estate. However, there is one situation in which an estate trust might be desirable, stemming from the requirement that, under a marital deduction power of appointment trust or a qualified terminable interest property trust (see below), all trust income must be paid to the surviving spouse for life. If the testator's estate includes *unproductive property*, a marital deduction power of appointment trust or QTIP trust must include a provision authorizing the surviving spouse to compel the trustee to (a) convert the unproductive assets to income-producing property or (b) pay the spouse a reasonable amount out of other trust assets to compensate for lost income. See Treas. Reg. §20.2056(b)-5(f)(5). This could raise a potentially serious problem if, for example, the testator owns closely held stock that does not pay dividends or owns unimproved real estate that is being held for future development. An estate trust might be useful in this situation.

(b) Limited survivorship exception. In drafting wills, it is a common practice to include a clause requiring that a legatee must survive the testator by a stated

period (for example, 30 or 60 days) in order to take under the will. The purpose of this type of condition is to avoid determining who survived in a common disaster. Section 2056(b)(3) provides that a devise with a limited survival requirement is deductible if (a) the condition of survival is for a period not exceeding six months and (b) the contingency (the spouse's death within the period) does not in fact occur. In short, a requirement of survival for up to six months can be attached to the interest passing to the spouse without disqualifying it for the marital deduction. (If the spouse does not survive for the stated period, no marital deduction will be available since no interest will actually pass from the decedent to the surviving spouse.)

Suppose *H* devises property to *W* "if she survives distribution of my estate." Does this qualify for the marital deduction? See Estate of Heim v. Commissioner, 914 F.2d 1322 (9th Cir. 1990).

(c) Life estate plus general power of appointment trust exception. In originally enacting the marital deduction in 1948, Congress permitted a trust to qualify for the marital deduction even if the surviving spouse is given only a life estate if the spouse is also given a general power of appointment over the property. Section 2056(b)(5) declares that the interest passing to the spouse qualifies for the marital deduction, provided that four technical requirements are met:

(1) The surviving spouse must be entitled to all income for life, payable annually or at more frequent intervals. (The trust property must be income producing.)

(2) The power of appointment must be exercisable in favor of the spouse or her estate, *that is,* a general power of appointment. The power may be exercisable during lifetime or by will.

(3) The power must be exercisable by the spouse "alone and in all events." A general testamentary power of appointment satisfies the "all events" requirement even though it cannot be exercised by the spouse during lifetime.

(4) The spouse's interest must not be subject to a power in anyone else to divert the property to someone other than the spouse. Thus, the trustee cannot be given a discretionary power to distribute trust corpus to, for example, the couple's children.

This important exception to the nondeductible terminable interest rule led to widespread use of the *life estate plus general power of appointment trust,* commonly referred to in the legal literature and in the practice as simply the *marital deduction power of appointment trust.*

In Estate of Foster v. Commissioner, 725 F.2d 201 (2d Cir. 1984), the testator, a dairy farmer, left his wife his property for her lifetime with power to invade principal "for her needs and the needs of my children as she in her discretion may deem necessary," with remainder over to the children. The court held the bequest did not qualify for the marital deduction because the wife's power to consume was not equivalent to a power to appoint "in all events." A power to consume is limited by a standard of good faith on the part of the donee of the power.

(d) Qualified terminable interest property (QTIP) trust exception. Until 1982, as a practical matter only three forms of transfer could be used to secure the marital deduction for an estate: an outright disposition, an estate trust, and a marital

deduction power of appointment trust. All of these forms of transfer had the effect of giving the surviving spouse the unrestricted power of disposition over the property, either during life or at death. When the unlimited marital deduction was enacted in 1981, Congress recognized that, under the existing law,

> the decedent cannot insure that the spouse will subsequently pass the property to his children. Because the maximum marital deduction is limited under present law to one-half of the decedent's adjusted gross estate, a decedent may at least control disposition of one-half of his estate and still maximize current tax benefits. However, unless certain interests that do not grant the spouse total control are eligible for the unlimited marital deduction, a decedent would be forced to choose between surrendering control of his entire estate to avoid imposition of estate tax at his death or reducing his tax benefits at his death to insure inheritance by the children. The committee believes that the tax laws should be neutral and that tax consequences should not control an individual's disposition of property. Accordingly, the committee believes that a deduction should be permitted for certain terminable interests. [H.R. Rep. No. 4242, 96th Cong., 2d Sess. 161 (1981).]

In 1981 Congress enacted §2056(b)(7), which allows a marital deduction for a *qualified terminable interest*. To qualify for the deduction under this section, two requirements must be met.

(1) The spouse must be entitled to all income for life, payable annually or at more frequent intervals. (The trust property must be income producing.)
(2) No person (including the spouse) can have the power to appoint the property during the spouse's lifetime to any person other than the spouse. The spouse may, but need not, be given a special power to appoint the property *by will*.

Since the purpose of the marital deduction is to permit deferral of estate taxes until the death of the surviving spouse, the allowance of a marital deduction for qualified terminable interest property (QTIP) is conditioned on an election to have the property taxed in the surviving spouse's estate. If it is a lifetime gift, the donor makes the election; if it is a death transfer, the decedent's executor makes the election. If such an election is made, the value of the property in which the spouse had an income interest is includable in the spouse's gross estate under §2044. To prevent the tax attributable to this interest from increasing the tax burden on the spouse's own heirs, the tax is borne by the persons receiving the qualified terminable interest property on the spouse's death. Thus, if a trust is involved, the tax attributable to the interest (measured by the difference between the estate tax actually paid in the spouse's estate and the tax that would have been due if the property had not been included in the spouse's gross estate) is paid out of the corpus of the trust.

Since the beneficiary of a QTIP trust is treated as owner for gift and estate tax purposes, if the surviving spouse makes a lifetime gift of his qualified terminable interest, the value of the entire property (and not just the value of the spouse's income interest) is treated as a taxable gift under §2519.

In comparing the QTIP trust with a marital deduction power of appointment trust, observe that both require that all income must be payable to the surviving spouse at least annually *for life*. If the spouse's income interest terminates on remarriage, this disqualifies both a marital deduction power of appointment trust and a QTIP trust. However, there are two important differences. In a power of appointment trust, the spouse must be given the power to appoint the property to anyone she wants, including either herself or her estate. In a QTIP trust, the remainder interest on the spouse's death can pass to any beneficiary designated by the settlor or to persons chosen by the spouse exercising a special power of appointment. Second, under a QTIP trust there can be no power in any person *including the spouse* to appoint the property to anyone other than the spouse during her lifetime. Invasions of trust principal by the spouse or by a trustee for the spouse are permitted.

The permissible terms of a QTIP trust are so attractive that the traditional marital deduction power of appointment trust will probably be far less frequently used in the future. A QTIP trust is particularly useful if the spouses have different natural beneficiaries (for example, children by a former marriage) or if the testator is concerned about the prospect that his spouse may remarry and then favor the new spouse.

The testator may direct his executor to elect to qualify a terminable interest trust for the marital deduction. Or the testator may direct his executor *not* to so elect. Or the testator may leave the election to the executor's discretion. If the testator leaves it up to the executor, the testator should be careful not to create any conflicts of interest so as to raise difficult questions of fiduciary obligations.

Estate of Rapp v. Commissioner
United States Court of Appeals, Ninth Circuit, 1998
140 F.3d 1211

FLETCHER, J.[20]   The executor of Mr. Bert Rapp's estate appeals the tax court's determination that a trust established by Mr. Rapp does not qualify as "qualified terminable interest property" (QTIP), as defined by 26 U.S.C. §2056(b)(7). As such, the value of the trust may not be deducted when determining federal estate taxes owed.

We have jurisdiction, 26 U.S.C. §7482, and we affirm.

I

The testator, Mr. Bert Rapp, died in February 1988. He was survived by his wife, Laura Rapp, and two children, Richard and David Rapp. Mr. Rapp willed his one-half of the community property to a trust.[21]

---

20. Judge Betty Binns Fletcher is a member of a prominent West Coast family with many connections to the law. Her father and grandfather were lawyers in Washington State. Her husband, Robert Fletcher, is a professor of law emeritus at the University of Washington. Her son William Fletcher, formerly a professor at UC Berkeley, now sits as a judge on the Ninth Circuit Court of Appeals. Her daughter Susan Fletcher French is a professor at UCLA Law School, Reporter for the Restatement of Servitudes, and mother of Sarah French, a Seattle-based lawyer. Judge Fletcher's brother, nephew, and several of her in-laws are also in the law business. — Eds.

21. By law of California, Mrs. Rapp received as her one-half of the community property, property valued at five million dollars.

Judge Betty Fletcher

Richard is the executor of the estate under Mr. Rapp's will and trustee of the trust. All relevant parties are citizens of California. The issue in this case is whether the trust created by Mr. Rapp's will constitutes a QTIP trust, qualifying it for the marital tax deduction. A QTIP is an exception to an exception. Generally, the value of property passed directly from a testator to a surviving spouse is deducted before computing federal estate taxes.[22] 26 U.S.C. §2056(a). However, if the interest passing to the spouse consists only of a life estate or other terminable interest, the value of that interest is not deducted when determining the tax owed. 26 U.S.C. §2056(b). If the terminable interest qualifies as a QTIP, however, the surviving spouse can elect the marital deduction as if the interest passed directly and without restraint to him or her.

The will left by Mr. Rapp did not create a QTIP trust; however, the will as reformed by the California probate court did create a QTIP trust. The primary issue in this case is the effect to be given to the California probate court's reformation.

A

In 1978, Laurence Clark, Mr. Rapp's attorney, prepared wills for both of the Rapps. Mr. Clark was not an estate attorney, but served as a consultant to Mr. Rapp in his business dealings. The 1978 wills were essentially identical to each other, and provided that household furnishings and other personal effects were to be given to the surviving spouse, and that all other property of the testator was to be held in trust during the life of the surviving spouse. The children were to be given the power as co-trustees to distribute such amounts from the principal and income of the trust as they determined necessary for the surviving spouse's health, education and support.[23] Any decision to do so would be in their "absolute discretion." Upon the death of the surviving spouse, the trust was to cease and the remaining assets were to be distributed to the two children or their living issue.

In 1986, Mr. Clark prepared new wills. These wills revoked the 1978 wills but were substantially similar. Again, Mr. and Mrs. Rapp's wills were nearly identical to

---

22. The tax deduction is in reality a tax deferral since the property is taxed when (or if) it becomes part of the surviving spouse's estate upon that spouse's death.

23. In this action, Richard is the sole trustee; David relinquished his position as co-trustee.

each other. The trust was to operate as previously described. Article Fifth (b) of Mr. Rapp's will stated:

> If at any time, in the absolute discretion of the Trustee or co-Trustees, my wife, LAURA B. RAPP, should for any reason be in need of funds for her proper health, education and support, the Trustee may in his absolute discretion pay to or apply for the benefit of my wife, such amounts from the principal and income of the trust estate, up to the whole thereof, as the Trustee from time to time may deem necessary or advisable for her use and benefit.

B

The 1986 will of Mr. Rapp was admitted to probate on May 5, 1988. Mrs. Rapp asked the probate court to modify her husband's will so that the trust created by the will would qualify for the marital deduction as a QTIP trust. Her petition to the probate court alleged:

> it was decedent's intention that the Trust created . . . for the benefit of Petitioner [i.e., Mrs. Rapp] during her lifetime was intended to qualify for the QTIP election and that decedent believed that the Trustees would pay all of the income from the Trust, at least annually, to or for the benefit of Petitioner during her lifetime.

She claimed that the trust was a "marital deduction gift" as defined by section 21520(b) of the California Probate Code.[24] Her petition relied upon the probate court's power to modify or terminate a trust upon consent of all parties, Cal. Prob. Code §15403, or its power to modify or terminate a trust due to changed circumstances, Cal. Prob. Code §15409(a).[25]

Oral argument was held before the probate court. A guardian ad litem was appointed to represent Richard Rapp's two minor children. No witnesses were called and no documents were introduced into evidence. Richard Rapp did not

---

24. California defines a "marital deduction gift" as a transfer of property that is intended to qualify for the marital deduction. Cal. Prob. Code §21520(a). A "marital deduction" is defined as that which meets the federal definition of a transfer under section 2056 of the Internal Revenue Code. Id. at §21520(a).
[Cal. Prob. Code §21522 provides:

> If an instrument contains a marital deduction gift:
> (a) The provisions of the instrument, including any power, duty, or discretionary authority given to a fiduciary, shall be construed to comply with the marital deduction provisions of the Internal Revenue Code.
> (b) The fiduciary shall not take any action or have any power that impairs the deduction as applied to the marital deduction gift.
> (c) The marital deduction gift may be satisfied only with property that qualifies for the marital deduction. — Eds.]

25. Cal. Probate Code §15403 provides:

> [Unless continuance of the trust is necessary to carry out a material purpose of the trust] if all beneficiaries of an irrevocable trust consent, they may compel modification or termination of the trust upon petition to the court.

Cal. Probate Code §15409 provides that a court may modify or terminate a trust if:

> owing to circumstances not known to the settlor and not anticipated by the settlor, the continuation of the trust under its terms would defeat or substantially impair the accomplishment of the purposes of the trust.

contest his mother's petition. He did not ask Mr. Clark, creator of the wills, to testify, and Mr. Clark did not appear.[26] The IRS did not receive notice of the hearing and did not appear. The guardian ad litem did not challenge Mrs. Rapp's petition.

The probate court granted Mrs. Rapp's petition. The court modified Article Fifth (b) to read:

> During the lifetime of my wife, LAURA B. RAPP, the Trustee or co-Trustee shall pay the net income from the corpus of the trust annually or at more frequent intervals to or for the benefit of LAURA B. RAPP, during her lifetime. . . . Any income accrued or held undistributed at the time of my wife's death shall be distributed to her estate.

and added the following provision:

> I authorize my executor to elect to treat the trust created under this Article FIFTH, or any portion thereof, as "qualified terminable interest property" in order to obtain the marital deduction for such property for federal estate tax purposes. Whether or not my executors make such an election, I hereby exonerate my executors from any liability resulting from making or failing to make such an election.

This order was entered October 31, 1988, and became final and unappealable as of April 30, 1989.

C

Shortly after the probate court's order was entered, the executor filed with the Internal Revenue Service (IRS) an application for extension of time to file a federal estate tax return. The return normally is due 9 months after a testator's death. The executor noted in his application that he intended to make an election under §2056 for QTIP exemption, but that he could not determine yet which portion of the estate was to be claimed as a QTIP deduction. He also sent a payment of $156,204 as an estimate of the taxes owed on the estate, but offered no explanation as to how he arrived at that figure.

In May 1989, after the probate court's reformation became final, the executor filed the final federal estate tax return. The executor elected to claim a marital QTIP deduction, but only with respect to as much of the estate as would reduce the total estate tax owed to $156,424, the amount that had been previously paid. Thus, the marital deduction claimed on the return totalled $3,683,899.38.

The IRS sent a notice of deficiency to the executor stating that he had failed to substantiate fully the marital deduction claimed. The IRS allowed the deduction only to the extent of the property that passed directly to Mrs. Rapp under Mr. Rapp's will, consisting of the household furnishings and other personal property valued at $435,262.50. The executor appealed the decision and his claim was heard before the tax court.

---

26. Mr. Clark initially was retained as counsel for the estate but was subsequently replaced. Although Mr. Clark did not testify at the reformation hearing, he did testify before the tax court at the behest of the government. He indicated that Mr. Rapp specifically intended to create a trust for his children's benefit, and did not wish to leave outright his money to Mrs. Rapp.

After hearing argument, the tax court held that the probate court's reformation order was not binding absent an affirmation by the California Supreme Court. In the absence of an affirmation by the California Supreme Court, the tax court considered itself authorized to determine whether the probate court's order was in conformity with California law. After reviewing California law, the tax court concluded that the probate court had erred in reforming Mr. Rapp's will because the will was not ambiguous and there was little or no evidence that Mr. Rapp intended to create a QTIP trust. As such, the tax court held that, for federal estate tax purposes, the trust created by Mr. Rapp was not a QTIP trust, and that the claimed deficiency was correct. . . .

III

The IRS argues, and the tax court agreed, that the probate court's reformation of Mr. Rapp's will is without binding effect for the purpose of determining federal estate taxes owed, unless California's highest court has affirmed the result. Both rely on Commissioner of Internal Revenue v. Estate of Bosch, 387 U.S. 456 (1967). We agree that *Bosch* is controlling.

A

In *Bosch*, the respondent, Mrs. Bosch, filed a federal estate tax return in which she claimed a marital deduction. Id. at 458. The IRS denied the deduction. Mr. Bosch's will had created a trust from which Mrs. Bosch was to receive all income and in which Mrs. Bosch had a general power of appointment. If she declined that appointment, however, half of the corpus of the trust was to go to Mr. Bosch's heirs.

The entire trust would qualify as tax exempt only if Mrs. Bosch retained the general power of appointment. Before Mr. Bosch died, Mrs. Bosch executed a release of her general power of appointment. Thus, whether or not the entire value of the trust was to be taxed depended upon the validity of the release. Before the tax court, Mrs. Bosch claimed that the release was invalid. While those proceedings were pending, Mrs. Bosch sought and received a determination from a New York state court that the release was a nullity under state law. The result was that a larger estate was to go to Mrs. Bosch as the surviving spouse, a diminished inheritance was to go to other beneficiaries, and a larger marital deduction could be claimed.

The issue before the Supreme Court was what effect was to be given to the state court's determination regarding the validity of the release. The Court first noted that neither res judicata nor collateral estoppel applied. Id. at 463. The Court then reviewed the legislative history of the marital deduction statute, and concluded that Congress did not intend state court actions to have a determinative effect on federal tax questions. It noted:

> [Congress] said that "proper regard," not finality "should be given to interpretations of the will" by state courts and then only when entered by a court "in a bona fide adversary proceeding." We cannot say that the authors of this directive intended that the decrees of state trial courts were to be conclusive and binding on the computation of the federal estate tax as levied by the Congress. If the Congress had intended state trial court determinations to have that effect on the federal actions, it certainly would have said so—which it did not do.

Id. at 464 (citations omitted). Relying on Erie R.R. Co. v. Tompkins, 304 U.S. 64 (1938), the Court stated:

> when the application of a federal statute is involved, the decision of a state trial court as to an underlying issue of state law should a fortiori not be controlling. . . . If there be no decision by [the State's highest court] then federal authorities must apply what they find to be the state law after giving the "proper regard" to relevant rulings of other courts of the State. In this respect, it may be said to be, in effect, sitting as a state court.

387 U.S. at 465.

This rule remains valid today. . . .

In this case, Mrs. Rapp sought modification in the probate proceeding for the sole purpose of reforming her husband's will so that the trust would qualify as a QTIP trust. As in *Bosch*, the state court proceedings were "brought for the purpose of directly affecting federal estate tax liability," and, as in *Bosch*, the issue before the state court was "determinative of federal estate tax consequences." *Bosch*, 387 U.S. at 462-463. Accordingly, the principle of *Bosch* applies here. The tax court correctly held that it was not bound by the California probate court's reformation of Mr. Rapp's will.

B

The executor does not argue that the tax court improperly applied California law. In fact, the executor concedes that the probate court's decision to reform Mr. Rapp's will was erroneous. Instead, the executor argues that the tax court was without power to ignore the California probate court decision to reform Mr. Rapp's will, i.e., that *Bosch* is inapplicable to the instant case. He argues that the tax court only needed to determine whether Mrs. Rapp had a QTIP trust as of the proper "measuring date." According to the executor, the proper measuring date is the date on which the executor elected a QTIP deduction, and as of that date, Mrs. Rapp had a QTIP trust because the probate court's order had become final. *Bosch*, he argues, cannot be read to stand for the proposition that a state court order affixing the property rights of a taxpayer may be ignored where the order becomes final and unappealable as of the relevant measuring date for federal tax purposes. . . .

Regardless of the proper measuring date, however, the executor's argument fails because, contrary to the executor's assertion, *Bosch* does stand for the proposition that a probate court decision may be ignored when determining federal tax consequences, even when that order is final, if the decision is contrary to state law.

The executor's argument that *Bosch* is inapplicable is unavailing. The executor argues that *Bosch* does not permit the tax court to ignore the import of a state court decision that has become final and unappealable, i.e., one that cannot be directly challenged. There is no language in *Bosch* or subsequent decisions, however, that would support this position. That the California Supreme Court itself can no longer overrule the probate court's decision is irrelevant. *Bosch* stands only for the proposition that the federal court is not bound by the state court proceedings for determining federal estate taxes; to this end, the tax court decision does nothing to upset the actual outcome of the probate court proceedings. Mrs. Rapp will still enjoy the benefits of the reformation for which she petitioned in probate court. The estate simply will not receive the federal tax benefits of a QTIP.[27]

C

Finally, contrary to the executor's assertion, affirming the tax court would not create a circuit split with the Fifth, Sixth, and Eighth Circuits. As the executor correctly notes, three circuits have held that the correct "measuring date" for determining whether a particular asset is considered part of a QTIP trust is the date of QTIP election, not the date of the testator's death. See Estate of Spencer v. Commissioner of Internal Revenue, 43 F.3d 226 (6th Cir. 1995); Estate of Robertson v. Commissioner of Internal Revenue, 15 F.3d 779 (8th Cir. 1994); Estate of Clayton v. Commissioner of Internal Revenue, 976 F.2d 1486 (5th Cir. 1992).

We need not decide whether these cases are analogous to the case at hand, or whether we agree with their resolutions.[28] We note instead that because the tax court was not bound by the California probate court's reformation of Mr. Rapp's will and because under California law Mr. Rapp's will should not have been reformed, Mrs. Rapp cannot establish for federal estate tax purposes that she had a QTIP trust at any time, either at her husband's death or at the time of QTIP election. Therefore, we need not decide the correct measuring date for QTIP election to resolve this case.

IV

The tax court properly held that it is not bound by the California probate court's reformation of Mr. Rapp's will as the decision was not affirmed by the California Supreme Court and is contrary to state law. For federal estate tax purposes, therefore, Mrs. Rapp at no time had a QTIP trust, and the deficiency is correct. . . .

We affirm.

27. To hold that the probate court's order is binding on the federal courts merely because no one appealed would be inconsistent with the underlying policy considerations behind *Bosch*, that is, to prevent collusive state court proceedings brought only to avoid federal estate taxes. See, e.g., Estate of Simpson v. Commissioner of Internal Revenue, T.C. Memo 1994-259, 67 T.C.M. (CCH) 3062 (1994) (noting that, "there are a number of aspects to a State court proceeding which can raise questions and cast doubt upon its bona fide, adversary character. . . . Taxpayers can achieve favorable but collusive results from State court proceedings in which the Commissioner has not been made a party or which appear to have been pursued for the purpose of affecting a Federal tax liability.").

28. In each of these cases, the testator's will created a QTIP trust, but left to the executor the decision regarding how much of the testator's property ultimately would be placed into the QTIP trust. The IRS challenged this "wait-and-see" approach, arguing that only property which had been designated as QTIP property as of the date of the testator's death could qualify for the tax deduction. . . .

The court agreed with the executor, holding that "since no property can be QTIP until the election is made, the proper date to determine if property satisfies the requirement of §2056(b)(7) is on the date of the election." Id. at 231. The court explicitly rejected the IRS' suggestion that property "satisfy every requirement for the QTIP counter-exception on the date of decedent's death." Id. In any event, we note that these cases are distinguishable because they involve the correct measuring date for deciding whether property meets the QTIP definition where the only issue at stake is not whether the trust created was a QTIP trust, but how much of the testator's property could be placed within that trust. [Treasury regulations follow these cases. See Treas. Reg. §§20.2044-1, 20.2056(b)-7, 20.2056(b)-10 (1997). — Eds.]

Pond v. Pond

Supreme Judicial Court of Massachusetts, 1997
424 Mass. 894, 678 N.E.2d 1321

LYNCH, J.   The plaintiff, trustee of the Sidney M. Pond Trust 1991, a revocable trust (trust), filed a complaint in the Probate and Family Court seeking reformation of the trust. The plaintiff alleges that, due to scrivener's errors in the form of omissions and ambiguities, the declaration of trust fails to give effect to the settlor's intent. At the request of the parties a Probate Court judge reserved and reported the case to the Appeals Court pursuant to G. L. c. 215, §13, and Mass. R. Civ. P. 64, 365 Mass. 831 (1974). We granted the plaintiff's application for direct appellate review. See Commissioner of Internal Revenue v. Estate of Bosch, 387 U.S. 456, 465 (1967) (Internal Revenue Service need not accept decisions other than those of State's highest court).

1.   BACKGROUND

We summarize the undisputed facts as presented by the plaintiff.[29] The settlor, Sidney M. Pond, executed his last will and testament on January 17, 1991. On the same day, the settlor executed a declaration of revocable trust, naming himself and his wife as trustees. Then, they transferred virtually all their assets, except the marital home, into the trust. The settlor died on February 26, 1996.[30]

The trust instrument provided that, during the settlor's lifetime, all of the annual income and such principal as the trustees deemed necessary was to be paid to the settlor and his wife. However, the trust made no provision for income or principal to be paid to his wife if she were to survive the settlor. The trust also provided that, on the death of the settlor and his wife, the trust shall terminate and its assets should be distributed in equal shares to their children. If one of the children predeceased the parents, the trust provided that the deceased child's share shall pass "equally and in equal shares to his/her issue by right of representation," when the issue reach the age of thirty.

In his will, the settlor bequeathed all his tangible personal property to his wife and the residue of his estate, both real and personal, to the trust. The tax clause in the will authorized his wife, as executrix, "in her sole, exclusive and unrestricted discretion, to determine whether to elect (under Sec. 2056[b][7] of the Internal Revenue Code of 1954, as amended, or any corresponding provision of state law) to qualify all or a specific portion of the SIDNEY M. POND REVOCABLE TRUST dated January 17, 1991 for the federal estate tax marital deduction and any marital deduction available under the law of the state in which I am domiciled at the time of my death." To qualify under §2056, however, the trust must provide the surviving spouse a "qualifying income interest for life." See §2056(b)(7)(B) of the Internal Revenue Code (I.R.C.). Without the marital deduction, the settlor's estate would have to pay $70,000 in otherwise avoidable taxes.

The plaintiff contends that scrivener's errors are apparent when the purposes of the trust are considered. The plaintiff avers that the settlor created the trust to

---

29. Notice of the proposed reformation was served on the Internal Revenue Service and the Attorney General. Neither the Commonwealth nor the IRS filed an appearance.

30. At the time of the settlor's death, the trust was valued at approximately $650,000.

satisfy the requirements for the marital deduction under §2056(b)(7) of the I.R.C. and the corresponding deduction under G. L. c. 65C, §3A. The plaintiff also contends that, pursuant to this estate plan, the settlor intended for the trust's assets to be used to support his surviving spouse. Due to the omission of an income provision for the surviving spouse, both objectives were thwarted because his wife was left with virtually no assets and the trust does not qualify for the marital deduction.

The plaintiff requests that the court reform the trust instrument to give effect to the settlor's intent. First, the plaintiff asks this court to insert a provision which would grant the surviving spouse the right to the trust's annual income, and discretionary principal payments, during her lifetime. Second, the plaintiff also asks this court to incorporate provisions which would correct the ambiguity in the termination provisions. The beneficiaries of the trust, who were named as defendants, assented to the proposed reformation.[31]

2. DISCUSSION

The modification of a trust agreement to conform with a settlor's intent with respect to the marital deduction is a matter of State law which this court may properly decide. See Loeser v. Talbot, 589 N.E.2d 301 (Mass. 1992); Berman v. Sandler, 399 N.E.2d 17 (Mass. 1980); Babson v. Babson, 371 N.E.2d 430 (Mass. 1977); Mazzola v. Myers, 296 N.E.2d 481 (Mass. 1973). When a trust instrument fails to embody the settlor's intent because of scrivener's error, it may be reformed on clear and decisive proof of mistake. Loeser v. Talbot, supra. To ascertain the settlor's intent, we look to the trust instrument as a whole and the circumstances known to the settlor on execution. Berman v. Sandler, supra.

The settlor's intent in creating the trust was clearly to qualify for the marital deduction under §2056(b)(7) of the I.R.C. The tax clause in the settlor's will, which was executed on the same day, demonstrates that the settlor thought that the trust qualified for the marital trust deduction.[32] To qualify, the trust must provide the surviving spouse a "qualifying income interest for life." §2056(b)(7)(B). This means the trust must pay income annually or more frequently to the surviving spouse. §2056(b)(7)(B)(ii). Because we read the trust as clearly manifesting an intent that it qualify for a marital deduction, it can only be a scrivener's error that caused a clause to be omitted that would have provided for income to be paid to his wife for life on the death of the settlor.

We are also convinced that the settlor did not intend to deny his wife discretionary use of the principal during her lifetime. The trust was an essential component in the settlor's estate plan. The settlor transferred virtually all his marital assets into this trust. The trust's income and principal were available to the settlor and his wife during his lifetime. The trust, however, omitted any provision for the surviving spouse after the settlor's death. Because we know that the settlor intended to provide income for his wife if he died first and since the trust

31. The guardians for the minor grandchildren also have assented to the proposed reformation.
32. Under §2056(b)(7) of the I.R.C., qualifying terminal interest property is eligible for a marital deduction in the estate of the settlor if the settlor's executrix so elects. If that election is made and the marital deduction is thus taken in the settlor's estate, the trust property must then be included in the estate of the surviving spouse for Federal estate tax purposes.

made principal available for as long as the settlor lived, we conclude that his intent to continue the same arrangement if he should die first is manifest. Babson v. Babson, 371 N.E.2d 430 (Mass. 1980) (considering will as a whole, testator intended to take maximum advantage of estate tax deductions even though word "maximum" not used). This conclusion is buttressed by the settlor's will bequeathing all his tangible property to his wife and naming her executrix of his estate. There is no indication that the settlor intended to deprive his surviving spouse of the trust's assets during her lifetime.

We conclude that there is clear and decisive proof of mistake due to scrivener's error. The settlor's intent was to minimize estate tax payable by establishing a qualifying terminal interest trust. To qualify under §2056, the trust must distribute income to the surviving spouse. While the discretionary principal payments are not required under §2056, the estate plan demonstrates an intent to treat both spouses equally. Thus, we agree that the trust should be reformed to give effect to the settlor's intent. . . .

The case is remanded to the Probate and Family Court for entry of a judgment of reformation consistent with this opinion.

So ordered.

NOTE AND PROBLEMS

1. *Post-mortem reformation to save taxes.* In Pond v. Pond, the court reformed a trust so as to obtain tax advantages lost, allegedly, by the faulty work of the lawyer. Judicial reformation is a new idea that has been pushed along by the threat of legal malpractice. Massachusetts has led the way in reforming trusts to obtain tax advantages lost through faulty drafting, a trend that, as discussed in Chapter 8 at page 579, has been embraced by Restatement (Third) of Property: Wills and Other Donative Transfers §12.2 (2003) and Uniform Trust Code §416 (2000). Note, however, that under Commissioner v. Estate of Bosch, 387 U.S. 456 (1967), the Internal Revenue Service is bound only by a construction or reformation approved by the state's highest court. Massachusetts has a special procedure permitting the parties to go directly from the probate court to the Supreme Judicial Court. Most states do not have such a summary appellate procedure. Most require appeal to a middle appellate court and then to the state supreme court, which takes time and money and requires jumping sundry procedural hurdles.

2. *H* by will creates a trust providing *W* with "so much of the net income as she may require to maintain her usual and customary standard of living." Does this qualify for the QTIP deduction? See Estate of Nicholson v. Commissioner, 94 T.C. 666 (1990). Suppose the trust gave the trustee the power to accumulate income in excess of the amount necessary for *W*'s "needs, best interests, and welfare." QTIP deduction? See Estate of Ellingson v. Commissioner, 964 F.2d 959 (9th Cir. 1992). Would it matter if the testator's will had stated that his intention was to qualify the trust for the marital deduction? See Wiseley v. United States, 893 F.2d 660 (4th Cir. 1990).

3. *W* has created a revocable trust for herself to avoid probate. The trust contains a provision that in the event of *W*'s incapacity the trustee may make gifts to members of the family qualifying for the annual $11,000 gift tax exclusion. *H* dies,

devising property to W's revocable trust. Does this qualify for the marital deduction?

4.   For criticism of the QTIP deduction as incompatible with the partnership theory of marriage, see page 429.

(3) Noncitizen spouses: qualified domestic trusts

The marital deduction allows a couple to defer all estate taxes until the death of the surviving spouse. The *quid pro quo* is that the property must be in the survivor's gross estate to the extent that it is not consumed or given away during the survivor's life. A surviving spouse who is not a citizen of the United States will not necessarily be subject to the federal estate tax at death. As a result, no marital deduction is allowed for property passing to a noncitizen spouse unless the property passes to a *qualified domestic trust*. I.R.C. §2056(d)(2). A qualified domestic trust (QDOT) is one where at least one trustee is a citizen of the United States or a domestic corporation. The trust instrument must give the U.S. trustee the right to withhold the deferred estate tax on the QDOT assets. In addition, the trust must qualify as a marital deduction power of appointment trust, a QTIP trust, or an estate trust. If the decedent did not create a QDOT, the noncitizen spouse or the decedent's executor may create a QDOT after the decedent's death. A court may also reform a trust to comply with the QDOT requirements. I.R.C. §2056(d)(5). To ensure the collection of the deferred estate tax, Treasury has issued regulations requiring a bond of an individual trustee and requiring securities to be kept in the United States. Treas. Reg. §26.2056A-2(d)(1)(B).

c.   Tax Planning

In a brief treatment of estate taxation such as this, we cannot cover in detail the more complicated tax avoidance devices developed for spouses. There is one basic strategy, however, with which all lawyers should be familiar — taking advantage of the unified credit available to both spouses. Drafting estate plans that use both unified credits (usually by means of testamentary or inter vivos trusts) is the most common form of planning for clients with potentially taxable estates. Failure to advise your clients of this strategy may well be malpractice.

Each spouse has an exemption from estate taxation, in the form of a unified credit, which is $2 million in 2006. It is possible for a spouse to leave his or her entire estate to the other spouse, deferring all taxation until the death of the surviving spouse. If this is done, however, the first spouse's exemption is lost since *all* of his or her assets will be subject to taxation on the surviving spouse's death. Thus:

> *Case 17.* W owns property worth $4 million. H owns no property. H and W have made no taxable gifts. W dies in 2006, devising all her property to H. Because of the unlimited marital deduction, no taxes are paid at W's death. At H's death a year later, H leaves an estate of $4 million; $2 million is exempt from taxation. An estate tax of $900,000 is payable on the remaining $2 million. (For ease of illustration, we keep the

asset values the same in the estates of *W* and *H* and ignore deductions for administration expenses, debts, and funeral expenses, and various credits.)

In Case 17, by devising everything to *H*, *W* did not use her $2 million exemption applicable to property taxable in her estate. To use this exemption, *W* must leave a taxable estate of $2 million, which means that $2 million worth of property should *not* qualify for the marital deduction. Case 18 illustrates how this can be done:

> *Case 18*. Refer back to Case 17. *W* dies, bequeathing $2 million in trust for *H* for life, remainder as *H* appoints by will among *W*'s issue, and in default of appointment to *W*'s issue per stirpes. This bequest would qualify for the marital deduction as a QTIP trust if *W*'s executor so elected, but *W*'s will directs her executor not to elect the marital deduction for this trust. This $2 million is taxable at *W*'s death, but because of *W*'s $2 million exemption in the form of a credit, no taxes are paid (hence this trust is known as a *credit shelter trust* or as a *bypass trust* because no taxes are payable at the spouse's death). The assets in the credit shelter trust are not taxable at *H*'s death because *H* has only a life estate coupled with a special power of appointment.
>
> *W*'s remaining assets (worth $2 million) are bequeathed outright to *H* by *W*'s residuary clause. These assets are taxable at *H*'s death, but no taxes are paid because the total is only $2 million.

By taking advantage of both spouses' exemptions, as is done in Case 18, at total of $4 million can be passed to the couple's children, free of estate taxation. If the spouses desire that the surviving spouse have all the income from the property, this can be arranged as in Case 18. The key to taking advantage of both exemptions is that $2 million worth of property must not qualify for the marital deduction in the estate of the first spouse to die. Putting $2 million in a credit shelter trust will reduce death taxes payable on the surviving spouse's death by an amount equal to at least 45 percent of the value of the trust assets on the surviving spouse's death. (If the value of the assets remains the same at the surviving spouse's death, the tax saving of the estate plan in Case 18, as compared to Case 17, is $900,000.)

The credit shelter trust does not, of course, have to give all the income to the surviving spouse. Case 18 is merely an illustration of a situation where the couple wants all the income to go to the surviving spouse. The credit shelter trust could give discretion to the trustee to spray the income among family members, thus reducing income taxes during the surviving spouse's remaining life. Or the first spouse to die could use his or her $2 million exemption by bequeathing that amount to children or persons other than the surviving spouse.

In discussing Case 17, we have assumed that *W*, the richer of the spouses, will die first. But suppose that *H* dies first. In that case, *H*'s exemption will be lost to the extent of $2 million because *H* owns nothing. At *W*'s death $2 million ($4 million minus *W*'s $2 million exemption) will be taxable. In order to take advantage of *H*'s exemption, *W* must transfer to *H* during life property worth $2 million. *W* can give *H* property outright or in a trust. The trust can be either a marital deduction power of appointment trust or a QTIP trust, which *W* elects to be taxable at *H*'s death. No gift tax is payable upon the transfer because any of these transfers qualifies for the gift tax marital deduction. Thus:

> *Case 19*. *W* creates an inter vivos QTIP trust with all income to be paid to *H* for his life and upon his death to pay the principal to *W*'s children. *W* transfers $2 million to

this trust and on her gift tax return elects to take the marital deduction. This results in the trust principal being taxable in *H*'s gross estate, but because of *H*'s exemption, no taxes are payable. *W* has reduced her taxable estate to $2 million, which is exempt from taxation. (If *W* wants to have the income on the $2 million come back to *W* after *H* dies, *W* can create an inter vivos marital deduction power of appointment trust with *H* as the beneficiary, and *H* by will can exercise the general power of appointment by appointing the trust funds to *W* for life, directing his executor not to elect the marital deduction.)

7. The Charitable Deduction

Decedents often want to leave assets to charity. Section 2055 of the Internal Revenue Code allows an unlimited deduction for transfers for public, charitable, or religious purposes. There is no limitation on the amount that can qualify for a charitable deduction.

A principal question is whether a particular bequest is for uses that qualify for the charitable deduction. The statute and regulations provide guidelines that, while taking care of the clear cases, leave the harder cases for resolution by revenue ruling or case decision. If a bequest is made to a corporation, to qualify as a *charity* the corporation must be

> organized and operated exclusively for religious, charitable, scientific, literary, or educational purposes, including the encouragement of art, or to foster national or international amateur sports competition (but only if no part of its activities involve the provision of athletic facilities or equipment), and the prevention of cruelty to children or animals, no part of the net earnings of which inures to the benefit of any private stockholder or individual, which is not disqualified for tax exemption under §501(c)(3) by reason of attempting to influence legislation, and which does not participate in, or intervene in (including the publishing or distributing of statements), any political campaign on behalf of any candidate for public office. [I.R.C. §2055(a)(2).]

IRS Publication 78 lists the official names of all charitable organizations exempt from taxation under the federal income tax. If the client wants to make a gift to a new charity not on the list, care must be taken to make sure the beneficiary qualifies for the deduction.

If a client wants to make a gift of a *remainder* to charity, special arrangements are required. Except for a remainder in a personal residence or in a farm, not in trust, a charitable deduction for a remainder is disallowed under the federal income, gift, and estate tax laws unless the remainder is in an *annuity trust* or a *unitrust* or unless the gift is to a *pooled income fund*. I.R.C. §§664(d), 2055(e)(2), and 2522(c)(2). A bequest in trust "to pay all the income to *A* for life, remainder to the *Y* charity" does *not* qualify for the charitable deduction because such a trust is not an annuity trust or a unitrust.

A charitable remainder *annuity trust* is one under which a fixed sum, which can be no less than 5 percent of the *original value* of the trust corpus, is paid at least annually to the private beneficiary or beneficiaries. The income beneficiary of an annuity trust thus receives a fixed and constant amount each year. A *unitrust* is one under which a fixed percentage, which cannot be less than 5 percent of the trust corpus, *valued annually*, is paid to the beneficiary. The income beneficiary of a unitrust thus will receive an annual amount that will fluctuate as the value of the trust changes. A *pooled income fund* is set up by a charitable organization to meet certain specific requirements of the Code. If the trustee or private beneficiary of an annuity trust, a unitrust, or a pooled income fund has a discretionary power to invade principal, the trust does not qualify for a charitable remainder deduction. The objectives of these rules are to reduce the uncertainty involved in valuing the future interest given to charity and to increase the likelihood that an interest will in fact pass to charity on the private beneficiary's death. However, the rules governing the drafting of these trusts are technical and stringent, and must be carefully followed.

We mention only one technicality to illustrate and underscore the need for caution in drafting gifts to charitable remainder trusts. If estate taxes may be paid from a charitable remainder trust, no charitable deduction is allowable. Rev. Rul. 82-128, 1982-2 C.B. 71. If taxes are apportioned by state law or by a clause in the decedent's will, a deduction may be denied. The will should provide that the charitable bequest pass free of all taxes.

PROBLEMS

1. *T* was unmarried. *T*'s will bequeaths his property to Princeton University and Johns Hopkins University. A codicil to his will grants *T*'s executors the discretion "to compensate persons who have contributed to my well-being or who have otherwise been helpful to me during my lifetime," providing that no single bequest should exceed 1 percent of the testator's gross estate. The executors determined that only two individuals met the definition of eligible persons and distributed $25,000 to them and the rest to the universities. Is the estate entitled to a charitable deduction? See Estate of Marine v. Commissioner, 990 F.2d 136 (4th Cir. 1993).

2. *W* bequeaths $500,000 in trust to pay the income to *H* for life, remainder to Smith College. The gift to Smith College does not qualify for the charitable deduction in *W*'s estate because the trust is not an annuity trust or a unitrust. *W*'s net estate is worth $2 million. *H* elects to take against the will a surviving spouse's elective share, which is one-half of *W*'s estate. *H*'s elective share is $1 million. What effect does *H*'s disclaimer of his life estate have on the charitable deduction? See First Natl. Bank of Fayetteville v. United States, 82-2 U.S. Tax Cas. (CCH) ¶13,478 (W.D. Ark. 1982). If *H* had not elected to take against the will and *W*'s executor had claimed the marital deduction for the trust as a QTIP trust, would a charitable deduction be allowed in *H*'s estate upon *H*'s death? See I.R.C. §2044.

3. Sometimes statutes or courts reform defective charitable remainder unitrusts to qualify under §2055 as a charitable unitrust, when the intent to obtain the charitable deduction is manifest. See, e.g., Putnam v. Putnam, 682 N.E.2d 1351 (Mass. 1997).

SECTION D.   THE GENERATION-SKIPPING TRANSFER TAX

1.   The Nature of the Tax

Until 1986, it was possible for wealthy persons to make transfers in trust, either during lifetime or by will, in a manner that would insulate the transferred property from estate or gift taxation over several generations. We call this a *dynasty trust*. For example, *O* might transfer property worth $5 million to a trust under which the income was payable to *O*'s children for *their lives*, then to the children's children for *their lives*, then to the grandchildren's children for *their lives*, and so on down the generations until the local version of the Rule against Perpetuities, if any, called a halt.

Under a dynasty trust, each beneficiary could be given, in addition to a share of the income, a power to consume principal measured by an "ascertainable standard," a "$5,000 or 5 percent" withdrawal power, and a special testamentary power of appointment over his share of the trust corpus, all without estate or gift tax cost to the beneficiary. In addition, an independent trustee could be given an unlimited power to distribute trust principal to the beneficiaries with no transfer tax consequences. As each beneficiary died, nothing would be taxed in the beneficiary's estate because the beneficiary held only a life estate and limited powers of appointment. See pages 595-597. Through careful drafting to comply with the Rule against Perpetuities, the trust might continue — and be removed from the transfer tax rolls — for several generations. When the assets resurfaced on termination of the trust, the new owners could turn around, pay a gift or estate tax on the value of the assets, and make another generation-skipping transfer for another long period of time.

In the Tax Reform Act of 1986, Congress put an end to this tax-avoidance technique by enacting what is titled a "Tax on Generation-Skipping Transfers."[33] In 2001, as a part of EGTRRA, Congress repealed the generation-skipping transfer (GST) tax along with the estate tax. However, this repeal does not take effect until 2010, and then, unless Congress makes the repeal permanent, the GST tax returns on January 1, 2011, as if nothing had happened. The future of this tax, like the estate tax, remains uncertain.

We assume, at least for the present, that the current GST tax will continue to exist in something approaching its current structure. Although the rules governing imposition of this tax can become enormously complicated, a general understanding is not difficult and is essential for the ordinary estate planner. Our treatment here is designed to give you a basic understanding. The fine details will have to be left to a course in tax planning.

The loophole in the estate and gift taxes that brought on the GST tax is the exemption of the life estate from transfer taxation at the death of the life tenant. The essential idea underlying the GST tax is that a transfer tax (gift, estate, or

---

33. The GST tax provisions, Chapter 13 of the Internal Revenue Code, comprise a separate and distinct tax from the estate tax (Chapter 11) and the gift tax (Chapter 12). The relevant sections are 2601-2663. Another version of the GST tax was enacted by Congress in 1976, but its effective date was annually postponed until 1986, when this earlier GST tax was retroactively repealed.

generation-skipping) should be paid *once each generation*, and that it should not be possible for an owner of property to avoid a transfer tax by giving the next generation only a life estate or skipping its members entirely. To implement this idea, the Code imposes a tax on any *generation-skipping transfer*, which is defined in §2611(a) as (1) a *taxable termination*, (2) a *taxable distribution*, or (3) a *direct skip*. Generally, a generation-skipping transfer is a transfer to a *skip person* (a new term invented by Congress in imposing this tax). A skip person is a grandchild, great-grandchild, or any other person assigned to a generation that is two or more generations below the transferor's generation (I.R.C. §2613(a)). A spouse or a child (or other person in the transferor's generation or the generation just below the transferor's) is a nonskip person. As you will see, it is transfers from a grandparent to a grandchild, either direct or as a future interest, which avoid estate taxation at the death of the donor's children, that are the central concern of the GST tax.

There are three types of generation-skipping transfers. A *taxable termination* is the

> termination (by death, lapse of time, release of power, or otherwise) of any interest in property held in a trust unless —
>   (A) immediately after such termination, a non-skip person has an interest in such property, or
>   (B) at no time after such termination may a distribution (including distributions on termination) be made from such trust to a skip person. [I.R.C. §2612(a)(1).]

Here is an example:

> *Case 20. T* bequeaths $5 million in trust for her son *A* for life, remainder to *A*'s children. At *A*'s death, a "taxable termination" takes place. *A*'s life interest terminates and only skip persons (*A*'s children) have an interest in the property. A GST tax must be paid. If the income were payable to *T*'s daughter *B* after *A*'s death, there would be no taxable termination upon *A*'s death; there would, however, be a taxable termination upon *B*'s death, when only skip persons would have an interest in the trust.

The purpose of the exceptions in the definition of a taxable termination ((A) and (B) above) is to limit to *one* the number of taxable terminations, per dollar of property, that can occur in each generation below the transferor's. Where, for example, *T* bequeaths the income from a trust to her children, with principal to be distributed to her grandchildren upon the death of her *last* surviving child, a taxable termination occurs only at the death of the last surviving child. On the other hand, if at the death of one child her share is distributed to her children, then a taxable termination of a fractional share of the trust principal has occurred (I.R.C. §2612(a)(2)). Each dollar of a generation-skipping transfer is to be taxed once a generation.

A *taxable distribution* takes place whenever any distribution is made from a trust to a skip person (other than a taxable termination or a direct skip). Thus, if in Case 20, *A* had a (special) power to distribute income or corpus to *A*'s children, a taxable distribution would take place when and if such distribution were made. In a discretionary trust, a taxable distribution takes place whenever a distribution is made to a skip person.[34]

---

34. An income tax deduction is provided for any GST tax imposed on any income distributions. This deduction prevents the same amount being subject to both income tax and the GST tax. But note that the GST tax rate is considerably higher than the income tax rate.

It is easy to see, from the explanation of a taxable termination and a taxable distribution, that the old-fashioned dynasty trust, described above in introducing the GST tax, generally will not work any longer in avoiding wealth transfer taxes. At the death of the transferor's children, holding life estates, or upon earlier distribution to the transferor's grandchildren, GST taxes must be paid. It is important to note, however, that the 1986 GST tax does not apply to any irrevocable trust created before the date of the act. All those trusts already established by the Rockefellers, the duPonts, and the Gettys, as well as lesser millionaires—with life estates and special powers of appointment in succeeding generations—will continue untaxed until after the termination of the trust.

To prevent the rich from bypassing one generation and making untaxed gifts to grandchildren or more remote descendants, Congress also has imposed a tax on direct skips. A *direct skip* is a transfer of property directly to a skip person. Case 21 illustrates a direct skip:

> *Case 21.* *T* leaves surviving her son *A* and *A*'s daughter *B*. *T* bequeaths $3 million to her granddaughter *B*. This is a direct skip. A GST tax (in addition to the estate tax payable on *T*'s death) is due on *T*'s death. This double taxation follows from the principle that a transfer tax must be paid once per generation. Similarly, if *T* had given *B* $3 million during life, a gift tax *and* a GST tax would be due.

Exceptions. Observe that the principle underlying taxation of a direct skip is that a transfer tax (be it an estate tax, gift tax, or GST tax) must be paid once a generation, *regardless of whether any person assigned to a particular generation has any present interest or power*. This principle has two important exceptions.

(a) *Multiple skips.* First, skipping over two or more generations is permitted with the payment of only one GST tax. An owner can transfer property to a great-grandchild, paying a GST tax for the direct skip. Although two generations are skipped over, only one tax is paid.

(b) *Predeceased child.* The second exception relates to transfers to descendants of predeceased children of the transferor. If a child of the transferor is dead at the time of the initial transfer, the children of that child are treated as the children of the transferor. Thus in Case 21 suppose that *A* had predeceased *T*. If this had happened, there would be no direct skip. The child of a predeceased child is treated as the child of the transferor; he is moved up a generation (I.R.C. §2651(e)). The children of this child (really *T*'s great-grandchildren) are treated as grandchildren. This makes sense. Since no estate taxes could be levied on this property at *A*'s death, prior to *T*'s death, a GST tax (the functional equivalent of an estate tax) should not be levied upon a gift by *T* to the children of *T*'s dead son.

If the transferor has no lineal descendants, this exception for persons with a predeceased parent applies to transfers to lineal descendants of the parent of the transferor (first line collaterals).

When the GST tax is imposed. No doubt you have observed one important difference between a direct skip on the one hand, and a taxable termination or distribution on the other. A direct skip occurs (and is taxable) on the day the transfer is effective; a taxable termination or taxable distribution occurs in the future, sometime after the original transfer in trust. In some cases, it will be certain when the trust is established that the trust will produce a GST tax in the future. In other cases, it will not be. Case 22 is an example.

Case 22. *T*'s will bequeaths property in trust to pay the income to *T*'s child *A* until *A* attains the age of 30, at which time the trustee is to distribute the trust principal to *A*. If *A* dies before reaching age 30, the trustee is to distribute the principal to *A*'s children in equal shares. Whether this trust will produce a generation-skipping transfer will turn on the events that actually occur—and for this purpose we wait to see what happens. If *A* lives to age 30 and receives the trust principal, it will turn out that *T* did not make a generation-skipping transfer. If *A* dies under age 30, and the trust principal is distributed to *A*'s children, a taxable termination will occur.

If a trust turns out to produce a generation-skipping transfer, the tax is payable in the future when such transfer occurs.

PROBLEM

If a person makes a qualified disclaimer (see page 635), for purposes of federal gift, estate, and GST taxes, the disclaimed interest in property is treated as if it had never been transferred to the person making the disclaimer. The disclaimant is *not* treated as having predeceased the transferor, as occurs under many state disclaimer statutes (see UPC §2-801(c), pages 133-134). *T* bequeaths $2 million to her son *A*. If *A* disclaims, is a GST tax imposed?

2. Rate and Base of Tax

Rate. All generation-skipping transfers are taxed at a flat rate, which is the highest rate applicable under the federal estate tax. The highest estate tax rate in 2006 is 46 percent (see page 850 for phased reductions in the top rate).

Base. The amount taxed and the person liable for the tax depend upon the type of transfer. Where there is a *direct skip*, the transferor must pay the tax on the amount received by the transferee. In this way, the direct skip resembles the gift tax. The base excludes the amount of tax levied; a direct skip is said to be "tax exclusive" (see page 852). Thus, for a transferor to pass $1 million directly to a grandchild, the transferor must part with $1,460,000, in addition to the gift or estate tax imposed. The gift tax is imposed on the amount of the gift and on the amount of the GST tax paid.

Taxable terminations and *taxable distributions* are treated differently. The tax in these events is imposed on a *tax-inclusive* basis (that is, the taxable amount includes the tax). In this respect, taxable terminations and distributions resemble the estate tax. Upon a taxable termination, the tax base is the entire property with respect to which the termination occurred. The tax is to be paid out of the trust.[35] Upon a taxable distribution, the tax base is the amount received by the beneficiary, who is liable for the tax. Thus, if a generation-skipping trust terminates and the taxable principal is $2 million, the trustee must pay $920,000 to Uncle Sam and $1,080,000 is distributed to the beneficiary. Similarly, if a trustee distributes $2 million to a skip person, the donee is liable for $920,000 in GST tax, leaving a net transfer of $1,080,000.

---

35. If the $2 million exemption is allocated to this at *T*'s death, no GST tax is payable at *A*'s death, even though the principal has appreciated. See discussion of exemption at page 923.

PROBLEM

O makes a $1 million gift to a grandchild, allocating no exemption to it. Assuming the maximum gift and estate tax rate of 46 percent is applicable, what is the cost of this transfer to *O*? To put the question a different way, how much does *O* have to part with to put $1 million in a grandchild's hands?

What would be the cost to *O* of a $1 million *bequest* to a grandchild?

3. Exemption and Exclusions

Exemption. Section 2631 provides an exemption of $2 million[36] in 2006-2008 for each person making generation-skipping transfers. In the case of inter vivos transfers by a married person, the transferor and her spouse may elect to treat the transfer as made one-half by each spouse (as under §2513 of the gift tax, see page 868). A husband and wife can give away $4 million in generation-skipping transfers in 2006 without incurring any tax. Thus:

> *Case 23.* During life *W* transfers $4 million to a trustee to pay the income to *W*'s children for their lives, then to distribute the principal to *W*'s grandchildren. *H* consents to treating this transfer as having been made half by him, thus using up his $2 million exemption. A gift tax is payable by *W* at the time of the transfer. At the death of *W*'s children, no GST tax is due.[37]

If, in Case 23, *W* had not made an inter vivos transfer but had bequeathed $4 million in trust, only $2 million would be exempt from GST tax. The split-gift provision applies only to inter vivos gifts. In case of a testamentary transfer, to take advantage of the spouse's GST tax exemption, it is necessary to make the spouse a "transferor" for estate tax purposes. This can be done by bequeathing the spouse outright ownership, or a life estate coupled with a general power of appointment, or a life estate in a QTIP trust. If, in Case 23, the trust had been a testamentary trust and *H* had been bequeathed a life estate in half of $4 million transferred by *W* into trust, *H*'s GST tax exemption of $2 million could be used up too.

If the transferor creates more than one generation-skipping trust, or makes generation-skipping transfers in excess of $2 million, the transferor or his personal representative can allocate the exemption as he sees fit. If not so allocated, §2632 provides some rather complex default rules. Generally, under these rules, the exemption is first allocated to direct skips and then to taxable terminations and taxable distributions. The exemption is allocated to the "property transferred" and not, in the case of taxable terminations and taxable distributions, to specific generation-skipping transfers that occur in the future. This means that with respect to trusts that might produce taxable terminations or taxable distributions, the entire exemption or a fraction thereof must be allocated to the trust *at the time of the transfer into trust*.

---

36. Originally, the exemption amount was $1 million to be increased by annual cost-of-living adjustments by the Treasury in multiples of $10,000. In 2001, however, Congress amended §2631 to provide that the GST tax exemption amount would be equal to the estate tax exemption amount.

37. Note that the gift tax exemption remains at $1 million while the estate and GST tax exemptions are $1.5 million in 2005, $2 million in 2006-2008, and $3.5 million in 2009.

The allocation, once made, is irrevocable. Therefore, it is important to allocate the exemption so as not to waste it on a trust that is uncertain to produce a generation-skipping transfer, when it could be allocated more effectively elsewhere. It is usually best to allocate the exemption first to direct skips, for this reason and for the additional reason that a tax postponed is better than a tax paid.

Under §2653(b)(1), the exempt fraction of the trust property — determined when the trust is created — remains the same for the duration of the trust. If the trust produces successive skips, the transferor's exemption can eliminate or reduce the GST tax generation after generation. If, for example, a trust provides for payment of income to *T*'s children for their lives, then to *T*'s grandchildren for their lives, and then to distribute the principal to *T*'s great-grandchildren, the transferor's $2 million exemption will shelter the trust, wholly or partially, from GST tax for its entire duration. This tax-shelter trust is known as a *dynasty trust*.

Exclusions. Certain transfers are excluded from the GST tax. Section 2642(c)(1) excludes any transfer not subject to the gift tax because of the annual exclusion (see page 857). Hence transfers of $11,000 or less annually to grandchildren will not produce a GST tax. Section 2611(b)(1) excludes from the term *generation-skipping transfer* any inter vivos transfers excluded under §2503(e) of the gift tax, relating to the direct payment of tuition and medical expenses (see page 858). Hence, a grandparent can pay tuition for a grandchild without making a generation-skipping transfer, or a trust can make tuition or medical payments for a skip person without subjecting such distributions to the GST tax.

PROBLEM

To reduce taxes, it is desirable for a child to be able to decide whether to pay an estate tax or to pay a GST tax on his death. This flexibility may give the child the advantage of making use of his and his spouse's exemptions, unified credits, and graduated rates. Can a parent pass property to the child in such a way as to give the child this option, to be elected as future events unfold? The answer is Yes. If *O* transfers property in trust for her son *A* for life, then to *A*'s children, and *O* gives *A* a special power to appoint the property to his wife or to one or more of *A*'s descendants, *A* has the choice of which tax to pay. If *A* wants the property in his federal gross estate at death, thereby avoiding GST tax, *A* can by will exercise the special power by creating a *general inter vivos* power in his wife. This exercise causes the property subject to the general power to be includable in *A*'s federal gross estate. For discussion, see Jonathan G. Blattmachr & Jeffrey N. Pennell, Adventures in Generation-Skipping, or How We Learned to Love the "Delaware Tax Trap," 24 Real Prop., Prob. & Tr. J. 75 (1989); Note: The "Delaware Tax Trap," page 694.

4. Definitions

To round out our picture of how the generation-skipping transfer tax operates, it is necessary to look at some definitions in the Code.

a.   Transferor

Generally, a transferor is a person who is treated as owner (or transferor) under the federal gift and estate taxes. A person transferring a fee simple is a transferor. A person who possesses a general power of appointment is a transferor when the power is exercised or when it lapses or is released. A person possessing a special power of appointment is not treated as a transferor. In case of a QTIP trust, the transferee spouse is the deemed transferor if the transferor spouse (or his executor) so elects. However, by a special provision in §2652(a)(3), the transferor spouse in a QTIP trust can elect to be the transferor for generation-skipping purposes (thus using his GST tax exemption), while at the same time electing to take the estate tax marital deduction. This has come to be called the *reverse QTIP election*.

As noted above, gift-splitting by married couples is permitted. Gift-splitting doubles the effect of any exemption or exclusion applicable to inter vivos transfers.

Successive skips. If a trust is created for several generations (for example, for children for their lives, then to grandchildren for their lives, then to great-grandchildren), a taxable termination occurs on the death of the first generation and again on the death of the second generation. This result follows from §2653(a), which provides that in such a trust, *after* a generation-skipping transfer at the death of the children, the "transferor" is dropped down to the children's level for any portion of the trust subject to GST tax.

However, any portion of the trust that has been allocated part of the original settlor's exemption remains exempt for the duration of the trust (see page 923). Thus a dynasty trust of $2 million, allocated the transferor's entire exemption, pays no GST tax for its duration. In a state that has abolished the Rule against Perpetuities, such a trust could continue, free from federal wealth transfer taxation, forever — a *perpetual dynasty trust*. See Robert H. Sitkoff & Max Schanzenbach, Jurisdictional Competition in Trust Law: An Empirical Analysis of Perpetuities and Taxes, 115 Yale L.J. (forthcoming 2005).

b.   Skip Person; Ascertaining Generations

Since a skip person is defined as an individual who is two or more generations below the transferor, it is necessary to define generations. With respect to descendants, the definition is naturally by generations. A grandchild or more remote descendant is a skip person. Similarly, for first and second line collaterals, the generations are natural. Nephews and nieces are treated as of the same generation as children; children of nephews and nieces are skip persons. I.R.C. §2651(b)(1). (See Table of Consanguinity, page 79, for a picture of second line collaterals who are on the same generational level as grandchildren.) Descendants and the first and second line collaterals of spouses of the transferor are assigned to the same generation they would be assigned to if related to the transferor. I.R.C. §2651(b)(2).

A person who has at any time been married to the transferor is assigned to the transferor's generation. A person who has been married to a descendant (or to a first or second line collateral) of the transferor or the transferor's spouse is assigned to the generation of the individual married. I.R.C. §2651(c).

With respect to a beneficiary who is not a lineal descendant of a grandparent of the transferor or of the transferor's spouse, §2651(d) provides for an assignment of generation based on the beneficiary's age in relation to that of the transferor. A person born not more than 12 1/2 years after the transferor is assigned to the transferor's generation. A person born more than 12 1/2 years but not more than 37 1/2 years after the transferor is assigned to the generation of the transferor's children. Thereafter, generation assignments are made in successive 25-year periods. Hence a gift to someone more than 37 1/2 years younger is treated the same as a gift to a grandchild (a skip person).

PROBLEMS

1. *T*, a bachelor, dies leaving a will that devises his residuary estate in trust, to pay the income to *T*'s sister, *S*, for life, and on *S*'s death to distribute the trust principal to *S*'s descendants then living per stirpes. Some years later, *S* dies; she is survived by a daughter and by three grandchildren, the children of her deceased son who died after *T* died. Does the GST tax apply?

2. *O*, your client, wants some advice. *O* wants to leave $2 million to her sister *S*. Is there any transfer tax advantage in leaving $2 million to *S* for life, remainder to *S*'s son *A*, rather than leaving $2 million to *S* outright?

c. Interest

In discussing generation-skipping transfers, we have noted above that a taxable termination occurs when an "interest" in property terminates and certain other conditions are present. A person has an interest if he has "a *right* (other than a future right) to receive income or corpus from the trust" or "is a *permissible current* recipient of income or corpus from the trust." I.R.C. §2652(c). A person who has a future interest, vested or contingent, does not have an interest for purposes of a taxable termination under the GST tax. When an owner of a future interest dies, no taxable termination takes place. Thus:

> *Case 24. T* bequeaths property in trust for her son *A* for life, remainder to *A*'s daughter *B* if *B* is then alive, and if *B* is not then alive, to *B*'s children (*T*'s great-grandchildren). Subsequently, *B* dies during the life of *A*. A GST tax is not levied at *B*'s death. Upon the subsequent death of *A*, a GST tax is levied, but a tax at *B*'s generation has been skipped.

A person who is a potential appointee (or object) of a power *currently* exercisable by another has an interest. A discretionary trust will illustrate this type of interest.

> *Case 25. T* bequeaths property in trust to pay income to *T*'s son *A* or *A*'s daughter *B* in such amount as the trustee shall determine, or accumulate it, and at the death of *A* and *B* to distribute the principal to *T*'s issue then living, per stirpes. At the death of *A*, a taxable termination occurs and a tax is due. So too at the death of *B*. If the trustee distributes income to *B* during *A*'s life, a taxable distribution occurs.

If the trust in Case 25 had been a discretionary trust for *T*'s issue until the perpetuities period expires, a taxable termination would occur upon the death of the last survivor of each generation. Under §2653(a), once a generation-skipping transfer occurs (at the death of the last survivor of *T*'s children), the transferor of the trust is then considered to be a member of the first generation above any person then having an interest in the trust (see page 925). In other words, the children are then treated as transferors, and the generation-skipping rules start over again.

Although the definitions of taxable termination and taxable distribution refer explicitly to property held in trust, which is the usual arrangement, the GST tax also applies to trust equivalents, such as legal life estates and remainders, estates for years, and insurance and annuity contracts. I.R.C. §2652(b).

5.   Tax Strategies

To reduce or avoid the generation-skipping tax, certain strategies are fairly obvious:

(a)   Use the annual gift tax exclusion of $11,000 per transferee ($22,000 for a married couple).[38] See page 857.

(b)   Use the gift tax exclusions for tuition and medical expense payments for grandchildren made directly to the educational institution or medical supplier. See page 858.

(c)   Use the predeceased child exception, if applicable to the particular family. See page 921.

(d)   Use the GST tax exemption. See page 923.

(e)   Arrange the assets of a married couple so as not to waste the GST tax exemption of either spouse. Where the couple's assets exceed $4 million, each spouse should be made the "transferor" of at least $2 million. To illustrate this, suppose *H* is very rich and *W* has no assets. *H* should transfer (at least) $2 million in a QTIP trust for *W* for life, then to *H*'s children for their lives, then to *H*'s grandchildren. This qualifies for the marital deduction *and* makes *W* the transferor for GST taxes. An estate tax will be payable at *W*'s death on the amount of property exceeding her unified credit, but no GST tax will be payable when the assets are distributed to the grand-children.

(f)   Make multiple skips in a direct skip, thus skipping more than one generation (for example, make gifts to great-grandchildren rather than grandchildren). See page 921.

(g)   Use the transferor's $2 million exemption ($4 million for a married couple) to establish a dynasty trust for successive generations for as long as the perpetuities period allows, thus avoiding GST tax for the duration of the trust. See page 925.

(h)   Give children enough property in a form subject to estate taxes in their estates to use up the $2 million exemption from estate tax (unified credit) each child has. Consider giving more property to children outright, subjecting property to estate taxes, rather than GST taxes, at their deaths. This

---

38. Gifts in trust that qualify for the gift tax annual exclusion do not automatically avoid the GST tax. To avoid this tax, the trust must be only for the benefit of one individual and must be in that individual's gross estate if that individual dies before the trust terminates. I.R.C. §2642(c)(2).

may produce these tax advantages at their deaths: lower graduated estate tax rates, a credit for previously taxed property, and the use of $2 million exemptions children have for generation-skipping transfers.

See generally Jon J. Gallo, Estate Planning and the Generation-Skipping Tax, 33 Real Prop., Prob. & Tr. J. 457 (1998).

SECTION E.   STATE WEALTH TRANSFER TAXES

Should decedents get a reduction in their federal estate taxes to reflect estate or inheritance taxes paid to a state, much as state income taxes are deductible on federal income tax returns? Before 2001, the federal estate tax included a credit for state death taxes. I.R.C. §2011. In the 1920s, when an effort was made to repeal the federal estate tax on the ground that this source of revenue should be reserved to the states, Congress enacted this credit. All states responded by enacting death taxes, some faster than others, to take full advantage of the credit, since it permitted diversion of federal revenues to the state without increasing the tax burden on the state's residents. Indeed, many states had only a *pick-up* (or *sponge*) tax that equaled the amount of the §2011 credit. Some states had an estate tax, but with their own rate schedule. And some states had both an inheritance tax—imposed on the recipients of legacies and devises—as well as an estate tax equal to any §2011 credit not offset by the inheritance tax.

The Economic Growth and Tax Relief Reconciliation Act of 1981 threw the state tax systems into turmoil by phasing out the §2011 credit as of January 1, 2005, and replacing it with a *deduction* for state death taxes. I.R.C. §2058. At the same time, the states have been confronted with the same political pressures to repeal their death taxes, tempered, however, by local budget crunches. States have reacted in two ways. Some have retained their estate taxes but have decoupled the rates from the federal estate tax credit. Others have done nothing, either waiting to see whether the repeal of §2011 will actually become effective or allowing their estate taxes to phase out along with the §2011 credit. See Jeffrey A. Cooper, John R. Ivimey & Donna D. Vincenti, State Estate Taxes after EGTRRA: A Long Day's Journey into Night, 17 Quinnipiac Prob. L.J. 317 (2004).

No one can predict the future of the federal estate tax. Its fate is bound up in politics, the economy, and federal budget battles. The fate of state wealth transfer taxes is equally uncertain. Only time will tell whether the federal system will rescue them, they will assume a life of their own, or they will die out.

TABLE OF CASES

Principal cases are indicated by italics.

929

AUTHOR INDEX

937

INDEX